KU-538-156

CONSTITUTIONAL AND ADMINISTRATIVE LAW

University of Liverpool

Withdrawn from stock

CONSTITUTIONAL AND ADMINISTRATIVE LAW

Seventeenth edition

A W Bradley MA, LLM, LLD, QC (Hon)

Emeritus Professor of Constitutional Law,
University of Edinburgh; Barrister, of the Inner Temple;
Institute of European and Comparative Law, Oxford

K D Ewing LLB, PhD

Professor of Public Law, King's College, London

C J S Knight MA, BCL

Barrister, of the Inner Temple

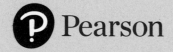 Pearson

Harlow, England • London • New York • Boston • San Francisco • Toronto • Sydney • Dubai • Singapore • Hong Kong
Tokyo • Seoul • Taipei • New Delhi • Cape Town • São Paulo • Mexico City • Madrid • Amsterdam • Munich • Paris • Milan

Pearson Education Limited
KAO Two
KAO Park
Harlow CM17 9NA
United Kingdom
Tel: +44 (0)1279 623623
Web: www.pearson.com/uk

First, second, third, fourth editions 1931, 1935, 1946, 1950 E C S Wade and G G Phillips (print)
Fifth and sixth editions 1955, 1960 E C S Wade (print)
Seventh and eighth editions 1965, 1970 E C S Wade and A W Bradley (print)
Ninth and tenth editions 1977, 1985 A W Bradley (print)
Eleventh, twelfth, thirteenth, fourteenth, fifteenth editions 1993, 1997, 2003, 2007, 2011 A W Bradley and K D Ewing (print)
Sixteenth edition 2015 A W Bradley, K D Ewing and C J S Knight (print and electronic)
Seventeenth edition published 2018 (print and electronic)

© Pearson Education Limited 2018 (print and electronic)

The rights of A W Bradley, K D Ewing and C J S Knight to be identified as authors of this work have been asserted by them in accordance with the Copyright, Designs and Patents Act 1988.

The print publication is protected by copyright. Prior to any prohibited reproduction, storage in a retrieval system, distribution or transmission in any form or by any means, electronic, mechanical, recording or otherwise, permission should be obtained from the publisher or, where applicable, a licence permitting restricted copying in the United Kingdom should be obtained from the Copyright Licensing Agency Ltd, Barnard's Inn, 86 Fetter Lane, London EC4A 1EN.

The ePublication is protected by copyright and must not be copied, reproduced, transferred, distributed, leased, licensed or publicly performed or used in any way except as specifically permitted in writing by the publishers, as allowed under the terms and conditions under which it was purchased, or as strictly permitted by applicable copyright law. Any unauthorised distribution or use of this text may be a direct infringement of the authors' and the publisher's rights and those responsible may be liable in law accordingly.

Contains public sector information licensed under the Open Government Licence (OGL) v3.0.
http://www.nationalarchives.gov.uk/doc/open-government-licence/version/3/

Contains Parliamentary information licensed under the Open Parliament Licence (OPL) v3.0.
http://www.parliament.uk/site-information/copyright/open-parliament-licence/

Pearson Education is not responsible for the content of third-party internet sites.

ISBN: 978-1-292-18586-6 (print)
    978-1-292-18584-2 (PDF)
    978-1-292-18585-9 (ePub)

British Library Cataloguing-in-Publication Data
A catalogue record for the print edition is available from the British Library

Library of Congress Cataloging-in-Publication Data
Library of Congress Cataloging-in-Publication Data
Names: Bradley, A. W. (Anthony Wilfred) author. | Ewing, K. D. (Keith D.),
    author. | Knight, Christopher (Lawyer), author.
Title: Constitutional and administrative law / A W Bradley MA, LLM, LLD, QC
    (Hon), Emeritus Professor of Constitutional Law, University of Edinburgh,
    Barrister of the Inner Temple, Institute of European and Comparative Law,
    University of Oxford; K D Ewing LLB, PhD, Professor of Public Law, King's
    College, London; C J S Knight, MA, BCL, Barrister of the Inner Temple.
Description: Seventeenth edition. | Harlow, United Kingdom ; New York :
    Pearson, 2018. | First edition, 1931, by E.C.S. Wade and G.G. Phillips. |
    Includes bibliographical references and index.
Identifiers: LCCN 2018008300| ISBN 9781292185866 (print) | ISBN 9781292185842
    (PDF) | ISBN 9781292185859 (ePub)
Subjects: LCSH: Constitutional law--Great Britain. | Civil rights--Great
    Britain. | Administrative law--Great Britain.
Classification: LCC KD3930 .W3 2018 | DDC 342.41--dc23
LC record available at https://lccn.loc.gov/2018008300

10 9 8 7 6 5 4 3 2 1
22 21 20 19 18

Cover image © iStock/Getty Images Plus/Yakovliev

Print edition typeset in 10/11.5 Ehrhardt MT Pro by iEnergizer Aptara®, Ltd.
Printed in Slovakia by Neografia

NOTE THAT ANY PAGE CROSS REFERENCES REFER TO THE PRINT EDITION

BRIEF CONTENTS

PART IV

Administrative law

CONTENTS

PART IV

Administrative law

PUBLISHER'S ACKNOWLEDGEMENTS

Extract on page 26 from *Vestey v Inland Revenue Commissioners* [1980] AC 1148,1173; Extract on page 54 from *Stella Madzimbamuto v D.W.Lardner-Burkeand Another (Southern Rhodesia)* [1969] 1 AC 645, 723; Extract on page 57 from *Per Willes J in Phillips v Eyre* (1870) LR 6 QB 1, 23; Extract on page 132 from [1983] 2 AC 771; Extract on page 133 from [1990] 2 AC 85,140; Extract on page 133 from [1990] 2 AC 85,143; Extract on page 134 from [1991] 1 AC 603 pp 658–9; Extract on page 136 from [1996] QB 404,at p 497; Extract on page 139 from *R (Schindler) v Chancellor of Duchy of Lancaster* [2016] [2017] QB 226; Extract on page 167 from *R (Woolas) v Speaker of the House of Commons* [2010] EWHC 3169 (Admin), [2012] QB 1, para 124; Extract on page 192 from Copyright Guardian News & Media Ltd, 9 November 2009; Extract on page 220 from *Pepper v Hart* [1993] AC 595, 645 (Lord Browne-Wilkinson); Extract on page 222 from *Church of Scientology of California v Johnson-Smith* [1972] 1 QB 522, 530 (Browne J); Extract on page 222 from *Hamilton v Al Fayed* [2001] 1 AC 395, 403; Extract on page 259 from *R v Criminal Injuries Compensation Board*, ex p Lain [1967] 2 QB 864, 886; Extract on page 263 from *Lord Advocate v Dumbarton Council* [1990] 2 AC 580; and ch 26; Extract on page 264 from *Burmah Oil Company (Burma Trading) Ltd. v Lord Advocate,* [1964] 2 W.L.R.1231,p 100; Extract on page 264 from *Burmah Oil Co Ltd v Lord Advocate* [1965] AC 75, 101; Extract on page 266 from *BBC v Johns* [1965] Ch 32,79; Extract on page 268 from *R v Home Secretary,* ex p Fire Brigades Union [1995] 2 AC 513; Extract on page 268 from *R v Secretary of State for the Home Department,* ex p. Northumbria Police Authority [1989] QB 26, at p 53; Extract on page 269 from *Burmah Oil Co Ltd v Lord Advocate* [1965] AC 75, Lord Pearce at p 143; Extract on page 270 from *Council of Civil Service Unions v Minister for the Civil Service* [1984]; Extract on page 315 from *TAMLIN v. HANNAFORD* [1950] 1 KB 18, 24 (Denning LJ); Extract on page 347 from *Attorney-General v English Lord Diplock* [1983] 1 AC 116, 141; Extract on page 359 from *Elguzouli-Daf v Metropolitan Police Commissioner* [1995] QB 335, at p 346; Extract on page 455 from *Douglas v Hello! Ltd,-* [2001] QB 967 above, at p 994.See also *A v B plc* [2002] EWCA Civ 337, [2003] QB 195, and now *PJS v News Group Newspapers Ltd* [2016] UKSC 26, specifically in relation to IPSO; Extract on page 467 from See *R v Broadcasting Standards Commission,* ex p BBC [2001] QB 885; Extract on page 475 from *R v Calder & Boyars Ltd* [1969] 1 QB 151, 168; Extract on page 478 from *Bonnick v Morris* [2002] UKPC 31, [2003] 1 AC 300; Extract on page 487 from *Attorney-General v Times Newspapers Ltd,* 2001 (No 4)- [2001] 1 WLR 885; Extract on page 501 from *NWL Ltd v Woods* [1979] ICR 867; Extract on page 506 from *R v Horseferry Road Metropolitan Stipendiary Magistrate,* ex parte Siadatan [1991] 1 All ER 324; Extract on page 506 from *R v Horseferry Road Metropolitan Stipendiary Magistrate,* ex parte Siadatan [1991] 1 QB 260, at p 266; Extract on page 521 from *REGINA V HOME SECRETARY,* EX PARTE HOSENBALL: CA 1977 [1977] 1 WLR 766; Extract on page 537 from *A-G v Leveller Magazine Ltd* [1979] AC 440; Extract on page 549 from *Conway v Rimmer* [1968] AC 910, at p 982; Extract on page 552 from *A-G for Northern Ireland's Reference* (No 1 of 1975) [1977] AC 105, at pp 136–7(Lord Diplock); Extract on page 585 from Lord Bingham's Eight Principles of the Rule of Law; Extract on page 638 from *R (Bradley) v Work and Pensions Secretary* [2008] EWCA Civ 36, [2009] QB 114, [139]; Extract on page 641 from *R v Environment Secretary,* ex p Hammersmith Council [1991] 1 AC 521, at 561 (Lord Donaldson MR); Extract on page 641 from *R v IRC,* ex p National Federation of Self-Employed [1982] AC 617, 640; Extract on page 645 from *Crédit Suisse v Allerdale Council* [1997] QB 306; Extract on page 647 from *Pearlman v Keepers and Governors of Harrow School* [1979] QB 56; Extract on page 648 from *R v Home Secretary,* ex p Khawaja [1984] AC 74, 108; Extract on page 648 from *Padfield v minister of agriculture fisheries and food* [1968] AC 997, 1030 (Lord Reid); Extract on page 649 from *R v Home Secretary,* ex p Venables [1998] AC 407, 518–19 (Lord Steyn); Extract on page 649 from *Council of Civil Service Unions v Minister for the Civil Service* [1985] AC 374; Extract on page 652 from *Congreve v Home Office* [1976] 1 QB 629; Extract on page 656 from *Council of Civil Service Unions v Minister for the Civil Service* [1985]

AC 374; Extract on page 656 from *R v Ministry of Defence*, ex p Smith [1996] QB 517, 554 (Sir Thomas Bingham MR); Extract on page 656 from *Education Secretary v Tameside Council* [1977] AC 1014, at 1064; Extract on page 661 from *R v Home Secretary*, ex p Brind [1991] 1 AC 696, 751 (Lord Templeman); Extract on page 663 from *A-G of Hong Kong v Ng Yuen Shiu* [1983] AC 629, 638 (Lord Fraser); Extract on page 664 from *R (Davies) v HMRC* [2011] UKSC 47, [2011] 1 WLR 2625 at [49] (Lord Wilson); Extract on page 667 from [1964] AC 40, 117 (Lord Morris of Borth-y-Gest); Extract on page 669 from *R v Gough* [1993] AC 646, 672 (Lord Woolf); Extract on page 670 from Ex p Pinochet Ugarte (No 2), at 139 (Lord Nolan). [2000] 1 AC 119; Extract on page 670 from *R v Sussex Justices*, ex p McCarthy [1924]; Extract on page 670 from *R v SUSSEX JUSTICES* ex p McCARTHY [1924] 1 KB 256; Extract on page 674 from *Lord Hodson in Ridge v Baldwin* [1964] AC 40, at 132; Extract on page 694 from *Anisminic Ltd v Foreign Compensation Commission* [1968] [1969] 2 AC 147; Extract on page 720 from *Stovin v Wise* [1996] AC 923, 958 (Lord Hoffmann); Extract on page 720 from *Barrett v Enfield Council* [2001] 2 AC 550 at 586; Extract on page 734 from *Woolwich Building Society v. Commissioners of Inland Revenue* [1993] AC 70, at 177; Extract on page 738 from *Duncan v Cammell Laird & Co.* [1942] AC 624, 642; Extract on page 739 from *Science Research Council v Nassé*, [1980] AC 1088; Extract on page 740 from *Science Research Council v Nassé*, [1980] AC 1090;D G T Williams [1980] CLJ 1; Extract on page 741 from *R v Chief Constable of West Midlands Police*, ex p Wiley [1995] 1 AC 274, 281 (Lord Templeman); Extract on page 742 from *R (Binyam Mohamed) v Foreign Secretary*, [2010] EWCA Civ 65 and [2010] EWCA Civ 158, [2011] QB 218.

PREFACE

We are living in a decade of political instability in which many of the apparently established features of the British constitution are under severe strain. The general election in 2010 saw the return of the first Coalition government since the Second World War, while nationalist sentiment led to a referendum on Scottish independence, the result of which could not be said to have been an overwhelming vote in favour of the Union.

Although the general election of 2015 nevertheless restored a government with a clear majority, this proved to be only a brief respite from the storms brewing around the Westminster model. These storms have been caused by yet another referendum, one which unlike the Scottish referendum went against the government, leading to a narrow vote in favour of Brexit, on a turnout of 72 per cent of those eligible to vote.

The referendum led to the resignation of the Prime Minister and a fresh general election not long thereafter in which the government increased its popular vote but lost its Commons majority. After 30 years of single-party governments mostly with clear Commons majorities, the Coalition thus has been followed by the first minority government since 1979, relying on the support of the Democratic Unionist Party, just as Brexit raised difficult questions affecting Northern Ireland.

At the time of writing, the minority British government is negotiating the UK withdrawal from the European Union, which is due to take effect on 29 March 2019. The process has already been difficult, with high-profile litigation leading to (i) what was in this country unprecedented abuse of the judges by sections of the media, and (ii) the strong reassertion of the principle of parliamentary sovereignty, which the same sections of the media had been campaigning to promote.

At the centre of these debates was the litigation in *R (Miller)* v *Secretary of State for Exiting the EU* [2017] UKSC 5 (in which one of us – CJSK – acted as counsel). That decision has important implications not only for the discussions of parliamentary sovereignty (Chapter 3), but also the role of constitutional conventions (Chapter 1) and the control of prerogative powers (Chapters 1 and 10), as much as it does for the operation of EU law in the United Kingdom (Chapter 6).

It is quite clear that we are in the early stages of what will be a long Brexit process as the constitutional and other problems continue to be exposed by intense parliamentary and public scrutiny. The European Union (Withdrawal) Bill, making domestic provision for leaving the EU and the body of EU law, has raised concerns about the relationship between government and Parliament, the implications of Brexit for devolution, and the loss of the EU Charter of Fundamental Rights.

As we deal with the Bill in a redrafted Chapter 6, the position of a minority government means it is unwise to assume that its contents will be reflected in the final Act of Parliament. It will be some time before the dust settles on the referendum of 2016, and subsequent editions of this book will likely need to respond to the evolving constitutional implications of a changing landscape, including our continuing relationship with the EU, whatever that may be.

But although Brexit is thus all-consuming, it is important in the meantime not to lose sight of the other changes that have taken place since 2014, as the United Kingdom's unique and dynamic constitution continues gradually to evolve. There have been notable developments on other issues affecting most chapters of this book, whether as a result of legislation or new jurisprudence, some of which have attracted intense media attention.

Apart from those already referred to, other changes dealt with in this edition are those relating to the Scottish and Welsh devolution settlements (Chapter 2); the modest yet significant 'reforms' to the House of Lords (Chapter 7); the new parliamentary procedures for dealing with English-only legislation (Chapter 8); and the role of the Fixed-term Parliaments Act 2011 in light of the 'snap election' called by the Prime Minister in 2017 (Chapter 10).

There is coverage of the Investigatory Power Act 2016 which extends State access to personal data (Chapter 16); the supervision of the press in the aftermath of the Leveson report (Chapters 16 and 17); and new counter-terrorism powers (Chapter 20). Also dealt with is the significant new case law on access to justice and the interplay between executive and judicial powers, as well as important procedural amendments to judicial review in both England and Scotland (Chapters 24 and 25).

This is the first edition for many years in which Tony Bradley has not been directly involved in the revision or the editing, and we have known since 2014 that the 16th edition would be his last. However, Tony remains the author of much of what follows, and his voice continues to be heard throughout. We are immensely grateful for his wisdom and continuing support. On this occasion, KDE has revised Chapters 6–8 and 10–20, and CJSK Chapters 1–5, 9 and 21–6.

As with earlier editions, case references are, where possible, to the official law reports, failing which to the WLR or All ER, failing which the more specialist law reports. For cases since 2001, the footnotes include the neutral case citation which enables cases to be read online on the website of the British and Irish Legal Information Institute (BAILII). The latter is a remarkable and important resource, much taken for granted, upon which we rely.

We continue to emphasise that the bibliography is not a complete a list of books in public law. It is a list of books cited, designed to enable the reader to follow up any discussion in the text. It does not include entries for the many journal articles cited, nor for official publications in the form of royal commission and select committee reports; though the latter, in particular, are invaluable sources that may be consulted on *www.parliament.uk*.

In preparing this and previous editions, we have benefited from the advice of many friends and colleagues, including Andrea Biondi, Nicola Countouris, Chris Himsworth, Richard Kay, Alastair Mowbray, Cesare Pinelli and Isobel Renzulli. In addition, CJSK is especially grateful for the support and tolerance of his wife, Charlotte, during the production of this edition, particularly as it reduced his capacity to assist in wedding planning.

Throughout, we have enjoyed the benefits of the Maugham Library at King's College London; the Bodleian Library, Oxford; the Squire Law Library, Cambridge; and the Inner Temple Library, London. We express our thanks to Pearson Education, in particular to Melanie Carter, Cheryl Stevart and Payal Rana, for their guidance and support in bringing this edition to publication.

We also thank Matthew Van Atta, the copy-editor; Nikhil Roshan, the proof-reader; and Vikas Makkar, who prepared the tables and index.

K D Ewing
C J S Knight
29 March 2018

TABLE OF LEGISLATION

Note The page numbers of the main legislative provisions and primary discussions are indicated in **bold**.

United Kingdom Statutes

United Kingdom Orders and Statutory Instruments

Legislation from other jurisdictions

Canada

European Union

Regulations

Directives

Treaties

Germany

India

Ireland

Scotland

TABLE OF CASES

Note: in this table, many of the longer entries have been shortened; thus the names of many public authorities and companies are not given in full. The abbreviation 'SSHD' has been used in place of 'Secretary of State for the Home Department' or 'Home Secretary'.

ABBREVIATIONS

In addition to the standard abbreviations used for the citation of reported cases, the following abbreviations are used for the principal journals and other sources cited.

ACD	*Administrative Court Digest*
AJCL	*American Journal of Comparative Law*
AJIL	*American Journal of International Law*
ALJ	*Australian Law Journal*
APS	*Acts of Parliament of Scotland*
BHRC	*Butterworths Human Rights Cases*
BNIL	*Bulletin of Northern Ireland Law*
BYIL	*British Yearbook of International Law*
CL	*Current Law*
CLJ	*Cambridge Law Journal*
CLP	*Current Legal Problems*
CJEU	*Court of Justice of the European Union*
CJQ	*Civil Justice Quarterly*
CMLR	*Common Market Law Reports*
CML Rev	*Common Market Law Review*
COD	*Crown Office Digest*
CPR	Civil Procedure Rules
Crim LR	*Criminal Law Review*
ECHR	*European Convention on Human Rights*
ECJ	*European Court of Justice*
ECtHR	*European Court of Human Rights*
Edin LR	*Edinburgh Law Review*
EHRLR	*European Human Rights Law Review*
EHRR	*European Human Rights Reports*
ELR	*Education Law Reports*
EL Rev	*European Law Review*
Harv L Rev	*Harvard Law Review*
HC	House of Commons (Paper)
HC Deb	House of Commons Debates (Hansard)
HEL	Sir William Holdsworth, *A History of English Law*
HL	House of Lords Paper
HL Deb	House of Lords Debates (Hansard)
HLE	*Halsbury's Laws of England* (5th edn, 2008 onwards)
HRLR	*Human Rights Law Review*
ICESCR	*International Covenant on Economic, Social and Cultural Rights, 1966*
ICLQ	*International and Comparative Law Quarterly*
ICON	*International Journal of Constitutional Law*
ILJ	*Industrial Law Journal*
JCHR	*Joint Committee on Human Rights*
J Civ Lib	*Journal of Civil Liberties*
JR	*Judicial Review*
JSSL	*Journal of Social Security Law*
Jur R	*Juridical Review*

Kilbrandon Report	Report of Royal Commission on the Constitution, vol. 1, Cmnd 5460, 1973
LQR	*Law Quarterly Review*
LS	*Legal Studies*
MLR	*Modern Law Review*
MPR	Report of Committee of Ministers' Powers, Cmd 4060, 1932
NDBP	*Non-Departmental Public Body*
NIJB	*Northern Ireland Judgment Bulletin*
NILQ	*Northern Ireland Legal Quarterly*
NLJ	*New Law Journal*
NMD	*Non-Ministerial Department*
OJLS	*Oxford Journal of Legal Studies*
PL	*Public Law*
SI	Statutory Instrument
SSI	Scottish Statutory Instrument
SLT	*Scots Law Times*
SO	Standing Order
TEU	Treaty on European Union
TFEU	Treaty on the Functioning of the European Union
WA	Written Answer
YBEL	*Yearbook of European Law*

PART I

Sources, structure and principles

CHAPTER 1

Constitutional law – its meaning and sources

> Unlike most countries, the United Kingdom does not have a constitution in the sense of a single coherent code of fundamental law which prevails over all other sources of law. Our constitutional arrangements have developed over time in a pragmatic as much as in a principled way, through a combination of statutes, events, conventions, academic writings and judicial decisions. Reflecting its development and its contents, the UK constitution was described by the constitutional scholar, Professor A.V. Dicey, as 'the most flexible polity in existence' —*Introduction to the Study of the Law of the Constitution, 8th edn (1915), p 87.*[1]

A. Constitutional law – its meaning and scope

The fundamental nature of constitutional law

At first sight, constitutional law may appear to be just one among many branches of law that must be studied by those who wish to make their living as lawyers, alongside subjects such as the law of civil wrongs (torts), company law, contract, crime, employment law, land law and taxation. But it has a deeper significance than this, since it is concerned with basic questions about the relations between individuals and the state in which they are citizens. In a society committed to values such as peace and good order, democracy and the rule of law, the existence and functions of the government and public bodies such as the police must be subject to law. And a basic principle in such a society is that those who govern must be accountable to those who are governed. But where does 'the law' come from, and what is the authority for it? Constitutional law may be said to be 'the law about law', a phrase that in turn raises questions about the ultimate authority of constitutional law.

In many countries (but not in the United Kingdom), there is a national constitution in writing that is regarded as providing the ultimate authority for all bodies that wield public power. By contrast, in the United Kingdom, some essential parts of the structure of government (in particular, the monarchy and Parliament) have taken their existence from history. This applies also to that part of the legal system that is termed the 'common law'. The common law derives its authority from the work of judges over the centuries, sitting to resolve disputes between contesting parties in accordance (so far as possible) with rules of law as they have been applied in earlier cases. By contrast, most public bodies today have been created by Parliament to exercise powers that are felt to be needed in the modern world. These include the Electoral Commission and the bodies which run the National Health Service, but countless other examples could be given.

Constitutional law not only recognises the existence of state power, which may be justified by reference to the wishes of the majority of the people, but it also seeks to protect individuals and minority groups against collective action that would ride roughshod over their rightful claim to live free from oppressive and intrusive conduct. The need to protect fundamental human rights is today recognised far more widely than it was in the early years of the 20th century, and it now plays a large part in our constitutional law.

---

[1] *R (Miller) v Secretary of State for Exiting the EU* [2017] UKSC 5, [2017] 2 WLR 583 at [40].

What is a constitution?

Applied to the system of law and government by which the affairs of a modern state are administered, the word constitution has two main meanings. In its narrower meaning, a constitution means a document having a special legal status which sets out the framework and principal functions of the organs of government and declares the principles or rules by which those organs must operate. In countries in which the constitution has overriding legal force, there is often a high-ranking court which applies and interprets the text of the constitution in disputed cases. Such a court is the Supreme Court in the United States, or the Federal Constitutional Court in Germany. In these countries, legislative or executive acts may be held by the court to be without legal force where they conflict with the constitution.

In this sense of the word, the United Kingdom of Great Britain and Northern Ireland has no constitution. There is no single document from which is derived the authority of the main organs of government, such as the Crown, the Cabinet, Parliament and the courts. No written text lays down the relationship of the primary organs of government one with another or with the people.[2] But the word constitution has a wider meaning. As Bolingbroke stated in 1733:

> By constitution we mean, whenever we speak with propriety and exactness, that assemblage of laws, institutions and customs, derived from certain fixed principles of reason, directed to certain fixed objects of public good, that compose the general system, according to which the community hath agreed to be governed.[3]

In 2001, the House of Lords committee on the constitution stated that the constitution means 'the set of laws, rules and practices that create the basic institutions of the state, and its component and related parts, and stipulate the powers of those institutions and the relationship between the different institutions and between those institutions and the individual'.[4] In this sense, the United Kingdom has a constitution since it has a complex and comprehensive system of government, which has been called 'one of the most successful political structures ever devised'.[5] The foundations for this system include Acts of Parliament, judicial decisions, political practice and also the procedures established by various organs of government for carrying out their own tasks, for example the law and custom of Parliament or the rules issued by the Prime Minister on the conduct of ministers.[6]

The wider sense of the word constitution necessarily includes a constitution in the narrower sense. In Canada, Germany, India, the United States and many other states, the written constitution occupies the primary place among the 'assemblage of laws, institutions and customs' which make up the constitution in the wider sense. But no written document alone can ensure the smooth working of a system of government. Around a written constitution will evolve a wide variety of customary rules and practices which adjust its working to changing

---

[2] For what such a document might contain on a purely descriptive basis, see Bogdanor, Vogenauer et al in Bryant (ed.), *Towards a New Constitutional Settlement*, p 152. For a more normative exercise as to what it should contain, see *The Constitution of the United Kingdom* (Institute for Public Policy Research, 1991); Gordon, *Repairing British Politics*; and Blick, *Beyond Magna Carta: A Constitution for the United Kingdom*. On the notion of a constitution, see King, *Does the United Kingdom Still Have a Constitution?* and *The British Constitution*; Loughlin, *The British Constitution: A Very Short Introduction*; G Marshall, 'The Constitution: Its Theory and Interpretation' in Bogdanor (ed.), *The British Constitution in the Twentieth Century*; Tomkins, *Our Republican Constitution*.

[3] From *A Dissertation upon Parties* (1733), reprinted in Bolingbroke, *Political Writings* (ed. Armitage), p 88.

[4] HL Committee on the Constitution (HL Paper 11, 2001–02), ch 2.

[5] Hailsham, *On the Constitution*, p 1. Other authors disagree: e.g. McLean, *What's Wrong with the British Constitution?* And see Bentham, *Handbook of Political Fallacies*, pp 154–63.

[6] See *Ministerial Code: A Code of Conduct and Guidance on Procedures for Ministers*; chs 5 and 11.

conditions.[7] These customary rules and practices may be more easily changed than the constitution itself: their continuing evolution will reduce the need for formal amendment of the written text. It has been said of the US constitution that '[the] governing Constitution is a synthesis of legal doctrines, institutional practices, and political norms'.[8] A perceptive study of the same constitution begins with the declaration that we can understand how it actually operates 'only by seeing it as a government fundamentally structured around . . . two nationally organised political parties'[9] – yet the existence of those parties is nowhere mentioned in the constitution itself.

In reality, a written constitution will often not contain all the rules upon which government depends. Thus, the scheme for electing the legislature may be found not in the constitution but in statutes enacted by the legislature. Such statutes can when necessary be amended by ordinary legislation, whereas amendments to the constitution may require a more elaborate process, such as a special majority in the legislature or approval by a referendum. Since the way in which the constitutional text operates is likely to depend on political practice, the process of constitutional change is not limited to the formal process of textual amendment.[10] Moreover, the making of comparisons is not straightforward, as we can see in an unexpected comment by an expert on the US constitution: 'Typically offered as a paradigm of a nation with a written constitution, the United States actually operates with a constitution that is more similar to than different from the paradigmatic unwritten constitution of the United Kingdom'.[11]

The making of written constitutions

It was in the late 18th century that the word constitution came to be identified with a single document, mainly as a result of the American and French Revolutions. The political significance of this new concept was stressed by the radical, Tom Paine:

> A constitution is a thing antecedent to a government, and a government is only the creature of a constitution . . . A constitution is not the act of a government, but of a people constituting a government, and government without a constitution, is power without a right.[12]

In today's world, the making of a constitution normally follows a fundamental political event – what Ackerman calls a 'constitutional moment'[13] – such as the conferment of independence on a former colony, a successful revolution, or reconstruction of a country's institutions following a war. The outcome of the process is likely to reflect the beliefs and political aspirations of those who have framed it. In the 1990s, after the collapse of communism, eastern and central Europe experienced an era of constitution-making, as the overthrow of socialist regimes led to the creation of new structures that embraced liberal and democratic values.

Within the United Kingdom, except between 1653 and 1660 when the country was ruled under Cromwell's 'Instrument of Government', political circumstances have never required the enactment of a code covering the whole of government. There have indeed been periods of political upheaval culminating in the reform of certain institutions; thus the 'Glorious Revolution' of 1688–9 was the final act of the constitutional conflicts of the 17th century.

---

[7] For the argument that all constitutions leave important things unsaid, see Foley, *The Silence of Constitutions*; and King, *Does the UK Still Have a Constitution?*, ch 1.

[8] Whittington, *Constitutional Construction*, p 3.

[9] Tushnet, *The Constitution of the USA*, p 5.

[10] See Oliver and Fusaro, *How Constitutions Change: A Comparative Study*.

[11] Tushnet, *The Constitution of the USA*, p 1.

[12] *The Rights of Man* (ed. Kuklick), pp 81 and 174.

[13] Ackerman, *We the People: Foundations*.

Later, there was the first major reform of the House of Commons in 1832 and the crisis over the Lords which led to the Parliament Act 1911. Both the union of England and Scotland in 1707 and the union of Great Britain and Ireland in 1800 were events that went to the heart of the entity known as the United Kingdom. And there was the abdication crisis affecting the monarchy in 1936. But these events did not lead to reconstruction of the whole system of government. Instead, a pragmatic approach has been adopted, with legislation being passed to give effect to the outcome of the political events. That legislation has intentionally avoided the difficult task of stating the foundational political beliefs and assumptions on which the system of government depends. After 1997, the government of Mr Blair was criticised for making extensive constitutional changes without placing them in an integrated programme of reform. In 2007, Mr Brown's government embarked on a new reform initiative,[14] but this fell far short of being a comprehensive programme of reform, and relatively little came of it. In 2010, the formation of the Coalition government led to numerous projected constitutional reforms being included in the *Programme for Government*[15] and placed under the responsibility of the Deputy Prime Minister. Few of those projected reforms eventuated either.

The referendum vote in 2016 in favour of the United Kingdom leaving the European Union, and the commencement of that process under the European Union (Notification of Withdrawal) Act 2017, will undoubtedly lead to one of the most significant constitutional upheavals in the modern era. It may lead to something akin to the reconstruction of large swathes of law. But even this process is being carried out in a piecemeal fashion, with little direct or overt consideration of the implications for the wider constitutional picture (although that is partly explicable by the sheer range of potential implications and the unknown quantity of the nature of the likely changes until the terms of withdrawal are finalised). We return to this topic in Chapter 6.

Nevertheless, what has often been called the Westminster system of government is compatible with a written constitution. Long before 1945, constitutions were framed for long established British territories overseas, such as Australia, Canada and New Zealand; some of these constitutions have stood the test of time, even though they did not guarantee the protection of fundamental human rights.[16] After 1945, as British colonies acquired their independence, numerous variants of the 'Westminster model' were created. It became common practice for guarantees of rights and broad political declarations to be included in the constitutions of the newly independent countries, as in 1979 when Rhodesia achieved independence as the republic of Zimbabwe.[17] Within the United Kingdom, there has usually been little political support for the idea of a written constitution.[18] However, because of devolution to Scotland, Wales and Northern Ireland, the Human Rights Act 1998 and changes in electoral law, as well as the emergence of documents such as the *Ministerial Code* and the *Code of Conduct for MPs*, many areas of government have become subject to written rules. The constitution is certainly not as unwritten as it was in the past.[19]

---

[14] See *The Governance of Britain*, Cm 7170, 2007; and *Constitutional Renewal*, Cm 7342, 2008. Also the Constitutional Reform and Governance Act 2010.

[15] Cabinet Office, 2010. And see the related agreement, *The Coalition Agreement for Stability and Reform* (Cabinet Office, 2010).

[16] In 1982, the last Canada Act to be passed at Westminster gave full powers of constitutional amendment to Canada and enacted the Charter of Rights and Freedoms as part of the Canadian constitution.

[17] Zimbabwe Constitution Order 1979, SI 1979 No 1600, part III. See de Smith, *The New Commonwealth and Its Constitutions*, ch 5, and Simpson, *Human Rights and the End of Empire*.

[18] See the arguments marshalled in N W Barber [2008] PL 11.

[19] See Bogdanor, *The New British Constitution*.

Legal consequences of the unwritten constitution

While the written constitutions of states are likely to contain some common ingredients (defining the identity of the state, formulating the aspirations of the people, and setting out the key structure of government), these contents assume a wide variety of forms. Within a federal constitution, the tasks of government are divided into two classes, those entrusted to the federal (or national) organs of government, and those entrusted to the various states or regions which make up the federation. Thus, in countries such as Australia, Canada, Germany and the United States, the constitution sets out in broad terms the powers that may be exercised by each level of government. Again, many constitutions give special protection to the fundamental rights of the citizen in the form of a 'Bill of Rights', for example by 'entrenching' these rights so that a special legislative procedure is needed if they are to be amended, or even by rendering certain rights in essence unalterable, as in Germany.[20] And many constitutions adopt a separation of powers, vesting legislative power in the legislature, executive power in the executive and judicial power in the courts.[21] In some cases, especially in the US constitution, this separation of powers is subject to an array of 'checks and balances'.

Within the United Kingdom, there is no written constitution to secure these objects or serve as the foundation of the legal system. The ensuing vacuum is occupied by the doctrines of the legislative supremacy of Parliament and the rule of law, their interrelation being a fundamental question of public law in Britain.[22] These doctrines will be examined later, but one result is that formal restraints on the exercise of power which exist elsewhere do not exist in the United Kingdom. For example, no truly federal system can exist so long as Parliament's legislative supremacy is maintained. Parliament passed the Government of Ireland Act 1920, devolving powers of self-government upon Northern Ireland, but in 1972 Parliament re-imposed direct rule on Northern Ireland.[23] For a formal federal system to be established, a written constitution would be needed to prevent the Westminster Parliament from taking back into its own hands powers that had been devolved to Edinburgh, Cardiff and Belfast.

Moreover, unlike the position in many written constitutions, the ultimate protection of fundamental rights is a matter for Parliament, not the courts. This remains the position in the United Kingdom, even though by enacting the Human Rights Act 1998, Parliament significantly extended the role of the courts in protecting human rights.[24]

The absence of a written constitution also means that there is no fixed procedure prescribed for legislation of constitutional importance. Referendums have been held in the United Kingdom (or parts of it) for political reasons, not because of a formal legal obligation binding on the government. Before the Republic of Ireland could join the European Communities in 1973, a constitutional amendment had to be approved by referendum of the people. In the United Kingdom, the European Communities Act 1972 was debated at length in Parliament, but was passed by a procedure in the same basic form as ordinary legislation. British membership of the European Communities was in 1975 subsequently confirmed by a consultative referendum, the holding of which was a consequence of political divisions in the Labour party rather than a legal requirement. Similarly, the choice of the United Kingdom to leave the European Union – formally notified under article 50 of the Treaty on European Union in March 2017 – was reached following the referendum vote on the subject in 2016, but could legally have occurred without such a vote. The 2014 Scottish independence referendum may have been politically necessary, but it was not legally required. There are some

---

[20] Basic Law of the Federal Republic of Germany, arts 19(2) and 79(3).
[21] Ch 4 C.
[22] See Allan, *Law, Liberty and Justice*; and Forsyth (ed.), *Judicial Review and the Constitution*.
[23] Ch 2 A.
[24] Ch 14.

notable exceptions to the lack of legal obligation for a referendum, neither of which have yet been triggered. The Northern Ireland Act 1998, s 1, has the effect that the status of the province as part of the United Kingdom cannot be altered without a 'poll' held for that purpose providing the consent of the majority of the people of Northern Ireland to a change in that status. Various provisions of the European Union Act 2011 would have required a referendum to be held in the event of certain types of further power being given to the EU; that legislation is of course shortly to be defunct. By amendments brought about in the Scotland Act 2016 and the Wales Act 2017, the Scottish Parliament and National Assembly for Wales (and the respective devolved governments) are now statutorily declared to be permanent and cannot be abolished save on the basis of a referendum result in the relevant territory in support of such a step: s 63A(3) of the Scotland Act 1998 (as amended) and s A1(3) of the Government of Wales Act 2006 (as amended).

By contrast with written constitutions, which may be described as *rigid* because of the special procedure required if they are to be altered, the United Kingdom has what in form is an extremely *flexible* constitution. It would seem that there is no aspect of our constitutional arrangements which could not be altered by Act of Parliament.[25] This quality of 'flexibility' is not without its dangers, and in 2011 the House of Lords' committee on the constitution struck a cautionary note in calling for more consultation to take place before a government embarks on constitutional reforms; the committee commented that fast-track legislation should not be used to make permanent constitutional changes.[26] Whether one sees the ease with which the process of withdrawal from the EU can be started – or Scotland leaving the Union altogether – as a vindication of the flexibility of the constitution, or an indictment of its lack of protections, is likely to depend in significant part on whether or not one approves of the destination.

Evolutionary development

To describe the British system of government as flexible means not that it is unstable but that, as we have seen, most of its principles and rules can be changed by legislation or by development of a new conventional rule or practice. Perhaps because of this flexibility, the United Kingdom has, at least since 1688–9, escaped those revolutionary convulsions which may occur in countries with more rigid constitutions but less stable political or social systems. Since the 17th-century settlement, there have been innumerable changes in the system of government, some freely conceded but many fought for by political action.[27] The result has been a complete change from personal rule by the monarch to the ascendancy of the Prime Minister, who leads the largest party in Parliament and is head of the executive branch of the state.

Some of the older features of government have survived from earlier times, and these (for instance, the Privy Council)[28] are tolerated or respected because they represent historic continuity. Writing in 1867, Walter Bagehot in *The English Constitution* distinguished between the *dignified* parts of the constitution 'which excite and preserve the reverence of the population' and the *efficient* parts, 'by which it, in fact, works and rules'.[29] Bagehot called it the characteristic merit of the constitution, 'that its dignified parts are very complicated and somewhat imposing, very old and rather venerable; while its efficient part, at least when in

---

[25] In *R (Jackson)* v *A-G* [2005] UKHL 56, [2006] 1 AC 262, Lord Steyn remarked that some fundamentals associated with the rule of law might be beyond the reach of Parliament. For an attempt to identify what those might be, see C J S Knight [2011] PL 89. pp 59–61.

[26] HL Paper 177 (2010–12), paras 37–46, 90, 99.

[27] I Cram (2016) 36 LS 75.

[28] Ch 10 C. For an entertaining account of the oddities of the Privy Council, see D Rogers, *By Royal Appointment*.

[29] *The English Constitution*, p 61.

great and critical action, is decidedly simple and rather modern.'[30] Because of the vast changes in the 'efficient parts' of the constitution that have occurred, it is misleading to claim, as a royal commission on the constitution said in 1973: 'The United Kingdom already possesses a constitution which in its essentials has served well for some hundreds of years.'[31] For a full understanding of the constitution, a sense of history is essential.[32]

The evolutionary nature of the constitution can be illustrated in many ways. While the monarch has lost the role of governing the country since 1688, further changes in the residual functions of the monarch may yet occur. Tension remains between the competing claims of Cabinet and Prime Ministerial (or presidential) government. And many questions remain about the accountability of Whitehall to Parliament. Despite the measures of constitutional reform that have been enacted since 1997, there is a continuing need to maintain and secure greater democratic accountability of government.

Constitutionalism[33]

The term 'constitutionalism' often appears in discussion of the relationship between state power, law, democracy and the preservation of liberal values,[34] but it is used with a wide variety of meanings. A Norwegian political scientist has said that constitutionalism 'is the doctrine that claims that political authority should be bound by institutions that restrict the exercise of power'.[35] A Hungarian jurist has written that constitutionalism 'is the set of principles, manners, and institutional arrangements' that have traditionally served to limit government.[36] And for an American commentator, '[the] special virtue of constitutionalism . . . lies not merely in reducing the power of the state, but in effecting that reduction by the advance imposition of rules'.[37]

The idea of constitutionalism is particularly associated with the existence of a written constitution from which the state's authority and legitimacy may be said to derive, and which may help to protect the rights of individuals and minorities. The façade of a written constitution may sometimes exist alongside the structure of a tyrannical state. However, the prevailing tradition in western liberalism assumes existence of a written constitution, along with a democratic parliament, respect for the law, and a system of courts that protect groups and individuals against the abuse of power.

In the United Kingdom the absence of formal limits upon state power has sometimes given rise to demands for a new 'constitutional settlement', including a new Bill of Rights to protect individual liberties.[38] Since the 1997 general election, numerous reforms of parts of

---

[30] Ibid, p 65.

[31] Kilbrandon Report, para 395.

[32] For two contrasting studies that reinforce this point, see Wicks, *The Evolution of a Constitution* and Allison, *The English Historical Constitution*.

[33] See Vile, *Constitutionalism and the Separation of Powers*; McIlwain, *Constitutionalism, Ancient and Modern*; Alexander (ed.), *Constitutionalism: Philosophical Foundations*.

[34] See J E K Murkens (2009) 29 OJLS 1. On 'common law constitutionalism', see T Poole (2003) 23 OJLS 435. Also King, *The British Constitution*, pp 12–13; and Ziegler, Baranger and Bradley, *Constitutionalism and the Role of Parliaments*, ch 1.

[35] Lane, *Constitutions and Political Theory*, p 19.

[36] Sajó, *Limiting Government: An Introduction to Constitutionalism*, p xiv.

[37] R Kay, in Alexander (ed.) above, pp 16, 23. See also S Holmes, in Rosenfeld and Sajó (ed.), *The Oxford Handbook of Comparative Constitutional Law*, ch 8.

[38] See Scarman, *English Law – The New Dimension*. Contrast the sparkling defence of the unwritten constitution as an expression of political culture in Thompson, *Writing by Candlelight*, pp 191–256. Works calling for reform include Brazier, *Constitutional Reform*; Foley, *The Politics of the British Constitution*; Mount, *The British Constitution*; and Oliver, *Constitutional Reform in the UK*.

the constitution have been carried through by successive governments, but all have stopped well short of creating a written constitution. In the United Kingdom today, there is widespread belief in the values of democratic and accountable government, and also much scepticism about the ability of the parliamentary process to protect the public against abuse of power, but these beliefs have not yet led to there being widespread support for the enactment of a written constitution. Given the real practical and theoretical difficulties involved, it is unsurprising that no government has wished to expend its political capital on such a divisive exercise.[39]

Constitutional law in the United Kingdom

As we have seen, the scope of constitutional law in the United Kingdom is necessarily affected by the absence of a written constitution. Constitutional law presupposes the existence of the state[40] and accordingly may be said to be that part of national law which governs the system of public administration and the relationships between the individual and the state.[41] One difficulty in defining the subject in the United Kingdom is that many of the rules and practices under which government operates do not have the force of law.[42] This means that knowledge of the legal rules alone gives an incomplete view of the subject. A distinction is sometimes made between what may be called the 'legal constitution', that emphasises the importance of judicial decisions and textual interpretation in the operation of government, and the 'political constitution', a term that stresses that the system depends on political culture and democratic process rather than on decisions taken by formal procedures that may not reflect public opinion today.[43] In reality, the distinction cannot be pressed too far, since all constitutions are political in content and no democracy can survive without a legal structure.

Another problem of definition is that, unlike systems in which the law is organised in the form of a series of codes administered by separate courts, there is no clear-cut demarcation in Britain between constitutional law and other branches of law. As a great legal historian observed: 'There is hardly any department of law which does not, at one time or another, become of constitutional importance.'[44] For example, in family law, important protection for family life is given by the European Convention on Human Rights;[45] in employment law, freedom of association and the law of picketing[46] are of constitutional importance; and innumerable issues of civil liberty arise out of criminal justice. Constitutional law does not comprehend the whole of the legal system, but the manner in which questions of rights, powers and duties are settled is a central aspect of the subject.[47]

In the past, constitutional law gave more emphasis to the role of the state in maintaining public order and national security than it did to the individual's ability to benefit from employment and housing, education, health services and conservation of the environment. The state today has important governmental functions in all these areas: how it carries out

---

[39] For some consideration of the difficulties, see: J Cornford (1991) 44 Parliamentary Affairs 558; R Brazier (1992) 13 Statute LR 104; and especially V Bogdanor and S Vogenauer [2011] PL 38.

[40] For the impact of the changing concept of the state, see N MacCormick (1993) 56 MLR 1; C M G Himsworth [1996] PL 639; MacCormick, *Questioning Sovereignty*; and N W Barber, *The Constitutional State*.

[41] HLE, vol 8 (2), para 1; and see Marshall, *Constitutional Theory*, ch 1.

[42] See section C below.

[43] See the seminal analysis by J A G Griffith in (1979) 42 MLR 1. Also Whittington, *Constitutional Construction*, ch 1; Bellamy, *Political Constitutionalism*; K D Ewing [2000] PL 405; G Gee and G Webber (2010) 30 OJLS 273; and a symposium on the 'political constitution' in (2013) 14 *German Law Journal* (available online).

[44] Maitland, *Constitutional History*, p 538.

[45] Arts 8 and 12. Ch 14 C.

[46] Ch 18.

[47] Cf the approach to the constitution taken in D Feldman [2005] CLJ 329.

these functions is of concern to the public at large. Through social services and economic regulation, individuals come into contact more often with officials than with judges. *Administrative law* is a close relation of constitutional law, since it deals with the powers of government and with the remedies (whether political or judicial) that are open to someone who is affected by the decisions of public officials.[48] Not surprisingly, there is no sharp demarcation between constitutional and administrative law.[49] A rough distinction might be that constitutional law is mainly concerned with the structure of the primary organs of government, whereas administrative law is concerned with the role of official agencies in providing services and in regulating the activities of citizens. But it is an essential feature of a constitutional state that use or misuse of executive power can be questioned, whether by political or judicial means.

There is also a close relationship between constitutional law and *public international law*, which is the system of law whose primary function is to regulate the relations of states with one another, through such matters as the conduct of diplomacy, the making of treaties, membership of international organisations, and formalities such as the sending of ambassadors.[50] International law thus deals with the *external* relations of a state with other states; constitutional law concerns the *internal* structure of the state and its relations with those persons who are within its jurisdiction.[51] Each in its own way is concerned with subjecting to law the power that states wield, but how does one relate to the other? In answering this question, the *monist* tradition seeks to assimilate the national and international legal systems. But in the *dualist* tradition, which the United Kingdom has generally observed, national and international law operate at two distinct levels. Hence, action by a state (for instance, the use of armed forces abroad) may be lawful in national law but in breach of international law; moreover, when a state is in breach of an obligation at international law, the state may not plead in an international forum that its government had no power under national law to take action required by international law. In matters of fundamental human rights, it is desirable for both systems to have the same rules, so that an official decision may be lawful or unlawful in both.[52] Since 1945, under the aegis of the United Nations, international organisations have established many forms of cooperation between states, and multilateral treaties have set standards of conduct for the world community, for example, in respect of war crimes, genocide and torture. International law is increasingly concerned with protecting human rights, to the extent of permitting international intervention in a state's affairs on matters that would once have been considered to be solely within the sovereignty of that state. Because of the evolving interface between constitutional law and international law, courts in the United Kingdom are increasingly dealing with the effects of what has been called 'the internationalisation of public law'.[53]

The dualist tradition of British law was the basis for the litigation in *R (Miller)* v *Secretary of State for Exiting the EU*.[54] The reason why the government believed and argued that it was entitled to exercise the royal prerogative, without the need for statutory authority, to leave

---

[48] See chs 21–26.

[49] Maitland, *Constitutional History*, pp 528–35, and Craig, *Public Law and Democracy in the UK and the USA*, pp 1–3.

[50] See Brownlie, *Principles of Public International Law*; Clapham, *Brierly's Law of Nations*; and Shaw, *International Law*. Also C Greenwood in Rawlings, Leyland and Young (eds), *Sovereignty and the Law*, ch 14.

[51] On the different meaning of a state's jurisdiction in European human rights law, see *Bancovic* v *Belgium* (2001) 11 BHRC 435, *Al-Skeini* v *UK* (2011) 30 BHRC 561, and *Smith* v *Ministry of Defence* [2013] UKSC 41, [2014] AC 52.

[52] See e.g. *Al-Jedda* v *Home Secretary* [2013] UKSC 62, [2014] AC 253 (unlawful to use statutory power to revoke British citizenship where effect is to create statelessness).

[53] See Jowell and Oliver (eds), *The Changing Constitution* (7th edn, 2011), ch 5 (D Feldman).

[54] [2017] UKSC 5, [2017] 2 WLR 583.

the EU was because a notification of withdrawal is an act under the international treaty which forms part of the constitutional law of the EU.[55] Dualism means that an act on the international law plane is, in general terms, irrelevant in domestic law. The counter-argument was that while that may well be the ordinary case, the particular nature and incorporation of EU law into domestic law meant that it would in fact have very significant potential ramifications on the domestic law plane, and so required statutory authority.

For present purposes, the *Miller* case is an important reminder that the EU is an international law organisation, entered into by the member states of the European Community. However, the EC was from its inception different from other international organisations, being equipped with legislative, administrative and judicial powers that were exercised with direct effect in member states. The unique nature of the EU's powers, competences and methods for securing the achievement of its objectives within its member states mean that it has always had a degree of constitutional implication quite unlike any other international law organisation (including the United Nations).[56]

As a system of government, the EU already has a 'constitution' based on the treaties that created it, on decisions by the Court of Justice of the European Union interpreting the treaties, and on a complex structure of agreements and practices by which the EU functions.[57] Such a constitution comes within Bolingbroke's use of that term, mentioned earlier, to refer to the 'assemblage of laws, institutions and customs' by which states forming the EU have agreed to be governed. In 2005, an ambitious attempt to provide the EU with a formal 'European Constitution' by that name failed, when it was rejected by referendums in the Netherlands and France. A further attempt at EU reform was made in the form of the Lisbon Treaty, which retained many of the changes of the 'Constitution' but without the political sensitivity caused by the use of that term.[58] It too required ratification by all member states; this came into effect in December 2009, after it was approved (at the second time of asking) by a referendum held in Ireland, and the final ratification by a member state was given to it by the Czech Republic.

B. The formal sources of constitutional law

If the United Kingdom possessed a written constitution, the main rules of constitutional law would be contained within it. Alterations to these rules would be made by the procedure laid down for amending the constitution. Parliament would be likely to have power to legislate on such matters as the machinery of elections and the structure of the courts; and in disputed cases the courts would probably have the authority to determine the meaning of the constitution. The formal sources of constitutional law would comprise: (*a*) the constitution itself, and amendments made to it; (*b*) Acts of Parliament dealing with matters of constitutional importance; (*c*) judicial decisions interpreting the constitution. In the absence of a written constitution, the two main sources of constitutional law in the United Kingdom are the same as those of law in general, namely:

(a) *Legislation* (or enacted law) including: Acts of Parliament; legislation made by ministers and other authorities on whom Parliament has conferred power to legislate;[59] exceptionally,

---

[55] Specifically, the Treaty on European Union.

[56] Ch 6.

[57] See e.g. S Douglas-Scott, *Constitutional Law of the European Union*.

[58] Properly speaking, the Lisbon Treaty is actually two separate treaties: the Treaty on European Union and the Treaty on the Functioning of the European Union.

[59] Ch 22.

legislative measures issued by the Crown under prerogative powers;[60] and, from 1973 until 'exit day', legislation enacted by organs of the EU.[61]

(b) *Judicial precedent* (or case law), being the decisions of the courts expounding the common law or interpreting legislation. Currently, this includes decisions of the Court of Justice in relation to EU law; and the Human Rights Act 1998 requires all courts and tribunals to take account of relevant decisions of the European Court of Human Rights.[62]

A lesser-known branch of constitutional law is found in the 'law and custom of Parliament' (*lex et consuetudo Parliamenti*), which derives from the authority inherent in each House of Parliament to regulate its internal affairs.[63]

Legislation

There are few topics of constitutional law which are not affected by legislation. Unlike some branches of private law, for example the law of contract, a study of constitutional law involves frequent recourse to the statute book. The statutes which deal with constitutional topics do not form sections of a complete code. If a collection were made of all the legislation (from medieval charters to the present day) that deals with the form and functions of government, the result would present a very unwieldy but incomplete picture of the constitution.[64] While these enactments can each be repealed or amended by further Acts, a few statutes have special constitutional significance.

1 *Magna Carta*.[65] Magna Carta was granted in 1215 by King John under pressure from the nobles at Runnymede. In varying forms, the charter was confirmed by later kings with the approval of the English Parliament; it appears on the statute book in the form confirmed by Edward I in 1297. It contained a statement of grievances, formulated on behalf of important sections of the community, which the King undertook to redress. The charter set out the rights of various classes of the medieval community according to their different needs. The Church was to be free; London and other cities were to enjoy their liberties and customs; merchants were not to be subject to unjust taxation. Although both trial by jury and the writ of habeas corpus owe their origins to other sources, chapter 29 declared that no man should be punished except by the judgment of his peers or the law of the land, and that to none should justice be denied. These clauses embodied a protest against arbitrary punishment and asserted the right to a fair trial and a just legal system. Today, few provisions of Magna Carta remain in force, but it has been called 'the nearest approach to an irrepealable "fundamental statute" that England has ever had'.[66]

2 *Petition of Right*. A document adopted by the English Parliament at a much later period of conflict is the Petition of Right 1628, enrolled on the statute book as 3 Car 1 c 1.[67] This contained protests against taxation without consent of Parliament, arbitrary imprisonment, the

---

[60] Ch 10 D.

[61] Ch 6 A, B.

[62] Ch 14 C.

[63] See p 19 below and p 19.

[64] See the four volumes under the title 'Constitutional Law' in *Halsbury's Statutes*, 4th edn, vol 10 (2013 reissue).

[65] For an historical account, see Holt, *Magna Carta*; Carpenter, *Magna Carta*; and Arlidge and Judge, *Magna Carta Uncovered*.

[66] Pollock and Maitland, *History of English Law*, vol I, p 173. See also *R v Home Secretary, ex p Phansopkar* [1976] QB 606; *R v Foreign Secretary, ex p Bancoult* [2001] QB 1067; A Tomkins [2001] PL 571; and R Hazell and J Melton (eds), *Magna Carta and Its Modern Legacy*.

[67] *Halsbury's Statutes*, vol 10 (1), p 109.

use of commissions of martial law in time of peace and the billeting of soldiers upon private persons. To these protests the King yielded, though the effect of the concession was weakened by the view Charles I held that his prerogative powers were not thereby diminished.

3 *Bill of Rights and Claim of Right.* The 'Glorious Revolution' of 1688 brought about the downfall of James II of England and James VII of Scotland from his two thrones, and the restoration of monarchy in the two kingdoms on terms laid down by the English and Scottish Parliaments, respectively. These terms were accepted by the incoming joint monarchs, William and Mary. In England it was the House of Lords and the remnants of Charles II's last Parliament that in 1689 approved the Bill of Rights, which was later confirmed by the post-revolution Parliament.[68] This laid the foundations of the modern constitution by disposing of the more extravagant claims of the Stuarts to rule by prerogative right.

Its principal provisions ('articles'), many of which are still in force in English law, declared:

(1) That the pretended power of suspending of laws or the execution of laws by regal authority without consent of Parliament is illegal.

(2) That the pretended power of dispensing with laws or the execution of laws by regal authority, as it hath been assumed and exercised of late, is illegal.

(3) That the commission for erecting the late Court of Commissioners for Ecclesiastical Causes, and all other commissions and courts of like nature, are illegal and pernicious.

(4) That the levying money for or to the use of the Crown by pretence of prerogative, without grant of Parliament, for longer time, or in other manner than the same is or shall be granted, is illegal.

(5) That it is the right of the subjects to petition the king, and all commitments and prosecutions for such petitioning are illegal.

(6) That the raising or keeping of a standing army within the kingdom in time of peace, unless it be with consent of Parliament, is against law.

(7) That the subjects which are Protestants may have arms for their defence suitable to their conditions and as allowed by law.

(8) That election of members of Parliament ought to be free.

(9) That the freedom of speech and debates or proceedings in Parliament ought not to be impeached or questioned in any court or place out of Parliament.

(10) That excessive bail ought not to be required, nor excessive fines imposed, nor cruel and unusual punishments inflicted.

(11) That jurors ought to be duly impannelled and returned.

(12) That all grants and promises of fines and forfeitures of particular persons before conviction are illegal and void.

(13) And that for redress of all grievances, and for the amending, strengthening and preserving of the laws, Parliaments ought to be held frequently.[69]

The Scottish Parliament enacted the Claim of Right in 1689. Its contents followed those of the Bill of Rights, with certain modifications; for example, the distinction between the suspending

---

[68] Ibid, p 116.

[69] Cases on the Bill of Rights include: *Fitzgerald* v *Muldoon* [1976] 2 NZLR 615 (art 1); *Congreve* v *Home Office* [1976] QB 629 (art 4); *Williams* v *Home Office (No 2)* [1981] 1 All ER 1211 (art 10); and *R* v *Home Secretary, ex p Herbage (No 2)* [1987] QB 1077 (art 10). Art 7, sometimes cited by the gun lobby, had no effect on the Firearms (Amendment) Act 1997. Art 9 was amended by the Defamation Act 1996; see chs 9 A and 17 F. On the Bill of Rights, see Wicks, *The Evolution of a Constitution*, ch 1.

and dispensing powers was not made, but all proclamations asserting an absolute power to 'cass [quash], annul or disable laws' were declared illegal.[70] Many provisions of the Claim of Right are still in force within Scotland.

4 *The Act of Settlement.* The Act of Settlement 1700, enacted by the English Parliament, not only provided for the succession to the throne but also added important provisions complementary to the Bill of Rights, especially:

> That whosoever shall hereafter come to the possession of this Crown shall join in communion with the Church of England as by law established. . . .
>
> That no person who has an office or place of profit under the King or receives a pension from the Crown shall be capable of serving as a member of the House of Commons.
>
> That . . . judges' commissions be made quamdiu se bene gesserint [so long as they are of good behaviour], and their salaries ascertained and established, but upon the address of both Houses of Parliament it may be lawful to remove them.
>
> That no pardon under the great seal of England be pleadable to an impeachment by the Commons in Parliament.[71]

The Bill of Rights and the Act of Settlement marked the victory of Parliament over the claim of the Stuart kings to govern by the prerogative. There was, however, nothing in these statutes to secure the responsibility of the King's ministers to Parliament. That principle of parliamentary government developed in the 18th century and later, a product of constitutional practice rather than legislation.[72] This enabled the exercise by ministers of many prerogative powers of the Crown to survive into the 21st century.[73]

5 *Other statutes of constitutional importance.* Other statutes that form part of constitutional law include the Act of Union with Scotland 1707, the Parliament Acts 1911 and 1949, the Crown Proceedings Act 1947, the European Communities Act 1972 and the British Nationality Act 1981. Those enacted since 1997 include the Scotland Act 1998, the Government of Wales Act 1998, the Northern Ireland Act 1998, the Human Rights Act 1998, the House of Lords Act 1999, the Constitutional Reform Act 2005, the Constitutional Reform and Governance Act 2010, the Scotland Act 2016, the Wales Act 2017 and the European Union (Notification of Withdrawal) Act 2017. Any future Act making provision for the treatment of EU law after exiting the EU will be of fundamental constitutional importance.

If the United Kingdom had a written constitution, this would be likely to provide a special procedure for making amendments to the constitution. As it is, in two respects a distinction is sometimes drawn between constitutional and other legislation. First, the House of Commons may refer Bills of constitutional significance for detailed examination to a committee of the whole House rather than to a Public Bill committee,[74] but not all Bills with a constitutional content are treated in this way. Second, by the doctrine of implied repeal, a later Act prevails over an earlier Act which is inconsistent with the later Act; however, the courts are sometimes reluctant to hold that a statute of special significance has been repealed or amended by a later Act. In 2002, it was held, controversially, that 'constitutional' statutes (those that govern relations between citizen and state 'in some general, overarching manner' or affect the scope of fundamental constitutional rights) are unlike 'ordinary' statutes in that the former

---

[70] APS IX, 38.

[71] *Halsbury's Statutes*, vol 10 (1), p 126.

[72] Ch 5.

[73] Ch 10 D.

[74] See p 196. And R Hazell [2006] PL 247.

may not be impliedly repealed, but they may be repealed when the actual intention of a later Parliament is stated expressly.[75]

A different question is whether the electorate should be consulted by a national referendum when major constitutional changes are proposed. The practice of holding such a referendum has developed since 1973. A referendum was held in 1975 to confirm continued membership of the EU, and to confirm the desire of the majority to withdraw from the EU in 2016. Referendums were held on devolution to Scotland and Wales in 1979 (rejecting it) and 1997 (supporting it), as well as a further referendum in Wales in 2011 on increasing devolved powers (in favour). Northern Ireland has held referendums on whether to remain part of the United Kingdom in 1973 and whether to approve the Good Friday peace agreement, the basis of which was continued membership of the United Kingdom, in 1998. A referendum on the reform of the electoral system was held in 2011 as required by the coalition agreement between the Conservatives and Liberal Democrats, which rejected the introduction of the alternative vote system. In September 2014, a referendum was held in Scotland on whether Scotland should become an independent country. On that occasion, independence was rejected; but since the EU referendum result, there has been an increased desire on the part of many Scots to hold a further vote on independence. There is no general consensus as to when such referendums should be held. But if a future government wished to abolish the Scottish Parliament or the National Assembly for Wales, which were both established after referendums in those countries, a prior referendum is now required by statute.[76]

Case law

The other main source of legal rules is found in decisions of the superior courts, stated in authoritative form in the law reports. Under the doctrine of precedent, or '*stare decisis*' (i.e. the duty of courts to observe decided cases), these decisions are binding on inferior courts and may, according to the relative status of the courts in question, bind other superior courts.[77] Judge-made law takes two principal forms.

1 *The common law.* This consists of the rules and customs which have long been declared to be law by the judges in deciding cases before them. In reports of these cases are found authoritative expositions of the law relating to prerogatives of the Crown,[78] remedies of the subject against illegal acts by public authorities and officials, including habeas corpus,[79] which in English law protects individuals against unlawful detention. Such decisions established the principle that 'from its very earliest days', the common law 'set its face firmly against the use of torture'.[80]

Examples of judicial decisions are *Entick* v *Carrington*, which held that a Secretary of State had no power to issue general warrants for the arrest and search of those publishing seditious papers;[81] and, in modern times, *Burmah Oil Co* v *Lord Advocate*, which held that the Crown

---

[75] *Thoburn* v *Sunderland City Council* [2002] EWHC 195 (Admin), [2003] QB 151 (the metric measures case, concerning the status of the European Communities Act 1972). On implied repeal, see ch 3 C.

[76] See p 8 above. It is highly likely, at least politically, that a referendum would have been required even without the statutory promise of one.

[77] See Cross and Harris, *Precedent in English Law*.

[78] Ch 10 E.

[79] Ch 26 D.

[80] *A* v *Home Secretary (No 2)* [2005] UKHL 71, [2006] 2 AC 221 paras [11], [12] (Lord Bingham).

[81] (1765) 19 State Tr 1029. And see ch 4 A.

must compensate the owners of property taken in the exercise of prerogative powers,[82] *Conway* v *Rimmer*, which held that the courts had power to order the production as evidence of documents for which Crown privilege had been claimed,[83] and *M* v *Home Office*, holding that the Home Secretary had committed contempt of court in not obeying a judge's order to bring a deported Zairean teacher back to the United Kingdom.[84] Such decisions declare important rules of public law which often would not have been enacted by Parliament. In the absence of a written constitution, such decisions provide what have been called the legal foundations of British constitutionalism.[85] Even so, they are not binding for all time, since they may be set aside or amended by Parliament, even retrospectively.[86]

The final court of appeal formerly took the form of the 'Law Lords' sitting as a committee of the House of Lords, but in October 2009, these twelve full-time judges became Justices of the Supreme Court for the United Kingdom. As the final court of appeal, the Law Lords could in exceptional circumstances review and, if necessary, alter the law laid down by their earlier decisions,[87] and the position of the Supreme Court is the same. Judicial decisions are the basis for such principles as the legislative supremacy of Parliament and judicial review of executive action.[88] But even such fundamental principles may be affected by European law. When a case concerns EU law, the decision by a UK court may be referred to the Court of Justice at Luxembourg.[89] In cases concerning rights under the European Convention on Human Rights, the European Court of Human Rights at Strasbourg may consider whether the national decision conflicts with the Convention.[90]

2 Interpretation of statute law. As a general rule, the courts have no authority to rule on the validity of an Act of Parliament (although they may rule on the validity of subordinate legislation),[91] but they have the regular task of interpreting all manner of legislation where the meaning of an Act is disputed. Important issues of public law may arise from the interpretation of statutes. In a leading decision under the Human Rights Act 1998, the Law Lords held that a power conferred by Parliament in 2001 to detain foreigners suspected of involvement with terrorist acts infringed their right to liberty and could not be used to bring about their indefinite imprisonment without charge or trial; such imprisonment, said Lord Nicholls, 'is anathema in any country which observes the rule of law'.[92] Another decision concerned the power of the Environment Secretary, under an Act of 1985, to make regulations restricting increases in certain residential rents. He used this power to protect tenants against increases resulting from judicial decisions on the assessment of rents; but landlords claimed that the power could be used only as a measure against inflation. In upholding the regulations, the judges discussed their approach to deciding the meaning of the 1985 Act. Lord Bingham

---

[82] [1965] AC 75; ch 10 E.

[83] [1968] AC 910; ch 26 D.

[84] [1994] 1 AC 377; chs 13 C, 25 D.

[85] See Allan, *Law, Liberty and Justice*, chs 1, 4. Also S Sedley, in Richardson and Genn (eds), *Administrative Law and Government Action*, ch 2; and (1994) 110 LQR 270.

[86] The War Damage Act 1965 reversed the *Burmah Oil* decision.

[87] *Practice Statement (Judicial Precedent)* [1966] 1 WLR 1234. For review of a previous decision for due process reasons, see *R* v *Bow Street Magistrate, ex p Pinochet Ugarte (No 2)* [2000] 1 AC 119.

[88] Ch 3 and chs 24, 25.

[89] For the *Factortame* litigation, see ch 6 D.

[90] Ch 14 B.

[91] Ch 22.

[92] *A* v *Home Secretary* [2004] UKHL 56, [2005] 2 AC 68, [74].

said, 'the overriding aim . . . must always be to give effect to the intention of Parliament as expressed in the words used'.[93] And Lord Nicholls said:

> The task of the court is often said to be to ascertain the intention of Parliament expressed in the language under consideration. This is correct and may be helpful, so long as it is remembered that the 'intention of Parliament' is an objective concept, not subjective. The phrase is a short-hand reference to the intention which the court reasonably imputes to Parliament in respect of the language used. It is not the subjective intention of the minister or other persons who promoted the legislation. Nor is it the subjective intention of the draftsman, or of individual members or even of a majority of individual members of either House.[94]

In seeking the meaning of the words used by Parliament, the courts employ established principles of interpretation as useful guides and, if necessary, use internal aids (found in the rest of the Act) or external aids (for example, material outside the Act) to identify the mischief that the statute is intended to cure and the purpose of the legislation.

Since most powers of government are derived from statute, the judge-made law which results from interpretation of statutes is of great importance in administrative law. The principles (or presumptions) of statutory interpretation are seldom conclusive and sometimes point in opposite directions.[95] The task of the court in discovering the meaning of words used by Parliament always requires analysis of the text itself. But if the policy or purpose of a statute can be determined, it may be possible to give an interpretation consistent with that. There was formerly a rule that the courts could not look at Hansard (the record of debates in Parliament) to discover the meaning of legislation, although limited use might be made of documents such as reports of royal commissions and parliamentary committees as an aid to identifying the mischief which legislation was intended to remedy.[96] However, Hansard was used to discover the intention of Parliament in approving regulations which gave effect to a decision of the European Court of Justice.[97] And in 1992, the former rule against reading Hansard was changed: a court may now use Hansard as an aid to statutory construction where the legislation is ambiguous or obscure and the material relied on consists of clear statements made by a minister or other promoter of the Bill.[98]

Some presumptions of interpretation are of constitutional importance. Thus, many Acts do not bind central government, since the Crown is presumed not to be bound by legislation, unless this is expressly stated or necessarily implied.[99] It has often been presumed that Parliament does not intend to take away common law rights by implication, as distinct from express words. Thus, the courts have held that Parliament does not intend to take away the property of a subject without compensation,[100] or to deprive a subject of access to the courts,[101] and have interpreted penal statutes strictly in favour of the citizen: thus a statute creating a criminal offence will not in the absence of express words be held to be retrospective.[102] In recent decisions, the

---

[93] *R v Environment Secretary, ex p Spath Holme Ltd* [2001] 2 AC 349, 388.

[94] Ibid, 396.

[95] Marshall, *Constitutional Theory*, ch 4; Cross, *Statutory Interpretation*; Bennion, *Statutory Interpretation*.

[96] *Black-Clawson International Ltd v Papierwerke AG* [1975] AC 591; *Davis v Johnson* [1979] AC 264.

[97] *Pickstone v Freemans plc* [1989] AC 66.

[98] *Pepper v Hart* [1993] AC 593. On use of Hansard, see *R v Environment Secretary, ex p Spath Holme Ltd* (above); and *Wilson v First County Trust Ltd (No 2)* [2003] UKHL 40, [2004] 1 AC 816. Also Lord Steyn (2001) 21 OJLS 59 and ch 9.

[99] *Lord Advocate v Dumbarton DC* [1990] 2 AC 580; *R (Black) v Justice Secretary* [2017] UKSC 81; ch 10 D, 26 D.

[100] *Central Control Board v Cannon Brewery Co* [1919] AC 744, 752.

[101] *Chester v Bateson* [1920] 1 KB 829.

[102] *Waddington v Miah* [1974] 2 All ER 377.

courts have used these presumptions to develop the idea of common law constitutional rights, such as the right of access to a court, which may be abrogated but only by express words or necessary implication.[103] As Lord Hoffmann has said: 'The principle of legality means that Parliament must squarely confront what it is doing and accept the political cost. Fundamental rights cannot be overridden by general or ambiguous words.'[104]

It is in keeping with this approach that, under the Human Rights Act 1998, all legislation, whenever made, must, 'so far as it is possible to do so', be read and given effect in a way that is compatible with the rights protected by the European Convention on Human Rights. This duty on the courts (which turns on how the courts interpret the phrase 'so far as it is possible') may lead to an outcome far beyond any interpretation that would have been acceptable in the past, and the effect may be to amend the statute.[105]

British membership of the European Union, while it continues, directly affects the courts' traditional approaches to interpretation, since in most European countries methods of legislative drafting and rules of interpretation are different from those in Britain. Where it is necessary for a European treaty or regulation to be interpreted in a British court, a procedure for seeking a preliminary ruling enables the question of interpretation to be settled by the Court of Justice.[106] British courts must follow that court's practice by giving a purposive construction to domestic legislation intended to comply with EU directives.[107]

It is an essential principle of the rule of law that legislation should be interpreted by judicial bodies independent of the legislature which made the law.[108] While the courts must be able to act independently of the executive in interpreting legislation, their duty is to decide what Parliament must be taken to have intended; they are not free merely to decide what they believe may be in the public interest.[109]

The law and custom of Parliament

Legislation enacted by Parliament and decisions of the courts are sources of law with which every lawyer is familiar. The same cannot be said of the law and custom of Parliament. In earlier days, reference was often made to the 'High Court of Parliament'.[110] Although the notion of Parliament as a court is now obsolete,[111] each House has for centuries had certain privileges, including power over its own procedure. A striking illustration of this power is found in the rules of each House that determine the successive stages by which a Bill is considered by the House. Other rules of constitutional importance are contained in the standing orders of the two Houses, in resolutions of each House and in rulings by the Speaker of the Commons. The inherent authority of each House to control its own affairs is respected by the

---

[103] *R v Lord Chancellor, ex p Witham* [1998] QB 575. Also *R v Home Secretary, ex p Pierson* [1998] AC 539; and *R v Home Secretary, ex p Simms* [2000] 2 AC 115.

[104] *R v Home Secretary, ex p Simms*, at p 131.

[105] The leading case on interpretation under the Human Rights Act is *Ghaidan v Godin-Mendoza* [2004] UKHL 30, [2004] 2 AC 557; and see ch 14 C.

[106] Ch 6 A.

[107] *Litster v Forth Dry Dock and Engineering Co Ltd* [1990] 1 AC 546; *R (IDT Card Services Ireland Ltd) v HMRC* [2006] EWCA Civ 29, [2006] STC 1252 at [69]–[92] (Arden LJ).

[108] See: *R (Evans) v Attorney General* [2015] UKSC 21, [2015] AC 1787.

[109] *Duport Steels Ltd v Sirs* [1980] 1 All ER 529.

[110] Sir Edward Coke CJ, Co Inst I, 109b: Parliament is 'the highest and most honourable and absolute court of justice in England'. See too the effect of *Case of the Sheriff of Middlesex* (1840) 11 A & E 273.

[111] Although for a different view with relevance to sovereignty, see C J S Knight [2009] CLJ 361.

courts. Each House has now adopted a 'Code of Conduct' for its members. Under the codes, all members have to register their financial and other interests, and compliance with the codes is enforced by each House.[112] The Commons retains its ancient power to expel or suspend an MP who is in serious breach of the House's rules of conduct.

In addition to formal rules that govern parliamentary procedure, many informal practices and understandings are observed between the parties in the Commons, and between the front benches and the backbenchers. Such matters are not found in the House's standing orders. They resemble the customary practices and understandings (or 'conventions') outside Parliament that are examined in the next section of this chapter. For one party to depart from these practices could cause other parties to react adversely: this might lead to the withdrawal of cooperation between government and opposition parties (on such matters as pairing between absent MPs or timetabling of Bills), or eventually to changes in the rules of procedure.

C. Other rules and principles, including constitutional conventions

Many rules of constitutional behaviour which are observed by the Queen, ministers, members of Parliament, judges and civil servants are contained neither in Acts nor in judicial decisions. Disputes which arise from these rules rarely lead to action in the courts, and judicial sanctions are not applicable if the rules are broken. The Supreme Court in the *Miller* case explained the legal limits on constitutional conventions as follows:

> Judges therefore are neither the parents nor the guardians of political conventions; they are merely observers. As such, they can recognise the operation of a political convention in the context of deciding a legal question (as in the Crossman diaries case . . .), but they cannot give legal rulings on its operation or scope, because those matters are determined within the political world. As Professor Colin Munro has stated, 'the validity of conventions cannot be the subject of proceedings in a court of law'.[113]

These rules have been described in many ways, for instance as the 'unwritten maxims' of the constitution,[114] rules for ensuring political accountability[115] and as 'a whole system of political morality, a whole code of precepts for the guidance of public men'.[116] Dicey referred to them as:

> conventions, understandings, habits or practices which, though they may regulate the conduct of the several members of the sovereign power . . . are not in reality laws at all since they are not enforced by the courts.[117]

Under Dicey's influence, the most common term for them is constitutional convention, which has a meaning quite different from a convention in international law (which refers to a treaty between states).

The notion of conventional conduct includes a strong element of what is customarily expected, in the sense of ordinary or regular behaviour. In social terms, unconventional conduct departs from accepted patterns of behaviour, rather than being in breach of any rule as to how we should

---

112 Ch 9 B.

113 *R (Miller) v Secretary of State for Exiting the EU* [2017] UKSC 5, [2017] 2 WLR 583 at [146]. The quote from Professor Munro is cited from (1975) 91 LQR 218, 228.

114 Mill, *Representative Government*, ch 5.

115 Marshall, *Constitutional Conventions: The Rules and Forms of Political Accountability*.

116 Freeman, *Growth of the English Constitution*, p 109, quoted in Dicey, p 418. Cf O Hood Phillips (1966) 29 MLR 137.

117 Dicey, *Law of the Constitution*, p 24.

behave. In considering constitutional conventions, we will find a continuing tension (that may cause much uncertainty in practice) between regarding conventions as (*a*) *descriptive* statements of constitutional practice, based on knowledge and observation of what actually happens; or as (*b*) *prescriptive* statements of what ought to happen, based in part on observation but also on constitutional principle: normative expressions of constitutional values.[118] We return later to the choice between these two approaches;[119] but at present we will assume that conventions are concerned with matters of obligation, and we will explore the nature of that obligation. First, examples will be given of conventional rules that affect constitutional behaviour, and in each case relevant legal rules will be mentioned.

Conventional rules of the constitution: some examples

1 It is a rule of common law that the royal assent must be given before a Bill which has been approved by both Houses of Parliament can become an Act of Parliament.[120] The manner in which the royal assent may be given is now regulated by statute, and in certain circumstances the royal assent may be signified by others on behalf of the Queen.[121] These rules deal with a vital matter of legal form. But a more important conventional rule is that the royal assent is granted by the Queen on the advice of her ministers. Where a Bill has been passed by both Houses of Parliament, the royal assent is given as a matter of course. The monarch's legal power to refuse assent was last exercised by Queen Anne in 1708, when (apparently with the approval of her ministers and without objection by Parliament) assent was refused to the Scottish Militia Bill.[122] In the Irish crisis of 1912–14, the Unionists suggested to George V that he should withhold assent from the Bill to give home rule to Ireland. The Liberal Prime Minister, Asquith, advised the King against this and the royal assent was granted.[123] While the Queen may not of her own initiative refuse the royal assent, the position might be different if ministers advised her to do so, although this advice would have to be defended in Parliament and, depending on the circumstances, could be highly controversial.[124]

2 In law the Queen has unlimited power to appoint whom she pleases to be her ministers. Statutes provide for the payment of salaries to ministers and limit the number of appointments which may be made from the House of Commons.[125] There is no rule of law which prevents the monarch appointing to ministerial office a person who is outside Parliament. But all such appointments are made on the advice of the Prime Minister, and the principle of ministerial responsibility[126] requires that a minister should belong to one or other House of Parliament. If a non-member is appointed a minister, the non-member will receive a life peerage: the earlier practice of expecting such a person to enter the Commons at an early by-election (last seen in 1965) has lapsed, since no government today willingly causes a by-election to be held in one of its own seats.

---

[118] A McHarg (2008) 71 MLR 853, 857.

[119] Marshall (above) describes this as the difference between positive morality and critical morality: pp 11–2. An example of the former approach would: Wheare, *Modern Constitutions*. An example of the latter approach would be: Jennings, *The Law and the Constitution*.

[120] Ch 3 C, 8 D.

[121] Royal Assent Act 1967, Regency Acts 1937–53. And see R Brazier (2013) 129 LQR 184 and G J Wheeler (2016) 132 LQR 495.

[122] Hearn, *The Government of England*, p 61.

[123] Jennings, *Cabinet Government*, pp 395–400. Cf Brazier, *Constitutional Practice*, pp 193–6.

[124] The highly acclaimed 2014 play by Mike Bartlett, *Charles III*, has as its premise King Charles III exercising his refusal of assent to a Bill limiting press freedom, with significant consequences.

[125] Ch 7 C.

[126] Ch 5.

3 Although the conduct of a general election is governed by detailed statutory rules,[127] no legal rule regulates the conduct of the Prime Minister when the result of the election is known. But by a long-standing conventional rule, the government must have the confidence of a majority in the Commons. When it is clear from election results that the Prime Minister who decided to call the election has been defeated and another party has won, the Prime Minister must resign immediately without waiting for the new Parliament to meet.[128] Where the result of the election gives no party an overall majority in the Commons, the Prime Minister may continue in office for so long as is necessary to discover whether that person can govern with the support of other parties on a formal or informal basis, as happened in June 2017; or, as happened in May 2010, a coalition may be formed that will command a majority in the Commons.

4 High Court judges in England and Wales hold their offices by statute during good behaviour, subject to a power of removal by the Queen on an address presented to her by both Houses; by statute they are disqualified from membership of the Commons.[129] Before appointment as a judge, a lawyer may have been active in party politics (and, although rarely today, may have been an MP before being appointed a judge); but if so, a conventional rule requires the judge to sever all links with the party which the judge had formerly supported. This convention is now incorporated in the Guide to Judicial Conduct, which states it to be a specific application of the principle that judges must avoid extra-judicial activities that may give rise to 'a reasonable apprehension of bias'.[130]

5 Under the Scotland Act 1998 as amended, the Scottish Parliament has power to legislate on many devolved matters, but the Westminster Parliament retains, in s 28(7), full power to legislate for Scotland. By what is known as the 'Sewel convention', that is based on an agreement between the government in London and the Scottish Executive, the Westminster Parliament will not normally legislate for Scotland on devolved matters except with the agreement of the Scottish Parliament; that agreement is given by a 'legislative consent motion' adopted by the Scottish Parliament (although the convention itself does not provide how consent is to be signified).[131] By s 2 of the Scotland Act 2016, s 28 was amended to include a statutory form of the Sewel convention; s 107 of the Government of Wales Act 2006 was amended by the Wales Act 2017, s 2, to the same effect.

6 The legal opinions which the Law Officers of the Crown (who include the Attorney General and the Solicitor General) give to the government are in law confidential and are protected by legal privilege from being produced as evidence in court proceedings. They may, however, be published by the government or quoted from in Parliament if (as rarely happens) a minister considers it expedient that the Commons should be told of their contents.[132] During the Westland affair in 1986, the Secretary of State for Trade and Industry (Mr Brittan) authorised civil servants to leak to the press extracts from a confidential letter to him from the Solicitor General, without first seeking the latter's consent. 'Cover' but not approval for the leak was sought from the Prime Minister's Office. Under a storm of criticism, Mr Brittan resigned. This resignation reinforced the authority of the rule which the Law Officers sought to defend.[133] The code of conduct for ministers now states: 'The fact that the Law Officers have

---

[127] Ch 7 D.

[128] Ch 10 B.

[129] Ch 7 G, 13 B.

[130] See *Guide to Judicial Conduct* (revised version, 2008), para 3.3.

[131] See HL Deb, 21 July 1998, col 791; Cm 4444 (1999), para 13. Also ch 2 B.

[132] Edwards, *The Law Officers of the Crown*, pp 256–61. See too the discussion in *Savic v Information Commissioner and Attorney General's Office* [2016] UKUT 534 (AAC).

[133] See Linklater and Leigh, *Not Without Honour*, ch 11; and G Marshall [1986] PL 184.

advised or have not advised and the content of their advice must not be disclosed outside Government without their authority'.[134] In a very controversial decision, the Blair government at first refused to publish an opinion given by the Attorney General on 7 March 2003, regarding the legality of an invasion of Iraq by American and British forces. The Attorney General published a brief summary of his opinion a few days later, but the full opinion was eventually published only after extensive extracts had been leaked to the press.[135] In September 2015, Prime Minister Cameron took the unusual step of departing from the convention by confirming to the House of Commons that the Attorney General had provided legal advice supporting a lethal strike from an unmanned aerial vehicle (or drone) on a British national in Syria, believed to have been a member of Daesh and planning terror attacks on the United Kingdom. The confirmation was not a breach of the convention because it had been authorised by the Attorney.[136]

Many more examples of conventional rules could be given.[137] Such rules develop under every system of government, whether a written constitution exists or not. It is through such rules and practices that the system of government in Britain has developed and continues to evolve. With such a diversity of subject matter, what general characteristics, if any, do these rules possess?

General characteristics[138]

The starting point for whether or not a convention exists is usually the tripartite test proposed by Sir Ivor Jennings: 'first, what are the precedents; secondly, did the actors in the precedents believe that they were bound by a rule; and thirdly, is there a reason for the rule?'[139] This approach is, of course, contested; certainly all of the stages of the test contain important ambiguities or disguise value judgments.[140] It is highly unlikely that all conventions require all limbs of the test to be satisfied, at least not in the same way or to the same extent: the Sewel convention noted above, for example, came into being effectively immediately without the need for historic precedent.[141] Other long-established conventional rules have great authority and are universally known. Many have developed out of a desire to avoid the formality, explicitness and publicity associated with changes in the law. The role of the monarch in the conduct of government has almost disappeared since the 18th century without a series of statutes removing one royal power after another. In the same way, powers have been acquired by the Prime Minister by operation of convention rather than as the result of legislation. Conventional rules may be used for discreetly managing the internal relationships of government while the outward legal form is left intact.

The informality of such rules is often accentuated by the fact that the rules themselves are not formulated in writing, but this is not always the case. As we have seen, the rule that judges should not undertake political activities is now in a written form. In 2011, the government

---

[134] *Ministerial Code* (2016), para 2.13; and see ch 5 C and ch 11 C.

[135] The documents are in Sands, *Lawless World*, Apps X, XI.

[136] HC Deb, 7 September 2015, cols 25–7. See too: *Corderoy v Information Commissioner and Attorney General's Office* [2017] UKUT 495 (AAC)

[137] For examples applicable to the legislative process, such as the Salisbury–Addison convention, see ch 8 D.

[138] A full discussion by the Supreme Court of Canada is in *Reference re Amendment of the Constitution of Canada* (1982) 125 DLR (3d) 1. See also C R Munro (1975) 91 LQR 218; Marshall (above); R Brazier (1992) 43 NILQ 262; G Wilson's postscript to Nolan and Sedley, *The Making and Remaking of the British Constitution*, pp 95–133; and D Feldman in Qvortrup (ed.), *The British Constitution: Continuity and Change*, ch 6.

[139] Jennings, *The Law and the Constitution*, pp 119–20.

[140] For just one example of critical engagement with Jennings, see Jaconelli in Qvortrup (ed.), *The British Constitution: Continuity and Change*, ch 7.

[141] Although there is an analogy with the Westminster Parliament not normally legislating for Commonwealth countries except at their request or with their consent.

issued *The Cabinet Manual*, which derived from a similar document prepared previously in New Zealand, as 'a guide to laws, customs and rules on the operation of government'.[142] The booklet covers all the machinery of central government in an informative way, but it is essentially descriptive; it does not claim any special authority (it has not been approved by Parliament), and the government reserves the right to change the practices that are described. In reality, some of the practices are too well-established to be changed (for instance, the rule that the Queen's speech in opening a session of Parliament is written by the government).

The development of unwritten rules is often an evolutionary process that occurs before clear rules of conduct emerge. In retrospect, we can identify when (for instance) a member of the House of Lords last held office as Prime Minister (1902). But because such an occurrence is impossible today, we cannot conclude that this has always been the case since 1902. At any given time, it may be difficult to tell whether practice on a certain matter has hardened into a rule, particularly when the practice is negative in character. Before the Constitutional Reform Act 2005, which took away the judicial role of the Lord Chancellor, there was uncertainty over the extent to which the Lord Chancellor, as a government minister, might properly sit as a judge to decide appeals in the House of Lords.[143]

As with all forms of rules, disputes may arise about the meaning and effect of conventional rules, particularly when they have no definitive written form. The enforcement of many conventions depends essentially on the force of public and political opinion. If many legal rules have an 'open texture',[144] how much more 'open' will be the texture of non-legal rules where there is no definite procedure for resolving disputes about their existence and content. The vaguer the convention – perhaps better expressed as a principle than a rule – the harder it will be to show consensus as to its boundaries, unless there is a single authoritative figure who can enforce it (such as the Prime Minister with the Ministerial Code).

In the past, accounts of constitutional conventions often concentrated on the rules by which powers vested in the monarch came to be exercised by ministers of the Crown. Dicey considered that conventions were 'rules intended to regulate the exercise of the whole of the remaining discretionary powers of the Crown'.[145] It is more accurate to say that conventional rules regulate the conduct of all those holding public office. Different roles in government are played by the monarch, ministers, judges, civil servants and so on. Anyone who would play one of these roles must observe the restraints which apply to that office. It is the roots of the convention in constitutional tradition (either based upon precedent or upon principle or values) which form the critical guide to the formation of, continuity and compliance with constitutional conventions.

Why are conventional rules observed?

Dicey, writing as a lawyer in a period dominated by Austinian jurisprudence according to which laws were observed because they could be enforced by the coercive power of the state, said:

> the sanction which constrains the boldest political adventurer to obey the fundamental principles of the constitution and the conventions in which these principles are expressed, is the fact that the breach of these principles and of these conventions will almost immediately bring the offender into conflict with the courts and the law of the land.[146]

---

[142] Cabinet Office, 2011.
[143] As he did in *Boddington v British Transport Police* [1999] 2 AC 143.
[144] See Hart, *The Concept of Law*, pp 121–32.
[145] Dicey, p 426.
[146] Dicey, pp 445–6.

To support this view, Dicey argued that Parliament meets at least once a year because the government would be compelled to act unlawfully if this did not happen. This argument was shown to be much weaker than Dicey had supposed.[147] In any event, the rule which the supposed sanction supports is antiquated. Today, Parliament is in session at Westminster for about 34 weeks in the year, interspersed with holidays, the summer recess and the party conferences. During these weeks, there is a customary pattern of work to be done, for which purpose it is expected that Parliament will meet. The Provisional Collection of Taxes Act 1968[148] imposes certain constraints upon the timetable of Parliament, but this in itself does not explain why Parliament meets regularly throughout the year.

It is nearer the mark to say, as did Sir Ivor Jennings, that conventions are observed because of the political difficulties which arise if they are not.[149] As these rules regulate the conduct of those holding public office, possibly the most acute political difficulty for such a person is to be forced out of office. In a moment of personal crisis, a minister may choose to resign rather than wait to be dismissed by the Prime Minister. However, an explanation merely in terms of political difficulties is inadequate, since not every event which gives rise to political difficulties (for example, an unpopular Bill) is a breach of a conventional rule. Nor are conventions always concerned with continued holding of office: the Sewel convention, for example, is not likely to result in resignations were it to be breached, even if there were party political difficulties. The Supreme Court of Canada stated that the main purpose of conventions is to ensure that the legal framework of the constitution is operated in accordance with the prevailing constitutional values of the period.[150] On this basis, conventions are observed both for the positive reason that they express prevailing constitutional values and for the negative reason of avoiding the difficulties that may follow from 'unconstitutional' conduct.

Formulating rules of good government

It is sometimes said that, as conventions derive neither from legislation nor from decisions of the courts, they are essentially uncertain and are not backed up by any obligation. Indeed, so long as the obligations owed by ministers to Parliament or to the Prime Minister rested on shared understandings of what the political game required, those understandings might change, and their content could be disputed.

Today, in many areas of government, particularly regarding standards of integrity in public life, written codes of behaviour exist – for the civil service, for ministers, for members of Parliament and for public authorities. These codes may not be authorised by legislation or enforced by the courts, but it would be wrong to claim that the codes lack any authority. An important rule in the *Ministerial Code*[151] is that ministers should give accurate and truthful information to Parliament, and that ministers who knowingly mislead Parliament will be expected to offer their resignation to the Prime Minister. It is up to each House to ensure that this rule is observed.[152] A minister in breach of the *Ministerial Code* knows that a refusal to resign may lead to a dismissal. Under the same code, ministers must 'ensure that no conflict arises, or appears to rise, between their public duties and their private interests, financial or otherwise'. Enforcement of this duty is essentially for the Prime Minister, acting in the light of

---

[147] See Jennings, *The Law and the Constitution*, pp 128–9.

[148] Ch 8 B.

[149] *The Law and the Constitution*, p 134. See J Jaconelli (1999) 19 LS 24 and [2005] CLJ 149.

[150] *Reference re Amendment of the Constitution of Canada* (1982) 125 DLR (3d) 1, 84; *Miller* (above), at [141]–[143] citing the Supreme Court of Canada. See, too, Feldman in Qvortrup, *The British Constitution*, ch 6.

[151] See ch 11 C. N W Barber (2009) 125 LQR 294, argues persuasively that the *Ministerial Code* is an instance of how some conventional rules 'are in the process of crystallisation' and acquire greater formality.

[152] The courts may not question the truth of statements in Parliament: Article 9, Bill of Rights; ch 9 A.

public and parliamentary opinion. Other rules of 'good government' that may have a potentially similar effect are the rules of public accounting,[153] and the principles of good administration upheld by the Parliamentary Ombudsman.[154] And there is now a statutory basis for the operation of disciplinary rules and procedures affecting various levels of judges.[155]

What we can identify here is an evolving regulatory process. The starting point is power to direct or oversee an organ of government: the need to regulate the conduct of its members leads in time to the emergence of principles, guidance as to best practice, and ultimately a code of rules. The outcome of this process may be little different in legal terms from a code of practice authorised by statute.[156]

The meaning of 'unconstitutional'

Where a written constitution ranks as fundamental law, acts which conflict with the constitution may be held unconstitutional and thus illegal. In the United Kingdom, the term 'unconstitutional' has no defined content. For Freeman, writing in the 19th century, unconstitutional conduct was conduct contrary to 'the undoubted principles of the unwritten but universally accepted constitution'.[157] Where conduct breaches a written constitution, 'unconstitutional' is likely to mean 'unlawful'; where it breaches unwritten principles of government, the term may mean simply 'wrong' or 'unwise'. The two senses of 'unconstitutional' were illustrated in the Canadian controversy of 1981–2, when the Supreme Court of Canada dealt separately with the issues of whether it would be (*a*) illegal and (*b*) in breach of convention for the Federal Parliament to adopt resolutions requesting amendments to the constitution which were opposed by eight of the ten provinces.[158] On the first question, the court held (by seven to two) that such action would not be illegal, but on the second question, it held (by six to three) that it would be in breach of convention.

While conduct may be unconstitutional without being illegal, illegal acts are likely to be unconstitutional. British ministers who instigated or covered up criminal offences for political ends would be departing from the standards of behaviour recognised by public opinion, as well as being in breach of criminal law. There is an overriding obligation on government to conduct its affairs according to law. In relation to executive decisions, 'unconstitutional' implies that a decision is not merely incorrect in law but also contrary to fundamental principle, for example where a policy of the Inland Revenue involved 'taxation by self asserted administrative discretion and not by law'.[159] It is in this sense that exemplary damages may in exceptional cases be awarded in the law of tort when public authorities or officials commit wrongful acts that are 'oppressive, arbitrary or unconstitutional'.[160]

However, it may not be easy to determine whether the boundary between constitutional and unconstitutional conduct has been crossed. The political parties may take conflicting views of the propriety of the acts of a government. Unpopular proposals for new legislation are not in themselves unconstitutional, but a Bill which sought to destroy essential features of the electoral system or to give the Cabinet power to overrule decisions of the courts could rightly be described as unconstitutional.

---

[153] See *R* v *Foreign Secretary, ex p World Development Movement Ltd* [1995] 1 All ER 611.

[154] See ch 23 D.

[155] Constitutional Reform Act 2005, ss 108–21.

[156] The Civil Service Code is now issued under statute, not under the prerogative. See ch 11 D.

[157] Freeman, *The Growth of the English Constitution*, p 112.

[158] Note 150 above.

[159] *Vestey* v *Inland Revenue Commissioners* [1980] AC 1148, 1173.

[160] *Rookes* v *Barnard* [1964] AC 1129; *Kuddus* v *Chief Constable of Leicestershire* [2001] UKHL 29, [2002] 2 AC 122.

Another difficulty in determining what is constitutional in a given situation is that there may be no relevant precedent. When in 1932 the Cabinet of the National government agreed to differ on a major issue of economic policy, an attack on the government for unconstitutional conduct was met by the rejoinder:

> Who can say what is constitutional in the conduct of a National Government? It is a precedent, an experiment, a new practice, to meet a new emergency, a new condition of things.[161]

The existence of Coalition government between 2010 and 2015 enabled Conservative and Liberal Democrat ministers to disagree openly about the government's policies, in defiance of what would have been the ordinary approach to the convention on collective Cabinet responsibility. Within a single-party Cabinet, such open disagreements would be seriously damaging to its authority and would not be acceptable, but they could not be excluded so long as the partners to the coalition wished to retain their separate identities. The convention itself proved flexible enough to adapt to the political circumstances, reverting to its prior form upon the resumption of one-party government in 2015.

Consequences of a breach of convention

Various consequences may follow the breach of conventional rules. Loss of office or departure from public life is the severest consequence, as when a minister is forced to resign because of an open disagreement with stated government policy. The force of public opinion may compel the offender to acknowledge his or her error. In these instances, the outcome reinforces the established rule. A less serious consequence would be a warning not to act similarly in the future, given by someone in a position to enforce the rule. If no adverse consequences follow, the matter becomes more open. It may be expedient that, for instance, the Prime Minister should turn a blind eye to acts of colleagues that breach a rule for ministers: but if such acts are repeatedly condoned, it must be asked whether the rule has been modified or even abandoned.

As constitutional rules often give rise to reciprocal obligations, one consequence of a breach may be to release another office-holder from the normal constraints that would apply. When Ian Smith's Cabinet in 1965 unilaterally and unlawfully declared Rhodesia's independence, the immediate response of the UK government, conveyed through the Governor-General of Rhodesia, was to dismiss the entire Cabinet. This dismissal proved purely nominal. More significantly, the Southern Rhodesia Act 1965 was passed at Westminster to give the British government power to legislate for the domestic affairs of Rhodesia, overriding the previous convention that Westminster would not exercise its sovereignty in such matters except with the agreement of the Rhodesian government.[162]

Another consequence may be the passing of legislation to avoid a similar breach in the future. When, in 1909, the Lords rejected the Liberal government's Finance Bill, the crisis was resolved only by the Parliament Act 1911, which removed the power of the Lords to veto or delay money Bills. The 1911 Act contained other provisions intended to place the Lords–Commons relationship on a new footing, and these provisions led in turn to new conventions regarding the use by the House of Lords of its residual powers.[163] We will note in the next section what a Westminster committee said in 2006 about the possibility of 'codifying' these conventions.

----

[161] HC Deb, 8 February 1932, col 535 (Mr Baldwin).

[162] Cf *Madzimbamuto* v *Lardner-Burke* [1969] AC 645, 723. The Privy Council in that case affirmed that the convention was of no legal relevance to determining the validity of the competing legislative acts issued from Rhodesia and from Westminster.

[163] Ch 8 D.

Should all conventional rules be enacted as law?

In theory, all conventional rules of the constitution could be enacted by Parliament. Written constitutions in the Commonwealth have adopted various means of incorporating conventions: express enactment of the main rules, wholesale adoption by reference to practice in the United Kingdom and so on.[164]

If a written constitution were to be drafted for the United Kingdom, difficult decisions on these matters would have to be made. It would, for example, be far from easy to provide for every situation in which the appointment of a new Prime Minister might be required. Merely to declare that ministers are accountable to Parliament for their decisions would not achieve very much if it were left to Parliament to decide how to enforce that accountability. And to make ministerial responsibility enforceable by the courts would be to change its character entirely.[165]

There is little to be said for attempting to prepare a single document that would include *all* informal constitutional rules: this would be a huge task, and it might freeze evolving political practice at an arbitrary moment. But it may be useful to bring together rules on a defined subject matter, like the *Ministerial Code*. And a salutary contribution to promoting the health of democracy was made by the Nolan Committee in 1995,[166] which declared broad standards of integrity and honesty that should be observed in public life, and which led to more detailed rules of conduct being applied to many areas of government.

The development of new constitutional rules can be achieved without the formality and precision associated with legislation. Thus, it is now accepted that Parliament should give its approval before a government under the prerogative commits the armed forces to a new military policy abroad, but governments have resisted the argument that this should become a statutory requirement.[167]

In 2006, a joint committee of both Houses examined the conventions relating to the role of the House of Lords in the process of legislation, its remit being to 'consider the practicality of codifying the key conventions' in this highly political area. The committee flatly rejected the idea of codification, declaring that since conventions 'by their very nature, are unenforceable . . . codifying conventions is a contradiction in terms. It would raise issues of definition, reduce flexibility, and inhibit the capacity to evolve. It might create a need for adjudication . . .'.[168] However, despite rejecting 'codification', the committee stated that it would be useful for the House of Lords to adopt resolutions that would clarify the approach of the House to Bills that the government had promised in its election manifesto and also the need for the House to deal with government business 'in a reasonable time'.

In a democratic state that recognises executive accountability to Parliament, constitutional obligations exist that are based neither on legislation nor on decisions of the courts. Legal rules, whether stemming from the judges or from Parliament, may continue in force long after the original reasons for them are forgotten. The relative informality of many constitutional

---

[164] De Smith, *The New Commonwealth and its Constitutions*, pp 78–87. For an Australian exercise in restating the conventions, see C Sampford and D Wood [1987] PL 231.

[165] In 1996, Sir Richard Scott said that if ministers did not accept the obligations of accountability, a statutory duty requiring them to keep Parliament informed should be enacted and enforced by the courts: [1996] PL 410, 426. And see ch 5.

[166] Cm 2850-I, 1995.

[167] See ch 10 D. Also HL Constitution Committee, *Constitutional Arrangements for the Use of Armed Force* (HL Paper 46, 2013–14). When the Commons debated military deployment in Syria, the government motion proposing deployment was defeated by 285 to 272. HC Debs, 29 August 2013. The Prime Minister confirmed that he would abide by the vote, and the government did so until it obtained Commons authorisation in December 2015.

[168] Joint Committee on Conventions, *Conventions of the UK Parliament*, HL Paper 265-1, HC 1212-1, para 279. Adjudication need not, of course, necessarily be by a court.

rules makes for greater flexibility as circumstances change.[169] This does not mean that so long as the original circumstances continue, there is no rule or no obligation. The abdication of Edward VIII in 1936 and the reasons for it have had a continuing influence on later monarchs and their advisers. So, too, the process by which Conservative MPs caused Mrs Thatcher to resign as Prime Minister has implications for later Prime Ministers, however strong their majority in the Commons.

One lesson from previous events is that short-term political expediency may be a temptation that an experienced government ought to resist, and that constitutional principle may provide more reliable guidance. As Freeman wrote in 1872:

> Political men may debate whether such and such a course is or is not constitutional, just as lawyers may debate whether such a course is not legal. But the very form of the debate implies that there is a Constitution to be observed, just as in the other case it implies that there is a law to be observed.[170]

The motives for human conduct are usually mixed. If we seek to understand the conduct of a monarch, a politician or a judge, we may discover both enlightened self-interest and a strong perception of constitutional obligation. If that perception is shared by others in a similar position, as well as by informed commentators, it is difficult to explain this without reference to the perceived obligation. The fact that conventional rules may change without formal amendment does not mean that they are irrelevant to political behaviour.

The attitude of the courts

If, when a rule has been broken, a remedy is available in the courts for securing relief or penalising the wrongdoer, this indicates that the rule has the quality of law. Where an informal rule has been broken, no direct remedy is available in the courts. Often the citizen's only recourse will be political action – a complaint to an MP, a letter to the press, or a public demonstration. In view of the context of most conventions, the stress on political or parliamentary remedies is appropriate. Moreover, many conventions, for example those relating to the Cabinet, do not affect an individual closely enough for a judicial remedy to be justified.

The discussion so far has assumed that conventions are not capable of being enforced through due process of law. That assumption has been authoritatively affirmed by the Supreme Court in *Miller*, in which it was argued that to commence the process of withdrawal from the EU without statutory authority would be a breach of Sewel convention, because the legislative competences of the devolved administrations and legislatures would inevitably change as a result. The Court unanimously held that the 'operation or scope' of a convention, and even its interpretation, was a matter for the 'political world' only and not for the courts.[171] The Court expressly confirmed that even the inclusion of the Sewel convention within the Scotland Act itself did not mean that it was thereby rendered a justiciable issue; Parliament was simply recognising and entrenching the political convention as a convention, and not attempting to alter its status.[172] The Supreme Court drew further support from the particular context and wording of the convention itself; it concerned actions of Parliament, and so

---

[169] On the distinction between law and convention, see Jennings, *Law and the Constitution*, p 132; Mitchell, *Constitutional Law*, pp 34–8; Marshall, *Constitutional Theory*, pp 7–12. Also note 138 above.

[170] *The Growth of the English Constitution*, p 112; cf Loughlin, *Public Law and Political Theory*, p 53.

[171] *R (Miller)* v *Secretary of State for Exiting the EU* [2017] UKSC 5, [2017] 2 WLR 583 at [146], [148]. The Court affirmed the previous authority to this effect from the Privy Council: *Madzimbamuto* v *Lardner-Burke* [1969] AC 645, 723 (Lord Reid).

[172] *Miller* at [148]–[149]. (At the time, the Wales Act 2017 had not been passed so as to render the same effect in Wales.)

enforcing the convention would have trespassed into territory forbidden by article 9 of the Bill of Rights, and the language of 'it is recognised' and 'will not normally' did not indicate a legal norm capable of judicial enforcement.[173] The reasoning is orthodox, if brief, and an unprecedented unanimous decision from a Supreme Court of eleven Justices is not likely to be departed from. Conventions remain firmly affixed to the political rather than the legal constitution.

It may, however, be necessary for a court to take into account the existence of a conventional rule in making its decision on a legal dispute. This is likely to happen in administrative law, where the courts take judicial notice of the fact that civil servants take decisions in the name of ministers and that ministers may be called to account by Parliament for the decisions. But the courts are aware that such accountability may not provide an effective remedy for the individual.[174]

The Crossman diaries case, in which the Attorney General tried to prevent a newspaper publishing the diaries of a former Cabinet minister, is an outstanding illustration of the interrelation of legal and non-legal rules. In this case, an attempt was made by the Attorney General to prevent the breach of a conventional rule and to establish the existence of a legal obligation. The court held that former Cabinet ministers could be restrained by injunction from publishing confidential information which came to them as ministers: there was a legal duty to respect that confidentiality, and such a ban might be justified in the public interest (for instance, on grounds of national security) and to maintain the secrecy of current Cabinet discussions.[175] But the court did not thereby enforce the entire convention of collective responsibility, and the diaries were allowed to be published; the convention was thus no more than one material factor in establishing the limits of the legal doctrine of confidence. In the different context of the Canadian constitution, by a procedure which permits Canadian courts to give wide-ranging advisory opinions, the Supreme Court of Canada in 1981 gave an opinion on the existence of conventions governing the process of constitutional amendment.[176]

Nonetheless, developments in public law have broadened the scope for judicial decisions about the observance of conventions by public authorities. The GCHQ case concerned a decision by the Prime Minister (Mrs Thatcher) that was imposed on the civil servants without prior consultation; on the evidence, there was an invariable practice by government of consulting with civil service unions before changing conditions of employment.[177] If this practice had been viewed merely as a constitutional convention, the unions would have had no enforceable rights. But the House of Lords held that, as a matter of public law, the unions had a 'legitimate expectation' of being consulted that would have been protected,[178] had this not been overridden by national security considerations. As we have seen, many forms of ministerial conduct that formerly rested on unwritten rules are now contained in the *Ministerial Code*. Should someone be adversely affected by the breach of a minister's duties under the Code, an argument based on legitimate expectations might succeed that would have been certain to fail if phrased in terms of breach of a constitutional convention.

Legal and constitutional literature

In English law, no legal textbook has inherent authority as a source of law: the authority of the most eminent text is confined to the extent to which a court considers that it accurately reproduces the law enacted by the legislature or decided by earlier courts. Where a statute has not yet been judicially interpreted, or where no court has pronounced on a matter of common law, the opinions of textbook writers and academic authors may be of great value when a case arises

---

[173] *Miller* at [145], [148].
[174] *Carltona Ltd v Commissioners of Works* [1943] 2 All ER 560.
[175] *A-G v Jonathan Cape Ltd* [1976] QB 752; ch 11 B.
[176] Note 138 above. Cf *Adegbenro v Akintola* [1963] AC 614.
[177] *CCSU v Minister for the Civil Service* [1985] AC 374.
[178] See ch 24 B.

for decision.[179] Such writing is also of value when questions of constitutional principle have to be decided. Dicey's *Law of the Constitution* has profoundly influenced many aspects of constitutional law since its publication in 1885. In recent decades, the development of administrative law has owed much to the work of the late Professors Stanley de Smith and Sir William Wade.

In Scots law, the position is different as regards the past. A series of eminent legal authors between the mid-17th and early 19th centuries, including Stair, Erskine and Hume, are known as the institutional writers. Their work expounded the private law and criminal law of Scotland in a systematic manner derived from the institutional writers of Roman law: in the absence of other authority, a statement in their works may be taken as settling the law.[180] The approach of the Scottish legal system was seen in *Burmah Oil Co* v *Lord Advocate*,[181] relating to the Crown's prerogative: the case having reached the House of Lords on appeal from Scotland, counsel and judges referred extensively to the civilian writers of earlier centuries, in a manner untypical of the English common law.

Legal writers on the constitution are handicapped by the unreality of many of the terms which they must sometimes employ.[182] Statements about the prerogative powers of the Crown may seem to be conferring despotic powers upon the monarch, until it is realised that they concern powers of government exercised by ministers and civil servants.

In some areas of the constitution, books such as Jennings's *Cabinet Government*, Mackintosh's *The British Cabinet*, Hennessy's *Cabinet* and Brazier's *Constitutional Practice* are a valuable record of practice. Since they are founded both on historical sources and on contemporary political accounts, works on the British government are seldom unanimous in their description of controversial events (for example, the differing interpretations of the political crisis in 1931 which led to the formation of the National government).[183] Moreover, historical precedents are often of doubtful relevance to present issues, especially with the increasing pace of change in political and governmental practice. There is, however, much more openness about the Cabinet system today than in the past: it is remarkable that, until 1992, even the structure of Cabinet committees and the rules of conduct for ministers were regarded as secret.

In the field of parliamentary procedure, a work with special authority is Erskine May's *Parliamentary Practice*. First published in 1844, this is revised regularly under the editorship of the Clerk to the House of Commons.[184] It is an invaluable guide to the sources of parliamentary procedure, which are found in standing orders, in resolutions of the House and in rulings given by the Speaker and recorded in Hansard.

Finally, there is an unending flow from government and Parliament of reports by such bodies as royal commissions, departmental committees, committees at Westminster and ministerial inquiries. Some of these reports have concerned important constitutional topics, the most notable in recent years being the first report of the (Nolan) committee on standards in public life, Sir Richard Scott's massive report on the 'arms for Iraq' inquiry, and Lord Butler's inquiry into the use of intelligence about weapons of mass destruction in Iraq.[185] As well as the innumerable reports by select committees of the Commons into the activities of government departments,[186] some committees at Westminster have a special concern for constitutional affairs.[187]

....

[179] For recognition of this by the House of Lords, see *Woolwich BS* v *IRC (No 2)* [1993] AC 70, 163-4 (Lord Goff).

[180] See *Stair Memorial Encyclopedia, The Laws of Scotland*, vol 22, pp 212–19.

[181] [1965] AC 75; ch 10 E.

[182] Cf Bagehot, *The English Constitution*, pp 99–100. The point is made strongly by Lady Hale in *R (Quark Fishing Ltd)* v *Foreign Secretary* [2005] UKHL 57, [2006] 1 AC 529, at [94]–[95].

[183] See Bassett, *1931: Political Crisis*.

[184] See the 24th edn by M Jack, 2011.

[185] Respectively Cm 2850-1, 1995, HC 115 (1995–6) and HC 898 (2003–4).

[186] Ch 8 E.

[187] In particular, in the Commons, the Political and Constitutional Reform Committee and in the Lords, the Constitution Committee.

CHAPTER 2

The structure of the United Kingdom

A. The historic structure

While the external identity of a state is a matter for international law, it is constitutional law which regulates the internal relationships of the various territories which make up the state. In the past, writers often used the word 'English' in referring to the constitution. Dicey and Bagehot, for example, wrote about the English constitution when they were dealing with the British constitution or, to be completely accurate, with what was then the constitution of the United Kingdom of Great Britain and Ireland. The active political consciousness of Ireland since the 19th century, and that of Scotland and Wales more recently, means that today constitutional lawyers must choose their geographical adjectives with care. When in 1969 a royal commission on the constitution was appointed, among its duties was 'to examine the present functions of the central legislature and government in relation to *the several countries, nations and regions* of the United Kingdom'.[1] Some of the deliberate vagueness of the words in italics was dispelled when the commission's report referred to England, Scotland, Wales and Northern Ireland as the four countries which make up the United Kingdom of Great Britain and Northern Ireland.

The United Kingdom has often been described as a unitary state, since there is no structure of federalism. But while the authority of the Crown and Parliament extends to all the United Kingdom, three legal systems exist, each with its own courts and legal profession, namely (*a*) England and Wales, (*b*) Scotland and (*c*) Northern Ireland. A unifying influence is that the Supreme Court for the United Kingdom is the final court of appeal from all three jurisdictions, except for criminal cases in Scotland. When Parliament legislates, it may do so for all the United Kingdom (for example, on income tax or immigration), for Great Britain (for example, on social security or trade union law), or separately for one or more of the countries within the United Kingdom.

Legal definitions

In law, the expression 'United Kingdom' means Great Britain and Northern Ireland; it does not include the Channel Islands or the Isle of Man.[2] For purposes of international relations, however, these islands are represented by the UK government. So are the remaining overseas territories of the United Kingdom, such as Bermuda, the Falkland Islands and Gibraltar.[3] The term 'British Islands' is defined in the Interpretation Act 1978 as meaning the United Kingdom, the Channel Islands and the Isle of Man. The Republic of Ireland is of course outside the United Kingdom and now a completely separate state. 'Great Britain' refers to England, Scotland and Wales: these became a single kingdom by virtue of the Treaty of Union between England and Scotland in 1707. The Wales and Berwick Act 1746 provided,

---

[1] See section B in this chapter.

[2] Interpretation Act 1978, Sch 1. By the British Nationality Act 1981, s 50 (1), the United Kingdom includes the Channel Islands and the Isle of Man for purposes of nationality law. They are today referred to as Crown Dependencies: see HC 56 (2009–10).

[3] For a recent account, see Hendry and Dickson, *British Overseas Territories Law*.

curiously to our eyes today, that where the expression 'England' was used in an Act of Parliament, this should be taken to include the dominion of Wales and the town of Berwick-upon-Tweed. But by the Welsh Language Act 1967, s 4, references to England in future Acts do not include Wales.[4]

The adjective 'British' is used in common speech to refer to matters associated with Great Britain or the United Kingdom. It has no single legal connotation, and the term 'British law' is best avoided. In legislation 'British' is sometimes used with reference to the United Kingdom, particularly in the context of nationality.[5]

Historical development of the United Kingdom

1. Wales[6]

While there is no need to summarise the lengthy history by which England became a single entity, it is worthwhile briefly to examine the historical formation of the United Kingdom. The military conquest of Wales by the English reached its culmination in 1282, when Prince Llywelyn was killed and his principality passed by conquest to King Edward I of England. Thereafter the principality (which formed only part of what is now Wales) was administered in the name of the Prince, but the rest of Wales was subjected to rule by a variety of local princes and lords; at this period English law was not extended to Wales, where the local customs, laws and language prevailed. From 1471, a Council of Wales and the Marches brought Wales under closer rule from England, and the accession of the Tudors did much to complete the process of assimilation. In 1536, an Act of the English Parliament united Wales with England, establishing an administrative system on English lines, requiring the English language to be used, and granting Wales representation in the English Parliament.[7] In 1543, a system of Welsh courts (the Courts of the Great Sessions) was established to apply the common law of England. The Council of Wales and the Marches was granted a statutory jurisdiction which it exercised until its abolition in 1689. In 1830, the Courts of the Great Sessions were replaced by two new circuits that operated as part of the English court system. After the union with England, Acts of Parliament applying exclusively to Wales were rare.[8]

The mid-19th century saw the beginning of a political and educational revival and occasional Acts of Parliament applying only to Wales began again to be passed.[9] In 1906 the Welsh Department of the Board of Education was established, the first central department created specifically to administer Welsh affairs.[10] In 1914 was passed the Welsh Church Act, which disestablished and disendowed the Church of England in Wales. From time to time, the identity of Wales was recognised as new administrative arrangements were made.[11] In 1964, the post of Secretary of State for Wales was established and the Welsh Office emerged as a department of the UK government. Thereafter administration of Wales through the Welsh Office was to an extent based on the model of the Scottish Office.[12] Wales and England

---

[4] On the boundary between England and Wales, see Local Government Act 1972, ss 1(12), 20(7) and 269; Interpretation Act 1978, Sch 1.

[5] British Nationality Act 1981.

[6] Kilbrandon Report, ch 5, and Andrews (ed.), *Welsh Studies in Public Law*, especially chs 2 (D Jenkins), 3 (H Carter) and 4 (I L Gowan).

[7] 27 Hen VIII, c 26. The Statute Law Revision Act 1948 called this the Laws in Wales Act 1535, but recent Welsh writers have called it the Act of Union of 1536: *Welsh Studies*, p 28.

[8] See e.g. Welsh Bible and Prayer Book Act 1563: *Welsh Studies*, pp 38–9.

[9] See e.g. Sunday Closing (Wales) Act 1881: *Welsh Studies*, p 48.

[10] *Welsh Studies*, p 49.

[11] E.g. creation of the Welsh Economic Planning Council in 1966.

[12] See *Welsh Studies*, ch 4 (I L Gowan); and HLE, vol 8(2), pp 50–4.

share a common legal system,[13] but some statutes make special provision for Wales. By the Welsh Language Act 1967, the Welsh language may be spoken in any legal proceedings within Wales, by any person who desires to use it; and Welsh versions of any official document or form may be used. The Welsh Language Act 1993 created the Welsh Language Board, to further the principle in Wales that public authorities and the courts should treat the English and Welsh languages on a basis of equality.

2. Scotland[14]

Unlike Wales, Scotland maintained its independence of England during the Middle Ages. Scotland retained its own monarchy and only in the 16th century did the two royal lines come closer with the marriage of Henry VII's daughter, Margaret, to James IV of Scotland. On the death of Elizabeth I in 1603, James VI of Scotland, great-great-grandson of Henry VII, became James I of England. This personal union of the two monarchies had the legal consequence that persons born in England and Scotland after the union both owed allegiance to the same King.[15] During the conflicts of the 17th century, there was a brief period under Cromwell when the Commonwealth of England, Scotland and Ireland was subject to a single legislature and executive. But apart from this, and despite the personal union of the monarchies, the constitutions of the two countries were not united and the English and Scottish Parliaments maintained separate existences.[16] Following the ousting of James II/VII in 1688, the Scottish Parliament for the first time asserted independence of the royal will (see, in particular, the Claim of Right Act 1689). There followed a contest of wills between the English and Scottish Parliaments, marked by religious disputation and by keen rivalry to profit from expanding ventures in world trade, against a deeply insecure European background. In 1704, the Scottish Parliament went so far as to provide that if Anne died without heirs, the Parliament would choose her successor, 'provided always that the same be not successor to the Crown of England', unless in the meantime acceptable conditions of government had been established between the two countries.[17] Following a strong initiative from the English government, the two Parliaments authorised negotiations between two groups of commissioners representing each Parliament but appointed by the Queen. The Treaty of Union was drawn up by them and was approved by Act of each Parliament together with an Act to maintain Presbyterian Church government within Scotland.[18]

The Treaty of Union came into effect on 1 May 1707: it united the two kingdoms of England and Scotland into one by the name of Great Britain; the Crown was to descend to the Hanoverian line after Anne's death; there was to be a Parliament of Great Britain including 16 Scottish peers and 45 elected members in the Commons. Extensive financial and economic terms were included in the Treaty. Guarantees were given for the continuance of Scottish private law (art 18) and the Scottish courts (art 19), as well as for the maintenance of the feudal jurisdictions in Scotland and the privileges of the royal burghs in Scotland. The Act to maintain the Presbyterian Church in Scotland was incorporated in the Treaty and it provided for the maintenance of the Scottish universities. The Treaty was described as an incorporating union: it did not establish a federal system and did not maintain any role for

---

[13] See e.g. Constitutional Reform Act 2005, ss 7–9.

[14] Kilbrandon Report, ch 4; Donaldson, *Scotland: James V–James VII*; Ferguson, *Scotland, 1689 to the Present*; HLE, vol 8(2), pp 54–72 and Devine, *The Scottish Nation 1700–2000*, pt 1. Also Wicks, *The Evolution of a Constitution*, ch 2.

[15] *Calvin's* case (1608) 7 Co Rep 1a. And see C Russell [2005] PL 336.

[16] See Donaldson, ch 15, and Terry, *The Scottish Parliament 1603–1707*.

[17] APS XI, 136.

[18] Scottish Act: APS XI, 406, English Act: 6 Anne c 11; *Halsbury's Statutes*, vol 10(1), 4th edn, 2013 reissue, p 136. On the making of the union, see Riley, *The Union of England and Scotland* and Devine, ch 1.

the previous Scottish and English legislatures. But it gave extensive guarantees to Scottish institutions. Guarantees of a similar kind for English institutions were not required as it was obvious that the English would be predominant in the new Parliament of Great Britain.[19]

In the years after 1707, the new unity of Great Britain was challenged by the Jacobite uprisings in 1715 and 1745 but without success. Various expedients were resorted to for governing Scotland from London and, from time to time, new laws were made for Scotland by the Parliament of Great Britain. Some of these, for example abolition of the Scottish feudal jurisdictions in 1747, were considered in Scotland to be a breach of the Treaty of Union. The Scottish Privy Council having been abolished in 1708, for much of the 18th and 19th centuries the Lord Advocate, the chief law officer in Scotland, occupied the primary role in politics and government, managing affairs in Scotland on behalf of the Crown. In 1885, a post of Secretary for Scotland was created, and in 1928 this was raised to Cabinet status with the title of Secretary of State for Scotland. Demands for home rule for Scotland were expressed from the late 19th century onwards: the response of the government was to develop the Scottish Office as the department responsible for Scottish affairs.[20] Political demands for a Scottish legislative assembly were firmly resisted, although greater use was made of committees of Scottish MPs in the Commons. After 1707, Parliament often legislated separately for the English and Scottish legal systems. In particular, the structure of private law, the criminal law, the courts, education and local government in Scotland has always differed from the English pattern.

From 1945 to 1999 the Scottish Office comprised four or five departments of the UK government, located in Edinburgh but headed by the Secretary of State for Scotland.[21] The officials in these departments were members of the British civil service. The functions entrusted to the Scottish Office included agriculture and fisheries, education, health, housing, local government, police, prisons, social services, transport (except road freight and rail) and town planning. Other functions (such as inland revenue, social security, employment and control of immigration) were exercised in Scotland by British or UK departments. As well as having direct responsibility for the Scottish Office, the Secretary of State had an indirect interest in all matters affecting Scotland, enabling a Scottish view to be heard in a wide variety of decisions made in Whitehall.

Although the direction of government remained centralised in the Cabinet, the Scottish Office system enabled much Scottish business to be handled by civil servants resident in Scotland and, latterly, some financial autonomy was conferred on Scottish ministers. On many matters, uniform social and economic standards were maintained throughout Great Britain (for example, financing of higher education), but in some services higher levels of expenditure in Scotland were accepted. One drawback was that subjects requiring separate legislation for Scotland had to compete for a place in Westminster's legislative programme. The political legitimacy of the system was brought into question whenever, as from 1970 to 1974 and from 1979 to 1997, the majority of MPs from Scotland were in the Opposition at Westminster. For instance, despite the fact that only ten Conservative MPs (out of 72) were elected from Scotland at the 1987 election, the Conservative government in 1989 abolished domestic rates for financing local government in favour of the notorious poll tax (community charge), one year earlier in Scotland than in England and Wales.[22] Although the Scottish Office system was sometimes referred to as 'administrative devolution', it was in essence a form of direct rule of Scotland by the UK government.

....

[19] On the legal effect of these guarantees, see ch 3 D and J D Ford [2007] CLJ 106. Also E Wicks (2001) 117 LQR 109; and (same author), *The Evolution of a Constitution*, ch 2.

[20] See H J Hanham in Wolfe (ed.) *Government and Nationalism in Scotland*, ch 4.

[21] See Drucker (ed.) *Scottish Government Yearbook 1980*, ch 8 (M Macdonald and A Redpath); Keating and Midwinter, *The Government of Scotland*; Milne, *The Scottish Office*. And HLE, vol 8(2), pp 69–71.

[22] See C M G Himsworth and N C Walker [1987] PL 586 and authorities cited in ch 3, note 195.

The place of Scotland within the Union remains hotly contested. The Scottish National Party – whose ideological lodestar is independence for Scotland – has been the dominant political party in Scotland for a decade, forming the Scottish government (as either a minority or majority government) since 2007 and returning the largest number of MPs for Scottish seats in Westminster in both the 2015 and 2017 general elections. The SNP announced in January 2012 that it wished to hold a referendum on Scottish independence, and later that year the British government at Westminster agreed to make provision for that referendum.[23] The referendum was held on 18 September 2014, after a lengthy campaign which saw opinion polling figures considerably narrow and the SNP publish detailed plans for what independence might look like (including retaining the monarchy, the currency and the BBC).[24] Concerns of unionist parties about the level of support for independence caused the leaders of the Conservative, Labour and Liberal Democrat parties to jointly vow in the closing stages of the campaign to devolve greater powers to the Scottish Parliament. The final result was that 55 per cent of Scots voted 'no' to the proposition: 'Should Scotland be an independent country?'.[25] Although it was assumed at the time of the referendum that the outcome would settle the issue for the foreseeable future, the result of the referendum on Britain's membership of the European Union – in which the country as a whole voted to leave, but Scotland voted to remain by 62–38 per cent – has reignited talk of a further independence referendum. The degree of popular support for a second bite at the independence cherry may partly depend upon the terms upon which Britain exits and the nature of its agreed future relationship with the EU.

3. Northern Ireland[26]

The history of Northern Ireland is inextricably linked with that of Ireland itself. As an entity, Northern Ireland dates only from the partition of Ireland in the early 1920s. Ireland itself came under English influence in the 12th century when Henry II of England became Lord of Ireland. As settlers came from England, courts modelled on those in England were established. While an Irish Parliament began to develop, some English legislation was extended to Ireland by ordinance of the King of England. In 1494, the Irish Parliament passed the statute known as Poyning's Law, which required that all Irish Bills be submitted to the King and his Council in England; only such Bills as the English Council approved were returned for the Irish Parliament to pass. In 1541, the title of Lord of Ireland was changed to King of Ireland. During the 17th century, Ireland had its share of religious bitterness and conflict. William of Orange defeated the former King James II at the Battle of the Boyne in 1690. To resolve a dispute over the power of the Irish House of Lords to hear appeals from Irish courts, the British Parliament in 1720 declared that it retained full power to legislate for Ireland and deprived the Irish House of Lords of all its judicial powers. Pressure from Ireland for greater autonomy led in 1782 to repeal of the Declaratory Act of 1720 and to the recognition by the British Parliament of the Irish Parliament's legislative independence, although there was no

---

[23] After some dispute as to whether or not the Scottish Parliament could legislate to hold the referendum itself (see N Aroney [2014] PL 422), the British government made the Scotland Act 1998 (Modification of Schedule 5) Order 2013, permitting the Scottish Parliament to do so. The Scottish Parliament subsequently passed the Scottish Independence Referendum Act 2013 and the Scottish Independence Referendum (Franchise) Act 2013.

[24] Scottish Government, *Scotland's Future* (2013). The document is some 650 pages long.

[25] A Tomkins (2014) 130 LQR 215; S Tierney [2015] PL 633.

[26] For the earlier history, see Donaldson, *Some Comparative Aspects of Irish Law*; for the 1920 Constitution, Calvert, *Constitutional Law in Northern Ireland*, and Kilbrandon Report, ch 6. Also Hadfield, *The Constitution of Northern Ireland*; Hadfield (ed.), *Northern Ireland: Politics and the Constitution*; C McCrudden, in Jowell and Oliver (eds), *The Changing Constitution*, 3rd edn, ch 12; Morison and Livingstone, *Reshaping Public Power*; HLE, vol 8(2), pp 72–93.

change in the position of the monarchy.[27] But legislative independence was short-lived, and after the rising of the United Irishmen in 1798, the British government proceeded to a legislative union with Ireland.

The Union agreement between the two Parliaments was broadly similar to the Union with Scotland, although fewer guarantees were given to Ireland than had been given to Scotland. Article 1 created the United Kingdom of Great Britain and Ireland and arts 3 and 4 provided for Irish representation in the Parliament of the United Kingdom. Article 5 provided for the (Protestant) United Church of England and Ireland, whose continuance was stated to be an essential and fundamental part of the Union. Within the enlarged United Kingdom, all trade was to be free; the laws in force in Ireland were to continue, subject to alteration by Parliament from time to time. As with the Scottish Union, the terms of the Union were separately adopted by Act of each of the two Parliaments concerned.[28]

The Irish Union with Britain was less stable than the Union of 1707. For much of the 19th and 20th centuries, the Irish question was one of the most difficult political and constitutional issues within the United Kingdom. Catholic emancipation in 1829 opened the way for demands for further reform, often associated with militant action and violence. The Irish Church was disestablished in 1869 despite the guarantee for its existence contained in the Act of Union.[29] Gladstone's two Home Rule Bills in 1886 and 1893 were both defeated in Parliament, the first in the Commons, the second in the Lords. After the Parliament Act 1911 had taken away the power of the Lords to veto legislation,[30] the Government of Ireland Act 1914 became law, but it never came into effect because of the outbreak of world war; its parliamentary history had been marked by the extreme determination of Ulster Protestants not to be separated from Britain.

The Easter rising in Dublin in 1916 was further evidence of nationalist feeling in Catholic Ireland. In 1919, the Sinn Fein movement established a representative assembly for what was proclaimed to be the Irish Republic. In 1920, the Government of Ireland Act was passed by the UK Parliament, providing for two Parliaments in Ireland, one for six northern counties and one for the remainder of Ireland, with cooperation between the two to be maintained by means of a Council of Ireland. The Act was ignored by Sinn Fein and, after a period of bitter civil war, an Anglo-Irish Treaty was formally concluded in 1922. This recognised the existence of the Irish Free State (excluding the six northern counties), on which Westminster conferred what was described as the status of a self-governing dominion within the British Empire.

The dominion status of the Irish Free State proved no more than a transitional stage, and the Irish Constitution of 1937 declared that Eire was a sovereign independent state. During the Second World War, Eire was neutral. In 1949, the state became the Republic of Ireland. The UK Parliament at last recognised that Eire had ceased to be part of Her Majesty's dominions although it was, perhaps anomalously, also declared that Ireland was not to be regarded as a foreign country.[31]

Under the Government of Ireland Act 1920, a scheme of devolution was created for the six counties of Northern Ireland that featured an executive (Governor, Prime Minister and Cabinet) and a legislature of two houses sitting at Stormont.[32] Subject to the legislative supremacy of Westminster and except for many matters that were reserved to Westminster,

---

[27] Cf *Re Keenan* [1972] 1 QB 533.

[28] For the Union with Ireland Act 1800, see *Halsbury's Statutes*, vol 32 (2011 reissue), p 49.

[29] *Ex p Canon Selwyn* (1872) 36 JP 54.

[30] Ch 8 D.

[31] Ireland Act 1949, ss 1(1) and 2. And see Roberts-Wray, *Commonwealth and Colonial Law*, pp 32–5.

[32] See note 26. Also Birrell and Murie, *Policy and Government in Northern Ireland*; Buckland, *The Factory of Grievances*; Lawrence, *The Government of Northern Ireland*, ch 10.

the Stormont Parliament had power 'to make laws for the peace, order and good government of Northern Ireland'.[33] If an Act of the Stormont Parliament exceeded its competence (for example, by legislating with respect to the armed forces),[34] it could be held invalid, but the courts rarely had to interpret the Act of 1920.[35] Since the (Protestant) Unionist party was in power throughout the life of Stormont, the Catholic community was in a permanent minority and their accumulated grievances led to serious unrest from 1968 onwards.[36] In 1972, direct rule of Northern Ireland from London was resumed; the 1920 constitution was suspended, and brought to an end one year later.[37] There followed nearly three decades in which various attempts were made to establish a new Assembly, elected by proportional representation, and a new form of executive based on the concept of power-sharing. These attempts included the Sunningdale agreement (to which the Dublin government was a party) in 1974, an increase in Northern Ireland's representation at Westminster from 12 to 17 seats,[38] and in 1985 the Anglo-Irish Agreement signed by the British and Irish Prime Ministers at Hillsborough.[39] The 1985 Agreement led Unionists to protest at the recognition of the Dublin government's interest in Northern Ireland.[40]

Both direct rule and terrorist activity continued during most of the 1990s. In 1993, the 'Downing Street Declaration' of the two Prime Ministers renewed the assurance that the status of Northern Ireland would not be changed without majority consent and confirmed that the British government would not oppose a united Ireland for which there was popular consent.[41] But only after the general election in 1997 was a more fruitful initiative taken, in the form of the Belfast (or Good Friday) Agreement reached on 10 April 1998.[42] Strand One of the agreement provided for an elected Assembly in Northern Ireland of 108 members. Strand Two created a North/South Ministerial Council, representing the Northern Ireland and Irish governments and with machinery for implementing policies agreed by the Council. Strand Three provided for a British–Irish Council, representing the British and Irish governments, as well as the devolved governments of Northern Ireland, Scotland and Wales, and also a British–Irish Inter-governmental Conference to discuss Northern Ireland matters that were not devolved, such as policing. In this elaborate way, the Good Friday Agreement made possible a scheme of devolution for Northern Ireland.

In the next section, we examine aspects of the current devolution legislation applying to Scotland, Wales and Northern Ireland. Emphasis will be given to structural issues, rather than the detail of how these schemes of devolution are operating.[43]

---

[33] Government of Ireland Act 1920, s 4(1).

[34] See *R (Hume)* v *Londonderry Justices* [1972] NILR 91; Northern Ireland Act 1972.

[35] See *Londonderry CC* v *McGlade* [1925] NI 47; *Gallagher* v *Lynn* [1937] AC 863; *Belfast Corporation* v *OD Cars Ltd* [1960] AC 490.

[36] See Cmnd 532, 1969 (the Cameron report).

[37] Cmnd 5259, 1973; Northern Ireland Assembly Act 1973; Northern Ireland Constitution Act 1973.

[38] House of Commons (Redistribution of Seats) Act 1979.

[39] Cmnd 9690. And see Hadden and Boyle, *The Anglo-Irish Agreement*.

[40] For an unsuccessful legal challenge, see *Ex p Molyneaux* [1986] 1 WLR 331.

[41] Cm 2442, 1994.

[42] *The Belfast Agreement: An Agreement Reached at the Multi-Party talks on Northern Ireland*, Cm 3383, 1998; B Hadfield [1999] PL 599 and D O'Sullivan [2000] Dublin Univ LJ 112. On subsequent events, see Jowell and Oliver (eds), *The Changing Constitution* (6th edn, 2007), ch 10 (C McCrudden).

[43] See the Constitution Unit's series on this subject, including Hazell (ed.) *The State of the Nations 2003*; Trench (ed.) *Has Devolution made a Difference?*, *The Dynamics of Devolution* and *The State of the Nations 2008*. Also Hazell and Rawlings, *Devolution, Law Making and the Constitution*; Mitchell, *Devolution in the United Kingdom*; Bogdanor, *Devolution in the United Kingdom*; and symposium 'Devolution, Ten Years On' (2010) 63 *Parliamentary Affairs* 85–172.

B. Devolution of government

The Labour government elected in 1997 was committed to securing devolution of government to both Scotland and Wales and to renewing efforts to establish peace and order in Northern Ireland. This commitment caused Westminster in 1998 to legislate separately for Scotland, Wales and Northern Ireland.[44] It is an indication of the asymmetric structure of the United Kingdom that differences between the three schemes are almost greater than the similarities, although the positions of Scotland and Wales have been steadily moving closer over the subsequent 20 years.

Devolution is not a term of art in constitutional law. Unlike federalism, its nature within the United Kingdom depends not on a written constitution, but on the devolution legislation and on the operation of the new structures. It can mean what the respective parties to it need and want it to mean at any given time. In essence, devolution denotes the vesting of legislative and executive powers in elected bodies in Scotland, Wales and Northern Ireland, who have political responsibility for the devolved functions. The legislation specifies the areas of government that are devolved, arrangements for funding, and measures to ensure legal and political accountability. The scope of devolution, and even the models of it, have substantially evolved since 1998; like the remainder of the constitution, devolution is a flexible rather than a fixed element. Despite the devolution of many functions, the Parliament and government in Westminster retains ultimate authority over all of the United Kingdom.

Precursors to devolution in 1998

The schemes of devolution created in 1998 were influenced by the abortive attempt in the 1970s to establish devolved government for Scotland and Wales. In 1973, the Royal Commission on the constitution (the Kilbrandon report)[45] made proposals for devolution that were far from unanimous. For Scotland, eight of the 13 members recommended legislative devolution, but only six members favoured a similar scheme for Wales. Nonetheless, the Labour government decided to create a Parliament for Scotland and an Assembly for Wales. The Scotland Act 1978 and the Wales Act 1978 were eventually enacted, but in referendums in March 1979 the scheme for Wales was heavily defeated; the Scottish scheme was approved by a small majority of those voting, but their number did not satisfy the controversial '40 per cent rule' that had been applied to the referendum to guard against a low turnout of voters.

Between 1979 and 1997, the Conservative government opposed all proposals for devolution within Great Britain, apart from minor changes in Scottish business at Westminster.[46] The Labour and Liberal Democrat parties supported the Scottish Constitutional Convention, a non-governmental body endorsed by many groups and organisations in Scotland. In 1995, the Convention proposed a scheme of devolution which sought to improve on the Scotland Act 1978.[47] In 1997, the Labour and Liberal Democrat parties agreed that there would be an early referendum in Scotland on the Convention's scheme. For Wales, they favoured an elected assembly to oversee Welsh affairs.

The Referendums (Scotland and Wales) Act 1997 authorised referendums in Scotland and Wales on the government's schemes for devolution.[48] In 1997, of the 60 per cent who voted in Scotland, 74 per cent supported the proposed Parliament and 63.5 per cent agreed

---

[44] Scotland Act 1998; Government of Wales Act 1998; and Northern Ireland Act 1998.

[45] Cmnd 5460, 1973. And see T C Daintith (1974) 37 MLR 544.

[46] See HC S0 94A–94H (1995); HC Deb, 29 November 1995, col 1228, and 19 December 1995, col 1410.

[47] *Scotland's Parliament, Scotland's Right* (1995); J McFadden [1995] PL 215; D Millar (1997) 1 Edin LR 260.

[48] *Scotland's Parliament*, Cm 3658, 1997; and *A Voice for Wales*, Cm 3718, 1997.

that the Parliament should be able to vary the basic rate of income tax for Scottish taxpayers. In Wales, only 50 per cent of the electorate voted, of whom no more than 50.3 per cent supported the proposed Assembly. Yet legislation to implement both schemes was enacted and elections to the Parliament and Assembly were held in May 1999.

Devolution to Scotland[49]

Under the Scotland Act 1998, there is a unicameral Parliament of 129 members: 73 are elected from single-member constituencies by simple majority vote and 56 are elected from regions under an 'additional member' system of proportional representation.[50] Elections are held every four years (s 2), but elections may exceptionally be held at other times, for example if two-thirds of the members vote for a resolution dissolving the Parliament (s 3). The electoral system is less likely than a 'first past the post' system to give an absolute majority to a single party. In 2007, the Scottish National Party won the largest number of seats (47) and formed a minority government, but in 2011 the party won an absolute majority of seats (69). Members of the Scottish Parliament (MSPs) are not barred by law from being members of the House of Commons or the Lords, or of the European Parliament.

The Scottish Parliament has a broad power to make laws for Scotland, known as Acts of the Scottish Parliament (s 28(1)), but this power does not extend to matters reserved to Westminster. 'Reserved matters' include the Crown, the Union, foreign affairs, the civil service, defence and the armed forces, and a long list of domestic matters under 11 headings, including finance and the economy, aspects of home affairs (such as misuse of drugs, data protection and immigration), trade and industry, energy, social security, regulation of the professions, employment, broadcasting and equal opportunities.[51] The Act provides for the list of reserved matters to be amended by an Order in Council, made with the approval of the Houses at Westminster and the Scottish Parliament (s 30(2)). The Scotland Act 2012 extended further powers, particularly in respect of taxation and borrowing, implementing recommendations of the Calman Commission.[52] Following the independence referendum vote, and the promises made by the main Westminster parties for greater Scottish devolution, a further report was issued by the Smith Commission recommending substantial amendments to the 1998 Act settlement.[53] These recommendations were implemented in the Scotland Act 2016, which devolved: the rates and bands of income tax, air passenger duty and the assignment of VAT revenues; increased responsibility for welfare policy and delivery in Scotland; increased devolution in a variety of areas ranging from oil and gas extraction to road signage; and gave the Scottish Parliament greater autonomy over its own powers and procedures. It also increased the financial accountability of the Scottish Parliament alongside an amended fiscal framework. The Scotland Act 2016 also legislated for some political commitments, addressed below.

The fundamental architecture of the 1998 Act, however, remains in place. If the Scottish Parliament were to legislate on a 'reserved matter', that provision would not be law (s 29(1)). Other limits on its competence are that a Scottish Act may not affect the law of any country outside Scotland and may not conflict with European Union law or with the European Convention on Human Rights (s 29(2)(a), (d)).

---

[49] Himsworth and Munro, *The Scotland Act 1998*; Jowell and Oliver (eds), *The Changing Constitution* (6th edn, 2007), ch 9 (B K Winetrobe); Himsworth and O'Neill, *Scotland's Constitution: Law and Practice*, chs 4–6.

[50] The size of the Parliament was originally linked to the number of Westminster MPs from Scotland, but that link was removed by the Scottish Parliamentary Constituencies Act 2004.

[51] Schedule 5 to the 1998 Act contains general and specific reservations; detailed provisions modify the effect of the general headings. See Himsworth and O'Neill, pp 119–40.

[52] *Serving Scotland Better: Scotland and the United Kingdom in the 21st Century* (2010).

[53] *Report of the Smith Commission for Further Devolution of Powers to the Scottish Parliament* (2014).

By Part 2 of the 1998 Act, the Scottish Government (as the 2012 Act re-named the Scottish Executive) comprises the First Minister, other ministers and the law officers (the Lord Advocate and the Solicitor-General for Scotland) (s 44). The First Minister is appointed by the Queen after having been nominated by the Parliament (ss 45, 46). The First Minister and other ministers must be MSPs, and the nomination of other ministers must be approved by the Parliament before their formal appointment (s 47). All ministers must resign if the Parliament resolves that the Government no longer enjoys its confidence (ss 45(2), 47(3)(c), 48(2)). The Government is thus accountable to the Parliament, which may scrutinise acts of the ministers and civil servants who staff the Scottish Administration (s 51). For this purpose, the Parliament has a system of committees, dealing with all aspects of the work of the Government.

The Government's powers are based on a transfer of functions from the UK government. It exercises the powers of the Crown in Scotland, including prerogative powers, unless they are reserved to Westminster (s 53). In general, these functions relate to matters within the Parliament's legislative competence. Like the Parliament, the Government may not take decisions that are contrary to EU law or conflict with Convention rights (s 57).

The bulk of the income of the Scottish Administration comes in a block grant from Westminster (Parts 3 and 4 of the 1998 Act). The grant is calculated on the basis of the 'Barnett formula', which produces a sum that is treated as Scotland's share of public expenditure.[54] Within that total, the Scottish Government may set its priorities for expenditure: thus it has adopted its own policy on university tuition fees and on personal care for the elderly.[55] The Scottish Government has yet to fully employ its tax varying powers under any of the Acts which have steadily increased those powers.

While it is inherent in the devolution of powers that the Scottish authorities should make their own decisions (one of the most controversial being the decision by the Minister of Justice in 2009 to permit a Libyan prisoner convicted of complicity in the Lockerbie air-disaster to return to Libya), there are safeguards against decisions that would be outside the devolved powers. When a Bill is introduced, the minister and the presiding officer must separately consider whether it is within the competence of the Parliament (s 31); the Supreme Court for the United Kingdom may be asked to decide whether a Bill is within competence (s 33). The 1998 Act also provides for the decision of 'devolution issues' (Schedule 6). Such issues arise when a Scottish Act or an executive decision is challenged on the ground that it is not within the devolved powers, including questions as to compatibility with the European Convention on Human Rights. A devolution issue that arises in any court or tribunal may be referred to the Court of Session or the High Court of Justiciary; a further appeal may lie to the Supreme Court. In such cases, interpretation of the 1998 Act (as amended) has constitutional significance.[56] Since these Acts impose many limitations on the powers of the Scottish authorities, the range of questions that may have to be decided is potentially very wide, and the Scottish Parliament has actively legislated across varied areas. Many cases have concerned the question of compliance with the European

----

[54] The formula, dating from 1979, is used to calculate a population-based proportion of future expenditure for each of Scotland, Wales and Northern Ireland, reflecting proposed changes in spending on comparable services in England: see HM Treasury, *Funding the Scottish Parliament, National Assembly for Wales and the Northern Ireland Assembly* (2000); Trench (ed.), *The Dynamics of Devolution*, ch 8 (D Bell and A Christie); House of Commons Library Research Paper 07/91, *The Barnett Formula* (2007) and *Serving Scotland better: Scotland and the UK in the 21st Century*, 2009 (the Calman report), ch 3.

[55] On the latter, see Hazell (ed.), *The State of the Nations 2003*, ch 9 (R Simeon).

[56] See P Craig and M Walters [1999] PL 274; S Tierney (2001) 5 Edin LR 49; Himsworth and O'Neill, *Scotland's Constitution: Law and Practice*, pp 395–410.

Convention on Human Rights.[57] Some have concerned compliance with EU law.[58] Relatively few cases have arisen from other provisions of the 1998 Act.[59] In 2011, in *AXA General Insurance Ltd, Petitioners*,[60] insurance companies challenged the validity of the Damages (Asbestos-related conditions) (Scotland) Act 2009: the Act made it easier for those claiming for personal injuries caused by exposure to asbestos at work to claim compensation from the former employers' insurers. The companies claimed unsuccessfully both that the legislation deprived them retrospectively of their possessions (thus breaching ECHR, First Protocol, art 1) and, relying on common law grounds of judicial review,[61] that the Act was irrational, unreasonable or arbitrary. If reliance on those common law grounds had succeeded, this would have been a serious limitation on the authority of the Parliament imposed by the judges. The Supreme Court held that while the 1998 Act had not excluded the supervisory jurisdiction of the courts, and that an Act of the Scottish Parliament was not to be equated with primary legislation of the Westminster Parliament, it would have to be a very extreme case in which review at common law should be applied to the work of a democratically elected legislature.

The Edinburgh Parliament has been an active legislature. Moreover, Westminster retains power to legislate for Scotland (s 28(7)) and it has done so frequently. On devolved matters, there is a firm convention, known as the 'Sewel convention', that Westminster will not normally legislate on devolved matters without the prior consent of the Scottish Parliament. The consent is given in the form of a 'legislative consent motion', the form of which is not itself part of the convention. This use of Westminster's continuing supremacy has sometimes been controversial but is often convenient.[62] One of the recommendations of the Smith Commission, enacted in the Scotland Act 2016, was to place the Sewel convention on a legislative footing: see now s 28(8). We have seen in Chapter 1 how the Supreme Court unanimously held that this legislative step did not render the convention legally enforceable, but was rather a purely political commitment.[63]

Critics of devolution have argued that it is an essentially unstable structure that creates the risk of conferring too little autonomy to be worthwhile or of fuelling a desire for ever increasing powers. In 2009, a cross-party commission chaired by Sir Kenneth Calman reported on the need for changes in the system of Scottish devolution.[64] The report concluded that devolution had been a 'real success' and that it was to Scotland's advantage that the United Kingdom, despite the asymmetry of its union structure, enjoyed a highly integrated economy. It would appear that the decisive rejection of independence in the 2014 referendum indicates an

---

[57] These include *Brown v Stott* [2003] 1 AC 681 (car owner's duty to inform police of identity of driver); *R v Lord Advocate* [2002] UKPC D3, [2004] 1 AC 462 (duty of court to stay delayed prosecution); *Cadder v Lord Advocate* [2010] UKSC 43, [2010] 1 WLR 2601 (police questioning of suspect in absence of lawyer). And see Reed and Murdoch, *A Guide to Human Rights Law in Scotland*.

[58] *Moohan v Lord Advocate* [2014] UKSC 67, [2015] AC 901 (prisoners not being enfranchised in the independence referendum); *Scotch Whiskey Association v Lord Advocate* [2016] CSIH 77, 2016 SLT 1141 (minimum alcohol pricing).

[59] But see *Whaley v Lord Watson* 2000 SC 340, *Adams v Scottish Ministers* 2004 SC 665 and *Martin v Lord Advocate* [2010] UKSC 10, 2010 SLT 412. On the difficult overlap between devolution issues and claims under the Human Rights Act, see *Somerville v Scottish Ministers* [2007] UKHL 44, [2007] 1 WLR 2734; and now Scotland Act (2012), s 14 and part 4. See also *H v Lord Advocate* [2012] UKSC 24, [2013] 1 AC 413 and *Kinloch v HM Advocate* [2012] UKSC 62, [2013] 2 AC 93.

[60] [2011] UKSC 46, 2011 SLT 1061. See C Himsworth [2012] PL 205; A Page (2012) *Juridical Review* 225; and A McHarg (2012) 16 Edin L R 224.

[61] See ch 24.

[62] For the 'Sewel convention', see Himsworth and O'Neill, pp 140–3; *Memorandum of Understanding* (Cm 4444, 1999), para 13; A Page and A Batey [2002] PL 501; Hazell and Rawlings, ch 2 (B Winetrobe).

[63] *R (Miller) v Secretary of State for Exiting the EU* [2107] UKSC 5, [2017] 2 WLR 583; see pp 29–30 above.

[64] See *Serving Scotland Better: Scotland and the UK in the 21st Century*, June 2009.

essential agreement with that proposition. However, the febrile political and constitutional atmosphere engendered by the Brexit referendum and process means that devolution – even the extensive further devolution provided in the Scotland Act 2016 – cannot provide a sufficient answer alone. Leaving the EU will require careful consideration of the domestic constitutional settlement; there will be an immediate issue of whether and how repatriated areas of competence from the EU are to be devolved, and a longer-term concern about whether Scotland will be content to remain within a United Kingdom no longer a full member of the EU.

What is apparent is the effective permanence of the Scottish Parliament and the Scottish Government. Its precise forms and the extent of its competencies have varied, but there has been no suggestion by any mainstream political party that the process of devolution should be reversed. It is presently almost inconceivable that the British government at Westminster would seek to abolish the devolution regime in Scotland without a clear mandate from the (Scottish) public to do so. In that political context, it is unsurprising that the recommendation of the Smith Commission that there be a formal legal statement of the permanence of the devolved institutions in Scotland was readily provided for in the Scotland Act 2016. That introduced a new s 63A into the 1998 Act having affirmed the permanence of the Scottish Parliament and Government and the commitment of the British Parliament and government to them. It also expressly requires a referendum of the people of Scotland to support abolition of either. Section 63A is purely political window-dressing. The Westminster Parliament retains the ability to repeal those provisions at any time as the supreme legislature. The devolution settlement is ultimately a matter of politics, a political constitution, provided for within a legal framework.

Devolution to Wales[65]

Although both schemes were created in 1998, devolution to Wales differed markedly from devolution to Scotland. Under the opaque and bureaucratic Government of Wales Act 1998, the National Assembly for Wales had no general power to make laws and was seen as a kind of executive body, limited to making secondary (or delegated) legislation by transfer from the Secretary of State for Wales. In composition, the Assembly was and remains a smaller version of the Scottish Parliament: 40 members are elected in single-member constituencies by simple majority, and 20 members by regions under proportional representation. In 2004, a commission appointed by the Assembly, chaired by Lord Richard, recommended that the Assembly should have a broad power to make laws for Wales and that there should be a clear distinction between legislative and executive powers.[66]

What emerged in 2006 was a second Government of Wales Act, re-enacting much of the 1998 Act but containing new provisions. Assembly elections are held every four years, except that an extraordinary election may be held if at least two-thirds of all members vote for it, or if the Assembly fails to nominate a First Minister within the requisite time (2006 Act, s 5). No person may be nominated on a party's regional list of candidates who has been nominated for election in an Assembly constituency (s 7). The Assembly has a broad power to appoint committees and sub-committees (s 28). Since the Assembly under the 2006 Act initially had no general legislative power, the Act enabled it to be consulted each year before the UK government settled its legislative programme (s 33), and some laws were made in this way to meet Welsh needs.[67]

[65] See Jowell and Oliver (eds), *The Changing Constitution* (6th edn), ch 11 (B Hadfield); A Trench [2006] PL 687. On the Government of Wales Act 1998, see Rawlings, *Delineating Wales: Constitutional, Legal and Administrative Aspects of National Devolution*.
[66] Commission on the Powers and Electoral Arrangements of the National Assembly for Wales, 2004; R Rawlings [2005] PL 824.
[67] E.g. Public Services Ombudsman (Wales) Act 2005 and Commissioner for Older People (Wales) Act 2006.

Executive powers are vested in the Welsh Ministers: the 'Welsh Assembly Government' (s 45) comprises the First Minister, the Welsh Ministers, deputy ministers, and the Counsel General to the Welsh Government, who is legal adviser to ministers and the Assembly (s 49). The Assembly may scrutinise the activities of Welsh public bodies.

The model of Welsh devolution was different from that in Scotland; instead of general competence unless a subject matter was reserved, the Welsh Assembly and government only had power where it had been specifically devolved to it. This significant difference was altered by the Wales Act 2017, which has moved Wales to a reserved powers model, but with a greater list of reserved matters than applies in Scotland.

Legislation by the Assembly is now contained in Bills, which when approved become 'Acts of the Assembly'. The first legislation to be enacted by this procedure (the Local Government Byelaws (Wales) Bill) was referred to the Supreme Court, when it was argued that a simpler procedure for making local byelaws in Wales proposed in the Bill could not dispense with the need for certain byelaws to be confirmed by the Secretary of State for Wales. The argument was rejected by the Court, and the validity of the Bill was upheld.[68]

Despite the widening of its powers since 2006, the Assembly remains subject to many restrictions on its competence, for instance it may not breach international or European obligations of the United Kingdom (the latter will change after Brexit), and may not act inconsistently with the Human Rights Act 1998. As with Scotland, the Assembly is primarily funded by an annual block grant from Westminster calculated with reference to the Barnett formula, and within this figure it can set its expenditure priorities. Unlike the Scottish Parliament, and despite the 2017 Act amendments, the Assembly has no power to vary the basic rate of income tax, but has acquired new borrowing powers, and power over landfill charges and stamp duty on property transactions.[69]

The Wales Act 2017 also enacted equivalent political commitments to the permanence of the Welsh devolution institutions, and the Sewel convention. Those provisions are the subject of precisely the same conclusions as their equivalents in the Scotland Act 2016, discussed above.

Devolution to Northern Ireland

The Belfast Agreement was endorsed on 22 May 1998 by separate referendums in both parts of Ireland and elections for the new Assembly were held in June 1998. By the Northern Ireland Act 1998, Northern Ireland will remain part of the United Kingdom until a majority of the electorate, voting in a poll held for the purpose, decide to the contrary (s 1); in that event, the Secretary of State shall lay proposals to give effect to the majority wish before the Westminster Parliament. The Assembly is, in principle, elected every four years. The electoral system is that of the single transferable vote, with each of the 18 Westminster constituencies returning six members.

A complex scheme of power sharing between the main parties provides for key decisions to be taken on a cross-community basis, either by parallel consent of a majority of unionist and nationalist designations or by a weighted majority (60 per cent) of members present and voting, including at least 40 per cent of unionist and nationalist designations. These key decisions include election of the Assembly chair, the First Minister and the Deputy First Minister. The Executive Committee of the Assembly comprises the First Minister, the Deputy First Minister

---

[68] *A G's Reference, re Local Government Byelaws (Wales) Bill 2012* [2012] UKSC 53, [2013] 1 AC 792. For subsequent challenges see: *AG for England and Wales v Counsel General for Wales* [2014] UKSC 43, [2014] 1 WLR 2622 and *Re Recovery of Medical Costs for Asbestos Diseases (Wales) Bill* [2015] UKSC 3, [2015] AC 1016; and for comment on the need for judges to interpret the devolution legislation to protect Welsh devolution see Dame Mary Arden [2014] PL 189.

[69] *Empowerment and Responsibility: Financial Powers to Strengthen Wales*, November 2012.

and other ministers appointed by a formula that divides ministries between the main parties on the basis of voting at the previous election. All ministers must take the prescribed pledge of office.[70] The First Minister and Deputy First Minister must represent the largest and second-largest parties, which has operated – as anticipated – to mean a Unionist First Minister and a Nationalist Deputy. The Assembly is, however, a power-sharing system in its true sense: if the parties cannot agree to share power and govern together, the Assembly cannot function, and direct rule is restored to Westminster. In early 2017, a significant fallout between the DUP and Sinn Fein following a number of scandals around DUP ministerial competence effectively brought power sharing to a standstill. The tensions were not eased by the DUP entering into a formal confidence and supply agreement with the Conservative government at Westminster, whose role was to broker an agreement to restore devolved power sharing.

Certain matters (such as the Crown, defence, immigration, elections and political parties) are *excepted* from devolution (s 4 and Sch 2). Other matters (including civil aviation, law, emergency powers, telecommunications, consumer protection and data protection) are *reserved* from devolution (s 4 and Sch 3). *Transferred* matters, which fall within the scheme of devolution, are neither excepted nor reserved. The Assembly may make laws on transferred matters, but this does not affect the power of Westminster to make laws for Northern Ireland (s 5). The Assembly may not adopt measures that would extend outside Northern Ireland, would be incompatible with the Human Rights Act 1998 or EU law (for the moment) or would discriminate on grounds of religious belief or political opinion (s 6). As in Scotland, there are safeguards against the Assembly exceeding its competence (ss 11, 14) and provision for the decision of 'devolution issues' (s 79, Sch 10).

The 1998 Act gives effect to other aspects of the Belfast Agreement, such as the North/South Ministerial Council and the British–Irish Council and the appointment in Northern Ireland of a Human Rights Commission (ss 68–70) and an Equality Commission (s 73). All public authorities must promote equality of opportunity (s 75) and it is unlawful for a public authority to discriminate on grounds of religious belief or political opinion (s 76).

The progress of devolution was impeded by continuing difficulties in the peace process, in particular as regards decommissioning of arms and other aspects of the security situation. For many months between 2000 and 2007, the Assembly was suspended while Northern Ireland returned to direct rule by the Secretary of State. Since elections in 2003, the Democratic Unionist Party and Sinn Fein were the leading parties from the two communities. Disagreements between them after 2003 prevented the Assembly from resuming its operations, and UK ministers became responsible for all Northern Ireland departments. In July 2005, the Provisional IRA announced the end of its armed campaign and the independent international commission on decommissioning (formed in 1997) reported that the Provisional IRA had decommissioned all its weapons. In October 2006, the St Andrews Agreement was concluded between the two governments and the major parties in Northern Ireland, and a timetable was set for elections, the formation of a four-party power-sharing government, and the return of devolution.[71] Devolved government under the (amended) Northern Ireland Act 1998 was restored in May 2007, with the Northern Ireland Executive Committee comprising the First Minister, the Deputy First Minister and ten departmental ministers. Debate continued into 2010 over devolving the sensitive function of policing and justice.[72] Agreement having at last been reached between the representatives of the two communities, policing and justice were devolved in April 2010.[73] A Minister of Justice with

---

[70] See Northern Ireland Act 2000.

[71] Northern Ireland Act 2006, Northern Ireland (Miscellaneous Provisions) Act 2006 and Northern Ireland (St Andrews Agreement) Act 2007.

[72] See Northern Ireland Act 2009, and the Hillsborough Castle Agreement of 5 February 2010.

[73] Northern Ireland Act 1998 (Devolution of Policing and Justice Functions) Order 2010; SI 2010/976.

responsibility for policing and justice was elected by a cross-community vote in the Assembly; but the direction and control of the Police Service of Northern Ireland remain with the chief constable of Northern Ireland. Notwithstanding these governmental changes, there have continued to be difficulties over the control of sectarian parades and the flying of the Union flag from public buildings.

C. Government in England

Devolution within the United Kingdom is asymmetrical. The position in England presents a sharp contrast to Scotland, Wales and Northern Ireland. With the possible exception of Greater London, which enjoys a form of regional government in transport, economic and environmental matters,[74] democratic decision-making has not been devolved to a regional level. In 1994 Whitehall divided England outside London into eight regions for official purposes,[75] but in 2004, in a referendum in north-east England held by postal ballot, 78 per cent of those voting rejected the proposal for a regional assembly of 25–35 members elected by proportional representation: the scale of the defeat ensured that the referendum would be the last of its kind.[76]

There is not the space in a book of this nature to attempt to detail the extraordinarily complicated thicket of legislation governing the powers and duties of local government in England, or even the various layers of metropolitan, county, district and parish councils. While much of the broad structure remains set out in the Local Government Act 1972, Parliament has legislated on substantive and procedural areas of local government in England (and Wales) in 1974, 1978, 1982, 1986, 1988 1989, 1992, 1999, 2000, 2003, 2009, 2010, 2011, 2012 and 2016. That list is by no means complete, and some years included more than one statute. Much of it has concerned the almost impenetrable workings of local government finance. The breadth of legislation is important: local authorities have responsibility for housing, libraries, adult and child social services, public health, planning and some education functions. A considerable proportion of the interaction between the citizen and the state concerns matters which are the responsibility of local, rather than national, government. Indeed, there are few Acts of Parliament passed which do not have some impact on local government functions.

Major changes have been made in recent years. The Local Government Act 1999 allows the Secretary of State to take over control of some or all of a local authority's functions where he believes the authority is failing to perform efficiently and effectively.[77] The Localism Act 2011 radically overhauled the nature of local authority governance and standards, introduced referendums on council tax rises, as well as making significant policy changes in the planning and housing fields. The Health and Social Care Act 2011 imposed new public health functions on local authorities as it reorganised the National Health Service. The Police Reform and Social Responsibility Act 2011 abolished local police authorities (largely populated by local councillors) and introduced directly elected police and crime commissioners to set strategic policing

---

[74] Trench (ed.) *Has Devolution made a Difference?*, ch 6 (M Sandford) and *The Dynamics of Devolution*, ch 5 (M Sandford and P Hetherington).

[75] Regional Development Agencies Act 1998.

[76] See Cm 5511, 2002 and the Regional Assemblies (Preparations) Act 2003. See Trench (ed.), *The Dynamics of Devolution*, ch 5 (M Sandford and P Hetherington).

[77] These powers (see s 15 in particular) have been exercised in relation to Doncaster Metropolitan Borough Council following repeated failings and allegations of corruption, Rotherham Metropolitan Borough Council following child sexual abuse scandals and the London Borough of Tower Hamlets following various concerns about the elected mayor's grant of public contracts.

priorities for their local police forces. The Local Democracy, Economic Development and Construction Act 2009 and the Cities and Local Government Devolution Act 2016 have introduced an ability for local authorities to combine into a single regional authority, adopt an elected mayor model (who also acts as the police and crime commissioner) and have, as a consequence, greater powers devolved to them from central government. This regional government model is explicitly modelled (as it had been in the late 1990s and early 2000s) on the successfully embedded creation of an elected mayor for Greater London exercising considerable powers under the Greater London Authority Act 1999. In 2017, six regions elected a mayor to be responsible for a new combined authority with devolved powers: Greater Manchester, Liverpool, Tees Valley, West Midlands, West of England and Cambridgeshire and Peterborough. Each of those new authorities has a different devolution settlement and a different set of powers and responsibilities. Regional devolution remains highly fragmented.

Nor has an answer been found to the 'West Lothian question' or, as it is sometimes called, the 'English question'.[78] This question takes the form of asking why Scottish MPs may debate and (more importantly) vote at Westminster on, for instance, issues about the NHS, housing policy or education in England, when English MPs are barred from considering these matters in Scotland (or Wales or Northern Ireland, as the case may be). The short answer is that Westminster serves both as the Parliament for the United Kingdom and for England: but how can it best fulfil these two functions?

In 2013, an independent commission, chaired by Sir William McKay, a former Clerk to the Commons, failed to find a clear solution to this question.[79] In examining the consequences of devolution for the Commons, the commission considered how in the light of powers devolved to Scotland, Northern Ireland and Wales the House might best deal with legislation that affected only England. The commission formulated the principle that decisions at the UK level that had a separate effect on England should normally be taken only with the consent of a majority of MPs for England: the principle should be adopted by resolution of the Commons, but the right of the whole House to decide on legislation should remain. The commission rejected the idea that MPs elected for constituencies that were not directly affected by a Bill should be barred from voting on it. The underlying political difficulty is that a government with a majority in the whole House may not have a majority if MPs from devolved areas are barred from voting on certain topics. Immediately following the Scottish independence referendum, Prime Minister Cameron announced a desire to implement a system of 'English votes for English laws', which was subsequently given effect through a series of complex Standing Orders of the House of Commons in 2015. The details of those are discussed in Chapter 8.[80]

D. Conclusion

It might be said that three of the four countries that make up the United Kingdom each now has a written constitution. But each of these 'constitutions' gives no more than a partial account of the government of these countries. For one thing, their operation cannot be understood without reference to the elaborate array of 'Concordats', namely, the agreements reached between Whitehall departments and the devolved executives as to how the two levels of government should relate to each other.[81] Important functions are still exercised by the

----

[78] B Hadfield [2005] PL 288; Hazell (ed.), *The English Question*.

[79] Report, *The Consequences of Devolution for the House of Commons* (May 2013).

[80] See pp 199–200 below.

[81] See *Memorandum of Understanding and Supplementary Agreements*, Cm 4444, 1999, and works cited in note 43 above. Also R Rawlings (2000) 106 LQR 257 and J Poirier [2001] PL 134.

Westminster Parliament and by Whitehall. The Secretaries of State for the three countries remain in being, albeit with far fewer functions than before devolution, and the activities of each Secretary of State are overseen by a select committee of the Commons. Westminster retains power to alter the present arrangements (and it frequently has, although so far only to increase devolution), but use of that power cannot ignore the politics of devolution.

Whether or not the devolution legislation renders the institutions it created and regulates a permanent legal feature of the constitutional landscape, it is presently hard to envisage circumstances in which Westminster would legislate to remove them, even if Westminster might wish to do so, without at the very least clear popular support. If Westminster took such a step, it is highly likely that the Union would fall as a result. As Lord Denning MR once put it in relation to Westminster having removed its own power to legislate for various colonies in 1931, 'freedom once given cannot be taken away'.[82]

Is devolution leading to the break-up of the United Kingdom, as some of its opponents predicted?[83] The position of Northern Ireland must be set on one side, since there is general agreement that the future of the six counties must be decided by their people. The SNP's campaign for Scottish independence has plainly been assisted by the party's success in elections for the Edinburgh Parliament (and the Westminster Parliament in 2015 and 2017), but the referendum in September 2014 did not support independence, and in 2017 polling figures have not significantly altered, even in the light of Brexit. While in neither Scotland nor Wales will devolution be put into reverse, one effect has been increased complexity in the making of statute law, and in the administrative structure that underlies the political process.[84] One important aspect of devolution is the developing network of governmental relationships, both within the United Kingdom and extending into Europe.[85] At one time devolution was defined as involving 'the delegation of central government powers without the relinquishment of sovereignty'.[86] That conclusion is not sustainable today except on a simple view of sovereignty that leaves out of account both Europe and the new centres of political power in the United Kingdom.[87]

---

[82] *Blackburn v AG* [1971] 1 WLR 1037, 1040.

[83] E. g. Dalyell, *Devolution, the End of Britain?*

[84] See HL Paper 192 (2003–4), App 1 (C M G Himsworth); Hazell and Rawlings, *Devolution, Law Making and the Constitution*. Also A Ross and H Nash [2009] PL 564 (examining the ways in which EU environmental law is implemented within Great Britain).

[85] See *Devolution: Inter-institutional Relations in the United Kingdom*, (HL Paper 28, 2002–3); and Trench (ed.) *The Dynamics of Devolution*, ch 7 (A Trench) and ch 9 (C Jeffery). Also R Rawlings, 'Cymru yn Ewrop: Wales in Europe', in Craig and Rawlings (eds), *Law and Administration in Europe*, ch 13.

[86] Kilbrandon Report, para 543.

[87] MacCormick, *Questioning Sovereignty*, p 74, says in respect of Scotland: 'The unitary sovereignty of the incorporating union agreed in 1707 seems to be at best in its twilight.'

CHAPTER 3

Parliamentary supremacy

> the most fundamental rule of UK constitutional law is that the Crown in Parliament is sovereign and that legislation enacted by the Crown with the consent of both Houses of Parliament is supreme . . . Parliament can, by enactment of primary legislation, change the law of the land in any way it chooses.[1]

It is a fundamental principle of democratic government that there should be an elected assembly representing the people, and that this assembly should have authority to make laws that apply to the entire population. But there is no universal agreement that such an assembly should have an absolute and unlimited power to make laws of whatever kind and subject matter. In many national constitutions both the existence of the assembly and the extent of its powers are set out in the constitution itself. Without such a constitutional text, are there limits on legislative authority and, if so, where may they be found? And should measures enacted by Parliament prevail over all other rules of law?

This chapter examines the extent of the legislative authority exercised today by the Westminster Parliament. We first consider briefly the stages by which that authority was established, since in the absence of a written constitution, the historical background to the authority of Parliament has great significance.

A. The growth of the legislative authority of Parliament

The year 2015 marked the 750th anniversary of the Parliament assembled by Simon de Montfort in 1265 to give counsel to Henry III, which for the first time included representatives of the shires, cities and boroughs of England as well as the feudal barons. But to become a legislature in a modern sense, the enlarged royal council had to acquire a regular existence as a body with power to legislate and with settled procedure; and the measures which emerged from that procedure had to be accepted as law. By 1485, it was accepted that measures that had been considered by Parliament and enacted by the monarch could change the common law. With the English Reformation, there disappeared the belief that Parliament could not affect the authority of the Roman Church. Henry VIII and Elizabeth I made the Crown of England supreme over all persons and causes and used the English Parliament to attain this end.

Although wide authority was attributed to acts of the 'King in Parliament', two views were held as to the justification for this.[2] The royalist view grounded legislative authority in the King, acting as Sovereign in exercise of divine right, but with the approval of Lords and Commons. By contrast, the parliamentarian view stressed the role of the two Houses, acting on behalf of the nobility and the common people, in exercising supreme authority with the monarch. There continued to be a view that certain natural laws could not be changed, even

---

[1] *R (Miller)* v *Secretary of State for Exiting the EU* [2016] EWHC 2768 (Admin), [2017] 2 WLR 583 at [20] (and see in the Supreme Court [2017] UKSC 5 at [43]).

[2] For historical attitudes to the authority of Parliament, see Goldsworthy, *The Sovereignty of Parliament*, ch 4. Also P Craig [2000] PL 211.

by the King in Parliament.[3] To set against this view, there was much authority in the law reports and in political writing which indicated that the courts had no power to review the validity of Acts of Parliament.[4]

The struggle for supremacy

Legislative supremacy involves not only the right to change the law but also that no one else should have that right. At the heart of the conflicts in the 17th century that led to the civil war, Charles I's execution, Cromwell's Protectorate and the restoration of the monarchy in 1660, lay the question whether the King could use his prerogative powers to govern without Parliament. In 1603, the King's prerogatives were undefined. Despite the existence of Parliament and the common law courts, the King, through his Council, exercised not only full executive powers but also a residue of legislative and judicial power. Acts of Parliament which sought to take away any of the 'inseparable' prerogatives of the Crown were considered invalid.[5] Four instances of the struggle for authority between Crown and Parliament may be mentioned.

1. Ordinances and proclamations

A clear distinction between statutes of the English Parliament and ordinances of the King in Council was lacking long after the end of the 13th century. The Statute of Proclamations 1539 declared that Henry VIII had wide powers of legislating by proclamation without reference to Parliament. This statute did not give the King and Council power to legislate, but sought to clarify the position of the authority possessed by proclamations. It safeguarded the common law, existing Acts of Parliament and rights of property, and prohibited infliction of the death penalty for breach of a proclamation.[6] 'Its chief practical purpose was to create machinery to enforce proclamations.'[7] Despite repeal of the statute in 1547, Mary and Elizabeth continued to resort to proclamations. The judicial powers of the Council, in particular of the Court of Star Chamber, were available to enforce proclamations. The scope of the royal prerogative to legislate remained undefined. James I made full use of this power, and in 1611 Chief Justice Coke was consulted by the Council, along with three of his brother judges, about the legality of proclamations. The resulting opinion is to be found in the *Case of Proclamations*:

(1) The King by his proclamation cannot create any offence which was not one before; for then he might alter the law of the land in a high point; for if he may create an offence where none is, upon that ensues fine and imprisonment.

(2) The King hath no prerogative but what the law of the land allows him.

(3) But the King for the prevention of offences may by proclamation admonish his subjects that they keep the laws and do not offend them upon punishment to be inflicted by law; the neglect of such proclamation aggravates the offence.

(4) If an offence be not punishable in the Star Chamber, the prohibition of it by proclamation cannot make it so.[8]

---

[3] See *Bonham*'s case (1610) 8 Co Rep 114a, quoted below in text at note 72.

[4] Goldsworthy (passim); and Gough, *Fundamental Law in English Constitutional History*.

[5] 'No Act of Parliament can bar a King of his regality': *The Case of Ship Money* (1637) 3 St Tr 825, Finch CJ, at 1235. For the leading 17th-century cases on prerogative, see Keir and Lawson, *Cases in Constitutional Law*, ch II. Also Tomkins, *Our Republican Constitution*, ch 3.

[6] HEL, vol IV, pp 102–3.

[7] G R Elton, in Fryde and Miller, *Historical Studies of the English Parliament*, II, p 206.

[8] (1611) 12 Co Rep 74. This case was applied by the Court of Session in *Grieve v Edinburgh and District Water Trustees* 1918 SC 700.

A definite limit was thus put upon the prerogative, the full force of which was effective only when Star Chamber and other conciliar tribunals were abolished in 1640. The gist of the *Case of Proclamations* is that the King's prerogative is under the law and that Parliament alone can alter the law which the King is to administer.[9] This was a critical principle of law which the majority of the Supreme Court applied in the Brexit challenge, holding by reference to the *Case of Proclamations* that the prerogative (including the power to negotiate and enter into international treaties) could not be used in a manner which would alter statute or common law, and could not be used to bring about a 'far reaching change to the UK constitutional arrangements' that withdrawing from the EU would amount to, without the authorisation of Parliament.[10]

2. Taxation

If the imposition of taxes is to be lawful, it must be authorised by legislation. But this basic principle was the subject of a long-running dispute between Parliament and the Stuart kings, who claimed that the Crown had a prerogative right to levy certain forms of taxation without the consent of Parliament. It had been conceded by the time of Edward I that the consent of Parliament was necessary for direct taxation. The history of indirect taxation is more complicated, since the regulation of foreign trade was a part of the royal prerogative relating to foreign affairs. There was no clear distinction between the imposition of taxes in the form of customs duties and the exercise of prerogative powers over foreign trade and defence of the realm:

> In the *Case of Impositions (Bate's Case)*,[11] John Bate refused to pay a duty on imported currants imposed by the Crown on the ground that the imposition was contrary to the statute 45 Edw 3 c 4 which prohibited indirect taxation without the consent of Parliament. The Court of Exchequer unanimously decided in favour of the Crown. The King could impose what duties he pleased for the purpose of regulating trade, and the court could not go behind the King's statement that the duty was in fact imposed for the regulation of trade.

> In the *Case of Ship Money (R v Hampden)*,[12] John Hampden refused to pay ship money, a tax levied by Charles I for the purpose of furnishing ships in time of national danger. Counsel for Hampden accepted that sometimes the existence of danger would justify taking the subject's goods without his consent, but only in actual as opposed to threatened emergency. The Crown conceded that the subject could not be taxed in normal circumstances without the consent of Parliament, but contended that the King was the sole judge of whether an emergency justified use of his prerogative power to raise funds to meet a national danger. A majority of the Court of Exchequer Chamber gave judgment for the King.[13]

---

[9] The Crown retains broad prerogative power to make laws for a few overseas territories, but this power is not unlimited: *Campbell* v *Hall* (1774) 1 Cowp 204; cf *R (Bancoult)* v *Foreign Secretary (No 2)* [2008] UKHL 61, [2009] 1 AC 453. And see ch 10 D.

[10] *R (Miller)* v *Secretary of State for Exiting the EU* [2017] UKSC 5, [2017] 2 WLR 583 at [44], [50] and [81]-[82].

[11] (1606) 2 St Tr 371; G D G Hall (1953) 69 LQR 200.

[12] (1637) 3 St Tr 825.

[13] For a full analysis, see D L Keir (1936) 52 LQR 546.

The *Ship Money* decision was reversed by the Long Parliament,[14] and this aspect of the struggle for supremacy was concluded by the Bill of Rights, art 4, which declared that it was illegal for the Crown to seek to raise money without parliamentary approval.[15] This has been a regularly reiterated principle of the constitution.[16]

3. Dispensing and suspending powers

The power of the Crown to dispense with the operation of statutes (for instance, by declaring that a statute need not be applied in a certain situation) may at one time have been necessary because of the form of ancient statutes and the irregular meetings of Parliament. So long, however, as the limits on the dispensing power were not clearly defined, this constituted a potential threat to the legislative authority of Parliament. In *Thomas v Sorrell*,[17] the court took care to define the limits within which the royal power to dispense with laws was acceptable. But in *Godden v Hales*, an unduly compliant court upheld a dispensation from James II to Sir Edward Hales excusing him from taking religious oaths and fulfilling other obligations imposed by the Test Act; it was held that it was an inseparable prerogative of the King to dispense with penal laws in particular cases and upon necessary reasons of which the King was sole judge.[18]

Thus encouraged, James II proceeded to set aside statutes as he pleased, granting a suspension of the penal laws relating to religion in the Declarations of Indulgence in 1687 and 1688. These acts of James were an immediate cause of the revolution of 1688. The Bill of Rights abolished the Crown's alleged power of suspending laws and prohibited the Crown's power to dispense with the operation of statutes, except where this was authorised by Parliament.[19] Similar provision was made in the Scottish Claim of Right.[20] A modern example of a breach of this basic principle may be seen in the New Zealand case of *Fitzgerald v Muldoon*, in which the Prime Minister attempted, by means of a press release, to abolish a pension scheme for civil servants established by primary legislation. The Chief Justice declared that the press release was an unlawful breach of the prohibition on dispensing powers in the Bill of Rights.[21] Similarly, when a claim sought to compel the Director of Public Prosecutions to specify in guidance the circumstances he would not prosecute individuals for the offence of assisting another person to commit suicide, the House of Lords noted that it was constitutionally impermissible for a public official to give an effective grant of immunity from the criminal law.[22]

4. The independence of the judiciary

As was shown by *Godden v Hales*, so long as judges could be removed from office at pleasure of the Crown, there was a continuing risk of their being subservient to the King in cases in which he had a direct interest. To ensure that English judges should not serve at the pleasure of the Crown, the Act of Settlement 1700 provided that they should hold office *quamdiu se bene*

---

[14] Ship Money Act 1640.

[15] Page 13 above.

[16] *Congreve v Home Office* [1976] QB 629, 652 (Lord Denning MR) (in which the revocation of valid television licences in order to charge higher licence fees was held to be an attempt to levy money without parliamentary approval).

[17] (1674) Vaughan 330.

[18] (1686) 11 St Tr 1165. The judges were hand-picked by James II, and gave cursory reasons for the decision: see A W Bradley [2008] PL 470.

[19] Articles 1 and 2 of the Bill of Rights, p 14 above. The Bill of Rights did not curtail the prerogative of pardon or the power to enter a nolle prosequi.

[20] Pages 14–5 above.

[21] [1976] 2 NZLR 615

[22] *R (Pretty) v DPP* [2002] 1 AC 800 at [39] (Lord Bingham).

gesserint (during good behaviour) but subject to a power of removal upon an address from both Houses of Parliament.[23]

Growth of ministerial responsibility

The Bill of Rights and the Act of Settlement established the legislative authority of the English Parliament vis-à-vis the Crown, while not affecting prerogatives of the Crown which had not been called in question. The settlement reflected the fact that the common lawyers had joined with Parliament to defeat the Crown's claim to rule by prerogative; and it is often said that the common lawyers thereby accepted that legislation by Parliament was of overriding authority as a source of law.[24] However, executive power itself was left in the hands of the monarch and a more democratic base for government was established only by degrees during the two centuries after the Act of Settlement. The changed role of the monarch has been summarised in this way:

> The position of affairs has been reversed since 1714. Then the King or Queen governed through Ministers, now Ministers govern through the instrumentality of the Crown.[25]

The development of Cabinet government and the creation of a democratic electoral system eventually ensured that the political authority of Parliament is pre-eminent in relation to the monarch, but government ministers still exercise many powers for which it is difficult to achieve democratic accountability. In the next section, we consider the nature of the legislative authority of Parliament, which is not necessarily justified in constitutional terms by the argument that the most recent general election will have given a mandate to the party (or parties) with a majority of seats in the Commons.

B. Meaning of legislative supremacy

The legal doctrine of the legislative supremacy of Parliament is referred to by many writers, notably by Dicey, as the sovereignty of Parliament. New constitutional developments are often debated in terms of their supposed effect on the sovereignty of Parliament. Thus, in the debate about British membership of the European Communities, those opposed to British membership proposed, without success, an amendment to the Bill which became the European Communities Act 1972 declaring that British membership would not affect the sovereignty of Parliament.[26] Critics of British membership of the EU complain both at the loss of national sovereignty and at erosion of the sovereignty of Parliament; this was a significant feature of the Brexit referendum campaign in 2016. There is no doubt that Britain's membership of the EU affected the role of Parliament, since many laws were made at a European level, under the relevant treaties, as a result. But the same applies to every state that is a member of the EU. Moreover, many states (including the United States) enjoy sovereignty in international law without having a 'sovereign' legislature. In this chapter, the expression legislative supremacy will be used, partly because it is less likely to be confused with national sovereignty, and also to stay clear of the jurisprudential doctrine of John Austin and his

---

[23] See now Senior Courts Act 1981, s 11(3); Constitutional Reform Act 2005, s 33. Also ch 13 B.

[24] This also seems to be the view of the majority of the Supreme Court in *Miller* (above) at [43], which refers to this legislation as having 'conclusively established' Parliamentary sovereignty as a 'fundamental principle of the UK constitution'.

[25] Anson, *Law and Custom of the Constitution*, vol II, p 41.

[26] HC Deb, 5 July 1972, cols 556–644; HL Deb, 7 August 1972, cols 893–914. And see ch 6.

successors that in every legal system there must be a sovereign.[27] The chapter will concentrate on the fundamental legal elements of legislative supremacy, but the concept has significant political implications which come into play in any discussion of the desirability of retaining that supremacy.

At its simplest, the supremacy of Parliament means that there are no legal limitations on the power of Parliament to legislate. Parliament here does not refer to the two Houses separately, for neither House may legislate on its own, but to the constitutional entity known as the Queen in Parliament: namely the process by which a Bill approved by Lords and Commons receives the royal assent and thus becomes an Act of Parliament. Thus defined, said Dicey, Parliament has 'under the English constitution, the right to make or unmake any law whatever; and further . . . no person or body is recognised by the law of England as having a right to override or set aside the legislation of Parliament'.[28] Dicey was writing at a time when England was often used as a loose synonym for Great Britain or the United Kingdom,[29] and today it is necessary to discuss whether the law on this matter is the same throughout the United Kingdom.[30] But the positive and negative aspects of the doctrine emerge clearly from Dicey's formulation, namely that Parliament has power to legislate on any matter whatsoever and that there exists no competing authority with power to legislate for the United Kingdom or to impose limits upon the competence of Parliament.

British membership of the European Union has given rise to the difficult issue of competing supremacies, the supremacy of Parliament on the one hand and the supremacy, or primacy, of EU law, on the other. This question – shortly to be largely historic in nature – will be considered later,[31] but we first examine the issue of supremacy in terms of the law of the United Kingdom alone.

Legal nature of legislative supremacy

This doctrine consists essentially of a legal rule which governs the relationship between the courts and the legislature, namely that the courts must apply the legislation made by Parliament and may not hold an Act of Parliament to be invalid or unconstitutional. As was at one time said, 'All that a court of law can do with an Act of Parliament is to apply it.'[32] In *Madzimbamuto* v *Lardner-Burke*, which concerned the effect of the unilateral declaration of independence in 1965 by the Rhodesian government on the Westminster Parliament's power to legislate for Rhodesia, Lord Reid said:

> It is often said that it would be unconstitutional for the United Kingdom Parliament to do certain things, meaning that the moral, political and other reasons against doing them are so strong that most people would regard it as highly improper if Parliament did these things. But that does not mean that it is beyond the power of Parliament to do such things. If Parliament chose to do any of them, the courts could not hold the Act of Parliament invalid.[33]

While the doctrine of legislative supremacy has great political significance, the legal rule defines the outcome of the process of legislation; it is not concerned with whether that process

---

[27] Austin, *The Province of Jurisprudence Determined*, Lecture 6. See MacCormick, *Questioning Sovereignty* and (same author) (1993) 56 MLR 1; P Eleftheriadis (2009) 22 Canadian Jl of Law & Jurisprudence 367. On sovereignty in Commonwealth law, see Oliver, *The Constitution of Independence*, chs 1, 3, 4, 11, 12.

[28] Dicey, *The Law of the Constitution*, pp 39–40.

[29] Ch 2 A.

[30] Section D in this chapter.

[31] Page 72 and ch 6.

[32] Keir and Lawson, *Cases in Constitutional Law*, p 72. For the position where an Act conflicts with EU law, see p 72 below; and where an Act is incompatible with Convention rights, p 74 below.

[33] [1969] 1 AC 645, 723. And see *Manuel* v *A-G* [1983] Ch 77.

is controlled by the governing party, the Cabinet or the Prime Minister. Certainly, how Parliament exercises its authority is of great importance in the debate about whether its supremacy should be retained or modified. Craig has argued that Dicey's exposition of sovereignty was advanced on the basis of assumptions about representative democracy which (in Craig's view) were flawed even in 1885 and cannot be made today.[34] However, we must distinguish as far as possible between analysing the present law and considering how it should develop in future. Changes in the legislative process do not in themselves alter the legal effect of that process, although they might affect the case for further development of the law.

Only an Act of Parliament is supreme

An Act of Parliament has a legal force which the courts are not willing to ascribe to other instruments which for one reason or another fall short of that pre-eminent status. Thus the following instruments do not enjoy legislative supremacy and the courts will if necessary decide whether or not they have legal effect:

(*a*) a resolution of the House of Commons;[35]

(*b*) a proclamation issued by the Crown under prerogative powers for which the force of law is claimed;[36]

(*c*) a treaty entered into by the government under prerogative powers which seeks to change the law within territory subject to British jurisdiction;[37]

(*d*) subordinate legislation which appears to be issued under the authority of an Act of Parliament by a minister or government department,[38] whether or not this has been approved by resolution of each House of Parliament;[39]

(*e*) an act of a subordinate legislature,[40] such as the Scottish Parliament or the Northern Ireland Assembly;[41]

(*f*) by-laws made by a local authority or other public body;[42]

(*g*) prerogative Orders in Council made for overseas territories, and laws purporting to be made under powers conferred by such Orders.[43]

In all these cases, the courts must consider whether the document for which legislative force is claimed is indeed legally binding.[44] So, too, when a litigant relies on an Act of Parliament, the court must if necessary decide whether the provision in question has been brought into force.

---

[34] In *Public Law and Democracy*, ch 2, Craig argues that Dicey's notion of sovereignty was 'firmly embedded within a conception of self-correcting majoritarian democracy' (p 15) since, in Dicey's words, 'The electors can in the long run always enforce their will'; further, that the British system 'became one dominated by the top, by the executive and the party hierarchy' (p 42) and that the danger has always been one of majoritarian tyranny.

[35] *Stockdale* v *Hansard* (1839) 9 A & E 1; *Bowles* v *Bank of England* [1913] 1 Ch 57.

[36] *Case of Proclamations* (note 8 above); *The Zamora* [1916] 2 AC 77.

[37] *A-G for Canada* v *A-G for Ontario* [1937] AC 326; *JH Rayner (Mincing Lane) Ltd* v *Department of Trade and Industry* [1990] 2 AC 418, 500 (Lord Oliver).

[38] E.g. *Chester* v *Bateson* [1902] 1 KB 829; ch 22.

[39] *Hoffmann-La Roche* v *Secretary for Trade & Industry* [1975] AC 295.

[40] *Belfast Corpn* v *OD Cars Ltd* [1960] AC 490.

[41] *AXA General Insurance* v *HM Advocate* [2011] UKSC 46, [2012] 1 AC 868.

[42] E.g. *Kruse* v *Johnson* [1898] 2 QB 91.

[43] *R* v *Foreign Secretary, ex p Bancoult (No 2)* (note 9 above); and *R* v *Foreign Secretary, ex p Bancoult* [2001] QB 1067.

[44] As was done in *R (Jackson)* v *A-G* [2005] UKHL 56, [2006] 1 AC 262 (p 69 below).

The difference between an Act of Parliament and lesser instruments is reflected in a distinction drawn by the Human Rights Act 1998 between 'primary legislation' and 'secondary legislation'. Unfortunately, the line drawn in the 1998 Act does not coincide with the distinctions just drawn. Thus various measures (including prerogative Orders in Council) are treated by the Act as primary legislation.[45]

Position different under written constitution

The doctrine of legislative supremacy distinguishes the United Kingdom from those countries in which a written constitution imposes limits on the legislature and entrusts the ordinary courts or a constitutional court to decide whether acts of the legislature comply with the constitution. In *Marbury* v *Madison*, the US Supreme Court held that the judicial function vested in the court necessarily carried with it the task of deciding whether an Act of Congress was or was not in conformity with the constitution.[46] In a legal system which accepts judicial review of legislation, legislation may be held invalid on a variety of grounds: for example, because it conflicts with the separation of powers where this is a feature of the constitution,[47] infringes human rights guaranteed by the constitution,[48] or has not been passed in accordance with the procedure laid down in the constitution.[49] By contrast, in the United Kingdom the legislative supremacy of Parliament appears to be the fundamental rule of constitutional law, and this supremacy includes power to legislate on constitutional matters. In so far as constitutional rules are contained in earlier Acts, there seems to be no Act which Parliament could not repeal or amend by passing a new Act. The Bill of Rights of 1689 could in law be repealed or amended by an ordinary Act of Parliament. This was done in the Defamation Act 1996, section 13 of which amended article 9 of the Bill of Rights regarding the freedom of speech in Parliament.[50]

Legislative supremacy illustrated

The apparently unlimited powers of Parliament may be illustrated in many ways. The Tudor kings used Parliament to legalise the separation of the English Church from the Church of Rome. In 1715, Parliament passed the Septennial Act to extend the life of Parliament (including its own) from three to seven years, because it was desired to avoid an election so soon after the Hanoverian accession and the 1715 uprising in Scotland. In vain did opponents of the Act argue that the supreme legislature must be restrained 'from subverting the foundation on which it stands'.[51] Less controversially, during the two world wars, Parliament prolonged its own life by amending the rule in the Parliament Act 1911 that a general election must be held at least every five years.

Parliament has altered the succession to the throne (in the Act of Settlement 1700 and His Majesty's Declaration of Abdication Act 1936); reformed the composition of both Houses of Parliament; dispensed with the approval of the House of Lords for certain Bills (the Parliament Acts 1911 and 1949); enabled British membership of an international organisation exercising powers of extraordinary breadth and scope (the European Communities Act 1972); given effect to the Scottish and Irish Treaties of Union and later departed from those treaties,

---

[45] Human Rights Act 1998, s 21(1). See ch 14 C; and P Billings and B Pontin [2001] PL 21.

[46] 1 Cranch 137 (1803).

[47] *Liyanage* v *R* [1967] 1 AC 259; *Hinds* v *R* [1977] AC 195 and see ch 4 C.

[48] E.g. *Aptheker* v *Secretary of State* 378 US 500 (1964) (Act of US Congress refusing passports to communists held an unconstitutional restriction on right to travel).

[49] *Harris* v *Minister of Interior* 1952 (2) SA 428. Generally see de Visser, *Constitutional Review in Europe*.

[50] See ch 9 A.

[51] Quoted in Marshall, *Parliamentary Sovereignty and Commonwealth*, p 84.

including by devolving some of its own legislative power within certain territories (i.e. Scotland, Wales and Northern Ireland);[52] and altered the territorial limits of the United Kingdom.[53] Since 1997, there has been a flurry of constitutional legislation, including the Scotland Act 1998, the Human Rights Act 1998, the House of Lords Act 1999, the Constitutional Reform Act 2005, the Constitutional Reform and Governance Act 2010 and the Fixed-term Parliaments Act 2011.

Indemnity Acts and retrospective legislation

Parliament has exercised the power to legalise past illegalities and to alter the law retrospectively. This power has been used by a government with a secure majority in Parliament to reverse inconvenient decisions made by the courts.[54] Retrospective legislation was passed after both world wars, protecting various illegal acts committed in the national interest.[55] Retrospective laws are, however,

> contrary to the general principle that legislation by which the conduct of mankind is to be regulated ought . . . to deal with future acts and ought not to change the character of past transactions carried on upon the faith of the then existing law . . . Accordingly the court will not ascribe retrospective force to new laws affecting rights unless by express words or necessary implication it appears that such was the intention of the legislature.[56]

The rule of interpretation is that a statute will not be read as having a retrospective effect that impairs an existing right or obligation unless this result is unavoidable.[57] The Immigration Act 1971 was held to empower the Home Office to deport Commonwealth citizens who had entered in breach of earlier immigration laws but against whom no such action could have been taken at the time the 1971 Act came into effect:[58] but the Act did not make punishable by criminal sanctions conduct which had occurred before the Act was passed.[59] Although art 7 of the European Convention on Human Rights provides that no one shall be held guilty of a criminal offence for conduct which did not constitute an offence at the time when it was committed,[60] Parliament has power to legislate retrospectively in breach of this. However, 'It is hardly credible that any government department would promote or that Parliament would pass retrospective criminal legislation.'[61] Legislation which authorises payments to be made to individuals in respect of past events is also retrospective,[62] but it may be objectionable if it restricts existing claims or is discriminatory.

....

[52] Ch 2, and section D in this chapter.

[53] Island of Rockall Act 1972.

[54] War Damage Act 1965 (*Burmah Oil Co* v *Lord Advocate* [1965] AC 75); Northern Ireland Act 1972 (*R (Hume* et al.) v *Londonderry Justices* [1972] NILR 91); Education (Scotland) Act 1973 (*Malloch* v *Aberdeen Corpn* 1974 SLT 253); National Health Service (Invalid Direction) Act 1980 (*Lambeth BC* v *Secretary of State* (1980) 79 LGR 61).

[55] Indemnity Act 1920 and War Charges Validity Act 1925; Enemy Property Act 1953, ss 1–3.

[56] Per Willes J in *Phillips* v *Eyre* (1870) LR 6 QB 1, 23. On retrospectivity in general, see Lord Rodger of Earlsferry (2005) 121 LQR 57; and Sampford, *Retrospectivity and the Rule of Law*.

[57] *Yew Bon Tew* v *Kenderaan Bas Mara* [1983] 1 AC 553, 558. And see *Plewa* v *Chief Adjudication Officer* [1995] 1 AC 249 (common law presumption applied to recovery of overpaid benefits).

[58] *Azam* v *Home Secretary* [1974] AC 18.

[59] *Waddington* v *Miah* [1974] 2 All ER 377, 379 (Lord Reid).

[60] Ch 14 B. On the War Crimes Act 1991, A T Richardson (1992) 55 MLR 73, 76–80; S N McMurtrie (1992) 13 *Statute Law Review* 128. On retrospective penalties, *R* v *Pora* [2001] 2 NZLR 37; A Butler [2001] PL 586.

[61] [1974] 2 All ER 377, 379; and see *R* v *Home Secretary, ex p Bhajan Singh* [1976] QB 198.

[62] E.g. Employment Act 1982, s 2 and Sch 1.

Legislative supremacy and international law

There are many reasons why Parliament should take into account the United Kingdom's obligations at international law when it legislates, but the courts may not hold an Act void on the ground that it contravenes general principles of international law.

> The Herring Fishery (Scotland) Act 1889 authorised a fishery board to make by-laws prohibiting certain forms of trawling within the Moray Firth, an area which included much sea that lay beyond British territorial waters. The Danish master of a Norwegian trawler was convicted in a Scottish court for breaking these by-laws. The High Court of Justiciary held that its function was confined to interpreting the Act and the by-laws, and that Parliament had intended to legislate for the conduct of all persons within the Moray Firth, whatever might be the position in international law. 'For us an Act of Parliament duly passed by Lords and Commons and assented to by the King is supreme, and we are bound to give effect to its terms.'[63]

Nor may the courts hold an Act invalid because it conflicts with a treaty to which the United Kingdom is a party.

> An assessment to income tax was challenged on the ground that part of the tax raised was used for the manufacture of nuclear weapons, contrary to the Geneva Convention Act 1957. It was held that the unambiguous provisions of a statute must be followed even if they are contrary to international law. Regarding an argument that tax had been imposed for an improper purpose, the judge said: 'What the statute itself enacts cannot be unlawful, because what the statute says and provides is itself the law, and the highest form of law that is known to this country.'[64]

However, there is a principle of statutory interpretation that Parliament has intended to legislate in a manner which does not place the United Kingdom in breach of its international law obligations, and the courts will expend a considerable effort attempting to construe legislation so as to achieve this outcome.[65]

As far as UK courts are concerned, there are no territorial restrictions on the legislative competence of Parliament. Sir Ivor Jennings famously stated that Parliament could, *as a matter of law*, legislate to prohibit smoking on the streets of Paris if it so wished.[66] Generally Parliament legislates only in respect of its own territory or in respect of the conduct of its own citizens when they are abroad, but occasionally legislation is intended to operate outside the United Kingdom: thus the Continental Shelf Act 1964 vested in the Queen the rights of exploration and exploitation of the continental shelf; the Act provided for the application of

---

[63] Lord Dunedin in *Mortensen* v *Peters* (1906) 8 F(J) 93, 100. The Trawling in Prohibited Areas Prevention Act 1909 later made it an offence to land fish caught in prohibited areas of the sea, thus limiting the extra-territorial effect of the earlier ban.

[64] Ungoed-Thomas J in *Cheney* v *Conn* [1968] 1 All ER 779, 782; and see *Inland Revenue Commissioners* v *Collco Dealings Ltd* [1962] AC 1.

[65] *R* v *Lyons* [2003] 1 AC 976 at [27]-[28] (Lord Hoffmann); *Assange* v *Swedish Prosecution Authority* [2012] UKSC 22, [2012] 2 AC 471.

[66] Jennings, *The Law and the Constitution*, p 170. The fact that no one in France would enforce the law is not the point, as Jennings explained at p 171.

criminal and civil law in respect of installations placed in the surface waters above the continental shelf. A few serious crimes committed abroad by British citizens are justiciable in British courts, such as treason, murder, bigamy and some revenue offences; all torture, wherever it takes place, is a crime in UK law.[67] The courts apply a rule of interpretation that statutes will not be given extraterritorial effect, unless this is expressly provided or necessarily implied.[68] In general, Parliament does not pass laws which would be contrary to the comity of nations. Yet national law does not always keep pace with Britain's changing international obligations. While the government under the royal prerogative may enter into treaties, treaties must be adopted by Act of Parliament if national law is to be altered.[69] The ratification of a treaty by the government may in some instances create a legitimate expectation that the government will act in accordance with the treaty,[70] but such an expectation does not oblige Parliament to implement the treaty in national law.

No legal limitations on Parliament

Many illustrations may be given of the use which Parliament has made of its legislative supremacy in legislating on constitutional matters, retrospectively, in breach of international law, and so on. It does not follow from a recital of this kind that the powers of Parliament are unlimited. As Calvert said:

> No one doubts that the powers of the UK Parliament are extremely wide . . . But that is not what is in issue. What is in issue is whether those powers are unlimited and one no more demonstrates this by pointing to a wide range of legislative objects than one demonstrates the contrary by pointing to matters on which Parliament has not, in fact, ever legislated.[71]

There is much evidence from the law reports that, at least since 1688, judges have been strongly inclined to accept the legislative omnicompetence of Parliament. Yet this has not always been the judicial attitude. In his note on *Dr Bonham*'s case, Coke CJ said:

> In many cases, the common law will control Acts of Parliament, and sometimes adjudge them to be utterly void: for when an Act of Parliament is against common right and reason, or repugnant, or impossible to be performed, the common law will control it, and adjudge such Act to be void.[72]

While English judges made similar statements only rarely after 1688,[73] it is not possible from reported cases alone to demonstrate that they have utterly lost the power to 'control' an Act of Parliament – or to show that a judge who is confronted with a statute repugnant to moral or constitutional principle (for example, a law condemning all of a certain race to be executed) must either apply the statute or resign from office.[74] Support for this has come

---

[67] Criminal Justice Act 1988, s 134; see *R v Bow Street Magistrate, ex p Pinochet Ugarte (No 3)* [2000] 1 AC 147.

[68] *Treacy v DPP* [1971] AC 537, 552; and Jones, *Bennion's Statutory Interpretation*, pp 371–8. On the extraterritorial effect of the Human Rights Act 1998, see *Smith v Ministry of Defence* [2013] UKSC 41, [2014] AC 52.

[69] *R (Miller) v Secretary of State for Exiting the EU* [2017] UKSC 5, [2017] 2 WLR 583; note 37 above. And see Constitutional Reform and Governance Act 2010, part 2 for the procedural rules about drawing Parliament's attention to treaties entered into by the Crown.

[70] See *R v Uxbridge Magistrates' Court, ex p Adimi* [2001] QB 667.

[71] *Constitutional Law in Northern Ireland*, p 14.

[72] (1610) 8 Co Rep 113b, 118a. For an argument that 'void' meant something closer to an interpretative exercise in the language of the time, see: I Williams (2006) 27 J Legal History 111. See also: S E Thorne (1938) 54 LQR 543; Goldsworthy, *The Sovereignty of Parliament*, pp 111–17; and Gough, *Fundamental Law*, pp 35–40.

[73] E.g. Holt CJ, *City of London v Wood* (1702) 12 Mod 669, 687.

[74] Cf Jennings, *The Law and the Constitution*, pp 159–60. For the attitude of British courts to foreign legislation which infringes fundamental rights, see *Oppenheimer v Cattermole* [1976] AC 249 and F A Mann (1978) 94 LQR 512.

from New Zealand, where Lord Cooke of Thorndon urged that within the common law the judges exercise authority which extends to upholding fundamental values that might be at risk from certain forms of legislation.[75] Lord Mance has queried in passing whether 'it were to be possible at all' for even primary legislation to require internment without the ability to challenge basis of it.[76] In 1995, Lord Woolf argued that 'if Parliament did the unthinkable' and legislated without regard for the role of the judiciary in upholding the rule of law, the courts might wish to make it clear that 'ultimately there are even limits on the supremacy of Parliament which it is the courts' inalienable responsibility to identify and uphold'.[77] Laws LJ explained that parliamentary supremacy is *conditional* on there being an authoritative and independent judicial source of interpretation of the law.[78] Lord Steyn has said that the courts might have to revisit the principle of parliamentary supremacy, if Parliament sought 'to abolish judicial review of flagrant abuse of power by a government or even the role of the ordinary courts in standing between the executive and citizens'; in such circumstances, the courts might have to 'qualify' the supremacy of Parliament, 'a principle established on a different hypothesis of constitutionalism'.[79] In a challenge to the exclusion of Scottish prisoners from voting in the 2014 independence referendum, Lord Hodge commented that:

> While the common law cannot extend the franchise beyond that provided by parliamentary legislation, I do not exclude the possibility that in the very unlikely event that a parliamentary majority abusively sought to entrench its power by a curtailment of the franchise or similar device, the common law, informed by principles of democracy and the rule of law and international norms, would be able to declare such legislation unlawful.[80]

Short of such an extreme situation, it is not at all likely that the courts would of their volition exercise power derived solely from common law to review the validity of Acts of Parliament. Nor is there widespread academic support for their doing so,[81] still less on what basis and in which cases.[82] Where in countries judicial review of legislation takes place, this is generally derived from a written constitution.[83] But it has been said that the rule that the courts enforce without question all Acts of Parliament is the one rule of the common law which Parliament may not change:[84] parliamentary supremacy is the fundamental constitutional principle because the *common law* holds it to be so. A number of the Law Lords made this observation in *Jackson* (on which, see further below).[85] The attractiveness of this analysis for some is that rules of the common law can be changed by the courts: the acceptance of absolute parliamentary supremacy may fall to be revised if it were necessary to ensure

---

[75] See *Taylor* v *New Zealand Poultry Board* [1984] 1 NZLR 394, 398; also J L Caldwell [1984] NZLJ 357 and R Cooke [1988] NZLJ 158.

[76] *Ahmed* v *HM Treasury* [2010] UKSC 2, [2010] 2 AC 534 at [249].

[77] Lord Woolf [1995] PL 57, 69. Cf Lord Irvine [1996] PL 59, 75–8.

[78] *R (Cart)* v *Upper Tribunal* [2009] EWHC 3052 (Admin), [2010] 2 WLR 1012 at [36]–[39]. This reasoning was not adopted by the Court of Appeal or the Supreme Court, but nor was it addressed. For Sir John's extra-judicial work, see Laws [1995] PL 72, 81–93.

[79] *R (Jackson)* v *A–G*, [102], note 141 below. See too *AXA General Insurance Ltd* v *HM Advocate* [2011] UKSC 46, [2012] 1 AC 868 at [51] (Lord Hope).

[80] *Moohan* v *Lord Advocate* [2014] UKSC 67, [2015] AC 901 at [35] (a majority judgment in which four other Justices joined).

[81] The most high-profile supporter, on a rule of law basis, being T R S Allan in *Law, Liberty and Justice*; *Constitutional Justice: A Liberal Theory of the Rule of Law*; and *The Sovereignty of Law*.

[82] For attempts to answer these two questions, see C J S Knight [2009] CLJ 361; [2011] PL 90.

[83] Israel is an apparent exception: I Zamir [1991] PL 523, 529–30, C Klein (1996) 2 *European Public Law* 225. Also Navot, *The Constitutional Law of Israel*, pp 57–63, 156–67.

[84] H W R Wade [1955] CLJ 172, 187–9; and (1996) 112 LQR 568.

[85] [2005] UKHL 56, [2006] 1 AC 262 at [102] (Lord Steyn), [126] (Lord Hope), [168] (Lord Carswell).

compliance with other paramount constitutional principles, such as the rule of law. For precisely this reason, the common law source of parliamentary supremacy is by no means universally accepted. The majority's judgment in *Miller* appeared to suggest that parliamentary supremacy was established *in statute*,[86] and particularly the legislation which cemented the role of Parliament during and following the Glorious Revolution: the Bill of Rights and the Acts of Settlement.[87] A more orthodox approach is summarised by Lord Bingham as follows:

> It is true of course that the principle of parliamentary sovereignty cannot without circularity be ascribed to statute, and the historical record in any event reveals no such statute. But it does not follow that that the principle must be a creature of the judge-made common law which the judges can alter: if it were, the rule could be altered by statute, since the prime characteristic of any common law rule is that it yields to a contrary provision of statute. To my mind, it has been convincingly shown that the principle of parliamentary sovereignty has been recognised as fundamental in this country not because the judges invented it but because it has for centuries been accepted as such by judges and others officially concerned in the operation of our constitutional system. The judges did not by themselves establish the principle and they cannot, by themselves, change it.[88]

The UK Parliament, though, enjoys an unlimited power to legislate on constitutional matters. Is it therefore possible that, *on the initiative of Parliament itself*, the courts could exercise a power of judicial review derived from constitutional legislation passed by Parliament? This possibility has often been dismissed out of hand by invoking the principle that no Parliament may bind its successors. But, it has been asked, 'Why cannot Parliament change that rule; since all other rules of the common law are subject to its sovereignty?'[89] It is to this difficult and fundamental question that we now turn.

C. The continuing nature of parliamentary supremacy

Within a modern legal system, enacted laws remain in force until they are repealed or amended, unless by the inclusion of a 'sunset clause' they are declared when enacted to have a limited life.[90] It is inherent in the nature of a legislature that it should be free to make new laws. The fact that legislation about, say, divorce or abortion was enacted five or 25 years ago does not prevent fresh legislation on the same subject being enacted today: even if social conditions have not changed, the legislature may wish to adopt a new approach. When Parliament does so, it is convenient if the new Act expressly repeals the old law or states the extent to which the old law is amended. Suppose that this is not done and the new Act conflicts with an older Act but does not expressly repeal it. There now appear to be two inconsistent statutes on the statute book. How is the apparent conflict to be resolved?

[86] *Miller* (above), at [43].

[87] See p 53 above.

[88] Lord Bingham, *The Rule of Law*, p 167. Lord Bingham's reference to the orthodox approach being 'convincingly shown' is too the work of H L A Hart in *The Concept of Law*, discussing an ultimate rule of recognition which relevant actors (in this context, politicians, judges, civil servants) accept shows the ultimate source of authority. See, to, Goldsworthy, *The Sovereignty of Parliament*, ch 10.

[89] E C S Wade, Introduction to Dicey, p lv.

[90] This has always been the position in English law (Greenberg, *Craies on Legislation*, p 483). But Scottish Acts passed before 1707 may by the doctrine of desuetude cease to be law through non-use and change of circumstances: *M'Ara* v *Magistrates of Edinburgh* 1913 SC 1059; Mitchell, *Constitutional Law*, pp 21–2. An example of legislation with a 'sunset clause' was the Data Retention and Investigatory Powers Act 2014; see s 8.

The doctrine of implied repeal

It is for the courts to resolve this conflict because they must decide the law which applies to a given situation. If the conflict cannot be resolved in any other way, the courts apply the later Act; the earlier Act is taken to have been repealed by implication to the extent of the inconsistency.

> If two inconsistent Acts be passed at different times, the last must be obeyed . . . Every Act is made either for the purpose of making a change in the law, or for the purpose of better declaring the law, and its operation is not to be impeded by the mere fact that it is inconsistent with some previous enactment.[91]

This doctrine is found in many legal systems, but in Britain the operation of the doctrine is sometimes considered to have special constitutional significance.

> Before 1919, many public and private Acts of Parliament empowered public authorities to acquire land compulsorily and laid down differing rules of compensation. In 1919, the Acquisition of Land (Assessment of Compensation) Act was passed to provide a uniform code of rules for assessing the compensation to be paid in future. Section 7(1) provided: 'The provisions of the Act or order by which the land is authorised to be acquired, or of any Act incorporated therewith, shall . . . have effect subject to this Act, and so far as inconsistent with this Act those provisions shall cease to have or shall not have effect.' The Housing Act 1925 sought to alter the 1919 rules of compensation by reducing the compensation payable in respect of slum-housing. In *Vauxhall Estates Ltd* v *Liverpool Corporation*,[92] it was held that the provisions of the 1925 Act must prevail over the 1919 Act so far as they were inconsistent with it. The court rejected the ingenious argument of counsel for the slum-owners that s 7(1) (and especially the words 'or shall not have effect') had tied the hands of future Parliaments so that the later Parliament could not (short of express repeal) legislate inconsistently with the 1919 Act. In a similar case, *Ellen Street Estates Ltd* v *Minister of Health*, Maugham LJ said: 'The Legislature cannot, according to our constitution, bind itself as to the form of subsequent legislation, and it is impossible for Parliament to enact that in a subsequent statute dealing with the same subject matter there can be no implied repeal. If in a subsequent Act Parliament chooses to make it plain that the earlier statute is being to some extent repealed, effect must be given to that intention just because it is the will of Parliament.'[93]

The correctness of these two decisions is not in doubt, for there were very weak grounds for suggesting that in 1919 Parliament had been attempting to bind its successors. But Maugham LJ went far beyond the actual situation in saying that Parliament could not bind itself as to the *form* of subsequent legislation. He would have been closer to the facts of the case had he said that Parliament could not bind itself as to the *contents* of subsequent legislation.[94] However, these cases, which illustrate the doctrine of implied repeal, have been used to support a broad constitutional argument that Parliament may never bind its successors.[95]

---

[91] Lord Langdale, in *Dean of Ely* v *Bliss* (1842) 5 Beav 574, 582. See also *Thoburn* v *Sunderland Council* [2002] EWHC 195 (Admin), [2003] QB 151; Jones, *Bennion's Statutory Interpretation*, pp 315–20; Young, *Parliamentary Sovereignty and the Human Rights Act*, ch 2.

[92] [1932] 1 KB 733.

[93] [1934] 1 KB 590, 597.

[94] H R Gray (1953) 10 Univ of Toronto LJ 54, 67.

[95] Cf H W R Wade [1955] CLJ 172, 187.

Can Parliament bind its successors?

The rule that Parliament may not bind its successors (and that no Parliament is bound by Acts of its predecessors) is often cited both as a limitation on legislative supremacy and as an example of it. To adopt for a moment the language of sovereignty: if it is an essential attribute of a legal sovereign that there should be no legal restraints upon her, then, by definition, the rules laid down by a predecessor cannot bind the present sovereign, for otherwise the present holder of the post would not be sovereign. Dicey, outstanding exponent of the sovereignty of Parliament, accepted this point:

> The logical reason why Parliament has failed in its endeavours to enact unchangeable enactments is that a sovereign power cannot, *while retaining its sovereign character*, restrict its own powers by any parliamentary enactment.[96] (italics supplied)

Thus to state that no Parliament may bind its successors is to assume that all future Parliaments must have the same attribute of sovereignty as the present Parliament. But why must this be so? The problem is less intractable than the comparable conundrum of whether an omnipotent deity can bind itself,[97] for even sovereign Parliaments are human institutions; and there is nothing inherently absurd in the idea of a supreme Parliament having power to make fresh constitutional arrangements for the future. To state that Parliament may not bind its successors leaves unclear both the nature of the obligation which a present Parliament cannot impose on its successors and also the meaning of 'successors'.[98] Indeed, the doctrine that Parliament may not 'bind' its successors is an over-simplification.

(*a*) Some matters authorised by legislation are of such a kind that, once done, they cannot be undone by a later Act. Thus, over 60 years after Parliament approved the cession of Heligoland to Germany in 1890, Parliament repealed the statute by which cession was approved,[99] but no one expected that this would recover the territory for the United Kingdom. On the many occasions after 1960 when independence was conferred on an overseas territory, it was the practice for Parliament to provide that no future Act of the UK Parliament 'shall extend or be deemed to extend' to the independent country as part of its law; and that the UK government should thereafter have no responsibility for the government of the country in question.[100] Earlier Independence Acts were less categorical, since it was thought that it might sometimes be convenient for the Westminster Parliament to continue to legislate at the request of the territory concerned.[101] At one time it was suggested that provisions conferring independence could be revoked by the Westminster Parliament,[102] but in reality 'freedom once conferred cannot be revoked'.[103] Thus, by ceding territory or conferring independence, Parliament may restrict the geographical area over which future Parliaments may legislate effectively. In the Canada Act 1982, which conferred full power of constitutional amendment on Canada, it was provided that no subsequent Act of the UK Parliament 'shall extend to Canada as part of its law'. If Westminster in future should attempt to legislate for Canada, Canadian courts would ignore the attempt, unless the Canadian Parliament had authorised

---

[96] Dicey, p 68.
[97] Cf Hart, *The Concept of Law*, p 146; Marshall, *Parliamentary Sovereignty and the Commonwealth*, p 13.
[98] R Stone (1966) 26 Louisiana LR 753, 755.
[99] Anglo–German Agreement Act 1890, repealed by Statute Law Revision Act 1953, s 1.
[100] E.g. Kenya Independence Act 1963, s 1; and see Roberts-Wray, *Commonwealth and Colonial Law*, p 261.
[101] Statute of Westminster 1931, s 4 and e.g. Ceylon Independence Act 1947, s 1.
[102] *British Coal Corpn* v *R* [1935] AC 500, 520.
[103] *Ndlwana* v *Hofmeyr* 1937 AD 229, 237; *Ibralebbe* v *R* [1964] AC 900, 923; *Blackburn* v *A–G* [1971] 2 All ER 1380.

them to apply the legislation from Westminster. But British courts would be bound to give effect to the Westminster legislation so far as it lay within their jurisdiction to do so.[104]

(*b*) In a different way, Parliament may bind future Parliaments by altering the composition of the two Houses or the succession to the throne. In 1832, when Parliament reformed the House of Commons to secure more democratic representation, later Parliaments were bound by that legislation inasmuch as the only lawful House of Commons was one elected in accordance with the 1832 Act. The present House was elected under election laws that are different from what they were in 1900 or in 1945. As for the Lords, in 1958 authority was given for life peerages, and in 1999 all but 92 hereditary peers were removed from the House. Every change in composition of the Lords must either be approved by that House (as constituted for the time being), or in the absence of such approval be enacted under the Parliament Acts 1911 and 1949.[105] In 1936, His Majesty's Declaration of Abdication Act altered the line of succession to the throne laid down by the Act of Settlement 1700, by removing Edward VIII from the throne: if a later Parliament had wished the throne to revert to him, the assent of the monarch (George VI or his descendant) would have been required, just as Edward VIII's assent was needed for the Abdication Act itself. Thus, Parliament may alter the rules that determine who the successors of the component parts of Parliament will be.

By contrast, when Westminster creates an assembly or parliament with devolved power to make law for part of the United Kingdom, its current practice is to ensure that this does not limit its own power to legislate for the whole United Kingdom. The Scotland Act 1998, s 28, empowered the Scottish Parliament to make laws on devolved matters; but the Act stated that conferment of that power to make laws 'does not affect the power' of the UK Parliament to make laws for Scotland (s 28(7)). A similar provision is found in the legislation for Wales and Northern Ireland.[106] When the Government of Ireland Act 1920 established a parliament for Northern Ireland, s 75 provided that the 'supreme authority' of the UK Parliament 'shall remain unaffected and undiminished over all persons, matters and things' in Northern Ireland. That authority was exercised in 1972, when Westminster abolished the Stormont Parliament. On the Diceyan view of supremacy, it is not necessary in law to include express provision in a devolution Act to preserve Westminster's legislative powers. But such provision serves a political purpose, if only to forestall any challenge to the continuing authority of Westminster to legislate even on devolved matters.[107] Similarly, in the amendments in the Scotland Act 2016 and Wales Act 2017 to expressly state in legislation that the Scottish Parliament and Scottish government, and the National Assembly for Wales and the Welsh government, were to be permanent is no more binding on a future Parliament than before the amendment was made.[108] There is nothing to stop Parliament in 2019 from repealing both changes; indeed if Scotland does become an independent country, the various Scotland Acts doubtless will be repealed. Unusually, the purely political purpose of the 'permanence' amendments is expressly signalled in the legislation itself: they are directly included to 'signify the commitment of the Parliament and Government of the United Kingdom' to the devolution settlement.[109]

The rule that Parliament may not bind its successors presents difficulties for certain constitutional reforms (for example, the creation of an entrenched Bill of Rights, discussed below). But it presents no obstacle to the adoption of a new constitutional structure for the United Kingdom.

---

[104] *Manuel* v *A-G* [1983] Ch 77, 88.

[105] Ch 8 D.

[106] Government of Wales Act 2006, s 93(5); Northern Ireland Act 1998, s 5(6).

[107] And see ch 2 B.

[108] See now: s 63A of the Scotland Act 1998 and s A1 of the Government of Wales Act 2006.

[109] See: s 63A(2) of the Scotland Act 1998 and s A1(2) of the Government of Wales Act 2006.

As was said about Gladstone's first Home Rule Bill for Ireland, 'if the Irish Government Bill had become law the Parliament of 1885 would have had no successors'.[110] Dicey described it as a 'strange' and 'clearly untenable' dogma that a sovereign power 'can never by its own act divest itself of sovereignty'.[111] The object of ensuring that no subsequent Parliament enjoyed legislative supremacy could be achieved in various ways, for example by creating a federal system in the United Kingdom under which England, Scotland, Wales and Northern Ireland each had its own legislature and executive; these bodies, together with a federal legislature and executive, would all be subject to the constitution. Such a system would be inconsistent with the continuing supremacy of the Westminster Parliament. The legislative ground for the new constitution would be laid by the supreme Parliament before it put an end to its own existence.[112]

With the possible exception of the Union between Scotland and England in 1707 and the Union between Ireland and Great Britain in 1800,[113] no reforms have been intended to go as far as this. However, as with British membership of the EU,[114] problems may arise where the clear intention of Parliament to divest itself of legislative supremacy is not expressed and it may be argued that the supremacy has not been affected. The question is not, 'May a supreme Parliament bind its successors?' but 'What must Parliament do (a) to express the definite intention that future Parliaments should not be supreme and (b) to ensure (by express direction and/or structural changes) that the courts will give effect to that intention?' The second part of the question is important: for if the matter were to rest merely on the stated intention of the present Parliament, it is likely (in the absence of structural changes) that the courts would hold that a later Parliament would be free to depart from that intention. An example of legislation, outside the devolution context, that is intended to have a lasting effect is the Fixed-term Parliaments Act 2011, which requires general elections to be held at regular five-year intervals and no longer at the discretion of the Prime Minister. The Act contains no protection against its amendment or repeal by Parliament, should a new government decide to change from the five-year rule.[115]

But does the fact that the legislation deals with important matters of constitutional law mean that it should be afforded special protection? On an orthodox view of supremacy and of implied repeal, there is no difference between the Act of Union and the Dentists Act. But this does not reflect reality, and the common law has gradually recognised that not all statutes – or at least not all provisions of all statutes – are equal, and that 'constitutional' legislation is immune from implied repeal: a supreme Parliament may repeal it but must do so expressly or by necessary implication, and not by an accidental sidewind. This concept of 'constitutional statutes' was first seen in relation to the European Communities Act 1972[116] and has been repeatedly endorsed by the Supreme Court in relation to that, and other, legislation which shapes the constitutional structure and principles of the United Kingdom.[117] No court has,

....
[110] W R Anson (1886) 2 LQR 427, 436.

[111] Dicey, p 68.

[112] And see Dicey, p 69.

[113] Ch 2 A and section D in this chapter.

[114] Ch 6 C, D.

[115] And see ch 10 B. It has remained in place despite the general election of 2017 being precisely the sort of exercise the Act was designed to prevent.

[116] *Thoburn* v *Sunderland CC* [2002] EWHC 195 (Admin), [2003] QB 151.

[117] *R (HS2 Alliance)* v *Transport Secretary* [2014] UKSC 3, [2014] 1 WLR 324 at [207], referring to Magna Carta, the Petition of Right 1628, the Bill of Rights and the Claim of Rights Act 1689, the Act of Settlement 1701 and the Act of Union 1707, the European Communities Act 1972, the Human Rights Act 1998 and the Constitutional Reform Act 2005. See also: *R (Miller)* v *Secretary of State for Exiting the EU* [2017] UKSC 5, [2017] 2 WLR 583. Whether or not the devolution legislation has acquired this classification is not absolutely clear, but as a matter of principle it should do so: see *H* v *Lord Advocate* [2012] UKSC 24, [2013] 1 AC 413 (Scotland Act 1998).

however, sought to define the content of the protected category or the principles upon which its content can be discerned.[118]

It is worth distinguishing at this stage between formal requirements as to subsequent amendment or repeal of legislation, and statutory provisions which are intended to avoid the implied repeal rule and apply presumptions even to future legislation. The former are unknown, but there are examples of the latter, which may be thought of as a 'soft' form of affecting successor Parliaments (subject always to express repeal). The Interpretation Act 1978 sets numerous interpretative presumptions which apply to all legislation which both pre- and post-dates it (s 22(1)). Both the European Communities Act 1972 (s 2(1)) and the Human Rights Act 1998 (s 3) require past and future legislation to be interpreted in accordance with the principles to which they give effect.

We must at this point examine more fully a question which has already been mentioned, namely the need for legal rules identifying the measures which are to be accepted as Acts of Parliament.

What is an Act of Parliament?[119]

In an extremely simple community, where all powers within the human group are exercised by one person recognised as sovereign, no legal problems of identifying acts of the sovereign arise. But, as R T E Latham said:

> Where the purported sovereign is anyone but a single actual person, the designation of him must include the statement of rules for the ascertainment of his will, and these rules, since their observance is a condition of the validity of his legislation, are rules of law logically prior to him.[120]

Latham pointed out that Parliament, regarded only as an assembly of human beings, was not sovereign. 'It can only be sovereign when acting in a certain way prescribed by law. At least some rudimentary "manner and form" is demanded of it: the simultaneous incoherent cry of a rabble, small or large, cannot be law, for it is unintelligible.'[121]

In the absence of a written constitution to guide the courts in identifying an Act of Parliament, the definition of such an Act is primarily a matter of common law.[122] The long-standing rule is that for a Bill to become law, it must have been approved by Lords and Commons and have received the royal assent. In the ordinary case, this simple test will be satisfied by a rapid inspection of the Queen's Printer's copy of an Act of Parliament which will bear at its head formal words of enactment.[123] When Acts of Parliament have been challenged on the ground of procedural defects during their passage through Parliament, the judges have laid down the 'enrolled Act' rule.

....

[118] D Feldman (2013) 129 LQR 343; (same) (2014) 130 LQR 473; F Ahmed and A Perry [2014] CLJ 514; (same) (2017) 37 OJLS 461.

[119] R T E Latham (1939) *King's Counsel* 152; G Marshall (1954) 2 *Political Studies* 193.

[120] *The Law and the Commonwealth*, p 523; compare Hart's 'rule of recognition', *The Concept of Law* (pp 75, 245 and ch 6). And see on Latham, P Oliver (2002) 2 *King's College Law Journal* 153.

[121] (1939) *King's Counsel*, 153, quoted in Heuston, *Essays in Constitutional Law*, pp 7–8.

[122] Sir Owen Dixon (1957) 31 ALJ 240. And see *Prince's Case* (1606) 8 Co Rep 1, 20b; also *R (Jackson)* v *A-G*, discussed below. Note that the practical issue of a definition of legislation may be different from the common law being the ultimate source of approval for parliamentary supremacy (see note 88 above).

[123] Interpretation Act 1978, s 3. And see *Manuel* v *A-G* [1983] Ch 77, 87.

In *Edinburgh & Dalkeith Railway* v *Wauchope,* a private Act which adversely affected Wauchope's rights against a railway company was challenged by him on the ground that notice of its introduction as a Bill into Parliament had not been given to him, as required by standing orders of the Commons. The court rejected this challenge. Lord Campbell said: 'All that a court of justice can do is to look to the Parliament roll: if from that it should appear that a Bill has passed both Houses and received the Royal Assent, no court of justice can inquire into the mode in which it was introduced into Parliament, or into what was done previous to its introduction, or what passed in Parliament during its progress in its various stages through both Houses.'[124] And in *Lee* v *Bude & Torrington Railway Co* it was said: 'If an Act of Parliament has been obtained improperly, it is for the legislature to correct it by repealing it; but, so long as it exists as law, the courts are bound to obey it.'[125]

This principle was re-affirmed in 1974, when the House of Lords in *Pickin* v *British Railways Board* held that a local or private Act of Parliament was binding whether or not the standing orders of each House had been complied with.

Private Acts of 1836 and 1845 authorised the taking of land for a railway and provided that, if the line were ever abandoned, the land should vest in the owners of the adjoining land. In 1968, another private Act was passed, promoted by the British Railways Board, which abolished this rule. In 1969, Pickin bought a small piece of adjoining land and, when the railway was closed, claimed that under the 1836 and 1845 Acts he was entitled to a strip of the old line. He alleged that the board had fraudulently misled Parliament when promoting the 1968 Act, and had not complied with the standing orders of each House requiring individual notice to be given to owners affected by private legislation. Although the Court of Appeal held that these allegations raised a triable issue,[126] the House of Lords held that the courts had no power to disregard an Act of Parliament, whether public or private, nor to examine proceedings in Parliament to determine whether an Act had been obtained by irregularity or fraud.[127]

There are several reasons why the courts do not inquire into the internal procedures of Parliament. One important reason is the privilege of each House to regulate its own proceedings.[128] Thus for officers of Parliament to give evidence in a court about the internal proceedings of Parliament would create a danger of the court infringing art 9 of the Bill of Rights.[129] On many matters of parliamentary procedure, the courts have declined to intervene whether or not alleged breaches of statute were involved.[130] Moreover, the rule that a Bill must be read three times in each House is not a requirement of the common law but is part of the 'law and

---

[124] (1842) 8 Cl and F 710, 725.

[125] (1871) LR 6 CP 577, 582 (Willes J).

[126] [1973] QB 219.

[127] [1974] AC 765.

[128] Ch 9 A. The Scottish Parliament does not enjoy this privilege (*Whaley* v *Lord Watson of Invergowrie* 2000 SC 125) but by the Scotland Act 1998, s 28(5), the validity of an Act of that Parliament is not affected by any invalidity in proceedings leading to its enactment.

[129] Page 14 above.

[130] *Bradlaugh* v *Gossett* (1884) 12 QBD 271; *Bilston* v *Wolverhampton Corpn* [1942] Ch 391; *Harper* v *Home Secretary* [1955] Ch 238; *Rediffusion (Hong Kong) Ltd* v *A–G of Hong Kong* [1970] AC 1136 (O Hood Phillips (1971) 87 LQR 321). And see B Beinart [1954] SALR 135.

custom of Parliament' on which the standing orders of each House are based. If one House altered the requirement, say by abolishing the third reading, this change would not affect the duty of the courts to apply the 'enrolled Act' rule.

But some comments must be made on the 'enrolled Act' rule. First, there is today no Parliament roll: in case of necessity, all that a court could inspect is the two vellum prints of an Act which since 1849 have been signed by the Clerk of Parliaments and preserved in the National Archives and the House of Lords Record Office.[131] Second, the rule is reinforced by the provision in the Interpretation Act 1978 that every Act passed after 1850 shall be a public Act and judicially noticed as such, unless the contrary is expressly provided by the Act.[132] However, if it should appear that a measure has not been approved by one House, then (unless the Parliament Acts 1911–49 apply) the measure is not an Act.[133] Where there is a written constitution, this may lay down the procedure to be followed before a Bill can become an Act. In South Africa, the pre-apartheid constitution provided that certain entrenched rights could be revoked only by legislation adopted at a joint sitting of both Houses of the South African Parliament, voting by a two-thirds majority: when this procedure was not followed, the result was not a valid Act.[134]

Could the 'enrolled Act' rule be changed by Act of Parliament? To an extent this has already occurred. Thus the Regency Acts 1937–53 make permanent provision for the infancy, incapacity or temporary absence abroad of the monarch.[135] A regent appointed under these Acts may exercise all royal functions, including assenting to Bills, except that he or she may not assent to a Bill for changing the order of succession to the Crown or for repealing or altering the Act of 1707 securing Presbyterian church government in Scotland. If, which is unlikely, a regent did assent to a Bill for one of these purposes, the courts ought not to regard the resulting measure as an Act of Parliament.

Similarly, the Parliament Acts 1911–49[136] provide that in certain circumstances a Bill may become an Act without having been approved by the Lords. The 1911 Act lays down special words of enactment which refer to the Parliament Acts (s 4(1)) and provides that the Speaker's certificate that the requirements of the Acts have been complied with shall be conclusive for all purposes (s 3). But this procedure does not apply to a Bill to extend the life of Parliament or to private or local Bills. If it were attempted to extend the life of Parliament by a measure which had not been approved by the Lords, a court should decline to regard the result as an Act of Parliament: the 'conclusiveness' of the Speaker's certificate would not bar such a decision by the court.[137]

In respect of the Regency Acts and the Parliament Acts, it has been argued that measures which become law thereunder are Acts of a subordinate legislature to which the supreme Parliament has made a limited delegation of its powers; such measures must therefore be regarded as delegated legislation.[138] In other contexts, courts have been reluctant to apply to a legislature the principle that delegated power may not be sub-delegated (*delegatus non potest delegare*)[139] and a contrasting view is that, except for the excluded purposes, Parliament has

---

[131] Heuston, *Essays in Constitutional Law*, p 18; and Erskine May, *Parliamentary Practice*, p 660.

[132] For an explanation of this rule, see *Craies on Legislation*, pp 26–7.

[133] *The Prince's Case* (1606) 8 Co Rep 1a.

[134] *Harris* v *Minister of Interior* 1952 (2) SA 428. See Marshall, *Parliamentary Sovereignty and the Commonwealth*, part 3; Loveland, *By Due Process of Law*, chs 7 and 8.

[135] See R Brazier [2005] CLJ 352.

[136] Ch 8 D.

[137] Section 3 of the 1911 Act requires that the Speaker's certificate shall be given 'under this Act'; in interpreting this section, a court could hold that the test of ultra vires had not been ousted: cf *Minister of Health* v *R* [1931] AC 494 and *Anisminic Ltd* v *Foreign Compensation Commission* [1969] 2 AC 147; ch 25 C.

[138] H W R Wade [1955] CLJ 172, 193–4 and *Constitutional Fundamentals*, pp 27–8.

[139] *R* v *Burah* (1878) 3 App Cas 889 and *Hodge* v *R* (1883) 9 App Cas 117.

provided a procedure for legislation which is alternative to legislation by the supreme Parliament.[140] This question arose in the unusual case of *R (Jackson) v Attorney-General*.[141]

> The Hunting Act 2004, which made fox hunting with dogs unlawful and had been strongly opposed in the Lords, had been enacted under the Parliament Act 1911, as amended by the Parliament Act 1949. Supporters of hunting claimed that the Hunting Act was invalid; they argued that the Parliament Act 1949 was invalid as it had not been passed by the supreme Parliament, yet it had amended the conditions on which power to legislate without the approval of the Lords had been created in 1911 (by reducing the delaying power of the Lords from two years to one). The Court of Appeal had held that 'major constitutional changes' could not be made under the Parliament Act 1911, but that the reduction in the period of delay was not a major change. The nine Law Lords who heard the appeal *held*, unanimously, that both the 1949 Act and the Hunting Act were valid. The broad consensus that emerged from eight separate judgments was that in 1911 Parliament had intended to restrict the powers of the Lords by enabling the Commons and monarch to legislate without the Lords' approval. The procedure was an alternative to the usual process of legislation, and a measure passed under the Parliament Acts was primary (not delegated) legislation. The power to enact legislation in this way was not subject to implied exceptions but, as expressly stated in the 1911 Act, the life of Parliament could not be extended without consent of the Lords. A majority of the judges held obiter that the Parliament Act procedure could not be used to remove this exception from the 1911 Act.

In the course of his judgment, Lord Steyn questioned whether Dicey's account of the 'pure and absolute' nature of parliamentary supremacy was 'out of place in the modern United Kingdom'. Taken with similar comments by Lord Hope and Lady Hale, this raised the possibility of a situation in which a court might refuse to apply a statute that breached a fundamental constitutional principle, for instance by seeking to abolish judicial review of executive decisions.[142] For present purposes, *Jackson* decided that the definition of an Act of Parliament differs according to whether it has been enacted with the consent of both Commons and Lords, or with consent of the Commons alone. The judges accepted that legislation by means of the Parliament Acts may include matters of constitutional importance (for instance, changes in functions of the Lords), although there was disagreement about the extent of this power. Further, despite hesitation by some judges, on an issue that in this case was not contested by the Attorney General, *Jackson* confirms that the courts have jurisdiction to decide whether an instrument relied on in litigation is or is not an Act of Parliament, at least where the issue turns on a matter of statutory interpretation. In 1974, a different view had been expressed by Lord Morris in *Pickin*'s case:

> It must surely be for Parliament to lay down the procedures which are to be followed before a Bill can become an Act. It must be for Parliament to decide whether its decreed procedures have been followed.[143]

---

[140] P Mirfield (1979) 95 LQR 36, 47–50.

[141] [2005] UKHL 56, [2006] 1 AC 262. See A Young [2006] PL 187, A McHarg, [2006] PL 539, Lord Cooke of Thorndon (2006) 122 LQR 224, M Plaxton (2006) 69 MLR 249, R Ekins (2007) 123 LQR 91. Also HL Committee on the Constitution, HL Paper 141 (2005–6), App 3 (A W Bradley).

[142] On what Lord Steyn might have meant by 'a different hypothesis of constitutionalism', see J Jowell [2006] PL 562.

[143] [1974] AC 765, 790. There is an ambiguity here: does 'Parliament' refer to an Act of Parliament, or to a decision made by resolution of one or both of the Houses?

That was said in the context of an alleged departure from the standing orders of the Commons, where the issue was rightly held to be a matter of internal procedure. But *Jackson* confirms that, in the rare situation where the status of a legislative instrument is disputed, the court must decide whether that document satisfies the 'enrolled Act' rule at common law, or any other rule that a statute may have laid down for the enactment of legislation.

In the light of *Jackson*, we may consider a question that has been much discussed,[144] namely whether a parliament with supreme legislative authority may bind itself by laying down rules that determine the 'manner and form' of future legislation. Although the case concerned a subordinate legislature, *A-G for New South Wales* v *Trethowan*[145] illustrates issues that may arise when a legislature departs from rules governing the process of legislation which it had itself enacted.

> Under the Colonial Laws Validity Act 1865, the legislature of New South Wales had power to make laws respecting its own constitution and procedure, provided that these laws were passed 'in such manner and form' as might be required by a law for the time being in force in the state. In 1929, an Act provided that the upper House of the legislature should not be abolished until a Bill approved by both Houses had been approved by a referendum of the electorate; the requirement of a referendum applied also to amendments of the 1929 Act. Following a change of government, a Bill passed through both Houses which sought to abolish both the upper House and the requirement of a referendum. The government did not intend to submit the Bill to a referendum. An injunction was granted by the New South Wales court to restrain the government from presenting the Bill for the royal assent unless a majority of the electors had approved it. On appeal, the Privy Council held that the requirement of a referendum was binding on the legislature until it had been abolished by a law passed in the 'manner and form' required by law for the time being, i.e. with the approval of a referendum.

One view of *Trethowan*'s case is that it depended solely on the fact that the legislature was a subordinate legislature, subject to the rule in the Colonial Laws Validity Act that a constitutional amendment had to be enacted 'in such manner and form' as the law required from time to time. On this view, *Trethowan* is not relevant to the Westminster Parliament.[146] Another view is that there is a rule at common law that legislation may be enacted only in such manner and form as is laid down, that this rule applies to the UK Parliament, and that the 1865 Act put into statutory form a rule that is fundamental to the court's task of deciding whether a measure has the force of law.[147] The judgments in the Hunting Act case support the view that identifying an Act of Parliament depends on the rules as to 'manner and form' currently required of legislation. But they are not conclusive of how a future court would resolve a dispute concerning the Westminster Parliament on facts resembling those in *Trethowan*.[148]

....

[144] The work of Jennings, Latham, Marshall and others is examined in Oliver, *The Constitution of Independence*, ch 4, and in Gordon, *Parliamentary Sovereignty in the UK Constitution*. See also M Gordon [2009] PL 519; H-R Zhou (2013) 129 LQR 610; A W Bradley in Jowell and Oliver (eds), *The Changing Constitution* (7th edn), ch 2.

[145] [1932] AC 526. See Marshall, *Parliamentary Sovereignty and the Commonwealth*, ch 8; Oliver, *The Constitution of Independence*, pp 72–5.

[146] H W R Wade [1955] CLJ 172, 183, E C S Wade, Introduction to Dicey, *Law of the Constitution*, pp lxxiii–v.

[147] E.g. Jennings, *The Law and the Constitution*, p 153; R T E Latham (1939) *King's Counsel* 152, 161; O Dixon (1935) 51 LQR 590, 603.

[148] See in particular in *R (Jackson)* v *A-G*, Lady Hale's observations at [160]–[163].

The Human Rights Act 1998 provides an example of a change in procedure that might give rise to a 'manner and form' argument. By s 19, a minister in charge of a Bill in Parliament must, before it is debated on second reading, state either that the Bill is compatible with the rights protected by the 1998 Act or, if it is not so compatible, that the government wishes the Bill to proceed. Would failure by a minister to make such a statement affect the validity of the resulting Act? For several reasons, the answer to this question is no. The requirement of a ministerial statement would be seen as an internal procedure, enforceable only by Parliament. And a court would be unlikely to hold that in enacting s 19, Parliament was intending to alter the 'enrolled Act' rule.[149]

We have seen that the doctrine of implied repeal has been used in support of the argument that Parliament may not bind its successors. Has Parliament the power to modify the doctrine of implied repeal itself? Two developments suggest that it can. The first, the 'metric measures' case,[150] concerned the relation between EU law and English law. The court held that Parliament could not abandon its sovereignty by stipulating that a statute may not be repealed. However, it also held that where (as with the European Communities Act 1972) Parliament legislates on a subject with 'overarching' constitutional importance, such an Act (unlike an 'ordinary' statute) is not subject to implied repeal; it may be repealed only where a later Parliament declared expressly that this is its intention.[151] Second, the scheme of the Human Rights Act 1998 in effect excludes the ordinary operation of implied repeal: if Parliament wishes in future to legislate in breach of the Convention rights protected by that Act, it will succeed in doing so only if it uses express words or in some other way makes absolutely clear its intention to legislate with that effect.[152]

Summary

The argument in this chapter may be summarised as follows. In principle, a legislature must remain free to enact new laws on matters within its competence: if a conflict occurs between the laws enacted at different times, the courts apply the later of the two laws. The authority of Parliament includes power to legislate on constitutional matters, including both the composition of Parliament and the 'manner and form' by which new legislation may be made. While the courts may not of their own accord review the internal proceedings of Parliament, the scope for judicial decision could be extended if, by statute, Parliament altered the common law rules according to which the courts recognise or identify an Act of Parliament. The doctrine of parliamentary supremacy is no bar to the adoption of a written constitution for the United Kingdom which imposes judicially enforceable limits upon a future legislature, at least if such structural changes are made so that the new legislative process is materially different from the present process involving Lords, Commons and royal assent. However, if changes were *not* made in the structure of the legislature but an attempt were made to limit the powers of Parliament, the courts would be unlikely to regard the purported limits ousting the continuing legislative supremacy of Parliament. It is not possible to predict the outcome of changes made by Parliament to the 'manner and form' of the legislative process since, depending on the nature and reasons for such changes, the courts might still be influenced by a deep-seated belief in the proposition that Parliament cannot bind itself.

These general principles will now be discussed briefly in relation to some specific constitutional issues.

---

149 See N Bamforth [1998] PL 572, 575–82, citing *Mangawaro Enterprises* v *Attorney-General* [1994] 2 NZLR 451.
150 *Thoburn* v *Sunderland Council* [2002] EWHC 195 Admin, [2003] QB 151.
151 *Thoburn* v *Sunderland Council* at [63].
152 This effect arises from the novel duty of interpretation imposed by the Human Rights Act 1998, s 3; and see ch 14 C. For a different view, see Young, *Parliamentary Sovereignty and the Human Rights Act*, ch 2.

1. *Constitutional guarantees for Northern Ireland*[153]

An account is given elsewhere of the events by which the Irish Republic broke from the United Kingdom.[154] In the Ireland Act 1949, it was declared that 'in no event' would Northern Ireland 'or any part thereof' cease to be part of the United Kingdom 'without consent of the Parliament of Northern Ireland'.[155] However, the 1949 Act did not guarantee the continued existence of the Parliament of Northern Ireland. When that Parliament was abolished in 1973 by Westminster, a new guarantee was given that Northern Ireland would not cease to be part of the United Kingdom without consent of the majority of the people.[156]

Today, the Northern Ireland Act 1998, s 1, declares that Northern Ireland 'in its entirety remains part of the United Kingdom and shall not cease to be so without the consent of a majority of the people of Northern Ireland' voting in a poll held for the purpose. The guarantee is of great political significance. But has Parliament fettered itself from, say, ceding a border area to the Republic without first obtaining the consent of a majority of the people of Northern Ireland? Or could Parliament at a future date repeal the 1998 Act and provide nothing in its place? The strongest legal argument for the proposition that Parliament could not breach the guarantee takes the form that for the purposes of legislating for the future status of Northern Ireland, Parliament has redefined itself so that an additional stage, namely approval by a border poll, is mandatory. But would the courts hold that this intention had been so clearly expressed that a subsequent Parliament had lost the legal capacity to repeal the 1998 Act, expressly or by implication? It has been suggested that the Northern Ireland guarantee is an example of a limitation which Parliament may impose on itself, but which does not ultimately incapacitate Parliament from acting.[157] In reality, the political constraints against breach of the guarantee provide a much greater safeguard for the Unionists in Northern Ireland than reliance on litigation to establish that in 1998 Parliament had limited the powers of future Parliaments.

2. *British membership of the European Union*

The United Kingdom continues, in the short term at least, to be a member of the European Union during the period of negotiating its exit, and EU law continues to take effect domestically. Chapter 6 will discuss the relationship between national law and EU law, as well as its effect on the supremacy of Parliament, in more detail. EU law has been held by the Court of Justice of the European Union to prevail over any inconsistent provisions of the national law of the member states:

> the law stemming from the Treaty, an independent source of law, cannot because of its very nature be overridden by rules of national law, however framed . . . without the legal basis of the Community itself being called into question.[158]

The European Communities Act 1972 gave effect within the United Kingdom to those provisions of EU law which were, according to the European treaties, intended to have direct

---

[153] Calvert, *Constitutional Law in Northern Ireland*, pp 23–33; Heuston, *Essays in Constitutional Law*, ch 1; Hadfield, *The Constitution of Northern Ireland*, pp 104–5.

[154] Ch 2 A.

[155] For an analogous provision in Gladstone's first Home Rule Bill, see Marshall, *Parliamentary Sovereignty and the Commonwealth*, pp 63–6.

[156] Northern Ireland Constitution Act 1973, s 1.

[157] Mitchell, *Constitutional Law*, p 81. See also *Re McCord's Application for Judicial Review* [2016] NIQB 85, [2017] 2 CMLR 7 at [154], in which Maguire J indicated that the Westminster Parliament had retained to itself the power to legislate for Northern Ireland without the need for any special procedure, save where it might be required for the purposes of s 1.

[158] *Case 11/70, Internationale Handelsgesellschaft* case [1970] ECR 1125, 1134. And see ch 6 B.

effect within member states. This applied both to existing and future treaties and regulations. The EU organs therefore legislate for the United Kingdom, as they do for all member states. While Britain remains a member of the EU, the Westminster Parliament is not the sole body with power to make new law for the United Kingdom.[159] The 1972 Act imported, or permitted the import of, a new source of law.[160] Nor can EU law appropriately be described as delegated legislation.[161]

The extent to which EU law overrides national law was seen in *R* v *Transport Secretary, ex p Factortame Ltd*:[162]

Spanish fishing interests that had formed companies registered in the United Kingdom challenged the Merchant Shipping Act 1988 as being contrary to EU law. This Act, by defining the term 'British fishing vessels' in a restrictive way, sought to prevent non-British interests from having access to the British fishing quota. In interim proceedings to protect Spanish interests pending decision of the substantive case, the Court of Justice held that a national court must set aside a rule of national law if this was the sole obstacle to the granting of temporary relief to protect EU rights. Thus the British courts must disregard s 21 of the Crown Proceedings Act 1947 (no injunctions to be granted against the Crown)[163] and must not apply the Merchant Shipping Act 1988. Lord Bridge challenged the view that 'this was a novel and dangerous invasion by a Community institution of the sovereignty of the United Kingdom Parliament'. He stated that long before the United Kingdom joined the EU, the supremacy of EU law over the laws of member states was well established. 'Thus whatever limitation of its sovereignty Parliament accepted when it enacted the European Communities Act 1972 was entirely voluntary.'[164]

In *R* v *Employment Secretary, ex p EOC*,[165] the House of Lords declared that provisions in the Employment Protection (Consolidation) Act 1978, making protection for part-time workers (who were mainly female) subject to conditions that did not apply to full-time workers (who were mainly male), were incompatible with the right of female workers under EU law to equal treatment with male workers.

Accordingly, the British courts must not apply national legislation, whether enacted before or after the European Communities Act 1972, if to do so would conflict with EU law. In Sir William Wade's view, decisions such as *Factortame* effected a 'constitutional revolution' by holding that Parliament in 1972 did bind its successors.[166] A narrower explanation is that the 1972 Act created a rule of construction requiring the courts to apply UK legislation consistently with EU law, except where an Act expressly overrides EU law.[167] Whichever explanation is preferred, the primacy of EU law is an inescapable consequence of membership of the EU.

In *Miller* (discussed in more detail in this respect in Chapter 6), the Supreme Court held that nothing in EU law altered the ultimate supremacy of Parliament, which could repeal the 1972 Act

---

[159] EU law may require extra procedures to be observed before an Act of the UK Parliament is fully enforceable: see *R* v *Budimir* [2010] EWCA Crim 1846, [2011] 3 All ER 206.

[160] *R (Miller)* v *Secretary of State for Exiting the EU* [2017] UKSC 5, [2017] 2 WLR 583.

[161] Cf Cmnd 3301, 1967, para 22.

[162] [1990] 2 AC 85 and (the same) (*No 2*) [1991] 1 AC 603. See also ch 6 C.

[163] See ch 26 D.

[164] [1991] 1 AC at 659. And see *Thoburn* v *Sunderland Council* [2002] EWHC 195 Admin, [2003] QB 151 (upholding the sovereignty of Parliament but giving broad effect to the European Communities Act 1972).

[165] [1995] 1 AC 1.

[166] (1996) 112 LQR 568.

[167] P Craig (1991) 11 YBEL 221, 251. And ch 6 C.

and so remove that source of law at any time; rejecting Wade's view, nothing in the ultimate source of constitutional authority, or rule of recognition, had been altered by EU law and the 1972 Act.[168] Rather more controversially, the majority also held that, although as a matter of form, EU law only enjoys its effect domestically because of the 1972 Act passed by a supreme Westminster Parliament, the 'realistic' picture of substance is that EU law is 'an independent and over-riding source of domestic law'.[169] This is not at all consistent with the Court's rejection of any change in the rule of recognition,[170] nor is it consistent with the emphasis of the Supreme Court in the *HS2* case that the effect of EU law can only be addressed by reference to the 1972 Act.[171]

Section 18 of the European Union Act 2011 declared that EU law has effect in the United Kingdom only by reason of the European Communities Act 1972 or any other UK Act. This confirmed the long-established rule based on the 'dualism' of national and international law, by which treaties entered into by the government have effect in national law only when Parliament has authorised this.[172] The need for this declaratory statement was much debated.[173] The government claimed that it was needed to guard against any argument that EU law constituted a new autonomous legal order that might be binding on Parliament; possibly it served a political purpose as a limited concession to Eurosceptics that would not prejudice British membership of the EU. Certainly it had no legal effect, and the Supreme Court confirmed in *Miller* that it merely confirmed the position which had been effective since 1973.[174]

3. The Human Rights Act 1998

The doctrine that Parliament may not bind its successors is a major obstacle to enactment of a Bill of Rights intended to protect human rights against legislation by later Parliaments. In outlining its scheme for the Human Rights Act, the government in 1997 denied that it was trying to transfer power from future Parliaments to the courts:

> To make provision in the Bill for the courts to set aside Acts of Parliament would confer on the judiciary a general power over the decisions of Parliament which under our present constitutional arrangements they do not possess, and would be likely on occasions to draw the judiciary into serious conflict with Parliament. There is no evidence to suggest that they desire this power, nor that the public wish them to have it. Certainly this Government has no mandate for any such change.[175]

This stance applied to both existing and future Acts of Parliament, although Parliament in 1998 undoubtedly could have provided that the rights protected by the Human Rights Act should prevail over all *existing* statutes. On whether those rights should be entrenched against *subsequent* legislation, the government mentioned the procedure for amending the US constitution and stated:

> an arrangement of this kind could not be reconciled with our own constitutional traditions, which allow any Act of Parliament to be amended or repealed by a subsequent Act of Parliament. We do not believe that it is necessary or would be desirable *to attempt to devise such a special arrangement* for this Bill.[176]

---

[168] *R (Miller)* v *Secretary of State for Exiting the EU* [2017] UKSC 5, [2017] 2 WLR 583 at [60].

[169] *Miller*, at [65], [80] and [81].

[170] See further M Elliott [2017] CLJ 257.

[171] *R (HS2 Alliance)* v *Transport Secretary* [2014] UKSC 3, [2014] 1 WLR 324.

[172] Note 69 above.

[173] See *The EU Bill and Parliamentary Sovereignty*, European Scrutiny Committee, 10th report (HC 633, 2010–11) vols 1 and 2.

[174] *Miller* (above), at [66]

[175] *Rights Brought Home*, Cm 3872 (1997), para 2.13. And see ch 14 C.

[176] Ibid, para 2.16 (emphasis supplied). Note use of the word 'attempt' in the italicised phrase.

Certainly, if a wholly new constitution for the United Kingdom were to be created, it could include entrenched fundamental rights. Short of that, are there ways in which fundamental rights could be protected against infringement by a future Parliament? In 1979, a committee of the House of Lords, considering the desirability of a Bill of Rights for the United Kingdom, said:

> there is no way in which a Bill of Rights could protect itself from encroachment, whether express or implied, by later Acts. The most that such a Bill could do would be to include an interpretation provision which ensured that the Bill of Rights was always taken into account in the construction of later Acts and that, so far as a later Act could be construed in a way that was compatible with a Bill of Rights, such a construction would be preferred to one that was not.[177]

As will be seen later, the Human Rights Act did not attempt to bind future Parliaments from legislating in breach of rights protected by the Act. Instead, the Act (s 3) imposed a new duty on the courts to interpret all legislation, whatever its date, consistently with the Convention, *if such an interpretation is possible.*[178] If such an interpretation is not possible, the conflicting provision remains in effect, but it may be declared by a superior court to be incompatible with Convention rights, in which case the government may make a 'remedial order' removing the incompatibility.[179] This scheme preserves the formal authority of Parliament, while extending the powers of the judiciary to subject Parliament's work to detailed scrutiny. As Judge LJ said in 2001, 'The Act is carefully drafted to ensure that the court cannot and must not strike down or dispense with any single item of primary legislation.'[180] Yet under the scheme of the Act, all other Acts of Parliament (regardless of their date) are subject to judicial scrutiny to determine whether they are compatible with the Convention rights.

4. Abolition of the House of Lords

In Chapter 8 we examine the role of the House of Lords both in legislation generally and under the Parliament Acts 1911 and 1949. Here we deal only with whether the legislative authority of Parliament extends to abolishing one component part of the supreme legislature (not with whether this would be a desirable change). If, as suggested earlier, the legislative supremacy of Parliament is founded to some extent on decisions of the courts, the change to a unicameral Parliament or the replacement of the Lords by an elected Senate would not necessarily require the courts to accept that the newly constituted legislature had unlimited power to legislate. Arguably the change could be regarded as a legal revolution or a breach in legal continuity,[181] but would this be accurate if the courts were simply to give full effect to a change authorised by the former legislature?

Several practical issues might arise. First, it might be argued politically that the reconstruction of Parliament would be so radical as to require the approval of the electorate given by referendum. Second, would the new legislation include any answer to the question we are considering? For instance, if that legislation were to include a Bill of Rights that was declared to be incapable of amendment by the new legislature, the courts must then choose between (*a*) giving effect to that declaration by the former legislature, or (*b*) holding that the new legislature was as legislatively supreme as its predecessor (contrary to that declaration). It could also be relevant whether the legislation provided any procedure for enabling the Bill of Rights to be amended or suspended in the event of emergency.

---

[177] HL 176 (1977–8), para 23. Contrast the view of the Northern Ireland Standing Advisory Committee on Human Rights in 1977: Cmnd 7009, 1977.

[178] As to which see *Ghaidan* v *Godin-Mendoza* [2004] UKHL 30, [2004] 2 AC 557.

[179] Human Rights Act 1998, ss 4, 5 and 10.

[180] *Re K* (*a child*) [2001] Fam 377, para 121.

[181] For the main arguments, see P Mirfield (1979) 95 LQR 36 and G Winterton (1979) 95 LQR 386. And Dicey, *The Law of the Constitution*, pp 64–70.

Another question is whether the House of Lords could be lawfully abolished against the wishes of that House, by use of the Parliament Acts 1911 and 1949? In *Jackson*, it was held that the Parliament Acts could be used to achieve major constitutional changes without consent of the upper House.[182] The rejection of the 'delegated legislation' argument in that case strengthens the view that these major changes include abolition of the Lords. But the question did not arise for decision, and most of the judgments do not deal with it.[183]

D. The Treaty of Union between England and Scotland

In section C, we discussed whether the Westminster Parliament may impose legal limitations upon its successors. The Anglo-Scottish Union of 1707 raises the different question, 'Was the United Kingdom Parliament born unfree?'[184] The main features of the Treaty of Union have already been outlined.[185] Now we examine more closely provisions of the Treaty concerning the power to legislate after the Union. The Treaty contemplated that the new Parliament of Great Britain would legislate both for England and Scotland; but no grant of general legislative competence to Parliament was made. Article 18 provided that the laws concerning regulation of trade, as well as customs and excise duties, should be uniform throughout Britain; subject to this, all other laws within Scotland were to remain in force,

> but alterable by the Parliament of Great Britain, with this difference betwixt the laws concerning public right, policy, and civil government, and those which concern private right; that the laws which concern public right, policy and civil government may be made the same throughout the whole United Kingdom, but that no alteration be made in laws which concern private right except for evident utility of the subjects within Scotland.

By art 19, the Court of Session and the Court of Justiciary were to remain 'in all time coming' within Scotland as then constituted and with the same authority and privileges as before the Union, 'subject nevertheless to such regulations for the better administration of justice as shall be made by the Parliament of Great Britain'. Other courts were to be subject to regulation and alteration by Parliament. No causes in Scotland were to be capable of being heard by the courts of Chancery, Queen's Bench, Common Pleas (or any other court in Westminster Hall). An Act for securing the Protestant religion and Presbyterian Church government in Scotland was passed at the same time by the English and Scottish Parliaments and was declared to be a fundamental and essential condition of the Treaty of Union 'in all time coming'.

While the framers of the Union intended the new Parliament to be the sole legislature, they distinguished between matters on which Parliament would be free to legislate, matters on which it would have limited authority to legislate, and matters which were declared fundamental and unalterable. The Treaty made no provision for future amendment of itself or for future renegotiation of the Union. The former English and Scottish Parliaments ceased to exist. No machinery was provided for applying the distinction in art 18 between laws concerning 'public right, policy and civil government' and laws concerning 'private right' or, in the latter case, for discovering what changes might be for 'evident utility' of the Scottish people.

---

[182] In 2000, the royal commission on reform of the House of Lords recommended that the Parliament Acts be amended to prevent them being further amended by use of the Parliament Acts: Cm 4534, para 5.15.

[183] But note, at para [101], Lord Steyn's observations (obiter) on this point.

[184] Mitchell, *Constitutional Law*, pp 69–74; T B Smith [1957] PL 99; D N MacCormick (1978) 29 NILQ 1. Also Munro, *Studies in Constitutional Law*, pp 137–42; M Upton (1989) 105 LQR 79; *Stair Memorial Encyclopedia: The Laws of Scotland*, vol 5, pp 137–62 (T B Smith) and 2002 reissue, pp 29–83 (N Walker); HLE, vol 8(2), pp 54–8; MacCormick, *Questioning Sovereignty*, ch 4.

[185] Ch 2 A.

The argument that the Union imposed limitations upon the new Parliament can be summarised as follows: the new Parliament came into being by virtue of the Union; its powers were limited by the guarantees in the Treaty, which had been enacted by the separate Parliaments before the united Parliament was born. Even if both the English and Scottish Parliaments were supreme before 1707,[186] each abolished themselves in favour of a common heir with limited powers. The Treaty of Union, concludes the argument, is a fundamental constitutional text which prevents the British Parliament from itself enjoying the attribute of legislative supremacy. When, as in *Cheney v Conn*, an English judge remarks, 'what the statute says and provides is the highest form of law that is known to this country',[187] a Scots lawyer might reply: 'Not so: the Treaty of Union is a higher form of law and may prevail over inconsistent Acts of Parliament.'

This argument is subject to both theoretical and historical difficulties. First, no legislature other than the British Parliament was created. If circumstances changed, and amendments to the Union became desirable, how could they be made except by Act of Parliament? Thus in 1748, the heritable jurisdictions were abolished and, when Scottish local government was reformed in 1975, the royal burghs were abolished.[188] In 1853, the Universities (Scotland) Act abolished the requirement that professors in the ancient Scottish universities should be members of the Church of Scotland, thus repealing an 'unalterable' provision of the Act for securing the Presbyterian Church. Second, the distinction between laws concerning 'public right, policy and civil government' and laws concerning 'private right' is a difficult one. For example, power to tax private property or to acquire land compulsorily for public purposes concerns both public and private right; and is the law of education a matter of public or private right? Third, the test of 'evident utility' for changes in the law affecting private right is obscure: who is to decide – Scottish MPs, the Westminster Parliament, Scottish ministers, the courts or other bodies in Scotland?[189]

Moreover, after the Union the Westminster Parliament conducted its affairs exactly as before, subject only to its enlargement by members from Scotland.[190] As dominant partners in the Union, the English assumed that continuity from pre-Union days was unbroken. On a matter left silent by the Treaty of Union, the House of Lords in its judicial capacity formerly heard appeals from Scotland in civil cases, following the case of *Greenshields* in 1709 (the House of Lords was not a court within Westminster Hall within the meaning of art 19 of the Union) but it had no jurisdiction in Scottish criminal cases, a position that is to an extent maintained in the jurisdiction of the present Supreme Court.[191] Finally, even if the framers of the Union intended there to be limitations on the British Parliament, was this sufficient to empower the courts to hold Acts of Parliament invalid that conflicted with the Treaty? In Dicey's view, the subsequent history of the Union 'affords the strongest proof of the futility inherent in every attempt of one sovereign legislature to restrain the action of another equally sovereign body'.[192]

These matters have been debated in several Scottish cases.

....

[186] On whether the Scottish Parliament was supreme before 1707, Donaldson, *Scotland: James V–James VII*, ch 15; Dicey and Rait, *Thoughts on the Union between England and Scotland*, pp 19–22, 242–4.

[187] Note 64 above.

[188] Cf arts 20 and 21 of the Treaty of Union.

[189] The court was prepared to find a statute to be of 'evident utility' in *Laughland v Wansborough Paper Co* 1921 1 SLT 341, but cf *Gibson v Lord Advocate* (below).

[190] Hence the comment by Bryce, *Studies in History and Jurisprudence*, vol 1, p 194, that in 1707 England altered the constitution of the enlarged state no further than by admitting additional members to Parliament and suppressing certain offices in Scotland.

[191] Constitutional Reform Act 2005, s 40(3).

[192] Dicey, *The Law of the Constitution*, p 65; and cf Dicey and Rait, p 252.

In *MacCormick* v *Lord Advocate*,[193] the Rector of Glasgow University challenged the Queen's title as 'Elizabeth the Second', on the grounds that this was contrary to historical fact and contravened art 1 of the Treaty of Union. At first instance, Lord Guthrie dismissed the challenge for the reason, among others, that an Act of Parliament could not be challenged in any court as being in breach of the Treaty of Union or on any other ground. In the Inner House of the Court of Session, the First Division dismissed the appeal against Lord Guthrie's decision, but on narrower grounds. After holding that MacCormick had no legal title or interest to sue, that the royal numeral was not contrary to the Treaty, and that the Royal Titles Act 1953 was irrelevant, Lord President Cooper said: 'The principle of the unlimited sovereignty of Parliament is a distinctively English principle which has no counterpart in Scottish constitutional law.' He had difficulty in seeing why it should have been supposed that the Parliament of Great Britain must have inherited all the peculiar characteristics of the English Parliament but none of the Scottish Parliament. He could find in the Union legislation no provision that the Parliament of Great Britain should be 'absolutely sovereign' in the sense that it should be free to alter the Treaty at will. He reserved opinion on whether breach of such fundamental law as is contained in the Treaty would raise a justiciable issue; in his view there was no precedent that the courts of Scotland or England had authority to determine 'whether a governmental act of the type here in controversy is or is not conform to the provisions of a Treaty, least of all when that Treaty is one under which both Scotland and England ceased to be independent States and merged their identity in an incorporating union'. Lord Russell, who concurred, suggested that a political remedy would be more suitable for MacCormick than a judicial remedy.

Lord Cooper's judgment went beyond what was necessary for decision of the case and uncertainty remained on some key issues. In particular, the denial that the courts have jurisdiction to decide whether 'a governmental act of the type here in controversy' conformed to the Treaty must be read in relation to the disputed royal title, which did not concern matters of private right in Scotland.

In 1975, a Scottish fisherman unsuccessfully claimed that British membership of the European Community was incompatible with the Treaty of Union.

In *Gibson* v *Lord Advocate*, Gibson claimed that an EC regulation granting EC nationals the right to fish in Scottish waters and the European Communities Act 1972, which gave this legal effect in Britain, were contrary to art 18 of the Union, since this was a change in the law concerning private right which was not for the 'evident utility' of the Scottish people. Lord Keith held that control of fishing in territorial waters was a branch of public law, which might be made the same throughout the United Kingdom and was not protected by art 18. Obiter, he said that the question whether an Act of Parliament altering Scots private law was for the 'evident utility' of the Scottish people was not a justiciable issue. 'The making of decisions upon what must essentially be a political matter is no part of the function of the court.'[194]

Both in *MacCormick* and in *Gibson* the question was held open of the validity of legislation seeking to abolish the Court of Session or the Church of Scotland, both being institutions safeguarded by the Union. Short of such an extreme situation, the Scottish courts are reluctant to

[193] 1953 SC 396.
[194] 1975 SLT 134.

claim a power to review the validity of Acts of Parliament. This attitude was maintained when the Court of Session declined to hold that the community charge (or poll tax) legislation, which applied to Scotland a year earlier than in England and Wales, was contrary to art 4 of the Treaty of Union.[195]

The Scotland Act 1998 conferred on the courts jurisdiction to decide 'devolution issues', namely questions as to the powers of the Scottish Parliament and Executive.[196] But this jurisdiction does not enable any court to review the validity of Acts of the Westminster Parliament. A related question is whether the Scotland Act affected the historical jurisdiction of the Scottish courts. To avoid any doubt on this point, section 37 of the 1998 Act declares that the Union with Scotland Act 1706 and the Union with England Act 1707 shall 'have effect subject to this Act'. This provision aims 'to ensure that neither the Scotland Act 1998 nor legislation or actions authorised under its terms should be vulnerable to challenge on the ground of their inconsistency with the Acts of Union'.[197]

E. Conclusions

This chapter has examined whether there are legal limits on the legislative supremacy of Parliament, in particular whether there are, or could be, any limits capable of being enforced judicially. While British tradition has been strongly against judicial review of primary legislation, the courts must if necessary decide whether a document for which legislative authority is claimed is indeed an Act of Parliament.[198] While the basic rule of legislative supremacy is a matter of common law that has political significance, it cannot be demonstrated from existing precedents that under no circumstances could this rule be qualified by judicial decision – still less that the rule could not be changed by Act of Parliament. It is therefore not possible to assert dogmatically that the legislative supremacy of Parliament will continue to be the primary rule of constitutional law in the United Kingdom. According to Lord Hope in *R (Jackson)* v *Attorney-General*, 'Our constitution is dominated by the sovereignty of Parliament. But parliamentary sovereignty is no longer, if it ever was, absolute.'[199] Indeed, the impact of European integration has made extensive inroads into Dicey's doctrine of legislative supremacy. The Human Rights Act stops short of enabling the courts to set aside an Act of Parliament, but it authorises them to review legislation for compliance with the European Convention on Human Rights. And the advent of devolution means that Westminster is not the only legislature in the United Kingdom.

Political significance of legislative supremacy

It is not easy to assess the political significance of the legislative supremacy of Parliament. For one thing, constitutional and legal rules tend to reflect political facts, but sometimes only with a considerable time lag. Moreover, the doctrine has always been affected by a tinge of

....
[195] *Pringle, Petitioner* 1991 SLT 330 and *Murray* v *Rogers* 1992 SLT 221. See N C Walker and C M G Himsworth [1991] JR 45; D J Edwards (1992) 12 LS 34; and *R (Jackson)* v *A-G*, note 141 above at para [106] (Lord Hope).

[196] See ch 2 B.

[197] Himsworth and Munro, *The Scotland Act 1998*, p 52. In 1999, the HL Committee of Privileges decided that removal of Scottish peers from the House of Lords under what became the House of Lords Act 1999 would not breach the Treaty of Union, art 22: *Lord Gray's Motion* [2000] 1 AC 124; and Himsworth and O'Neill, pp 112–13.

[198] This function was performed in *R (Jackson)* v *A-G*, note 141 above.

[199] Ibid, para [104].

unreality since it would empower Parliament to do many unlikely, immoral or undesirable things which no one wishes it to do. Does Parliament really need power to condemn all red-haired males to death or to make attendance at public worship illegal?

Yet it would be wrong to ignore the political argument for retaining supremacy, particularly when the wishes of a newly elected House of Commons can be identified with the will of the majority. Legislative supremacy is well suited to a centralised, unitary system of government in which the policies of the executive are supported by the dominant political voice in Parliament, and in which the judiciary exercise an important but subordinate role. Even in such a system, there are many factors that limit the use to which the executive can put Parliament's legislative powers. Dicey suggested that political sovereignty, as opposed to legislative sovereignty, lay in the electorate and that ultimately the will of the electorate would prevail on all subjects determined by the British government.[200] Certainly, the electoral system influences the use of legislative powers, but this influence is generalised and sporadic in its effect: and this depends in turn on the political parties, on the media, on economic and social groups and on other means by which public opinion is expressed. Moreover, the electoral system produces a House of Commons which does not accurately reproduce the distribution of views among the electorate and provides only weak protection for unpopular minorities. Dicey's view is far too optimistic, but the placing of supreme power in the hands of unelected judges instead is not necessarily the appropriate response.

Parliament and the electorate

Under the British system, the electorate takes no direct part in legislative decision-making, save by electing the House of Commons. Where major political issues are concerned, the outcome of a general election may indicate the degree of popular support for key changes. In 1910, two elections were held because of the legislative veto of the Lords and the need to gain support for overcoming that veto. In general, however, it is difficult to decide from the result of a general election the state of opinion on particular issues. Since the party which wins an election can claim to have a mandate to implement its manifesto, a government cannot be criticised for carrying out its election programme. But this does not prevent a government from carrying out major reforms which have not been put to the electorate, or indeed reforms flatly contrary to their manifesto (as with the introduction of university tuition fees by Labour).

Dicey famously observed that the 'judges know nothing about any will of the people except in so far as that will is expressed by an Act of Parliament'.[201] In some constitutions, for example in Ireland and Australia, constitutional amendments take effect only if they are approved by referendum. In other constitutions (for example, Denmark and Switzerland) legislative proposals may be subject to referendum. Until 1975, the United Kingdom found no place for direct democracy, apart from the border poll in Northern Ireland.[202] Even when exercises in direct democracy are conducted, their meaning is by no means as clear as the binary question posed might suggest: did the rejection of the alternative vote system signify love for the existing system or just a dislike of the offered alternative, and when a majority voted to leave the EU, the referendum itself told politicians nothing about what the majority saw as the appropriate form of the future British relationship with the EU. While advisory referendums do not directly affect the authority of Parliament, it would affect the position of Parliament if referendums were to become mandatory for certain purposes. In one case, the alternative vote referendum, the outcome was not advisory: had a majority voted in favour, s 8 of the Parliamentary Voting and Constituencies Act 2011 required ministers to implement

---

[200] Dicey, *The Law of the Constitution*, p 73.
[201] Ibid, p 72.
[202] Page 72 above.

the referendum by secondary legislation. Infamously, no such provision was included in the European Union Referendum Act 2015. It has been argued that referendums should be used 'as an extra check against government, an additional protection to that given by Parliament'.[203] What aspects of the constitution should be protected in this way? There is a case to be made for requiring a referendum whenever it is proposed to transfer the powers of Parliament; as John Locke said, 'it being but a delegated power from the People, they who have it cannot pass it to others'.[204] There is, however, little sign of a more considered structural use of referendums, recent use of which has been on an ad hoc basis, with the ground rules and consequences being laid down afresh for each referendum.

Summary

The view taken in this chapter has been that Parliament's legislative authority includes power to make new arrangements under which future Parliaments would not necessarily be supreme. The argument for retaining legislative supremacy is strengthened if it can be shown that the political system provides safeguards against legislation which would be contrary to fundamental constitutional principle or basic human rights. It is, however, doubtful whether the political system does adequately protect individuals or minority groups who may be vulnerable to oppressive action by the state. In reality, Parliament's role within British government depends less on exercising absolute legislative power than on its effectiveness as a forum in expressing public opinion and in exercising control over government.

---

[203] Bogdanor, *The People and the Party System*, p 69.
[204] *Second Treatise on Civil Government*, quoted in Bogdanor, p 77.

CHAPTER 4

The rule of law

> The concept of the rule of law is not fixed for all time . . . But in a world divided by differences of nationality, race, colour, religion and wealth it is one of the greatest unifying factors, perhaps the greatest, the nearest we are likely to approach to a universal secular religion. It remains an ideal, but an ideal worth striving for, in the interests of good government and peace, at home and in the world at large.[1]

During 1971, at what we now know was an early stage of open strife between the communities in Northern Ireland, the IRA increased the ferocity of its campaign of violence in Northern Ireland, shooting soldiers and police and blowing up buildings. Early in August, the government of Northern Ireland, after consulting with the UK government, decided to exercise the power of internment available to it under the Civil Authorities (Special Powers) Act (Northern Ireland) 1922.[2] This power could be used against persons suspected of having acted or being about to act in a manner prejudicial to the preservation of peace or the maintenance of order. On 9 August, 342 men were arrested. By November 1971, when the total arrested had risen to 980, 299 of those arrested were being interned indefinitely; the remainder were held under temporary detention orders or had already been released.

The security forces saw in internment an opportunity of obtaining fresh intelligence about the IRA. Fourteen detainees were interrogated in depth. The procedures of interrogation included keeping the detainees' heads covered with black hoods; subjecting them to continuous and monotonous noise; depriving them of sleep; depriving them of food and water, except for one slice of bread and one pint of water at six-hourly intervals; making them stand facing a wall with legs apart and hands raised.

In November 1971, after these facts had been established, three Privy Counsellors were asked to consider whether the procedures 'currently authorised' for interrogating persons suspected of terrorism needed to be changed. They produced two reports.[3] Two members, a former Lord Chief Justice and a former Conservative Cabinet minister, recommended that the procedures could continue to be used subject to certain safeguards, including the express authority of a UK minister for their use, the presence of a doctor with psychiatric training at the interrogation centre, and a complaints procedure. This report did not express any view on the legality of the interrogation procedures, but stated that valuable information about the IRA had been discovered through the interrogation.

The minority report, by Lord Gardiner, a former Labour Lord Chancellor, held that the interrogation procedures had never been authorised:

> If any document or minister had purported to authorise them, it would have been invalid because the procedures were and are illegal by the domestic law and may also have been illegal by international law.

Should legislation be introduced enabling a minister in time of emergency to fix in secret the limits of permissible ill-treatment to be used in interrogating suspects? Lord Gardiner viewed

---

[1] Lord Bingham, *The Rule of Law*, p 174.

[2] The power did not survive into the Terrorism Act 2000; see ch 20 C. On the internments in 1971–6, see R J Spjut (1986) 49 MLR 712.

[3] Cmnd 4901, 1972 (Parker Report).

with abhorrence any proposal that a minister should be empowered to make secret law. Nor could he agree that a minister should fix secret limits without the authority of Parliament, 'that is to say illegally', and then if found out ask Parliament for an Act of Indemnity: that, he said, would be a flagrant breach of the whole basis of the rule of law and of the principles of democratic government.

The government accepted Lord Gardiner's report and Prime Minister Heath stated that the interrogation procedures would not be used again. When those who had been interrogated sued the government for damages for their unlawful treatment, liability was not contested and substantial awards of damages were made. The European Commission on Human Rights held that the interrogation procedures amounted to inhuman and degrading treatment and also torture, contrary to art 3 of the European Convention on Human Rights. When the Irish government referred the case to the European Court of Human Rights, the court held that the procedures were inhuman and degrading treatment but did not amount to torture.[4]

No clearer illustration could be given of the need to adhere to the rule of law if citizens are to be protected against arbitrary and harsh acts of government. However lawless may have been the acts of the IRA, and however seriously those acts infringed life and liberty, government must not retaliate with measures which are not only unlawful but also are of such a nature that it would be impossible on moral and political grounds to make them lawful. Controversial as the power of internment was, it was authorised by the legislature and its use was a matter of public knowledge and admitted political responsibility. But in law the power to intern does not include power to interrogate or to administer physical ill-treatment or torture.

Northern Ireland has, happily, entered a more peaceful stage in its history. But the issues the internment example gives rise to are not confined to Northern Ireland, nor to history. Depressingly, it remains an intensely relevant example.[5] The role of the law in policing the state's security efforts, and holding it to a higher standard than those of its enemies, is as crucial today as ever. Since the 9/11 atrocities in the United States, many urgent questions have been raised as to the legality (in national and international law) of measures taken in the 'war against terrorism'. One aim of the Bush administration in establishing a detention centre at the Guantanamo Bay naval base on Cuba was to place detainees outside the protection of any legal system, but in 2004 the US Supreme Court held that this had not been achieved.[6] There can now be no doubt that procedures amounting to torture were authorised by the Bush administration.

....

[4] *Ireland* v *UK* (1978) 2 EHRR 25; and see ch 14 B. In 2004, Lord Hope wrote: 'It seems likely that the mixture of physical and psychological pressures that were used in the case of the IRA suspects would now be regarded as torture . . .': (2004) 53 ICLQ 807, 826. The UN Convention against Torture was signed by the United Kingdom in 1984 and ratified in 1988 after enactment of the Criminal Justice Act 1988, s 134.

[5] The above account of interrogation of IRA suspects first appeared in this book in 1977. It should by 2013 have been possible to relegate this to the pages of history, since a government assurance was given in 1972 (HC Debs, 2 March 1972, col 743), repeated by the Attorney General in 1977, that the unlawful techniques had been prohibited. Sadly, events involving the death of an Iraqi citizen while in the custody of British troops in Basra caused serious concern at Westminster regarding 'discrepancies' in evidence from military sources on use of the techniques: Joint Committee on Human Rights, 28th report (2007–8), HL Paper 157, HC 527; 23rd report (2008–9), HL Paper 153, HC 553. And see *R (Al-Skeini)* v *Defence Secretary* [2007] UKHL 26, [2008] AC 153 and *Al-Skeini* v *United Kingdom* (2011) 30 BHRC 561. A document-based inquiry led by Sir Peter Gibson into issues of interrogation and rendition found there to be many matters needing further investigation: *Report of the Detainee Inquiry* (Cabinet Office, 2013, and HC Debs, 19 December 2013, col 913).

[6] *Rasul* v *Bush* 124 S Ct 2686 (2004); *Hamdi* v *Rumsfeld* 124 S Ct 2633 (2004); *Boumediene* v *Bush* 128 S Ct 2229 (2008). See D Golove (2005) 3 Int Jl of Const Law 128; S Hannett [2008] PL 636. Also Lord Steyn (2004) 53 ICLQ 1; Sands, *Lawless World* and (same author) *Torture Team*.

In the United Kingdom, two particularly significant decisions have arisen from the 'war against terror': (1) indefinite detention without trial under the Anti-Terrorism, Crime and Security Act 2001 was held to breach the European Convention on Human Rights;[7] and (2) evidence obtained or likely to have been obtained by torture committed abroad by a foreign state's agents was held to be inadmissible in proceedings before the Special Immigration Appeals Commission.[8] The decisions underline the continuing relevance of values associated with the 'rule of law'. In the first case, Lord Nicholls said that 'indefinite imprisonment without charge or trial is anathema in any country which observes the rule of law';[9] Lord Hoffmann said that there was 'nothing more antithetical to the instincts and traditions of the people of the United Kingdom'.[10] A Court of Appeal judge has written of this decision: 'It is a powerful statement by the highest court in the land of what it means to live in a society where the executive is subject to the rule of law.'[11]

A. Historical development

In a review of the history of political philosophy, Anthony Quinton has written: 'In all its historical variations the state has sought to discharge two connected functions: the maintenance of order within its domain by the promulgation and enforcement of law and the defence of the nation against external enemies'.[12] To perform these functions, the state possesses coercive powers that may be used to oppress the people as well as confer benefits upon them. Law is an instrument for exercising state power that in some circumstances is also a means of protecting the people against arbitrary or abusive government. Aristotle argued that government by laws was superior to government by men.[13] But one dominant theme in the story of western civilisation in the last 500 years has been the struggle for liberty and rights against absolutism in its several forms, including the absolutism of the state and its use of law.[14]

Bracton, in the 13th century, maintained that rulers were subject to law: 'The King shall not be subject to men, but to God and the law: since law makes the King.'[15] Magna Carta and its later confirmations expressed the principle that justice according to law was due both to the ruler and to other classes in the feudal hierarchy. When renaissance and reformation in the 16th century weakened the idea of a universal natural law, emphasis shifted to the function of law as an aspect of the sovereignty of the state.[16] In Britain, the 17th-century constitutional settlement rejected the claims of absolute monarchy based on the divine right of kings, in favour of a mixed system of government that relied on the authority of the Houses of Parliament and the common law courts.

---

[7] *A v Home Secretary* [2004] UKHL 56, [2005] 2 AC 68.

[8] *A v Home Secretary (No 2)* [2005] UKHL 71, [2006] 2 AC 221. At [101], Lord Hope said: '[In times of emergency] where the rule of law is absent, or is reduced to a mere form of words to which those in authority pay no more than lip service, the temptation to use torture is unrestrained.'

[9] *A v Home Secretary* (above) at [74].

[10] Ibid, at [86].

[11] M Arden (2005) 121 LQR 604, 622.

[12] Kenny (ed.) *The Oxford History of Western Philosophy*, ch 6 (A Quinton), p 296.

[13] d'Entrèves, *The Notion of the State*, p 71.

[14] See Grayling, *Towards the Light*.

[15] Maitland, *Constitutional History*, pp 100–4; McIlwain, *Constitutionalism Ancient and Modern*, ch 4.

[16] For the rule of law in 16th-century England, see Elton, *Studies in Tudor and Stuart Politics and Government*, vol 1, p 260.

The Bill of Rights in 1689 affirmed that the monarchy was subject to the law.[17] Not only did it force the Crown to govern through Parliament, but it also established the right of individuals to challenge unlawful interference in respect of their life, liberty and property.

> In *Entick* v *Carrington*, two King's Messengers were sued for having unlawfully broken into the plaintiff's house and seized his papers: the defendants relied on a warrant issued by one of the Secretaries of State ordering them to search for Entick and bring him with his books and papers before the Secretary of State for examination. The Secretary of State claimed that the power to issue such warrants was essential to government, 'the only means of quieting clamours and sedition'. The court *held* that, in the absence of a statute or judicial precedent upholding the legality of such a warrant, the practice was illegal. Lord Camden CJ said: 'What would the Parliament say if the judges should take upon themselves to mould an unlawful power into a convenient authority, by new restrictions? That would be, not judgment, but legislation . . . And with respect to the argument of State necessity, or a distinction that has been aimed at between State offences and others, the common law does not understand that kind of reasoning, nor do our books take notice of any such distinction.'[18]

The 'general warrant' cases sought to protect rights to liberty and property, but such rights were not absolute. In 1772 Lord Mansfield held that the common law did not recognise the right of a slave-owner to enforce ownership of a slave brought from Jamaica to England.[19] The procedure by which individual liberty was protected was that of habeas corpus, a common law writ which had been rendered more effective by statute.[20] Formal adherence to the law was one of the public values of 18th-century Britain, although not all the people gained equally from it.[21] Economic and social developments since 1765 have qualified the forthright declaration of Lord Camden that in the absence of precedent no common law powers of search and seizure will be recognised,[22] but *Entick* v *Carrington* still exercises influence on judicial attitudes to the claims of government.

Dicey's exposition of the rule of law

One reason for this is found in the work of A V Dicey, whose lectures at Oxford were first published in 1885 under the title, *Introduction to the Study of the Law of the Constitution*.[23] Dicey's aim was to introduce students to 'two or three guiding principles' of the constitution, foremost among these being the rule of law. The spirit of *Entick* v *Carrington* seems to run through Dicey's arguments, but he expressed the doctrine of the rule of law in the form of

---

[17] See too: *R (Miller)* v *Secretary of State for Exiting the EU* [2017] UKSC 5, [2017] 2 WLR 582 at [41]–[42].

[18] (1765) 19 St Tr 1030, 1067, 1073. And see *Wilkes* v *Wood* (1763) Lofft 1. See the fascinating collection of essays celebrating *Entick* and its impact on the law in Tomkins and Scott, *Entick v Carrington: 250 Years of the Rule of Law*.

[19] *Somersett* v *Steuart* (1772) 20 St Tr 1. See for Scotland: *Knight* v *Wedderburn* (1778) Mor 14545.

[20] See ch 25 D.

[21] Thompson, *Whigs and Hunters*, pp 258–69. And see Tomkins, *Our Republican Constitution*. In the age of colonialism, British rule was not always characterised by adherence to law: see Kostal, *A Jurisprudence of Power*, examining the impact on opinion in London of atrocities during the Jamaica uprising in 1865.

[22] *Malone* v *Metropolitan Police Commissioner* [1979] Ch 344.

[23] The main text was settled by Dicey in 1908; it appears in the 10th edn (with introduction by E C S Wade). See also Cosgrove, *The Rule of Law: Albert Venn Dicey, Victorian Jurist*, and the symposium of articles at [1985] PL 587.

several statements describing the English constitution, some of them derived from authors who immediately preceded him.[24] Dicey gave to the rule of law three meanings:

> It means, in the first place, the absolute supremacy or predominance of regular law as opposed to the influence of arbitrary power, and excludes the existence of arbitrariness, of prerogative, or even of wide discretionary authority on the part of the government . . . ; a man may with us be punished for a breach of law, but he can be punished for nothing else.

Thus no one could be made to suffer penalties except for a distinct breach of law established before the ordinary courts. In this sense Dicey contrasted the rule of law with systems of government based on the exercise by those in authority of wide or arbitrary powers of constraint, such as a power of detention without trial.

Second, the rule of law meant

> equality before the law, or the equal subjection of all classes to the ordinary law of the land administered by the ordinary law courts.

In Dicey's view, this implied that no one was above the law; that officials like private citizens were under a duty to obey the same law; and that there were no 'administrative courts' to decide claims by citizens against the state or its officials.

Third, the rule of law meant

> that with us the law of the constitution, the rules which in foreign countries naturally form part of a constitutional code, are not the source but the consequence of the rights of individuals, as defined and enforced by the courts; that, in short, the principles of private law have with us been by the action of the courts and Parliament so extended as to determine the position of the Crown and of its servants; thus the constitution is the result of the ordinary law of the land.[25]

So the rights of the individual were secured not by guarantees in a formal document but by the ordinary remedies of private law available against those who unlawfully interfered with someone's liberty, whether they were private citizens or officials.

Assessment of Dicey's views[26]

These three statements about the rule of law raise many questions. In the first, what is meant by 'regular law'? Does this include, for example, social security law, anti-discrimination law or anti-terror laws? Does 'arbitrary power' refer to powers of government that are so broad they could be used for a wide variety of different purposes; powers that are capable of abuse if they are not properly controlled; or powers that directly infringe individual liberty (for example, power to detain a citizen without trial)? If 'arbitrary power' and 'wide discretionary authority' alike are unacceptable, how may the limits of acceptable authority be settled? If it is contrary to the rule of law that discretionary authority should be given to government departments or public officers, then the rule of law applies to no modern constitution. Today the state regulates national life in multifarious ways. Discretionary authority in most spheres of government is inevitable. While there are still certain powers which we are unwilling to trust to the executive (for example, the power to indefinitely detain individuals without trial) except when national emergencies dictate otherwise, attention has to be given not so much to attacking the

---

[24] H W Arndt (1957) 31 ALJ 117.

[25] Dicey, pp 202–3.

[26] See Jennings, *The Law and the Constitution*, ch 2 and app 2; F H Lawson (1959) 7 *Political Studies* 109, 207; H W Arthurs (1979) Osgoode Hall LJ 1; Lord Bingham [2002] PL 39; Craig, *Public Law and Democracy*, ch 2; Loughlin, *Public Law and Political Theory*, ch 7. For endorsement of Dicey's approach, see Allan, *Law, Liberty and Justice*, ch 2, and *Constitutional Justice*, ch 1. A devastating dissection of Dicey's methodology is in Allison, *The English Historical Constitution*, ch 7.

existence of discretionary powers as to establishing legal and political safeguards by which the use of such powers may be controlled.[27] Doubtless Dicey would have regarded as arbitrary many powers of government on which social welfare and economic regulation now depend.

Dicey's second meaning stresses the equal subjection of all persons to the 'ordinary law'. The 14th Amendment to the US Constitution provides that no state shall 'deny to any person within its jurisdiction the equal protection of the law', a provision which has been a fertile source of constitutional challenges to discriminatory state legislation. Similar provisions are in the constitutions of India, Germany and Canada.[28] In fact, the legislature must frequently distinguish between categories of person by reference to economic or social considerations or legal status. Landlords and tenants, employers and employees, company directors and shareholders, British citizens and aliens – these and innumerable other categories are subject to differing legal rules. What a constitutional guarantee of equality may achieve is to enable legislation to be invalidated which distinguishes between citizens on grounds which appear irrelevant, unacceptable or offensive (for example, discrimination between persons on grounds of sex, race, origin or colour).[29] Dicey had in mind no such jurisdiction. The specific meaning he attached to equality before the law was that all citizens (including officials) were subject to the ordinary courts should they transgress the law which applied to them, and that there should be no separate administrative courts, as in France, to deal with unlawful conduct by officials.[30] He believed that *droit administratif* in France favoured the officials and that English law through decisions such as *Entick* v *Carrington* gave better protection to the people. These views of Dicey long impeded the proper understanding of administrative law. Today the need for such law cannot be denied. Administrative courts in most European countries, including France, protect the individual against unlawful acts by public bodies.

Dicey's third meaning of the rule of law expressed the view that the principles of common law declared by the judges are the basis of the citizen's rights and liberties. Dicey had in mind the fundamental political freedoms – freedom of the person, freedom of speech, freedom of association. Someone whose freedoms were infringed could seek a remedy in the courts and did not need to rely on constitutional guarantees. Dicey believed that the common law gave better protection to the citizen than a written constitution. The Habeas Corpus Acts, which made effective the remedy by which persons unlawfully detained might be set free, were 'for practical purposes worth a hundred constitutional articles guaranteeing individual liberty'.[31] Today, we cannot share Dicey's faith in the common law as the primary means of protecting our liberties against the state. First, liberties at common law may be eroded by Parliament and thus they have a residual character (namely, what is left after all statutory restrictions have taken effect). Second, the common law does not assure the economic or social well-being of the people. Third, there is now wide support in many countries both for a formal declaration of basic rights (such as is provided by the European Convention on Human Rights) and for the creation of judicial procedures for protecting those rights.[32] That is not to say that a written guarantee of specified rights is sufficient. Some of the most tyrannical regimes have had, on paper, fulsome rights afforded to their citizens which were, in practice, wholly illusory.[33]

Dicey's view of the rule of law, like his view of parliamentary sovereignty, was based on assumptions about the British system of government that no longer apply. Although he did

---

[27] Davis, *Discretionary Justice*.

[28] India, 1949 Constitution, art 14; Federal Republic of Germany, Basic Law, art 3; Canadian Charter of Rights and Freedoms, s 15.

[29] Ch 14 A; and Feldman, *Civil Liberties and Human Rights*, ch 3.

[30] See Brown and Bell, *French Administrative Law*; and ch 21.

[31] Dicey, p 199. And see ch 25 D.

[32] Ch 14.

[33] The constitution of the Union of Soviet Socialist Republics was a classic example of this genre.

not satisfactorily resolve the potential conflict between the two notions of the rule of law and the supremacy of Parliament,[34] a judicial formulation of the relationship implies the need for equilibrium and balance rather than conflict:

> The maintenance of the rule of law is in every way as important in a free society as the democratic franchise. In our society the rule of law rests upon twin foundations: the sovereignty of the Queen in Parliament in making the law and the sovereignty of the Queen's courts in interpreting and applying the law.[35]

We have seen that Dicey's views on the sovereignty of Parliament remain influential today. The same cannot be said of his treatment of the rule of law. But this is no reason for assigning the rule of law and its meaning today to the margins of legal debate. Indeed, in the Constitutional Reform Act 2005 (s 1), Parliament declared (without offering a definition) that the Act 'does not adversely effect . . . the existing constitutional principle of the rule of law'. The next section seeks to explore the main aspects of the rule of law today, in a discussion which is not cast in the Diceyan mould.

B. The rule of law and its implications today

Emphasis will be placed on three related ideas. First, statements of the rule of law embody a preference for orderly life within an organised community, rather than a situation of anarchy or strife in which there is no security for persons, their well-being or their possessions. Some stability in society is a precondition for the existence of a legal system. Second, the rule of law expresses the fundamental principle that government must be conducted according to law and that in disputed cases, what the law requires is declared by judicial decision. This principle is manifest in innumerable decisions of the courts, and represents existing law. Third, the rule of law refers to a rich body of opinion on matters such as the powers that the state should or should not have (for example, whether ministers should have power to detain without trial), the procedures to be followed when action is taken by the state (for example, the right to a fair hearing in criminal trials), and the values inherent in a system of justice. This third idea is relevant to debates about what the law should be, particularly when our lives are challenged by events such as unrest on the streets or international terrorism, whether these debates occur in Parliament or in a court when new issues are confronted by the judges.

The relation between the second and third ideas may be put in this way. The requirement that government be conducted according to law (the principle of legality) is a necessary condition for the rule of law; but insistence on legality alone does not ensure that the state's powers are consistent with values such as liberty and due process. This emphasis is found in case law of the European Court of Human Rights.[36]

These three aspects of the rule of law are now examined in more depth.

Three aspects of the rule of law

1. Law and order better than anarchy

In the limited sense of law and order, the rule of law may appear to be preserved by a dictatorship or a military occupation as well as by a democratic form of government. Under a

---

[34] Dicey, ch 13. For an approach that sees no such conflict, see Allan, *Law, Liberty and Justice*, chs 3, 11; and (same author) *Constitutional Justice*, ch 7.
[35] *X* v *Morgan-Grampian Ltd* [1991] AC 1, 48 (Lord Bridge).
[36] See ch 14 B.

government which is not freely elected, courts of law may function, settling disputes between private citizens and such disputes between citizens and government officials as the regime permits to be so decided. However, constitutionalism and the rule of law will not thrive unless legal restraints apply to the government. The maintenance of law and order and the existence of political liberty are not mutually exclusive, but interdependent. As the Supreme Court of Canada has said, 'democracy in any real sense of the word cannot exist without the rule of law.'[37] The Universal Declaration of Human Rights states: 'It is essential if man is not to be compelled to have recourse, as a last resort, to rebellion against tyranny and oppression, that human rights should be protected by the rule of law.'[38] In a democracy, it must be possible by political means to change a government without threatening the existence of the state. Unless this possibility exists, the state becomes identified with coercive might and the role of law within the state is emptied of moral content, for 'the State cannot be conceived in terms of force alone'.[39]

2. Government according to law

The principle of legality requires that the organs of the state operate through law. If the police need to detain a citizen or if taxes are levied, the officials concerned must be able to show legal authority for their actions. In Britain, their authority may be challenged before a court of law. Acts of public authorities which are beyond their legal powers may be declared ultra vires and quashed by the courts.[40] In a striking instance, the High Court held (30 years after the event) that the enforced removal of some 1,000 British citizens from the Chagos islands in the Indian Ocean to make way for the US military base on Diego Garcia had lacked legal authority.[41] It is because of the principle of legality that legislation by Parliament is necessary if (for instance) the police are to have additional powers to combat crime; and for this reason the rule of law serves as a buttress for democracy.[42]

In the British tradition of government according to law, it is from the ordinary courts that a remedy for unlawful acts of government may be obtained: the Human Rights Act 1998 extended this jurisdiction by requiring all courts where possible to interpret legislation in conformity with the European Convention on Human Rights.[43] In many European legal systems, jurisdiction in public law is assigned to administrative courts. Such courts vary greatly in structure and procedure, but their power to review the legality of executive acts has much in common with the work of the Administrative Court.

Public authorities and officials must be subject to effective sanctions if they depart from the law. Often the sanction is that their acts are declared invalid by the courts. The idea within the rule of law that the state – and everyone else – is bound by and accountable to the law only holds good if there is a mechanism by which alleged infringements of the law can be tested and established. This is why the courts have repeatedly reiterated that access to justice is integral to the rule of law; Dicey's second principle is meaningless if it cannot be adjudicated upon and enforced (not necessarily in all instances by a judicial body). This point was

---

[37] *Reference Concerning Certain Questions Relating to the Secession of Quebec* (1998) 161 DLR (4th) 385, 416–17.

[38] Preamble, 3rd para.

[39] d'Entrèves, *The Notion of the State*, p 69.

[40] Ch 24.

[41] *R v Foreign Secretary, ex p Bancoult* [2001] QB 1067; A Tomkins [2001] PL 571. According to Ewing and Gearty, *The Struggle for Civil Liberties*, ch 1, the principle of legality is the essence of the rule of law. And see *R v Home Secretary, ex p Pierson* [1998] AC 539, 587–9 (Lord Steyn).

[42] On the relevance of the rule of law to government, see Jowell and Oliver (eds), *The Changing Constitution*, 7th edn, ch 1 (J Jowell). In the case of the Chagos islands (previous note) further 'powers of government' were conferred not by Parliament, but by the secret procedure of a prerogative Order in Council: *R v Foreign Secretary, ex p Bancoult (No 2)* [2008] UKHL 61, [2009] 1 AC 453.

[43] Ch 14 C.

made in stirring language by Lord Reed in the Supreme Court's decision quashing the imposition of unjustifiably high fees to bring various sorts of claims in employment tribunals:

> At the heart of the concept of the rule of law is the idea that society is governed by law. Parliament exists primarily in order to make laws for society in this country. Democratic procedures exist primarily in order to ensure that the Parliament which makes those laws includes Members of Parliament who are chosen by the people of this country and are accountable to them. Courts exist in order to ensure that the laws made by Parliament, and the common law created by the courts themselves, are applied and enforced. That role includes ensuring that the executive branch of government carries out its functions in accordance with the law. In order for the courts to perform that role, people must in principle have unimpeded access to them. Without such access, laws are liable to become a dead letter, the work done by Parliament may be rendered nugatory, and the democratic election of Members of Parliament may become a meaningless charade. That is why the courts do not merely provide a public service like any other.[44]

In Britain, government departments are liable to be sued for their wrongful acts under the Crown Proceedings Act 1947.[45] That Act preserved the personal immunity of the Sovereign, an immunity which in other legal systems is enjoyed by the head of state. Thus in the United States, the President in office is immune from liability for his unlawful acts and he is irremovable except on a successful impeachment. If the President is removed, he can then be sued or prosecuted for unlawful acts which he may have committed. Even a President in office may not disregard the law.

In the course of criminal investigations into the Watergate affair, the special prosecutor appointed by the Attorney General requested President Nixon to produce tape-recordings of discussions which the President had had with his advisers. When presidential privilege was claimed for the tapes, the US Supreme Court held that the claim had to be considered 'in the light of our historic commitment to the rule of law'. The court rejected the claim and ordered the tapes to be produced, since 'the generalised assertion of privilege must yield to the demonstrated, specific need for evidence in a pending criminal trial'.[46]

Nixon then resigned rather than face impeachment proceedings before a hostile Congress. In 1998–9, when President Clinton was impeached, he was acquitted by the Senate on charges that included one of giving false testimony to a federal grand jury in the Lewinsky affair.[47] In 1999, presidential immunity of a different kind came before the House of Lords: General Pinochet, former President of Chile, was held liable to be extradited to Spain to stand trial on charges of conspiring to commit torture contrary to international law, relating to events while he was in office.[48] No general immunity applies to government ministers. In 1993, the Law Lords held that the Home Secretary was liable for contempt of court, in that he failed to order the return to the United Kingdom of a Zairean teacher who had claimed refugee status, despite an order by a High Court judge that this should be done. Lord Templeman said: 'For the purpose of enforcing the law against all persons and institutions, . . . the courts are armed with coercive powers exercisable in proceedings for contempt of court.'

----

[44] *R (Unison)* v *Lord Chancellor* [2017] UKSC 51, [2017] 3 WLR 409 at [68].
[45] Ch 26.
[46] *US* v *Nixon* 418 US 683 (1974); for public interest immunity in Britain, see ch 26 D.
[47] Gerhardt, *The Federal Impeachment Process*, ch 14. And see Berger, *Impeachment*.
[48] *R* v *Bow Street Magistrate, ex p Pinochet Ugarte (No 3)* [2000] 1 AC 147.

The Home Secretary's argument that the courts had no such powers against ministers 'would, if upheld, establish the proposition that the executive obey the law as a matter of grace and not as a matter of necessity, a proposition which would reverse the result of the Civil War'.[49]

In a system in which Parliament is supreme, and so long as the Cabinet has a majority in the Commons, legal authority for new powers may not be difficult for the government to obtain, and fundamental rights are not protected against legislative invasion. The supreme Parliament may grant the executive powers which drastically affect individual liberty, as it did in 2001 when it authorised the indefinite detention without trial of foreign nationals suspected of terrorist involvement.[50] If all that the rule of law means is the purely formal idea that official acts must be clothed with legality, this gives no guarantee that other fundamental values are not infringed.

3. The rule of law as a broad doctrine affecting the making of new law

If law is not to be merely a means of achieving whatever ends a particular government may favour, the rule of law must go beyond the principle of legality. The experience and values of the legal system are relevant not only to the question, 'What legal authority *does* the government have for its acts?' but also to the questions, 'What powers *ought* the government to have? And how *ought* those powers to be exercised?' If, for example, the government wishes to introduce penal sanctions for conduct contrary to its economic or social policies, the new legislation ought to respect principles of fair criminal procedure. That obligation is reinforced by the Human Rights Act 1998 and the right to a fair trial under the European Convention on Human Rights, art 6.

As a broad principle influencing development of the law, the content of the 'rule of law' has been much debated. What *are* the essential values which have emerged from centuries of legal experience? Are they absolute values, or are there circumstances in which political necessity justifies the legislature in departing from them? To revert to the example of interrogation in depth with which this chapter began, could it ever be justified to use such methods to compel those suspected of terrorist activities to reveal information? Could there be legislation to authorise this that would not also open the way for measures amounting to torture or degrading treatment in breach of art 3, ECHR?

Since 2001, there have been many claims that measures amounting to torture have been used by states against suspected terrorists. In 2005, as we have seen, the Law Lords held that evidence that might have been obtained by means of torture committed abroad is inadmissible in special immigration proceedings. Having surveyed national and international rules against torture, Lord Bingham said:

> it would of course be within the power of a sovereign Parliament (in breach of international law) to confer power on [a tribunal] to receive third party torture evidence. But the English common law has regarded torture and its fruits with abhorrence for over 500 years, and that abhorrence is now shared by over 140 countries which have acceded to the Torture Convention.[51]

For legislation to connive at the use of torture would indeed be to erode the rule of law. The same may be said of proposals to administer justice in secret, especially if the aim is to prevent sensitive evidence being made known to an accused person and his or her legal representatives. Yet a controversial result of the present role of the security and intelligence agencies is that a majority ruling by the UK Supreme Court that the courts have no inherent

---

[49] *M v Home Office* [1994] 1 AC 377, 395.
[50] See *A v Home Secretary* (note 7 above) and ch 20 D.
[51] *A v Home Secretary (No 2)* (note 8 above), [51].

authority to permit civil justice in secret without disclosure to one of the parties was soon followed by legislation to permit this, albeit subject to certain safeguards in the legislation.[52]

There may of course be room for disagreement over the 'rule of law' aspects of a particular situation. In 2008, the Divisional Court relied on the rule of law in holding that the Director of the Serious Fraud Office acted unlawfully in dropping an investigation into charges of bribery against BAE Systems plc, in the light of threats from Saudi Arabia to take action that would damage UK security, if the investigation continued. The Law Lords disagreed, holding that the Director's decision had been properly made and that the ordinary principles of judicial review gave effect to the rule of law.[53]

Is the rule of law then in this broad sense too subjective and uncertain to be of any value? Would discussion of changes in the law be clearer if the 'rule of law' were excluded from the vocabulary of debate? As Toulson LJ colourfully put it in the context of the press seeking access to the court file in extradition proceedings: 'The rule of law is a fine concept but fine words butter no parsnips'.[54]

One attempt to ascertain the values inherent in law was made by Lon Fuller, who argued that the enactment of secret laws would be contrary to the essential nature of a legal system, as would heavy reliance on retrospective legislation or on legislation imposing criminal sanctions for conduct which is not defined but may be deemed undesirable by an official.[55]

By contrast, Joseph Raz argues that the term 'rule of law' should be limited to formal values associated with the legal system. Thus, laws should be prospective, open, certain and capable of guiding human conduct; judges should be independent and the courts accessible; and litigants should receive a fair hearing. While these standards may ensure formal conformity to the rule of law, Raz emphasises that they do not ensure that the substance of the law meets the needs of the people; and that conformity to legal values is a matter of degree, to be balanced against competing claims.[56]

While Raz regards the rule of law as dealing with matters of form, other jurists favour a more substantive concept.[57] But the distinction between form and substance is not always clear-cut (is the case against 'arbitrary power' based on matters of form or substance or both?). For Raz, the rule of law is 'compatible with gross violations of human rights', but he also argued that 'deliberate disregard for the rule of law violates human dignity'.[58] He rightly warns against identifying the rule of law with utopia. But is the rule of law observed under a dictatorship in which the judges diligently apply the dictator's edicts, including one that permits indefinite detention without trial for those suspected of undesirable activity?

Many would conclude that the rule of law in a strong sense thrives only alongside values of human dignity, liberty and democracy. This view was shared by the late Lord Bingham,

---

[52] *Al Rawi* v *Security Service* [2011] UKSC 34, [2012] 1 AC 531; and Justice and Security Act 2013, part 2 (and see ch 26 D). Cf *Home Office* v *Tariq* [2011] UKSC 35, [2012] 1 AC 452 (closed procedure authorised by regulations, no breach of EU law or art 6 ECHR). See also *A* v *United Kingdom* (2009) 26 BHRC 1 and *A* v *Home Secretary (No 3)* [2009] UKHL 28, [2010] 2 AC 269.

[53] *R (Corner House Research)* v *Director of SFO* [2008] UKHL 60, [2009] AC 756. See J Jowell [2008] JR 273 and Lord Steyn [2009] PL 338.

[54] *R (Guardian News and Media)* v *City of Westminster Magistrates' Court* [2012] EWCA Civ 420, [2013] QB 618 at [1].

[55] Fuller, *The Morality of Law*. Allan, *Constitutional Justice* endorses Fuller's approach. For a vivid illustration of the perversion of legal process, see Lord Steyn's quotation from Kafka's *The Trial* in *R (Roberts)* v *Parole Board* [2005] UKHL 45, [2005] 2 AC 738, [95].

[56] J Raz (1977) 93 LQR 195. See also Raz, *Ethics in the Public Domain*, ch 16.

[57] See P Craig [1997] PL 467 and (the same) in Feldman (ed.), *English Public Law*, ch 13 B.

[58] J Raz (1977) 93 LQR 195, 204 and 205.

for many years the presiding Law Lord; his book *The Rule of Law* identified eight principal ingredients of the concept:[59]

(1) The law must be accessible and so far as possible intelligible, clear and predictable.

(2) Questions of legal right and liability should ordinarily be resolved by application of the law and not the exercise of discretion.

(3) The laws should apply equally to all, save to the extent that objective differences justify differentiation.

(4) Public officers at all levels must exercise their powers in good faith, fairly, for the purposes for which the powers are conferred, without exceeding the limits of such powers and not unreasonably.

(5) The law must afford adequate protection for fundamental human rights.

(6) Means must be provided for resolving, without excessive cost or delay, civil disputes which the parties themselves cannot resolve.

(7) Adjudicative procedures provided by the state should be fair.

(8) The state must comply with its obligations in international law as in national law.

Among British judges there is an important vein of belief in the values to be upheld in a legal system. The nature of these values can be discovered from judicial decisions[60] and from many articles and lectures by judges.[61]

International aspects of the rule of law

Since 1945, there have been constant efforts to further the rule of law in international relations and to secure respect for human rights. The Universal Declaration of Human Rights, adopted in 1948, was followed by the European Convention on Human Rights (ECHR), signed at Rome in 1950.[62] The Convention recognised that European countries have 'a common heritage of political traditions, ideals, freedom and the rule of law' and created machinery for protecting certain human rights. In *Golder*'s case, upholding the right of a convicted prisoner in the United Kingdom to obtain legal advice regarding a civil action against the prison authorities, the European Court of Human Rights said, 'in civil matters one can scarcely conceive of the rule of law without there being a possibility of having access to the courts'.[63]

   Both the Convention and the case law of the Strasbourg Court support the analysis of the rule of law made in this chapter.[64] The Convention seeks to protect individuals against the arbitrary or unlawful exercise of state power, and it requires national legal systems to bear the primary burden of protecting Convention rights. In respect of those Convention rights

---

[59] See also his analysis of the rule of law at [2007] CLJ 67.

[60] See D Feldman (1990) 106 LQR 246. On the power of the court to stay proceedings which 'have only been made possible by acts which offend the court's conscience as being contrary to the rule of law', see *R v Horseferry Road Magistrates, ex p Bennett* [1994] 1 AC 42, 76 (Lord Lowry).

[61] Articles by senior judges include: J Laws (1994) 57 MLR 213, [1995] PL 72, [1996] PL 622, [1997] PL 455, [1998] PL 221; R Scott [1996] PL 410 and 427; S Sedley (1994) 110 LQR 260; Lord Steyn [1997] PL 84, (2004) 53 ICLQ 1; and Lord Woolf [1995] PL 57, [2004] CLJ 317.

[62] Ch 14 B. For the background, see Simpson, *Human Rights and the End of Empire*.

[63] *Golder* v *UK* (1975) 1 EHRR 524.

[64] Although the background to the term 'rule of law' is the common law, French law knows the term 'état de droit' and German law the concept of 'rechtsstaat'. The three concepts are the subject of a rich comparative analysis in Heuschling, *État de droit, Rechsstaat, Rule of Law*.

that (unlike the right not to be tortured) are not absolute, any restrictions in the public interest must (among other things) satisfy the test of being 'prescribed by law'. This test means (in outline) that (1) the restriction must be authorised in national law and (2) the 'quality' of the national law must be compatible with the Convention.[65] In English law, it was formerly held that public authorities might do anything which did not interfere with the rights of individuals, even if they had no express authority for such action.[66] This approach is not acceptable where Convention rights are concerned.

The ECHR, established through the Council of Europe, is one of many multilateral treaties that encourage states to protect human rights. Treaties adopted under the United Nations include the International Covenant on Civil and Political Rights, the International Convention on the Elimination of all Forms of Racial Discrimination and the Convention against Torture.

Social and economic aspects of the rule of law

The rule of law movement has broadened to include social and economic goals which lie far beyond the typical values associated with the courts, legal process and the legal profession. Such a broadening of the 'rule of law' raises issues that often arise from government policies in relation to the economy and social welfare. One extreme view is that individual autonomy and the ability to plan one's affairs will be prejudiced if governments retain powers to intervene in social and economic affairs.[67] Now certainty and predictability are values often associated with law. In a different context, Lord Diplock said in 1975: 'The acceptance of the rule of law as a constitutional principle requires that a citizen, before committing himself to any course of action, should be able to know what are the legal consequences that will flow from it.'[68] But, however desirable it may be that discretionary powers of government should be controlled by rules,[69] the principle is difficult to apply to the state's responsibilities for the economic and social well-being of its people.

A related question is whether legal protection for classic civil and political rights (such as personal liberty, freedom of expression and the right to vote) can or should be extended to economic and social rights (such as rights relating to employment, social security, health care and housing).[70] Protection for rights of these kinds is found in the national constitutions of many EU member states, and in other countries where new constitutions have recently been adopted. Some economic and social rights are, however, subject to problems of definition, implementation and enforcement, while others (such as employment rights) are addressed to private law relationships as well as the relationship between the individual and the state. But it is certainly arguable that individuals ought to have enforceable rights to the delivery of some public goods, such as education or medical care. In South Africa, constitutionally protected social rights (including rights to housing, health care, food and shelter) are enforceable by the Constitutional Court.[71]

---

[65] See *Sunday Times* v *UK* (1979) 2 EHRR 245; *Malone* v *UK* (1984) 7 EHRR 14. Harris, O'Boyle and Warbrick, *Law of the European Convention on Human Rights*, pp 344–8. For a rather stricter version of the test applied in at least some situations, see the discussion in *R (T)* v *Chief Constable of Greater Manchester* [2014] UKSC 35, [2015] AC 49.

[66] *Malone* v *Metropolitan Police Commissioner* [1979] Ch 344; cf *R* v *Somerset CC, ex p Fewings* [1995] 3 All ER 20.

[67] See the analysis of rule of law concepts in Hayek, *The Constitution of Liberty*; for a critique, see Loughlin, *Public Law and Political Theory*, pp 84–101.

[68] *Black-Clawson International Ltd* v *Papierwerke AG* [1975] AC 591, 638.

[69] Davis, *Discretionary Justice*, ch 3.

[70] See S Fredman and M Wesson in Feldman (ed.), *English Public Law*, ch 10. Also K D Ewing (2001) 5 Edin LR 297; G van Beuren [2002] PL 456 and [2013] PL 821; and in Rosenfeld and Sajó (eds), *Oxford Handbook of Comparative Constitutional Law*, ch 49 (D M Davis) and ch 50 (K D Ewing).

[71] See *Government of Republic of South Africa* v *Grootboom* 2001 (1) SA 46 (CC); M Wesson [2007] PL 748; and E Cameron and M Taylor [2017] PL 382.

Within the Council of Europe, there has since 1995 been a collective complaints procedure to enable cases to be taken to the Social Rights Committee by organisations claiming that a member state is in breach of an obligation under the European Social Charter. The United Kingdom has ratified the Social Charter of 1961, but not the collective complaints protocol, nor the Revised Social Charter of 1996, in which the collective complaints procedure is also included.[72] Otherwise, the Social Charter has become an important source used by the Strasbourg court in the interpretation of Convention rights (particularly in relation to articles 4 and 11).[73] In the United Kingdom, much detailed social legislation has long existed, and individuals may usually enforce rights under that legislation by appealing to the appropriate tribunal (where one exists) or, where there is no right of appeal, by recourse to judicial review.[74]

However, questions of how appropriate it is for unelected courts to determine such rights arise particularly starkly in the context of social and economic rights; why is it legitimate for a court to require the allocation of scarce resources – which such rights invariably require – in a way which Parliament, or an elected and/or accountable official, has not? Are judges well-placed or well-qualified to say that more money should be spent on x, even if it reduces the amount that can be spent on y and z? Social and economic rights are especially likely to give rise to such concerns, which are commonly known as polycentricity issues (i.e. where there are a number of interlocking and interacting interests and considerations). This is an important part of why courts have been traditionally less comfortable or confident in addressing such rights.[75]

Conclusion

In his study of the rule of law, Lord Bingham concluded that the core of the principle is 'that all persons and authorities within the state, whether public or private, should be bound by and entitled to the benefit of laws publicly made, taking effect (generally) in the future and publicly administered in the courts.'[76] Surrounding this core are many principles of legal, political and democratic significance. A government's developing response to changing social needs may require these principles to be re-assessed, but no government should suppose that new areas of public action (such as the regulation of public utilities) can be insulated from the scope of law and subjected only to administrative or political controls.

Challenges to the orderly working of law and society are presented by phenomena such as hijacking, urban terrorism, direct action by militant groups, civil disobedience, and violent demonstrations. All these are sometimes described indiscriminately as a threat to the rule of law (by which may be meant a challenge to the authority of established institutions). There are many distinctions to be drawn between these different forms of political or criminal action. But, if we leave aside acts of criminal violence at one end of the scale and peaceful political action at the other, do acts of non-violent civil disobedience endanger the legal system? In particular, does the rule of law require obedience to the law at all times from all citizens and organisations?[77] It may be argued both that in a democracy there are important

---

[72] See Harris and Darcy, *The European Social Charter*. The EU Charter of Fundamental Rights (2000) includes both civil and political rights, and social and economic rights, and it seeks to break down the traditional distinction between the two: Fredman and Wesson (above), pp 473–8. See also ch 6 B.

[73] *Demir and Baycara* v *Turkey* [2008] ECHR 1345, (2009) 48 EHRR 54.

[74] Chs 23 A and 24.

[75] J W F Allison [1994] CLJ 367; (same) [1994] PL 452; J A King [2008] PL 101; Fredman and Campbell (eds), *Social and Economic Rights and Constitutional Law*; Palmer, *Judicial Review, Socio-Economic Rights and the Human Rights Act*.

[76] *The Rule of Law*, p 8.

[77] Marshall, *Constitutional Theory*, ch 9; Dworkin, *Taking Rights Seriously*, ch 8; Allan, *Law, Liberty, and Justice*, ch 5.

reasons for obeying the law which do not exist in other forms of government, and that there are forms of principled disobedience that do not run counter to the general justification for obedience. The last point applies particularly to actions that are planned to improve the working of democratic decision-making.[78] The claims of the state are not absolute, and individuals may be driven by their conscience to resist a law that they regard as unjust or immoral. Such action does not conflict with there being a general obligation to obey the law, including legal rules with which an individual disagrees.

Modern society requires willingness from most people for most of the time to observe the law, even law that is unpopular. It deserves to be remembered that law, like the democratic process, may protect the weaker and underprivileged sections of society against those who can exercise physical or economic force.

C. The separation of powers

In this section, we examine a principle which is found, in one form or another, in most modern constitutions. The need for some 'separation of powers' within the state is essential both in the interests of democracy and also for the legal system, where an independent judiciary is essential if the rule of law is to have any substance.[79]

The need for the separation of powers in what may be called a strong sense of the term has often been downplayed in respect of the United Kingdom. Thus Dicey referred in passing to the doctrine as being 'the offspring of a double misconception'.[80] In 1995, Lord Mustill sought to recognise its significance:

> It is a feature of the peculiarly British conception of the separation of powers that Parliament, the executive and the courts have each their distinct and largely exclusive domain. Parliament has a legally unchallengeable right to make whatever laws it thinks right. The executive carries on the administration of the country in accordance with the powers conferred on it by law. The courts interpret the laws, and see that they are obeyed.[81]

This model for the exercise of legislative, executive and judicial powers may be seen at work in such fields as the law of taxation, criminal law and administrative law. In reality, the validity of the model is more complex than the quotation suggests. Three questions need to be asked:

(*a*) to what extent are the three functions (legislative, executive and judicial) distinguishable?

(*b*) how and why should these three functions be 'separated'?

(*c*) to what extent are these functions exercised separately in the United Kingdom?

---

[78] Singer, *Democracy and Disobedience*. The Strasbourg Court has recognised that direct action may involve Convention rights to freedom of expression and association: *Steel* v *UK* (1998) 28 EHRR 603. See H Fenwick and G Phillipson [2000] PL 627 and (2001) 21 LS 535.

[79] Vile, *Constitutionalism and the Separation of Powers*; Allan, *Law, Liberty and Justice*, chs 1, 3, 8 and Allan, *Constitutional Justice*, ch 2. Also Mount, *The British Constitution Now*, pp 81–92; N W Barber [2001] CLJ 59 and Barber, *The Constitutional State*, ch 3.

[80] Dicey, *Law of the Constitution*, p 338. For a critical analysis, see Jennings, *Law and the Constitution*, pp 18–28 and App 1. Robson, a contemporary of Jennings, called separation of powers 'that antique and rickety chariot . . . , so long the favourite vehicle of writers on political science and constitutional law for the conveyance of fallacious ideas': *Justice and Administrative Law*, p 14.

[81] *R* v *Home Secretary, ex p Fire Brigades Union* [1995] 2 AC 513, 567. For an interesting analysis of the use of the separation of powers by the courts, see R Masterman and S Wheatle [2017] PL 469.

To what extent are the three functions (legislative, executive and judicial) distinguishable?

The *legislative function* involves the enactment of general rules determining the structure and powers of public authorities and regulating the conduct of citizens and private bodies. We have seen that supreme legislative authority in the United Kingdom is exercised by Parliament, generally on the proposal of the government, but not all new laws are made directly at Westminster. Parliament has created devolved assemblies in Scotland, Wales and Northern Ireland and frequently confers legislative powers on executive bodies such as ministers, government departments and local authorities. Under the European Communities Act 1972 (while it remains in force), some legislative authority for all EU member states, including the United Kingdom, is exercised at the European level. Despite the severe limits placed by history on the authority of the Crown to legislate without Parliament, a few legislative powers of the Crown have survived. An attempt by the government to use such a power to pre-empt legislation by Parliament was the subject of judicial review in 1995,[82] and the Brexit litigation concerned the ability of the Crown to act in a manner which could frustrate legislation or remove legislative rights derived from EU law.[83] As regards legislation by Parliament, the courts decide the effect of that legislation by the process of interpretation; and in the area of the common law the courts still exercise a role that may involve the making of new law. Moreover, in most areas of government, ministers and departments regularly formulate policies for the exercise of statutory powers and apply those policies to specific individuals: the power to make general rules and policies carries with it the power to make sub-rules and more detailed policies and may often become blurred with the making of decisions based on a person's individual circumstances.

The *executive function* is more difficult to define, since it broadly comprises the whole body of authority to govern, other than that involved in the legislative functions of Parliament and the judicial functions of the courts. The authority to govern includes such matters as initiating and implementing legislation, maintaining order and state security, promoting social welfare and the economy, and conducting the external relations of the state. Historically, the executive was identified with the monarch, but today the executive in a broad sense comprises all ministers, officials and public authorities by which functions of government are exercised. Executive functions are also performed by devolved authorities in Scotland, Wales and Northern Ireland, by local authorities and at a European level by the EU.

The primary *judicial function* is to determine disputes in accordance with the laws made by Parliament and decisions of the superior courts, and extends to matters of private and public law. It is exercised in the civil and criminal courts and in tribunals.

How and why should the functions be 'separated'?

Within a system of government based on law, the primary organs for performing legislative, executive and judicial functions are respectively the legislature, the executive and the courts. As a legal historian remarked:

> This threefold division of labour, between a legislator, an administrative official, and an independent judge, is a necessary condition for the rule of law in modern society and therefore for democratic government itself.[84]

In Britain, Parliament, the courts and central government all owe their historical origin to the monarchy. Before these institutions developed as distinct entities, the King and his

---

[82] *R v Home Secretary, ex p Fire Brigades Union* [1995] 2 AC 513 (E Barendt [1995] PL 357).
[83] *R (Miller) v Secretary of State for Exiting the EU* [2017] UKSC 5, [2017] 2 WLR 583.
[84] Henderson, *Foundations of English Administrative Law*, p 5.

Council dealt variously with legislative, executive and judicial work. Today these tasks are all performed in the name of the Crown, but with a differentiation of process and personnel: it is the relationships between these three distinct institutions that are of concern for present purposes.[85]

The doctrine of separation is associated particularly with the French jurist Montesquieu (1689–1755), who based his exposition on an idealised view of the English constitution in his day. For him, the essence of the doctrine was the achievement of liberty.

> When legislative power is united with executive power in a single person or in a single body of the magistracy, there is no liberty . . . Nor is there liberty if the power of judging is not separate from legislative power and from executive power. If it were joined to legislative power, the power over the life and liberty of the citizens would be arbitrary, for the judge would be the legislator. If it were joined to executive power, the judge could have the force of an oppressor.[86]

The framers of the US constitution of 1787 were fully aware of these implications for liberty. In a famous paper James Madison described the need for separation as a political truism:

> The accumulation of all powers, legislative, executive, and judiciary, in the same hands, whether of one, a few, or many, and whether hereditary, self-appointed, or elective, may justly be pronounced the very definition of tyranny.[87]

But Madison's aim was to show that complete separation between legislature, executive and judiciary was neither possible nor desirable, and he defended the 1787 constitution for the manner in which it provided an elaborate structure of mutual restraints and influences ('checks and balances') between Congress, the President and the courts.

Not only the separation of powers is a prominent feature of the US constitution, but so also is the structure of checks and balances that it created. Legislative power is vested in Congress, consisting of the Senate and House of Representatives (art 1), executive power in the President (art 2) and judicial power in the Supreme Court and such other federal courts as might be established (art 3). The President holds office for a term of four years and is elected separately from Congress, so he may be of a different party from that which has a majority in either or both Houses. Neither the President nor members of his Cabinet may sit or vote in Congress; they have no direct power of initiating Bills or securing their passage through Congress. While the President has a power to veto legislation passed by Congress, his veto may be overridden by a two-thirds vote in each House of Congress. Some key executive powers, such as the negotiation of treaties and the appointment of federal judges, are subject to approval or confirmation by the Senate. The President is not directly responsible to Congress: in normal circumstances he is irremovable, but the constitution enables the President to be removed from office by impeachment at the hands of the Senate, 'for treason, bribery, or other high crimes and misdemeanours' (art 2(4)). Once appointed, the Supreme Court justices are independent of Congress and the President: they serve for life, but they too may be removed by impeachment. In one of its earliest decisions, *Marbury* v *Madison*, the Supreme Court assumed the power to declare acts of Congress and the President to be unconstitutional should they conflict with the constitution.[88]

---

[85] See Vile, note 79 above, for reassessment of the link between legal values and separation of powers; also Marshall, *Constitutional Theory*, ch 5; Munro, *Studies in Constitutional Law*, ch 9; and Masterman, *The Separation of Powers in the Contemporary Constitution*.

[86] Montesquieu, *The Spirit of the Laws* (ed. Cohler, Miller and Stone), book XI, ch 6.

[87] *The Federalist*, no 47.

[88] 1 Cranch 137 (1803). Cf *US* v *Nixon* 418 US 683 (1974). On separation of powers issues under the US constitution, see Tribe, *Constitutional Choices*, part II. For reassessment of US-style separation of powers as a constitutional model, see B Ackerman (2000) 113 Harv LR 634.

While most written constitutions contain separate chapters dealing with legislative, judicial and executive powers, they display no uniformity in the interrelation of the institutions that exercise these powers. In France, for instance, the doctrine of separation has manifested itself very differently from the American version. Thus it is considered to flow from the separation of powers that the ordinary courts should have no jurisdiction to review the legality of acts of the legislature or executive.[89] The constitutions of countries in the Commonwealth likewise vary widely in maintaining a 'separation' of powers. Under the Australian constitution, for example, delegation of legislative powers to executive agencies has been accepted more readily than the delegation to them of judicial powers.[90] The former constitution of Sri Lanka was held to be based on an implied separation of powers, so that legislation to provide special machinery for convicting the leaders of an unsuccessful coup infringed the principle that judicial power was vested only in the courts.[91] Where the constitution is based on an express or implied separation of powers, the courts may have to decide whether a power created by new legislation should be classified as legislative, executive or judicial.[92] British courts do not have this task, since there is no constitutional restraint to prevent Parliament from vesting in executive bodies powers that are in essence legislative or judicial.[93]

A comprehensive analysis of the separation of powers would have to deal with at least three meanings of the concept of 'separation'. First, that the same persons should not form part of more than one of the three branches (for example, that ministers as members of the executive should not sit in the legislature); second, that one branch of the state should not directly control the work of another (for example, that the executive should not be able to interfere in judicial decisions); and third, that one branch should not exercise the functions of another (so, for example, ministers should not have power to create criminal offences or to commit offenders to prison).

To what extent are these functions exercised separately in the United Kingdom?

Against this background, some features of the separation of powers are plainly incompatible with parliamentary government. Writing in 1867, Bagehot described the 'efficient secret' of the British constitution as 'the close union, the nearly complete fusion, of the legislative and executive powers'.[94] Bagehot's critics have rejected the concept of fusion, arguing that the close relationship between executive and legislature does not negate the constitutional distinction between the two. The fact that today all government ministers are required to be members of the Commons or the Lords has not taken away the distinction between the two institutions of government and Parliament.[95] For instance, there is a statutory limit on the number of ministers who may be members of the Commons.[96] Most persons who hold positions within the executive (including the civil service, the armed forces and the police) are disqualified from the

---

[89] See Bell, *French Constitutional Law*. The important powers of the Conseil d'Etat and the Conseil Constitutionnel over executive and legislative measures respectively are exercised outside the jurisdiction of the civil and criminal courts.

[90] Lumb, Trone and Moens, *The Constitution of the Commonwealth of Australia*, pp 23–7.

[91] *Liyanage* v *R* [1967] 1 AC 259.

[92] *Hinds* v *R* [1977] AC 195 (Jamaica). And see *DPP of Jamaica* v *Mollinson* [2003] UKPC 6, [2003] 2 AC 411, para [13].

[93] But see European Convention on Human Rights, art 6(1) (below).

[94] Bagehot, *The English Constitution*, p 65.

[95] Amery, *Thoughts on the Constitution*, p 28: also Vile, *Constitutionalism and the Separation of Powers*, pp 224–30, and Mount, *The British Constitution Now*, pp 39–47.

[96] Ch 7 G.

Commons. Only ministers are key figures in both Parliament and the executive. Moreover, the processes of the two Houses are very different from decision-making in Whitehall. No formula based on separation of powers can provide a lasting answer to the questions that arise from this relationship, but there are democratic reasons why a balance between government and Parliament should be achieved. In 1978, the Select Committee on Procedure concluded that

> the balance of advantage between Parliament and Government in the day to day working of the Constitution is now weighted in favour of the Government to a degree which arouses widespread anxiety and is inimical to the proper working of our parliamentary democracy.[97]

That report led directly to the creation of the system of department select committees, that has done much to increase the accountability of government to Parliament, and in the 1990s some measures were taken to modernise the procedures of the Commons. More recent reforms have concentrated on the need to strengthen the position of the House vis-à-vis the executive and on the need for the House to gain more control over its business.[98] But it has been commented that within the British system, the public at large see 'no visible distinction' between Parliament and government.[99]

Turning to the judicial branch, it must be stressed that independence of the judiciary calls for a strong form of separation between the courts on the one hand and the legislature and executive on the other. An obvious breach of that separation continued so long as the Lord Chancellor was both a senior Cabinet minister and head of the judiciary in England and Wales; and another breach continued so long as a committee of the House of Lords served as the final court of appeal. Under the Constitutional Reform Act 2005, the Lord Chief Justice became head of the judiciary in England and Wales, and the Supreme Court in 2009 took over the appellate function of the Lords. The courts are dependent on Parliament for their funding, but they must be able to function independently both of government and Parliament. Since the Act of Settlement 1700, the senior English judges have held office during good behaviour, not at pleasure of the executive. In 2005, Parliament declared that all ministers of the Crown 'and all with responsibility for matters relating to the judiciary . . . must uphold the continued independence of the judiciary'.[100] The need for judicial independence is reinforced by the European Convention on Human Rights, art 6(1) of which declares that 'in the determination of his civil rights and obligations, or of any criminal charge against him, everyone is entitled to a fair and public hearing within a reasonable time by *an independent and impartial tribunal* established by law' (emphasis supplied). Under the Tribunals, Courts and Enforcement Act 2007,[101] the judicial role of tribunal members has been recognised and their independent status enhanced.

The importance of judicial independence was reinforced in *M v Home Office*, when it was held that ministers are subject to the contempt jurisdiction of the courts: the Home Secretary was in contempt of court when he disobeyed a judge's order to return to London a Zairean teacher who had sought asylum in England.[102] A perceptive summary of the position was given by Nolan LJ:

> The proper constitutional relationship of the executive with the courts is that the courts will respect all acts of the executive within its lawful province, and that the executive will respect all decisions of the courts as to what its lawful province is.[103]

---

[97] HC 588–1 (1977–78), p viii.

[98] See report of House of Commons Reform Committee (Wright committee), HC 1117, 2008–9; and HC 82, 2013–14.

[99] HC 1117, 2008–9, p 9, quoting evidence by the Parliamentary Ombudsman.

[100] Constitutional Reform Act 2005, s 3(1).

[101] See ch 23 A.

[102] [1994] 1 AC 377; see G Marshall [1992] PL 7; M Gould [1993] PL 568.

[103] *M v Home Office* [1992] QB 270, 314.

An unusual trespass onto the territory of the separation of powers is contained in the Freedom of Information Act 2000. Section 53 contains a so-called 'executive override', allowing a minister in specified circumstances to override a decision notice (under s 50) of the Information Commissioner which has been served on a government department, or, more significantly, a judicial decision on an appeal against such a decision notice. This power – to be exercised by means of a ministerial certificate which must be laid before Parliament – reflects the government's belief that 'there will be certain cases dealing with the most sensitive issues where a senior member of the Government, able to seek advice from his Cabinet colleagues, should decide on the final question of public interest in relation to disclosure'.[104] This is a unique provision: it is always open to Parliament to legislate to overturn a judicial decision, but it is a basic principle of the rule of law, as we have seen, that when the courts deliver a judgment the executive respects and complies with it. That is doubtless why something like s 53 is so unusual, and why the Lord Chief Justice described it as a 'constitutional aberration'.[105]

In a lengthy judgment the Upper Tribunal had held that it was in the public interest that certain correspondence from the Prince of Wales to government departments advocating particular causes be disclosed.[106] The Attorney General disagreed, and exercised the s 53 override power, which was then judicially reviewed.[107] The case placed the rule of law – with its emphasis on the separation of powers and independence of the judiciary – in conflict with parliamentary supremacy, as Parliament had expressly authorised such a power in s 53. Two of the Supreme Court Justices (Lords Wilson and Hughes) held that Parliament had been sufficiently clear in what it wanted, and it was entitled to provide for an exception to the separation of powers if it wished. Three of the Justices (in a judgment of Lord Neuberger) considered that s 53 was contrary to the rule of law, and Parliament had not been sufficiently clear to allow such an outcome, meaning that the power could only be used in highly restrictive circumstances. The remaining two Justices (Lord Mance and Baroness Hale) appeared to agree with Lords Wilson and Hughes that s 53 had a wider scope than Lord Neuberger was prepared to give it, but found against the Attorney General on the basis that his reasoning was not nearly clear or compelling enough to rationally justify overturning the Upper Tribunal. All of the judgments encapsulate the critical difficulties in our key constitutional concepts, and how contested they are. They ask whether Parliament can depart from important elements of the rule of law and the separation of powers; how clear it must be to do so; what role the judges have in policing that departure; and how we prioritise Dicey's conflict between supremacy and the rule of law.[108]

As for the relationship between the judiciary and the legislature, judges of the superior courts may be removed by the Crown on an address from both Houses, but only once since the Act of Settlement has Parliament exercised the power of removal.[109] Rules of Commons procedure protect judges from certain forms of criticism. The doctrine of legislative supremacy generally protects Acts of Parliament from being questioned in the courts but, as we have seen, the European Communities Act 1972 and the Human Rights Act 1998 have extended the jurisdiction of the courts.[110] The effect of their decisions may be altered by Parliament, both prospectively and also if necessary retrospectively. Because of the doctrine of precedent,

[104] HL Deb, 14 November 2000, col 258.

[105] *R (Evans)* v *Attorney General* [2013] EWHC 1960 (Admin), [2013] 3 WLR 1631 at [2] (Lord Judge CJ).

[106] *Evans* v *Information Commissioner* [2012] UKUT 313 (AAC).

[107] *R (Evans)* v *Attorney General* [2015] UKSC 21, [2015] 1 AC 1787.

[108] For an introductory overview, see C J S Knight (2015) 131 LQR 548; for greater detail, see: M Elliott [2015] PL 529; T R S Allan [2016] CLJ 38.

[109] Ch 13 B.

[110] And see chs 6 C and 14 C.

the judicial function of declaring and applying the law enables the superior courts to make law by their decisions. But this power is much narrower than the ability of Parliament to legislate, since Parliament is unrestricted in its power to change established rules of law.

D. Conclusion

In the absence of a written constitution, there is no formal separation of powers in the United Kingdom. No legislation may be challenged on the ground that it confers powers in breach of the doctrine. The functions of legislature and executive are closely interrelated, and ministers are members of both. Yet '[it] is a feature of the peculiarly British conception of the separation of powers that Parliament, the executive and the courts each have their distinct and largely exclusive domain'.[111]

The formal process of legislation is different from the day-to-day conduct of government. Parliament frequently delegates power to legislate upon the executive, but it retains oversight of such delegated powers.[112] However close the relationship between Parliament and the executive may be, the continuing independence of the judiciary is a constitutional fundamental. If government is to be based on law, the constitutional structure must distinguish between the primary functions of law-making, law-executing and law-adjudicating. If these distinctions are abandoned, the concept of law itself can scarcely survive.[113]

---

[111] *R v Home Secretary, ex p Fire Brigades Union* [1995] 2 AC 513, 567 (Lord Mustill).

[112] Ch 22.

[113] See Allan, *Constitutional Justice*: 'When the idea of the rule of law is interpreted as a principle of constitutionalism, it assumes a division of governmental powers or functions that inhibits the exercise of arbitrary state power' (p 31).

CHAPTER 5

Responsible and accountable government

A. The background

Within a democracy, those who govern must be accountable, or responsible, to those whom they govern. The power to govern derives directly from the votes of the electors, and from their continuing willingness to have their lives and well-being overseen by the government. Between general elections, one function of the elected representatives is to call the government to account openly for its acts and policies. This both requires government to justify its decisions by giving reasons for them, and enables decisions that appear unjustified or mistaken to be criticised. The process enables electors at their next opportunity to vote to make an informed appraisal of the government's record; until then it influences the formation of public opinion regarding the government.

In ordinary speech, the words 'responsible' and 'accountable' have several meanings; and the concept of responsible government takes several forms.[1] During the 1990s, because of some serious failures of accountability, attempts were made to identify the essential meaning of accountable government. In 1996, the Scott report on the 'arms for Iraq' affair contained penetrating criticism of incomplete and misleading answers given by ministers in Parliament to questions about the government's policy.[2] In the same year, a report by the Public Service committee of the House of Commons, while affirming that ministerial responsibility 'is a central principle of the British Constitution', examined the difficulties inherent in the principle.[3] In 2001, an independent committee urged that Parliament must be at the apex of the system of scrutiny of the executive and must develop both a culture of scrutiny and more effective methods of securing accountability.[4] In 2007, the Public Administration Committee of the Commons referred to the 'robust system of political accountability' in the United Kingdom, but urged that the relationship between ministers and the civil service should ensure the 'ultimate accountability of the government' to the electorate.[5]

This chapter examines the political responsibility of government to Parliament, including both collective and individual responsibility. Another form of responsibility is the responsibility in law of ministers and officials for their acts. Whereas legal responsibility is ultimately a matter for the courts, political responsibility is enforced primarily through Parliament. A government's relationship with Parliament is too complex to be the subject of a complete code, but at the heart of that relationship are obligations which ought to be observed by every government. A guide to these obligations may now be found in two related documents, the *Ministerial Code* and the *Civil Service Code*,[6] as well as in resolutions of each House at Westminster.

---

[1] Related principles include popular control of decision-making and political equality: see Weir and Beetham, *Political Power and Democratic Control in Britain*, ch 1. Tomkins, *Our Republican Constitution*, p 1, emphasises that the government is responsible *to Parliament*. For discussion of a much broader concept of accountability, see Bamforth and Leyland (eds), *Accountability in the Contemporary Constitution*.

[2] HC 115 (1995–6), vol IV, section K.8, pp 1799–1806; and see R Scott [1996] PL 410.

[3] HC 313–I (1995–6). For the government's response, see HC 67 (1996–7).

[4] Hansard Society, *The Challenge for Parliament: Making Government Accountable* (the Newton report). See also HC 300 and 748 (1999–2000), Cm 4737, 2000, HC 321 (2000–1) and D Oliver [2001] PL 666.

[5] HC 122 (2006–7). For the government's response, see HC 1057 (2007–8).

[6] See respectively ch 11 C and E.

Origins of responsible government

So long as government was carried on by the King, the nature of monarchy made it difficult to establish any responsibility for acts of government. In medieval times, the practice developed by which the royal will was signified in documents bearing a royal seal, and applied by one of the King's ministers. In this practice lay 'the foundation for our modern doctrine of ministerial responsibility – that for every exercise of the royal power some minister is answerable'.[7] With the responsibility of ministers came a specific understanding of the rule that 'the King can do no wrong'. This meant not that everything done on behalf of the King was lawful, but that the King's advisers and ministers were punishable for illegal measures that occurred in the course of government.[8] Today responsibility for an Order in Council made by the Queen is borne by the Cabinet minister whose department decided that the order should be made.[9]

This responsibility was at one time enforced by the English Parliament through impeachment. Officers of state were liable to be impeached by the Commons at the bar of the House of Lords for the treason, high crimes and misdemeanours they were alleged to have committed. In the 17th century, impeachment became a political weapon wielded by Parliament for striking at unpopular royal policies.[10] Following the granting of a royal pardon to Danby in 1679 to forestall his impeachment, the Act of Settlement provided that a royal pardon could not be pleaded in bar of an impeachment. The last instance of a purely political impeachment came when the Tory ministers who in 1713 negotiated the Peace of Utrecht were later impeached by a Whig House of Commons. Thereafter, only two impeachments occurred, of Warren Hastings between 1788 and 1795 for misgovernment in India and of Lord Melville in 1806 for alleged corruption. The power of impeachment is still in theory available to Parliament: but more modern means of achieving ministerial responsibility have rendered it obsolete in the United Kingdom.[11]

The legal responsibility of government

The principle that government must be conducted according to law has already been discussed.[12] The Queen may not herself be sued or prosecuted in the courts. But servants or officers of the Crown who commit crimes or civil wrongs are, and always have been, subject to the jurisdiction of the courts. This jurisdiction extends to contempt of court.[13] Superior orders or state necessity are no defence to such proceedings.[14] Public authorities other than the Crown are at common law liable for the wrongful acts of their officials or servants.[15] The departments of central government became liable to be sued under the Crown Proceedings Act 1947 and their decisions are subject to control by means of judicial review.[16] It is with political responsibility that this chapter is concerned.

---

[7] Maitland, *Constitutional History*, p 203. Cf art 106 of the Belgian Constitution (1994).

[8] Chitty, *Prerogatives of the Crown*, p 5. For rules on the use of seals and recording of decisions, see Anson, *Law and Custom of the Constitution*, vol II, part I, pp 62–72; HLE, vol 8(2), pp 233, 518–19.

[9] See *R (Bancoult)* v *Foreign Secretary (No.2)* [2008] UKHL 61, [2009] 1 AC 453.

[10] Maitland, *Constitutional History*, pp 317–18; Taswell-Langmead, *English Constitutional History*, pp 164–5, 353–4, 529–38; Clayton Roberts, *The Growth of Responsible Government in Stuart England*; Berger, *Impeachment*, ch 1.

[11] See Carnall and Nicholson (eds), *The Impeachment of Warren Hastings*, ch 7 (A W Bradley). Cf Dicey, *The Law of the Constitution*, p 499.

[12] Ch 4.

[13] *M* v *Home Office* [1994] 1 AC 377.

[14] Smith and Hogan, *Criminal Law*, pp 425–7; Dicey, pp 302–6; *Entick* v *Carrington*, p 85 above.

[15] *Mersey Docks and Harbour Board Trustees* v *Gibbs* (1866) LR 1 HL 93.

[16] Chs 24, 25 and 26.

Development of responsibility to Parliament

After 1688 the doctrine of collective responsibility developed in fits and starts as the Cabinet system came into being.[17] For much of the 18th century the Cabinet was a body of holders of high office whose relationship with one another was ill-defined; the body as a whole was not responsible to Parliament. Although the King rarely attended Cabinet meetings after 1717, it was the King's government in fact as well as in name, and the King could act on the advice of individual ministers. Under Walpole, the first 'Prime Minister', ministries were relatively homogeneous. Other Cabinets in the century were less united. Parliament could force the dismissal of individual ministers who were unpopular, but could not dictate appointments to the King. The King sometimes consulted those who were out of office without the prior approval of his ministers. There was no clear dividing line between matters dealt with by individual ministers and matters dealt with in the Cabinet. As late as 1806, it was debated in the Commons whether ministers must accept collective responsibility for the general affairs of government or whether only those ministers who carried policies into execution were individually responsible.[18]

By the early 19th century, as the scope for personal government by the Sovereign sharply declined, the tendencies towards the collective responsibility of the Cabinet became more marked. After 1832, it became evident that the Cabinet must retain the support of the majority in the House of Commons if it wished to continue in office. Just as it had earlier been recognised that a single minister could not retain office against the will of Parliament, so it was realised that all ministers must stand or fall together in Parliament, if the Cabinet were to function effectively.

By the mid-19th century, ministerial responsibility was the accepted basis of parliamentary government in Britain.[19] Critics of the rule of Cabinet unity were reminded that 'the various departments of the Administration are but parts of a single machine . . . and that the various branches of the Government have a close connection and mutual dependence upon each other'.[20]

The development of collective responsibility was accompanied by an expansion in government, not least in the period after 1832 when new central agencies were created to oversee areas of social administration, such as the reformed poor law and public health. After some experimenting with appointed public boards that were not directly responsible to Parliament and had no one in Parliament to defend them against their critics,[21] a strong preference was expressed for vesting the new powers in a minister who sat in Parliament and could account to Parliament for what was done. The development of parliamentary procedures for financial scrutiny and for obtaining information through questions addressed to ministers enabled members to influence matters within the minister's responsibility.[22] The corollary of this, as the civil service itself was reformed following the Northcote–Trevelyan report of 1854, was the anonymity and permanence of the civil servants who administered the new departments under the control or oversight of ministers.[23]

The modern form of ministerial responsibility to Parliament is also partly a result of, or at least conditioned by, the growth over the 19th century of party politics within the Houses of Parliament. A critical part of *how* ministers are rendered responsible, and held to account, is through the role of Her Majesty's Loyal Opposition; an officially recognised (and funded) role within the constitutional structure to ensure critical scrutiny of the Crown's ministers.[24]

---

[17] Mackintosh, *British Cabinet*, ch 2.

[18] Williams, *The 18th Century Constitution*, pp 123–5.

[19] For a notable summary, see Grey, *Parliamentary Government*, p 4.

[20] Grey, p 57.

[21] F M G Willson (1955) 33 *Public Administration* 43.

[22] Chester and Bowring, *Questions in Parliament*, ch 2.

[23] Parris, *Constitutional Bureaucracy*, ch 3.

[24] See ch 8; G Webber (2017) 37 OJLS 357.

B. Collective responsibility

The meaning of collective responsibility

The doctrine of collective responsibility was stated in absolute terms by Lord Salisbury in 1878:

> For all that passes in Cabinet every member of it who does not resign is absolutely and irretrievably responsible and has no right afterwards to say that he agreed in one case to a compromise, while in another he was persuaded by his colleagues . . . It is only on the principle that absolute responsibility is undertaken by every member of the Cabinet, who, after a decision is arrived at, remains a member of it, that the joint responsibility of Ministers to Parliament can be upheld and one of the most essential principles of parliamentary responsibility established.[25]

It is now customary for an incoming Prime Minister to issue the *Ministerial Code*, that lays down the rules and principles that ministers must observe. The version that was issued after the formation of the Coalition government in May 2010 stressed at the outset the principle of collective responsibility. Prime Minister Cameron's statement took this form:

> The principle of collective responsibility, *save where it is explicitly set aside*, requires that Ministers should be able to express their views frankly in the expectation that they can argue freely in private while maintaining a united front when decisions have been reached. This in turn requires that the privacy of opinions expressed in Cabinet and Ministerial Committees, including in correspondence, should be maintained.[26]

The italicised words were introduced into the Code in 2010 because, under the terms of the Coalition Agreement, the two coalition parties expressly reserved the right to differ on some aspects of the coalition programme. These included the holding of a referendum on the electoral system, a projected reduction in the size of the House of Commons and the question of a British Bill of Rights.[27] The inserted wording was removed again in the version of the Code re-issued by Prime Minister Cameron in October 2015, following the election of a majority Conservative government and has not reappeared in Prime Minister May's December 2016 Code.[28]

Today, collective responsibility embodies a number of related aspects. Like other principles of government, it is neither static nor unchangeable and may give way before more pressing political forces.

(1) The Prime Minister and other ministers are collectively responsible to Parliament, and to the Commons in particular, for the conduct of national affairs. In practice, so long as the governing party retains its majority in the House and the Prime Minister retains the confidence of her party, the Prime Minister is unlikely to be forced (at least by the opposition) to resign or to seek a dissolution of Parliament.

(2) When a Prime Minister dies or resigns, then even if the same party (or parties) continues in power, all ministerial offices are at the disposal of the new Prime Minister.

(3) Although ministers are individually responsible to Parliament for the conduct of their departments, if members of the Commons seek to censure an individual minister, the government often will seek to resist this, so that collective responsibility may be a means of defending an incompetent or unpopular minister.

---

[25] *Life of Robert, Marquis of Salisbury*, vol II, pp 219–20.
[26] *Ministerial Code* (Cabinet Office, 2010), para 2.1 (emphasis supplied). See also *Cabinet Manual* (2011), ch 4.
[27] And see 'Agreements to Differ' below.
[28] For the most recent version, see *Ministerial Code* (Cabinet Office, 2016).

(4) Subject to any contrary provisions during a coalition government or specific agreements to differ (see below), all ministers while in office share in the government's collective responsibility. As the Ministerial Code states bluntly: 'Decisions reached by the Cabinet or Ministerial Committees are binding on all members of the Government.'[29] All ministers are expected to support the government by voting in Parliament. Cabinet ministers who were also members of the National Executive Committee of the Labour party were in 1974 told by the Prime Minister that they must observe the conventions of collective responsibility at Executive meetings.[30]

(5) In principle, secrecy attaches to Cabinet proceedings, especially to what is said during a Cabinet discussion, but this does not prevent information about the subjects considered being made public. At this level of government, the Freedom of Information Act has made little difference, since the Cabinet Office's 'working assumption' is that Cabinet papers are not released in response to FoI requests 'to protect the confidential nature of collective decision-making'.[31] Exceptionally, a minister who has resigned may explain in detail the reasons for this decision, both in Parliament and the press.[32]

(6) To a lesser extent, secrecy attaches to dealings between departments. Decisions reached by the Cabinet or ministerial committees are 'normally announced and explained as the decision of the Minister concerned'.[33] While it may generally be convenient to the government that the internal processes by which decisions are made should be protected from disclosure, again an element of concealment is involved in trying to maintain that different departments always agree with each other; the reality, especially in a period of coalition or minority government, may be very different.

Collective responsibility serves a variety of political uses. As most governments are drawn from one party, it reinforces party unity and helps to maintain government control of the House of Commons. But some purposes served by the doctrine are controversial, in particular as regards the protection which should be given to the secrecy of decision-making, the authority of the Prime Minister[34] and the need for the appearance of external unanimity. In some open processes of government, especially public inquiries, the separate views of government departments are regularly made public.[35] But there is an obvious advantage to the leaders of any political party in being able to present an outward appearance of unity. It also ensures that the civil service can be more confident that a policy should be developed and implemented, because it requires a collective decision to overturn it. In the view of the Lords Constitution Committee in 2014 at least, the convention also leads to better decision-making.[36]

As is clear from the *Ministerial Code*,[37] many important government decisions are taken outside Cabinet meetings, whether by the department primarily concerned or after various forms of consultation between departments. According to the Code, 'No definite criteria can be given for issues which engage collective responsibility'.[38] Even questions which raise major issues of policy may be settled outside the Cabinet by a few ministers in consultation

---

[29] *Ministerial Code*, para 2.3.
[30] Wilson, *The Governance of Britain*, pp 74–5, 191–3; and see D L Ellis [1980] PL 367, 379–83.
[31] *Guide to Cabinet and Cabinet Committee Business* (2010, Cabinet Office), p 23; cf observations in *Cabinet Office* v *Information Commissioner* [2014] UKUT 461 (AAC) in the context of freedom of information.
[32] See R Brazier [1990] PL 300.
[33] *Ministerial Code*, para 2.3.
[34] See ch 11 A.
[35] Ch 23 B.
[36] HL 130 (2013–14).
[37] *Ministerial Code*, para 2.2.
[38] *Ministerial Code*, para 2.4.

with the Prime Minister. The best-known examples of this include the decisions to manufacture the British atomic bomb,[39] to mount the Suez operation in 1956 and to devalue the pound in 1967.[40] Made in a similar fashion were the decisions to ban trade union membership for staff at Government Communications Headquarters,[41] and to give the Bank of England responsibility for setting interest rates in 1997. When Mr Blair was Prime Minister, he appears to have made little use of the Cabinet for collective decision-making. Robin Cook, a former senior Cabinet minister before he resigned over Iraq in 2003, wrote, 'Tony does not regard the Cabinet as a place for decisions. Normally he avoids discussions in Cabinet until decisions are taken and announced to it.'[42] Although Cook said that policy in relation to Iraq was often discussed in Cabinet during 2002,[43] the Butler review of intelligence on weapons of mass destruction in Iraq criticised the informality with which Cabinet discussion took place, difficult questions of policy being aired without circulation of relevant papers.[44] Different views have been expressed at different times by different individuals on the extent to which Cabinet decision-making has returned to favour under Mr Blair's successors. In the modern political era, with permanent media scrutiny and the need for 'news', the temptation for Prime Ministers to control both the substance and circulation of decisions is understandable if also regrettable.

Whether decisions are taken by the Cabinet or are merely reported to it, a minister may at any time resign in protest against decisions with which he or she disagrees. Such resignations may indicate a deep disagreement over the way in which the Prime Minister is conducting government.

Agreements to differ

In some circumstances, it may be politically impossible for the Cabinet to maintain a united front on all issues. In 1932, the Coalition or 'National' government, formed in 1931 to deal with the economic crisis, adopted an 'agreement to differ'. The majority of the Cabinet favoured the adoption of a general tariff of 10 per cent, against the strong opposition of three Liberal ministers and one National Labour minister. It was announced that the dissenting ministers would be free to oppose the majority's proposals by speech and vote, both in Parliament and outside. When the Labour opposition criticised the government for violating 'the long-established constitutional principle of Cabinet responsibility', the motion of censure was defeated by an overwhelming majority.[45] Eight months later, the dissenting ministers resigned on the related issue of imperial preference. This short-lived departure from the principle of unanimity took place in the circumstances of a Coalition government formed to deal with a serious national crisis.

In 1975, for different political reasons, the Labour Cabinet agreed to differ over Britain's continued membership of the European Communities, an issue on which the Labour party was divided. Party unity had been maintained in two general elections in 1974 by an undertaking from Prime Minister Wilson to renegotiate the terms of British membership and to submit the outcome to the people for decision, either at a general election or by referendum. When in April 1975 the renegotiation of terms was completed and a referendum was held,

---

[39] See Hennessy, *Cabinet*, ch 4.

[40] Wilson, *The Labour Government 1964–70*, ch 23.

[41] See *CCSU v Minister for the Civil Service* [1985] AC 374.

[42] Cook, *The Point of Departure*, p 115. And see Foster, *British Government in Crisis*, p 291: 'Power has drained from Parliament, Cabinet and civil service into the PM and those around him.'

[43] *The Point of Departure*, p 116.

[44] HC 898 (2003–4), paras 610–11. And see ch 11 B.

[45] Jennings, *Cabinet Government*, pp 279–81.

the Cabinet by 16–7 decided to recommend continued membership to the electorate. It was agreed that ministers who opposed this policy should be free to speak and campaign against it, but only outside Parliament.[46] When a junior minister, Eric Heffer, insisted on opposing Britain's membership in the Commons,[47] he had to resign from office.

The precedent of 1975 was applied again in the 2016 referendum on continued membership of the EU, for very similar party political reasons. The governing Conservative party was seriously split on the issue (and indeed, the party itself remained formally neutral), whilst the government of Prime Minister Cameron adopted a strong policy stance in favour of remaining within the EU. Following a degree of internal party machinations, and threats of substantial backbench rebellions, it was agreed that collective responsibility would be suspended for the duration of the referendum campaign to allow ministers to campaign in favour of leaving the EU.[48] The suspension was only in effect for that element of government policy, but the extremely hostile nature of the campaign led to a number of senior ministers, including Cabinet members, attacking their colleagues in often vituperative language over matters of wider government policy for which they remained formally responsible.[49]

In 2010, the coalition agreement between the Conservative and Liberal Democrat parties included various issues on which the parties agreed to differ. A procedural agreement entitled *Coalition Agreement for Stability and Reform*[50] set out the agreed methods in Whitehall and at Westminster for ensuring that the government retained the support of a majority in the Commons. This is a good example of customary practices in government (conventions) being adjusted to take account of a changed political situation. If conventions are observed because of the political difficulties which follow if they are not,[51] then in situations where no single party has a majority in the Commons, it may be less difficult to depart from Cabinet unanimity than to seek to enforce it.[52]

Other aspects of collective responsibility

In any government there are more ministers outside the Cabinet than within it. Some have heavy departmental duties; others are concerned only with a narrow range of subjects.[53] These ministers are bound by Cabinet decisions and must refrain from criticising them in public. On some constituency matters a minister may make his or her views clearly known to the responsible minister,[54] but on all other matters the principle of collective responsibility requires ministers to ensure that their public statements are consistent with government

---

[46] See Cmnd 6003, 1975; HC Deb, 23 January 1975, col 1745; HC Deb, 7 April 1975, col 351 (WA). And Wilson, *The Governance of Britain*, pp 194–7.

[47] HC Deb, 9 April 1975, cols 1325–32.

[48] Office of the Prime Minister, 'Letter by the Prime Minister to Ministerial Colleagues: EU Referendum', 11 January 2016.

[49] For an extraordinarily detailed account of the referendum campaign, from which no particular individual emerges with great credit, see Shipman, *All Out War*. The dominance of the internal Conservative party disputes in the coverage of the referendum is probably partly explained by Mr Cameron's direct and close involvement in the campaign, in contrast to the example of Harold Wilson in 1974, who maintained a largely neutral and silent stance and therefore avoided becoming the target of his colleagues' attacks.

[50] Cabinet Office, 2010.

[51] Page 25 above.

[52] Cf the free vote allowed to Labour MPs on the European Assembly Elections Bill during a minority government: HC Deb, 23 March 1977, col 1307; and D L Ellis [1980] PL 367, 388. A free vote is allowed on some social or ethical issues, when MPs including ministers may vote in accordance with their conscience (as e.g. with capital punishment, see HC Deb, 13 July 1983, col 972).

[53] *Ministerial Code*, paras 4.6, 4.7.

[54] *Ministerial Code*, paras 6.5, 6.6.

policy.[55] The policy content and timing of all major speeches by ministers 'should, where possible' be cleared 24 hours in advance with the No 10 Press Office.[56]

Another restraint is that ministers 'may not, while in office, write and publish a book on their ministerial experience'.[57] In 1969, a parliamentary secretary resigned to publish a book on the economy and the machinery of government. Refusing him permission to publish the book and remain a minister, Harold Wilson publicly stated that he had no choice as Prime Minister but to apply the principle of collective responsibility.[58] Collective responsibility can thus be invoked by the Prime Minister to control the behaviour of ministers. The obligation to support government policy extends to those backbench MPs who act as unpaid parliamentary secretaries to ministers, and may be dismissed for stepping out of line.[59]

C. Individual responsibility of ministers

Operation of individual responsibility today[60]

Ministerial responsibility remains important, but structural changes in government have affected its application. During the 20th century, as the tasks of the state expanded and vast Whitehall departments were created, officials continued to act in their minister's name, but the ability of ministers to oversee their work declined. The state's economic and social functions led to the creation of non-departmental bodies, public corporations and other agencies. Many of these (especially the boards of the nationalised industries after 1945) were intended to operate beyond the reach of ministerial responsibility, at least for day-to-day decisions. By contrast, the executive agencies created since 1988 under the 'Next Steps' initiative were intended to achieve effective delegation of managerial power, without necessarily reducing overall ministerial control.[61]

In the tradition of parliamentary government, a minister answers to Parliament for his or her department. Praise and blame are addressed to the minister, not to civil servants; and as a general rule ministers may not excuse the failure of policies by turning on their advisers and officials. Attempts to do so may damage the minister's reputation, as the Home Secretary (Michael Howard) discovered in 1995: after intervening repeatedly in the operation of the Prison Service, Howard denied responsibility for defects in prison security and dismissed the Service's director, Derek Lewis, saying that the defects had been an operational matter entrusted to the director.[62] More recently, ministers whose departments are faring badly have been willing to identify the key administrators who may be to blame.[63] Apart from these

[55] *Ministerial Code*, para 8.3.

[56] *Ministerial Code*, para 8.2.

[57] *Ministerial Code*, para 8.9. Once out of office, the convention has less force, although the confidentiality aspect of it arguably remains in place. However, the memoirs and autobiographies of former Cabinet ministers now routinely reveal the substance of government policy and decision-making, including individual differences, sometimes only a very short time after the event.

[58] See the reports in *The Times*, 26 and 29 September 1969.

[59] *Ministerial Code*, paras 3.6–3.10.

[60] Marshall, *Constitutional Conventions*, ch 4; Brazier, *Ministers of the Crown*, ch 15; Woodhouse, *Ministers and Parliament*; and (the same) in Bogdanor (ed.) *The British Constitution in the 20th Century*, ch 8.

[61] See chs 11 D and 12 E.

[62] See HC Deb, 16 October 1995, col 30 and 19 October 1995, col 502, and ch 13 D. Also A Barker (1998) 76 *Public Administration* 21 and C Polidano (2000) 71 *Political Quarterly* 177.

[63] See the troubled history of the UK Borders Agency, disbanded in 2013 when ministers resumed direct control of the immigration and visa service, as described by the Home Affairs Committee: HC 587 (4th report), HC 907 (9th report), HC 1497 (15th report) and HC 1722 (21st report).

instances, the corollary of the minister's responsibility is that civil servants are not directly responsible to Parliament for government decisions, although they are responsible *to ministers* for their own actions and conduct. In 1996 the government defended 'the fundamental principle that civil servants are servants of the Crown, accountable to the duly constituted government of the day, and not servants of the House'.[64]

Much of the work of Parliament rests on this basis. Government Bills are drafted on the instructions of ministers. Question time in the Commons emphasises the responsibility of ministers.[65] Although civil servants have no voice in most parliamentary proceedings, they appear before select committees to give evidence on departmental policies and decisions. In giving such evidence, they do so 'as representatives of their Ministers' and their purpose 'is to contribute to the process of Ministerial accountability not to offer personal views or judgements on matters of political controversy'.[66] In 2014, the Cabinet Office amended its approach to civil service evidence by including within the category of civil servants who could be expected to account to Parliament 'senior responsible officers' for major projects, along with the formally designated 'accounting officer' for each department.

The sanctions for individual responsibility

What are the sanctions which underlie this general practice of Parliament? The system assumes that ministers fulfil their parliamentary duties, such as introducing legislation and answering questions. By a rota system, departments are assigned days for answering questions and a minister could not refuse to appear on the assigned day. Ministers may refuse to answer a question if they consider that it does not fall within their responsibility, that it would be contrary to the public interest to answer the question or that the expense of obtaining the information requested would be excessive.[67] These grounds are similar to some of the grounds that exempt from disclosure under the Freedom of Information Act 2000.[68] If a minister persistently refused to answer questions that were properly asked and antagonised many MPs in so doing, that minister would risk losing the support of the Prime Minister. Situations may occur in which a Prime Minister is unable to protect a minister from pressure to resign. In 1986, the Westland affair caused the Trade and Industry Secretary (Mr Brittan) to resign for having released to the press a confidential letter from the Solicitor General. Mr Brittan refused to answer questions from the Commons Defence Committee about the matter.[69] However, as a matter of general practice today, select committees in the Commons may inquire into the conduct of ministers and their questions may relate directly to the duties of ministers under the Ministerial Code.[70]

---

[64] HC 67 (1996–7), app, para 10. See also *Cabinet Manual*, para 7.1 and ch 11 D.

[65] Ch 8 E. Chester and Bowring, pp 251–68, and app II; Franklin and Norton (eds), *Parliamentary Questions*.

[66] *Departmental Evidence and Response to Select Committees (the 'Osmotherly Rules')* (Cabinet Office, 2014), paras 4–5. The rules should be treated as applying to non-departmental public bodies and arms-length bodies (para 8).

[67] And see Erskine May, pp 360–70. Since 1993, the House of Commons Table Office has rejected questions only when a minister has refused to answer them in the same session: Erskine May, pp 363–4; HC 313–I (1995–6), para 39; and R Scott [1996] PL 410, 416–17. On ministerial accountability and parliamentary questions, see HC 820 (1997–8), HC 821 (1998–9), HC 61 (2000–1), HC 1086 (2001–2), HC 355 (2003–4), HC 449 (2004–5) and HC 853 (2005–6) (reports by Public Administration Committee).

[68] See ch 11 F; and HC 449 (2004–5). In HC 853 (2005–6), the government explained why Freedom of Information Act grounds for refusing disclosure in the public interest could not be applied to parliamentary questions.

[69] HC (1985–6) 519; HC Deb, 29 October 1986, col 339; also A Tomkins (1996) 16 LS 63, 76–7.

[70] Ch 8 E.

Ministerial responsibility for departmental maladministration

Ministers are, or ought to be, responsible to Parliament for their own decisions and policies and for the work of their departments. The position in respect of the errors of civil servants is less clear. Two questions arise: (*a*) to what extent is a minister responsible for acts of maladministration in the department? (*b*) if serious maladministration occurs, does such responsibility involve a duty to resign? The Crichel Down affair has long been a starting point for discussion of these questions.

Farmland in Dorset known as Crichel Down had been acquired under compulsory powers from several owners by the Air Ministry in 1937. After the war, the land was transferred to the Ministry of Agriculture, for whom it was administered by a commission set up under the Agriculture Act 1947. While the future of the land was being considered, Marten, whose wife's family had previously owned much of the land, asked that it be sold back to the family. Misleading replies and false assurances were given when this and similar requests were refused, and an inaccurate report was prepared by a civil servant which led the ministry to stick to a scheme which it had prepared for letting all the land to a single tenant. When Conservative MPs took up Marten's case with the Minister of Agriculture, Sir Andrew Clark QC was appointed to hold an inquiry. His report established that there had been muddle, inefficiency, bias and bad faith on the part of some officials named in the report.[71] A subsequent inquiry to consider disciplinary action against the civil servants reported that some of the deficiencies were due as much to weak organisation within the ministry as to the faults of individuals.[72]

During a Commons debate on these reports, the Minister of Agriculture, Sir Thomas Dugdale, resigned. Speaking in the debate, the Home Secretary, Sir David Maxwell Fyfe, reaffirmed that a civil servant is wholly and directly responsible to his minister and can be dismissed at any time by the minister – a 'power none the less real because it is seldom used'. He outlined several categories where differing considerations apply.

(1) A minister must protect a civil servant who has carried out his explicit order.

(2) Equally a minister must defend a civil servant who acts properly in accordance with the policy laid down by the minister.

(3) Where an official makes a mistake or causes some delay, but not on an important issue of policy and not where a claim to individual rights is seriously involved, the Minister acknowledges the mistake and he accepts the responsibility although he is not personally involved. He states that he will take corrective action in the Department.

(4) Where action has been taken by a civil servant of which the minister disapproves and has no previous knowledge, and the conduct of the official is reprehensible, there is no obligation on a minister to endorse what he believes to be wrong or to defend what are clearly shown to be errors of his officers. He remains however, 'constitutionally responsible to Parliament for the fact that something has gone wrong', but this does not affect his power to control and discipline his staff.[73]

This statement and the implications of the Crichel Down affair have been much discussed.[74] Was the resignation due to the part which the minister had played, or to the unpopularity of

---

[71] Cmd 9176, 1954.

[72] Cmd 9220, 1954.

[73] HC Deb, 20 July 1954, cols 1286–7.

[74] See e.g. J A G Griffith (1955) 8 MLR 557; (1954) 32 *Public Administration* 385 (C J Hamson) and 389 (D N Chester). For a reinterpretation, see Nicolson, *The Mystery of Crichel Down*.

the department's policy among Conservative MPs, or was he accepting vicarious responsibility for the civil servants? Maxwell Fyfe's analysis sought to identify situations in which a minister must 'accept responsibility' for the acts of civil servants. The analysis did not state that a minister's duty to accept responsibility carried with it a duty to resign.[75]

Subsequent events confirmed that there is no 'duty' on a minister to resign because of misconduct by officials within the minister's department,[76] and today there is no expectation that this will occur. Different considerations apply where the personal conduct of a minister is an issue: the Chancellor of the Exchequer's inadvertent disclosure of a Budget secret caused him to resign in 1947;[77] and in 1963 the Secretary of State for War resigned for having lied to the Commons in a personal statement.[78] Other resignations because of personal misconduct have occurred from time to time.[79] Resignations are unavoidable if a minister's own conduct makes it too difficult for the individual to perform his or her duties faced with continuing criticism in the media[80] (a convenient formula that is often used to explain a forced resignation). In some situations, it may be that events in a department call into question the manner in which a minister has been heading the department. Publicity given to serious departmental errors (such as the discovery in April 2006 that the Home Office had released over 1,000 foreign prisoners at the end of their prison sentences rather than considering them for deportation)[81] may force the Prime Minister to make an immediate Cabinet reshuffle in which the minister leaves the government. On rare occasions a senior minister may resign because they do not consider themselves up to the job.[82]

In considering some past instances of practice in this area, we must remember that, 40 years ago, British government was marked by a degree of secrecy that would not be accepted today. The only information known about decision-making in Whitehall was that given by ministers; unauthorised disclosures ran the risk of prosecution under the draconian Official Secrets Act 1911. Crichel Down was unusual in that a public inquiry exposed the acts of officials to the light of day. In 1968, the first major investigation by the newly created Parliamentary Ombudsman found that there had been maladministration by the Foreign Office in the Sachsenhausen affair.[83] The Foreign Secretary (George Brown) 'assumed personal responsibility' for decisions made in the Foreign Office, while reluctantly agreeing to provide compensation for the claimants. But he also said: 'We will breach a very serious constitutional position if we start holding officials responsible for things that are done wrong . . . If things are wrongly done, then they are wrongly done by ministers.'[84] This statement failed to recognise that an investigation by the Ombudsman into a complaint of maladministration

---

[75] And see Sir R Scott [1996] PL 410 at 412–13.

[76] S E Finer (1956) 34 *Public Administration* 377, analysed the political factors that may be in play.

[77] HC 20 (1947–8).

[78] HC Deb, 22 March 1963, col 809; 17 June 1963, cols 34–170; and Cmnd 2152, 1963.

[79] In June 2009, several ministers left office in a Cabinet reshuffle caused in part by concern about their claims for parliamentary expenses. Ministers who have resigned because of questions about their conduct include David Laws (Chief Secretary to the Treasury) in 2010 and Liam Fox (Defence Secretary) in 2011. Andrew Mitchell (Chief Whip) resigned in 2012 following strongly disputed allegations that he had sworn at a police officer in Downing Street and called him a 'pleb'. With tedious predictability, the matter quickly acquired the moniker 'Plebgate'.

[80] See D Woodhouse, *Ministers and Parliament*; (1993) 46 *Parliamentary Affairs* 277, and (2004) 82 *Public Administration* 1.

[81] See HC Deb, 26 April 2006, col 573 and 3 May 2006, col 969 (statements by Charles Clarke MP).

[82] The Education and Skills Secretary, Estelle Morris, resigned on this basis in 2002, feeling that she had been better suited to a more junior ministerial role. The occasions on which a minister has been dismissed because the Prime Minister feels that they are not up to the job are doubtless rather more numerous.

[83] Ch 23 D, and see G K Fry [1970] PL 336.

[84] HC Deb, 5 February 1968, col 112.

must inevitably probe behind statements by the minister. However, creation of the Ombudsman did not mean an overnight change in the relationship between ministers and the civil service; ministers continued to insist that it followed 'from the principle that the minister alone has responsibility for the actions of his department' that individual civil servants should remain anonymous.[85]

In April 1982, the Argentine invasion of the Falkland Islands caused the Foreign Secretary, Lord Carrington, and two Foreign Office ministers to resign. They 'accepted responsibility' for the conduct of policy on the Falkland Islands, and insisted on resigning, against the express wishes of the Prime Minister. A committee of privy counsellors later reviewed government actions occurring before the invasion, found that the Foreign Office had misjudged the situation, and recommended changes in the intelligence organisation. But no blame was attached to individuals, nor did the committee consider that criticism for the events leading to the invasion could be attached to the government.[86]

In 1996, the report by the judge, Sir Richard Scott, on the 'arms for Iraq' affair found that on numerous occasions ministers failed to inform Parliament adequately about their policy on exporting arms and machine tools to Iraq and did not reveal changes they had made in the policy. The answers by ministers to repeated questions had been misleading,[87] but ministers persuaded the inquiry that they had not intentionally misled Parliament. However, as Scott observed, without the provision of full information Parliament cannot

> assess what consequences, in the form of attribution or blame, ought to follow . . . A failure by Ministers to meet the obligations of Ministerial accountability by providing information about the activities of their departments undermines . . . the democratic process.[88]

When the report was debated in the Commons, the government survived by one vote. No ministers resigned.[89]

Failings in a different context were revealed by the massive inquiry conducted by another judge (Lord Phillips) and two scientists into the response of five government departments to the problems for health and agriculture posed by BSE and variant CJD.[90] The Phillips report examined in detail the actions of ministers, civil servants and scientific advisers from 1986 to 1996. It was much less critical in tone than the Scott report, and no question of resignations had arisen. What is certain is that a fact-finding judicial inquiry, with access to relevant material in Whitehall, enables informed conclusions to be drawn that will not easily emerge from the political process in Parliament. When an inquiry into a departmental affair is made by a Commons committee, this is likely to be less effective than an independent inquiry.[91] But even a judicial inquiry will not settle the political verdict on a controversial affair.

In 2003, a senior judge, Lord Hutton, conducted an inquiry into the tragic suicide of the scientist Dr David Kelly under the pressure of events relating to the government's 'dodgy dossier' on Iraq. The inquiry itself was notable for the mass of evidence that came from Whitehall and was placed on the internet. The Hutton report did not convince informed opinion that its conclusions in the dispute between the BBC and the government were

---

[85] HC 350 (1967–8), para 24 (the Attorney General, Sir Elwyn Jones).

[86] Cmnd 8787, 1983.

[87] See e.g. the summary at HC 115 (1995–6), vol IV, pp 1799–1800.

[88] HC 115 (1995–6), vol IV, p 1801.

[89] HC Deb, 26 February 1996, col 589. On the Scott report, see articles at [1996] PL 357–507; Thompson and Ridley (eds), *Under the Scott-light*; Tomkins, *The Constitution after Scott*.

[90] HC 887–1 (1999–2000).

[91] See C Polidano (2001) 79 *Public Administration* 249, discussing inquiries into the Sandline affair: HC 1016 (1997–8), HC 116–I (1998–9).

well-founded.[92] But the report of the Butler inquiry in 2004 by a committee of privy counsellors into what was known about weapons of mass destruction before Britain went to war in Iraq was widely accepted in its serious criticism of the style of decision-making in Mr Blair's government.[93] In 2009, Sir John Chilcot and other privy counsellors were appointed by the Prime Minister, after consulting opposition parties, to examine British involvement in Iraq from 2001 until July 2009, resulting in the third inquiry into the circumstances of the Iraq war. The inquiry did not publish its report until 2016 but again made substantial criticisms of both the political and military aspects of decision-making.[94] The length of time the inquiry took – partially explained by the extensive process of giving those criticised the chance to comment on drafts, and by the need to agree with the government as to what primary documentation could be published – was nonetheless a substantial source of criticism.

Responsibility and accountability restated

A central theme in this area is the tension between government power and democratic accountability. In 1986, responding to a parliamentary inquiry into the Westland affair, the head of the civil service restated the duties of ministers towards Parliament;[95] in a revised form, the statement was later given to other Commons committees and the Scott inquiry.[96] The statement contrasted 'accountability' (in its non-financial sense) with 'responsibility'. A minister is '*accountable*' to Parliament for everything which occurs in a department: the duty, which may not be delegated, is to *inform* Parliament about policies and decisions of the department, except in rare cases where secrecy is an overriding necessity (as with sensitive questions of defence secrets). If something goes wrong, the minister owes it to Parliament to find out what has happened, ensure necessary disciplinary action and take steps to avoid a recurrence.

By contrast, a minister is said to be '*responsible*' only for broad policies, the framework of administration and issues in which he or she has been involved, not for all departmental affairs. The emphasis is on matters for which the minister may be personally praised or blamed. Since decision-making may be delegated, the minister is *not* responsible for what is done or decided by civil servants (for example, by the chief officer of an executive agency) within the authority assigned to them.[97]

This distinction between accountability and responsibility requires close scrutiny, since it provides a means by which a minister may avoid liability for unpopular or mistaken decisions; and it opens up potential areas of government for which no one is 'responsible' to Parliament, even though a minister remains 'accountable'. In 1996, the Public Service Committee of the Commons insisted that no clear dividing line can be drawn between accountability and responsibility, and that the two main aspects of ministerial responsibility are (i) the duty to give an account and (ii) the liability to be held to account.[98] In 2012, the Constitution Committee of the Lords concluded: 'In our view there is no constitutional difference between the terms responsibility and accountability'.[99] There is much to be said for this avoidance of technical distinctions.

....

[92] See HC 247 (2003–4). See R P Kaye (2005) *Parliamentary Affairs* 171, 172–6; Rogers (ed.), *The Hutton Inquiry and its Impact*. In defence of his report, see Lord Hutton [2006] PL 807.

[93] See HC 898 (2003–4). Also Runciman (ed.), *Hutton and Butler: Lifting the Lid on the Workings of Power*.

[94] HC 264 (2016–7).

[95] HC 92–II (1985–6). And Cmnd 9916, 1986, para 40.

[96] E.g. HC 390 (1992–3), para 25; HC 27 (1993–4), paras 118–20; Cm 2748, 1995, para 16; HC 313–I (1995–6), paras 15–18. See also the Scott report, HC 115 (1995–6), vol IV, pp 1805–6.

[97] On executive agencies, see ch 11 D.

[98] HC 313 (1995–6), paras 21 and 32. For the BSE inquiry's views on ministerial accountability, see HC 887 (1999–2000), vol 15, paras 8.7, 8.8.

[99] HL Paper 61 (2012–13), para 17. This report provides an excellent survey of the accountability of civil servants.

There has long been a view that both ministerial responsibility and accountability are so ineffective and fictional as to be worthless,[100] but this largely depends on what outcomes one expects to result from the doctrines. If it is expected that accountability will always result in resignations or dismissals, then – as the limited historical examples set out above suggest – the doctrines tend to fall a long way short. But accountability does not and should not always be equated to the reaction that 'heads must roll'.[101] Accountability includes much more basic things: answering questions about particular issues, explaining where things went wrong if they did and how such errors can be avoided in the future, and even correcting public misinterpretations of situations. In the heat of a party political clash at Westminster, opposition parties will see the claiming of a ministerial scalp as a victory, and anything less as a failure of responsibility. But there is no constitutional reason to see things in such binary terms. Good administration requires more thoughtful and considered responses to policy failures. We shall see in Chapter 8 how the role of parliamentary committees can scrutinise government, and how practical change can be effected through that more detailed examination, even if it does not acquire the media spotlight that a ministerial resignation does.

One outcome of the Scott inquiry was that in 1997 both Houses adopted a resolution stating the principles that must govern the conduct of ministers in relation to Parliament. These principles are now included in the *Ministerial Code* issued by the Prime Minister:

(a) the principle of collective responsibility, save where it is explicitly set aside, applies to all Government Ministers;

(b) Ministers have a duty to Parliament to account, and be held to account, for the policies, decisions and actions of their departments and agencies;

(c) it is of paramount importance that Ministers give accurate and truthful information to Parliament, correcting any inadvertent error at the earliest opportunity. Ministers who knowingly mislead Parliament will be expected to offer their resignation to the Prime Minister;

(d) Ministers should be as open as possible with Parliament, refusing to provide information only when disclosure would not be in the public interest, which should be decided in accordance with the relevant statutes and the Freedom of Information Act 2000;

(e) Ministers should similarly require civil servants who give evidence before Parliamentary Committees on their behalf and under their direction to be as helpful as possible in providing accurate, truthful and full information in accordance with the duties and responsibilities of civil servants as set out in the Civil Service Code.[102]

These principles are not enacted as legislation but, having been endorsed by both Houses and by successive Prime Ministers, they have great weight as rules that are fundamental to the relationship between executive and Parliament.[103] Moreover, for a minister or civil servant knowingly to mislead Parliament is a contempt of Parliament.[104]

Inevitably, difficulties remain in the way of achieving a more open system of governance. One is the government's relatively restrictive approach to the giving of evidence by civil servants to

---

[100] G Drewry in Jowell and Oliver (eds), *The Changing Constitution* (7th ed., 2011), p 211; compare P Norton in Jowell, Oliver and O'Cinneide (eds), *The Changing Constitution*, ch 6.

[101] For precisely this view in a civil service context, see *R (Shoesmith) v Ofsted* [2011] EWCA Civ 642, [2011] PTSR 1459 at [66] (Maurice Kay LJ).

[102] *Ministerial Code* (2010), para 1.2. For the original Commons resolution, see HC Deb, 19 March 1997, col 1046.

[103] On their status and enforceability, see ch 1 C.

[104] Ch 9 A. In 2013, the Commons Home Affairs Committee found that it had repeatedly been supplied with incorrect immigration statistics by the UK Borders Agency: HC 792 (2012–13), ch 2.

select committees:[105] should ministers be able to censor evidence as to matters of fact which civil servants give at Westminster, particularly where those civil servants may, in reality, be much more informed on the detail of particular issues than their ministers? Another is the government's power to control the timing and manner in which reports on inquiries that are critical of government policies and decisions are published.[106]

In 2007, the Public Administration Committee of the Commons urged that the discharge of responsibilities by ministers and civil servants should reflect the way in which decisions are in fact taken, and that the civil service's responsibilities should include 'responsibility to Parliament and the constitution'. In the committee's view, greater transparency in government need not prejudice the political accountability of ministers to Parliament.[107] In its reply, the government argued for a more traditional framework:

> Civil servants are accountable to Ministers, who in turn are accountable to Parliament. It is this line of accountability which makes clear that ultimately Ministers are accountable to the electorate.[108]

One parliamentary body that especially since 2010 has enabled there to be informed criticism of government failings is the Public Accounts Committee of the House of Commons: its reports are based both on the work of the National Audit Office and on the evidence given to the committee.[109] The committee's forthright interrogation of officials is one indication of the tension that often arises between the actual operations of government and the emphasis on retaining ministers as the link between executive and Parliament. It now seems remarkable that the doctrine of ministerial responsibility was used as an argument *against* creating the Parliamentary Ombudsman in 1967,[110] and *against* adoption of the present select committees of the Commons in 1979 – fortunately, on each occasion without success. The principle of accountable government is ultimately more important than ministerial responsibility. If there is any conflict between the two, the former principle ought to apply.

Ministerial responsibility and the courts

In a system of parliamentary government, the procedures for securing the accountability of ministers to Parliament and the extent of that accountability are essentially matters for the two Houses. Neither they nor the courts wish to see judicial processes used to review procedures at Westminster. The desire to keep courts well away from the internal affairs of the two Houses is seen as a reason why parliamentary practice should not be embodied in legislation.[111] In part 4 of this text, we examine the manner in which the courts by judicial review exercise control over many acts and decisions of the executive. Where statutory powers are in issue, a central justification for judicial review of executive decisions is that this is an important means of ensuring that in law the government makes proper use of powers conferred by Parliament.

When executive decisions are challenged by judicial review, the courts must decide whether any legal grounds have been shown which make the decision vulnerable to judicial review.[112] For

---

[105] See the Osmotherly Rules, note 66 above; and HL Paper 61, note 99 above, ch 4.

[106] For a clear abuse of this power, see the manner in which the Scott report was published in 1996.

[107] See *Politics and Administration: Ministers and Civil Servants*, HC 122, 2006–7. Annexed to the report is a 'Compact between Ministers and the Home Office Board' (January 2007) which states that officials who head Home Office services (i.e. the executive agencies) have the function of 'increasingly answering *externally* for operational matters for which they are responsible' (emphasis supplied).

[108] Government Response, HC 1057, 2007–8.

[109] See ch 8 E.

[110] Ch 23 D.

[111] See *Conventions of the UK Parliament*, HL Paper 265, HC 1212 (2004–5), paras 279, 285.

[112] See ch 24.

much of the 20th century, before judicial review took its present form, the evolution of administrative law was impeded by the fact that some courts relied on ministerial responsibility to Parliament as a reason for not reviewing the legality of ministers' decisions.[113] It is arguable that the rapid evolution of administrative law after 1980 was influenced by the failure of Parliament to take adequate steps to enforce the accountability of ministers.[114] Today, it is generally accepted that judicial review and ministerial responsibility serve different purposes and are not mutually exclusive.[115] Moreover, the scope and intensity of judicial review were extended by the Human Rights Act 1998: the courts must now form judgments about executive decisions on grounds that in the past would have been regarded as falling within the area of ministerial responsibility to Parliament.[116] One particular oddity of the Brexit litigation was the use by the claimants of judicial review to require Parliamentary involvement in a process which Parliament itself had shown no inclination of securing for itself.[117] Indeed, during the hearing in the Supreme Court, the House of Commons positively endorsed by resolution that the process of Brexit be commenced on the government's timetable without any indication in the resolution that it should proceed only by way of primary legislation.[118] Whether this is indicative of the inherent weakness of a party political Parliament to secure outcomes required by constitutional principle, or the courts stepping too far into the political arena, is a matter of debate in each individual case. Certainly that particular instance is a stark reminder of how important judicial review can be as a tool in aid of an ultimately political campaign when the political process is unwilling or unable to support that viewpoint.

Two other instances of the impact on ministerial responsibility of judicial review may be given: (*a*) in the case of a large and unwieldy bureaucracy (such as the Home Office) with powers that affect countless individuals, the ministers themselves may be unable to ensure that the policies they have publicly adopted are known to and observed by all the officials in the department;[119] and (*b*) in the highly complex schemes for public services today (for instance, regarding social security and welfare), Whitehall departments sometimes adopt rules by executive decision that should properly be made by procedures subject to parliamentary approval.[120] These instances suggest that judicial review usually helps to promote and not to restrict the accountability of ministers to Parliament.

Devolution and ministerial responsibility

This chapter has dealt with current practice relating to the responsibility of UK ministers at Westminster. What has been described here does not necessarily apply to the Scottish Parliament or the Assemblies in Wales and Northern Ireland. As we have seen, the three forms of devolution differ both from each other and from the Westminster model.[121] In Scotland, where the structure is closest to that at Westminster, the Scottish ministers may

---

[113] See J D B Mitchell [1965] PL 95; and Dicey, *Law of the Constitution*, app 2.

[114] See *R v Home Secretary, ex p Fire Brigades Union* [1995] 2 AC 513, 572–3, 575 (Lord Mustill).

[115] See e.g. *R v IRC, ex p National Federation of Self-Employed* [1982] AC 617, 644.

[116] Ch 14 C. And see e.g. *A v Home Secretary* [2004] UKHL 56, [2005] 2 AC 68 and *R (Quila) v Home Secretary* [2011] UKSC 45, [2012] 1 AC 621.

[117] *R (Miller) v Secretary of State for Exiting the European Union* [2017] UKSC 5, [2017] 2 WLR 583.

[118] See *Miller* at [162] (Lord Reed).

[119] See e.g. *R (Lumba) v Home Secretary* [2011] UKSC 12, [2012] 1 AC 245; *R (Kambadzi) v Home Secretary* [2011] UKSC 23, [2011] 4 All ER 975.

[120] See *R (Reilly) v Work and Pensions Secretary* [2013] UKSC 68, [2014] AC 453. Cf the contrasting outcomes in *R (Munir) v Home Secretary* [2012] UKSC 32, [2012] 4 All ER 1025 and *R (Alvi) v Home Secretary* [2012] UKSC 33, [2012] 4 All ER 1041.

[121] Ch 2 B.

not continue in office if the Parliament resolves that it has lost confidence in the Executive;[122] and Parliament has its own procedures for calling the ministers to account for their departmental functions. The original position in Wales was very different, when executive powers were vested in the Assembly itself, but the Government of Wales Act 2006 created a ministerial structure that comes closer to that in Scotland. In Northern Ireland, government is based on an elaborate scheme of power-sharing and this necessarily affects the accountability of the ministers to the Assembly, along with the particular partisan nature of politics in that region.

---

[122] Scotland Act 1998, s 45(2). See the *Scottish Ministerial Code* (2016) and *Guide to Collective Decision Making* (2008); Himsworth and O'Neill, *Scotland's Constitution: Law and Practice*, pp 167–76 and ch 9.

CHAPTER 6

United Kingdom and the European Union

On 23 June 2016, the British people voted by a narrow margin in favour of withdrawal from the European Union (EU), opening a new chapter in the United Kingdom's troubled relationship with Brussels, and with it a new range of knotty constitutional questions to be carefully unravelled. At the time of writing the United Kingdom has given notice to leave the EU but remains in membership, as sometimes fraught negotiations around the terms of withdrawal are undertaken.

While these negotiations take place and until the United Kingdom ceases to be a member of the EU, EU law continues to apply in this country. However, if events unfold as planned, it is likely that EU law will have ceased to apply in the United Kingdom by the time most of the undergraduates reading this text begin life in legal practice. As a result, while it is important that the existing legal framework is known and understood, the level of detail that may have been necessary in the past may not be as necessary now.

What is necessary, however, is an understanding of the constitutional context within which Brexit is taking place, as well as the constitutional questions that it has generated and is likely to continue to generate. In order fully to understand current problems, it is thus essential to understand how we arrived at the position we are in today, a journey that has been dominated by arguments about parliamentary sovereignty, which has been a contentious question throughout the period of Britain's membership of the EU.

Parliamentary sovereignty is a dominant theme of this chapter, which explores the constitutional relationship between Britain and the EU, from the time of (i) the United Kingdom's joining what at the time was the European Economic Community (EEC) on 1 January 1973, to (ii) the Prime Minister's notification of withdrawal from what had become the EU on 29 March 2017.[1] We examine the evolving constitutional relationship between London and Brussels in the intervening 44 years, and the claims about EU membership on British constitutional law.

These claims were greatly exaggerated, and a better understanding of the legal and constitutional position may well have led to a different outcome at the referendum on 23 June 2016, which was dominated in part by arguments about sovereignty. It is nevertheless clearly the case that the EU of 28 member states was a very different organization from the EEC of six members which the United Kingdom joined at the same time as Denmark and Ireland, in what was the first of several subsequent enlargements.

---

[1] There have of course been a number of stages in between, with a number of treaty amendments along the way: for example, the Single European Act of 1986, the Maastricht Treaty in 1992, the Nice Treaty in 2001, and the Lisbon Treaty in 2007. These expanded the powers of what were then the 'Community' institutions, and enabling an expanding volume of what was then 'Community' law to be made on the basis of qualified majority voting rather than the agreement of all member states. The Lisbon Treaty arose from the ashes of ambitious plans for a European Constitution, as designed by the Convention on the Future of Europe in 2003, under the chairmanship of a former French President.

A. Joining the EEC

The white paper

Britain's application for membership was made in 1967, the Treaty of Accession signed on 22 January 1972,[2] without a referendum before entry.[3] The constitutional implications of EEC membership were addressed in a white paper published in 1967, which formed an important basis for the European Communities Act 1972.[4] Here, two types of EEC obligations were addressed: those intended to have direct effect, and those requiring implementing legislation. So far as the former are concerned (mainly obligations arising under the EEC Treaty following important decisions of the European Court of Justice, which are discussed below):[5]

> legislation would be needed, because, under our constitutional law, adherence to a treaty does not of itself have the effect of changing our internal law even where provisions of the treaty are intended to have direct internal effect as law within the participating states.[6]

The white paper further pointed out that 'legislation would have to cover both provisions in force when we joined and those coming into force subsequently as a result of instruments issued by the Community institutions'. Although 'no new problem would be created by the provisions which were in force at the time we became a member of the Communities', a constitutional innovation would lie 'in the acceptance in advance as part of the law of the United Kingdom of provisions to be made in the future by instruments issued by the Community institutions – a situation for which there is no precedent in this country'. These instruments were implausibly equated with ordinary delegated legislation, which was said to 'derive [its] force under the law of the United Kingdom from the original enactment passed by Parliament'.[7]

Quite whether this constitutional innovation could be successfully implemented is a question not resolved before the introduction of the European Communities Act 1972. The 1967 white paper simply noted:

> The Community law having direct internal effect is designed to take precedence over the domestic law of the member states. From this it follows that the legislation of the Parliament of the United Kingdom giving effect to that law would have to do so in such a way as to override existing national law so far as inconsistent with it.[8]

But this merely restated rather than resolved the problem: what happens if Parliament should legislate deliberately or otherwise in a manner inconsistent with the directly effective terms of the Treaty?

---

[2] A challenge to the treaty on the ground that it would undermine parliamentary sovereignty was rebuffed in *Blackburn* v *A-G* [1971] 1 WLR 1037 (ch 10 below), while a claim that it violated the Treaty of Union with Scotland was likewise rebuffed in *Gibson* v *Lord Advocate* 1975 SLT 134. See subsequently on further treaty extensions: *R* v *Foreign Secretary, ex p Rees-Mogg* [1994] QB 552; *R* v *Foreign Secretary, ex p Southall* [2003] 3 CMLR 562; and *R (Wheeler)* v *Office of Prime Minister* [2008] EWHC 1409 (Admin).

[3] A referendum was held shortly after membership, mainly to address splits within the ruling Labour Party which had won power at the general elections in 1974. The Party leadership was in favour of membership. See Referendum Act 1975. See also Cmnd 5925, 1975 and 6251, 1975.

[4] Cmnd 3301, 1967.

[5] The EEC Treaty (the Treaty of Rome of 1957) gave way in due course to the EC Treaty, and in turn after Lisbon to the Treaty on European Union (TEU), and the Treaty on the Functioning of the European Union (TFEU).

[6] Cmnd 3301, 1967, para 22.

[7] Ibid. Today this analogy is seen to be badly misconceived. Delegated legislation (see ch 22) does not give rise to an autonomous body of law claiming supremacy over the source of its legal authority in domestic law.

[8] Cmnd 3301, 1967, para 23.

The answer, it seemed, was that 'within the fields occupied by Community law Parliament would have to refrain from passing fresh legislation inconsistent with that law as for the time being in force', although this 'would not however involve any constitutional innovation', for 'many of our treaty obligations already impose such restraints – for example, the Charter of the United Nations, the European Convention on Human Rights and GATT'.[9] But this did not provide an answer either: what would be the position of a post-accession statute that was incompatible with a subsequently introduced regulation having direct effect or a statute introduced to comply with the Treaty, the terms of which were expanded in a novel and unpredictable way by the ECJ/CJEU?

In this context, the examples of the UN Charter or the ECHR are beside the point, for unlike what was then the EEC Treaty, these provisions do not seek to create directly effective obligations that would operate over inconsistent domestic legislation (whenever passed), but rely instead on implementing legislation for any obligations they generate. In any event, the real problem was whether Parliament could legislate in a manner expressly in defiance of EEC law, while Britain remained a member. Should that happen, how should the UK courts respond? It is on this question that the politicians abdicated all responsibility in the pre-accession debates. The point was made by the Lord Chancellor in 1967:

> There is in theory no constitutional means available to us to make it certain that no future Parliament would enact legislation in conflict with Community law. It would, however, be unprofitable to speculate on the academic possibility of a future Parliament enacting legislation expressly designed to have that effect. Some risk of inadvertent contradiction between United Kingdom legislation and Community law could not be ruled out.[10]

European Communities Act 1972

The accession treaty was implemented by the European Communities Act 1972.[11] This deals with two central questions identified above, which were said to be 'fundamental to the structure and contents' of the Act,[12] the first being those provisions intended to embody in domestic law the provisions of EEC (now EU) law designed to have direct effect, and the second being the provisions which did not have direct effect but where action was necessary for their implementation. So far as the former is concerned, s 2(1) of the 1972 Act, said to be 'at the heart of the Bill',[13] provides:

> All such rights, powers, liabilities, obligations and restrictions from time to time created or arising by or under the Treaties, and all such remedies and procedures from time to time provided for by or under the Treaties, as in accordance with the Treaties are without further enactment to be given legal effect or used in the United Kingdom shall be recognised and available in law, and be enforced, allowed and followed accordingly.

What this does is to provide that in so far as EEC/EU law has direct effect, it is enforceable in the UK courts. It is also designed to ensure that directly effective EEC/EU obligations take precedence over national law. But it does not address the question of what should happen

---

[9] Ibid.

[10] HL Deb, 8 May 1967, col 1203.

[11] This has been amended on several occasions since. On the interaction of some of these amending measures, see *R* v *Foreign Secretary, ex p Rees-Mogg* [1994] QB 552.

[12] HC Deb, 15 February 1972, col 271.

[13] Ibid, col 650.

where there is a statute inconsistent with directly effective EEC/EU obligations. This, however, is addressed by s 2(4) which provides (inter alia):

> any enactment passed or to be passed [i.e. by the Westminster Parliament], other than one contained in this part of this Act, shall be construed and have effect subject to the foregoing provisions of this section.

Together with s 2(1), this is expressly designed to mean that 'the directly applicable provisions ought to prevail over future Acts of Parliament in so far as they might be inconsistent with them'.[14] As such, s 2 is an attempt by one Parliament to fetter the continuing supremacy of another by providing that, while future Parliaments may legislate in breach of EEC (now EU) law, the courts must (to the extent of any inconsistency) deny it any effect.[15]

The provisions of EEC (now EU) law that do not have direct effect were addressed in two ways by the 1972 Act. The first was by making a number of amendments to existing legislation to bring it into line with EEC (now EU) law; and the second was by introducing a general power to make subordinate legislation to implement future as well as some existing Community instruments. Although there was concern about the new power to make subordinate legislation, the government did not expect the power to be frequently used,[16] an expectation which was clearly unfulfilled. By s 2(2) of the 1972 Act, regulations may be introduced by a designated minister for the purpose of implementing any EEC/EU obligation. This is subject to Sched 2, which provides that regulations may not be used for a number of specified purposes.

These latter purposes are (i) an imposition of or increase in taxation; (ii) a provision having retrospective effect; (iii) a power delegating legislative authority; and (iv) in some cases a measure creating a new criminal offence punishable with imprisonment. The power to make regulations under these provisions is otherwise exercisable by statutory instrument, which if not made following a draft being approved by resolution of each House of Parliament, is subject to annulment by either House.[17] Although the power has been widely construed,[18] the government must indicate in clear terms what (if any) primary legislation is being repealed or amended when this procedure is invoked.[19]

The provisions of the 1972 Act are in addition to delegated powers that exist in other legislation and which may be used to implement EU law, as well as for other purposes.[20]

B. Legal obligations of membership

Supremacy of EEC/EU law

The first of four major legal obligations of EEC membership is the acknowledgement of the principle established by the ECJ that that the EU is 'more than an agreement which

---

[14] Ibid, col 278.

[15] See S A de Smith (1971) 34 MLR 597, H W R Wade (1972) 88 LQR 1, J D B Mitchell et al. (1972) 9 CML Rev 134, F A Trindade (1972) 35 MLR 375, G Winterton (1976) 92 LQR 591.

[16] HC Deb, 15 February 1972, col 282.

[17] For parliamentary scrutiny of delegated legislation, see ch 22 C.

[18] See *R v Trade and Industry Secretary, ex p UNISON* [1997] 1 CMLR 459.

[19] *R (Orange Personal Communications Ltd) v Trade and Industry Secretary* [2001] 3 CMLR 36.

[20] See for example, SI 2006 No 246 (Regulations made under the authority of both the 1972 Act, s 2, and the Employment Relations Act 1999, s 38).

merely creates mutual obligations between the contracting states'. Indeed, according to the Court:

> By contrast with ordinary international treaties, the EEC Treaty has created its own legal system which, on the entry into force of the Treaty, became an integral part of the legal systems of the member states and which their courts are bound to apply. By creating a Community of unlimited duration, having its own institutions, its own personality, its own legal capacity and capacity of representation on the international plane and, more particularly, real powers stemming from a limitation of sovereignty or a transfer of powers from the states to the Community, the member states have limited their sovereign rights, albeit within limited fields, and have thus created a body of law which binds both their nationals and themselves.[21]

The implications of this were clearly established in *Case 6/64, Costa v ENEL*,[22] where Mr Costa claimed that he was not obliged to pay for electricity supplied to him by ENEL on the ground that the supplier was an entity which had been nationalised in 1962 in breach of provisions of what was then the EEC Treaty. The Italian court (the Giudice Conciliatore of Milan) referred to the European Court of Justice (ECJ) for consideration whether Italian law violated the Treaty in the manner suggested, only to be faced with the argument by the Italian government that the reference was 'absolutely inadmissible' inasmuch as the national court was obliged to apply a national law and for that reason could not make the contested reference.[23] In rejecting this argument, the ECJ held:

> The integration into the laws of each member state of provisions which derive from the Community, and more generally the terms and the spirit of the Treaty, make it impossible for the states, as a corollary, to accord precedence to a unilateral and subsequent measure over a legal system accepted by them on a basis of reciprocity. Such a measure cannot therefore be inconsistent with that legal system. The executive force of Community law cannot vary from one state to another in deference to subsequent domestic laws, without jeopardising the attainment of the objectives of the Treaty.[24]

This case thus unequivocally reinforced the supremacy of EEC – and now EU – law over inconsistent domestic law, including in particular domestic law introduced after accession.[25] It was since established that EU law takes priority even over the national constitutional law of member states, the leading case (*Case 11/70, Internationale Handelsgesellschaft v Einfuhrund Vorratsstelle für Getreide und Futtermittel*[26]) concerned with regulations which required applicants for export and import licences to pay a deposit forfeited if terms of the licence were violated. The German authorities were of the view that the system of licences violated certain

---

[21] *Case 26/62, Van Gend en Loos v Nederlandse Administratie der Belastingen* [1963] ECR 1. The point was reinforced forcefully in *Case 6/64, Costa v ENEL* (below), and reflected in the Declaration concerning primacy annexed to the Lisbon Treaty (Declaration 17), which provides that 'In accordance with well settled case law of the Court of Justice of the European Union, the Treaties and the law adopted by the Union on the basis of the Treaties have primacy over the law of member states, under the conditions laid down by the said case law'.

[22] [1964] ECR 585.

[23] On the procedures by which this was done, see pp 129–30. below.

[24] [1964] ECR 585, pp 593–4. The ECJ further asserted that 'the laws stemming from the Treaty, an independent source of law, could not, because of its special and original nature, be overridden by domestic legal provisions, however framed, without being deprived of its character as Community law, and without the legal basis of the Community itself being called into question' (ibid, p 594).

[25] See also *Case 106/77, Amministrazione delle Finanze dello Stato v Simmenthal SpA* [1978] ECR 629.

[26] [1970] ECR 1125.

principles of German constitutional law 'which must be protected within the framework of the German Basic Law'. But the ECJ disagreed and held:

> Recourse to the legal rules or concepts of national law in order to judge the validity of measures adopted by the institutions of the Community would have an adverse effect on the uniformity and efficacy of Community law. The validity of such measures can only be judged in the light of Community law. In fact, the law stemming from the Treaty, an independent source of law, cannot because of its very nature be overridden by rules of national law, however framed, without being deprived of its character as Community law and without the legal basis of the Community itself being called into question.[27]

Further, 'the validity of a Community measure or its effect within a member state cannot be affected by allegations that it runs counter to either fundamental rights as formulated by the constitution of that state or the principles of a national constitutional structure'.[28] Although Community law thus prevails over even fundamental rights guaranteed by national constitutions, the ECJ did, nevertheless, hold that 'respect for fundamental rights forms an integral part of the general principles of law protected by the Court of Justice', and that 'protection of such rights, whilst inspired by the constitutional traditions common to the member states, must be ensured within the framework of the structure and objectives of the Community'.[29] On the facts it was held that the system of licences in question did not violate any such rights.

Direct effect of EEC/EU law

The second obligation of EEC membership is the principle of the direct effect of EEC law, for which express provision is made in the 1972 Act, s 2(1) above, with the decision as to what provisions of EEC/EU law are to have direct effect being one for the ECJ alone. The highest form of EEC/EU law is the relevant treaty (initially the Treaty of Rome, now the Treaty on European Union (TEU) and the Treaty on the Functioning of the European Union (TFEU)), which not only set out the constitution of the EU but also deal with substantive matters, some of which give rise to rights which have direct effect in national courts. *Case 26/62, Van Gend en Loos* v *Nederlandse Administratie der Belastingen*[30] was concerned with the interpretation of what was then art 12 of the EEC Treaty, this requiring member states to refrain from introducing between themselves new customs duties, or increasing those already in force, in trade with each other. In a seminal decision, the ECJ held that:

> Independently of the legislation of member states, Community law . . . not only imposes obligations on individuals but is also intended to confer upon them rights which become part of their legal heritage. These rights arise not only where they are expressly granted by the Treaty, but also by reason of obligations which the Treaty imposes in a clearly defined way upon individuals as well as upon the member states and upon the institutions of the Community.[31]

---

[27] Ibid, p 1134.

[28] See also *Case 44/79, Hauer* v *Land Rheinland-Pfalz* [1979] ECR 3727, and more recently *Case C-438/05, International Transport Workers' Federation and Finnish Seamen's Union* v *Viking Line ABP* [2007] ECR I-10779.

[29] [1970] ECR 1125, 1134. See now the EU Charter of Fundamental Rights adopted at Nice in 2000 and given legal effects at Lisbon in 2008. For a full discussion of the Charter, see HL Paper 62-I (2007–8), paras 5.84–5.111; also *R (AB)* v *Home Secretary* [2013] EWHC 3453 (Admin), esp paras 10–16. See further TEU, art 6(3) (European Convention on Human Rights) and *Opinion 2/13* [2014] ECLI:EU:C 2454. For more detail on the Charter, see pp 130–1 below.

[30] [1963] ECR 1.

[31] Ibid, p 12.

Where a treaty provision does have direct effect, in some cases it may be relied on by one private party against another, in which case it is said to have 'horizontal' direct effect. A provision that can be relied upon only against the state is said in contrast to have 'vertical' direct effect. Among the cases in which the ECJ has held that treaty provisions have horizontal direct effect, *Case 43/75, Defrenne v Sabena*[32] was concerned with the then art 119 (thereafter art 141, now TFEU, art 257). This provides that 'each member state shall during the first stage ensure and subsequently maintain the application of the principle that men and women should receive equal pay for equal work'. The principle of equal pay formed part of 'the foundations of the Community', and art 119 was held to have direct effect even though its complete implementation 'may in certain cases involve the elaboration of criteria whose implementation necessitates the taking of appropriate measures at Community and national level'.[33]

But it is not only the treaties that may have direct effect in the sense that they may be enforced in the domestic courts. So too does some EU legislation, with regulations having 'general application', in the sense that they are binding in their entirety and directly applicable in all member states.[34]

Case 93/71, Leonesio v Italian Ministry of Agriculture[35] was concerned with an EEC regulation of 1969 providing a subsidy for those who slaughtered milk cows. The question for the ECJ was whether the regulation conferred on farmers a right to payment of the subsidy enforceable in national courts. In holding that it did, the Court held that, as a general principle, 'because of its nature and its purpose within the system of sources of Community law', a regulation 'has direct effect and is, as such, capable of creating individual rights which national courts must protect'. It was no excuse in this case that the national Parliament had not allocated the necessary funds to meet the costs of the subsidy, for to hold otherwise would have the effect of placing Italian farmers in a less favourable position than their counterparts elsewhere 'in disregard of the fundamental rule requiring the uniform application of regulations throughout the Community'.[36]

Like some provisions of the Treaty, regulations may have horizontal as well as vertical direct effect.[37]

Directives are another form of EU legislation. They generally require implementing legislation by a member state before they give rise to enforceable obligations in the member state in question, the TFEU providing that directives are binding 'as to the result to be achieved', the national authorities being left 'the choice of form and methods'.[38] So 'where different options

---

[32] [1976] ECR 455.

[33] *Case 43/75, Defrenne v Sabena* was relied upon by the ECJ in the controversial decision in *Case C-438/05, International Transport Workers' Federation and Finnish Seamen's Union v Viking Line*, above, in holding that a company can proceed against a trade union where the company's right to freedom of establishment (under what is now TFEU, art 49) was allegedly impeded by the industrial action organised by the defendant organisation based in London (which is why this case was a reference from the Court of Appeal).

[34] TFEU, art 288.

[35] [1972] ECR 287.

[36] See also *Case 128/78, Re Tachographs: Commission v UK* [1979] ECR 419.

[37] *Case C-253/00, Antonio Muñoz y Cia SA v Frumar Ltd* [2003] Ch 328.

[38] TFEU, art 288.

are available for and effective to achieve the objects of the Directive it is for member states to choose between them'.[39] But directives also may have vertical direct effect,[40] 'wherever the provisions of a directive appear, as far as their subject matter is concerned, to be unconditional and sufficiently precise.'[41] As a general rule, however, directives do not have horizontal direct effect.

> In *Case 152/84, Marshall v Southampton and South West Hampshire AHA*,[42] it was held that art 5(1) of the Equal Treatment Directive (76/207/EEC) was directly effective, thereby allowing a woman (who had been dismissed at the age of 62 in circumstances where men would not have been dismissed until the age of 65) to bring proceedings in domestic law for sex discrimination on an issue to which domestic legislation did not then apply. It was held that although directives have only 'vertical' rather than 'horizontal' direct effect, a directive nevertheless may be relied on against the state 'regardless of the capacity in which the latter is acting, whether employer or public authority'.[43]

Indirect effect of EEC/EU law

Where EEC/EU legislation (notably directives) did/does not have direct effect, self-evidently it cannot be enforced in domestic courts. The third obligation of EEC/EU membership, however, is acceptance of the principle that the courts may nevertheless still have to apply EEC/EU law, the ECJ having developed a number of doctrines to ensure that the intended beneficiaries of such legislation have an opportunity to rely on them in domestic legal proceedings, and to ensure that beneficiaries do not suffer as a result of any default by governments which are obliged fully to implement directives. In the United Kingdom, implementation would be by primary legislation, or by secondary legislation under either the 1972 Act or other delegated powers. The question which arises, however, is what happens when governments (whether deliberately or inadvertently) failed properly to implement the requirements of a directive, or produced an ambiguous legislative result. Here we encounter the indirect effect of EU law.

In one case (*Von Colson*),[44] a question arose about the relationship between German national law and the Equal Treatment Directive (76/207/EEC). According to the ECJ, 'in applying the national law and in particular the provisions of a national law specifically introduced in order to implement [a directive], national courts are required to interpret their national law in the light of the wording and the purpose of the directive'. *Von Colson*

---

[39] *Wilson v St Helens Borough Council* [1999] 2 AC 52, per Lord Slynn.

[40] *Case 41/74, Van Duyn v Home Office* [1974] ECR 1337.

[41] *Case 8/81, Becker v Finanzamt Münster-Innenstadt* [1982] ECR 53.

[42] [1986] ECR 723. See A Arnull [1987] PL 383.

[43] *Marshall*, at p 749. The Area Health Authority was a public authority (or emanation of the state) for this purpose. See further *Case C-222/84, Johnston v Chief Constable of the RUC* [1987] QB 129 (police authority); *Case 188/89, Foster v British Gas* [1991] 2 AC 306 (nationalised industry); and *Griffin v South West Water* [1995] IRLR 15 (privatised water company). It has also been said that a directive may be 'relied on against organisations or bodies which are subject to the authority or control of the state or have special powers beyond those which result from the normal rules applicable to relations between individuals, such as local or regional authorities or other bodies which, irrespective of their legal form, have been given responsibility by the public authorities and under their supervision, for providing a public service': *Joined Cases C-253/96 to C-258/96, Kampelmann v Landschaftsverband Westfalen-Lippe* [1997] ECR 6907.

[44] *Case 14/83, Von Colson and Kamann v Land Nordrhein-Westfalen* [1984] ECR 1891.

was followed in *Marleasing*,[45] where the ECJ took a wider view of the application of directives, concluding now that:

> in applying national law, whether the provisions in question were adopted before or after the directive, the national court called upon to interpret it is required to do so, as far as possible, in the light of the wording and the purpose of the directive in order to achieve the result pursued by the latter.

In other words, legislation whenever passed is to be construed consistently with the terms of a directive with which it implements or overlaps.

In the United Kingdom, the duty to construe domestic law consistently with EU law is to be found in the 1972 Act, s 2(4), above. This provides the peg on which to hang the principle of indirect effect, which is now applied consistently with the spirit of *Marleasing* despite an initially cautious approach by the House of Lords.[46] In *Webb* v *EMO Air Cargo (UK) Ltd*[47] (following *Marleasing*), it was accepted that an English court should construe a statute to comply with a directive regardless of whether the statute was passed before or after the directive was made. Indeed, it is recognised that 'the obligation on the English courts to construe domestic legislation consistently with Community law obligations is both broad and far-reaching'. To this end, the relevant principles of interpretation applicable in these cases was helpfully summarised in the following manner, where referring to the latter obligation it was said that:

> (a) It is not constrained by conventional rules of construction; (b) It does not require ambiguity in the legislative language; (c) It is not an exercise in semantics or linguistics; (d) It permits departure from the strict and literal application of the words which the legislature has elected to use; (e) It permits the implication of words necessary to comply with Community law obligations; and (f) The precise form of the words to be implied does not matter.[48]

This principle of the indirect effect of directives was, however, stretched still further in *Pfeiffer*,[49] where the ECJ said in a case about the scope of the Working Time Directive that 'a national court is required, when applying the provisions of domestic law adopted for the purpose of transposing obligations laid down by a directive, *to consider the whole body of rules of national law* and to interpret them, so far as possible, in the light of the wording and purpose of the directive in order to achieve an outcome consistent with the objective pursued by the directive'.[50] Nevertheless, the obligation is not unconditional: where a directive is implemented at national level after its prescribed commencement date, domestic courts are not required to construe the implementing legislation retrospectively to cover the period of the delay.[51] Any such obligation would conflict with 'general principles of law, particularly those of legal certainty'.[52]

In addition to the foregoing, under the so-called *Francovich* principle, it may be possible in appropriate cases to bring an action against a national government for damages where an

---

[45] *Case 106/89, Marleasing SA v La Comercial Internacional de Alimentación SA* [1990] ECR I-4135. See now *Cases C-397–403/01, Pfeiffer v Deutches Roles Kreuz, Kreisverband Waldshut eV* [2004] ECR I-8835 (S Prechal (2005) 42 CMLR 1445), *Case C-212/04, Adeneler v Ellinikos Organismos Galaktos* [2006] ECR I-6057, and *Case C-268/06, IMPACT v Minister for Agriculture and Food* [2008] ECR I-02483.

[46] *Duke v Reliance Systems Ltd* [1998] AC 618.

[47] [1992] 4 All ER 929. See N Gravells [1993] PL 44.

[48] *Vodafone 2 v Revenue and Customs Commissioners* [2009] EWCA Civ 446, [2010] Ch 77, para 37 (references omitted). Also *Swift v Robertson* [2014] UKSC 50, [2014] 1 WLR 3438; *United States v Nolan* [2015] UKSC 65, [2015] 1 WLR 1105.

[49] *Cases C-397–403/01, Pfeiffer v Deutches Roles Kreuz, Kreisverband Waldshut eV*, above.

[50] See also for a strong expression of this obligation, *Case C-555/07, Kücükdeveci v Swedex GmbH & Co KG* [2010] All ER (EC) 867.

[51] *Case C-268/06, IMPACT v Minister for Agriculture and Food*, above. See also *Churchill Insurance Co Ltd v Fitzgerald* [2012] EWCA Civ 1166, [2012] 3 CMLR 1165, para 48.

[52] *IMPACT*, above, para 100.

individual has suffered loss as a result of a failure properly to implement a directive.[53] Any such action would be brought in the national courts.[54]

Role of the European Court of Justice

Finally, a fourth obligation of membership is acceptance of the dominant role of the European Court of Justice/Court of Justice of the European Union. The function of the Court (ECJ/CJEU) is to 'ensure that in the interpretation and application of the Treaties the law is observed'.[55] It consists of one judge for each member state and may sit in chambers (normally of 5 judges) or in a Grand Chamber (of 13 judges), as provided by its own statute which is annexed as a protocol to the treaties. Judges are appointed from among people who are eligible for the highest judicial offices in their respective countries and appointments are made 'by common accord of the Governments of the member states for a term of six years'.[56]

Cases may be brought before the CJEU in one of a number of ways:

- The Commission may bring proceedings against a member state, where it considers that the state has failed to comply with a Treaty obligation.[57] If the Commission considers that a member state has failed to fulfil a Treaty obligation, it must first deliver a reasoned opinion on the matter after giving the state concerned an opportunity to submit its observations. It is only if the state does not comply with the opinion that the Commission may bring the matter before the Court.[58]

- One state may initiate proceedings against another where the former considers that the latter has failed to comply with a Treaty obligation.[59] Before this is done the matter must first be referred to the Commission, which will deliver a reasoned opinion in this situation as well. Where the court finds that a state has failed to comply with a Treaty obligation, 'the state shall be required to take the necessary measures to comply with the judgment of the Court',[60] and failure to do so could lead to a financial penalty on the state.[61]

It may also be possible for one member state to challenge the legality of a legal instrument in proceedings against an EU institution, as in *Case C-84/94, UK v EU Council*,[62] where the British government unsuccessfully contested the legal basis of the Working Time Directive (93/104/EC), as exceeding powers under what was then TEC, art 118a.

Apart from the foregoing, the Court also has jurisdiction to give preliminary rulings concerning the interpretation of the Treaties, as well as the validity and interpretation of acts of

---

[53] *Cases C-6&9/90, Francovich and Bonifaci v Italy* [1991] ECR I-5357 (R Caranta [1993] 52 CLJ 272). Also *Case C-91/92, Faccini Dori v Recreb Srl* [1994] ECR I-3325; *Case C-261/95, Palmisani v INPS* [1997] ECR I-4025; *Case C-224/01, Gerhard Köbler* [2003] ECR I-10239. For a valuable account of the application of *Francovich* in different member states, see M-P F Granger (2007) 32 EL Rev 157.

[54] See *Spencer v Secretary of State for Work and Pensions* [2008] IRLR 911.

[55] TEU, art 19.

[56] TFEU, art 253.

[57] TFEU, art 258. Liability under the latter arises whatever the agency of the state whose action or inaction is the cause of the failure to fulfil its obligations, even in the case of a constitutionally independent institution: *Case 77/69, EC Commission v Belgium* [1970] ECR 237 (difficulty in securing parliamentary approval because Parliament had been dissolved).

[58] TFEU, art 258. See *Case 293/85, EC Commission v Belgium* [1988] ECR 305, and *Case 74/82, EC Commission v Ireland* [1984] ECR 317.

[59] TFEU, art 259. See *Case 141/78, France v UK* [1979] ECR 2923, *Case C-364/10, Hungary v Slovakia*, 16 October 2012.

[60] Ibid, art 260(1). In the *Factortame* affair (pp 133–6. below), secondary legislation was introduced to remove the discriminatory effect of the vessel registration scheme set out in the Merchant Shipping Act 1988.

[61] TFEU, art 260(2).

[62] [1996] 3 CMLR 671.

the institutions, bodies, offices or agencies of the Union.[63] A national court or tribunal may seek a preliminary ruling where it 'considers that a decision on the question is necessary to enable it to give judgment'.[64] In the case of a court or tribunal 'against whose decisions there is no judicial remedy under national law', the court or tribunal must bring before the CJEU for a ruling any question on a matter which is necessary for it to give judgment.[65] According to the CJEU, a reference is not required where the question of EU law is irrelevant, or the matter has already been decided by the CJEU, or the position is 'so obvious as to leave no scope for any reasonable doubt'.[66]

Where a reference is made, the court will request an answer to specific questions by the CJEU;[67] the latter is not empowered to resolve the dispute between the parties, it being for the national court to apply the ruling to the facts of the case before it.[68] By these different means the ECJ/CJEU nevertheless has been in a position not only to ensure the consistent application of EU law throughout member states, but also in the process effectively to enforce the supremacy of EEC/EU law. The Court thus has the power to determine the scope of the competence of the EU vis-à-vis member states; to determine the relationship between EU law and national law; and to determine or give guidance on whether national law is compatible with EU law. As a result, the reasoning and decisions of the Court have helped to forge a clearer European legal identity, and may be the focus of disquiet as a result particularly in those member states not wholly committed to the European project.

Also important in forging a European legal identity is the EU Charter of Fundamental Rights, adopted at Nice in December 2000.[69] This is a wide-ranging document, particularly important for its commitment to 'the indivisible, universal values of human dignity, freedom, equality and solidarity'. A document of 54 articles, the Charter is divided into seven chapters, entitled respectively: dignity (articles 1–5); freedoms (articles 6–19); equality (articles 20–6); solidarity (articles 27–38); citizens' rights (articles 39–46); justice (articles 47–50); and general provisions (articles 51–4).

The Charter draws freely on other texts for its contents, including the ECHR and the Council of Europe's Social Charter, as well as the Community's Charter of the Fundamental Social Rights of Workers of 1989. The Nice Charter is addressed to the institutions and bodies of the Union and to the member states only when they are implementing Union law.[70] Where the EU Charter includes rights which are also to be found in the ECHR, 'the meaning and scope of those rights shall be the same as those laid down' by the Convention, thereby minimising the possibility of conflicting interpretations of Convention rights by the two highest courts in the European legal order.[71]

---

[63] TFEU, art 267. This has been said to be 'an instrument of cooperation between the Court of Justice and national courts' (*Case C-313/07, Kirtuna SL v Red Elite de Electrodomesticos SA* [2009] 1 CMLR 14, at para 25).

[64] TFEU, art 267.

[65] Ibid. This would apply to the House of Lords and now the Supreme Court of the United Kingdom (but see *R v Employment Secretary, ex p EOC* [1995] 1 AC 1).

[66] *Case 283/81, CILFIT v Ministry of Health* [1982] ECR 3415.

[67] The questions will normally be agreed with the parties in advance: see *Marks and Spencer plc v Customs and Excise Commissioners* [2005] UKHL 53, [2005] STC 1254.

[68] The ECJ/CJEU 'has consistently held that under [TFEU, art 267] it has no jurisdiction to rule on the compatibility of national measures with Community law': *Case C-458/93, Saddik* [1995] ECR I-511.

[69] See A Arnull [2003] PL 774, S Douglas-Scott [2004] EHRLR 37, and Peers and Ward (eds), *The EU Charter of Fundamental Rights*. The Charter had been seen as 'a prelude to a European constitution' (F Jacobs (2001) 26 EL Rev 331).

[70] On which, see *Case C-617/10, Aklagaren v Fransonn*, 26 February 2013, and *Case C 399/11, Melloni v Ministerio Fiscal*, 26 February 2013. See also *R (Sandiford) v Foreign Secretary* [2013] EWCA Civ 581, [2013] 1 WLR 2938.

[71] On the relationship between the two courts, see *Bosphorus Hava Yollari Turizm v Ireland* (2005) 42 EHRR 1. See generally, S Douglas-Scott (2006) 43 CML Rev 629; G Harpaz (2009) 46 CML Rev 105.

The legal status of the EU Charter was transformed by the Lisbon Treaty, with the TEU, art 6 now also providing that the Charter 'shall have the same legal value as the Treaties',[72] albeit not integrated into the treaties. In the case of the United Kingdom (and Poland), however, Protocol No 30 provides that the Charter does not extend the ability of the ECJ (or of any domestic court) to find that any provision of domestic law is inconsistent with its terms; the Protocol also provides 'for the avoidance of doubt' that nothing in title IV of the Charter (dealing with certain trade union freedoms and employment rights) creates justiciable rights applicable to the United Kingdom.[73]

From the time it was agreed, doubts have been raised about the effectiveness of Protocol 30. These doubts appear to have been vindicated by a passage from the decision of the CJEU in a reference from the United Kingdom.[74] According to the Court, Protocol 30 'does not intend to exempt the Republic of Poland or the United Kingdom from the obligation to comply with the provisions of the Charter or to prevent a court of one of those member states from ensuring compliance with those provisions'.[75] It has been said subsequently that the 'constitutional significance of this decision can hardly be overstated'.[76]

Thus, 'Notwithstanding the endeavours of our political representatives at Lisbon', according to Mostyn J, 'it would seem that the much wider Charter of Rights is now part of our domestic law', and that it operates as such independently of the ECHR, which it significantly expands upon,[77] not least in the provision of potentially more powerful remedies.[78] Whatever the substance in these claims, it is uncertain whether they take fully on board those provisions of the Charter that make clear that the latter is 'addressed to the institutions and bodies of the Union with due regard for the principle of subsidiarity and to the member states only when they are implementing Union law' (art 51).[79]

C. Constitutional implications of membership

Parliamentary sovereignty

As we have seen, the questions of parliamentary supremacy presented by Britain's membership of the EEC/EU were identified but not resolved in the pre-accession era. We have seen the obligations of EU membership and the expectations of the ECJ, which appeared to be faithfully reflected in the 1972 Act, s 2 purporting to give full effect to EU law. But how would the British courts respond to a conflict between EU law and an Act of Parliament, in light of the doctrine

---

[72] But see also Protocol 7, which is said to make it 'absolutely clear that the contracting parties agreed that the Charter did not create one single further justiciable right in our domestic courts': *R(AB)* v *Home Secretary* [2013] EWHC 3453 (Admin), para 12.

[73] For a full discussion, see HL Paper 62-I (2007–8), paras 5.84–5.111. But see now *R(AB)* v *Home Secretary*, above, esp paras 10–16.

[74] *Joined Cases C-411/10 and C-493/10, NS* v *Home Secretary*, 21 December 2011.

[75] Ibid, para 120.

[76] *R(AB)* v *Home Secretary*, above, para 14.

[77] Moreover, engaging with another debate (on which see ch 14 below), Mostyn J said that the 'much wider Charter of Rights would remain part of our domestic law even if the Human Rights Act were repealed' (para 14).

[78] Unlike a declaration of incompatibility under the Human Rights Act 1998, s 4 to reflect a breach of the ECHR, a breach of the Charter can require the domestic courts to disapply primary legislation: see for example, *Benkharbouche* v *Foreign Secretary* [2017] UKSC 62, para 78; and *Google* v *Vidal-Hall* [2015] EWCA Civ 311, [2016] QB 1003.

[79] As the court made clear in *Joined Cases C-411/10 and C-493/10, NS* v *Home Secretary*, above. See also *Rugby Football Union* v *Consolidated Information Services Ltd* [2012] UKSC 55, [2012] 1 WLR 3333, para 28.

of parliamentary sovereignty covered in Chapter 5 above? There would be no problem where the conflict arose between an Act of Parliament passed before 1972, which would be impliedly repealed by the 1972 Act. But what about an Act of Parliament passed after 1972 which conflicts with a directly effective EEC/EU obligation which the 1972 Act was designed to entrench?

For the first decade after the passing of the 1972 Act, the courts vacillated between mutually conflicting positions. In *Felixstowe Dock and Railway Co v British Transport Docks Board*,[80] Lord Denning commented that once a Bill 'is passed by Parliament and becomes a statute, that will dispose of all discussion about the Treaty. These courts will then have to abide by the statute without regard to the Treaty at all'.[81] Only three years later, Lord Denning appeared to change his mind. In *Macarthys Ltd v Smith*,[82] questions arose about the compatibility of the Equal Pay Act 1970 (which did not come into force until 1975) with the EEC Treaty, art 119. The Court of Appeal was divided in whether a woman could use as her equal pay comparator someone who was no longer engaged by her employer (Lord Denning dissenting in favour of the woman). The claim would not have been possible under the Equal Pay Act 1970, and a preliminary ruling on the meaning of EEC law was sought.

The ECJ confirmed the interpretation of EEC law that had been suggested by Lord Denning,[83] following which the Court of Appeal sought to make it plain that the provisions of the Treaty 'take priority over anything in our English statute on equal pay which is inconsistent with art 119 (now TFEU, art 157)', this priority having been 'given by our own law'. According to Lord Denning:

> Community law is now part of our law: and, whenever there is any inconsistency, Community law has priority. It is not supplanting English law. It is part of our law which overrides any other part which is inconsistent with it.[84]

But although Lord Denning appeared thus to have changed his mind, he also observed:

> Thus far I have assumed that our Parliament, whenever it passes legislation, intends to fulfil its obligations under the Treaty. If the time should come when our Parliament deliberately passes an Act – with the intention of repudiating the Treaty or any provision in it – or intentionally of acting inconsistently with it – and says so in express terms – then I should have thought that it would be the duty of our courts to follow the statute of our Parliament.[85]

On this basis the European Communities Act 1972, s 2, effected only a limited form of entrenchment: it would have the effect that Community law (now EU law) will apply in preference to any post-1972 statute and to that extent Parliament would have bound its successors. In these cases the courts would assume that Parliament had not intended to depart from EEC/EU obligations. But Lord Denning left open the possibility that Parliament might wish to assert its supremacy by stating clearly that a domestic statute is to apply notwithstanding Community law (now EU law). In this case the domestic statute would displace to that extent s 2 of the 1972 Act. Further support for the view that the 1972 Act only qualified the supremacy of Parliament was provided by *Case 12/81, Garland v British Rail Engineering Ltd*,[86] where Lord Diplock raised the question whether:

> having regard to the express direction as to the construction of enactments 'to be passed' ... contained in section 2(4), anything short of an express positive statement in an Act of Parliament passed after January 1, 1973, that a particular provision is intended to be made in breach of an obligation assumed

[80] [1976] 2 Ll L. Rep 656.

[81] Ibid, p 663.

[82] [1979] ICR 785. See T R S Allan (1983) 3 OJLS 22.

[83] *Case 129/79, Macarthys Ltd v Smith* [1981] 1 QB 180.

[84] [1981] 1 QB 180, 200. See also Cumming Bruce LJ, at p 201.

[85] [1979] ICR 785, 789.

[86] [1983] 2 AC 751.

by the United Kingdom under a Community treaty, would justify an English court in construing that provision in a manner inconsistent with a Community treaty obligation of the United Kingdom.[87]

Factortame (No 1)

Despite the foregoing, the debates relating to a conflict between an Act of Parliament and EU law are dominated by the inconclusive *Factortame* series of cases,[88] in which the company challenged the Merchant Shipping Act 1988 and regulations made thereunder, on the ground that they violated provisions of the EEC Treaty, including arts 7 and 52 (now TFEU, arts 26 and 46 respectively).[89] The Act had been introduced to prevent what was called 'quota hopping', and amended the rules relating to the licensing of fishing vessels by providing that only British-owned vessels could be registered, a requirement which excluded the Spanish-owned vessels of the applicants.

In judicial review proceedings in *Factortame (No 1)*, the Divisional Court made a reference under EEC Treaty, art 177 (now TFEU, art 267) for a preliminary ruling on the issues of Community law raised by the proceedings, and ordered by way of interim relief that the application of the 1988 Act should be suspended as regards the applicants. This latter order was set aside by the Court of Appeal on the ground that the court had no power to suspend the application of an Act, since 'it is fundamental to our (unwritten) constitution that it is for Parliament to legislate and for the judiciary to interpret and apply the fruits of Parliament's labours'.[90] By the time the case reached the House of Lords, however, the question of parliamentary sovereignty had been diluted, although not completely displaced.

It was said by Lord Bridge (in upholding the Court of Appeal's refusal to grant interim relief to restrain the operation of the Merchant Shipping Act 1988 pending the outcome of the art 177 (now TFEU, art 267) reference that s 2(4) was to be regarded as having

> precisely the same effect as if a section were incorporated in Part II of the Act of 1988 which in terms enacted that the provisions with respect to registration of British fishing vessels were to be without prejudice to the directly enforceable Community rights of nationals of any member state of the EEC.[91]

The House of Lords held, nevertheless, that it had no jurisdiction to grant the interim relief sought, Lord Bridge continuing:

> If the applicants fail to establish the rights they claim before the ECJ, the effect of the interim relief granted would be to have conferred upon them rights directly contrary to Parliament's sovereign will and correspondingly to have deprived British fishing vessels, as defined by Parliament, of the enjoyment of a substantial proportion of the United Kingdom quota of stocks of fish protected by the common fisheries policy. I am clearly of the opinion that, as a matter of English law, the court has no power to make an order which has these consequences.[92]

87 Ibid, p 771.
88 For the *Factortame* litigation, see *R v Transport Secretary, ex p Factortame Ltd (No 1)* [1989] 2 CMLR 353 (CA), [1990] 2 AC 85 (HL); *Case C-213/89, R v Transport Secretary, ex p Factortame Ltd (No 2)* [1991] AC 603 (ECJ and HL); *Case C-221/89, R v Transport Secretary, ex p Factortame Ltd (No 3)* [1992] QB 680 (ECJ); *Case C-48/93, R v Transport Secretary, ex p Factortame Ltd (No 4)* [1996] QB 404 (ECJ); *R v Secretary of State for Transport, ex p Factortame (No 5)* [2000] 1 AC 524. For proceedings by the Commission under art 169 (now TFEU, art 226) see *Case C-246/89, Commission v UK* [1991] ECR I-4585. For the sequel, see Merchant Shipping Act 1988 (Amendment) Order 1989, SI 1989 No 2006. For an account of the costs of the *Factortame* case, see HL Deb, 4 July 2000, WA 132.
89 On the question of parliamentary sovereignty, see P P Craig (1991) 11 YBEL 221; N Gravells [1989] PL 568, [1991] PL 180; and H W R Wade (1991) 107 LQR 1, (1996) 112 LQR 568.
90 [1989] 2 CMLR 353, 397 (Lord Donaldson MR).
91 [1990] 2 AC 85, 140.
92 Ibid, p 143. It was also held that under English law it was not possible (at that time) to grant an interlocutory injunction against the Crown.

This, however, was not the view of the ECJ in the preliminary reference proceedings in relation to the position under European law, 'the full effectiveness' of which would be impaired 'if a rule of national law could prevent a court seised of a dispute governed by Community law from granting interim relief in order to ensure the full effectiveness of the judgment to be given on the existence of the rights claimed under community law'. It therefore followed that 'a court which in those circumstances would grant interim relief, if it were not for a rule of national law, is obliged to set aside that rule'. As a result EC law (now EU law) must take priority over domestic legislation, even if this means that the British courts are required to set aside a fundamental constitutional principle, in this case the sovereignty of Parliament.

Factortame (No 2)

When the matter returned to the House of Lords, interim relief was granted, thereby restraining the operation of the Merchant Shipping Act 1988 in relation to the plaintiffs pending the final resolution of the case.[93] In a much-quoted passage in *Factortame (No 2)*, Lord Bridge said:

> Some public comments on the decision of the European Court of Justice, affirming the jurisdiction of the courts of member states to override national legislation if necessary to enable interim relief to be granted in protection of rights under Community law, have suggested that this was a novel and dangerous invasion by a Community institution of the sovereignty of the UK Parliament. But such comments are based on a misconception. If the supremacy . . . of Community law over the national law of member states was not always inherent in the EEC Treaty it was certainly well established in the jurisprudence of the European Court of Justice long before the UK joined the Community. . . . Thus, whatever limitation of its sovereignty Parliament accepted when it enacted the European Communities Act 1972 was entirely voluntary. Under the terms of the Act of 1972 it has always been clear that it was the duty of a UK court, when delivering final judgment, to override any rule of national law found to be in conflict with any directly enforceable rule of Community law. Similarly, when decisions of the European Court of Justice have exposed areas of UK statute law which failed to implement Council directives, Parliament has always loyally accepted the obligation to make appropriate and prompt amendments. Thus there is nothing in any way novel in according supremacy to rules of Community law in those areas to which they apply and to insist that, in the protection of rights under Community law, national courts must not be inhibited by rules of national law from granting interim relief in appropriate cases is no more than a logical recognition of that supremacy.[94]

In this way, the House of Lords appeared to have effected a form of entrenchment of s 2(4) of the 1972 Act which thereby does what no statute has done before, namely fetter the continuing supremacy of Parliament.[95] The late Sir William Wade referred to this as a constitutional revolution: 'The Parliament of 1972 had succeeded in binding the Parliament of 1988 and restricting its sovereignty, something that was supposed to be constitutionally impossible.'[96] But although this may be necessary as a matter of European integration, it is unclear whether the House of Lords in *Factortame (Nos 1 and 2)* satisfactorily dealt with the issue as

---

[93] [1991] 1 AC 603.

[94] Ibid, pp 658–9.

[95] See also *R v Employment Secretary, ex p EOC* [1995] 1 AC 1 where declarations were made that provisions of the Employment Protection (Consolidation) Act 1978 were incompatible with art 119 (now art 141) of the EEC Treaty and Council Directive 75/117/EEC and that other provisions of the Act were incompatible with the latter. For subsequent developments, see D Nicol [1996] PL 579.

[96] (1996) 112 LQR 568. See also Bogdanor, *The New British Constitution*, p 28 (cited with approval in *R v Budimir* [2010] EWCA Crim 1486, [2011] 3 All ER 206). But the claim about the revolutionary nature of *Factortame* seems wide of the mark, as would any suggestion of Brexit being counter-revolutionary. See also J Eekelaar (1997) 113 LQR 185 and T R S Allan (1997) LQR 443.

a matter of domestic constitutional law; nor is it clear that the decisions answered all the questions which arise. Indeed, it is open to question whether the decisions advance the matter much beyond the Court of Appeal decision in *Macarthys Ltd* v *Smith*.[97]

It is, however, unfortunate that in a case of such constitutional significance, the full range of constitutional authorities was not addressed in the course of argument, even if it would have been difficult for the defendants to have mounted a full frontal attack on the constitutional implications of s 2(4). In terms of unanswered questions, what would be the position in the (admittedly unlikely) event that Parliament should say expressly (or by clear implication) that a statutory provision should apply notwithstanding any EU obligation to the contrary? Wade argued that: 'If there had been any such provision in the Act of 1988 we can be sure that the European Court of Justice would hold that it was contrary to Community law to which by the Act of 1972 the Act of 1988 is held to be subject.'[98]

But does it follow that in such a case national courts would be required to give effect to the 1972 Act rather than the 1988 Act? As a matter of British constitutional law (and regardless of what the ECJ might say), it would appear that in such an eventuality Parliament had repudiated the 'voluntary' 'limitation of its sovereignty', which it accepted when it enacted the 1972 Act (at least insofar as the 1988 Act is concerned). This is not to deny that such a decision would give rise to serious political and constitutional problems at EU level. But it would be for the Commission to take appropriate action by way of enforcement proceedings or otherwise, and it is perhaps in that way that any problems should be resolved rather than in the British courts. More recent decisions of the Supreme Court incline towards this view.[99]

Some of these matters were considered in *Thoburn* v *Sunderland City Council*[100] (the so-called 'Metric Martyrs' case) where the appellant had been convicted for breaching the Weights and Measures Act 1985 by selling fruit in imperial rather than metric measurements. As originally enacted the 1985 Act had permitted fruit to be sold in either measure, but the Act had been amended by regulations and now required fruit to be sold in metric measures only. These regulations, made partially under the authority of the European Communities Act 1972, s 2(2), had been introduced in order to comply with the EC Metrication Directive. The appeal failed, with the Administrative Court rejecting on a number of grounds the argument that the Weights and Measures Act 1985 impliedly repealed the European Communities Act 1972, s 2(2), to the extent of any inconsistency. But in the course of his judgment Laws LJ made a number of important observations about the relationship between British and EC law.

According to Laws LJ, the House of Lords in *Factortame (No 1)* (above) had effectively accepted that s 2(4) of the 1972 Act could not be impliedly repealed ('albeit the point was not argued'). In this way the common law had created an exception to the doctrine of implied repeal (an exception which in the view of Laws LJ should be extended to all 'constitutional statutes', of which the European Communities Act 1972 was an example).[101] This did not mean that the 1972 Act could not be repealed or modified. But it did mean that repeal or modification could be achieved only by 'express words in the later statute, or by words so specific that the inference of an actual determination to effect the result contended for was

---

[97] [1979] ICR 785.

[98] (1996) 112 LQR 568, p 570.

[99] *HS2* and *Miller* respectively, below.

[100] [2002] EWHC 195 (Admin), [2003] QB 151 (D Marshall and J Young [2002] PL 399, G Marshall (2002) 118 LQR 493, and A Perreau-Saussine [2002] CLJ 528).

[101] See ch 3 above on this aspect of the case.

> irresistible'. By these means the courts were said to 'have found their way through the *impasse* seemingly created by two supremacies, the supremacy of European law and the supremacy of Parliament'. It is important to emphasise that in *Factortame* the House of Lords held that an Act of Parliament in breach of EU law was to be disapplied, not that it was a nullity.

Parliamentary sovereignty in flux

From the standpoint of EEC/EU law, there was nothing novel about the ECJ decision in *Factortame (No 1)*, the court having held on a number of occasions that the supremacy of Community law (now EU law) applies even in respect of provisions of national constitutional law. The position was reinforced by *Factortame (No 4)*, where the ECJ held that the British government was liable to pay damages to the applicants for financial losses suffered[102], even though the losses in question were the consequence of legislation.[103] As a result, in *Factortame (No 5)*, the House of Lords held that the 'deliberate adoption of legislation which was clearly discriminatory on the ground of nationality and which inevitably violated [what was then] article 52 of the Treaty' was a sufficiently serious breach to give rise under Community law to a right to compensatory damages.[104] This clearly reinforced the sense of a lost of sovereignty, with which it is hard to argue if damages have to be paid at the insistence of a court for harm caused by an Act of Parliament.

Yet as we have seen, from the standpoint of domestic law, it remained unresolved whether Parliament could assert its ultimate sovereignty by making clear its intention not to be bound by EU law. But that uncertainty appeared never to have been properly understood, least of all by the politicians who made much of the loss of legal sovereignty post *Factortame* and beyond. Nevertheless, it is undeniable that as the legal competences of the EU expanded, so the impact of EU law on domestic law grew as a result, as did the influence of the CJEU.[105] Responding to growing concerns about EU expansion particularly in light of changes introduced following the Lisbon Treaty in particular[106], the European Union Act 2011 was passed to ensure that the United Kingdom would not agree to any further amendment of the EU treaties or any further expansion of powers without both express legislative approval and approval by the people in a referendum. Although constitutionally significant in light of Brexit, these are powers that are unlikely now to be exercised.[107]

---

[102] [1996] QB 404. Although the government moved quickly to repair the legislation, losses were sustained from the time the 1988 Act came into force (31 March 1989) until the offending discrimination was removed (2 November 1989).

[103] [1996] QB 404, at p 497.

[104] *R v Secretary of State for Transport, ex p Factortame Ltd (No 5)* [2000] 1 AC 524, at p 545 (Lord Slynn). See A Cygan (2000) 25 EL Rev 452. Article 52 is now TFEU, art 43.

[105] The point is well-made in the Brexit White Paper: 'The extent of EU activity relevant to the UK can be demonstrated by the fact that 1,056 EU-related documents were deposited for parliamentary scrutiny in 2016. These include proposals for EU Directives, Regulations, Decisions and Recommendations, as well as Commission delegated acts, and other documents such as Commission Communications, Reports and Opinions submitted to the Council, Court of Auditors Reports and more': Department for Exiting the EU, *The United Kingdom's Exit from and New Partnership with the European Union*, Cm 9417 (2017), para 2.1.

[106] See *R (Wheeler)* v *Office of Prime Minister* [2008] EWHC 1409 (Admin) – no legal obligation to hold a referendum on the treaty. For a full analysis of the Lisbon Treaty, see HL Paper 62-I (2007–8).

[107] On the 2011 Act, see M Gordon and M Dougan (2012) 27 ELR 3; Gordon, *Parliamentary Sovereignty in the UK Constitution* (2015), ch 6.

The 2011 Act was notable also for the so-called 'sovereignty clause' in s 18,[108] which appears designed principally to pacify Eurosceptics on the government's backbenches. It provides that:

> Directly applicable or directly effective EU law (that is, the rights, powers, liabilities, obligations, restrictions, remedies and procedures referred to in section 2(1) of the European Communities Act 1972) falls to be recognised and available in law in the United Kingdom only by virtue of that Act or where it is required to be recognised and available in law by virtue of any other Act.

It is doubtful, however, whether this adds anything to the existing law,[109] though it seems to have been designed to counter arguments that EU law constitutes 'a new higher autonomous legal order derived from the EU treaties or international law and principles which has become an integral part of the UK's legal system independent of statute'.[110] This refers to an argument by counsel rejected by Laws LJ in *Thoburn* v *Sunderland Council*.[111]

The 2011 Act was thus a response to a growing discontent with the EU, though neither the promise of a referendum before any future expansion would be supported, nor the sovereignty clause in s 18 was enough to pacify the sceptics who demanded a fresh referendum on whether the United Kingdom should remain in membership. Nor were the sceptics pacified by what seemed to be a formal judicial acknowledgement that the constitutional relationship between the United Kingdom and the EU was much more subtle than the sceptics portrayed, even if politically it would be difficult in practice for national sovereignty to prevail in the event of a conflict with the EU in relation to the use of existing powers. In *HS2 Action Alliance*,[112] Lords Neuberger and Mance suggested that there were certain implied limitations in the 1972 Act, when they said that it was

> certainly arguable (and it is for United Kingdom law and courts to determine) that there may be fundamental principles, whether contained in other constitutional instruments or recognised at common law, of which Parliament when it enacted the European Communities Act 1972 did not either contemplate or authorise the abrogation.[113]

One of these principles would be of course the sovereignty of the Westminster Parliament, which was powerfully restated in the *Miller* case discussed below and elsewhere in this text.[114]

In *R (HS2 Alliance Ltd)* v *Transport Secretary*,[115] one of the questions was whether the proposed authorisation for the high-speed rail link between London and the North of England could be authorized by a hybrid Act of Parliament while complying with the Environmental Impact Assessment Directive,[116] which called for effective public participation in the approval process. The Supreme Court held that the parliamentary procedure would allow the environmental issues to be adequately considered and that it was not a requirement of EU law that national courts should scrutinize the procedures of national legislatures.

---

[108] Ibid, p 8.

[109] According to the majority in *Miller* (note 114, below), it 'simply confirmed the position as it had been since the beginning of 1973' (para 66).

[110] Explanatory Notes to the European Union Act 2011, para 120.

[111] [2002] EWHC 195 (Admin) [2003] QB 151.

[112] *R (HS2 Alliance Ltd)* v *Transport Secretary* [2014] UKSC 3, [2014] 1 WLR 324.

[113] Ibid, para 207.

[114] *R (Miller)* v *Secretary of State for Exiting the EU* [2017] UKSC 5, [2017] 2 WLR 583. See pp 141–2 below.

[115] [2014] UKSC 3, [2014] 1 WLR 324.

[116] Directive 2011/92/EU.

Although the issue was not raised directly by the parties, Lord Reed pointed out that if such an obligation did exist, this would 'impinge upon long-established constitutional principles governing the relationship between Parliament and the courts, as reflected for example in article 9 of the Bill of Rights 1689, in authorities concerned with judicial scrutiny of Parliamentary procedure'.[117] According to Lord Reed, were it to arise, 'that question cannot be resolved simply by applying the doctrine developed by the Court of Justice of the supremacy of EU law, since the application of that doctrine in our law itself depends upon the 1972 Act'.

In a passage reinforcing the words of Lords Neuberger and Mance above, Lord Reed continued by saying that 'If there is a conflict between a constitutional principle, such as that embodied in article 9 of the Bill of Rights, and EU law, that conflict has to be resolved by our courts as an issue arising under the constitutional law of the United Kingdom. Nor can the issue be resolved, as was also suggested, by following the decision in *R* v *Secretary of State for Transport, Ex p Factortame Ltd (No 2)* [1991] 1 AC 603, since that case was not concerned with the compatibility with EU law of the process by which legislation is enacted in Parliament'.[118]

D. Leaving the EU

Referendum

As already pointed out, the 2011 Act failed to satisfy demands for a referendum. The demand was not for a referendum on EU expansion but for a referendum on EU membership. By way of response, David Cameron as Conservative party leader fought the general election in 2015 with a promise that – if elected – the Conservatives would offer a referendum on the United Kingdom's continued membership of the EU.[119] It is unclear if the Conservatives (then leading a Coalition government) expected to win the general election in 2015. It is clear, however, that having committed to hold the referendum, Mr Cameron expected the country to vote in favour of remaining in the European Union.

As pointed out, however, the people voted by 51.89 per cent to 48.11 per cent to leave (on a 72 per cent turnout, which meant that less than 40 per cent of those eligible to vote did so in favour of leaving the EU).[120] The result was complicated not only by its narrow margin but also by the fact that a majority of those in Scotland, Northern Ireland and Gibraltar respectively voted to remain. The referendum was held under the authority of the European Referendum Act 2015, and conducted in accordance with the principles in the Political Parties, Elections and Referendums Act 2000, which is considered in chapter 7. The Conservative government, the two main opposition parties, and the SNP and Plaid Cmyru campaigned to remain, though the Conservative party took a formal position of neutrality in the light of significant internal division.

---

[117] Here he cited (at para 78) *Edinburgh and Dalkeith Railway Co* v *Wauchope* (1842) 8 Cl & F 710, *Lee* v *Bude and Torrington Junction Railway Co* (1871) LR 6 CP 576, *Pickin* v *British Railways Board* [1974] AC 765 and *Wilson* v *First County Trust Ltd (No 2)* [2003] UKHL 40; [2004] 1 AC 816.

[118] [2014] UKSC 3, [2014] 1 WLR 324, para 79 (Lord Reed).

[119] Conservative Party, *Strong Leadership, A Clear Economic Plan, A Brighter, More Secure Future* (2015), p 72: 'We will hold that in-out referendum before 2017 and respect the outcome'.

[120] This is significant not only because it was the threshold required at the 1978 devolution referendums, but also because it was subsequently required for some trade union industrial action ballots by the Trade Union Act 2016.

The referendum raised important questions about eligibility to vote, which was restricted to the parliamentary franchise, which meant in turn that a number of British citizens resident overseas were denied the right to vote, an exclusion keenly felt especially by British citizens resident in other European countries. In *Schindler* it as held that the rules relating to the franchise did not breach EU law relating to freedom of movement, Elias LJ concluding that 'EU law can have no part to play in the decision whether a state chooses to remain in the EU',[121] having doubted whether

> purely as a matter of domestic law, Parliament would have intended section 2(1) to apply so as to give primacy to EU law where the very question in issue is whether the UK should remain bound by EU law. The effect of section 2(1) is to bind the UK to the rules of the club whilst it remains a member; but I do not think it can have been intended to bind the UK to those rules when the very question is whether it should be bound by those rules. Parliament agreed to join the EU by exercising sovereign powers untrammeled by EU law and I think it would expect to be able to leave the EU in the exercise of the same untrammeled sovereign power, whether the later legislation expressly dis-applies section 2(1) or not. It is not, in my view, a question of implied repeal but rather a question of the scope of section 2(1). Parliament would not have intended that the UK should give precedence to EU law when the very question to be decided is whether the UK should continue to give precedence to EU law.[122]

Apart from questions about the conduct of the campaign, the other major issue related to the effect of the result. Governments are resorting to referendums more frequently when dealing with difficult questions (devolution, and the electoral system, and the EU). There is, however, no consistent approach to the legal effects of referendums, with different legislation authorising referendums sometimes silent on the legal effects and sometimes explicit on legal consequences.[123] The 2015 Act fell into the former category which led some to conclude that it was advisory only, though as has been said in other contexts in relation to other matters, legal principle has no bearing on political reality.

Article 50

The process of leaving the EU is governed by the TEU, art 50, which provides that

(1) Any member state may decide to withdraw from the Union in accordance with its own constitutional requirements.

(2) A member state which decides to withdraw shall notify the European Council of its intention. In the light of the guidelines provided by the European Council, the Union shall negotiate and conclude an agreement with that State, setting out the arrangements for its withdrawal, taking account of the framework for its future relationship with the Union. That agreement shall be negotiated in accordance with Article 218(3) of the Treaty on the Functioning of the European Union. It shall be concluded on behalf of the Union by the Council, acting by a qualified majority, after obtaining the consent of the European Parliament.

There are no precedents to govern the exercise of this power, and despite the silence of the European Referendum Act 2015 on the legal effect of the referendum and the narrow vote in favour of Brexit, the government expressed the view immediately afterwards that it had

---

[121] *R (Schindler) v Chancellor of Duchy of Lancaster* [2016] EWCA Civ 469, [2017] QB 226, para 60.

[122] Ibid, para 58. For comment, see B Davies [2016] 27 KLJ 323.

[123] Compare and contrast the Parliamentary Voting System and Constituencies Act 2011, s 8, and the European Referendum Act 2015, s 1. The 2015 Act said simply that 'A referendum is to be held on whether the United Kingdom should remain a member of the European Union'. See further, K Ewing (2017) 80 MLR 711.

authority under Article 50 to notify the Commission of the United Kingdom's intention to leave by invoking prerogative powers.[124]

This meant, according to the government, that it did not need statutory authority to invoke the political authority of the referendum. This view was, however, challenged in litigation on the ground that the prerogative did not authorize the government's proposed action mainly because Brexit would directly affect statutory rights, which only an Act of Parliament can abrogate. The statutory rights in question include those that have direct effect in the United Kingdom as a result of the European Communities Act 1972 as described above, rights which would automatically cease to have effect two years after the Article 50 procedure was invoked. This view was accepted in judicial review proceedings, the High Court in *Miller* holding that the government had no prerogative authority to invoke Article 50, granting a declaration to this effect.[125]

The hostile press reaction to that decision – including the infamous claim that the judges were 'enemies of the people' – is considered in Chapter 13. It was nevertheless upheld by the Supreme Court by a majority of 8–3, in a case in which all eleven justices sat for the first time.[126] The majority decision was notable for its strong defence of parliamentary sovereignty, which the majority appeared to suggest had not been surrendered by EU membership after all, in the sense that it had always been possible for Parliament to legislate contrary to EU law, legislation to which the courts would give effect. However, *Miller* was concerned principally with a different point, the majority concluding that invoking Article 50 would not only affect directly effective rights derived from statute, but also an entire source of law (that is to say, the application of EU law in the United Kingdom).[127]

As a result of the Supreme Court decision, the government introduced the EU (Notification of Withdrawal) Bill,[128] a simple measure of only 57 words authorising the Prime Minister to 'notify the United Kingdom's intention to withdraw from the EU'. The Bill was passed without amendment, and the government duly gave notice of its intention to withdraw from the EU on 29 March 2017. This means that subject to the subsequent negotiations between the EU and the United Kingdom and the provisions of the TEU Article 50, the United Kingdom will cease to be a member of the EU on 29 March 2019, with the possibility of a soft landing by means of a short transition period thereafter.

It is uncertain whether as a matter of law the notice could be unilaterally withdrawn by the United Kingdom, for which Article 50 makes no express provision.[129] In the event of any such withdrawal, it must be likely that political reality would resolve any legal uncertainty.

----

[124] HC 431, 2016–17, Oral evidence, Q 86.

[125] *R (Miller)* v *Secretary of State for Exiting the EU* [2016] 2768 (Admin). This contradicted an earlier decision in Northern Ireland, which also held that there was no need for the approval of the Northern Ireland Assembly: *Re McCord's Application* [2016] NIQB 85. On the constitutional and legal implication in the aftermath of the High Court decision, see (2016) 27(3) *King's Law Journal* 289 (Special Issue on Brexit with articles on constitutional aspects by T Tridimas, V Bogdanor, B Davies, M Gordon, F Davis, C McCorkindale and M Kendrick).

[126] For a full account, see (2017) 80 MLR 685–745 (Special section on *Miller*, articles by J Murkens, T Poole, K Ewing and M Aroney), and *Public Law Brexit Special Extra Issue* (2017, articles by M Barczentewicz, R Craig, P Craig, P Daly and P O'Brien). Also J Grant (2017) 28 *King's Law Journal* 35.

[127] *Miller*, note 114 above, para 93.

[128] This was followed shortly by the Brexit White Paper (above) which reads as if it was hastily rewritten in the wake of the strong commitment to parliamentary sovereignty in the *Miller* case, note 114 above. See below, pp 142–3.

[129] Litigation was commenced in Ireland to seek a reference on the point, but was withdrawn. In December 2017 it was announced that litigation would be commenced in Scotland.

The *Miller* case

Before considering the next step in the withdrawal process, it is necessary to dwell on the *Miller* case, the strong re-assertion of parliamentary sovereignty by the majority catching the government by surprise. Thus in the White Paper published shortly thereafter to outline the government's ambitions for a future relationship with the EU, it was said that

> The sovereignty of Parliament is a fundamental principle of the UK constitution. Whilst Parliament has remained sovereign throughout our membership of the EU, it has not always felt like that'.[130]

But apart from asserting constitutional orthodoxy in relation to parliamentary sovereignty and holding that the prerogative did not provide sufficient authority to trigger Article 50, *Miller* was important for two other reasons. The first related to the referendum: did this not provide sufficient authority for the government to trigger Article 50? Was it not evidence that Parliament had redefined itself upwards as Baroness Hale had suggested in *Jackson* v *Attorney General*?[131]

The answer from the UK Supreme Court was a resounding 'No'. The referendum may have provided a political imperative for government action, but it created no legal authority for such action. This highlighted the chaotic nature of referendum law in the United Kingdom referred to above. Although there are general principles regulating the conduct of referendums (introduced ironically in anticipation of a referendum to join the euro),[132] the legal effects of referendums are determined on a case-by-case basis in the legislation by which the referendum in question is authorized. The legislation varies from the devolution legislation in the 1970s, which sought approval by referendum for the implementation of legislation (legal effect), to the devolution referendums in the 1990s, which sought approval by referendum for the introduction of legislation (political effect).[133] The EU referendum was at the latter end of the scale.

The other issue highlighted by the EU referendum and the decision to withdraw related to devolution, and in particular the question whether Parliament could legislate to authorize Brexit without the consent of the Scottish Parliament. This question arises in light of the Sewel convention, and in particular its reduction to legislative form in the Scotland Act 2006, which provides that the Westminster Parliament will not normally legislate on a devolved matter without the consent of the Scottish Parliament.[134] But although Brexit would clearly affect devolved matters, the UKSC in *Miller* nevertheless held that there was no legal duty to secure the prior approval of the Scottish Parliament, the court taking the view that the Sewel convention was not legally binding despite its statutory nature.

This was perhaps the most unsatisfactory aspect of the reasoning in *Miller*. It is not the case that the courts cannot rule on the meaning of a convention, particularly in exceptional circumstances (and few would argue that the issues in *Miller* were not exceptional – the assembling of 11 judges was itself exceptional), even though any such ruling may not have any binding effect.[135] More importantly, however, it can be argued strongly that having been reduced to statute, the nature of the convention changed, now embedded as the highest legal form our legal system acknowledges, the supremacy of which the *Miller* case went a long way to re-assert. The question for the Court – having taken the route that it did – was to determine whether these were 'normal' circumstances in accordance with the Scotland Act 1998, as amended.

---

[130] Department for Exiting the EU, *The United Kingdom's Exit from and New Partnership with the European Union*, Cm 9417 (2017), para 2.1.

[131] [2005] UKHL 58, para 163. See ch 3 above.

[132] Political Parties, Elections and Referendums Act 2000, Part VII. See Ewing [2001] PL 542.

[133] Compare also the Parliamentary Voting System and Constituencies Act 2011, s 8 referred to at note 123 above, the strong legal effects of which did not have to be invoked following the referendum result. See ch 7 F below.

[134] On the Sewel convention, see ch 2 B above.

[135] See *Re Resolution to amend the Constitution* [1981] 1 SCR 753. On conventions, see ch 1 C above.

It is unlikely that this would have led to a different outcome, but it may have produced what some may have regarded to be more palatable and consistent reasoning.[136]

'Great Repeal Bill'

Having (i) held the referendum and (ii) given notice of withdrawal, the next step in the process was (iii) to deal with the immediate implications of withdrawal. What will happen to the vast areas of political, economic and social life that are underpinned by EU law following Brexit? Will that law cease to apply? If so what will be the consequences? Or would it make sense to retain existing EU law, and if so: in what form, for how long, and with what effect? These questions are addressed in the European Union (Withdrawal) Bill 2017 which by proposing to repeal the European Communities Act 1972 also makes the questions all the more urgent in view of the fact that the 1972 Act gives effect to EU law, or enables EU law fairly easily to have effect.

The Bill was introduced into the House of Commons on 13 July 2017, and the discussion here reflects its terms as originally drafted. But given the considerable complexity of the issues, the very narrow majority of the government and the wide array of opposition and criticism in various respects, it is highly unlikely that the Bill will be enacted without significant amendments, even though a measure of this kind is an essential part of the process of Brexit. As drafted, however, it is proposed that any EU law – including the TEU and the TFEU as well as any new laws – will not apply in the United Kingdom from Brexit day.[137] On the other hand, it is also provided that existing EU law is to continue to be applicable for the time being, giving the government the opportunity to assess in the long term which EU-derived law it wishes to retain and which it wishes to amend or repeal.

In what is in effect a statutory novation, the European Union (Withdrawal) Bill 2017 thus provides for two different types of EU law:

- EU-derived domestic legislation, as it has effect in domestic law immediately before exit day, will continue to have effect in domestic law on and after exit day. This applies principally (though not only) to any secondary legislation introduced under the 1972 Act to give effect to EU law.

- Direct EU legislation, so far as operative immediately before exit day, will form part of domestic law on and after exit day. This applies principally to regulations which have not yet been implemented by domestic legislation, but not to directives, even those that have direct effect.

Provision is also made thirdly for 'any rights, powers, liabilities, obligations, restrictions, remedies and procedures which, immediately before exit day (a) are recognised and available in domestic law by virtue of section 2(1) of the European Communities Act 1972, and (b) are enforced, allowed and followed accordingly'.

These latter rights, powers, liabilities, obligations, restrictions, remedies and procedures are to continue on and after exit day to be recognised and available in domestic law (and to be enforced, allowed and followed accordingly). It appears that this may include directives

---

[136] For further discussion of this issue, see K Ewing (2017) 80 MLR 711. But compare Grant, above, who cites an article by D Feldman (2015) 37 *Statute Law Review* 212 to the effect that not all legislation gives rise to legal consequences. However, the examples given by the latter are unpersuasive: no government could expressly repudiate a statutory duty no matter how silly, inconvenient or aspirational it might be. A better comparison would be the enactment of the conventions relating to the House of Lords in the Parliament Acts 1911–1949, which clearly have binding legal effects. Note 1911 Act, s 3 (Speaker's certificate expressly stated to be non-justiciable).

[137] The United Kingdom will also cease to be represented in the European Parliament and cease being represented in the other EU institutions, including the CJEU.

which on withdrawal day have been held by the CJEU to have direct effect, though it is expressly provided that there will be no right to bring *Francovich* claims in respect of losses caused by a failure properly to implement these directives.[138] There will be no references to the CJEU for a preliminary ruling on what will now be British laws with an EU origin, though it may be difficult to shake off the continuing role of the CJEU completely. Issues are likely to arise about the meaning of any withdrawal agreement, and there is already a suggestion that the CJEU will have a role in protecting the rights of EU citizen residents in the United Kingdom at the time of Brexit.

Issues relating to the continuing significance of CJEU jurisprudence on EU derived law operating in the United Kingdom at the time of Brexit are considered below. A distinction is drawn between cases relating to EU-derived law which are decided before and after Brexit.

E. The emerging legal implications of Brexit

Legislative implications

According to the House of Lords Constitution Committee, the Bill raised 'a series of profound, wide-ranging and interlocking constitutional concerns',[139] though we should not overlook the influence of politics in shaping these concerns. The issues are broadly of two kinds, one relating to legislation, claims having been made that the government is using Brexit to enhance its power at the expense of Parliament. This is seen in the provisions of the Bill that

> A Minister of the Crown may by regulations make such provision as the Minister considers appropriate to prevent, remedy or mitigate (a) any failure of retained EU law to operate effectively, or (b) any other deficiency in retained EU law.

This means that ministers will be able to rewrite EU-based legislation to ensure that it continues to operate meaningfully in the United Kingdom, for example to remove any provisions which are redundant as a result of Brexit.

This has given rise to claims about the government taking power to rewrite domestic legislation and by-passing Parliament in the process.[140] It is nevertheless the case that the legislation to be amended will typically have been made by the same process under the European Communities Act 1972 to implement EU law in the first place (albeit to implement standards that set an irreducible EU-based minimum). It is also true that the proposed power to amend legislation by way of regulations restricts but does not remove the role of Parliament; that there are limits proposed on how this power can be used; and that there are time limits on its operation.[141] Misuse of the power will be subject to judicial review if not used for the statutory purposes or in breach of the statutory limits. The proposed executive power does nevertheless apply to primary legislation.[142]

---

[138] On *Francovich*, see pp 138–9. above.

[139] HL Paper 19 (2017–19).

[140] HL Paper 22 (2017–19) (Delegated Powers and Regulatory Reform Committee): proposed powers said to be notable for their 'width, novelty and uncertainty' (para 15).

[141] The powers may not be used to create a tax, introduce a new criminal offence or amend or repeal the Human Rights Act 1998. The powers will lapse two years after exit day.

[142] It will also allow for the amendment of those measures created by a combination of both primary and secondary legislation, on which see *United States v Nolan* [2015] UKSC 65, [2015] 1 WLR 1105. The *Nolan* case highlights the need for care in the exercise of the proposed powers in the EU Withdrawal Bill, to avoid amending provisions in primary legislation that were intended to implement EU obligations while going beyond what EU law required.

Related to the foregoing is the issue of devolution, the Scottish and Welsh governments in particular claiming that the Bill represents a 'power grab' by Whitehall, with the Westminster government proposing that all EU powers will revert to Westminster immediately after Brexit.[143] Indeed, the Bill provides expressly that 'an Act of the Scottish Parliament cannot modify, or confer power by subordinate legislation to modify, retained EU law', with similar provisions applying to restrict the powers of the devolved legislatures in Wales and Northern Ireland. This appears to mean that any retained EU law may be modified only by the Westminster Parliament, even where it relates wholly or mainly to devolved matters, quite apart from the fear that matters within devolved competence will not revert directly to the devolved legislatures.

It is hard to tell whether this is as serious a concern as has been claimed, though the Scottish and Welsh governments in particular are surely right to be anxious. From a technical point of view, however, it is perfectly reasonable to see Brexit not as an event, but as a process taking place in the dark, in which civil servants and politicians are cautiously feeling their way. In that context it is equally perfectly reasonable in the first instance for EU-retained law made by the Westminster Parliament to be returned to the Westminster Parliament whence it initially came, with decisions as to the final destination of these reclaimed laws to be made in the years that follow. That said, 'the political and constitutional implications of proceeding with the Bill' without the consent of the devolved institutions 'would be significant and potentially damaging'.[144]

Rule of law implications

The other group of concerns are what might be referred to as rule of law concerns, including the issue raised by the Labour shadow minister for Brexit that the EU Charter of Fundamental Rights will not continue to operate after Brexit day; indeed, the Charter has been expressly excluded, the government apparently believing it to be unnecessary.[145] At first sight it is difficult to see how the Charter could be relevant in British law given that we will no longer be members of the EU. On reflection, however, it will potentially be applicable in relation to retained EU law, so long as the retained EU law remains in force. It is perfectly reasonable to claim that the Charter should continue to apply to help with the interpretation of that law, while remedies under the Charter are also important where there is a conflict.

But again, it is not clear how big a problem this really is. As the government has pointed out, the European Convention on Human Rights will continue to apply post-Brexit, and Convention rights will be enforceable in the domestic courts. Although it is true that there have been significant decisions of the CJEU using the Charter, it is also true that the outcome of some of these cases was driven as much by the ECHR as by the EU's instrument.[146] In any event, the EU Charter is not free from difficulty, and it is curious that the Labour party in particular should want it retained. One of the rights included in the EU Charter which is not in the ECHR is the right to conduct a business (art 16), which in some circles notoriously has been seen as a productive restraint on the social rights of workers.[147]

On an altogether different note, concerns have been expressed by senior judges about the position relating to CJEU jurisprudence post Brexit. According to Lord Neuberger (then

---

[143] *The Guardian*, 14 July 2017.

[144] HL Paper 19 (2017–19), para 76.

[145] Cm 9446 (2017), paras 2.21–2.25.

[146] See *Joined Cases C-293/12 and 594/12, Digital Rights Ireland and Seitlinger*, 8 April 2014. Though this is not to deny that the CJEU has left open the possibility that the Charter could be read to provide more extensive protection than the ECHR: *Joined Cases C-203/15 and C-698/15, Home Secretary v Watson*, 21 December 2016, para 129.

[147] *Case C-426/11, Alemo Herron v Parkwood Leisure Ltd*, 18 July 2013.

President of the UK Supreme Court), there was a need for the government to be clear about the continuing role of the CJEU in British law:

> If [the government] doesn't express clearly what the judges should do about decisions of the ECJ after Brexit, or indeed any other topic after Brexit, then the judges will simply have to do their best. But to blame the judges for making the law when Parliament has failed to do so would be unfair'.

Lord Neuberger is also reported as saying the instructions judges would be expected to follow after Brexit should be spelled out in statute.[148]

This no doubt reflects acute anxiety on the part of the judges, much more exposed to public criticism following the unrestrained abuse to which they were subject following the *Miller* decision at first instance in particular. But again, it is nevertheless difficult to assess the nature of the problem. The Bill makes it clear that the domestic courts will be (i) bound to follow the *pre-Brexit* decisions of the CJEU unless overruled by the UKSC, and (ii) to take into account ('have regard' to) (but not necessarily follow) *post-Brexit* decisions of the CJEU on the meaning of EU-derived law.[149] This is in addition to the provisions of the Bill making clear post-Brexit that there will be no references to the CJEU in relation to EU-retained law, which will now be British law over which the UK Supreme Court (or exceptionally the High Court of Justiciary in Scotland) must now have the last word.

It is not clear how appropriate it would be for Parliament to give any more direct guidance to the courts, without encountering claims about improper interference by government with the judicial role (and the rule of law).[150]

F. Conclusion

Although the United Kingdom is set to withdraw from the European Union, at the time of writing it is unclear what this will mean in practice. While the people voted narrowly in the referendum in 2016 in favour of Brexit, the referendum result did not give any guidance about the type of Brexit the people had in mind. Since the referendum, we have as a result become (i) familiar with a new vocabulary, including 'Soft Brexit' and 'Hard Brexit', and various stages in between, (ii) much better informed about organisations such as the Economic Free Trade Area (EFTA) and the European Economic Area (EEA), and (iii) more familiar with issues around the Single Market and the common customs union.

Post-Brexit options for the United Kingdom's future relationship included:

- Membership of the European Free Trade Area/European Economic Area, which includes all member states of the EU plus Iceland, Norway, Switzerland and Liechtenstein. This would provide access to the European Single Market but would also require the United Kingdom to allow free movement of workers, comply with a substantial body of EU law (over the making of which it would have no formal role), and be subject to the jurisdiction of the EFTA Court, which some would see (incorrectly) as the CJEU in another form.

---

[148] As reported widely in the press, including *The Guardian*, 8 August 2017.

[149] In its interim report on the Bill, the House of Lords Constitution Committee concluded that the Bill 'provides some welcome clarity regarding judgments of the Court of Justice of the European Union', though it was 'at least arguable that the Bill should provide more guidance to the courts': HL Paper 19 (2017–19), para 70.

[150] Compare the formula used in the Human Rights Act 1998, s 2, in relation to the jurisprudence of the European Court of Human Rights. See ch 14 C.

- A 'bespoke' arrangement whereby the United Kingdom concludes some kind of continuing arrangement with the EU which is not as formal as EEA or EFTA membership, but which takes the form of a social, economic and political relationship and a level of co-operation and mutual obligation that is greater than that implied by a free trade agreement of the kind described immediately below. This would be the 'fudge' option, which would also reflect the need to deal with the particular problem of Northern Ireland.

- A free trade agreement with the EU, the United Kingdom being a third country for EU purposes, with the same kind of relationship with the EU as Korea, Canada and Japan, also party to bilateral free trade agreements with the EU. For both sides this would be one of only a number of bilateral free trade agreements with countries all over the world. In the case of the United Kingdom, one such agreement is proposed with the United States, a move calculated to create fresh political and constitutional problems.

It is difficult to predict at the time of writing which if any of these options is most likely to prevail at a time of what is also one of great political uncertainty, with one Prime Minister having resigned within a year of the general election in 2015, and the authority of his successor greatly diminished by an ill-fated though perhaps not unnecessary general election in 2017. Some even question whether Brexit will happen, while others point to the likelihood of a long transition period (though a transition from EU membership to what?), while others still speak about a future of regulatory alignment (but not regulatory convergence). Whatever happens, Brexit is unlikely to resolve the constitutional fall-out from Mr Cameron's manifesto commitment to hold an 'in-out' referendum, fall-out that will not be confined to the issues around the European Union (Withdrawal) Bill.

Viewed with considerable anxiety by many, Brexit is nevertheless the culmination of a process that saw the United Kingdom a reluctant and truculent member of the EU for some 45 years, unwilling initially to embrace the social agenda (which it did much thereafter to dilute) and unwilling ever to accept the single currency, which following the European Union Act 2011 would require not only parliamentary approval but also a referendum. It is unlikely nevertheless that the European Union (Withdrawal) Bill will take us into a state of permanent detachment, as a new relationship with the EU is forged and takes shape. In the meantime, however, the latter Bill should be recognised for what it is, despite the inevitable (and appropriate) high politics and intense drama with which it is associated. It is no more and no less than:

(i) adjectival law to facilitate a process,

(ii) a process which will assert the sovereignty which in the *Miller* case we are told Parliament had never in any event lost, but

(iii) a process that may nevertheless lead in due course to a divergence from the EU in the standards currently set by substantive law, though for good or ill this was surely the purpose of Brexit to enable.

Although this is neither the time nor the place for speculation, the proposal that EU membership should be replaced by multiple free trade agreements (with the EU itself and with many other third countries as well) will create many constitutional objections as great as those associated with membership of the EU, including questions relating to the rule of law and parliamentary sovereignty. The ill-fated Transatlantic Trade and Investment Partnership (TTIP – a proposed free trade agreement between the EU and the United States) was strongly opposed simply because it would empower foreign companies (investors) to challenge domestic legislation (parliamentary sovereignty) in secret arbitration forums (rule of law).

We may be about to move from one area of conflict about the nature of the legal and political sovereignty of Parliament to another, with altogether different challenges relating to legality, transparency and sovereignty.

PART II

The institutions of government

CHAPTER 7

Composition of Parliament

In this and the two following chapters, we examine the structure of Parliament, the functions of the two Houses and their privileges. Although both the House of Commons and the House of Lords meet in the palace of Westminster, they sit separately and are constituted on entirely different principles. The process of legislation is a matter in which both Houses take part and the two-chamber structure is an integral feature of the parliamentary system.

Within Parliament the House of Commons is the dominant House, as it is on the ability to command a majority in the Commons that a government depends for holding office. Under the Parliament Acts of 1911 and 1949, the formal power of the Lords in legislation is limited to imposing a temporary veto on public Bills, a power which may sometimes be an effective check on controversial legislation. The role of the Lords as a revising chamber is important, especially for securing amendments to Bills which have been subjected to timetabling in the Commons,[1] and the House serves other constitutional purposes.

The Queen is formally also part of Parliament: she opens each session of Parliament and the royal assent is necessary for primary legislation. These functions are performed on the advice of the government, but in very rare circumstances the Queen may have a personal discretion to exercise in relation to Parliament.

A. The electoral system

Acts for widening the franchise were passed in 1832, 1867, 1884, 1918, 1928, 1948 and 1969, until today the total parliamentary electorate is over 46 million.[2] The details of the earlier Acts have passed into history. In 1918 a uniform franchise based on residence was established for county and borough constituencies.[3] Votes for women over 30 were introduced in 1918 and in 1928 for women over 21, reversing the common law rule that men only were to take part in the election of members of Parliament.[4]

The voting age for men and women is now 18, though it has now been lowered to 16 for Scottish elections.[5] After 1918 various categories of person had the right to vote more than once either by reason of occupying land for business purposes or because of the right of graduates to vote in separate constituencies representing the universities. These elements of plural voting were abolished in 1948.

---

[1] Ch 8.

[2] According to the Office for National Statistics, the local government electorate is slightly higher.

[3] See Butler, *The Electoral System in Britain since 1918* and, for the law and practice today, Price, De Silva and Clayton (eds), *Parker's Law and Conduct of Elections*; also Morris, *Parliamentary Elections, Representation and the Law*.

[4] *Nairn v St Andrews University*, 1907 SLT 471, at p 473 (Lord Salvesen). See Scutt, *Women and the Magna Carta*.

[5] Scottish Elections (Reduction of Voting Age) Act 2015.

The franchise

The law is now contained in Part I of the Representation of the People Act 1983,[6] which consolidated earlier legislation and which has itself been heavily amended, notably in 1985 when the right to vote was extended to certain British citizens resident outside the United Kingdom.[7] As amended in 2000, s 1 of the 1983 Act provides that the right to vote at parliamentary elections is exercisable by all Commonwealth citizens (which in law includes all British citizens and British subjects),[8] and citizens of the Republic of Ireland who are (*a*) registered in the register of electors for the constituency in which they wish to vote; (*b*) not subject to any legal incapacity to vote (on which see below); and (*c*) of voting age (now 18 years or over).[9]

Under the 1983 Act a person is entitled to be registered in a constituency if that person is resident there and is otherwise entitled to vote.[10] There is not now a qualifying period of residence before an elector may register in a particular constituency (except in Northern Ireland where the elector must be resident in the Province – not necessarily a particular constituency – for at least three months);[11] and it is no longer necessary to be resident in the constituency on a particular date (which until the 2000 amendments used to be 10 October, which was referred to as the qualifying date). The meaning of residence for electoral purposes is governed by the 1983 Act, s 5 (as amended).[12]

No one may vote more than once at a parliamentary election.[13] The parliamentary franchise may not be exercised by:

(*a*) persons who are subject to legal incapacity (such as those who because of mental illness, drunkenness or infirmity lack the capacity at the moment of voting to understand what they are about to do);[14]

(*b*) persons who are neither Commonwealth citizens nor citizens of the Republic of Ireland;[15]

(*c*) persons who have not attained the age of 18 by the date of the poll;[16]

---

[6] The Act has been heavily amended since enactment, notably by the Representation of the People Act 2000, the Political Parties, Elections and Referendums Act 2000, the Electoral Administration Act 2006, the Political Parties and Elections Act 2009 and the Recall of MPs Act 2015. Although the amendments are taken in below, the specific sources of the amendments are not identified.

[7] Representation of the People Act 1985, s 1; amended by the Political Parties, Elections and Referendums Act 2000 (PPERA), s 141, reducing from 20 to 15 years the period during which British citizens formerly resident in this country may continue to be registered to vote. See *R (Preston)* v *Wandsworth LBC* [2012] EWCA Civ 1378, [2013] QB 687 (loss of vote after 15 years not a breach of EU freedom of movement principles), and *Shindler* v *United Kingdom*, Application 19840/09, 9 September 2013 (loss of vote after 15 years not a breach of ECHR). Also *R (Shindler)* v *Chancellor of Duchy of Lancaster* [2016] EWCA Civ 469, [2017] QB 226 (referendum).

[8] See British Nationality Act 1981, s 37.

[9] Representation of the People Act 1983 (RPA), s 1.

[10] Ibid, s 4 (as amended).

[11] Ibid.

[12] On which see *Scott* v *Phillips* 1974 SLT 32 (ownership of a country cottage as a second home may not be enough to make the owner resident there); and *Hipperson* v *Newbury Registration Officer* [1985] QB 1060 (Greenham Common women at peace camp held to be resident for electoral purposes).

[13] RPA, s 1(2).

[14] Ibid, s 1(1)(b) (as amended). Nor may anyone vote on behalf of someone disqualified for lack of capacity: Mental Capacity Act 2005, s 29.

[15] RPA, s 1(1)(c) (as amended). Citizens of the European Union resident in the United Kingdom may vote and stand in local government elections and in elections to the European Parliament.

[16] RPA Act, s 1(1)(d) (as amended).

(*d*) persons convicted of a criminal offence and detained in a penal institution in pursuance of a sentence.[17] Remand prisoners may vote if they are on the register, and at the general election in 2005 prisoners who were part of an intermittent custody scheme were also permitted to vote;[18]

(*e*) persons detained in mental hospitals under statutory authority, including the Mental Health Act 1983 and the Criminal Procedure (Insanity) Act 1964;[19]

(*f*) persons who are members of the House of Lords. Hereditary peers were previously disqualified; but they may now vote in a parliamentary election unless they have retained a place in the Lords by virtue of the House of Lords Act 1999;[20]

(*g*) persons convicted of corrupt or illegal practices at elections, the extent of disqualification depending on the nature of the offence.[21]

The most controversial of these disqualifications is (*d*): it is not clear why convicted prisoners should automatically be denied the right to vote.[22] Although the domestic courts held that the restriction did not breach the Human Rights Act,[23] in *Hirst* v *United Kingdom (No 2)*[24] the Strasbourg court found that the blanket disqualification of convicted prisoners breached art 3 of the First Protocol to the Convention, noting that it applied automatically irrespective of the length of the prisoner's sentence, and irrespective of the nature and gravity of the offence.[25] But although the Strasbourg court has re-affirmed the position since *Hirst (No 2)*,[26] successive governments have been unwilling to comply with Convention obligations, and at the time of writing the disqualification of prisoners remains in force.[27] Art 3 of Protocol 1 does not apply to referendums.[28]

---

[17] Ibid, s 3.

[18] RPA, s 7A (inserted by RPA 2000, s 5) – place of detention to be treated as a place of residence.

[19] Ibid, s 3A (as amended).

[20] House of Lords Act 1999, s 3. If a retained hereditary peer either resigns or is expelled, the disqualification from the franchise (and membership of the House of Commons) will cease to apply: House of Lords Reform Act 2014. See p 185 below.

[21] RPA, ss 160, 173.

[22] For the position in Canada, see *Sauve* v *Canada (No 1)* [1992] 2 SCR 438, and *Sauve* v *Canada (No 2)* [2002] SCR 519.

[23] *R (Pearson)* v *Home Secretary, The Times*, 17 April 2001.

[24] Application No 74025/01.

[25] *Hirst* v *United Kingdom (No 2)* [2005] ECHR 681, (2006) 42 EHRR 41. See also *Smith* v *Scott* 2007 SLT 137 (declaration of incompatibility re RPA, s 3). But see *R (Chester)* v *Lord President of the Council* [2013] UKSC, [2013] 3 WLR 376 (accepted that UK law in breach of ECHR, but no need for a fresh declaration of incompatibility in light of *Smith* v *Scott*, above; see ch 14 below for fuller consideration of this important case).

[26] *Greens* v *United Kingdom* [2010] ECHR 868; *Scoppola* v *Italy (No 3)* [2012] ECHR 868. But see *Firth* v *United Kingdom* [2014] ECHR 274 and *McHugh* v *United Kingdom* [2015] ECHR 155 (breach re-affirmed, no compensation and no costs), which effectively ends the matter.

[27] But see HL Paper 103, HC 924 (2013–14): 'all prisoners serving sentences of 12 months or less should be entitled to vote in all UK parliamentary, local and European elections; and moreover that prisoners should be entitled to apply, up to 6 months before their scheduled release date, to be registered to vote in the constituency into which they are due to be released' (Joint Committee on the Draft Voting Eligibility (Prisoners) Bill 2013 – Report). Subsequent developments are outlined in HC Library, *Prisoners' Voting Rights: Developments since May 2015* (CBP 7461, 2016).

[28] *Moohan* v *United Kingdom*, Appn No 22962/15, 13 June 2017 (ban from voting in Scottish independence referendum not a breach), upholding majority in *Moohan* v *Lord Advocate* [2014] UKSC 67.

The register of electors

As already pointed out, it is a condition precedent to exercising the vote that the elector should be entered in the register of electors. The register is prepared by the registration officer of each constituency, who in England and Wales is appointed by each district council or London borough.[29] Each registration officer was traditionally required to conduct an annual canvass of the area to determine who is entitled to be on the register, and to take all necessary steps to maintain the register in what was a system of household voter registration, whereby every household is responsible for registering the electors in the household in question.

The canvass for any year was typically conducted between October and December, and a revised version of the register was then published in December each year.[30] But it was also possible for an elector to be added to the register between annual canvasses. The principle of the 'rolling register' was introduced in 2000, designed to remove obstacles to registration and voting. We have thus moved from what was referred to as a 'fixed register' (amended annually) to a 'rolling register' (amended constantly): the former may be said to be more sensitive to the needs of the administration responsible for maintaining the register; and the latter more responsive to the interests of electors. Although a long-established practice, household voter registration is, nevertheless, susceptible to electoral fraud.

In their programme for government in 2010, the Conservative–Lib Dem Coalition undertook to 'reduce electoral fraud by speeding up the implementation of individual voter registration'.[31] Initiatives to promote this undertaking are to be found in the Electoral Registration and Administration Act 2013, which sets in train the move towards individual rather than household registration of electors (s 1). This, however, is not a wholly uncontroversial initiative, as it is thought by some that individual registration will lead to fewer people being registered, and to fewer people being eligible to vote as a result. The Electoral Registration and Administration Act 2013 does, nevertheless, retain the annual canvass of households at least for the time being, with the Act also conferring a power on the appropriate Minister to abolish it by order (s 7(2)).

While the duty to carry out the annual canvass continues, the registration officer must invite people in his or her area to apply for registration, 'if (a) the officer is aware of the person's name and address, (b) the person is not registered in the register, and (c) the officer has reason to believe that the person may be entitled to be registered in the register' (RPA, s 9E). In a notable provision, the Act also provides that a registration officer may follow an 'invitation to register' with a 'requirement to register', after complying with prescribed requirements set out in regulations (ibid, s 9E(6)(b)) Failure to comply with the requirement to register may lead to the registration officer imposing a civil penalty (ibid, s 9E(7)), in accordance with a procedure to be set out in regulations, with a right of appeal to the First-tier tribunal.[32]

Conduct of elections

The proceedings at parliamentary elections are conducted in accordance with the Parliamentary Elections Rules in Schedule 1 of the 1983 Act. These detailed rules deal with the nomination of candidates, as well as the procedure to be followed at the polling station and in particular the secrecy of the ballot. Normally voting takes place in person at a convenient polling station allotted by the returning officer.[33] In 2014 the Electoral Commission

---

[29] RPA, s 8.
[30] Ibid, s 13 (as amended).
[31] See also Cm 8108, 2011.
[32] RPA, s 9E was inserted by Electoral Registration and Administration Act 2013, s 5.
[33] RPA, Sch 1(25).

recommended that electors should be required to present an acceptable form of identity at polling stations.[34]

The registration officer must grant an application to vote by proxy where the applicant is a registered service voter; blind or suffers another physical disability; is unable to attend the polling station because of work or educational commitments; or unable to go to the polling station in person without making a journey by sea or air (as in the case of overseas voters).[35] The Representation of the People Act 2000 relaxed the rules with the aim of enabling more people to vote by post if they so wish. Under the existing rules, the registration officer must grant an application to vote by post if satisfied that the elector is registered,[36] and otherwise meets prescribed statutory requirements.[37] The increased use of postal voting has been controversial. Apart from the failures of the postal system,[38] it has given rise to concerns about irregularity, and fraud, leading to claims about the harvesting of votes.[39]

Responsibility for the official conduct of an election in each constituency rests with the returning officer, who in England and Wales in the case of a county constituency wholly contained within the area of a county council is the sheriff, and in the case of a borough constituency wholly contained within a local government district is the chairman of the district council.[40] Most functions of the returning officer are, however, discharged by the registration officer or by an appointed deputy. Certain matters, for example the declaration of the poll, may be reserved for the returning officer. The official costs of an election, as distinct from the expenses of the candidates, are paid out of public funds in accordance with a scale prescribed by the Treasury.

In the past, office-holders who conducted elections did not always exercise their functions impartially. In the great case of *Ashby* v *White*, the Mayor of Aylesbury as returning officer wrongfully refused to allow Ashby to vote, and Ashby sued him for damages. The House of Lords upheld the view of Holt CJ (dissenting in the Queen's Bench) that the remedy of damages should be given. In Holt's words: 'To allow this action will make public officers more careful to observe the constitution of cities and boroughs, and not to be so partial as they commonly are in all elections.'[41] Today, officials concerned with the conduct of elections are required to carry out their duties impartially and are subject to criminal penalties if they do not, but they cannot be sued for damages if breach of official duty is alleged.[42]

B. Distribution of constituencies

Before 1832, the composition of the unreformed House of Commons was based on the general principle that every county and borough in England and Wales was entitled to be represented by two members. A similar principle applied to Scottish representation at Westminster, subject to the limit of numbers imposed in the Treaty of Union, which led to the grouping of certain shires and royal burghs for this purpose. Representation thus depended on the status

---

[34] Electoral Commission, *Electoral Fraud in the UK* (2014). Also E Pickles, *Securing the Ballot* (2016).
[35] RPA, Sch 4(3).
[36] Representation of the People Act 2000, Sch 4(3).
[37] SI 2001 No 341, Part IV.
[38] *Knight* v *Nicholls* [2004] EWCA Civ 68, [2004] 1 WLR 1653 (election not invalidated by late arrival of voting papers).
[39] See *R (Afzal)* v *Election Court* [2005] EWCA (Civ) 647. A number of anti-fraud measures were introduced by the Electoral Administration Act 2006, s 14.
[40] Ibid, s 24(1).
[41] (1703) 2 Ld Raym 938, 956.
[42] RPA, s 63.

of the unit of local government and bore no regard to population. Counties such as Cornwall, which contained many tiny boroughs, were grossly over-represented by comparison with areas of rapidly growing industrial population.

From the Reform Act 1832 onwards, successive measures of redistributing constituencies to remove glaring differences were undertaken, usually at the same time as reforms in the franchise were made.[43] Only since 1917 has there been general acceptance of the principle of broad mathematical equality in the size of constituencies,[44] and only since 1945 has there been permanent machinery to enable boundaries to be adjusted from time to time to take account of the shifting population and to avoid excessive disparities developing between constituencies. The legislation has sought to establish impartial machinery, but in practice the system has not operated without controversy.

The current system does not try to achieve strict arithmetical equality between constituencies, but lays emphasis also on the territorial aspect of representation, on the link between the elected member and his or her constituency, and on the desirability of parliamentary boundaries not clashing with local government boundaries. The degree of discretion built into the system of electoral apportionment makes it particularly necessary to ensure that the machinery is impartial and charges of gerrymandering are avoided. As the late Aneurin Bevan once said, there was 'nothing that could undermine the authority of Parliament more than that people outside should feel that the constitutional mechanism by which the House of Commons is elected has been framed so as to favour one party in the State'.[45]

Boundary review

By the Parliamentary Constituencies Act 1986, there are four permanent boundary commissions, for England, Wales, Scotland and Northern Ireland. These commissions are 'independent, non-political, and impartial' bodies which 'emphasise that the results of previous elections do not, and should not, enter into [their] considerations'.[46] The Speaker is the chairman of each commission but in practice does not sit, and a judge from the appropriate High Court (in Scotland, from the Court of Session) is appointed deputy chairman of each commission. Each commission includes two other members, those for England being appointed by ministers, as well as two official assessors, those for England being the Registrar General and the Director General of Ordnance Survey.

The commissions must undertake a general review of constituencies in that part of the United Kingdom assigned to them, at intervals of what is now no more than five years, having initially been 10–15 years under the 1986 Act (s 3(2)).[47] There is an additional power 'from time to time' to address concerns relating to any particular constituency (s 3(3)). Notice must be given to the constituencies affected by any provisional recommendations (s 5(2)). If objections to the proposed changes are received from an interested local authority or from a body of at least 100 electors, a local inquiry must be held into the recommendations (s 6), which may lead to the preliminary recommendations being varied.

The 1986 Act, by s 3(5), imposes a duty on the Secretary of State, 'as soon as may be after a Boundary Commission has submitted a report', to lay the report before Parliament together with a draft Order in Council for giving effect, with or without modifications, to the recommendations

---

[43] Butler, note 3 above, app II.
[44] Report of Speaker's Conference, Cd 8463, 1917; Report of Committee on Electoral Machinery, Cmd 6408, 1943.
[45] HC Deb, 15 December 1954, col 1872.
[46] Boundary Commission for England, *Annual Report 2008/2009* (2009), p 4.
[47] Boundary Commissions Act 1992, and subs Parliamentary Voting System and Constituencies Act 2011, and the Electoral Registration and Administration Act 2013, on both of which see below.

in the report (reasons must be given to Parliament for any modifications). The draft Order must be approved by resolution of each House before the final Order can be made by the Queen in Council. The validity of any Order in Council which purports to be made under the 1986 Act and recites that approval was given by each House is not to be called into question in any legal proceedings.[48]

The 1986 Act contains the rules which the commissions must observe in redistributing seats. At the time of writing the Act states that there shall be 600 constituencies, though there are in fact 650.[49] Following devolution, it is no longer the case that Scotland must be represented by at least 71 seats,[50] and in 2005 Scottish representation at Westminster was reduced from 72 to 59,[51] in the process reducing the number of seats in the House of Commons from 659 to 646 (restored to 650 in 2010). The legislation provides for the calculation of a separate electoral quota for each of England, Scotland, Wales and Northern Ireland, the quota to be determined by dividing the total electorate by the number of constituencies at the time the review begins.

Until the changes introduced by the Coalition government (see below), each commission was bound to secure that the electorate of a constituency was as near the relevant electoral quota as practicable, having regard to certain other rules, for example, that parliamentary constituencies should as far as practicable not cross certain local government boundaries. Strict application of these principles could be departed from for geographical reasons; and account was to be taken of inconveniences that could follow the alteration of boundaries. The commissions thus had a broad discretion to decide how much priority should be given to achieving arithmetical equality between constituencies.[52]

The politics of boundary review

General reviews were completed by the four boundary commissions in 1954, 1969, 1982, 1994 and 2006. In 1954 the review resulted in the abolition of six constituencies and the creation of 11 new ones, all in England, to bring membership of the House up to 630. As well as other difficulties experienced by the English commission,[53] the method of calculating the electoral quota for England under what was then the House of Commons (Redistribution of Seats) Act 1949 resulted in the draft Orders in Council being challenged in the courts. In *Harper* v *Home Secretary*,[54] however, the Court of Appeal expressed reluctance to interfere in these matters, though such intervention was not ruled out where the commissions had made recommendations manifestly in complete disregard of the Act, which was not the position in this case. In 1954 the government gave effect without modification to the recommendations of the four commissions.

Events took a different turn in 1969 when the next general review was completed. The commission for England proposed major changes to 271 constituencies and five new constituencies for England. At the time the commissions submitted their reports, a radical reorganisation of local government in England (outside Greater London) and in Wales was in train, and the Labour government decided that revision of parliamentary boundaries should

....
[48] 1986 Act, s 4(7).

[49] Ibid, Sch 2. This was to be reduced to 600 by the Parliamentary Voting System and Constituencies Act 2011, subject to the Electoral Registration and Administration Act 2013, on which see below.

[50] Scotland Act 1998, s 86.

[51] SI 2005 No 250 (S1).

[52] *R* v *Boundary Commission for England, ex p Foot* [1983] QB 600.

[53] D E Butler (1955) 33 *Public Administration* 125.

[54] [1955] Ch 238, 251. See also Marshall and Moodie, *Some Problems of the Constitution*, ch 5; and S A de Smith (1955) 18 MLR 281.

wait until local government had been reorganised. The government therefore delayed laying the commissions' reports in Parliament and instead introduced a Bill which gave effect only to the changes affecting Greater London and a few abnormally large constituencies elsewhere. The government thus sought by legislation to depart from its obligations under the House of Commons (Redistribution of Seats) Acts 1949 and 1958.

The Bill passed the Commons against severe criticism but was drastically amended by the Lords, and was abandoned by the government when in October 1969 that House refused to give way to the Commons. An elector for the borough of Enfield then sought an order of mandamus from the High Court requiring the Home Secretary to perform his statutory duty of laying before Parliament the commission reports together with draft Orders in Council.[55] Thereupon the Home Secretary laid before Parliament the reports and the draft Orders in Council, but invited the Commons to reject them, using the government majority for this purpose. By this tangled course of events, the Labour government succeeded in postponing the much-needed adjustments of constituency boundaries until after the 1970 general election, following which the new Conservative government promptly secured parliamentary approval to the changes recommended in 1969.

Some MPs complained that Parliament had fettered its hands by setting up the boundary commissions and argued that Parliament must retain the right to make the final decisions. But the Conservative Home Secretary in the 1970s considered it 'enormously important' that Parliament comply with the impartial recommendations of the four commissions.[56] In 1983 the general review again led to extensive changes in constituencies, with seats in Great Britain being increased by ten and the total in the House rising to 650. The Labour party leader challenged the English changes in the High Court, but with no success.[57] There were no legal challenges to either the fourth or fifth reviews completed in 1994 and 2006 respectively, the latter leading to the House of Commons membership being restored to 650, after having been reduced since 1983.

The current uncertainty

The Parliamentary Voting System and Constituencies Act 2011 radically amended the Parliamentary Constituencies Act 1986 by proposing to increase the frequency of boundary reviews, from periods of between eight and twelve years, to a period of every five years. In proposing to reduce the number of parliamentary constituencies to 600, the Parliamentary Voting System and Constituencies Act 2011 also introduced new principles to secure a more equal distribution of constituencies, which was to be completed by October 2013. This reflected a much cherished ambition on the part of the Conservative party in particular to create electoral boundaries that would place greater emphasis on numerical equality at the expense of geographical logic, reflecting a concern that the existing arrangements gave an undue advantage to the Labour party.

The implementation of these measures was, however, thwarted by the withdrawal of support for them by Liberal Democrats in the Coalition government. This followed a disagreement between the two governing parties about the implementation of the government's agreed proposals for constitutional reform, the Liberal Democrat resistance to boundary change being seen as retaliation for Conservative resistance to House of Lords reform (on which see below). The 2015 and 2017 general elections were thus fought on the old boundaries, which in the former case at least did not appear seriously to impair the Conservatives, who

---

[55] *R* v *Home Secretary, ex p McWhirter*, *The Times*, 21 October 1969. The application was dismissed in view of the Home Secretary's action in October 1969 in laying the reports and draft Orders in Parliament.

[56] HC Deb, 28 October 1970, col 241 ff.

[57] *R* v *Boundary Commission for England, ex p Foot* [1983] QB 600.

were thought to be the most likely beneficiaries of a smaller House of Commons based on more equal electoral boundaries.

This disagreement found formal expression in the Electoral Registration and Administration Act 2013, which by s 6 amends the Parliamentary Voting System and Constituencies Act 2011 by providing that there should be no boundary review until 2018. The process by which the latter provision was introduced was thought to be significant constitutionally, the government splitting on party lines in voting for (Liberal Democrat) and against (Conservative) it. In supporting an amendment to a government Bill, this was 'the first time in [the] Parliament [elected in 2010] that ministers in either house have voted against the government'. The Prime Minister's spokesman was also reported as having said that 'the application of collective responsibility has been set aside' for the Electoral Registration and Administration Bill.[58]

The Electoral Registration and Administration Act 2013, s 6, did not repeal the changes introduced by the 2011 Act: it simply postponed their implementation until after the general election in 2015. It was expected that the provisions of the 2011 Act would be fully brought into force if the Conservative party won a majority at that election, but that it would be either repealed or heavily amended if the Labour party had been successful. In the event, the Conservative party majority was squandered at the unexpected election in 2017, raising fresh doubts about whether the 2011 Act will now be implemented, even though at the time of writing the Boundary Commissions have completed draft reviews under the new principles.[59]

C. Political parties

Central to the role of modern democracy are political parties: they provide the policies and personnel of government (and opposition) and have other important functions as well.[60] Although electors vote for individuals to represent them in Parliament, the candidates will typically be chosen by a political party. It is unusual for a candidate who is not representing one of the established parties to be elected to Parliament,[61] or for an independent to be elected.[62] The parties also dominate appointments to the House of Lords.

Yet political parties remain voluntary associations in the eyes of the law: bodies exercising a public function but governed by private law.[63] The relationship between a political party and its members is one based on contract, and the contract may be enforced in the courts by an aggrieved member.[64] Cases arise from time to time from individuals disputing (i) internal elections;[65] (ii) their expulsion from the party in breach of its rules; and (iii) the selection of a party's

---

[58] *The Guardian*, 29 January 2013. The Deputy Prime Minister was reported earlier as having said that 'conventions mutate and change over time': *Daily Telegraph*, 3 September 2012.

[59] *The Guardian*, 6 September 2017.

[60] See Fisher, *British Political Parties*, pp 194–9, and Webb, *The Modern British Party System*.

[61] In 2001 and again in 2005 a seat was won by a party registered as the Independent Hospital and Health Concern, while in 2005 a seat was won by Respect, a new party.

[62] In 1997 the broadcaster Martin Bell was famously elected as an independent for Tatton, while in 2005 Peter Law was elected as an independent for Blaenau Gwent. The last time an independent was elected was Dai Davies at a by-election (also Blaenau Gwent) in 2006.

[63] But see on the special and complex position of the Conservative Party, *Conservative and Unionist Central Office* v *Burrell* [1982] 2 All ER 1.

[64] See *Foster* v *McNichol* [2016] EWHC 1966 (QB) (unsuccessful attempt by a member to challenge right of Mr Corbyn to stand as Labour leadership candidate). And subsequently, *Evangelou* v *McNichol* [2016] EWHC 2058 (QB) (on right to vote in the leadership election)..

[65] *Foster* and *Evangelou*, ibid.

candidate for election to public office.[66] In one case it was held that all-women shortlists for the selection of parliamentary candidates were contrary to the Sex Discrimination Act 1975.[67]

All-women shortlists had been introduced by the Labour party for the selection of some candidates in order to increase the number of women MPs, and the practice was restored following the Sex Discrimination (Election Candidates) Act 2002, the provisions of which now expire in 2030 unless renewed. Provisions in the Equality Act 2010 allow political parties more generally to take steps to promote the candidature of under-represented groups within the party. Otherwise, however, discrimination by political parties in the selection of candidates is likely to be unlawful under the Equality Act 2010, as it was under the legislation that the latter replaced.[68]

Registration of political parties

Provision for the registration of political parties was first made in 1998,[69] and is now to be found in the Political Parties, Elections and Referendums Act 2000.[70] Registration was first introduced in anticipation of the elections to the European Parliament for which a new electoral system was introduced by the European Elections Act 1999. This was known as a party list system whereby members are elected from large regional constituencies in proportion to the votes cast in favour of the different parties in the region in question. For this system to work effectively, it was thought that only registered political parties should take part.

Registration is now important for other reasons. Only candidates representing a registered party may be nominated for election; other candidates must be nominated as independents or without description.[71] This overcomes an irritant of British elections whereby individuals would present themselves in a manner calculated to confuse electors, as in one case where a candidate stood as a Literal Democrat, causing confusion with the Liberal Democrat.[72] The other principal reason why registration is important relates to party political broadcasts, which broadcasters now may carry only if made by registered parties.[73]

It is important to stress that registration of political parties is not compulsory, but that it is necessary in order to enjoy a number of prescribed benefits. There is no definition of a political party for this purpose, with registration being open to any association that declares that it intends to contest one or more 'relevant elections' in Great Britain or Northern Ireland.[74] There are separate registers for Great Britain and Northern Ireland. A party seeking registration must register its principal office-holders (including its leader and treasurer) and its financial structure.[75] The latter obligation is in pursuance of a requirement that the parties adopt a scheme approved by the Electoral Commission which 'sets out the arrangements for regulating the financial affairs of the party'.[76]

---

[66] *Lewis* v *Heffer* [1978] 1 WLR 1061; *Weir* v *Hermon* [2001] NIJB 260; *Mortimer* v *Labour Party*, *The Independent*, 28 February 2000; and *Donaldson* v *Empey* [2004] NIJB 1.

[67] *Jepson* v *Labour Party* [1996] IRLR 116.

[68] *Ahsan* v *Watt* [2007] UKHL 51, [2008] AC 696.

[69] Registration of Political Parties Act 1998; for comment, see O Gay [2001] PL 245.

[70] For a fuller account of the Act (hereafter PPERA), see K D Ewing [2001] PL 542.

[71] PPERA, ss 22 and 28.

[72] *Sanders* v *Chichester* (1994) SJ 225.

[73] PPERA, s 37.

[74] Ibid, ss 22 and 28.

[75] Ibid, ss 24–7.

[76] Ibid, s 26(2). Where the party is composed of a number of separate 'accounting units' (such as the headquarters and each constituency party or association, as is the practice with the main parties), the treasurer of each accounting unit must also be registered (s 27).

An application for registration must be made to the Electoral Commission and must be granted unless the proposed name (i) is the same (or sufficiently similar to cause confusion) as that of a party already registered; (ii) comprises more than six words; (iii) is obscene or offensive; (iv) includes words which if published would be likely to amount to the commission of an offence; (v) includes any script other than Roman; or (vi) includes any words or expression prohibited by order made by the Secretary of State.[77] A registered party may also register three emblems to be used on ballot papers.[78] At the general election in 2010, no fewer than 134 registered parties fielded a total of 4,152 candidates,[79] which in both cases represented an increase on the election in 2005.

Funding of political parties

The funding of political parties has been a constant source of controversy.[80] The obligations of parties are such that it is not possible for them to rely on the subscriptions of members alone. Concern is frequently expressed about large private donations to political parties, which are sometimes associated with allegations of corruption.[81] There are also concerns that governments intervene in ways designed to secure partisan advantage. These concerns resurfaced with the enactment of the Trade Union Act 2016,[82] which changes the rules regulating the way trade unions collect contributions to their political funds, in a way calculated to ensure that trade unions will have less money available to support the Labour party.[83]

All donations to a political party in excess of £7,500 nationally, and £1,500 locally must be reported to the Electoral Commission on a quarterly basis,[84] with the names of donors and the amount of donation published by the Electoral Commission.[85] Donations may only be received from a permissible donor, defined to mean individuals who are on the electoral register in this country, or organisations (such as companies and trade unions) that are based here and conduct business and activity here.[86] The aim is to stop the foreign funding of British political parties, although as we have seen it is possible to be resident overseas and yet be on the electoral register, while it is also possible to be a resident in the United Kingdom and yet not be on the electoral register.[87]

....

[77] Ibid, s 28(4).

[78] Ibid, s 29.

[79] But many of these parties will have fielded candidates in only a small number of constituencies.

[80] See Ewing, *The Funding of Political Parties in Britain*, Ewing, *The Cost of Democracy*, and Pinto–Duschinsky, *British Political Finance 1830–1980*.

[81] Under the Honours (Prevention of Abuses) Act 1925 it is an offence to make or receive a donation in return for an honour. But the problems of proof are overwhelming.

[82] K D Ewing and J Hendy (2016) 45 ILJ 391.

[83] For background, see House of Lords Select Committee on Trade Union Political Funds and Political Party Funding, HL Paper 106 (2015–16).

[84] Political Parties, Elections and Referendums Act 2000, ss 62, 63. The Act was passed to implement the recommendations of the Committee on Standards in Public Life, Cm 4057, 1998. See L Klein (1999) 31 *Case Western Reserve Journal of International Law*. Before the changes made by the Political Parties and Elections Act 2009, the reporting thresholds were £5,000 and £1,000 respectively.

[85] Ibid, ss 69, 149. The information is made available by the Electoral Commission on its website: www. electoralcommission.org.uk. It is possible to track the main donors to the parties. The information is also reported in the press on a quarterly basis.

[86] PPERA, s 54. Additional restrictions were introduced by the Political Parties and Elections Act 2009 (ss 10, 11) prohibiting donations (and loans) from persons not resident in the United Kingdom for income tax purposes (so-called 'non-doms').

[87] *R (Electoral Commission)* v *City of Westminster Magistrates' Court and UKIP* [2010] UKSC 40, [2010] 3 WLR 705, where it was held by a majority that impermissible donations under PPERA, s 58 need not be forfeited where the donor was an eligible voter who was not on the electoral register (and thus an impermissible donor) by virtue of an administrative oversight.

A major political storm broke early in 2006 relating to the funding of political parties, when the Labour and Conservative parties were forced to reveal that they had accepted secret loans to finance their general election campaigns in 2005. In the case of the Labour party, 12 wealthy businessmen had loaned just under £14 million, while the Conservatives revealed loans of just under £16 million from 12 individuals and one company, and repaid another £5 million to anonymous lenders who did not wish publicly to be identified. The Liberal Democrats also admitted to having received loans, though on a much smaller scale. Apart from the secrecy of the loans, allegations were made that loans to the Labour party in particular had been made in return for the promise of a peerage.

Indeed, four of Labour's lenders were nominated for peerages without the House of Lords Appointments Commission being informed of the loans. Three of the nominees were vetoed by the Commission on other grounds; a fourth was rejected when the Commission was made aware of the undisclosed loan. The 'cash for honours' affair sparked a highly controversial police investigation into whether there had been a breach of the Honours (Prevention of Abuses) Act 1925 or the Political Parties, Elections and Referendums Act 2000. Although there were no prosecutions under either Act, the affair did, nevertheless, lead to (i) a change in the law, so that political parties must (under the Electoral Administration Act 2006) now report loans as well as donations to the Electoral Commission, and perhaps to (ii) a more active approach by the Commission in its supervision of the political parties.

State support for political parties

In many countries, political parties receive annual subventions of public funds to enable them more effectively to perform their functions without the need for excessive reliance on wealthy private donors.[88] In other countries the parties are assisted by the provision of income tax relief for donations to political parties, designed to encourage more people to make small donations. A scheme for public funding of political parties was proposed by the Houghton committee as long ago as 1976 but never implemented;[89] and proposals by the Committee on Standards in Public Life (Neill committee) in 1998 for income tax relief for small contributions to political parties were rejected by the government.[90] Media disquiet about large donations to the parties periodically revives interest in public funding, to relieve the parties of the need to rely on such donations.

The case for public funding of political parties was rejected by the Electoral Commission in 2004, mainly for lack of public support and because of opposition from the two main parties.[91] Nevertheless, fresh proposals for public funding of political parties were made several years later by Sir Hayden Phillips, a retired civil servant who had been appointed by the then Prime Minister to look at the matter again in the light of the 'cash for honours' crisis. But although producing a well-thought-out scheme,[92] like others before and since, Sir Hayden was unable to secure all-party agreement for his proposals. At a time of public funding cuts, financial support for political parties is unlikely to be a popular priority for any government in the near future.[93]

---

[88] Ewing and Issacharoff (eds) *Party Funding and Campaign Financing in International Perspective* (chapters on New Zealand, Australia, Canada, United States and Japan), and Ewing, Rowbottom and Tham (eds), *The Funding of Political Parties – Where Now?* (chapters on EU members states, United States, Canada, United Kingdom, Australia and New Zealand).

[89] Cmnd 6601, 1976.

[90] HC Deb, 10 January 2000, col 114 (Mr Mike O'Brien).

[91] Electoral Commission, *The Funding of Political Parties* (2004).

[92] Sir Hayden Phillips, *Strengthening Democracy: Fair and Sustainable Funding of Political Parties* (2007). See also HC 163 (2006–7).

[93] Nevertheless fresh proposals for public funding – building on Hayden Phillips – were later made by the Committee on Standards in Public Life: Cm 8208, 2011. But these too failed to win the necessary support.

This is not to say that there is no state support for political parties in Britain, although it is limited when compared to some other countries. Parliamentary candidates are provided with free postage for one election communication and are permitted to use school halls for election meetings free of charge,[94] though in practice the latter appears rarely to be taken up in an era when there are more effective ways of reaching the electorate. Free time is made available to the political parties for party political broadcasts and party election broadcasts by both the BBC and the independent broadcasters, a facility which in the latter case exists as a matter of statutory obligation.[95] The amount of time made available for the parties is determined by the broadcasters in consultation with the parties.[96]

Finally, public money is made available to the opposition parties in Parliament to assist them in the performance of their parliamentary activities;[97] and a relatively small sum of money (£2m) is now available for distribution to eligible parties (those with parliamentary representation) to assist with policy development.[98] In the case of the former the amounts involved are not inconsiderable, the principal opposition party now receiving in excess of £6.5m annually,[99] with correspondingly smaller sums being made available to the other opposition parties in Parliament.[100] The Public Administration Select Committee expressed concern about the lack of effective scrutiny to ensure that the money is spent only for parliamentary purposes,[101] and the audit and accounting procedures have been tightened up as a result.[102]

There is also provision for the public funding of campaign groups (up to £600,000 for each side) in the event of a national referendum.[103] This did not apply to the Scottish independence referendum in 2014, but it did apply to the Brexit referendum in 2016.

D. The conduct of elections

There is now a substantial body of law to regulate both local and national election campaigns. There are a number of objectives which legislation must promote, with the overriding objective being the need to maintain public confidence in the fairness and integrity of the electoral process.[104] So it is necessary to ensure that neither electors nor candidates are subject to improper influences or pressures, and necessary also to ensure that there is a measure of

---

[94] RPA, ss 91, 95.

[95] Communications Act 2003, s 333. See pp 164–6 in this chapter.

[96] For an account of the arrangements, see L Klein at note 84 above.

[97] These are the so-called Short and Cranborne monies for the House of Commons and House of Lords respectively. See Cm 4057, 1998, ch 9.

[98] PPERA, s 12.

[99] This includes an allowance of £789,146 for the Leader of the Opposition (as at 1 April 2017). Ten parties qualify overall, at a total cost of just over £9 million. Just under £1m is allocated to the Labour, Liberal Democrat and Cross Bench peers under the Cranborne scheme.

[100] A similar scheme operates in the Scottish Parliament: SI 1999 No 1745.

[101] HC 238 (1999–2000); HC 293 (2000–1). There is also uncertainty about what is covered by the term parliamentary purposes.

[102] See now R Kelly, *Short Money* (House of Commons Library Briefing Paper 1663 (2016)), pp 15–16.

[103] PPERA, s 110. Provision is also made for referendum campaign broadcasts (ibid). Cf on the latter, *Wilson v IBA* 1979 SC 351.

[104] For a powerful case arguing the need to re-assess electoral law as an autonomous body of law, see H Green (2017) 27 *King's Law Journal* 173.

equality of arms between candidates representing major strands of opinion. In addition, it has been acknowledged judicially that there is a need

> to achieve a level financial playing field between competing candidates, so as to prevent perversion of the voters' democratic choice between competing candidates within constituencies by significant disparities of local expenditure. At the constituency level it is the voters' perception of the personality and policies of the candidates, and the parties which they represent, which is intended to be reflected in the voting, not the weight of the parties' expenditure on local electioneering.[105]

It is important also that no party is able to secure an electoral advantage because of its greater financial resources or because it has better access to radio and television. British law has thus developed detailed (yet not always effective) rules to help promote electoral fairness between the main parties and to reduce the influence of money in electoral politics. But because campaigning is expensive (yet of contestable effect), money cannot be removed completely from the conduct of campaigns. There will thus inevitably be disagreements about the content of some of the regulatory means which have been chosen to control its influence.

Local spending limits

Under the Representation of the People Act 1983, Part II, every candidate must appoint an election agent; a candidate may appoint himself or herself to act in that capacity. There are now restrictions on who may donate to candidates,[106] but the most important control is the limit on candidates' election expenses in the 1983 Act, s 76, knowingly to breach which is an illegal practice. First introduced in 1883, the amount that may be spent by a candidate 'on account of or in respect of the conduct or management of the election' depends on the number of electors in the constituency and on whether it is a borough or county constituency. But in 2017 a maximum sum of £13,000 in a median constituency with an electorate of 72,000 would be about right.[107] As a result of changes introduced in 2000, the limit applies only during the period an individual declares himself or herself to be a candidate, which means that there were no limits on prospective candidates' spending before the announcement.

Steps to address this problem were taken by the Political Parties and Elections Act 2009 (s 21), which applies an additional spending limit to people who are to become candidates. This very complicated limit is designed to deal with spending in the six months or so before an election when the campaign heats up, but before the candidate formally declares. However, the limit applies only from the 55th month of an existing Parliament, which means that while they applied at the general election in 2015, they did not apply at the general election in 2017. The permitted expenditure in this period between the 55th month and 60th month of a Parliament which is not dissolved beforehand is based on a formula that would yield a sum of about £45,000 in the median constituency in 2015. The period before the individual formally becomes the candidate is referred to as the 'long campaign'; the period which attracts the limit of £13,000 above after the candidature has been formally announced is referred to as the 'short campaign'.[108] Election agents must submit a

---

[105] *R v Jones* [1999] 2 Cr App R 253, at p 255.

[106] RPA, s 71A, as inserted by PPERA, s 130 and Sch 16.

[107] A much higher level of expenditure is permitted at by-elections. In 2001, this was set at £100,000.

[108] In addition to these limits on the amount of permitted expenditure, certain forms of expenditure are forbidden. These include the payment to an elector for the display of election posters unless payment is made in the ordinary course of the elector's business as an advertising agent; and payments to canvassers (RPA, ss 109, 111). Corrupt practices include bribery and treating (ibid, s 113, 114).

return of their candidate's election expenses to the returning officer within 35 days of the result being declared.[109]

Also important is the Representation of the People Act 1983, s 75, which imposes controls on the election expenses of third parties. These third parties may be local businesses, trade unions or local interest groups who believe that their cause would be well served by the election of one particular candidate or poorly served by the election of another. They may wish as a result to campaign in the election and in the absence of controls could, in theory, exceed the permitted expenditure of the candidates themselves. It is thus a corrupt practice under the widely construed s 75 to (i) incur an election expenditure with a view to promoting or procuring the election of a candidate, (ii) on account of holding public meetings, issuing advertisements or circulars or otherwise presenting the candidate or his views to the electorate, (iii) except with the authority of the candidate (in which case the authorised expenditure falls to be treated as part of the candidate's expenses).[110]

The foregoing controls on third parties are subject to an exception for the media to ensure that press and broadcasting activity is not inadvertently caught, though this is by no means uncontroversial. Another exception permitted a third party to spend up to £5 without committing a corrupt practice. The £5 limit was found by the European Court of Human Rights in *Bowman* v *United Kingdom* to be too low, and a violation of art 10 of the ECHR.[111] Following an amendment introduced by the Political Parties, Elections and Referendums Act 2000,[112] the limit is now £500, which means that individuals and campaign groups may spend up to £500 each promoting or attacking candidates without any candidate having to account for the expense. However, they must do so in independent campaigns and must not collude with candidates or pool resources with other third parties.

National spending limits

Since 2001, the spending limits on candidates have been accompanied by spending limits on the national election spending incurred by political parties and others during a general election campaign. It was for a long time the case that, although the expenditure of candidates was subject to limits, there was no corresponding limit on the national election campaigns of the parties.[113] These campaigns were becoming more sophisticated and more expensive: at the general election in 1997 the Conservative and Labour parties were thought to have spent £28 and £26.5m respectively, which in each case was more than double the amount they spent at the general election in 1992.

The Committee on Standards in Public Life (the Neill Committee as it then was) recommended that national spending should be limited,[114] and this recommendation forms the basis of Part V of the Political Parties, Elections and Referendums Act 2000 (with corresponding limits on national referendum expenditure in Part VII). This imposes a limit on the campaign expenditure of political parties,[115] the limit depending on the number of constituencies contested by

---

[109] RPA, s 81 (as amended). The return, which must now also include a statement of donations to the candidate (Sch 2A), must be accompanied by a declaration made by the agent and the candidate that the return is a true record of expenses incurred. For a high-profile but unsuccessful prosecution of a candidate for allegedly making a false declaration, see *R* v *Jones* [1999] 2 Cr App R 253.

[110] In *DPP* v *Luft* [1977] AC 962 it was held that expenditure on negative publicity aimed at preventing the election of a candidate was covered by this provision, as well as expenditure on positive promotional material aimed at procuring the election of a candidate.

[111] *Bowman* v *UK* (1998) 26 EHRR 1.

[112] PPERA, s 131.

[113] *R* v *Tronoh Mines Ltd* [1952] 1 All ER 697.

[114] Cm 4057, 1998, ch 10.

[115] For the definition of campaign expenditure, see PPERA, s 72 and Sch 8.

party candidates.[116] But a national party which puts up a candidate in every constituency would be able to spend up to about £19.5m to promote the electoral success of the party. This is in addition to the amounts that may be spent by each candidate under the Representation of the People Act 1983 on the conduct or management of his or her campaign. The statutory spending limits on political parties for referendum campaigns is £5m for each of the largest in a national referendum.[117]

It is not only the national campaigns of political parties that are subject to restrictions. Spending limits are also imposed on the campaigns of so-called third parties, such as trade unions, companies and pressure groups.[118] These bodies may take part in an election by incurring expensive national advertising to promote particular issues that may tend to benefit one party at the expense of the others. Under Part VI of the 2000 Act,[119] third parties may incur 'controlled expenditure' of up to £20,000 in England and £10,000 in each of Scotland, Wales and Northern Ireland without restraint. 'Controlled expenditure' is defined to mean expenses incurred in connection with the production or publication of election material that is made available to the public at large or any section of the public (s 85).

A third party wishing to spend more than the foregoing amounts must register with the Electoral Commission to become a 'recognised third party'. A recognised third party may incur controlled expenditure of up to £450,000, though within this overall limit there are separate limits for England (£319,800), Scotland (£55,400), Wales (£44,000) and Northern Ireland (£38,000). A recognised third party must also submit an election return after the election, giving details of income received and controlled expenditure incurred. This reduces by about a half the amount of money that could be spent by third parties under the 2000 Act when first introduced, the restrictions even tighter by virtue of the fact that within these overall limits there are restrictions on what is referred to as 'targeted expenditure'. There were 48 recognised third parties in 2017, concerned with a wide range of causes.

Broadcasting and elections

Political broadcasting at election times has also given rise to difficulties. It is an illegal practice for any person to procure the use of transmitting stations outside the United Kingdom with intent to influence voters at an election.[120] The Office of Communications (OFCOM) is under a statutory duty to review and revise standards designed to ensure that news programmes are accurate and impartial and that due impartiality is preserved in political programmes.[121] Political advertising is banned on ITV and on commercial radio stations,[122] a measure justified judicially as being necessary to prevent elections from becoming 'auctions' and to stop wealthy interests dominating a scarce medium of communication.[123] Although far-reaching, this

---

[116] Ibid, s 79 and Sch 9.

[117] PPERA, Part VII. There are also limits on campaign groups and others. See Ewing, *Cost of Democracy*, note 80 above, ch 7 for fuller treatment of this issue.

[118] The electoral activity of pressure groups tends to reflect the dominant political issues of the moment, which at the time of writing is EU membership, with lobby groups on both sides of the remain/leave debate.

[119] As amended by the Transparency of Lobbying, Non Party Campaigning and Trade Union Administration Act 2014.

[120] RPA, s 92.

[121] Communications Act 2003, s 319. The BBC, which exists under royal charter, seeks to maintain due impartiality but it is not subject to statutory restrictions.

[122] Communications Act 2003, ss 319–21. A Geddis [2002] PL 615.

[123] *R (Animal Defenders International)* v *Secretary of State for Culture, Media and Sport* [2008] UKHL 15, paras [28], [29] (Lord Bingham). For a robust academic defence of these measures, see J Rowbottom, in Ewing and Issacharoff (eds), note 88 above, ch 5.

restriction on political advertising (which applies not only to political parties and not only at election time) was found narrowly by the European Court of Human Rights to be a proportionate restriction on freedom of expression.[124] But as already pointed out, free time is provided to the parties by the broadcasters for party election broadcasts. These broadcasts must comply with the various obligations of the broadcasters relating to matters such as taste and decency.[125]

The allocation of time is now governed by rules developed by OFCOM (which now apply also to the BBC).[126] At the general election in 2017, the Labour party and the Conservative party were allocated five broadcasts each in England, and the Liberal Democrats and UKIP three. There were separate allocations in Scotland and Wales where the nationalist parties were given equal time with Labour and the Conservatives. The Green party qualified for broadcasts in England and Wales. Other smaller parties may qualify if they contest at least one-sixth of the parliamentary seats in a particular nation, which means that a party contesting seats in England would have to stand in 89 constituencies to be eligible for an election broadcast, which is an expensive way to secure air time. Disputes about allocation are dealt with by OFCOM's election committee, and legal challenges to allocations under the current or earlier rules have usually been unsuccessful.[127]

The other major issue relating to broadcasting concerns the ability of the broadcasters to report about activities in particular constituencies. The curious effect of the Representation of the People Act 1983, s 93, was that if a candidate took part in an item about a constituency election, the item could not be broadcast without the candidate's consent; and it was an offence for a candidate to take part in such an item for the purpose of promoting his or her election unless the broadcast had the consent of every other candidate for the constituency.[128] To 'take part' in a constituency item meant to participate actively, for example in an interview or discussion; a candidate could not prevent the BBC from filming while the candidate was campaigning in streets.[129] These measures – which effectively gave individual candidates a veto over what might be broadcast – were widely criticised, and they were replaced by the Political Parties, Elections and Referendums Act 2000.

The Representation of the People Act 1983, section 93 now provides that each broadcasting authority must adopt a code of practice to deal with 'the participation of candidates at a parliamentary or local government election in items about the constituency'. Before drawing up the code, the broadcasters must 'have regard' to any views expressed by the Electoral Commission. The broadcasters thus now have a freer hand, perhaps inevitably after the Human Rights Act 1998. The OFCOM Broadcasting Code provides that a candidate may take part in a broadcast about his or her constituency only if the candidates of each of the other major parties are also offered an opportunity to take part.[130] If, however, another candidate is unable or refuses to take part, the broadcast may nevertheless go ahead.

There is in contrast no effective regulation of internet-based electoral activity, the exiting legislation having been drafted pre-internet, which appears to have provided opportunities

---

[124] *Animal Defenders International* v *United Kingdom* [2013] ECHR 362, (2013) 57 EHRR 21.

[125] *Pro-Life Alliance* v *BBC* [2003] UKHL 23, [2004] 1 AC 185.

[126] For the OFCOM rules in force at the time of writing, see OFCOM, *Rules on Party Political and Referendum Broadcasts* (2017).

[127] See *Grieve* v *Douglas-Home* 1965 SLT 186, *R* v *Broadcasting Complaints Commission, ex p Owen* [1985] QB 1153 and *R* v *BBC and ITC, ex p Referendum Party* [1997] COD 459. Also *R (Pro-Life Alliance)* v *BBC* [2003] UKHL 23, [2004] 1 AC 185. Cf *Wilson* v *IBA* 1979 SC 351 (restraints on referendum broadcasts; see now PPERA, s 110).

[128] RPA, s 93(1).

[129] *Marshall* v *BBC* [1979] 3 All ER 80. And see *McAliskey* v *BBC* [1980] NI 44.

[130] OFCOM, *Broadcasting Code* (2017), para 6.9.

for improper interference in elections by both foreign governments and wealthy individuals in a manner calculated to subvert existing regulation. Needless to say, this is a matter in urgent need of attention.[131]

E. Supervision of elections

If elections are to be conducted according to law, there must be effective machinery for investigating alleged breaches of the law and for imposing appropriate sanctions. Since the House of Commons has a direct interest in its own composition, it formerly claimed as a matter of privilege the right to determine questions of disputed elections.

The Commons exercised the right to determine such questions from 1604 to 1868; and objected, not always with success, to breaches of election law being raised in the ordinary courts.[132] From 1672 election disputes were decided by the whole House, but the growth of party government resulted in disputes being settled by purely party voting. In 1868, Parliament entrusted the duty of deciding disputed elections to the courts.[133]

The matter is now governed by the Representation of the People Act 1983, which provides a procedure for contesting elections and for these contests to be dealt with in the courts. Also important, however, is the Electoral Commission established under the Political Parties, Elections and Referendums Act 2000.[134] Apart from supervising the regulatory regime introduced by the latter Act, the Commission has wide-ranging responsibilities for the conduct of elections.

Election petitions

The principal way of challenging an election is by way of an election petition.[135] This can be done only to challenge the election of a candidate: there is no way by which a general election result can be challenged. Within 21 days of the official return of the result of an election, an election petition complaining of an undue election may be presented by a registered elector for the constituency in question, by a person who claims the right to have been elected at the election, or by any person claiming to have been validly nominated as a candidate.[136] The petition may raise a wide variety of issues, including the improper conduct of the election by officials,[137] the legal qualification of the successful candidate to be a member of the Commons,[138] and the commission of election offences such as unauthorised election expenditure.[139]

The petition is heard by an Election Court consisting of two judges of the Queen's Bench Division in England or of the Court of Session in Scotland. The Election Court, which 'has the authority of the High Court and is a court of record,'[140] has a wide range of powers,

---

[131] K D Ewing and J Rowbottom, in Ewing, Rowbottom and Tham (eds), *The Funding of Political Parties – Where Now?*, ch 5; C Torres-Spelliscy (2017) 28 *King's Law Journal* 239.

[132] *Ashby* v *White* (1703) 2 Ld Raym 938; *R* v *Paty* (1704) 2 Ld Raym 1105.

[133] On problems relating to which, see R Grist [2015] PL 375.

[134] For the Commission, see www.electoralcommission.org.uk.

[135] For less formal ways of correcting any mistakes in the conduct of elections, see *Gough* v *Local Sunday Newspapers (North) Ltd* [2003] EWCA Civ 297, [2003] 1 WLR 1836.

[136] See *Ahmed* v *Kennedy* [2002] EWCA Civ 1793, [2003] 1 WLR 1820.

[137] *Re Kensington North Parliamentary Election* [1960] 2 All ER 150.

[138] *Re Parliamentary Election for Bristol South East* [1964] 2 QB 257.

[139] *Grieve* v *Douglas-Home* 1965 SC 186.

[140] *Attorney-General* v *Jones* [2000] QB 66, at p 69.

including the power to order a recount or a scrutiny of the votes. The court determines whether the person whose election is complained of was duly elected and whether any alleged corrupt or illegal practices at the election were proved. If the court finds the candidate to have been disqualified from membership of the House, the court may, if satisfied that the cause of the disqualification was known to the electorate, deem the votes cast for him or her to be void and declare the runner-up to have been elected.[141] If the election has not been conducted substantially in accordance with the law or if there have been irregularities which have affected the result, the court must declare the election void and require a fresh election to be held.[142] If the candidate was disqualified from membership of the House, the court may deem the votes cast for him or her to be void and declare the runner-up to have been elected.

An important reminder of the severe consequences of breaching electoral law is provided by *Watkins* v *Woolas*,[143] where a Labour MP was unseated for violating the Representation of the People Act 1983, s 106. The latter provides that it is an offence to make or publish any false statement of fact in relation to a candidate's personal character or conduct, where this is done for the purpose of affecting the return of a candidate at the election. In the *Watkins* case, Mr Woolas was found by an Election Court to have made three such false statements in relation to his Liberal Democrat rival whom he had defeated with a majority of only 103 votes. The statements in question 'were a serious personal attack on a candidate by saying he condoned violence by extremists and refused to condemn those who advocated violence'.[144] By virtue of the Representation of the People Act 1983, s 159, Mr Woolas' election was held to be void, and as a result of having thus been found to have committed an illegal practice, he was barred from standing for Parliament. This proved to be a rather pyrrhic victory for Mr Watkins, losing to the Labour candidate at the subsequent by-election by over 2,000 votes.

Although decisions of the Election Court are not subject to appeal, Mr Woolas challenged the foregoing decision in judicial review proceedings, in a case acknowledged to have raised important constitutional questions about the susceptibility of the Election Court (which consists of High Court judges) to judicial review by the Administrative Court (which consists of a panel of other High Court judges).[145] In holding that the latter has the power to review the former in order to prevent any mistakes of law from going unchecked, the Administrative Court overturned one of the findings against Mr Woolas, but not the other two. The case also raised important questions about the relationship between the Representation of the People Act 1983, s 106, and Convention rights, notably art 10. But according to Thomas LJ:

> Freedom of political debate must allow for the fact that statements are made which attack the political character of a candidate which are false but which are made carelessly. Such statements may also suggest an attack on aspects of his character by implying he is a hypocrite. Again, imposing a criminal penalty on a person who fails to exercise care when making statements in respect of a candidate's political position or character that by implication suggest he is a hypocrite would very significantly curtail the freedom of political debate so essential to a democracy. It could not be justified as representing the intention of Parliament. However imposing such a penalty where care is not taken in making a statement that goes beyond this and is a statement in relation to the personal character of a candidate can only enhance the standard of political debate and thus strengthen the way in which a democratic legislature is elected.[146]

---

[141] As in the *Bristol South East* case, above.

[142] *Morgan* v *Simpson* [1975] QB 151; *Ruffle* v *Rogers* [1982] QB 1220 (local election cases).

[143] [2010] EWHC 2702 (QB).

[144] *R (Woolas)* v *Speaker of the House of Commons* [2010] EWHC 3169 (Admin), [2012] QB 1, para 125.

[145] Ibid.

[146] Ibid, para 124.

Election offences

Apart from an election petition, the other way by which election law can be enforced is by a criminal prosecution.[147] A person convicted on indictment of a corrupt practice is liable normally to imprisonment of up to one year and a fine; summary conviction carries a lesser penalty that may still lead to six months' imprisonment.[148] Conviction for an illegal practice carries a penalty of a fine not exceeding level 5 on the standard scale.[149] Equally important, conviction brings certain political disabilities, in the sense that a person found guilty of a corrupt or illegal practice is disqualified from being registered as an elector, 'or voting at any parliamentary election in the United Kingdom or at any local government election in Great Britain',[150] or of holding elective office.

Anyone elected to the House of Commons who is subsequently found to have committed a corrupt or illegal practice, is required to vacate his or her seat.[151] In the case of a conviction for a corrupt practice the disqualification is for five years, and three years in the case of an illegal practice. Similar disqualifications may face anyone found to have committed a corrupt or illegal practice by an election court following an election petition. Prosecutions must be brought within a year of the alleged offence being committed.[152]

In *Attorney-General* v *Jones*,[153] the defendant – the Labour member for Newark – had been convicted of the corrupt practice of knowingly making a false declaration of her election expenses. As a result her seat became vacant by the operation of s 160(4) of the 1983 Act. The conviction was reversed on appeal, at which point it was held that the seat ceased to be vacant, and that the existing member was entitled to resume her seat.

Following this case the law was changed so that where a sitting member is convicted of a corrupt or illegal practice, the seat does not become vacant until the end of the period within which an appeal may be lodged against the conviction. If notice of appeal is given, the seat becomes vacant three months after the conviction, unless the appeal is withdrawn or is unsuccessful (in which case it is vacated immediately), or unless the appeal is heard and succeeds (in which case the seat is not vacated). Where a seat is vacated and the appeal ultimately succeeds, this will not entitle the member to resume his or her seat.[154]

Failure to comply with the provisions of the Political Parties, Elections and Referendums Act 2000 has altogether much less dramatic consequences, although these are not to be underestimated. So far as elections are concerned, the main provisions here are the national spending limits that apply to political parties and third parties. Although it recommended that such limits should be introduced, in doing so the Committee on Standards in Public Life thought it 'wholly unrealistic' to suppose that a general election could be set aside and 'the runner-up party to be declared the winner' where the winning party exceeded the

---

[147] See *Attorney-General* v *Jones* [2000] QB 66, at p 69. Also, on a controversial matter, *Erlam* v *Rahman* [2015] EWHC 1215 (QB), which also raises question about the corrupt practice of 'undue spiritual influence', addressed by A McColgan (2017) 28 *King's Law Journal* 279.

[148] RPA, s 168.

[149] Ibid, s 169.

[150] Ibid, s 173.

[151] Ibid, s 173(1)(b).

[152] Ibid, s 176.

[153] [2000] QB 66.

[154] RPA s 173 (as amended).

national limit.[155] The 'only realistic sanction' was thought to be the imposition of a 'heavy financial penalty' on the defaulting party, along with the adverse publicity that any such default would inevitably generate.[156]

It is the criminal law that must thus bear the greater part of the burden of enforcing the limits in the 2000 Act, although financial penalties are combined with the possibility of imprisonment of party officials in the event of a breach. So in the event of expenditure in excess of the statutory maximum, an offence is committed by both the party and the treasurer who authorised the expenditure, in this case the penalty on the party being an unlimited fine.[157] But it is the treasurer who must accept responsibility for any failure to deliver a return of campaign expenditure to the Commission or for making a false declaration about its contents.[158] The general election of 2015 led to allegations following a Channel 4 investigation that the Conservative party was using national expenditure to subsidise local campaigns, in breach of the local spending limits. The matter was investigated by the police, but no charges were brought on the central allegations.[159]

The Electoral Commission

One of the other major innovations of the Political Parties, Elections and Referendums Act 2000 was the creation of the Electoral Commission, with a wide range of functions. It must publish a report on the conduct of elections and referendums, and keep under review a number of electoral matters (including political party income and expenditure and political advertising in the broadcast media). The Commission must also be consulted about any changes to electoral law,[160] and is empowered to give advice and assistance (but not financial assistance) to registration officers, returning officers, political parties and others.[161] This advice may be sought during election campaigns about election law. The Commission also administers the £2m made available to the political parties by the government for policy development, the money distributed in accordance with a scheme drawn up by the Commission and approved by the Ministry of Justice, which is the government department responsible for elections.[162]

As we have also seen, the Electoral Commission plays a crucial part in the administration of the law relating to donations to political parties and electoral expenditure. Under s 145 of the 2000 Act the Commission has a general duty to monitor compliance not only with the provisions of the Political Parties, Elections and Referendums Act, but also 'the restrictions and other requirements imposed by other enactments' relating to 'election expenses incurred by or on behalf of candidates at elections', which extends obviously to the Representation of the People Act 1983.[163] It has a similar administrative and supervisory role in relation to the conduct of referendums, which includes the distribution of state funding to referendum participants. But although the Commission has wide powers of investigation, it bears no responsibility for the prosecution of offenders.

The Political Parties and Elections Act 2009 introduced a number of important changes relating to the Electoral Commission, including its powers to monitor, investigate and enforce

---

[155] Cm 4057, 1998, para 10.25.

[156] Ibid, para 10.26.

[157] PPERA, s 79(2).

[158] Ibid, ss 80–3.

[159] CPS Statement on Election Expenses, 10 May 2017.

[160] PPERA, s 7.

[161] Ibid, s 9.

[162] PPERA, ss 11 and 12. The Commission also has an important educational function regarding the electoral systems (s 13).

[163] With the exception of Scottish local government elections, unless the Scottish ministers so provide (s 145(2)).

the law. The main impact of the changes was to introduce a more flexible enforcement regime, including a greater power to use civil sanctions.[164] There were also changes to its composition, with provision being made for the political parties to nominate four (out of nine or ten) Commissioners. The three largest parliamentary parties are each entitled to nominate a Commissioner, with the fourth place to be allocated to one of the other parliamentary parties, provided it has at least two MPs.[165] This is a change which had been recommended by Sir Hayden Phillips in the wake of the cash for honours affair, when it was felt that the Commission was not sufficiently aware of how political parties operate.[166]

It is unclear, however, whether political commissioners are a desirable or a necessary response to that crisis (especially as the performance of the Electoral Commission appears greatly to have improved): the new provisions challenge the political independence of the Commission, they favour the established national political parties at the expense of the others (notably the nationalist parties which compete in elections in different parts of the country), and there was already provision in the Political Parties, Elections and Referendums Act 2000 for a parliamentary parties panel to be an effective channel of communication between the Electoral Commission and the political parties. Apart from the foregoing, the 2009 Act relaxed the political restrictions on Electoral Commission staff: the old rule whereby staff had to be free of political activity for ten years preceding their appointment was replaced by a restriction of five years.[167]

F. Electoral systems and electoral reform

Under the present electoral system in the United Kingdom, each constituency returns a single member. Each elector can vote for only one candidate, and the successful candidate is the one who receives the highest number of valid votes. This system of 'first past the post' is known as the relative majority system since whenever there are more than two candidates in a constituency, the successful candidate may not have an absolute majority of votes but merely a majority relative to the vote of the runner-up.

This system is simple, but as a means of providing representation in Parliament it is very crude. It makes no provision for the representation of minority interests, nor does it ensure that the distribution of seats in the Commons is at all in proportion to the national distribution of votes. In Britain, the general tendency of the system has been to exaggerate the representation of the two largest parties and to reduce that of the smaller parties; but even for the larger parties there is no consistent relation between the votes and the seats they obtain. The distortion felt by some is illustrated – for example – by the general elections of 2015 and 2017, when the Conservative party saw its share of the vote increase from 36.9 per cent of the vote to 45.6 per cent, but the number of seats won decline from 331 to 297, losing its majority in the process.

The advantages claimed for the system include the simplicity of the voting method, the close links which develop between the member and his or her constituency, and its tendency to produce an absolute majority of seats in the House of Commons out of a large minority of votes. In defence of the system it is claimed that the function of a general election is to elect a government as well as a Parliament, and that the system typically produces strong government. This last claim needs to be examined with care, particularly in the light of the 2010

---

[164] 2009 Act, ss 1–3.
[165] Ibid, s 5.
[166] Sir Hayden Phillips, above, p 21.
[167] 2009 Act, s 7.

election which produced the first Coalition government since 1945, and the 2017 election which led to a minority government. The system also distorts the influence on electoral outcomes of a relatively few marginal constituencies.

Other voting systems

Other electoral systems have long been devised with a view to securing better representation of minorities and a distribution of seats which bears a less haphazard relation to the votes cast. Many different systems are used in other countries.[168] One method, the alternative vote system which operates in Australia (where it is known as preferential voting), retains single-member constituencies but allows the elector to express a choice of candidates in order of preference. If no candidate has an absolute majority of first preferences, the lowest on the list is eliminated and his or her votes are distributed according to the second preference shown on the voting papers. The procedure continues until one candidate obtains an absolute majority. This system eliminates the return of a candidate on a minority vote when account is taken of second and later preferences, but it would not necessarily secure representation in the Commons proportional to the first preferences of the electorate on a national basis.

Other systems have been designed to secure representation in Parliament directly proportional to the national voting strengths of the parties. Thus by the list system, as used in Israel and South Africa, voting for party lists of candidates takes place in a national constituency, with each party receiving that number of seats which comes closest to its share of national votes; this system does not provide for any directly accountable local links between voters and their representatives. In Germany, a mixed system is used by which each elector has two votes, one to elect a candidate in a single-member constituency, the other to vote for a party list; the list seats are assigned to parties to compensate for disproportionate representation arising from the constituency elections, but a party must record 5 per cent of the national vote or win three constituencies to gain any list seats. A similar system to replace first past the post was introduced in New Zealand in 1993 where it is known as mixed member proportional.[169]

The system which is likely to produce a reasonably close relationship between votes and seats while maintaining a local basis for representation is that of the single transferable vote. This method has been used within the United Kingdom for several purposes.[170] It would require the country to be divided into multi-member constituencies, each returning between three and, say, seven members. Every elector would have a single vote but would vote for candidates in order of preference. Any candidate obtaining the quota of first preferences necessary to guarantee election would be immediately elected, the quota being calculated by a simple formula: in a five-member constituency, this quota would be one vote more than one-sixth of the total votes cast.[171] The surplus votes of a successful candidate would be distributed to other candidates proportionately according to the second preference expressed; any candidate then obtaining the quota would be elected and a similar distribution of the surplus would follow.

If at any count under the single transferable vote no candidate obtained the quota figure, the candidate with the lowest number of votes would be eliminated and all his or her preferences distributed among the others. Under this scheme, parties would both nationally and

---

[168] Bogdanor, *The People and the Party System*, parts III–V; and Blackburn, above, ch 8.

[169] On the New Zealand experience, see A Geddis and C Morris (2004) 32 *Federal Law Review* 451.

[170] E.g. for university constituencies between 1918 and 1948; in Northern Ireland for elections to Stormont in 1922–8, to the Assembly in 1973 and 1982, to the Constitutional Convention in 1975 and to the European Parliament. Its use for electing assemblies in Scotland and Wales was proposed by the Royal Commission on the Constitution in 1973 (Cmnd 5460, 1973, paras 779–88), but this proposal was not adopted either in 1978 or in 1998.

[171] See the formula in SSI 2007 No 42, Sched 1, paras 46–55 (STV for Scottish local government elections).

locally be likely to secure representation according to their true strength; minority parties and independent candidates would stand a better chance of election; and the number of ineffective votes would be reduced. Within the constituency, electors could in their order of preference choose between candidates from the same party and could base their choice of candidates on non-party considerations. Unless voting habits were to change, one party would be less likely to secure an absolute majority of seats in the Commons than at present; and Britain would have to get used to periods of minority or coalition government,[172] which would become the norm rather than so far an unusual consequence of the sometimes unpredictable first past the post system.

Electoral reform

The case for electoral reform has been examined many times and a number of different electoral systems have been introduced in Britain since 1997. Under the Scotland Act 1998, a form of the additional member system has been adopted for elections to the Scottish Parliament, which contains 73 constituency members and 56 regional members.[173] Registered parties may submit lists of candidates to be regional members for a particular region, with up to 12 names on each party list, although only seven may be elected.[174] Electors have two votes: one for a constituency member; and the other for regional members to be exercised by voting for a political party which has submitted a regional list.[175] Constituency members are to be elected by first past the post as is currently the case for Westminster elections, and a measure of proportionality is secured by the regional member seats.

The latter are allocated to the parties on the basis of a complex formula that allocates seats according to votes cast for the party in the region.[176] The regional member constituencies are the same constituencies that existed for the purposes of the European Parliament, before the European Parliamentary Elections Act 1999. The new electoral system for European Parliament elections was very different (based on closed party lists in much larger regional constituencies) and will end with Brexit. A system similar to the Scottish system is in place for the National Assembly for Wales.[177] In the case of both Scotland and Wales the electoral system tends to ensure that no one party has a majority of seats in the devolved legislatures; and in the case of Scotland, after the election in 2007 the SNP first assumed office with only 47 of the 129 seats, the defeated Labour administration securing 46 seats.

Different systems have been adopted for the Northern Ireland Assembly and the Greater London Authority. In the case of the former, the single transferable vote is used to elect six candidates from each of the parliamentary constituencies for Northern Ireland.[178] The single transferable vote is defined in the Act as a vote (*a*) 'capable of being given so as to indicate the voter's order of preference for the candidates for election as members for the constituency', and (*b*) 'capable of being transferred to the next choice when the vote is not needed to give a prior choice the necessary quota of votes or when a prior choice is eliminated from the list of candidates because of a deficiency in the number of votes given for him'.[179] In the case of

---

[172] Ch 10.

[173] Scotland Act 1998, s 1. This contrasts with the first past the post system which had been proposed in the Scotland Act 1978. See Cmnd 6348, 1975, p 9.

[174] Scotland Act 1998, s 5(6).

[175] Ibid, s 6.

[176] Ibid, s 1; Sch 1.

[177] Government of Wales Act 1998, Part 1. This contrasts with the first past the post system which had been proposed in the Wales Act 1978.

[178] Northern Ireland Act 1998, s 34.

[179] Ibid, s 34(3).

London, the system is different again. An elector has three votes: one for a mayoral candidate; one (a constituency vote) for an Assembly candidate; and one (a London vote) for a registered party or an individual candidate standing for election as London member.[180]

Mayoral candidates are elected by simple majority unless there are more than two in which case the supplementary vote system is used: this means that where none of the candidates has a majority of the votes cast, all but the first two are eliminated with the second preference votes of the eliminated candidates then distributed to the candidates still in the contest.[181] The Assembly is elected on the basis of a variation of the additional member system used in Scotland and Wales.[182] There are thus three or four electoral systems operating in different parts of the country for the purposes of different elections, with still more variety introduced when STV was adopted for Scottish local authority elections in 2007.[183] This gave rise to considerable confusion when the new system was introduced for local authority elections held on the same day as the Scottish Parliament elections with a different electoral system.[184]

Electoral reform and Westminster

There are thus new electoral systems for the European Parliament, the devolved bodies and local government (in some parts of the country). But what about Westminster? There have been many proposals for reforming the Westminster system, one of the earliest being a recommendation by a royal commission in 1910 for the introduction of the alternative vote.[185] This was followed in 1917 by the recommendations of a Speaker's Conference on electoral reform for the adoption of the single transferable vote.[186] But after some vacillation Parliament refused to accept either this or the alternative vote. The second Labour government revived the matter in 1929,[187] and a Bill proposing to introduce the alternative vote was passed by the Commons but abandoned when the government fell in 1931. The Speaker's Conference on electoral reform in 1944 rejected by a large majority proposals for change, as did a similar conference in 1967.[188]

Electoral reform nevertheless continued to have its strong advocates, with few countries electing their legislatures on the basis of first past the post and with all the new electoral regimes adopted in Britain in recent years rejecting it in favour of a system perceived to be fairer in terms of producing a more representative outcome. Before the general election in 1997, the Labour and Liberal Democrat parties agreed that an early referendum should be held on electoral reform and a commitment to this effect was included in the Labour party's general election manifesto of that year. In acknowledgement of the manifesto commitment, in December 1997 the Prime Minister appointed the Independent Commission on the Voting System under the chairmanship of Lord Jenkins to consider and recommend alternatives

---

[180] Greater London Authority Act 1999, s 4(1).

[181] The candidate with the largest number of first preference votes and distributed second preferences from the other candidates is the winner. See Greater London Authority Act 1999, s 4(3).

[182] Ibid, s 4(4) (Assembly members elected under simple majority system) and s 4(5) (London members elected from party lists in a single London-wide constituency). It is in this latter respect (one rather than several additional member constituencies) that London differs from Scotland and Wales.

[183] SSI 2007 No 42.

[184] See Electoral Commission, *Independent Review of the Scottish Parliamentary and Local Government Elections, 3 May 2007* (2007) – a stinging review by Ron Gould, a senior Canadian election administrator. For comment, see N Ghaleigh (2008) 12 Edin LR.142, and H Lardy [2008] PL 214.

[185] Cd 5163, 1910.

[186] Cd 8463, 1917 and Representation of the People Act 1918, s 20. See Butler, above, part 1.

[187] Cmd 3636, 1930.

[188] Cmd 6534, 1944; Cmnd 3202, 1967.

for Westminster elections. But although the report and its proposals were widely praised for their elegance and subtlety, no referendum on these or any other proposals was ever held until the formation of the Coalition government in 2010.

The Liberal Democrats have a particularly strong long-standing interest in electoral reform. This is because under the first past the post electoral system, they are typically under-represented in terms of seats in proportion to the number of votes they manage to win. At the general election in 2010, for example, the Liberal Democrats won 23 per cent of the vote but less than 10 per cent of the seats in the House of Commons. However, in proposing electoral reform, the Coalition programme for government made provision for an electoral system (the alternative vote) that was the least likely to deliver a legislature reflecting the national vote. As explained above, under the alternative vote the country would still be divided into single member constituencies. As mentioned, the only major country to use this system is Australia, where it is said to produce the strongest two-party system in the world, with small parties having even greater difficulty of breaking through in the House of Representatives than under the first past the post system in the United Kingdom.[189] The extent to which small parties and independents are represented in Australia is due in large part to the different electoral arrangements used for election to the Senate.

Nevertheless, the Parliamentary Voting System and Constituencies Act 2011 imposed a duty to bring forward an order to change the existing electoral law if 'more votes are cast in [a] referendum in favour of the answer "Yes" than in favour of the answer "No"'.[190] The referendum was duly held on 5 May 2011, with a large vote in favour of the status quo: 6.1 million voted in favour of change and 13 million against. Most people appeared to be indifferent, with a turnout of only 41.9 per cent, which means that a change to the voting system was supported by only a small percentage of those eligible to vote. A majority in favour was recorded in only 10 out of 500 voting centres (including Cambridge and Oxford). As a result, it is likely to be a long time before serious attempts are made to change the voting system. Despite its failure to produce a Parliament representative of the nation as a whole; despite its failure to produce MPs who have majority support in their own constituency; and despite the barriers it presents to new parties and small parties from breaking through, first past the post has the virtue of simplicity, even if many now consider it to old-fashioned. It is not clear if the 2011 referendum result would have been different if a different kind of electoral reform had been chosen, but it seems unlikely.

G. Membership of the House of Commons

The following are the main categories of persons who are disqualified from sitting and voting in the House of Commons.[191]

(a) Both by common law and by statute, aliens are disqualified;[192] 'qualifying' Commonwealth citizens and citizens of the Republic of Ireland are not disqualified.[193]

---

[189] See G Orr and K D Ewing, Written Evidence to Political and Constitutional Reform Committee on Parliamentary Voting System and Constituencies Bill, HC 437 (2010–11).

[190] Parliamentary Voting System and Constituencies Act 2011, s 8.

[191] For greater detail, see Erskine May, *Parliamentary Practice*, ch 3.

[192] See for example, Act of Settlement 1700, s 3. For discussion, see *Re Canavan* [2017] HCA 45, dealing with the provisions of the Australian Constitution, which by s 44 excludes those who are subjects or citizens of a foreign power from membership of the Commonwealth Parliament. This led to the unseating of a number of high-profile members, including the Deputy Prime Minister (who was one of seven members affected).

[193] British Nationality Act 1981, Sch 7; Electoral Administration Act 2006, s 18.

(*b*) Persons under 18 on the day they are nominated as candidates.[194]

(*c*) Peers and peeresses. But following the House of Lords Act 1999, hereditary peers are no longer disqualified unless they are one of the 92 hereditary peers (on which see below) who has retained his or her membership of the House under s 2 of the Act. And anyone who ceases to be a member of the House of Lords by virtue of the House of Lords Reform Act 2014 or the House of Lords (Expulsion and Suspension) Act 2015 (see below) is not disqualified from being a member of the House of Commons.

(*d*) Bankrupts. Under the Insolvency Act 1986, s 426A, a person who is subject to a bankruptcy restriction order is disqualified from membership of the Commons. Where a sitting member is adjudged bankrupt, his or her seat becomes vacant and if he or she stands for re-election, his or her return shall be void should he or she be re-elected. Where a court makes a bankruptcy restriction order on a sitting MP, it must inform the Speaker.[195]

(*e*) Persons guilty of corrupt or illegal practices, under the Representation of the People Act 1983. A person found to have committed a corrupt practice is disqualified from being elected to the Commons for five years; and anyone found to have committed an illegal practice is disqualified for three years.[196]

(*f*) Under the Forfeiture Act 1870, a person convicted of treason is disqualified from membership until expiry of the sentence or receipt of a pardon.

(*g*) A person convicted of an offence and sentenced to prison for more than a year by a court in the United Kingdom or elsewhere is, while detained in the British Isles or in the Republic of Ireland or unlawfully at large, disqualified from being nominated and from being a member. If he or she is already a member, the seat is vacated.[197]

It is within the disciplinary powers of the House to expel a member, but expulsion does not prevent him or her from being re-elected.[198] Formerly a person who held contracts with the Crown for the public service was disqualified from membership. But this disqualification was abolished in 1975 along with the disqualification of those who held pensions from the Crown. It was also the case that ordained clergy and ministers of the Church of Scotland were disqualified from membership of the House of Commons.[199] But these disqualifications were removed in 2001,[200] although it is still provided that a person is disqualified from being or being elected as a member of the House of Commons if a Lord Spiritual (that is to say, one of the Bishops of the Church of England who is a member of the House of Lords). More recently still, disqualification from membership of the House of Commons on grounds of mental illness was removed by the Mental Health (Discrimination) Act 2013.

Disqualification of office-holders

In addition to the above, there are a number of office-holders who are disqualified from membership of the House of Commons, the law governing disqualification having emerged from

---

[194] Electoral Administration Act 2006, s 17.

[195] Insolvency Act 1986, s 426A(5).

[196] RPA, ss 160, 173.

[197] Representation of the People Act 1981; and see C P Walker [1982] PL 389.

[198] Ch 9.

[199] House of Commons (Clergy Disqualification) Act 1801, Roman Catholic Relief Act 1829, s 9. There was no similar disqualification from membership of the European Parliament, the Scottish Parliament, the National Assembly for Wales or the Northern Ireland Assembly.

[200] House of Commons (Removal of Clergy Disqualification) Act 2001. The Act implements a recommendation of the Home Affairs Committee (HC 768-I (1997–8), para 127).

the ancient conflicts between the Crown and Commons. During the early 17th century, the House secured recognition of the right to control its own composition. In particular, the House asserted the principle that a member could not continue to serve when appointed by the Crown to a position the duties of which entailed prolonged absence from Westminster. After 1660, the House feared that the Crown would exercise excessive influence over it by the use of patronage and sought to avert a situation in which members held positions of profit at pleasure of the Crown. This fear led in 1700 to a provision in the Act of Settlement to the effect that no one who held an office or place of profit under the Crown should be capable of serving as a member of the House.

This latter provision would have excluded ministers from the Commons. It was, however, repealed before it took effect. In its place, the Succession to the Crown Act 1707 enabled certain ministers to retain their seats in the House, subject to re-election after appointment, but excluded those who held office of a non-political character, for example in what today would be regarded as the civil service. But much legislation was necessary to establish the distinction between ministerial, or political, office-holders, who were eligible for membership, and non-political office-holders, who were ineligible and excluded. Moreover, it was necessary to restrict the number of people appointed to ministerial office from the Commons, in order to avoid a situation in which the executive (now in the form of the Prime Minister) exercised excessive control by patronage over the House. The position is now governed by the House of Commons Disqualification Act 1975.

The latter replaced disqualification for holding 'an office or place of profit under the Crown' by disqualification attached to the holding of specified offices. There are three broad reasons for disqualification: (1) the physical impossibility for certain office-holders of attendance at Westminster, (2) the risk of patronage and (3) the conflict of constitutional duties. Under s 1 of the 1975 Act, the disqualifying offices fall into the following categories:

(*a*) Lords spiritual (that is to say the 26 bishops who are also members of the House of Lords);

(*b*) A great variety of judicial offices, listed in Sch 1 of the Act, including judges of the Supreme Court of the United Kingdom; judges of the Court of Appeal, High Court and circuit judges in England and Wales; and judges of the Court of Session and sheriffs in Scotland, as well as the holders of less senior judicial office. The principle is that no person may hold full-time judicial office and be a practising politician. Lay magistrates are not affected.

(*c*) Employment in the civil service of the Crown, whether in an established or temporary capacity, whole time or part time. The disqualification extends to members of the civil service of Northern Ireland and the diplomatic service. Civil servants who wish to stand for election to Parliament are required by civil service rules to resign before becoming candidates.[201] This applies also to civil servants in the politically free group of civil servants, who are required to resign on being nominated as a candidate.[202]

(*d*) Membership of the regular armed forces of the Crown. Members of the reserve and auxiliary forces are not disqualified if recalled for active service. Members of the armed forces, like civil servants, must resign before becoming candidates for election to Parliament and they may apply for release to contest an election. A spate of such applications in 1962 led to the appointment of an advisory committee of seven members to examine the credentials of applicants and to test the sincerity of their desire to enter Parliament.[203]

---

[201] Servants of the Crown (Parliamentary, European Assembly and Northern Ireland Assembly) Order 1987, *Civil Service Management Code*, paras 4.4.20–4.4.21.

[202] *Civil Service Management Code*, ibid, para 4.4.20. On the politically free category, see ch 11.

[203] HC 111 and 262 (1962–3); HC Deb, 18 February 1963, col 163.

(*e*) Membership of any police force maintained by a police authority.

(*f*) Membership of the legislature of any country or territory outside the Commonwealth, except – following the Disqualifications Act 2000 – in the case of the Republic of Ireland. It is likely that members of a legislature other than that of the Irish Republic would be debarred by their status as aliens from membership of the Commons.

(*g*) A great variety of disqualifying offices arising from chairmanship or membership of commissions, boards, agencies, administrative tribunals, public authorities and undertakings; in a few cases the disqualification attaches only to particular constituencies (Sch 1, Parts 2–4). As these offices cover such a wide range, each office is specified by name. The Schedule may be amended by Order in Council made following a resolution approved by the House of Commons (s 5). This power – which is frequently used – avoids the need for amendment by statute as and when new offices are created.

For one purpose alone acceptance of an office of profit continues to disqualify. From early times a member of the House was in law unable to resign his or her seat and acceptance of an office of profit under the Crown was the only legal method of release from membership. The offices commonly used for the purpose were the office of Steward or Bailiff of the Chiltern Hundreds or of the Manor of Northstead. Under the Act of 1975 these offices are disqualifying offices (s 4). Appointment to them is made by the Chancellor of the Exchequer on the request of the member concerned.

Other matters

1. *Ministers in the House of Commons*

British practice requires that the holders of ministerial office should be members of either the House of Commons or the House of Lords and that the great majority should be drawn from the Commons. But it has long been necessary for limits to be imposed on the number of ministers who may sit in the Commons, lest excessive powers of patronage be exercised by the Prime Minister over the House. The present law is found partly in the House of Commons Disqualification Act 1975 and partly in the Ministerial and other Salaries Act 1975.

Section 2 of the House of Commons Disqualification Act 1975 allows no more than 95 holders of ministerial office (whether paid or unpaid, it would seem) to sit and vote in the Commons; this limit had been raised from 70 to 91 in 1964,[204] and to 95 in 1975.[205] If more members of the Commons are appointed to ministerial office than are allowed by law, those appointed in excess must not sit or vote in the House until the number has been reduced to the permitted figure (s 2(2)).

The Ministerial and other Salaries Act 1975 (as amended) sets out the salaries payable to various categories of ministerial office, these salaries being subject to revision.[206] Schedule 1 to the Act imposes limits on the total number of such salaries payable at any one time to the various categories. Thus, in category 1 (holders of posts in the Cabinet apart from the Lord Chancellor), not more than 21 salaries are payable. Not more than 50 salaries are payable to posts in category 1 taken together with category 2 (ministers of state and departmental ministers outside the Cabinet).

Not more than 83 salaries are payable to posts in categories 1, 2 and 4 (parliamentary secretaries) taken together. In addition, salaries are paid to the law officers of the Crown (category 3), to five Junior Lords to the Treasury (government whips in the Commons) and to

---

[204] Ministers of the Crown Act 1964, noted by A E W Park (1965) 28 MLR 338.

[205] Ministers of the Crown Act 1974, repealed and replaced by the House of Commons Disqualification Act 1975.

[206] See Ministerial and other Salaries Act 1997.

seven assistant whips in the Commons, as well as to various political posts in the royal house-hold, some of which may be held only by members of the Lords. Provision is also made for the payment of salaries to the Leader of the Opposition and to the Opposition whips (s 2).

2. *Effects of disqualification*

If any person is elected to the House while disqualified by the House of Commons Disqualification Act 1975 Act, the election is void (s 6(1)) and this could be so determined on an election petition. If a member becomes disqualified after election, his or her seat is vacated and the House may so resolve. The House may, however, direct by order that a disqualification under the 1975 Act which existed at the material time be disregarded if it has already been removed (for example, by the member's resignation from the office in question) (s 6(2)).

Thus a new election is unnecessary where the House itself has dispensed with the consequences of the disqualification, but no such order can affect the proceedings on an election petition (s 6(3)). Disputed cases of disqualification are in general determined by the House after consideration by a select committee. Thus in 1961 the Committee of Privileges reported that Mr Tony Benn was disqualified because he had succeeded to his father's peerage while a member of the Commons.[207]

While disputes under the 1975 Act as to disqualifying offices arise rarely, the Judicial Committee of the Privy Council has jurisdiction to declare whether a person has incurred a disqualification under that Act (s 7). Any person may apply to the Judicial Committee for a declaration of disqualification but must give security for costs. Issues of fact may on the direction of the Judicial Committee be tried by the High Court in England, the Court of Session in Scotland or the High Court in Northern Ireland (s 7(4)).

A declaration may not be made if an election petition is pending, if one has been tried in which disqualification on the same grounds was in issue, nor where the House has given relief by order (s 7(5)). This procedure has yet to be used.[208] Another procedure open where there is a dispute over disqualification is for the Commons to petition the Crown to refer the matter to the Judicial Committee of the Privy Council for an advisory opinion on the law.[209]

3. *Recall of MPs*

An important initiative albeit of limited scope is the provision for the recall of MPs introduced by the Recall of MPs Act 2015. This reflects the principle that constituents who are dissatisfied with an MP's performance (because of idleness, misconduct, failures in office) should not be required to wait until a general election to secure his or her removal, and should be free if there is a sufficient demand to do so to require the MP to account for his or her conduct at an early election. This would also be a valuable device in those rare cases where the MP crosses the floor to join the other party.

Although the recall is accepted in other jurisdictions (reflecting the principle that the mandate is conditional and revocable), it has not been a feature of the British system of parliamentary representation and sits ill at ease with notions of representation developed by Edmund Burke.[210] It appears, however, that the idea was stimulated by the national disquiet following disclosures in 2009 about the abuse of parliamentary allowances and expenses by many MPs. The 2015 Act reflects these origins by eschewing a general right of electors to demand a recall, insisting instead that a recall may only be triggered by one of a number of events. These are (i) conviction of an offence followed by a custodial sentence; (ii) suspension

---

[207] HC 142 (1960–61).
[208] Erskine May, above, p 41.
[209] Under the Judicial Committee Act 1833, s 4; and see *Re MacManaway* [1951] AC 161.
[210] See *Amalgamated Society of Railway Servants v Osborne* [1987] AC 87.

from the House for more than 10 days following a report by the Committee on Standards; and (iii) conviction for offences relating to parliamentary expenses (whether or not the conviction leads to imprisonment). In any of these cases, the Speaker must notify the petition officer for the constituency,[211] who must then open a petition for six weeks to allow electors to support the recall. The petition – which must be supported by at least 10 per cent of the electors – can be curtailed by a number of events, including the MP's resignation.

Provision is made in the 2015 Act to regulate the expenditure of money during the petition period, in which it is anticipated that there will be campaigns on both sides – for and against the petition. Those who wish to spend up to £10,000 must register as an accredited campaigner with the Electoral Commission, while others may spend up to £500 each. Only those falling with the list of permitted donors may make donations to petition campaigners. Should both the triggering requirement and the threshold be met, the MP will lose his or her seat, and there would then follow a by-election, at which the deposed MP is permitted to stand as a candidate.

H. The House of Lords

Historically, membership of the House of Lords was confined to hereditary peers and the bishops of the Church of England.[212] The former inherited their status and a considerable body of law has developed to regulate title to the peerage.[213] The latter held their position ex officio and ceased to occupy a seat in the Lords on resignation or retirement.

In 1876, provision was made for the appointment of Lords of Appeal in Ordinary to conduct the judicial business of the House;[214] and in 1958 the Life Peerages Act allowed for the appointment of others to the peerage for life, without the conferring of a title which would pass to succeeding generations. Membership of the House of Lords was thus confined to those who inherited their position or who were appointed by the Crown (in the case of the bishops, the law lords, and the life peers).

The House of Lords Act 1999 broke the link between the hereditary peerage and membership of the House of Lords;[215] until then all hereditary peers were entitled to a seat in the Lords. There continue to be four categories of members of the House of Lords, although the effect of the House of Lords Act 1999 and the Constitutional Reform Act 2005 has been greatly to alter the balance between the different categories, with hereditary peers displaced by the life peers as the largest group. The four categories of membership are as follows:

(*a*) Life peers created under the Life Peerages Act 1958.

(*b*) Law Lords appointed under the Appellate Jurisdiction Act 1876.

(*c*) Lords Spiritual, being 26 senior clergy of the Church of England.

(*d*) Hereditary peers, as provided by the House of Lords Act 1999.

---

[211] Under the 2015 Act, this will be the returning officer, who is required to designate up to ten places where the petition can be signed, and to send notice of the petition to electors.

[212] A good history is provided by Lowell, *The Government of England*, ch 21. See also Maitland, *The Constitutional History of England*, pp 166–72.

[213] See the 12th edition of this work, pp 164–6.

[214] Appellate Jurisdiction Act 1876.

[215] House of Lords Act 1999, s 1: 'No one shall be a member of the House of Lords by virtue of a hereditary peerage.' This is subject to s 2, on which see below.

Life peers

In 1856 it was decided that the Crown, although able to create a life peerage, could not create such a peerage carrying with it the right to a seat in the House of Lords.[216] If life peers were to be created to sit in the Lords, legislation was thus necessary. The Life Peerages Act 1958 both strengthened the Lords and weakened the hereditary principle. The Act enabled the Queen by letters patent to confer a peerage for life with a seat in Parliament on a man or woman. It did not restrict the power of the Crown to confer hereditary peerages, although it made it unnecessary for new hereditary peerages to be created. In fact very few hereditary peerages have since been created, although Mrs Thatcher revived the practice of making such appointments when she nominated Viscount Whitelaw and Speaker Thomas in 1983.[217]

Life peers may not vote in House of Commons elections and they may not stand as parliamentary candidates. They may vote and stand for election to the devolved parliament and assemblies, but not the European Parliament.[218] An appointment under the 1958 Act is irrevocable: unlike a hereditary peerage, a life peerage cannot be disclaimed (though peers may now resign or effectively be expelled from membership of the House of Lords),[219] and there are no limits to the number of peers who may be appointed. In 2017, there were 799 life peers (an increase from 601 in March 2009), of whom 209 were women (compared to 145 in 2009), giving rise to concerns about the unsustainable increase in the size of the House, as each Prime Minister appoints more members to redress the balance in the interests of his or her own party.

There is a great deal of criticism that the system of appointment on the recommendation of the Prime Minister is an inappropriate way to recruit a legislative chamber, and that it allows too much patronage on the part of the Prime Minister. In order to address such criticism, Mr Blair (when Prime Minister) established the House of Lords Appointments Commission which is a non-statutory, non-departmental public body, attached to the Cabinet Office.[220] It is chaired by a peer and its members include nominees of the three main national political parties and three independent members. The role of the Commission is to make recommendations for non-political peers and to vet all nominations for peerages by the political parties on grounds of propriety.

It is important to point out that although recommendations for the peerage are made by the Prime Minister, he or she will act on the advice of party leaders when nominating members from political parties other than his or her own. It appears, however, that it is for the Prime Minister to decide how many new opposition peers may be created at any one time, there being no clear formula to provide guidance for this purpose. All parties need constantly to refresh their active membership in the House of Lords, in the government's case to ensure that its business is carried forward, and in the opposition's case to expose weaknesses and propose amendments. It remains the case that although Canada also has a nominated second chamber (the Senate), this is nevertheless a very unusual method for selecting a parliamentary chamber.[221]

Law Lords and Lords Spiritual

The peers appointed under the Appellate Jurisdiction Act 1876 to perform the judicial functions of the House of Lords were styled Lords of Appeal in Ordinary. They could sit and

---

[216] *Wensleydale Peerage case* (1856) 5 HLC 958.

[217] See Brazier, *Constitutional Practice*, p 241.

[218] See p 151 above.

[219] See p 185 below.

[220] Full details of the activities of the Commission are to be found on its website. For proposals to enhance the status and role of the Commission, see HC 153 (2007–8); HC 137 (2008–9) (Public Administration Committee).

[221] For a full account, see Russell, *Reforming the House of Lords*.

vote for life, notwithstanding resignation or retirement from their judicial appointment. In 2009 (the year of the opening of the UKSC), 22 members of the House of Lords had been appointed under the 1876 Act. Since the creation of the Supreme Court, however, the House of Lords ceases to have a judicial function, and the Appellate Jurisdiction Act 1876 has been repealed. Supreme Court judges are ineligible to sit in the House of Lords, and while the Lords of Appeal in Ordinary at the time of the creation of the Supreme Court were by statute to become the first justices of the Supreme Court,[222] they no longer sit and vote in the House of Lords or its committees.

Supreme Court judges appointed to the peerage under the 1876 Act are able to resume their parliamentary activities following their retirement from judicial office, though several who are eligible to do so have also retired from the House and no longer sit. All holders of judicial office are now disqualified from taking part in the activities of the House of Lords,[223] which means that the need for legal expertise to carry out its scrutiny work must be met by the appointment as life peers under the Life Peerages Act 1958 of lawyers who do not hold judicial office. The judicial members of the Lords had in the past taken a particular interest in the scrutiny of EU law, the reform of the legal profession,[224] the privileges of the House, and human rights.[225]

The Lords Spiritual are 26 bishops of the Church of England; they hold their seats in the Lords until they resign from their episcopal office. The Archbishops of Canterbury and York and the Bishops of London, Durham and Winchester have the right to a seat. The remaining Lords Spiritual are the 21 other diocesan bishops having seniority of date of appointment, with the exception of the Bishop of Sodor and Man who may not take a seat. When a bishop with a seat in the Lords resigns or retires, the place in the Lords is taken by the next senior diocesan bishop.[226] In 1847, it was enacted that the number of bishops sitting in Parliament should not be increased whenever a new diocesan bishopric is created.[227] The Lords Spiritual (Women) Act 2015 acknowledges the creation of female bishops, and at the request of the Church of England makes provision to accelerate their appointment to the House of Lords.

Although justified historically, such representation is bound to be closely questioned in an age which is simultaneously both more multicultural and more secular. It is possible for members and clergy of other churches and faiths to be appointed under the Life Peerages Act 1958, in the case of those churches and faiths which do not prohibit their senior clergy from accepting positions of political authority.[228] But this is not the same as an entitlement to a guaranteed number of places. It is striking nevertheless that the House of Lords Reform Bill introduced by the Coalition government in 2012 proposed to retain the Lords Spiritual in what would have been a predominantly elected House. The government's ill-fated Bill proposed gradually to reduce the number of Lords Spiritual from its current 26 to 12 over a period of 15 years.

Hereditary peers

It was previously the case that a hereditary peerage carried with it the right to a seat in the House of Lords. The House of Lords Act 1999 now provides that hereditary peers are no

---

[222] Constitutional Reform Act 2005, s 24.

[223] Ibid.

[224] See HL Deb, 7 April 1999, cols 1307–1480.

[225] Particularly on the proceedings relating to the Human Rights Bill: see K D Ewing (1999) 62 MLR 79.

[226] Under the Ecclesiastical Offices (Age Limit) Measure 1975, bishops retire from their sees, and therefore from membership of the House, at age 70. Retired bishops are entitled to use the facilities of the House available to members of the House outside the Chamber.

[227] Ecclesiastical Commissioners Act 1847, s 2; Bishoprics Act 1878, s 5.

[228] For a valuable account of religious representation in the House of Lords, see C Smith [2002] PL 674, and A Harlow, F Cranmer and N Doe [2008] PL 490.

longer entitled to membership of the Lords. But hereditary peers have not been excluded altogether. In order to expedite the passing of the House of Lords Act 1999, the government accepted an arrangement whereby 90 hereditary peers (plus the Earl Marshal and the Lord Great Chamberlain)[229] would remain in the Lords until the process of reform was completed.[230] These 90 are elected in accordance with the standing orders of the House. In 2013, the House of Lords was thus still graced by one duke, one marquess, 21 earls and countesses and 18 viscounts.

The removal of the hereditary peers was nevertheless challenged as breaching the Treaty of Union, which provides a guarantee that 16 Scottish peers would be accepted into membership of the House of Lords. But this was rejected by the House of Lords Committee of Privileges, which concluded that the Treaty of Union did not provide an unalterable restraint on the power of Parliament.[231] Hereditary peers are now eligible to vote and to stand for election to the House of Commons, unless they are members of the House of Lords by virtue of the new procedures.[232]

Under the standing orders of the House governing the election of hereditary peers,[233] 15 of the 90 places were set aside for those hereditary peers who were office-holders in the House: deputy speakers and deputy chairmen of committees. They were elected by the whole House, the remaining 75 places being elected by the hereditary peers to reflect the strength of the different parties from among their number. So, 42 places were allocated to the Conservatives; three to the Liberal Democrats; two to Labour; and 28 to the cross benchers. These members were elected from constituencies of their own party or group (so that, for example, only Conservative hereditary peers elected the 42 Conservatives),[234] though hereditary peers supporting other parties may stand as candidates in these elections.

A peerage cannot be alienated or surrendered, although under the Peerages Act 1963 a hereditary peer may disclaim his or her title for life.[235] The primary purpose of granting this right was to enable hereditary peers to sit in the Commons, following an unsuccessful action by Tony Benn, then Viscount Stansgate by succession, who challenged the existing law

---

[229] The Earl Marshal has responsibility for ceremonial matters, while previous editions of the *Companion to the Standing Orders and Guide to the Proceedings of the House of Lords* referred to the Lord Chamberlain as 'the hereditary officer of state to whom the sovereign entrusts the custody and control of those parts of the Palace of Westminster not assigned to the two Houses' (such as the Queen's Robing Room). This passage has been removed from the current edition of the *Companion*.

[230] House of Lords Act 1999, s 2. For an account of how these figures were arrived at, see R Brazier, House of Lords Act 1999, *Current Law Statutes 1999*. In addition to the places reserved to hereditary peers by the House of Lords Act 1999, another ten were made life peers to enable them to remain. These were mainly hereditary peers of first creation. Another two hereditary peers reverted to sitting under the authority of life peerages which they already had.

[231] *Lord Gray's Motion* 2000 SC (HL) 46.

[232] House of Lords Act 1999, s 3.

[233] HL SO 9.

[234] Should a vacancy arise, provision is made in Standing Order 10 for a by-election, at which only those hereditary peers who remain in membership of the House may vote. So only the 41 remaining Conservative hereditary peers could vote in a by-election for a new Conservative hereditary peer to become a member of the House. See A Murphy (2003) 71 *The Table* 11.

[235] Under the 1963 Act existing peers were given 12 months from royal assent to disclaim and new peers were given 12 months from the date of their succession (s 1). This still applies unless the peer is excepted from s 1 of the 1999 Act by s 2 of the same Act. A sitting member of the Commons was given one month from the death of his predecessor in which to disclaim (1963 Act, s 2); but this has been repealed by the 1999 Act. Where a peer disclaims his title, it could not be restored to him, although the title would pass to the next generation following the death of the person who disclaimed. A person who disclaimed could be restored to the House of Lords by a life peerage under the 1958 Act. It would presumably be possible – if unlikely – for a new hereditary peerage to be conferred on the person who disclaimed.

which disqualified members of the Lords from standing for election to Parliament.[236] Like other peers, hereditary peers may resign or cease to be members under the House of Lords Reform Act 2014 and the House of Lords (Expulsion and Suspension) Act 2015, in which case fresh by-elections under the procedure for hereditary peers, described above, would need to be held. Specific provision to this effect is made in the 2014 Act.

I. Membership of the House of Lords

Although there are thus a number of different routes to membership of the House of Lords, a member may not take his or her seat until he or she has obtained a writ of summons, which is issued by direction of the Lord Chancellor, from the office of the Clerk of the Crown in Chancery (a senior officer of the House). New writs are issued before the meeting of each Parliament to all Lords – temporal and Spiritual – who are entitled to receive them.[237] Writs are also issued to peers newly created during the life of a Parliament. But no writs are issued to any peer who is known to be disqualified.

There are currently several categories of disqualification:[238]

aliens;[239]

those under the age of 21;[240]

those in respect of whom a bankruptcy restriction order has been made;[241]

those convicted of treason (until they have served their sentence or been pardoned);[242]

those who hold judicial office of certain kinds, which includes not only those who hold judicial office and who have been made life peers under the Appellate Jurisdiction Act 1876, but also those who hold less senior judicial office but who have been made life peers under the Life Peerages Act 1958;[243]

those who are members of the European Parliament;[244]

those who retire, or cease to be members under the House of Lords Reform Act 2014 (exclusion for non-attendance or conviction for serious offence and imprisonment for more than a year);

those who are expelled from membership following general powers of expulsion introduced by the House of Lords (Expulsion and Suspension) Act 2015.[245]

It is also necessary for a new peer to be formally introduced into the House. A day for this purpose is fixed by the Speaker and by custom not more than two introductions may take

---

[236] *Re Parliamentary Election for Bristol South East* [1964] 2 QB 257. It was under the 1963 Act that the Earl of Home disclaimed his title on being appointed Prime Minister in 1963 in succession to Mr Harold Macmillan.

[237] House of Lords, *Companion to the Standing Orders and Guide to the Proceedings of the House of Lords* (2017), para 1.07.

[238] The Peerage Act 1963, s 6 removed the disqualification on peeresses in their own right to receive a writ of summons. See *Viscountess Rhondda's Claim* [1922] 2 AC 339.

[239] Act of Settlement 1700, s 3 (as amended by the British Nationality Act 1981, Sch 7).

[240] HL SO 2.

[241] Insolvency Act 1986, s 426A.

[242] Forfeiture Act 1870.

[243] Constitutional Reform Act 2005, s 137.

[244] SI 2008 No 1647.

[245] HL SO 12 – expulsion only to take place after a recommendation from the Committee for Privileges and Conduct following a breach of the *Code of Conduct for Members of the House of Lords* (2017).

place on any one day. Lords are normally introduced by two peers 'of the same degree in the House'.[246] It is not to be overlooked that despite the manner of its composition and the formality of its proceedings, the House of Lords exists principally to transact political business. This gives rise to questions about the political balance of the chamber and the obligations of its members.

The political composition of the House of Lords

The effect of the House of Lords Act 1999 was significantly to reduce the size of the House of Lords: in 1999, there were 1,295 members who were culled to 695 by October in the following year. The House of Lords was nevertheless by some way still one of the largest parliamentary chambers in Europe, and since then its numbers have continued to grow, as successive governments have made a large number of appointments to redress the political balance inherited from previous administrations. It appears to be accepted that pending more radical reform of the House, (i) no one party should have an overall majority in the Lords (as was previously the case when the large body of hereditary peers gave the Conservatives a guaranteed majority), but (ii) the governing party should be the largest party, with the political composition of the Lords to be broadly reflective of 'the share of the vote secured by the political parties in the last general election'.[247]

But although admirable, this principle will be difficult to implement in a system where existing members can be removed only by retirement, non-attendance or misconduct, and where balance can be achieved only by new appointments. Thus, although the House has been reformed by the 1999 Act and although a large number of Labour peers were created, it was not until 2005 that Labour became the largest party, despite Labour having been in government since 1997. Similarly, although Labour lost the election in 2010, by 2013 it was still the largest party in the House, with 213 members, compared to the Conservatives of whom there were 160, the Liberal Democrats of whom there were 85, and 'other parties' of whom there were 12. The remaining places were occupied by 151 'crossbenchers' (who sit as independents), 21 peers who were said to be 'non-affiliated', and 24 (not 26) Bishops. By 2017 the Conservatives were again the largest party but with only 252 members in a House of some 799 members in total.

The legislative role of the House of Lords makes it inevitable that the government should have some presence in the chamber, to ensure that business is conducted efficiently and that an account is given of government proposals. In recent years the practice has been for only two or three Cabinet ministers to be drawn from the House of Lords, though these do not now necessarily include the Lord Chancellor. By convention the Prime Minister must be a member of the House of Commons, and the same is true of other senior Cabinet posts: it is inconceivable in particular that the Chancellor of the Exchequer could be a member of the House of Lords.[248] But there is no reason in principle why other ministers should not be based in the Lords, and the life peerage provides an opportunity for the Prime Minister to bring into his or her government an individual who may not be a member of Parliament (as in the case of Lord Mandelson by Mr Brown).

The 1958 Act also provides an opportunity for the Prime Minister to retain the services of a minister who may have lost his or her Commons seat in a general election (as in the case

---

[246] House of Lords, *Companion to the Standing Orders and Guide to the Proceedings of the House of Lords*, above, para 1.11.

[247] HM Government, *The Coalition: Our Programme for Government* (2010), p 27.

[248] Lord Carrington was Foreign Secretary in the House of Lords in Mrs Thatcher's government until he resigned in 1982 following the invasion of the Falkland Islands.

of Mrs Lynda Chalker who lost her seat in 1992 but who was elevated to the peerage, retaining her position as minister for overseas development in Mr Major's government). In 2017 there were in fact 15 ministers who held seats in the Lords, with the ministerial teams of many departments including a member of the Lords. However, only one of these was a member of the Cabinet (the Leader of the House). There are also nine government whips in the Lords, this position sometimes combined with junior ministerial responsibilities. Previous governments in contrast have tended to draw more freely on the House of Lords for recruitment to the Cabinet, and it is perhaps paradoxical that as the size of the Lords increases, so the number of House of Lords ministers declines.

Obligations of membership

Unlike the House of Commons, many members of the House of Lords are not engaged full time in the business of the House or activities incidental thereto. Indeed, it is one of the strengths of the House that its many part-time members are occupied in other pursuits, on the experience of which they may draw in their work in the upper chamber. But there must be some obligation of attendance and participation, particularly on the part of the life peers who have voluntarily assumed the benefits of office, and complaints are sometimes made that not all members play as full a part in the work of the House as they should. House of Lords Standing Order 23 – introduced on 16 June 1958 – provides that 'Lords are to attend the sittings of the House or, if they cannot do so, obtain leave of absence, which the House may grant at pleasure'.

At a time of concern about the expanding size of the House of Lords, steps were taken in the modest but grandly titled House of Lords Reform Act 2014 to allow for peers to resign – an irrevocable event which means they may not sit at any time in the future. The Act also provides for the automatic expulsion of peers who not having obtained leave of absence fail to attend the House in the session in question. In both cases – retirement and expulsion – the individual in question does not lose his or her title, the 2014 Act the latest uncoupling of the peerage from automatic membership of the Lords. There appears to be no way by which a peerage granted under the Life Peerages Act 1958 can be revoked, but the gradual uncoupling of membership of the House from the status as a peer is welcome.[249]

The same process can be seen at work in the provisions of the 2014 Act (as well as those of the House of Lords (Expulsion and Suspension) Act 2015) which allow for the removal of those who commit a serious offence or act in breach of the House of Lords Code of Conduct. The House previously had no power to expel a member, though it did have the power to suspend for breach of the rules governing conduct.[250] This power was exercised in 2009 in relation to two Labour peers who had been reported by the *Sunday Times* as being willing to use their position to promote commercial interests for financial advantage.[251] More recently a number of other peers were suspended in 2010 and 2011 following irregularities over expenses, in the latter case the suspensions coinciding with the imprisonment of the members in question.[252]

Since 1957 a daily attendance allowance has been paid and travel costs are met; attending peers also receive allowances for overnight stays away from home, as well as for secretarial

---

[249] See also House of Lords Act 1999 (removal of hereditary peers) and Constitutional Reform Act 2005 (removal of Supreme Court judges).

[250] HL 87 (2008–09). Powers of expulsion were included in the government's Constitutional Reform and Governance Bill 2009. But they were not enacted.

[251] HL 88 (2008–9). And see ch 9.

[252] The length of the suspensions varied, but one case was until the end of the parliamentary session in question and another was for 12 months, in that case coinciding with a prison sentence relating to the same matter.

and research assistance. It was the breach of the rules relating to these allowances that led to the disciplinary suspensions referred to above. These allowances notwithstanding, there is a sense that membership of a part-time legislative chamber on an unpaid basis is difficult for people from outside London and the south-east. To this end, it is noteworthy that the ill-fated House of Lords Bill 2012 (on which see below) proposed that peers (whether elected or nominated under the scheme in the Bill) should be paid. Remarkably, however, it also proposed that payment should be linked to the member's participation in the work of the House, with a determination to be made by Independent Parliamentary Standards Authority as to what counts as participation for these purposes. Members of the House of Lords continue to be unpaid.

Further reform

The House of Lords Act 1999 was designed to be only the first step in the process of reform. But as was discovered by the Royal Commission on the Reform of the House of Lords which reported in 2000, it is difficult to produce a solution for a reformed House which commands agreement across the political spectrum.[253] Democratic instinct suggests that the only credible solution is a wholly or largely elected (directly or indirectly) Upper House (perhaps one renamed as a Senate).[254] But the difficulty with this is that it could end up with a House wholly dominated by the political parties and, depending on election results, with the same party in control of both the Commons and the Lords. In that case, there would be little prospect of effective scrutiny or revision of government business. Conversely, election could lead to a House with a majority different from that of the Commons, leading to the alternative result of stalemate or gridlock in the legislative process.

It is thus a curious paradox that a nominated House without an electoral mandate is able to produce a revising chamber which simultaneously provides a greater measure of independent scrutiny of government than the House of Commons, without at the same time undermining the political supremacy of the House of Commons, or unduly impeding or frustrating the implementation of the government's programme.[255] Any change to these arrangements ought logically to begin by asking what it is we expect the House of Lords to do and to tailor composition to function. If the purpose is to act as a restraint on government, the case for an elected chamber would be irresistible (provided election were guaranteed to produce a House with a different political majority from the Commons). If, however, the purpose is (as currently) that of revision and scrutiny, there may be a case for other methods of composition, which is not to say that the current arrangements for the nominated house can easily be justified.

It has, however, proved to be impossible to build a consensus around the next stage of reform, perhaps because there is no consensus on the role of a second chamber in the British constitution. Deep divisions were on display in 2007 when the Commons voted for a wholly or largely (80 per cent) elected House of Lords, to be followed only a few days later by the House of Lords voting for a wholly nominated chamber.[256] A House of Lords Reform Bill was introduced in 2012, all three main political parties having promised further House of Lords reform in the general election campaign in 2010. The latter measure provided for the phased introduction of a

---

[253] For good accounts of the difficulties, see Bogdanor, *Politics and the Constitution*, ch 14; Brazier, *Constitutional Reform*, ch 11; and Shell, *The House of Lords*.

[254] See Richard and Welfare, *Unfinished Business*. See also R Blackburn, in Blackburn and Plant, *Constitutional Reform*, ch 1 and Billy Bragg, *A Genuine Expression of the Will of the People*.

[255] The elected option was rejected by the Royal Commission on the Reform of the House of Lords which had been appointed in 1999, although it did recommend that there should be an elected element: Cm 4534, 2000.

[256] HC Deb, 6 March 2007, col 1389, 7 March 2007, col 1524; HL Deb, 12 March 2007, col 451, 13 March 2007, col 626.

second chamber of 360 directly elected members, plus 90 appointed members, 12 Bishops and an indefinite number of 'ministerial members'. The elected members would be directly elected by a system of proportional representation for terms of 15 years each, with elections taking place every five years for a third of the seats in the reformed Chamber.

It was not proposed under these plans to affect the primacy of the House of Commons, or alter the powers of the House of Lords. Indeed, it was expressly provided that the Parliament Act 1911–1949 would remain in force, a provision that seemed unnecessary in the light of the lack of any intention to repeal them.[257] The electoral system would be similar to that used for European parliamentary elections, with Great Britain being divided into ten regional constituencies from which members would be elected from party lists (and in Northern Ireland by single transferable vote from a single constituency). But although a government Bill designed to implement a provision in the Coalition agreement, this apparently well-thought-out and elegant solution to an intractable problem was withdrawn after Second Reading, in the face of strong opposition from Conservative backbenchers.

J. Conclusion

The Coalition government attempted unsuccessfully to change the rules relating to the composition of Parliament, ostensibly to make the House of Commons more representative of popular opinion, and to make the House of Lords more democratic. The failure of both initiatives – for different reasons – may make it difficult to revive campaigns for electoral reform or an elected House of Lords, at least for the foreseeable future.

The United Kingdom thus unusually retains a legislature in which the lower house is elected by first past the post in single member constituencies, and the upper house is wholly unelected. In this broad sense, the United Kingdom thus began the 21st century with a legislature similar in structure to the one in which it began the 20th century. Yet behind these formal structures a great deal has changed, with universal suffrage for the House of Commons creating controversial and politically loaded problems about eligibility to vote, the registration of electors, the distribution of boundaries, and the regulation of candidates and political parties.

The position of the House of Lords is no less controversial or politically loaded. The removal of the great bulk (but not all) of the hereditary peers has been accompanied by a large increase in the number of peers appointed under the Life Peerages Act 1958 in order to create a House more representative of party strength in the country. While this is a laudable goal, the current method by which it is advanced is unlikely to be sustainable for long.

---

[257] On the continuing significance of the Parliament Acts, see Pannick [2012] PL 230.

CHAPTER 8

Role of Parliament

In this chapter we move from a consideration of the composition of Parliament to an assessment of its role and functions in the modern constitution. At a simplistic level, Parliament's role and purpose seem obvious: it is the body that makes the laws by which we are governed. Of course, it does not make all the laws by which we are governed: many laws were made by the institutions of the EU, and others still are the product of the common law and as such they are made by judges. Nevertheless, EU law applied in the United Kingdom by virtue of an Act of Parliament, while Parliament always has the authority to change common law rules and frequently does so, with legislation having displaced the common law in most areas where the latter had generally prevailed.

In performing its law-making function, Parliament purports to be broadly representative of the mood of the nation, as determined at the most recent general election. Law will thus have a partisan edge, being the product of the political process. But beyond this rather simple account, Parliament has many other functions the scope and content of which are unclear, as would be expected of an institution that has no expressly defined role, and which has had an existence for an unbroken period of many hundreds of years. Although we live in a more democratic age, Parliament existed in pre-democratic times; it had a role and functions before the emergence of the democracy that it helped to create, and of which it is now the living embodiment, in what is a dynamic and evolving process.

A. The functions of Parliament

Contemporary discussions of the place of Parliament in the Westminster system might begin with its role in (i) providing the personnel of government, as (ii) the institution through which the government in turn must govern to secure its money and its business, while (iii) having a responsibility to hold the government to account in the conduct of the nation's affairs. The effectiveness of these sometimes-conflicting roles depends to some extent on the adversarial nature of Parliament, which – although sometimes apparently unattractive to many – is a necessary feature of the Westminster system if its contradictions are to be reconciled: one side of the House supplies the government and will generally ensure safe passage of its measures; the other will principally be responsible for scrutiny and accountability. Both are important.

A classic statement of the importance of parliamentary control of government and its limitations was made by the political philosopher, John Stuart Mill:

> Instead of the function of governing, for which it is radically unfit, the proper office of a representative assembly is to watch and control the government; to throw the light of publicity on its acts; to compel a full exposition and justification of all of them which anyone considers questionable; to censure them if found condemnable, and, if the men who compose the government abuse their trust, or fulfil it in a manner which conflicts with the deliberate sense of the nation, to expel them from office, and either expressly or virtually appoint their successors.[1]

[1] Mill, *Representative Government*, ch 5.

This high-principled analysis is still of value, and finds an echo in the important report of the House of Commons Reform Select Committee that 'Government should get its business, the House should get its scrutiny and the public should get listened to'.[2] Analysis of this kind also has important implications for Parliament: if it is a duty of the House to find out about, scrutinise and influence the many acts of government agencies, two consequences follow. First, the House needs procedures and resources to match the scale of the task; second, the members of the House who do not hold ministerial office need the political will to do more than simply sustain the government in office while voting through the measures laid before them. There is a need for committed parliamentarians as much as for committed ministers.

In this chapter we concentrate on three major areas of Parliament's work. We begin with its role in voting supply, which Parliament is expected both to scrutinise and authorise simultaneously. We begin with supply because of its importance: without money the government would be unable to do very much. Thereafter we consider the legislative process, and the means by which the government gets its business through a Parliament where government business has priority over that of private members. Finally, we examine the role of Parliament in the scrutiny of government, and the different procedures that have been adopted for this purpose. In all of these areas, significant procedural changes have taken place or have been proposed in recent years, often in response to criticism of parliamentary shortcomings.

In concentrating on these three core functions, we do not suggest that they exhaust the functions of Parliament. Thus, Parliament also has an important role to play in the redress of individual grievances, which is an aspect of the scrutiny of administration generally. Also relevant is the Parliamentary Ombudsman, whose work will be considered in Chapter 23 D. Parliament's other main role is to act as a constitutional watchdog, and to this end influential select committees dealing with constitutional questions have been formed by both the House of Commons and the House of Lords. This is a matter to which we return later in this chapter, while the related work of the Joint Committee on Human Rights is addressed in Chapter 14.

Beyond that, it is sometimes said that Parliament represents the 'conscience of the nation',[3] which places it in a unique legal and political position. In the United Kingdom, unlike in other countries, it is Parliament that has the last word on controversial moral questions, and it is to Parliament that the courts look for guidance and leadership.[4] Thus, as pointed out in the Court of Appeal, 'the circumstances in which a pregnancy may be terminated were decided by Parliament', while 'the abolition of the death penalty following the conviction for murder was, similarly, decided by Parliament'.[5] The same is true of homosexuality law reform, also initiated in the 1960s by a progressive backbencher.

B. Authorising expenditure and providing income[6]

No government can exist without raising and spending money. In the Bill of Rights 1689, art 4, the levying of money for the use of the Crown without grant of Parliament was declared illegal. Relying on the principle that the redress of grievances preceded supply, the Commons

---

[2] HC 1117 (2012–13), para 20.

[3] *R (Nicklinson)* v *Ministry of Justice* [2013] EWCA Civ 961, [2013] WLR(D) 326, para 155. See subs appeal at [2014] UKSC 3.

[4] Ibid, para 112.

[5] Ibid, para 155.

[6] See also J F McEldowney, in Jowell, Oliver and O'Cinneide (eds), *The Changing Constitution* (8th edn), ch 13. We refer to earlier iterations of this unique and valuable essay as it appeared in earlier editions of the foregoing title in the pages that follow.

could after 1689 insist that the Crown pursued acceptable policies before granting the taxes or other revenue that the Crown needed. It has been said of the financial procedure of Parliament that the Crown requests money, the Commons grants it, and the Lords assents to the grant.[7] Today, the assent of the Lords is only nominal, and it is generally regarded as vital to a government's existence that its financial proposals be accepted by the Commons. It is unlikely that a government would accept that the Commons should modify its expenditure proposals, and it is likely that a government that failed to ensure supply would have to resign.[8]

It is important to emphasise that Parliament has two roles: the first is to authorise the government's proposed expenditure; and the second is to authorise the raising of money (through taxation) to pay for it. Both require legislation. It is important also to emphasise that it is a fundamental constitutional principle that no payment out of the national Exchequer may be made without the authority of an Act of Parliament, and then only for the purposes for which the statute has authorised the expenditure.[9] Taxpayers and certain interest groups may have a sufficient interest in an expenditure decision to seek judicial review of its legality.[10] It is an equally fundamental constitutional principle that no charges by way of taxation may be imposed by the government on the citizen without the authority of an Act of Parliament, a principle that gives the citizen protection in the courts against unauthorised tax or other charges.[11]

Basic principles and rules of financial procedure

The financial procedures of the Commons are intricate and can only be outlined here, the basic principles of financial control by, and accountability to, Parliament forming part of a broader public expenditure process, which has helpfully been described as having four stages: (i) expenditure planning by the executive; (ii) parliamentary debate and approval of the executive's request for supply; (iii) spending by the executive of the money voted by Parliament; and (iv) accounting for the money spent.[12] Our concern in this chapter is principally with the second of these steps in the process. But although the 'power of the purse' is 'central to the ability of Parliament to call government to account',[13] it ought not to be assumed that Parliament has developed adequate methods for this purpose.

It has been pointed out that in reality, 'little substantial scrutiny is involved' in these procedures, for 'the policy objectives on which the money is spent are not determined by the Commons but by the government'.[14] Indeed, one prominent backbencher referred to the 'charade' of the House of Commons 'rubber stamping tablets of stone handed down by the executive of the day'.[15] This is perhaps inevitable in a parliamentary democracy which operates generally on the basis of a mandate claimed by government for a range of actions: the government can normally expect that its electoral promises will not be frustrated by the Commons.

---

[7] Erskine May, *Parliamentary Practice*, p 711.

[8] Hence the need for a general election after the Lords had rejected the Liberal government's Finance Bill in 1909. In 1975, the failure of the Prime Minister of Australia to ensure supply (because of opposition from the Australian Senate to two Appropriation Bills) was the reason given by the Governor General for dismissing him.

[9] *Auckland Harbour Board* v *R* [1924] AC 318.

[10] *R* v *Foreign Secretary, ex p World Development Movement* [1995] 1 All ER 611: decision to finance Pergau Dam in Malaysia declared to be ultra vires the Overseas Development and Cooperation Act 1980. The government made up the money from other public funds: HC Deb, 13 December 1994, col 773.

[11] And see *Congreve* v *Home Office* [1976] QB 629; *Woolwich Building Society* v *IRC* (*No 2*) [1993] AC 70.

[12] White and Hollingsworth, *Audit, Accountability and Government*, p 1.

[13] Ibid.

[14] J F McEldowney, in Jowell and Oliver (5th edn), p 381.

[15] HC Deb, 3 December 2002, col 871 (Andrew Mackinley).

Yet although government can properly claim the opportunity to implement its mandate, this ought not to be at the expense of rigorous and effective financial scrutiny of how money is to be spent. As the Clerk of Supply has pointed out, it is for the members of Parliament themselves to determine 'the extent to which the process of authorising public expenditure constitutes a rubber stamp'.[16]

According to Erskine May, three key rules govern the present procedure.[17] For the purpose of these rules, the word 'charge' includes both charges upon the public revenue, i.e. expenditure, and charges upon the people, i.e. taxation:

(1) A charge 'whether upon public funds or upon the people' must be authorised by legislation;[18] it must generally originate in the Commons, and money to meet authorised expenditure must be appropriated in the same session of Parliament as that in which the relevant estimate is laid before Parliament.

(2) A charge may not be considered by the Commons unless proposed or recommended by the Crown. The latter requirement is expressed in House of Commons Standing Orders, dating in part from 1713: 'This House will receive no petition for any sum relating to public service or proceed upon any motion for a grant or charge upon the public revenue . . . unless recommended from the Crown.'[19] The government thus has formal control over almost all financial business in the Commons, the ability of Opposition and backbenchers to propose additional expenditure or taxation correspondingly subject to serious restrictions.

(3) A charge must first be considered in the form of a resolution passed by the House, which forms an essential preliminary to the Bill or clause by which the charge is authorised. Certain financial Bills must be preceded by such a resolution before they can be read a second time. But for most Bills, whether the main object or an incidental object is the creation of a public charge, the financial resolution normally follows the second reading and must be proposed by a minister.[20]

The work of the Commons is conducted on a sessional basis. Following the Fixed-term Parliaments Act 2011, each session now runs for a year from early May, having previously run from November. However, the government's financial year runs from April, thereby still (just) crossing two parliamentary sessions. The result is a complex annual financial cycle, which will now be described – first in relation to the authorisation of expenditure (supply), and second in relation to taxation. The elaborate system of authorising expenditure discussed below still owes much to reforms linked with Gladstone's tenure of office as Chancellor of the Exchequer in the 1860s, though they have since been overhauled, most notably by the Government Resources and Accounts Act 2000.[21]

The system of supply: government estimates

Funds are requested by the government by means of estimates. These are prepared in government departments and examined by the Treasury to ensure that they are consistent with the government's overall spending plans. After scrutiny by and debate in Parliament, the estimates are approved by a resolution of the House of Commons. Scrutiny of individual

---

[16] C Lee (2004) 72 *The Table* 14.
[17] Erskine May, ch 32. For discussion of earlier forms of the rules, see Reid, *The Politics of Financial Control*, and M Ryle, in Walkland (ed.), ch 7.
[18] Erskine May, p 713.
[19] HC SO 48. For background, see Reid, pp 35–45.
[20] HC SO 50.
[21] See HC 841 (1999–2000), Annex A; and HC 426 (2007–8), paras 15–22.

departmental estimates is now mainly undertaken as a 'core task' of select committees,[22] which may take evidence from ministers and officials (but there is no suggestion that the estimates should be 'cleared' by the select committees before being put to the House for approval).[23] Although select committees may receive advance copies of the estimates in draft, it has been claimed that they may have only between two and four weeks at most to consider them.[24] However, there is also an opportunity for the House as a whole to debate and vote on individual estimates on three estimates' days set aside for this purpose under the Commons standing orders.[25]

These debates in principle are informed by the reports of the select committees, with the time allocated on the basis of advice given by the chairman of the Liaison Committee (the committee of select committee chairmen).[26] As suggested above, however, serious questions have been raised about the adequacy of the procedures, having regard to the sums of money involved, the resources at the disposal of the House, and the time available to it.[27] According to one leading parliamentarian when in opposition:

> Select committees need to exercise more oversight of departments' spending. Most now look at annual reports and spending plans. But few get into the detail of their department's budget, and there's no real link between the government's estimates and the committee responsible, other than the nomination by the liaison committee of a handful of reports for debate on the floor of the house.[28]

While at times difficult to comprehend, the financial procedure of the House remains crucially important: the scrutiny of government spending (and the attendant authorisation for the raising of taxes) is one of the most important functions of Parliament. The current procedure provides that once the House of Commons has agreed the grants set out in the estimates, the Supply and Appropriation (Main Estimates) Bill is introduced and passed through all stages before the summer recess. Once passed, the Act (known until recently as the Appropriation Act) will do the following:

(*a*) authorise the issue from the Consolidated Fund of the balance of the grant of the estimates for the current financial year.[29] Some money will already have been voted on account to meet departmental expenditure. This is because – as already indicated – the Supply and Appropriation (Main Estimates) Act will not normally be passed until after the financial year has started, which means that unless some other method were available to supply money to the departments, they would be unable to carry out their business. So in the Supply and Appropriation (Anticipation and Adjustments) Act passed earlier in the session (but in the previous financial year), money will be provided by a vote on account to fund activities pending the enactment of the Supply and Appropriation (Main Estimates) Act.[30]

(*b*) specify in a detailed schedule to the Act the total net resources, the net capital, and the net cash authorised for each department or service in the year in question. In relation to each

---

[22] HC 514 (2008–9).

[23] HC 426 (2007–8), para 68. See also HC 321 (2000–1), para 5.

[24] *The Guardian*, 9 December 2009 (Michael Fallon).

[25] HC SOs 54, 55. It has been proposed that this should be extended to five days. See HC 426 (2007–8) and HC 1117 (2008–9).

[26] HC SO 145(3). See HC 514 (2008–9).

[27] HC 426 (2007–8).

[28] *The Guardian*, 9 November 2009 (Michael Fallon). For proposals that answer such concerns, see HC 426 (2007–8).

[29] The Consolidated Fund is the government's account into which revenue derived from taxation is paid.

[30] The vote on account was typically 45 per cent of the amount voted to the service or activity in the year to which it is to apply. See HC 1235 (2004–5), para 3.

department or agency, there is also a brief description in the Schedule of the ways in which this money is to be used. But this description is in the most general terms, there being no detailed breakdown of how the allocated cash is to be distributed between identified uses. In the case of the Department of Work and Pensions, less than a page explains how just under £83 billion is to be spent on social security benefits.[31] Nevertheless, in this way, the Supply and Appropriation (Main Estimates) Act specifies both the use and expenditure of money as well as the general purposes for which it may be spent.

There will not normally be a debate on the Supply and Appropriation (Main Estimates) Act.

Although the Supply and Appropriation (Main Estimates) Act will authorise the bulk of expenditure for the current year, there are, nevertheless, two wrinkles that may need to be ironed out. First, a department may exceed its estimated expenditure during the current financial year – because of unforeseen circumstances or a new policy initiative; in that case supplementary estimates will have to be approved, usually towards the end of the financial year in question.[32] Secondly, there is also the possibility that a department may spend more than provided for in the annual estimate, but has been unable to cure the excess before the end of the financial year. This will have to be authorised after the event by what is referred to as an excess vote (usually in an Act of Parliament in the next financial year, though sometimes later still) to authorize the expenditure retrospectively. These matters are usually addressed in a separate Supply and Appropriation Act.

The system of supply: statutory authorisation

The three principal statutes in a typical financial year for the grant of supply are thus:

- the Supply and Appropriation (Anticipation and Adjustments) Act (passed in March) to provide money on account to fund activities from the start of the new financial year;

- the Supply and Appropriation (Main Estimates) Act (passed in July) to deal with the main estimates for the new financial year; and

- the Supply and Appropriation (Anticipation and Adjustments) Act (passed in the following March) to deal with supplementary estimates in the financial year about to end, and excess spending in the previous financial year.

Any excesses for the year just ending will be dealt with in the Supply and Appropriation (Anticipation and Adjustments) Act in the following March (and perhaps in the March after that).

By way of illustration, between March 2016 and March 2017, the three pieces of financial legislation crossing the boundaries of two parliamentary sessions provided as follows:

(1) The Supply and Appropriation (Anticipation and Adjustments) Act 2016 received the royal assent on 16 March 2016. This authorised on account the use of resources for the service of the following financial year (ending on 31 March 2017) and the issuing of money from the Consolidated Fund for these purposes. The sums involved were £258.3 billion and £222.9 billion respectively. The same Act also authorised the use of additional resources in the current financial year (ending 31 March 2016) of £139.9 billion for purposes specified in the Schedule, and a much smaller sum to cover excesses in the previous year 2014–15.

....
[31] See Supply and Appropriation (Main Estimates) Act 2016, Schedule.
[32] See HC 1005 (2013–14) (Justice Committee, expressing concern about the amount of the supplementary estimate, which should be drawn to the attention of the House).

(2) The Supply and Appropriation (Main Estimates) Act 2016 received the royal assent on 20 July 2016, well into the financial year. This authorised the use of additional resources of £292.7 billion for the service of the year ending 31 March 2017. It also authorised the Consolidated Fund to pay out up to an additional £259.4 billion to meet this authorisation, the sums being appropriated under many separate headings. Together the Supply and Appropriation (Anticipation and Adjustments) Act 2016 and the Supply and Appropriation (Main Estimates) Act 2017 thus authorised a total of £551.2 billion to be paid from the Consolidated Fund in the financial year 2016–17.[33]

(3) The Supply and Appropriation (Anticipation and Adjustments) Act 2017 received the royal assent on 16 March 2017. Apart from providing money on account for the financial year 2017–18 in the manner described above, the Act also made supplementary provisions for 2016–17 (of up to £87.9 billion). These supplementary measures related to several departments. The 2017 Act in addition made provision for an excess vote for 2015–16 (of £290 million), as well as for late excesses for the year before that.

This, however, will not be the whole of it; other government expenditure is authorised by what are referred to as Consolidated Fund standing services: these charges have separate statutory authority and do not need annual approval. This form of public spending is used for matters such as the Civil List, judicial salaries, and payments to the European Union,[34] and accounts for another substantial expenditure.[35] An additional standing charge was introduced by the Banking Act 2009 in the wake of the global banking crisis. If the Treasury is satisfied that the need for the expenditure is too urgent for arrangements to be made for the provision of money by Parliament, it may be met by payments from the Consolidated Fund.[36] Where money is paid in reliance of this remarkable power, the Treasury must report to Parliament specifying the amount paid ('but not the identity of the institution to or in respect of which it is paid').[37]

And this still is not the whole of it, for there is also a Contingencies Fund which may be used to meet unforeseen government expenditure,[38] the fund being of an amount equal to 2 per cent of the net cash requirement for the previous year.[39] Although the Fund may not be drawn upon for any purpose for which legislation is necessary until a second reading has been given to the Bill in question, the existence of the Fund is a striking exception to the principle that parliamentary authority should be obtained before expenditure is incurred; effective scrutiny of the Fund depends on the Treasury, backed up by the Comptroller and Auditor General's powers of audit.[40] The legality of payments from the Fund appears uncertain, but is not likely to arise for decision in the courts.[41] Indeed, decisions of the courts that certain government expenditure is unlawful may lead to the Fund being used to underwrite the contested expenditure.[42]

---

[33] As might be expected, the largest appropriations were to the large spending departments, such as Health, Work and Pensions, Defence and Local Government.

[34] See HC 185 (2016–17) (Consolidated Fund Account).

[35] See HC 484 (2004–5). This contributes to what has been said to be 'more than a third of government spending included in budgets' which is not voted in Estimates: HC 426 (2007–8), para 28. In 2015–16, £15.9 billion was accounted for as the UK contribution to the EU budget: HC 475 (2016–17).

[36] Banking Act 2009, s 228(5).

[37] Ibid, s 228(6). But even this latter obligation can be dispensed with on public interest grounds: s 228(7).

[38] See J F McEldowney [1988] PL 232.

[39] Miscellaneous Financial Provisions Act 1946; Contingencies Fund Act 1974.

[40] A statement of the account is laid annually before Parliament. See HC 185 (2016–17), with details of how the money was spent.

[41] HC 118–1 (1980–1), p xiv; HC 137 (1981–2), app 20; HC 24–1 (1982–3), p xliii. And see J F McEldowney, in Jowell and Oliver (6th edn), pp 367–8.

[42] See McEldowney, ibid, pp 367, 370 citing *R* v *Foreign Secretary, ex parte World Development Movement* [1995] 1 All ER 611 (Pergau Dam).

The raising of money: taxation and the budget

Government expenditure must be paid for from taxation, which must in turn be authorised by Parliament.[43] While many forms of revenue, such as customs and excise duties, are raised under legislation that continues in force from year to year, some taxes, notably income tax and corporation tax, are authorised from year to year. The machinery for the collection of these taxes is permanent but Parliament must approve each year the rates of tax. In recent years the Budget had been presented in the Spring, until Mrs May's government revived the practice of an Autumn Budget to tie in better with the parliamentary timetable.

The contents of the budget are kept secret until the speech is delivered. While the government is collectively responsible for the budget speech and the Chancellor prepares it in close consultation with the Prime Minister, the contents are traditionally made known to the Cabinet only on the previous day or even on the morning of the speech. The brief period of Coalition government made it necessary to ensure that both parties in government were fully aware of Budget proposals, and it was important to this end that a Liberal Democrat occupied the position of Chief Secretary to the Treasury. The Chancellor may find it necessary to announce changes in indirect taxation and expenditure decisions at other times in the year.

As soon as the Chancellor's speech is completed, the House passes formal resolutions that enable immediate changes to be made in the rates of existing taxes and duties, and give renewed authority for the collection of the annual taxes. These resolutions are confirmed by the House at the end of the budget debate. The taxing resolutions are later embodied in the annual Finance Act. The effect of any changes made by the Finance Act may be made retrospective to the date of the budget or any selected date. It was for long the practice to begin at once to collect taxes under the authority of the budget resolutions alone. But in *Bowles* v *Bank of England*,[44] Bowles successfully sued the Bank for a declaration that it was not entitled to deduct any sum by way of income tax from dividends, until such tax had been imposed by Act of Parliament.

This latter decision illustrates the principle in *Stockdale* v *Hansard*,[45] that no resolution of the House of Commons can alter the law of the land. The decision made it necessary to pass a law which has now been re-enacted in the Provisional Collection of Taxes Act 1968, which gives statutory force for a limited period to resolutions of the House varying an existing tax or renewing a tax imposed during the preceding year. The Act was amended by the Finance Act 2011 to take account of the Fixed-term Parliaments Act 2011.[46] The effect of these latter amendments is that a resolution can be carried over from one parliamentary session to another (as the new parliamentary calendar requires), and that an Act confirming the resolutions must become law within seven months of the date of the resolution.[47]

Because the Finance Bill must become law by a set date, the government must ensure that it is passed by the Commons and sent to the Lords as quickly as possible. Although the House of Lords generally debates the Finance Bill on its second reading, its passage through the Lords is unopposed. Unlike the Appropriation Bills, the Finance Bill is not always certified as a 'money Bill' for the purposes of the Parliament Act 1911. Nevertheless, it would be a serious challenge to the financial privileges of the Commons for the Lords to seek to amend a Finance Bill, which comes within the hallowed class of 'Bills of Aids and Supplies',[48]

[43] See *Congreve* v *Home Office* [1976] QB 629.
[44] [1913] 1 Ch 57.
[45] (1839) 9 A & E 1; ch 9 A.
[46] HMRC, Provisional Collection of Taxes Act 1968: Amendments to Section 1 (2011).
[47] As now amended the Act applies to income tax and corporation tax, as well as a range of other taxes and duties. For details, see Erskine May, pp 778–9.
[48] Erskine May, p 795.

amendments to which the House of Commons typically opposes without any reason being given, in circumstances where the House of Lords would always give way.[49]

C. Enacting legislation – House of Commons procedure

In Chapter 3, we saw that the legislative supremacy of Parliament does not mean that the whole work of legislating is carried on within Parliament or that the parliamentary stage is the most formative stage in the process of legislation. Many government policies can be achieved within the framework of existing legislation: for example, by the provision of more money for certain purposes or by the use of existing powers to direct local authorities. But other policies require legislation, and most legislation is initiated by the government. The scope for legislative initiatives by individual MPs is severely limited, both because of restricted parliamentary time, and because of the tight hold the government maintains over departmental action.

The process by which government policies are turned into law falls into three broad stages:

(*a*) before publication of the Bill;

(*b*) the passage of the Bill through Parliament;

(*c*) after the Bill has received the royal assent.

In this section, emphasis is placed on the second of these stages. But stages (*a*) and (*c*) are both important to an understanding of the legislative process.

The process of legislation, like most aspects of parliamentary procedure, is complicated.[50] A distinction must be drawn between public and private Bills. A public Bill seeks to alter the general law and is introduced into Parliament under the standing orders of the two Houses relating to public business. A private Bill is a Bill relating to a matter of individual, corporate or local interest and is subject to separate standing orders relating to private business.[51] A private Bill must not be confused with a public Bill introduced by a private member, which is known as a private member's Bill.[52]

In this chapter we are concerned only with public Bills.[53]

Origins of legislation and pre-legislative scrutiny

A Bill will typically be included in a government's legislative programme, which will be announced in the Queen's Speech, delivered at the beginning of each parliamentary session. The history of a Bill will, however, usually have begun long before this, originating perhaps in the efforts of a pressure group to get the law changed. Public authorities may have experienced difficulties in administering the existing law and may seek wider powers. Bodies such as the Law Commissions or the Committee on Standards in Public Life may have published reports recommending law reform, while a decision of the courts (including the European Court of Human Rights and the European Court of Justice) may have shown the need for legislation.[54] There may also be obligations to change the law as a result of a new international treaty.

---

[49] House of Lords Constitution Committee, HL Paper 97 (2010–12), App 2 (Commons Financial Privilege).

[50] The authoritative work on legislative procedure is Erskine May, above. See also Griffith, *Parliamentary Scrutiny of Government Bills*, and Griffith and Ryle, *Parliament*, ch 6. See also HC 538 (1970–1); HC 1097 (2005–6).

[51] Provision must be made to publicise local Bills, and an opportunity provided by members of the public to petition against any such Bill.

[52] See pp 202–3 below.

[53] For an account of private bills, see Erskine May, above, and earlier editions of this book.

[54] See *R (Miller)* v *Secretary of State for Exiting the EU* [2017] UKSC 5; [2017] 2 WLR 583, leading to the European Union (Notification of Withdrawal) Act 2017.

The most likely source of legislation, however, will be the election manifestos of the political parties, which set out the steps they will take if elected to government. In the modern era governments can be expected to carry out manifesto pledges, with the manifesto providing governments with both an obligation and a defence to justify their actions. In the case of the Coalition government that assumed office in 2010, however, compromises had to be made by both sides, with neither in a position fully to implement its own manifesto commitments. These compromises were set out in an agreement between the two Coalition parties (said to be the 'contract that underwrites this government'), followed by a comprehensive programme for government, which in turn was the subject of a 'mid-term review'.

Once it is decided to proceed with a Bill, it is for the department primarily concerned to determine precisely what it should contain, and these instructions are conveyed to Parliamentary Counsel who are responsible for drafting all government Bills. While a Bill is being drafted, extensive consultation may take place with other departments affected and successive revisions of the draft Bill will be circulated confidentially within government. There may also be consultation with organisations outside government representing the interests primarily affected, but until recently it was uncommon for a draft Bill to be disclosed. These consultations will normally cover both the general principles of the Bill as well as some of its more detailed provisions, especially where they are contentious.

Modern governments have adopted the practice of publishing a number of Bills in draft form, a practice welcomed by the now defunct House of Commons Modernisation Committee in 2002, as providing a 'real chance for the House to exercise its powers of pre-legislative scrutiny in an effective way'.[55] In an important report on the *Legislative Process*, the Modernisation Committee returned to the theme in 2006 and announced that pre-legislative scrutiny of draft Bills was 'one of the most successful Parliamentary innovations of the last ten years', and 'should become more widespread, giving outside bodies and individuals a chance to have their say before a bill is introduced and improving the quality of the bills that are presented to Parliament'.[56] Only a minority of Bills are published in Draft, and it is for government to choose which are most suitable for this purpose.

Parliamentary procedure

In the case of government Bills, the sponsoring minister presents the Bill to the Commons; it receives a formal first reading and is then printed and published. There follows the **second reading** of the Bill, when the House may debate its general proposals. If the second reading is opposed, a division may take place on an opposition amendment to postpone the second reading for three or six months, or (more usually) on a reasoned amendment opposing the Bill. For a government Bill to be lost on second reading would be a serious political defeat, to be generally avoided. One of the most famous examples of a Bill being lost at this stage was under the Thatcher government in 1986 when the Shops Bill, to reform the law on Sunday opening of shops, was defeated on second reading in the Commons by 296 votes to 282.[57]

The amount of time devoted to the second reading of a Bill will vary, though modern practice has been to schedule all second reading debates to last for no more than a day.[58] Where a Bill involves new public expenditure or new taxation, the Commons must approve a financial resolution on the proposal of a minister before the clauses concerned may be considered in

---

[55] HC 1168 (2001–2). For an account of scrutiny of draft Bills, see A Kennon [2004] PL 477.

[56] HC 1097 (2005–6).

[57] HC Deb, 14 April 1986, cols 584–702. See Brazier, *Constitutional Practice*, pp 219–20. On the willingness of MPs to rebel, see Cowley, *The Rebels*.

[58] HC 1096 (2005–6), paras 41–5. It has been suggested that this is too long for some Bills and too short for others, and that more flexibility is required by the business managers in the House (ibid).

committee; the financial resolution is approved immediately after a Bill's second reading.[59] Provision is made in the Standing Orders for the second reading to take place in some cases in the Scottish Grand Committee,[60] or the Welsh Grand Committee,[61] but there is no recent experience of this having been done. In exceptional circumstances non-controversial Bills may be taken in a second reading committee,[62] while a separate expedited procedure exists for Consolidation Bills.[63]

After second reading, a Bill is normally referred for detailed consideration to a **public bill committee**, consisting of between 16 and 50 members nominated by the Committee of Selection.[64] The Committee of Selection must have regard to the qualifications of the members and to the composition of the House, which means in practice that the parties are represented as nearly as possible in proportion to their parliamentary representation. If the government came into office with an overall majority over other parties and later lost that majority, questions would arise about its continuing majorities on public bill committees.[65] Following the House of Commons Modernisation Committee's report on the *Legislative Process*, public bill committees may now receive both written and oral evidence from interested parties as part of their examination of a Bill.

Instead of referring a Bill to a public bill committee, the House may commit the Bill to a committee of the whole House,[66] for which purpose the Speaker's place is taken by the Chairman of Ways and Means, or by one of the deputy chairmen. In practice this happens only on the proposal of the government, whether for minor Bills on which the committee stage is purely formal, conversely for Bills of outstanding political or constitutional importance, or for Bills which the government wishes to see become law as soon as possible.[67] Occasionally the committee stages of parts of a Bill will be dealt with in a committee of the whole House, with the other parts being dealt with in a public bill committee.

Whether a Bill is considered in a public bill committee or in a committee of the whole House, the object of the committee stage is to consider the individual clauses of the Bill and to enable amendments to be made. While general approval has been given to the Bill on second reading, members opposed to the Bill may use the committee stage to propose amendments narrowing its scope, or in other ways rendering it more acceptable to them. Members may be able to persuade the minister in charge of the Bill to reconsider a specific point, but the government expects to maintain its majority in committee and an amendment is not often made against the wishes of the government. On one notable occasion, however, a committee of the whole House inflicted the first Commons defeat on the post-1997 Labour government when it accepted an amendment to reject proposals for the detention without charge of terrorist suspects for up to 90 days.[68]

....

[59] Erskine May, ch 34; Griffith and Ryle, p 324.

[60] HC Standing Orders (HC SOs) 92 9. See C M G Himsworth (1996) 1 Edin LR 79.

[61] HC SOs 102–8.

[62] HC SO 90; Griffith and Ryle, p 323.

[63] HC SO 140. See Lord Simon of Glaisdale and J V D Webb [1975] PL 285.

[64] HC SOs 84, 86; Griffith and Ryle, pp 325–30.

[65] See Erskine May, p 860, footnote 2.

[66] HC SOs 63, 66.

[67] It is a 'long-standing convention of the House' that 'bills of first class constitutional importance' should 'have all their stages on the floor of the House'. This is said to derive from a memorandum submitted by the Labour government to the Procedure Committee in 1945. See HC 190 (1997–8), paras 74–5. Major Bills taken in committee of the whole House have included the Bills for the European Communities Act 1972, the Scotland Act 1998, the Government of Wales Act 1998, the Northern Ireland Act 1998, the Human Rights Act 1998, the House of Lords Act 1999, the Representation of the People Act 2000 and parts of the Political Parties, Elections and Referendums Act 2000, the Political Parties and Elections Act 2009 and the European Union (Notification of Withdrawal) Act 2017.

[68] HC Deb, 9 November 2005, col 386.

On completion of the committee stage, the Bill is reported as amended to the whole House. At that stage, ministers may propose further amendments to the Bill, sometimes to give effect to undertakings they have made in committee, sometimes to remove amendments made in committee but not accepted by the government. The Opposition may use the report stage to propose further amendments, though it is rare for these amendments to succeed and the Speaker has the discretion to select the amendments which will be debated.[69] A Bill committed to the whole House and not amended in committee is not considered by the House on report. After a Bill has been considered on report, it receives its third reading; only verbal amendments may be made to a Bill at this stage.[70]

Bills relating only to England or England and Wales

Responding to concerns about the impact of devolution on England and the lack of a distinctively English voice in the legislative process, the government announced in 2014 a plan for the introduction of a parliamentary procedure that would reserve to English MPs (i) the right to sit and vote on Bills and clauses in Bills that affect England only, on (ii) subjects which had they related to Scotland, Northern Ireland or Wales would have fallen within the powers of one or other of the devolved bodies. The idea here is that only English MPs should sit and vote on matters that affect England only, the principle being implemented by complex new Standing Orders introduced in 2015.[71] These adapt existing procedures and introduce new procedures for legislation which has been certified by the Speaker as (i) relating exclusively to England or to England and Wales, and (ii) is within devolved legislative competence.[72]

If a Bill is certified under this procedure (which applies only to government Bills, and in relation to which there are a number of minor exceptions), the Public Bill Committee will be composed only of MPs from English (or English and Welsh) constituencies, depending on whether the Bill applies to England or to England and Wales respectively.[73] Where the Bill is referred to a Committee of the Whole House, only MPs from English (or English and Welsh) seats will take part.[74] Otherwise, all members are entitled to sit and vote at Second Reading and on Report. After the Bill is reported and if it has been amended, it will be considered again by the Speaker, to determine whether the new procedures continue to apply.[75] A new stage has been introduced for those Bills to which the procedure does continue to apply, in the form of the Legislative Grand Committee (England) and the Legislative Grand Committee (England and Wales).[76]

After the report stage, the Bill will be considered in Legislative Grand Committee, a step that takes place on the floor of the House. It may be necessary for parts of the same Bill to be dealt with in two different Legislative Grand Committees if aspects deal with England only and other aspects deal with England and Wales only. All MPs may participate in the proceedings of the Legislative Grand Committees, but voting is restricted in the case of the Legislative Grand Committee (England) to all MPs from English seats, and in the case of the Legislative Grand Committee (England and Wales) to all MPs from English and Welsh seats as the case may be. At this stage (which should take place as soon as possible after the Report

---

[69] HC SO 32(1).

[70] HC SO 77.

[71] HC SO 83J–83X.

[72] HC SO 83J.

[73] HC SO 86(2)(iv).

[74] In some cases, the procedure applies also to legislation applying only to England, Wales and Northern Ireland, and the following account should be adapted accordingly.

[75] HC SO 83L.

[76] HC SO 83W, 83X.

stage), a consent motion is required to approve the Bill, and another opportunity will be provided for amendments to be made.

This, however, is only the first of three potential new stages for English-only or English and Welsh-only Bills, though the two subsequent stages arise only if the Bill is rejected by the Legislative Grand Committee which seems unlikely to happen very often, at least where the government has a majority in both the House overall and in English or English and Welsh constituencies. If the Legislative Grand Committee rejects the Bill, the next stage is for the Bill to be reconsidered by the whole House (which approved the Bill at Second Reading), with a view to resolving the differences between the House and the Committee. It is expected that this would lead to amendments to the Bill, which would then have to be agreed by the Legislative Grand Committee. Failure to agree would mean that the Bill would be lost, or that contested clauses of the Bill would be lost; though, as already indicated, neither seems likely to happen often.

Where, however, there *is* an irreconcilable failure to agree, a third new stage is referred to as 'Consequential consideration' and involves examination of the Bill by the whole House to make technical amendments to tidy up the Bill following the rejection of any part of it. When these stages are completed, the Bill would then proceed to third reading, which would normally take place immediately after the Legislative Grand Committee. One final procedural change relates to Lords amendments to a Bill which deals with certified matters. In these situations, the amendments will now be required to be approved not only by the whole House, but separately also by members of the House representing English or English and Welsh constituencies as the case may be. If the amendments are not approved in this way, they will be treated as not having been accepted, and the Bill will be sent back to the Lords.

This is an altogether complex procedure to give effect to a simple idea that in the post-devolution age English (or English and Welsh) laws should be made by English (or English and Welsh) MPs. In its current form the procedure is not so much a distinct process for making law as a process for giving English MPs collectively the power to veto laws approved by the House as a whole. Together with the administratively awkward manner of its operation, this has led to serious criticism by the House of Commons Procedure Committee in 2016, which complained that 'the attempt to combine the twin functions of voice and veto in a single legislative stage is not delivering significant and worthwhile benefits to Members representing constituencies in England and Wales'.[77] Although they had been used in relation to a significant number of Bills,[78] the arrangements did not 'command the respect and support' that they should.[79]

Programme orders and guillotines

In the legislative work of the Commons, the time factor is always of importance both to the government, which wishes to see its Bills pass through Parliament without delay, and to the

---

[77] HC 189 (2016–17), para 45 (Procedure Committee).

[78] Between October 2015 (when the procedures were introduced) and December 2016 (when the House of Commons Procedure Committee reported), the new procedures were applied to seven Commons Bills and five Lords Bills. Legislative Grand Committees had met to give consent to the certified provisions of ten bills. The Legislative Grand Committee (England, Wales and Northern Ireland) had met once; the Legislative Grand Committee (England and Wales) had met on seven occasions and the Legislative Grand Committee (England) had met on seven occasions. According to the Procedure Committee (on which the foregoing draws), the total time taken in all legislative grand committees was one hour and 23 minutes, the Committee adding that 'besides Ministers, five Members have spoken. On each occasion Ministers have invited the Committee to consent to the certified provisions of the Bill, and on each occasion the motion has been agreed to without a division': ibid, para 10.

[79] Ibid, para 76. In addition, 'Genuine debate in such committees has been so scarce as to be almost non-existent': ibid, para 32.

Opposition and backbench MPs, who may seek to prolong proceedings as a means of persuading the government to make concessions. As well as the power of the Speaker or chair to require a member to discontinue speaking who persists in irrelevance or tedious repetition,[80] various methods of curtailing debates have been adopted by the House, of which the most important are now programme orders, whereby a fixed amount of time is allocated in advance to each stage of a Bill in the House of Commons.[81]

Programming (which we deal with below) has largely (though not wholly) displaced the other means available to the government to curtail debates. These include closure motions, by which any member (in practice usually a government whip) may, either in the House or in Committee, move that 'the question be now put'.[82] The chair may refuse to put the motion on the ground that it is an abuse of the rules of the House or an infringement of the rights of the minority; but if the chair does not so decide, the motion must be put forthwith and voted upon without debate. The motion can be carried only if at least 100 members vote for it, and if it is carried, the debate to which it relates must be brought to an end and voted upon. Although not now widely used, this procedure has nevertheless been thought still to be important.

Other means available to curtail debates include the 'guillotine', which may also be moved by a minister with a view to allotting a specified number of days or portions of days to the consideration of a Bill in committee of the whole House or on report.[83] The difference between this and a programme order is that the latter is moved after the second reading, while the guillotine motion will be moved at a later stage if the government believes that a Bill is being held up deliberately.[84] The guillotine motion may be debated for no more than three hours, and if it is carried, it is the duty of the Business Committee, which consists of the Chairman of Ways and Means and up to eight other members nominated by the Speaker, to divide the Bill into parts and to allot to each part a specified period of time.[85] The effect of a guillotine motion is that at the end of each allotted period, the portion of the Bill in question is voted on without further discussion.

Turning to programme orders, their effect is to 'provide for the allocation of time for any proceedings on a Bill'.[86] A programme motion may be moved only by a minister before second reading, with the vote on the motion taking place immediately after second reading. Although this seems a rather obvious way to conduct legislative business, it is a fairly recent innovation, being first used in 1998 following a recommendation of the Modernisation Committee.[87] It also remains a mildly controversial innovation, with the Modernisation Committee addressing concerns that a good idea had been corrupted in practice, and that programming was undermining the rights of backbenchers by squeezing them out of debates. Acknowledging these concerns, the Committee nevertheless noted that programming 'has become much less prescriptive and is used to ensure full debate', while the government 'works hard to make programming consensual' and that 'opposition to programming has decreased'.[88]

---

[80] HC SO 42.

[81] HC SO 83A–83I. See Griffith and Ryle, p 416.

[82] HC SO 36 and 37.

[83] See HC SOs 82 and 83.

[84] It may also be used to deal with Lords amendments, an unfortunate use of the procedure given that the Lords stage is often used by government to introduce its own amendments to Bills incomplete at the time of their introduction in the Commons, which means that measures will be enacted without debate in the Commons.

[85] For the history, see Jennings, *Parliament*, pp 241–6; for more recent practice, Griffith and Ryle, pp 413–18.

[86] HC SO 83A(6).

[87] See HC 190 (1997–98). See also HC 589 (1999–2000), HC 382 (2000–1), HC 1222 (2002–3), and HC 1097 (2005–6).

[88] HC 337 (2006–7), paras 120–2. For continuing problems, see HC 767 (2013–14).

Although initially opposed by the Conservatives when in opposition, the programming of Bills is now well established. It is recognised as a way of ensuring that the government's business is conducted in a timely manner, while also ensuring that time is allocated in such a way that enables all provisions of a Bill to be properly considered, with programming also applying in committee. However, not all Bills are subject to programming. The procedure does not apply to Bills for which it is unnecessary (for example, because the Bill is uncontroversial), to appropriation Bills (expressly exempt by Standing Orders), or to a number of other specific categories of Bill where there are special parliamentary procedures (such as consolidation Bills). Otherwise, the government may choose not to use programming for fast-track Bills where it wishes to restrict the time at second reading, the procedure not applicable at this early stage in the life of a Bill.

Programming has, however, been extended to the new procedures introduced for English (or English and Welsh laws), with time allocated in the initial programme motion after second reading, and also in supplementary programme motions. However, the former will typically require the Report stage and the Legislative Grand Committee stage to be concluded by a particular time, which may mean that proceedings on Report may leave no room for debate in the Legislative Grand Committee. Although this problem can be avoided by supplementary programme motions, the Procedure Committee also identifies a need for more precise programming to ensure consideration in Legislative Grand Committee of both the need for consent to the Bill generally as well as for consideration of amendments.[89] In practice it appears that only about an hour is allocated to the Legislative Grand Committee, which at least as currently operating appears to be ample time in view of the 'apparent lack of appetite for debate in that forum.[90]

Private members' Bills

The bulk of the legislative programme is taken up by government Bills, with only a small albeit significant part consisting of Bills introduced by backbench MPs. Although standing orders generally give precedence to government business, HC Standing Order 14 provides that 13 Fridays in each session are set aside for private members' Bills. On the first seven of these Fridays, precedence is given to the second reading of Bills presented by members who have secured the best places in the ballot for private members' Bills held at the beginning of each session. On the remaining Fridays, precedence is given to the later stages of those Bills which received their second reading earlier in the session.[91] As with government Bills, private members' Bills are referred to a public bill committee, the composition of a public bill committee usually reflecting the voting of the House on second reading, so that the supporters of the Bill form a majority.

Otherwise, a member may seek leave under HC Standing Order 23 to introduce a Bill under the 'ten-minute rule' procedure (on Tuesdays and Wednesdays only), and may speak briefly in support of the Bill, while an opponent may reply, and the House may then divide on the issue.[92] There may also be an opportunity under HC Standing Order 57 for a private member simply to present a Bill for its first reading, after giving notice, but without previously obtaining the leave of the House.[93] Under each of these latter procedures, the chances of a Bill proceeding further depend on whether it is completely unopposed, or on whether some time can be found for a second reading debate and later stages, either by the government or on a

---

[89] HC 189 (2016–17) (Procedure Committee).
[90] Ibid, para 39.
[91] HC SO 14(4), (5).
[92] HC SO 23.
[93] HC SO 57(1).

Friday devoted to private members' business. These are nevertheless valuable ways of giving publicity to a question about which a backbencher feels strongly, and by seeking leave to introduce a Bill there may be no need to have a Bill to present.

Surprisingly, in the 25-year period between 1983 and 2008, some 230 private members' Bills were enacted. Even more surprisingly, while most of these (179) originated under HC Standing Order 14, a significant minority nevertheless originated under the HC Standing Order 23 and 57 procedures. Private members' Bills are used for a variety of purposes, including matters of social reform (such as abortion, gay rights and the abolition of capital punishment) which were too divisive for the government to wish to take the initiative, matters of special interest to minority groups and topics of law reform which may be useful but have too low a priority to find a place in the government's programme.[94] A private member may not, however, propose a Bill the main object of which is the creation of a charge on the public revenue,[95] and where a Bill proposes charges on the revenue which are incidental to its main object, a financial resolution moved by a minister is needed before the financial clauses can be considered in committee.

It is not the practice for the government to use its majority to defeat a private member's Bill.[96] Indeed, the government has undertaken 'to make available the resources of parliamentary counsel whenever it appears that a Bill is likely to pass', whether or not the government supports the Bill.[97] Nevertheless, the sponsors of private members' Bills face considerable obstacles if they are to get their measure through, and this is true of those MPs who succeed in the annual ballot for time on Fridays for the introduction of their measure. Allocation of time orders are not applicable (whether in the form of programme motions or the guillotine, even if the Bill has government support), and the closure of debate needs the support of 100 members, which may not be easy to achieve on a Friday.

Concern has been expressed in recent years that the procedures need to be overhauled if this form of legislation is to survive.[98] However, important proposals for reform have been resisted by the government,[99] these proposals designed to ensure that backbench Bills with cross-party and public support have a greater chance of being passed.

D. Enacting legislation – House of Lords and after

Before it can be presented for the royal assent, a Bill must be approved by both Houses of Parliament. In practice, however, the two Houses do not have the same political composition, so that it cannot today be assumed that the Lords will always acquiesce with the wishes of the Commons. Historically this was not a problem for the Conservative party, as traditionally it enjoyed a large in-built majority as most of the hereditary peers tended to be Conservatives. But it was a problem for Labour governments, even after the Life Peerages Act 1958 allowed for life peers to be appointed. Since the House of Lords Act 1999 the hereditary peers have all but gone, and no one party has a majority in the House of Lords, which is now a problem for all governments. The formal position is that the House of Lords has the power to reject

....

[94] See Richards, *Parliament and Conscience*, and (same author) in Walkland (ed.), *The House of Commons in the Twentieth Century*, ch 6; Bromhead, *Private Members' Bills in the British Parliament*; Griffith and Ryle, pp 539–58; and Cowley (ed.), *Conscience and Parliament*.

[95] HC SO 48.

[96] Richards, *Parliament and Conscience*, p 27, describes this as a 'strong convention'.

[97] HC 610 (2003–04), para 20. Also HC Deb, 23 June 2008, col 10W.

[98] HC 684 (2015–16) (Procedure Committee).

[99] HC 701 (2016–17).

any Bill which is presented to it, regardless of whether it is a government Bill, and regardless of whether it has been approved by the House of Commons.

The House of Lords also has the power to make whatever amendments it likes to Bills and to insist that these amendments are included in the Bill as a condition of its acceptance. In practice, however, the relationship between the two Houses is regulated by law (the Parliament Acts 1911–49) and by convention (the so-called Salisbury–Addison Convention), both designed to affirm the supremacy of the House of Commons as the democratically elected chamber. But although subordinated to the Commons in these ways, it would be a grave mistake to under-estimate the very real political power retained by the House of Lords, and a mistake also to under-estimate its willingness to use that power.[100] In 2002–3, for example, the government was defeated 88 times on 14 separate Bills. This was 'more than in any one session since 1975–76'.[101] The Labour governments were defeated thereafter on no fewer than 278 times in the seven sessions beginning in 2003–4, while the Coalition was defeated on 75 occasions between 2010 and 25 June 2013.

Legislative procedure[102]

Except under the Parliament Acts 1911 and 1949, which are considered later, a Bill may be presented for the royal assent only when it has been approved by both Houses. After a public Bill has had its third reading in the Commons, it will be introduced into the Lords. The various stages in the Lords are broadly similar to those in the Commons, although they are governed by separate standing orders. The main difference has been that the committee stage of Bills is usually taken in committee of the whole House. In 1995, for the first time, the 'committee of the whole House' sat in a separate room at Westminster to consider the Children (Scotland) Bill, enabling the House itself to deal with other business.[103] Bills not considered in a 'committee of the whole House' may be considered instead by a Grand Committee which is a committee unlimited in number and which all members of the House are entitled to attend.[104]

In committee, there is no provision for the selection of amendments so that any amendments tabled may be moved. Even if no amendments are made in committee, there may be a report stage; although there is no limitation on the amendments which may be moved at the third reading, the House normally resolves major points of difference by the end of the Report stage, and to use Third Reading for tidying up the Bill. It is generally accepted that the House must consider government business within a reasonable time, but whether in fact this occurs often gives rise to disagreement. Exceptionally, a Bill or parts thereof may be referred to a select committee after second reading as in the case of the controversial Constitutional Reform Bill in 2004, which was so referred against the wishes of the government.[105]

The distinctive procedures of the House, in contrast with those of the Commons, facilitate the submission and consideration of amendments.[106] While some Bills coming from the

---

[100] Between 1970 and 1995, there were 603 government defeats in the Lords: HL Deb, 16 October 1995, col 90 (WA) and 27 November 1995, col 23 (WA), an average of 24 per session.

[101] P Cowley and M Stuart (2004) 57 *Parliamentary Affairs* 301, at p 304. See also P Cowley and M Stuart (2005) 58 *Parliamentary Affairs* 301.

[102] Griffith and Ryle, ch 12; Shell, *The House of Lords*, chs 5 and 6.

[103] HL Deb, 6 June 1995, col CWH 1.

[104] Erskine May, ch 28. But there are no votes in this committee, which can proceed only on the basis of unanimity.

[105] See HL 125 (2003–4). For an account, see R Walters (2005) 73 *The Table* 87. See also Trade Union Bill 2016: House of Lords Select Committee on Trade Union Political Funds and Political Party Funding, HL Paper 106 (2015–16).

[106] See D N Clarke and D Shell [1994] PL 409, 412.

Commons are approved by the Lords unchanged and with little debate, it is more usual for Bills to be considered in detail by the Lords and amendments made. This is particularly valuable when the effect of timetabling has been that only part of a Bill has been considered in detail by the Commons. The government itself tables many amendments in the Lords, some in response to undertakings given in the Commons. The passage of a Bill through the Lords thus enables the drafting of Bills to be improved as well as substantial amendments to be made and new material introduced. While the foregoing account has assumed that Bills are always introduced in the Commons, in principle Bills may originate in either House.

The major exception is that by ancient privilege of the Commons, Bills of 'aids and supplies', i.e. those which relate to national taxation and expenditure or to local revenues and charges upon them, must begin in the Commons.[107] Moreover, the democratic character of the Commons and the fact that most ministers are MPs mean that Bills of major political importance usually start there. These factors often mean that early in a session the Lords have too little legislative work and have too much later in the session when a load of Bills approved by the Commons reaches them. In 1972 a standing order was adopted by the Commons which relaxed the extent of the Commons' financial privilege in the case of government Bills and made it easier for Bills with financial provisions to begin in the Lords.[108]

Parliament Acts 1911–49

The immediate origin of the Parliament Act 1911 was the crisis caused when the House of Lords rejected Lloyd George's 'People's Budget' in 1909. However, conflict between the two houses had been simmering for some time,[109] and it was unsurprising that the matter would reach boiling point as a Liberal government with a popular mandate from an ever-widening franchise confronted a second chamber with a permanent majority of Conservative hereditary peers. The budget crisis of 1909 was resolved only when, after two general elections in 1910, the Liberal government made known George V's willingness on the Prime Minister's advice to create over 400 new Liberal peers to coerce the Lords to accept formal restraints on its powers.[110] Rather than have their control of the House of Lords overturned by the influx of a large number of new peers, the Conservative majority accepted a reduction in their powers.

The 1911 Act, which did not alter the composition of the upper House, made three main changes: (*a*) it reduced the life of Parliament from seven to five years; (*b*) it removed the power of the Lords to veto or delay money Bills; and (*c*) in the case of other public Bills, apart from a Bill to prolong the life of Parliament, the veto of the Lords was abolished and there was substituted a power to delay legislation for two years. But the period of delay the Lords could impose meant that in the fourth and fifth years of a Parliament the Lords could hold up a Bill knowing that it could not become law until after a general election. After 1945, faced with a massive programme of nationalisation to get through Parliament, the Labour government proposed to reduce the period of delay from two years to one year. After extensive discussions on the reform of the House of Lords, which broke down on the period of delay, the Parliament Act 1949 became law under the 1911 Act procedure.

Under the Parliament Acts 1911–49, Bills may in certain circumstances receive the royal assent after having been approved only by the Commons. This may happen (*a*) if the Lords fail within one month to pass a Bill which, having passed the Commons, is sent up at least one

---

[107] Erskine May, p 526; HC 538 (1970–71), paras 19–21. And see M Ryle, in Walkland (ed.), above, pp 355–9.

[108] HC Deb, 8 August 1972, col 1656; Erskine May, pp 526, 629–30, 780–90.

[109] See Lowell, *The Government of England*, ch 22.

[110] See Jenkins, *Mr Balfour's Poodle*; Nicolson, *King George V*, chs 9 and 10; Jennings, *Cabinet Government*, pp 428–48. For an account of why the 1911 Act took the form it did, see J Jaconelli (1991) 10 *Parliamentary History* 277. See also *R (Jackson)* v *A-G* [2005] UKHL 56, [2006] 1 AC 262, discussed more fully below.

month before the end of the session and is endorsed by the Speaker as a money Bill (s 1);[111] or (*b*) if the Lords refuse in two successive sessions, whether of the same Parliament or not, to pass a public Bill (other than a Bill certified as a money Bill or a Bill to extend the maximum duration of Parliament beyond five years) which has been passed by the Commons in those two sessions, provided that one year has elapsed between the date of the Bill's second reading in the Commons in the first of those sessions, and the date of its third reading in that House in the second of those sessions (s 2).[112]

A money Bill is a public Bill which, in the opinion of the Speaker, contains only provisions dealing with: the imposition, repeal, remission, alteration or regulation of taxation; the imposition of charges on the Consolidated Fund, or the National Loans Fund or on money provided by Parliament for the payment of debt or other financial purposes, or the variation or repeal of such charges; supply; the appropriation, receipt, custody, issue or audit of public accounts; or the raising or guarantee or repayment of loans. Bills dealing with taxation, money or loans raised by local authorities or bodies for local purposes are not certifiable as money Bills.[113] The statutory definition has been so strictly interpreted that many annual Finance Bills have not been endorsed with the Speaker's certificate.[114] However, Consolidated Fund Bills are invariably certified as money Bills.[115]

Where a Bill is presented for the royal assent under s 2 of the 1911 Act, it must be endorsed with the Speaker's certificate that s 2 has been complied with. As the Speaker must certify that it is the same Bill that has been rejected in two successive sessions, there are strict limits on the alterations which may be made to a Bill between the first and second sessions. But the Bill in the second session may include amendments which have already been approved by the Lords and, in sending up the Bill in the second session, the Commons may accompany it with further suggested amendments without inserting them into the Bill.[116] Any certificate of the Speaker given under the 1911 Act 'shall be conclusive for all purposes, and shall not be questioned in any court of law',[117] a formula which seeks to exclude any challenge to the validity of an Act passed under the Parliament Acts based on alleged defects in procedure.

Apart from not applying to Bills which seek to extend the maximum duration of Parliament beyond five years, the Parliament Acts do not apply to local and private legislation or to public Bills which confirm provisional orders. Nor do they apply to delegated legislation: here the formal powers of the Lords will depend on whether the parent Act expressly empowers the Lords to approve or disapprove of the delegated legislation in question.[118] This power of the Lords to veto delegated legislation is not insignificant, and although proposals have been made to subject it to some kind of procedure similar to that in the Parliament Acts 1911–49, none of these proposals has been implemented. The matter was not addressed in the ill-fated House of Lords Reform Bill 2012, which generally proposed to retain the status quo on Lords' powers.

---

[111] The original s 1 has only been lightly amended, but not in a way relevant here.

[112] As amended by the Parliament Act 1949.

[113] Ibid, s 1 (as amended by the National Loans Act 1968). See D Morris (2001) 22 Statute LR 211.

[114] Erskine May, p 796, footnote 50; and Jennings, *Parliament*, pp 416–19. Before giving the certificate, the Speaker must, if practicable, consult two members appointed from the chairmen's panel each session by the Committee of Selection of the House of Commons.

[115] Erskine May, p 796, footnote 50.

[116] 1911 Act, s 2(4). The procedure was used in relation to the Bill which became the Trade Union and Labour Relations (Amendment) Act 1976.

[117] 1911 Act, s 3.

[118] Ch 22.

Parliament Acts in operation

Apart from the Welsh Church Act 1914 and the Government of Ireland Act 1914, only the Parliament Act 1949 became law under the Parliament Act procedure before the War Crimes Act 1991. The War Crimes Bill proposed retrospectively to authorise prosecutions in Britain in respect of war crimes in Germany between 1939 and 1945 by persons who had become British citizens. It had not been part of the Conservative programme at the 1987 election and was carried on free votes in the Commons. It was, however, twice defeated on second reading in the Lords: following the second such defeat, the royal assent was given to it. The debates in the Lords on the War Crimes Bill were confused on the constitutional issues,[119] but those peers who voted against the Bill on the second occasion knew that their action would not prevent the Bill from becoming law.

The willingness on the part of the House of Lords more readily to challenge the Commons led to the Parliament Acts being used on several occasions since 1997: on one occasion following the defeat of the European Parliamentary Election Bill, and on another following the defeat of the Sexual Offences (Amendment) Bill. Most controversially, the Parliament Acts were used to secure the enactment of the Hunting Bill in 2004. Recent events have also revealed some of the limitations of the Parliament Acts: they do not apply to Bills which begin in the Lords (and so could not be invoked when the Lords voted down the Criminal Justice (Mode of Trial) Bill);[120] or – as we have seen – to secondary legislation (and so could not be invoked when the Lords rejected the Greater London Authority (Election Expenses) Order 2000 – the first time an affirmative order had been rejected by the Lords since 1968).[121]

These limiting features of the Parliament Acts were acknowledged by the (Wakeham) Royal Commission on House of Lords Reform, as were others: it had been argued that it should be possible for the Commons to amend a Bill before presenting it to the Lords on the second occasion without the Bill losing the protection of the Parliament Acts; at present the Commons may only 'suggest' amendments. But such technical questions were not thought by the Royal Commission to have given rise to any 'real difficulty in practice'[122] and no amendment to the Act was proposed, although it was proposed that the House of Lords should lose its power to veto secondary legislation, a recommendation accepted by the government.[123] This recommendation was renewed by Lord Strathclyde in 2016 in a report commissioned by the government following the Lords' rejection of Draft Tax Credits (Income Thresholds and Determination of Rates) (Amendment) Regulations 2015.[124]

The Wakeham Commission had also broadly endorsed the present statutory procedures and conventional practices relating to the distribution of powers between the two Houses. But the Commission apparently felt it unnecessary to address the argument that the Parliament Act 1949 is invalid since the Parliament Act procedure was never intended to be used

[119] G Ganz (1992) 55 MLR 87.

[120] One practical effect of this is that the House of Lords has an absolute veto over Commons amendments to Lords Bills.

[121] HL Deb, 22 February 2000, cols 134–82. On the same day the Lords also, for the first time, rejected an instrument subject to an annulment (Greater London Authority Election Rules 2000). See HL Deb, 22 February, cols 182–5. Note also the rejection of the Draft Tax Credits (Income Thresholds and Determination of Rates) (Amendment) Regulations 2015, said to be all the more significant for the fact that it related to a 'matter contained in the budget which was central to the Government's fiscal policy': Cm 9177, 2015.

[122] Cm 4534, 2000, p 36.

[123] Ibid, pp 77–8.

[124] For the Strathclyde Report, see Cm 9177, 2015; for the government's response see Cm 9363, 2016. The government stated that it had no intention to implement this aspect of the Strathclyde Report but was 'prepared to act if the primacy of the Commons is further threatened'.

for amending the 1911 Act itself, and since a delegate may not use delegated authority to increase the scope of his or her power.[125] While there are indeed limits on the Bills which may become law under the Parliament Act procedure, the argument that the 1949 Act is invalid depended on the view that measures passed by the Commons and the Crown alone should be regarded as delegated legislation: yet the interpretation of Commonwealth constitutions suggests that a legislature is not subject to the limitations implied by the maxim *delegatus non potest delegare*.[126]

The issue was considered in *R (Jackson) v Attorney-General*[127] where it was argued that the Hunting Act 2004 was invalid because it had been passed by using the Parliament Acts 1911–49, the contention being that the 1949 Act was invalid. But in a unanimous decision, this was rejected as implausible by the House of Lords. According to Lord Bingham, for 'the past half century, it has been generally, if not universally, believed that the 1949 Act has been validly enacted, as evidenced by the use made of it by governments of different political persuasions'. In his opinion that belief was 'well-founded'. The unanimous decision of nine judges in the *Jackson* case tended to confirm the view expressed in earlier editions of this text that arguments about the invalidity of the Parliament Act 1949 are more appropriate for the classroom than the courtroom. It seems unlikely that any court would take this argument seriously.[128]

Quite apart from the problems already identified, there are a number of other problems associated with the Parliament Acts, though these have yet to be confronted. Thus, at what stage has a Bill 'not been passed' by the Lords subsequently, once it has been given a second reading? In the event of conflict, it is not clear how such problems could be resolved, given the well-established common law rule that matters of parliamentary procedure are for Parliament alone to decide. Where, however, the source of conflict relates to primary legislation that purports to regulate such procedural matters, it may be thought that it is the courts that would be best placed to resolve such questions. The decision in *Pickin v British Railways Board*[129] suggests, nevertheless, that the latter cannot be taken for granted, though it does seem the most appropriate solution.

Salisbury–Addison and other conventions

The supremacy of the House of Commons is not based on legislation alone, and indeed it would be impractical if all Bills had to go through the lengthy process to be found in the Parliament Acts before being enacted. For much of the interwar period the problem of conflict between the two houses was contained by the fact that the Conservative party was in government for much of the period. In 1945, however, the Labour party won a landslide victory at the general election, standing on a platform of radical reform, including the nationalisation of many industries and the creation of a national health service.

Although the government was poorly represented in the House of Lords, the Conservative leader in the Lords (Lord Salisbury) nevertheless announced that Bills anticipated by the Labour party election manifesto would be accepted by the Lords as having been approved by the people; but that the Conservative peers 'reserved full liberty of action' as to measures that had not been in the election manifesto.[130] This became known as the Salisbury convention,

---

[125] Hood Phillips and Jackson, *Constitutional and Administrative Law*, pp 79–81; Hood Phillips, *Reform of the Constitution*, pp 18–19, 91–3.

[126] *R v Burah* (1878) 3 App Cas 889; *Hodge v R* (1883) 9 App Cas 117.

[127] [2005] UKHL 56, [2006] 1 AC 262.

[128] Compare Pannick [2012] PL 230.

[129] [1974] AC 763.

[130] HL Deb, 4 November 1964, col 66; Griffith and Ryle, pp 708–11; and see HL Deb, 19 May 1993, col 1780.

more recently referred to as the Salisbury–Addison convention,[131] and was designed to avoid direct confrontation between the Lords and the Commons, the general practice of the Lords being to allow a second reading to Bills coming from the Commons. This important convention reflects 'the status of the House of Commons as the United Kingdom's pre-eminent political forum', and the 'fact that general elections are the most significant expression of the political will of the electorate'.[132]

The convention was reviewed along with others by a joint committee of both Houses in 2006, which had been established at the invitation of the government to 'consider the practicality of codifying the key conventions on the relationship between the two Houses . . . which affect the consideration of legislation'. The committee saw its main task as being 'to seek consensus on the conventions applicable [to the legislative process], and to consider the practicality of codifying them'.[133] The key question was whether the formal position of the Lords as a legislative body had been moderated by conventions reflecting the primacy of the Commons. The evidence showed that, particularly since the exclusion of most hereditary peers in 1999, the House has become more assertive of its authority.

While this was acceptable to opposition parties, the government was not so happy, arguing that the Lords had recently moved too far beyond the limited role of the House under the Salisbury–Addison convention. Although the government wished the convention to be restated in terms supporting this view, the committee found that the Salisbury–Addison convention had changed since 1945, and particularly since 1999. In its current form, the convention required that every 'manifesto Bill' should receive a second reading in the Lords; such Bills should not be subject to 'wrecking amendments' that departed from the government's manifesto intention; and they should be passed and sent to the Commons in time for that House to consider the Bill with amendments proposed by the Lords.

In its unanimous report, the joint committee found that there would be value in the upper House adopting resolutions concerning manifesto Bills and the need to consider government business in reasonable time, on the understanding 'that conventions as such are flexible and unenforceable, particularly in the self-regulating environment of the House of Lords'. In making these recommendations, the joint committee stated its complete opposition to legislation on such matters. It did not support conventions to be turned into rules, nor for there to be any scope for judicial review of parliamentary procedures.[134] The government's response to this report insisted that the Commons must maintain its primacy in Parliament, and that the Lords must not exercise its power as a revising chamber in a way that undermines the Commons.[135]

The formation of the Coalition government in 2010 created further uncertainty, on the ground that it was difficult to argue that any government Bill was a 'manifesto Bill'. The matter was addressed by the Select Committee on Political and Constitutional Reform, as part of a wide-ranging inquiry on the formation of the new government. In evidence to the inquiry, the Opposition leader in the House of Lords (Baroness Royall) claimed that the Salisbury–Addison Convention applies only to Bills that were independently in the manifestos of both parties.[136] This is unsatisfactory if understandable, and there is much to be said for the view

---

[131] See Cm 4534, 2000, pp 39–40 for a discussion of the origins and purpose of the Convention. It is sometimes referred to as the Salisbury–Addison convention, as it is based on an understanding between Viscount Cranborne (the fifth Marquess of Salisbury) and Viscount Addison (the Leader of the Lords): HL Paper 265, HC 1212 (2005–6) (Report of Joint Committee on Conventions), para 63.

[132] Report of Joint Committee on Conventions, ibid, para 72.

[133] HL Paper 189, HC 1151 (2005–6) (Special Report of Joint Committee on Conventions).

[134] 'The courts have no role in adjudicating on possible breaches of parliamentary conventions. Parliament is accountable to the electorate, not to the judiciary': ibid, para 285.

[135] Cm 6997, 2006.

[136] HC 528-ii (2010–11), Ev w11, para 22 et seq.

that the Convention should cover all government Bills. The conclusion of the Committee was equally unsatisfactory:

> Members of the House of Lords may not feel bound to apply the Salisbury–Addison convention to policies contained in a coalition government's programme for government.[137]

Royal assent and post-legislative scrutiny

Parliament cannot legislate without the concurrence of all its parts, and therefore the assent of the Queen is required after a Bill has passed through both Houses. The Queen does not attend Parliament to assent in person, since an Act of 1541 authorised the giving of the assent by commissioners in the presence of Lords and Commons and this became the invariable practice. Formerly, the business of the Commons was interrupted to enable the Commons to attend the Lords for the purpose. But by the Royal Assent Act 1967, the assent, having been signified by letters patent under the Great Seal signed by the Sovereign, is notified separately to each House by its Speaker.[138] The traditional procedure has not, however, been abolished. In giving the royal assent ancient forms are used.[139]

A public Bill, unless dealing with finance, as also a private Bill other than one of a personal nature, is accepted by the words '*La Reyne le veult*'. A financial Bill is assented to with the words '*La Reyne remercie ses bons sujets, accepte leur benevolence et ainsi le veult*'. The formula for the veto was '*La Reyne s'avisera*'. The right of veto has not been exercised since the reign of Queen Anne. The veto could now only be exercised on ministerial advice and no government would wish to veto Bills for which it was responsible or for the passage of which it had afforded facilities through Parliament.[140] The consent of the Queen is requested before legislation which affects any matter relating to the royal prerogative is debated. Although the seeking of such consent may today be no more than an act of courtesy so far as government Bills are concerned, the need for this consent presents a potential obstacle for a private member's Bill which seeks to abolish one of the Queen's prerogatives, since it enables the government to prevent the House considering any such proposals.[141]

While the royal assent concludes the formal process by which Bills become law, it would be wrong to assume that the assent also marks the end of the legislative process. The royal assent may bring the Act into force immediately,[142] but the operation of all or part of an Act is often suspended by provisions in the Act itself. Thus the Act may specify a later date on which it is to come into force or may give power to the government by Order in Council or to a minister by statutory instrument to specify when the Act, or different parts of it, will operate.[143] Moreover, many Acts confer powers on the government to regulate in detail topics indicated only in outline in the Acts. Exercise of these powers is primarily a matter for the executive, subject to scrutiny by Parliament.[144] Parliamentary interest in what happens after

---

[137] HC 528-i (2010–11), para 54.

[138] See HL Deb, 2 March 1967, col 1181.

[139] Erskine May, pp 642–5 for details.

[140] See ch 10. On the question whether the royal assent could be refused by a monarch in the exercise of his or her human rights (such as the right to freedom of conscience in art 9 of the ECHR), see R Blackburn [2003] PL 205.

[141] Erskine May, 22nd edn, pp 603–5.

[142] Acts of Parliament (Commencement) Act 1793 and Interpretation Act 1978, s 4: Acts deemed in force at beginning of day on which royal assent given, if no other provision made.

[143] Even if power to bring an Act into force has not been exercised, existence of the power may prevent the minister from acting under the prerogative to make provision inconsistent with the Act: *R v Home Secretary, ex p Fire Brigades Union* [1995] 2 AC 513; and E Barendt [1995] PL 357.

[144] Ch 22.

a Bill becomes law is not confined to delegated legislation, but traditional procedures are not designed for enabling MPs to monitor the operation of legislation.

As far back as 1971, the Select Committee on Procedure recommended that use should be made of 'post-legislation' committees. These committees would examine the working of a statute within a short period of its enactment and would consider whether there was a need for early amending legislation to deal with difficulties arising in the administration of the Act.[145] Support for such scrutiny was subsequently expressed by other select committees of both Houses as well as by the Law Commission,[146] and in 2008 the Leader of the House issued a cautious statement of government support for scrutiny by Select Committees rather than a dedicated new committee as proposed by the Law Commission.[147] Most recently, post-legislative scrutiny of the Flood and Water Management Act 2010 by the Environment, Food and Rural Affairs Committee reinforced concerns about its shortcomings, with recommendations for reform of the Act.[148]

E. Scrutiny of the administration

In Chapter 5, the principle of responsible government was discussed. We are now concerned with the procedures within the Commons by which the conduct of the administration may be scrutinised by the House. The financial and legislative procedures of Parliament have strongly influenced the means by which Parliament finds out about the work of government. But certain procedures have an importance related neither to finance nor to legislation. As we saw in the quotation from Mill at the beginning of this chapter, it is an important function of Parliament to 'watch and control the government; to throw the light of publicity on its acts; to compel a full exposition and justification of all of them which anyone considers questionable; [and] to censure them if found condemnable'.

The financial and legislative procedures already discussed provide an opportunity for these roles to be performed, but they do not provide a full opportunity for MPs to examine the way in which the government carries out its business. For these purposes a number of procedures have emerged to enable Parliament more effectively to hold the government to account. Here we concentrate on the three most important: questions to obtain information and explanation, debates to ventilate concerns and require reasoned responses, and select committees to penetrate more deeply into the conduct of departments. In considering how effectively Parliament scrutinises the government, we need to recall that the House of Commons also has a duty to sustain the government.

Parliamentary questions[149]

According to Erskine May, parliamentary questions 'should relate to matters for which those Ministers are officially responsible. They may be asked for statements of their policy or

---

[145] HC 538 (1970–1), pp vii–ix; and HC 588–1 (1977–8), p xxvii.

[146] See respectively HC 190 (1997–8) and HC 1097 (2005–6) (Modernisation Committee); HC 558 (2002–3) (Liaison Committee); HL Paper 173 (2003–4) (Constitution Committee); and Law Commission, Cm 7170, 2007 (Law Commission, which had been asked by the government to undertake the inquiry).

[147] Cm 7320, 2008 (Response to the Law Commission, ibid).

[148] HC 990 (2016–17). For an account of recent post-legislative scrutiny, see R Kelly, *Post Legislative Scrutiny* (HC Library, 2013) (only four cases between 2010 and 2013). See also HC 639 (2013–14) (Justice Committee post-legislative scrutiny of the Serious Crime Act 2007).

[149] Chester and Bowring, *Questions in Parliament*; Franklin and Norton (eds), *Parliamentary Questions*; Griffith and Ryle, pp 519–29; HC 859 (2008–9); HC 129 (2009–10); HC 1095 (2012–13); Erskine May, pp 352–40.

intentions on such matters, or for administrative or legislative action'.[150] The regular questioning of the Prime Minister receives much attention in the media and the use of 'open' questions to the Prime Minister (for example, asking her to list her engagements for the day) is permitted as a device for enabling a wide range of supplementary questions to be asked. In May 1997, the allocation for questions to the Prime Minister was changed from 15 minutes every Tuesday and Thursday to 30 minutes every Wednesday.

So far as other ministers are concerned, an hour is set aside each day the House is sitting (except Fridays) to enable members to question ministers. Departmental ministers attend for questioning by rota (the Order of Oral Questions), in what has been said to be pre-eminently a device for emphasising the 'individual responsibility of ministers'.[151] However, many more questions are tabled than can possibly be answered in the time available, so questions are chosen by the Speaker on a random basis. In order to ensure that they can be printed and circulated, and to give the relevant department an opportunity to prepare a response, questions must be tabled at least three days before the question is to be answered. Longer notice is required in the case of oral questions to the Secretaries of State for Northern Ireland, Scotland and Wales.[152]

Members may ask questions for written answer at any time, and questions tabled for oral answer which are not taken will also receive a written answer. Written answers are published in Hansard. While ministers customarily answer questions which have been accepted as being in order by the clerks of the House, acting under the Speaker's direction, it is for the minister to decide whether and how to reply to questions: 'An answer to a question cannot be insisted upon, if the answer be refused by a minister.'[153] As might be anticipated, there are a number of grounds on which information sought may be withheld: for example, if the cost of obtaining the information would be excessive, or if it would be contrary to the public interest for the information to be given (for example, matters relating to Cabinet proceedings, or to the security and intelligence services).

The quality and timeliness of answers are now monitored by the Procedure Committee, which may summon ministers to explain poor departmental performance.[154] Because of the existence of question time, however, matters concerning their constituencies may be raised by members in correspondence with ministers, who know that an unsatisfactory reply may lead to the tabling of a question. Partly for this reason, questions are used more for concentrating public attention on topics of general concern than for securing the redress of individual grievances. Questions may be ruled out of order or refused an answer if they relate to matters for which the ministers are not responsible, including decisions by local authorities, the BBC, courts and tribunals, the universities, trade unions and so on.

In 1996, the Scott report on 'arms for Iraq' extensively criticised attitudes within government to the answering of questions.[155] Civil servants are now instructed that in preparing answers they must be as open as possible with Parliament, although ministers are entitled to present government actions in a positive light; information should not be omitted merely because disclosure could lead to political embarrassment; and answers should be avoided 'which are literally true but likely to give rise to misleading inferences'.[156] When a question to a minister concerns a matter assigned to an executive agency set up under the 'next steps'

[150] Erskine May, p 360.
[151] Chester and Bowring, p 287.
[152] HC SO 22. Longer notice is also required for questions to the Advocate General for Scotland.
[153] Erskine May, p 364.
[154] HC 191 (2016–17).
[155] HC 115 (1995–6), esp vol IV, section K.8.
[156] See HC 671 (1996–7), annex C. See also *Civil Service Code* (civil servants not to mislead Parliament or ministers). See further ch 11.

initiative,[157] it is generally answered by a letter to the MP from the agency's chief executive (the minister may be consulted on what is said).[158] MPs may require a ministerial response if they are dissatisfied with the chief executive's reply.

The marked increase in the number of questions asked for written answer in recent years, which is linked with the use by some MPs of research assistants, is not considered to make necessary any limit on the number of questions which MPs may ask.[159] However, the effectiveness of parliamentary questions as a means of securing information which the government does not wish to make available has often been doubted.[160] In addition to oral and written questions, Standing Orders also make provision for urgent questions (known previously as Private Notice Questions).[161] MPs may also use the Freedom of Information Act 2000 to obtain information from government departments, though in principle this ought not to be necessary, and the use of the latter Act by MPs is perhaps an unflattering reflection on the operation of parliamentary questions.[162]

Debates

At the end of every day's public business, when the adjournment of the House is formally moved, half an hour is available for a private member to raise a particular issue and for a ministerial reply. Members periodically ballot for the right to initiate an adjournment debate, and advance notice of the subject is given so that the relevant minister may reply. While this gives more time for discussion of an issue than is possible in question time, the minister's reply, which often consists of a reasoned defence of the department's decision, may not advance the matter very far. During the debate, incidental reference to the need for legislation may be permitted by the Speaker. These brief debates are not followed by a vote of the House.[163]

More substantial debates may be held at short notice under HC Standing Order 24 for the purpose of discussing a specific and important matter that should have urgent consideration (so-called emergency debates). The Speaker must be satisfied that the matter is proper to be discussed under the urgency procedure, and either the request must be supported by at least 40 members or leave for the debate must be given by the House, if necessary upon a division. In deciding whether the matter should be debated, the Speaker considers the extent to which it concerns the administrative responsibilities of ministers or could come within the scope of ministerial action, but the Speaker does not give reasons for the decision. In recent years, 'such applications have only rarely been successful'.[164]

---

[157] Ch 11.

[158] See P Evans, in Giddings (ed.), *Parliamentary Accountability*, ch 7. Also HC 178 (1990–1) and HC 14 (1996–7).

[159] HC 859 (2008–9). According to the Modernisation Committee, 'The average number of questions appearing on the notice paper each day increased from 414 in 2007 to 434 in 2008, and had reached 514 by March 2009. This is a significant rise from the average figure of about 350 WPQs per day that persisted between 2002 and 2005' (ibid, para 5).

[160] See B Hough [2003] PL 211. But see HC 859 (2008–9), where it is said by the Procedure Committee that 'WPQs are highly valued by Members as a means of scrutinising government and obtaining information' (para 6). On concerns about unsatisfactory answers, see HC 1095 (2012–13).

[161] HC SO 21(2). These must relate to matters of public importance.

[162] See *Office of Government Commerce* v *Information Commissioner* [2008] EWHC 737 (Admin), [2010] QB 98.

[163] See HC SO 9(7); Erskine May, pp 340–42.

[164] Erskine May, p 342. See also Griffith and Ryle, p 378, who claim that the procedure has 'almost fallen into extinction' (p 497). For an outstanding example of such a debate, see that on the Westland affair on 27 January 1986. But only nine such debates took place between then and August 2009. See generally HC 337 (2006–7), paras 65–71.

In recent times a number of other opportunities have been provided for the opposition and for backbenchers wishing to raise matters in debate. In each session 20 days in the whole House are allotted for Opposition business,[165] 17 at the disposal of the Leader of the Opposition and three at the disposal of the leader of the second-largest opposition party.[166] The existence of Opposition days is thought to be one of the reasons why the emergency debate procedure referred to above is not now used more frequently. But although very important, it is also the case that the Opposition days do not necessarily satisfy the needs of backbenchers who are looking for 'effective ways of bringing a constituency problem or some other topic to the personal attention of Ministers and putting to them a case to which they have both an opportunity and an obligation to make a full reply'.[167]

So far as backbenchers are concerned, in November 2000 a parallel chamber was established in Westminster Hall to help meet backbench demand. As a result of recent changes, the forum is now used for a number of purposes: (*a*) to consider e-petitions (on which see below) selected by the Backbench Business Committee for debate; (*b*) to debate issues of concern to members; and (*c*) to consider Select Committee reports (on which see below). Westminster Hall debates last between three and four-and-a-half hours in total, with debates on several topics in each session,[168] and are said by the then government to have 'greatly widened the opportunities for members to raise matters of concern to them'.[169] The Backbench Business Committee plays a key role in selecting matters for debate.[170]

But despite these and other opportunities for members to debate the administration of government departments (including debates on the Queen's Speech), all such debates are limited by the adversary framework in which they are often held, and individual members may have no means of probing behind the statements made by ministers. These limitations continue to give rise to demands for better procedures to enable the House to inform itself more directly of the work of government. The continuing pressure for more backbench time has most recently seen the amendment of the Standing Orders to allow for a minimum of 27 days being allocated each session for the exclusive purpose of backbench business on the floor of the House itself. This is in addition to the Westminster Hall procedure.[171]

The government decides when in the course of the parliamentary calendar the debates will be held, but not the subject-matter of the debates. The latter is the responsibility of the Backbench Business Committee, from which ministers are excluded.[172] The Committee considers formal requests from members for time to be allocated for a debate on their particular interest, and there are many more requests than there are spaces available. Requests are granted having regard to a range of criteria, including the topicality of the subject matter, the level of interest amongst MPs as a whole, and the possibility of the debate taking place under different parliamentary procedures. The Backbench Business Committee also has the power to call a debate on 'a matter of regional, national or international importance'.[173]

---

[165] HC SO 14(2).

[166] During the period of Coalition government after 2010, these latter three days were shared between the Democratic Unionist Party, the SNP and Plaid Cymru.

[167] HC 194 (1998–9), para 24.

[168] HC SO 10; Erskine May, pp 322–5.

[169] HC 440 (2001–2) (Memorandum by the Leader of the House), para 8, and HC 337 (2006–7), para 124 respectively.

[170] HC SO 10.

[171] HC SO 14(4).

[172] HC SO 152J.

[173] HC SO 24A.

Select committees

Select committees were much used to investigate social and administrative problems in the 19th century. A group of MPs would examine a topic of current concern, with power on behalf of the House to take evidence from witnesses with first-hand knowledge of the issues. Their report, published with the supporting evidence, might convince the House of the need for legislative reforms. The use of select committees declined as departments grew in strength and resources, as the primary initiative for legislation moved to the government, and as the party system established stricter control over backbench MPs.

The experience of the select committee on the Marconi scandal, when Liberal ministers were accused of reaping financial rewards through their prior knowledge of a government contract, showed that a select committee was not appropriate for investigations directly involving the reputation of Cabinet ministers.[174] On the other hand, the Public Accounts Committee has since 1861 had the task of reporting to the House on the financial and accounting practices of departments.[175] In the period after 1945, however, little use was made of committees for scrutinising the administration, apart from specialist committees dealing with government finance, the technical scrutiny of delegated legislation by the committee on statutory instruments,[176] and (from 1956 to 1979) the work of the select committee on nationalised industries.

One obstacle to the development of such committees was the fear that their investigations would interfere with the running of departments and conflict with ministerial responsibility. In 1959 the Select Committee on Procedure rejected a proposal for a committee on colonial affairs, on the ground that this was 'a radical constitutional innovation': 'there is little doubt that the activities of such a committee would be aimed at controlling rather than criticising the policy and actions of the department concerned. It would be usurping a function which the House itself has never attempted to exercise.'[177] By the mid-1960s the mood of the Commons had changed. In 1965, the Committee on Procedure declared that lack of knowledge of how the executive worked was the main weakness of the House.[178]

Some limited reforms were made in 1966–8 while Richard Crossman MP was Leader of the House. Two specialised committees were created in 1966, one to consider the activities of a department (the Ministry of Agriculture, Fisheries and Food), the other to consider the subject of science and technology. The latter committee was regularly reappointed, but the Committee on the Ministry of Agriculture survived only for two sessions. Other committees established piecemeal at this time included committees to examine the activities of two departments (Education and Science, and Overseas Development respectively), race relations and immigration, and Scottish affairs. During the 1970s, such committees existed alongside the Expenditure Committee and its sub-committees.[179]

In 1978, an influential report by the Select Committee on Procedure recommended a complete reorganisation of the select committees to produce a more rational structure and to provide means by which MPs could regularly scrutinise the activities of the main departments.[180] The incoming Conservative government moved with notable speed to adopt these

---

[174] Donaldson, *The Marconi Scandal*; and ch 11.

[175] The PAC is said to be the 'doyen' of select committees: J F McEldowney, in Jowell and Oliver (eds), above (3rd edn), ch 7.

[176] Ch 22.

[177] HC 92–1 (1958–9), para 47; Crick, *The Reform of Parliament*, ch 7.

[178] HC 303 (1964–5).

[179] See Morris (ed.), *The Growth of Parliamentary Scrutiny by Committee*.

[180] HC 588–1 (1977–8), chs 5–7; and see HC Deb, 19 and 20 February 1979, cols 44, 276.

recommendations.[181] Now embodied in the House's standing orders,[182] the system of select committees is directly related to the principal government departments. Select committees are appointed for the life of a Parliament to examine the 'expenditure, administration and policy' of the main departments,[183] though a few – such as the Public Accounts Committee – have a wider remit that cuts across departmental boundaries. Each committee typically has 11 or 14 members, and each may appoint a sub-committee.

As well as examining the work of the principal department specified for the committee, each committee has power to look at 'associated public bodies', that is, executive agencies, public corporations, boards and advisory bodies in the relevant field. Consistently with the idea of Parliament as the 'conscience of the nation', however, some committees take a very wide view of their brief, examining the conduct of banks during the financial crisis, large employers where bad employment practices have been alleged, and even the internal affairs of political parties.[184] There are also a number of joint select committees composed of members drawn from both Houses, in addition to a number of select committees in the House of Lords. The joint committees include the JCHR, which examines proposed legislation to consider its compatibility with obligations under international human rights law, including the ECHR.

The work of the select committees

Standing Orders provide for 20 Commons select committees related to government departments, with a number of others governed by separate Standing Orders. Until 2010, committee chairs and members were appointed by the Committee of Selection, which is dominated by party whips. Perhaps predictably, this gave rise to difficulty, with governments apparently keen to control appointments to these key positions. As long ago as 2001, the House of Commons Modernisation Select Committee concluded that the existing method of filling positions by the Committee of Selection no longer enjoyed the confidence of the House.[185] Proposals for reform were made in the well-received report of a select committee that had been appointed in 2009 specifically to consider House of Commons Reform. Since 2010 chairs of select committees are elected in a secret ballot by MPs, while members are elected following nomination of the Committee of Selection.[186]

Only backbench MPs serve on select committees. Each committee typically has a majority of members from the government side of the House,[187] but Standing Orders require a proportion of the committees to be chaired by Opposition members.[188] The committees are serviced by House of Commons clerks and they may appoint specialist advisers, often academics with specialist knowledge. Within its subject area, each committee may choose the topics for

[181] HC Deb, 25 June 1979, col 33. The literature on the select committees includes Drewry (ed.), *The New Select Committees*; Englefield (ed.), *Commons Select Committees*; Griffith and Ryle, ch 11; and N Johnson, in Ryle and Richards (eds), *The Commons under Scrutiny*, ch 9. Also A Kelso, in Flinders *et al.* (eds), *The Oxford Handbook of British Politics*, ch 13.

[182] HC SOs 121–152K.

[183] For an account of the 'core tasks' of select committees, see HC 697 (2012–13).

[184] See respectively HC 144 (2008–9), HC 219 (2016–17), HC 136 (2016 –17), in which some non-governmental characters were given a rough ride, and in some cases reputations tarnished.

[185] HC 224 (2001–2), para 6. It was said that the Committee of Selection had 'come to interpret its role as limited to confirming the proposals put to it by the front benches on both sides' (ibid, para 9). See D Oliver [2001] PL 666.

[186] See HC SO 121, 122B. For background see HC 1117 (2008–9), paras 43–94; HC 1573 (2010–12).

[187] The Exiting the EU Select Committee established in 2016 is unusual not only for its size (21 members), but also because the government does not have a majority.

[188] HC SO 122B.

investigation, subject only to the avoidance of duplication with other committees. The topics investigated by select committees vary widely, ranging from major subjects that may take a year or longer to complete, to the latest departmental estimates, and issues of topical concern which a committee may seek to influence by holding public hearings and publishing the evidence with a report and recommendations.

The freedom for a committee to decide for itself what to investigate is very important, and no government approval is needed. The reports of select committees would be valueless if they merely reproduced the government's justification of its policies. The committees are aware that, even though they do not often change government decisions, as all-party committees they exercise an important critical function. Voting on party lines can occur when a committee is deciding the contents of its report, but this is exceptional and not the rule. For criticism of the government to be made, such criticism typically would have to be supported in the committee by one or more MPs from the government side. Committee reports contain only the majority view; but the extent of unity or division is revealed in the minutes of proceedings that are published with the report. Each committee will conduct many investigations and publish several reports on a wide range of subjects every parliamentary session.[189]

In 1979, some MPs believed that such committees might detract from the adversarial quality of parliamentary procedure, might develop overly consensus politics, might develop too close a relationship with the departments concerned, and so on. These fears have not been borne out in practice. The government undertook at an early stage to cooperate fully with the committees,[190] and it lays down the rules by which civil servants may give evidence; these rules seek to protect from investigation the process of decision making within government.[191] Some committees have occasionally encountered difficulties in securing evidence, whether from ministers who refused to attend;[192] individuals prohibited by government from attending; or departments that refused to release documents.[193] But these difficulties are not commonplace, and it is now claimed that:

> select committees are seen as a key part of the constitutional framework, successful in influencing both Government and external bodies, and a leading forum for public debate; they also greatly extend the engagement of the public with Parliament in a positive way. Committees' legitimacy in the eyes of the public, their profile in the media, and their self-confidence is growing.[194]

This is not to say that the system does not need to be improved, and many proposals to this effect have been made for the best part of 20 years. As long ago as 2001, the Liaison Committee made a number of recommendations in an important report for the committees to be more effective and independent.[195] Concern was expressed about the system for the nomination of members, which was then 'too much under the control of the Whips', with members kept off or removed 'on account of their views'. The committee also recommended that more time should be spent on the floor of the House considering select committee reports. Although

---

[189] Each Select Committee has a website which contains reports as well as written and oral evidence.

[190] HC Deb, 25 June 1979, col 45; and 16 January 1981, col 1697.

[191] See ch 11 where this matter is more fully explored.

[192] See HL 152, HC 230 (2008–9), esp para 51 where the JCHR reported repeated attempts to request oral evidence from ministers on the question of British government complicity in the torture of terrorist suspects. It is clear from the Committee's reports that such a refusal was rare to the point of being unique, leading the committee to reflect that 'the constitutional significance of the ministers' refusal should not be under-estimated' (ibid).

[193] HC 321 (2000–1), paras 118–26. Difficulties have also arisen in relation to a witness who refused to answer questions put to him by a Committee: see HC 1044 (2002–3).

[194] HC 697 (2012–13), para 135 (Liaison Committee). See also HC 321 (2000–1), para 2, and HC 224 (2001–2), para 2.

[195] HC 321 (2000–1). See Oliver, *Constitutional Reform in the UK*, ch 9.

Westminster Hall enables debates on committee reports to take place, this was thought not to be a substitute for 'debating time on the floor of the House, on substantive motions'.

Further proposals for reform were made by the Modernisation Committee in 2002, the Committee having expressed concern that the select committees generally were 'much poorer in the resources they can command than in other parliaments and they have a weak record of stability of membership. They also have a much more marginal role in scrutinising legislation, which is the principal function of the parallel committees in some other parliaments.'[196] The matter was revisited in *Rebuilding the House*, the important report of the House of Commons Reform Committee, which in 2009 made a number of well-received proposals, these complementing the earlier proposals of the Liaison Committee, renewing the recommendation that select committees should be elected by the House and not selected by the party whips.

F. Conclusion

The apparently contradictory roles of Parliament in the Westminster system of government identified in the introduction to this chapter create a constant tension between the demands of the government to secure safe passage for its business, and the demands of the Opposition that the government's business should be subject to proper scrutiny. It also creates a constant tension for backbenchers, with a responsibility to their party to support or oppose the government as the case may be, but also with a responsibility to the House to exercise independent judgment on the issues of the day. These tensions – felt more keenly by some members than by others – are on display in each of the three areas examined in this chapter, in relation to all of which significant procedural reforms have taken place in recent years. Although dry procedural matters, these reforms are of great constitutional importance, addressing fundamental questions about the legitimacy of government and the 'effectiveness' of Parliament.[197]

According to the House of Commons Procedure Committee, 'in the last twenty years or so the House has seen something of a revolution in its procedures', highlighting 'the creation of sittings in Westminster Hall, programming of virtually all government legislation, the re-invention of backbench business, and most recently the introduction of the elaborate machinery of English votes for English laws'.[198] However, the tension between the different roles of Parliament is a continuing one, with the case for an even stronger Parliament hard to refute. These begin with financial procedures and the case made by the Liaison Committee in *Recreating Financial Scrutiny*,[199] where in addition to simplification of government finances and better-quality information for Parliament, it was argued that there was a need for

(*a*) the ability to engage with financial issues under discussion within government before decisions are made;

---

[196] HC 224 (2001–2), para 4.

[197] We should not overlook the suggestion that the government's commitment to *modernisation of the legislative process* (if not to some of the other initiatives discussed in this chapter) 'always owed more to its desire to secure the passage of its business than a desire to improve the effectiveness of parliamentary scrutiny': P Cowley and M Stuart (2001) 54 *Parliamentary Affairs* 238. Nor should we overlook the fact that the 'effectiveness' of Parliament is in the eye of the beholder. Supporters of the government will emphasise its legislative role as the means through which the government governs. Supporters of the opposition in contrast will emphasise its scrutiny function. Neither are likely to be satisfied. On 'effectiveness' from a government perspective, see K D Ewing (2017) 28 *King's Law Journal* 343.

[198] HC 701 (2016–17) (Procedure Committee), para 37.

[199] HC 426 (2007–8).

(*b*) adequate opportunities to debate and vote on financial decisions, including specific spending proposals, after the government has made them; and

(*c*) expert assistance for members on financial matters.[200]

Otherwise, concern has been expressed about the reluctance of governments to implement other reforms that had been proposed in *Rebuilding the House* in 2009, including in particular the establishment of a House Business Committee in which members would play a greater part in determining the order of business, as an assertion of the principle that all time is 'the House's time'.[201] This has not been accepted by governments, to the evident disappointment of the Political and Constitutional Reform Select Committee in *Revisiting Rebuilding the House*.[202] The latter report also repeated proposals for the pre-legislative scrutiny of all public Bills and the election of members to public bill committees, following similar recommendations relating to the select committees. The most excoriating criticisms, however, have come from the Procedure Committee in relation to government resistance to reforming the procedures relating to backbench legislation, which:

> have remained in their current state, resting on procedural practices and assumptions which would be familiar to Members of a century, if not two centuries, ago. There are arguments to be made for tradition, but they are unconvincing when adherence to past rituals makes the House look ridiculous, puny and ineffectual.[203]

One final matter to have attracted attention in recent years has been how better to involve the public in the parliamentary process. There is now a streamlined 'collaborative' e-petition procedure whereby members of the public may petition online on any matter for which the government is responsible.[204] If the petition secures 100,000 signatures, the newly established Petitions Committee will consider requesting time for debate in Westminster Hall, and in some cases on the floor of the House.[205] Other initiatives are designed to enhance public engagement directly with the legislative process, including a public reading day at the committee stage of public Bills.[206] However, the latter has been used infrequently, though in the case of the Children and Families Bill 2013, it 'involved hosting an online forum for members of the public to leave their views on the Bill, with a summary of comments then made available to members of the Public Bill Committee considering the Bill'.[207]

---

[200] Ibid, para 62. The main issue in relation to (*a*) was the government's multi-year spending review, which set out the government's spending plans for the next three years. See subsequently, Study of Parliament Group, Written and Oral Evidence, 4 May 2016 (HC 190, 2016–17) (Procedure Committee).

[201] HC 1117 (2008–9), para 129. A commitment to such an initiative was made in the Coalition *Programme for Government* but has not been implemented: The Coalition, *Our Programme for Government* (2010), p 27.

[202] HC 1062 (2012–13).

[203] HC 701 (2016–17) (Procedure Committee), para 37.

[204] See HC 235 (2014–15) (Procedure Committee).

[205] See the House of Commons Petitions Committee website for full details.

[206] HM Government, The Coalition: *Our Programme for Government* (2010), p 27.

[207] L Petrie and J Mulley, Evaluation of the Public Reading Pilot (Scrutiny Unit, 2013): http://www.parliament.uk/documents/commons/Scrutiny/SU-PRS-Evaluation-FINAL-June-2013-JNM.PDF

CHAPTER 9
Privileges of Parliament

> Parliamentary privilege consists of the rights and immunities which the two Houses of Parliament and their members and officers possess to enable them to carry out their parliamentary functions effectively. Without this protection members would be handicapped in performing their parliamentary duties, and the authority of Parliament itself in confronting the executive and as a forum for expressing the anxieties of citizens would be correspondingly diminished.[1]

At the height of the revelations about parliamentary expenses in 2009, the term 'parliamentary privilege' was likely at best to be greeted with cynicism. In fact, as a joint committee of the two Houses in 1999 emphasised in the above words, parliamentary privilege is part of the framework which enables each House and its members to fulfil their duties. This principle was re-affirmed by another joint committee in 2013, which explained that 'in brief, [privilege] comprises the right of each House to control its own proceedings and precincts, and the right of those participating in parliamentary proceedings, whether or not they are Members, to speak freely without fear of legal liability or other reprisal.'[2] The privileges of each House have both external and internal aspects: they protect it against attempts from outside to interfere in its proceedings; and they require its members to refrain from abusing their privileged position.

As a vital part of the law and custom of Parliament, privilege has evolved over centuries in response to changed circumstances. It has considerable roots in the clashes between the Crown and Parliament leading to the Civil War, and then to the Glorious Revolution; but to the extent that parliamentary privilege is a protection against the overwheening powers of the monarch, such a basis has little modern relevance. In the 21st century, questions of privilege are much more likely to arise as a potential limit on the judicial role. Neither House can by its own resolution create new privileges. When a matter of privilege is disputed, 'it is for the courts to decide whether a privilege exists and for the House to decide whether such privilege has been infringed.'[3]

This chapter does not discuss the application of privilege to the Scottish Parliament and the Assemblies for Wales and Northern Ireland. These bodies enjoy rights and immunities enacted by legislation,[4] but they do not share in Westminster's privileges.[5] Emphasis will be placed on the House of Commons, but questions of privilege also arise in relation to the Lords.

---

[1] Report of joint committee on parliamentary privilege (HL Paper 43-I, HC 214-I, 1998–9), para 3 (cited here as the 'Nicholls report'). And see Erskine May, chs 12–17; Griffith and Ryle, *Parliament*, ch 3; Horne, Drewry and Oliver (eds), *Parliament and the Law*, chs 1–4.

[2] Report of joint committee on parliamentary privilege (HL Paper 30, HC 100, 2013–14) (cited here as the 'Brabazon report'), para 3.

[3] *Pepper* v *Hart* [1993] AC 595, 645 (Lord Browne-Wilkinson). See generally: Lord Lisvane [2016] PL 72.

[4] See e.g. Scotland Act 1998, ss 22 and Sch 3 (standing orders), ss 23–6 (witnesses and documents), 39 (members' interests), 41 (defamatory statements), 42 (contempt of court), and 43 (corrupt practices).

[5] See *Whaley* v *Lord Watson of Invergowrie* 2000 SLT 475. And C R Munro [2000] PL 347. On the European Parliament, see Protocol on the Privileges and Immunities of the European Union (16 December 2004), arts 7–9; C-200/07 *Marra* v *De Gregorio* [2009] 1 CMLR 15; and *Barron* v *Collins* [2016] EWHC 3350 (QB) in which a claim for immunity from libel proceedings in reliance on European Parliamentary privilege was considered and rejected.

A. House of Commons

Certain privileges and immunities have long been attached to the House and its members. At the opening of each Parliament, the Speaker claims for the Commons 'their ancient and undoubted rights and privileges' and, in particular, 'freedom of speech in debate, freedom from arrest, freedom of access to Her Majesty whenever occasion shall require; and that the most favourable construction should be placed upon all their proceedings.' Two of these freedoms need to be discussed.

Freedom from arrest[6]

The ancient privilege of freedom from *civil* arrest enabled members to attend the House at a time when imprisonment was a common means of enforcing payment of debts. Today, an MP is protected against committal for contempt of court where this is sought to compel performance of a civil obligation.[7] Members have no immunity from having civil actions brought against them,[8] but it is a contempt of the House to serve a writ on a member within the precincts of the House.[9] Members are not protected against bankruptcy proceedings, and are no longer exempt from jury service.[10] In 1999 and again in 2013, it was recommended that any surviving freedom from civil arrest should be abolished.[11]

As regards *criminal* law, members have no immunity from arrest. In *R* v *Chaytor*,[12] when former MPs were prosecuted for submitting false claims for expenses, the Supreme Court held that MPs are fully subject to the criminal law, even for conduct in the House of Commons itself when this is not protected by the privilege that attaches to 'proceedings in Parliament'. The absence of immunity was seen earlier, when Damian Green MP, then Conservative shadow Home Secretary, was arrested at his home in November 2008 while police investigated a series of leaks from the Home Office to the press that had led the Cabinet Office to call in the police. That affair raised many questions, and it was not obvious that the leaks constituted criminal offences at all.[13] The police made an unprecedented search of Mr Green's office at Westminster, seizing documents, computers and other materials, on the basis of a consent-form that the police had caused the Serjeant at Arms to sign, which she did without getting the approval of senior House authorities. The Speaker (Michael Martin MP) responded by instructing that no future search of an MP's office could take place without a warrant, but this itself raised questions about the impact of parliamentary privilege on police powers and the right of the House to resist intrusive police action.[14]

Members may be required to give surety to keep the peace or security for good behaviour, and may (except where their freedom of speech protects them) be committed for contempt of court where the contempt has a criminal character.[15] An MP was held in preventive detention under defence regulations during the Second World War.[16] The House insists on receiving

---

6 Erskine May, ch 14; Nicholls report, paras 325–8; Brabazon report, paras 254–7.
7 As in *Stourton* v *Stourton* [1963] P 302. Erskine May, pp 246–7.
8 *Re Parliamentary Privilege Act 1770* [1958] AC 331.
9 HC 221 (1969–70) and HC 144 (1972–3).
10 Insolvency Act 1986, s 427; Criminal Justice Act 2003, s 9 and Sch 1, pt 3.
11 Note 6 above.
12 [2010] UKSC 52, [2011] 1 AC 684; and see below, pp 225–6.
13 In view of the Official Secrets Act 1989; ch 19 D.
14 See HC 157 and HC 1026 (2008–9); also Sir Denis O'Connor, *Review of Lessons Learned from the Metropolitan Police Service's Investigation* (October 2009). For a full account, see report of the Campbell committee (HC 62, 2009–10); and A W Bradley [2012] PL 396.
15 Ch 13 C. And see note 6 above.
16 HC 164 (1939–40) (Captain Ramsay's case).

immediate information of the imprisonment of a member, with reasons for the detention. While a member awaiting trial may carry out many duties as a constituency representative, a member who is imprisoned after conviction may do so only if granted exceptional concessions under prison rules.[17] A term of imprisonment for more than a year causes the seat to be vacated,[18] but a member who is convicted of a crime involving dishonest or immoral conduct is likely to resign from Parliament whatever the sentence.[19]

Freedom of speech[20]

Freedom of speech is the most substantial privilege of the House. Its essence is that no penal or coercive action should be taken against members for what is said or done in Parliament. Claims for the privilege were regularly made by the Speaker from the end of the 16th century. The right of the Commons to criticise the King's government was called in question in 1629 when Eliot, Holles and Valentine were convicted by the Court of King's Bench for seditious words spoken in the Commons and for tumult in the House.[21] This judgment was reversed in 1668 by the House of Lords on the ground that words spoken in Parliament could be judged only in Parliament. In art 9 of the Bill of Rights 1689, it was declared 'that the freedom of speech and debates or proceedings in Parliament ought not to be impeached or questioned in any court or place out of Parliament'.[22] Article 9 is generally accepted to reflect a fundamental constitutional principle, sufficiently important to give rise to a suggestion that it may even take priority over EU law.[23]

The most important consequence of this declaration is that no member may be made liable in the courts for what is said or written in course of parliamentary proceedings. Thus members who speak in the House are immune from the law of defamation.[24] Nor can what is said in Parliament be examined by a court for the purpose of deciding whether it supports a cause of action in defamation which has arisen outside Parliament: 'a member must have a complete right of free speech in the House without any fear that his motives or intentions or reasoning will be questioned or held against him thereafter'.[25] Moreover, the courts may not receive in any proceedings 'evidence, questioning or submissions designed to show that a witness in parliamentary proceedings deliberately misled Parliament'.[26]

Since 1818, leave of the House has been required before officers of the House may give evidence in court of proceedings in the Commons. In 1980, the House relaxed its practice by giving general permission for reference to be made in court to Hansard and to the published evidence and reports of committees.[27] This change did not diminish the effect of art 9 of the Bill of Rights, nor did it alter the rule that Hansard could not be used in court as an aid to statutory interpretation. In 1993, the Law Lords changed the latter rule, holding that

---

[17] HC 185 (1970–1). And see G J Zellick [1977] PL 29.

[18] See Representation of the People Act 1981, s 1; and ch 7 G.

[19] For example, Chris Huhne resigned his seat in 2013 upon pleading guilty at trial to a charge of perverting the course of justice. Nigel Evans did not resign upon being charged with rape and sexual assault, and was acquitted at trial in 2014, remaining an MP.

[20] Erskine May, ch 13; Nicholls report, paras 36–134, 189–228; Brabazon report, ch 6.

[21] *Eliot*'s case (1629) 3 St Tr 294.

[22] And see *Re Parliamentary Privilege Act 1770*, note 8 above.

[23] *R (Buckinghamshire County Council)* v *Transport Secretary* [2014] UKSC 3, [2014] 1 WLR 324 at [202]–[208] (Lords Neuberger and Mance).

[24] *Lake* v *King* (1667) 1 Saunders 131; *Dillon* v *Balfour* (1887) 20 LR Ir 600. And see *A* v *UK* (2003) 36 EHRR 917 (MP's immunity from defamation compatible with arts 6(1) and 8, ECHR).

[25] *Church of Scientology of California* v *Johnson-Smith* [1972] 1 QB 522, 530 (Browne J).

[26] *Hamilton* v *Al Fayed* [2001] 1 AC 395, 403 (Lord Browne-Wilkinson).

[27] HC Deb, 3 December 1979, col 167, and 31 October 1980, col 879; HC 102 (1978–9); and P M Leopold [1981] PL 316.

courts may use ministerial statements in Hansard to resolve ambiguities in legislation; such use does not 'impeach or question' freedom of speech in the Commons.[28] Use of Hansard may only be used to clarify the meaning of an ambiguous statutory expression, not to clarify the scope of a discretionary ministerial power.[29] It may be used to identify the mischief at which the statute was directed, but not to discover the government's intentions from statements of ministers.[30]

More controversially, ministerial statements in Parliament announcing new policies or explaining executive decisions are sometimes used as evidence in judicial review proceedings; they may be in substance the decision under challenge.[31] The justification for this is that such statements may cast light on the motivation for executive action that ministers have taken outside the House, and may show that the action involved the improper exercise of power.[32] On occasion, it may involve an extremely detailed consideration of both the statement and the wider context of the debate or occasion in which it is made.[33] But a statement in Parliament of an intention, for example to consult, cannot form the basis of a legal duty or a legitimate expectation that that political statement will be carried out.[34] In 1999, the Nicholls committee concluded that privilege was not a reason for restricting judicial review of executive decisions and that statements in the House could be used even to question the minister's good faith.[35] But the Brabazon committee in 2013 disagreed with this, taking the view that it was 'constitutionally inappropriate' for the courts to rely on such material as select committee reports in judicial review cases, since such reliance 'risks having a chilling effect upon parliamentary debate'.[36] The High Court has held that proceedings in Parliament are admissible as to historical facts or events (i.e. that something was said or passed), but they may not be questioned.[37] It is accordingly difficult for a party in proceedings to rely upon an opinion expressed by a select committee, because it will place either the other party, or the court, in the position of approving or disapproving of that opinion.[38]

Nor may the courts grant any relief which trespasses on the role of Members of Parliament. It cannot require a minister, in his role as a Member of Parliament, to introduce primary or secondary legislation into the House.[39] It cannot forbid a minister to take a legislative step in Parliament.[40] Nor, it has been stated on more than one occasion, can the courts even declare that the introduction of legislation into Parliament is required.[41] In the Brexit

---

[28] *Pepper* v *Hart* [1993] AC 593; and ch 1 B. This change, and its limits, remains controversial: Lord Steyn (2001) 21 OJLS 59; Vogenauer (2005) 25 OJLS 629; Sales (2006) OJLS 585.

[29] *R (Spath Holme Ltd)* v *Environment Secretary* [2001] 2 AC 349.

[30] *The Presidential Insurance Co Ltd* v *Resha St Hill* [2012] UKPC 33; *R (Jackson)* v *Attorney General* [2005] UKHL 56, [2006] 1 AC 262 at [97]–[97] (Lord Steyn). See too: *R (Henley-Smith)* v *Justice Secretary* [2017] EWHC 1948 (Admin).

[31] *Pepper* v *Hart* [1993] AC 593, 639 (Lord Browne-Wilkinson); *R* v *Home Secretary, ex p Brind* [1991] 1 AC 696.

[32] *Toussaint* v *A-G of St Vincent* [2007] UKPC 48, [2008] 1 All ER 1.

[33] A particularly extensive example of which may be seen in *R (Justice for Health Ltd)* v *Health Secretary* [2016] EWHC 2338 (Admin).

[34] *R (Wheeler)* v *Office of the Prime Minister* [2008] EWHC 1409 (Admin); *R* v *Education Secretary, ex p Begbie* [2000] 1 WLR 1115; *R (Henley-Smith)* v *Justice Secretary* [2017] EWHC 1948 (Admin).

[35] Nicholls report, paras 46–55.

[36] Brabazon report, paras 118–36.

[37] *Office of Government Commerce* v *Information Commissioner* [2008] EWHC 774 (Admin), [2010] QB 98.

[38] Ibid., at [57]–[59] (Stanley Burnton J).

[39] *R (Wheeler)* v *Office of the Prime Minister* [2008] EWHC 1409 (Admin); *R* v *HM Treasury, ex p Smedley* [1995] QB 657.

[40] *R (Unison)* v *Health Secretary* [2010] EWHC 2655 (Admin).

[41] *R (Wheeler)* v *Office of the Prime Minister* [2008] EWHC 1409 (Admin) at [49] (Richards LJ); *R (Henley-Smith)* v *Justice Secretary* [2017] EWHC 1948 (Admin) at [53] (Lang J); *Wheeler* v *Office of the Prime Minister* [2014] EWHC 3815 (Admin).

litigation the Divisional Court expressed the clear view during argument – as is clear from the published transcripts – that it must be able to declare that the Prime Minister could not commence the process of leaving the EU without the authorisation of primary legislation where the question was justiciable, and the issue was not pressed by the government.[42] Although the magnitude of the issue was obviously distinctive, it is not immediately obvious why a declaration which had the direct effect of requiring legislation to be introduced into Parliament was more acceptable in Bill of Rights terms than in the previous cases in which the courts have held that such a step is constitutionally impermissible.

However, when a court has to decide whether a statute is compatible with rights under the Human Rights Act 1998, it may read Hansard to find out the background to the legislation, the problem at which it was aimed and its likely effect, although the admissibility of such material to determine matters such as the proportionality of the statute is less clear.[43]

The protection of members for words spoken extends to criminal as well as civil liability, even for words that if used outside Westminster could lead the speaker to being prosecuted for such offences as incitement to racial hatred.[44] Disclosures to Parliament may not be made the subject of prosecution under the Official Secrets Acts,[45] although the MP concerned may be liable to the disciplinary jurisdiction of the House. Speeches or questions in Parliament may be in breach of the House's *sub judice* rule if they concern pending judicial proceedings, but they may not be held to be in contempt of court.[46]

In protecting MPs from liability for speaking in Parliament, one indirect effect of the Bill of Rights was to restrict the ability of MPs to sue in defamation. The reason for this was that if an MP sued a newspaper for a defamatory report about the MP's conduct, art 9 of the Bill of Rights prevented the newspaper from showing that the report was true by bringing evidence of what had been said or done in Parliament: in the interests of justice, the court would require the case to be stayed.[47] In 1996, concern at 'cash for questions' allegations led Parliament hastily to amend the Bill of Rights to enable Neil Hamilton MP to sue *The Guardian*: by s 13 of the Defamation Act 1996, any individual (whether an MP or not) may waive parliamentary privilege so that an action can proceed.[48] This was an unsatisfactory change in the law. In 1999, the Nicholls committee recommended that s 13 of the 1996 Act be replaced by the grant of power to each House to waive privilege in court proceedings, subject to safeguards to maintain protection of the Bill of Rights for individuals.[49] In 2013, the Brabazon committee went further by simply recommending the repeal of s 13, without any replacement.[50]

---

[42] *R (Miller)* v *Secretary of State for Exiting the European Union* [2016] EWHC 2768 (Admin), [2017] 1 All ER 158 at [109]. The form of declaration granted by the Divisional Court was: 'The Secretary of State does not have power under the Crown's prerogative to give notice pursuant to Article 50 of the Treaty on European Union for the United Kingdom to withdraw from the European Union.'

[43] *Wilson* v *First County Trust Ltd* [2003] UKHL 40, [2004] 1 AC 816 takes a relatively restrictive approach, emphasising, quite correctly, that proportionality is a question for the courts. But in other cases, the courts have engaged in detailed consideration of the Parliamentary involvement as relevant to the degree of deference to be afforded to Parliament's judgment on proportionality: e.g. *R (Animal Defenders International)* v *Culture Secretary* [2008] UKHL 15, [2008] 1 AC 1312. See also: T Lewis [2006] PL 209; A Kavanagh (2014) 34 OJLS 443.

[44] See ch 17 D below.

[45] *Duncan Sandys* case, HC 101 (1938–9). On liability for criminal conspiracy, see *Ex p Wason* (1869) LR 4 QB 573.

[46] E.g. the disclosure of Colonel B's identity on 20 April 1978; HC 667 (1977–8) and 222 (1978–9). And see report of HC Procedure Committee, HC 125 (2004–5) and Brabazon report, paras 158–60.

[47] *Prebble* v *Television New Zealand Ltd*; see ch 17 F below and P M Leopold (1995) 15 LS 204.

[48] By using s 13, Mr Hamilton later sued Mr Al Fayed over allegations already examined by a Commons committee: *Hamilton* v *Al Fayed* [2001] 1 AC 395 (and see A W Bradley [2000] PL 556). See also ch 17 F.

[49] Nicholls report, paras 60–82.

[50] Brabazon report, para 170.

A slightly different element of the protections afforded to MPs is known as the 'Wilson Doctrine'. This arises from a statement by the Prime Minister, Harold Wilson, in 1966 that it was government policy that the intelligence agencies were not to tap the telephones of MPs or members of the House of Lords, and that any change in that policy would be announced to Parliament.[51] Successive governments have repeated that stance, despite recommendations by successive Interceptions of Communications Commissioners.[52] The intelligence agencies have internal codes and guidance which permit the interception of an MP's communications only in exceptional cases as a result of warrants granted by the Secretary of State under the Regulation of Investigatory Powers Act 2000. In the context of a challenge brought by Caroline Lucas MP in the Investigatory Powers Tribunal, the IPT held that the Wilson Doctrine had never been absolute and could not override the general warrant-making powers Parliament itself had given the Secretary of State, that it had never been intended to rule out incidental interception of communications (such as through internet monitoring), and that the Doctrine was not enforceable in English law as a matter of legitimate expectations or otherwise because it had no legal effect.[53] Under the Investigatory Powers Act 2016, any warrant which authorises the targeting of equipment or communications of any member of Parliament, the devolved assemblies or the European Parliament, will require the authorisation of the Prime Minister and a judicial commissioner: sections 26 and 111.

The meaning of 'proceedings in Parliament'

We have seen that art 9 of the Bill of Rights protects 'the freedom of speech and debates or proceedings in Parliament'. It plainly applies to what members say in debates in the House, but how far does this protection extend? And who may decide the extent of protection? In 1939, the House of Commons resolved that it covers asking questions, giving written notice of questions and 'everything said or done by a member in the exercise of his functions as a member in a committee in either House, as well as everything said or done in either House in the transaction of parliamentary business'.[54] On this basis, protection extends to officials of the House in performing their duties (for example, when a clerk advises a member on the draft of a question to be asked of a minister), as well as to witnesses giving evidence to committees of the House. But this does not mean that privilege applies to every casual conversation in the corridors or over a drink at Westminster. If the extent of the privilege is disputed, this is a matter for decision by the courts.

Following the scandal in 2009 regarding MPs' expenses and allowances,[55] several former MPs and a member of the Lords, who had claimed for items such as fictitious mortgage payments and travel expenses, were prosecuted for having made false statements to officials of the House contrary to the Theft Act 1968, s 17. To the indignation of the media, they submitted that (i) the claims for expenses were 'proceedings in Parliament' and within article 9 of the Bill of Rights; and (ii) the claims were within the internal proceedings of Parliament, over which each House has sole jurisdiction.[56]

----

[51] HC 730 (1966), cols 42–43.

[52] See, in particular, the detailed argument of Sir Swinton Thomas in the *Annual Report of the Interception of Communications Commissioner 2005-06*, HC 315 (2006–7), pp 12–14.

[53] *Lucas v Security Service* [2017] 1 All ER 283.

[54] HC 101 (1938–9).

[55] See below, section B.

[56] Below, p 229.

In *R v Chaytor*,[57] a nine-judge Supreme Court unanimously rejected the claim of privilege. It was held that claiming for allowances and expenses did not form part of, nor was incidental to, the core or essential business of Parliament. For MPs to be prosecuted for false claims would not inhibit freedom of speech and debate in Parliament. Lord Rodger found that there was nothing in the charges 'which relates in any way to the legislative or deliberative processes of the House of Commons, however widely construed'.[58] Lord Phillips cited the dictum of Stephen J, in *Bradlaugh v Gossett*[59] that he knew of 'no authority for the proposition that an *ordinary crime* committed in the . . . Commons would be withdrawn from the ordinary course of criminal justice' (emphasis supplied).[60] The defendants argued that to make false claims might be a contempt of the House, but denied that it was an 'ordinary crime'. But the court held that the making of claims for allowances and expenses was not within the 'exclusive jurisdiction' that each House enjoyed over its own procedures.[61] While the House might take disciplinary proceedings for any contempt, the courts must deal with charges of criminal conduct where these are outside article 9.

The Supreme Court's decision rejecting the claim of privilege was inevitable given the historical justification for protecting the freedom of 'speech and debate' in Parliament. It upholds the long-standing rule that MPs at Westminster have no general immunity from the criminal law, unlike their counterparts in many European countries.[62]

The publication of parliamentary proceedings

The courts have long exercised their authority to decide disputes about the extent of parliamentary privilege when claims by the Commons would have an adverse effect on the rights of persons outside the House. In 1839, the question arose as to the authority of the House to publish outside Parliament debates and reports of its committees. A lengthy dispute between the Commons and the courts led to the ruling that at common law the authority of the House was no defence when defamatory material was published outside the House and, more fundamentally, that the House could not create a new privilege by its own resolution.

In *Stockdale v Hansard*,[63] Hansard printed and sold to the public by order of the Commons a report by the inspectors of prisons which stated that an indecent book published by Stockdale was circulating in Newgate Prison. When Stockdale sued in defamation, the case was decided for Hansard on the ground that the statement in the report was true. When Stockdale sued again, after the report had been republished, Hansard was ordered by the House to plead only that he had acted under an order of the Commons, a body that was superior to any court of law; that each House was the sole judge of its own privileges; and that a resolution of the

---

[57] [2010] UKSC 52, [2011] 1 AC 684.

[58] Ibid, para [122].

[59] See below, p 232.

[60] (1884) 12 QBD 271, 283. The notion of an 'ordinary crime' was not applicable to the alleged conduct of Mr Damian Green MP (above, p 221).

[61] Findings by the Parliamentary Commissioner for Standards are not subject to judicial review: *R v Parliamentary Commissioner for Standards, ex p Al Fayed* [1998] 1 All ER 93.

[62] See S Hardt, *Parliamentary Immunity*.

[63] (1839) 9 A & E 1. For the background, see P and G Ford (eds), *Luke Graves Hansard's Diary 1814–1841*, and E Stockdale [1990] PL 30.

House declaring its privileges could not be questioned. The court rejected this defence, holding that only the Queen and both Houses of Parliament could make or unmake laws; when it was necessary to decide the rights of persons outside Parliament, the courts must determine the nature and existence of privileges of the Commons; and the House had no privilege to permit publication of defamatory matter outside the House.

In the light of this clear-cut decision, legislation by Parliament was necessary. By s 1 of the Parliamentary Papers Act 1840, any civil or criminal proceedings arising out of the publication of papers, reports, etc., made by the authority of either House must be stayed on the production of a certificate of such authority from an officer of the House. The Act thus gave the protection of absolute privilege to parliamentary papers. The official report of debates in the House (Hansard) has absolute privilege under the 1840 Act and so have documents (such as committee reports) that are published as *House of Commons papers*.[64]

Section 3 of the 1840 Act protects the publication of 'any extract from or abstract of' papers published under the authority of Parliament, but the burden of showing that publication was in good faith and not affected by malice is placed on the defendant (unlike the rule that applies to qualified privilege in the law of defamation). This limited protection has been extended to radio and television,[65] but the 1840 Act does not apply to most media reports of debates, as these are based not on Hansard but on the reporter's own notes. The 1840 Act needs to be replaced by new legislation, providing for the levels of privilege that are acceptable today.[66] While MPs who speak in the House are protected by art 9 of the Bill of Rights from liability for defamation, they are not generally so protected if they repeat their remarks outside the House (for example, in a broadcast interview) and even if they simply affirm what was said in the House.[67]

In the 18th century, the House maintained the right to control publication of its debates outside Parliament, and even declared that any publication in the press of speeches by members was a breach of privilege. In modern times, this declaration bore no relation to reality. On 16 July 1971, the House resolved that in future it would entertain no complaint of contempt or breach of privilege regarding the publication of debates in the House or its committees, except when the House or a committee sat in private session. The House thus retains the power to protect committees and sub-committees that wish to meet in private.[68] While select committees generally take evidence in public, their deliberations, especially when a draft report is being considered, are in private. Premature reporting of these proceedings may be regarded as a serious breach of privilege,[69] but the reporting of evidence taken at public sittings of committees is not restricted.[70]

The public interest in reports of parliamentary proceedings has long been recognised in the defence of qualified privilege in the law of defamation that attaches to a fair and accurate

---

[64] But *Command papers* (published by the government) are not protected in this way: see Cmnd 5909, 1975, p 55; P M Leopold [1990] PL 183; Nicholls report, paras 343–54.

[65] Defamation Act 1952, s 9(1); Broadcasting Act 1990, s 203(1) and Sch 20, para 1.

[66] Brabazon report, paras 195–6.

[67] *Buchanan* v *Jennings* [2004] UKPC 36; [2005] 1 AC 115. The Court of Appeal was willing to accept exceptions to the *Buchanan* approach in narrow cases, where there was a sufficiently close nexus between what was said inside and outside Parliament that repetition was reasonably foreseeable and that the public interest favoured applying the privilege: *Makudi* v *Triesman* [2014] EWCA Civ 179; [2014] QB 839.

[68] HC 34 (1966–7), paras 116–29.

[69] E.g. HC 357 (1967–8), debated on 24 July 1968; HC 185 (1969–70); HC 180 (1971–2); and HC 22 (1975–6), debated on 16 December 1975.

[70] HC Deb, 31 October 1980, col 917; and HC SO 136.

report of proceedings in Parliament.[71] Today there is statutory qualified privilege, without explanation or contradiction, for 'a fair and accurate report of proceedings in public of a legislature anywhere in the world'.[72]

Sound broadcasting of proceedings in both Houses began in 1978. Debates in the Lords were first televised in 1985 and in the Commons in 1989. It is likely that those who broadcast such debates are protected against liability for defamation by the common law defence of qualified privilege and by the Parliamentary Papers Act 1840, s 3 of which was extended to radio broadcasting in 1952 and to television in 1990.[73] But if the 1840 Act is to be replaced, the new legislation should give absolute privilege to broadcasts by authority of either House and should confirm that 'broadcasts' include all electronic forms of communication.[74]

Parliamentary privilege and the functions of members

We have seen that in 1939 the House of Commons took the view that privilege extends to 'everything said or done by a member in the exercise of his functions,' whether in either House or in a committee. This is a very broad test, and the Supreme Court in *R* v *Chayter* rejected the argument that to make a claim for expenses or allowances came within privilege. A member's functions today include the sending of correspondence to ministers and constituents about constituency issues and about other issues of public concern. However, since 1958, such correspondence has been regarded by the Commons as not being a 'proceeding in Parliament'.

> G R Strauss MP had written to the minister responsible for the electricity industry, complaining of the methods of disposal of scrap cable adopted by the London Electricity Board. When the board heard of the letter, Strauss was threatened with a libel action unless he withdrew and apologised. The Committee of Privileges concluded that the MP's letter to the minister was a 'proceeding in Parliament' and that the threat of a libel action was to 'impeach or question' Strauss's freedom of speech in Parliament. But on 8 July 1958, the House decided by 218 to 213 to disagree with the committee, and resolved that (*a*) the original letter was not a proceeding in Parliament and (*b*) nothing in the subsequent correspondence was a breach of privilege.[75] In support of the majority view, it was argued that members should not widen the scope of absolute parliamentary privilege and should rely on the defence of qualified privilege in the law of defamation.

Certainly, a complaint addressed by an MP to a minister on an issue of public concern in which the minister has an interest is protected by qualified privilege.[76] But qualified privilege may be rebutted by proof of malice, and it might be held to constitute malice if a member forwarded to a minister without making any inquiry a letter from a constituent containing defamatory allegations. The position of an MP is much stronger if he or she can rely on absolute privilege.

[71] *Wason* v *Walter* (1868) LR 4 QB 73. Also *Cook* v *Alexander* [1974] QB 279 (qualified privilege for a 'parliamentary sketch').

[72] Defamation Act 1996, s 15, sch 1, para 1 (and see paras 3, 7 and 9).

[73] Nicholls report, paras 355–75. Also HC 376 (1981–2) and P M Leopold [1987] PL 524, (1989) 9 LS 53 and [1999] PL 604, 614.

[74] Brabazon report, para 196.

[75] HC 305 (1956–7); *Re Parliamentary Privilege Act 1770* [1958] AC 331; HC 227 (1957–8). Also S A de Smith (1958) 21 MLR 465; D Thompson [1959] PL 10.

[76] See *Beach* v *Freeson* [1972] 1 QB 14 (MP forwarding complaint about solicitors to the Law Society and Lord Chancellor); and ch 17 F.

Despite the narrowness of the vote in 1958 (and such a decision does not have the force of law), the view that absolute privilege should not be extended to all letters between MPs and ministers was upheld in 1999 by the Nicholls committee, and again in 2013 by the Brabazon committee.[77] In the Damian Green affair, the question arose during the investigation whether parliamentary material was in law subject to search and seizure by the police, but the issue did not reach a court. Potential whistleblowers might feel more secure in approaching an MP if they knew that their letters would be protected by absolute privilege. But where an MP takes up an issue with a minister and intends to raise it in the House, especially when advised on how to proceed by a clerk in the House, the proposed action would by then be likely to have become a 'proceeding in Parliament'. If there were to be a statutory definition of 'proceeding in Parliament', as in Australia,[78] it would be desirable to clarify when the protection of parliamentary privilege begins to apply to an MP's correspondence.

One common situation on which there is no precedent at Westminster arose in New Zealand, when a civil servant was sued in defamation for briefing a minister on the reply to a parliamentary question: the court applied the test of whether absolute parliamentary privilege was 'necessary' to the working of Parliament, and decided that it was not, holding that the defence of qualified privilege at common law was sufficient.[79] The decision is not binding on UK courts, and it has been criticised on the ground that such briefings by officials are necessarily antecedent to proceedings in Parliament.[80] A decision by an English judge that the register of MPs' interests is not a 'proceeding in Parliament' has been strongly criticised.[81] By contrast, a decision by the Speaker to withhold facilities from Sinn Fein members who refused to take their seats at Westminster was held to be probably a 'proceeding in Parliament', but that in any event the decision was within the 'exclusive cognizance' of the Commons, and was not subject to judicial review.[82]

An issue not addressed in the Strauss case in 1958 was whether for someone to sue an MP for defamation in respect of a proceeding in Parliament is itself a breach of privilege. One view is that MPs should leave it to the courts to reject such an action as being bound to fail, and that the House should not treat the action itself as a breach of privilege,[83] but this view would not be shared by many MPs.

Right to control internal proceedings

The House is entitled to control its proceedings and to regulate its internal affairs without interference by the courts. This right to 'exclusive cognisance' of its proceedings is one reason why the courts refuse to examine alleged defects of procedure when the validity of an Act of Parliament is challenged on this ground.[84] For the same reason, the court refused to enforce a contract between two local authorities by which one council had promised not to oppose in Parliament a Bill promoted by the other council;[85] and the courts will not consider whether the report of a Commons committee is invalid because

---

[77] See Nicholls report, paras 103–12, and Brabazon report, paras 235–42.

[78] See Parliamentary Privileges (Australia) Act 1987, s 16(2); and Nicholls report, Annex B.

[79] *A-G v Leigh* [2011] NZSC 106; cf *Canada (House of Commons) v Vaid* [2005] SCC 30.

[80] Brabazon report, para 248.

[81] *Rost v Edwards* [1990] 2 QB 460. See *Prebble*'s case [1995] 1 AC 321, 337; P M Leopold [1990] PL 475; Nicholls report, paras 122–3; Brabazon report, paras 233–4.

[82] *Re McGuinness's application* [1997] NI 359.

[83] S A de Smith (1958) 21 MLR 465, 468–75. Lord Denning's unpublished dissent in *Re Parliamentary Privilege Act 1770* (above) is at [1985] PL 80.

[84] *Pickin v British Railways Board* [1974] AC 765. And see Erskine May, pp 227–33.

[85] *Bilston Corpn v Wolverhampton Corpn* [1942] Ch 391.

of procedural defects.[86] However, the MPs charged with making false claims for parliamentary expenses failed in their argument that the House had 'exclusive cognisance' over the claims such that they were outside the reach of criminal law.[87]

The House is also considered, in archaic language, to have the right 'to provide for its own constitution as established by law'.[88] This no longer includes the right to decide disputed elections (these are now decided by the courts).[89] But the House retains the right (*a*) to order the issue of a warrant by the Speaker for a writ for a by-election;[90] (*b*) to determine whether a member is qualified to sit in the House and to declare a seat vacant if she is not so qualified;[91] and (*c*) to expel a member whom it considers unfit to continue as a member. Expulsion is the ultimate disciplinary sanction which the House can exercise over its members. In 1947, Mr Allighan MP had published an article that accused MPs of disclosing when drunk or for payment the proceedings of confidential party meetings held in the precincts of the House. The MP failed to substantiate these allegations, and his conduct was considered to be a gross contempt of the House justifying expulsion.[92]

By contrast with the position in the United States,[93] no court in Britain may review the legality of a resolution of the House to exclude or expel a member. One safeguard against abuse of this power is that a constituency may re-elect an expelled member, as in the case of John Wilkes in the 18th century and Charles Bradlaugh a century later. Today, a member who commits severe misconduct is more likely to resign or undertake not to stand at the next general election than to be expelled.[94] In certain, narrow, circumstances, the Recall of MPs Act 2015 allows for by-elections to be triggered by petition.

This right of the House to regulate its proceedings includes the right to maintain order and discipline during debates. A member guilty of disorderly conduct who refuses to withdraw may, on being named by the Speaker, be suspended from the House either for a specified time or for the remainder of the session.[95] In *Eliot*'s case[96] the question of whether the courts could deal with an assault on the Speaker committed in the House was left open when the judgment was declared illegal by resolutions of both Houses. We have seen that in principle criminal acts in the precincts of Parliament may be dealt with in the ordinary courts, even when they also constitute a contempt of the House. In the case of a statutory offence, the prosecutor must be able to show that the statute applies to the Palace of Westminster.[97]

Breaches of privilege and contempt of the House

Subject to the limitation that the House may not by its own resolution create a new privilege, the House has inherent power to protect its privileges, though the extent of this power over

---

[86] *Dingle* v *Associated Newspapers Ltd* [1961] 2 QB 162.

[87] *R* v *Chaytor*, above, note 57.

[88] Erskine May, pp 216–7.

[89] Ch 7 E.

[90] Erskine May, p 25.

[91] Cf *A-G* v *Jones* [2000] QB 66 (Speaker asked court to decide whether an MP whose seat was vacated on her conviction for an election offence, reverted to her when she won her appeal against conviction.) This situation will not recur: see Political Parties, Elections and Referendums Act 2000, s 136.

[92] HC 138 (1946–7).

[93] *Powell* v *McCormack* 395 US 486 (1970).

[94] For the case of the disappearing MP, John Stonehouse, who was eventually convicted of fraud and resigned, see HC 273, 357, 373, 414 (1974–5), and HC Deb, 11 June 1975, col 408.

[95] HC SOs 45, 45A.

[96] *Eliot*'s case (1629) 3 St Tr 294.

[97] *R* v *Graham-Campbell, ex p Herbert* [1935] 1 KB 594 (Commons bar not subject to Licensing Acts). Cf Nicholls report, paras 240–51; Brabazon report, paras 226–7.

members of the general public (including the media) is doubtful. The House has power to order the offender to be reprimanded by the Speaker. Moreover, members of the Commons may be suspended or expelled; officers of the House may be dismissed; and non-members such as lobby correspondents, who are granted facilities in the Palace of Westminster, may have those facilities withdrawn.[98] Although the House has no power to impose a fine, it has an ancient power to commit a person to the custody of its own officers until the end of the session, but this has not been exercised since 1880. Today, arrests for criminal conduct in the House such as an assault are made by the police officers on duty at Westminster.

The term 'breach of privilege' is not synonymous with contempt of the House, and someone could be guilty of contempt who had not infringed any privilege of the House.[99] Contempt of the House, like contempt of court, is a very wide concept. In Erskine May's words:

> any act or omission which obstructs or impedes either House of Parliament in the performance of its functions, or which obstructs or impedes any member or officer of such House in the discharge of his duty, or which has a tendency, directly or indirectly, to produce such results may be treated as a contempt even though there is no precedent of the offence.[100]

Contempt has been held to include: disorderly conduct within the precincts of the House; interference with the giving of evidence to a committee;[101] obstruction of a member in coming to and from the House;[102] uttering lies in a personal statement to the House; molesting a member on account of conduct in the House (for example, when a newspaper invited readers to telephone a member at his home to express their views about a question which he had tabled);[103] premature disclosure of the proceedings of a committee;[104] and secret recording by a journalist of conversations with MPs at Westminster while trying to persuade them to accept cash for asking questions.[105] The hacking of MPs' mobile phones could be a contempt if its effect or motivation was to interfere with their parliamentary duties.[106] Action by the police or prison officers to prevent a constituent communicating with her MP could also be a contempt, even if the communication would not itself be a 'proceeding in Parliament'.

The fact that certain action may be regarded as a contempt does not mean that the House will take action against the offender. In 1978, it was agreed that the House should use its penal jurisdiction sparingly and only when the House

> is satisfied that to do so is essential to provide reasonable protection for the House, its members or its officers, from such improper obstruction or attempt at or threat of obstruction as is causing or is liable to cause, substantial interference with the performance of their respective functions.[107]

Civil servants are subject to direction by ministers in giving evidence to select committees,[108] but this does not apply to members of non-departmental public bodies: when a member of

---

[98] Cf HC 22 (1975–6).

[99] In *Allighan*'s case, above, the false reports about party meetings at Westminster involved an affront to the House but not a breach of privilege as such.

[100] Erskine May, p 251; see HC 34 (1967–8), pp xi–xviii and 95–101; Nicholls report, paras 262–70. For the precedents and full references, see Erskine May, ch 15.

[101] The House resolved in 1688 that all witnesses summoned to the House should have the privilege of the House 'in coming, staying and returning'; and see the Witnesses (Public Inquiries) Protection Act 1892.

[102] Cf *Papworth* v *Coventry* [1967] 2 All ER 41.

[103] The *Daily Graphic* case, HC 27 (1956–7).

[104] See note 69 above.

[105] HC 351-I (1994–5).

[106] HC 628 (2010–12).

[107] HC 34 (1967–8), para 15; HC Deb, 6 February 1978, cols 1155–98.

[108] See the *Osmotherly Rules* (p 111 above). And see ch 11 D.

one such body (CAFCASS) gave evidence to a Commons committee about its poor adminis-tration, other members of CAFCASS and the Lord Chancellor were held to have acted in contempt of the House in taking action against her because she had given that evidence.[109]

Parliamentary privilege, contempt and the courts

Although it is now accepted that the courts have jurisdiction to decide the existence and extent of privileges of the House, it remains a matter for the House to decide what constitutes a contempt and, when there has been a contempt, what action to take. One difficulty is that, apart from the power of the House to impose sanctions (such as suspension or expulsion) on its own members or officials, the sanctions which can be imposed on a non-member (for instance, for refusing to give evidence to a committee) are very uncertain.[110] The ancient power to detain persons for contempt is effectively obsolete, except for the power to detain briefly anyone who tries to disrupt a sitting of the House. For this reason, we need not here consider whether by seeking habeas corpus someone detained by order of the House could ask the courts to intervene.[111] Today, the imposition of lesser penal sanctions on members of the public (such as a financial penalty) would be vulnerable to challenge on grounds arising from the European Convention on Human Rights (in particular art 6, the right to a fair hear-ing by a court before criminal sanctions are imposed).[112] In 2013, the Brabazon committee concluded that committees should have the powers they need to function effectively, but hoped that, without legislation to criminalise specific contempts, it might be possible to achieve due standards of fairness of procedure.[113]

As we have seen, questions of privilege used to be a source of conflict between the Com-mons and the courts.[114] Another illustration of the relationship between courts and Parlia-ment is provided by complex events in the 1880s relating to the radical Charles Bradlaugh, an atheist who was elected MP for Northampton but was prevented by the House from taking the oath as required by the existing legislation. In outline, the court first held Bradlaugh sub-ject to penalties payable to a member of the public (common informer) who sued him to enforce the Parliamentary Oaths Act 1866.[115] Later, following his re-election to Parliament, the dispute continued, and the House resolved that the Serjeant at Arms should exclude Bradlaugh from the House. Bradlaugh challenged this resolution, but in *Bradlaugh* v *Gossett* it was held that, since this was a matter relating to internal management of the House, the court had no power to interfere. Lord Coleridge CJ said, 'If injustice has been done, it is injustice for which the courts of law afford no remedy.'[116]

Because of the potential for disputes between the courts and the Commons, it was for-merly said that there might at any one time be 'two doctrines of privilege, the one held by the courts, the other by either House'.[117] Today, there is much greater regard for inter-institutional

---

[109] See HC 210, 447 and 1055 (2003–4).
[110] See Gordon and Street, *Select Committees and Coercive Powers – Clarity or Confusion?* Also P M Leopold [1992] PL 516.
[111] See *Paty*'s case (1704) 2 Lord Raymond 1105; *Burdett* v *Abbot* (1811) 14 East 1; and *Case of the Sheriff of Middlesex* (1840) 11 A & E 273. In this sequel to *Stockdale* v *Hansard*, the Commons committed for con-tempt of the House the sheriffs who were attempting to enforce the judgment given in favour of Stockdale. And see E Stockdale [1990] PL 30.
[112] Cf *Demicoli* v *Malta* (1992) 14 EHRR 47.
[113] Brabazon report, ch 3. The Nicholls report in 1999 had recommended legislation to enable the courts to fine non-members for contempt of Parliament (paras 300–14).
[114] Erskine May, ch 17.
[115] *Clarke* v *Bradlaugh* (1881) 7 QBD 38. And see Arnstein, *The Bradlaugh Case*.
[116] (1884) 12 QBD 271, 277.
[117] Keir and Lawson, *Cases in Constitutional Law*, p 255.

comity,[118] and it is accepted that new privileges, for example, the absolute privilege which an MP has in forwarding a citizen's complaint to the Parliamentary Ombudsman,[119] must be created by statute and not by resolution of the House. However, there is still scope for conflict between the courts and Parliament, or at least between the courts and some parliamentarians. This was evident when some MPs used their freedom of speech in the House to circumvent the effect of court orders, naming individuals whose identity was protected by an injunction: this action would have been in contempt of court if they had been named outside Parliament. This occurred at a time when in sections of the media there was concern that the courts were issuing 'super-injunctions' to prevent any disclosure of the fact that an injunction had been obtained.[120] In 2013, a joint committee stressed the importance of freedom of speech in Parliament, urged that MPs should take such action nullifying a court order only when they can show that it is in the public interest to do so, and concluded that it was not necessary for the Houses to create new procedures for preventing members revealing information subject to privacy injunctions.[121]

Procedure

When a possible breach of privilege or contempt comes to the notice of a member, the member must give written notice of it to the Speaker as soon as is reasonably practicable. If the Speaker decides that the complaint should not have precedence over other Commons business, the MP is told this by letter, and it is then up to the member (if he or she can) to find another way of bringing the matter to the House. If the Speaker decides that the complaint should have priority over other business, this decision is announced to the House, and the member may table a motion for the next day proposing that the matter be referred to the Committee on Privileges. The motion is then debated and voted on by the House. In 1995, the examination of complaints of privilege was linked with the enforcement of MPs' standards of conduct (discussed in section B), but in 2013 the two functions were separated. The Committee on Privileges comprises ten members of the House and decides on the procedure for investigating a complaint remitted to it by the House. It is not usual to permit the person complained against to be represented by counsel. After examining witnesses and being advised by the Clerk of the House on relevant precedents, and if necessary by the Attorney General on matters of law, the committee reports to the House and may recommend action by the House. The House need accept neither the conclusions nor the recommendations. The party whips are not applied on privilege issues,[122] but nonetheless voting may be affected by party political considerations.

This procedure has been criticised for providing inadequate procedural safeguards to the individual complained against. In 1999, the Nicholls committee set out what procedural fairness requires, referred to the right to a fair hearing under art 6 ECHR and urged that the then Committee on Standards and Privileges should devise an appropriate procedure.[123] In 2013, the Brabazon committee rejected the idea of entrusting the courts with jurisdiction over contempts of Parliament and recommended the adoption by the Commons of new

---

[118] Brabazon report, paras 115–17.

[119] Parliamentary Commissioner Act 1967, s 10(5); ch 23 D.

[120] Joint Committee on Privacy and Injunctions (HL Paper 273, HC 1443, 2010–12).

[121] The same, ch 9; and see Brabazon report, para 160.

[122] In 1996, a junior whip resigned after seeking to exercise improper pressure on the former Committee on Members' Interests: HC 88 (1996–7).

[123] Nicholls report, paras 280–92, citing *Demicoli* v *Malta* (note 112 above). See HC 403 (2002–3) replying to the report of the Committee on Standards in Public Life (Cm 5663) urging procedural reforms. For earlier recommendations, see HC 34 (1967–8) and HC 417 (1976–7).

resolutions and Standing Orders that would explain the House's contempt powers and the procedures to be adopted on allegations of contempt or breach of privilege.[124]

B. Financial interests and payment of members

It is one thing to assert the principle that MPs should have complete freedom of speech in Parliament, but another to ensure that they are, in fact, free of undue influence from financial and business interests outside the House and do not abuse their public office for private gain. In this section we examine (*a*) the regulation by the House of MPs' external financial interests; (*b*) the dramatic issues exposed by the media in 2009 relating to MPs' expenses and allowances; and (*c*) the response to those issues since 2009.

Two preliminary points may be made. First, it was in 1911 that MPs who did not hold ministerial office first received a salary. Payment of salaries became essential once the Law Lords had held that the use of trade union funds for political purposes was ultra vires and illegal,[125] thus preventing unions from paying salaries to the MPs whom they supported. Today, it is accepted that salaries should be paid to MPs, but difficulties have often arisen as to how much they should be paid. With effect from 2012, responsibility for deciding the level of salaries was taken from the House and given to the Independent Parliamentary Standards Authority (IPSA).[126] That body is also responsible for determining and providing the expenses and allowances that MPs need to enable them to perform their duties. Secondly, MPs have never been required to give up their existing business or professional interests when they are elected to the House, and some may acquire new sources of income in the world of business or the media[127] while at Westminster; but for practical reasons many must cut down the time they formerly gave to such interests, and others leave their previous employment completely.

Payments and rewards to Members of Parliament from external sources

Every MP is expected to take an active interest in questions that directly affect their constituency and their constituents. At the national level, numerous interest groups (professional associations, trade unions, companies and voluntary organisations) seek to influence the government and to win support in Parliament. Many groups consider it worthwhile to obtain advice from MPs and to ensure that opportunities of promoting their cause in Parliament are taken. Where an MP gives time and effort to helping a constituent, no question of additional remuneration arises. But where an MP takes an interest in other matters, may the MP expect to be rewarded for this? And how is a line to be drawn between payments and rewards that are acceptable, and those that are not?

As long ago as 1695, the House resolved that 'the offer of any money, or other advantage, to any member of Parliament for the promoting of any matter whatsoever depending or to be transacted in Parliament is a high crime and misdemeanour'. In 1858, the House resolved that it was improper for a member to promote or advocate in the House any proceeding or measure in which he was acting for pecuniary reward. In 1945, it was considered that, in

---

[124] Brabazon report, Annexes 2 and 3.
[125] *Amalgamated Society of Railway Servants* v *Osborne* [1910] AC 87. Under the Trade Union and Labour Relations (Consolidation) Act 1992, unions may contribute to the expenses of parliamentary candidates from separate political funds.
[126] For this body, see below, p 238. For the history of members' salaries, see Erskine May, pp 52–4.
[127] Such as appearing on *I'm a Celebrity: Get Me Out of Here*: see 4th report of Committee on Standards (HC 806, 2013–14), concerning Ms Nadine Dorries MP.

accordance with the resolution of 1695, it would be a breach of privilege for money or other advantage to be offered to a member, or to a local party or a charity, to induce the member to take up a question with a minister.[128]

By an old rule of the House, no member who has a direct pecuniary interest in a question may vote upon it. But this rule was narrowly interpreted: Speaker Abbot declared in 1811 that the rule applied only where the interest was a 'direct pecuniary interest and separately belonging to the persons . . . and not in common with the rest of His Majesty's subjects, or on a matter of state policy'. The rule was applied only to private legislation and never to voting on a public Bill.[129] By custom of the House, members had to declare their direct pecuniary interest when speaking in a debate, but this did not apply to question time or to letters sent by a member to a minister.[130]

There have long been difficulties when members took paid employment outside the House or acted as advisers or consultants to commercial or other bodies, arising from the inevitable lack of transparency when payments from those outside sources related to actions of the member in Parliament, and when the outside body would directly or indirectly expect to see some return for payments made.[131] In 1947, after an acrimonious dispute in which a civil service union was dissatisfied with the way their 'parliamentary general secretary', W J Brown MP, had dealt in Parliament with questions relating to the union, the House resolved that it was improper for an MP

> to enter into any contractual agreement with any outside body, controlling or limiting the Member's complete independence and freedom of action in Parliament or stipulating that he shall act in any way as the representative of such outside body in regard to any matters to be transacted in Parliament; the duty of a Member being to his constituents and to the country as a whole, rather than to any particular section thereof.[132]

This was to an extent an important statement of principle, but it left the door wide open for the growth of what came to be called 'parliamentary consultancies', a door which in 1995 the Nolan committee said must be closed.[133] Further action to compel MPs to disclose their financial and business interests was needed after the collapse in 1972 of the business network associated with the architect, John Poulson. Bankruptcy proceedings revealed that the network had largely been built up through bribing officials in central and local government, police committees and health authorities. Three MPs, including a member of the shadow Cabinet, had used their position to promote Poulson's business without disclosing benefits which they were receiving from him. The conduct of one of these MPs, who had raised matters in the House for reward, was held to be a contempt of the House.[134] The duty to disclose private interests became a rule of the House on 25 May 1974, when it was resolved:

> That in any debate or proceedings of the House or its committees or transactions or communications which a member may have with other members or with Ministers or servants of the Crown, he shall disclose any relevant pecuniary interest or benefit of whatever nature, whether direct or indirect, that he may have had, may have or may be expecting to have.

This resolution governs all parliamentary proceedings, but it does not in its terms apply to dealings which MPs have with local councils, public corporations or foreign governments.

---

128 *Henderson*'s case, HC 63 (1944–5). See also *Robinson*'s case HC 85 (1943–4).
129 HC 57 (1969–70), p xii; Griffith and Ryle, *Parliament*, p 97.
130 See *Boothby*'s case, HC 5 (1940–1).
131 See First Report of the (Nolan) Committee on Standards in Public Life, Cm 2850-I (1995); and HC 637 (1994–5).
132 HC Deb, 15 July 1947, col 284.
133 Cm 2850-I (1995), pp 24–32.
134 See HC 490 (1976–7); HC Deb, 26 July 1977, col 332; and G J Zellick [1978] PL 133.

The Transparency of Lobbying, Non-Party Campaigning and Trade Union Administration Act 2014 introduced a controversial new requirement that all 'consultant lobbyists' be registered on a central register of lobbyists. A consultant lobbyist is defined in s 2 as a person who makes communications to a minister (or senior civil servant) concerning legislation or government policy. The breadth of the Act's provisions caused much debate, because of their being likely to catch most charitable campaigns and the work of non-governmental organisations. It also has the potential to catch some of the wider work of MPs, and in August 2017 the Labour MP Barry Sheerman became the first MP to register as a consultant lobbyist.

One matter that has had much attention concerns the law relating to an MP who corruptly provides services in Parliament in return for payment. Some serious difficulties have been thought to arise from art 9 of the Bill of Rights in applying to MPs the law of corruption.[135] In the light of *R* v *Chayter*,[136] MPs have no immunity from the 'ordinary' criminal law, but this does not mean that a court may rely on what was said in Parliament to prove commission of an offence.

Register of members' financial interests

It will be evident that MPs were very slow to accept the need for a systematic method of making their interests more transparent: another result of the Poulson affair was that in 1975 the House established a compulsory register of members' financial interests.[137] The aim was to publish information of any pecuniary interest or benefit which might affect the conduct of members, or influence their actions, speeches or vote in Parliament. The register was maintained by a senior clerk of the House and supervised by a select committee. In 1990 an MP who failed to register his financial interests was suspended from the House for 20 days.[138] And in 1995, two MPs were found to have been prepared to accept £1,000 from a *Sunday Times* reporter posing as a businessman, in return for asking a parliamentary question. Although the reporter was held to have committed a contempt of the House by secretly recording his conversations at Westminster with the MPs, the two MPs were suspended from the House, for 10 and 20 days respectively.[139]

This 'cash for questions' affair was one reason for the appointment of the Nolan Committee on Standards in Public Life. In its first report,[140] the committee restated seven key principles of conduct in public life (summarising these principles as selflessness, integrity, objectivity, accountability, openness, honesty and leadership). Applying these principles to MPs, the Nolan committee said that MPs should be barred from selling their services to firms engaged in lobbying on behalf of clients, but the committee was against placing the rules of conduct for MPs on a statutory basis. Accordingly, measures adopted by the House in 1995[141] included appointment of a new officer of the House, the Parliamentary Commissioner for Standards, to maintain the Register of Members' Interests, and to investigate complaints about MPs' conduct.[142] The Committee on Standards and Privileges was created to oversee the work of the Commissioner, to consider matters relating to the conduct of

[135] See Cmnd 6524 (Salmon report); GJ Zellick [1979] PL 31; Nicholls report, paras 135–42; *R* v *Greenway* (1992, at [1998] PL 356); report of joint committee on draft Bribery Bill (HL Paper 115, HC 430 (2008–9), ch 13. The Bribery Act 2010 made no special provision for the conduct of MPs.
[136] Above, section A; and see Brabazon report, paras 137–56.
[137] See HC 57 (1969–70); and HC 102 (1974–5).
[138] See HC 135 (1989–90) and HC Deb, 7 March 1990, col 889. Also M Ryle [1990] PL 313; Griffith and Ryle, *Parliament*, pp 80–102.
[139] HC 351-I (1994–5) and HC Deb, 20 April 1995, col 350.
[140] Cm 2850-I, 1995. And see ch 12 D.
[141] HC 637 and 816 (1994–5); HC Deb, 18 May 1995, col 481.
[142] See HC SO 150.

members referred to it by the Commissioner, and issues of privilege referred to it by the House. Stricter rules were adopted as to the categories of interests to be registered. The revised rules now include company directorships, employment, profession and vocation; services to clients arising from the member's position as MP; financial sponsorships, whether as a candidate for election or as a member; gifts, benefits and hospitality relating in any way to membership; overseas visits; foreign benefits and gift; land and property of substantial value; shareholdings; family members remunerated through parliamentary allowances; and a residual category of any interest or benefit received which might reasonably be thought by others to influence the member's actions in Parliament.[143] Where an MP enters into an agreement to provide services as a member, the full agreement must be registered with the Commissioner.

Also in 1995, a code of conduct for members was adopted,[144] and the 1947 resolution[145] was restated by the House, with addition of the following words:

> in particular, no Members . . . shall, in consideration of any remuneration, fee, payment, or reward or benefit in kind, direct or indirect . . .
>
> (a) advocate or initiate any cause or matter on behalf of any outside body or individual, or
>
> (b) urge any other Member of either House . . . including Ministers, to do so, by means of any speech, Question, Motion, introduction of a Bill or amendment to a Motion or Bill.[146]

The Code of Conduct also provides that the acceptance by a member of a bribe to influence his or her conduct as a member is 'contrary to the law of Parliament'.

Between 1997 and 2005, the Committee on Standards and Privileges issued almost 100 reports, many of which concerned failure by MPs to register relevant interests. When a serious failure was shown to have occurred, the Committee recommended that the MPs in question be suspended from the House for a stated period.[147] The most substantial inquiry made by the first Commissioner, Sir Gordon Downey, upheld allegations that Neil Hamilton MP received undisclosed payments from Mr Al Fayed for lobbying services and undisclosed hospitality, including a stay at the Ritz Hotel in Paris.[148] In such serious cases of misconduct, an adverse report may cause the MP to resign or to leave Parliament at the next election. In the light of events in 2009, we may note that the Committee's reports in this period often concerned alleged mistakes or abuse arising from allowances or expenses payable to MPs.[149]

With the aim of strengthening the registration of interests, some changes were made to the House's standing orders in 2003. The Parliamentary Commissioner for Standards was authorised not to report to the Committee a minor failure to register an interest where the matter had been rectified, and provision was made for an investigatory panel to deal with difficult factual disputes. Another change was to protect the Commissioner from being removed from office, except for unfitness or inability to act; and future appointments were to be made for a single period of five years, not renewable.[150]

....

[143] The current register may be read on the Commons website, as may the latest version of *The Code of Conduct, together with the Rules Relating to the Conduct of Members*.

[144] HC 688 (1995–6); and HC Deb, 24 July 1996, col 392.

[145] See text at note 132 above.

[146] HC Deb, 6 November 1995, cols 604, 661.

[147] See HC 260 (1999–2000) (untruthful denial of connections with offshore companies, intended to deceive Committee); and HC 297 (2001–2) (inadequate replies to questions from Commissioner and Committee).

[148] See HC 30, 261 (1997–8); and HC Deb, 17 November 1997, cols 81–121. Mr Hamilton later sued Mr Al Fayed for libel without success (see note 48 above).

[149] See e.g. HC 435, 946, 947 (2002–3), HC 71, 189, 233 (2004–5) and HC 419 (2005–6).

[150] See Nicholls report, pp 77–8; Cm 5663; HC 403 (2002–3); HC Deb, and cols 1239–58 (26 June 2003). The rules of appointment were changed to prevent a repeat of the unfortunate manner in which the appointment of the second Commissioner (Ms Elizabeth Filkin) was not renewed in 2001.

MPs' expenses and allowances

As well as their salaries, MPs have long been able to claim allowances for their costs in respect of such matters as travel, constituency expenses, and staff to do research and handle dealings with constituents. In 1971, MPs from constituencies outside London became able to claim an 'additional costs allowance' to compensate them for *'expenses wholly, exclusively and necessarily incurred* when staying overnight away from their main UK residence . . . for the purposes of performing Parliamentary duties' (italics supplied). Thereafter the scope of the allowance grew until by 2008, a maximum tax-free payment of £23,083 per year could be charged for such items as interest on a second mortgage, rent, furnishings, home maintenance and a food allowance (£400 per month).[151] The system was overseen by the Members' Estimate Committee and the Committee on Members' Allowances, the former being chaired by the Speaker and having the same membership as the House of Commons Commission.[152]

When in 2005 the Freedom of Information Act 2000 came into effect, attempts were made to discover details of expenses claimed by leading MPs, but this was resisted by the Commons authorities. In 2008, the Divisional Court agreed with the Information Tribunal that there was a direct public interest in knowledge of the scheme being available: the court referred to 'the absence of a coherent system for the exercise of control' over a 'deeply flawed' scheme.[153] An attempt in Parliament to exempt the Commons from the Freedom of Information Act did not succeed. In May 2009, *The Daily Telegraph* began publishing leaked details of claims by and payments to every MP.[154] These revelations were based on material obtained by the newspaper before the House authorities published the redacted information about allowances they had been required to publish under the Act of 2000.

It was clear from these sensational reports that MPs' claims spanned a very wide range, including claims for non-existent second mortgages and the opportunist 'flipping' of allowances between two homes to get maximum financial advantage, and other claims that were clearly outside the stated aims of the scheme. Knowledge of these payments caused widespread public anger. Some ministers resigned over claims they had made, other MPs were disciplined by their parties or decided to leave Parliament, and the Speaker (Michael Martin MP) resigned, mainly because of his weak leadership in the complex wrangling over publication of the expenses. Eventually, as we have seen, the Supreme Court in *R* v *Chaytor* held that parliamentary privilege did not protect from criminal liability those who had made false claims.[155] The government decided that self-regulation of MPs' expenses must end, and asked the Committee of Standards in Public Life to make an urgent review of these matters.[156]

The Parliamentary Standards Act 2009

Legislation was hastily enacted to provide a new structure for salaries and allowances that would be independent of the House. The Parliamentary Standards Act 2009 (as amended within a year) provided a new structure for salaries and allowances. The aim of the Act, which does not apply to the House of Lords (s 2(1)), was to end self-regulation of these matters by the Commons and to create a new regulatory body, the Independent Parliamentary

---

[151] Details of the scheme were contained in the *Green Book* issued from time to time to MPs.
[152] See House of Commons (Administration) Act 1978.
[153] *Corporate Officer of the House of Commons* v *Information Commissioner* [2008] EWHC 1084 (Admin), [2009] 3 All ER 403.
[154] See the *Daily Telegraph*'s booklet, *The Complete Expenses File* (20 June 2009) and P Leyland [2009] PL 675.
[155] Above, note 57.
[156] See Cm 7274 (the Kelly report), November 2009.

Standards Authority (IPSA) (s 3, and sched 1). The five members of IPSA must include a retired senior judge, an auditor and a member who was formerly an MP, but no serving MPs may be appointed. Members are formally appointed by the Queen on an address from the Commons, having been selected 'on merit on the basis of fair and open competition' by a committee of eight MPs and three other persons chaired by the Speaker (sched 1, para 2; sched 3, as amended). IPSA reports annually to each House, but its independent status means that it is not directly accountable for its decisions to the Commons. IPSA is charged with paying salaries and allowances to MPs in accordance with schemes of salaries and allowances that are adopted by IPSA itself after consultation with interested persons, including all MPs, the Committee on Standards in Public Life and the Review Body on Senior Salaries (ss 4, 5, as amended). Allowances may be paid only when they have been claimed by an MP, and MPs have a right to appeal against decisions made by IPSA, first to a Compliance Officer and then to a tribunal (s 6A).

To ensure that the scheme is properly administered, a Compliance Officer is appointed by IPSA (s 3(3) and sched 2, as amended). The Officer serves for one term of not more than five years, may not be re-appointed, and may be removed from office only for unfitness or inability to carry out his duties. If the Compliance Officer discovers that an MP was wrongly paid an allowance, the over-payment may be recovered from the recipient. A civil penalty may be imposed on an MP who fails to comply with the Compliance Officer's requirements. It is a criminal offence for an MP to provide false or misleading information when making a claim for an allowance (s 10). These measures exist alongside the disciplinary powers of the House's Committee on Standards. IPSA and the Compliance Officer must prepare a scheme for co-operating with the Parliamentary Commissioner for Standards, the Director of Public Prosecutions and the police (s 10A).

The 2009 Act includes a declaration (s 1) that the Act shall not affect the protection for proceedings in Parliament given by the Bill of Rights, art 9. Despite its constitutional significance, the Act was enacted in great haste.[157] Many provisions of the Act were amended by the Constitutional Reform and Governance Act 2010, which restored power to the House to determine the code of conduct on MPs' financial interests, but removed from the House the power to determine MPs' salaries. Some critics of the 2009 Act feared that it would lead to judicial review of decisions made in the House of Commons. However, it is not the first time that Parliament has conferred one of its historic functions on an independent body.[158] While the practical operation of IPSA is unpopular with some MPs, the legislation created a more acceptable and transparent regime for MPs' expenses than the scheme that brought the House into such low repute in 2009.[159]

C. House of Lords

By comparison with the Commons, questions of privilege seldom arise in the Lords, but events in 2009 showed that the House needs disciplinary powers equivalent to those of the Commons, and that the payment of allowances to members for attending at Westminster

---

[157] HL Committee on the Constitution, HL Papers 130 and 134 (2008–9). For the committee's criticism of high-speed legislation in general, see HL Paper 116 (2008–9).

[158] Disputes over election results used to be decided by the Commons, but since 1868 they have been decided by the Election Court (see ch 7 E).

[159] Separate schemes exist in the devolved parliaments: see the Members' Expenses Scheme for the Scottish Parliament, administered by the Scottish Parliamentary Corporate Body; and the National Assembly for Wales Remuneration Board, Determination on Members' Pay and Allowances, July 2013.

needed to be revised. The ancient privileges of the House to freedom from civil arrest and freedom of speech are in essence the same as those of the Commons and are not discussed again here. Three House of Lords Standing Orders referring to obsolete privileges were repealed in 2013.[160] The House itself decides, through the Committee for Privileges, the right of newly created peers to sit and vote. Claims to disputed hereditary peerages formerly came before that committee,[161] but such questions are of little importance today.

The power of the House to commit a person for a definite term has not been exercised in modern times, and in the past the House claimed a power to impose fines. In 2009, the question arose as to the sanctions that the House could apply in case of misconduct by its members. It was alleged by the *Sunday Times* that some peers had told journalists that parliamentary services to commercial interests could be provided by them in return for payment. The Committee for Privileges found that two peers had breached the House's code of conduct, and the conduct of two other peers was criticised.[162] The committee reported that the House has always had power to discipline its members: the House (unlike the Commons) may not expel a member, but it has an inherent power to suspend a member for a period not exceeding the life of the current Parliament.[163] This was considered an appropriate sanction to be exercised today, unlike the power of the House to detain or to fine someone who had breached privileges of the House. Two peers were suspended for the rest of the session for their misconduct, and two apologised to the House. Several peers who made false or exaggerated claims for allowances have been suspended, for periods of up to 18 months.[164]

Financial interests of peers

The House of Lords has not always been under the same pressure as the Commons concerning disclosure of interests. At one time the view was held that peers ought not to have to account publicly for their interests in the same manner as elected MPs. Yet peers can influence the legislative process, and many have access to government; they cannot expect to observe lower standards of conduct than MPs. In 1995, the House resolved that its members should act always on their personal honour and should never accept a financial benefit in return for exercising parliamentary influence; peers with a direct interest in lobbying ought not to speak, vote or otherwise use their office on behalf of clients. The House created a register of peers' consultancies and similar interests in lobbying for clients, but this was of much narrower scope than the Commons register.[165] In 2000, the Committee on Standards in Public Life recommended that the House should adopt a Code of Conduct, extending the registration and declaration of a wider range of interests. The Code first came into effect in 2002.[166] Complaints of failure to register an interest were heard by a sub-committee on registration of interests, with an appeal to the House's Committee for Privileges.

Events in 2009 caused the House to return to the matter, and in November 2009 a new Code of Conduct was adopted that requires the registration of all relevant interests and bars peers from undertaking 'parliamentary consultancies' and receiving payment for advice on lobbying.[167] In June 2010 the House appointed a retired chief constable as House of Lords

---

[160] See Cm 8318, paras 328–42; HL Procedure Committee, 5th report, HL Paper 150 (2012–13), paras 8–17; Brabazon report, para 228.

[161] See e.g. *The Ampthill Peerage* [1977] AC 547.

[162] HL Committee for Privileges (2nd report, HL Paper 88, 2008–9).

[163] See HL Committee for Privileges, *The Powers of the House of Lords in Respect of Its Members* (1st report, HL Paper 87, 2008–9).

[164] Brabazon report, annex 1, para 8.

[165] See HL 90 and 98 (1994–5); HL Deb, 1 November 1995, col 1428, and 7 November 1995, col 1631.

[166] Cm 4903, 2000; HL 68 (2000–01); HL Deb, 2 July 2001, col 630 and 24 July 2001, col 1849.

[167] See *Code of Conduct* for Members of the House of Lords and *Guide to the Code of Conduct* (2nd edn, 2011).

Commissioner for Standards, who investigates complaints of alleged breaches of the Code and reports on investigations to a sub-committee on Lords' Conduct of the House's Committee for Privileges and Standards.

Peers receive no salary, but they are entitled to an allowance for each day on which they attend the House and undertake parliamentary work, and they may claim travelling and overnight expenses and for secretarial assistance. The increased openness in publication of MPs' allowances and expenses led in 2009 to publication of the payments made to every peer. Although the Parliamentary Standards Act 2009 does not apply to the Lords, the House decided in December 2009 to approve a new scheme for providing members with financial support that would ensure greater accountability and openness.[168]

---

[168] See report of HL House Committee (HL Paper 12, 2009–10) and Senior Salaries Review Body, *Review of Financial Support for Members of the House of Lords*. Also HL Deb (14 Dec 2009), col 1317 ff. In May 2014, having previously served a sentence of imprisonment resulting from the expenses scandal, Lord Hanningfield was suspended from the House for the rest of the session for having repeatedly claimed the daily allowance while performing no parliamentary duties: see HL Privileges and Conduct Committee, 14th report, HL Paper 181 (2013–14).

CHAPTER 10

The Crown and royal prerogative

It is still formally the case that executive power in the United Kingdom is vested in the Crown, however little this may reflect the reality of modern government. The Queen may reign, but it is the Prime Minister and other ministers who rule. Yet within the executive in Britain, it is not possible to dismiss the position of the monarch as an anachronism since the monarch as head of state performs some essential functions. The fact that central government is carried on in the name of the Crown has left its mark on the law, which has never developed a notion of 'the state'.[1]

Although it is common to speak of state schools, state regulation and so on, until recently legislation rarely referred to the state as such.[2] Instead, the 'Crown' developed as 'a convenient symbol for the State',[3] though it is unclear whether the two terms can always be used as synonyms.[4] One distinction refers to 'the Sovereign' in matters concerning the personal conduct or decisions of the monarch (though that too is misleading in a country where legal sovereignty is acknowledged to rest with Parliament),[5] and to 'the Crown' as the collective entity which in law may stand for central government.

A. The monarchy[6]

Most advanced liberal democracies have moved to a republican system of government, sometimes with an elected president as head of state, the best-known examples being France and the United States. But Britain is by no means alone in having a hereditary monarch as head of state, an institution which is to be found in other G7 countries (notably Canada, which shares the same monarch) as well as other European Union countries (notably Sweden and Spain).

If there was a written constitution for the United Kingdom, the role and functions of the monarch as head of state would be set down, as they are in Spain. There the constitution provides by art 54 that the King's role is largely symbolic and representative – he is the symbol of unity and permanence, and assumes the highest representation of the state in international relations.

---

[1] The provisions of the Transparency of Lobbying, Non-Party Campaigning and Trade Union Administration Act 2014, Sch 1 referring to service as the Registrar of Consultant Lobbyists as not being 'the civil service of the State' are thus very unusual.

[2] See now Constitutional Reform and Governance Act 2010, part 1. See discussion in *Chandler* v *DPP* [1964] AC 763 (on Official Secrets Act 1911, s 1).

[3] G Sawer's phrase, quoted in Hogg, *Liability of the Crown* (1st edn), p 10; and see Marshall, *Constitutional Theory*, ch 2.

[4] See Commissioners for Revenue and Customs Act 2005, which provides for the appointment of Commissioners to act on behalf of the Crown (s 1(1)) but to serve in the civil service of the State (s 1(5)).

[5] See ch 3 above.

[6] For a fuller account of the law relating to the monarchy (dealing with styles and titles, royal marriages, accession and coronation, minority and incapacity and illness and incapacity), see the 12th edn of this work, pp 255–8. On regency, see J Jaconelli [2002] PL 449.

In the United Kingdom the role of the monarchy has evolved over many years, and we can say that it has a number of symbolic and ceremonial duties which bring dignity and solemnity to constitutional government. But the monarchy also has representative and practical duties to perform, which in the latter case may be desirable for the continuity and stability of constitutional government. As the experience of other countries demonstrates, these different roles need not be performed by a hereditary monarch, with those other countries relying on other symbols or institutions.

Title to the Crown

In 1689, the Convention Parliament (summoned by Prince William of Orange at the request of an improvised assembly of notables) filled the constitutional vacuum which arose on the departure of James II by declaring the Throne vacant and inviting William of Orange and his wife Mary jointly to accept the vacancy.[7] These events finally confirmed the power of Parliament to regulate the succession to the Crown as it should think fit.[8] Today title to the Crown is derived from the Act of Settlement 1700, subsequently extended to Scotland in 1707 and to Ireland in 1800 by the Acts of Union. By the Act of Settlement, the Crown shall 'be remain and continue to the said most excellent Princess Sophia' (the Electress of Hanover, granddaughter of James I) 'and the heirs of her body being Protestant'.[9]

The limitation to the heirs of the body, which has been described as a parliamentary entail, means that the Crown descended in principle as did real property under the law of inheritance before 1926.[10] The latter inter alia gave preference to males over females and recognised the right of primogeniture. However, the position is to be altered by the Succession to the Crown Act 2013, which removes the preference for males over females in determining the succession to the Crown, providing that 'the gender of a person born after 28 October 2011 does not give that person, or that person's descendants, precedence over any other person (whenever born)'.[11] It is likely to be some time before the effect of this change will be felt in practice if the current heir inherits the Throne, and if in due course his heir does the same.

The Act of Settlement disqualifies from the succession Roman Catholics and those who marry Roman Catholics; the Sovereign must swear to maintain the Churches of England and Scotland and must join in communion with the former Church. This restriction has been questioned in recent years as being not easily justifiable in an increasingly multicultural and secular society. Under the Succession to the Crown Act 2013, however, a person is no longer disqualified 'from succeeding to the Crown or from possessing it as a result of marrying a person of the Roman Catholic faith'.[12] This applies in relation to marriages that took place before the Act came into force, as well as those that take place afterwards. The 2013 Act does not, however, alter the restriction on persons of the Roman Catholic faith from succeeding to the Throne, or the duty of the monarch to join in communion with the Church of England.[13]

Since 1714, when the Hanoverian succession took effect under the Act of Settlement, the line of hereditary succession has been altered only once: it was provided by His Majesty's Declaration of Abdication Act 1936 that the declaration of abdication by Edward VIII should

---

[7] Maitland, *Constitutional History*, pp 283–5; Taswell-Langmead, *English Constitutional History*, pp 443–8.
[8] Taswell-Langmead, p 504.
[9] See *A–G v Prince Ernest Augustus of Hanover* [1957] AC 436, for construction of Princess Sophia Naturalization Act 1705 (repealed by British Nationality Act 1948) which entitled to British nationality all non-Catholic lineal descendants of Princess Sophia.
[10] On which, see C d'O Farran (1953) 16 MLR 140.
[11] Succession to the Crown Act 2013, s 1.
[12] Ibid, s 2(3).
[13] For background, see A Twomey [2011] PL 378.

have effect; that the member of the royal family then next in succession to the Throne should succeed (thus Edward VIII's brother became King George VI); and that Edward VIII, his issue, if any, and the descendants of that issue should not thereafter have any right to the succession. The eldest son of a reigning monarch was traditionally heir apparent to the Throne; he is Duke of Cornwall by inheritance and is invariably created Prince of Wales.[14]

Financing the monarchy[15]

In the 17th century, when the monarch personally carried out the functions of government, the revenue from the taxes which Parliament authorised was paid over to the monarch and merged with the hereditary revenues already available to him. Today a separation is made between the expenses of government and the expenses of maintaining the monarchy. Since the time of George III, it has been customary at the beginning of each reign for the monarch to surrender to Parliament for his or her life the ancient hereditary revenues of the Crown, including the income from Crown lands.[16] Provision is then made by Parliament for meeting the salaries and other expenses of the royal household.

The Sovereign Grant Act 2011 introduced a new regime for financing the monarchy. The first of two key features of the replaced regime is that it was 'reign specific', in the sense that provision was made for the monarch at the beginning of his or her reign that would continue until death. The other is that the support consisted of separate allowances, notably the civil list to meet the salaries and other expenses of the royal household,[17] and the grants in aid for the purposes of royal travel (from the budget of the Department of Transport), and the maintenance of the royal palaces (from the budget of the Department of Culture, Media and Sport). According to the Explanatory Notes accompanying it, the Sovereign Grant Act 2011 'develops a new streamlined system of support for Royal Household expenditure'.

The Sovereign Grant was set at £76 million for the year 2017–18,[18] with the annual amount determined by the royal trustees in accordance with a formula set out in the Sovereign Grant Act 2011, s 6 (as amended in 2017).[19] The Sovereign Grant is paid from money provided by Parliament,[20] and there are now formal statutory obligations on the Royal Household to keep proper accounting records, which must be examined annually by the Comptroller and Auditor General,[21] with a copy of the latter's report on the accounts (together with a statement of the accounts) to be submitted to Parliament by the Treasury.[22] A Reserve Fund has been created, into which the Grant may be carried forward if unspent, and conversely from which any overspending can be drawn. There is no parliamentary annuity for the Prince of Wales.

The monarch also holds property in a personal capacity and derives income from this. The extent of this private wealth is unknown, though it is sometimes emphasised that there is a need to distinguish private wealth from that held in trust by the Queen as Sovereign and

....

[14] On the constitutional role of the Prince of Wales, see R Brazier [1995] PL 401. See also Blackburn, *King and Country: Monarchy and the Future King Charles III.*

[15] For a good account, see Bogdanor, *The Monarchy and the Constitution,* ch 7.

[16] Under the Crown Estate Act 1961, the Crown Estate Commissioners are responsible for administering the Crown Estate: for the history, see HC 29 (1971–2), app 18. The Commissioners have wide powers under the Act. See *Walford* v *Crown Estate Commissioners* 1988 SLT 377.

[17] Civil List Act 1952, amended by Civil List Act 1972.

[18] Sovereign Grant Act 2011, s 1(3); See Report of the Royal Trustees on the Sovereign Grant for 2017–18 (2017).

[19] SI 2017 No 438.

[20] 2011 Act, s 1(6).

[21] On which see 15th ed, pp 356–8.

[22] Ibid, s 2.

Head of State, and not as an individual. Unlike other members of the royal family, the Queen benefits from the principle that the Crown is not liable to pay taxes unless Parliament says so either expressly or by necessary implication.[23] In 1992, however, it was announced that the Queen had undertaken to pay tax on her private income with effect from 1993,[24] but this does not extend to inheritance tax. The Prince of Wales has also agreed on a voluntary basis to pay tax on income derived from the Duchy of Cornwall.[25]

Duties of the monarch

It would be difficult to list the full duties that fall to the Queen to perform in person.[26] Many formal acts of government require her participation. State documents may require her signature, and she receives copies of all major government papers, including reports from ambassadors abroad and their instructions from the Foreign Office, as well as minutes of Cabinet meetings and other Cabinet papers. 'There is therefore a continuing burden of unseen work involving some hours reading of papers each day in addition to Her Majesty's more public duties.'[27] The Queen gives frequent audiences to the Prime Minister and visiting ministers from the Commonwealth, receives foreign diplomatic representatives, holds investitures, and personally confers honours and decorations. She receives visits to this country by the heads of foreign states and makes state visits overseas. She attends numerous state occasions, for example to deliver the Queen's Speech at the opening of each session of Parliament, while her formal consent is needed for appointments made by the Crown on the advice of the Prime Minister, the Lord Chancellor and other ministers.

A catalogue of official duties does not reveal what influence, if any, the monarch has on the political direction of the country's affairs. In general, the monarch is bound to act on the advice of the Prime Minister or other appropriate minister, for example, the Home Secretary in respect of the prerogative of mercy. The monarch cannot reject the final advice that ministers offer to her without the probable consequence of bringing about their resignation and their replacement by other ministers, thereby drawing the monarchy into controversy. But to what extent may the Queen offer her ministers guidance from her own fund of experience in public affairs? Bagehot described the monarch's rights as being the right to be consulted, the right to encourage, and the right to warn.[28] While this may entitle the monarch to express personal views on political events to the Prime Minister, these views may have little influence over the whole range of the government's work.[29] However, both Mr Major and Mr Blair each paid tribute to the advice received from the Queen during their time as Prime Minister.[30]

Much light was thrown upon the role of the monarch in the 20th century by Sir Harold Nicolson's biography of George V and by Sir John Wheeler-Bennett's biography of George VI. Thus it appears that the monarch, even before the days when Cabinet conclusions were regularly recorded by the Cabinet secretariat, could insist on the advice of the Cabinet being given in written form, if he felt that it was dangerous or opposed to the wishes of the people.

---

[23] HC 29 (1971–2), app 12; and ch 8.

[24] HC Deb, 26 November 1992, col 982.

[25] HC 464 (1992–3). See also HC 313 (2004–5).

[26] See HC 29 (1971–2), paras 16–17 and evidence by the Queen's Private Secretary, pp 30–41 and app 13. See also generally Pimlott, *The Queen: A Biography of Elizabeth II*.

[27] HC 29 (1971–2), para 17.

[28] *The English Constitution*, p 111. See also Brazier, *Constitutional Practice*, p 185.

[29] Although it has been said as a result that 'the Sovereign may have a marginal but beneficial influence on governmental decisions' (Brazier, ibid, p 185).

[30] R Blackburn [2004] PL 546, at p 558, note 40.

This was so that the King could record in writing the misgivings and reluctance with which he followed the advice of his Cabinet.[31] The clear impression is given in these two biographies that the monarch is far from being a mere mouthpiece of his constitutional advisers. In more recent times, the advice of Queen Elizabeth II was said to be particularly valuable in relation to Commonwealth affairs where she was considered by Mr Major to have an 'encyclopaedic knowledge'.[32] But it would be wrong to suppose that the right to be consulted, to encourage and to warn applies to all areas of policy-making, in many of which the monarch will have had no relevant experience.

The Private Secretary to the Queen plays a significant role in conducting communications between the monarch and her ministers and, in exceptional circumstances where this is constitutionally proper, between the monarch and other political leaders. Occasionally, the Queen's Private Secretary may be drawn into public controversies. In 1986, Sir William Heseltine, the Queen's Private Secretary, wrote to *The Times* following alleged disagreements between the Prime Minister (Mrs Thatcher) and the Queen on policy matters. Sir William made three points which he considered axiomatic:

(1) The Queen has the right – indeed, the duty – to counsel, encourage and warn her government. She is thus entitled to have opinions on government policy and to express them to her chief minister.

(2) Whatever personal opinions the Queen may hold or may have expressed to her government, she is bound to accept and act on the advice of her ministers.

(3) The Queen is obliged to treat her communications with the Prime Minister as entirely confidential between the two of them.[33]

Sir William asserted that it was preposterous to suggest that the Queen would suddenly depart from these principles.

Reform of the monarchy

Unlike many of the other parts of the constitution, the monarch largely survived the reforming and modernising zeal of the 1990s. Indeed, in its election manifesto of 1997, which was the basis of much of the constitutional reform in the modern era, the Labour party announced: 'We have no plans to replace the monarchy.'[34] Although this 'fell considerably short of a ringing endorsement of the institution of monarchy',[35] it remains the case that there has been little serious debate about the desirability of retaining a hereditary monarch as head of state in a modern democracy. In the 1990s, the monarchy weathered a lot of unwanted publicity about the private lives and business activities of some of its senior figures, and was subject to public criticism following the premature death of the Princess of Wales in 1997.[36]

Greater public exposure and a less deferential media have at most ignited concerns for a more responsive monarchy, not its replacement. The difficulties of reform of the latter kind were highlighted by the referendum in Australia in 1999 where the people voted to retain the monarchy when given the option of a republic instead. So the Queen remains the Head of State in Australia and indeed in a number of other prominent Commonwealth countries. One of the problems facing the republican campaigners in Australia was the division among the

---

[31] Nicolson, *George V*, p 115.
[32] Major, *The Autobiography*, p 508.
[33] *The Times*, 29 July 1986. See G Marshall [1986] PL 505.
[34] Labour Party, *New Labour: Because Britain Deserves Better* (1997), p 33.
[35] Blackburn and Plant (eds), *Constitutional Reform*, p 139.
[36] On which see Barnett, *This Time: Our Constitutional Revolution*.

anti-monarchists about how the head of state in a republic should be chosen. Those who favoured a directly elected president (on the Irish model) were unhappy with the choice in the referendum between retaining the monarchy or moving to a president elected by Parliament.[37]

B. Personal prerogatives of the monarch

It is commonplace to distinguish between prerogative powers that are exercised by the monarch, and those that are exercised by ministers in her name. The former are referred to as personal prerogatives, and the latter as the 'prerogative powers of ministers'.[38] The existence of personal prerogatives – as they were referred to by Jennings – implies an element of personal discretion on the part of the monarch in the exercise of these powers.

This approach, however, has been disputed as being contrary to political reality and constitutional sense. It has been claimed that these prerogatives should be understood 'not as personal discretionary powers of the monarch, nor as matters over which the monarch has any independent personal rights', but as 'clearly circumscribed constitutional duties to be carried out on the advice of the Prime Minister'. The removal of the residue of personal and unaccountable power from a hereditary head of state is thought by some to be important to maintain the political neutrality of the monarchy, which in turn must be the 'golden rule' for its continuity.[39]

Appointment of Prime Minister[40]

In appointing a Prime Minister, the monarch must appoint that person who is in the best position to command the support of the majority in the House of Commons. This does not involve the monarch in making a personal assessment of leading politicians, since no major party could fight a general election or govern without a recognised leader. There are, however, two circumstances where the monarch may have to intervene in the choice of Prime Minister: after an election, especially if the result is inconclusive; and during the lifetime of a Parliament if the incumbent Prime Minister resigns or dies in office.

1. After an election

Where an election produces an absolute majority in the Commons for one party, the leader of that party will be invited to become Prime Minister or, if already Prime Minister, that person will continue in office. In these circumstances, the Queen 'has no choice whom he or she should appoint as Prime Minister, and it is obvious who should be called to the Palace'.[41] By modern practice, a defeated Prime Minister resigns from office as soon as a decisive result of the election is known.

Where after an election no one party has an absolute majority (as in 1923, 1929, February 1974, 2010 and 2017), the Prime Minister in office may decide to wait until Parliament resumes to see whether he or she can obtain a majority in the new House with support from another party (as Baldwin did after the 1923 election, only to find that he could not). Or the

---

[37] See C Munro [2000] PL 3. Also J Uhr [2000] 11 *Public Law Review* 7.
[38] HC 422 (2003–4), para 1.
[39] R Blackburn [2004] PL 546; also (in reply) R Brazier [2005] PL 45.
[40] See Jennings, *Cabinet Government*, ch 2; Brazier, chs 2, 3; and Bogdanor, ch 6.
[41] Bogdanor, p 84.

Prime Minister may resign without waiting for Parliament to meet (as did Baldwin in 1929, Heath in 1974, and Brown in 2010). When the Prime Minister has resigned, the Queen will send for the leader of the party with the largest number of seats (as in 1929, 1974 and 2010) or with the next largest number of seats (as in January 1924 after Baldwin had been defeated by combined Labour and Liberal votes).[42]

The inconclusive general election in 2010 gave rise to much discussion of these practices, and to a post-mortem about the right of the incumbent Prime Minister to remain in office as well as his or her duty to do so until a new government can be formed.[43] An attempt to crystallise practice in the interests of clarity in the so-called *Cabinet Manual* proved to be controversial,[44] the latter taking a view which is different and perhaps less prescriptive than the foregoing account. According to the latter, a special responsibility falls on the Prime Minister as 'the Crown's principal adviser', who 'at the time of his or her resignation may also be asked by the Sovereign for a recommendation on who can best command the confidence of the House of Commons in his or her place'.[45]

However, there is no sense in which such advice can be binding, the view having been expressed from another quarter that 'the established convention seems to be that the Monarch is not obliged to take the advice of the outgoing Prime Minister, and may take advice from other sources'.[46] Any such advice and any decision based on that advice should be based in turn on the precedents referred to above, consistently with a less contentious passage in the *Cabinet Manual* that emphasises 'the responsibility of those involved in the political process, and in particular the parties represented in Parliament, to seek to determine and communicate clearly to the Sovereign who is best placed to be able to command the confidence of the House of Commons'.[47]

Thus, where an election produces a clear majority for one party, the Queen has no discretion to exercise. Even where the election fails to produce a clear result, it will usually be very clear who should be appointed Prime Minister. Despite her government losing its majority at the election in 2017, Mrs Theresa May was nevertheless able to continue in office as the leader of the largest party with the support of the Democratic Unionist Party, this in the circumstances being the only credible option. It would only be where there was no obvious solution to an electoral impasse that the Queen would have any discretion, in which case she would have to initiate discussions between the parties to discover whether a government could be formed by a politician who was not a party leader, or whether a coalition government could be formed.[48]

Even then, as the *Cabinet Manual* now makes clear, it would be the responsibility of the politicians to save the Queen from any embarrassment.[49]

2. Resignation or death of a Prime Minister

Where a Prime Minister resigns because of ill-health or old age or dies while in office, a new leader of the governing party must be found and a new Prime Minister appointed. In the case

---

[42] The precedents thus showed a preference for 'minority government' rather than 'majority coalition' (Bogdanor, p 253).

[43] See HC 528, 734 (2010–12).

[44] On the *Cabinet Manual*, see below, p 281. On this point, See *Cabinet Manual* (2011), paras 2.12–2.17. For consideration of the provisions relating to the formation of government after a general election, see HC 734 (2010–12), paras 64–79.

[45] *Cabinet Manual*, ibid, para 2.9.

[46] HC 528 (2010–12), para 28.

[47] *Cabinet Manual*, above, para 2.9.

[48] See Brazier, ch 3; Butler, *Governing without a Majority*, ch 5; and Bogdanor, *Multi-party Politics and the Constitution*, chs 5, 6.

[49] *Cabinet Manual*, above, para 2.10.

of the Liberal and Conservative parties, at one time this was a situation in which the monarch was required to exercise a discretion, to invite a person to be Prime Minister who would command general support within the governing party, as happened in 1957 and 1963. The parties now choose their own leader in accordance with their own rules. It was initially the case that the leader of the Conservative party was chosen by the party's MPs, and it was under these rules that Mr Major replaced Mrs Thatcher as leader of the party in 1990,[50] following which Mrs Thatcher resigned as Prime Minister.[51]

The current leadership rules of the Conservative party provide for the leader to be elected by the members of the party in a postal ballot.[52] The rules provide, however, that the candidates for election are to be chosen by the 1922 Committee, which is a committee of Conservative MPs. It is also provided that 'the procedure by which the 1922 Committee selects candidates for submission for election shall be determined by the Executive Committee of the 1922 Committee'. It was under these procedures that Mrs Theresa May was elected Conservative party leader in 2016. There were five candidates at that election, and under the applicable procedures Conservative MPs took part in several votes to reduce the number of candidates to two – Mrs May and Mrs Andrea Leadsom, with the latter withdrawing without the need for a ballot of members to be held.

In the case of the Labour party, the right to vote in the election of leader was formerly confined to Labour MPs, but in 1981 the party changed its constitution and standing orders to provide for the leader and deputy leader to be elected by an electoral college at a party conference.[53] Under rules introduced in 2014, the party leader is now elected by members, registered supporters and members of affiliated organisations on the basis of one member, one vote. An incumbent can be challenged and an election triggered by someone who has the support of 20 per cent of the Parliamentary Labour Party and European Parliamentary Party combined. Where there is no incumbent (because of death or resignation), any candidate must be nominated by at least 15 per cent of the PLP and the EPLP combined. It was under these rules that Mr Corbyn was elected and re-elected party leader.

In 1990, the Conservative party removed Mrs Thatcher as party leader against her wishes while she was also Prime Minister, her replacement by Mr Major representing the first occasion in modern times that a serving peacetime Prime Minister has been forcibly removed from office by her party. And in 1995, Mr Major resigned as leader of the Conservative party, thereby forcing an election for party leader, in which he was a candidate. He did not resign as Prime Minister, though presumably he would have done so had he not succeeded in being re-elected as party leader. More recently, the leadership rules of both parties (including their earlier iterations) have allowed for the orderly transition of party leadership where an incumbent Prime Minister has resigned, as when Mr Blair stood down to be replaced by Mr Brown in 2007, and when Mr Cameron did the same to be replaced by Mrs May in 2016.

While therefore under stable political conditions the Queen will not need to exercise a personal discretion in selecting a Prime Minister, circumstances could nevertheless arise in which it might become necessary for her to do so.[54] First, since the election of a new leader

---

[50] See R K Alderman [1992] PL 30.

[51] Major, *The Autobiography*, p 199.

[52] For background, see K Alderman (1999) 52 *Parliamentary Affairs* 260.

[53] The electoral college for leadership elections was in three sections, Labour MPs and constituency parties each having one-third of the votes and affiliated organisations also having one-third (mainly trade unions, who balloted their members for this purpose).

[54] Cf R Blackburn [2004] PL 546, at p 552. The position is very different in Scotland in relation to the First Minister under the Scotland Act 1998, s 45. See Himsworth and O'Neill, *Scotland's Constitution: Law and Practice*, where it is said that the Queen has 'only the formal role of accepting the recommendations made to her. It would be unconstitutional for her to do otherwise' (p 193).

may take some weeks, the appointment of an acting Prime Minister might well be needed if, unlike the position in 1976, the outgoing Prime Minister had died or was too ill to continue in office. Presumably a senior member of the Cabinet would be so appointed.[55] Moreover, there could well be circumstances in which reliance on normal party procedures would not produce an immediate solution: for example, where a party holding office broke up after serious internal dissensions; or where no party had a majority in the House and there was a deadlock between the parties as to who should form a government; or where a coalition agreement had broken down.[56]

In such situations, the Queen could not avoid taking initiatives to enable a new government to be formed, for example by calling inter-party discussions. Perhaps the closest we have come to unstable political circumstances of this kind was in 1931, when Ramsay MacDonald and the Labour Cabinet resigned because of serious disagreement within the Cabinet over the steps that should be taken to deal with the international financial crisis. After consulting with Conservative and Liberal leaders, George V invited MacDonald to form a 'National Government' with Liberal and Conservative support. The extreme bitterness which MacDonald's defection caused in the Labour party led to criticism of George V's conduct as unconstitutional. Although such criticism seems unjustified,[57] the National Government was not a great success and was politically damaging for many of those involved.[58]

Dissolution of Parliament[59]

Introduced to cement the Coalition between the Conservatives and the Liberal Democrats after the general election in 2010, the Fixed-term Parliaments Act 2011 was designed to transform the prerogative power to dissolve Parliament. In order fully to understand the 2011 Act, it is necessary to explain the arrangements that it replaced, while it may also be the case that the exercise of the prerogative power in relation to dissolution is constrained rather than removed by the 2011 Act. Notwithstanding the latter Act, there are circumstances whereby Parliament could be dissolved without serving a full term, as indeed revealed by the 'snap' general election in 2017, which took place before the Parliament elected in 2015 had run its course.

1. *Prerogative power*

Before the Fixed-term Parliaments Act 2011 introduced a fixed term for the life of Parliament, the Queen could in principle dissolve Parliament by prerogative, and cause a general election to be held at any time in the five-year life of a Parliament. In practice, however, the Queen acted on the advice of the Prime Minister and granted a dissolution when requested. Since 1918, it had also become established practice that a Cabinet decision was not necessary before the Prime Minister could seek a dissolution, although members of the Cabinet might

---

[55] Cf Brazier, p 17. Under the Labour party rules, when the party is in government and the leader becomes 'permanently unavailable', 'the Cabinet shall in consultation with the National Executive Committee appoint one of its members to serve as party leader until a ballot … can be carried out'. Some Prime Ministers appoint a Deputy Prime Minister. While such a person may be a suitable interim Prime Minister where the government has a majority, he or she may be less attractive where the leader of a minority party in a Coalition. It is difficult to contemplate Conservative party backbenchers accepting Mr Clegg as interim Prime Minister had the issue arisen during the Coalition government from 2010 to 2015.

[56] See R Brazier [1986] PL 387.

[57] A full account is in Bassett, *1931: Political Crisis*. See also Mackintosh, *British Cabinet*, pp 419–20, and Middlemas and Barnes, *Baldwin*, ch 23.

[58] For further consideration of issues raised in this section, see P Norton [2016] PL 18.

[59] Forsey, *The Royal Power of Dissolution in the British Commonwealth*; Markesinis, *The Theory and Practice of Dissolution of Parliament*; Marshall, *Constitutional Conventions*, ch 3; R Blackburn [2009] PL 760.

be consulted in advance.[60] Are there circumstances in which the Sovereign could have been justified in refusing a dissolution, or was it automatic that the Sovereign should grant a dissolution when requested?

It is doubtful whether there could be grounds for the refusal of a dissolution to a Prime Minister who commanded a clear majority in the Commons.[61] Political practice accepted that a Prime Minister could choose the time for a general election within the five-year life of Parliament prescribed by the Parliament Act 1911. If the Queen did refuse dissolution to a Prime Minister who commanded a majority in the House, and the Prime Minister then resigned from office with the Cabinet, any other politician invited to be Prime Minister (for example, the Leader of the Opposition) would presumably have had no prospect of a majority at Westminster until an election had been held. The Queen would therefore have been faced with an early request for a dissolution from the new Prime Minister and with inevitable criticism of political bias if the request were granted.

Where a minority government held office, the position would have been more complicated, but here again it is likely that the Prime Minister could choose the time for an election. Much may have depended on the circumstances in which the minority government had come about and on how recently a general election had been held. Thus a Prime Minister who had been granted one dissolution and failed to get a majority at the ensuing election may not necessarily have been able to insist on a second dissolution immediately. Indeed, it might have been argued that there would be a duty to resign and to give the leader of another party the opportunity of forming a government. Where a Prime Minister had been in office for a considerable period (for example, some months) since the previous election and was then defeated on an issue of confidence in the House, he or she would then have a choice between resigning or, as MacDonald did in 1924, seeking a dissolution.

The issue arose in 1950, during discussion of the problems caused by the Labour government's small majority after the election of that year. Sir Alan Lascelles, Private Secretary to George VI, wrote to *The Times*, under a pseudonym, to outline the circumstances in which he believed the monarch could properly refuse a dissolution when requested by the Prime Minister. According to Sir Alan, the monarch could properly refuse a dissolution if he were satisfied that (*a*) the existing Parliament was still 'vital, viable, and capable of doing its job', (*b*) a general election would be detrimental to the national economy, and (*c*) he could rely on finding another Prime Minister who could carry on his government for a reasonable period with a working majority.[62] It would be seldom that all these conditions could be satisfied, and it might even be argued that these were eminently matters for the Prime Minister in office to decide.

In the last 100 years there are no known instances of the monarch having refused a dissolution in the United Kingdom. However, the controversy between the 'automatic' and 'discretionary' views of the prerogative of dissolution arose afresh in 1974. After the election in February of that year, when no party had an absolute majority, questions were asked in Parliament whether Mr Wilson as Prime Minister was entitled to a dissolution if his government were defeated by a combined opposition vote. In reply, the Lord President of the Council, Mr Edward Short, told them: 'Constitutional lawyers of the highest authority are of the clear opinion that the Sovereign is not in all circumstances bound to grant a Prime Minister's

---

[60] Jennings, pp 417–19; Mackintosh, pp 453–5; Markesinis, ch 5 A.

[61] Markesinis, pp 84–6; Forsey, p 269. If an opportunist Prime Minister decided to take advantage of the death of the Leader of the Opposition to seek an immediate dissolution, knowing that the rules of the opposition party required the election of a new leader to take a month, could the Queen insist on delaying the election so that the parties could campaign on more equal terms?

[62] For this pseudonymous letter to *The Times*, see Markesinis, pp 87–8 and app 4.

request for dissolution'; it was impossible to define in advance the circumstances in which the Queen's discretion to refuse a request for a dissolution might be exercised.[63]

The matter was left unresolved, the government refusing to allow the matter to be debated in the Commons. Indeed the resolution of such a question in any particular case would have depended on the political circumstances of the time. In the event, when Mr Wilson sought a dissolution in September 1974, this was granted without question by the Queen. That the monarch should not refuse a Prime Minister's request for dissolution except for very strong reasons is obvious. In practice, the political significance of the Prime Minister's power to decide when Parliament should be dissolved was much greater than the possibility of the Queen's refusal of a dissolution. But the view that the monarch's reserve power could serve to restrain a Prime Minister who otherwise might be tempted to abuse his or her position was an argument for maintaining the reserve power as a potential restraint, not for abolishing it.[64]

2. Fixed-term Parliaments Act 2011

The Conservative party and the Liberal Democrats made an agreement for government and negotiated a programme for government in the aftermath of the inconclusive general election in 2010.[65] At the heart of that agreement and programme was an unusual – if not unique – undertaking that the newly elected Parliament would serve a full parliamentary term of five years. This would prevent either party from collapsing the Coalition at a time that seemed politically opportunistic, and would require both sides to enter into a constructive long-term relationship. The agreement led to the Fixed-term Parliaments Act 2011,[66] which not only declared that the date of the next general election was to be 7 May 2015 (s 1(2)), but also that all future general elections are to be held at fixed five yearly intervals thereafter (s 1(3)).

This important measure appears in principle to remove the right of the Prime Minister to determine the date of the general election. However, as events in 2017 clearly displayed, it does not mean that there cannot be an early election. The Act provides that such an election may be held following a House of Commons motion that there should be an early election if the motion is carried with the support of two-thirds of MPs (s 2(1), (2)). This effectively means that an early election may be held if sufficient opposition parties in the House of Commons agree. Otherwise, the Act also provides that an early election can be held when the government loses a confidence motion in the House of Commons (s 2(3), (4)).[67] This would be on the basis of a simple majority of those voting, which happened in 1979 but which is unlikely to happen where the government has a working majority.

In the event of a vote of no confidence taking place (but not in the event of a motion for an early parliamentary election with the support of at least two-thirds of those eligible to vote), the motion does not take immediate effect. The Act expressly provides for the possibility of an alternative government being formed, and allows 14 days for this to be done. If in that time a new Prime Minister is appointed and he or she is able to form a government, the House of Commons may then resolve that it has confidence in the new government, thereby nullifying the need for an immediate election. The new government would serve until the end of the five-year term of the Parliament in question, subject of course to a subsequent motion for an early election under s 2(1), or a subsequent motion of confidence in the new government under s 2(3). Only once since 1945 has a government lost a confidence vote.

Although a major negotiating achievement of the Liberal Democrats and their leader Nick Clegg, who became Deputy Prime Minister in the Coalition, it is nevertheless unclear

---

[63] *The Times*, 11 May 1974.
[64] For a robust defence of the reserve power, see G Marshall [2002] PL 4.
[65] H M Government, The Coalition: *Our Programme for Government* (2010).
[66] See M Ryan [2012] PL 213.
[67] As in 1979 when the Callaghan government resigned following a vote of no confidence.

whether the 2011 Act provides a significant restraint on Prime Ministerial power to call an election in more typical political circumstances where there is not a Coalition government (itself a rare event). On 18 April 2017, the then Prime Minister (Theresa May) announced in Downing Street that she intended on the following day to seek parliamentary approval for an early election on 8 June 2017.[68] The circumstances revealed that whatever the legal position, it would be very difficult in practice for an Opposition party to resist a Prime Ministerial demand, even when the party of Opposition is ill-prepared for an election.

It is the stated ambition of all Leaders of the Opposition to be Prime Minister, and it is likely to be only rarely that opposition leaders could oppose a prime ministerial request, regardless of how ill-judged their agreement may be. No party can afford to look ill-prepared for an election, and no party leader unwilling to contest it. So although the 2011 Act has been controversial, it is uncertain what would be the benefits of its repeal. It is important to point out that the Act is an ordinary Act of Parliament that can be repealed in the same way as any other Act of Parliament. Although there is a need for a special majority to depart from the fixed-term requirement, there is no need for a special majority to repeal the Act. But if the benefits of repealing the Act are unclear, so are the advantages of its retention. In the event of the 2011 Act's repeal, it would presumably form a template for a negotiated agreement between two or more governing parties in a future Coalition government.

That said, the Fixed-term Parliaments Act 2011 resolves any dispute about a reserve power of the monarch to require a dissolution and a general election to provide a clear mandate for a particularly controversial government proposal. The last known example of a British monarch requiring a general election is in 1910, when George V insisted that a general election be held on the Liberal proposal to remove the veto of the House of Lords, before he would create enough new Liberal peers to pass the Parliament Bill through the Lords against Conservative opposition; this requirement was accepted by the Prime Minister, and an election was duly held. Such a demand could now be made only with the consent of a special majority in the House of Commons under the 2011 Act, which might thus be seen not only as a restraint on the power of the Prime Minister, but also on the power of the monarch.

The dissolution of Parliament is now governed principally if not exclusively by statute, not prerogative.

C. The Queen in Council

The Tudor monarchs governed mainly through the Privy Council, a select group of royal officials and advisers, having recourse to Parliament only when legislative authority was considered necessary for matters of taxation or to give effect to royal policies. The Privy Council survived the 17th-century conflicts, although its judicial arm, the Court of Star Chamber, was abolished in 1641. But in the 50 years after the restoration of the monarchy in 1660, the Privy Council lost its position as the main political executive and its numbers grew, many becoming members because of other offices which they held.

As the Cabinet system developed, so did the English Privy Council lose its policy-making and deliberative role.[69] Soon after the union of England and Wales and Scotland in 1707, the Scottish Privy Council was abolished and its functions were assumed by the Privy Council for Great Britain.[70] In a formal sense the Council remained at the centre of the administrative machinery of government, but despite an attempt by Parliament in the Act of Settlement to

---

[68] HC Debs, 19 April 2017, col 624.
[69] For the history of this period, see Mackintosh, ch 2.
[70] See Devine, *The Scottish Nation*, pp 18, 21.

insist that the Privy Council should exercise its former functions, the Council had lost its political authority. Significantly, politicians began to remain members of the Council after they had ceased to be ministers, a practice which has continued until today.

Privy Counsellors and Orders in Council

Membership of the Privy Council is now a titular honour. Appointments are made by the Queen on ministerial advice. By convention all Cabinet ministers become Privy Counsellors. Members of the royal family and holders of certain high offices of a non-political character, such as archbishops and Lord Justices of Appeal, are appointed members of the Council. As in recent years have the leaders of the opposition parties 'so that they can be given classified information on "Privy Counsellor terms" should the need arise on a matter affecting national security'. In the 1970s, Len Murray, general secretary of the TUC, was made a Privy Counsellor to facilitate consultation on government policy,[71] though this was in a very different era.

The office is a recognised reward for public and political service, members entitled to the prefix, 'Right Honourable'. They take an oath on appointment which binds them not to disclose anything said or done 'in Council' without the consent of the Sovereign. As all members of the Cabinet are also Privy Counsellors, it has been considered that it is this oath which, in addition to their obligations under the Official Secrets Acts 1911–89, binds to secrecy all present and past Cabinet ministers, who may disclose Cabinet proceedings and other confidential discussions only if so authorised by the Sovereign; but little reliance was placed on this oath in the *Crossman Diaries* case,[72] and its wording does not seem apt to include Cabinet proceedings. Aliens are disqualified, but on naturalisation an alien becomes qualified for membership.[73]

Despite the many powers conferred by statutes on individual ministers, the Order in Council remains an important method of giving the force of law to acts of the government, especially the more significant executive orders. A royal proclamation is issued when it is desired to give wide publicity to the action of the Queen in Council, as in summoning Parliament (to which the statutory underpinning of dissolution under the Fixed-term Parliaments Act 2011 does not apply). Orders in Council are approved by the Queen at a meeting of the Council to which only four members are normally summoned. No discussion of substance on the merits of an instrument takes place at these meetings, and the acts of the Council are mainly formal.

Orders in Council are made either under the prerogative, or under an Act of Parliament, as for example, any orders exercising powers to make regulations under the Civil Contingencies Act 2004.[74] Prerogative orders are treated as equivalent to primary legislation, and are regarded as such for the purposes of the Human Rights Act 1998 (but not for the purposes of the Civil Contingencies Act 2004), while statutory Orders in Council are generally subject to the Statutory Instruments Act 1946.[75] Legislation made in the Channel Islands must be sanctioned by Order in Council before it comes into force.

Judicial and other functions

In 1833, the Judicial Committee of the Privy Council was set up by statute to exercise the jurisdiction of the Council in deciding appeals from colonial, ecclesiastical and admiralty

[71] Hennessy, *Whitehall*, pp 350–1.
[72] *A-G v Jonathan Cape Ltd* [1976] QB 752.
[73] *R v Speyer* [1916] 2KB 858.
[74] ch 20.
[75] ch 14.

courts.[76] In the heyday of the British Empire, the Judicial Committee was indeed an imperial court exercising what was potentially a vast jurisdiction over much of the globe. Today, its role as an appeal court within the Commonwealth has much declined, as leading members, such as Australia, Canada, India, Pakistan and South Africa, no longer – or do not – permit appeals to the Privy Council. Nevertheless, a steady flow of cases continues to be heard from other Commonwealth countries,[77] while the Privy Council remains the final court of appeal from British Overseas Territories (such as Gibraltar) and Crown dependencies (such as the Channel Islands and the Isle of Man).[78]

A matter may also be referred to the Privy Council by the Crown for an advisory opinion, an interesting but rarely used procedure established by s 4 of the Judicial Committee Act 1833,[79] which has survived the creation of the Supreme Court of the United Kingdom. The devolution legislation extended the Privy Council's jurisdiction by providing initially for it to be the final court of appeal on the powers of the devolved Parliament and assemblies. But this was short-lived, with jurisdiction being transferred to the Supreme Court of the United Kingdom when it was established in 2009. The composition of the Judicial Committee is governed by the 1833 Act: cases are usually heard by three or five Supreme Court justices or other senior judges in what is a 'strictly judicial proceeding'.[80]

So far as other functions are concerned, issues of constitutional importance are sometimes referred to ad hoc committees of Privy Counsellors, as, for example, the legal basis of the practice of telephone tapping and matters affecting state security.[81] Similarly, a committee of five Privy Counsellors was appointed to review the collection, assessment and use of intelligence prior to the invasion of Iraq in 2003.[82] In 2009, a committee under the chairmanship of Sir John Chilcot was established to examine the circumstances surrounding the more recent invasion of Iraq and its aftermath.[83] Unusually and controversially, in 2013 the Privy Council was charged with the responsibility of developing a Royal Charter for regulating the newspaper industry, after a high-profile investigation of the latter by Sir Brian Leveson had revealed poor ethical standards.[84]

The functions of the Privy Council are quite distinct from those of the Cabinet. The first gives legal form to certain decisions of the government; the second exercises the policy-making function of the executive in major matters. There is, however, an overlap between the Cabinet and the Privy Council: decisions of the latter are normally taken by ministerial members, while the Lord President of the Council is usually a senior member of the Cabinet. He or she in the past has acted as chairman of Cabinet committees, and the position may be held with the office of Leader of the House of Commons or Leader of the House of Lords. Much of the work of the Privy Council is spent dealing with institutions and companies established by Royal Charter, of which there are in excess of 900.

---

[76] Judicial Committee Act 1833.

[77] For the background, see L P Beth [1975] PL 219. See also Swinfen, *Imperial Appeal.*

[78] On the nature of this jurisdiction, see *Chief Justice of Cayman Islands* v *Governor of Cayman Islands* [2012] UKPC 39, [2013] 3 WLR 457; J Restano [2013] PL 477.

[79] See *Re MacManaway* [1951] AC 161; *Re Parliamentary Privilege Act 1770* [1958] AC 331. For a rare recent example, see *Hearing on the Report of the Chief Justice of Gibraltar* [2009] UKPC 43.

[80] *Hull* v *McKenna* [1926] IR 402.

[81] ch 16.

[82] HC 898 (2003–4).

[83] Report of the Iraq Inquiry, HC 264 (2015–16). It is not clear if this over long report was ever intended to be read. For a good follow up on the issues raised, see HC 656 (2015–16). See ch 11 below.

[84] HC 780 (2012–13). On litigation subsequently, see *R (Press Standards Board of Finance Ltd)* v *Culture, Media and Sport Secretary* [2013] EWHC 3814 (Admin), and for fuller consideration, ch 17 below.

D. The royal prerogative

Both the monarch, as head of state, and the government, as personified for many purposes by the Crown, need powers to be able to perform their constitutional functions. The rule of law requires that these powers are grounded in law and are not outside or above the system of law which the courts administer.

In Britain, the powers of the monarch and the Crown must be either derived from an Act of Parliament or recognised as a matter of common law, for there is no written constitution to confer powers on the executive. In the 17th-century constitutional settlement, it was established that the powers of the Crown were subject to law and that the Crown had no powers that could not be taken away or controlled by statute. Once that position had been achieved against the claims of the Stuarts, the courts thereafter accepted that the monarch and the Crown enjoyed certain powers, rights, immunities and privileges which were necessary to the maintenance of government and which were not shared with private citizens.

Acknowledged to be 'a notoriously difficult concept to define adequately',[85] the term prerogative is used as a collective description of these matters. Blackstone referred to the prerogative as 'that special pre-eminence which the King hath, over and above all other persons, and out of the ordinary course of the common law, in right of his royal dignity'.[86] A modern definition would stress that the prerogative has been maintained not for the benefit of the monarch but to enable the government to function, and that prerogative is a matter of common law, which does not derive from statute. Thus Parliament may not create a new prerogative, although it may confer on the Crown new rights or powers which may be very similar in character to prerogative power.

History of the prerogative[87]

The medieval King was both feudal lord and head of the kingdom. He thus had all the rights of a feudal lord and certain exceptional rights above those of other lords. Like other lords, the King could not be sued in his own courts; as there was no lord superior to the King, there was no court in which the King could be sued. In addition, the King had powers accounted for by the need to preserve the realm against external foes and an 'undefined residue of power which he might use for the public good'.[88] We have already seen that medieval lawyers did not regard the King as being above the law.[89] Moreover, certain royal functions could be exercised only in certain ways. The common law courts were the King's courts, and only through them could the King decide questions of title to land and punish felonies. Yet the King possessed a residual power of doing justice through his Council where the courts of common law were inadequate.

In the 17th century, the main disputes arose over the undefined residue of prerogative power claimed by the Stuart kings.[90] Those common lawyers who allied with Parliament in resisting the Stuart claims asserted that there was a fundamental distinction between what was called the ordinary as opposed to the absolute prerogative. The ordinary prerogative meant those royal functions which could only be exercised in defined ways and involved no

[85] HC 422 (2003–4), para 3.

[86] Blackstone, *Commentaries*, I, p 239. Cf Wade, *Constitutional Fundamentals*, pp 45–53.

[87] A valuable account is in Keir and Lawson, *Cases in Constitutional Law*, part II. See also Heuston, *Essays*, ch 3, and more recently, Tomkins, *Our Republican Constitution*, ch 3.

[88] Keir and Lawson, p 70.

[89] ch 3.

[90] Ibid.

element of royal discretion. Thus the King could not himself act as a judge; he must dispense justice through his judges. In 1607 James, who had by then also become King James I of England, claimed the right in England to determine judicially a dispute between the common law courts and the ecclesiastical courts. In the case of *Prohibitions del Roy*, it was decided by all the common law judges, headed by Coke, that the right of the King to administer justice no longer existed.[91]

By contrast, the absolute or extraordinary prerogative meant those powers which the King could exercise in his discretion. They included not only such powers as the right to pardon a criminal or grant a peerage, but also the King's undoubted powers to exercise discretion in the interest of the realm, especially in times of emergency. It was these powers on which Charles I relied in seeking to govern without Parliament. The conflict was resolved only after the execution of one King and the expulsion of another. But the particular disputes often gave rise to cases in the courts, in which the rival political theories were expressed in legal argument. Where the judges accepted the Crown's more extreme claims, their decisions had subsequently to be reversed by Parliament.

> As well as the cases on taxation and the dispensing power,[92] another outstanding case was *Darnel's* or *The Five Knights'* case,[93] where it was held that it was a sufficient answer to a writ of habeas corpus to state that a prisoner was detained *per speciale mandatum regis* (by special order of the King). Thus the King was entrusted with a power of preventive arrest which could not be questioned by the courts and which in *Darnel's* case was used to enforce taxation levied without the consent of Parliament. This arbitrary power of committal was declared illegal by the Petition of Right 1628, and in 1640 the subject's right to habeas corpus against the King and his Council was guaranteed by statute.[94]

The problem of the prerogative was confronted in two stages. The first was that of the 17th-century struggle culminating in the Bill of Rights 1689, which declared illegal certain specific uses and abuses of the prerogative.[95] The second stage was the growth of responsible government and the establishment of a constitutional monarchy.[96] It became established that prerogative powers could be exercised only through and on the advice of ministers responsible to Parliament. Nonetheless, the ability of ministers to rely on prerogative powers gives rise to continuing problems of accountability.

The prerogative today

The greater part of government depends on statute. But certain powers, rights, immunities and privileges of the monarch and of the Crown, which vary widely in importance, continue to have their legal source in the common law. Where these powers or rights are common to all persons, including the Crown (for example, the power to own property or enter into contracts), they are not described as matters of prerogative;[97] but the term royal prerogative is

---

[91] (1607) 12 Co Rep 63. See also *Case of Proclamations* (1611) 12 Co Rep 74, ch 3.
[92] ch 3.
[93] (1627) 3 St Tr 1.
[94] Habeas Corpus Act 1640.
[95] ch 3.
[96] chs 3 and 5.
[97] And see B V Harris (1992) 108 LQR 626.

properly applied to those legal attributes of the Crown which the common law recognises as differing significantly from those of private persons.

Except in those special instances where prerogative powers involve the personal discretion of the Queen, prerogative powers are exercised by or on behalf of the government of the day. For their exercise, just as for the use of statutory powers, ministers are responsible to Parliament, and questions may be asked of ministers about the exercise of prerogative power. Where a matter does not fall within the province of a departmental minister, questions may be addressed to the Prime Minister. To this rule there are certain exceptions: for example, the Prime Minister may not be questioned in the Commons as to the advice that may have been given to the Queen regarding the grant of honours or the ecclesiastical patronage of the Crown.[98] Although an Act of Parliament may abolish or curtail the prerogative, the prior authority of Parliament has traditionally not been required for the exercise of a prerogative power.

That said, certain prerogative powers could be exercised only if the government was confident that it would thereafter have the support of Parliament should this be necessary. Although signing or ratifying a treaty did not formally require parliamentary approval, the treaty would have no domestic legal effects until enacted in legislation. Similarly, where the government proposed to engage in military conflict, it would have had to be confident that Parliament would vote the supply necessary to meet the costs of the conflict. Nevertheless, growing pressure for better parliamentary scrutiny of the exercise of prerogative powers has led in recent years to a number of important changes, including the emergence of a convention – considered more fully below – that Parliament should be consulted about proposed military operations. There is, however, little prospect of the prerogative being abolished, as was proposed by one former senior Cabinet minister shortly before he joined the government.[99]

Nevertheless, steps were taken under the last Labour government to place at least some prerogative powers on a statutory footing, as with the regulation of civil servants. Before the Constitutional Reform and Governance Act 2010, the legal relationship between the Crown and Crown servants was an aspect of the prerogative, which differed markedly from the normal contractual relationship between employer and employee, though the tendency in recent years has been to move civil service employment more closely in line with the standard employment model. The other notable initiative of the last Labour government was to put in place statutory procedures to be followed before the prerogative foreign affairs power was exercised. Thus, the Constitutional Reform and Governance Act 2010 in some cases requires treaties to be laid before Parliament before being ratified, the legislation substantially replacing a convention to similar effect.

The extent of the prerogative today

Because of the diverse subjects covered by prerogative and because of the uncertainty of the law in many instances where an ancient power has not been used in modern times, it is not possible to give a comprehensive catalogue of prerogative powers.[100] Instead the main areas in which the prerogative is used today will be mentioned briefly; most of these are discussed more fully in other chapters.

---

[98] Erskine May, p 360.

[99] Jack Straw, MP, 'Abolish the Royal Prerogative' in A. Barnett (ed.), *Power and the Throne: The Monarchy Debate* (1994): '[t]he royal prerogative has no place in a modern western democracy. . . [The prerogative] has been used as a smoke-screen by Ministers to obfuscate the use of power for which they are insufficiently accountable' (p 129).

[100] For a review of the scope of the prerogative, see HC Deb, 21 April 1993, col 490. See also HC 422 (2003–4) (Memorandum by Treasury Solicitor's Department).

1. Powers relating to the legislature

It is by virtue of the prerogative that the Queen summons and prorogues Parliament.[101] (Dissolution is now governed principally by statute.)[102] The prerogative power to create hereditary peers has been diminished in practice, first by the Life Peerages Act 1958 and then by the House of Lords Act 1999. But it is presumably possible in principle for the Queen to confer hereditary titles on her subjects (presumably also on the advice of her Prime Minister), who would not as a result be entitled to membership of the House of Lords,[103] though this is a power that seems likely to fall into abeyance as inappropriate in modern times. It is under the prerogative that the Queen assents to Bills.

The Crown retains certain powers to legislate under the prerogative by Order in Council or by letters patent. Described as an 'anachronistic survival',[104] this power remains in use for the surviving overseas territories[105] and the Channel Islands. While the Crown may not create new criminal offences or impose new obligations upon citizens,[106] it may under the prerogative create schemes for conferring benefits upon citizens provided that Parliament appropriates the necessary money to pay for these benefits; thus concerning the Criminal Injuries Compensation scheme, set up by means of a non-statutory document noticed to Parliament, Diplock LJ said:

> It may be a novel development in constitutional practice to govern by public statement of intention made by the executive government instead of by legislation. This is no more, however, than a reversion to the ancient practice of government by royal proclamation, although it is now subject to the limitations imposed on that practice by the development of constitutional law in the 17th century.[107]

2. Powers relating to the judicial system[108]

The Crown can no longer by the prerogative create courts to administer any system of law other than the common law.[109] This restriction had its roots in the common lawyers' distrust of the prerogative courts of the Star Chamber and the High Commission. Its effect today is that new courts and tribunals may be created only by Act of Parliament, but this does not prevent the Crown under prerogative from establishing a body to administer a scheme for conferring financial benefits on individuals.[110] But such procedures are better done by statute. The Crown also exercises many functions in relation to criminal justice.

Thus, in England and Wales prosecutions on indictment may be stopped by the Attorney General entering a *nolle prosequi*,[111] a power exercisable even in the case of those prosecutions over which he or she has no power of superintendence, as in the case of prosecutions by HM Revenue and Customs.[112] It has been explained that 'a *nolle prosequi* acts as a stay upon the proceedings', and 'puts an end to a prosecution but does not operate as a bar or discharge or

---

[101] Parliamentary Constituencies Act 1986, s 6(4).
[102] Fixed-term Parliaments Act 2011, s 3. Previously dissolution was a prerogative matter.
[103] House of Lords Act 1999, s 1.
[104] *R (Bancoult) v Foreign Secretary (No 2)* [2008] UKHL 61, [2009] 1 AC 453, at para [69] (Lord Bingham).
[105] Roberts-Wray, *Commonwealth and Colonial Law*, ch 5. And see *R (Bancoult) v Foreign Secretary*, above.
[106] *Case of Proclamations* (1611) 12 Co Rep 74.
[107] *R v Criminal Injuries Compensation Board, ex p Lain* [1967] 2 QB 864, 886; cf Wade, pp 47–8. See also *R v Home Secretary, ex p Harrison* [1988] 3 All ER 86, and *R v Home Secretary, ex p Fire Brigades Union* [1995] 2 AC 513.
[108] ch 13.
[109] *Re Lord Bishop of Natal* (1864) 3 Moo PC (NS) 115.
[110] *R v Criminal Injuries Compensation Board, ex p Lain* [1967] 2 QB 864.
[111] On which see *Allen* (1862) 1 B&S 850.
[112] HC 115 (1995–6) (Scott Report), para C 3.10.

acquittal on the merits', which means in principle that the accused could be re-indicted. The power is rarely used, and the last Labour government proposed its abolition. A *nolle prosequi* application will normally be made to the Attorney General by the defendant, and the power is most likely to be used 'when the defendant cannot attend court for plea or attend trial because of physical or mental incapacity, which is expected to be permanent'.[113]

The Crown may also pardon convicted offenders,[114] though under the Criminal Appeal Act 1995 the Home Secretary may seek the advice of the Criminal Cases Review Commission.[115] Pardons may take three forms – as a special remission granted after a prisoner has been released early by mistake, as a conditional pardon to commute a sentence (such as the death penalty to life imprisonment) or as a free pardon to address a miscarriage of justice.[116] Most recently, pardons (including posthumous pardons for thousands of men convicted of historic homosexual offences) were granted by statute.[117] In civil matters the Attorney General represents the Crown as *parens patriae* to enforce matters of public right.[118] In this capacity the Attorney General has the power to seek an injunction to restrain a breach of the criminal law, but cannot be required to exercise the power if he or she chooses not to do so.[119]

In 1991, the Court of Appeal held that the Crown, unlike ministers and servants of the Crown, was not subject to the contempt jurisdiction vested in the courts.[120]

3. Powers relating to foreign affairs

The conduct of foreign affairs by the government is carried on mainly by reliance on the prerogative. The prerogative includes power to acquire additional territory; thus by royal warrant in 1955, the Crown took possession of the island of Rockall, subsequently incorporated into the United Kingdom as part of Scotland by the Island of Rockall Act 1972. It is doubtful whether the Crown may by treaty cede British territory without the authority of Parliament, and modern practice is to secure parliamentary approval,[121] but it seems that the prerogative includes power to declare or to alter the limits of British territorial waters.[122]

The phrase 'act of state' is often used to refer to acts of the Crown in foreign affairs: while these acts would often fall within the scope of the prerogative, the concept of the prerogative is best confined to powers of the Crown exercised in relation to its own subjects, and 'act of state' should apply only to a limited plea to the jurisdiction of the British courts, in respect of acts of the Crown performed in foreign territory in relation to aliens.[123] There is no prerogative power to expel British subjects or forcibly to remove them to another part of the country

---

[113] HC Deb, 5 March 2004, col 1202 W.

[114] *R v Home Secretary, ex p Bentley* [1994] QB 349; *R (Shields) v Secretary of State for Justice* [2008] EWHC 3102 (Admin), [2010] QB 150.

[115] 1995 Act, s 16. See HC 850 (2014–15), para 29.

[116] For a good discussion, see Ministry of Justice, *Review of the Executive Royal Prerogative Powers – Final Report* (2009), pp 15–18.

[117] Policing and Crime Act 2017, s 164.

[118] *Gouriet v Union of Post Office Workers* [1978] AC 435.

[119] Criminal Appeal Act 1995, s 16.

[120] *M v Home Office* [1992] QB 270. The House of Lords held the same, for other reasons: [1994] 1 AC 377.

[121] Anson, *Law and Custom of the Constitution*, II, ii, pp 137–42; and Roberts-Wray, ch 4. The Hong Kong Act 1985 provides that 'As from 1st July 1997 Her Majesty shall no longer have sovereignty or jurisdiction over any part of Hong Kong' (s 1(1)).

[122] *R v Kent JJ, ex p Lye* [1967] 2 QB 153; cf W R Edeson (1973) 89 LQR 364.

[123] See the varying opinions on the application of prerogative abroad in *Nissan v A-G* [1970] AC 179. See now *Rahmatullah v Ministry of Defence* [2017] UKSC 1 (no liability in tort in claim by foreign national for acts done overseas as part of a military campaign). But note *Belhaj and Rahmatullah v Straw* [2017] UKSC 3 (claims of UK complicity for unlawful detention and mistreatment overseas at the hands of foreign state officials are nevertheless properly triable in the English courts).

for the purposes of internal exile, though the position may be different under the prerogative in relation to an overseas territory.[124] By means of the writ *ne exeat regno*, the Crown could restrain a person from leaving the realm when the interests of state so demanded, but it is doubtful whether the power would be exercised today.

In time of war the Crown may possibly under the prerogative restrain a British subject from leaving the realm or recall him or her from abroad, but during modern wars entry and exit have been controlled by statutory powers. Although the Crown has power under the prerogative to restrain aliens from entering the United Kingdom, it is uncertain whether it has a prerogative power to expel aliens who have been permitted to reside here. Today, powers over aliens are exercised under the Immigration Act 1971, although that Act expressly reserves such prerogative powers as the Crown may have (s 33(5)).[125] The issue of passports to citizens is based on the prerogative, as are the conditions under which such passports are held, though there are now also statutory powers authorizing ministers to require passports to be surrendered.[126]

4. Powers relating to treaties

As we have seen, the making of treaties is done under the authority of the prerogative. In the United States the constitution vests the treaty making power in the President 'by and with the advice of the Senate'. Ratification of a treaty requires the concurrence of two-thirds of the Senate, following which a treaty will have a status equal to that of domestic law. In both of these respects, the position in the United Kingdom under the prerogative has been very different: no parliamentary approval has been required before a treaty may be ratified, and no treaty may be enforced in the domestic courts until formally implemented by legislation. The latter principle reflects the nature of the treaty-making process: it is an act of the executive, not an act of Parliament.

As suggested above, however, in recent years there has been growing pressure for greater parliamentary involvement in the making of treaties. It was already the case that under the so-called Ponsonby rule,[127] treaties once signed by ministers must be laid before Parliament for 21 days before being ratified (except in cases of urgency). Dating from the first Labour government in 1924, this convention was designed both to inform Parliament and to provide it with an opportunity to debate the treaty.[128] That convention was given statutory force by the Constitutional Reform and Governance Act 2010, which provides the House of Commons with a veto over the government's treaty-making powers in some circumstances. According to the Act, 'a treaty is not to be ratified' unless it has been laid before Parliament for at least 21 days, and neither House has resolved during that time that the treaty in question should not be ratified (s 20).

Where the House of Commons does so resolve, the minister in question may explain why in his or her view the treaty nevertheless should be ratified (s 20(4)). The House must then be given another opportunity to consider it, and may resolve again that the treaty ought not to be ratified. The House of Lords has no comparable veto: although it may resolve that a treaty

---

[124] See *Bancoult*, note 104 above. See also Sibley and Jeffries, *The Shameful Deportation of a Trade Union Leader* (on the removal of trade union leader Albert Fava from Gibraltar to England after the Second World War). Legislation may, however, confer statutory powers on ministers to proscribe where individuals may live. See Counter-Terrorism and Security Act 2015, s 16 (ch 20 below).

[125] See *R (Munir)* v *Home Secretary* [2012] UKSC 32: prerogative power applies only to aliens but not to Commonwealth citizens.

[126] Counter-Terrorism and Security Act 2015, s 1 (ch 20 below).

[127] HC Deb, 1 April 1924, cols 2001–4.

[128] Some international obligations require treaties to be laid before Parliament, even though the treaties have not yet been signed by the government: ILO Constitution (1919), art 19.

may not be ratified, this may be overruled by the government unless the House of Commons has passed a similar resolution (s 20(8)). It is expressly provided, however, that the foregoing provisions do not apply where the minister takes the view that 'exceptionally, the treaty should be ratified without the requirements of [section 20] being met' (s 22). In these cases, the minister must lay the treaty before Parliament, with an explanation of the exceptional circumstances (s 20(3)). There are also exceptions for certain EU treaties for which there are separate requirements of parliamentary approval.[129]

The 2010 Act does not affect the principle that a ratified treaty is unenforceable in domestic law without an Act of Parliament.

5. Powers relating to war and the armed forces

It is under the prerogative that the government may declare war, said by some to be 'the most significant of the prerogative powers'.[130] In modern times, however, it has not been the practice to make a formal declaration of war before commencing military activity, as in the case of the invasion of Iraq in 2003, or the military operations in Afghanistan. Such military activity is also authorised by the prerogative.

Both by prerogative and by statute the Queen is commander-in-chief of the armed forces of the Crown. The Bill of Rights 1689 prohibited the keeping of a standing army within the realm in time of peace without the consent of Parliament; thus the authority of Parliament is required for the maintenance of the army, the Royal Air Force and other forces serving on land. It has been pointed out that while the army and the RAF are now governed by statute, 'the Royal Navy is still maintained by virtue of the prerogative'.[131] Although many matters regarding the armed forces are thus regulated by statute, their control, organisation and disposition are within the prerogative and cannot be questioned in a court.[132]

In 2006 the House of Lords Constitution Committee proposed a new convention to determine the role of Parliament before British troops were deployed for the purposes of armed conflict outside the United Kingdom.[133] The government made a similar proposal in 2008 in the White Paper *Constitutional Renewal*, and it was suggested most recently that the armed forces should not be deployed overseas without Parliament being given an opportunity to debate and vote on the matter.[134] The invasion of Iraq in 2003 was preceded by such a vote,[135] while military operations in Libya in 2011 were also approved overwhelmingly by a Commons resolution.[136] The crystallisation of the convention appeared to be complete when in August 2013 the Coalition government felt compelled to withdraw support for military operations in Syria following a defeat in the House of Commons.[137]

6. Patronage, appointments and honours[138]

On the advice of the Prime Minister or other ministers, the Queen appoints ministers, judges and many other holders of public office, including the members of royal commissions to

---

[129] Constitutional Reform and Governance Act 2010, s 23, as amended by the European Union Act 2011, s 14.

[130] HC 422 (2003–4), para 18. See Joseph, *The War Prerogative*.

[131] HC 422 (2003–4), para 9. See now Armed Forces Act 2006.

[132] *China Navigation Co Ltd* v *A-G* [1932] 2 KB 197; *Chandler* v *DPP* [1964] AC 763; Crown Proceedings Act 1947, s 11.

[133] HL Paper 35 (2005–6).

[134] HL Paper 46 (2013–14), para 63.

[135] HC Deb, 18 March 2003, cols 760–911. The House of Commons voted by 412–149 to support a detailed government motion that authorised the 'use of all means necessary' to ensure the disarmament of Iraq's weapons of mass destruction. No such weapons have ever been found.

[136] HC Deb, 21 March 2011, cols 700–802.

[137] HC Deb, 29 August 2013, cols 1425–51.

[138] Jennings, ch 14; Richards, *Patronage in British Government*, ch 10; Walker, *The Queen Has Been Pleased*.

inquire into matters of controversy.[139] The Queen is the sole fountain of honour and alone can create peers, confer honours and decorations,[140] grant arms and regulate matters of precedence.[141] Honours are generally conferred by the Queen on the advice of the Prime Minister. In the case of peerages, the formal position is that the House of Lords Appointments Commission advises the Prime Minister about the non-political nominations, and the Prime Minister passes these on to the Queen.[142]

The Commission also advises the Prime Minister about party political nominees, performing a task previously performed by the Political Honours Scrutiny Committee, which is to vet all nominations to ensure the highest levels of propriety. The Political Honours Scrutiny Committee (a committee of three Privy Counsellors), which also advised on the suitability of those who are recommended for other political honours. has been abolished,[143] though a number of Honours Committees within the Cabinet Office now advise on a wide range of distinctions. Certain honours are in the personal gift of the Queen.[144]

7. Immunities and privileges

It is a principle of interpretation that statutes do not bind the Crown except by express statement or necessary implication.

> In *Lord Advocate* v *Dumbarton Council*, the Ministry of Defence decided to erect an improved security fence at its submarine base at Faslane, Dunbartonshire. Part of the fence ran alongside the A814 road and when the roads authority (Strathclyde Council) discovered that the Ministry intended to place temporary works on part of the road, they notified the Ministry that it would require their consent under the Roads (Scotland) Act 1984. The Ministry replied that these provisions did not bind the Crown and contractors took possession of a one-mile stretch of part of the road by erecting a temporary fence.
>
> Thereupon the roads authority (Strathclyde) and the planning authority (Dumbarton) gave various notices under statutes to stop the work. The Lord Advocate sought judicial review of the councils' conduct, alleging that the statutes in question did not bind the Crown. Although the Crown's immunity was restricted by the Inner House of the Court of Session, the wider immunity was restored by the House of Lords. In the view of Lord Keith, 'the Crown is not bound by any statutory provision unless there can somehow be gathered from the terms of the relevant Act an intention to that effect. The Crown can be bound only by express words or necessary implication.' At the same time, Lord Keith rejected as no longer tenable the view that 'the Crown is in terms bound by general words in a statute but that the prerogative enables it to override the statute'.[145]

Tax is not payable as a matter of law on income received by the monarch as such, neither in respect of Crown property, nor on income received on behalf of the Crown by a servant of the Crown in the course of official duties.[146] But as we have seen, the Queen has undertaken

---

[139] On judicial appointments, see ch 13.
[140] On which see for example Cm 6936, 2006 (Iraq medal).
[141] A Wagner and G D Squibb (1973) 80 LQR 352.
[142] See ch 7.
[143] See Cmd 1789, 1922; and Cm 4057-1, 1998. It is an offence to trade in honours: Honours (Prevention of Abuses) Act 1925.
[144] Namely the Order of the Garter, the Order of the Thistle, the Royal Victoria Order (for personal services to the Queen) and the Order of Merit.
[145] [1990] 2 AC 580; and ch 26.
[146] *Bank voor Handel en Scheepvaart NV* v *Administrator of Hungarian Property* [1954] AC 584.

to pay tax on her private income since 1993, and it is claimed on the official royal website that her private income is taxable 'as for any taxpayer', though it does not say at what rate.[147] Many of the immunities of the Crown in civil litigation were removed by the Crown Proceedings Act 1947, but the Crown and government departments still have certain privileges.

Thus the 1947 Act preserved the personal immunity of the Sovereign from being sued.[148] The question has arisen whether the Crown enjoys immunity from criminal liability. During the Spycatcher affair in the mid-1980s, a retired MI5 officer, Mr Peter Wright, alleged that members of the Security Service had been engaged in surveillance operations which included burgling premises in London. The Home Secretary announced that the government had never asserted that actions 'could lawfully be done under the prerogative when they would otherwise be criminal offences'.[149] The security and intelligence services may now engage in activity with the authority of a warrant granted with statutory authority that could otherwise give rise to criminal liability.[150]

8. The prerogative in time of emergency

The extent of the prerogative in times of grave emergency cannot be precisely stated. That prerogative powers were wide was admitted by Hampden's counsel in the *Case of Ship Money*. Save in regard to taxation, they were not abridged by the Bill of Rights. In 1964, Lord Reid said: 'The prerogative certainly covers doing all those things in an emergency which are necessary for the conduct of war'; but he added that there was difficulty in relating the prerogative to modern conditions since no modern war had been waged without statutory powers:

> The mobilisation of the industrial and financial resources of the country could not be done without statutory emergency powers. The prerogative is really a relic of a past age, not lost by disuse but only available for a case not covered by statute.[151]

According to the old law, in time of sudden invasion or insurrection, the King might demand personal service within the realm.[152]

Either the Crown or a subject might invade the land of another to erect fortifications for the defence of the realm.[153] But it is not certain whether this should be regarded as an aspect of the prerogative since it was a duty shared by the Crown with all its subjects. Extensive emergency powers have now been granted by Parliament, and these confer authority on ministers to make regulations that provide for the confiscation of private property, with or without compensation.[154] But if, for example, an emergency arose in which it was necessary for the armed forces to take immediate steps against major terrorist action within the United Kingdom, it is conceivable that private property needed for this purpose could be occupied under prerogative, and (as will be considered below) that compensation would at common law be payable to the owners.

In these circumstances, however, there are likely to be serious legal hurdles to cross, and extensive statutory powers exist to deal with terrorism. That said, judicial tolerance of prerogative powers in relation to police powers and in relation to terrorist-related activity is not to be overlooked.[155]

---

[147] See also on royal finances, pp 244–5 above.

[148] ch 26.

[149] HC Deb, 29 January 1988, col 397 (WA). Cf *A–G v Guardian Newspapers Ltd (No 2)* [1990] 1 AC 109, 190. See now Intelligence Services Act 1994, s 7.

[150] See ch 18.

[151] *Burmah Oil Co Ltd v Lord Advocate* [1965] AC 75, 101.

[152] Chitty, p 49.

[153] *Case of the King's Prerogative in Saltpetre* (1607) 12 Co Rep 12.

[154] Civil Contingencies Act 2004, ss 18–22.

[155] *R v Home Secretary, ex p Northumbria Police Authority* (below), and *R (XH) v Home Secretary* (below).

9. Miscellaneous prerogatives

Other historic prerogative powers concerning matters which are today largely regulated by statute relate to: the granting of a royal charter to professional bodies and charities;[156] the right to mine precious metals; coinage; the grant of franchises, for example, markets, ferries and fisheries;[157] the right to treasure trove;[158] the sole right of printing or licensing others to print the Authorised Version of the Bible,[159] the Book of Common Prayer and state papers;[160] and the guardianship of infants (a prerogative jurisdiction said to be delegated to the courts).[161] The courts may interfere 'for the protection of infants, qua infants, by virtue of the prerogative which belongs to the Crown as parens patriae'.[162]

Although potentially wide in scope,[163] this latter jurisdiction is, however, 'carefully and cautiously applied by judges in circumstances in which the welfare of those to whom the inherent jurisdiction applies positively require its exercise for their protection'.[164] When a court is exercising this paternal jurisdiction, it is empowered to exclude the public from the hearing of the case where it is necessary to do so.[165] In *R* v *Central Television plc*,[166] however, it was held that the power could not be invoked to obscure the pictures of a man in a television programme imprisoned for indecency with young boys, on the ground that his identification would cause harm to his child: the programme had nothing to do with the care or upbringing of the child.

E. The royal prerogative and the courts

Some prerogative acts are unlikely to give rise to the possibility of challenge in the courts, for example the conferment of an honour or the summoning of Parliament. But where an act purporting to be done under the prerogative directly affects the rights or interests of an individual, the courts may be asked to determine a number of issues.

---

[156] See *R (Project Management Institute)* v *Minister for the Cabinet Office* [2016] EWCA Civ 21; [2016] 1 WLR 1737: the granting of a royal charter is subject to judicial review, though in this case the application by a rival organization was unsuccessful. On the BBC, see Ministry of Justice, *Review of the Executive Royal Prerogative Powers – Final Report*, above, p 23, and ch 17 below.

[157] Cf *Spook Erection Ltd* v *Environment Secretary* [1989] QB 300 (beneficiary of market franchise not entitled to Crown's exemption from planning control).

[158] Treasure trove, i.e. gold or silver objects that have been hidden and of which no owner can be traced, is the property of the Crown: *A-G of Duchy of Lancaster* v *G E Overton (Farms) Ltd* [1982] Ch 277. See now Treasure Act 1996.

[159] *Universities of Oxford and Cambridge* v *Eyre & Spottiswoode Ltd* [1964] Ch 736 (royal prerogative did not extend to New English Bible).

[160] Copyright, Designs and Patents Act 1988, s 163.

[161] *Butler* v *Freeman* (1756) Amb 302; and *Wellesley* v *Duke of Beaufort* (1827) 2 Russ 1.

[162] *In re Spence* (1847) 2 Ph 247 (Lord Cottenham, LC), cited with approval by Lord Denning (*In re L (An Infant)* [1968] P 119), cited with approval in turn by Dame Elizabeth Butler-Sloss (*In re a Local Authority* [2003] EWHC 2746 (Fam), [2004] Fam 96). The jurisdiction also applies to adults who lack sufficient capacity: *E* v *Channel Four* [2005] EWHC 1144 (Fam), [2005] UKHRR 789, *PS* v *City of Sunderland* [2007] EWHC 623 (Fam), [2007] 2 FLR 1083.

[163] See from Australia, *Re Beth* [2013] VSC 189.

[164] *In re a Local Authority*, above, para 61. And see *Re T* [2001] NI Fam 4.

[165] *Scott* v *Scott* [1913] AC 417.

[166] [1994] Fam 192.

The existence and extent of a prerogative power

In principle the courts will not recognise the existence of new prerogative powers. In *Entick v Carrington*, in which the court held that the mere plea of state necessity would not protect anyone accused of an unlawful act, Lord Camden CJ said, 'If it is law, it will be found in our books. If it is not to be found there, it is not law.'[167] And in 1964 Diplock LJ said,

> It is 350 years and a civil war too late for the Queen's courts to broaden the prerogative. The limits within which the executive government may impose obligations or restraints on citizens of the United Kingdom without any statutory authority are now well settled and incapable of extension.[168]

But some prerogative powers are very wide, and difficulties arise when the courts are asked to decide whether an ancient power applies in a new situation; for example, whether the prerogative right to intercept postal communications justifies the tapping of telephones;[169] or most controversially whether the prerogative relating to foreign affairs could be used to give notice of withdrawal from the EU in circumstances that would affect rights conferred by Parliament.[170]

When difficult questions of these kinds arise, it may not be easy to distinguish between creating a new prerogative and applying an old prerogative to new circumstances.

In *R v Home Secretary, ex p Northumbria Police Authority*,[171] the Home Secretary made available CS gas and baton rounds to the police to deal with situations of serious public disorder, notwithstanding the objections of the local police authority. The police authority sought a declaration that the Home Secretary had no power to provide the equipment without their consent, save in a situation of grave emergency. The Court of Appeal held that the provision of the equipment was authorised by the Police Act 1964, but also by the royal prerogative. In so concluding, the court had first to determine that there did in fact exist a 'prerogative to enforce the keeping of what is popularly called the Queen's peace within the realm'. Although the court had difficulty in finding authority for such a power, Croom-Johnson LJ nevertheless concluded that such a general power is bound up with the Crown's 'undoubted right to see that crime is prevented and justice administered'. The supply of baton rounds and CS gas was held to fall within the scope of the prerogative, since it is open to the Home Secretary 'to supply equipment reasonably required by police forces to discharge their functions'.

A related question is whether the courts have power to rule that an ancient prerogative has become so unsuited to modern conditions that it can no longer be relied on by the Crown. In general, rules of common law do not lapse through desuetude.[172] But it is difficult to see why a court should be required to give new life to an archaic power which offends modern constitutional principles, merely because its existence had been recognised several centuries ago.

---

[167] (1765) 19 State Tr 1029, 1066: ch 16. *Entick*'s case was distinguished in *Malone* v *Metropolitan Police Commissioner* [1979] Ch 344 (no evidence of unlawful act in tapping telephones); ch 16.

[168] *BBC* v *Johns* [1965] Ch 32, 79.

[169] Cf Cmd 283, 1957. In *Malone*'s case, no claim of prerogative power was made.

[170] *R (Miller)* v *Secretary of State for Exiting the EU* [2017] UKSC 5, [2017] 2 WLR 583. See ch 6 above.

[171] [1989] QB 26, criticised by A W Bradley [1988] PL 297.

[172] Maitland, *Constitutional History*, p 418; cf *Nyali Ltd* v *A-G* [1956] 1 QB 1, and *McKendrick* v *Sinclair* 1972 SC (HL) 25, at pp 60–1.

The difficulty of applying the old common law in contemporary circumstances was evident in *Burmah Oil Company* v *Lord Advocate*.[173]

In 1942 extensive oil installations were destroyed by British troops in Rangoon, not accidentally as a result of fighting but deliberately so as to prevent the installations falling into enemy hands. One day later, the Japanese army entered Rangoon. After receiving some £4 million from the British government as an ex gratia payment, the company sued the Lord Advocate representing the Crown in Scotland for over £31 million. It was agreed that the destruction had not been ordered under statutory authority and the company claimed compensation for the lawful exercise of prerogative power. The House of Lords held (a) that, as a general rule, compensation was payable by the Crown to the subject who was deprived of property for the benefit of the state, by prerogative act in relation to war, and (b) that the destruction of the refineries did not fall within the 'battle damage' exception to the general rule. But the House left open the basis on which compensation should be assessed.

This decision established that where private property was taken under the prerogative, the owner was entitled at common law to compensation from the Crown; but the War Damage Act 1965 retrospectively provided that no person should be entitled at common law to receive compensation in respect of damage to or destruction of property caused by lawful acts of the Crown 'during, or in contemplation of the outbreak of, a war in which the Sovereign is or was engaged'. This Act prevented the Burmah Oil Company's claim from succeeding, but its effect was limited to acts of the Crown which destroyed property during or in contemplation of a war; the principle that the Crown is obliged to pay compensation for property taken under the prerogative for use of the armed forces otherwise still seems to apply.[174] Thus the Crown may under prerogative requisition British ships in time of urgent national necessity, but compensation is payable, as it was in 1982 when British ships were requisitioned for use in the recapture of the Falkland Islands.[175] By the right of angary, the Crown may in time of war appropriate the property of a neutral which is within the realm where necessity requires, but compensation must be paid.[176] In both world wars, statutory powers of requisitioning property were conferred on the Crown and compensation was paid.

The effect of statutes upon prerogative powers

Parliament may abolish or restrict prerogative powers expressly or by necessary implication, whether or not coupling this with the grant of statutory powers in the same area of government. But often Parliament has not expressly abolished prerogative powers and has merely created a statutory scheme dealing with the same subject. Where this is the case, as a general principle, must the Crown proceed under the statutory powers or may it rely instead upon the prerogative?

---

[173] [1965] AC 75, discussed by A L Goodhart (1966) 82 LQR 97; T C Daintith (1965) 14 ICLQ 1000; and (1966) 79 Harv LR 614.

[174] E.g. *Nissan* v *A-G* [1970] AC 179, 229 (Lord Pearce).

[175] Requisitioning of Ships Order 1982. And see *Crown of Leon* v *Admiralty Commissioners* [1921] 1 KB 595; W S Holdsworth (1919) 35 LQR 12.

[176] *Commercial and Estates Co of Egypt* v *Board of Trade* [1925] 1 KB 271. And see W I Jennings (1927) 3 CLJ 1.

In *Attorney-General v De Keyser's Royal Hotel*[177] a hotel was required for housing the administrative staff of the Royal Flying Corps during the First World War. The Army Council offered to hire the hotel at a rent but, negotiations having broken down, a letter was sent on the instruction of the Army Council stating that possession was being taken under the Defence of the Realm Acts and Regulations. A petition of right was later brought against the Crown claiming compensation as of right for the use of the hotel by the authorities.

It was argued for the Crown that there was a prerogative power to take the land of the subject in case of emergency in time of war; that no compensation was payable as of right for land so taken; and that this power could be exercised, notwithstanding provisions of the Defence Act 1842 which had been incorporated into the Defence of the Realm Acts and provided for statutory compensation as of right to the owners. The argument for the owners of the hotel was that the Crown had taken possession under the statutes and so could not fall back on the prerogative.

The House of Lords rejected the argument of the Crown, holding that on the facts the Crown had taken possession under statutory powers. The House also held that the prerogative had been superseded for the time being by the statute. The Crown could not revert to prerogative powers when the legislature had given to the Crown statutory powers which covered all that could be necessary for the defence of the nation, and which were accompanied by important safeguards to the individual. Thus for the duration of the statutory powers, the prerogative was in abeyance. The House therefore did not have to decide whether the Crown had a prerogative power to requisition land in time of war without paying compensation, but serious doubts were expressed about this claim.[178]

The principle in this case, that the 'executive cannot exercise the prerogative in a way which would derogate from the due fulfilment of a statutory duty',[179] is subject to a number of refinements. First, it applies only when Parliament has not given an express indication of its intention. Thus the Immigration Act 1971 provided that the powers which it conferred should be additional to any prerogative powers (s 33(5)), as did the Emergency Powers (Defence) Act 1939.[180] Second, there are suggestions that it may apply only where the statute confers rights or benefits on the citizen which would be undermined were the Crown to retain the right to use the prerogative power. In the *Northumbria Police* case, the Court of Appeal held that the supply of baton rounds and CS gas was authorised by the Police Act 1964, s 41, but also by the prerogative power to maintain the peace. Was the prerogative power displaced by the statute, or could both exist and operate simultaneously?

In opting for the latter position, Purchas LJ said:

It is well established that the courts will intervene to prevent executive action under prerogative powers in violation of property or other rights of the individual where this is inconsistent with statutory provisions providing for the same executive action. Where the executive action is directed towards the benefit or protection of the individual, it is unlikely that its use will attract the intervention of the courts . . . [B]efore the courts will hold that such executive action

---

[177] [1920] AC 508.

[178] See subsequently the *Burmah Oil* case, p 267 above. See also *C O Williams Construction Ltd v Blackman* [1995] 1 WLR 102, at p 108; *R v Home Secretary, ex p Fire Brigades Union* [1995] 2 AC 513; and *Attorney-General v Blake* [2001] AC 268. For a modern consideration of *De Keyser*, see *R (Alvi) v Home Secretary* [2012] UKSC 33, [2012] 1 WLR 2208.

[179] *R v Home Secretary, ex p Fire Brigades Union* [1995] 2 AC 513.

[180] ch 20.

is contrary to legislation, express and unequivocal terms must be found in the statute which deprive the individual from receiving the benefit or protection intended by the exercise of prerogative power.[181]

In the *Northumbria Police* case, even if the statute had not provided the necessary authority, the court was unable to find 'an express and unequivocal inhibition sufficient to abridge the prerogative powers, otherwise available to the Secretary of State, to do all that is reasonably necessary to preserve the peace of the realm'. Third, where the statute restricting the prerogative is repealed, 'the prerogative power would apparently re-emerge as it existed before the statute'.[182] This is subject to 'words in the repealing statute which make it clear that the prerogative power is not intended by Parliament to be revived or again brought into use'.[183]

The manner of exercise of a prerogative power

Although the courts have long had the power to determine the existence and extent of a prerogative power, traditionally they have had no authority to regulate the manner of its exercise. This contrasts with statutory powers of the executive, which the courts have held must generally be exercised in accordance with the rules of natural justice and in accordance with the so-called *Wednesbury* principles.[184] Thus, the courts have held that the courts cannot question whether the Crown has wisely exercised its discretionary power regarding the disposition of the armed forces;[185] nor could the courts say whether the government should enter into a particular treaty;[186] nor whether the Home Secretary had properly advised the Queen regarding the prerogative of mercy.[187] In *Gouriet* v *Union of Post Office Workers*[188] the House of Lords held that the exercise of the Attorney General's discretion in giving consent to the bringing of relator actions could not be reviewed by the courts.

But when this last decision was made, there were already some indications of a more flexible approach by the courts.[189] Although it may not have been fully appreciated at the time,[190] *R* v *Criminal Injuries Compensation Board, ex p Lain*[191] was to prove an important landmark, where it was held that the High Court had the power to review the activities of the board, a body set up under the royal prerogative to administer benefits for the victims of criminal injury. Lord Parker CJ could see no reason why a body set up by prerogative rather than by statute should be any less amenable to judicial review for that reason alone.[192] The position is now governed by the House of Lords decision in *Council of Civil Service Unions* v *Minister of State for Civil Service*.[193]

---

[181] [1989] QB 26, at p 53. See also *R (XH)* v *Home Secretary* [2017] EWCA Civ 41, [2017] 2 WLR 1437 (also distinguishing *De Keyser*, prerogative power to withdraw passport not lost by the Terrorism Prevention and Investigation Measures Act 2011 providing statutory authority authorising the same). But see now the wider powers in the Counter-Terrorism and Security Act 2015, s 1.

[182] *Burmah Oil Co Ltd* v *Lord Advocate* [1965] AC 75, Lord Pearce at p 143.

[183] *R* v *Foreign Secretary, ex p CCSU* [1984] IRLR 309, at 321 (Glidewell J).

[184] See ch 24 A on the latter.

[185] *China Navigation Co Ltd* v *A-G* [1932] 2 KB 197; *Chandler* v *DPP* [1964] AC 763; Crown Proceedings Act 1947, s 11.

[186] *Blackburn* v *A-G* [1971] 1 WLR 1037. Also *R* v *Foreign Secretary, ex p Rees-Mogg* [1994] QB 552.

[187] *Hanratty* v *Lord Butler* (1971) 115 SJ 386, discussed by A T H Smith [1983] PL 398, 432. Cf B V Harris [1991] PL 386. But see *R* v *Home Secretary, ex p Bentley* (note 196 below).

[188] [1978] AC 435.

[189] See *Chandler* v *DPP* [1964] AC 763, 810 (Lord Devlin).

[190] See C P Walker [1987] PL 62.

[191] [1967] 2 QB 864.

[192] See also *Laker Airways Ltd* v *Department of Trade and Industry* [1977] QB 643 (Lord Denning).

[193] [1985] AC 374. See H W R Wade (1985) 101 LQR 180.

In January 1984, the Foreign Secretary announced the government's decision to exclude trade unions from Government Communications' Headquarters (GCHQ). This would be done under an Order in Council of 1982 authorising the Minister for the Civil Service to give instructions regulating the terms and conditions of civil service employment. The instructions given directed that staff at GCHQ would no longer be permitted to be members of the civil service unions, but only to join an officially approved staff association. These steps had been taken because of earlier industrial action at GCHQ.

In deciding whether the government's decision was reviewable by the courts, a majority in the House of Lords held that the courts could review the manner of exercise of discretionary powers conferred by the prerogative just as they could review the manner of exercise of discretionary powers conferred by statute. Lord Diplock could 'see no reason why simply because a decision-making power is derived from a common law and not a statutory source, it should for that reason only be immune from judicial review'. It does not follow, however, that all prerogative powers would be subject to review in this way. According to the House of Lords, it depends on the nature of the power, and in particular whether the power in question is justiciable, i.e. whether it gives rise to questions which are capable of adjudication in a court of law.

It was not clear which powers are justiciable, though Lord Roskill gave many examples of those which are not, including the making of treaties, the disposition of the armed forces, the granting of honours and the dissolution of Parliament. Litigation arising from the events in Iraq in 2003 was a sobering reminder that despite the *CCSU* decision, by no means all decisions under the prerogative are subject to judicial review. In a challenge to the legality of British involvement in the hostilities brought by CND, it was argued that the action was being taken without a clear UN mandate. But this was unsuccessful, with the Divisional Court (of three members) applying the *CCSU* decision to hold that such matters were not justiciable.[194] Indeed, it is difficult to see how a court could realistically be expected to challenge such intensely political decisions in such circumstances.

Nevertheless, one effect of the *CCSU* decision was that the prerogative power to regulate terms of employment in the civil service was now subject to judicial review, though the power in question has since been displaced by statute following the enactment of the Constitutional Reform and Governance Act 2010. Otherwise, it was quickly accepted that the power to issue a passport is subject to judicial review (in the event of the passport being withheld or revoked),[195] and also that 'some aspects of the exercise of the Royal Prerogative [of mercy] are amenable to the judicial process'.[196] In *R v Home Secretary, ex p Fire Brigades Union*,[197] it was held to be an 'abuse of the prerogative' when the Home Secretary failed to implement a statutory scheme to compensate the victims of crime and chose instead to reintroduce a less favourable scheme by relying on common law powers.[198] It does not follow, however, that because a power is amenable to judicial process, the courts will therefore be willing to intervene.

---

[194] *CND* v *Prime Minister* [2002] EWHC 2759 (QB), *The Times*, 27 December 2002.

[195] *R* v *Foreign Secretary, ex p Everett* [1989] QB 811; *R (XH)* v *Home Secretary*, above (application failed).

[196] *R* v *Home Secretary, ex p Bentley* [1994] QB 349. See subsequently, *R* v *Bentley* (2001) 1 Cr App Rep 307. Compare *Hanratty* v *Lord Butler* (1971) 115 SJ 386, and *de Freitas* v *Benny* [1976] AC 239.

[197] [1995] 2 AC 513; T R S Allan [1995] CLJ 489.

[198] The case was thought not to involve an application of the *De Keyser* principle (above, p 268), because the statutory provisions (Criminal Justice Act 1988) had not been brought into force and thus had 'no legal significance of any kind'.

Thus, in *R (Bancoult)* v *Foreign Secretary (No 2)* the House of Lords went further than in *CCSU* by holding that the making of an Order in Council could be reviewed, as well as the manner of exercise of the power it conferred (the *CCSU* case being concerned only with the latter).[199] On the facts of that case, however, an Order in Council preventing displaced Chagos Islanders from returning home was upheld, the House of Lords (by a majority) accepting government arguments based on cost and security. On a different matter, the Foreign Office has a policy for providing support for British citizens facing capital punishment abroad, the policy expressly excluding the provision of legal representation. Unlike in the case of discretionary powers conferred by statute (which cannot be fettered by a rigid rule),[200] there is no obligation on the part of the government to consider departing from its established practice under the prerogative to meet the justice of a particular case.[201] According to Lords Carnwath and Mance, 'prerogative powers have to be approached on a different basis from statutory powers'.[202]

In *Youssef* v *Foreign Secretary*,[203] the appellant had been placed on a UN sanctions list as a terrorist suspect by the decision of a committee in which the Foreign Secretary had participated. The powers of the Foreign Secretary were governed by the foreign affairs prerogative, which although not 'immune from judicial review', is 'an area in which the courts proceed with caution'. In this case the minister's conduct was clearly justiciable as bearing directly on the interests of the appellant.

The appeal failed, the Supreme Court holding that the Foreign Secretary had not acted unlawfully. One of the grounds of challenge was that the minister had participated in a process in which other countries may have been influenced by evidence tainted by torture. Although the use of torture evidence could not be supported, in the exercise of his prerogative powers it was the responsibility of the minister to ensure that his participation was not influenced by evidence tainted by torture, but he could not be responsible for the conduct of the others.

Questions relating to treaties

As indicated above, the decision to enter into a treaty is not justiciable.[204] Nor can the treaty be enforced in the domestic courts until enacted in legislation.[205] Notwithstanding these rules, however, once made, a treaty may nevertheless have legal consequences. First, the courts increasingly will refer to treaties in the interpretation of legislation,[206] a process encouraged by the Human Rights Act and the duty to have regard to Strasbourg jurisprudence.[207] It is certainly the case that the ECtHR freely refers to a wide range of international sources in construing Convention rights, arguing that it has a duty under the Vienna Convention on the Law of Treaties to 'take into account any relevant rules and principles of international law'.[208] That this is rubbing off on the domestic courts is vividly illustrated by

---

[199] [2008] UKHL 61, [2009] 1 AC 453.

[200] See ch 24 below.

[201] *R (Sandiford)* v *Foreign Secretary* [2014] UKHL 44; [2014] 1 WLR 2697.

[202] Ibid, para 62. The possibility was raised, however, of prerogative powers being reviewable on grounds of irrationality in exceptional cases, contrary to the views expressed by Lord Diplock in *CCSU*, above: ibid, para 66.

[203] [2016] UKSC 3.

[204] *Blackburn* v *Attorney General* [1971] 1 WLR 1037.

[205] *R* v *Home Secretary, ex p Brind* [1991] 1 AC 696. But see *Minister of State for Immigration* v *Teoh* (1995) 128 ALR 353 (High Court of Australia held that a treaty could give rise to a legitimate expectation that the executive would act in accordance with the treaty).

[206] See *R (Adams)* v *Justice Secretary* [2011] UKSC 18, [2012] 1 AC 48.

[207] Human Rights Act 1998, s 2. See ch 14.

[208] *Demir* v *Turkey* [2008] ECHR 1345, (2009) 48 EHRR 54, para 67, referred to in *R(SG)* v *Work and Pensions Secretary*, below.

RMT v *Serco*,[209] where the Court of Appeal was presented with the task of construing legislation consistently with Convention rights. In the course of doing so, Elias LJ took into account the relevant provisions of the Council of Europe's Social Charter of 1961, as well as ILO Conventions 98 and 151.[210]

Secondly, although a treaty (or other international agreement) itself is not enforceable in domestic law, it may nevertheless give rise to rights and obligations that are so enforceable. The principle is illustrated well by the important decision in *Rahmatullah* v *Foreign Secretary*,[211] even though on the facts the application failed. In the latter case, British forces had detained the applicant in Iran in 2004. He was handed over to the Americans and taken to Afghanistan where he had been detained ever since. Habeas corpus proceedings were brought on his behalf in the English courts,[212] a central element in the case being a Memorandum of Understanding (MOU) concluded between the Australian, British and US governments relating to the transfer of prisoners. This provided for the treatment of prisoners in accordance with the Geneva Conventions, and the return of British prisoners such as Rahmatullah by the United States 'without delay upon request' by the United Kingdom.

The seven judges in the Supreme Court held unanimously that there was prima facie evidence that Rahmatullah had been illegally detained and that, even though the respondents did not have physical control over him, there were grounds under the MOU whereby they could assert control with a reasonable prospect of producing him to the court. A major concern for the Supreme Court, however, was whether they were being drawn into the 'forbidden territory' of diplomatic affairs and foreign policy. But in dismissing this concern, Lord Kerr said that

> the Secretaries of State were not required to make any particular diplomatic move. Because they appeared [by virtue of the MOU] to have the means of securing Mr Rahmatullah's production on foot of the writ of habeas corpus, they were required to bring that about or to give an account of why it was not possible.[213]

Having thus established that the MOU provided the basis for the action, a majority (5–2) held (in the face of a strong dissent) that the government had done enough to answer the application, in the light of US insistence that Rahmatullah was lawfully detained under US law, and the absence of any indication from the US authorities 'that there would be any opportunity for discussion of that question'.[214]

Apart from the foregoing, a third example of the growing importance of treaties in litigation is provided by *Hounga* v *Allen*,[215] which related to the development of the common law and the willingness of the Supreme Court to adapt the private law rules relating to public policy to reflect the changing public policy demands expressed in modern treaties. *Hounga* was concerned with the public policy rule that prevents the enforcement of contracts tainted by illegality, in this case a relationship in breach of immigration law between a young woman and her 'employer' in which the former was held in conditions of domestic servitude. In

[209] [2011] EWCA Civ 226, [2011] ICR 848.
[210] See also *R(SG)* v *Work and Pensions Secretary* [2015] UKHL 16 (UN Convention on the Rights of the Child); and *Mathieson* v *Work and Pensions Secretary* [2015] UKSC 47 (UN Convention on the Rights of the Child and UN Convention on Rights of Persons with Disabilities).
[211] [2012] UKSC 48, [2013] 1 All ER 574.
[212] On habeas corpus, see ch 25 below.
[213] *Rahmatullah* (note 123 above), para 68.
[214] Ibid, para 84. See subsequently in relation to other claims arising from the same incidents, *Rahmatullah* (note 123 above), and *Belhaj and Rahmatullah* v *Straw* (note 123 above), above.
[215] [2014] UKSC 47; [2014] 1 WLR 2889. See A Bogg and V Mantouvalou, 'Illegality, Human Rights and Employment: A Watershed Moment for the United Kingdom Supreme Court?' *UK Const L Blog* (13 March 2014).

taking into account Council of Europe and ILO Conventions against trafficking and forced labour, it was held that

> the decision of the Court of Appeal to uphold Mrs Allen's defence of illegality to her complaint runs strikingly counter to the prominent strain of current public policy against trafficking and in favour of the protection of its victims. The public policy in support of the application of that defence, to the extent that it exists at all, should give way to the public policy to which its application is an affront; and Miss Hounga's appeal should be allowed.[216]

The boundaries between municipal and international treaties are thus much more fluid than they were in the past, and although this is generally a progressive development, it is nonetheless paradoxical to the extent that the courts are thereby giving effect to prerogative acts at a time when they are simultaneously engaging in closer scrutiny of the exercise of prerogative power.[217]

The prerogative and the Human Rights Act

The growing willingness of the courts to review the exercise of prerogative powers is reinforced by the Human Rights Act 1998 which gives the courts even greater powers of review. Under the Human Rights Act, Orders in Council made under the authority of the royal prerogative are deemed to be primary legislation[218] and must be read and given effect to in a way compatible with Convention rights (s 3).[219] Where the terms of such an Order in Council breach Convention rights, the courts are empowered to declare the Order in Council incompatible with Convention rights, although they are bound to continue to apply it until it is revoked or revised (s 4).

A more likely source of challenge to the exercise of prerogative powers arises as a result of the Human Rights Act 1998, s 6, which provides that it is unlawful for a public authority to act in a way that is incompatible with Convention rights. The right to enforce Convention rights against an exercise of prerogative power does not formally depend on the power in question being justiciable. But in view of the fact that many prerogative powers deal with issues such as defence of the realm and national security, it may be expected that the courts would exercise caution in response to any claim under the Act.[220]

So much is confirmed by *R (Abbasi) v Foreign Secretary*[221] which was concerned with the detention of British citizens by the US government in Guantanamo Bay in circumstances described by Lord Steyn extra-judicially as being a 'legal black hole'.[222] Arguing that the detention violated their Convention rights, the claimants sought to require the British government to take all reasonable steps to require the US government to release them. But the action failed, with the Court of Appeal holding that the British government is not under a duty to take positive action to prevent violations of human rights that occur outside the jurisdiction and for which it has no responsibility.

---

[216] *Hounga*, ibid, para 52 (Lord Wilson).
[217] For further consideration of the power of the courts to use treaties in adjudication, including unratified treaties imposing no obligation on the United Kingdom, see E Bjorge [2017] PL 571.
[218] On which see P Billings and B Pontin [2001] PL 21.
[219] For a full account of the Act, see ch 14 below.
[220] See generally R Moosavian [2012] PL 124.
[221] [2002] EWCA Civ 1598, [2002] All ER (D) 70. Also *R(al Rawi) v Foreign Secretary* [2006] EWCA Civ 1279; [2008] QB 289.
[222] Lord Steyn (2004) 53 ICLQ 1. See also *Abbasi*, ibid, at para 66.

Similarly, in *R (Gentle)* v *Prime Minister*[223] it was held that the mothers of two soldiers killed in Iraq had no right under article 2 of the ECHR (which protects the right to life) to require the government to establish a public inquiry to consider whether the decision to go to war in 2003 was consistent with international law. The House of Lords concluded that article 2 imposes no duty to ensure that the country does not go to war contrary to international law. It could not therefore be said that there was 'an independent duty to use reasonable care to ascertain whether the war would be contrary to [international law] or not'.[224]

F. Conclusion

For many years the law relating to the prerogative was fairly stable. The prerogative gave great power to government across a number of important areas of activity and in the exercise of that power the government was largely unencumbered by the need for parliamentary approval or the fear of judicial review. But as should be clear from this chapter, much is changing, with the law relating to the prerogative being swept up with other aspects of constitutional and administrative law in the fast pace of reform that has been taking place generally.

So far as the prerogative is concerned, there are three major developments to note. The first of these has been the removal of civil service employment from regulation by prerogative to regulation by statute, though the legislation in question continues to give extremely wide powers to the government. Given that the prerogative power relating to the civil service was in any event already subject to judicial review, this important initiative from the perspective of principle may be of limited practical significance. This is a matter considered more fully in Chapter 11.

Secondly, steps have been taken by statute and other means to displace both personal and governmental prerogative power, though in no case has the prerogative power been removed altogether. The power of dissolution of Parliament has been largely displaced by the Fixed-term Parliaments Act 2011, while the exercise of the treaty-making power is now the subject of parliamentary approval by virtue of the Constitutional Reform and Governance Act 2010. This is in addition to the emergence of a convention (of indeterminate scope) requiring parliamentary approval before the authorisation of military operations.

Thirdly, at the same time, we see an increase in the willingness of lawyers to try to develop means of holding government to account in the courts for the exercise of prerogative powers. These initiatives have been taken partly as a result of controversial military intervention in Iraq and Afghanistan, and they serve to shine a bright light on the human costs of these campaigns. But they have also been taken most spectacularly in relation to Brexit, with the Supreme Court holding that the government had no power under the prerogative to give notice of withdrawal from the EU, as a result of which it was necessary for legislation hastily to be prepared.[225]

It seems unlikely that these initiatives by lawyers will cease, as efforts continue to be made to create new and wider exceptions to existing rules.

---

[223] [2008] UKHL 20, [2008] 1 AC 1346.
[224] Ibid, para 16 (Lord Hoffmann).
[225] *Miller*, above.

CHAPTER 11

Cabinet, government departments and civil service

As organs of government, the Cabinet and the office of Prime Minister have evolved together since the 18th century. Their existence is recognised in occasional statutes (for example, the Ministerial and other Salaries Act 1975), but their powers of government derive neither from statute nor from common law administered in the courts. Parliament could confer powers directly on the Prime Minister or on the Cabinet. In practice this does not often happen, statutory powers being conferred either on specific ministers or on the Queen in Council. Yet the Prime Minister and the Cabinet occupy key places at the heart of the political and governmental system.[1]

As the Prime Minister provides the individual leadership of the majority party in the House of Commons, so the Cabinet provides the collective leadership of that party.[2] If national affairs are to be directed in any systematic way, and if deliberate choices in government between competing political priorities are to be made, these decisions can be made only by the Prime Minister and the Cabinet. In the past, descriptions of the British system of government often labelled it Cabinet government. As L S Amery wrote:

> The central directing instrument of government, in legislation as well as in administration, is the Cabinet. It is in Cabinet that administrative action is co-ordinated and that legislative proposals are sanctioned. It is the Cabinet which controls Parliament and governs the country.[3]

In recent years, more emphasis has been placed on the role of the Prime Minister and less on the Cabinet itself. In 1963, when he had not yet served as a Cabinet minister, Richard Crossman wrote: 'The post-war epoch has seen the final transformation of Cabinet government into Prime Ministerial government', arguing that the Cabinet had joined the Crown and the House of Lords as one of the 'dignified' elements in the constitution.[4] This judgment appears to have been reinforced in the 1980s when it is claimed that 'members of Mrs Thatcher's Cabinets had allowed the usual forms of Cabinet government to be displaced by imperious prime ministerial rule'.[5]

A 'presidential' style of government is also associated with Mr Blair,[6] and there seems little doubt that the grip of the Prime Minister tightened during his tenure in office.[7] But

---

[1] Bagehot's celebrated description of the Cabinet in *The English Constitution*, pp 65–9, must still be read, though his definition of the Cabinet as 'a committee of the legislative body selected to be the executive body' is misleading. For general accounts, see Jennings, *Cabinet Government*; Mackintosh, *The British Cabinet*; Gordon Walker, *The Cabinet*; Wilson, *The Governance of Britain*; Hennessy, *Cabinet*; Hennessy, *The Prime Minister*; and James, *British Cabinet Government*.

[2] Gordon Walker, p 56.

[3] *Thoughts on the Constitution*, p 70. This orthodoxy is reproduced today in the *Ministerial Code*, which provides that 'the business of the Cabinet and Ministerial Committees consists in the main of (*a*) questions which significantly engage the collective responsibility of the Government because they raise major issues of policy or because they are of critical importance to the public; and (*b*) questions on which there is an unresolved argument between departments': *Ministerial Code* (2016), para 2.2.

[4] Introduction to Bagehot, pp 51, 54. See also Berkeley, *The Power of the Prime Minister*, and Mackintosh, ch 24; cf A H Brown [1968] PL 28, 96.

[5] R Brazier (1991) 54 MLR 471, 476.

[6] See Foley, *The Rise of the British Presidency*.

[7] Foster, *British Government in Crisis*, esp Part 4.

Mr Blair was blessed with a very large parliamentary majority, a well-disciplined government and a relatively united party. Subsequent Prime Ministers were not so fortunate: Mr Brown's authority was diminished by a series of personal miscalculations and political crises; Mr Cameron's tenure was spent mainly as head of a Coalition government; and Mrs May had the misfortune of losing her government's majority in the face of an insurgent opposition and a divided parliamentary party.

A. The Prime Minister[8]

The nature of the office

Like the Cabinet, the office of Prime Minister has evolved as a matter of political expediency and constitutional practice rather than of law. Although he did not recognise the title, Robert Walpole is now regarded as having been the first Prime Minister when he was First Lord of the Treasury, from 1721 to 1742. William Pitt the Younger did much to create the modern office of Prime Minister in the years after 1784. In fact the post acquired its present form only with the advent of the modern party system and the creation of the present machinery of government.

For most of its history, the office of Prime Minister has been held along with a recognised post, usually that of First Lord of the Treasury. Between 1895 and 1900 Lord Salisbury was both Prime Minister and Foreign Secretary, and between 1900 and 1902 he was Prime Minister and Lord Privy Seal; during these years A J Balfour was First Lord of the Treasury and Leader of the Commons. Since 1902, the offices of Prime Minister and First Lord of the Treasury have always been held together by a member of the Commons.

In 1905, by act of the prerogative, the Prime Minister was given precedence next after the Archbishop of York,[9] and as already mentioned the existence of the office is recognised increasingly by statute.[10] Since 1937 statutory provision of a salary and a pension has assumed that the Prime Minister is also First Lord of the Treasury. In the latter capacity, the Prime Minister is one of the Treasury ministers, although the financial and economic duties of the Treasury are borne primarily by the Chancellor of the Exchequer.

Exceptionally, the Prime Minister may decide also to hold another office: Ramsay MacDonald was both Prime Minister and Foreign Secretary in the first Labour government in 1924. During the Second World War, Churchill assumed the title of Minister of Defence, although without a separate ministry and without his duties being defined. The Prime Minister is also minister for the civil service,[11] though there is now also a Minister for the Cabinet Office who has day-to-day responsibility for civil service matters.

The Prime Minister is responsible for the appointment of commissioners to oversee the interception of communications and the work of the intelligence services.[12] The approval of the Prime Minister is also required for appointment of the most senior civil servants. Important Crown appointments are filled on his or her nomination, for example, the senior judges, the bishops, the chairman of the BBC Board and the Parliamentary Ombudsman. The Prime Minister also still advises the Queen on new peerages,[13] on appointments to the

---

[8] For a good account of the office and recent incumbents at the time the book was written, see Hennessy, *The Prime Minister*.
[9] *London Gazette*, 5 December 1905.
[10] E.g. Chequers Estate Act 1917; Chevening Estate Act 1959; Ministerial and other Pensions and Salaries Act 1991; Political Parties, Elections and Referendums Act 2000; Constitutional Reform Act 2005; and Investigatory Powers Act 2016.
[11] See *CCSU v Minister for the Civil Service* [1985] AC 374.
[12] Investigatory Powers Act 2016, s 227. For details, see ch 16.
[13] See ch 7.

Privy Council and the grant of honours,[14] and the filling of those university chairs which are in the gift of the Crown.

In these appointments, the Prime Minister's freedom of action may to a greater or lesser extent be restricted by conventions requiring prior consultation with or deference to the interests affected; or by the Public Appointments Order in Council 2016.[15] In the case of peerages, some nominations are now made by the House of Lords Appointments Commission, which also considers the Prime Minister's nominations;[16] in the case of judges, appointments to the Supreme Court of the United Kingdom are determined largely by ad hoc Supreme Court Selection Commissions.[17] Nonetheless, the Prime Minister's extensive patronage continues to give rise at least to the possibility that non-political appointments could be used for political purposes.[18]

Powers of the Prime Minister in relation to the Cabinet

Although each Prime Minister must adopt his or her own style of leadership, he or she is in a position to exercise a dominant influence over the Cabinet, having powers that other ministers do not have, however senior and experienced they may be. This is not to say that the Prime Minister has unlimited power, with his or her position contingent on retaining the confidence of both the Cabinet and his or her parliamentary party, as the downfall of Mrs Thatcher spectacularly revealed.[19] The rare cases until now of minority or coalition government will impose additional restraints on the power of the Prime Minister, as the experiences of Mr Cameron and Mrs May respectively make clear. But minority and coalition government aside, the following considerations have tended to reinforce prime ministerial power in the post-war era:

1 The Prime Minister effectively makes all appointments to ministerial office, whether within or outside the Cabinet. He or she may ask ministers to resign, recommend the Queen to dismiss them or, with their consent, move them to other offices. The Prime Minister settles the order of precedence in the Cabinet, and may name one of the Cabinet to be Deputy Prime Minister,[20] or First Secretary of State. In forming his or her first Cabinet, a new Prime Minister will be expected to appoint from the senior members of the party; and a leading politician may be able to stipulate the Cabinet post which he or she is prepared to accept.

In the case of Labour, party rules at one time provided that on taking office the Prime Minister must appoint existing members of the Shadow Cabinet, provided they retained their seats in the new Parliament. This constraint has now been abolished, the Labour leader free to choose both Cabinet and Shadow Cabinet members.[21] Although there have never been similar constraints on Conservative party leaders, they too will nevertheless normally rely on an established team when assuming the responsibilities of office.[22] But as the tenure of the Prime Minister extends, constraints of this kind will begin to wane: only nine members of

---

[14] Some honours are granted on the advice of other ministers, e.g. the Foreign Secretary and the Defence Secretary. Some appointments are made on the recommendation of other bodies such as the House of Lords Appointments Commission (some life peers).

[15] See ch 12 below.

[16] ch 7.

[17] ch 13.

[18] Cf T Benn (1980) 33 *Parl Affairs* 7, still a classic.

[19] R Brazier (1991) 54 MLR 471, 477. For an assessment of the relationship between Prime Ministers and their Cabinets, see S James (1994) 47 *Parl Affairs* 613, and Hennessy, *The Prime Minister*.

[20] In 1951, George VI refused to appoint Eden to this 'non-existent' office: Wheeler-Bennett, *King George VI*, p 797. But see Brazier, *Constitutional Practice*, pp 78–81.

[21] Labour Party Rules (2016), Clause VII.

[22] See Brazier, above, pp 61–7.

Mr Blair's first Cabinet appointed in 1997 (including Mr Blair himself) were still Cabinet ministers in 2001; by 2005 that had fallen to seven.

2 The Prime Minister controls the machinery of central government in that he or she decides how the tasks of government should be allocated to departments and whether departments should be created, amalgamated or abolished. A good example in 2009 relates to further reorganisation which consolidated changes Mr Brown had made in 2007 on assuming office, when the large Department for Business, Innovation and Skills (BIS) was created, with 10 ministers, three of whom could attend Cabinet. Subsequent re-structuring under Mr Cameron led to the BIS behemoth becoming the Department of Business, Energy and Industrial Strategy (BEIS), with six ministers of whom only the Secretary of State attended Cabinet.

Most Prime Ministers must take a special interest in foreign affairs, the economy and defence. He or she is also likely to take the lead on major issues, such as the strategy and the conduct of negotiations relating to Brexit following the referendum on 23 June 2016. In consultation with individual ministers, the Prime Minister may take decisions or authorise them to be taken without waiting for a Cabinet meeting. According to a Committee of Privy Counsellors in 2004, in the period before the invasion of Iraq in 2003, it was a 'small number of key Ministers, officials and military officers most closely involved' who 'provided the framework of discussion and decision-making within Government'.[23]

3 As head of government, the Prime Minister is able to determine and present the priorities of his or her government, with government policy being directed from No 10, which houses the Prime Minister's Private Office. According to its website, the latter 'helps the Prime Minister to establish and deliver the government's overall strategy and policy priorities, and to communicate the government's policies to Parliament, the public and international audiences'. It has appeared increasingly to be the case that the Prime Minister and his or her close colleagues determine policy, with departments being responsible principally for its implementation.

At a more mechanical level, control of the machinery of government also means that the Prime Minister presides at Cabinet meetings, again important following the informality of the Blair years and the criticisms such informality attracted.[24] This enables the Prime Minister to dominate Cabinet discussions and the process of decision-making, by settling the order of business, by deciding which items are to be discussed,[25] and by taking the sense of the meeting rather than by counting the votes of Cabinet members. While the Cabinet Secretariat provides services for the whole Cabinet, it owes a special responsibility to the Prime Minister.

4 The doctrine of collective responsibility helps to reinforce the powers of the Prime Minister. The effect of the doctrine is that ministers must not criticise government policy in public and if necessary must be prepared to defend it. This means that – depending on the political

---

[23] Lord Butler (Chair), Review of Intelligence on Weapons of Mass Destruction: Report of a Committee of Privy Counsellors (HC 898, 2004), para 610. It was suggested that the role of Cabinet as a forum for the discussion of policy had been significantly reduced generally: meetings were shortened and major decisions were taken by the Prime Minister in consultation with a small group of senior colleagues (paras 606–11). See subsequently HC 656 (2015–16).

[24] HC 656 (2015–16).

[25] Mackintosh, p 449, asserts that the Prime Minister can keep any item off the agenda indefinitely, but the examples he gives do not support this. Cf Wilson, p 47.

circumstances (which for a Prime Minister may not always be propitious) – if the firm hand of the Prime Minister is guiding that policy, there will be no public criticism from the most influential and informed people in the government. The importance of the doctrine for silencing potential criticism is underlined by the fact that – as we have seen – many decisions of government are not taken by the Cabinet as a whole, but by the Prime Minister in consultation with a few key colleagues.

This was true, for example, of an important decision such as transferring to the Bank of England in 1997 the responsibility for the setting of interest rates.[26] It was also the case in relation to the decision to go to war in Iraq in 2003, Mr Blair strongly criticized for telling President Bush that 'I will be with you whatever', against advice and without 'the explicit agreement of his key ministers'.[27] The influence of this convention during the lifetime of a coalition or a minority government is clearly much less strong, where the reality may be that in such circumstances conventions may be set aside, either formally on specific issues, or informally because they are unenforceable in light of Prime Ministerial weakness to insist that they are respected.[28]

5 Compared to other ministers, the Prime Minister has a more regular opportunity to present and defend the government's policies in Parliament and elsewhere.[29] He or she is available for questioning in the Commons on Wednesdays (admittedly not always an unmixed blessing for a Prime Minister whose political authority is waning, as in the case of Mrs May), and he or she may choose when to intervene in debates.[30] The Prime Minister is also in a position to dominate if not control the government's communications to the press, and to disclose information about government decisions and Cabinet business.[31]

Alone among Cabinet ministers, the Prime Minister has regular meetings with the Queen and is responsible for keeping the Queen informed of the Cabinet's handling of affairs. Quite how significant this is in practice in reinforcing the power of the Prime Minister over the Cabinet and Parliament is contestable, given the limited political influence of the monarch in British politics. It does nevertheless serve an important symbolic function and reinforces the view that the Prime Minister occupies a pre-eminent position in the British system of government.

As already suggested, the foregoing considerations are most likely to be most relevant in the context of stable government where one party holds a majority of seats and governs on its own, the typical outcome of general elections since 1945. Different considerations may apply in the context of coalition or minority governments when the position of the Prime Minister may be much more vulnerable. This seems to be particularly true of the position of Mrs May, whose loss of a parliamentary majority at a general election in 2017 left her dependent controversially on the support of the Democratic Unionist Party.

....

[26] See Hennessy, *The Prime Minister*, pp 480–1.
[27] HC 656 (2015–16), para 53. This was said to be 'just one of a number of examples identified by the Iraq Inquiry of the breakdown of collective ministerial decision-making over the development of UK policy on Iraq before the invasion', the HC Public Administration and Constitutional Affairs Committee concluding that it is 'no longer acceptable that the present arrangements should continue without stronger means to prevent key ministers, or even the whole Cabinet, from being side-lined' (ibid).
[28] See ch 5 B.
[29] But see P Dunleavy, G W Jones *et al.* (1993) 23 *British Journal of Political Science* 267 on the declining accountability of the Prime Minister to Parliament. But Parliament draws its strength from its composition, and much depends on the size of the Prime Minister's majority and the unity and/or discipline of his or her own parliamentary party.
[30] On Prime Minister's question time, see R K Alderman (1992) 45 *Parl Affairs* 66.
[31] See Margach, *The Abuse of Power*.

B. The Cabinet

Composition of the Cabinet

A modern Cabinet usually consists of 22 or 23 members (including the Prime Minister). No statute regulates the composition of the Cabinet, but there are both administrative and political constraints on the Prime Minister's freedom of choice. Thus in peacetime it is impossible to exclude certain offices, such as the Home Secretary, the Foreign Secretary and the Chancellor of the Exchequer. New offices may be created to deal with specific temporal problems of a significant nature, such as the Secretary of State for the Withdrawal from the EU.

In addition to those attending as full Cabinet members, a number of other ministers may attend Cabinet meetings, although not formally members of the Cabinet. In the Coalition government there were ten ministers in this position, including the Leader of the House of Commons and the Chief Whip. Since 1951 the government chief whip in the Commons, whose formal title is Parliamentary Secretary to the Treasury, has regularly attended Cabinet. The Law Officers of the Crown[32] are not appointed to the Cabinet but, like other ministers outside the Cabinet, the Attorney General may attend Cabinet meetings for particular matters.

In the post-Coalition era the number of ministers attending Cabinet though not members of the Cabinet has declined sharply. Nevertheless the practice still continues, for one of several possible reasons, one of which is that the number of salaried Cabinet posts is limited by statute. Apart from the Prime Minister and the Lord Chancellor, not more than 20 salaries may be paid to Cabinet ministers at one time.[33] Political necessity requires all members of the Cabinet to be members of the Commons or the Lords, unless a minister is actively seeking election to the Commons at a by-election or is to be created a life peer.[34]

It is no longer necessary for the Lord Chancellor to be a member of the House of Lords, but it is normal for at least some ministers to be drawn from the upper House, though it would be undesirable for many senior positions to be held by peers. Under the Coalition government, only one member of the House of Lords (the Leader of the House) was a member of the Cabinet, and this was true of more recent Conservative governments. The amalgamation of departments to form larger departments which took place during the 1960s[35] meant that all major departments were placed under the supervision of a Cabinet minister, and this continues to be the case.

Cabinet committees[36]

The increase in the scale of government since 1900 has not been matched by a corresponding increase in the size of the Cabinet. The government could not have kept abreast of its work had there not developed under its umbrella a complicated structure of committees, which are acknowledged to reduce the burden on government by enabling collective decisions to be taken by a smaller group of ministers. Although once secret and controversial, the Cabinet committee system is now transparent and necessary.

The composition and terms of reference of Cabinet committees are matters for the Prime Minister. The committee structure may as a result vary from government to government, and it appears to be the case that some of the committees established by the Brown government

---

[32] ch 13.
[33] Ministerial and other Salaries Act 1975. See ch 7.
[34] ch 5.
[35] Section C below.
[36] Jennings, pp 255–61; Mackintosh, pp 521–9; Gordon Walker, pp 38–47; Wilson, pp 62–8; Hennessy, *The Prime Minister*, pp 482–3.

have been abolished. As explained in the *Ministerial Code*, decisions reached by Cabinet committees are 'binding on all members of the Government'.[37] Committee size varies, with the Economy and Industrial Strategy (Economic Affairs) sub-committee having 20 members, even though the Economy and Industrial Strategy Committee has only 14 members.

There were 23 Cabinet Committees and sub-committees in Mrs May's first government (2016–17), 12 of which were chaired by the Prime Minister herself. Notable Cabinet committees under the May government included the Economy and Industrial Strategy Committee, the EU Exit and Trade Committee and the Social Reform Committee, as well as a number of 'Implementation Taskforces' (dealing with matters as varied as childcare, digital infrastructure and modern slavery). Most governments also need a Parliamentary Business and Legislation Committee to manage the implementation of their legislative programmes.

Otherwise, most governments also have to deal with a core set of problems relating to the economy, foreign affairs and national security, and whatever their composition, most governments will need a committee structure that incorporates such matters. The committees nevertheless give some sense of the ideological direction of government, as well as the priorities and immediate concerns of a particular administration, and the interests of a particular Prime Minister. Under the May government, one of the Economy and Industrial Strategy sub-committees was concerned with 'Reducing Regulation', while four of the Committees and sub-committees were concerned with Brexit.

Cabinet Secretary and Cabinet Office[38]

In 1917, to enable the War Cabinet and its system of committees to function efficiently, a Secretary to the Cabinet was appointed to be present at meetings of the Cabinet and its committees, to circulate minutes of the conclusions reached, to communicate decisions rapidly to those who had to act on them and also to circulate papers before meetings. The conclusions prepared by the Secretary to the Cabinet and circulated to the Queen and Cabinet ministers continue to be the only official record of Cabinet meetings. This account is designed to record agreement and not controversy.

Differences of opinion in discussion are not attributed to individuals, although the arguments for and against a decision may be summarised: 'behind many of the decisions lay tensions and influences which are not reflected in the official records'.[39] However, if a minister expressly wishes his or her dissent to be recorded, then this will be done.[40] An important recent initiative of the Cabinet Secretary was the production of the *Cabinet Manual*, which sets out the rules and procedures by which the government operates, an initiative that provoked lively parliamentary interest and some mild controversy, raising doubts about its success.[41]

Proposals have been made in the aftermath of the Chilcott report on the Iraq war which would more formally clarify the position of the Cabinet Secretary.[42] The latter is no longer also the Permanent Secretary of the Cabinet Office, the primary responsibility of which is to

---

[37] *Ministerial Code* (2016), para 2.3.
[38] Jennings, pp 242–5; Gordon Walker, pp 47–55; Mosley, *The Story of the Cabinet Office*; Wilson, *The Cabinet Office to 1945*.
[39] Wilson, *The Cabinet Office to 1945*, p 4. At p 142 are printed instructions on minute-taking current in 1936. Crossman's comment 30 years later was that the minutes 'do not pretend to be an account of what actually takes place in the Cabinet' (p 198).
[40] It was the alleged failure to follow this convention that added to the drama surrounding the resignation of Mr Michael Heseltine in the so-called Westland affair in 1986.
[41] See the critical account in HC 233 (2014–15). There is in particular a concern about the contested rules of constitutional behaviour being drafted by civil servants and others without parliamentary involvement or approval.
[42] HC 656 (2015–16).

support the Prime Minister and, according to its website, to ensure the effective running of government. To this end, the Cabinet Office has a number of specific duties, including the development, coordination and implementation of government policy; and the promotion of 'efficiency' in government, which in the present economic climate generally means making savings on procurement, and operating with fewer civil servants.

The Cabinet Office also supports the National Security Council and the Joint Intelligence Organisation, as well as having responsibility for constitutional and political reform. Largely because of political differences between the two parties, the Coalition government was unable to make much progress on the latter, with plans for electoral reform and House of Lords reform both having failed. Since then the Cabinet Office has scaled down its concerns about constitutional reform, dealing with matters such as the House of Lords veto over secondary legislation,[43] and voter fraud in elections to the House of Commons.[44]

The day-to-day direction of the Cabinet Office is the responsibility of the Minister for the Cabinet Office (who attends but is not a member of the Cabinet).

Cabinet secrecy

The operation of the Cabinet system is surrounded by considerable secrecy.[45] It is the 'working assumption' of government that most Cabinet papers are protected from disclosure under the Freedom of Information Act 2000,[46] only to be made available as historical records for public inspection in the National Archives after 30 years.[47] Many Cabinet decisions are notified to Parliament or otherwise made public, but the doctrine of collective responsibility throws a heavy veil over decision-making in Cabinet. That veil is only rarely pierced, as when Lord Hutton laid bare the internal workings of the Cabinet in his report on the circumstances surrounding the death of Dr David Kelly, a senior civil servant who took his own life in 2003.[48]

One justification for Cabinet secrecy is the view that anything which damages the collective unity and integrity of the Cabinet damages the good government of the country.[49] Certainly the public interest in national security requires that some information about defence and external relations must be kept secret by those in government. But the 'good government' argument goes very much further than national security since it seeks to preserve the process of decision-making within government from scrutiny by those outside. Some critics argue, on the contrary, that 'good government' in a democracy requires that more light be thrown on political decision-making and that government be more open.

One important practice is that the ministers in one government do not have access to the papers of an earlier government of a different political party. On a change of government, the outgoing Prime Minister issues special instructions about the disposal of the Cabinet papers of his or her administration. The practice applies to papers of the Cabinet and ministerial committees, as well as departmental papers that contain the private views of ministers and advice given by officials. The main reason for the practice is to prevent a minister from one

---

[43] Cm 9117, 2016.

[44] Cabinet Office, *A Democracy that Works for Everyone: A Clear and Secure Democracy* (2016).

[45] Williams, *Not in the Public Interest*, ch 2; Gordon Walker, pp 26–33, 164–8; Report on Section 2 of Official Secrets Act 1911, Cmnd 5104, 1972, ch 11; Report on Ministerial Memoirs, Cmnd 6386, 1976.

[46] See Section F below.

[47] See Freedom of Information Act 2000, ss 35, 36, 63–7; and Public Records Act 1958, s 5 (amended by the Freedom of Information Act 2000, s 67).

[48] Lord Hutton, Report of the Inquiry into the Circumstances Surrounding the Death of Dr David Kelly CMG (2004). See also Butler Report, above, and the evidence given in public by Cabinet ministers and senior civil servants to the Chilcott inquiry of 2010 into the events leading up to the invasion of Iraq in 2003.

[49] Cmnd 5104, 1972, p 68.

party having access to 'matters that the previous administration had been most anxious to keep quiet'.[50] Former ministers retain the right of access to documents that they saw in office.

Before access to Cabinet papers or other ministerial documents of a former government can be given to third persons, the present Prime Minister must seek the agreement of the former Prime Minister concerned or the current leader of his or her party. Thus, when a committee of privy counsellors was appointed to review British policy towards the Falkland Islands before the Argentine invasion, five former Prime Ministers agreed to the relevant documents being seen by the committee.[51] Ministers relinquishing office without a change of government 'should hand back to their department any Cabinet documents and/or other departmental papers in their possession'.[52]

Cabinet secrecy and the courts

Cabinet documents are protected to some extent from (*a*) production as evidence in litigation by public interest immunity, which authorises non-disclosure of documents which it would be injurious to the public interest to disclose,[53] and (*b*) examination by the Parliamentary Ombudsman;[54] they may also (*c*) be protected by the Official Secrets Acts,[55] and – as we shall consider – (*d*) be exempt from disclosure under the Freedom of Information Act 2000.[56] Political sanctions also operate: a serving Cabinet minister would be liable to lose office if he or she could be shown improperly to have revealed the details of Cabinet discussions.

But is a former Cabinet minister, who may be subject to no political sanction, under a legal obligation not to reveal such secrets? The question arose for decision in *Attorney-General* v *Jonathan Cape Ltd*.[57]

Richard Crossman kept a political diary between 1964 and 1970 while a Labour Cabinet minister. After his death in 1974, his diary for 1964–66 was edited for publication and, as was customary, submitted to the Secretary to the Cabinet. He refused to consent to publication, since the diary contained detailed accounts of Cabinet discussions, reports of the advice given to ministers by civil servants and comments about the suitability of senior civil servants for promotion. When Crossman's literary executors decided to publish the diary, the Attorney General sought an injunction to stop them.

Lord Widgery CJ held that the court had power to restrain the improper publication of information which had been received by a Cabinet minister in confidence, and that the doctrine of collective responsibility justified the court in restraining the disclosures of Cabinet discussions; but that the court should act only where continuing confidentiality of the material could clearly be shown. On the facts, he held that publication in 1975 of Cabinet discussions during the period 1964–66 should not be restrained. In this decision, no reliance was placed either upon the Privy Counsellor's oath of secrecy or upon the Official Secrets Acts.

---

[50] HC Deb, 8 July 1982, col 474 (Mr M Foot).
[51] HC Deb, 1 July 1982, col 1039; 8 July 1982, col 469. See Lord Hunt [1982] PL 514.
[52] *Ministerial Code* (2016), para 2.7. And see R Brazier [1996] CLJ 65, on the sale of the Churchill papers in 1995.
[53] ch 26. On the relationship between the Cabinet and the courts, see M C Harris [1989] PL 251.
[54] Parliamentary Commissioner Act 1967, s 8(4); ch 23.
[55] ch 19.
[56] Section F below.
[57] [1976] QB 752; Young, *The Crossman Affair*.

This decision established the power of the courts to restrain publication of Cabinet secrets but gave no clear guidance as to when the power should be exercised. The problems of memoirs of ex-Cabinet ministers were subsequently considered by a committee of Privy Counsellors.[58] The committee distinguished between secret information relating to national security and international relations, on which an ex-minister must accept the decision of the Cabinet Secretary, and other confidential material about relationships between ministers or between ministers and civil servants. In the latter case there should be no publication within 15 years, except with clearance from the Cabinet Secretary.

In the event of a dispute between the minister and the Cabinet Secretary, it must in the last resort be for the ex-minister to decide what to publish. Advice given by a civil servant to a minister should not be revealed while the adviser is still a civil servant. The latter committee recommended against legislation, preferring to suggest a clear working procedure which would be brought to the attention of every minister on assuming office. The committee's recommendations were accepted by the government in 1976 and have been maintained by subsequent governments. There has since been a spate of ministerial memoirs,[59] though the last Labour government thought that the existing procedures generally work well in practice.[60]

C. Ministers and departments

Ministerial offices

Some ministerial offices have a much longer history than the office of Prime Minister, others have been created more recently. The office of Lord Chancellor goes back to the reign of Edward the Confessor and was of great political and judicial significance for several centuries after the Norman conquest. The office of Lord Privy Seal dates from the 14th century and in a later period was often held by leading statesmen; but the historic duties in respect of the Privy Seal were abolished in 1884 and the office now carries no departmental responsibilities.

The office of Lord President of the Council was created in 1497 and became important during the period of government through the Council under the Stuarts. The office of Secretary of State has almost as long a history, acquiring its political significance in the Tudor period, particularly during the tenure of the Cecils under Elizabeth I. It came to be recognised as the means by which communications could take place between citizen and monarch.[61] From the 17th century, two and sometimes three Secretaries of State were appointed who divided national and foreign affairs between them.

In 1782 a different division of functions vested in one Secretary of State responsibility for domestic affairs and the colonies, and in the other Secretary responsibility for foreign affairs. Thus were created the offices of Home Secretary and Foreign Secretary. In 1794 a Secretary of State for War was appointed and thereafter, from time to time, additional Secretaryships (for example, for the Colonies, for India, for Scotland, for Exiting the EU) were created and

---

[58] Cmnd 6386, 1976 (Radcliffe Report). For more recent considerations of this issue, see HC 689 (2005–6); HC 664 (2007–8); HC 428 (2008–9).

[59] The *Ministerial Code* requires former ministers to submit their manuscript to the Cabinet Secretary and to conform to the principles set out in the Radcliffe Report (para 8.10).

[60] HC 428 (2008–9). The current position is set out in the *Ministerial Code* (2016), which provides that 'Former Ministers intending to publish their memoirs are required to submit the draft manuscript in good time before publication to the Cabinet Secretary and to conform to the principles set out in the Radcliffe report of 1976 (Cmnd 6386)' (para 8.10).

[61] For the history of the Secretaries of State, see Anson, *The Law and Custom of the Constitution*, vol II, i, pp 172–84.

abolished as the need arose. Appointments are now made on the advice of the Prime Minister who decides what offices are needed, and what departments should be created to support the office holders.[62]

When statutory powers are conferred on a Secretary of State, it is usual for the statute to designate him or her as 'the Secretary of State'; it will also usually be obvious from the context which Secretary of State is intended to exercise the new functions.[63] In law the duties of Secretaries of State are interchangeable, but in practice each Secretary's functions are limited to those related to his or her own department. As pointed out above, one Secretary of State may be named as First Secretary; while this makes no legal difference to the office, it determines precedence in the Cabinet.

Government departments

While the term 'government department' has no precise meaning in law, it usually refers to those branches of the central administration staffed by civil servants, paid for out of exchequer funds and headed by a minister responsible to Parliament. A single minister may be responsible for more than one department: thus the Chancellor of the Exchequer is responsible for the Treasury as well as HM Revenue and Customs. Moreover, one person may hold two offices: in 2005, the Secretary of State for Transport was also the Secretary of State for Scotland, while the Secretary of State for Northern Ireland was also the Secretary of State for Wales. Exceptionally, there are departments which for constitutional reasons do not have a ministerial head: thus the National Audit Office is headed by the Comptroller and Auditor General.[64]

For the purposes of legal proceedings against the Crown, a list of departments is maintained under the Crown Proceedings Act 1947.[65] For the purposes of investigation by the Parliamentary Ombudsman, a statutory list of departments is maintained, and this is revised as new departments are established.[66] There are many public bodies with governmental functions, including local authorities; regulatory bodies such as the OFCOM and OFGEM; and a wide range of other bodies with policy-making and advisory functions, often resembling the executive agencies closely linked to government departments (on which see below), but usually classified in a different way.[67] Often such bodies are financed from central government funds. These bodies are considered more fully in Chapter 12 below.

The creation of new departments and the appointment of a Secretary of State are prerogative acts. The role of the prerogative is to be seen in the Defence (Transfer of Functions) Act 1964, where s 1 refers to Her Majesty being pleased to make arrangements for one of Her Principal Secretaries of State to be charged with general responsibility for defence. Other matters are governed by statute. These include the transfer of functions to the new department, the legal status of the Secretary of State, the transfer of property to the new department, the adaptation of any legislation relating to the work of the department, and the substitution of the new Secretary of State as a party in current legal proceedings. The relevant statute for this purpose is the extensively used Ministers of the Crown Act 1975.[68]

---

[62] HC 540 (2008–9).
[63] By the Interpretation Act 1978, unless the contrary intention appears, 'Secretary of State' means 'one of Her Majesty's Principal Secretaries of State'. See *Agee* v *Lord Advocate* 1977 SLT (Notes) 54.
[64] ch 12.
[65] ch 26.
[66] ch 23.
[67] See ch 12.
[68] For an illustration of a notable exercise of this power, see SI 2016 No 992.

The latter authorises the Crown, by Order in Council, to transfer to any minister functions previously exercised by another minister; to provide for the dissolution of a government department and for the transfer to other departments of the functions previously exercised by that department; and to direct that functions shall be exercised concurrently by two ministers. Consequential steps may also be authorised, such as the transfer of property from one department to another and changes in the title of ministers. While it is important that the structure of government should not be ossified, it is equally important that the capacity to engineer radical structural change is subject to meaningful parliamentary scrutiny,[69] though recommendations to this effect have not been met with great enthusiasm in Whitehall.[70]

Ministers of the Crown[71]

According to one statutory definition, minister of the Crown means 'the holder of any office in Her Majesty's Government in the United Kingdom, and includes the Treasury . . . and the Defence Council'.[72] In a less technical sense, ministers are those members or supporters of the party in power who hold political office in the government. They are all appointed by the Crown on the advice of the Prime Minister, and their offices are at the disposal of an incoming Prime Minister. They do not include members of the civil service or the armed forces, who continue in office despite a change of government; or special advisers to ministers, who may be paid salaries and are temporarily attached to departments but who lose their position when a minister leaves office; or members of regulatory bodies; and so on.

Unlike most of these other office-holders, ministers are not disqualified from membership of the House of Commons. Indeed, it is a convention that ministerial office-holders should be members of one or the other House of Parliament. This is widely thought to be essential for the effective operation of the principle of ministerial responsibility, one of the core principles of the constitution, albeit one often overlooked by public lawyers. There is, however, no law that a minister must be in Parliament, and the possibility of recruiting ministers from outside is sometimes discussed. But this could only be done if the individuals in question could be made responsible to Parliament other than by membership, and although there are unlikely to be insuperable barriers, it may not be good practice.

If a Prime Minister wishes to appoint to ministerial office someone who is not already in Parliament, the current practice is to confer a life peerage on the individual in question so that he or she may take a seat in the Lords, though not many Cabinet offices are held by members of the Lords. There are no legal limits on the number of ministers which the Crown may appoint, assuming that they are not to receive a salary and do not sit in the House of Commons. However, as already pointed out, there are statutory limits on the number of ministers who may be members of the Commons and on the number of salaries payable to holders of ministerial office.[73] Ministerial salaries are now governed by a formula set out in the Ministerial and Other Salaries Act 1975.

There are thus various grades of ministerial appointment today, but they may be grouped into three broad categories: (*a*) Cabinet ministers, who may or may not have departmental responsibilities; (*b*) departmental ministers and ministers of state who are outside the Cabinet, the duty of a minister of state being to share in the administration of a

---

[69] HC 672 (2006–7); HC 160 (2007–8) (Public Administration Select Committee).
[70] HC 514 (2007–8); HC 540 (2008–9) (government response).
[71] See Brazier, *Ministers of the Crown*, for a full account.
[72] Ministers of the Crown Act 1975, s 8(1).
[73] See pp 175–8 above.

department headed by a Cabinet minister; and (*c*) parliamentary secretaries, whose duty it is to assist in the parliamentary work of a department and who may also have some administrative responsibility. The two Law Officers of the Crown for England and Wales (Attorney General and Solicitor General) are within category (*b*), but the government whips have no departmental responsibilities. As indicated, all are recruited from Parliament, normally the House of Commons.

The *Ministerial Code*

The conduct of ministers is governed by the *Ministerial Code*, now 'an integral part of the new constitutional architecture'.[74] The Code – which is not legally binding – was first compiled by Attlee in 1945, although some of its provisions go back further.[75] It deals with a range of matters applying to the relationship between ministers and the government, Parliament and the civil service. It also deals with ministers' private interests. Previously known as *Questions of Procedure for Ministers* (QPM), the Code was first made public by Mr Major in 1992, and was revised following the recommendations of the Committee on Standards in Public Life,[76] before being reissued by each of his successors.[77] The current code was issued by Mrs May in 2016, retaining a style based more on principles and less on procedures.[78]

Section 1 reminds ministers that they are 'expected to behave in a way that upholds the highest standards of propriety'. In particular, they are required to observe the ten principles of ministerial conduct that are set out in the Code. These include a duty to uphold the principle of collective responsibility, which applies to all ministers; a requirement to account to Parliament for the activities of their departments and executive agencies; and an obligation to 'give accurate and truthful information to Parliament, correcting any inadvertent error at the earliest opportunity'. Ministers who 'knowingly mislead Parliament will be expected to offer their resignation to the Prime Minister'. There are those who feel that the word 'knowingly' should be removed from the text.[79]

In addition to the duty not to mislead Parliament, the *Ministerial Code* also advises ministers of the need to be 'as open as possible with Parliament and the public, refusing to provide information only when disclosure would not be in the public interest'. This should be determined in accordance with 'the' relevant statutes (which are not specified) and the Freedom of Information Act 2000.[80] One of the other key principles provides that ministers should require civil servants who give evidence before select committees 'on their behalf and under their direction', to be as 'helpful as possible in providing accurate, truthful and full information in accordance with the duties and responsibilities of civil servants as set out in the *Civil Service Code*'.

Otherwise, the Code deals with ministerial conflicts of interest (on which see below) and a prohibition on using government resources for party political purposes. Ministers are also required to uphold the political impartiality of the civil service, and they are reminded of their responsibility 'for justifying their actions and conduct to Parliament and the public', and that they can 'remain in office [only] for so long as they retain the confidence of the Prime Minister', who is 'the ultimate judge of the standards of behaviour expected of a Minister and the appropriate

---

[74] HC 235 (2000–1), para 15.
[75] Ibid.
[76] Cm 2850-I, 1995.
[77] The Code is set out in full on the government website.
[78] See HC 381, 1056 (2007–8).
[79] Section F below.
[80] See A Tomkins [1996] PL 484. Cf HC 115 (1995–6), para K8.5.

consequences of a breach of those standards'. Where a breach of the Code is alleged, the Prime Minister may refer the matter to the Independent Adviser on Minister's Interests.[81]

Financial interests of ministers

Because of their office, many ministers take decisions which have a direct financial effect on particular businesses, sections of industry and land values. They also have access to confidential information about future decisions which could be put to financial profit. The Marconi affair of 1912 involved three leading members of the Liberal government who were alleged to have made use of secret information about an impending government contract to make an investment in Marconi shares: an inquiry by a parliamentary committee established that they had bought shares not in the company to which the contract was about to be awarded, but in a sister company.[82]

In 1948 the Lynskey Tribunal of Inquiry reported on allegations that ministers and other public servants had been bribed in connection with the grant of licences by the Board of Trade; a junior minister, who later resigned from Parliament, was found to have received presents of wine and spirits and other gifts, knowing that they had been made to secure favourable treatment by the department of applications for licences.[83] While such conduct could give rise to criminal proceedings, additional safeguards are required if ministers are to avoid suspicion. In 1952 the rules then in force were published in a parliamentary written answer.[84]

These rules remain in operation, although they have been amended and are now to be found in the *Ministerial Code*. The overriding principle is that ministers must ensure that no conflict arises, or could reasonably be perceived to arise, between their private interests and their public duties. This conflict could arise if a minister took any active part or had a financial interest in any undertaking that had contractual or other relations (for example, receiving a licence or a subsidy) with his or her department. Under the current rules, ministers should, on assuming office, provide their Permanent Secretary with a full list of interests that might be thought to give rise to a conflict.

Ministers' interests are now published on the government website, which is updated from time to time and includes interests of a varied nature. Where necessary, a minister will be advised by the Permanent Secretary and the Independent Adviser on Ministers' Interests about which interests need to be disposed of.[85] The government now publishes details of gifts and other benefits to ministers as well. In addition, the *Ministerial Code* reminds ministers of the restrictions that apply to accepting appointments within two years of leaving office, on which they must seek advice from the Advisory Committee on Business Appointments.[86]

D. Civil service: organisation and accountability

Legal base

The departments of central government are staffed by administrative, professional, technical and other officials who constitute the civil service, which performs many functions, from the development to the implementation of government policy. Traditionally governed by royal

---

[81] For background, see HC 1457 (2005–6); HC 381, 1056 (2007–8); HC 1761 (2010–12); HC 976 (2012–13). See also HC Deb, 13 June 2012, col 315 et seq.

[82] See Donaldson, *The Marconi Scandal*.

[83] Cmd 7616, 1949.

[84] HC Deb, 25 February 1952, col 701; and 20 March 1980, col 293 (WA).

[85] See HC 381, 1056 (2007–8).

[86] See HC 651, 1087 (2006–7).

prerogative, fresh ground was broken by the Constitutional Reform and Governance Act 2010, which succeeded in putting the management of the civil service on a statutory footing.[87] The Act also made provision for the Civil Service Commission, which is primarily responsible for developing recruitment principles based on fair and open competition. But in giving power of management to the Minister for the Civil Service, the Act does nothing to structure or constrain that power, which appears to be just as wide as the prerogative power it apparently replaced.

It has been said to be 'common ground that the civil service defies an easy universally applicable definition' and that 'a civil servant has no specific legal status'.[88] In the absence of an adequate legal definition,[89] a civil servant has been described as 'a servant of the Crown working in a civil capacity who is not: the holder of a political (or judicial) office; the holder of certain other offices in respect of whose tenure of office special provision has been made; a servant of the Crown in a personal capacity paid from the Civil List'.[90] This definition excludes ministers of the Crown, members of the armed forces (who are Crown servants but are not employed in a civil capacity), the police and those employed in local government and the National Health Service, even though they are all engaged in public services.[91]

There are now about 385,000 civil servants,[92] though the numbers are falling. As far as their employment position is concerned, there is a sharp contrast between legal doctrine and practical reality. It is true that although civil servants were traditionally regarded as having been appointed under the royal prerogative, the courts nevertheless have gradually recognised that they may have terms of service 'which are contractually enforceable'.[93] But while recognising the existence of a contract, the courts seem unwilling to challenge the traditional rule that civil servants are employed at the pleasure of the Crown,[94] which means that they may be dismissed without a common law remedy for wrongful dismissal.[95] Moreover, although the management of the civil service has been placed on a statutory footing,[96] the Cabinet Office still claims the prerogative power to dismiss at pleasure, a claim that now seems implausible.

Despite apparently having no right to notice on termination, the *Civil Service Management Code* provides minimum notice periods for civil servants which 'in practice' departments and agencies 'will normally apply'.[97] More importantly, it is also the case that civil servants are deemed by statute to be employed under contracts of service for some employment protection purposes, and will normally be able to bring an action for unfair dismissal as a result.[98] Other employment protection rights typically also apply now to civil servants, reflecting what has been a trend towards providing civil servants with the same formal protections as

---

[87] This was a long time coming: for background, see Cm 4587-I, 2000, HC 128 (2003–4), and Cm 6373, 2004.

[88] This is probably inaccurate: the civil servant does have a legal *status* different in law from that of other employees. It might be more accurate to say that the civil servant has no accepted legal *definition*.

[89] The Constitutional Reform and Governance Act 2010 unhelpfully defines the civil service to mean 'the civil service of the State', with some exceptions.

[90] HC 390-II (1992–3), p 261.

[91] For a somewhat similar definition, see Crown Proceedings Act 1947, s 2(6). See ch 26.

[92] This is the full-time equivalent in December 2016. The number of civil servants is falling as the number of workers generally (c 31 million) is increasing.

[93] *McLaren v Home Office* [1990] IRLR 338, 341; *R v Lord Chancellor's Department, ex p Nangle* [1992] 1 All ER 897; and *R (Patel) v HMRC* [2009] EWHC 3731 (Admin). See S Fredman and G Morris [1991] PL 485.

[94] See *Civil Service Management Code*, s 11.1.1. Compare *Wells v Newfoundland* [1993] 3 SCC 199.

[95] *Dunn v R* [1896] 1 QB 116; *Riordan v War Office* [1959] 1 WLR 1046. And see ch 26.

[96] Constitutional Reform and Governance Act 2010, s 3.

[97] *Civil Service Management Code*, s 11.1.

[98] Employment Rights Act 1996, s 191.

their counterparts in the private sector. But whatever the precise legal nature of their relationship with the Crown, it is an important constitutional principle that civil servants should, in fact, enjoy a tenure of office by which they may serve successive ministers of different political parties.

Civil service structure

The structure of the civil service has undergone a great deal of change since the 1980s, reflecting growing Treasury concerns about cost and efficiency.[99] The starting point is the publication in 1988 of a report to the Prime Minister by Sir Robin Ibbs, entitled *Improving Management in Government: The Next Steps.*[100] This was a most far-reaching and fundamental review of the civil service, and led to the most radical changes since 1854.[101] The report expressed concern that the civil service (then with over 600,000 staff) was too big and too diverse to be managed as a single organisation, and recommended that attempts should be made to establish a different way of conducting the business of government.

It was suggested that the central civil service should consist of a relatively small core engaged in the function of servicing ministers and managing departments, which would be the main sponsors of particular government policies and services. Responding to these departments would be a range of agencies employing their own staff, concentrating on the delivery of their particular service, with responsibilities clearly defined between the Secretary of State and the Permanent Secretary on the one hand, and the chairman and chief executive of the agency on the other.[102]

The proposals were largely accepted by the government, and by 2000, 137 agencies had been created (accounting for some 80 per cent of the civil service), though the number of such agencies has declined in more recent years. Each agency has a defined task, or range of tasks, which are set out in its published framework document. In addition, 'key performance targets – covering financial performance, efficiency and service to the customer – are set out by ministers annually. Each agency has a chief executive, normally directly accountable to ministers and with personal responsibility for the success of the agency in meeting its targets.'[103] Like other government bodies, executive agencies may be subject to judicial review.[104]

Alongside the delegation of tasks to the agencies has been the delegation to the agencies and departments of responsibility for the pay and working conditions of staff. The process of delegation in the setting of working conditions (with an emphasis on performance-related incentives) was facilitated by the Civil Service (Management of Functions) Act 1992. In 1996 the long-established central pay bargaining arrangements were entirely replaced by a system that delegated to the departments and agencies the authority to make their own pay arrangements, 'albeit within the overall Treasury limits on running costs'.[105]

---

[99] For a full account, see HL Paper 55 (1998). See also G Drewry, in Jowell and Oliver (eds), *The Changing Constitution* (6th edn), ch 7.

[100] The report had been commissioned in 1986. For the reaction to it, see Hennessy, *Whitehall*, pp 620–1, and Lawson, *The View from No 11*, pp 391–3. See also Woodhouse, *Ministers and Parliament*, chs 11, 12.

[101] See respectively Cmnd 3638, 1968 (Fulton Committee) and Northcote–Trevelyan Report (reprinted in app B of the Fulton Report).

[102] For the previous consideration of this option with reference particularly to Sweden, see Cmnd 3638, 1968, paras 188–91.

[103] Cm 2750, 1994, p ii.

[104] *R (National Association of Health Stores) v Department of Health* [2003] EWCA Civ 3133.

[105] HL 55 (1997–8), para 94. See also Cm 4310, 1999, p 58.

The civil servant within the department

The senior civil servant within a department is the Permanent Secretary,[106] below whom in descending order of seniority are directors general, directors and assistant directors. These posts together form what is known as the 'Senior Civil Service', an entity created in 1996.[107] Special advisers to ministers – whose numbers have grown in recent years – also play a key role.[108] Where schemes of delegation exist within a department, they do not generally affect the legal position of the department or of outsiders dealing with it. Where the power to make a discretionary decision affecting an individual is vested in a minister, an official within the department may in general take that decision on behalf of the minister (the *Carltona* principle),[109] unless there are express or implied limitations in the statute conferring the power.[110]

The latter principle is illustrated by a number of important cases, since it emerged in *Carltona* itself. In a criminal case in which it was claimed that the Home Secretary had never approved a breathalyser device as required by the Road Safety Act 1973, Widgery LJ said: 'The minister is not expected personally to take every decision entrusted to him by Parliament. If a decision is made on his behalf by one of his officials, then that constitutionally is the minister's decision.'[111] In regard to the Secretary of State's powers under the Immigration Act 1971, it was held that immigration officers (in whom certain functions are expressly vested by the Act) were also entitled by virtue of the *Carltona* principle to exercise decision-making powers in regard to deportation on behalf of the Secretary of State.[112]

New questions about departmental delegation arise following the introduction of the executive agencies. But despite initial doubts to the contrary,[113] it is now clear that the *Carltona* principle is sufficiently flexible to accommodate these new developments, one court accepting that 'the Highways Agency is the alter ego of the Department for Transport in the areas for which the Secretary of State accepts responsibility in Parliament, just as he does for the actions of civil servants housed under his departmental roof'.[114] However, prison governors may not by virtue of *Carltona* exercise powers of prison discipline vested by legislation in the Home Secretary, the relationship between the two bearing 'no resemblance to those governing the relationship between a minister and his departmental officials'.[115]

It is important to stress that the framework documents establishing the agencies typically make clear that it is the minister who has ultimate responsibility for determining the policy and financial framework within which the agency operates, and that it is the minister who is accountable to Parliament for all matters concerning the agency, even though he or she is not normally involved in its day-to-day running. The framework documents typically also provide that the agency chief executive will represent the minister at parliamentary committees

---

[106] For a study of permanent secretaries, see K Theakston and G K Fry (1989) 67 *Public Administration* 129.
[107] HL 55 (1997–8). On the continuing influence of the civil service in the legislative process, see E C Page (2003) 81 *Public Administration* 651. See also HC 74 (2013–14) for claims of civil service obstruction of government.
[108] See HC 238 (1999–2000); and HC 423-I (2003–4), Q 63. On special advisers, see T Daintith [2002] PL 13.
[109] *Carltona Ltd* v *Commissioners of Works* [1943] 2 All ER 560. See ch 5.
[110] *R* v *Home Secretary, ex p Oladehinde* [1991] 1 AC 254, at p 282.
[111] *R* v *Skinner* [1968] 2 QB 700, 707. See also *Copeland* v *H M Advocate* 1988 SLT 249, and *R* v *Home Secretary, ex p Doody* [1994] 1 AC 531, at p 566. And see ch 5.
[112] *R* v *Home Secretary, ex p Oladehinde* [1991] 1 AC 254.
[113] See M R Freedland [1996] PL 19. Also M R Freedland, in Sunkin and Payne (eds), *The Nature of the Crown*, ch 5.
[114] *Castle* v *DPP* [2014] EWHC 587 Admin, [2014] 1 WLR 4279, relying on *R* v *Social Security Secretary, ex p Sherwin* (1996) 32 BMLR 1.
[115] *R (Bourgass)* v *Justice Secretary* [2015] UKSC 54.

and answer questions on his or her behalf, an arrangement previously reinforced by Cabinet Office rules relating to evidence to select committees. The latter made clear that chief executives give evidence 'on behalf of the minister to whom they are accountable and are subject to that minister's instruction'.[116]

Civil servants and ministerial responsibility

The principle of responsibility through ministers to Parliament is one of the most essential characteristics of the civil service. In a memorandum to the House of Commons Treasury and Civil Service Committee in the early 1990s, the Cabinet Office asserted that,

> The Minister in charge of a department is the only person who may be said to be ultimately accountable for the work of his department. It is usually on the Secretary of State as minister that Parliament has conferred powers, and Parliament calls on ministers to be accountable for the policy, actions and resources of their departments and the use of those powers. While ministers may delegate much of the day to day work of their departments, often now to agencies, they remain ultimately accountable to Parliament for all that is done under their power. Civil servants, except in those particular cases where statute confers powers on them directly, cannot take decisions or actions except insofar as they act on behalf of ministers. Civil servants are accountable to ministers, ministers are accountable to Parliament.[117]

According to the Cabinet Office, ministerial responsibility has often been used to describe this process. In recent years, however, there has been a significant refinement of the principle, the government taking the view that ministers are 'accountable' to Parliament for the work of their department, but are not 'responsible' for all the actions of civil servants in the sense of being blameworthy. There appears as a result to be a greater willingness to attribute responsibility for operational matters to individual civil servants. Although the distinction has been strenuously defended, there are those who remain sceptical, yet it remains unclear how far the distinction expresses anything which is qualitatively different from what was expressed by Sir David Maxwell-Fyfe in the aftermath of the Crichel Down affair in the 1950s.[118]

This is a question that has been brought sharply into focus as a result of the creation of the executive agencies. Although ministers are formally accountable for the work of the agencies, there is nevertheless concern that there is now a responsibility gap, as ministers are able to deflect blame onto the shoulders of chief executives.[119] These concerns were highlighted following difficulties in the Prison Service which led to the dismissal in October 1995 of its chief executive, Mr Derek Lewis, by the Home Secretary, Mr Michael Howard. Mr Lewis is not the only chief executive to lose office because of failure within an agency,[120] but his departure has been the most controversial. It followed the report of a review of security procedures in prisons by General Sir John Learmont, conducted after the escape of three prisoners from Parkhurst Jail on the Isle of Wight.

The latter report made a number of criticisms of Parkhurst and its security, but also claimed that some of the problems could be 'traced along the lines of communication to Prison Service headquarters'.[121] In the words of the Home Secretary, Learmont did not find that 'any policy decision of [his], directly or indirectly, caused the escape'.[122] Mr Lewis was

[116] Cabinet Office, *Departmental Evidence and Response to Select Committees* (2005, re-issued 2010), para 50. This passage has been deleted from the current text (2014).
[117] HC 27-II (1993–4), p 188.
[118] HC Deb, 20 July 1954, cols 1285–7. And see ch 5.
[119] HC 27-II (1993–4), p 189.
[120] See *The Guardian*, 17 November 2004 (resignation of Chief Executive of the Child Support Agency).
[121] HC Deb, 16 October 1995, col 31.
[122] Ibid.

dismissed, although not without complaining of ministerial interference in operational matters, and not without a substantial settlement being made in his favour for the premature termination of his appointment.[123] In the controversy that followed this dismissal, the Home Secretary declined to accept responsibility for the agency failures. In his view there was a distinction between policy and operations, a distinction said to be 'reflected in the framework document that established the Prison Service as an Executive Agency'.[124]

Civil servants and select committees

Select committees are now an important channel for ministerial accountability.[125] Although it is the departmental minister who is responsible to Parliament, the select committees nevertheless may wish to take evidence from civil servants within the minister's department, sometimes for a more informed and detailed account of the issues which the department may be dealing with. A question to have arisen is whether select committees can summon and require the attendance of named officials,[126] or whether a minister can instruct the official not to attend and thereby potentially frustrate a select committee's investigation. During the Westland affair in 1985–6, the House of Commons Defence Committee wished to examine five named officials, three from the Department of Trade and Industry and two from the Prime Minister's Office. The government took the view that because these officials had participated in an internal departmental inquiry, it would be neither fair nor reasonable to expect them to submit to a second round of detailed questioning.

The Defence Committee nevertheless asserted that 'its power to secure the attendance of an individual *named* civil servant is unqualified',[127] and that it was unacceptable for the government to prevent these officials from attending, a power which the same committee reasserted in 1994.[128] Although such instances are rare, Westland is not unique: in 1992, the Ministry of Defence frustrated efforts by the Trade and Industry Committee's inquiry into arms to Iraq (following allegations that British companies had sold arms to Iraq), the Committee having wished to take evidence from recently retired officials.[129] In a decision which was subsequently criticised by Sir Richard Scott (a Lord Justice of Appeal who had been appointed by the government to investigate the allegations of arms for Iraq), the Ministry refused to help contact the officials in question on the ground that 'retired officials are not normally given access to departmental papers'.[130]

Sir Richard, in fact, proposed that in the interests of full and effective accountability, select committees should not be hindered by the government in summoning named officials to appear before them, as did the Public Service Committee in 1996 which proposed that 'there should be a presumption that Ministers accept requests by Committees that named individual civil servants give evidence to them'.[131] The government agreed that 'where a Select Committee indicates that it wishes to hear evidence from named civil servants, Ministers should normally accept such a request',[132] and the rules have been amended

---

[123] *The Times*, 17 October 1995.
[124] HC Deb, 19 October 1995, col 519.
[125] See ch 8 E above.
[126] See also p 287 above.
[127] HC 519 (1985–6).
[128] HC 27-I (1993–4). But this was contested by the government, which pointed out that it was ministers who were ultimately accountable to Parliament 'for the whole range of a department's business', even though this did not mean that 'Ministers must be expected to be personally responsible, in the sense of being creditworthy or blameworthy, for every act of their department' (Cm 2627, 1994, p 28).
[129] HC 86 (1991–2).
[130] HC 115 (1995–6), para F4.64.
[131] HC 313-I (1995–6), para 83.
[132] HC 67 (1996–7), p x.

accordingly.[133] But these rules – sometimes known as the Osmotherly Rules – also provide that ministers retain the right to suggest an alternative official to that named by the committee if they feel that the former is better placed to represent them.[134] The rules further provide that it is not the role of a select committee to act as a disciplinary tribunal and that a minister may wish to suggest someone else where the named official is likely to be exposed 'to questioning about their personal actions or the allocation of blame as between them and others'.[135]

But as the amended rules also make clear: 'If a Committee nonetheless insists on a particular official appearing before them, contrary to the Minister's wishes, the formal position remains that it could issue an order for attendance, and request the House to enforce it.'[136]

> In 2003, the Foreign Affairs Committee summoned Dr David Kelly, a distinguished weapons inspector seconded to the Defence Science and Technology Laboratory (a trading fund of the Ministry of Defence). There had been much political controversy arising from a claim by a BBC journalist that the government had exaggerated Saddam Hussain's military capabilities in the run-up to the war in Iraq. Dr Kelly had been disclosed as the source of the journalist's claim, and the Defence Secretary agreed to the Foreign Affairs Committee's request to take evidence from Dr Kelly in the light of an inquiry they had recently concluded on the war in Iraq. Despite the provisions of the Osmotherly Rules (and what is now para 35 (previously para 46) in particular), Dr Kelly was questioned not about government policy but about his own role in the preparation of the dossier and his relationship with journalists. It was felt by at least one member of the committee that Dr Kelly had been 'thrown to the wolves'. Dr Kelly took his own life two days later. The Defence Secretary had agreed to the Committee's request that Dr Kelly appear as a witness despite the fact that he was 'a relatively junior official', unaccustomed 'to being thrust into the public eye'. In the subsequent inquiry into the circumstances surrounding Dr Kelly's death, Lord Hutton concluded that 'there would have been a serious political storm' if the Defence Secretary had refused to permit Dr Kelly to appear before the Committee. The decision to agree to the request that Dr Kelly should appear was not one that could be 'subject to valid criticism'.[137]

E. Civil service: ethics and standards

Civil Service Code

A statement of the ethical standards by which the civil service should be bound is to be found in the *Civil Service Code*, which now has a statutory basis in the Constitutional Reform and Governance Act 2010.[138] The Code states explicitly that it forms part of the

---

[133] Cabinet Office, *Giving Evidence to Select Committees – Guidance for Civil Servants* (2014). The rules now provide that 'Where a Select Committee indicates that it wishes to take evidence from a particular named official, including special advisers, the presumption should be that the minister will [seek to] agree such a request' (para 12). The words in brackets did not appear in the earlier version (2010).

[134] Cabinet Office, *Giving Evidence to Select Committees*, above, para 12.

[135] Ibid, para 35.

[136] Ibid, para 13. The House of Commons Liaison Committee (the Committee of Select Committee chairs) has said that the Osmotherly rules 'should [not] have any bearing on whom a select committee should choose to summon as a witness. The Osmotherly rules are merely internal for Government. They have never been accepted by Parliament' (HC 697 (2012–13)).

[137] See HC 390-I (2003–4) (Foreign Affairs Committee) and Lord Hutton, Report of the Inquiry into the Circumstances Surrounding the Death of Dr David Kelly, CMG, above.

[138] 2010 Act, s 5. Earlier versions of the code were made in 1996 and 2006, under different legal authority.

contractual relationship between the civil servant and his or her employer, and that it creates an expectation of 'high standards of behaviour'.[139] Now a slight and insubstantial document of 'core values', the Code is by no means exhaustive of the obligations of civil servants, with individual departments imposing additional requirements. The Code declares that civil servants are expected to carry out their role 'with dedication and a commitment to the Civil Service and its core values: integrity, honesty, objectivity and impartiality'.

This means that civil servants are expected to put the obligations of public service above their own personal interests, to be truthful and open, to base their advice and decisions on rigorous analysis of the evidence, and to 'act solely according to the merits of the case', serving equally well 'Governments of different political persuasions'. Apart from laying out the various duties of the civil servant, the *Civil Service Code* includes a procedure for civil servants to raise concerns where they believe that they are being required to act in a way that contradicts the Code, or if they believe that others are acting contrary to the Code. The final stage in the procedure involves the Civil Service Commission for those who remain unsatisfied by a response given at a lower level.[140] Criminal or other unlawful activity may be reported to the police or other appropriate authorities. But there is no right, far less any duty, to bring wrongdoing to public notice.[141]

Significant provisions of the Code under the rubric of *integrity* require the civil servant to make sure that public money is used 'properly and efficiently', deal with the public fairly and promptly, and comply with the law and uphold the administration of justice. Under the rubric of *honesty*, civil servants are required to set out facts and issues truthfully, use resources only for the public purposes for which they are provided, and refrain from deceiving or knowingly misleading ministers, Parliament or others. So far as *objectivity* is concerned, this is stated to mean that the civil servant must provide accurate and evidence-based advice to ministers and others, take due account of expert and professional advice, and must not frustrate the implementation of policies once decisions have been taken.

Impartiality means that the civil servant must carry out his or her responsibilities in a way that is fair, just and equitable and does not unjustifiably favour or discriminate against particular individuals or interests. The Code also addresses specifically the question of political impartiality, and provides that civil servants must serve governments of whatever political persuasion to the best of their ability, regardless of their own political beliefs, acting in a way that retains the confidence of ministers, while ensuring that they will be able to establish a similar relationship with the members of a future government. It is specifically provided that civil servants must not act in a way that is determined by party political considerations, use official resources for party political purposes, or allow personal views to determine advice or actions.

Financial interests of civil servants

We have seen that ministers are subject to rules enforced by the Prime Minister that are intended inter alia to ensure that they do not profit improperly from their public position.[142] The *Civil Service Code* informs civil servants that they should not 'misuse [their] official position, for example by using information acquired in the course of [their] official duties to further [their] private interests or those of others'. Nor should they place themselves in a

---

[139] The Code also states that it applies to all Home civil servants, and that those working for the Scottish Executive and the Welsh Assembly will have their own versions of the Code, as will the Executive Agencies.

[140] The Civil Service Commissioners were set up in 1870 with the rather different task of promoting competitive entry into the civil service on the principle of intellectual merit. There is no provision in the Code addressing the powers of the Commissioners in these circumstances.

[141] The issue was considered – albeit inconclusively – by the Public Service Committee in HC 313-I (1995–6).

[142] Section C in this chapter.

position that 'might reasonably be seen to compromise [their] personal judgment or integrity'. The separate and much larger *Civil Service Management Code* provides further that civil servants must have departmental permission before engaging in any occupation which might affect their work.

The latter *Code* also requires civil servants to disclose any directorships or shareholdings that could be advanced by their official position, and to accept any instruction as to their retention, disposal or management. There are strict rules about civil servants entering into business relationships with government departments (such as letting property or buying surplus stock), as well as about the acceptance of gifts or hospitality which might compromise the civil servant's judgment or integrity. Breach of the *Civil Service Management Code* could give rise to contractual sanctions (including dismissal in appropriate cases), though in some cases, a failure of duty could also give rise to prosecution. The Bribery Act 2010 applies to civil servants, and the *Civil Service Management Code* requires its provisions to be notified to staff.[143]

The public interest in integrity needs also to address the positions held by officials after they leave the civil service. Suspicions may be aroused – for example – where a civil servant with responsibility for defence procurement is employed by a weapons' manufacturer following retirement from the service. How can we be sure that the official was not moved by considerations of personal interest when making major decisions before retirement? The Business Appointment Rules provide for the scrutiny of appointments which former civil servants propose to accept in the first two years after they leave the service. The aim of the rules is to avoid any reasonable concerns that the advice and decisions of a serving officer 'might be influenced in carrying out his or her official duties by the hope or expectation of future employment with a particular firm or organisation'.

Another purpose of the Business Appointment Rules is to avoid the risk that 'a particular firm or organisation might gain an improper advantage by employing someone who, in the course of their official duties, has had access to [information about government policy that may] affect the prospective employer or any competitors'. In some cases permission is required before the civil servant accepts any new appointment or employment within two years of leaving the civil service. In many cases permission will be granted without condition, while in other cases a waiting period or other conditions may be imposed. The process is supervised by the Advisory Committee on Business Appointments, an independent body appointed by the Prime Minister whose members have experience of the relationship between the civil service and the private sector.[144] The Public Administration Select Committee proposed radical reforms to the procedures in 2013.[145]

Political activities of civil servants

Servants of the Crown are prohibited from parliamentary candidature and disqualified from membership of the Commons.[146] But should civil servants be subject to additional limitations, to secure the political impartiality of the civil service as a whole? The *Civil Service Management Code* points out that 'from the nature of the work which a civil servant is required to do and the context in which he has to do it, there must be certain restrictions on

---

[143] The foregoing provisions are drawn from *Civil Service Management Code*, ch 4. See also pp 297–8 below, on links with lobbyists.

[144] See HC 651 (2006–7), and the government's response (HC 1087 (2006–7)). The current rules from which the foregoing is drawn are to be found in the *Civil Service Management Code*, Section 4.3, Annex A. They are also to be found in the Annual Reports of the Advisory Committee on Business Committees, which helpfully provide an account of the advice it has given in individual cases. See http://acoba.independent.gov.uk.

[145] HC 404 (2012–13).

[146] See ch 7.

the type of political activities in which a civil servant is allowed to participate and the extent to which he may do so will, of course, depend on his position and seniority'.[147] Formal restrictions to give effect to this principle were first brought into force in 1954.[148]

The current procedures recognise that the political neutrality of the civil service is fundamental, but that the rules need not be the same for all members of the service. The position was fully reviewed by the Armitage Committee in 1978, in response to requests from the civil service unions for greater political freedom for civil servants. The committee reasserted the constitutional importance of the political neutrality of the civil service. It recommended that the scheme then in force should continue subject to substantial changes in its operation, the effect of which would be to reduce the number of civil servants in the 'restricted' category.[149] In 1984 these recommendations were adopted after extensive discussion between government and the civil service unions.[150]

Participation in national political activities (for example, holding office in a political Party; or expressing public views on matters of national political controversy) is barred to the Senior Civil Service and other senior grades. This 'politically restricted' category must seek permission to take part in local political activities and must comply with any conditions laid down by their department or agency. A second 'intermediate' category may, with the leave of their departments, take part in national or local activities, although some grades have a mandate to take part in such activities without the need for permission. In cases where there is no mandate, permission will normally be refused only where civil servants are employed in sensitive areas where the impartiality of the civil service is most at risk.

A post is regarded as sensitive for these purposes if it is closely engaged in policy assistance to ministers; it is in the private office of a minister; it requires the post-holder to speak regularly for the government; the post-holder represents the government in dealing with overseas governments; or the post-holder is involved in regular face-to-face contact with the public. The third 'politically free' category combines industrial and non-office grades: they are free to engage in all political activities, national and local, except when on duty, or on official premises, or while wearing their uniform. These procedures are reinforced by the *Civil Service Code* which provides that civil servants must comply with political restrictions that apply to them.[151] The foregoing provisions are unlikely to violate Convention rights.[152]

Civil servants and lobbyists

In 1998 new guidelines about contacts with lobbyists were issued to civil servants. These followed a press report that a journalist posing as an American businessman had been introduced by a lobbyist to a senior Downing Street official. In a disputed remark, the official is reported to have said to the putative businessman: 'Just tell me what you want, who you want to meet and . . . I will make the call for you.'[153] As we have seen in Chapter 9 B, the Cash

---

[147] *R v Civil Service Appeal Board, ex p Bruce* [1988] 3 All ER 686, at p 690 (May LJ). The arrangements are set out in *Civil Service Management Code*, Section 4.4.

[148] See Cmd 7718, 1949, and Cmd 8783, 1953.

[149] Cmnd 7057, 1978.

[150] HC Deb, 26 March 1981, col 1186; 4 March 1982, col 503; 19 July 1984, col 272 (WA).

[151] Apart from personal involvement in political activities, civil servants may wish to participate in political action through their trade unions. Civil service unions may establish political funds under what is now the Trade Union and Labour Relations (Consolidation) Act 1992 (as amended by the Trade Union Act 2016) to enable them more effectively to represent their members by campaigning politically. None is affiliated to any political party (although there are no legal restrictions on such affiliation), but several are affiliated to the TUC.

[152] *Ahmed* v *United Kingdom* (2000) 29 EHRR 1 (no violation of Convention rights in relation to similar restrictions applying to local government officers).

[153] *The Observer*, 5 July 1998. The allegations were strongly denied: HC Deb, 8 July 1998, col 1065.

for Questions affair in the 1990s led to the creation of the Committee on Standards in Public Life and tighter rules to regulate the relationship between MPs and lobbyists. But at the time of 'Lobbygate', as this incident was known, there was no regulation of civil service contact with lobbyists.

Guidelines drafted in response adopt a minimalist approach[154] and reflect the view in the first report of the Committee on Standards in Public Life that 'it is the right of everyone to lobby Parliament and ministers, and it is for public institutions to develop ways of controlling the reaction to approaches from professional lobbyists in such a way as to give due weight to their case while always taking care to consider the public interest'.[155] The government's approach in the guidelines is thus not to ban contacts between civil servants and lobbyists, but 'to insist that wherever and whenever they take place they should be conducted in accordance with the *Civil Service Code*, and the principles of public life set out by the Nolan Committee', which are considered in Chapter 12.

The guidelines are drawn from the principles in the *Civil Service Code* that civil servants should conduct themselves with honesty and integrity. Some activities are said to be 'completely unacceptable' and to be serious disciplinary offences which could lead to dismissal. These are the leaking of confidential or sensitive material (especially market-sensitive material) to a lobbyist and deliberately helping a lobbyist to attract business by arranging for clients to have privileged access to a minister or undue influence over policy. Other situations are to be handled with care, although again any misjudgment could lead to disciplinary action. A number of basic rules are set out, including a requirement that civil servants should not grant a lobbyist preferential or premature access to information.

Otherwise, the rules provide that civil servants should not meet one group making representations on a particular issue without offering other groups a similar opportunity; accept gifts from a lobbyist; do anything which might breach parliamentary privilege (for example, by revealing the contents of a report not yet published); use knowledge of the workings of government to impress a lobbyist; help a lobbyist to obtain a benefit to which he or she is not entitled; or give the impression of offering a lobbyist preferential access to ministers. Civil servants should also declare to their department any family or business interests which may create a conflict of interest with departmental work; and take care in accepting hospitality from a lobbyist. Although meetings between civil servants and lobbyists are now recorded,[156] the government rejected proposals that these records should be published.[157]

There is now a statutory register of consultant lobbyists, designed to enhance transparency of those lobbying ministers and civil servants on behalf of third parties.[158]

Assessing 'reform'

The large-scale changes to the civil service since 1988 have given rise to a great deal of discussion. In a major report in 1998, the House of Lords Select Committee on Public Service concluded that the changes represented a 'radical' and 'fundamental revolution' in public administration. But the committee accepted that there had been 'little open or public debate about the extent of the structural changes being made', and expressed itself as being not satisfied that 'the constitutional implications of the changes were fully thought through' before they were introduced. There was a tension between the

---

[154] Cabinet Office, *Guidance for Civil Servants: Contact with Lobbyists* (2010).
[155] Cm 280-I, 1995, para 72. Indeed, the Guidelines referred to in the text acknowledge that lobbyists are 'a feature of our democratic system'.
[156] See Cm 4557-I, 2000, R 28; and HC 1058 (2008–9).
[157] See HC 36 (2008–9), and the government's response HC 1058 (2008–9).
[158] Transparency of Lobbying, Non-Party Campaigning and Trade Union Administration Act 2014. Part 1.

(economic) justification for change based on efficiency, effectiveness and value for money, on the one hand, and traditional (political) concerns based on responsibility and accountability, on the other.

The creation of the executive agencies was not thought, in a constitutional sense, to 'recast the architecture of the state', 'but only so long as accountability of Ministers to Parliament for the work of executive agencies remains the same as their accountability for any other aspect of their Department's work'. The committee was concerned that 'the devolution to executive agencies was contributing to a sense of disunity in the Civil Service', although not yet to fragmentation. There was a need to determine how far this process of reducing the role of the core civil service should go and a need for 'open and public debate' about the irreducible nucleus of functions which must be carried out by the core civil service: this is as much 'a matter for the governed as for the governors'.

The process of civil service reform continued under the Labour government elected in 1997 and has taken on a new dimension.[159] In the white paper, *Modernising Government*, it was announced in 1999 that permanent secretaries and heads of department would have performance targets 'for taking forward the government's modernisation agenda and ensuring delivery of the government's key targets'.[160] There is now great emphasis not only on the public service values of impartiality, objectivity and integrity, but also on the need for 'greater creativity, radical thinking, and collaborative working', as well as efficiency in the delivery of public services.[161] The pace of change continued under the Coalition with a *Civil Service Reform Plan* announcing a reduction in the number of civil servants to 380,000 by 2015 (the lowest since the Second World War),[162] a target which as we have seen seems largely to have been met.

The pace of change in the civil service since the *Next Steps Report* in 1988 has been extraordinary. Yet there has been no serious attempt to assess the benefits or impact of these changes, which have been driven as much by cost as the need for organizational efficiency and service delivery. An attempt to undertake such a task by the Public Administration and Constitutional Affairs Committee was cut short by the general election in 2017, and it may be that the work already started will be continued by a successor committee. The initial work of the PACAC also suggested, however, that the work of the reformer's scalpel has not yet finished, with the Committee beginning an unprecedented examination of the relationship between ministers and their Permanent Secretaries, inviting the possibility of better guidelines being issued to deal with this most sensitive interface between the political and official arms of government.[163]

F. Open government and freedom of information

Background

Discussion of the structure of the civil service and transparency of lobbying leads directly to a consideration of open government and the public right of access to official information. Historically there was no such right in the United Kingdom, in contrast to the position in other parliamentary democracies (notably Australia, Canada and New Zealand) where the

---

[159] On the implementation of these reforms, see C D Foster (2001) 79 *Public Administration* 725. For further analysis, see Hennessy, *The Prime Minister*, ch 18. For a full account of civil service reform, see Bogdanor (ed.), *The British Constitution in the Twentieth Century*, ch 7.

[160] See Cm 4310, 1999.

[161] Cabinet Office, *Civil Service Reform – Delivery and Values* (2004).

[162] HM Government, *Civil Service Reform Plan* (2012), p 11.

[163] HC 263 (2016–17) ('The Work of the Civil Service – Key Themes and Preliminary Findings').

right of access to information was introduced much earlier than in Britain.[164] Such access is important for a number of reasons, not least because of the insights it provides into the conduct of government and the enhanced opportunities it provides for politicians, the press and the public more effectively to hold government to account. In 1979 a green paper on open government was published by the then Labour government, offering modestly a non-binding code of practice on access to official information.[165]

But electoral defeat meant that these proposals were never implemented. Although campaigners for open government were thus disappointed, important initiatives in the direction of reform were nevertheless taken in the 1980s and 1990s. Apart from a number of specific statutory provisions,[166] these included the *Citizen's Charter* introduced in 1991, providing that every citizen is entitled to expect openness and stating unequivocally that there should be no secrecy about how public services are run, how much they cost, who is in charge, and whether or not they are meeting their standards.[177] This was followed in 1993 by the white paper, *Open Government*, which revived the idea of a non-binding code of practice. Such a code was, in fact, introduced in 1994 and revised in 1997,[168] allowing for complaints to be made to the Ombudsman (through the medium of a member of Parliament) that information had been unreasonably withheld.[169]

It was the Labour government's turn to publish a white paper ('with green edges') on freedom of information in 1997.[170] The original plan was to replace existing open government initiatives (including the Code of Practice) 'with clear and consistent requirements which would apply across government'.[171] The white paper proposed the introduction of 'a right, exercisable by any individual, company or other body to records or information of any date held by the public authority concerned in connection with its public functions'.[172] The presumption would be that information should be released unless disclosure would cause harm to one or more specified interests or would be contrary to the public interest. But these original proposals were abandoned and responsibility for open government transferred from the Cabinet Office to the Home Office (said to be 'one of the most overworked and accident-prone departments of government').[173]

A diluted measure was subsequently introduced, this forming the basis of what is now the Freedom of Information Act 2000,[174] which was not brought fully into force until 1 January 2005, along with a separate regime for access to environmental information held by public authorities.[175] Although the Act gives a legal right of access to official information, it was

---

[164] Open government was actively discouraged by the Official Secrets Act 1911, esp s 2 by which it was an offence for a civil servant to communicate any information to a member of the public without authorisation. There was no right to information and no right to disclose it. Section 2 of the 1911 Act was repealed by the Official Secrets Act 1989. See ch 19.

[165] Cmnd 7520, 1979.

[166] Access to Personal Files Act 1987, Access to Medical Reports Act 1988, Access to Health Records Act 1990, Environmental Information Regulations 1992, SI 1992 No 3240. Also important was the Data Protection Act 1984 (now Data Protection Act 1998). See ch 16.

[167] Cm 1588, 1991. See C Scott [1999] PL 595; G Drewry [2002] PL 12.

[168] Cm 2290, 1993.

[169] See Birkinshaw, *Freedom of Information*.

[170] *Your Right to Know: Freedom of Information*, Cm 3818, 1997. For comment, see P Birkinshaw [1998] PL 176.

[171] Cm 3818, 1997, para 1.6.

[172] Ibid, para 2.6.

[173] HL Deb, 20 April 2000, col 836.

[174] For a valuable account, see S Palmer, in Beatson and Cripps (eds), *Freedom of Expression and Freedom of Information*, ch 15. Also P Birkinshaw, in Jowell and Oliver (eds), *The Changing Constitution*, ch 14.

[175] SI 2004 No 3391, implementing EC Directive 2003/4/EC. These regulations revoked the earlier SI 1992 No 3240.

nevertheless criticised for being too restrictive in a number of key respects, these criticisms being voiced on two occasions by the Public Administration Committee of the House of Commons.[176] The government openly acknowledged some of these criticisms,[177] and responded by having 'some of that diluting removed'.[178] A similar regime was introduced in Scotland by the Freedom of Information (Scotland) Act 2002, and the Environmental Information (Scotland) Regulations 2004.[179]

Scope of the Act

The Freedom of Information Act has been described as 'a landmark enactment of great constitutional significance for the United Kingdom'.[180] It 'creates a general right of access to information upon written request made to a public authority'.[181] Any person making a request for information is entitled (a) to be told in writing by the authority whether it holds information of the type specified in the request, and if so (b) to have that information communicated to him or her (s 1). A public authority's duty to comply with (a) is referred to as 'the duty to confirm or deny'. The public authorities to which the Act applies are listed in Schedule 1: there are over 400 such bodies,[182] a list which may be added to by order of the Secretary of State for Justice (now the minister responsible for freedom of information) (s 4).[183] The list – amended as new legislation creates new public authorities – includes central government departments, local authorities, national health service bodies, schools and educational institutions, and the police.

In this respect the Act contrasts sharply with the Human Rights Act 1998, which also applies to public authorities. There is no definition of a public authority in the Human Rights Act (save to make clear that a court is a public authority), the scope of the Act being left to the courts to determine.[184] Although there ought thus to be less room for uncertainty about the application of the Freedom of Information Act 2000, tortuous difficulties have arisen about the nature of its application to bodies like the BBC.[185] The BBC is one of a few bodies listed only in relation to some information they hold: for example, the Act applies to the BBC 'in respect of information held for purposes other than those of journalism, art or literature'. The only information the BBC can be required to disclose is that held exclusively for non-journalistic purposes, a position justified on grounds of freedom of expression.[186]

---

[176] HC 570-I (1998–9); HC 78 (1999–2000).

[177] HL Deb, 20 April 2000, col 824.

[178] Ibid, col 831. The Act was the subject of post-legislative scrutiny by the Justice Select Committee: HC 96 (2012–13).

[179] SSI 2004 No 520.

[180] *Kennedy* v *Charity Commission* [2014] UKSC 20, [2015] 1 AC 455, para 153.

[181] *R(Ofcom)* v *Information Commissioner* [2008] EWHC 1445 (Admin), para 5.

[182] Although there are over 400 bodies listed in the Act, some of these are listed collectively (such as NHS bodies, universities and local authorities). As a result there are very many more individual bodies to which the Act applies.

[183] The Act also allows an order to be made bringing in private bodies exercising public functions, such as companies running prisons and the British Board of Film Classification: HL Deb, 20 April 2000, col 825.

[184] See ch 14.

[185] *BBC* v *Information Commissioner* [2009] UKHL 9, [2009] 1 WLR 430; *Sugar* v *BBC* [2012] UKSC 4, [2012] 1 WLR 439. For an example concerning a body only partially designated as a public authority by an Order, see *University and Colleges Admissions Service* v *Information Commissioner and Lord Lucas* [2014] UKUT 557 (AAC).

[186] *Sugar* v *BBC*, above.

A request for information is to be made in writing to the relevant public authority (s 8), which may (but need not) charge a fee for the information in accordance with regulations (s 9).[187] The fee may be not insignificant, and may be charged at a rate of up to £25 an hour.[188] Requests are to be dealt with promptly and within 20 working days of receipt (s 10). There is a right only to have access to information: there is no right to have access to documents (s 11),[189] though there is now a right to have datasets provided electronically (s11(A)).[190] The authority may refuse to comply with a request for information where the cost would be excessive (s 12), or where the application is vexatious (s 14). The public authorities to which the Act applies must provide advice and assistance to persons who propose to make or who have made requests under the Act (s 16).

Where an application for information is refused, the public authority must issue the applicant with a notice explaining the grounds for the refusal (s 17). In addition, publication schemes must be approved by the Information Commissioner (s 19), who is also required to produce model publication schemes (s 20). The publication scheme should specify the classes of information that the authority in question publishes or intends to publish, specifying the manner in which information of each class is to be published, indicating whether a charge is made. It has been said that 'the requirement for all public authorities to apply a scheme for publication – in effect to say what, when and how information will be published – is probably the most powerful push to openness in the [Act]'.[191] These schemes will help to guide citizens through the freedom of information process.

Exemptions

It is almost certainly the case that 'no legislation which any responsible government could introduce would completely satisfy [the more ardent advocates of freedom of information]'.[192] Nevertheless, it is a striking feature of the FOI regime that there are so many categories of exempted information. Many of the 24 sections of exempt information (ss 21–44) are wholly predictable, with the exemptions falling into two groups: those which carry absolute exemption, and those which do not (s 2). In the latter case, the exemption applies only where the public interest in maintaining the exclusion of the duty to confirm or deny (s 1(1)(a)), or in withholding the information (s 1(1)(b)) outweighs the public interest in disclosing whether the public authority holds the information or in communicating it to the person seeking access, as the case may be (s 2(1),(2)).[193]

Information which will be absolutely exempt (and which therefore does not need to be disclosed) includes that which is reasonably accessible to the public by other means (s 21), information which relates to bodies dealing with security matters (s 23), information relating to court records, or to the conduct by public authorities of inquiries held under

---

[187] The regulations provide a limit of £600 or £450 depending on the nature of the public authority: SI 2004 No 3244.

[188] See SI 2004 No 3244. In practice, very few public authorities charge fees for the overwhelming majority of information requests.

[189] In practice documents will often be produced: *Home Office* v *Information Commissioner* [2009] EWHC 1611 (Admin), para 8. In some cases, the original documents will be the only way of conveying all of the information they reveal: *Independent Parliamentary Standards Authority* v *Information Commissioner & Leapman* [2015] EWCA Civ 388, [2015] 1 WLR 2879. Compare TFEU, art 15: any citizen of the Union, and any natural or legal person residing or based in the Union, has a 'right of access' to documents of the Union institutions. See Regulation 1049/2001/EC.

[190] Inserted by Protection of Freedoms Act 2012, s 102.

[191] HL Deb, 20 April 2000, col 826 (Lord Falconer).

[192] HL Deb, 20 April 2000, col 863.

[193] See *Home Office* v *Information Commissioner*, above: a broad judgment is required to determine where the public interest lies (para 25), citing *Office of Communications* v *Information Commissioner* [2009] EWCA Civ 90.

statute (s 32),[194] information which consists of personal data the release of which would violate the data protection principles (s 40),[195] information obtained in confidence (s 41), and information the disclosure of which is prohibited by statute, incompatible with an EU obligation, or would constitute a contempt of court (s 44).

The larger category of information to which an absolute exemption does not apply (and the withholding of which therefore has to be justified on public interest grounds) includes information which is held by the authority with a view to its future publication (s 22), information required for the purpose of safeguarding national security (s 24), information relating to defence (s 26), information the disclosure of which would prejudice international relations (s 27), information the disclosure of which would prejudice relations between Whitehall and the devolved administrations or between the devolved administrations (s 28), and so on at some length.

Among the other noteworthy categories of information not subject to absolute exemption are information which if disclosed would or would be likely to prejudice the economic interests of the United Kingdom or any part thereof or any administration in the United Kingdom (s 29);[196] information relating to criminal investigations conducted by a wide range of statutory agencies (s 30) or law enforcement bodies (s 31); information relating to the formulation or development of government policy (s 35);[197] as well as information held by a public authority which, in the reasonable opinion of an appropriately qualified person (such as a minister), if disclosed could prejudice the effective conduct of public affairs (s 36). Notably, many of these exemptions apply on the low threshold that publication would cause 'prejudice'. It was felt by some that the higher standard of 'substantial prejudice' or 'necessity' would be more appropriate.

Public interest considerations

Since the Act was introduced, there have been several notable decisions in which government departments have challenged rulings that they release information. Many of these have been contested on public interest grounds, which on some occasions concerned important constitutional principles and practices not always consistent with freedom of information. In *HM Treasury* v *Information Commissioner*,[198] it was held that the convention that the law officers' advice to ministers (in this case the Attorney General's advice on the compatibility of the Financial Services and Markets Act 2000 with the Human Rights Act 1998) had not been given sufficient weight by the Information Tribunal in ordering its release.

This latter convention had been breached on only five occasions since 1968, and in the view of Blake J, it had not been modified by the 2000 Act. It had rather been preserved but rendered 'amenable to being out-weighed by greater considerations of the public interest requiring disclosure of information'. Section 35(1)(c) of the 2000 Act specifically refers to 'the provision of advice by any of the Law Officers or any request for the provision of such advice' as information exempt from disclosure, and the tribunal was found to have erred by 'failing to conclude that Parliament intended real weight should continue to be afforded to [the] Law Officers' Convention'.[199]

---

[194] On which see *Kennedy* v *Charity Commission* [2012] EWCA Civ 317, [2012] 1 WLR 3524.

[195] These principles are set out in the Data Protection Act 1998 (see ch 16). On how personal data protected by the 1998 Act might be rendered suitable for release under the FOI Act 2000, see *Common Services Agency* v *Scottish Information Commissioner* [2008] UKHL 47, [2008] 1 WLR 1550, and *South Lanarkshire Council* v *Scottish Information Commissioner* [2013] UKSC 55.

[196] On the purpose of this exemption, see HL Deb, 19 October 2000, col 1287.

[197] This includes advice provided by the law officers, and information to which the convention of Cabinet collective responsibility applies

[198] [2009] EWHC 1811 (Admin).

[199] See also *Savic* v *Information Commissioner and Attorney General's Office* [2016] UKUT 534 (AAC) (similar reiteration of the weight to be given to information falling within the law officers' convention in an appeal concerning legal advice about NATO's military action in Kosovo).

On the other hand, in *House of Commons* v *Information Commissioner*,[200] there was no question of parliamentary privilege standing in the way of a request for information about MPs' allowances,[201] which had been required by the Information Commissioner and the Information Tribunal (which at that time dealt with appeals under the Act). In a strong judgment it was held by a three-member Administrative Court that the 'legitimate public interest engaged by these applications [was] obvious', with questions relating to MPs' allowances having 'a wide resonance throughout the body politic', and to 'bear on public confidence in the operation of our democratic system at its very pinnacle'.

Also, in *Evans* v *Information Commissioner*[202] the Upper Tribunal upheld an appeal from an Information Commissioner's decision that the substance of correspondence between the Prince of Wales and seven government departments should not be disclosed on public interest grounds. In this important decision, the tribunal weighed up competing public interest considerations based principally on arguments about constitutional conventions. But it was held that advocacy by the Prince could not be protected by the conventions relating to the constitutional role of the monarch, which might otherwise have tended towards non-disclosure. In a bold decision the tribunal said that:

> none of the Departments' contentions persuades us that, in the absence of special circumstances, as regards advocacy correspondence it is appropriate to give correspondence between ministers and Prince Charles greater protection from disclosure than would be afforded to correspondence with others who have dealings with government in a context where those others are seeking to advance the work of charities or to promote views.[203]

Enforcement and remedies

Enforcement of the Act is the initial responsibility of the Information Commissioner (s 18). A complaint may be made to the Commissioner that a public authority has failed to comply with the requirements of Part I of the Act, and if the complaint is upheld, the Commissioner may issue a decision notice specifying steps to be taken to comply with the Act (s 50). These notices are published on the Commission's website, and there is now a significant volume of them that – along with the other enforcement responsibilities of the Commissioner – still awaits full academic analysis. The Commissioner is also empowered to issue an enforcement notice (s 52), failure to comply with which may lead to the matter being referred to the High Court or Court of Session to be punished as a contempt of court (s 54).

The right of appeal to the Information Tribunal against a decision of the Commissioner (s 57) has been transferred to the unified tribunal system in England and Wales,[204] with a further appeal on a point of law from the Upper Tribunal to the Court of Appeal (s 59).[205] Under s 60, the Tribunal (which in some cases will be the First-tier Tribunal but in others the Upper Tribunal) has been given powers to quash a ministerial certificate protecting national security information from disclosure. As an expert body, the tribunal 'is not required to defer to the views of Ministers or civil servants' when exercising its powers

---

[200] [2008] EWHC 1084 (Admin). See P Leyland [2009] PL 675.

[201] But compare *Office of Government Commerce* v *Information Commissioner* [2008] EWHC 737 (Admin). See ch 9 above.

[202] [2012] UKUT 313 (AAC).

[203] Ibid, para 211.

[204] Tribunals, Courts and Enforcement Act 2007; see ch 23 below. The appeal system under the Freedom of Information (Scotland) Act is different: a challenge to a decision notice of the Scottish Information Commissioner (a different entity) may only be made on a point of law to the Court of Session.

[205] An appeal to the Tribunal against a decision notice under s 57 is a full merits appeal; the Tribunal is not restricted by the reasoning of, or the evidence available to, the Information Commissioner (s 58).

under the Act,[206] though as already indicated the courts have emphasised on several occasions the need to take seriously government claims that information must be withheld in particular cases on public interest grounds,[207] and particularly in cases where the tribunal or courts have a reduced institutional competence.[208] It is an offence to destroy or tamper with information, but only if this is done after a request for disclosure has been made (s 77).

Although she has wide powers under the Act, the government has nevertheless been reluctant to leave the last word to the Commissioner (or the tribunals or courts), taking the highly unusual view that it would be 'profoundly undemocratic' to permit the Commissioner to have the final say on what should be disclosed. Section 53 thus contains a so-called 'executive override', a 'kind of nuclear option for the Government',[209] allowing a minister in some limited circumstances to override a decision notice (under s 50) or an enforcement notice (under s 52) of the Commissioner which has been served on a government department.[210] This power – to be exercised by means of a ministerial certificate which must be laid before Parliament – reflects the government's belief that 'there will be certain cases dealing with the most sensitive issues where a senior member of the Government, able to seek advice from his Cabinet colleagues, should decide on the final question of public interest in relation to disclosure'.[211]

The power was used in 2007 to prevent the publication of minutes of two Cabinet meetings in March 2003 (relating to the Iraq war), and again in 2009 to prevent the publication of minutes of Cabinet sub-committee meetings in 1997 (relating to devolution). On this latter occasion, the Justice Secretary claimed that 'disclosure of the information in this case would put the convention [of collective responsibility] at serious risk of harm'.[212] The consistent use of the override in relation to Cabinet minutes (suggesting the existence of a policy) seems calculated to be tested in judicial review proceedings at some point. Most controversially, however, the power was used to veto the decision in the *Evans* case discussed above, thereby saving the Prince of Wales the embarrassment of his correspondence to government departments being made public. In subsequent judicial review proceedings, the Supreme Court quashed the Attorney General's certificate on what, as a matter of strict *ratio*, were very narrow grounds concerning the quality of the Attorney's reasoning.[213]

Although the statutory information access regimes are undoubtedly the most practically significant, it is important to note the potential breadth of the Supreme Court's judgment in *Kennedy* v *Charity Commission*.[214] That was a case which originated under the Freedom of Information Act 2000, but the Court discerned an alternative to the legislation. It was held by the majority that a request for information could have been made to the Charity Commission and considered by the Commission by reference to the statutory regime under the Charities Act 1993, challengeable by way of judicial review. It need not have been pursued under the Freedom of Information Act at all.

The reasoning of the majority strongly indicates that a similar analysis would have applied to other public authorities, including by reference to common law (or third source) powers to

[206] *Home Office* v *Information Commissioner* [2009] EWHC 1611 (Admin), at para 29.
[207] See also *Common Services Agency* v *Scottish Information Commissioner*, above, para [4].
[208] *All Party Parliamentary Group on Extraordinary Rendition* v *Information Commissioner & Ministry of Defence* [2011] UKUT 153 (AAC).
[209] HL Deb, 22 November 2000, col 843.
[210] The power applies only to decisions taken in relation to exempt information.
[211] HL Deb, 14 November 2000, col 258.
[212] *BBC News*, 10 December 2009.
[213] *R (Evans)* v *Attorney General* [2015] UKSC 21, [2015] 1 AC 1787. See C Knight (2015) 131 LQR 548.
[214] [2014] UKSC 20, [2015] 1 AC 455.

disclose information in the interests of transparency. This common law right of access to official information had not previously been the subject of any serious judicial consideration, and it has not yet resulted in the sort of vindication apparently anticipated by the Court in other cases. The 'discovery' of this right was partly driven by the Supreme Court's reluctance to accept that Article 10 ECHR contained an analogous right of access to official information,[215] but the Grand Chamber of the European Court of Human Rights has subsequently recognised exactly that (albeit in a limited form).[216] The interaction between Article 10, the *Kennedy* decision and the Freedom of Information Act 2000 awaits further judicial consideration.

G. Conclusion

This chapter has been concerned principally with the structure of government and the constitutional foundations on which it is based. In the United Kingdom, questions of government structure are largely a matter of convention, from the existence of various offices and institutions (such as the Cabinet and Prime Minister), to the way in which they should conduct themselves (such as the requirement of collective responsibility). The formation of a Coalition government in 2010 took place within these structures, which required little adaptation or amendment, and although it did serve significantly to reduce the power of the Prime Minister in a number of areas, this proved to be only a brief hiatus with perhaps few (if any) long-term consequences.

A second theme to emerge in this chapter is that behind the façade of the traditional constitution has been a process of perpetual change. This is particularly marked in relation to the civil service, which has undergone major organisational re-structuring, alongside which the relationship of civil servants to ministers and to Parliament is also changing. Senior civil servants are now much more visible, and partly because of the work of the House of Commons Select Committees in particular they are also much more accountable for the conduct of their departments. Although the deflection of responsibility from ministers may be regretted, this is a process that nevertheless helps to shine a brighter light on the workings of government.

A third theme to emerge in this chapter is the proliferation of codes of conduct – such as the *Ministerial Code* and the *Civil Service Code* – to govern the behaviour of those engaged in central government. It is a short step from the introduction of codes to a more formal arrangement in which codes of conduct have a statutory base, as is now the case in relation to the *Civil Service Code*. This is a process that will have longer-term implications, with demands already emerging for more statutory regulation of those involved in government. A notable example is the Public Administration Select Committee's recommendation that the existing business appointment rules for civil servants should be replaced by statute.[217]

The final theme to emerge from the foregoing has been the persistent push from Parliament and elsewhere to open up the process of government to greater scrutiny and accountability. These steps in the direction of more open and accountable government are calculated only to grow louder, notwithstanding attempts such as those on display after the *Evans* case to frustrate the operation of freedom of information principles. However, the resounding comments of Lord Neuberger in the latter case about the inconsistency of an executive override of a judicial decision on the one hand with the rule of law on the other, suggests that there may now be very little practical scope for the use of the s 53 power.

[215] As to which, see: C Knight [2013] PL 468.
[216] *Magyar Helsinki Bizottság* v *Hungary* (App No 18030/11, 30 November 2016).
[217] HC 404 (2012–13).

CHAPTER 12

Public bodies and public appointments

Chapters 10 and 11 give a very incomplete account of the structure and powers of government in the United Kingdom. They tell us about the Crown, the Prime Minister and the Cabinet, as well as government departments, civil servants and executive agencies. But they tell us nothing about the role of what are loosely referred to as public bodies,[1] which exercise various governmental functions, sometimes independently of government. An outline of the role of these public bodies will help us to give a fuller account of the Executive in modern Britain, the importance of which is reflected in the scrutiny to which they are increasingly subjected.[2]

Public bodies – which range in scope from the Bank of England to the Low Pay Commission – raise important constitutional questions, partly because they have policy-making functions or are otherwise influential, yet with members who are appointed rather than elected, who in the course of their tenure frequently manage large budgets. According to the Public Accounts Committee:

> there are 467 arm's-length bodies spending some £250 billion of taxpayers' money. Three of these bodies—HM Revenue & Customs, NHS England and the Skills Funding Agency—account for more than £200 billion. The scale of arm's-length bodies varies hugely, from large executive agencies to smaller, non-departmental public bodies. But they are often vital to delivering departments' strategic objectives, and provide critical services to the public. Arms-length bodies operate with varying degrees of independence, but in all cases departmental Accounting Officers remain ultimately accountable to Parliament for the bodies they oversee.[3]

In this chapter we address a feature of modern public administration which is routinely condemned and denigrated by many governments, but which all governments discover they cannot manage without. So although the government elected in 2010 sought to cull public bodies, nevertheless it also created new ones, as did its successors.[4] The first task then is to trace the origins of such bodies and to explain why they are thought to be necessary, a process that reveals that the shape and form of such bodies continues to evolve, to reflect the changing nature of the state in modern British society.

It is important also to emphasise the lack of homogeneity around the structure and functions of public bodies: they come in several different shapes and forms (which continue to metamorphose),[5] and perform different kinds of functions. Although by no means exhaustive

---

[1] It appears increasingly the practice in government to refer to these bodies as 'arms-length bodies', which includes not only the bodies referred to in this chapter, but also Executive Agencies referred to in ch 11 D.

[2] G Grimstone, *Better Public Appointments* (2016); Comptroller and Auditor General, *Departments' Oversight of Arm's-Length Bodies: A Comparative Study*, HC 507 (2016–17); HC 488 (2016–17) (Public Accounts Committee); HC 495 (2016–17) (Public Administration and Constitutional Affairs Committee).

[3] HC 488 (2016–17), para 2. HM Revenue and Customs is a Non-Ministerial Department; NHS England is a Non-Departmental Public Body; and the Skills Funding Agency is an Executive Agency. In this chapter we are not concerned with Executive Agencies, though their importance in this context is to be acknowledged.

[4] See Budget Responsibility and National Audit Act 2011 (Office for Budget Responsibility), Groceries Code Adjudicator Act 2013, Transparency of Lobbying, Non-Party Campaigning and Trade Union Administration Act 2014 (Registrar of Consultant Lobbyists); Enterprise Act 2016 (Small Business Commissioner), and Higher Education and Research Act 2017 (The Office for Students).

[5] See Energy Act 2016, which establishes the Oil and Gas Authority (previously an Executive Agency) as a government company with a minister the sole shareholder: see Oil and Gas Authority, *OGA Overview* (2017).

and although by no means an official classification, there are bodies which now perform a policy-making function, others that have a service delivery function, others a regulatory function, others an enforcement function, and others still an advisory function. In the case of at least some advisory bodies, there appears to be an expectation that their advice will be followed.

These bodies are thus important for a host of reasons, not least because their work may bear on the lives of citizens just as directly as will the work of ministers and government departments. One question raised by such bodies relates to their appointment. If such bodies are not elected, how do we avoid the risk of nepotism and the abuse of patronage, or what is referred to in some countries as the development of the 'party state', in which major positions are gifted to leading supporters of the party in power? And if they are not elected, how do we ensure that they are fully accountable, and to whom, and why?

One final question to be considered in this chapter is the attempts by the Coalition government from 2010 to 2015 to reduce the number of public bodies. Extensive powers were taken for this purpose in the Public Bodies Act 2011, a measure giving wide powers to ministers with limited parliamentary oversight, to enable changes to be made as quickly as possible. This reflects the commitment made in the Coalition's programme for government to reduce the number and cost of public bodies, as well as to enhance the transparency of their operation.[6]

A. Origins

Purpose

The work of many public bodies could be performed just as easily by government departments, for which ministers would be directly responsible to Parliament. Thus the enforcement work of the Health and Safety Executive could be done by inspectors employed by a Ministry of Labour, as could the work of the Gangmasters and Labour Abuse Authority, one of the functions of which is to register and supervise the suppliers of labour in some sectors of the economy.[7] Indeed the now privatised Post Office was until 1969 a government department headed by a minister of Cabinet rank – the Postmaster General – who was responsible to Parliament.

There are several reasons why governments may seek less involvement over certain questions.[8] One is to reduce the scope for direct political control or interference over some decisions. At times the reasons are fully understandable, in cases – such as the BBC – where political independence is essential to the integrity of the service in question. It is hardly conceivable that a non-partisan public service broadcaster could be organised in the form of a government department, headed by a Cabinet minister directly responsible to Parliament.

Sometimes the reason is less understandable, as in the case of decision of the government in 1997 to transfer responsibility for interest rates – a key economic lever – from the Treasury to the Bank of England. Apart from the fact that key decisions relating to economic management might be thought to be the direct responsibility of the government, there is no way by which the Monetary Policy Committee of the Bank of England can be as directly accountable to Parliament for its decisions as would be the Chancellor of the Exchequer, no matter how intense the scrutiny.

Otherwise, it is not always clear why certain activities are allocated to departments, and others to executive agencies or public bodies of the kind encountered in this chapter, and the

---

[6] The Coalition, *Our Programme for Government* (2010), p 16.
[8] See also HC 488 (2016–17), para 3.
[7] Gangmasters (Licensing) Act 2004 (as amended by Immigration Act 2016).

quest for rational explanation is likely to prove elusive.[9] Nor is it always clear why a particular form of public body is chosen for a particular task. Whatever the explanations, ministers should not absolve themselves of responsibility for the composition, activities or funding of public bodies, nor seek to deflect blame when things go wrong. Not all attempts to take sensitive questions 'out of politics' by entrusting them to a public body have been successful.[10]

Evolution

The creation of specialised public agencies that are not government departments is not new. In the 18th century, there were innumerable bodies of commissioners created by private Acts, which exercised limited powers for purposes such as police, paving, lighting, turnpikes and local improvements. Through the curtailment of the powers of the Privy Council in the previous century, they were free from administrative control by central government, but in England they were subject to legal control by means of the prerogative writs issued by the Court of King's Bench.

These bodies were essentially local in character. In the period of social and administrative reform that followed the reform of Parliament in 1832, experiments were made in setting up national agencies with powers covering the whole country. One of the most notable experiments occurred in 1834 when the English Poor Law was reformed. The Poor Law Commissioners enforced strict central control on the local administration of poor relief, by means of rules, orders and inspection. Yet no minister answered for the commissioners in Parliament, to defend them against political attack or to control their decisions.

In 1847, the experiment gave way to a system based on a minister responsible to Parliament but similar experiments occurred, such as the General Board of Health in 1848.[11] By the late 19th century, it was accepted that the vesting of public powers in departments of central government had the great constitutional advantage of securing political control through ministerial responsibility.[12] As Chester remarked, the House of Commons has never found a way of making anybody other than ministers accountable to it (an assessment that may need to be revised in light of the introduction and development of select committees).[13]

In the 20th century, new public bodies were created as the state took wide-ranging powers to intervene more extensively in social and economic affairs, to improve the general well-being of the population. Steps were taken to regulate working conditions (and to create trade boards and wages councils for this purpose); new national insurance and social security systems were created (with different boards and commissions established to manage the various schemes); and a national health service was set up (along with various bodies to administer its operation).

Nationalisation

In addition to the foregoing, the Labour governments from 1945 onwards adopted a programme of nationalisation of many key areas of the economy, leading to the creation of public corporations like the National Coal Board and British Rail to administer the industries taken

---

[9] See also the Public Accounts Committee referring to Cabinet Office evidence in a review of public bodies), ibid: 'the landscape of arm's-length bodies was "not particularly clear across government", "very messy", and to some degree "an accident of history"' (para 5).

[10] As with financial relief for the unemployed in 1934: see Millett, *The Unemployment Assistance Board*.

[11] Administration by the board system was much used in Scotland and in Ireland.

[12] See also ch 5 above and, for rise and fall of the board system, F M G Willson (1955) 33 *Public Administration* 43, and Parris, *Constitutional Bureaucracy*, ch 3.

[13] D N Chester (1979) 57 *Public Administration* 51, 54. See below, pp 324–5.

into public ownership. In theory, the tasks entrusted to public boards and agencies could also have been undertaken directly by civil servants working in government departments, although this would mean a vast increase in the civil service and the adoption by it of new methods.

Indeed as we have already seen, postal and telephone services were for very many years provided by the Post Office as a government department.[14] But the existence of public corporations affords strong evidence for the view that departmental administration of major industries was thought likely to be less efficient and flexible than management by a public board. Ministers would no doubt also wish to avoid the levels of parliamentary scrutiny and responsibility associated with direct departmental administration.

The post-war nationalisation legislation thus sought to apply the concept of the public corporation associated with the leading Labour politician Herbert Morrison.[15] Under these arrangements, the relevant ministers were given important powers relating to the boards but were not expected to become concerned with day-to-day management of the industries. These general powers were infrequently used, though it was claimed that ministers could not avoid responsibility for the general inefficiency of a board, as illustrated by a variety of incidents in its day-to-day administration.[16]

The nationalisation model nevertheless presented problems of parliamentary accountability, given the nature of the British system which presumed that a public authority can be controlled by Parliament only through a responsible Minister of the Crown.[17] One solution was the creation of a Select Committee in 1956 to examine the reports and accounts of the nationalised industries, the latter a step in the journey that led to the Select Committee system created in 1979 and now operating with such conspicuous success.[18] It was also a step in a journey which has led to individuals other than ministers being accountable to Parliament.

Privatisation

Conservative governments after 1979 introduced a policy of privatisation of public corporations, whereby the ownership of many state-controlled enterprises was transferred to the private sector. In an important report by the Public Accounts Committee published in 1998, it was stated that:

> During that time over 150 United Kingdom businesses have been privatised, ranging from major undertakings with billions of pounds to small loss-making enterprises. In the process, the proportion of Gross Domestic Product accounted for by state-owned businesses has fallen from 11 per cent to 2 per cent. These privatisations have shared a number of overall objectives, including improving the efficiency of the business concerned, promoting the development of a market economy, reducing state debt and increasing state revenues.[19]

The privatisation programme took several forms, including the denationalisation and breakup of state corporations such as British Gas, British Telecom, British Airways, British Coal and British Rail;[20] the disposal of shares in companies previously owned by the

---

14 See now Postal Services Act 2011.
15 See Morrison, *Government and Parliament*, ch 12.
16 E C S Wade and G G Phillips (7th ed by E C S Wade and A W Bradley, 1965), p 288.
17 Ibid, p 289.
18 See ch 8 above.
19 HC 992 (1997–8).
20 See Gas Act 1986, Civil Aviation Act 1980, Telecommunications Act 1984, Railways Act 1993 and Coal Industry Act 1994. Other major privatisations included water (Water Act 1989) and electricity (Electricity Act 1989).

government (such as Jaguar, Rolls-Royce, Amersham International, British Nuclear Fuels Ltd, and Cable and Wireless);[21] and the sale of government holdings in companies such as British Petroleum.[22] Two hotly contested privatisations, for different reasons, were of the water supply industry in England and Wales, and the Trustee Savings Bank.[23]

Two politically symbolic privatisations were those of the coal industry and the railways, both of which had been nationalised by the post-war Labour government. Yet this programme of privatisation has not removed the need for public bodies, but to the emergence of different kinds of bodies to regulate rather than manage the public utilities. These include the Gas and Electricity Markets Authority established under the Utilities Act 2000, with similar bodies having been created by the legislation privatising telecommunications, water and the railways, as well as in a number of other public services.

It is important to emphasise that public bodies do not exist simply to manage public utilities or public services. And as already pointed out, it is important also to emphasise that public bodies also perform a regulatory function. Changing ideas about the role of the state partially dictate the changing role of such bodies and the nature of the activities in which they are engaged. Despite the apparent 'hollowing out' of the state since the 1980s, the role of public bodies remains and is calculated always to be wide ranging and far reaching. It seems that even free markets cannot be trusted to operate without regulatory supervision.

B. Categories of public body

Non-ministerial departments (NMDs)

Public bodies take a number of forms, beginning now with NMDs. According to the Cabinet Office, there were 20 NMDs in 2017, in contrast to 26 ministerial departments.[24] These NMDs are at best a constitutional curiosity,[25] and as their name suggests, NMDs are not led by a minister for the department's activities, but in the case of the National Crime Agency, for example, by a Director General appointed by the Home Secretary.[26] NMD staff are civil servants, and NMDs differ from executive agencies to the extent that they are independent departments rather than agencies with an arm's-length relationship with departments.[27] As discussed below, there may not be much to distinguish some NMDs from other categories (such as NDPBs).[28]

The 21 NMDs include the utility regulators, such as the Gas and Electricity Markets Authority and the Water Services Regulation Authority (OFWAT), considered more fully below. But they also include other important bodies encountered at various points in the text,

21 See Atomic Energy (Miscellaneous Provisions) Act 1981 (Amersham, BNFL); British Telecommunications Act 1981, s 79 (Cable and Wireless). See also Atomic Energy Authority Act 1995. For the developments in the motor industry, see A A McLaughlin and W A Maloney (1996) 74 *Public Administration* 435.

22 On this form of state intervention (the mixed enterprise), see pp 309–10 of the 10th edn of this book.

23 See *Ross* v *Lord Advocate* [1986] 1 WLR 1077; and M Percival (1987) 50 MLR 231.

24 https://www.gov.uk/government/organisations.

25 J Rutter, *The Strange Case of Non Ministerial Departments* (Institute for Government, 2013) (describing NMDs as a 'oxymoronic anomaly').

26 Crime and Courts Act 2013, Sch 1.

27 As already pointed out, they continue to be created, as in the case of the National Crime Agency: Crime and Courts Act 2013.

28 Two recently created NMDs – the National Crime Agency and the Competition and Markets Authority – were created to replace pre-existing NDPBs (the Serious Organised Crime Agency, and the Competition Commission respectively, though the Competition and Markets Authority also inherited work previously performed by the Office of Fair Trading, also an NMD).

such as the CPS (Chapter 13) and (as already mentioned) the National Crime Agency (Chapter 15), as well as HMRC, the National Archives, the UK Statistics Authority and agencies like the Food Standards Agency. Curiously, the Supreme Court of the United Kingdom is classified as an NMD, as is the Government Legal Department. Scope for parliamentary accountability is unclear, the government claiming that it is the minister in the department with whom the NMD works who will be accountable to Parliament.[29]

NMDs are creatures of statute, though the statutes creating them do not make use of the term 'non-ministerial department', which appears to be an administrative rather than a legal designation. There may be legal clues as to this status in the legislation establishing these bodies, but if so they are deeply buried, for there may be little formally to distinguish an NMD from an NDPB (on which see below).[30] To this end, a comparison of two bodies operating in two quite different fields is quite striking. Thus while both ACAS (in the field of industrial relations) and the NCA (in the field of policing) are appointed by ministers, exercise their functions on behalf of the Crown[31] and are staffed by civil servants, the former is an NDPB and the latter an NMD.

Just to add to the confusion, an NDPB may also be regarded as if it were a government department for the purposes of the Crown Proceedings Act 1947.[32] Otherwise, NMD members will normally be expressly disqualified from membership of the House of Commons, as in the case for example of the members of the Food Standards Agency and the National Crime Agency.[33] In this sense NMDs differ from ministerial departments at least to the extent that the minister must by convention be a member of Parliament (even if departmental staff as civil servants are disqualified).[34] It is an open question, however, whether NMDs really differ from NDPBs in this respect, given that at least in some – if not all – cases there is a similar disqualification.[35]

Non-departmental public bodies (NDPBs)

There is no legal definition of an NDPB. For administrative purposes, however, an NDPB is defined as a 'body which has a role in the processes of national government, but is not a government department, or part of one, and which accordingly operates to a greater or lesser extent at arm's length from ministers'.[36] They are distinguished from executive agencies, which are 'clearly designated (and financially viable) business units within departments which are responsible for undertaking the executive functions of that department, as distinct from giving policy advice', with 'a clear focus on delivering specified outputs within a framework of accountability to Ministers'.[37]

---

[29] See Cabinet Office, *Classification of Public Bodies: Guidance for Departments* (2016), part 2.4. This would be true also of NDPBs. Select committees provide the only real opportunity to hold NMDs to account. See below, pp 324–5.

[30] The main clue will be that the NMD has its own estimate voted by Parliament annually.

[31] Crime and Courts Act 2013, Sch 1(1).

[32] Health and Safety at Work Act 1974, s 10 (Health and Safety Executive).

[33] Food Standards Act 1999, Sch 1, para 7. Similar provision is made in the case of other NMDs. See generally ch 7 above.

[34] See ch 7 G.

[35] Equality Act 2006, Sch 1. Although there is no statutory disqualification of ACAS council or HSE board members, it is nevertheless difficult to see how membership of these bodies could be performed by someone who was also an MP.

[36] Cabinet Office, *Categories of Public Bodies: A Guide for Departments* (2013), p 16. The definition is still in use: Cabinet Office, *Classification of Public Bodies*, above, part 2.3. See also HC 488 (2016–17), para 5.

[37] Cabinet Office, *Classification of Public Bodies*, ibid, part 2.3.

Despite their role in national government, it is said to be atypical for NDPBs to be 'part of the Crown', and to be usual for them to have their own legal personality.[38] In addition, it may be expressly stated that members of the NDPB in question are not to be 'regarded as the servant or agent of the Crown'.[39] Yet there is no consistency: although the NDPB in question may be a 'body corporate', in the case of ACAS it is one that is stated expressly to perform its functions 'on behalf of the Crown'.[40] This is qualified so as not 'to make [ACAS] subject to directions of any kind from any Minister of the Crown as to the manner in which it is to exercise its functions under any enactment'.[41]

The Cabinet Office reported in 2013 that there were 497 NDPBs, this by far the largest category of public bodies (though there are many fewer now).[42] Within this category there were reported to be:

- Executive NDPBs, which carry out administrative, regulatory and executive functions. Examples of such bodies include the Advisory Conciliation and Arbitration Service (ACAS), the Equality and Human Rights Commission, the Higher Education Funding Council, the Care Quality Commission, and the Independent Police Complaints Commission.

- Advisory NDPBs set up to 'provide independent and expert advice to ministers on particular topics of interest'. Included in this category are, the Commission on Human Medicines, the Low Pay Commission, the Committee on Fuel Poverty, the Regulatory Policy Committee, and the Office for Budgetary Responsibility.

In addition to the Executive and Advisory NDPBs, there are also Tribunal NDPBs sponsored by individual departments, though this anachronistic classification is being phased out. Some of these tribunals deal with important economic and political questions, in some cases raising sensitive human rights questions, and their members may include senior judges, raising questions about why this particular form is adopted for such purposes. Examples from diverse fields include the Central Arbitration Committee, the Competition Appeal Tribunal, the Copyright Tribunal, the Insolvency Practitioners Tribunal, and (even more curiously) the Investigatory Powers Tribunal (on which see Chapter 19 below).

Public corporations

Public corporations are a dwindling and motley category of public bodies that in the past included a number of nationally significant institutions, such as the National Coal Board, the British Railways Board, and the British Gas Corporation. Although the category is now greatly diminished, it still includes bodies such as the BBC, Channel 4 and the Civil Aviation Authority, and a few more besides. The idea of a public corporation is one that has an important historical and political resonance, and refers back to the post-war era of nationalisation, from which – perhaps regrettably – all political parties have sought to distance themselves.

---

[38] Cabinet Office, *Categories of Public Bodies: A Guide for Departments*, above, p 15; Cabinet Office, *Classification of Public Bodies*, ibid, part 2.3.

[39] Equality Act 2006, Sch 1, para 42(1)(a) (Equality and Human Rights Commission).

[40] Trade Union and Labour Relations (Consolidation) Act 1992, s 247(3). The Health and Safety Executive, also created to exercise functions previously exercised by departments, is also stated to perform its functions on behalf of the Crown: Health and Safety at Work etc. Act 1974, s 10(7).

[41] Ibid. See also Equality Act 2006: the minister 'shall have regard to the desirability of ensuring that the [Equality and Human Rights] Commission is under as few constraints as reasonably possible in determining (a) its activities . . .' (Sch 1, para 42(3)).

[42] Cabinet Office, *Public Bodies – Summary Data* (2014)

Nevertheless, public corporations still exist, in some – though not all – cases as a creature of statute (the BBC and the BBC World Service being notable exceptions). Public corporations – which are thought to be most appropriate where they can operate commercially – are likely to work at a greater distance from ministers than other public bodies. Thus, the Civil Aviation Authority is expressly stated 'not to be regarded as the servant or agent of the Crown or as enjoying any status, privilege or immunity of the Crown'. Nor is its property to be regarded as Crown property.[43]

But distance does not mean complete autonomy, and the distinction from NDPBs may not be easy to draw. Before the abolition of the Audit Commission in 2015,[44] the Secretary of State was empowered to 'give the Commission directions as to the discharge of its functions and the Commission shall give effect to any such directions'.[45] The Commission was obliged to provide the Secretary of State with 'such information relating to the discharge of its functions as he may require', and for that purpose the Commission must permit 'any person authorised by [the minister] to inspect and make copies of any accounts or other documents of the Commission'.[46]

It is notable that when a number of failing banks had to be rescued by being taken into public ownership during the banking crisis in 2008, no attempt was made to use the classic public corporation model for this purpose. Thus, when the (Labour) government stepped in with a financial rescue package, it did so by securing shareholdings in the banks in question. These shareholdings were then managed on behalf of the 'taxpayer as shareholder' (an implausible notion) by UK Financial Investments Ltd, a company established under the Companies Act, with the Treasury being the sole shareholder.[47]

Parliamentary bodies

A new category of public body to have emerged in recent years has been referred to as parliamentary bodies, by virtue of the fact that the bodies in question are not only created by Parliament but are also accountable directly to Parliament rather than a minister. These include the Parliamentary Commissioner for Administration, the National Audit Office, the Electoral Commission, and the Independent Parliamentary Standards Authority. There is also a separate category of independent office-holders, such as the Commissioner for Public Appointments considered below.

Reinforcing the sense that they appear to be designed to be independent of the government of the day, these bodies are not to be regarded as servants or agents of the Crown, or as enjoying any status, immunity or privileges of the Crown. Nor are their staff, who are to be appointed on terms determined by the body in question, though in the case of the Electoral Commission, 'the Commission shall have regard to the desirability of keeping the remuneration and other terms and conditions of employment of its staff broadly in line with those applying to persons employed in the civil service of the State'.[48]

---

[43] Civil Aviation Act 1982, s 2(4).

[44] Local Audit and Accountability Act 2014, s 1. The Audit Commission was also improbably classified as a public corporation, though it was very different from the great institutions created after World War II to run the public utilities.

[45] Audit Commission Act 1998, Sch 1, para 3(1). The Audit Commission's role is now performed by Public Sector Audits Ltd, an independent company limited by guarantee incorporated by the Local Government Association, exercising powers delegated to it under statute.

[46] Audit Commission Act 1998, Sch 1, para 3(2). But 'no direction shall be given by the Secretary of State and no information shall be required by him under this paragraph in respect of any particular body subject to audit' (ibid, para 3(3)).

[47] In other words, it was the Treasury, not the taxpayer, that was the shareholder.

[48] Political Parties, Elections and Referendums Act 2000, Sch 1, para 11(5).

As suggested, a distinguishing feature of these bodies is that they are directly responsible to Parliament, and not indirectly responsible through an appropriate minister as appears generally to be the case in relation to NMDs and NDPBs, as explained above. In the case of the Electoral Commission, this responsibility is via the cross-party Speaker's Committee,[49] which has important responsibilities for the budget of the Commission. Although it is inevitable that ministers should have a say in the appointment of Commissioners, their influence is limited by a statutory duty to consult the leaders of other political parties.[50]

Similar arrangements apply in relation to the National Audit Office,[51] with slight variations (there is no Speaker's committee). The NAO is not the servant or agent of the Crown, nor are its employees, though there is a requirement to have regard to the desirability of maintaining pay parity with the civil service. The Prime Minister nominates the chair of the NAO, and in doing so must have the agreement of the chair of the Public Accounts Committee and thereafter the approval of the House of Commons. Other members are appointed by and may be removed by the Public Accounts Commission.[52]

C. Status, functions and powers

Status

Except where statutes provide otherwise, departments of central government share in the legal status of the Crown and may benefit from certain privileges and immunities peculiar to the Crown.[53] But local authorities, statutory bodies set up for local commercial purposes and privately owned companies do not benefit from Crown status.[54] Into which category do other public bodies fall?

> In *Tamlin* v *Hannaford*, it had to be decided whether, after nationalisation of the railways, a dwelling-house owned by the British Transport Commission was subject to the Rent Restriction Acts or was exempted from them by virtue of being Crown property. After examining the Transport Act 1947, the Court of Appeal rejected the view that the Commission was the servant or agent of the Crown, even though the Ministry of Transport had wide statutory powers of control over the Commission:
>
> 'In the eye of the law, the corporation is its own master and is answerable as fully as any other person or corporation. It is not the Crown and has none of the immunities or privileges of the Crown. Its servants are not civil servants and its property is not Crown property . . . It is, of course, a public authority and its purposes, no doubt, are public purposes, but it is not a government department nor do its powers fall within the province of government.'[55]

---

[49] Ibid, s 2.

[50] Ibid, s 3.

[51] The NAO has responsibility for the scrutiny of government finances on behalf of Parliament.

[52] Budget Responsibility and National Audit Act 2011, Sch 2. The Public Accounts Commission is a cross-party committee of senior MPs established by the National Audit Act 1983 with responsibility to keep the work of the NAO under review.

[53] Chs 10 D and 26 D.

[54] *Mersey Docks and Harbour Trustees* v *Gibbs* (1866) LR 1 HL 93; ch 26 A.

[55] [1950] 1 KB 18, 24 (Denning LJ).

It would seem that this decision would govern the status of other public corporations, unless they are expressly made to act by and on behalf of the Crown or are directly placed under a minister of the Crown. In *Pfizer Corpn* v *Ministry of Health*,[56] it was held that, since a hospital board was acting on behalf of the then Minister of Health, the treatment of patients in NHS hospitals was a government function and thus the use of drugs was use 'for the services of the Crown'; the Crown could therefore make use of its special rights under patent law for importing drugs.[57] NHS immunities were later removed by statute.[58]

It is not clear how helpful the distinctions drawn in the *Tamlin* case would be today. If we take the National Crime Agency as an example, as an NMD it is notionally an independent body, but the Home Secretary sets its strategic priorities. In the absence of legislation putting the question beyond doubt, is it part of the Crown or not following the *Tamlin* test? For this reason the modern practice of making clear in statute whether the body in question is part of the Crown or not is a good one. In this case it is stated expressly that the NCA operates 'on behalf of the Crown'.[59]

But if the function of the body and its relationship to government may not now provide a clear answer to questions of this kind, nor will the status of the body in question. Although it might be expected that NMDs would be treated as part of the Crown, there is often very little to distinguish an NMD from an NDPB. Yet while it might be assumed from the nature of their activities that the latter would invariably be part of the Crown, this is not normally the government's intention, to clarify which legislation is required in the way outlined above. As we have seen, that legislation does not always make consistent provision for NDPBs.

Policy-making and regulatory functions

As suggested in the introduction to this chapter, public bodies can be said to be set up to perform a number of overlapping functions.[60] The first is **policy-making**, the Bank of England being perhaps the best-known example, with a number of responsibilities that have evolved over its long history.[61] These include acting as banker to the government and to the clearing banks; the implementation of monetary policy; and the issue of currency.[62] A major initiative introduced in 1997 was to give the Bank operational responsibility to set interest rates.[63] This was done 'to ensure that decision-making on monetary policy was more effective, open, accountable, and free from short-term political manipulation'.[64]

Under the Bank of England Act 1998 the Bank is responsible for monetary policy within the objectives set out in the Act: these are to maintain price stability and to support the economic policy of the government, 'including its objectives for growth and employment' (s 11). It is the

[56] [1965] AC 512.
[57] By contrast, in the BBC were held not to be entitled to benefit from the Crown's immunity from taxation in *BBC* v *Johns* [1965] Ch 32, since broadcasting had not become a function of the central government. It was strange that financial considerations led the BBC in this case to argue its close dependence upon the Crown and central government, whereas usually the BBC is anxious to stress its independence.
[58] National Health Service and Community Care Act 1990.
[59] Crime and Courts Act 2013, Sch 1.
[60] Many of these bodies have multiple functions. For example, according to its website, the role of the Care Quality Commission is to 'monitor, inspect and regulate'.
[61] The government previously classified the Bank of England as a public corporation. It was then treated sui generis as a 'central bank', and now as one several hundred 'agencies and other public bodies'.
[62] Responsibilities for the management of government debt were transferred to the Treasury (HC Deb, 20 May 1997, col 509) and for the supervision of other banks and financial institutions to the Financial Services Authority (Bank of England Act 1998, s 21).
[63] HC Deb, 6 May 1997, col 509; also HC Deb, 20 May 1997, col 507 et seq.
[64] HC Deb, 20 May 1997, col 508 (Mr Gordon Brown).

specific responsibility of the Monetary Policy Committee of the Bank of England to formulate monetary policy. The committee consists of the governor and the deputy governors, two senior Bank officials with responsibility for monetary policy and market operations, but also 'four other expert members appointed from outside the Bank by the government'.[65]

Apart from policy-making, public bodies have a prominent **regulatory role**, notably in relation to public utilities.[66] The key to the regulatory model initially adopted for this purpose is the 'single independent regulator for each industry, operating without undue bureaucracy and supported by a small staff', the government rejecting regulatory systems found overseas, 'in favour of a quicker and less bureaucratic system of regulation'.[67] This model was strongly criticised by the Comptroller and Auditor General, who raised questions about 'the over-concentration of power in one pair of hands', leading him to consider whether there might be a case for 'possible alternatives to the current system of industry-specific regulation by single regulators'.

The gas and electricity regulators – OFGAS and OFFER – were merged in 1999 to become OFGEM (the Office of Gas and Electricity Markets), which operates under the direction of the Gas and Electricity Markets Authority.[68] In taking these steps, the government explained that the task of regulation was becoming increasingly complex, with the interests of what are now hundreds of licensees to be considered and balanced. It thus is accepted that regulatory responsibilities can best be undertaken by a regulatory authority, to ensure that regulatory decisions are 'less dependent on the personality of a single regulator', thereby ensuring in turn greater continuity and consistency in decision-making.[69]

Supervisory and advisory functions

A different role performed by public bodies is in **supervising various regulatory regimes**, usually to ensure that minimum standards are followed in the area within which the body in question operates. The Information Commissioner's Office is a good example, with responsibility for the Data Protection Act 1998 and the Freedom of Information Act 2000. Under the former, the Commissioner manages a scheme whereby those who process personal data must register with the ICO in accordance with statutory requirements. The ICO also has power to ensure that data are not unlawfully processed, and to take action against those who are alleged to be acting in breach of the Act.

Another example is the Gangmasters and Labour Abuse Authority, which supervises the supply of labour in (mainly food processing) sections of the economy, where workers have been found to be particularly vulnerable to exploitation. The labour suppliers in these sectors (known as gangmasters) must obtain a GLAA licence, and in order to do so they must meet various licence conditions relating to wages, health and safety, and accommodation for the workers in question. It is an offence to operate without a licence, and the GLAA enforcement officers have a duty to conduct investigations, as well as wide powers to investigate offences, including powers of arrest (on which see below).[70]

---

[65] Ibid. The Treasury has reserve powers to give the Bank directions relating to monetary policy in 'extreme economic circumstances' (s 19). The government expected this power to be used 'rarely, if at all' (HC Deb, 20 May 1997, col 509).

[66] Important contributions are Graham, *Regulating Public Utilities*, Prosser, *Laws and the Regulators*, and T Prosser, in Jowell, Oliver and O'Cinneide (eds), *The Changing Constitution* (8th ed), ch 12, which give a good insight into the scale and scope of regulatory activity in contemporary Britain.

[67] A Carlsberg (1992) 37 *New York Law School Law Rev* 285.

[68] Utilities Act 2000. For background see Cm 3898, 1998; T Prosser (1999) 62 MLR 196.

[69] HL Deb, 4 May 2000, col 1141.

[70] Gangmasters (Licensing) Act 2004, amended by the Immigration Act 2016.

Turning from supervisory to **advisory functions**, it is important to note here that advice in this context has a scale of meanings, from the non-prescriptive (in the sense that it need only to be considered) to the highly prescriptive (in the sense that there is an expectation that it will normally be acted upon). The Low Pay Commission is an advisory body operating at the higher end of the scale, with a responsibility under the National Minimum Wage Act 1998 to set the level of the national minimum wage. If the minister decides not to act on the recommendations of the LPC, he or she must report to both Houses of Parliament his or her reasons for doing so.[71]

The LPC is an advisory NDPB, as is the Police Remuneration Review Body, which replaced the Police Negotiating Board in 2014.[72] Before making regulations for police pay and conditions of service, the Home Secretary must normally seek and consider the advice of the PRRB, the chair of which is appointed by the Prime Minister and the members of which are appointed by the Home Secretary. Before making any decision on the advice of the PRRB, the Home Secretary must consult organisations representing police officers. In some circumstances the Home Secretary may make a decision without referring the matter to the PRRB.

Powers

It has already been suggested that some public bodies have significant powers in terms of the functions they perform. Some perform multiple roles, of what might be referred to as roles of a legislative, executive or judicial (or quasi-judicial) nature, and they are equipped with the capacity to perform these different roles. Among NMDs this is particularly true of the utility regulators, with the Gas and Electricity Markets Authority having the power to make statutory instruments (a legislative power); to issue licences, vary the terms of licences and regulate the activities of licence holders (an executive power); and deal with complaints from consumers (a quasi-judicial power).

Under the Utilities Act 2000, the regulator also has the power to impose financial penalties on licence holders who have breached a licence condition, a power which has given rise to questions about compliance with art 6 of the ECHR (which guarantees the right to a fair trial in the determination of civil rights and obligations):

> How can the regulator, who determines the penalty, be an independent and impartial tribunal? The regulator decides whether he will pursue the licensee. He assesses whether the licensee has broken the terms of his licence. He then decides what the penalty is. He is an individual appointed by the executive . . . he is legislator, prosecutor and judge, all rolled into one.[73]

There are also examples of NDPBs having a wide range of powers of this kind, though perhaps not on this scale.[74]

While public bodies are curious institutions for the blend of powers they may have, the same is true of the nature of some of their powers. As an NMD, the National Crime Agency has powers that perhaps no government department – ministerial or otherwise – ought to have. Notable in this respect is the power of the Director General of the NCA to designate

---

[71] National Minimum Wage 1998, s 1(4).

[72] Anti-social Behaviour, Crime and Policing Act 2014, amending the Police Act 1996.

[73] HL Deb, 4 May 2000, col 1171 (Lord Kingsland). There is, however, a right of appeal against the imposition of a penalty and against the amount of the penalty: Gas Act 1986, s 30E, as inserted by Utilities Act 2000, s 95.

[74] The Certification Officer for Trade Unions and Employers' Associations is perhaps an example of such a body with a blend of 'legislative', executive and quasi-judicial functions: see Collins, Ewing and McColgan, *Labour Law*, ch 13. These powers were greatly strengthened by the Trade Union Act 2016: S Cavalier and R Arthur (2016) 45 ILJ 363.

NCA officers as having the powers and privileges of a constable; an officer of Revenue and Customs; and/or an immigration officer.[75] It is then provided that

If an NCA officer (other than the Director General) is designated as a person having the powers and privileges of a constable, the NCA officer has –

(a) in England and Wales and the adjacent United Kingdom waters, all the powers and privileges of an English and Welsh constable;

(b) in Scotland and the adjacent United Kingdom waters, all the powers and privileges of a Scottish constable;

(c) in Northern Ireland and the adjacent United Kingdom waters, all the powers and privileges of a Northern Ireland constable; and

(d) outside the United Kingdom and the United Kingdom waters, all the powers and privileges of a constable that are exercisable overseas.[76]

But it is not only NMDs that have powers of this kind. NDPBs with enforcement functions are also likely to have extensive powers, as in the case of the Gangmasters and Labour Abuse Authority, which is authorised to appoint enforcement and compliance officers respectively to ensure the Act is followed. These officers have wide powers 'for the purposes of the Act' to demand (i) the production of documents (including access to computers), (ii) explanations about the documents, (iii) the provision of information, as well as (iv) to enter private property without a warrant. Additional powers authorise GLAA officers to apply for search warrants to enter and search private property where unlicensed activities are suspected to be taking place,[77] and the Home Secretary is now empowered to extend all police powers in the Police and Criminal Evidence Act 1984 to labour abuse prevention officers.[78]

D. Appointments to public bodies

Committee on Standards in Public Life

The members of public bodies exercise a government function, yet are appointed by ministers or civil servants rather than elected. Not surprisingly, political patronage of this kind has given rise to concern and was fully addressed by the Committee on Standards in Public Life (CSPL),[79] itself an advisory NDPB established in 1995. The first report of the Committee is famous for having developed seven principles for the conduct of public life (selflessness, integrity, objectivity, accountability, openness, honesty and leadership).[80]

Also in its first report, the CSPL found no evidence of political bias in public appointments, and rejected calls for an impartial and independent body to be given the responsibility

---

[75] Crime and Courts Act 2013, s 10.

[76] Ibid, Sch 5, para 10. This is subject to a number of limitations and qualifications relating to Scotland and Northern Ireland in particular. Tucked away in the Crime and Courts Act 2013, Sch 5 are provisions making it an offence to resist, wilfully obstruct or assault a designated NCA officer: ibid, Sch 5, paras 21–4.

[77] Gangmasters (Licensing) Act 2004, ss 15–17. For similar provisions in a wholly different field, see Health and Social Care Act 2008, ss 62–5 (Care Quality Commission). Workplace health and safety inspectors have also long had powers of entry.

[78] Immigration Act 2016, s 12, inserting new PACE 1984, s 114B.

[79] Cm 2850-I, 1995. One complaint was that public bodies were ceasing to be representative and were increasingly dominated by business people. However, it was to a businessman that the government turned to review the procedures rather than the CPSL: Grimstone, *Better Public Appointments*, above.

[80] These are the so-called 'Nolan principles' after the Committee's first chair (Lord Nolan).

for making appointments, recommending that 'ultimate responsibility for appointments should remain with ministers'. But it did not follow that ministers 'should act with unfettered discretion', and it was proposed that existing procedures should be 'substantially improved' in order to ensure that they were 'sufficiently robust'.

The first of two safeguards proposed by the CSPL (or Nolan Committee as it was sometimes called) was that appointments should embrace: the principle of appointment on merit; the principle that 'selection on merit should take account of the need to appoint boards which include a balance of skills and backgrounds'; and the principle that appointments should be made only after advice from a panel or committee which included independent members, who would normally account for at least one-third of the membership.

Apart from 'the establishment of [these] clear published principles governing selections for appointment, the second safeguard against abuse proposed by Nolan was the more effective external scrutiny of appointments. This latter safeguard was to be achieved principally by the appointment of a Commissioner for Public Appointments to 'monitor, regulate, and approve departmental appointments procedures', and to draw up a Code of Practice for public appointments procedures.

Commissioner for Public Appointments

The Nolan recommendations were accepted by the government of the day, and a Commissioner for Public Appointments was appointed (under the prerogative rather than statute) by an Order in Council in November 1995. The role of the Commissioner was to oversee the way public appointments are made to the executive departmental bodies, a term defined then to include only 274 NDPBs and NHS bodies. The jurisdiction of the Commissioner has since been extended and now covers NMDs, NDPBs, health bodies, public corporations, public broadcasting authorities and utility regulators. Although there are still a number of exempt posts, it is thought that the process now covers tens of thousands of positions.

Until 2016 the Commissioner was responsible for both providing the guidance to be followed in the making of public appointments, and in monitoring the application of the guidance. However, the procedures were radically reformed in 2016, following a review of the appointments procedure by a leading businessman appointed by the Cabinet Office. In an oft-quoted passage the review found that 'too many public appointments take far too long to conclude which is both inefficient and can deter good candidates from applying'.[81] Controversially, however, the review also recommended changes to the role of the Commissioner, which caused 'disquiet' and led to parliamentary criticism.[82]

Public appointments are now governed by the Public Appointments Order in Council 2016, which applies in relation to the large number of public bodies listed in a Schedule. It is the responsibility of the Minister for the Cabinet Office to prepare, publish and keep under review a governance code for public appointments, displacing what previously had been the responsibility of the Commissioner to 'prescribe and publish' a code of practice for this purpose. The governance code must set out the 'principles of public appointments' and the practices to be followed in making these appointments. The role of the Commissioner is to ensure that appointing authorities act in accordance with the code and the principles of public appointment.

The Commissioner – who continues to be appointed under the prerogative[83] – must be consulted about the content of the code. Otherwise, he is empowered to audit the procedures and practices followed by appointing authorities; conduct investigations into any aspect of

---

[81] Grimstone, *Better Public Appointments*, above, para 3.31
[82] HC 495 (2016–17).
[83] Public Appointments Commissioner Order in Council 2016.

public appointments with a view to improving their quality; and conduct an inquiry into any particular public appointment, following a complaint or otherwise. The Commissioner is also required to publish an annual report which must include details of any audit or inquiry conducted in the year in question. The Commissioner has been subject to scrutiny by select committees,[84] as well as the Committee on Standards in Public Life.[85]

Governance Code on Public Appointments

The Governance Code on Public Appointments has replaced the OFCA Code of Practice which had been rewritten in 2012, and is now a short document of only eight pages replacing an over-lengthy text of 126 pages which had been drafted in 2002. The redrafting of the OFCA Code had been applauded by the Public Administration Select Committee,[86] the current code eschewing detail in favour of general principles to be followed in the making of public appointments. The relatively short principles-based text also includes general guidance about the procedures to be followed in making appointments.

The Governance Code sets out eight principles of public appointments. The first principle is ministerial responsibility, with ministers ultimately accountable to Parliament for selections made. The second principle of selflessness means that ministers making these appointments should act solely in the national interest, while by the third principle of integrity ministers must not put themselves under obligation to people who may 'try inappropriately to influence them in their work'. Nor should they take decisions to gain benefits for themselves or their families, while any conflicts of interest must be declared and resolved.

Otherwise, perhaps the most important of the principles is the fourth, which provides that all public appointments should be made on 'merit', with the remaining four principles emphasizing the need for 'openness', in the form of open and transparent appointment procedures; 'diversity' to include a balance of skills and backgrounds; 'assurance', meaning processes with appropriate checks and balances; and 'fairness', with each candidate to be assessed on the basis of the same criteria for the position in question. The role of the Commissioner is highlighted especially in relation to providing 'independent assurance'.

So far as the process of public appointments is concerned, the Governance Code outlines the responsibilities of departments, ministers and the Commissioner respectively. It also provides that ministers should be assisted in making appointments by an Advisory Assessment Panel which should include a departmental official and an independent member. In the case of 'significant appointments' to be agreed between departments and the Commissioner, the Advisory Assessment Panel must include a Senior Independent Panel Member who is familiar with senior recruitment.

Political activists and ministerial involvement

A particularly important issue in dealing with the potential problem of patronage and cronyism is the political background of individual applicants. This is a tricky question, because although there may be a need to stop the abuse of patronage by filling public bodies with political placemen, it is also the case that individuals should not be denied the opportunity to serve on public bodies by virtue of their political views, while there are also cases where the

---

[84] Notably the Public Administration Select Committee: HC 165-I (2002–3); HC 122 (2006–7); HC 152 (2007–8); HC 1389 (2010–12). See also HC 495 (2016–17) (Public Administration and Constitutional Affairs Committee) (scrutinizing government changes rather than the work of the OCPA, though giving much weight to the views of the then Commissioner).

[85] See Cm 6704, 2005; and Cm 6723, 2005 (government's response).

[86] HC 1389 (2010–12).

nature of the appointment is such that it requires someone with a partisan political background (as with the political members of the Electoral Commission or the CSPL).

The solution adopted in the Governance Code is that political activity does not bar public appointment (or membership of an Advisory Assessment Panel, though it does bar membership of a Senior Independent Panel). Candidates are no longer required to declare 'any significant political activity',[87] though panel members and successful candidates are required to disclose if 'in the last five years, [they have] been employed by a political party, held a significant office in a party, [have] stood as a candidate for a party in an election, [have] publicly spoken on behalf of a political party, or [have] made significant donations or loans to a party'.

The other important question to arise relates to ministerial involvement in the appointments process. As with the previous code, the Governance Code provides too much scope for ministerial involvement, the ultimate responsibility of ministers meaning that they must be:

- involved at the beginning of the competition, when they must be asked to agree the selection process, selection criteria and publicity strategy, and to suggest potential candidates to be invited to apply;

- 'must agree the composition of Advisory Assessment Panels' which must 'actively inform Ministers of progress at every stage throughout the competition'; and

- at the end of the process, are not bound by the advice of the Advisory Assessment Panels, and may require a competition to be re-run or appoint someone judged not appointable by the panel (in which case the Commissioner must be consulted).

A final safeguard is that some senior appointments are now subject to scrutiny by select committees, a practice which is acknowledged in the Guidance Code.[88] This is an important part of the work of many select committees, and it is by no means the case that this process is a formality. Ministers are not bound by the assessments or recommendations of select committees, though a nominee who continued to appointment in the face of parliamentary concern about their suitability for office would be placed in a very difficult position. Understandably, such criticism may cause some to withdraw.[89]

E. Legality and accountability

Judicial review and NMDs

NMDs are generally created by statute, and they exercise authority on behalf of the Crown. As such there seems to be little doubt that they would be subject to judicial review, and in recent years judicial review proceedings have been initiated against NMDs as diverse as HM Revenue and Customs, the Charity Commission, the Food Standards Agency[90] and the UK Statistics Authority, in the last case unsuccessfully raising important questions relating to Convention rights (especially art 8) in relation to the conduct of the national census.[91]

---

[87] As they had been under the OCPA Code of Practice.

[88] Cm 7170, 2007, pp 28–9. See L Maer, *Pre-Appointment Hearing* (House of Commons Library SN/PC/04387 (2015)).

[89] For a very full account of pre-appointment scrutiny by select committee, see Maer, ibid.

[90] *R (Newby Foods Ltd) v Food Standards Agency* [2016] EWHC 408 (Admin).

[91] *R (Thames Water Utilities) Ltd v Water Services Regulation Authority* [2012] EWCA Civ 218; *R (Ali) v Minister for Cabinet Office and Statistics Board* [2012] EWHC 1943 (Admin).

The role of judicial review has been controversial in relation to the activities of the utility regulators. Questions were raised at an early stage about the suitability of judicial review, it being questioned whether it was 'always appropriate' or 'a substitute for proper political supervision and well thought-out decision-making procedures'.[92] Other questions related to its effectiveness, on the ground that the courts are unprepared 'to question the quality of the regulator's decision or require that the evidence underpinning the decision be examined'.[93]

In addition, at least one regulator (OFGAS) went to considerable lengths to avoid judicial review by adopting a 'deliberate policy' of refusing to give reasons for decisions and by failing to keep adequate records of reasons for decisions (in this case relating to the adoption of a particular price control). This was strongly deprecated by the Public Accounts Committee, which considered it 'essential that public bodies keep adequate records of the reasons for their decisions, to help ensure the proper conduct of public business and accountability'.[94]

The utility regulators have wide powers in relation to the utility companies, and the Utilities Act 2000 requires reasons to be given for a wide range of decisions taken by both the Gas and Electricity Markets Authority and the Secretary of State.[95] There is now an appeal from many of the decisions of the utility regulators to the Competition Appeal Tribunal (a tribunal NDPB in the Department for Business, Energy and Industrial Strategy), and from the latter tribunal to the Court of Appeal. The CAT also hears appeals from OFCOM (which deals with broadcasters).

Judicial review and NDPBs

The scope for the judicial review of NDPBs might depend on the manner and formality of their creation. Sedley LJ has already raised questions in the Court of Appeal that might apply in the context of legal proceedings against executive agencies, and in particular whether they had sufficient legal personality.[96] Similar questions could conceivably arise in the case of some NDPBs not created by statute, about which there is often little published information. Where, however, the NDPB is set up by statute, it seems unlikely that there could be any doubt about it being subject to judicial review.[97]

It is true that the founding statute will sometimes provide – as in the case of public corporations[98] – that the body in question does not act on behalf of the Crown. But this formula – used as we have seen in the case of the Equality and Human Rights Commission[99] – is not used in relation to all NDPBs.[100] In any event, although this form of words may seek to emphasise distance from ministers, it remains unequivocally the case that an NDPB is a public authority for the purposes of judicial review.[101] Whether or not the NDPB is subject to review or not will thus depend on what it does and how it does it.

As a result of the nature of their activity, some NDPBs are more likely to be subject to judicial review than others. And because of the manner of their composition and the subject

---

[92] A McHarg [1995] PL 539, at p 550.

[93] HC 481-iii (1994–5), p 77 (memorandum submitted by National Power plc). For fuller treatment of judicial review in this context, see Graham, pp 68–75.

[94] HC 37 (1996–7).

[95] Utilities Act 2000, s 87, amending Gas Act 1986, s 38A.

[96] *R (National Association of Health Stores) v Department of Health* [2003] EWCA Civ 3133, para 41.

[97] *R (JBol) Ltd v Health Protection Agency* [2011] EWCA Civ 1 (Laws LJ). See also *R (Allensway Recycling Ltd) v Environmental Agency* [2015] EWCA Civ 1289, and *R (Mott) v Environment Agency* [2016] EWCA Civ 564.

[98] On which, see *Charles Roberts and Co Ltd v British Railways Board* 1964] 3 All ER 651. See also *NUM v National Coal Board* [1986] ICR 736.

[99] Equality Act 2006, Sch 1, para 42(1)(a).

[100] As in the case of ACAS, on which see *Grunwick Processing Laboratories Ltd v ACAS* [1978] AC 655.

[101] See ch 25 below.

matter they deal with, the courts may be more or less likely to subject the body in question to intense scrutiny. So a Tribunal NDPB like the Central Arbitration Committee is by its activity (the recognition of trade unions by employers) clearly the subject of judicial review, but by virtue of the expertise of its tripartite specialist membership also shown a measure of deference by the High Court.[102]

Rather different considerations applied to the Serious Organised Crime Agency, which was an NDPB (unlike the National Crime Agency, an NMD by which it was replaced), which had the power to apply for a search warrant, and 'for these purposes [had] identical powers to those of the police'.[103] It was held in *Cook* that SOCA could not – by virtue of the Police and Criminal Evidence Act 1984 – retain documents that had been obtained as a result of a defective search warrant.[104] But in a case acknowledged by the court to be of 'real importance', the claimants had no right to the return of copies made of the documents.

Select committees and NMDs

Moving from legality to accountability, privatisation has obviously eliminated the need for scrutiny of the former nationalised industries by the select committees. But parliamentary accountability of public bodies continues to be important, and scrutiny has by no means disappeared. Both the Public Accounts Committee and the Trade and Industry Committee (as it then was) have conducted a number of enquiries into the work of the utility regulators, who have been 'fairly regular witnesses' before select committees.[105]

The Public Accounts Committee has been concerned to ensure that OFGEM (the gas regulator) maintained pressure on the gas companies to reduce their prices,[106] while the Trade and Industry Committee has in the past examined the annual reports of OFGAS,[107] and investigated the work of OFGAS and more recently OFGEM.[108] These investigations have dealt with a range of issues, although a constant refrain has related to the role of the regulator in promoting price competition on the one hand, and protecting the 'fuel poor' on the other.[109]

The select committees have also examined the work of other regulators, including OFCOM, OFWAT and the Rail Regulator,[110] while the investigation by the Culture, Media and Sport Committee into the National Lottery included an examination of the work of the National Lottery Commission.[111] Select committees have proposed important reforms to the regulatory framework,[112] including reforms to the structure and powers of the select committees, proposed by both witnesses and committees themselves.[113]

....

[102] See *R (BBC) v Central Arbitration Committee* [2003] EWHC 1375 (Admin), [2003] ICR 1542, per Moses J, esp paras 14 and 15.

[103] *R (Cook) v Serious Organised Crime Agency* [2010] EWHC 2119 (Admin), [2011] 1 WLR 144, para 1 (Leveson LJ).

[104] Ibid. On PACE 1984, see ch 15 below.

[105] HC 193-i (1999–2000), p i.

[106] HC 171 (1999–2000).

[107] HC 646 (1994–5). OFGAS is the former gas regulator.

[108] HC 185 (1993–4); HC 193-i, ii (1999–2000).

[109] HC 174 (1998–9); HC 171 (1999–2000); HC 193-ii (1999–2000); HC 206 (2003–4); HC 297 (2004–5); and HC 422 (2004–5).

[110] See HC 407 (2004–5); HC 463 (2003–4); and HC 205 (2003–4).

[111] HC 56, 57 (2000–1). The committee lamented the lack of 'relevant skills or experience on the part of the Commission', and questioned whether the body selecting the licence holder should also be the regulator. See also HC 196 (2003–4).

[112] HC 481 (1994–5).

[113] HC 646 (1994–5) (calls from gas regulator for separate select committee for the 'regulation and regulators'); HC 536 (1999–2000) (need for committee to take evidence from previous regulators where incumbent unable to explain decisions of predecessor).

Apart from investigating the utility regulators, the select committees have also examined the utility companies, and their practices, as well as the problems of fuel debt and the practice of disconnection by the gas and electricity providers. But although there is a case for greater co-ordination, proposals by the House of Lords Constitution Committee to establish a joint committee of both Houses to scrutinise 'the regulatory state' failed to secure government support.[114]

Select committees and NDPBs

In contrast to the one-time intense (though perhaps now declining) scrutiny of the NMDs (and the utility regulators in particular), select committee scrutiny of NDPBs is sporadic, being one of many tasks which fall to select committees. It is true that there have been a number of important select committee inquiries and reports into NDPBs. The Work and Pensions Select Committee inquiry into the Health and Safety NDPBs is both a case in point and a good example of the select committee system working well.[115]

But for the most part, there are too many NDPBs, and too many other demands on the time of select committees, for this to be a serious form of intense or regular scrutiny. There must be dozens of NDPBs whose work has never been examined by any select committee, and almost as many whose work is never likely to be. Indeed, in the Parliaments elected since 2010, the attention of select committees was not on the work of selected NDPBs but on whether the government had made a case for their abolition under the Public Bodies Act 2011 (below).

Such parliamentary scrutiny that does take place thus tends to be reactive, usually in response to a crisis reported in the press. The extent to which NDPBs are subject to scrutiny depends also on the priorities of the Committee in question. In the case of the Health Select Committee, since 2010 scrutiny appears to have been a high priority, with important accountability work being done in relation to the Care Quality Commission,[116] and other bodies. But there are other committees that appear to have undertaken very little or no scrutiny work of this kind.

In the Parliament elected in 2010, the Health Select Committee initiated annual accountability sessions that included NDPBs, the Committee unusually aware of the constitutional significance of NDPB scrutiny, drawing attention curiously to one NDPB as being 'independent of government and directly accountable to Parliament'.[117] Although this was a good model for other committees to follow, it was not continued by the Health Committee after the general election in 2015, and the initiative has not been followed so far by other committees.

F. Reform

Public Bodies Act 2011

On assuming office in 2010 the Coalition government embarked on a programme to overhaul the number of public bodies operating in the United Kingdom, starting with the presumption that 'if a public function is needed then it should be undertaken by a body that is

---

[114] HL Paper 68 (2003–4), and for the government's response see HL Paper 150 (2003–4). It was also proposed that 'select committees consider expanding their terms of reference to include a requirement routinely to consider and react to regulators' annual reports, and monitor the use of resources. These activities would be in addition to the *ad hoc* inquiries they undertake from time to time'.

[115] HC 246 (2007–8).

[116] HC 761 (2013–14) – a good example of the select committee system. See also HC 7779 (2010–12) – scrutiny of the Care Quality Commission by the Public Accounts Committee.

[117] HC 1431 (2010–12), para 1. Monitor is a regulatory body in the health service. See page 312 above.

democratically accountable at either national or local level'.[118] With this in mind, the government concluded that 'a body should only exist at arm's length from government if it performs a technical function; its activities require political impartiality; or it needs to act independently to establish facts'.[119]

As a result, a review of all NDPBs as well as some NMDs and public corporations led to proposals to reduce the number of public bodies from what was said then to exceed over 900 such bodies, with 200 to be abolished, and 170 to be merged into fewer than 80, leading eventually to a total reduction of about 300. Powers to enable this to be done quickly were taken in the Public Bodies Act 2011, in cases where change could only take place as a result of legislation because the bodies in question had been created by statute.

The 2011 Act gave remarkable powers to ministers to abolish by order any of the 34 bodies or categories of bodies specified in Schedule 1 of the Act (s 1), while power was also given by order to merge groups of bodies specified in Schedule 2 (such as the DPP and the Director of Revenue and Customs Protections) (s 2). In addition, power was given in sections 3 and 4 to modify by order the constitutional and/or funding arrangements of other groups of bodies listed in Schedules 3 and 4, and in s 5 to modify the functions of a number of bodies listed in Schedule 5. Together this accounted for 285 public bodies in total.

Some bodies – including the Equality and Human Rights Commission and the Administrative Justice and Tribunals Council – appeared in several Schedules, thereby giving the minister wide discretionary powers in terms of how to deal with them. The Equality and Human Rights Commission could have its constitutional arrangements, its funding arrangements, and its functions modified, and the same was true of the Administrative Justice and Tribunals Council, which could also be abolished, as a body falling within Schedule 2, as well as Schedules 3–5.

Conditions and procedures

Before these powers could be exercised, however, the minister was required to 'consider' (a very weak standard doubtless to protect against judicial review) that the order would serve the purpose of improving the exercise of public functions, having regard to efficiency, effectiveness, economy, and securing appropriate accountability to ministers (s 8(1)). All these conditions had to be met, and the minister would doubtless have been required to have reasonable grounds to consider that they had been met in any particular case.[120] It was an additional qualification that an order did not 'remove any necessary protection' (s 8(2)(a)).[121]

Ministers were required to consult with a range of interested parties before an order was made under sections 1–5. As might be expected, the parties in question included 'the body or the holder of the office to which the proposal relates', as well as others appearing to the minister 'to be representative of interests substantially affected by the proposal' (s 10). Thereafter, the minister could lay a draft order along with an explanatory document before Parliament for the purposes outlined in sections 1–5 above, which could be done after 12 weeks beginning with the start of the consultation (s 11).

The explanatory document should give reasons for the order and explain why the conditions in s 8 were met, and give an account of the representations received during the consultation process. The committee of each House responsible for scrutiny of the order (select committees in the Commons, and the Secondary Legislation Scrutiny Committee in the

---

118 Cabinet Office, *Public Bodies Reform* (2013).
119 Ibid.
120 See ch 24 below. For comment on the 2011 Act, see also ch 22 B.
121 It is also provided that the order 'does not prevent any person from continuing to exercise any right or freedom which that person might reasonably expect to continue to exercise' (s 8(2)(b)).

Lords) had 30 days to consider and clear the order (s 11(5)). The draft order was scrutinised to ensure that the foregoing statutory tests for making the order in question were met, and that the order served the purpose of improving the exercise of public functions.

If the draft order was cleared, it would then be debated with a view to approval by both Houses of Parliament. This would be done 40 days after it was laid, enabling the minister then to make an order in terms set out in the draft. If, however, the scrutiny committee had concerns, an enhanced scrutiny procedure could be invoked, permitting the period of scrutiny to be increased by another 30 days (which meant that there would be 60 days scrutiny in total). This enabled the appropriate committee to make representations to the minister, before the order was debated (with or without amendment) after 60 days.[122]

Use of other powers

It is important to note that the 2011 Act did not provide the only means for the 'culling' of public bodies. Not all public bodies are statutory bodies: those established without the formality of statute could be abolished by the same means as those by which they were created. In other cases, the powers under the 2011 Act were eschewed in favour of primary legislation, even though the 2011 Act expressly made provision to abolish or merge the bodies in question.

The latter is true, for example, of the Competition Commission and the Office of Fair Trading, which were merged by the Enterprise and Regulatory Reform Act 2013 to become the Competition and Markets Authority. It is also true of the Agricultural Wages Board which set minimum terms and conditions of employment for farm workers, and was also abolished by the 2013 Act. It is not altogether clear why the government proceeded in this way, though there may be a number of explanations.

First, it would be reasonable to conclude that in some cases it would be especially inappropriate to abolish or merge by order. The establishment of the Competition and Markets Authority is perhaps a case in point, given the importance of its role as a 'super-regulator'. This argument would not be as persuasive for some in the case of the Agricultural Wages Board, but here there may have been concerns about problems that might have been encountered in Parliament if the 2011 Act had been used.[123]

In by-passing the 2011 Act, the use of primary legislation did not guarantee that the abolition or merger of a public body would be more fully considered by Parliament. In the case of the last-mentioned Board, it has been pointed out that the relevant abolition provisions were tabled as a Lords amendment, and guillotined in the Commons by which they were never considered.[124] One other consequence of using primary legislation would be to frustrate any legal challenge to abolition based on Convention rights.[125]

Impact of the 2011 Act

The bodies listed in the Schedules to the Act were automatically removed five years and two months after the Act came into force, which means that ministers had 62 months to exercise

---

[122] Two qualifications need to be added to the outline of the 2011 Act provided above. The first is that the consent of the Scottish Parliament and the Northern Ireland and Welsh Assemblies is required where the body in question falls within the legislative competence of the devolved body in question (s 9). In addition, some of the powers under the Act were expressly devolved to the Welsh ministers insofar as these relate to bodies operating only in Wales, or to national bodies with certain functions devolved to Wales (ss 13–15).

[123] 2011 Act, s 8 may have given rise to particular problems.

[124] *Farmers' Guardian*, 18 April 2013.

[125] Concerns were expressed by the JCHR about the government's failure to provide it with an assessment of the human rights implications of this amendment: HL Paper 157, HC 107 (2012–13), para 83. The ECtHR found that there was no breach of the ECHR, art 11: *Unite the Union* v *UK*, Application No 65397/13.

powers in relation to these bodies, failing which any such power would lapse. The Act was intended to deal with what is referred to as the 2010–15 Public Bodies Reform Programme', though the Act and its powers are not completely redundant following the sun-setting on Schedules 1–5. However, any future use of the Act will depend upon public bodies being made expressly subject to its terms by new primary legislation.

The Act thus remains in force though the bodies to which it originally applied have been removed from its grip. In including so many bodies in the first place, it appears that the then government was over-ambitious and that the Act failed to deliver what had been expected. According to a government review, the Public Bodies Reform Programme led to a reduction in the number of public bodies by more than 190 and to the merger of over 165 into fewer than 70, while more than another 130 were 'substantially reformed'. It is clear nevertheless that the changes were only to a limited extent made under the 2011 Act.

No more than 33 orders were made under the Act, leading to the reform of no more than 52 public bodies, the government offering a number of explanations for this limited effect. These included the use of the other legislative powers to which we have referred. Otherwise, many of the bodies initially targeted for abolition or reform were retained following a change of government policy, or because on close inspection they were found to serve a useful purpose and provide value for money. In other cases restraint was due to the complex problems associated with abolition, while in other cases still the 2011 Act was found to be unsuitable.[126]

A 'bonfire of the quangos' may be good rhetoric, but it is not necessarily good politics. And in the case of the 2011 Act it produced neither satisfactory nor effective legislation, the powers contained in which were the subject of constant criticism. Nevertheless, the May government claimed in its post-legislative scrutiny that the 2011 Act 'was an important legislative vehicle for the delivery of public body reform', and that 'it has been a central element of the reform programme [enabling] a great deal of change to be executed in a consistent manner'.[127]

G. Conclusion

There is now a mosaic of bodies at the heart of government responsible for a wide range of activities. In this chapter we have encountered the central bank, non-ministerial departments, non-departmental public bodies, public corporations and parliamentary bodies. To this list might be added health service bodies (not dealt with in this chapter) and the executive agencies discussed in Chapter 11. It is a mosaic that does not appear to take any rational form, a concern which is being increasingly highlighted.[128]

There are otherwise problems with administration by public body, these bodies not guaranteed to provide any greater independence from government than if the work were undertaken by civil servants in government departments with security of tenure. There are also serious problems of the parliamentary accountability of government departments that have no ministerial head (as in the case of NMDs), or public bodies that are at some length removed from their sponsoring department (as in the case of NDPBs).

Complaints are made from time to time about the politicisation of appointments (and more usually re-appointments) to these bodies, it sometimes being alleged that governments try to ensure that government supporters are appointed to public positions. It is partly to prevent the scourge of favouritism, cronyism and nepotism that the rules relating to public

---

[126] Minister for the Constitution, Post Legislative Scrutiny of the Public Bodies Act 2011, Cm 9367, 2016,
[127] Ibid, para 122.
[128] HC 110 (2014–15), referring to inconsistency, overlaps, confusion and clutter.

appointments have been introduced, and these rules ought also to prevent public appointments from being used as a reward for services rendered or donations made.

The positions to which these procedures apply are important and many have a bearing on the lives of millions of citizens. Although complaints of impropriety are made from time to time in the appointments process, it is difficult to judge whether what one side sees as an abuse is a crude attempt at balance by the other side enjoying the spoils of office. But so long as the procedures continue to provide for appointments by ministers, these questions will continue to be raised and suspicions will continue to be aroused.

There are thus legitimate questions about the proliferation of these many bodies and the constitutional status they are given, and equally legitimate questions about appointments. But there are also questions about the manner of their reform under the Public Bodies Act 2011, even if the instinct behind the reform process is sound: without descending into populism, policy-making and other activities should be undertaken so far as possible by those who are elected and accountable for the policies they make and the decisions they take.

CHAPTER 13

Courts and the administration of justice

In this chapter we address a number of constitutional questions relating to the judiciary and the administration of justice. First, we consider the procedures for the appointment of judges, and the measures designed to protect their independence; secondly, we examine the steps taken to ensure that litigants have a right to a fair trial, and the circumstances in which that right may collide with the rights of others; and thirdly we deal with the role of the executive in the administration of justice, concentrating on the position of the Lord Chancellor and the Ministry of Justice, together with the procedures for the prosecution of offenders.

These are all areas where in recent years extensive changes have been made, the most important of these being introduced by the Constitutional Reform Act 2005, particularly notable for establishing the Supreme Court of the United Kingdom.[1] Designed to reinforce both the rule of law and the independence of the judiciary, the Act proved to be highly controversial and many of its provisions were hotly contested. An important driving force behind the Act was a belief in the principle that the judicial function should be institutionally distinct from the legislative function, and that the highest court should not be based in the legislature.[2]

A. Judiciary and judicial appointments

Judicial appointments in the United Kingdom are a matter for the executive, the Queen's judges being appointed on the advice of the Queen's ministers. Supreme Court appointments are made by the Queen on the advice of the Prime Minister. Other senior positions (including Lord Chief Justice, Master of the Rolls, and President of the Family Division) are made on the advice of the Prime Minister and Lord Chancellor, while High Court judges, circuit judges and recorders are appointed by the Queen on the advice of the Lord Chancellor.[3] The advice of ministers is, however, now effectively constrained by the appointments commissions discussed below.[4]

Judges of the Court of Session (as well as sheriffs principal and sheriffs) are now appointed by the Queen on the recommendation of the First Minister, who must consult the Lord President before making a recommendation. The Lord President of the Court of Session and the Lord Justice Clerk (also in the Court of Session) are appointed by the Queen on the recommendation of the Prime Minister, who in turn must recommend the persons nominated

---

[1] The process is ongoing: Crime and Courts Act 2013, extensively amending the Constitutional Reform Act 2005. For a summary of the 2005 Act and the issues raised by it, see A W Bradley, HL 83, 2005–6 (Appendix 1), and for a positive assessment of its operation, see R Hazell [2015] PL 198.

[2] See ch 4 C above.

[3] Senior Courts Act 1981, s 10. On the legal status of recorders for the purposes of EU employment law, see *O'Brien* v *Ministry of Justice* [2013] UKSC 6 (treated as being in an 'employment relationship' for the purposes of EU law and as 'workers' for the purposes of implementing domestic law, in a dispute about the discrimination of part-time recorders in relation to pensions). For round two, see *O'Brien* v *Ministry of Justice* [2017] UKSC 46 (reference to CJEU on a point of EU law).

[4] Magistrates are appointed by the Lord Chancellor.

by the First Minister.[5] The First Minister must consult the Lord President and the Lord Justice Clerk (unless in either case the office is vacant) before making a nomination.

Unlike in the United States, there is no requirement anywhere in the United Kingdom that executive nominees should be subject to scrutiny and confirmation by Parliament (or the Scottish Parliament), and the Constitutional Reform Act 2005 did not introduce such a procedure.[6]

Qualifications for appointment

By statute, minimum qualifications for appointments must be observed. Before the Courts and Legal Services Act 1990, judges of the High Court had to be of at least ten years' standing as a barrister. Since the 1990 Act, however, it is now possible for solicitors with rights of audience in the High Court and for circuit judges of at least two years' standing to be appointed.[7] As far as the Court of Appeal is concerned, candidates for appointment as a Lord Justice of Appeal had previously to be of at least 15 years' standing as a barrister or already to have been a High Court judge.[8] Since the 1990 Act, this has been reduced to ten years and extended to include solicitors.

In general, however, appointments to the superior courts are made only from successful legal practitioners, and the experience of those appointed is generally well above the legal minimum. In Scotland, membership of the Court of Session is regulated by a rule of five years' standing as a member of the Faculty of Advocates.[9] In 1990, however, the rules were relaxed, with eligibility being extended to sheriffs principal and sheriffs (who must have held office for at least five years) and solicitors, who must have had a right of audience in the Court of Session for at least five years.[10] There are also rules of standing for members of the lower judiciary.

Appointment to the more senior positions (Court of Appeal and Supreme Court) is normally by way of promotion, and it remains exceptional for someone to be appointed to a senior judicial position without coming through the traditional channels. Although there have been a few appointments of academics to judicial office in recent years, those appointed from such a background must also satisfy the standard requirements of office, which emphasise the need for many years of practical experience. A major innovation has been the advertisement of some vacancies up to the level of the High Court.

In other countries experience as a legal practitioner is not the only route to a career on the Bench, with civil law countries in particular providing opportunities for recruitment at a young age into a career judiciary, with opportunities to progress through the various layers in the court structure. Without removing the scope for appointment of legal professionals, arrangements of this kind would help to ensure that there is no single route to appointment, nor a monopoly of the appointment process by one particular interest group, and may help also to overcome some of the problems of diversity addressed below.[11]

Judicial Appointments Commission

In the Constitutional Reform Act 2005 (as amended), the government yielded to growing concern about the process of judicial appointment, previously criticised for its secrecy and

---

[5] Scotland Act 1998, s 95. In making his nomination, the First Minister must have regard to the recommendations of a panel established under the Judiciary and Courts (Scotland) Act 2008, s 19 and Sch 2.
[6] For discussion of this issue, see K D Ewing, in Flinders *et al.* (eds), *The Oxford Handbook of British Politics*, pp 275–7.
[7] Courts and Legal Services Act 1990, s 71.
[8] Senior Courts Act 1981, s 10(3).
[9] Treaty of Union 1706, art 19.
[10] Law Reform (Miscellaneous Provisions) (Scotland) Act 1990, s 35.
[11] See K D Ewing (2000) 38 *Alta Law Rev* 708.

lack of transparency. The creation of the Judicial Appointments Commission, which was formally launched in April 2006, followed the formation of a Judicial Appointments Board in Scotland in 2001,[12] albeit on a non-statutory basis, and the creation of a Commission for Judicial Appointments for England and Wales in the same year. Established by Order in Council, the latter was empowered only to review rather than recommend appointments, though even in this limited capacity it did cause some discomfort by reporting on the role of the Lord Chancellor in some judicial appointments.[13]

The Commission established for England and Wales under the 2005 Act has a much wider remit than the non-statutory body which preceded it, and consists of a lay chairman,[14] as well as a number of other Commissioners as determined by regulations made by the Lord Chancellor with the agreement of the Lord Chief Justice (who is now Head of the Judiciary of England and Wales).[15] Although judges are appointed to serve on the Commission, the majority of members must not be holders of judicial office, with provision made for the appointment of legal practitioners and non-lawyers. Amendments made in 2013 also require regulations to deal with a range of matters relating to Commissioners, including eligibility, regional balance, terms and conditions of employment, and the maximum length of tenure of Commissioners.[16]

Different procedures apply for different appointments. The first relate to the senior posts of Lord Chief Justice, Master of the Rolls, President of the Queen's Bench Division, President of the Family Division and Chancellor of the High Court: in the event of a vacancy arising in one of these posts, the Lord Chancellor may ask the Commission to convene a selection panel. The panel must consist of five members, of whom at least two are not legally qualified, and at least two must be judges.[17] At least two members of the panel must be members of the Commission,[18] which means in effect that the Commission is represented on the selection panel it has convened, but that it is not directly responsible for making the recommendation. In the case of the appointment of the Lord Chief Justice the panel must be chaired by a non-lawyer.[19]

Turning from the Lord Chief Justice and the Heads of Division, the procedure for the Court of Appeal is similar to that described above, though there are a number of small variations following the Judicial Appointments Regulations 2013.[20] The position is different in the case of High Court judges, in relation to whom it is a Judicial Appointments Commission panel that makes the recommendation, after consulting the Lord Chief Justice and another High Court judge. It is important to note, however, that in all appointments referred to here, the JAC process leads to a recommendation to the Lord Chancellor who may ask the panel to reconsider its recommendation or reject it altogether.[21] The government thus has the last word: the Commission may be independent and may be an executive NDPB,[22] but it does not necessarily have the final say.

[12] There is now a statutory Judicial Appointments Board for Scotland: Judiciary and Courts (Scotland) Act 2008, Part 2.

[13] See Commission for Judicial Appointments, *Annual Report 2005*, para 2.44; Commission for Judicial Appointments, *Review of the Recorder 2004/05 Competition* (*Midland Circuit*) (2005), pp 89–90.

[14] On which see K Malleson [2004] PL 102.

[15] The role of Head of the Judiciary is one previously performed by the Lord Chancellor.

[16] Constitutional Reform Act 2005, Sch 12 (as amended by the Crime and Courts Act 2013).

[17] Ibid, s 70 (as amended). See also s 71A. The precise composition of the panels is set out in SI 2013 No 2192.

[18] Constitutional Reform Act 2005, s 70 (as amended).

[19] Ibid.

[20] Ibid, s 79. SI 2013 No 2192.

[21] SI 2013 No 2192, regs 8 (Lord Chief Justice), 14 (Heads of Division), 20 (Senior President of Tribunals), 26 (Lord Justice of Appeal), 32 (High Court judge).

[22] On which see Ch 12 above.

Supreme Court of the United Kingdom

The foregoing procedures do not apply to the Supreme Court of the United Kingdom, which acquired the existing appellate jurisdiction of the House of Lords, as well as the devolution jurisdiction of the Privy Council.[23] The Constitutional Reform Act 2005 (as amended) provides that the court is to consist of the equivalent of 12 full-time judges, who (with the exception of the President and Deputy President) are styled Justices of the Supreme Court. The founding members of the Court were the Law Lords in post at the time the Court was created. These members retained their titles as Lords of Appeal in Ordinary (which under the 1876 Act cannot be revoked, though they may now resign their membership of the Lords);[24] but as discussed below, serving justices of the Supreme Court are prohibited from taking an active part in the work of the legislature, from which they had largely withdrawn even before the Supreme Court was established.

The Supreme Court was established on 1 October 2009. Appointments since that date are governed by the Constitutional Reform Act 2005 (as amended), with the qualifications for appointment being similar to those under the (repealed) Appellate Jurisdiction Act 1876.[25] It is not necessary to have prior judicial experience, and unusually Lord Sumption was appointed to the Court in 2012 under the new procedures straight from the Bar, the first time it is thought such an appointment has been made to the highest court since Lord Radcliffe was appointed to the House of Lords in 1949. Appointment to the Supreme Court will not, however, bring a peerage (though justices appointed under the 2005 Act are given the courtesy title 'Lord'). There is no reason why retired justices of the Supreme Court could not be made life peers under the Life Peerages Act 1958, so long as the House of Lords remains a wholly or partially nominated body.

When a vacancy arises on the Supreme Court, the 2005 Act requires the Lord Chancellor to convene an ad hoc Supreme Court Selection Commission, the process for initiating the establishment of such a Commission depending on whether the vacancy relates to the President or Deputy President of the Court on the one hand, or its remaining members on the other. In the case of vacancies apart from President or Deputy President of the court, the initiative to convene a selection commission may be taken by the senior judge on the Court at the time. In all cases the Commission is to consist of five members, one of whom must be a member of the Supreme Court, one of whom must be a lay member, with the other three being drawn from the Judicial Appointments Commission, and its Scottish and Northern Irish equivalents.[26]

Once a recommendation has been made, the Lord Chancellor is then under a statutory duty to consult various parties about the recommendation.[27] A reserve power authorizes the Lord Chancellor to (i) require a Supreme Court Selection Commission to reconsider its recommendation, or (ii) reject it altogether.[28] So although the Lord Chancellor no longer selects candidates for presentation to the Prime Minister (as was the case in relation to House of Lords appointments under the Appellate Jurisdiction Act 1876), he or she nevertheless retains a veto on who may be nominated, though reasons must be given in the event of this power being exercised. But it is surely only in the most exceptional and improbable circumstances that such a reserve power could legitimately be used.

---

[23] Constitutional Reform Act 2005, s 40.

[24] On resignation, see House of Lords Reform Act 2014, s 1; ch 7 I above.

[25] Constitutional Reform Act 2005, s 25.

[26] Further provision about the membership and procedures of the selection commission is to be found in the Supreme Court (Judicial Appointments) Regulations 2013: SI 2013 No 2193.

[27] SI 2013 No 2193, reg 19.

[28] Constitutional Reform Act 2005, s 27A(2); SI 2013 No 2193, reg 20.

Diversity of judicial composition

Should the judiciary be 'representative', and if so, what does this mean? The idea that the judiciary should be 'representative of the community' was repudiated by the Home Affairs Committee and by the Lord Chancellor's Department, on behalf of which it was asserted in 1996 that:

> It is not the function of the judiciary to reflect particular sections of the community, as it is of the democratically elected legislature. The judges' role is to administer justice in accordance with the laws of England and Wales. This requires above all professional legal knowledge and competence. Any litigant or defendant will usually appear before a single judge and it is of paramount importance that the judge is fully qualified for the office he or she holds, and is able to discharge his or her functions to the highest standards. Social or other considerations are not relevant for this purpose; the Lord Chancellor accordingly seeks to appoint, or recommend for appointment, those who are the best qualified candidates available and willing to serve at the time.[29]

This is not a view that is often heard today, it now being recognised that the judiciary should at least 'more closely' reflect the make-up of society as a whole. The Constitutional Reform Act 2005 requires the Judicial Appointments Commission to have regard to 'the need to encourage diversity in the range of persons available for selection for appointments' (s 64).[30] But although there has been some improvement in recent years,[31] women and members of the ethnic minority communities remain poorly represented on the Bench, particularly at its highest levels. On 31 May 2017 only one member of the Supreme Court was female, and all the heads of division were men. Moreover, although the number of female judges in the Court of Appeal was growing, on the same date, it remained the case that only eight of the 40 members of that court were female. The great bulk of High Court judges were men.

Apart from the chronic under-representation of women (particularly at the highest level), ethnic minorities continue to be even more poorly represented.[32] As the Judicial Appointments Commission has pointed out, however, the judiciary 'will always be dependent on the diversity of the legal profession' (at least so long as judges continue to be recruited from experienced legal practitioners), where there is an issue about the lack of diversity at the more senior levels. In 2009, the Commission pointed out, for example, that only 20–25 per cent of partners in solicitors' firms are women, though women make up a majority of those entering the profession; and that only 10 per cent of QCs are women, though women account for 49 per cent of pupils. Only 4 per cent of QCs are from black and ethnic minority backgrounds.[33] Diversity cannot be separated from methods of recruitment and barriers – formal and informal – to career progression.

Nevertheless, the Crime and Courts Act 2013 makes a number of notable amendments to the Constitutional Reform Act 2005, particularly in relation to the question of diversity. Thus, in making judicial appointments 'solely on merit',[34] it is now provided expressly that the relevant appointments commission may make a choice between two candidates of equal merit 'for the purpose of increasing diversity' within the court to which the appointment is to

---

[29] HC 52-II (1995–6), p 130.

[30] For a contemporary examination of this issue, see Gee and Rackley (eds), *Debating Judicial Appointments in an Age of Diversity*.

[31] See Lord Chief Justice and Senior President of Tribunals, *Judicial Diversity Statistics 2016* (2016), where it is reported that the representation of women is higher in lower courts, and that the majority of recent appointments to judicial office of people under the age of 40 have been women.

[32] Ibid.

[33] Judicial Appointments Commission, *Annual Report 2008/09*, p 38.

[34] Constitutional Reform Act 2005, s 63(2).

be made.[35] That is to say, where there are two equally meritorious candidates, one may be preferred on grounds of sex or race, though there is no obligation to use this power in any appointment recommended by the appointment commission in question. In addition, a new statutory duty requires both the Lord Chancellor and the Lord Chief Justice to 'take such steps' as they consider 'appropriate for the purpose of encouraging judicial diversity'.[36]

B. Independence of the judiciary

The principle of judicial independence is now formally recognised in legislation, the Constitutional Reform Act 2005 introducing a legal duty to 'uphold' the continued independence of the judiciary.[37] The duty is addressed to the Lord Chancellor, other government ministers, and anyone else 'with responsibility for matters relating to the judiciary or otherwise to the administration of justice'.[38] Compliance with this obligation relies heavily on self-restraint by ministers, while its enforcement relies heavily on a Lord Chancellor capable of rising above partisan interest. This general obligation to uphold judicial independence is strengthened by specific obligations addressed personally to the Lord Chancellor.

Thus, the Lord Chancellor must have regard to (i) the need to defend judicial independence, (ii) the need for the judiciary to have the support necessary to carry out its functions, and (iii) 'the need for the public interest in regard to matters relating to the judiciary or otherwise to the administration of justice to be properly represented in decisions affecting those matters' (s 3(6)). There is, however, no definition of judicial independence in the 2005 Act, though the principle has been re-invigorated also by the Human Rights Act 1998. It has been said that the Lord Chancellor's duty requires him or her to draw to the attention of the Cabinet any proposed legislation that would undermine the independence of the judiciary, and that it obliges him or her to deal with any ministers who indulge in personal attacks on judges.[39]

It is important to note that the duty of the Lord Chancellor is of a general nature, which means that there is a duty to protect the independence of the judiciary not only from being undermined by ministers, but also more widely.[40] It is thought that the Lord Chancellor failed to fulfil this duty when three High Court judges (including the Lord Chief Justice) were the subject of highly charged personal abuse by newspapers following their decision in *R (Miller)* v *Secretary of State for Exiting the EU*.[41] These thoughts found expression in evidence by the Lord Chief Justice to the House of Lords Constitution Committee when he

----

[35] Ibid, s 27A (as amended) (Supreme Court), 63(4) (as amended) (other appointments). Also s 137A below.

[36] Ibid, s 137A (as amended). On the initiatives taken by the JAC to promote diversity, see Judicial Appointments Commission, Annual Report 2016 (2016), ch 5.

[37] For comparable provisions in Scotland, see Judiciary and Courts (Scotland) Act 2008, s 1.

[38] Constitutional Reform Act 2005, s 3. See HL Paper 151 (2006–7), para 39.

[39] HL Paper 151 (2006–7), paras 38–40. The Act expressly provides that the Lord Chancellor and other ministers must not seek to influence particular judicial decisions through any special access to the judiciary (s 3(5)).

[40] It is strongly arguable that the Lord Chancellor is under a duty to intervene to remind ministers of their statutory duty relating to judicial independence and if necessary to rebuke those who may be thought to fall short of expectations if not obligations. It is not clear to what extent this is done privately, in circumstances where there is no public response from the Lord Chancellor, as where the Home Secretary took to *The Daily Mail* to accuse 'judges of "subverting" British democracy and making the streets of Britain more dangerous by ignoring rules aimed at deporting more foreign criminals': *The Guardian*, 17 February 2013.

[41] [2016] EWHC 2768 (Admin); subs *R (Miller)* v *Secretary of State for Exiting the EU* [2017] UKSC 5, [2017] 2 WLR 583.

'severely criticised' the Lord Chancellor for having failed adequately to protect the judges from such abuse, a failure which he thought was 'constitutionally absolutely wrong'.[42]

Protection of judges from political pressure

Judicial independence requires that judges should be protected from political pressure to reach decisions which suit the government or other powerful interests. In recent years, however, there has been an erosion of the long-standing convention that ministers do not criticise the judiciary or judicial decisions. For example, in 2003 the sentence imposed on a convicted paedophile by the Recorder of Cardiff attracted criticism from the then Home Secretary (and a junior minister), which in turn fanned a hostile press response addressed to the courts. Concern was compounded by a feeling that the Lord Chancellor had been too slow to defend the judge (against whose decision there was no appeal by the Attorney General).[43] This latter affair led to calls for the *Ministerial Code* to be amended to include 'strongly worded guidelines setting out the principles governing public comment by ministers on individual judges'.[44]

No less contentious were comments made by the Prime Minister in 2005 which were seen as being designed to put pressure on the courts generally in cases about the extradition of foreign terrorist suspects. After noting that each tightening of the terrorism laws had met 'fierce opposition in the courts', and that the 'rules of the game are changing', the Prime Minister continued by saying that should legal obstacles arise in the future, the government 'will legislate further including, if necessary, amending the Human Rights Act in respect of the interpretation of the European Convention on Human Rights'.[45] Although the Prime Minister's comments were not seen to impugn an individual judge, it is nevertheless difficult to recall circumstances in which a Prime Minister has informed the judiciary in advance of any litigation that the law will be changed if the government is unhappy with the result.

Members of Parliament are also subject to restraints in their criticism of judges. There is a long-standing rule of the House that unless the discussion is based on a substantive motion, reflections must not be cast on the conduct of judges or upon judges generally.[46] Another parliamentary rule seeks to protect the principle of a fair trial rather than the status of the judges: by the *sub judice* rule, matters awaiting the adjudication of a court may not be raised in debate. The rule – which was codified for the first time in 1963 and updated in 1972, and again in 2001[47] – is designed to ensure that there is no interference with the right to a fair trial. In this sense the rule complements (though it does not overlap precisely with) the Contempt of Court Act 1981, which is designed to protect the integrity of legal proceedings from improper influence by the press. Considered in the following section, the 1981 Act does not apply to parliamentary proceedings.

The *sub judice* rule is also designed to acknowledge the respective roles of judiciary and Parliament: if the role of the former is to be discharged effectively, the judges 'should not only be, but also be seen to be, the only constitutional body for determining issues which come before the courts'.[48] Under the terms of the rule, matters which are the subject of legal

---

[42] House of Lords Constitution Committee, Oral Evidence Session with the Lord Chief Justice, 22 March 2017, Q4.

[43] HL Paper 151 (2006–7), paras 45–9. The Lord Chancellor would now have a duty under the Constitutional Reform Act 2005 to intervene.

[44] Ibid, para 49.

[45] As expressed on the No 10 website on 2 November 2005.

[46] Erskine May, pp 396 and 443–4.

[47] See HC Deb, 23 July 1963, col 1417 and HC Deb, 28 June 1972, col 1589. For the text of the current rule, see HC Deb, 15 November 2001, col 1012. Also HL Deb, 11 May 2000, cols 1725–6. For the report of the Joint Committee on Parliamentary Privilege, see HC 214-I–III (1998–9) and HL 43-I–III (1998–9).

[48] HC 125 (2004–5), para 13, citing evidence of Lord Nicholls.

proceedings may not be referred to in any motion, debate or question. This is subject to a discretion on the part of the Speaker to permit such a reference 'where a ministerial decision is in question', or where the case 'concerns issues of national importance such as the economy, public order or the essential services'. The reason for this relaxation is to permit some parliamentary discussion of ministerial decisions or other major issues of public concern, notwithstanding the fact that legal action may have been instituted.[49] Nevertheless, the operation of the rule continues to give rise to frustration on the part of MPs.[50]

Protection of judges from dismissal

At the apex of the principle of judicial independence is security of tenure: judges cannot be dismissed because they are unpopular with the government. Judges of the Supreme Court, Court of Appeal and High Court hold office during good behaviour, subject to a power of removal by the Queen on an address presented by both Houses of Parliament.[51] These statutory rules clearly prevent a judge from being removed at the pleasure of the Crown, but their meaning is not wholly certain. The wording of the provision in the Act of Settlement, from which these rules derived,[52] suggests that the intention of Parliament was that, while a judge should hold office during good behaviour, Parliament itself should enjoy an unqualified power of removal.

Assuming that there was no intention to alter the effect of the Act of Settlement by the revised wording now contained in modern legislation, it is thus theoretically possible for a judge to be dismissed not only for misconduct, but also for any other reason which might induce both Houses to pass the necessary address to the Crown. This appears to have been the position of the Ministry of Justice, which understood that it appointed judges on the condition that they could be removed from office by the Lord Chancellor for misbehaviour or inability, with the concurrence of the Lord Chief Justice. This is reinforced by the Constitutional Reform Act 2005, which clearly recognises that judges may be removed by an Address, presumably for reasons other than misbehaviour or inability (s 109).

But whatever the theoretical position, there are a number of reasons which help to explain why these latter powers are unlikely ever to be used, with the security of judicial tenure relying not so much on legal rules as on a shared constitutional understanding which these rules reflect. In Scotland, these understandings are reinforced by legislation that gives the Scottish judge greater formal security then his or her English counterpart. The historic tenure on which Scottish judges hold office is *ad vitam aut culpam*, which means that they cannot be removed except on grounds of misconduct.[53] Judges of the Court of Session now hold office until retirement, and may be removed by Her Majesty following a recommendation by the First Minister, who may make a recommendation only with the authority of the Scottish Parliament.[54]

Before the First Minister seeks parliamentary authority to recommend the removal of a Court of Session judge, he or she must appoint a tribunal (to be chaired by a judicial member of the Privy Council), to investigate whether the judge in question is unfit for office by reason of 'inability, neglect of duty or misbehaviour'.[55] A sheriff may be removed from office only

---

[49] See e.g. debate on the thalidomide cases, HC Deb, 29 November 1972, col 432.
[50] HC 125 (2004–5). The rule does not affect the power of Parliament to legislate.
[51] Constitutional Reform Act 2005, s 33; Senior Courts Act 1981, s 11(3).
[52] Ch 1.
[53] Claim of Right 1689, art 13; *Mackay and Esslemont* v *Lord Advocate* 1937 SC 860.
[54] Scotland Act 1998, s 95.
[55] Ibid, s 95(8). See now Judiciary and Courts (Scotland) Act 2008, ss 35–9.

after a tribunal constituted by the First Minister (to include senior judicial as well as lay representation) has established unfitness for office due to inability, neglect of duty or misbehaviour. The sheriff may be removed by the First Minister by statutory instrument, after the tribunal's report has been laid before the Scottish Parliament.[56] Judges lower down the pecking order in England and Wales may be removed from office for incapacity or misbehaviour.[57]

Use of judges for extra-judicial purposes

Judges have often been called on by the government to preside over royal commissions, departmental committees and inquiries conducted under the Tribunals of Inquiry (Evidence) Act 1921 (now replaced by the Inquiries Act 2005). It has been claimed that there were 366 major commissions and inquiries throughout the 20th century, as well as another 1,000 or so departmental inquiries. Thirty per cent of these major commissions and inquiries are said to have been conducted by a judge.[58] These have included matters as diverse as safety at sports grounds, prison riots, the collapse of an international bank, the so-called Arms for Iraq affair, the future of legislation against terrorism, and the Bloody Sunday killings in 1972.

An emerging theme of some significance has been the appointment of senior judges as commissioners to oversee and to report annually to the Prime Minister about the operation of surveillance powers created by legislation such as the Investigatory Powers Act 2016,[59] though the practice has changed in recent years in the sense that these roles are now generally performed by retired rather than serving judges. Also important was the appointment of Lord Nolan in 1994 to examine concerns about standards of conduct in public life.[60] Many judges are well suited to this work but there are potential dangers to judicial independence, especially when matters of acute political controversy are referred to a judge for an impartial opinion.[61]

Particularly controversial references in the past were the investigations conducted by Lord Denning on the request of the Prime Minister into the security aspects arising out of the resignation of a minister (John Profumo) in 1963; by the Lord Chief Justice, Lord Widgery, in 1972 into deaths in Londonderry; and by Lord Bridge in 1985 into allegations of improper telephone tapping of trade unionists and peace activists by members of the security service.[62] Such references may give rise to allegations that the government is using the judiciary for its own ends; and they may expose the judge in question, particularly if he or she is the sole member of the inquiry, to political or personal criticism by those who disagree with his or her report. The report by Lord Hutton in 2004 about the circumstances surrounding the death of a government scientist (Dr David Kelly) attracted a great deal of media criticism.[63]

---

[56] Courts Reform (Scotland) Act 2014, ss 21–5.

[57] Courts Act 1971, s 17(4). Lay magistrates may be removed from office for incapacity, misbehaviour, incompetence or neglect of duty: Courts Act 2003, s 11. District judges (magistrates' courts) may be removed for incapacity or misbehaviour (s 22(5)). On the procedure to be followed, see Constitutional Reform Act 2005, s 108.

[58] J Beatson (2005) 121 LQR 221.

[59] See ch 16 D.

[60] HC Deb, 25 October 1994, col 757. Lord Nolan was also a commissioner under the Interception of Communications Act 1985. And see ch 16 D.

[61] See also Beatson, above.

[62] See respectively Cmnd 2152, 1963; HC 220 (1971–2); and *The Times*, 7 March 1985.

[63] I Steele [2004] PL 738.

Before a judge is appointed to an inquiry, ministers would normally consult with senior judges about the appointment, a practice which is now sometimes mandatory.[64] It needs to be stressed that such work is not the primary task of the judges and that the government cannot assume that the services of a judge will be available whenever an awkward political situation might be eased by an impartial inquiry. There may also be concerns about judges being too intimately involved with the operation and needs of government, particularly in cases where they are drawn on to give advice on a matter about which they are subsequently called upon to adjudicate, albeit in a different context.[65] Nevertheless, judges continue to be deployed to conduct high-profile inquiries, as in the Prime Minister's appointment of Sir Brian Leveson in 2011 to examine the culture, practices and ethics of the press.

Judges in the political process

The role of judges acting at the behest of the executive in the manner described above is increasingly anomalous in a constitution which now embraces a stronger formal commitment to judicial independence, and to a greater separation of powers. That such activity should continue is all the more anomalous for the fact that judicial involvement in the political process generally has greatly receded in recent years. It is true that by a strong convention mentioned in Chapter 1 C, the judges must not be seen to be engaged in party political activity, a convention now expressed by the Judicial Appointments Commission to mean that judges 'must expect to forgo any kind of political activity and be on their guard against circumstances arising in which their involvement in any outside activity might be seen to cast doubt on their judicial impartiality'.

It is true that this convention did not in the past prevent Law Lords from participating in the political work of the House of Lords, when they felt inclined to do so. Judicial members of the House of Lords took part in debates on a number of Bills covering a wide range of issues, by no means all of which were uncontroversial. As a result, judges were responsible for a number of important amendments, which improved measures such as the Contempt of Court Act 1981, with s 10 on journalists' sources being an amendment tabled by Lord Scarman. Another example is the Police and Criminal Evidence Act 1984, with s 78 on the admissibility of evidence also being a Scarman amendment. In addition, the Law Lords (serving and retired) played a prominent part in the debates relating to the Human Rights Bill.[66]

But that is in the past. As explained above, these opportunities for parliamentary participation by judges have been brought to an end by the Constitutional Reform Act 2005, with Supreme Court justices being prohibited from sitting in the House of Lords. Members of the House of Lords who are appointed as Supreme Court justices (notably the Law Lords in post at the time the Supreme Court was created) will be entitled to receive a writ of summons at the beginning of each session (and presumably to attend the House), but not to sit or vote in its proceedings or those of its committees.[67] Despite the removal of the

----

[64] Inquiries Act 2005, s 10.

[65] See K D Ewing, in Campbell, Ewing and Tomkins (eds), *The Legal Protection of Human Rights: Sceptical Essays* (highlighting the role of Lord Radcliffe as reviewer of official secrets legislation following security lapses and the adjudicator on the meaning of the Official Secrets Act 1911, s 1 within a short period thereafter.

[66] See K D Ewing (1999) 62 MLR 79.

[67] Constitutional Reform Act 2005, s 137. The individuals in question are, however, excluded from the list of members of the House of Lords and appear on a separate list of ineligible members. By the same token, it will be possible (if unlikely) for (*a*) a serving Justice of the Supreme Court to be made a life peer, or (less unlikely) (*b*) an existing life peer (suitably qualified) to be made a justice of the Supreme Court, but subject to provisions of the CRA, s 137 by which they would be unable to sit or vote until retirement from the Bench.

platform provided by the House of Lords, it is implausible to believe that the senior judges will cease to be engaged in public affairs, or that they will be able to ignore demands for greater accountability.

As they are subjected to more media attention, senior judges may feel obliged to explain their role in various forums.[68] Apart from exceptional provisions in the Constitutional Reform Act 2005,[69] there are no formal channels for this to be done, though judges are increasingly responding to events by way of unattributed interviews in the press, speeches and lectures reported in the press and elsewhere,[70] and media interviews in the case of retired judges. Select committees provide another important forum for senior judges to make their views known, though there are sensitive constitutional issues to be considered when judges appear before such bodies.[71] But if these can be overcome, the select committees provide an opportunity for structured dialogue between legislature and judiciary, which may be of benefit to both.[72]

C. Administration of justice and contempt of court

Article 6 of the ECHR provides that the individual has the right to a fair and public hearing within a reasonable time by an independent and impartial tribunal. There are a number of legal rules designed to maintain the quality of justice in the courts. In principle trials are conducted in open court and the proceedings may be reported by the press,[73] though there are concerns about magistrate court procedures whereby

> uncontested cases involving adults charged with summary-only, non-imprisonable offences may be dealt with on the papers by a single magistrate, supported by a legal adviser, without attendance by the prosecutor or defendant.[74]

---

[68] See HL Deb, 12 February 2004 (Lord Hoffmann responding to the 'unconstitutional, inexcusable behaviour' of Mr Blunkett, then Home Secretary).

[69] The 2005 Act, s 5, provides that 'The chief justice of any part of the United Kingdom may lay before Parliament written representations on matters that appear to him to be matters of importance relating to the judiciary, or otherwise to the administration of justice, in that part of the United Kingdom.' But this seems designed as a 'nuclear option' signalling a serious breakdown in relations between the government and the judiciary collectively.

[70] See for example Lord Woolf [2004] CLJ 317. See also *The Guardian*, 15 September 2005 (Lord Bingham responding robustly to criticism of the judiciary). For consideration of this form of judicial activity, see K D Ewing, 'Judges and Free Speech in the United Kingdom', in Lee (ed.), *Judiciaries in Comparative Perspective*, ch 12.

[71] HL 66-iii, HC 332-iii (2000–1), Q 77.

[72] The Senior Law Lord, the Lord Chief Justice and the Master of the Rolls appeared together before the Joint Committee on Human Rights in 2000–1: HL 66, HC 133 (2000–1). A particularly notable appearance was that of the Lord Chief Justice before the House of Lords Constitution Committee on 22 March 2017 referred to above. For guidance to judges appearing before Committees, see Judicial Executive Board, *Guidance to Judges on Appearances before Select Committees* (2012), and for an assessment of this 'dialogue' see R Hazell and P O'Brien [2016] PL 54.

[73] See *Scott* v *Scott* [1913] AC 417; and now *In re Guardian News and Media Ltd* [2010] UKSC 1, [2010] 2 AC 697; *Marine A* v *Guardian News and Media* [2013] EWCA Crim 2367; *A* v *BBC* [2014] UKSC 25, 2014 SC (UKSC) 151; *Khuja* v *Times Newspapers Ltd* [2017] UKSC 49.

[74] HC 165 (2016–17), para 21 (Justice Committee).

Moreover, cases exceptionally may be heard ex parte or in camera (under common law,[75] or statutory authority);[76] witnesses may be permitted to give evidence anonymously;[77] and restrictions may be imposed on reporting legal proceedings.[78]

The rules of evidence, particularly in criminal trials before a jury,[79] exclude material that might be unfairly prejudicial to an accused. To the extent that legal representation contributes to the quality of justice, there are also schemes to enable people with limited means to be defended by a lawyer in criminal proceedings and to seek redress through the civil courts, though these have been seriously compromised in recent years.[80] The other issue is the cost of access to justice,[81] the Supreme Court intervening notably in *R (Unison) v Lord Chancellor*,[82] to strike down prohibitive fees imposed by secondary legislation in order to enforce employment rights. In the words of Lord Reed:

> In order for the courts to perform [their] role, people must in principle have unimpeded access to them. Without such access, laws are liable to become a dead letter, the work done by Parliament may be rendered nugatory, and the democratic election of Members of Parliament may become a meaningless charade.[83]

As we will see, there are several areas where the right to a fair trial will overlap with the right to freedom of expression, and where judgments have to be made about which has priority. There is – most notably – a difficult tension between the right to a fair trial and the right to freedom of expression when newspapers publish material that might prejudice the position of an accused person by influencing a jury.[84] One of the functions of the law of contempt of court is to manage this tension,[85] although it also has other functions; these include protecting the dignity of the court and generally safeguarding the administration of justice.

[75] *Guardian News and Media Ltd* v *Incedal* [2014] EWCA Crim 1861 (interesting for allowing the presence of a few accredited journalists in the *in camera* proceedings). But see the extraordinary restrictions in *R (Yang Wam)* v *Central Criminal Court* [2015] UKSC 76.

[76] Official Secrets Act 1911, s 8(4); Children and Young Persons Act 1933, s 37; Justice and Security Act 2013. Pt 2. The 2013 Act allows for 'closed material procedures' to be adopted in civil litigation essentially to protect evidence that if disclosed would damage national security. This reverses the decision in *Al Rawi* v *Security Service* [2011] UKSC 34, [2012] 1 AC 531, and means that information or evidence may be withheld from a party to the proceedings whose interests will be represented by a special advocate appointed by the court. See pp 570–1 below. On the operation of this power, see *In Re Gallacher* [2016] NIQB 95.

[77] *R* v *Lord Saville of Newdigate ex p A* [1999] 4 All ER 860 (B Hadfield [1999] PL 633); *R (Al-Fawwaz)* v *Governor of Brixton Prison* [2001] UKHL 69, [2002] 1 AC 666; and *In re Times Newspapers Ltd* [2008] EWCA Crim 2396, [2009] 1 WLR 1015. See now Criminal Justice and Courts Act 2015, s 78 (lifetime reporting restrictions in criminal proceedings).

[78] For example, Judicial Proceedings (Regulation of Reports) Act 1926, on which see *Gilchrist* v *Scott* 2000 SCCR 28; Children and Young Persons Act 1933, s 39, on which see *In re S (A Child)* [2004] UKHL 47, [2004] 4 All ER 683, and *Aitken* v *DPP* [2015] EWHC 1079 (Admin); [2016] 3 All ER 45; Youth Justice and Criminal Evidence Act 1999, s 46. See also *A G's Reference No 3 of 1999: Reporting Restriction Order* [2009] UKHL 34, [2010] 1 AC 145. In addition, 'super-injunctions' may exceptionally prevent the existence of the injunction being published. See pp 487–8 below.

[79] On which, see Ch 15.

[80] See HC 311 (2014–15).

[81] See HC 167 (2016–17) (Justice Committee).

[82] [2017] UKSC 51.

[83] Ibid, para 68.

[84] See *Miami Herald* v *Tornillo* 418 US 241 (1974).

[85] See *Attorney-General* v *BBC* [2007] EWCA Civ 280.

Contempt in the face of the court

All superior courts have power to punish summarily by fine or imprisonment violence committed or threats uttered in face of the court. Thus the judge may punish an attack on anyone in court or restrain the use of threatening words or scurrilous abuse. The issue whether an act constitutes a contempt is for the judge alone. If the act is committed in court, the judge is in a sense prosecutor, chief witness, judge and jury.[86]

In *Morris v Crown Office*,[87] a group of students demonstrated in support of the Welsh language by interrupting a sitting of the High Court in London, where they sang, shouted slogans and scattered pamphlets. After order was restored, the trial judge sentenced some of the students to prison for three months and fined others £50 each.

On appeal, the Court of Appeal, Civil Division, held that a High Court judge still had power at common law to commit instantly to prison for criminal contempt; and that the requirement under the Criminal Justice Act 1967 that prison sentences under six months be suspended did not apply to committal for contempt.

The court did not consider the prison sentences to be excessive, but, having regard to all the circumstances, allowed the appeal against sentence and bound over the appellants to be of good behaviour for one year.

Contempt in the face of the court includes insulting behaviour,[88] disregard of a judge's ruling,[89] photographing legal proceedings,[90] and refusal by a witness to give evidence or to answer questions which he or she is required to answer.[91]

In *Attorney-General v Mulholland and Foster*,[92] two journalists refused to disclose their sources of information to a tribunal of inquiry appointed after an Admiralty clerk, Vassall, had been convicted of espionage. The tribunal had by statute the powers of the High Court in examining witnesses.[93]

On appeal against a prison sentence imposed by the High Court, to which the tribunal had reported the journalists, it was held that journalists had no legal privilege to refuse to disclose sources of information given to them in confidence, where the information was relevant and necessary to the trial or inquiry.

[86] See *European Asian Bank* v *Wentworth* (1986) 5 NSWLR 445, at p 452.

[87] [1970] 2 QB 114.

[88] See *R* v *Powell* (1994) 98 Cr App R 224. For a fuller account of the type of conduct that may constitute contempt in the face of the court, see Law Commission, *Contempt of Court* (Consultation Paper No 209 (2012)), para 5.5. See also Magistrates Courts Act 1980, s 12.

[89] *H M Advocate* v *Howden* 2015 SCCR 418 (disregarding instruction not to look at Facebook in relation to the trial). For England and Wales, see now Juries Act 1974, s 20C (as inserted by Criminal Justice and Courts Act 2015, s 73, on which see A T H Smith (2015) *Crim Law Rev* 845).

[90] *Solicitor General* v *Cox* [2016] EWHC 1241 (QB). Photography is also an offence under the Criminal Justice Act 1925, s 41.

[91] *R* v *Montgomery* [1995] 2 Cr App R 23.

[92] [1963] 2 QB 477. And see *Senior* v *Holdsworth* [1976] QB 23.

[93] Ch 23 C.

So too, in *British Steel Corporation* v *Granada Television Ltd*,[94] the House of Lords ordered the Granada company to reveal the name of an employee of the corporation who had passed secret documents to Granada that were then used in a programme about the corporation. Although failure by Granada to comply with this order would have constituted contempt, the matter was resolved when the employee concerned made his identity known.

In the Contempt of Court Act 1981, the power of the court to demand information was limited by s 10. The court may not now request a person to disclose the source of information contained in a publication for which he or she is responsible, unless the court is satisfied that disclosure is necessary in the interests of justice, or national security, or for the prevention of disorder or crime.[95] If cases such as *Mulholland* and *British Steel Corporation* were to occur today, the statutory test of necessity would have to be applied before the court decided to require disclosure, but the outcome might still be the same.

In *Secretary of State for Defence* v *Guardian Newspapers Ltd*,[96] a junior civil servant delivered anonymously to the *Guardian* newspaper confidential documents addressed to Cabinet ministers by the Secretary of State for Defence. The documents related to the arrival of US cruise missiles at Greenham Common airbase.

The Ministry of Defence sought to recover the documents to help them identify the person responsible for the leak. The House of Lords held that s 10 of the 1981 Act was a valid defence not only where a journalist was asked a direct question in court, but also in an action for recovery of property where the property once recovered would help to reveal the newspaper's source. But the House also held (Lords Fraser and Scarman dissenting) that it was necessary to recover the documents and identify the source of the leak in the interests of national security.

The minister had expressed concern that a significant document relating to the defence of the realm had found its way to a national newspaper. This was of grave importance for national security, since Britain's allies could not be expected to continue to entrust the government with secret information if it was liable to unauthorised disclosure.

Guardian Newspapers is only one of a number of cases in which the courts at the highest levels have been willing to order the disclosure of journalists' sources by applying a low threshold which applicants need cross.[97] The more robust view of the European Court of Human Rights on this issue has led to conflict between that body and the domestic courts.[98] The domestic courts nevertheless appear willing to require the disclosure of sources where this will help an employer to identify an employee within an organisation who has leaked commercial information, or confidential medical information about a patient.[99] But the courts may refuse to order the disclosure of sources where the applicant's interests will be adequately protected

---

[94] [1981] AC 1096.

[95] Contempt of Court Act 1981, s 10.

[96] [1985] AC 339.

[97] *Maxwell* v *Pressdram Ltd* [1987] 1 All ER 656; *Re an Inquiry under the Company Securities (Insider Dealing) Act 1985* [1988] AC 660; and *X* v *Morgan Grampian (Publishers) Ltd* [1991] 1 AC 1. See T R S Allan [1991] CLJ 131; S Palmer [1992] PL 61.

[98] *Goodwin* v *UK* (1996) 22 EHRR 123, concluding that the decision in *Morgan Grampian* contravened ECHR, art 10. Also, *Financial Times* v *UK* [2009] ECHR 2065, (2010) 50 EHRR 46. But see *Hourani* v *Thomson* [2017] EWHC 173 (QB) (sources protected).

[99] See *Camelot Group* v *Centaur Ltd* [1999] QB 124, and *Ashworth Hospital Authority* v *MGN* [2002] UKHL 29; [2002] 1 WLR 2033.

by an injunction,[100] or where in the circumstances the applicant has not tried to find the source of the disclosure by other means first.[101]

Strict liability rule

Until the Contempt of Court Act 1981, it was on the basis of the common law that penalties were imposed on those whose publications were prejudicial to a fair trial or to civil proceedings.[102] The law was reformed in 1981, following recommendations of the Phillimore committee,[103] and the decision of the European Court of Human Rights in the *Sunday Times* case.

Nearly 400 claims against Distillers Ltd, the manufacturers of thalidomide, were pending when the *Sunday Times* published an article which inter alia urged the company to make a generous settlement. Later it proposed to publish an article examining the precautions taken by the company before the drug was sold. On the Attorney General's request, the Divisional Court granted an injunction to restrain publication of the article, holding that it would create a serious risk of interference with the company's freedom of action in the litigation. The Court of Appeal discharged the injunction, on the grounds that the article commented in good faith on matters of outstanding public importance and did not prejudice pending litigation since the litigation had been dormant for some years.

The House of Lords restored the injunction, holding that it was a contempt to publish an article prejudging the merits of an issue before the court where this created a real risk that a fair trial of the action would be prejudiced; the thalidomide actions were not dormant, since active negotiations for a settlement were going on. It was a contempt to use improper pressure to induce a litigant to settle a case on terms to which he or she did not wish to agree, or to hold a litigant up to public obloquy for exercising his or her rights in the courts.[104] Thereafter the *Sunday Times* claimed that the decision of the House of Lords infringed the freedom of expression protected by art 10 of the European Convention on Human Rights. Before the European Court of Human Rights, the main issue was whether, under art 10, the ban on publication was 'necessary in a democratic society . . . for maintaining the authority and impartiality of the judiciary'. By 11 to 9 votes, the court held that the ban had not been shown to be necessary for this purpose.[105]

The Contempt of Court Act 1981 was designed to bring British law into line with the requirements of the *Sunday Times* decision,[106] and is now recognised as reconciling the

---

[100] See *Saunders* v *Punch Ltd* [1998] 1 WLR 986.

[101] *John* v *Express Newspapers* [2000] 1 WLR 1931, and *Broadmoor Hospital* v *Hyde*, *The Independent*, 4 March 1994.

[102] Leading cases arising out of criminal litigation before 1981 include *R* v *Bolam, ex p Haigh* (1949) 93 SJ 220; *R* v *Evening Standard Co Ltd* [1954] 1 QB 578; *R* v *Thomson Newspapers Ltd, ex p A–G* [1968] 1 All ER 268; and *Stirling* v *Associated Newspapers Ltd* 1960 JC 5. In relation to civil litigation, see *Vine Products Ltd* v *Green* [1966] Ch 484.

[103] Cmnd 5794, 1974.

[104] *A–G* v *Times Newspapers Ltd* [1974] AC 273.

[105] *Sunday Times* v *UK* (1979) 2 EHRR 245.

[106] See S Bailey (1982) 45 MLR 301.

competing rights in articles 6 (fair trial) and 10 (freedom of expression) of the ECHR.[107] The courts have emphasised that in enacting the Contempt of Court Act 1981,

> Parliament was thereby recognising the need to ensure that restrictions should be placed on media coverage of court proceedings only to the extent that it could be shown to be necessary and proportionate to the need to protect the administration of justice.[108]

Under the Act, liability for contempt is based on the 'strict liability rule', defined to mean 'the rule of law whereby conduct may be treated as a contempt of court as tending to interfere with the course of justice in particular legal proceedings regardless of intent to do so' (s 1). By s 2, the strict liability rule applies to any publication that creates 'a substantial risk that the course of justice in the proceedings in question will be seriously impeded or prejudiced'.

The strict liability rule applies to both civil and criminal proceedings. According to the Law Commission in a recent consultation paper canvassing options for the reform of the law relating to contempt of court (on which see below), 'section 2 involves a test with two benchmarks: the level of risk must be substantial; the degree of prejudice or impediment likely to be caused must be serious'.[109] The questions of 'substantial risk' and 'serious prejudice' are to be determined 'as at the date of publication', the questions to be examined from a practical rather than a theoretical perspective.[110] In emphasising the predictive nature of this task, the courts have also pointed out that it must be 'proved to the criminal standard and separately in relation to each defendant',[111] 'that there was a significant risk that the potentially highly prejudicial articles would seriously prejudice the course of justice',[112] and that 'the circumstances of the publication actually gave rise to a substantial risk of serious prejudice'.[113]

The other requirement of s 2 is that the proceedings in question must be 'active', governed by Sch 1, which lays down in detail when civil or criminal proceedings begin to be active. Criminal proceedings become active when an individual is arrested or orally charged or when an arrest warrant is issued (whereas at common law liability for contempt could arise where criminal proceedings were imminent).[114] Civil proceedings become active not when the writ is served but when the action is set down for trial. In some cases, proceedings may be instituted at common law to deal with publications which are likely to prejudice the outcome of proceedings not yet active within the statutory definition.[115] Proceedings remain active in criminal cases until concluded by acquittal, sentence or discontinuance, and in other cases until the proceedings are disposed of, discontinued or withdrawn.[116] Apart from criminal liability, it may be possible to restrain a publication in breach of the strict liability rule by injunction, though this will be difficult if the information is already in the public domain.[117]

---

[107] See *Attorney General* v *MGN Ltd* [2011] EWHC 2074 (Admin), [2012] 1 WLR 2408; and *Attorney General* v *Times Newspapers Ltd* [2012] EWHC 3195 (Admin).

[108] *Attorney General* v *Times Newspapers Ltd*, ibid, citing Lord Hailsham, HL Debs 9 December 1980, col 660.

[109] Law Commission, note 88 above, para 2.45.

[110] *Attorney General* v *MGN Ltd*, above, para 17.

[111] Ibid.

[112] *Attorney General* v *Times Newspapers Ltd*, above, para 38.

[113] Ibid, para 35.

[114] *R* v *Savundranayagan* [1968] 3 All ER 439; *R* v *Beaverbrook Newspapers Ltd* [1962] NI 15.

[115] *A-G* v *News Group Newspapers* [1989] QB 110. Cf *A-G* v *Sport Newspapers Ltd* [1991] 1 WLR 1194.

[116] On the question of appeals against sentence and 'misguided' press campaigns, see *R* v *Vano*, *The Times*, 29 December 1994.

[117] *Attorney-General* v *BBC* [2007] EWCA Civ 280; *Attorney General* v *Random House Group Ltd* [2009] EWHC 1727 (QB), [2010] EMLR 9.

Application of strict liability rule

The question whether there is a substantial risk that the course of justice in particular legal proceedings will be seriously impeded or prejudiced is ultimately one of fact; this will depend primarily on whether the publication will bring influence to bear which is likely to direct the proceedings in some way from the course which they would otherwise have followed.[118] Many of the cases on contempt of court are concerned with pre-trial publicity that may influence the jury, though questions such as the impact of publication on an ongoing police investigation are also relevant.[119] In recent years, however, it appeared that the Act was not vigorously applied and that a great deal of press reporting and speculation was taking place that would not have been tolerated in the past. Indeed, it appears to have been accepted that much of the concern about pre-trial publicity might be exaggerated. In the typical case someone would be arrested and there would be much coverage of the individual in question. But except in notorious cases,[120] memory of such reporting would be likely to fade by the time of the trial, while other steps would be taken by the judge to ensure the integrity of the jury's deliberations.[121]

Yet perhaps reflecting the general decline in press standards on the one hand, and a tightening up by the Attorney General on the other, there has been a spate of contempt cases in recent years. In *Attorney General v MGN Ltd*,[122] a man was arrested on suspicion of a murder he plainly did not commit. He was then the subject of the most appalling vilification in the press before being released by the police. Although the man in question was not prosecuted, the abuse took place at a time when proceedings were active, and it was held that the vilification of a suspect 'readily' fell within s 2(2) of the 1981 Act, not least because it would discourage witnesses coming forward in his defence. And in *Attorney General v Associated Newspapers Ltd*,[123] a man was found guilty by a jury of the murder of a young woman that had attracted a great deal of media attention. The jury announced its verdict in this case while still considering its verdict in another murder case involving the same man. While the latter was under consideration, several newspapers published an account of the conviction in the first case that included material that had never been put to the jury. This was held to be contempt, and indeed the proceedings in the second case had to be discontinued.

There are nevertheless a number of defences to the strict liability rule, including the defence of innocent publication (1981 Act, s 3), where the person responsible for the publication can prove that, having taken all reasonable care, he or she did not know that relevant

---

[118] *Re Lonrho* [1990] 2 AC 154.

[119] See *A-G v News Group Newspapers Ltd* [1986] 2 All ER 833; *A-G v ITN Ltd* [1995] 2 All ER 370; *A-G v BBC* [1997] EMLR 76; *A-G v MGN Ltd* [1997] 1 All ER 456 (no contempt where trial would not take place for several months and where already saturation coverage); *A-G v Birmingham Post and Mail Ltd* [1999] 1 WLR 361; *A-G v Associated Newspapers Ltd* [2011] EWHC 418 (Admin), [2011] 1 WLR 2097. For Scotland, see *HM Advocate v Caledonian Newspapers Ltd* 1995 SCCR 330; *Cox and Griffiths, Petitioners* 1998 SCCR 561; *Al Megrahi v Times Newspapers Ltd* 1999 SCCR 824; *HM Advocate v The Scotsman Publications* 1999 SLT 466; *Scottish Daily Record v Thompson* 2009 SLT 363.

[120] *Attorney-General v Times Newspapers Ltd*, *The Times*, 12 February 1983, is one notorious case where it has been accepted that the 'fade factor' would not work in favour of the defence. That case concerned reports carried by newspapers about a man who had intruded into the Queen's bedroom at Buckingham Palace. The man in question was awaiting trial on a number of counts, including the theft of a bottle of wine. It was held that a newspaper report that he had admitted the theft was a contempt, since it was difficult to see how an assertion that an accused person had admitted the very fact that was in issue could do otherwise than cause a very substantial risk that the trial might be prejudiced. It is also the case that pre-trial publicity is unlikely to be a contempt in proceedings pending before an appeal court: *Re Lonrho plc* [1990] 2 AC 154.

[121] See *Attorney General v Times Newspapers Ltd* [2012] EWHC 3195 (Admin).

[122] [2011] EWHC 2074 (Admin), [2012] 1 WLR 2408.

[123] [2012] EWHC 2029 (Admin).

legal proceedings were active.[124] The second is the 'fair and accurate report of legal proceedings held in public, published contemporaneously and in good faith' (s 4(1)). However, a court may order the publication of reports to be delayed – but not prevented indefinitely[125] – where necessary to avoid a substantial risk of prejudice to the administration of justice (s 4(2)). 'In forming a view whether it is necessary to make an order for avoiding such a risk a court will inevitably have regard to the competing public interest considerations of ensuring a fair trial and of open justice.'[126] More recently, it has been said that a s 4(2) order should only be made 'as a last resort', and should not be used to impose a permanent ban on the reporting of a trial, or aspects relating thereto.[127] Before granting an order under s 4(2), the magistrates are entitled to hear representations from the press that the order should not be granted.[128]

The third defence is where the publication contains a good faith discussion of public affairs if the risk of prejudice to particular legal proceedings is merely incidental to the discussion (s 5). In *Attorney-General* v *English* Lord Diplock noted that s 5 does not take the form of an exception to s 2, but stands on an equal footing with it: 'It does not set out exculpatory matter. Like s 2(2) it states what publications shall *not* amount to contempt of court despite their tendency to interfere with the course of justice in particular legal proceedings.'[129]

In *Attorney-General* v *English, The Daily Mail* published an article in support of a woman standing for election to Parliament as an independent pro-life candidate, one of her aims being to stop the alleged practice in hospitals whereby newly born disabled babies were allowed to die. At the time the article was published a well-known paediatrician was standing trial, accused of murdering a three-day-old boy with Down's syndrome, by allowing him to die of starvation.

The House of Lords held that this did not amount to a contempt of court; although the publication of the article on the third day of the trial was capable of prejudicing the jury, the publication was a discussion in good faith on a matter of wide public interest and the risk of prejudice was incidental to the discussion. To hold otherwise 'would have prevented [the candidate] from . . . obtaining publicity for what was a main plank in her election programme and would have stifled all discussion in the press . . . about mercy killing from the time that [the doctor] was charged in the magistrates' court in February 1981 until the date of his acquittal [in] November of that year.'[130]

---

[124] See also *HM Advocate* v *Express Newspapers plc* 1998 SCCR 471.

[125] *BBC, Petitioners* 2002 SLT 2; *In re Times Newspapers Ltd* v *R* [2007] EWCA Crim 1925, [2008] 1 WLR 234.

[126] *R* v *Central Criminal Court Ex parte Telegraph plc* [1993] 1 WLR 980; [1993] 2 All ER 971, at 975. See *R* v *Horsham Justices, ex p Farquharson* [1982] QB 762 (M J Beloff [1992] PL 92); *Marine A* v *Guardian News and Media*, above (applying *Independent Publishing Co Ltd* v *A-G of Trinidad and Tobago* [2004] UKPC 26, [2005] 1 AC 190 and important for emphasizing that the s 4(2) balancing will require also a balancing of competing Convention rights, such as those arising under arts 2, 6 and 10).

[127] *R (Press Association)* v *Cambridge Crown Court* [2012] EWCA Crim 2434, [2013] 1 WLR 1979, at para 13. It was explained there that these orders are typically used to prevent any prejudice to proceedings in a subsequent trial involving the same parties or witnesses, or to prevent the publication of evidence or argument before the judge in the absence of the jury, or where there has been a successful appeal against conviction, to avoid prejudice to any retrial. See also *Re X and Y* [2012] EWCA Civ 1500 (no reporting of oral argument in sensitive case to prevent counsel from being inhibited in argument). But see *MGN Ltd (Application for Leave to Appeal)* [2011] EWCA Crim 100, (2011) Cr App Rep 31. On the right of appeal against an order issued under s 4(2), see Criminal Justice Act 1988, s 159. For Scotland, see *Scottish Daily Record, Petitioner* 1998 SCCR 626; *Galbraith* v *HM Advocate* 2001 SLT 465; and *BBC, Petitioners* 2002 SLT 2

[128] *R* v *Clerkenwell Metropolitan Magistrate, ex p The Telegraph plc* [1993] QB 462.

[129] [1983] 1 AC 116, 141.

[130] [1983] 1 AC 116, at 144 (Lord Diplock).

The strict liability rule does not apply to the good faith reporting of proceedings of the Scottish Parliament or Welsh Assembly.[131] Nor does it apply to tribunals which do not exercise the 'judicial power of the state'.[132]

Other acts interfering with the course of justice

Nothing in the Contempt of Court Act 1981 is designed to restrict liability for contempt of court in respect of conduct intended to impede or prejudice the administration of justice (s 6(2)). Many other acts are punishable as contempts, some of them also being criminal offences in their own right, for example attempts to pervert the course of justice or interference with witnesses.[133] A prison governor who, acting under prison rules, obstructed a prisoner's communication with the High Court was held to be in contempt.[134] It is a contempt to punish or victimise a witness for evidence which has already been given, even in proceedings which have concluded, since this might deter potential witnesses in future cases.[135] It may be a contempt of court for a solicitor to disclose to a journalist documents relating to litigation.

A prisoner challenged the legality of a Home Office decision to set up a 'control unit' for prisoners considered to be troublemakers. An order for discovery of documents being made against the Home Office, a large number of official documents were made available to the prisoner's solicitor. She undertook that the documents would be used only for the case in hand, but she later allowed a journalist to see documents which had been read out in open court.

The journalist published an article based on these documents. The House of Lords held (by three to two) that although the documents had been read in court, and could have been reported by journalists present, the solicitor was guilty of contempt since she had used the documents for a purpose which was not necessary for the conduct of her client's case, and had broken her implied undertaking to the court that had ordered discovery.[136]

Interference with the work of a jury may constitute contempt, whether before, during or after a trial.[137] By s 8 of the Contempt of Court Act 1981, it is a contempt of court to solicit, obtain or disclose details of any statements made or votes cast by jurors during their deliberations in any legal proceedings.[138] This reversed a decision in 1980 that a magazine article

---

[131] Scotland Act 1998, s 42; and Government of Wales Act 2006, s 43.

[132] Contempt of Court Act 1981, s 19. See *Pickering* v *Liverpool Daily Post plc* [1991] 2 AC 370 and *General Medical Council* v *BBC* [1998] 1 WLR 1573. For background, see *AG* v *BBC* [1981] AC 303.

[133] See *Peach Grey & Co* v *Sommers* [1995] 2 All ER 513.

[134] *Raymond* v *Honey* [1983] AC 1.

[135] *A-G* v *Butterworth* [1963] 1 QB 696; *Moore* v *Clerk of Assize, Bristol* [1973] 1 All ER 58.

[136] *Home Office* v *Harman* [1983] AC 280. Subsequent proceedings under the European Convention on Human Rights were the subject of a friendly settlement. In 1987 the decision was largely reversed by an amendment to the Rules of the Supreme Court, which released parties from any undertaking once the material has been read in open court.

[137] See *Attorney General* v *Fraill* [2011] EWCA Crim 1570, (2011) Cr App R 21; *Attorney General* v *Dallas* [2012] EWHC 136 (Admin), [2012] 1 WLR 991; and *Attorney General* v *Davey* [2013] EWHC 2317 (Admin).

[138] It is an offence for a jury member to write to a relative of a convicted person to expose unfairness by jurors (*A-G* v *Scotcher* [2004] UKHL 36, [2005] 1 WLR 1867), but it is not an offence to raise such concerns with the court (*R* v *Mirza* [2004] UKHL 2, [2004] 1 AC 1118). It is also an offence for a newspaper to publish jury deliberations: *A-G* v *Associated Newspapers* [1994] 2 AC 238. On the compatibility of s 8 with the ECHR, art 10, see *Scotcher*, above, and now *Seckerson* v *United Kingdom* [2012] ECHR 241, (2012) 54 EHRR SE 19.

disclosing aspects of the jury's deliberations during the trial of Mr Jeremy Thorpe was not a contempt of court.[139] Section 8 still applies in Scotland and Northern Ireland but has been replaced in England and Wales by an amendment to the Juries Act 1974.[140] The latter is similar in terms to s 8, but contains a number of exceptions designed principally to permit disclosures that expose juror misconduct.

The dynamic nature of the law of contempt has been well demonstrated by decisions arising out of important disputes between the courts and the press. It is a contempt for a newspaper to disregard a judge's directions that the names of prosecution witnesses in blackmail cases should not be published.[141] But the power to issue such directions is not limited to blackmail cases.

> In *Attorney-General* v *Leveller Magazine Ltd* a magazine published the name of a prosecution witness at an official secrets trial, who had been described in court as Colonel B. The House of Lords held that it was contempt of court to publish a witness's name if this interfered with the administration of justice. But on the facts no contempt had occurred, since inter alia, no clear direction against publication had been given by the magistrates; and Colonel B's identity could have been discovered from evidence given in open court.[142]

The uncertainties left by this decision were reduced by the Contempt of Court Act 1981. By s 11, where a court has the power to withhold evidence from the public (although the court is sitting in public) and allows the name of a witness or other matter to be withheld, it may restrict publication accordingly.[143] Although the courts should be careful about exercising this power (which should not be used to protect privacy or avoid embarrassment),[144] nevertheless it would be a contempt of court to publish information, even though the identity of the witness could be discovered from evidence given in open court, as in the *Leveller Magazine* case. However, a court cannot prohibit the press from reporting names which are mentioned in court unless there has first been a direction that these names should be withheld from the public.[145] Nor can an order be issued under section 11 to prevent *speculation* about what may have been said in camera, with section 11 applying only to prohibit the publication of a *name or matter*.[146] And although it clearly affects freedom of expression, a restriction order under section 11 does not violate the Convention rights of the press in a case where making the order was 'overwhelming'.[147]

It may also be contempt to publish material which has been the subject of an injunction against another party.[148] A third party who knowingly acts in breach of the terms of the

---

[139] *A-G* v *New Statesman Publishing Co* [1981] QB 1.

[140] As inserted by Criminal Justice and Courts Act 2015, s 74.

[141] *R* v *Socialist Worker Ltd, ex p A-G* [1975] QB 637. But magistrates cannot withhold their identity from the public or the press: *R* v *Felixstowe JJ, ex p Leigh* [1987] QB 582.

[142] [1979] AC 440.

[143] On the circumstances in which a court has the power to withhold evidence from the public, see *In re Times Newspapers Ltd* [2008] EWCA Crim 2396, [2009] 1 WLR 1015.

[144] *R* v *Westminster City Council, ex p Castelli, The Times*, 14 August 1995. Also *Trustor AB* v *Smallbone* [2000] 1 All ER 811. This applies particularly where anonymity is sought by one of the parties to litigation rather than by a witness: *R* v *Legal Aid Board, ex p Kaim Todner* [1999] QB 966.

[145] *R* v *Arundel Justices, ex p Westminster Press* [1985] 2 All ER 390.

[146] *Times Newspapers Ltd* v *R* [2007] EWCA Crim 1925, [2008] 1 WLR 234. The Court of Appeal warned, however, that such speculation might constitute a contempt of court at common law, which is expressly preserved by the 1981 Act (s 6(c)). For full consideration of this case, see Ewing, *Bonfire of the Liberties*, ch 5.

[147] *A* v *BBC*, above. It was also held in the latter case that the provisions of the Human Rights Act 1998, s 12 do not apply to s 11 orders. See pp 389–390. below.

[148] *A-G* v *Times Newspapers Ltd* [1992] 1 AC 191. See also *A-G* v *Observer* [1988] 1 All ER 385.

injunction may be in contempt even though he or she is not a party to the proceedings and indeed may not have had an opportunity to make representations in these proceedings:

> In 1986 interlocutory injunctions were granted against two newspapers, *The Guardian* and *The Observer*, restraining them from publishing material from the book *Spycatcher*, by Mr Peter Wright, pending a full trial of the action in which the Attorney General sought permanent injunctions on the ground that the information was confidential. While interlocutory injunctions were still in force, extensive extracts from the book were published in other newspapers, including the *Sunday Times*. The House of Lords held that these publications amounted to a contempt of court, even though the injunctions had not been issued against these newspapers in the first place.
>
> In the view of the House, where a party (C) knowingly does something which would if done by B be a breach of an injunction obtained by A against B, C is guilty of contempt of court if this conduct interferes with the administration of justice between A and B. In this case the publication by C (the *Sunday Times*) did interfere with proceedings between A (the Attorney General) and B (*The Guardian* and *The Observer*). The consequence of the publication by the *Sunday Times* before the main *Spycatcher* trial was to nullify, in part at least, the purpose of such a trial, because it put into the public domain part of the material which the Attorney General claimed should remain confidential.

The principle in the latter case is sometimes referred to as the 'Spycatcher principle', for obvious reasons. The Court of Appeal has since been unwilling to accept that 'conduct by a third party which is inconsistent with a court order in only a trivial or technical way should expose a party to conviction for contempt'.[149] However, the importance of the principle is not to be under-estimated, nor is the willingness of the courts to enforce it:

> In *AG v Punch Ltd*[150] an interlocutory injunction was granted to restrain Associated Newspapers Ltd (proprietors of the *Mail on Sunday*) from publishing any information obtained from Mr David Shayler which was obtained by him in the course of or as a result of his employment in the security service. Mr Shayler subsequently started to write a weekly column for *Punch*, the aim of the column being to criticise the performance of the security service.
>
> Following the publication of an article about an IRA bombing in London, the Attorney General brought contempt proceedings against *Punch*. The Court of Appeal overturned the first instance decision that there had been a contempt, the court accepting that the editor 'thought that the purpose of the [injunction] was to restrain material dangerous to national security' which it was not his intention to publish. But on an appeal by the Attorney General, the original decision was restored.
>
> According to Lord Nicholls, the editor of *Punch* knew that the action against Shayler raised confidentiality issues relating to national security: 'He must, inevitably, have appreciated that by publishing the article he was doing precisely what the order was intended to prevent, namely, pre-empting the court's decision on these confidentiality issues. That is knowing interference with the administration of justice.'[151]

---

[149] *A-G v Newspaper Publishing plc* [1997] 1 WLR 926 (Lord Bingham CJ). Also *Harrow LBC v Johnstone* [1997] 1 WLR 459.

[150] [2002] UKHL 50, [2003] 1 AC 1046.

[151] Ibid, at para 52.

Reform

The current legal framework on the law of contempt was drafted in a very different era. Although the 1981 Act was a response to the decision of the Strasbourg court in the *Sunday Times* case, the law now in force pre-dates the modern human rights era, which has raised questions about the balance struck in 1981 between competing interests. The law developed in 1981 also predates the internet and other modern means of communication, as well as what some might see as a declining newspaper industry revealed by experience to be much less respectful of others than may have been the case even in 1981.

The Attorney General in the Coalition government (Dominic Grieve) appeared to have taken a much greater interest in the law of contempt than his Labour predecessors, and with it a greater willingness to confront the press, which may also explain a recent spate of prosecutions for contempt covering a wide range of issues. It may also explain his request that the Law Commission should give priority to this question in its current work programme, which has already led to the removal of liability for scandalising the judiciary, a form of contempt that hitherto had been thought to have fallen into disuse.[152]

In a consultation paper issued in 2012, the Law Commission identified a number of other areas of difficulty. The first relates to contempt in the face of the court, where concern was expressed about the uncertain scope of the offence, the inconsistency between courts in dealing with it, and the compatibility of existing law with ECHR, art 6. The second relates to the strict liability rule, with one of a number of concerns being whether the 'threshold of *serious* prejudice or impediment is too high and that *any* prejudice or impediment caused by a publication should be sufficient to be in contempt'.[153] The third is that the current law was introduced in a very different era, pre-internet.

These concerns were expressed well by the Law Commission in its consultation paper on contempt. There it is cogently argued that while 'prejudicial information may historically have faded with the newspaper print, as well as from our collective memory, as data it is now processed, archived and is retrievable for very much longer periods of time'.[154] Attention was also drawn to growing concern about juror 'misconduct' – relating particularly to the problem of jurors communicating with third parties or seeking information about defendants on the internet,[155] now largely addressed by amendments to the Juries Act 1974.[156]

D. The executive and the machinery of justice[157]

Questions about the court structure, the buildings in which the courts should be housed, and how the courts should be funded, are questions for the government that cannot be decided by the judges and lawyers (though they may be consulted about such decisions). Before 2007, the Lord Chancellor's Department (latterly the Department for Constitutional Affairs) and the Home Office were the government departments principally responsible for such matters.

---

[152] Crime and Courts Act 2013, s 33. For a recent and unusual revival of this head of liability in Northern Ireland in proceedings brought against a former Cabinet minister (Peter Hain) for comments in his autobiography, see *The Guardian*, 17 May 2012. See generally on this head of liability, the 13th edn of this book, pp 378–9.

[153] Law Commission, above, para 2.45, citing *Worm v Austria* (1997) 25 EHRR 454.

[154] Ibid, para 3.1.

[155] See respectively *Attorney General v Fraill* [2011] EWCA Crim 1570, (2011) Cr App R 21; and *Attorney General v Dallas* [2012] EWHC 136 (Admin), [2012] 1 WLR 991 (contempt of court for interfering with administration of justice). See also *Attorney General v Davey* [2013] EWHC 2317 (Admin).

[156] As inserted by Criminal Justice and Courts Act 2015, ss 71–3.

[157] See Brazier, *Constitutional Practice*, ch 12.

These matters are now the responsibility of the Ministry of Justice, which as one of the biggest departments in government inherited the duties of the Department for Constitutional Affairs as well as duties performed hitherto by the Home Office.[158] The birth of the Ministry of Justice proved to be controversial, mainly because of the way in which the new Ministry was established, drawing criticism of the government from the House of Lords Constitution Committee (and from the House of Commons Constitutional Affairs Committee).[159]

It was a particular concern of the foregoing critics that the government had failed to consult the judiciary in good time about its plans, the Lords Committee advising that the government must learn to treat the judges as a constitutional partner rather than merely the subjects of change. The Lord Chancellor and Secretary of State for Justice is the ministerial head of the Ministry of Justice. The position is different in Scotland, where there is a Secretary for Justice in the Scottish Government.

Lord Chancellor

The office of Lord Chancellor was regarded as one of the great offices of state with an unbroken pedigree stretching back to 1068, the position having been held in that time by some notable historical figures, including Thomas Becket, Thomas Wolsey and Sir Thomas More. Apart from being a member of the Cabinet as political head of an important government department, the Lord Chancellor was also the Speaker of the House of Lords, for which a portion of his salary was paid by the House of Lords. On appointment, moreover, the Lord Chancellor took the judicial oath and was entitled to preside over the House of Lords in its judicial work and the Judicial Committee of the Privy Council.

Thus, Lord Mackay sat on 67 occasions (House of Lords and Privy Council) between 1987 and 1994, while Lord Hailsham sat 68 times as Lord Chancellor between 1979 and 1987.[160] Lord Irvine also took part in a number of cases,[161] though he was the last to do so. The role of the Lord Chancellor has been radically redefined since 2003, with the Constitutional Reform Act 2005 giving effect to a series of changes that were under way before the Act was passed. The Lord Chancellor has ceased to be a judge and no longer takes the judicial oath,[162] with a new oath for the Lord Chancellor being introduced by the Constitutional Reform Act 2005.[163] Also, the Lord Chancellor is no longer the Speaker of the House of Lords, which now elects its own presiding officer.[164]

Unusually for a government minister, there are statutory provisions relating to eligibility for appointment of the Lord Chancellor. The Constitutional Reform Act 2005 provides that a person may not be recommended for appointment as Lord Chancellor unless 'qualified by experience', which includes experience as a minister, a member of either House of Parliament, a legal practitioner, a university law teacher, and anything else the Prime Minister 'considers relevant'.[165] None of the foregoing factors is a requirement or condition of appointment, and in particular the Lord Chancellor need no longer be legally qualified. Nor is it necessary for the Lord Chancellor now to be a member of the House of Lords, with the first incumbent under the new regime (Jack Straw) being a member of the House of Commons.

[158] The creation of a Ministry of Justice had been proposed by the Haldane Committee on the Machinery of Government as long ago as 1918: Cd 9230, 1918.
[159] See HL Paper 151 (2006–7), and HC 466 (2006–7). See further A W Bradley [2008] PL 470.
[160] HL Deb, 24 October 1994, col 395 (WA). Also HL Deb, 20 October 1992, col 82 (WA).
[161] See for example *DPP* v *Jones* [1999] 2 AC 240 (ch 18); and *National Power plc* v *Carmichael* [1999] ICR 1227.
[162] Constitutional Reform Act 2005, s 17.
[163] Ibid, amending the Promissory Oaths Act 1868.
[164] Constitutional Reform Act, s 18.
[165] Ibid, s 2.

Some of the responsibilities previously discharged by the Lord Chancellor have been reassigned, many going to the Lord Chief Justice whose administrative role as Head of the Judiciary in England and Wales has been greatly enhanced by the Constitutional Reform Act 2005 (as amended in 2013).[166] So while the Lord Chancellor still remains concerned with virtually all judicial appointments at the level of the High Court and above, responsibility for judicial appointments below that level has been re-assigned. Although senior appointments now fall within the scope of the Judicial Appointments Commission, it remains the case nevertheless that the Lord Chancellor retains a potentially important role in advising the Queen on judicial appointments at different levels of seniority.[167] It is not clear, nevertheless, whether the office continues to be necessary.[168]

Ministry of Justice

Despite the apparent diminution in the role and status of the Lord Chancellor, he or she remains head of what is claimed to be one of the largest government departments, with a wide range of responsibilities. These relate principally to the administration of justice in its widest sense (including the courts, prisons and probation services), as well as constitutional matters (including human rights). Some of these responsibilities are underpinned by statute in the sense that the Lord Chancellor has a statutory duty to ensure that there is an efficient and effective system to support the carrying on of the business of the courts.[169] This includes the appointment of staff and the provision of accommodation,[170] and the appointment of court security officers with powers of search, as well as powers of exclusion, removal and restraint.[171]

As pointed out, the creation of the Ministry of Justice was controversial, and led to a souring of relations between government and judiciary. One concern of the judges was that funding for the courts, tribunals and legal aid might be put at risk by having to compete in the Ministry of Justice with expenditure needed for prisons. The impasse was resolved when the Lord Chancellor and the Lord Chief Justice agreed to establish an executive agency,[172] Her Majesty's Courts Service. Unlike other executive agencies, the latter was to be based on a 'partnership model', an approach adopted because the courts 'are by their nature a shared endeavour between the judiciary, who are responsible for the judicial function to deliver justice independently, and the government, which has overall responsibility for the justice system'.

In April 2008, details of the agreement between the Lord Chancellor and the Lord Chief Justice were laid before Parliament in the form of HM Courts Service Framework Document.[173] In outline, the Lord Chancellor and the Lord Chief Justice undertook jointly to agree the aims and objectives for the Courts Service, and the priorities for funding within the Service. The Courts Service was replaced by HM Courts and Tribunals Service, which was established in 2011 on the same partnership model as its predecessor, though now including the Senior President of Tribunals along with the Lord Chancellor and the Lord Chief Justice.[174] The role

---

[166] Ibid, ss 12, 13; Sch 1, 2.

[167] See above, section A. Some responsibilities have been assigned to the Senior President of Tribunals: see ch 23 A.

[168] Contrast G Gee [2014] PL 11.

[169] Courts Act 2003, s 1.

[170] Ibid, s 3. Although employed as civil servants, court service staff may be regarded by the courts as part of the judicial arm of the state, as in *Quinland* v *Governor of Swaleside Prison* [2002] EWCA Civ 174, [2003] QB 306.

[171] Courts Act 2003, ss 51–7.

[172] See ch 11 A on executive agencies.

[173] Cm 7350, 2008.

[174] Cm 8043, 2011.

of HM Courts and Tribunals Service is to 'run an efficient and effective courts and tribunals system, which enables the rule of law to be upheld and provides access to justice for all'.[175]

The Courts and Tribunal Service Framework Agreement makes clear that it is to be reviewed every three years, and that while it may be amended before the mandatory review, any such amendment will require the agreement of all parties.[176] Provision is made for the Lord Chancellor to override the need for consent where it is necessary to do so to enable him to carry out duties under the Courts Act 2003 and the Tribunals, Courts and Enforcement Act 2007. On the other hand, the Lord Chief Justice may terminate the partnership if he concludes that 'it is no longer compatible with his constitutional position or the independence of the judiciary'.[177] If the partnership is terminated, governance of the Service will revert to a conventional executive agency model reporting directly to the Lord Chancellor, until a new model is agreed.[178]

Law Officers of the Crown[179]

The Attorney General and Solicitor General are the law officers of the Crown, ministerial positions to which the incumbents are appointed by the Prime Minister. Their historic role is to represent the Crown in the courts, and they now act as legal advisers to the government on important matters, though ministers may also receive legal advice from within their own departments. Serviced by the Attorney General's office, the Law Officers operate independently of the Ministry of Justice and have a number of responsibilities. These include leading for the Crown in major prosecutions (especially in trials involving state security or official secrecy) or in major civil actions to which the Crown is a party (such as litigation relating to Brexit).[180]

In other cases (the great bulk), the Law Officers will be responsible for recruiting and appointing counsel who appear on behalf of the government in legal proceedings; appointing a special advocate to represent the interests of a party who cannot for security or other reasons be fully informed of all the material relied on against him or her;[181] and lodging an appeal against sentences which are considered to be unduly lenient. The Attorney General's consent is also needed for relator actions, with decisions granting or refusing such consent not yet subject to review by the courts.[182] Otherwise, the Law Officers have parliamentary responsibilities, which includes giving advice to parliamentary committees (notably the Standards and Privileges Committee).

It has been said that in the exercise of these many different functions, 'the Attorney General acts not as a minister of the Crown (although he is of course such) and not as the public officer with overall responsibility for the conduct of prosecutions, but as independent, unpartisan guardian of the public interest in the administration of justice'.[183] It had been the practice since the reign of George III for the Attorney General to be an MP, though between 1999 and 2010

---

[175] Ibid, para 2.2.

[176] HM Courts and Tribunals Service Framework Document (2014).

[177] Ibid, para 10.5.

[178] On the relationship between the Ministry of Justice and the Lord Chief Justice, see HC 97 (2012–13), paras 115–19 (Justice Committee).

[179] Edwards, *The Law Officers of the Crown*, and (same author), *The Attorney General, Politics and the Public Interest*.

[180] See *R (Miller) v Secretary of State for Exiting the EU* [2017] UKSC 5, [2017] 2 WLR 583.

[181] See *R v H* [2004] UKHL 3, [2004] 2 AC 134.

[182] *Gouriet v Union of Post Office Workers* [1978] AC 435; Chs 10, 25. On the requirement of Attorney General consent under the Charities Act 2011, s 325, see M Synge [2016] PL 409.

[183] *R v H*, above, per Lord Bingham, at para 46.

the office was held by life peers.[184] In view of his or her duties in connection with prosecutions, it is thought preferable that the Attorney General should remain outside the Cabinet, attending particular Cabinet meetings when summoned.

After a detailed examination of the role of the Law Officers carried out in 2007–8, the government concluded that the Attorney General should continue as the law officer and as a minister responsible to Parliament, rejecting a suggestion that the work of the Attorney should be carried out by an official outside party political life.[185] The government did, however, propose that the independence of the office should be strengthened by a new oath, committing the incumbent to uphold the rule of law, while the government also seemed open to the possibility of greater parliamentary scrutiny of the office.[186] A recent holder of the office (Dominic Grieve) played a prominent part in revitalising the law relating to contempt of court, appearing in a number of high-profile prosecutions.

Law Officers' advice

The invasion of Iraq in 2003 gave rise to a number of political concerns, not the least of which was the legal basis for the government's action, it being widely believed in this country that the action did not have the necessary authority under international law. Related to this were questions about the advice which the government received from the Attorney General, and the extent to which that advice was made fully available to the Cabinet as a whole. There were also queries about the circumstances – if any – in which the advice might be made available to Parliament and the public, either at the time it was given, or after the event when questions were raised about the legality of the government's conduct. Erskine May refers to a 'long-standing convention, observed by successive governments', that 'the fact of, and substance of advice from, the law officers of the Crown is not disclosed outside government'.

Erskine May also explains that 'the purpose of this convention is to enable the government to obtain full and frank legal advice in confidence'.[187] This is not to say that the advice may not be disclosed, but it does mean that it will not be laid before Parliament or quoted from in debate, unless a minister considers it expedient to do so;[188] even then it may be appropriate to make disclosure only with the consent of the law officer concerned. Indeed, according to the *Ministerial Code*, 'the fact that the Law Officers have advised or have not advised and the content of their advice must not be disclosed outside government without their authority'.[189] Breach of this principle may lead to the resignation of a minister, as during the Westland affair in 1985–6 when a Cabinet minister resigned following the leak to the media of a confidential letter of advice from the Solicitor General to other ministers.

The disclosure of the advice given by the Law Officers thus takes place very infrequently, despite the highly charged circumstances in which advice may sometimes have to be given. It has been said by one authority that there is 'an impregnable moat around the Law Officer's opinions',[190] and acknowledged judicially that

there are only five occasions in the 40 years before 2008 when the government of the day decided that the public interest favoured disclosure of such advice. These were: 1971, when the substance of the advice was disclosed but not the actual advice relating to the United Kingdom's

---

[184] For a critique of this departure from long established practice, see *The Guardian*, 21 November 2005 (editorial), and for a defence, see Lord Goodhart, *The Guardian*, 22 November 2005 (letter to the editor).

[185] For a more recent assessment, see G Appleby [2016] PL 573.

[186] Cm 7342, 2008, paras 91–8. Compare HC 306 (2006–7); HL Paper 93 (2007–8).

[187] Erskine May, p 447.

[188] See HC Deb, 17 March 2003, col 515 (WA).

[189] *Ministerial Code*, para 2.13. And see pp 287–8 above.

[190] Edwards, *The Attorney General, Politics and the Public Interest*, p 226.

obligations to supply arms to South Africa under the Simonstown Agreement [*sic*]; 1986: the disclosure of a letter of advice in respect of issues arising under the so-called Westland Affair, there having been an unauthorised partial leak of advice; 1992: the advice of the Law Officers regarding the legal regime governing arms sales to Iraq was disclosed to the Scott Enquiry following the collapse of the Matrix Churchill trial; 1997: the advice of the Law Officers was disclosed in connection with the government's liabilities for breaching community law in the Factortame litigation; 2003 and 2006: the advice of the Attorney General on the legality of the use of force against Iraq was disclosed in March 2003 in part and subsequently in May 2006 in whole.[191]

The then government's review of the office of Attorney General in 2007–8 did not lead it to recommend that the current arrangements should be changed, taking the view (in accordance with a majority of respondents to its consultation exercise) that 'the benefits, which would come from regular disclosure (transparency and accountability)', would be 'vastly outweighed by the downsides (adverse impact on the openness of communications between client and lawyer)'.[192] The government would continue to provide Parliament and the public with an explanation of why a particular course of action is lawful, acknowledging that any such explanation must be consistent with the advice received, and 'must not dishonestly represent that advice'.[193] In 2011 the Coalition government published a summary of the Attorney General's advice in advance of the UN-led invasion of Libya, but consistently with past practice refused to publish the full advice.[194]

E. Prosecution of offenders and miscarriages of justice

In practice, the great majority of criminal prosecutions are initiated by the police; others are instituted by government departments (for example, HM Revenue and Customs for evasion of tax) or local authorities (for example, for breach of by-laws). The position regarding criminal prosecutions in England and Wales was overhauled by the Prosecution of Offences Act 1985, which introduced the Crown Prosecution Service.[195]

The philosophy of the Act was 'to separate the functions of the investigation of crime, that being the responsibility of the police, and the prosecution of offences, that being the responsibility of a single national prosecution service'.[196] It has been emphasised that prosecution is a quasi-judicial act which requires 'the evaluation of the strength of the evidence and also a judgment about whether an investigation and/or prosecution is needed in the public interest'.[197] Prosecutors are thus expected to take decisions in 'a fair and impartial way, acting at all times in accordance with the highest ethical standards and in the best interests of justice'.[198]

In principle, private persons may institute prosecutions in English law for any criminal offence unless by statute this has been excluded,[199] a potentially important safeguard against

---

[191] *HM Treasury* v *Information Commissioner* [2009] EWHC 1811 (Admin), [2010] QB 563, at para [9].

[192] Cm 7342, 2008, para 66.

[193] Ibid, para 68.

[194] See HC 950 (2010–12), para 24 (Defence Committee).

[195] See Report of Royal Commission on Criminal Procedure, Cmnd 8092, 1981, part II.

[196] *Elguzouli-Daf* v *Metropolitan Police Commissioner* [1995] QB 335, at p 346.

[197] Protocol between the Attorney General and the Prosecuting Departments (2012), para 4.1.

[198] Ibid.

[199] For the procedural rights of a private prosecutor, see *R* v *George Maxwell (Developments) Ltd* [1980] 2 All ER 99; *R* v *DPP, ex p Hallas* (1988) 87 Cr App Rep 340. See also *R (Lowden)* v *Gateshead Magistrates' Court)* [2016] EWHC 3436 (Admin); and *R (al Rabbat)* v *Westminster Magistrates' Court* [2017] EWHC 1969 (Admin) (failed attempt to bring private prosecution against Tony Blair and former senior ministers in his government at the time of the Iraq war).

abuse on the part of the prosecuting authorities. The position has traditionally been very different in Scotland where prosecutions are under the control of the Lord Advocate and where private prosecutions are extremely rare.

Crown Prosecution Service

The Crown Prosecution Service is 'an autonomous and independent agency' though 'not a body corporate but a collection of individuals with statutory functions to perform'.[200] It is under the central direction of the Director of Public Prosecutions, an office created in 1879. A barrister or solicitor of at least ten years' standing, the DPP is appointed by the Attorney General to work under his or her general superintendence. Apart from the DPP, other key personnel in the Crown Prosecution Service are the Chief Crown Prosecutors (appointed by the DPP to supervise the work of the CPS in geographical areas), and Crown Prosecutors (barristers or solicitors who conduct proceedings under the direction of the DPP).[201] The CPS reviews cases submitted by the police for prosecution and conducts prosecutions on behalf of the Crown.

The Service also institutes proceedings in difficult or important cases and gives advice to the police on all matters relating to criminal offences. Although the CPS is under a duty to take over all legal proceedings instituted by the police, it is not required to but may take over proceedings begun by others (such as private prosecutions). Having taken over such proceedings, the CPS may discontinue them if the evidence is insufficient, if the proceedings would be contrary to the public interest, to avoid duplication, or for any other good reason.[202] If it is too late to discontinue, the prosecutor may offer no evidence, so that an acquittal automatically follows. The Attorney General has a separate prerogative power to stop a prosecution on indictment by issuing a nolle prosequi. This power is rarely used today,[203] and the Brown government proposed that it should be abolished.[204]

The Prosecution of Offences Act 1985 requires the DPP to issue a Code for Crown Prosecutors,[205] an initiative acknowledged judicially as being important to ensure consistency in prosecuting decisions.[206] In setting out the principles governing prosecutions, the Code for Crown Prosecutors makes it clear that there is no duty to bring criminal proceedings against a person suspected of having committed an offence.[207] Although the Code has been revised, it is still the general rule that proceedings will be brought only when (*a*) there is enough evidence to provide a realistic prospect of conviction, and (*b*) it is in the public interest to prosecute; the Code gives guidance on the factors to be weighed in making this judgment.[208] As a document issued under statutory authority, the Code has been said by the House of Lords to

---

[200] *Elguzouli-Daf*, above, at pp 346, 351. It is in fact a non-ministerial department (ch 12), unlike HM Courts and Tribunals Service (above), which is an executive agency (ch 11).

[201] Surprisingly, the dismissal of a Crown Prosecutor from his or her employment is not normally subject to judicial review: *R v Crown Prosecution Service, ex p Hogg*, The Times, 14 April 1994.

[202] See *R (Gujra) v Crown Prosecution Service* [2012] UKSC 52, [2012] 3 WLR 1227.

[203] For examples of its use in relation to customs prosecutions (where the Attorney General had no duty of superintendence), see HC 115 (1995–6) (Scott Report), para C 3.10.

[204] Cm 7342, 2008, paras 93–4.

[205] CPS, Code for Crown Prosecutors (2013). The DPP may also make a public statement on his or her prosecuting policy other than in the Code for Crown Prosecutors: *R (Pretty) v DPP* [2001] UKHL 61, [2002] 1 AC 800, at para 39; *R (Purdy) v DPP* [2009] UKHL 45, [2010] 1 AC 345, at para 54. The Lord Advocate exercises such a power in Scotland: *Pretty*, above, esp Lord Hope at paras 79–82.

[206] *Purdy*, above.

[207] As explained by Sir Hartley Shawcross QC when Attorney General: 'It has never been the rule in this country – I hope it never will be – that suspected criminal offences must automatically be the subject of prosecution' (HC Deb, 29 January 1951, col 681). See *Smedleys Ltd v Breed* [1974] AC 839.

[208] CPS, Code for Crown Prosecutors, above, paras 4.7–4.12.

constitute 'law' for the purposes of the ECHR, which means that it must meet Convention standards of accessibility and foreseeability.

Although the Code appears generally to meet these standards, it was held in one case attracting great media interest to have given insufficient information about prosecution decisions in the case of assisted suicide. As a result, the DPP was instructed by the House of Lords to issue a policy to identify the facts and circumstances he would take into account in deciding whether to consent to a prosecution for assisting a suicide.[209] While there is no duty to prosecute in every case, equally the DPP does not have the power to grant an immunity from prosecution: 'The power to dispense with and suspend laws and the execution of laws without the consent of Parliament was denied to the Crown and its servants by the Bill of Rights 1688.'[210] A decision not to prosecute is subject to judicial review,[211] although the power of judicial review in such circumstances is 'sparingly exercised'.[212]

Role of the Attorney General in prosecutions

What opportunities are there for political considerations to be brought to bear in the prosecution of offenders? The question arises because (i) prosecution policy generally is under the superintendence of a government minister (the Attorney General) and therefore liable in principle to interference; (ii) some prosecution decisions require the consent of the Attorney General, for example under the Official Secrets Act 1911, the Theatres Act 1968 and the Public Order Act 1986; and (iii) the Attorney General has the power to intervene to discontinue prosecutions. Concern about the appearance of possible opportunities for political interference is compounded by the fact that in recent years some very high-profile investigations of a highly political nature have not been followed through to the stage of prosecution, these including the cash for honours affair in 2005–6 and the investigation of alleged corruption by a British company in 2007.

In the first case, prosecutions under the Honours (Prevention of Abuses) Act 1925 did not require the consent of the Attorney General, and in any event the CPS had been unable to find sufficient evidence on which to base a prosecution. But it would have been acutely embarrassing for the Attorney General if those for whom he was accountable (the CPS) were in a position of having to decide whether it was in the public interest to prosecute members of the governing political party, including the Prime Minister.[213] In the second case, an investigation by the Serious Fraud Office into allegations of corruption by a British company was brought to an end, following intervention by the Prime Minister who advised that the proceedings would damage national security and could lead to a refusal by the Saudi government to provide sensitive information needed for counter-terrorism purposes. The investigation was discontinued, the House of Lords holding that the SFO was entitled to bring it to an end in such circumstances.[214]

It is perhaps unsurprising that proposals should be made from time to time to remove ministerial involvement in prosecution decisions. However, although it has been suggested

---

[209] *R (Purdy)* v *DPP*, above.

[210] *R (Pretty)* v *DPP*, above, at para 39 (Lord Bingham).

[211] *R* v *DPP, ex p C* (1995) 1 Cr App R 136. But the decision to prosecute is not, 'absent dishonesty, mala fides or an exceptional circumstance': *R (Pretty)* v *DPP* above, at para 67, applying *R* v *DPP, ex p Kebeline* [2000] 2 AC 326. See also *Pretty* v *United Kingdom* (2002) 35 EHRR 1.

[212] *R* v *DPP, ex p Manning* [2001] QB 330, at p 343.

[213] See CPS Decision: 'Cash for Honours' Case – Explanatory Document (2007). The Attorney had previously intervened under the Contempt of Court Act 1981 to restrain the publication of evidence relating to the case that had been leaked to the BBC: *Attorney-General* v *BBC* [2007] EWCA Civ 280.

[214] See *R (Corner House Research)* v *Director of the Serious Fraud Office* [2008] UKHL 60, [2009] 1 AC 756. Although the decision was that of the Director General, the Attorney General was also involved.

that the Attorney General's consent should no longer be required for prosecutions, it has also been proposed that it should be retained for cases involving national security.[215] The current guidelines emphasise that 'it is a constitutional principle' that the Attorney General 'acts independently of government' when taking decisions about prosecutions, but that unless expressly required to do so by statute, he or she should not normally be consulted about decisions which are politically sensitive (because they relate to MPs, political parties or the conduct of elections). They also make it clear that the Attorney may exceptionally direct that a prosecution is not started or discontinued where such intervention is necessary 'for the purpose of safeguarding national security'.[216]

The procedures adopted in such circumstances were fully canvassed in the *Corner House* case,[217] where it was pointed out that before intervening to prevent or discontinue a prosecution, the Attorney may engage in what is called a 'Shawcross exercise', so called because it is based on a statement made to the House of Commons in 1951 by the then Attorney General (Sir Hartley Shawcross).[218] The essence of the statement is that 'when deciding whether or not it is in the public interest to prosecute in a case where there is sufficient evidence to do so the Attorney General may, if he chooses, sound opinion among his ministerial colleagues, but that the ultimate decision rests with him alone and he is not to be put under pressure in the matter by his colleagues'.[219] Where the Attorney General intervenes in this way, a statement will be made to Parliament giving reasons for his or her action.[220]

Accountability of the Crown Prosecution Service

The creation of the Crown Prosecution Service in 1988 brought into prominence both the scope for central influence over the criminal justice system, which had previously been exercised without publicity, and the question of accountability for the abuse of power by public prosecutors. It has been acknowledged judicially that 'by convention the Attorney General is answerable to Parliament for general prosecution policy and for specific cases where the Attorney General and the Director of Public Prosecutions intervenes'.[221] But because both the Attorney and the DPP should be free from extraneous political interference in their work, there is inevitably a limit to what Parliament can do,[222] and it may not, for example, give directions to the Law Officers about the conduct of particular cases.

Nevertheless, parliamentary accountability is not to be under-estimated: it was an alleged political interference in a prosecution decision in 1924 that led to the defeat of the first Labour government on an opposition vote of no confidence.[223] In brief, the Attorney General, Sir Patrick Hastings, who was experienced in advocacy but not in ministerial work, authorised the prosecution of J R Campbell, acting editor of the *Workers' Weekly*, for having

[215] Cm 7342 (2008), paras 85–9.

[216] Protocol between the Attorney General and the Prosecuting Departments (2012), para 4(b)1.

[217] Above, note 214.

[218] HC Deb, 29 January 1951, col 681. See *R (Corner House Research)* v *Director of the Serious Fraud Office*, above, para 6.

[219] *Corner House*, ibid, para 6.

[220] It is in order for questions to be asked in Parliament about particular decisions made by the Attorney General: how much information the Attorney General gives in reply is a matter for his or her own discretion. Cf Edwards, *Law Officers of the Crown*, p 261.

[221] *Elguzouli-Daf* v *Metropolitan Police Commissioner* [1995] QB 335, at p 346.

[222] 'Parliament can usually only call the Attorney General to account after a prosecution has run its course' (ibid).

[223] Edwards, *Law Officers of the Crown*, chs 10 and 11; Edwards, *The Attorney General, Politics and the Public Interest*, pp 310–17; F H Newark (1969) 20 NILQ 19; Ewing and Gearty, *The Struggle for Civil Liberties*, ch 3. For the censure debate, see HC Deb, 8 October 1924, col 581.

published an article which apparently sought to seduce members of the armed forces from their allegiance to the Crown. A few days later, the prosecution was withdrawn in circumstances suggesting that political pressure had been brought to bear on the Attorney General. The true facts are not easy to establish, but the Cabinet appears thereafter to have courted further controversy by requiring the Attorney to seek its prior approval before initiating prosecutions of a political character, a requirement that was of doubtful constitutionally propriety.

But although the work of the Law Officers may thus have dramatic and far-reaching consequences, rarely will accountability lead to the fall of a government as it did in 1924. Apart from parliamentary accountability on this or a less dramatic scale, there are other ways of holding the prosecuting authorities to account. The role of the Attorney General in the Matrix Churchill affair in the 1990s was closely reviewed and sharply criticised by Sir Richard Scott's inquiry into the export of arms for Iraq. Sir Richard found that the decision to prosecute three executives of the company was taken by the Commissioners of Customs and Excise (now HM Revenue and Customs) following the advice of Treasury counsel. In this decision the Attorney General was not consulted and indeed he was not kept informed of important Customs prosecutions, having no duty of superintendence of such prosecutions, although he did have 'an overall purview of prosecutions brought by the Crown by any authority'.

The Attorney's position was nevertheless called into question as a result of his conduct in relation to public interest immunity (PII) certificates dealing with the granting of export licences to Matrix Churchill and other companies. Although a number of ministers had signed such certificates, the President of the Board of Trade (Mr Heseltine) refused to do so, on the ground that the interests of justice required the disclosure of many of the documents in question. Nevertheless, the Attorney General informed Mr Heseltine that he was under a legal duty to sign the certificates,[224] but that his reservations could be put to the judge. In the event Mr Heseltine's reservations were not even disclosed to the prosecution legal team, an omission that drew a strong rebuke from Sir Richard Scott. Sir Richard also repudiated the belief of the Attorney General that he was personally, as opposed to constitutionally, blameless for the inadequacy of the instructions sent to prosecuting counsel.[225]

Miscarriages of justice

One of the most regrettable features of the criminal justice system in the 1970s and 1980s was the number of miscarriages of justice, particularly the number of people who were wrongly convicted for offences they did not commit.[226] Some of these cases arose out of terrorist incidents, most notably the pub bombings at Guildford and Birmingham in 1974,[227] although there were many other cases unrelated to acts of terrorism, including that of the so-called 'Bridgewater Three'.[228] A number of different factors were responsible for these events, not the least significant of which were the serious shortcomings of the police and the prosecuting authorities.[229] The matter was reviewed by the Royal Commission on Criminal Justice appointed in 1991, with terms of reference that required it to consider 'whether changes were

---

[224] *Makanjuola* v *Metropolitan Police Commissioner* [1992] 3 All ER 617. On the law of public interest immunity, see ch 26 D and especially *R* v *Chief Constable of the West Midlands Police, ex p Wiley* [1995] 1 AC 274, where the House of Lords overruled *Makanjuola*. Compare HC 115 (1995–6) (Scott Report), para G 59.

[225] See further A W Bradley [1996] PL 373.

[226] For a wider definition of the term, see HC 419 (1993–4). For a detailed examination of miscarriages of justice, see Nobles and Schiff, *Understanding Miscarriages of Justice*.

[227] See *R* v *Richardson*, *The Times*, 20 October 1989; *R* v *McIlkenny* [1992] 2 All ER 417; *R* v *Maguire* [1992] QB 936. And note *R* v *Ward* [1993] 1 WLR 619.

[228] See *The Times*, 21 and 22 February 1997.

[229] See on specific aspects, I H Dennis [1993] PL 291.

needed in the arrangements for considering and investigating allegations of miscarriages of justice when appeal rights have been exhausted'.[230]

The procedures then in force were governed by the Criminal Appeal Act 1968, s 17, which authorised a reference to the Court of Appeal by the Home Secretary. According to the royal commission, however, the Home Secretary operated within 'strict self-imposed limits', and would not refer cases to the Court of Appeal merely to enable it to reconsider matters it had already considered; but would 'normally only refer a conviction if there is new evidence or some other consideration of substance which was not before the trial court'. The Home Office adopted this approach 'not only because they have thought that it would be wrong for ministers to suggest to the Court of Appeal that a different decision should have been reached by the courts on the same facts', but also because there was 'no purpose' in referring a case where there was 'no real possibility of the Court of Appeal taking a different view than it did on the original appeal because of the lack of fresh evidence or some other new consideration of substance'.[231]

These arrangements were criticised both by Sir John May (who had been asked to inquire into two miscarriages of justice)[232] and by the Royal Commission on Criminal Justice,[233] and a new procedure was proposed for the referral of cases. This would require the creation of a new body, independent of both the government and the courts, for dealing with allegations that a miscarriage of justice had occurred, reflecting concern that the Home Secretary should not be 'directly responsible for the consideration and investigation of alleged miscarriages of justice as well as being responsible for law and order and for the police'.[234] The Criminal Appeal Act 1995 addressed the incompatibility of these procedures 'with the constitutional separation of powers as between the courts and the executive',[235] and made provision for the appointment by the Queen (on the advice of the Prime Minister) of a Criminal Cases Review Commission (s 9).

The Commission is empowered to refer to the Court of Appeal (following the conviction of an offence on indictment) any conviction or sentence where it considers that 'there is a real possibility that the conviction, verdict, finding or sentence would not be upheld were the reference to be made' (s 13): this is a 'judgment entrusted to the Commission and to no one else'.[236] The Act also introduces for the first time a power (on the part of the Commission) to refer convictions or sentences arising from cases tried summarily (s 11), in this case to the Crown Court, subject to the same conditions as apply in the case of references to the Court of Appeal following a conviction on indictment (which include convictions by court-martial).[237] The Commission has wide powers to obtain documents and to appoint investigating officers to carry out inquiries in relation to a case under review,

---

[230] Cm 2263, 1993.

[231] Ibid, pp 181–2. The propriety of this approach was called into question in *R v Home Secretary, ex p Hickey (No 2)* [1995] 1 All ER 490, where it was suggested that the Secretary of State should ask another question: could the new material reasonably cause the Court of Appeal to regard the verdict as unsafe? If it could, the matter should then have been referred without more ado.

[232] HC 296 (1992), pp 93–4.

[233] Cm 2263, 1993, pp 181–2.

[234] Ibid, p 182.

[235] Ibid. And see HC Deb, 6 March 1995, col 32.

[236] *R v Criminal Cases Review Commission, ex p Pearson* [1999] 3 All ER 498, at p 505. For concerns that the Commission may be applying the test too strictly, see HC 106 (1998–9), para 30, and more recently for concerns addressed to both the Commission and the Court of Appeal, see HC 850 (2014–15). For clarification of the powers of the Commission, see Criminal Cases Review (Insanity) Act 1999.

[237] *R v Blackman* [2017] EWCA Crim 190.

although these will generally be carried out by the police rather than by the Commission's own officers (ss 17–20 as amended).[238]

Compensation is payable for a miscarriage of justice under the Criminal Justice Act 1988, though 'only if the new or newly discovered fact shows beyond reasonable doubt that the [applicant] did not commit the offence.'[239]

F. Conclusion

The courts play a critical constitutional role in a democracy in upholding the rule of law, and in ensuring that governments do not exceed the limits of the powers granted to them by Parliament.[240] In performing this role it is important that judges command public confidence, and are seen to be independent of the governments by whom they are appointed. Concerns about judicial independence have led to the creation of new procedures for the selection of judges, at a time when the judiciary is being invited to address other principles of general constitutional importance. Questions about the representativeness of the judiciary have led to growing awareness of the need for diversity on the Bench, a matter now taken more seriously than in the past. At the same time, questions about accountability of the judiciary are leading to more light being shed on the way in which the courts operate.[241]

In a democracy it is right that citizens should have a full understanding of the way legal and political institutions operate. To this extent the televising of Supreme Court proceedings is welcome.[242] It is right also that people should know more about those who sit in judgment of disputes between fellow citizens, or between citizens and the State. But as has been shown in this chapter, judges are only one (albeit one essential) cog in the much larger machinery that sustains the courts and the administration of justice generally. It is thus also fundamental to the rule of law that the government plays its part not only in obeying the law, but also in ensuring that there is proper support and funding for the courts, whose duty it is to ensure that governments meet their legal obligations. Although the foregoing may seem rich in irony, the rule of law also requires the government to ensure that the law is applied equally to everyone; there should be no political indulgence.[243]

---

[238] The CCRC was the subject of review by the House of Commons Justice Committee: HC 850 (2014–15). For an inside account of the work of the Commission, see G Zellick (2005) *Amicus Curiae*, May/June, p 2; and [2005] Crim LR 937. For an account of the work of its Scottish counterpart, see P Duff (2009) 72 MLR 693. See also R Nobles and D Schiff (2008) 71 MLR 464.

[239] This qualification was inserted by the Anti-Social Behaviour, Crime and Policing Act 2014, with a claim that it violated Convention rights resisted in *R (Hallam) v Justice Secretary* [2016] EWCA Civ 355.

[240] For a powerful restatement of that role, see *R (Unison) v Lord Chancellor*, above, esp per Lord Reed, paras 66–85, inadvertently raising questions (for discussion elsewhere) about the legitimacy of law making in a democracy by the random process of litigation (paras 67, 69 and 70).

[241] See Paterson, *Final Judgment: The Last Law Lords and the Supreme Court*. Also B Dickson (2007) 123 LQR 571.

[242] Crime and Courts Act 2013, s 31, amending Contempt of Court Act 1981, s 9.

[243] But see *R (Corner House Research) v Director of the Serious Fraud Office*, above.

PART III

Personal liberty and human rights

CHAPTER 14

Human Rights Act

This chapter is concerned with the protection of human rights. The first task is to determine what is meant by human rights: there is a great deal of terminological inconsistency in this area, with a number of terms frequently used – human rights, civil liberties, fundamental rights – often referring to the same thing.

For our purposes, human rights take two forms. On the one hand, there are the classical civil and political rights – the right to liberty of the person, the right to form political parties and to participate in elections, and the rights to freedom of conscience, religion and expression. On the other hand, there are social and economic rights – the right to employment, health care, housing and income maintenance during periods of ill health, unemployment or old age. Human rights lawyers have traditionally confined their concerns to the former category, to the exclusion of the latter, even though social and economic security is indispensable to effective participation in the civil and political life of the community.

Yet although there are several international treaties promoting social and economic security,[1] the boldness of their aspirations is generally matched only by the difficulties in their enforcement, and few democracies in the common law tradition take them seriously as fundamental rights. The position is different with regard to so-called civil and political rights. One international treaty in particular – the European Convention on Human Rights[2] – has had a significant influence on British law and practice, with the British government having been held in violation of its terms on numerous occasions and having been required on many occasions now to introduce legislation to give effect to specific rulings of the European Court of Human Rights.

Many countries give constitutional protection to civil and political rights, often in a Bill of Rights embedded in a written constitution with which in some cases both executive and legislative measures must comply, failing which they may be struck down by the courts. Legal protection of human rights in Britain is now to be found in the Human Rights Act 1998, which enables the Convention rights to be enforced in the British courts.[3]

A. The classical approach

The traditional British approach to the protection of civil liberties and human rights has been greatly influenced by Dicey.[4] For him there was no need for any statement of fundamental

---

[1] These include the Conventions of the International Labour Organization, a United Nations agency based in Geneva, set up to promote the interests of working people. Also important is the Council of Europe's Social Charter of 1961 and the Revised Social Charter of 1996, while the EC Charter of the Fundamental Social Rights of Workers of 1989 has contributed to the development of social law. There is also the EU Charter of Fundamental Rights, adopted at Nice in December 2000. On the Council of Europe's Social Charter, see Harris and Darcy, *The European Social Charter*. On the EC Charter, see Bercusson, *European Labour Law*, and on the EU Charter, see Peers and Hervey, *The EU Charter of Fundamental Rights*.

[2] Cmd 8969, 1953.

[3] See section C below.

[4] Dicey, *The Law of the Constitution*. And see ch 4.

principles operating as a kind of higher law, because political freedom was adequately protected by the common law and by an independent Parliament acting as a watchdog against any excess of zeal by the executive.[5]

Under the common law, a wide measure of individual liberty was guaranteed by the principle that citizens are free to do as they like unless expressly prohibited by law. So people already enjoy the freedom of religion, the freedom of expression and the freedom of assembly, and may be restrained from exercising these freedoms only if there are clear common law or statutory restrictions. This approach is illustrated most famously by *Entick* v *Carrington*[6] where the Secretary of State issued a warrant to search the premises of John Entick and to seize any seditious literature. When the legality of the conduct was challenged, the minister claimed that the existence and exercise of such a power were necessary in the interests of the state. But the court upheld the challenge on the ground that there was no authority in the common law or in statute for warrants to be issued in this way.[7]

A more recent example of liberty being protected by the common law is *A* v *Home Secretary (No 2)*[8] where the issue was whether evidence obtained by torture could be admitted by the Special Immigration Appeal Commission. In a case said by Lord Hoffmann to be of 'great importance' to the 'reputation of English law', the House of Lords held unanimously that such evidence could not be admitted, with Lord Bingham saying that common law principles 'compel the exclusion of third party torture evidence as unreliable, unfair, offensive to ordinary standards of humanity and decency and incompatible with the principles which should animate a tribunal seeking to administer justice'. However, the House divided on the standard of proof required before such evidence should be excluded.

Although there are thus important illustrations of the principle, it is open to question whether this approach is an adequate basis for the protection of liberty. In the first place, the common law rule that people are free to do anything which is not prohibited by law applied (it would seem) equally to the government. As a result, the government could violate individual freedom even though it was not formally empowered to do so, on the ground that it was doing nothing which was prohibited by law. So in *Malone* v *Metropolitan Police Commissioner*[9] the practice of telephone tapping was exposed as being done by the executive without any clear lawful authority. But when Mr Malone sought a declaration that the tapping of his telephone was unlawful, he failed because he could not point to any legal right of his which it was the duty of the government not to invade.

A second difficulty with the traditional British approach is that the common law merely recognises the freedom to do anything that is not unlawful, but is powerless to prevent new

---

[5] For a vivid expression of this view, see *Wheeler* v *Leicester City Council* [1985] AC 1054, at 1065 (Browne-Wilkinson LJ). For a powerful critique, see Craig, *Public Law and Democracy*.

[6] (1765) 19 St Tr 1030; ch 4. See also *Beatty* v *Gillbanks* (1882) 9 QBD 308, on which see ch 18.

[7] It is to be emphasised, however, that although concerned with freedom of expression and state power, *Entick* v *Carrington* was relied on in *Youssef* v *Foreign Secretary* [2016] UKSC 3, [2016] 3 WLR 157 for the principle that interference by the State with individual property rights cannot be justified by the exercise of prerogative powers, unsupported by specific statutory authority (ibid, para 31).

[8] [2005] UKHL 71, [2006] 1 All ER 575. See also *Al Rawi* v *Security Service* [2011] UKSC 34, [2012] 1 AC 531 (assertion of common law rules to prevent the use of closed procedure material in a civil claim for damages where no statutory authority; see ch 26). Compare *Home Office* v *Tariq* [2011] UKSC 35, [2012] 1 AC 452; see ch 26.

[9] [1979] Ch 344.

restrictions from being enacted by the legislature. It is also the case that many restrictions on liberty are imposed by the common law, for it is sometimes convenient for the executive to avoid seeking new powers from Parliament.[10] In this way the authorities may seek a decision of the courts that will develop the law restrictively and create a precedent of general application. Thus in *Moss* v *McLachlan*[11] the Divisional Court created, from the common law powers of the police to control and regulate public assemblies, an extended right to prevent people from assembling in the first place. And in the *Spycatcher* and other cases, it was held that injunctions could be granted to the Attorney General to restrain the publication of confidential government secrets.[12]

B. European Convention on Human Rights[13]

The protection of human rights, which is primarily a matter for the state in whose territory the rights may be enjoyed, cannot today be confined within national boundaries. The European Convention on Human Rights was signed at Rome in 1950, was ratified by the United Kingdom in 1951, and came into force among those states which had ratified it in 1953. The Convention is a treaty under international law and its authority derives solely from the consent of those states who have become parties to it. Now one of a number of human rights treaties, which include the International Covenant on Civil and Political Rights of 1966,[14] the making of the ECHR was a direct result of the movement for cooperation in Western Europe, which in 1949 led to the creation of the Council of Europe.

Inspiration for the Convention came from the wide principles declared in the United Nations Universal Declaration of Human Rights in 1948. The Convention declares certain human rights that are or should be protected by law in each state. It also provides political and judicial procedures by which alleged infringements of these rights may be examined at an international level. In particular, the acts of public authorities may be challenged even though they are in accordance with national law. The Convention thus provides a constraint under international law on the legislative authority of national parliaments, including that at Westminster. These constraints are a matter of growing controversy in the United Kingdom, as the Strasbourg process increasingly becomes the subject of political debate.

The scope of the Convention

The Convention does not cover the whole field of human rights. As already suggested, it does not expressly include economic and social rights, and is confined to certain basic rights and liberties which the framers of the Convention considered would be generally

[10] Cf Lord Browne-Wilkinson [1992] PL 397, and Sir J Laws [1993] PL 59.
[11] [1985] IRLR 76, and now *Austin* v *Metropolitan Police Commissioner* [2009] UKHL 5, [2009] 1 AC 564 (and subsequently *Austin* v *United Kingdom* [2012] ECHR 459, (2012) 55 EHRR 14); and *R (Hicks)* v *Metropolitan Police Commissioner* [2017] UKHL 9. See ch 18 below.
[12] *A-G* v *Guardian Newspapers Ltd* [1987] 1 WLR 1248, [1990] 1 AC 109.
[13] The extensive literature includes Amos, *Human Rights Law*; Harris, O'Boyle and Warbrick, *Law of the European Convention on Human Rights*; Jacobs, White and Ovey, *The European Convention on Human Rights*; Janis, Kay and Bradley, *European Human Rights Law: Text and Materials*; Mowbray, *Cases and Materials on the European Convention on Human Rights*. Also Bates, *The Evolution of the European Convention on Human Rights*, and Simpson, *Human Rights and the End of Empire*.
[14] On the ICCPR, see D Fottrell [2002] PL 485.

accepted in the liberal democracies of Western Europe. These rights and liberties are as follows:

the right to life (art 2);

freedom from torture, or inhuman or degrading treatment or punishment (art 3);

freedom from slavery or forced labour (art 4);

the right to liberty and security of the person (art 5), including the right of one who is arrested to be informed promptly of the reason for his or her arrest, and of any charge against him or her;

the right to a fair trial by an impartial tribunal of a person's civil rights and obligations and of criminal charges against him or her (art 6), including the right to be presumed innocent of a criminal charge until proved guilty, and the right to be defended by a lawyer and to have free legal assistance 'when the interests of justice so require';

the prohibition of retroactive criminal laws (art 7);

the right to respect for a person's private and family life, his or her home and correspondence (art 8);

freedom of thought, conscience and religion (art 9) and freedom of expression (art 10);

freedom of peaceful assembly and of association with others, including the right to form and join trade unions (art 11);

the right to marry and found a family (art 12).

By art 14, the rights declared in the Convention are to be enjoyed

without discrimination on any ground such as sex, race, colour, language, religion, political or other opinion, national or social origin, association with a national minority, property, birth or other status.

All persons within the jurisdiction of the member states benefit from the Convention regardless of citizenship, although a state may restrict the political activities of aliens.

Many of these rights are subject to exceptions or qualifications. Thus art 5 sets out the grounds on which a person may lawfully be deprived of his or her liberty; these include the lawful arrest of a person to prevent his or her entering the country without authority and the lawful detention 'of persons of unsound mind, alcoholics or drug addicts or vagrants' (art 5(1)(f)). So too the right to respect for private and family life under art 8 is protected from interference by a public authority

except such interference as is in accordance with the law and is necessary in a democratic society in the interests of national security, public safety or the economic well-being of the country, for the prevention of disorder or crime, for the protection of health or morals, or for the protection of the rights and freedoms of others.

Clearly, it is essential that such restrictions should not be interpreted so widely that the protected right becomes illusory. Member states may derogate from most but not all of their obligations under the Convention in time of war or other public emergency (and the United Kingdom has on occasion done so in respect of Northern Ireland and other anti-terrorist legislation), but they must inform the Secretary General of the Council of Europe of the measures taken and the reasons (art 15).[15]

---

[15] See *Lawless* v *Ireland* (1961) 1 EHRR 15; *Brannigan* v *UK* (1993) 17 EHRR 539; *Aksoy* v *Turkey* (1996) 23 EHRR 553; and *Marshall* v *UK* (10 July 2001, Application No 41571/98). More recently, see *A* v *Home Secretary* [2004] UKHL 56, [2005] 2 AC 68 (esp per Lord Bingham), and *A* v *United Kingdom* [2009] ECHR 301, (2009) 49 EHRR 29.

The scope of the Convention was extended by the First Protocol concluded as an addendum to the Convention in 1952 and ratified by the United Kingdom. By this protocol, every person is entitled to the peaceful enjoyment of his or her possessions (art 1); the right to education is protected and states must respect the right of parents to ensure education of their children in conformity with their own religious and philosophical convictions (art 2);[16] and the right to take part in free elections by secret ballot is declared (art 3).[17] The Fourth Protocol to the Convention, concluded in 1963, guarantees freedom of movement within a state and freedom to leave any country; it also precludes a state from expelling or refusing to admit its own nationals. This protocol – which has not been ratified by the United Kingdom – has been very important in constraining the scope of ECHR, art 5, with the European Court of Human Rights drawing a contentious distinction between restrictions on liberty and restrictions on movement.[18]

The Sixth Protocol provides for the abolition of the death penalty, thereby qualifying the terms of art 2 of the Convention itself. Under the terms of the protocol, which is now ratified by the United Kingdom, no one is to be condemned to death or executed, with the only exception being made for times of war. The Seventh Protocol (not ratified by the United Kingdom) deals mainly with appeals procedures in criminal cases, although it also provides (in art 5) for 'equality of rights and responsibilities of a private law character' between spouses. Of the remaining protocols, the Eleventh and Twelfth are among the most significant. The former is dealt with below and the latter (which has not been ratified by the United Kingdom) contains a general prohibition against discrimination.[19] The Thirteenth Protocol makes final provision for the abolition of the death penalty in all circumstances, and has been ratified by the United Kingdom, as has the Fourteenth, also dealt with below. Not yet in operation, the Fifteenth Protocol seeks to limit the power of the European Court of Human Rights,[20] while the Sixteenth will permit national courts to seek advisory opinions from the European Court of Human Rights.

Institutions and procedure

One novel feature of the Convention was the right extended to individuals to complain of breaches of the Convention by the states party to it. The enforcement procedure initially made use both of the Committee of Ministers of the Council of Europe (a committee of political representatives of the member states) and of two institutions created by the Convention: (*a*) the European Commission of Human Rights, which comprised individual members, elected by the Committee of Ministers but in office acting independently; and (*b*) the European Court of Human Rights, comprising judges elected by the Consultative Assembly of the Council of Europe. No two members of the Commission or the Court respectively could be citizens of the same state.

Although these procedures have been replaced (see below), the decisions taken thereunder remain authoritative.[21] So it is necessary to have a basic knowledge of how they operated. The function of the Commission was to receive and inquire into alleged breaches of the

---

[16] The United Kingdom accepted the latter principle 'only so far as is compatible with provision of efficient instruction and training, and the avoidance of unreasonable public expenditure'; see *Campbell and Cosans* v *UK* (1982) 4 EHRR 293.

[17] See *Liberal Party* v *UK* (1982) 4 EHRR 106 (simple majority electoral system not a breach of Convention), *Matthews* v *UK* (1998) 28 EHRR 361 (exclusion of residents of Gibraltar a breach of art 3).

[18] *Austin* v *UK*, above.

[19] See U Khaliq [2001] PL 457 on the Twelfth Protocol.

[20] See below, pp 378–9.

[21] See for example *Copsey* v *WWB Devon Clays Ltd* [2005] EWCA Civ 932, [2006] ICR 55.

Convention either (*a*) at the request of any state party to the Convention which alleged that another state had breached the Convention (known as inter-state cases); or (*b*) where a state had recognised the competence of the Commission to receive such petitions, on the receipt of a petition from an individual or a non-governmental organisation alleging a violation of rights by the state in question.

Although not all states recognised the right of individuals to petition to the Commission, very many more individual petitions came to the Commission than inter-state cases. When an individual petition was received, the Commission had first to decide whether it was admissible under the Convention. If a petition cleared the hurdle of admissibility, the Commission had then to investigate the facts fully and offer its services to the parties with a view to securing a friendly settlement of the case. If such a settlement was not secured, a report on the case was sent by the Commission to the state or states concerned and to the Committee of Ministers. Thereafter the matter might be dealt in one of two ways. First, the matter could be disposed of politically, with the Committee of Ministers deciding by a two-thirds majority. Or secondly, the matter could be dealt with judicially, having been passed by the Committee of Ministers to the European Court of Human Rights.

Before the Eleventh Protocol introduced new procedures for enforcing Convention rights, a case could be brought before the Court only where the states concerned had accepted the compulsory jurisdiction of the Court or expressly consented to the case coming before it. As a general rule, only the Commission or a state concerned could refer a case to the Court: the individual applicant had only a limited right to do so.[22] Under the new procedures introduced by the Eleventh Protocol, however, this all changed, beginning with the abolition of the Commission and the creation of a full-time court. Although it has the same title as the old court it replaced, the new court is nevertheless 'an entirely different body with new functions, powers and composition'.[23] It is also the subject of perpetual reform.

Under the current arrangements, the court – which has made an important contribution to the development of the Convention[24] – consists of a number of judges equal to the number of states that are party to the Convention (art 20), with a judge from each country (art 22). By virtue of amendments introduced by the Fourteenth Protocol,[25] the judges now serve for non-renewable periods of nine years. The main effect of the Eleventh Protocol was to enable applicants complaining of a breach of the Convention to apply directly to the Court, and for this purpose (following changes introduced by the Fourteenth Protocol) the Court operates in a number of forms, the judges sitting in single-judge formation, committees of three judges, chambers of seven judges and the Grand Chamber of 17 judges (art 26).

Applications may continue to be made by one state against another (art 33) or by 'any person, non-governmental organisation or group of individuals claiming to be the victim of a violation' (art 34). There is still a requirement that an applicant should have exhausted all domestic remedies and have brought the complaint within six months of the final decision of the domestic authorities. The Court is required to declare inadmissible any application submitted under art 34 considered to be incompatible with the terms of the Convention, manifestly ill-founded, or an abuse of the right of individual application (art 35(1)). Following the Fourteenth Protocol, it is now possible for some cases to be struck out also because the applicant has not suffered a significant disadvantage (art 35(2)).

---

[22] See A R Mowbray [1991] PL 353.
[23] A R Mowbray [1994] PL 540 (and [1993] PL 419).
[24] For earlier valuable accounts of the role of the Court, see C A Gearty [1993] 45 CLJ 89, and A R Mowbray [2005] 5 HRLR 57. Also important is Mowbray, *The Development of Positive Obligations under the European Convention on Human Rights*.
[25] On which, see A R Mowbray [2002] PL 252; (2004) 4 HRLR 331.

Some of the changes introduced by the Fourteenth Protocol were a direct response to the massive increase in the workload of the Court as the Council of Europe has expanded since 1989. As a result of the changes, a single judge may now take admissibility decisions (art 27), while a committee of three judges may deal with both admissibility and the merits of a complaint at the same time, in cases where the matter in question is already the subject of well-established case law of the Court (art 28). Otherwise, a chamber of seven judges (though there is a procedure for committees to be composed of five rather than seven judges) will consider the merits of an application (art 29). On matters of particular importance, the chamber may relinquish jurisdiction in favour of a Grand Chamber of 17 judges (art 30).[26]

In some cases (such as those relating to admissibility), the decisions of single judges and committees are said to be final, as are some decisions of the merits. In other cases, however, there is a procedure for the referral of a chamber decision to the Grand Chamber (art 43). This procedure may be used by either party to a chamber decision (that is to say either the complainant or the government), though the hearing of such a case by the Grand Chamber needs the approval of five judges, and is reserved for serious cases affecting the interpretation of the Convention (or its protocols) or serious questions of general importance (art 43). It is a procedure that ought to be contemplated by governments with extreme caution; not only is it possible that the Grand Chamber will reach a similar decision to that of the chamber, but it is also likely that in doing so the Grand Chamber will deliver an outcome that is even more authoritative.[27]

By art 46, States undertake to abide by the final judgment of the Court in any case to which they are parties. This may mean compensating victims for losses suffered as a result of the violation of their rights, though it is likely also to have the more important effect of requiring domestic law to be changed to avoid any further violations.

Cases involving the United Kingdom

Under the original scheme of the Convention, enforcement depended essentially on a state recognising both the right of individuals to apply to Strasbourg, and the compulsory jurisdiction of the Court. In 1966, the British government first made the two optional declarations for which the Convention provided,[28] and these declarations were renewed at intervals thereafter.[29] One result of the changes made by the Eleventh Protocol is that member states today have no choice in these fundamental matters and must accept the right of individuals to apply to the Court. Since 1966 a wide variety of individual petitions have been brought against the UK government, and there have also been inter-state references to the Commission by the Republic of Ireland. Although individuals may now enforce Convention claims before the domestic courts,[30] applications continue to be made to Strasbourg, from the United Kingdom.

There is thus a significant body of jurisprudence which has helped to shape British law. Curiously, in the three years from 2002 to 2004,[31] the number of applications and decisions against the United Kingdom rose dramatically. No fewer than 4,287 applications were lodged, of which 179 were declared admissible,[32] the Court holding in 69 cases in that period

---

[26] See A Mowbray [2007] PL 507 for an account of the work of the Grand Chamber.

[27] An outstanding example of such governmental misjudgment is *Demir and Baycara* v *Turkey* [2008] ECHR 1345, (2009) 48 EHRR 54.

[28] For the making of the decisions involved, see A Lester [1984] PL 46 and [1998] PL 237.

[29] See HC Deb, 13 Dec 1995, col 647.

[30] section 3 below.

[31] The HRA came into force in 2000.

[32] Council of Europe, *European Court of Human Rights – Survey of Activities 2002–04*. See now M Amos [2007] PL 655.

that the United Kingdom had violated at least one provision of the treaty.[33] Since then, however, the number of applications and decisions against the United Kingdom have fallen just as dramatically, with the JCHR highlighting in 2015 in response to misleading press coverage 'the significant downward trend' in Strasbourg judgments against the United Kingdom from 30 in 2002 to only four in 2014.[34] Applications nevertheless continue to be made on important questions, such as prisoners' voting, the rights of terrorist suspects, and trade union freedom.[35]

The British cases before the Court have spanned a wide range of subjects. In *McCann v United Kingdom*,[36] it was held that art 2 (protecting the right to life) had been violated following the use of lethal force by members of the security forces in Gibraltar. In *Jordan v United Kingdom*,[37] a breach of art 2 was found where there had been no effective investigation into the circumstances surrounding the death of the claimant's son, who had been killed by the police.[38] But in *Da Silva v UK*,[39] it was held that there was no breach of art 2 where no one was prosecuted following the killing of an innocent man by police officers in brutal circumstances, the victim mistakenly believed to be a terrorist bomber. Questions concerning the interpretation of art 3 (protection against torture and inhuman or degrading treatment or punishment) arose in *Republic of Ireland v United Kingdom*[40] in relation to the interrogation of IRA suspects, in *Tyrer v United Kingdom*,[41] in relation to the corporal punishment of juveniles in the Isle of Man, and in *Soering v United Kingdom*[42] in relation to the request for the extradition of a German citizen to the United States to stand trial for murder with the risk of being sentenced to capital punishment and being kept on Death Row.

In *X v United Kingdom*[43] the Court held certain procedures for the compulsory detention of mental health patients to infringe art 5, a similar conclusion being reached in *Brogan v United Kingdom*[44] in relation to the provisions of the Prevention of Terrorism (Temporary Provisions) Act 1984 authorising the detention of suspects for up to seven days without judicial authority. The automatic denial of bail for certain offences in the Criminal Justice and Public Order Act 1994 was found to breach art 5 in *Caballero v United Kingdom*.[45] So far as art 6 is concerned, the Court held that there had been a breach in *V v United Kingdom*[46] following the conviction of two minors (for a notorious murder of a child) after a trial conducted in the full glare of highly charged media publicity. A breach of art 6 was found in another high-profile case in which two environmental activists were denied legal aid to defend themselves in an action for libel brought by a large multinational company (McDonald's), which

---

[33] Council of Europe, ibid.

[34] HL Paper 30, HC 1088 (2014–15).

[35] For recent cases in relation to the last of these matters, see K D Ewing and J Hendy QC [2017] EHRLR 356.

[36] (1995) 21 EHRR 97.

[37] (2003) 37 EHRR 52.

[38] See also *McShane v UK* (2002) 35 EHRR 593, and *Edwards v UK* (2002) 35 EHRR 487.

[39] [2016] ECHR 314.

[40] (1978) 2 EHRR 25.

[41] (1978) 2 EHRR 1. See also *Costello-Roberts v UK* (1995) 19 EHRR 112, and *A v UK* (1998) 27 EHRR 611 (child severely beaten by stepfather).

[42] (1989) 11 EHRR 439. See also *D v UK* (1997) 24 EHRR 423 (proposed removal of drug smuggler to St Kitts under the Immigration Act 1971. Applicant had AIDS and proposed removal found to be in breach of art 3).

[43] (1981) 4 EHRR 188.

[44] (1988) 11 EHRR 117; and see ch 20.

[45] (2000) 30 EHRR 643.

[46] (2000) 30 EHRR 121.

had the benefit of an experienced team of lawyers.[47] In *Ibrahim* v *UK*,[48] art 6 was breached by the withholding of access to a lawyer to an individual implicated in a failed London bombing in 2005.

In *Dudgeon* v *United Kingdom*,[49] legislation in Northern Ireland making homosexual conduct between adult males a crime was held to infringe the individual's right to respect for his private life under art 8. The practice of telephone tapping was held to infringe art 8 in *Malone* v *United Kingdom*[50] and in *Halford* v *United Kingdom*.[51] The law of contempt of court was held to infringe freedom of expression under art 10 in *Sunday Times Ltd* v *United Kingdom*,[52] but the English law on obscene publications survived scrutiny in *Handyside* v *United Kingdom*.[53] In three other landmark cases it was held that art 10 had been violated by (i) restraints on the publication by newspapers (the *Observer*, *Guardian* and *Sunday Times*) of the contents of a book (*Spycatcher*) by a retired security service officer;[54] (ii) a requirement imposed by a court that a journalist should disclose the confidential sources of an article he had written, publication of which had been restrained by the courts;[55] and (iii) the award of £1.5m damages to Lord Aldington for defamatory remarks contained in a pamphlet written by a historian.[56] Cases under art 10 have also called into question restrictions in electoral law,[57] and on the freedom of peaceful protest.[58]

In *Young, James and Webster* v *United Kingdom*[59] three former employees of British Railways, dismissed for refusing to join a trade union, established that their freedom of association had been infringed as a result of legislation on the closed shop initiated by a Labour government in 1974 and 1976: they were awarded substantial compensation. Conversely, in *Wilson* v *United Kingdom*[60] a former employee of the *Daily Mail* successfully claimed that art 11 had been breached in a case where he suffered discrimination because he refused to agree to new working practices whereby pay would be determined by individual rather than collective negotiation. In *Air Canada* v *United Kingdom* it was held that there was no breach of art 1 of the First Protocol where an aeroplane was seized by customs officers after it was found to be carrying cannabis.[61] Conversely, in *Nerva* v *United Kingdom*[62] it was held that there was no breach of art 1 of the First Protocol in circumstances where an employer was entitled to treat as wages the tips left by customers to waiters. More famously, in *Hirst* v *United Kingdom (No 2)*[63] the Court held that the total ban on prisoners voting was a breach of art 3 of the First Protocol.

---

[47] *Steel and Morris* v *UK* (2005) 41 EHRR 403. Cf *McVicar* v *UK* (2002) 35 EHRR 566.

[48] [2016] ECHR 750. Complaints by three applicants in that case were dismissed, with only the application by the fourth succeeding.

[49] (1981) 4 EHRR 149. See also *Smith* v *UK* (2000) 29 EHRR 493 (discharge of military personnel because they were homosexual found to be a breach of art 8). But cf *Laskey* v *UK* (1997) 24 EHRR 39 (conviction of homosexual men for sado-masochistic practices conducted in private not a breach of art 8).

[50] (1984) 7 EHRR 14.

[51] (1997) 24 EHRR 523.

[52] (1979) 2 EHRR 245; and see ch 13.

[53] (1976) 1 EHRR 737. See also *Wingrove* v *UK* (1996) 24 EHRR 1.

[54] (1991) 14 EHRR 153, 229.

[55] *Goodwin* v *UK* (1996) 22 EHRR 123.

[56] *Tolstoy Miloslavsky* v *UK* (1995) 20 EHRR 442.

[57] *Bowman* v *UK* (1998) 28 EHRR 1; C Gearty (2000) 51 NILQ 381. But compare *Animal Defenders International* v *United Kingdom* [2013] ECHR 362, (2013) 57 EHRR 21.

[58] *Steel* v *UK* (1999) 28 EHRR 603; and *Hashman* v *UK* (1999) 30 EHRR 241.

[59] (1981) 4 EHRR 38.

[60] (2002) 35 EHRR 523 (K D Ewing (2003) 32 ILJ 1).

[61] (1995) 20 EHRR 150.

[62] (2003) 36 EHRR 31.

[63] [2005] ECHR 681, (2006) 42 EHRR 41. But see *Moohan* v *United Kingdom*, Appn No 22962/15, 13 June 2017 (denial of prisoner voting in Scottish independence referendum not a breach of Art 3).

These decisions have often led to changes in the law intended to prevent future infringements of the Convention. Such legislative changes include the Contempt of Court Act 1981 (regulating the circumstances in which pre-trial publicity is unlawful), the Interception of Communications Act 1985 and the Investigatory Powers Act 2016 (regulating the circumstances in which telephone tapping may take place and giving individuals a right of redress against improper use) and the Homosexual Offences (Northern Ireland) Order 1982 (changing the law on homosexual conduct in Northern Ireland). Other significant consequences of Court decisions include the introduction of amendments to the procedures for detention and release of mental health patients following the decision in *X* v *United Kingdom*,[64] the issuing of new prison rules and changing practices in prisons following decisions on prisoners' correspondence, and the amending of employment legislation to protect employees from anti-union discrimination by employers. In some cases, however, the government has been unwilling to give effect to decisions of the European Court and has taken steps to avoid doing so.

In *Abdulaziz* v *United Kingdom*[65] the Court held that British immigration rules discriminated against women permanently settled in the United Kingdom because their husbands and fiancés were not entitled to enter, whereas the wives and fiancées of men settled here were entitled to enter. The government responded to this decision by amending the Immigration Rules to remove the entitlement of wives and fiancées to enter, thereby removing the source of discrimination. In *Brogan* v *United Kingdom*,[66] the government responded to the Court's decision, that the detention powers of the Prevention of Terrorism (Temporary Provisions) Act 1984 violated art 5, by declaring that the power was necessary on security grounds and by depositing at Strasbourg a limited derogation from the Convention to the extent that the legislation violated art 5. Government resistance to Strasbourg rulings is emerging as a more persistent problem, with the Court issuing a number of high-profile decisions against the government in recent years. There is a marked phenomenon of government delay in implementing decisions, in governments seeking to have Chamber decisions reconsidered by the Grand Chamber, and of minimalist implementation by legislation.[67]

The continuing importance of the Strasbourg process

As already pointed out, the Human Rights Act means that it is now possible to enforce Convention rights in the domestic courts without having to travel to Strasbourg. It is thus possible that many of the cases that went to the Strasbourg court in the past would now be resolved at 'home'. It is not always the case, however, that the Strasbourg process has been rendered redundant by the Human Rights Act, as some of the cases referred to in the previous section make clear. Although many of these decisions were made before the Human Rights Act came into force, it is also the case that several landmark decisions have been made since. By no means all of the applications are successful, the JCHR pointing to a significant level of failure in recent applications from the United Kingdom.[68] But the fact that this well-worn route continues to be trodden suggests a continuing need for such external supervision.

There are in fact a number of reasons why – despite the enactment of the Human Rights Act – applications will still have to be made to Strasbourg. The first is that, because of the

---

[64] (1981) 4 EHRR 188.
[65] (1985) 7 EHRR 471.
[66] (1988) 11 EHRR 117. See now ch 20.
[67] For consideration of the implementation of Strasbourg jurisprudence, see HL Paper 112, HC 555 (2006–7); HL Paper 173, HC 1078 (2007–8); HL Paper 85, HC 455 (2009–10), and HL Paper 130, HC 1088 (2014–15).
[68] HL Paper 130, HC 1088 (2014–15).

limitations of the Human Rights Act, the domestic courts are not in a position to enforce Convention rights. This is most likely to arise where the action complained of is authorised by legislation, which under the Human Rights Act the domestic courts are bound to enforce. An example is *ASLEF* v *United Kingdom*,[69] where the trade union alleged that its art 11 rights had been breached by statute. The latter prohibited trade unions from excluding or expelling from membership individuals who were members of the British National Party, in accordance with the policy of the union. In this case a BNP member successfully sued the union for wrongful expulsion, the employment tribunal being bound to uphold the statute notwithstanding its possible impact on the Convention rights of the union. A complaint to Strasbourg was upheld, and the law changed.[70] It is a striking feature of that case that the Strasbourg application was made following a decision of an employment tribunal (this being a sufficient exhaustion of domestic remedies for the purposes of the Convention).

In most cases where a conflict arises between Convention rights and a domestic statute, it will be open to the domestic court in some cases (though not employment tribunals in the above example) to make a declaration that the relevant provisions of the statute in question are incompatible with Convention rights. Although this may lead eventually to the statute in question being amended or repealed, it will not enable the applicant to secure redress for the violation of his or her Convention rights. For this purpose it will be necessary to proceed to Strasbourg to seek a remedy, as in the landmark *A* v *Home Secretary*.[71] There the House of Lords was confronted with the Anti-terrorism, Crime and Security Act 2001, which provided for the indefinite detention without trial of suspected international terrorists. It was held that these powers violated art 5 together with art 14, and a declaration of incompatibility was made. But the declaration had no legal effect on the validity of the statute, which remained in force, and it was necessary for the applicants to proceed to Strasbourg to vindicate their rights. The Strasbourg court agreed with the House of Lords, and the applicants were awarded compensation and costs.[72]

The foregoing are examples of cases where the relevance of Strasbourg continues because of the limitations of the Human Rights Act. A second and more important reason why Strasbourg continues to be important is because the domestic courts and the Strasbourg courts may disagree on the meaning of Convention rights. This is likely to be a common problem: a study of the jurisprudence of the House of Lords calculated that only one in three human rights cases leads to a finding that Convention rights have been violated.[73] Although it does not follow that the Strasbourg court will take a different view, it is understandable that disappointed litigants will want to take their case further. In *S and Marper* v *United Kingdom*,[74] the two applicants had been arrested by the police in unrelated incidents, after which they each had samples taken and entered on the DNA database. In one case the charges were dropped, and in the other the applicant (who was a child) was found not guilty. The House of Lords held that the retention of the DNA data did not violate Convention rights, even in the case of people who had not been convicted.[75] The Strasbourg court took a different view, the Grand Chamber holding unanimously that there had been a breach of art 8.[76]

....

[69] [2002] IRLR 568 (K D Ewing (2007) 36 ILJ 245).
[70] Employment Act 2008, s 19 (K D Ewing (2009) 38 ILJ 50).
[71] *A* v *Home Secretary* [2004] UKHL 56, [2005] 2 AC 68.
[72] *A* v *United Kingdom* [2009] ECHR 301. For other examples see Amos, note 13 above.
[73] T Poole and S Shah [2009] PL 347.
[74] [2008] ECHR 1581, (2009) 48 EHRR 50.
[75] *R (S)* v *South Yorkshire Chief Constable* [2004] UKHL 39, [2004] 1 WLR 2196. See ch 16.
[76] *S and Marper* v *United Kingdom* [2008] ECHR 1581, (2009) 48 EHRR 50.

Also falling into this category are high-profile cases such as *Hirst* v *United Kingdom (No 2)*,[77] where the domestic courts held the ban on voting by prisoners did not violate Convention rights. As we have seen, the Strasbourg court disagreed, being required to repeat its findings in the face of government defiance. In *Gillen and Quinton* v *United Kingdom*,[78] the House of Lords held that the wide police powers of stop and search in the Terrorism Act 2000 were Convention compliant. Again, the Strasbourg court disagreed, holding that there had been a breach of art 5, and on this occasion the law was changed. In *Abu Qatada* v *United Kingdom*,[79] the House of Lords held that there was no violation of Convention rights when the Home Secretary ordered the removal of the applicant to Jordan despite fears that he might be arrested and put on trial in circumstances where evidence obtained by torturing third parties might be used against him. The Strasbourg court held that removal in these circumstances would violate the applicant's rights under art 6, and the Home Secretary was prevented from proceeding with the removal until credible assurances were given by the Jordanian government that evidence obtained in such circumstances would not be used.

Finally, the Strasbourg applications will continue to be important in dynamic areas where the domestic courts appear reluctant to follow the lead of the Strasbourg court, or want more guidance or certainty before doing so. As with any other court, the jurisprudence of the European Court of Human Rights is not static but continues to evolve. It is not unknown for the Court formally to overrule previous decisions, a step which the Court nevertheless takes reluctantly because of rule of law concerns relating to 'legal certainty, foreseeability and equality before the law'.[80] But where the Court does take this step in a complaint against one country, its decisions will have implications for the rest of the Council of Europe, and domestic courts will understandably be concerned about the extent to which national law may have to change to adapt to any new line of authority. These concerns are most likely to arise when the question before them is not quite on point and where there is a perceived lack of clarity in the Strasbourg jurisprudence. Unlike EU law, there is currently no procedure under the ECHR whereby a domestic court can seek a preliminary ruling on a point that is unclear, though such a procedure is in the pipeline (in the Sixteenth Protocol).

This problem has arisen in relation to art 11 (freedom of association) where the Strasbourg court has most recently repudiated an established line of authority in which it had been held that the right to freedom of association did not include the right to bargain collectively or the right to strike. In a decisive rejection of that view, the Grand Chamber of the Strasbourg court unanimously changed its mind in 2008, holding that the right to freedom of association includes the right to bargain collectively in line with international labour standards.[81] In subsequent decisions, other chambers of the Court have extended protection to the right to strike under the umbrella of freedom of association, though they did not unequivocally state that the right to strike was protected.[82] When these developments were put to the Court of Appeal, it expressed some unease, especially in relation to the argument that art 11 now includes the right to strike, in view of what it regarded as a 'summary discussion of the point' in the Strasbourg case law.[83] A Strasbourg application by a British trade union appeared to vindicate the hesitancy of the domestic courts.[84]

---

[77] [2005] ECHR 681, (2006) 42 EHRR 41. And see subsequently, *Greens* v *United Kingdom* [2010] ECHR 868.

[78] [2010] ECHR 28, (2010) 50 EHRR 45.

[79] *Othman (Abu Qatada)* v *UK* [2012] ECHR 56, (2012) 55 EHRR 1.

[80] *Demir and Baykara* v *Turkey*, above, para 153.

[81] *Demir and Baykara*, ibid.

[82] See K D Ewing and J Hendy QC (2010) 39 ILJ 2 for full details.

[83] *Metrobus Ltd* v *Unite the Union* [2009] EWCA Civ 829, [2009] IRLR 851. Compare *RMT* v *Serco Ltd* [2011] EWCA Civ 226, [2011] 3 All ER 913.

[84] *RMT* v *United Kingdom* [2014] ECHR 366. See A Bogg and K D Ewing (2014) 43 ILJ 221.

The incorporation of Convention rights into domestic law (described perhaps optimistically as 'bringing rights home') may thus have the paradoxical impact of enhancing the role of the Strasbourg court in British law, for the three reasons suggested above: the limitations of the HRA, the gap between national and European standards, and the evolving nature of the Strasbourg case law. The continuing importance of the Strasbourg court is all the more likely for the fact that the House of Lords and the Supreme Court positioned themselves after the introduction of the HRA in such a way as to follow the standards set by the ECtHR rather than to develop an approach independently of it, despite a clear opportunity to do so presented by the Act itself. The growing presence of the Strasbourg court in British law has become a matter of acute political controversy, with the Conservative party in particular appearing to support proposals that some feel could lead to the removal of the United Kingdom from its jurisdiction, if implemented.

Controversy and change

There is thus strong political opposition to the ECHR generally (and to the Strasbourg court in particular) in some quarters, opposition that has largely centred on the evolving case law. The latter appears to raise the standard of human rights protection, and is claimed by some to go beyond what the authors of the treaty intended.[85] In addition to the criticisms that the Court was over-extending itself, there were criticisms of a different nature relating to the backlog of cases and the time taken for cases to be dealt with. It was estimated that at one time there were over 100,000 cases waiting to be heard, though that may say as much about the state of health of human rights in the Council of Europe as the procedures of the Court.

In direct response to these criticisms, one of the main thrusts of the High Level Conference on the Future of the European Court of Human Rights, which met at Brighton in 2012, was that more decisions on Convention rights should be taken by national courts.[86] The objective was to be met in a number of ways: first by revising the admissibility criteria; and secondly by amending the Treaty to underline the Court's obligation to reinforce the principle of subsidiarity, as well as the doctrine of the margin of appreciation in its jurisprudence. The latter change was to reflect the fact that 'the Convention system is subsidiary to the safeguarding of human rights at national level and that national authorities are in principle better placed than an international court to evaluate local needs and conditions'.

From the point of view of constitutional principle, however, particularly noteworthy was the proposal by the High Level Conference for 'dialogue' between the Court and State parties 'as a means of developing an enhanced understanding of their respective roles in carrying out their shared responsibility for applying the Convention'. This is to include 'dialogues between the Court and:

(i) the highest courts of the States Parties;

(ii) the Committee of Ministers, including on the principle of subsidiarity and on the clarity and consistency of the Court's case law; and

(iii) Government Agents and legal experts of the States Parties, particularly on procedural issues and through consultation on proposals to amend the Rules of Court'.

While some of the concerns addressed by the Brighton Declaration are unexceptional, it is perhaps thus unsurprising that the manner by which others were addressed were reported to

---

[85] See *Daily Telegraph*, 2 November 2013. Lord Chancellor accusing judges of the European Court of Human Rights of taking the Convention 'to places that the authors of the convention would never have imagined'. And see Straw, *Aspects of Law Reform: An Insider's Perspective*, ch 2.

[86] http://hub.coe.int/20120419-brighton-declaration. For discussion see, M Elliott [2012] PL 619.

have irritated the President of the Court, offended by politicians with a direct interest in the decisions of the ECtHR telling the judges how to carry out their duties.[87] Some of the proposals for 'dialogue' and 'clarification' certainly revealed a poor understanding of the principle of judicial independence, inconsistent with the spirit of the Council of Europe's Recommendation on Judicial Independence of 2010.[88] While the backlog in the Strasbourg court provides a compelling case for radical procedural reform, there is also a compelling need to ensure that administrative expediency is not advanced at the cost of constitutional principle, with the Court now exposed to the criticism of engaging in summary justice to reduce the list.[89]

Nevertheless, some of these outcomes of the Brighton Declaration were adopted in the Fifteenth Protocol which was drafted quickly thereafter. This includes in Art 1 the introduction of the following passage to the preamble to the ECHR:

> Affirming that the High Contracting Parties, in accordance with the principle of subsidiarity, have the primary responsibility to secure the rights and freedoms defined in this Convention and the Protocols thereto, and that in doing so they enjoy a margin of appreciation, subject to the supervisory jurisdiction of the European Court of Human Rights established by this Convention.[90]

This embraces two ideas (subsidiarity and the margin of appreciation), designed to encourage the Court to leave more room to the national authorities in the application of the Convention.[91]

The Fifteenth Protocol includes a number of other changes, notably the reduction from six to four months (from the date of the final decision of the domestic courts) for the bringing of applications (art 4). This was welcomed by the Court itself, which was surprisingly relaxed about the other changes. It approved the reference to subsidiarity, this having been 'a fundamental theme of the reform', which reflected 'the Court's pronouncements on the principle'. Although initially it had reservations about the reference to the margin of appreciation, in an opinion on the draft protocol the Court was content that 'there clearly was no common intention of the High Contracting Parties to alter either the substance of the Convention or its system of international, collective enforcement'.[92] The proposals for 'dialogue' are not in the protocol.[93]

At the time of writing, the Fifteenth Protocol is not yet formally in force.[94] It may be the case, however, that it is already being applied in practice, with the political pressure on the Court appearing to yield some rewards in relation to British cases in particular. There is an indication that the Court is willing on some matters to indulge the British

---

[87] J Rozenberg, 'Draft Brighton Declaration is a Breath of Fresh Air', *The Guardian*, 19 April 2012.

[88] Committee of Ministers, Judges: Independence, Efficiency and Responsibilities, Recommendation CM/Rec(2010)12 .

[89] K D Ewing and J Hendy QC (2017) 46 ILJ 435: ECtHR dismissing as inadmissible an important complaint challenging the compatibility of EU law with the ECHR without giving reasons.

[90] These treaty changes will have implications for the nature of human rights protection in the United Kingdom via the Human Rights Act (below), though it is unclear whether they will require implementing legislation.

[91] There is evidence of both of these principles at work in recent case law, *Austin* v *United Kingdom*, note 11 above, on the police practice of detaining protestors being a notable example.

[92] The Court's position is expressed in Opinion of the Court on Draft Protocol No 15 to the European Convention on Human Rights, 6 February 2013.

[93] But this does not mean that this rather troubling idea cannot be pursued by other less formal means.

[94] It has been signed and ratified by the United Kingdom. For background, see HL Paper, 71, HC 837 (2014–15).

government with a very generous margin of appreciation,[95] and an indication of weakness in the prisoners' voting issue, which caused such resentment in British governmental circles out of all proportion to the issues at stake. True, the Court has confirmed that a blanket ban on prisoner voting is a breach of Convention rights, but it has contrived to deny that authority of any normative impact by holding that there is no remedy for prisoners whose right has been denied, and no legal costs recoverable by those who seek to assert their Convention rights.[96]

In the same way, it is clear that the Court has been over-sensitive to government concerns in its treatment of trade union rights in Article 11. Since the Grand Chamber decision in *Demir and Baycara* v *Turkey* opening up the scope of the latter provision,[97] trade unions from countries as diverse as Croatia, Russia, Turkey and Ukraine have successfully brought such claims.[98] Five such cases have been brought from the United Kingdom, all dismissed as inadmissible (in some cases on flimsy grounds), or dismissed for reasons that reveal an inappropriate deference by a human rights court to political institutions.[99] Although it is possible that the approach detected recently in British cases is driven by a need for institutional self-preservation in a hostile climate (though, it should be stressed, not all cases are unsuccessful), there is a danger that respect for the Court (and the rule of law it is charged to uphold) will rapidly evaporate as a result.

C. The Human Rights Act 1998[100]

The Human Rights Act 1998 provides that Convention rights may now be enforced in the domestic courts. For the purposes of the Act, Convention rights are defined to mean arts 2–12 and 14 of the ECHR, arts 1–3 of the First Protocol and art 1 of the Thirteenth Protocol (s 1(1)). These are to be read with arts 16 and 17 of the Convention: the former permits the imposition of restrictions on the political activities of aliens; the latter deals with the abuse of rights by providing that no state, group or person has any right to engage in any activity or perform any act aimed at the destruction of any of the Convention rights. The main exclusions are thus arts 1 and 13.

Article 1 imposes a duty on the 'High Contracting Parties' to 'secure to everyone within their jurisdiction' the rights and freedoms set out in the Convention, an obligation that the government considers to have been met by the enactment of the Human Rights Act. The exclusion of art 13 in contrast was more controversial, this providing that everyone whose Convention rights and freedoms are violated 'shall have an effective remedy before a national

---

[95] *Austin* v *United Kingdom*, above; *RMT* v *United Kingdom*, above. See generally K D Ewing and J Hendy QC [2017] EHRLR 356.

[96] *McHugh* v *United Kingdom* [2015] ECHR 155.

[97] [2008] ECHR 1345, (2009) 48 EHRR 54.

[98] K D Ewing and J Hendy QC [2017] EHRLR 356; same authors (2016) 45 ILJ 391.

[99] [2017] EHRLR 356, ibid.

[100] There is a very full literature on the Act. The leading practitioners' works are Clayton and Tomlinson, *The Law of Human Rights*, and Lester, Pannick and Herberg, *Human Rights Law and Practice*. Notable academic studies include Brady, *Proportionality and Deference under the UK Human Rights Act*; Gearty, *Principles of Human Rights Adjudication*; Kavanagh, *Constitutional Review under the UK Human Rights Act 1998*; Leigh and Masterman, *Making Rights Real*; and Young, *Parliamentary Sovereignty and the Human Rights Act*. Also important is Dickson, *Human Rights and the United Kingdom Supreme Court*, and Young, *Democratic Dialogue and the Constitution*.

court'. Not everyone is prepared to accept that the contents of the Act fully satisfy this requirement, as the government also claimed.[101]

Convention rights and the Strasbourg case law

The incorporation of Convention rights raises questions about the substance of these rights, which are brought to life and given meaning by the case law of the European Court of Human Rights. Section 2 of the Human Rights Act requires a domestic court or tribunal when considering Convention rights to 'take into account' judgments, decisions, declarations or advisory opinions of the European Court of Human Rights. They must also take into account any opinion or decision of the now defunct European Commission of Human Rights as well as any decision of the Committee of Ministers (a political body). It is important to note that unlike decisions of the CJEU, which are binding on British courts on matters of EU law,[102] decisions of the Strasbourg bodies are only to be taken into account.

There has been much discussion about the impact of section 2, with Lord Irvine (who as Lord Chancellor was one of its authors) pointing out that its plain meaning does not require the courts to be bound by the Strasbourg jurisprudence.[103] This has emerged in the context of criticism that the domestic courts are too willing to follow the Strasbourg case law, rather than develop their own solutions more suited to national conditions, which may not require the same level of protection. But although the Strasbourg court could not object to the domestic courts setting higher human rights standards than the Convention requires, for obvious reasons it would be difficult for the domestic courts to set standards below those required by Strasbourg: to do so would be simply to invite litigants to proceed to Strasbourg. It is perhaps nevertheless surprising just how much weight is given to the Strasbourg jurisprudence, the domestic courts appearing unwilling to set higher standards of protection, and only exceptionally willing to set lower standards of protection.[104]

The starting point is *R (Ullah)* v *Special Adjudicator*[105] where Lord Bingham said that while 'not strictly binding' on the domestic courts, the courts should, 'in the absence of some special circumstances, follow any clear and constant jurisprudence of the Strasbourg court'.[106] According to Lord Bingham, this was said to reflect the fact that the Convention is an international instrument, 'the correct interpretation of which can be authoritatively expounded only by the Strasbourg court', with the result that 'a national court subject to a duty such as that imposed by section 2 should not without strong reason dilute or weaken the effect of the Strasbourg case law'. On the other hand, although – as explained above – it may be open in principle to member states to provide for rights more generous than those guaranteed by the Convention, according to Lord Bingham any such provision 'should not be the product of interpretation of the Convention by national courts, since the meaning of the Convention should be uniform throughout the states party to it'.

In Lord Bingham's view (and in the view of other judges) '[t]he duty of national courts is to keep pace with the Strasbourg jurisprudence as it evolves over time: no more,

---

[101] See HL Deb, 18 Nov 1997, cols 475–7. For a fuller discussion of points raised during the passing of the Act, see K D Ewing (1999) 62 MLR 79.

[102] ch 6 above.

[103] [2012] PL 237. But compare P Sales (2012) LQR 253, R Clayton [2012] PL 639.

[104] Compare J Wright [2009] PL 595 who failed to make good her claim that the courts have developed an indigenous meaning of Convention rights.

[105] [2004] UKHL 26, [2004] 2 AC 323 (R Masterman [2004] PL 725; J Lewis [2007] PL 720).

[106] Citing *R (Alconbury Developments Ltd)* v *Environment Secretary* [2003] 2 AC 295, para 26.

but certainly no less'. To the same effect, Baroness Hale said in a later case that 'we must interpret the Convention rights in a way which keeps pace with rather than leaps ahead of the Strasbourg jurisprudence as it evolves over time'.[107] *N v Home Secretary*[108] is a case that takes this to considerable lengths, the claimant having entered the country illegally and seeking asylum. Her application was refused and she was to be deported, despite the fact that she had AIDS for which she was being treated in the United Kingdom. The effect of her deportation to a country where she would not have had access to appropriate drugs would have been dramatically to shorten her life. Following a close textual analysis of the Strasbourg jurisprudence, it was found that there was no breach of the claimant's art 3 rights.[109]

Although reluctant to set a higher standard than Strasbourg requires,[110] the courts may be more willing to set what may appear to be a lower standard. In *R v Horncastle*,[111] the Supreme Court was faced with jurisprudence prohibiting the conviction of a suspect on the basis of hearsay evidence, where the latter was the 'sole or decisive' evidence against the accused. This was said to violate the right to a fair trial (art 6), and in particular the guarantee that the accused should have the right 'to examine or have examined witnesses against him and to obtain the attendance and examination of witnesses on his behalf under the same conditions as witnesses against him' (art 6(3)(d)). Although the Strasbourg court's decision had been most recently affirmed in a case from the United Kingdom only a few months earlier, the Supreme Court refused to follow it and upheld the convictions of appellants secured principally on the basis of hearsay evidence in circumstances clearly authorised by statute.

A unanimous bench of seven judges took the view that the existing procedures for the admission of such evidence adequately protected the right to a fair trial, and expressed concern that the rejection of hearsay evidence which was 'sole or decisive' would have drastic implications for the English criminal justice system. In rejecting the Strasbourg jurisprudence, Lord Philips said that

> The requirement to 'take into account' the Strasbourg jurisprudence will normally result in this Court applying principles that are clearly established by the Strasbourg Court. There will, however, be rare occasions where this court has concerns as to whether a decision of the Strasbourg Court sufficiently appreciates or accommodates particular aspects of our domestic process. In such circumstances it is open to this court to decline to follow the Strasbourg decision, giving reasons for adopting this course. This is likely to give the Strasbourg Court the opportunity to reconsider the particular aspect of the decision that is in issue, so that there takes place what may prove to be a valuable dialogue between this court and the Strasbourg Court. This is such a case.[112]

---

[107] *R (S) v South Yorkshire Chief Constable* [2004] UKHL 39, [2004] 1 WLR 2196, at para 78. Also *Brown v Scott* [2003] 1 AC 681; *R (Al Skeini) v Defence Secretary* [2007] UKHL 26, [2008] 1 AC 153; *R (Gentle) v Prime Minister* [2008] UKHL 20, [2008] 1 AC 1356, at para [56]; *R (RJM) v War Pensions Secretary* [2008] UKHL 63, [2009] 1 AC 311; *R (Black) v Justice Secretary* [2009] UKHL 1, [2009] 1 AC 949; *Smith v Ministry of Defence* [2013] UKSC 41, [2013] 3 WLR 69.

[108] [2005] UKHL 31, [2005] 2 AC 296. Compare *EM (Lebanon) v Home Secretary* [2008] UKHL 64, [2009] 1 AC 1198.

[109] The harshness of the *N* decision was compounded by the concession by Lord Nicholls that the Strasbourg jurisprudence 'lacks its customary clarity': ibid, at para 14.

[110] But see *Al Rawi v Security Service*, note 8 above.

[111] [2009] UKSC 14, [2010] 2 AC 373. For an earlier and much less high profile example, see *R v Spear* [2002] UKHL 31, [2003] 1 AC 734.

[112] *R v Horncastle*, ibid, para 11.

In *Al-Khawaja* v *United Kingdom*,[113] the ECtHR Grand Chamber appeared subsequently to relax the 'sole and decisive' test, to 'permit a conviction to be based on [hearsay] evidence [but] only if it is sufficiently reliable given its importance in the case'.[114]

Since *Horncastle*, there is evidence that some judges may not feel quite so constrained to follow the Strasbourg jurisprudence as *Ullah* might otherwise suggest (though the evidence should not be exaggerated). *Horncastle* was followed by *Manchester City Council* v *Pinnock*,[115] where Lord Neuberger said that the Supreme Court is not bound by every decision of the ECtHR. 'Not only would it be impractical to do so', but in his view 'it would sometimes be inappropriate, as it would destroy the ability of the court to engage in the constructive dialogue with the European court which is of value to the development of Convention law'.[116] The issue arose again in *R (Chester)* v *Justice Secretary*,[117] in which the Supreme Court was faced with the ban on prisoners' voting that had been held by the Strasbourg court on a number of occasions to be in breach of Convention rights,[118] and faced again with significant Strasbourg jurisprudence on the matter.

Here the Supreme Court repeated the line of argument developed in *Horncastle* and *Pinnock*, and said that there will 'be rare occasions' where the domestic court has concerns as to whether a decision of the Strasbourg court 'sufficiently appreciates or accommodates particular aspects of our domestic process'.[119] But although it was accepted that in these cases 'it is open to the domestic court to decline to follow the Strasbourg decision',[120] there are limits particularly where the matter has been already to a Grand Chamber (or in this case to two Grand Chambers). In these cases (of which *Chester* was not one):

> It would have then to involve some truly fundamental principle of our law or some most egregious oversight or misunderstanding before it could be appropriate for this Court to contemplate an outright refusal to follow Strasbourg authority at the Grand Chamber level.[121]

It has since been said, however, that these remarks are '[no] more than attempts at general guidelines', in a subsequent case where the UKSC refused to follow the ECtHR because it disagreed with the latter's interpretation of the Convention.[122]. The slow retreat from *Ullah* continues, as the British courts appear also to react to the politics of the ECHR.[123]

The Human Rights Act and parliamentary sovereignty

The structure of the Human Rights Act reflects the government's desire that 'courts should not have the power to set aside primary legislation, past or future, on the ground of

---

[113] [2011] ECHR 2127, (2012) 54 EHRR 23.

[114] Ibid, para 147. The safeguards in English law were said to ensure that such evidence was used only when reliable, and in *Al-Khawaja* it was held that there was no breach of ECHR, art 6 where the decisive evidence was a witness statement by someone who had died before the trial and who therefore could not be cross-examined.

[115] [2010] UKSC 45, [2011] 2 AC 104.

[116] Ibid, para 48.

[117] [2013] UKSC 63, [2013] 3 WLR 1076.

[118] See ch 7 A.

[119] *R (Chester)* v *Justice Secretary*, above, para 25, quoting Lord Phillips in *Horncastle*, above.

[120] Ibid.

[121] Ibid, para 27. This does not apply to single chamber decisions, in relation to which the Supreme Court feels less constrained: *Posteh* v *Kensington and Chelsea Royal Borough* [2017] UKSC 36, paras 36 and 37.

[122] *R (Hancy)* v *Whatton Prison Governor* [2014] UKSC 66, [2015] 1 AC 1344. The ECtHR decision was said to have been 'based on an over-expanded and inappropriate reading of the word "unlawful" in article 5(1) (a), which would not give rise to a sensible scheme' (para 33).

[123] Note also *Al-Waheed* v *Ministry of Defence* [2017] UKSC 2, para 48, and pp 392-3 below.

incompatibility with the Convention'. This was based on the continuing importance 'which the government attache[d] to parliamentary sovereignty'.[124] In practice many of the cases that had gone to Strasbourg in the past were not concerned with legislative action, so much as with executive or administrative action, and in some cases judicial action (relating to the operation of the common law). Nevertheless, this continuing commitment to parliamentary sovereignty distinguishes the regime established by the Human Rights Act from the practice in many other liberal democracies (including those in the Westminster tradition), where the courts have the power to strike down legislation on the ground of its incompatibility with constitutionally guaranteed fundamental rights or freedoms.[125]

But it does not follow from the foregoing that the courts have no powers in relation to statutes. In the first place, they are required to interpret legislation (primary and secondary) where possible in a manner consistent with the Convention (s 3(1)).[126] Section 3 has been considered by both the House of Lords and the Supreme Court on a number of occasions, and there has been a vigorous debate about the meaning of a provision accepted as 'a new rule of construction',[127] which applies if the Court has decided that there would otherwise be a breach of Convention rights.[128] It has been said judicially that s 3 is a 'strong adjuration',[129] and that it is 'a powerful tool whose use is obligatory'.[130] Thus, 'it is not an optional canon of construction. Nor is its use dependent on the existence of ambiguity'.[131] As a result, s 3 has been said by some to be a 'radical tool';[132] and by others to contain a power that is a significant limitation of Parliament's sovereign will.[133]

The mainstream position on the effect and proper scope of s 3 is best captured by *Ghaidan* v *Godin-Mendoza*.[134] According to Lord Nicholls, the courts may be required to construe legislation consistently with Convention rights even where there is no ambiguity in the legislation. That is to say, to give the statute a construction which is contrary to its clearly expressed meaning, and the 'unambiguous meaning the legislation would otherwise

---

[124] Cm 3782, 1997, para 2.13. See A W Bradley, in Jowell and Oliver (eds), *The Changing Constitution* (7th edn), ch 2; C O'Cinneide, in Jowell, Oliver and O'Cinneide (eds), *The Changing Constitution* (8th edn), ch 2; Young, *Parliamentary Sovereignty and the Human Rights Act*; and Young, *Democratic Dialogue and the Constitution*.

[125] The closest we come to such a power in the United Kingdom is in the devolution legislation. See for example the Scotland Act 1998, s 29, which limits the competence of the Scottish Parliament in the sense that it may not violate Convention rights. This is an important limitation of what is in effect primary legislative authority to make statutes that previously could only have been made at Westminster. For a vision of (i) how such a power would look in practice, (ii) the potential applicants in litigation and (iii) the type of legislation that would be challenged were such a power to constrain the Westminster Parliament, see *AXA General Insurance Ltd* v *Lord Advocate* [2011] UKSC 46. The case is significant also for the unconvincing claims by Lords Hope and Reed of an additional common law restraint on the power of the Scottish Parliament, quite apart from those contained in the Scotland Act 1998. These restraints were based on notions of the rule of law, and carry echoes of obiter remarks in *Jackson* v *Attorney General* [2005] UKHL 56 which were crushed extra-judicially by Lord Bingham (2008) 19 *King's Law Journal* 223.

[126] See A Lester [1998] EHRLR 520 and F Bennion [2000] PL 77.

[127] *R (Wardle)* v *Leeds Crown Court* [2001] UKHL 12, [2002] 1 AC 754.

[128] See A Lester [1998] EHRLR 665.

[129] *R* v *DPP, ex p Kebeline* [2000] 2 AC 326, at p 373 (Lord Cooke of Thorndon).

[130] *Re S (FC)* [2002] UKHL 10, [2002] AC 291, at para [37].

[131] Ibid, Lord Nicholls, para [37]. See also *R* v *A* [2001] UKHL 25, [2002] 1 AC 45, para [44] (Lord Steyn).

[132] F Klug and K Starmer [2001] PL 654, at p 664.

[133] T Campbell, in Campbell, Ewing and Tomkins (eds), *Sceptical Essays on Human Rights*, ch 2. Leading cases include *R* v *A*, above; *R* v *Lambert* [2001] UKHL 37, [2002] 2 AC 545; *Re S (FC)*, above; *R (Anderson)* v *Home Secretary* [2002] UKHL 46, [2003] 1 AC 837; *Ghaidan* v *Godin-Mendoza* [2004] UKHL 30, [2004] 2 AC 557.

[134] [2004] UKHL 30, [2004] 2 AC 557.

bear'.[135] This may mean that the courts must depart from the intention of Parliament in interpreting any contentious legislation, though this will only be permissible to the extent that in doing so the courts give effect to the intention 'reasonably to be attributed to Parliament' in enacting s 3 of the Human Rights Act. However, in determining what interpretation of legislation is possible notwithstanding its clear and unequivocal terms, Parliament is not to be taken to have empowered the courts to adopt a meaning inconsistent with a fundamental feature of the legislation.

In seeking to do what is possible, the courts are thus not empowered to construe legislation compatibly with the Convention at all costs. In an important passage, Lord Nicholls reminds the reader that Parliament has retained the right to enact legislation that is not Convention compliant. As a result, according to Lord Hope in *Hounslow LBC* v *Powell*,[136] 'for the courts to adopt a meaning inconsistent with a fundamental feature of legislation would be to cross the constitutional boundary that section 3 of the 1998 Act seeks to demarcate and preserve'.[137] But although s 3 must not be used to amend rather than construe legislation,[138] the power of interpretation has nevertheless been exercised on multiple occasions, according to one valuable study.[139] The power has been invoked by courts at all levels, in a number of areas of the law over a wide range of statutes.[140] In recent years the power has often been used to constrain the scope of discretionary authority, to ensure that the exercise of the latter is compatible with Convention rights.

Where it is not possible to construe legislation in a manner which is consistent with Convention rights, the High Court and superior courts (but not tribunals or inferior courts), after giving the Crown an opportunity to take part in the proceedings (s 5),[141] may make a declaration of incompatibility (s 4(2)). Such a declaration is stated not to be binding on the parties and does not affect the validity or operation of primary legislation (s 4(6)).[142] Opinion will differ as to whether this is a power 'extensively' used. By 2015, however, 29 statutory provisions had been declared incompatible, of which 20 had become final,[143] an average of more than one annually. In recent years the exercise of this power has declined, with the JCHR reporting that three declarations of incompatibility had been issued in the lifetime of the 2010–15 Parliament.[144] These were made by the High Court, the declarations upheld in two cases by the Court of Appeal, and given immediate effect by legislation in the other.[145]

---

[135] Ibid, at para 31. See *R* v *A*, note 131 above; and *R (Baiai)* v *Home Secretary* [2008] UKHL 53, [2009] 1 AC 287 (reading words into the Youth Justice and Criminal Evidence Act 1999, s 41, and the Asylum and Immigration (Treatment of Claimants etc.) Act 2004, s 19). Compare *R* v *Briggs-Price* [2009] UKHL 19, [2009] 1 AC 1026.

[136] [2011] UKSC 8, [2011] 2 AC 186.

[137] Ibid, at para 62.

[138] *Re S (FC)*, above. See also *R (Anderson)* v *Home Secretary*, above (D Nicol [2004] PL 274 and A Kavanagh [2004] PL 537).

[139] C Crawford (2014) 25 *King's Law Journal* 34.

[140] Ibid.

[141] *Wilson* v *First County Trust (No 2)* [2003] UKHL 40; [2004] 1 AC 816 (intervention by the Secretary of State for Trade and Industry).

[142] On which see *R (Reilly)* v *Work and Pensions Secretary* [2016] EWCA Civ 413, [2016] 3 WLR 1641.

[143] HL 151 (2006–7). App 6; see also *Ghaidan* v *Godin-Mendoza*, above (Appendix to Lord Steyn's speech) for an earlier account.

[144] HL Paper 130, HC 1088 (2014–15).

[145] Most of the declarations deal with legislation passed before the Human Rights Act was passed, though the power has now been used on five occasions in relation to post-HRA legislation: see *R (Wright)* v *Health Secretary* [2009] UKHL 3, [2009] 1 AC 739 (Care Standards Act 2000, s 82(4) – royal assent shortly before the Human Rights Act was brought into force); *A* v *Home Secretary* [2004] UKHL 56, [2005] 2 AC 68; *RCN* v *Home Secretary* [2010] EWCA Civ 2761 (aspects of the Safeguarding Vulnerable Groups Act 2006); and *R (Reilly)* v *Work and Pensions Secretary* [2016] EWCA Civ 413, [2016] 3 WLR 1641 (aspects of the Jobseekers (Back to Work Schemes) Act 2013).

It is a striking feature of this power, that the courts will go to considerable lengths to avoid using it.[146] According to Lord Steyn in *Ghaidan* v *Godin-Mendoza*, 'resort to s 4 must always be an exceptional course',[147] though it has been emphasised subsequently that the making of a declaration of incompatibility is for the discretion of the court.[148] Similarly, in *Home Secretary* v *Nasseri*,[149] Lord Hoffmann said that such a step should be a 'last resort', though he also raised the possibility of a declaration being made in cases where the respondent was not acting in breach of the applicant's Convention rights.[150] The discretionary and exceptional nature of the remedy was also emphasised in *R (Chester)* v *Justice Secretary*,[151] where the Supreme Court refused to make a declaration in circumstances where there would be 'no point' in doing so,[152] given that such a declaration had already been made by a Scottish court.

The highly risk-averse decision of the Supreme Court on this point in *Chester* – which won plaudits from the Prime Minister[153] – is open to criticism on a number of grounds, not least for giving the appearance that the Court had ducked a fast ball. Where, however, a declaration is made, it is for the government and Parliament to decide how to proceed – whether to amend the legislation or not. These procedures go about as far as possible without undermining Parliament's sovereignty and, in introducing the Human Rights Bill, the Home Secretary indicated that there were circumstances where the government would be unwilling to bring forward amending legislation to give effect to a declaration of incompatibility, citing abortion as an example.[154] It was probably not anticipated at the time of enactment of the Human Rights Act that prisoners' voting would be the issue on which government and Parliament would take a stand to protect the sovereignty of the latter.

When making declarations of incompatibility, judges have resisted requests to advise on what needs to be done to bring legislation into line with the Convention. Baroness Hale took the view that it is not for the judges to 'attempt to rewrite the legislation',[155] thereby tending to debunk the currently fashionable theory that judges and Parliament are engaged in some kind of 'dialogue' on Convention rights. When a declaration of incompatibility has been made, and the minister considers that there are 'compelling reasons' for doing so, the Human Rights Act empowers the minister to make a 'remedial order' for amending primary legislation so as to remove the incompatibility (s 10 and Sch 2). Although it is the practice for the government to respond to declarations of incompatibility by amending the legislation, this is not invariable, and it seems wishful thinking to suggest that there is now a convention that requires the government to seek by legislation to remove the incompatibility.

The Human Rights Act and public authorities

Sections 6 and 7 of the Human Rights Act are particularly important for the enforcement of Convention rights in the courts. The Act makes it unlawful for public authorities (including

---

[146] See notably *Home Secretary* v *MB* [2007] UKHL 47, [2008] AC 440 (K D Ewing and J-C Tham [2008] PL 668). See also *R(Haney)* v *Whatton Prison Governor*, above.

[147] Note 133 above. See also *R* v *A*, note 137, above; *Wilson* v *First County Trust*, note 141 above; and *R (Nasseri)* v *Home Secretary* [2009] UKHL 23, [2010] 1 AC 1, at para [18].

[148] *R (Rusbridger)* v *Attorney-General* [2003] UKHL 38, [2004] 1 AC 357. See also *Doherty* v *Birmingham City Council* [2008] UKHL 57, [2009] 1 AC 367.

[149] Note 147 above.

[150] Ibid, para 18.

[151] [2013] UKSC 63, [2013] 3 WLR 1076.

[152] Ibid, para 39 (Lord Mance).

[153] *The Guardian*, 16 October 2013.

[154] HC Deb, 21 October 1998, col 1301.

[155] *R (Wright)* v *Health Secretary*, [2009] UKHL 3, [2009] 2 WLR 267.

courts and tribunals) to act in a way incompatible with Convention rights, unless primary legislation permits no other course of action (s 6). This also applies to acts of persons other than public authorities, where those acts are done in exercise of 'functions of a public nature' but not if the 'nature of the act' is private (s 6(3)(b), (5)). A distinction between public and private bodies arises in other aspects of public law, notably in determining whether a body is subject to judicial review, and whether a body is an 'emanation of the State' for the purposes of the vertical direct effect of EU law.[156] However, the House of Lords counselled against relying on the jurisprudence under these different jurisdictions to guide the application of the Human Rights Act.[157]

Although the case law on judicial review may be 'helpful', the EU jurisprudence is 'not', and the matter must be examined under the Human Rights Act 'in the light of the jurisprudence of the Strasbourg court as to those bodies which engage the responsibility of the State for the purposes of the Convention'.[158] In the leading case on this question, *Aston Cantlow and Wilmcote with Billesley Parochial Church Council* v *Wallbank*,[159] it was acknowledged that s 6 applies to bodies 'whose nature is governmental in the broad sense of that expression, and would include government departments, local authorities, the police and the armed forces'.[160] But in addition to these 'core' public authorities, the Act is said to apply to 'hybrid' public authorities, that is to say non-governmental bodies carrying out governmental functions. Examples would include prisons run by private companies, though there is no clear test to decide if a body is public or private for these purposes.

The issue in the *Aston Cantlow* case was whether the applicants were liable as lay rectors to meet the costs of repairs to their parish church. Resisting the demand from the church, the Wallbanks argued that it was a violation of their Convention rights (private property – Protocol 1, art 1) on the part of a public authority (the parochial church council of the Church of England – the established church). However, the House of Lords held that the parochial parish council was not a core public authority, by reference to the text of the Convention itself and jurisprudence relating to religious bodies. It was also held that the parochial church council was not a hybrid public authority either, though this was a matter that had to be dealt with on a case-by-case basis. In this case the council was seeking to enforce the duty of the respondents to pay for repairs to the church, which according to Lord Hope was effectively a 'civil debt', an obligation said to be private rather than public.

The idea that the established church is not a public authority is perhaps a surprising one, not least because the Church, if not a law-making body, has obvious public functions. According to Lord Nicholls, however, this narrow approach is based on the idea that a core public authority is one 'established with a view to public administration as part of the process of government'. There was clearly a concern that if the Church were to be treated as a public authority for the purposes of an action brought against it by private parties like the Wallbanks, it would not then have been possible for the Church subsequently to rely on the Convention in an action brought to enforce violations of its Convention rights by the government. Under the scheme of the Convention, it appears that it is not possible to be both a core public authority for some purposes and a non-governmental organisation for others. This is an argument developed from the wording of ECHR, art 34, and the Human Rights Act, s 7.

The main concern with the meaning of public authority, however, arises as a result of the growth of the private sector and voluntary agencies to provide public services, under contract

---

[156] See chs 25 and 6 respectively.
[157] *Aston Cantlow and Wilmcote with Billesley Parochial Church Council* v *Wallbank* [2003] UKHL 37, [2004] 1 AC 546. See D Oliver [2000] PL 476, [2004] PL 329.
[158] *Aston Cantlow*, para [52] (Lord Hope).
[159] [2003] UKHL 37, [2004] 1 AC 546.
[160] Ibid, para [7] (Lord Nicholls).

with public authorities. Some alarm was caused by a developing body of case law in which the Court of Appeal appeared to exclude the operation of the Act in such cases.[161] This line of authority was nevertheless confirmed in *YL v Birmingham City Council*,[162] a case concerned with a nursing home run by a large private company (Southern Cross), which cared for residents under a contract with a local authority. The issue arose when it was alleged that Southern Cross had violated the art 8 rights of an elderly resident by giving her 28 days' notice to quit following a disagreement with her family. The House of Lords held by a majority of 3–2 that even though most residents were placed in the company's nursing homes by local authorities under contract with the company, this did not make the company a public authority for the purposes of s 6.

This decision was a disappointment to the then government, which had expressed concerns about the narrow construction of s 6, even before the *YL* decision was published.[163] Nevertheless, the position was expressed clearly by Lord Scott who said that Southern Cross was

> a company carrying on a socially useful business for profit. It is neither a charity nor a philanthropist. It enters into private law contracts with the residents in its care homes and with the local authorities with whom it does business. It receives no public funding, enjoys no special statutory powers, and is at liberty to accept or reject residents as it chooses (subject, of course, to anti-discrimination legislation which affects everyone who offers a service to the public) and to charge whatever fees in its commercial judgment it thinks suitable. It is operating in a commercial market with commercial competitors.[164]

The decision was also a disappointment to the Joint Committee on Human Rights which had twice reviewed the meaning of public authority, expressing criticism of the lower courts, and concern that the decisions would undermine the purpose of the Human Rights Act in 'bringing rights home'.[165]

In both of these reports the JCHR explored a number of options to overcome the impact of the decisions, initially placing faith in litigation as a strategy in the hope that the House of Lords would reverse what were seen to be the unhelpful decisions of the Court of Appeal on the scope of the Convention. But after *YL* that strategy was in disarray, though it would be possible to seek a decision of the Strasbourg court, which for reasons considered above would have a decisive effect in resolving the matter. In the meantime, however, legislation enacted that privately run nursing homes were to be treated as public authorities for the purposes of the Human Rights Act where they provided care on behalf of public bodies.[166] But this was a sticking plaster solution to the *YL* case: even though the legislation has since been extended to cover a wider range of people who receive care,[167] it is hardly an adequate long-term response to the wider questions raised by the decision, and the earlier decisions of the Court of Appeal.[168]

---

[161] See *R (Heather) v Leonard Cheshire Foundation* [2002] EWCA Civ 366, [2002] 2 All ER 936; *R (Johnson) v Havering London Borough Council* [2007] EWCA Civ 26, [2008] QB 1. Compare *Poplar Housing Association Ltd v Donoghue* [2001] EWCA Civ 595, [2002] QB 48.

[162] [2007] UKHL 27, [2008] 1 AC 95.

[163] HC Debs, 15 June 2007, col 1045 (Solicitor General).

[164] *YL v Birmingham City Council*, above, para [26].

[165] See HL Paper 39, HC 382 (2003–4), HL Paper 77, HC 410 (2006–7). And see section D below.

[166] Health and Social Care Act 2008, s 145.

[167] See now Care Act 2014, s 73; SI 2015 No 914. For background, see HL Paper 121, HC 1027 (2013–14).

[168] A private members' bill introduced by the then Chairman of the JCHR in 2007 would have extended the scope of the Act by providing that 'a function of a public nature includes a function performed pursuant to a contract or other arrangement with a public authority which is under a duty to perform that function'. But the bill made no progress.

Legislation extending the HRA to bodies administering social care would of course have no impact on social housing, another major area where the private or third sectors provide public services. Although the *YL* decision reinforced doubts about the application of the Human Rights Act here too, the Court of Appeal revisited the matter in *R (Weaver)* v *London and Quadrant Housing Trust.*[169] There it was held (by a majority) that the Act applied in principle to the termination of a tenancy by the trust, which provided social housing supported by a public subsidy as part of the government's policy of providing low cost housing. True, the tenancy agreement was governed by contract. But

> if an act were necessarily a private act because it involved the exercise of rights conferred by private law, that would significantly undermine the protection which Parliament intended to afford to potential victims of hybrid authorities. Public bodies necessarily fulfil their functions by entering into contractual arrangements. It would severely limit the significance of identifying certain bodies as hybrid authorities if the fact that the act under consideration was a contractual act meant that it was a private act falling within section 6(5).[170]

The courts as public authorities

By virtue of s 7, an actual or potential victim of an unlawful act may bring proceedings in respect of the unlawful act or may rely on Convention rights in any legal proceedings (for example, as a defence to a prosecution). In particular, the actual or potential victim may apply for judicial review of the public authority's decision (s 7(3), (4)). So far as s 7 is concerned, an applicant is a victim only if he or she would be regarded as a victim for the purposes of ECHR, art 34. This provides that the ECtHR may receive applications from 'any person, non-governmental organisation or group of individuals claiming to be the victim of a violation by one of the High Contracting Parties of the rights set forth in the Convention or the Protocols thereto'. As pointed out above, this has been read to mean that applications may not be made by core public authorities, which cannot be victims. However, hybrid public authorities can be both perpetrator and victim.

By restricting applications to victims or potential victims, the Act effectively bars some public interest groups and others with standing (a 'sufficient interest') in judicial review proceedings from bringing claims that public authorities are violating Convention rights. A court or tribunal may provide 'such relief or remedy or make such order within its jurisdiction as it considers just and appropriate' (s 8(1)). However, damages for breach of Convention rights are available only in a civil court which otherwise has the power to award damages; and, in assessing damages, the civil court must take account of Strasbourg decisions awarding 'just satisfaction' under the Convention (s 8(2), (3)).[171] According to the House of Lords, 'the purpose of incorporating the Convention in domestic law through the 1998 Act was not to give victims better remedies at home than they could recover in Strasbourg but to give them the same remedies without the delay and expense of resort to Strasbourg'.[172]

Courts and tribunals are expressly stated to be public authorities. This means that courts and tribunals must conduct their affairs in a way that is consistent with Convention rights

---

[169] [2009] EWCA Civ 587, [2009] 4 All ER 865.

[170] Ibid, para 77 (Elias LJ). As in the case of social care, not all tenants would enjoy the benefit of the Human Rights Act; as Elias LJ pointed out it would depend on the lottery of their position being underpinned by the state in some way. This would mean that different tenants of the same landlord would be treated differently.

[171] See A R Mowbray [1997] PL 647. And see ch 26 A.

[172] *R (Greenfield)* v *Home Secretary* [2005] UKHL 14, [2005] 1 WLR 673, at para [19] (Lord Bingham). See now *R (Faulkner)* v *Justice Secretary* [2013] UKSC 23, [2013] 2 All ER 1013.

(such as the right to a fair trial (art 6) and the right to freedom of expression (art 10)). But it means much more, for it applies also to the remedies a court may order. So it would not be possible for a court to issue an injunction if to do so would violate the Convention rights of the defendant; or to fail to issue an injunction if to do so would violate the Convention rights of the applicant. But this cannot be pushed so far as to involve 'the Convention effectively being directly enforceable as between private citizens so as to alter their contractual rights and obligations'.[173] As was said in *McDonald* v *McDonald*:[174]

> although it may well be that article 8 is engaged when a judge makes an order for possession of a tenant's home at the suit of a private sector landlord, it is not open to the tenant to contend that article 8 could justify a different order from that which is mandated by the contractual relationship between the parties, at least where, as here, there are legislative provisions which the democratically elected legislature has decided properly balance the competing interests of private sector landlords and residential tenants.[175]

This question – the so-called horizontal status of the Convention – gave rise to a great deal of analysis in the literature, particularly in the period shortly after the Human Rights Act came into force.[176] The better view appears to be that (i) Convention rights may not be directly enforced by one private party against another, but that (ii) Convention rights may be relied on in an established cause of action to *extend* the rights of either party. More than that, (iii) Convention rights may be used to *transform* common law causes of action, so for example the law of breach of confidence has formed the foundation for a common law right to protection against the misuse of personal information based on ECHR, art 8.[177] By these means, the values embodied in art 8 are made applicable 'in disputes between individuals or between an individual and a non-governmental organisation', as well as in disputes between 'individuals and a public authority'.[178] In this example in particular, the courts have effectively created a new common law right to accommodate Convention obligations.[179]

Concerns that the Act might be used to extend existing or develop new causes of action in litigation between private parties gave rise to special measures relating to freedom of expression. There was concern in particular from the newspaper industry and its self-regulators (the Press Complaints Commission at the time) about the possible implications of the right to privacy in art 8. These and other concerns led to the inclusion of s 12, which applies where a court is considering whether to grant any relief that might affect the exercise of the Convention right to freedom of expression. In these cases, s 12 limits the circumstances in which a court may make interim injunctions, though in view of the inclusion of the courts as public authorities it may be questioned whether these special measures were strictly necessary.[180] The principal author of this provision has, however, complained that it has not been effective in preventing injunctions against newspapers in privacy cases, and has argued that the Human Rights Act should be amended to remove the industry from the supervision of the courts.[181]

---

[173] *McDonald* v *McDonald* [2016] UKSC 28, para 41.
[174] Ibid.
[175] Ibid, para 40.
[176] See M Hunt [1998] PL 423; G Phillipson (1999) 62 MLR 824; R Buxton (2000) 116 LQR 48; W Wade (2000) 116 LQR 217; A Young [2002] PL 232.
[177] *Douglas* v *Hello!* [2001] QB 967; *Venables* v *News Group Newspapers Ltd* [2001] Fam 430; *Campbell* v *MGN Ltd* [2004] UKHL 22, [2004] 2 AC 457; *PJS* v *News Group Newspapers Ltd* [2016] UKSC 26. See ch 16.
[178] *Campbell* v *MGN Ltd*, above, at para 17.
[179] See *Mosley* v *NGN Ltd* [2008] EWHC 1777 QB, [2008] EMLR 20.
[180] As pointed out in *PJS* v *News Group Newspapers Ltd*, above, 'freedom of expression is an important right for its own sake' (para 52).
[181] Lord Wakeham, *Daily Telegraph*, 24 May 2011.

This, however, would be to give the newspaper industry an immunity from legal liability and would be difficult to reconcile with constitutional principle. Short of such an immunity, the industry must make do with the special protection for freedom of expression enjoyed by everyone else. So, unless there are compelling circumstances, no interim injunction is to be granted without the respondent having been notified (s 12(2)), which means that there should not normally be any ex parte injunctions to restrain freedom of expression.[182] Moreover, no interim relief is to be granted – whether ex parte or inter partes – unless the court is satisfied that the applicant is likely to succeed at the full trial (s 12(3)). This qualifies the normal rules relating to interim injunctions as set out in *American Cyanamid Ltd* v *Ethicon Co*,[183] where the House of Lords held that in order to obtain interim relief the applicant need only show a serious issue to be tried and that the balance of convenience lies in favour of granting the injunction sought.

In typical civil proceedings the interim injunction thus 'holds the ring' until the full trial of the action, which may not take place until some considerable time in the future. In these interim proceedings, there is no need to show that a court is likely to grant the remedy sought at the eventual trial of the action, with questions of legality being weighed against other factors in the balance of convenience. This means that individuals may be restrained from doing something not because it is unlawful, but because it may be unlawful and subsequently shown to be lawful. Such a procedure gives rise to questions about the compatibility of procedural law with the rule of law, quite apart from its implications for human rights. It is thus important that a high bar is set for the likelihood of success test in s 12(3) to restrict the circumstances in which interim relief can be granted and to ensure that interim injunctions are not granted on flimsy grounds.

Section 12(3) has been read by the House of Lords at the higher end of the scale to mean that the applicant must show that he or she would probably (more likely than not) succeed at trial, in preference to the Court of Appeal's approach at the lower end of the scale that the applicant need only show a real prospect of success.[184] In addition, section 12(4) addresses more specifically the threat to freedom of expression created by the right to privacy and is a remarkable testament to concerns about the latter. Thus a court is to have particular regard to the importance of the Convention right to freedom of expression and in proceedings relating to journalistic material to 'any relevant privacy code'. The idea here is that no injunction should be granted to restrain a publication on the ground that it violates the privacy of the applicant if the respondent can show that it complies with 'relevant' privacy codes, intended at the time to mean the Codes of Practice of the Press Complaints Commission and OFCOM respectively.[185]

Section 13 contains special protection for religious bodies from the application of Convention rights that might undermine their doctrine and practices.[186]

---

[182] This does not apply, however, to applications that a name or other matter be withheld from the public in proceedings before the court under the Contempt of Court Act 1981, s 11: *A* v *BBC* [2014] UKSC 25. See further chs 13 C and 17 B.

[183] [1975] AC 396.

[184] *Cream Holdings Ltd* v *Banerjee* [2004] UKHL 44, [2005] 1 AC 253. See *Lachaux* v *Independent Print Ltd* [2017] EWCA Civ 1334, paras 47–9 (Davis LJ).

[185] This would now apply to both the Independent Press Standards Organisation (IPSO) and Impress codes respectively. As explained in ch 16, there are now two press codes which have replaced the Press Complaints Commission's Code: the revised self-regulatory scheme (IPSO), and the code introduced under the government's post – Leveson scheme (Impress). Although those who participate in the latter enjoy certain statutory privileges, there is no suggestion in the Royal Charter by which the latter is governed or legislation by which it is rewarded that the Human Rights Act 1998, s 12 applies only to those who participate in the government-backed code rather than the industry's own code.

[186] See P Cumper [2000] PL 254. Quite whether this and art 9 (protection of freedom of religion) is enough to meet the concerns of religious groups is unclear. See J Rivers (2012) 14 *Ecclesiastical Law Jo* 371: 'the law is coming to treat religions as merely recreational and trivial'.

Territorial scope of the Act

An important question to have arisen under the Human Rights Act is its scope of application. This has arisen particularly in the context of recent military activity involving the British armed forces overseas, and the liability if any of the British government for (i) the actions of military personnel and (ii) injuries suffered by military personnel while on active service. These questions are not likely to engage all Convention rights, and in the circumstances of military engagement or peace-keeping, the provisions most likely to be engaged are arts 2 (right to life), 3 (torture or inhuman or degrading treatment or punishment), 4 (forced labour), 5 (right to liberty), and 6 (right to a fair trial).

The legal starting point is ECHR, art 1 which provides that 'the High Contracting Parties shall secure to everyone within their jurisdiction the rights and freedoms defined in Section I of [the] Convention'. This is said to give rise to the principle that liability under the Convention can arise only in respect of conduct within the territory of the State in question.[187] In *Bankovic* v *Belgium* (where the victims of NATO bombing raids in the former Yugoslavia unsuccessfully sought relief under the Convention),[188] the Strasbourg court held that it was only in the most exceptional circumstances that a State could be liable under the Convention for extra-territorial events. These exceptions would arise where 'through the effective control of the relevant territory and its inhabitants abroad as a consequence of military occupation or through the consent, invitation or acquiescence of the Government of that territory, the respondent *exercises all or some of the public powers normally to be exercised by that Government*'.[189]

This principle was applied by the House of Lords in *Al-Skeini*,[190] where a number of Iraqi civilians were killed by British soldiers, one in a British military prison, and the others in circumstances following encounters with British troops in Basra. The question was whether under ECHR, art 2, the government was required to conduct an investigation into each of the deaths. Following the Strasbourg jurisprudence applicable at the time, the House of Lords held that there was no duty to conduct such an investigation in relation to the latter group of individuals, with Lord Brown holding that it would be 'too much' to expect that 'whenever a contracting state acts (militarily or otherwise) through its agents abroad, those affected by such activities fall within its article 1 jurisdiction'.[191] The position was different in relation to the civilian (Baha Mousa) killed while in custody, in respect of whom the Convention was said to have been engaged 'only on the narrow basis' that it was analogous with the extra-territorial exception for embassies.[192]

But that was not the end of it, the defeated applicants taking their case to Strasbourg, where the Court extended the circumstances in which the extra-territorial scope of the Convention would apply.[193] It acknowledged the principle that liability under the Convention may arise where 'as a consequence of lawful or unlawful military action, a Contracting State

---

[187] *Soering* v *United Kingdom* [1989] ECHR 14, (1989) 11 EHRR 439.
[188] [2001] ECHR 890, (2007) 44 EHRR SE5.
[189] Ibid, para 71. Emphasis added.
[190] *Al Skeini* v *Defence Secretary* [2007] UKHL 26, [2008] 1 AC 153.
[191] Ibid, para 127.
[192] Ibid, para 132.
[193] *Al Skeini* v *United Kingdom* [2011] ECHR 1093, (2011) 53 EHRR 18. In doing so it has been said that the Court 'adopted a radically different approach' to this question, Lord Sumption reading *Al-Skeini* to mean that 'the Convention was held to apply, so far as relevant, to extra-territorial military operations in any case where the agents of a Convention state exercised control and authority over an individual, even if they did not exercise governmental powers in the place where the relevant operations occurred': *al-Waheed* v *Ministry of Defence* [2017] UKSC 2, para 47.

exercises effective control of an area outside that national territory'.[194] And it held that having entered Iraq with the United States to remove the administration then in power, the British government was in effective control of the area where the alleged violations took place. Not only had the United Kingdom '*assumed in Iraq the exercise of some of the public powers normally to be exercised by a sovereign government*', but it also had 'assumed authority and responsibility for the maintenance of security in South East Iraq', sufficient to establish a jurisdictional link between the deceased and the United Kingdom.[195]

On the same day it issued the *al-Skeini* decision, the Grand Chamber also announced its decision in the parallel *al-Jedda* decision.[196] In that case the applicant complained of his internment for more than three years by British forces in Iraq, which he said was a violation of his right to liberty as protected by ECHR, art 5. This too followed an unsuccessful attempt to obtain relief in the domestic courts. It is true that the House of Lords (by a majority) rejected the argument of the government that the Convention did not apply because the British forces were under the effective control of the United Nations; this was simply not the case, the House of Lords noting that when they became occupying powers in Iraq, the coalition forces had no UN mandate. However, the House of Lords also held that the rights of the applicant under ECHR, art 5 were displaced by a UN Security Council resolution, which was said by the Lords to impose a duty to intern the applicant which prevailed over ECHR, art 5(1).[197]

The Strasbourg court agreed with the Lords on the jurisdictional point, holding that the 'internment took place within a detention facility in Basrah City, controlled exclusively by British forces, and the applicant was therefore within the authority and control of the United Kingdom throughout'.[198] On the substantive point, however, the Strasbourg court disagreed with the House of Lords, holding that in interpreting UN resolutions, 'there must be a presumption that the [UN] Security Council does not intend to impose any obligation on member states to breach fundamental principles of human rights'.[199] The Court continued by saying that 'in the event of any ambiguity in the terms of a Security Council Resolution, the Court must therefore choose the interpretation which is most in harmony with the requirements of the Convention and which avoids any conflict of obligations'.[200] In the absence of any explicit or implicit obligation to detain people indefinitely without charge, the obligations under ECHR, art 5 were not displaced.

The House of Lords having thus been overturned twice, this is a matter that risked conflict between the ECtHR and the UKSC. Lord Sumption expressed concern that the approach of the Strasbourg court went 'well beyond the ordinary concept of extra-territorial jurisdiction in international law', which was 'generally confined to territory where the state is the governmental authority or occupying power', and brought the ECHR into 'potential conflict with other sources of international law', while requiring 'the application of the Convention to the conduct of military operations for which it was not designed and is ill-adapted'.[201] Rather ominously, Lord Sumption continued by saying that it is 'ultimately a matter for the courts of the United Kingdom to decide the territorial ambit of the obligation of public authorities under section 6 to act compatibly with the Convention', and that they could not

[194] *Al Skeini*, Ibid, para 138.
[195] Ibid, para 149. Emphasis added.
[196] *Al-Jedda* v *United Kingdom* [2011] ECHR 292, (2011) 53 EHRR 23.
[197] *R (Al-Jedda)* v *Defence Secretary* [2007] UKHL 58, [2008] 1 AC 332.
[198] *Al-Jedda* v *United Kingdom*, above, para 85.
[199] Ibid, para 102.
[200] Ibid.
[201] *al-Waheed* v *Ministry of Defence* [2017] UKSC 2, para 48.

be 'bound by the view of the Strasbourg court' if 'satisfied that that view goes beyond what Parliament has enacted'.[202]

That said, any potential conflict appears to have been avoided by the most recent decision of the Strasbourg court in *Hassan* v *United Kingdom*,[203] in which the extra-territorial reach of the ECHR was confirmed but in the application of which Convention rights could be redefined to accommodate the different safeguards relating to armed conflict under international law. This revision by the Strasbourg court was seized with alacrity by the UKSC in *al-Waheed* v *Ministry of Defence*,[204] in which a majority led by Lord Sumption accepted the territorial claims of the Strasbourg court, but also the opportunity to interpret Convention rights in accordance with other international legal standards. This enabled the court to hold that the extended detention of the complainant in Iraq was lawful when necessary for 'imperative reasons of security', but not when done to interrogate for reasons of intelligence gathering. The complainant should also have been given an opportunity to challenge the lawfulness of his detention.[205]

These cases raised questions about the liability of the United Kingdom to the citizens of an occupied country.[206] But what about the liability to the soldiers or families of soldiers who are injured or killed while on active service in other countries, such as Iraq? This is an issue that has arisen in the context of ECHR, art 2, where the question is not only the duty to investigate the circumstances of someone's death but also the more far-reaching claim that art 2 is engaged by a failure of the military authorities to provide adequate equipment that would reduce the risk of being killed while in the theatre of war. The first case to reach the Supreme Court on this matter was *R (Smith)* v *Defence Secretary*,[207] a case involving a soldier who had died of heatstroke in Iraq. The issue was whether there was an obligation to investigate the death in a manner that met the procedural requirements set by ECHR, art 2. The Supreme Court held (by a 6–3 majority) that the Convention had no application in these circumstances.

The majority took this view on the ground that 'none of the exceptions recognised by the Strasbourg court, and there is no basis in its case law, or in principle, for the proposition that the jurisdiction which states undoubtedly have over their armed forces abroad both in national law and international law means that they are within their jurisdiction for the purposes of article 1'.[208] In *Smith* v *Ministry of Defence* three years later, however, the position had to change in the light of *al-Skeini*, the Supreme Court reversing the earlier *Smith* decision.[209] True, *al-Skeini* was not directly in point, while the Supreme Court also rehearsed concerns about not going beyond what Strasbourg requires. But it was recognised that the Convention was a 'living instrument', and it was admitted that the earlier *Smith* case was 'inconsistent with the guidance that the Grand Chamber [had] now given in *al Skeini*'.[210] As a result, 'the jurisdiction of the United Kingdom under art 1 of the Convention extends to securing the protection of art 2 to members of the armed forces when they are serving outside its territory'.[211]

[202] Ibid.
[203] [2014] ECHR
[204] [2017] UKSC 2.
[205] This reflecting the requirements of ECHR, art 5(4).
[206] On the continuing consequences of which in relation to ECHR, art 2 in particular, see *R (Mousa)* v *Defence Secretary* [2013] EWHC 1412 (Admin).
[207] [2010] UKSC 29, [2011] 1 AC 1.
[208] Ibid, para 307.
[209] *Smith* v *Defence Secretary* [2013] UKSC 41.
[210] Ibid, para 55 (Lord Hope).
[211] Ibid.

D. Enhanced parliamentary scrutiny

Although the courts are given significant powers by the Human Rights Act 1998, important questions also arise about the role of Parliament in scrutinising legislation on human rights grounds.[212] While lawyers tend to focus on the role of the courts, it is important that the contribution of Parliament is not overlooked, and indeed the nature of parliamentary scrutiny is a matter that will have legal consequences. The ECtHR has indicated that the extent of parliamentary scrutiny will be taken into account in deciding whether or not there has been a breach of Convention rights in contentious cases. This extensive scrutiny was an important factor in the decision of the majority in *Animal Defenders International* v *UK*,[213] that the ban on political advertising was consistent with ECHR, art 10.

So far as parliamentary scrutiny on human rights is concerned, the starting point is the Human Rights Act, s 19. This provides that a minister in charge of a Bill must make a statement to the effect that either (i) the Bill is in the minister's view compatible with Convention rights; or (ii) the government wishes the Bill to proceed even though the minister's is unable to make a statement of compatibility.[214] In practice, Bills generally contain a statement of compatibility on their face, though it is not unknown for a Bill to declare that the minister is unable to make a statement that it is compatible, as in the case of the Communications Bill 2002, which the government was concerned might breach art 10 of the Convention because of the ban on political advertising on television and radio.[215] In this case, however, both the House of Lords and (as we have seen) the ECtHR subsequently held that the ban was consistent with the right to freedom of expression.[216]

Also important in terms of parliamentary oversight is the creation of the Joint Committee on Human Rights, a select committee that came into operation in February 2001. This all-party committee has members drawn from both Houses of Parliament with terms of reference that include (i) an examination of ministerial statements of compatibility and (ii) remedial orders made under the HRA, s 10. A remedial order may be made following a declaration of incompatibility, or after a decision by the Strasbourg court in proceedings against the United Kingdom has indicated that primary legislation is incompatible with the Convention (s 10). In both cases a remedial order may be made only where a minister considers that there are 'compelling reasons' for doing so (s 10 and Sch 2).

The remedial order procedure is a controversial one that allows primary legislation to be amended by ministerial order, even though the order must be approved by a resolution passed by both Houses of Parliament, and even if the purpose appears to be benign, namely to enable an incompatibility with a Convention right to be removed from the statute book more quickly than if an amending Act of Parliament were needed.[217] In the first four years of the Parliament elected in 2010, the procedure was used only three times,[218] and it has not been used since. It is open to governments to use conventional legislative procedures to deal with declarations of incompatibility or rulings of the

---

[212] See M Ryle [1994] PL 192; K D Ewing, in Ziegler, Baranger and Bradley (eds), *Constitutionalism and the Role of Parliaments*, ch 14; and Hiebert and Kelly, *Parliamentary Bills of Rights* (an important study).

[213] [2013] ECHR 362, (2013) 57 EHRR 21. But see *R (Chester)* v *Justice Secretary*, above.

[214] Earlier versions of the *Ministerial Code* required ministers to consider the impact of the ECHR in preparing business for Cabinet.

[215] See HL Paper 50, HC 397 (2002–3).

[216] *R (Animal Defenders' International)* v *Culture, Media and Sport Secretary* [2008] UKHL 15, [2008] 2 WLR 781; *Animal Defenders International* v *UK*, above.

[217] For fuller details, see Ewing, note 101 above.

[218] HL Paper 54, HC 599 (2010–12), HL Paper 192, HC 1483 (2010–12), HL Paper 8, HC 166 (2012–13).

Strasbourg court, and there will be occasions where this is the more appropriate course of action.[219]

As a result, most of the work of the JCHR has been concerned with examining ministerial statements, and most of the Committee's time is spent examining Bills (and occasionally statutory instruments) to determine whether they meet Convention requirements. The Committee has been willing to challenge or to question ministers' claims that Bills are compatible with the ECHR,[220] and it has been prepared to test proposed legislation for compatibility with other international instruments,[221] drawing to the attention of Parliament any concerns that it may have.[222] But while its reports may inform debates in the House, the Committee is not always able to convince the government, which will have acted on legal advice of its own, legal advice that in all probability will have seen no reason for questioning the government's proposed action.

Nevertheless, the Committee has been particularly vocal about legislation proposed by the government to deal with the problem of terrorism, and has produced powerful critiques of the control order regime introduced by the Prevention of Terrorism Act 2005.[223] A more recent report of the Committee was notable for its trenchant criticism of the Transparency of Lobbying, Third-Party Campaigning and Trade Union Administration Bill in 2013.[224] The Committee expressed strong concern as much about parliamentary procedure as about the substance of the Bill, reporting that it was 'unacceptable' that it had been unable to report on the Bill until after it had left the Commons, particularly as there were no grounds for believing that it was an emergency measure.

In view of 'the rushed legislative time-table and lack of consultation and pre-legislative scrutiny', the Committee's primary recommendation was that the passage of the Bill should be 'paused' to allow for further scrutiny and consultation with interested parties who had expressed serious concerns about its contents.[225] These concerns – which the Committee also addressed – related principally to Part 2 of the Bill, which proposed far-reaching restrictions on political campaigning in the period before an election by organisations other than political parties. Part 2 of the Bill was in fact 'paused' briefly,[226] raising questions about whether the House of Commons Standing Orders should be amended to give to the Committee the formal power in all cases to delay measures on procedural and perhaps even substantive grounds.

Apart from its work in scrutinising legislation, the Committee has also conducted inquiries into topical issues and in this sense has operated like other select committees.[227] Among a

---

[219] The use of such legislation is not without its problems, giving rise to difficulties of effective legislative scrutiny in the case of fast track legislation; see HL Paper 130, HC 1088 (2014–15).

[220] See HL Paper 37, HC 372 (2001–2) (Anti-terrorism, Crime and Security Bill); HL Paper 68, HC 334 (2004–5) (Prevention of Terrorism Bill); and HL Paper 35, HC 283 (2004–5) (Identity Cards Bill).

[221] See HL Paper 30, HC 314 (2001–2) (Homelessness Bill: consideration given to compatibility with International Convention on the Elimination of all Forms of Racial Discrimination, and International Covenant on Economic, Social and Cultural Rights); HL Paper 96, HC 787 (2005–6) (Health Bill: consideration given to compatibility with the European Social Charter and the ICESCR); HL Paper 92, HC 630 (2015–16) (Trade Union Bill: consideration given to compatibility with ILO Conventions). In the last case the Committee was criticized for a lack of rigour in its engagement with the standards in question: K D Ewing and J Hendy QC (2016) 45 ILJ 391.

[222] See J Hiebert (2005) 68 MLR 676; (2006) 69 MLR 7; (2006) 4 *Int J of Const Law* 1; [2012] PL 27. Also D Feldman [2002] PL 323.

[223] Ewing, *Bonfire of the Liberties*, ch 8.

[224] HL Paper 61, HC 755 (2013–14).

[225] The Political and Constitutional Reform Select Committee also recommended a pause: HC 601 (2013–14).

[226] HC Debs, 5 Nov 2013, col 109, in response to a motion moved by a cross-bench peer.

[227] For background, see HL Paper 239, HC 1575 (2006–7). Its general select committee functions have also included scrutiny of the appointment of a new chair of the Equality and Human Rights Commission: HL Paper 145, HC 648 (2015–16).

number of notable reports are those dealing with (i) the rendition of terrorist suspects and the alleged complicity of British officials in the use of torture by foreign security and intelligence agencies;[228] (ii) the extent to which British businesses are complying with international human rights obligations, an investigation that required consideration of a wide range of international human rights other than the ECHR, including instruments produced by the OECD and the International Labour Organization;[229] and (iii) the human rights implications of the use of drones for targeted killing of British nationals.[230]

E. Conclusion

Human rights is an area that has proved to be remarkably controversial in recent years. As we have seen, the scheme of the HRA is such that within the British constitutional system the legal principle of parliamentary sovereignty has been preserved, with courts having powers that fall short of invalidating legislation on human rights grounds. But the debate has moved on, and is now dominated by general concerns about the extent to which the Convention and the jurisprudence of the Strasbourg court generally are a threat to Parliament's sovereignty in a political sense. As we have seen, this is a debate with which judges are beginning to engage,[231] some making the case for a more flexible approach on the part of the Strasbourg court, to permit differences to develop in the application of Convention rights at national level.

The latter is a controversial position for the judges to advance extra-judicially, and will lead to concerns that the Human Rights Act will become a vehicle in domestic law for the dilution rather than the strengthening of human rights standards. However, that may be a political price that has to be paid. It is no secret that 'human rights' is a subject about which the political parties are split. Many in the Conservative party appear hostile to both the ECHR and the HRA; the Labour party, the Liberal Democrats and nationalist parties generally appear strongly to support both. Nor is it a secret that within Whitehall the Home Office would like to diminish the risk of ECHR, art 8 causing immigration decisions to be reversed on Convention grounds: hence the clumsy attempts made in 2012 by amendments to the Immigration Rules to provide guidance to the judges on how art 8 should be interpreted more narrowly.[232]

An attempt to address some wider aspects of the 'human rights problem' was undertaken by the Coalition government, which established an all-party Commission to investigate the creation of a British Bill of Rights that 'incorporates and builds on all our obligations under the European Convention on Human Rights, ensures that these rights continue to be enshrined in British law, and protects and extends British liberties'.[233] During the lifetime of the Coalition government, however, the differences between the parties appeared to harden, with some Conservatives speaking openly (if implausibly) about withdrawing from the European Convention on Human Rights. Both the

---

[228] HL Paper 152, HC 230 (2008–9).
[229] HL Paper 5, HC 64 (2009–10). See subsequently on the same theme HL 153 Paper, HC 443 (2016–17).
[230] HL Paper 141, HC 174 (2015–16), HL Paper 49, HC 747 (2016–17).
[231] See pp 381–2, above.
[232] See for example *Home Secretary v Izuazu* [2013] UKUT 45, *MF (Nigeria) v Secretary of State for the Home Department* [2013] EWCA Civ 1192, [2013] WLR(D) 380; *MA (Somalia) v Secretary of State for Home Department* [2015] EWCA Civ 48; and *Suckoo v Home Secretary* [2016] EWCA Civ 38
[233] The Coalition, *Our Programme for Government* (2010), p 11.

ECHR and the Human Rights Act were also the target of extraordinary venom from the newspaper industry.[234]

In this febrile atmosphere it was highly unlikely that the Bill of Rights Commission would be able to resolve the sharp differences between the parties. Chaired by a retired senior civil servant and eventually composed exclusively of nine QCs, the Commission was unable to produce a unanimous report,[235] though it provided a blueprint for change that may be attractive to a Conservative government in the future for purely political reasons, in order to deal with what would be a largely presentational replacement of the HRA with an alternative that would be substantially similar. Paradoxically, however, Brexit appears to have diminished any immediate threat to the HRA; not because of a renewed commitment to European human rights in an era of Euroscepticism, but most likely because the government is heavily preoccupied with other matters.[236]

---

[234] Such rhetoric was fuelled by decisions of the ECtHR with which both the government and many newspapers strongly disagree. Particularly significant have been the decisions discussed above that require a relaxation of prisoners' voting restrictions (see above, p 376); as well as the decision preventing the extradition of the radical preacher Abu Qatada (*Othman (Abu Qatada)* v *United Kingdom* [2012] ECHR 56, (2012) 55 EHRR 1).

[235] The only non-QC member (apart from the Chair resigned before the Commission reported: *The Guardian*, 11 March 2012. For the report, see Commission on a Bill of Rights, *A UK Bill of Rights? – The Choice Before Us* (2012). For a good account of the complexity of some of the issues around the Commission's report and more generally, see H Fenwick, 'The Report of the Bill of Rights Commission: disappointing Conservative expectations or fulfilling them?', *UK Const L Blog* (21 March 2013) (available at http://ukconstitutionallaw.org).

[236] See Conservative Party, *Forward Together* (2017).

CHAPTER 15

Right to liberty and police powers

The preservation of law and order and the prevention and detection of crime are matters of great importance to government, taken very seriously by successive British governments. In 2008, the Home Affairs Select Committee reported that police expenditure in the United Kingdom (at 2.5 per cent GDP) is the highest in the OECD,[1] which by any account is a remarkable distinction. But while it is clearly important that such matters are taken seriously, it is equally important that these concerns should not be used to justify equipping the police with more power than is absolutely necessary, or in conferring power that is not subject to proper legal and political scrutiny, the determination of what is proper for these purposes being one that admittedly begs many questions.

Every power conferred on police officers inevitably means a corresponding reduction in the liberty of the individual, and brings us face to face with Convention obligations. As the European Court of Human Rights reminded us, protection from arbitrary interference by the state with an individual's liberty is 'a fundamental human right' and as such it is protected by art 5 of the ECHR.[2] This is a measure that has assumed greater significance with the enactment of the Human Rights Act 1998, although it is by no means the only Convention right which will have a bearing on the conduct of the police. As we shall see, arts 2 (the right to life), 3 (inhuman and degrading treatment), 6 (the right to a fair trial) and 8 (respect for private life, home and correspondence) may also be directly affected.

It is of course the case that the legal protection of the citizen from the misuse of police powers pre-dates the Human Rights Act 1998, with the right to liberty ingrained in the common law. The relationship between the police and the citizen is subject to detailed statutory regulation in the Police and Criminal Evidence Act 1984 (PACE), which despite being significantly amended on several occasions has nevertheless proved to be a remarkably robust legal framework. It is the various provisions of that Act (along with the Codes of Practice that accompany it) that form the basis of the bulk of this chapter.[3] The Act (as amended) regulates police powers of stop and search, police powers of arrest, police powers of detention and questioning, and police powers of entry, search and seizure, as well as much else besides.

But as already suggested, it is important that the police always act with legal authority and that chief constables and police officers should be fully accountable for their actions. It is fundamental to the rule of law that police officers should not exceed their powers in upholding the law, and that they should not enjoy any immunity when they do so. In this chapter we also consider some of the remedial and accountability mechanisms in place, without which policing within the law would be difficult to maintain. As it is, questions are constantly asked about the adequacy of these mechanisms, questions brought into even sharper focus by the report of the independent inquiry into the Hillsborough tragedy in 1989. This exposed not only police incompetence and corruption, but also failures in response thereto by all three branches of government.[4]

---

[1] HC 364 (2007–8), para 67.

[2] *Brogan* v *UK* (1989) 11 EHRR 117, at p 134.

[3] The Codes are issued under PACE, ss 66, 67. There are in fact eight codes (A–H), each dealing with different aspects of police practice, several of which are referred to below.

[4] Hillsborough Independent Panel, *Report*, HC 581 (2012–13).

A. Police powers short of arrest

At common law, the pre-arrest powers of the police are very limited: most police powers affecting the individual's liberty depend on an arrest having been made. There is no common law right to stop and question; to detain a suspect to help the police with their inquiries; or to detain a suspect pending an arrest.[5] Indeed in *Jackson* v *Stevenson*,[6] it was held to be contrary to constitutional principle and illegal to search someone to establish whether there are grounds for an arrest, unusually vivid language for the era in which these comments were made. If the police are to have such powers, they must be provided by Parliament, as they have been (often in controversial circumstances) for almost 200 years.[7] Stop and search powers have been used provocatively in a racially discriminatory way.[8]

Wide powers to stop and search are to be found in PACE 1984 s 1.[9] A constable may stop and search a person or vehicle, or anything which is in the vehicle, for stolen or prohibited articles. (The latter term is defined to include an offensive weapon, an article used for the purpose of burglary or related crimes, or an article for destroying or causing damage to property.) Section 1 has been amended so that the power of stop and search may also be used where someone is suspected of carrying a knife, or prohibited fireworks. Stop and search powers may be exercised only if the constable 'has reasonable grounds for suspecting that he will find stolen or prohibited articles' or any prohibited fireworks (s 1(3)), or that someone is carrying a knife or other sharp implement in a public place.

The Home Office Code A (Code of Practice for Statutory Powers of Stop and Search) gives some guidance as to reasonable grounds for suspicion. It emphasises that 'Reasonable suspicion cannot be based on generalisations or stereotypical images that certain groups or categories of people as more likely to be involved in criminal activity',[10] and was revised in 2014 following growing concerns about police misuse of the power.[11] If during a search a constable discovers articles to which the Act applies, they may be seized (s 1(6)). But before exercising these powers, a constable must (inter alia) inform the person to be searched of his or her name and police station, and of the grounds for the search.

PACE 1984 also requires a police officer to provide documentary evidence that he or she is a police officer if he or she is not in uniform (s 2). Details of the search must be recorded and if requested a copy must be supplied to the person searched (s 3). Failure to do so could render the action unlawful.[12] Reasonable force may be used by the police (s 117), but during any search made before an arrest a person may not be required to remove any clothing in public except for an outer coat, jacket or gloves (s 2(9)).[13] The safeguards in s 2 apply also to stop and search powers under the Misuse of Drugs Act 1971, s 23, which apply separately to anyone who is suspected on reasonable grounds to be in unlawful possession of a controlled drug.[14]

---

[5] See respectively *Kenlin* v *Gardner* [1967] QB 510, *R* v *Lemsatef* [1977] 2 All ER 835, and *R* v *Iqbal* [2011] EWCA Crim 273, [2011] 1 WLR 1541.

[6] (1879) 2 Adam 255.

[7] Cmnd 8427 (1981) (Scarman Report).

[8] Ibid.

[9] Note that they are powers of 'stop and search' not 'stop and account', on which see Ewing, *Bonfire of the Liberties*, pp 21–3. However, a person acting in an anti-social manner may be required to give his or her name and address to a constable in uniform (Police Reform Act 2002, s 50), a power exercisable also by designated community support officers (ibid, Sch 4, para 3). A police officer may also question individuals where it is possible to do so without detaining them: *Tester* v *DPP* [2015] EWHC 1353 (Admin).

[10] Code A, para 2.2B(b). The Code also deals with the 'recording of encounters not governed by statutory powers', only now to claim that there is no duty to record such encounters (para 4.12).

[11] *The Guardian*, 30 April 2014.

[12] *Osman* v *DPP* (1999) 163 JP 725.

[13] See further Code A, paras 3.1–3.7.

[14] See *Wither* v *Reid* 1979 SLT 192 (on the distinction between (*a*) arrest and (*b*) detention for search).

An important feature of the foregoing provisions is that they require the police officer to have 'reasonable suspicion' before exercising the powers in question. More recently, however, power has been given to the police in limited circumstances to conduct random or 'suspicion-less' searches,[15] as under the Criminal Justice and Public Order Act 1994 (prevention of violence and carrying offensive weapons), and the Terrorism Act 2000 (in relation to counter-terrorism).[16] Where authorisation is in place under the 1994 Act, a constable may 'stop any person or vehicle and make any search he thinks fit whether or not he has any grounds for suspecting that the person or vehicle is carrying weapons or articles of that kind' (s 60(5)).

These powers applied only when triggered by a senior police officer in response to a threat specified in the legislation in question. In relation to both of these categories of suspicion-less search powers, the House of Lords and subsequently the Supreme Court found them to be compatible with Convention rights,[17] in what appears to be a slip in the constitutional principles referred to in *Jackson* v *Stevenson* above. The ECtHR took a different view in relation to the provisions of the Terrorism Act 2000, and has yet to have an opportunity to consider the corresponding provisions of the CJPOA 1994. In *R (Roberts)* v *MPC*, however, the UKSC thought the latter powers to be sufficiently different from the former to be compatible with the ECHR.[18]

B. Police powers of arrest

Arrest with a warrant

Under the Magistrates' Courts Act 1980, s 1 (as amended), criminal proceedings may be initiated either by the issue of a summons, requiring the accused to attend court on a certain day, or, in more serious cases, by a warrant of arrest, naming the accused and the offence with which he or she is charged. A warrant is obtained from a justice of the peace after a written application (information) has been substantiated on oath.[19] A warrant may be executed anywhere in England or Wales by a police constable.[20] If the warrant is to arrest a person charged with an offence, it may be executed even when a constable does not have it in his or her possession, but the warrant must be shown on demand to the arrested person as soon as possible.[21]

Despite judicial dicta to the contrary,[22] a person arrested would seem entitled to know that the arrest is under a warrant (for if not, how can the person demand to see it?). Where a constable in good faith executes a warrant that seems valid on its face, the constable is protected from liability for the arrest by the Constables' Protection Act 1750 if it should turn out that the warrant was beyond the jurisdiction of the justice who issued it.[23] The requirement that the warrant be issued by a justice of the peace is thus as much

---

[15] B Bowling and E Marks (2017) 28 *King's Law Journal* 62.

[16] For full treatment of the latter, see ch 20 below.

[17] In relation to the 2000 and 1994 Acts respectively.

[18] [2015] UKSC 79.

[19] The exercise of the power may not be delegated: *R v Manchester Stipendiary Magistrate, ex p Hill* [1983] 1 AC 328.

[20] They may now be executed in Scotland: Criminal Justice and Public Order Act 1994, s 136. See also Magistrates' Courts Act 1980, s 126. Powers of arrest *without* a warrant for cross-border offences are to be found in the Criminal Justice and Public Order Act 1994, s 137A (as inserted by the Policing and Crime Act 2017, s 116).

[21] Magistrates' Courts Act 1980, s 125D; and cf *R v Purdy* [1975] QB 288.

[22] *R v Kulynycz* [1971] 1 QB 367, at p 372.

[23] See also *McGrath v RUC* [2001] 2 AC 731.

a safeguard for the police as it is for the person named on it. When an arrest warrant has been issued, a constable may enter and search premises to make the arrest, using such reasonable force as is necessary.[24]

Arrest without a warrant

The law on arrest without a warrant was revised and amended by the Serious Organised Crime and Police Act 2005, which generally sought to simplify the position.[25] PACE s 24 now provides that a constable may arrest without a warrant

(*a*) anyone who is about to commit an offence;

(*b*) anyone who is in the act of committing an offence;

(*c*) anyone whom the constable has reasonable grounds for suspecting to be about to commit an offence; and

(*d*) anyone whom the constable has reasonable grounds for suspecting to be committing an offence.

There are also powers of arrest where a constable (i) *suspects* an offence has been committed, and where (ii) an offence *has been* committed. In the former case, a constable may arrest anyone whom he or she has reasonable grounds to suspect of being guilty of the offence. In the latter case, the constable may arrest anyone who is guilty of the offence or anyone whom he or she has reasonable grounds for suspecting to be guilty of it.

These powers of arrest apply to any offence, no matter how trivial. But there is an important proviso in the sense that the arresting officer must have reasonable grounds for believing that it is *necessary* to make the arrest, for one of the reasons specified in s 24(5). The foregoing reasons are widely drafted and ought not to impose serious restraints on the power of summary arrest. They include the need to (i) ascertain the suspect's name or address; (ii) prevent the arrested person from causing harm to himself or herself or to others, committing an offence against public decency, or obstructing the highway; (iii) protect a child or other vulnerable person from the person arrested; (iv) allow the prompt and effective investigation of the offence; and (v) prevent a prosecution from being hindered by the disappearance of the suspect.[26]

In addition to these powers of arrest by a constable, s 24A of PACE provides that a person other than a constable may arrest without a warrant anyone who is in the act of committing an indictable offence, and anyone whom the arresting person has reasonable grounds for suspecting to be committing an indictable offence. Moreover, where an indictable offence has been committed, a person other than a constable may arrest without a warrant anyone who is guilty of the offence, or anyone whom he or she has reasonable grounds for suspecting to be guilty of it.[27] The fact that this universal power of summary arrest is confined to indictable offences is an important limitation, but most people will be unaware of which offences are indictable and which are not. Further limitations on this power (which may make its use by most people unwise) are to be found in s 24A(3).

The latter provides that the power may only be exercised where the person making the arrest has reasonable grounds for believing that any of the reasons mentioned in s 24A(4)

---

[24] Police and Criminal Evidence Act 1984, ss 17, 117.

[25] See *Shields* v *Merseyside Police* [2010] EWCA Civ 1281, for an account by Toulson LJ of the background to the 2005 amendments.

[26] See Code G (Code of Practice for the Statutory Power of Arrest by Police Officers, 2012, Revised) for guidance.

[27] See *Walters* v *W H Smith & Son Ltd* [1914] 1 KB 595, and *R* v *Self* (1992) 95 Cr App R 42.

apply to make it necessary to arrest the person in question, and it is not reasonably practicable for a constable to make the arrest. Section 24A(4) provides in turn that the reasons justifying the summary arrest are to prevent the person arrested causing physical injury to himself or herself or another person, suffering physical injury, causing loss or damage to property, or making off before a constable can assume responsibility for him or her. These are seriously circumscribed powers, and in practice they may empower community support officers rather than citizens with no connection with the police.[28]

Reasonable suspicion and necessity

In one of the leading cases on PACE, s 24 (as amended), it was explained that the amended statutory scheme 'is intended to be uniform, self-contained, *clear* and to strike an appropriate balance between, on one side, the need for protection of the public and proper enforcement of the criminal law and, on the other side, protection of the individual against undue interference with his liberty'.[29] It is nevertheless doubtful if the amendments have realised the ambitions of their authors, certainly in terms of clarity, with the legal anatomy of a lawful arrest both uncertain and complex. There are two areas of potential uncertainty, the first being that in some cases the power of arrest is conditional on the police officer having 'reasonable' grounds to suspect that the arrested person is about to commit, is committing, or has committed an offence.[30]

It was pointed out by the Court of Appeal in *Alanov* v *Sussex Chief Constable*[31] that 'the "threshold" for the existence of "reasonable grounds" for suspicion is low, meaning that the amount of material that is known to the arresting officer in order to found "reasonable grounds" for suspicion may be small, even sparse'.[32] One situation where an arrest might not satisfy this requirement is where an arresting officer acted at the request of another officer, but 'the information given to the arresting officer was too sparse to afford reasonable grounds for the necessary suspicion'.[33] It has been suggested also that an arrest would not be based on reasonable grounds if the police officer who carried out an arrest did so in bad faith, or in circumstances where the decision was irrational.

As we have seen, however, it is not enough that there should be reasonable grounds for an arrest: the powers in question should only be used when *necessary* to do so. This requirement has also attracted the attention of the Court of Appeal, this time in *Hayes* v *Chief Constable of Merseyside Police*.[34] There, a 'two stage test' was proposed to determine whether an arrest was necessary: (i) the constable making the arrest must actually believe that the arrest was necessary, and for a reason prescribed by s 24(5); and (ii) objectively that belief must be reasonable. In relation to the second limb it has been said that:

---

[28] Alongside the powers of arrest without a warrant under PACE, ss 24 and 24A, some residual common law powers continue in force. At common law, a police officer has a power to arrest without warrant anyone who commits a breach of the peace. For a fuller account, see the 15th edition of this work, ch 21; and see ch 18 below for the use of this power in the context of freedom of assembly.

[29] *Shields* v *Chief Constable of Merseyside Police* [2010] EWCA Civ 1281, para 12.

[30] PACE, s 24(1).

[31] [2012] EWCA Civ 235.

[32] Ibid, para 25.

[33] *Shields*, above, para 26, referring to *O'Hara* v *Chief Constable of RUC* [1997] AC 286. See also *Buckley* v *Thames Valley Chief Officer* [2009] EWCA Civ 356. The latter emphasises that 'an arresting officer may rely on what he had been told by others who may be civilian informants, reliable or unreliable, or other officers, providing that the information thus assembled provides reasonable grounds for suspicion' (Hughes LJ, para [9]). Also *Metropolitan Police Commissioner* v *Raissi* [2008] EWCA Civ 1237, [2009] QB 564.

[34] [2011] EWCA Civ 911, [2012] 1 WLR 517.

Insofar as the second limb deploys the adverb 'objectively', all that means is that this Court, in the exercise of its judicial function, applies independent, objective standards to its review of the Defendant's decision: in particular, the reasonableness of the grounds upon which that decision was founded. That review is carried out on the basis of information known to the decision-maker at the time it was made. Finally, the Court does not ask itself whether any police officer could rationally have made the decision under challenge; it directs itself to the particular decision maker and his grounds.[35]

In *TL*, the Court of Appeal also 'emphasised that the underlying concept in section 24(5) is that of necessity', which 'cannot be envisaged as a synonym for 'desirable' or 'convenient'. It was held (unusually) in that case that the arrest was unlawful on the ground that it was not necessary where the suspect had voluntarily undertaken to attend a police station for interview and where he had agreed not to contact the complainant in circumstances where there was no reason to doubt his word. It was also held not to be necessary for the effective investigation of the offence that the arrest would unlock police powers of enter and search of his premises under PACE, s 18 in circumstances where there was no urgent need to use such powers.

In a nutshell, there must be (i) reasonable grounds to believe that the arrested person is about to commit, is committing, or has committed an offence, and (ii) reasonable grounds to believe that it is necessary to invoke the statutory power of arrest.

Lord Hanningfield v *Essex Chief Constable*[36] is a notable case on the application of the powers of arrest conferred on police officers by PACE, s 24 (as amended). Not only were the limits of these powers of arrest tested, but they were found to have been exercised unlawfully.

The applicant had recently been released from prison following a conviction relating to parliamentary expenses. Shortly thereafter, he was visited at home by five police officers at 6.45 am and arrested, following which his house was searched, after which he was taken to a police station to be questioned about an offence relating to local government expenses when he had been leader of Essex County Council.[37]

According to Eady J in upholding Hanningfield's civil claim against the police for wrongful arrest, the proper test to be applied in determining whether an arrest is necessary for the purposes of PACE s 24 is to be found in *Hayes* v *Chief Constable of Merseyside Police*, above. In this case, Eady J held that 'the requirement of "necessity" as laid down by Parliament has not, on any realistic interpretation of the word, been met'.

The summary arrest was never going to have any impact on 'the prompt and effective investigation' of Lord Hanningfield's credit card expenses, and there were 'no solid grounds to suppose that he would suddenly start to hide or destroy evidence, or that he would make

---

[35] *R(TL)* v *Surrey Chief Constable* [2017] EWHC 129 (Admin). See also *R (B)* v *Chief Constable of the PSNI* [2015] EWHC 3691 (Admin), and *Fitzpatrick* v *Metropolitan Police Commissioner* [2012] EWHC 12 (Admin). The last is notable because the court rejected the argument that an arrest was lawful only if there was (*a*) reasonable suspicion, (*b*) necessity *and* (*c*) no abuse of the discretionary power to arrest within the meaning of the *Wednesbury* principles. According to the court, in relation to (*c*) that there was no separate *Wednesbury* inquiry to be conducted to determine the legality of an arrest, and that the *Wednesbury* test was 'for all material purposes subsumed within the new statutory test' (para 128). Earlier applications of *Wednesbury* to arrest were decided at a time when the necessity requirement did not apply: *Holgate-Mohammed* v *Duke* [1984] AC 437.

[36] [2013] EWHC 243 (QB), [2013] 3 WLR 3632.

[37] The allegations were not pursued.

inappropriate contacts'. There was no justification 'for by-passing all the usual statutory safeguards involved in obtaining a warrant', with the result that Lord Hanningfield succeeded in his civil claim for damages for wrongful arrest.

The wrongful nature of the arrest undermined both the legality of the search, as well as the legality of the detention at the police station.[38]

Manner of arrest

Although the first ingredient of a lawful arrest is the existence of lawful authority to make the arrest, it is not the only ingredient. The arrest must also be executed in a lawful manner, which means that the arrested person must be told of the fact of arrest (i.e. that he or she is under arrest) and also of the reasons for the arrest (PACE, s 28), measures 'laid down by Parliament to protect the individual against the excess or abuse of the power of arrest'.[39] The modern origin of the latter rule (requiring reasons to be given for the arrest) may be found in *Christie* v *Leachinsky*,[40] where the Liverpool police had purported to exercise a power of arrest contained in a local Act when they knew that the conditions for the arrest were not met.

When the officers concerned in the latter case were later sued for wrongful arrest and false imprisonment, it was argued that the arrest was lawful because at the time they had information about Leachinsky which would have justified his arrest for another offence. The House of Lords held that the arrest was unlawful, since it was a condition of a lawful arrest that the person arrested should be entitled to know the reason for it. An actual charge need not be formulated at the time of arrest, but 'the arrested man is entitled to be told what is the act for which he is arrested'. Indeed, it has been said that 'giving the correct information of the reasons for an arrest was of the utmost constitutional significance'.[41]

This information must be given at the time of arrest or as soon as practicable thereafter.[42] Otherwise the arrest is unlawful (PACE, s 28(1), (3)), although there is nothing laid down in the Act specifying how the information should be communicated to an arrested person.[43] The issue was considered by the Court of Appeal in *Taylor* v *Thames Valley Chief Constable*[44] where it was said that the 'relevant principles remain those set out in *Christie*'s case'.

In *Taylor*, a ten-year-old boy was arrested and was told that he had been arrested for violent disorder on 18 April at Hillgrove Farm (while he was attending an anti-vivisection protest with his mother). The arrest took place some six weeks later while the boy was taking part in another demonstration. It was held that the arrested person must be told 'in simple, non-technical language that he could understand, the essential legal and factual grounds for his arrest'.[45] It was also held that each case must depend on its own facts but that it has 'never been the law that an arrested person must be given detailed particulars

---

[38] It is reported that Lord Hanningfield was awarded damages of £3,500: *BBC News*, 15 February 2013.

[39] *Hill* v *Chief Constable of South Yorkshire* [1990] 1 All ER 1046.

[40] [1947] AC 573, 593 (Lord Simonds). But note that the 1984 Act goes beyond the common law position: see *Hill* v *Chief Constable of South Yorkshire* (note 39 above). On the continuing importance of *Christie* v *Leachinsky*, see *O'Loughlin* v *Chief Constable of Essex* [1998] 1 WLR 374, *R* v *Chalkley* [1998] QB 848, and *Taylor* v *Thames Valley Chief Constable* [2004] EWCA Civ 858, [2004] 1 WLR 3155.

[41] *Edwards* v *DPP* (1993) 97 Cr App R 301.

[42] See *Dawes* v *DPP* [1995] 1 Cr App R 65.

[43] See *Nicholas* v *Parsonage* [1987] RTR 199.

[44] See note 40 above.

[45] Ibid, at para [24] (Clarke LJ), citing *Fox* v *UK* (1991) 13 EHRR 157.

of the case against him'.[46] In this case it was accepted that the information provided at the time of the arrest was sufficient, though it was also accepted that in some cases 'it will be necessary for the officer to give more facts than in others'.[47]

In relation to the requirements of s 28 of PACE, two interesting questions have arisen. First, what happens if the police are unable to inform the arrested person of the fact and reasons at the time of arrest and then fail to do so as soon as it becomes practicable? Does this subsequent failure mean that the earlier arrest is unlawful? In *DPP* v *Hawkins*,[48] the court's answer was no:

When a police officer makes an arrest which he is lawfully entitled to make but is unable at the time to state the ground because it is impracticable to do so, . . . it is his duty to maintain the arrest until it is practicable to inform the arrested person of that ground. If, when it does become practicable, he fails to do so, then the arrest is unlawful, but that does not mean that acts, which were previously done and were, when done, done in the execution of duty, become, retrospectively, acts which were not done in the execution of duty.[49]

The second question relates to the position where the police have no reason to delay informing an arrested person of the fact and reasons for the arrest. Does this initial failure, rendering the arrest therefore unlawful, vitiate all the subsequent proceedings? Again, it seems not.

In *Lewis* v *Chief Constable of South Wales*,[50] two women were arrested for burglary but were not told why they were being arrested. They were then taken to a police station where they were informed of the reasons for the arrest, within (respectively) 10 minutes and 23 minutes after the time of arrest. Some five hours later both were released.

The women subsequently sued for wrongful arrest and false imprisonment and the question which arose was whether they were entitled to be compensated for 10 and 23 minutes respectively or for the entire five-hour period. The Court of Appeal agreed with the first instance decision that, although the initial arrest had been unlawful because the women had not been given the reasons for it, it ceased being unlawful when reasons were given. The court did not consider this result to be inconsistent with s 28(3) of PACE.

While a police officer may use reasonable force to make the arrest,[51] the use of unreasonable force does not necessarily make the arrest unlawful.[52] Unlike the police stop and search powers,[53] there is no statutory duty on police officers (even if not in uniform) to identify

---

[46] Ibid, at para [35]. See also *Chapman* v *DPP* (1989) 89 Cr App R 190, and *Shields*, above.

[47] See *Murphy* v *Oxford* [1985] CA Transcript 56 (as cited in *Taylor*, above) where 'a person arrested for burglary was told that he was being arrested on suspicion of burglary in Newquay. As Lord Donaldson MR put it, 'no mention was made either of the fact that the premises in Newquay were a hotel or of the date on which the offence was committed' (ibid).

[48] [1988] 3 All ER 673.

[49] Ibid, at p 674.

[50] [1991] 1 All ER 206.

[51] Police and Criminal Evidence Act 1984, s 117.

[52] *Simpson* v *Chief Constable of South Yorkshire Police*, *The Times*, 7 March 1991. Cf *Hill* v *Chief Constable of South Yorkshire*, note 39 above.

[53] See above, pp 399–400.

themselves as such to an arrested person. This seems curious, and perhaps could be justified on the ground that the power of stop and search is a power vested only in police officers, unlike the power of arrest, which is a power that may be exercised by anyone. That, however, does not provide a complete answer, for as we have seen, the police power of arrest is much greater than the power of arrest vested in others; it is hardly controversial to suggest that the citizen being arrested is entitled to know that the person making the arrest has the authority to do so.[54]

C. Detention and questioning of suspects

Detention of suspects

An arrested person must be brought to a police station as soon as practicable after the arrest (s 30), although this may be delayed if his or her presence elsewhere is necessary for immediate investigation (s 30(10)). These provisions were amended by the Criminal Justice Act 2003, which introduced an exception to the duty under s 30(1) where the arrested person has been granted bail by a police officer at any time before arriving at a police station (so-called 'street bail' (s 30A)). They were further amended by the Policing and Crime Act 2017, which requires people arrested elsewhere than at a police station to be released if neither continued arrest nor bail is justified.[55]

At every police station that is designated for such detention,[56] there must be a custody officer who must be a police officer of the rank of sergeant or above (s 36).[57] It is the duty of the custody officer to (i) release (with or without bail), (ii) charge, or (iii) authorise the detention of suspects, where 'necessary to secure or preserve evidence relating to an offence for which [they are] under arrest or to obtain such evidence by questioning [them]' (s 37(2)). The custody officer must ensure that the detention is carried out in accordance with the 1984 Act and the Home Office Code of Practice for the Detention, Treatment and Questioning of Persons by Police Officers (Code C) (s 39). In addition, a review officer is required by the Act to conduct regular reviews of detention.[58]

PACE allows the police to detain people who have been arrested but not yet charged. This may be for up to 24 hours in the first instance (s 41), a period which may be extended to 36 hours by an officer of the rank of superintendent or above where the offence is an indictable offence (s 42), which includes murder, rape, kidnapping and much else besides. In the case of indictable offences, the period of 36 hours may be extended by a warrant of further detention for up to 36 hours, if a magistrates' court (defined as a court of *two or more* justices of the peace,[59] a potentially important safeguard) on application by the police is satisfied that further detention is justified to secure or preserve evidence by questioning the detainee (s 43).

The detainee must be notified of the application to the magistrates, and may be legally represented at the hearing, which will not be heard in open court. The proceedings may also

---

[54] Compare Criminal Justice (Scotland) Act 2016, s 2(3) – identification to be shown but only if arrest made by officer not in uniform and only if requested. Compare also, PACE, s 2, above (identification mandatory in case of stop and search by constable not in uniform).

[55] See Policing and Crime Act 2017, s 52, amending PACE, ss 30 and 30A.

[56] See 1984 Act, s 35.

[57] On the limitations of this crucial measure designed 'to ensure that the welfare and interests of detained subjects are properly protected', see *Vince v Chief Constable of Dorset* [1993] 2 All ER 321.

[58] Failure to conduct a review at the proper time could render detention unlawful: *Roberts v Chief Constable of Cheshire* [1999] 1 WLR 662. The review may be conducted by telephone: 1984 Act, s 40A; also s 45A (video links).

[59] PACE, s 45, a safeguard so far to have survived.

be conducted by live video link if the justices so direct, subject to a number of statutory safe-guards being met (s 45ZA). If the court does not authorise further detention, the detainee must be released (with or without bail) or charged. A suspect released without bail should be informed in writing that he or she will not be prosecuted, where there is insufficient evidence to charge (s 43(21)). If the warrant for further detention is issued, it may be renewed, though it cannot extend beyond 96 hours from the time of arrest (or the time of arrival at a police station if earlier) (s 44).[60]

Securing and preserving evidence

The search of arrested or detained persons is authorised by s 54 of PACE which requires the custody officer to ascertain everything which the person has in his or her possession, and empowers the custody officer to make a record of such items. This may require the removal of clothing.[61] Any item may be seized and retained except for clothing and personal effects, which may be seized only if the custody officer has reasonable grounds to believe the item is evidence relating to an offence; or believes that the arrested person may use the items in question to cause physical injury personally or to another, damage property, interfere with evidence, or assist him or her to escape.[62]

Under PACE, section 54A, an officer of the rank of inspector may authorise a person detained in a police station to be searched or examined (or both) to establish whether he or she has any mark that would tend to identify him or her as a person involved in the commission of an offence.[63] Section 55 authorises intimate searches, i.e. the physical examination of a person's body orifices.[64] But this may be done only if it has been authorised by an officer of the rank of inspector or above, and there are reasonable grounds for believing that the person may have concealed on him or her either a Class A drug or an article which could be used to cause physical injury to himself or herself or others. X rays and ultra-sound scans may also be authorized (s 55A).

Section 61 of PACE (as amended) allows fingerprints to be taken without consent with the authority of a police inspector in a wide range of circumstances,[65] while s 61A allows the police to take impressions of footwear.[66] By s 62, intimate samples may also be required in more limited circumstances, an intimate sample being defined to include various bodily flu-ids, including blood and swabs from intimate parts of the anatomy (s 65), but not now swabs taken from the mouth.[67] Unlike fingerprints, however, intimate samples may be taken only with the consent of the detainee. However, a refusal without good cause to give consent may lead a court to 'draw such inferences from the refusal as appear proper' (s 62(10)).

A non-intimate sample (e.g. hair, a sample from under a nail, or a swab taken from the mouth) may, in contrast, be taken without consent, if authorised by an officer of the rank of

---

[60] A separate regime for the detention and questioning of terrorist suspects is to be found in the Terrorism Act 2000. See ch 20 below.

[61] *Davies* v *Merseyside Chief Constable* [2015] EWCA Civ 114. For the position at common law, see *Lindley* v *Rutter* [1981] QB 128; *Brazil* v *Chief Constable of Surrey* [1983] 3 All ER 537.

[62] On which see *Davies*, ibid (14-year-old arrestee stripped because deemed a suicide risk). No breach of ECHR, art 8, despite concern expressed by Pitchford LJ about the growing use of strip searching of children.

[63] Introduced by the Anti-terrorism, Crime and Security Act 2001, s 90. The new section permits any such mark to be photographed without the consent of the detainee.

[64] See *R* v *Hughes* [1994] 1 WLR 876 (an intimate search requires physical intrusion, not visual examination).

[65] The circumstances in which prints may be taken and the nature of the prints that may be taken were extended by amendments introduced by the Criminal Justice and Police Act 2001, s 78. Fingerprints are defined to include palm-prints.

[66] Serious Organised Crime and Police Act 2005, s 118.

[67] Criminal Justice and Public Order Act 1994, s 58, amending PACE, s 65. See now Serious Organised Crime and Police Act 2005, s 119.

inspector or above, if – as in the case of intimate samples – the offence for which the arrested person is being detained is a 'recordable' offence (s 63). Power also exists for the police to take non-intimate samples from persons from whom no such samples were taken at the time of their arrest (even though they were not prosecuted, or were found not guilty) (s 63(3ZA)). Apart from those arrested and detained on suspicion, a non-intimate sample may also be taken without consent from a person who has been charged with or convicted of a recordable offence.[68]

In some cases, those in police detention may also be tested for drugs,[69] and arrested suspects (and others) may be photographed without their consent.[70]

Safeguards for suspects

The detention and questioning of suspects should be carried out in accordance with the safeguards laid down in PACE and in Code C referred to above. The Act itself provides two safeguards. The first is the right not to be held incommunicado. A person who has been arrested and is held in custody in a police station is entitled on request to have a friend or relative (or some other person who is known to him or her) informed of the arrest, as soon as reasonably practicable (s 56).[71] The other safeguard provided by the Act is that arrested persons held in custody in a police station are entitled on request to consult a solicitor privately at any time (s 58).[72] It is for the person detained and not the police to decide who would be an appropriate solicitor for the purposes of giving advice.[73]

In some cases, the exercise of these rights may be delayed for up to 36 hours, where the arrest is for an indictable offence and where the delay has been authorised by an officer at least of the rank of inspector (in the case of s 56) or superintendent (in the case of s 58). This applies particularly where there is a risk of danger to evidence or witnesses.[74] These provisions do not apply to terrorism cases, which are now separately regulated, as a result of which the foregoing rights may be delayed for up to 48 hours.[75] There is no right to damages where the police act in breach of the duty to permit access to legal representatives,[76] though any evidence obtained from an accused person denied such representation may be inadmissible.[77]

So far as the right not to be held incommunicado is concerned, Code C provides that detained persons may receive visits at the custody officer's discretion and may speak on the telephone for a reasonable time to one person, although the call (other than to a solicitor) may be listened to and anything said used in evidence in any subsequent criminal proceedings (Code C, Part 5). As far as the right to legal advice is concerned, a person must be permitted

---

[68] PACE, s 63(3A), (3B).

[69] 1984 Act, s 63B.

[70] PACE, s 64A.

[71] See *R* v *Kerawalla* [1991] Crim LR 451.

[72] See *R* v *Samuel* [1988] QB 615; *R* v *Alladice* (1988) 87 Cr App R 380. See *R* v *South Wales Chief Constable, ex p Merrick* [1994] 2 All ER 560: s 58 does not apply to give the accused the right of access to a solicitor where he is in custody in a magistrates' court following the denial of bail. But there is a common law right to this effect 'which preceded the Act of 1984 and which [was] not abrogated by that Act' (p 572). This apparent common law right does not extend to having the solicitor present during police interviews: *R* v *Chief Constable of the RUC, ex p Begley* [1997] 1 WLR 1475. On the role of the solicitor, see *R* v *Paris* (1993) 97 Cr App R 99.

[73] *R (Thompson)* v *Chief Constable of Northumbria* [2001] 1 WLR 1342.

[74] Neither of the rights in ss 56 or 58 apply to persons arrested or detained under the Terrorism Act 2000, s 41 or Sch 8. See ch 20 below.

[75] Terrorism Act 2000, Sch 8, para 9.

[76] *Cullen* v *Chief Constable of the RUC* [2003] UKHL 39, [2003] 1 WLR 1763. This may have to be re-visited in light of *Ibrahim* v *United Kingdom* [2016] ECHR 750 (damages recoverable for denial of access to a solicitor in breach of Convention rights).

[77] *R* v *Samuel*, above, and see section E below.

to have his or her solicitor present while being interviewed by the police. The solicitor may be required to leave the interview only if his or her conduct is such that the interviewing officer is unable properly to put questions to the suspect (Part 6). The code also deals with the conditions of detention (Part 8) and the giving of cautions to detained persons (Part 10).

Regarding cautions, a suspected person 'must be cautioned before any questions about [the suspected offence] . . . are put to [him or her]' (Code C, para 10.1). The effect of the Criminal Justice and Public Order Act 1994 is that the caution should be in the following terms: 'You do not have to say anything. But it may harm your defence if you do not mention when questioned something which you later rely on in court. Anything you do say may be given in evidence.' In conducting interviews, officers should neither try 'to obtain answers or elicit a statement by the use of oppression', nor 'indicate, except to answer a direct question, what action will be taken by the police if the person being questioned answers questions, makes a statement or refuses to do either' (Code C, Part 11.5).[78] Interviews should be audio-recorded.[79]

Right to silence[80]

An important principle in criminal procedure is the right of a suspected or accused person to remain silent, a principle of the common law acknowledged by the Strasbourg court also to be 'at the heart' of the right to a fair trial in ECHR, art 6.[81] The main control over abuse at the stage of questioning, however, is exercised by the criminal courts,[82] it having long been established that a confession or statement by an accused person is not admissible unless it is voluntary, in the sense that it has not been obtained by fear of prejudice or hope of advantage, exercised or held out by a person in authority, or by oppression.[83]

Although the requirement that statements should be obtained voluntarily was reinforced by the 1984 Act (by providing for the exclusion of police evidence obtained oppressively), the right to silence has, however, been subject to erosion ever since, principally by measures that challenge the position accepted from time immemorial that the burden is on the police to obtain evidence of guilt, not on the suspect to prove innocence. Indeed, an early example of that erosion is to be found in the 1984 Act itself, which permits negative inferences to be drawn from an accused's failure to provide an intimate sample.

The drawing of negative inferences was extended further by the Criminal Justice and Public Order Act 1994, which permits the court in criminal proceedings to draw such inferences as appear to it to be proper where the accused failed to mention 'any fact relied on in his defence in these proceedings' when questioned by the police or on being charged with an offence, where the fact was one which in the circumstances 'the accused could reasonably have been expected to mention' (s 34).[84] The Act also permits a court or jury 'to draw such inferences as appear proper' from the failure of the accused to give evidence at his or her trial or without good cause to answer any question.

....

[78] In any 24-hour period, a detained person normally should be allowed a continuous period of at least eight hours for rest, free from questioning, travel or other interruption arising out of the investigation (Code C, Part 12).

[79] 1984 Act, s 60. See Code E (Code of Practice on Audio Recording Interviews with Suspects). There is no statutory duty to video-tape interviews, but it is encouraged by Code F (Code of Practice on Visual Recording with Sound of Interviews with Suspects).

[80] On the different meanings of the right to silence, see *R v Director of Serious Fraud Office, ex p Smith* [1993] AC 1, per Lord Mustill.

[81] See *Condron v UK* (2000) 31 EHRR 1, at p 20. The right to silence is not, however, an 'absolute right'.

[82] See *Lodwick v Sanders* [1985] 1 All ER 577, at pp 580–1 (Watkins LJ).

[83] *Ibrahim v R* [1914] AC 599. See now PACE 1984, ss 76, 78.

[84] For background to the changes, see Royal Commission on Criminal Justice, Cm 2263, 1993, which argued in favour of the right to silence. The provisions have since been extended to post-charge questioning under the Counter-Terrorism Act 2008, s 22.

The court or jury may, moreover, draw such inferences as appear proper in such circumstances in determining whether the accused is guilty of the offence charged. The accused is not, however, required to give evidence on his or her own behalf and is not guilty of contempt of court for failing to do so (s 35).[85] Subsequent amendments have confined the operation of these measures to situations where the accused has enjoyed the benefit of legal representation before remaining silent.[86] Although the drawing of adverse inferences is not itself a breach of the ECHR,[87] 'particular caution was required before a domestic court could invoke an accused's silence against him'.[88]

There is no breach of ECHR, art 6 when under the Road Traffic Act 1988 the owner of a vehicle is required to reveal the identity of its driver to a police officer.[89]

D. Police powers of entry, search and seizure

Police powers of entry

'By the law of England', said Lord Camden in *Entick* v *Carrington*,[90] 'every invasion of private property, be it ever so minute, is a trespass. No man can set foot upon my ground without my licence, but he is liable to an action though the damage be nothing.'[91]

There are, however, several circumstances in which the police may lawfully enter private property. One, as Lord Camden suggests, is with the consent of the owner or occupier.[92] Indeed, in *Robson* v *Hallett*[93] it was held that a police officer, like other members of the public coming to a house on lawful business, has an implied licence from the householder to walk to the front door and to ask whether he or she can come inside; and that the officer must be allowed a reasonable time to leave the premises before he or she becomes a trespasser.

Otherwise, the police may have statutory authority to enter private property even without the consent of the owner. Under the Police and Criminal Evidence Act 1984, a police officer may enter private premises to execute a search warrant (s 8). A police officer may also enter private premises without consent to execute an arrest warrant; arrest a person for an indictable offence;[94] arrest a person for certain public order, road traffic, animal welfare or property offences; recapture a person who is unlawfully at large (including specifically the breach of bail conditions);[95] save life and limb; or prevent serious damage to property (s 17).[96]

These s 17 powers are generally exercisable only if the officer has reasonable grounds for believing that the person sought is on the premises. There is a power to search the premises entered under the authority of s 17, but only a search that is reasonably required for the purpose for which the power to enter was exercised. So if the officer enters premises under

---

[85] See *R* v *Cowan* [1996] QB 373.

[86] Youth Justice and Criminal Evidence Act 1999, s 58; enacted in the light of *Murray* v *UK* (1996) 22 EHRR 29.

[87] *Condron* v *UK* (2001) 31 EHRR 1; *Averill* v *UK* (2001) 31 EHRR 839; *Beckles* v *UK* (2003) 36 EHRR 162; and *Murray* v *UK*, above. Also *R* v *Argent* [1997] 2 Cr App R 27.

[88] *Beckles* v *UK*, above.

[89] *Brown* v *Stott* [2001] 1 AC 681.

[90] (1765) 19 St Tr 1030, 1066; ch 16.

[91] See also *Davis* v *Lisle* [1936] 2 KB 434.

[92] See Code B (Code of Practice for Searches of Premises by Police Officers), Part 5.

[93] 1967] 2 QB 939.

[94] *Chapman* v *DPP* [1988] Crim LR 843.

[95] Amendments to s 17 mean that the power is not limited to situations where the police officer is *in pursuit* of someone unlawfully at large, as previously held in *D'Souza* v *DPP* [1992] 4 All ER 545.

[96] The power of entry to save life and limb or to prevent serious damage to property may also be exercised by designated community support officers: Police Reform Act 2002, Sch 4, para 8.

s 17 to arrest a person, he or she may search the premises to find that person, but may not under s 17 search for evidence relating to the offence. Other provisions of PACE confer this latter power.[97] Before exercising these powers of entry, the police should normally inform the occupant of the reasons for the entry.[98]

Apart from entry with consent or under statutory authority, a surviving power of entry may arise from common law. Although PACE, s 17(5), abolishes all common law rules authorising the entry of private premises by the police, it is expressly provided that this does not affect any power of entry to deal with or prevent a breach of the peace. The existence of such a power appears to have been recognised in *Thomas* v *Sawkins*,[99] although the ratio of that case is controversial.[100] The existence of the common law power has been accepted by the ECtHR as not violating Convention rights, though care needs to be taken before it is used.

In *McLeod* v *United Kingdom*,[101] the complainant argued that by forcibly entering her house, ostensibly to prevent a breach of peace, the police had violated her right to respect for her home and private life in art 8 of the ECHR. The police had entered to help the complainant's former husband to recover property while the complainant was absent.

The domestic courts held the entry to be lawful,[102] but the European Court of Human Rights upheld the complaint. The government argued that the entry could be justified under art 8(2). Although the Court accepted that the common law power was a power 'prescribed by law' for the purposes of art 8(2), it was held in this case that the exercise of the power could not be justified.

Search with a warrant

The effect of decisions such as *Entick* v *Carrington* was that, except for the power to search for stolen goods, for which a warrant could be obtained at common law from a magistrate,[103] statutory powers were needed if the police were lawfully to search private premises. These powers are to be found principally in PACE, s 8, authorising a search warrant to be granted by a justice of the peace on an application by a police constable (or designated investigating officer),[104] where there are reasonable grounds for believing that an indictable offence has been committed, and that there is material on the premises that is likely to be of substantial value in the police investigation.[105]

[97] 1984 Act, s 32(2)(b). For an example of other powers of entry without a warrant, see *Whitelaw* v *Haining* 1992 SLT 956.

[98] *O'Loughlin* v *Chief Constable of Essex* [1998] 1 WLR 374. It is only exceptionally that the power of entry must be exercised only by a constable in uniform.

[99] [1935] 2 KB 249; and see ch 18.

[100] See A L Goodhart (1936) 6 CLJ 22, and Ewing and Gearty, *The Struggle for Civil Liberties*, ch 6. The power is not confined to meetings. See *McLeod* v *Metropolitan Police Commissioner* [1994] 4 All ER 553.

[101] (1998) 27 EHRR 493.

[102] *McLeod* v *Metropolitan Police Commissioner*, note 100 above.

[103] See now Theft Act 1968, s 26.

[104] On the constitutional importance of the magistrate as a judicial officer in these circumstances standing between the citizen and the State, see *Attorney General of Jamaica* v *Williams* [1988] AC 351 referring to 'the independent scrutiny of the judiciary to protect the citizen against the excesses which would inevitably flow from allowing an executive officer to decide for himself whether the conditions under which he is permitted to enter on private property have been met' (Lord Hoffmann, p 358). Applied in *Haralambous* v *St Albans Crown Court* [2016] EWHC 916 (Admin), para 31.

[105] See also the conditions set out in PACE 1984, s 8(3), considered in *Redknapp* v *City of London Police Commissioner* [2008] EWHC 1177, [2009] 1 WLR 1177, and *Sweeney* v *Westminster Magistrates Court* [2014] EWHC 2068 (Admin).

A search warrant may now take one of two forms. A 'specific premises' warrant is one which specifies the premises to be searched, while an 'all premises' warrant applies to any premises occupied or controlled by the person named in the warrant.[106] The latter thus allows premises to be searched despite not being specified in the warrant, though these may be issued only where it is not reasonably practicable to specify all the premises of the person named in the warrant that may need to be searched. A warrant may now authorise multiple entries to the premises which it specifies,[107] though where a warrant authorises only one entry, the police may remain on the premises until their task is complete.[108]

This power of justices of the peace to grant a warrant does not apply to material which consists of or includes items subject to legal privilege, 'excluded material' or 'special procedure material' (s 9). Items subject to legal privilege include communications between a lawyer and his or her client (s 10),[109] while excluded material is defined to cover confidential personal records, human tissue or tissue fluid taken for purposes of medical treatment and held in confidence, and journalistic material which is held in confidence (s 11).[110] Special procedure material refers to other forms of journalistic material,[111] and also other material that is held in confidence or subject to an obligation of secrecy, and has been acquired in the course of any business, profession or other occupation (s 14).

No warrant can be issued in relation to material subject to legal privilege, but orders may be issued by a judge under Sch 1, para 4,[112] requiring excluded material or special procedure material to be delivered to a police constable or a designated investigating officer within seven days.[113] (Previously, an order under Sch 1, para 4 could be made only after an *inter partes* hearing, a condition that now applies exclusively in relation to journalistic material.)[114] If the order is not complied with, a judge may issue a warrant authorising a police officer or a designated investigating officer to enter and search premises and seize the material in question (Sch 1, para 12). A judge may issue both specific premises and all premises warrants for these purposes.

> In some circumstances, a warrant may be secured under Sch 1, para 12 without first seeking an order under para 4. This practice was, however, strongly deprecated in *R v Maidstone Crown Court, ex p Waitt*,[115] though at a time when the Sch 1, para 4 procedure was *inter partes* in all case.

---

[106] 1984 Act, s 8(1A).

[107] 1984 Act, s 8(1C).

[108] *Sher* v *Greater Manchester Police Constable* [2010] EWHC 1859 (Admin), [2011] 2 All ER 364.

[109] Cf *R* v *Central Criminal Court, ex p Francis and Francis* [1989] AC 346. See *R* v *R* [1994] 4 All ER 260, *R* v *Manchester Crown Court, ex p Rogers* [1999] 4 All ER 35, and *Fitzpatrick* v *Metropolitan Police Commissioner*, notable for appearing to set a high standard to be met before this exclusion can be met. Note also *R (Energy Financing Team Ltd)* v *Bow Street Magistrates Court* [2006] 1 WLR 1316 (duty of police to give full assistance to the court to ensure that material was not subject to legal privilege).

[110] Hospital records of patient admission and discharge are excluded material: see *R* v *Cardiff Crown Court, ex p Kellam*, *The Times*, 3 May 1993.

[111] On journalistic material, see 1984 Act s 13. Also *R* v *Bristol Crown Court, ex p Bristol Press Agency Ltd* (1987) 85 Cr App R 190; *R* v *Middlesex Crown Court, ex p Salinger* [1993] QB 564; *R* v *Manchester Stipendiary Magistrate, ex p Granada Television Ltd* [2001] 1 AC 300; and *R* v *Central Criminal Court, ex p Bright* [2001] 2 All ER 244.

[112] A judge for this purpose means a circuit judge, or a District Judge (Magistrates' Court): PACE 1984, Sch 1, para 17. As originally enacted, these powers were exercised only by circuit judges.

[113] The material may be surrendered voluntarily by the person who holds it without the consent of the person to whom it relates: *R* v *Singleton* (1995) 1 Cr App R 431.

[114] The law was changed – bizarrely – in the Deregulation Act 2015, s 82(3)(a).

[115] [1988] Crim LR 384.

It was said in *Waitt*: 'The special procedure under section 9 and schedule 1 is a serious inroad upon the liberty of the subject. The responsibility for ensuring that the procedure is not abused lies with circuit judges . . . The responsibility is greatest when the . . . judge is asked to issue a search warrant under paragraph 12. It is essential that the reason for authorising the seizure is made clear. The preferred method of obtaining material for a police investigation should always be by way of an *inter partes* order under paragraph 4, after notice of application has been served under paragraph 8. An *ex parte* application under paragraph 12 must never become a matter of common form and satisfaction as to the fulfilment of the conditions is an important matter of substance' (Lloyd LJ).

These cogent remarks make two points. The first is the question of principle about the special procedure, concerns adopted by other courts which have emphasised the need for 'great care and caution' by judges in the exercise of these powers.[116] The second is the practical question that para 12 should not be relied on in preference to para 4. In view of the amendments to Sch 1 whereby the former procedure is no longer to be treated as an *inter partes* one, this is a point that may be less cogent now than it was when made, given that the safeguards on which it was predicated have to some extent been removed. These changes make it all the more important that judges act with 'great care and caution' in dealing with Sch 1 applications.

Apart from thus extending the grounds for granting search warrants, the 1984 Act also introduced safeguards against misuse in the execution of a warrant.[117] These are found in ss 15 and 16, and they apply not only to search warrants issued under PACE, but also to warrants issued to a constable or a designated investigating officer 'under any enactment, including an enactment contained in an Act passed after this Act'.[118] An application, which is made ex parte, must be in writing and must explain the grounds for the application and the premises to be searched. The constable or designated investigating officer must answer on oath any question put by the justice of the peace or the judge. The warrant must specify the premises to be searched in a specific premises warrant, or in the case of an all premises warrant the identity of the person whose premises are to be searched.[119]

A search warrant must be executed within three months from the date of its issue. The application for and execution of a warrant may be timed, however, to enable the police to kill two birds with one stone. So in *R (Pearce)* v *Metropolitan Police Commissioner*,[120] the police obtained a warrant to search for stolen bicycles at an address in London. The effect of executing the warrant would be to disrupt a group of protesters who in turn had planned on the following day to frustrate royal wedding celebrations. In a case that has a whiff of the discredited *Elias* v *Pasmore* about it,[121] the execution of the warrant on the day before the royal wedding was held to be lawful because the dominant purpose of the searches was the one authorised by the warrants.

---

[116] *R* v *Crown Court at Lewes* (1991) 93 Cr App R 60 (Bingham LJ); *R (Faisaltex Ltd)* v *Crown Court at Preston* [2008] EWHC 2832 (Admin), [2009] 1 WLR 168.

[117] Further safeguards are in Code of Practice B above.

[118] Police and Criminal Evidence Act 1984, s 15(1). But note the Serious Crime Act 2015, s 52 (additional powers to issue and execute search warrants in relation to 'drug-cutting' equipment, with detailed procedures about applications and execution (Sch 2). Do these provisions complement or displace s 8 in this context?)

[119] PACE, s 15(6). On the importance of this provision, see *R(B)* v *Huddersfield Magistrates Court* [2014] EWHC 1089 (Admin), [2015] 1 WLR 4737.

[120] [2013] EWCA Civ 866.

[121] [1934] 2 KB 164. See E C S Wade (1934) 50 LQR 354, and Ewing and Gearty, *The Struggle for Civil Liberties*, ch 5.

Entry and search must be at a reasonable hour (though warrants will often be executed very early in the morning), and the police may be accompanied by non-police officers who may be required to provide technical assistance.[122] Where the occupier of the premises is present, the police officers or designated investigating officers must identify themselves, produce the warrant and supply a copy to the occupier.[123] When conducting a search, the police may detain individuals in one room while searching another room, and may use reasonable force to do so, if necessary.[124] If there is no person present, a copy of the warrant should be left in a prominent place on the premises. A search under the warrant does not authorise a general search of the premises, but only a search to the extent required for the purpose for which the warrant was issued (s 16). The police may (and do) use force to gain entry.

In *R v Longman*,[125] police officers with a search warrant effected entry to a house by deception, as a result of difficulties they had encountered in the past. A woman police officer in plain clothes pretended to deliver flowers. When the door was opened to her, other officers in plain clothes immediately entered the house, with one shouting 'Police, got a warrant' which he held in his hand.

The Court of Appeal held that this procedure complied with ss 15 and 16 of PACE. The court rejected the contention that '*before entering* the premises a police officer must not only identify himself but must produce his warrant card and . . . also the search warrant and serve a copy of the search warrant on the householder'. It is enough that these things are done *after entry* to the premises.

To hold otherwise, said Lord Lane CJ, would mean that the whole object of the more important type of search would be stultified.

There is no appeal against the issuing of a search warrant,[126] though an application for judicial review may be made to set aside a warrant irregularly obtained for any one of a number of reasons.[127] By these means the courts have created a common law right to see the information on which the application for a warrant was based, except where the information may be withheld on public interest grounds.[128]

---

[122] Criminal Justice Act 2003, s 2, amending PACE, s 16. See *Lord Advocate's Reference (No 1 of 2002)* 2002 SLT 1017 for the position in Scotland.

[123] See *R v Chief Constable of Lancashire, ex p Parker* [1993] QB 577 (the warrant and any schedule must be shown; an uncertified photocopy is impermissible). See also *Redknapp v City of London Police Commissioner*, above (copy of warrant must be left).

[124] *DPP v Meaden* [2003] EWHC 3005 (Admin), [2004] 4 All ER 75.

[125] [1988] 1 WLR 619. See also *Linehan v DPP* [2000] Crim LR 861.

[126] *R (Chaudhary) v Bristol Crown Court* [2014] EWHC 4096 (Admin).

[127] See *Haralambous v St Albans Crown Court* [2016] EWHC 916 (Admin), though in that case the application was unsuccessful. But see also *Redknapp v City of London Police Commissioner*, above; *R(B) v Huddersfield Magistrates Court*, above; and *Sweeney v Westminster Magistrates Court*, above. For warrants issued under other statutory powers, see also *R (Mills) v Sussex Police* [2014] EWHC 2523 (Admin); and *Hargreaves v Brecknock and Radmorshire Magistrates Court* [2015] EWHC 1803 (Admin). These cases have generally emphasized as a matter of principle the importance of the warrant as an instrument of last resort (esp *Mills*, per Elias LJ), and the procedural requirement as a result that 'all the material necessary to justify the grant of a warrant should be contained in the information provided on the form' (*Hargreaves*, para 34 (Thirlwall J)).

[128] *Haralambous v St Albans Crown Court*, ibid, para 34 for a discussion of the cases.

Search without a warrant

Police powers to search without a warrant arise in three circumstances. The first is the power to search a person following arrest. Section 32 allows a constable (but no one else) to search an arrested person, at a place other than a police station, 'if the constable has reasonable grounds for believing that the arrested person may present a danger to himself or others'. A constable (but no one else) may search an arrested person for anything which might be used to escape from lawful custody, or for anything which might be evidence relating to an offence (s 32(2)), although in both these cases the power to search is a power to search only to the extent that is reasonably required for the purpose of discovering 'any such thing or any such evidence' (s 32(3)).

The police power of search under PACE, s 32, does not authorise the police officer conducting the search to require a person to remove any item of clothing in public, except an outer coat, jacket or gloves (s 32(4)), but it does authorise the search of a person's mouth.[129] A police officer conducting a search under PACE, s 32, may seize any item which may cause physical injury, might assist in an escape from lawful custody, or is evidence relating to any offence (s 32(8)). The only items which may not be seized while conducting such a search are those subject to legal privilege (s 32(9)), although no such exception applies to excluded material or to special procedure material as described above.

The second power of search without a warrant is a power to search premises ancillary to arrest. At common law, the power to search premises incidental to arrest was a power to search at the time of the arrest. So in *McLorie* v *Oxford*[130] it was held that after having arrested a suspect and detaining him in custody, the police had no right to return to the house to search for the instruments of crime, even of serious crime; that is to say, no right to do so unless they could get a search warrant, although that would not have been available in all circumstances where it might have been necessary. In any event, it may not have been appropriate if the delay in obtaining the warrant meant that any evidence on the premises could be removed or destroyed in the meantime.

The position is now governed by PACE, s 32, so that after making an arrest for an indictable offence, a constable (but no one else) may enter any premises in which the person was when arrested or immediately before he or she was arrested. The constable may search the premises for evidence relating to the offence for which the person was arrested (s 32(2)(b)). This would allow the police to search the premises at the time of arrest where the arrest took place within or outside the premises. It is unclear whether, having made the arrest, this authorises the police to return to the scene to look for evidence.[131] Section 32 is open to the interpretation that the power of search may be, but need not be, contemporaneous with the arrest.[132]

The third power of search without a warrant is a power to search the home of the arrested person, even though he or she was not arrested there and even though he or she was not there immediately before arrest. At common law, the courts seemed reluctant to recognise any such power, though there were suggestions that such a search might be permitted where the house search was concerned with securing evidence relating to the offence for which the person had been arrested.[133] PACE, s 18, permits a constable or a designated community support

---

[129] Criminal Justice and Public Order Act 1994, s 59.

[130] [1982] QB 1290.

[131] As recently pointed out, however, the legality of a search under s 32(2)(b) will be undermined if the initial arrest is unlawful: *Lord Hanningfield* v *Chief Constable of Essex Police*, above, para 6 (Eady J).

[132] The power can be used only if the police officer has reasonable grounds for believing that there is evidence on the premises for which a search is permitted, and this must be the genuine reason for the entry: *R* v *Beckford* (1992) 94 Cr App R 43.

[133] *Jeffrey* v *Black* [1978] QB 490.

officer to enter and search any premises occupied or controlled by any person who is under arrest for an indictable offence, provided the statutory criteria for such a search are met.[134]

Thus, there must be reasonable grounds to suspect that there is on the premises evidence (other than items subject to legal privilege) relating to the indictable offence for which the suspect has been arrested or to a related indictable offence. However, the power can be used only in relation to premises actually owned or controlled by the arrested person, and not premises the police reasonably believe to be so owned or controlled.[135] The exercise of the power should normally be authorised in writing by an inspector or an officer of a higher rank, although the power can be used without first taking a suspect to the police station and securing authorisation, if this is necessary for the effective investigation of the offence.

Police powers of seizure

The powers of search discussed above are generally also associated with a power of seizure. However, the nature of that power varies from case to case. In the case of entry to search for an escaped person or to make an arrest (s 17), there is no power to seize and retain property. In the case of search with a search warrant (s 8), there is a power only to seize and retain 'anything for which a search has been authorised'.[136] The same is true of the power to enter and search an arrested person's premises after arrest (s 18).

In the case of a search of premises where the arrested person was at or immediately before the arrest (s 32), there is no power of seizure in the section itself, although in the case of a personal search there is a right to retain anything reasonably believed to be evidence of any offence, including an offence unrelated to the grounds for the arrest. What is the position if the police are on property for any of these purposes or if they are present with the consent of the owner or occupier and they stumble across something which may suggest that an offence has been committed? In what circumstances, if any, can the police seize that evidence? Clearly, they can do so if they are present with a search warrant and the material relates to the offence for which the warrant was granted. But what if it relates to some wholly unconnected offence? Similarly, what is the position if the police enter under s 17 to make an arrest and stumble across incriminating evidence?

The power of seizure is governed at common law by the Court of Appeal decision in *Ghani v Jones*,[137] where it was held that before seizing private property in the course of an investigation, the police must have reasonable grounds for believing (*a*) that a serious crime has been committed; (*b*) that the article is the instrument by which the crime was committed or is material evidence to prove commission of the crime; and (*c*) that the person in possession of the article is implicated in the crime. Where this power is exercised, (*d*) the police must not keep the article longer than is reasonably necessary; and (*e*) the lawfulness of the conduct of the police must be judged at the time and not (as in the earlier notorious decision of Horridge J in *Elias v Pasmore*) by what happens afterwards.[138] It was held in the latter case that the 'interests of the State' justified the police in seizing material that was relevant to the prosecution for any crime of any person, not only of the person who was arrested.

---

[134] On the uncertainty of whether someone occupies premises for these purposes, see *R(B) v Huddersfield Magistrates Court*, above.

[135] *Khan v Metropolitan Police Commissioner* [2008] EWCA Civ 723; if there is any doubt, the police can apply for a warrant.

[136] See *R v Chief Constable of Warwickshire, ex p Fitzpatrick* [1998] 1 All ER 65, and *R v Chesterfield JJ, ex p Bramley* [2000] 1 All ER 411.

[137] [1970] 1 QB 693.

[138] Cf *Frank Truman (Export) Ltd v Metropolitan Police Commissioner* [1977] QB 952; *Wershof v Metropolitan Police Commissioner* [1978] 3 All ER 540.

Additional powers of seizure and retention are in PACE, ss 19–22, and now the Criminal Justice and Police Act 2001, ss 50–70. These powers supplement but do not replace the common law powers (s 19(5)).[139] So to the extent that the statute is less extensive, the police may continue to rely on their common law powers as recognised by *Ghani* v *Jones*[140] and in subsequent cases.[141] The powers conferred by s 19 apply where a constable or a designated investigating officer is lawfully on any premises to make an arrest (in the case of a constable), or to conduct a search with or without a warrant.

In such circumstances material may be seized where the constable or the designated investigating officer has reasonable grounds to believe *either* that it has been obtained as a result of the commission of any offence (s 19(2)); *or* that it is evidence in relation to an offence which he or she is investigating, or any other offence (s 19(3)). In either case, seizure is permitted only where this is necessary to prevent the items from being concealed, lost, damaged, altered or destroyed. The only restriction on what may be seized relates to items reasonably believed to be subject to legal privilege (s 19(6)).

By PACE, s 21, a constable or a designated investigating officer who seizes anything is required, if requested, to provide a record of what is seized to the occupier of the premises or the person who had custody of it immediately before the seizure. In addition, the person who had custody or control of the item seized has a right of access to it under the supervision of the police, although this may be refused if the officer in charge of the investigation reasonably believes that access would prejudice the investigation.[142] One purpose of changes introduced in 2001 is to enable the police to seize material so that it can be examined elsewhere.[143]

E. Remedies for abuse of police powers

Self-defence and self-help

At the time of interference with person or property, the citizen may have some right of self-defence, and this can affect both civil and criminal liability. The point is acknowledged in the leading case, *Christie* v *Leachinsky*,[144] the ratio of which (as we have seen) forms the basis of what is now s 28(1) of PACE. There Lord Simonds said that 'it is the corollary of the right of every citizen to be thus free from arrest that he should be entitled to resist arrest unless that arrest is lawful'.[145] This tends to reinforce the view expressed above that police officers should be required to identify themselves as such when making an arrest.

In *Abbassy* v *Metropolitan Police Commissioner*,[146] Woolf LJ acknowledged that one of the reasons for the rule that a person is to be told the reason for his arrest is so that, if what he or she is told is not a reason which justifies his or her arrest, he or she can exercise '[his or her] right to resist arrest'.[147] On the other hand, under the Police Act 1996, s 89, it is an offence to

---

[139] On the continuing application of the common law, see *R (Rottman)* v *Metropolitan Police Commissioner* [2002] UKHL 20, [2002] 2 AC 692.

[140] [1970] 1 QB 693.

[141] See *Garfinkel* v *Metropolitan Police Commissioner* [1972] Crim LR 44.

[142] These provisions 'vest in the police no title to the property seized but only a temporary right to retain property for the specified statutory purposes': *Costello* v *Chief Constable of Derbyshire* [2001] 1 WLR 1437, at p 1441 (Lightman J).

[143] Criminal Justice and Police Act 2001, ss 50–70. For the position before the Act, see *R* v *Chesterfield JJ, ex p Bramley* [2000] QB 576. For the scope of the power, see *R (El-Kurd)* v *Winchester Crown Court* [2011] EWHC 855 (Admin).

[144] [1947] AC 573.

[145] Ibid, at p 591.

[146] [1990] 1 All ER 193.

[147] And see *Edwards* v *DPP* (1993) 97 Cr App R 301.

assault, resist or wilfully obstruct a constable in the execution of his or her duty. There are therefore hazards in the way of a citizen who uses force to resist what he or she believes to be an unlawful arrest by the police, whether of himself or herself or of a close relative.[148]

It has thus been pointed out that 'the law does not encourage the subject to resist the authority of one whom he knows to be an officer of the law'.[149] Although in *Kenlin* v *Gardiner* two boys were entitled to use reasonable force to escape from two constables who were seeking to question them,[150] in general it is inexpedient by self-defence to resist arrest by a police officer: if the arrest is lawful, the assault on the constable is aggravated because he or she is in execution of duty. Where however a defendant 'applies force to a police or court officer which would be reasonable if that person were not a police or court officer, and the defendant believes that he is not, then even if his belief is unreasonable he has a good plea of self-defence'.[151]

In *R* v *Iqbal*,[152] the accused was wanted by the police in relation to alleged drugs offences. He was seen by a constable attending the trial of a friend and was detained and handcuffed, being told these steps were being taken with a view to his subsequent arrest. Before he could be arrested, Iqbal broke free and escaped, and was later convicted for escaping from lawful custody.

The conviction was overturned on appeal on the ground that Iqbal had not been lawfully arrested and could not therefore escape from 'lawful' custody. According to the Lord Chief Justice: 'The common law offence of escape from custody does not cover those who escape from police restraint or control before they have been arrested. We cannot widen the ambit of this criminal offence by making it apply to those whose arrest has been deliberately postponed'.

Legal proceedings against the police

A person who claims to be the victim of unlawful police conduct may be able to bring an action for damages against the chief constable, who is vicariously liable for the unlawful acts committed by his or her officers.[153] An action may be for assault, wrongful arrest, false imprisonment or trespass to property or goods,[154] or may take the form of an action for the return of property which has been improperly seized.[155] Similarly, it is possible to bring an action for malicious procurement of a search warrant, though it is necessary to show malice in order to succeed,[156] and more usual now to seek to have the warrant quashed in judicial review proceedings.[157]

....
[148] *R* v *Fennell* [1971] QB 428.
[149] *Christie* v *Leachinsky* [1947] AC 573, 599 (Lord du Parcq).
[150] [1967] 2 QB 510. And see *Lindley* v *Rutter* [1981] QB 128; *Pedro* v *Diss* [1981] 2 All ER 59; and *Dawes* v *DPP* (1995) 1 Cr App R 65.
[151] *Blackburn* v *Bowering* [1994] 3 All ER 380, at p 384.
[152] [2011] EWCA Crim 273, [2011] 1 WLR 1541.
[153] Police Act 1996, s 88. See Clayton and Tomlinson, *Civil Actions against the Police*. On the liability of police civilian staff and the staff of private companies with police powers, see Police Reform Act 2002, s 42(7)–(10) (police authority a joint tortfeasor in the former case, the employer a joint tortfeasor in the latter case).
[154] See *O'Loughlin* v *Chief Constable of Essex* (note 98 above); *Abraham* v *Metropolitan Police Commissioner* [2001] 1 WLR 1257; and *Wood* v *DPP* [2008] EWHC 1056 (Admin).
[155] *Webb* v *Chief Constable of Merseyside Police* [2000] QB 427; *Costello* v *Chief Constable of Derbyshire* [2001] 1 WLR 1437. See now Criminal Justice and Police Act 2001, s 57.
[156] *Keegan* v *Merseyside Chief Constable* [2003] EWCA Civ 936, [2003] 1 WLR 2187; *Gibbs* v *Rea* [1998] AC 786 PC. According to *Fitzpatrick* v *Metropolitan Police Commissioner*, above, malice is one of four ingredients of the tort, following the latter two cases.
[157] See pp 412–3 above. If successful, this could potentially unlock other claims in tort.

An action for malicious prosecution may be maintained by any person who is prosecuted for a criminal offence maliciously and without reasonable and probable cause; but it is difficult to win such an action against the police.[158] In principle, public officials are personally liable for their own wrongful acts. But special protection is given to some officials against certain liabilities,[159] while there are also severe limits on the ability of convicted persons to bring civil proceedings for trespass to the person, in which it must be shown – inter alia – that the conduct of the police was grossly disproportionate.[160]

In addition to the foregoing, the police have a duty of care to those in their custody, breach of which may give rise to liability.[161] It may also be possible to seek judicial review against the police,[162] though perhaps not where there is a remedy in tort available.[163] Recent developments have opened up new areas of liability, as revealed in one important case where a boy badly treated by the police recovered not only for wrongful imprisonment, but also a failure by the police to make a reasonable adjustment to their procedures in their treatment of him under the Disability Discrimination Act 1995, and a breach of Convention rights (the police violating ECHR, arts 3 and 8).[164]

Civil liability may arise even where an arrest is lawful, as the subsequent detention as well as the initial arrest must be in accordance with law.[165] *Treadaway* v *Chief Constable of West Midlands*[166] is an extreme case, where damages of £50,000 (including £7,500 aggravated and £40,000 exemplary damages) were awarded to a claimant who had signed a confession, but 'only after he had been handcuffed behind his back and a succession of plastic bags had been placed over his head with the ends bunched up behind his neck causing him to struggle and pass out'.[167] Although now somewhat dated, *Treadaway* is nevertheless a reminder of the perils of police detention.

Nevertheless, in 1997 concern about the size of damages awards in civil actions against the police led to the Court of Appeal issuing guidelines on the level of exemplary damages in which an 'absolute maximum' of £50,000 should be awarded for particularly bad conduct by officers of at least the rank of superintendent.[168] This followed two cases in which awards of £302,000 and £220,000 respectively had been awarded to victims of police brutality.[169] Many of the actions initiated against the police are settled before they reach

[158] See *Glinski* v *McIver* [1962] AC 726; *Wershof* v *Metropolitan Police Commissioner* [1978] 3 All ER 540. Cf *Hunter* v *Chief Constable of West Midlands Police* [1982] AC 529. For a discussion of the purpose and scope of the law, see *Willers* v *Joyce* [2016] UKSC 43.

[159] See e.g. Constables' Protection Act 1750, s 6, relied on in *Williams* v *Dyfed and Powys Chief Constable* [2010] EWCA Civ 1627. The defence is not unlimited: see discussion in *Bell* v *Manchester Chief Constable* [2005] EWCA 902, and *Fitzpatrick* v *Metropolitan Police Commissioner*, above.

[160] Criminal Justice Act 2003, s 329; *Adorian* v *Metropolitan Police Commissioner* [2009] EWCA Civ 18, [2009] 1 WLR 1859.

[161] See *Kirkham* v *Chief Constable of Greater Manchester* [1990] 2 QB 283. See also *Reeves* v *Metropolitan Police Commissioner* [2001] AC 360 – House of Lords reduced damages by half on account of contributory negligence.

[162] See *R (Thompson)* v *Chief Constable of Northumbria* [2001] EWCA Civ 211, [2001] 1 WLR 1342.

[163] *Sher* v *Greater Manchester Chief Constable* [2010] EWHC 1859 (Admin), [2011] 2 All ER 364. Conversely, in some cases judicial review may be the only avenue (though to what effect?), with the House of Lords having held that there may be no liability in damages against the police who deny suspects certain statutory rights (*Cullen* v *Chief Constable of RUC* [2003] UKHL 39, [2003] 1 WLR 176).

[164] *ZH* v *Metropolitan Police Commissioner* [2013] EWCA 69, [2013] 1 WLR 3021.

[165] *Re Gillen's Application* [1988] NILR 40.

[166] *The Times*, 25 October 1994.

[167] See *Kuddus* v *Chief Constable of Leicestershire* [2001] UKHL 29, [2002] 2 AC 122 on exemplary damages, and now *Rowlands* v *Merseyside Chief Constable* [2006] EWCA Civ 1773, [2007] WLR 1065.

[168] *Thompson* v *Metropolitan Police Commissioner* [1998] QB 498.

[169] *The Guardian*, 20 February 1997.

the court, and in these cases the settlements are rarely published though the police may be required to make a public apology.[170]

Quite apart from civil proceedings, police forces or individual police officers may face criminal liability for unlawful conduct.[171] But this is unusual, and criminal wrongdoing is difficult to establish, as revealed in the case of a police constable who was acquitted on charges of manslaughter following an incident involving news-vendor Mr Ian Tomlinson at the G20 demonstration in 2009.[172] The police constable was, however, subsequently dismissed for gross misconduct by the Metropolitan Police,[173] which also issued a public apology to the family of Mr Tomlinson, who died shortly after the incident with the police constable in question.[174]

Complaints against the police

In addition to the foregoing, another form of redress is to complain to the police themselves. To command public confidence and to be effective, however, any such procedure needs to be independent and resilient (in the sense of being able to withstand pressure from the police). It is also necessary that those operating the procedure have the powers sufficient to address any abuses uncovered, whether in the form of providing redress to victims on the one hand or removing inadequate or corrupt police officers on the other. The Policing and Crime Act 2017 is the latest attempt to address these concerns in a significant shake-up of procedures introduced in 2002.

A Police Complaints Authority was first introduced in 1984, replaced in 2002 by the Independent Police Complaints Commission (IPCC). The creation of the IPCC was due in part to political pressure for a wholly independent police complaints machinery,[175] and to concerns expressed by the ECtHR about the independence of the Police Complaints Authority.[176] Essential features of the original police complaints procedures nevertheless remained in place, to the extent that in less serious cases the police investigate themselves. That apart, concerns were expressed about the effectiveness of the IPCC, at a time of 'doubt' about 'police integrity and competence',[177] which lamentably remain matters of concern.

Under the procedures introduced in 2017, police complaints are now the responsibility of the Independent Office for Police Conduct (IOPC), as the IPCC has been renamed and restructured.[178]

---

[170] *The Guardian*, 5 August 2013 (public apology by the Metropolitan police for the 'use of excessive and unlawful force' by a named police officer that 'caused' the death of news-vendor Mr Ian Tomlinson at the G20 demonstration in 2009.

[171] One of the most remarkable prosecutions occurred following the use of lethal force in 2005 against a young man (Jean Charles de Menenez) wrongly believed to be a terrorist suspect. He was shot dead by police officers at a Tube station in south London. This led in 2007 to the conviction of the Metropolitan Police for breach of the Health and Safety at Work Act 1974. No proceedings were brought against individual officers in this case. See, subsequently, *Da Silva* v *United Kingdom* [2016] ECHR 314, and *R (Duggan)* v *North London Assistant Deputy Coroner* [2017] EWCA Civ 142, [2017] 4 All ER 104.

[172] *The Guardian*, 19 July 2012. See also See *R* v *DPP, ex p Duckenfield* [2000] 1 WLR 55 (private prosecutions were brought against senior police officers following the Hillsborough stadium tragedy).

[173] *The Guardian*, 17 September 2012.

[174] *The Guardian*, 5 August 2013.

[175] HC 258 (1997–8), and Cm 4262, 1999, Recommendation 58 (*The Stephen Lawrence Inquiry* (Report by Sir William McPherson)).

[176] *Khan* v *UK* (2000) 8 BHRC 310.

[177] HC 494 (2012–13), para 42. The IPCC has twice been the subject of stinging criticism by the Home Affairs Committee: HC 366 (2009–10), and subsequently HC 494 (2012–13). It has also been criticized judicially for taking too narrow a view of its powers: *R (Reynolds)* v *IPCC* [2008] EWCA Civ 1160, [2009] 3 All ER 237.

[178] Policing and Crime Act 2017, s 33. It is to consist of a Director General and six other members to be appointed by the Queen.

A complaint is now defined to mean an 'expression of dissatisfaction' with a police force, which may be made in one of two circumstances. The first relates to the conduct of a person serving with the police, in which case the complainant must be a victim, or have been adversely affected by the conduct, or have witnessed it. The second relates to dissatisfaction unrelated to conduct, in which case the complaint may be made only by someone adversely affected by the matter in question.[179]

In addition to 'expressions of dissatisfaction', what are referred to as 'conduct matters' and 'death or serious injury matters' may also be the subject of investigation. These are matters which are not the subject of a complaint but which (a) give rise to an indication that a person serving with the police may have committed a criminal offence or behaved in a way that would justify bringing disciplinary proceedings;[180] or (b) are matters which relate to the death or serious injury (referred to as DSI) of someone in police custody.[181] It is to be noted that the IOPC has a duty to record deaths and serious injuries in police custody.

Although the grounds for making complaints has been extended, the system is still one whereby the great bulk of complaints are handled by the police themselves. This is either because cases are dealt with informally, or because even when dealt with under the formal procedures the local police force will be the 'appropriate authority' for dealing with the matter. Although serious cases must be referred to the IOPC, for the most part it operates as a supervisory body rather than a body which handles the complaints. Given the volume of complaints (37,105 in 2014–15), it is perhaps implausible to suggest that an independent agency should deal with them all.

It is nevertheless a major weakness of the complaints system that the police are responsible for investigating the complaints against themselves. The 2017 Act responds to these concerns in a number of ways, notably by empowering police and crime commissioners to replace the police as the appropriate authority to direct the investigation; and in giving the IOPC a greater role in the conduct of investigations. Also important are the new powers of the IOPC to initiate investigations, replacing restrictions that enabled it to investigate only those matters referred to it (albeit that there was a duty to refer serious complaints to the Commission).

In terms of redress, the official position is that a complaint 'should be upheld where the findings show that the service provided by or through the conduct of those serving with the police did not reach the standard a reasonable person could expect'.[182] This could have a number of consequences, from an apology, to a restorative conference between a police and a complainant, to action being taken against a police officer for unsatisfactory performance, to proceedings being initiated against an officer for misconduct.[183] The potential outcomes and consequences of a complaint are thus a mixture of the restorative and punitive but not compensatory.

Special provision is made for complaints that allege either discrimination on the part of the police, or a breach of Convention rights, especially articles 2 (right to life) and 3 (right not to suffer torture or inhuman or degrading treatment or punishment).[184] In the latter cases (which are likely in any event to involve very serious allegations even in the absence of Convention rights), the matter must be referred for investigation to the IOPC. Article 2 as interpreted requires a 'prompt and independent' investigation where someone dies while in police custody. This obligation is reinforced in the IOPC's official guidance.[185]

---

[179] Police Reform Act 2002, s 12 (as amended by the 2017 Act).
[180] Ibid, s 12(2).
[181] Ibid, s 12(2A)–(2D) (inserted by the Serious Organised Crime and Police Act 2005, s 160, Sch 12).
[182] IPCC, *Statutory Guidance to the Police Service* (2015), para 9.11.
[183] See SI 2012 No 1204.
[184] See *R (Reynolds)* v *IPCC*, above.
[185] See IPCC, above.

Exclusion of evidence

One of the potentially most effective ways of ensuring that the police respect the rights of the citizen is for the courts to rule inadmissible any evidence obtained as a result of such a violation. The position is governed by PACE, ss 76 and 78,[186] with s 76 providing that a confession made by an accused person may be given in evidence against him or her so far as it is relevant and is not excluded by the court exercising powers contained in s 76(2). This requires the court to exclude evidence obtained by oppression of the person who made it,[187] or 'in consequence of anything said or done which was likely, in the circumstances existing at the time, to render unreliable any confession which might be made in consequence thereof'.[188] Where a representation has been made to the court that a confession may have been secured in either of these ways, the onus is on the prosecution to establish otherwise (s 76(1)).

The term oppression is defined 'to include torture, inhuman or degrading treatment, and the use or threat of violence (whether or not amounting to torture)' (s 76(8)).[189] In *R v Fulling*,[190] the court said that otherwise 'oppression' should be given its ordinary meaning, that is to say, the exercise of authority or power in a burdensome, harsh or wrongful manner or giving rise to unjust or cruel treatment.[191] In that case it was held that there was no oppression where a confession had been made by a woman after being told by police of her lover's affair with another woman.[192] But although oppressive conduct by the police is thus discouraged by s 76, much of the impact of this is lost by s 76(4), which provides that the exclusion of a confession does not affect the admissibility in evidence of any facts discovered as a result of the confession. The fruit of the poison tree thus appears to be edible in English law.

Section 78, introduced as a result of pressure in the Lords from Lord Scarman and others, provides that in any proceedings the court may refuse to allow evidence on which the prosecution proposes to rely 'if it appears to the court that, having regard to all the circumstances, including the circumstances in which the evidence was obtained, the admission of the evidence would have such an adverse effect on the fairness of the proceedings that the court ought not to admit it'.[193] Despite the lack of clarity in its drafting, there is evidence to suggest that, together with s 76, this provision has helped to induce the judges to take a more assertive approach when faced with improper police practice. Thus in *R v Canale*,[194] the Court of Appeal held that the trial judge should not have admitted evidence of interviews which had not been contemporaneously recorded by the police officers conducting the interviews: they had been written up afterwards.[195]

---

[186] For background, see Cmnd 8092, 1981, pp 112–18. Together, PACE 1984, ss 76 and 78 are said to 'constitute a part codification of the law governing criminal evidence': *R v Hasan* [2005] UKHL 25, [2005] 2 AC 467. See also *Beeres v CPS* [2014] EWHC 283 (Admin), para 10 (Green J).

[187] On oppression, see *R v Fulling* [1987] QB 426. See also *R v Ismail* [1990] Crim LR 109, and *R v Hasan*, above.

[188] On unreliability, see *R v Goldenberg* (1988) 88 Cr App R 285, *R v Silcott, Braithwaite and Raghip, The Times*, 9 December 1991, and *R v Walker* [1998] Crim LR 211.

[189] Confession evidence may also be excluded under s 78 (see below). See *R v Mason* [1987] 3 All ER 481.

[190] [1987] QB 426.

[191] See also *R v Hasan*, above, para 53 (Lord Steyn).

[192] For a disturbing example of oppression which 'horrified' the Court of Appeal, and in which the accused was 'bullied and hectored', see *R v Paris* (1993) 97 Cr App R 99. ('The officers . . . were not questioning him so much as shouting at him what they wanted him to say. Short of physical violence, it is difficult to conceive of a more hostile and intimidatory approach by officers to a suspect'.)

[193] See K Grevling (1997) 113 LQR 667 for a full account.

[194] [1990] 2 All ER 187.

[195] See also *R v Keenan* [1990] 2 QB 54.

These breaches of Code C, as it was then drafted, were described by the Court of Appeal as 'flagrant', 'deliberate' and 'cynical'. In so holding, the Lord Chief Justice sharply observed:

> This case is the latest of a number of decisions emphasising the importance of the 1984 Act. If, which we find it hard to believe, police officers still do not appreciate the importance of that Act and the accompanying Codes, then it is time that they did.[196]

Apart from the conduct of interviews, another area where s 78 has been invoked successfully by defendants relates to the denial of access to a solicitor,[197] though it has been said not to be possible 'to give general guidance as to how a judge should exercise his discretion under section 78' on the ground that 'each case had to be determined on its own facts'.[198]

It does not follow that evidence obtained in breach of the codes of practice or in breach of the defendant's statutory rights will always be held to be inadmissible. In more recent cases the courts have taken a more cautious approach,[199] emphasising the literal provisions of s 78, so that neither the 'labelling of conduct as unlawful' nor the 'application to it of the epithet oppressive' 'automatically overrides the fundamental test of fairness in admission of evidence'.[200] Particular difficulties have arisen in connection with police undercover and surveillance work, the House of Lords having held that evidence obtained by means of an illegally placed surveillance device is admissible:[201] the fact that the conduct of the police amounted to an apparent or probable breach of the ECHR, art 8, was simply 'a consideration which may be taken into account for what it is worth'.[202]

Questions arise about the implications of ECHR, art 6 for the admissibility of evidence, particularly since the Human Rights Act was enacted.[203] But the European Court of Human Rights has also held that irregularly obtained evidence may be admitted,[204] and the view of the English courts is that the requirements of s 78 of the 1984 Act and art 6 are the same in this respect.[205] As a result, there is no need to modify s 78 in the light of the jurisprudence of the Strasbourg Court.[206] It is also important to note, however, that English law is now much more flexible than in the past, particularly in relation to entrapment. Referring to it as 'State-created crime' (though in a sense this is true of all crime), the House of Lords has indicated that in appropriate cases evidence obtained in this way should be excluded under s 78, or proceedings should be stayed as an abuse of process.[207]

---

[196] [1990] 2 All ER 187, 190 (Lord Lane CJ).

[197] *R v Samuel* [1988] QB 615; *R v Absolam* (1989) 88 Cr App R 332; *R v Beylan* [1990] Crim LR 185; *R v Chung* (1991) 92 Cr App R 314. But contrast *R v Ibrahim* [2008] EWCA Crim 880, [2009] 1 WLR 578, and *Beeres v CPS*, above.

[198] *R v Smurthwaite* [1994] 1 All ER 898.

[199] A Choo and S Nash [1999] Crim LR 929.

[200] *R v Chalkley* [1998] QB 848, at p 874 (Auld LJ). Also *R v Smurthwaite* (note 198 above) and *R v Cooke* [1995] 1 Cr App R 318.

[201] *R v Khan* [1997] AC 558. See now Police Act 1997, Part III. See ch 16 below. On the approach of the House of Lords to s 78, see also *R v Southwark Crown Court, ex p Bowles* [1998] AC 641, and *R v P* (1995) 2 All ER 58.

[202] At p 582 (Lord Nolan). It has been argued that the courts should take a more robust attitude to the exclusion of evidence obtained in breach of Convention rights: see D Ormerod [2003] Crim LR 61.

[203] See pp 381–2 above. See for example *R v Ibrahim* [2012] EWCA Crim 837.

[204] *Schenck v Switzerland* (1988) 13 EHRR 242. In *Teixeira de Castro v Portugal* (1998) 28 EHRR 101, the Court said that 'the admissibility of evidence is primarily a matter for regulation by national law and as a general rule it is for the national courts to assess the evidence before them. The Court's task under the Convention is not to give a ruling as to whether statements of witnesses were properly admitted as evidence, but rather to ascertain whether the proceedings as a whole, including the way in which evidence was taken, were fair' (at pp 114–15).

[205] See *R v Looseley* [2001] UKHL 53, [2001] 4 All ER 897, and *Attorney General's Reference (No 3 of 1999)* [2000] UKHL 63, [2001] 2 AC 91. See also *R v Hasan*, above, para 62 on the importance of s 78.

[206] *Looseley*, ibid.

[207] Ibid.

F. Accountability and control of the police[208]

Police and crime commissioners

The first source of police accountability is at local level, police forces still locally based. Local police authorities were abolished in 2012, following the creation of police and crime commissioners (PCCs).[209] There is a PCC for each of the 43 police areas in England and Wales. PCCs are directly elected (albeit on typically very low turnouts) and are therefore directly accountable to the communities they serve, in contrast to the local police authorities whose members were either indirectly elected or appointed. As such, the PCCs have inherited a number of the functions of the local police authorities and have a statutory duty to 'secure the maintenance of the police force' for their area, and 'secure that the police force is efficient and effective'.[210]

The PCC also has responsibility to hold the relevant chief constable to account, not only for the way in which he or she carries out his or her own functions, but also for the way in which people under the direction and control of the chief constable carry out their functions.[211] Apart from this general duty, the governing legislation imposes a number of specific duties of accountability on the PCC. These include holding to account the chief constable for (i) the implementation of the PCC's crime and police plan (on which see below), (ii) the way in which he or she has regard to the Home Secretary's strategic policing requirements, and (iii) the effectiveness of his or her engagement with local people.

Each PCC has a duty – as already indicated – to produce a local policing plan. The PCC must work collaboratively with local authorities and criminal justice agencies, and consult with the local population he or she serves. The role of the PCC is very significant, and includes the power to appoint the chief constable, as well as the power to suspend that person from office, along with the power to require him or her to resign.[212] Despite being directly elected, the PCC is nevertheless subject to scrutiny in the discharge of his or her functions by police and crime panels established and maintained by local authorities. The HAC has reported that PCCs have had 'beneficial effect on public accountability and clarity of leadership in policing'.[213]

The situation is different in London, where the Metropolitan Police Authority has been abolished, and the Mayor's Office for Policing and Crime established. The latter position is notionally held by the Mayor and is broadly similar in function to the PCC in the other 41 police forces (excluding the City of London where different arrangements also apply). One difference, however, is that the Metropolitan Police Commissioner is appointed by the Queen on the advice of the Home Secretary, though the latter must now have regard to any recommendation by the Mayor's Office. The power of the Mayor to suspend the Commissioner or require that person to resign may be exercised only with the Home Secretary's consent. Police and crime panel functions are conducted by the London Assembly.

Role of the Home Secretary

Although policing in England and Wales remains notionally a local matter, there is inevitably extensive government involvement, coordination and control, which in turn demands high levels of accountability from the Home Office in particular. Part II of the

---

[208] On police accountability see Jefferson and Grimshaw, *Controlling the Constable*; Reiner, *The Politics of the Police*; Walker, *Policing in a Changing Constitutional Order*.

[209] Police Reform and Social Responsibility Act 2011, s 1.

[210] Ibid, s 1(6).

[211] Ibid, s 1(7).

[212] The exercise of these powers was soon to cause concern: HC 487 (2013–14).

[213] HC 844 (2015–16) – a broadly sympathetic though not uncritical review.

Police Act 1996 is headed 'Central Supervision, Direction and Facilities' and is concerned principally with the national role of the Home Secretary in relation to local policing. It would be true to say, however, that some of the central direction and supervision of the Home Secretary has been revised following the introduction of the directly elected police and crime commissioners.

Prior to the police reforms of 2011, the Home Secretary had a duty to determine 'strategic priorities' for policing in all areas of police authorities, after consulting the Association of Police Authorities and the Association of Chief Police Officers.[214] Where strategic priorities were set in this way, the Home Secretary could then direct police authorities to establish performance targets, the minister having a wide discretion to issue a direction to one or more or to all police authorities, and a power to impose different conditions on different authorities.[215] The Home Secretary could also issue codes of practice relating to the discharge by police authorities of any of their functions.[216]

These powers have all gone, though the Home Secretary has a new duty introduced by the 2011 Act, to issue a document called the 'strategic policing requirement', which rather assumes that there will be a Home Office-led strategic policing requirement. Chief constables must have regard to this document, which addresses 'national threats' and local capabilities to address these threats.[217] The Home Secretary has also retained a number of powers existing pre-2011, including the power to intervene when satisfied that a police force is failing to discharge any of its functions effectively, in which case it can be directed to take 'specified measures'.[218]

The Home Secretary may make regulations for the government, administration and conditions of service of police forces, in particular with respect to ranks, qualifications for appointment and promotion, probationary service, voluntary retirement, discipline, duties, pay, allowances, clothing and equipment.[219] Otherwise, the Home Secretary may prescribe by regulation the equipment to be used by police forces, as well as require 'particular procedures or practices' to be adopted by all of them.[220] Her Majesty's Inspectors of Constabulary are appointed by and report to the Home Secretary, and may be directed by him or her to carry out an inspection of any force.[221]

Accountability to Parliament

MPs wishing to raise police subjects in Parliament may face the problem that that there is no direct ministerial responsibility for the acts of the police, despite the presence in the Home Office 'team' of a Minister for Policing, Fire and Criminal Justice. As we have seen, policing is a local matter, with responsibility through the police and crime commissioners and the

---

[214] Police Act 1996, s 37A (now repealed). Now the Association of Police and Crime Commissioners and the National Police Chiefs' Council respectively.

[215] Ibid, s 38 (now repealed).

[216] Ibid, s 39 (now repealed).

[217] Police Act 1996, s 37A (new), inserted by Reform and Social Responsibility Act 2011. See Home Office, *The National Policing Requirement* (2015); HC Debs, 3 March 2015 (WS 329).

[218] Police Act, 1996, s 40.

[219] Ibid, s 50.

[220] Ibid, s 53A. See also *R v Home Secretary, ex p Northumbria Police Authority* [1989] QB 28 (A W Bradley [1988] PL 298).

[221] Police Act 1996, s 54. In addition to these wide statutory powers, the Home Secretary exercises considerable financial control (albeit subject to Treasury agreement), with an annual grant being made for a service the cost of which has fallen as a result of the government's austerity programme: N Johnston and B Politowski, *Police Funding*, House of Commons Library Briefing Paper 7279 (2016). In determining how much an authority receives, the Home Secretary 'may exercise his discretion by applying such formulae or other rules as he considers appropriate' (Police Act 1996, s 46 (4)).

police and crime panels. There are, however, now much greater opportunities for police matters to be examined in Parliament following the introduction of the select committee system and the Home Affairs Select Committee (HASC) in particular. HASC examines a wide range of policing matters, ranging from the work of the Home Office to operational decisions by chief constables.

The work of the Home Office is examined in a number of ways. The Home Secretary will be invited in each session to appear before the Committee to account for the work of his or her department,[222] and the legislation produced by the Home Office may now be subject to pre-legislative scrutiny. In performing this latter role, the Committee has engaged constructively with the government, and as in the case of the (then) proposed legislation on police and crime commissioners made suggestions as to how the legislation could be improved.[223] In the case of the police and crime commissioners, HASC has also conducted a number of inquiries post-enactment, to highlight problems in the operation of the legislation and to suggest operational improvements.[224]

So far as operational matters as broadly defined are concerned, the Committee's work here has taken two forms, one being to consider controversial police methods, such as undercover policing, in the course of which evidence was taken from a Deputy Assistant Commissioner in the Metropolitan Police and a former undercover police officer, as well as victims of this particular form of policing.[225] Similarly, a number of senior police officers from a number of police forces throughout the country appeared with ministers and others in a large-scale HASC inquiry into the policing of large-scale disorder following disturbances in London and elsewhere in August 2011, in the course of which a number of people died and much damage was done to property.[226]

The latter report made some criticism of the police for failing to intervene early enough to prevent the situation from escalating. As such, however, it was focused more on the conduct of the police as a whole rather than on individual police officers. But in terms of operational responsibility, the Committee has also been willing to examine the conduct of individual officers and police forces. In July 2013 the Metropolitan Police Commissioner was asked to explain a briefing he had given to the press in relation to an affair dubbed 'Plebgate',[227] in which an altercation between a government minister and police officers in Downing Street led to the resignation of the former, at a time when the police version of events was being seriously questioned.

Role of the courts

It should be clear from the foregoing that the time-worn sentiment that a police officer possesses few powers not enjoyed by the ordinary citizen is seriously inaccurate, as is the view that a police officer is only 'a person paid to perform, as a matter of duty, acts which if he were so minded he might have done voluntarily'. Reflecting these views which were widely held, an important royal commission on the police reporting in 1962 came to an astonishing conclusion: 'The relation of the police to the courts is not . . . of any greater constitutional significance than the relation of any other citizen to the courts.'[228]

[222] See for example, HC 563 (2013–14).
[223] HC 836 (2012–13).
[224] See HC 69 (2013–14), HC 487 (2013–14) and HC 844 (2015–16).
[225] HC 837 (2012–13).
[226] HC 1456 (2010–12).
[227] HC 234-1 (2013–14). See also HC 629 (2014–15) ('inept handling' by South Yorkshire police of a raid on the home of Sir Cliff Richard, broadcast by the BBC while he was on holiday). As the Committee said, 'No citizen should have to watch on live television their home being raided in this way'.
[228] Cmnd 1728, p 34.

The corrective to this solecism was supplied by the Court of Appeal in *R* v *Metropolitan Police Commissioner, ex p Blackburn.*[229]

Under the Betting, Gaming and Lotteries Act 1963, certain forms of gaming were unlawful, and gaming clubs in London sought to avoid the Act. After legal difficulties in enforcing the Act had arisen, the Commissioner issued a secret circular to senior officers giving effect to a policy decision that no proceedings were to be taken against a gaming club for breach of the law, unless there were complaints of cheating or it had become the haunt of criminals.

Blackburn sought an order of mandamus against the Commissioner which in effect ordered him to reverse that policy decision. The circular was withdrawn before the case was concluded, but the Court of Appeal held that every chief constable owed a duty to the public to enforce the law. That duty could if necessary be enforced by the courts. Although chief officers had a wide discretion with which the courts would not interfere, the courts would control a policy decision which amounted to a failure of duty to enforce the law.

The court in this case left open whether Blackburn had a sufficient interest in the matter to ask for mandamus. In a later case brought by Blackburn to enforce the obscenity laws, the court held on the merits that the Commissioner was doing what he could to enforce the existing laws with the available resources and no more could reasonably be expected.[230]

The 'clear legal duty'[231] which the police owe the public to enforce the law is, however, subject to important limitations so far as the courts are concerned. Thus, in *Hill* v *Chief Constable of West Yorkshire*, it was held that the general duty of the police to suppress crime does not carry with it a liability to individuals for damage caused to them by criminals whom the police have failed to apprehend even in circumstances when it was possible to do so.[232] The courts take the view that it would not be in the public interest for the police to be liable for negligence in the investigation of crime, a position that has held firm despite claims that it violated Convention rights.[233]

The ECHR may, however, provide some opportunity to challenge operational failures by the police. In *Osman* v *United Kingdom*,[234] it was held that ECHR, art 2 requires the state 'to take preventive operational measures to protect an individual whose life is at risk from the criminal acts of another individual'.[235] But liability for breach of art 2 is hard to establish.[236] However, a duty arises under art 3 to takes steps properly to investigate crime, the negligent

[229] [1968] 2 QB 118.
[230] *R* v *Metropolitan Police Commissioner, ex p Blackburn (No 3)* [1973] QB 241. See also *R* v *Chief Constable of Devon and Cornwall, ex p CEGB* [1982] QB 458, and *R* v *Oxford, ex p Levey, The Times*, 1 November 1986.
[231] *R* v *Metropolitan Police Commissioner, ex p Blackburn* [1968] 2 QB 118, at p 138 (Salmon LJ).
[232] [1989] AC 53 (unsuccessful action in negligence brought by mother of a victim of the Yorkshire Ripper). Also *Brooks* v *Metropolitan Police Commissioner* [2005] UKHL 24, [2005] 2 All ER 289, and *Van Colle* v *Hertfordshire Chief Constable* [2008] UKHL 50, [2009] 1 AC 225. And see now *Michael* v *South Wales Chief Constable* [2015] UKSC 2, [2015] 2 WLR 343, and *Rathbone* v *Northumbria Chief Constable* [2016] EWHC 181 (QB).
[233] *Osman* v *United Kingdom* (2000) 29 EHRR 245; *Z* v *United Kingdom* (2002) 34 EHRR 97; *Van Colle* v *United Kingdom*, Application 7678/09, 13 November 2012.
[234] (2000) 29 EHRR 245; C A Gearty (2000) 64 MLR 179.
[235] It also 'requires by implication that there should be some form of effective official investigation when individuals have been killed as a result of the use of force', in order to ensure the accountability of State officials 'for deaths occurring under their responsibility': *Duggan*, above, para 37, applying *Jordan* v *United Kingdom* (2003) 37 EHRR 2.
[236] *Von Colle* v *Hertfordshire Chief Constable*, above; *Michael* v *South Wales Chief Constable*, above.

performance of which may give rise to liability to any subsequent victims following the failure.[237] Obvious difficulties are presented by the suggestion that a court should direct a chief constable at the instance of a member of the public.[238]

G. Conclusion

Whether in the field of maintaining public order or in the work of detecting and prosecuting crime, police decisions constantly involve the exercise of discretion, choice between alternative courses of action, and the setting of priorities for the use of limited resources. In a stable society it is easier for the police to seek to play an impartial and a non-political role, but even this role has latent political significance. In less stable conditions, issues of law and order acquire a more immediate political content. In the troubled 1980s, questions were often raised about the procedures for police accountability. Problems about police reaction to racial violence, to public demonstrations and to the events surrounding the miners' strike in particular all contributed to the concern, which persists to this day and were revealed most effectively in the report in 2012 of the independent inquiry on the Hillsborough tragedy in 1989.[239]

A complicating dimension is the movement towards greater centralisation of police work, which apart from the matters already discussed is reflected also in the role of the National Crime Agency, established by statute in 2013 to replace the Serious Organised Crime Agency but with a wider remit.[240] As with the creation of a national police force in Scotland,[241] we may be gradually approaching the position of having a national police force in England in all but name, with the Home Office controlling or dictating police finances, police strategy, and police priorities, as well as the working conditions of police officers. This drive for greater centralisation – masked but not seriously challenged by the optical illusion of local democracy with the election of police and crime commissioners – raises important questions about accountability, which the existing institutional structures may not be well suited to answer.

---

[237] *DSD* v *Metropolitan Police Commissioner* [2018] UKSC 11.

[238] It is one thing to strike down instructions by a chief constable that are plainly illegal; but another for a court to impose its own views on the use of police resources. See *R* v *Chief Constable of Sussex, ex p International Trader's Ferry Ltd* [1999] 2 AC 418. Also *E* v *RUC Chief Constable* [2008] UKHL 66, [2008] WLR (D) 351.

[239] HC 581 (2012–13).

[240] Crime and Courts Act 2013. Its duties relate mainly to combatting 'organised crime' and 'serious crime.

[241] Police and Fire Reform (Scotland) Act 2012.

CHAPTER 16

Right to privacy and surveillance powers

Part of the trouble with privacy is that it is notoriously difficult to define. It is largely for this reason that the Younger Committee on Privacy recommended against the introduction of any such right as long ago as 1972, in an influential report that was to shape the debate for a generation.[1] It was not until the Human Rights Act 1998 that a general right to privacy (or private life) was first formally recognised,[2] since when there have been extraordinary legal developments, confounding the concerns of Younger and his colleagues.

A second difficulty with the protection of privacy is in determining from whom the protection is needed. Many are agreed that the intrusive overtures of the state – which for some has lurid Orwellian overtures – ought to be contained. But many of the problems associated with the violation of privacy are perpetrated not by the state, but by other private parties – newspapers engaged in a desperate circulation war, or employers checking on employees (in one famous case to monitor calls to a solicitor by an employee who was suing her employer for sex discrimination).[3]

A third difficulty is that the fast development of new technology has provided fresh opportunities for the surveillance of individuals on a large scale by both state agencies (such as the police and security and intelligence services) and private parties (such as newspapers and employers). The risks associated with the former were brought to light by allegations in 2013, by a well-placed source, that the United Kingdom was a party with the United States to the large-scale but as yet indeterminate storage, analysis and exchange of the personal internet data of British citizens and others.

The risks associated with the latter were fully exposed in the 'phone-hacking' scandal, which revealed the widespread practice of 'hacking' into the voice-mail of media celebrities and others by some journalists. The affair was widely publicised by an inquiry led by Lord Justice Leveson, who had been appointed by the Prime Minister. It led also to the closure of the most successful Sunday newspaper, as well as to the prosecution of a number of high-profile newspaper editors and journalists for alleged offences relating to scandals in which it was alleged they had taken part.

This is not to suggest, of course, that there must be an unqualified right to personal privacy, the invasion of which by a range of devices is now seen to be a necessary or expedient weapon in the fight against organised crime and other unlawful acts which threaten public safety and national security.[4] But there are fewer issues that have given rise to as much controversy in recent years as the allegations that the state is intruding too much into the private lives of its citizens, and the accompanying allegations that newspapers, employers and others are not subject to proper and effective legal control.

---

[1] Cmnd 5012, 1972, especially paras 651–2. See also for a valuable early yet sceptical account, Wacks, *The Protection of Privacy*. Also, Wacks, *Personal Information*, especially ch 1.

[2] *Wainwright* v *Home Office* [2003] UKHL 53, [2004] AC 406.

[3] *Halford* v *UK* (1997) 24 EHRR 523.

[4] HC Deb, 6 March 2000, col 768 (Mr Jack Straw). These powers are now justified as being directed mainly at 'drug, terrorist, paedophilia and money-laundering crimes': ibid, col 834 (Mr Charles Clarke).

A. The case for protection

Privacy is a concept of indeterminate scope, closely related to concepts that might be encountered in the law of tort (trespass), equity (breach of confidence) or intellectual property (copyright). But it is important also for the public lawyer, at a time of growing anxiety about what is seen as the emergence and development of a 'surveillance society'.[5] Privacy is closely associated with liberty and with ideas about freedom from interference by the state.[6] As a principle, privacy is important also as a way of reinforcing other constitutional liberties – most notably the right to freedom of association and assembly.

One of the principal means of violating the liberty of those individuals and organisations who support unpopular causes is to monitor them, to keep them under surveillance, to maintain records about their members, and to circulate information about them – to provide the fuel for oppression and discrimination.[7] It is true that the concept of privacy as protected by the ECHR (art 8) and now the Human Rights Act 1998 extends some way beyond matters of this kind. But for the public lawyer the foregoing are core concerns which address fundamental issues about the political freedom of the individual in a democratic society.

New technologies that allow for even greater forms of surveillance make the case for some form of protection irresistible. But as suggested, there can be no case for an unqualified or an unlimited right to privacy. Privacy is a restraint on freedom of expression and as such gives rise to concerns when relied on by public officials and politicians who have something to hide, and who wish to prevent the disclosure of information that may expose hypocrisy or worse. It is also a restraint on the activities of the police and other authorities in the criminal justice system who are engaged in legitimate activities in the public interest to detect the drug dealers and other traffickers in human misery.

This is not to say, of course, that there should be no right to privacy: it is a case for balancing competing rights and interests. But where rights of privacy are restricted, there is a case for violations only where there is clear legal authority and only where there is a clear need for a legitimate purpose. And while it might be expected that the state would refrain from violating the privacy of the individual except where there is good cause to do so, equally it might be expected that the state would intervene to take steps to protect that privacy, particularly of the weak and vulnerable, from commercial exploitation and other forms of abuse by global media corporations and other powerful organisations.[8]

In this chapter we consider aspects of privacy relating specifically to various forms of surveillance of the individual, as well as the storage and processing of personal data. Underlying a great deal if not all of the discussion that follows are the requirements of ECHR, art 8, which has greatly informed both legislation and the common law in this field. It is important to acknowledge, however, that private life in art 8 is 'a broad term not susceptible to exhaustive definition', and that 'whether there has been an interference with the right to respect for a person's private life . . . will depend in each case on its own facts and circumstances'.[9] It is important also to acknowledge that not all forms of surveillance will constitute an interference with private life.

The violation of privacy in the so-called 'surveillance society' has been a highly contentious issue politically in recent years, and is addressed only to a limited extent in the Protection of

---

[5] See HC 58 (2007–8) (Home Affairs Select Committee); HL Paper 18 (2008–9) (House of Lords Constitution Committee).

[6] See Lustgarten and Leigh, *In from the Cold*, p 40. See also D Feldman [2000] PL 61.

[7] For the surveillance of the Communist Party of Great Britain, see Ewing and Gearty, *The Struggle for Civil Liberties*, ch 3.

[8] So much is required by the ECHR: see *Spencer* v *UK* (1998) 25 EHRR CD105; and by the Human Rights Act: see *Venables* v *News Group Newspapers Ltd* [2001] EWHC 32 (QB), [2001] Fam 430.

[9] *Kinloch* v *HM Advocate* [2012] UKSC 62, [2013] 2 WLR 141, para 18.

Freedoms Act 2012, the substance of which does not do justice to its exaggerated short title. As already pointed out, one of the gravest violations of privacy in modern times, however, was perpetrated not by the state but by news corporations, which were exposed as having 'hacked' personal phones on a massive scale. In view of its importance, we deal (albeit briefly) with aspects of interference with privacy by the press at appropriate points in this chapter.

B. Surveillance: acquiring information

The first way in which the privacy of the individual may be undermined is by different techniques of surveillance in order to obtain information about him or her.[10] This may be done in a number of ways – by the state, by the press and by others: it may involve breaking into a home and rifling through personal effects, it may involve the use of bugging devices or it may involve the interception of communications of various kinds.

As far as the common law is concerned, the placing of someone under surveillance is not in itself unlawful. But there are circumstances where various types of surveillance may be unlawful, although only where the surveillance involves an interference with existing rights already recognised by the law. The invasion of someone's privacy has not by itself given cause for the courts to intervene in the past.

Trespass

Perhaps the best-known example of common law protection for privacy is *Entick* v *Carrington*,[11] where John Entick's home was the subject of an illegal entry and his possessions the subject of an illegal search. Although clearly a violation of his home and his private life, Entick's action for damages succeeded because it was also a trespass to his property rights. In the memorable words of Lord Camden CJ, in one of the great judgments of the common law:

> No man can set his foot upon my ground without my licence, but he is liable for an action, though damage be nothing; . . . If he admits the fact, he is bound to show by way of justification, that some positive law has empowered or excused him.

It is true that the officers conducting the search were armed with a warrant issued by the Home Secretary. But this was no defence, because the Home Secretary had no legal authority to issue the warrant in the first place: such authority could be provided only by Parliament, save exceptionally in the case of warrants issued in relation to stolen goods. Parliament has not been slow in providing such power, it being claimed in the Explanatory Notes to the Protection of Freedoms Act 2012 that there were over 1,300 pieces of primary or secondary legislation authorising state officials to enter private premises.

In seeking to reduce the number of these provisions, the 2012 Act conferred power on the 'appropriate national authority', defined to mean a Minister of the Crown or the Welsh ministers. Under these measures, the 'appropriate national authority' may by order 'repeal any power of entry or associated power which the appropriate national authority considers to be unnecessary or inappropriate' (s 39). It may also add safeguards of various kinds to existing powers (s 40), and perhaps most remarkably 'rewrite' such powers (s 41). A Code of Practice has been issued to provide guidance relating to the power of entry (s 47).

Steps are also taken in Schedule 2 to repeal a number of existing powers of entry, though like probably most governments before it, the Coalition found it expedient

---

[10] See *Robertson* v *Keith* 1936 SLT 9, and *Connor* v *HM Advocate* 2002 SLT 671.
[11] (1765) 19 St Tr 1030.

to add to the existing powers of entry, notwithstanding the provisions of the Protection of Freedoms Act 2012. Thus, the Scrap Metal Dealers Act 2013 provides that 'A constable or an officer of a local authority may enter and inspect a licensed site at any reasonable time on notice to the site manager' (s 16(1)). It also contains powers of entry without prior notice (s 16(2)), and additional powers of entry with a warrant (s 16(3)). Old habits die hard.

Interference with property

The law of trespass took on a new role in relation to the use of listening devices by the police to record conversations involving people who were suspected of involvement in criminal activity.

> In *R* v *Khan*,[12] the accused was suspected of being involved in the importation of illegal drugs. The police placed a listening device on the outside of a house which he was visiting. This was done without any statutory authority, though in accordance with Home Office guidelines relating to the use of such devices. Nevertheless, it was accepted by the Crown that the conduct of the police involved both a trespass and damage to the property on which the device was placed.
>
> Khan was found guilty on charges relating to the importation of drugs, the evidence against him being found mainly in tape recordings acquired as a result of the listening device. He appealed against conviction and argued that the evidence should not have been admitted because it had been illegally obtained and had been obtained in breach of the ECHR, art 8. The appeal failed: in determining whether evidence should be admitted, the illegality of the means used is not decisive.
>
> The question was whether it was secured in circumstances which tainted the fairness of the proceedings. But although the House of Lords thought not, the case nevertheless exposed the illegality of this particular practice.[13]

The 'lack of a statutory system regulating the use of surveillance devices' by the police led to an expression of astonishment from the bench.[14] It was all the more remarkable for the fact that similar activity by the security service required the authority of a warrant from the Home Secretary under the Security Service Act 1989. (The position relating to the security service is now governed by the Regulation of Investigatory Powers Act 2000, which is considered in section D.) It was thus not surprising that the ECtHR should find English law and practice relating to the use of listening devices by the police to breach the ECHR, art 8.[15]

The use of bugging devices by the police is now governed by the Police Act 1997, Part III,[16] which proved to be extremely controversial at the time it was passed.[17] It provides that '[n]o entry on or interference with property or with wireless telegraphy shall be unlawful if it is authorised by an authorisation having effect under this Part' (s 92). Authorisation may be given to take action in respect of private property as may be specified in the authorisation, where the authorising officer believes that the action is necessary 'for the prevention or detection of serious crime'. It must also be shown that 'the taking of the action is proportionate to what the action seeks to achieve' (s 93(2)(b)).

....

[12] [1997] AC 558. See now *Khan* v *UK* (2001) 31 EHRR 1016.

[13] See also *R* v *Loveridge* [2001] 2 Cr App R 591, and *Teixeira de Castro* v *Portugal* (1998) 28 EHRR 101.

[14] [1997] AC 558, at p 582 (Lord Nolan).

[15] *Khan* v *UK*, note 12 above.

[16] For a good account, see Fenwick, *Civil Rights: New Labour, Freedom and the Human Rights Act*, pp 372–7.

[17] See Ewing and Gearty, *A Law Too Far: Part III of the Police Bill 1997*.

For these purposes, conduct is to be regarded as serious crime only if (*a*) 'it involves the use of violence, results in substantial financial gain or is conducted by a large number of persons in pursuit of a common purpose', or (*b*) the offence is one for which a person over the age of 18 with no previous convictions could reasonably expect to be jailed for at least three years (s 93(4)). (In the case of Northern Ireland, 'preventing or detecting serious crime' includes 'the interests of national security',[18] though there is hardly any need for such powers in Great Britain given the range of powers otherwise available to the police and the security and intelligence services.)

Authorisation may be given by a chief constable, or by one of a much-expanded number of other law enforcement agencies (s 93(5)), and in some cases, will not take effect until approved by a judicial commissioner appointed under the Investigatory Powers Act 2016 (IPA 2016).[19] Approval by a commissioner is required where any property specified in the authorisation is used as a dwelling, or as a bedroom in a hotel, or constitutes office premises. Approval is also required if it is likely to yield matters subject to legal privilege, confidential personal information or confidential journalistic material (s 97).[20]

If a judicial commissioner refuses to give his or her approval, or if an authorisation is quashed, the authorising officer may appeal to the Investigatory Powers Commissioner, who must allow the appeal unless there are no reasonable grounds for believing that the statutory conditions for seeking an authorisation have been met (s 104). The other party with an interest in these proceedings is, of course, the surveillance target, and here it is provided that in some cases complaints may be made to the Investigatory Powers Tribunal by those who are the subject of a s 93 authorisation, in the unlikely event that they even know that they are the target of surveillance.[21]

Surveillance and undercover operations

Additional measures relating to surveillance are to be found in the Regulation of Investigatory Powers Act 2000, Part II.[22] This applies to surveillance activities not only by the police, but also by a large number of other agencies which now play a part in law enforcement, including the security and intelligence services, HM Revenue and Customs and local authorities. But the Act does not by any means apply to all surveillance.[23] Although the RIPA 2000 deals with a wider range of activities than the use of bugging devices, it applies to this form of surveillance as well, and thus adds what is at times a confusing layer of regulation on top of the Police Act 1997, Part III, which remains in place

The RIPA 2000 deals with what are referred to as *directed surveillance*, *intrusive surveillance* and *the conduct and use of covert human intelligence sources*.[24] Surveillance is *directed* if it is covert but not intrusive and undertaken for the purposes of a specific operation to obtain private information about a person.[25] Surveillance is *intrusive* if covert and (*a*) carried out in relation to anything taking place on any residential premises or in a private vehicle, and (*b*) involves the presence of an individual on the premises (such as a paid informer or someone who is

---

[18] Police Act 1997, s 93(2A).

[19] See pp 441–2 below.

[20] These terms are defined in ss 98–100.

[21] Regulation of Investigatory Powers Act 2000, s 65(5)(f).

[22] For a fuller treatment, see Fenwick, above, pp 377–85. For the comparable provisions in Scotland, see Regulation of Investigatory Powers (Scotland) Act 2000.

[23] See p 458 below.

[24] RIPA 2000, s 26.

[25] Private information is defined to include any information relating to a person's private or family life: s 26(10). There will be circumstances where surveillance does not require authorisation: see Official Report, Standing Committee F, 30 March 2000, col 274.

concealed) or is carried out by means of a surveillance device. *Covert human intelligence sources* may be 'informants, agents [or] undercover officers'.[26]

These different forms of activity are uncovered from time to time in the reported cases.[27] But until the RIPA 2000 they were conducted without formal legal authority (with the exception of intrusive surveillance under the Police Act 1997). The 2000 Act is designed to ensure that practice in this area is brought into line with the ECHR by requiring that the different kinds of surveillance to which it applies are authorised in advance,[28] the authorisation in some cases now requiring judicial approval. There is also a right to complain to the Investigatory Powers Tribunal established under the Act about any authorisation.[29]

Directed surveillance may be authorised if necessary on one of several grounds (which include national security, the prevention or detection of crime, and the prevention of disorder), provided that the authorised surveillance is proportionate to the end to be achieved (s 28). The authorisation may be given internally by a designated person in one of a number of specified public authorities or types of public authority.[30] Predictably, these include the police and the intelligence services, but also various government departments (such as the Food Standards Agency), local authorities and other public bodies.

A similar regime operates for *covert human intelligence sources* (s 29), with the need for authorisation, to be given internally by a designated person. In the case of *covert human intelligence sources*, however, the authorisation may be given by agencies that do not also have the power to conduct directed surveillance, such as the Health and Safety Executive. Subsequent amendments require local authority authorisations (but inexplicably not others) to be approved by a justice of the peace (in England and Wales), or a sheriff (in Scotland). These amendments apply to the authorisation of both the use of covert human intelligence sources and directed surveillance.[31]

Covert human intelligence sources is the term used for undercover police officers. The Home Affairs Select Committee examined serious concerns about the practice of undercover officers, who were revealed by legal proceedings to have infiltrated protest groups and to have become deeply embedded within them.[32] These concerns related in part to claims that police officers had taken the identities of dead children, had participated in unlawful activities,[33] and had forged close personal relationships with members of the groups infiltrated, on at least one occasion fathering a child with a partner unaware of the real identity of her lover.

Although the use of undercover officers is regulated by statute (in the sense that RIPA 2000 requires authorisation), the conduct of such officers is governed only by the Home Office Code of Practice on Covert Human Intelligence Sources. Full investigation of this matter by the Home Affairs Select Committee has been postponed pending the outcome of

---

[26] Official Report, Standing Committee F, 30 March 2000, col 274 (Mr Charles Clarke).

[27] See *R* v *Smurthwaite* [1994] 1 All ER 898; *R* v *Latif* [1996] 1 WLR 104; *R* v *Khan*, above; *Connor* v *HM Advocate*, above; *Kinloch* v *H M Advocate*, above.

[28] HC Deb, 6 March 2000, col 767 (Mr Jack Straw).

[29] RIPA 2000, s 65(5), though the problem with this complaints procedure as well is that people will be unaware that they are or have been under surveillance; without that knowledge they will be in no position to make a complaint.

[30] SI 2003 No 3171, SI 2010 No 521.

[31] RIPA 2000, s 32A–32B, amended by Protection of Freedoms Act 2012, s 37.

[32] *R* v *Barkshire* [2011] EWCA Crim 1885, [2012] Crim LR 453.

[33] In *Barkshire*, ibid, it was said that the evidence 'appeared to show him as . . . arguably, an agent provocateur' (para 18).

legal proceedings (i) by five of the 'victims' of undercover police officers alleging violations of Convention and common law rights;[34] and (ii) by an undercover officer claiming that the police as employer had failed in breach of its duty of care to him.

The Home Affairs Select Committee nevertheless insisted that undercover officers should not 'enter into intimate, physical sexual relationships while using their false identities undercover without clear, prior authorisation, which should only be given in the most exceptional circumstances', concluding also that it was 'unacceptable that a child should be brought into the world as a result of such a relationship and this must never be allowed to happen again'. The use of dead children's identities was strongly condemned as 'ghoulish and disrespectful' and the practice 'must never be followed in the future'.

According to the Committee the current legal framework 'fails adequately to safeguard the fundamental rights of the individuals affected', concluding that 'there is a compelling case for a fundamental review of the legislative framework governing undercover policing', in the light of the lessons learned from these cases.[35] In 2015, the then Home Secretary announced the appointment of a judge-led inquiry under the Inquiries Act 2015, to investigate and report on undercover police operations by police forces in England and Wales since 2015.[36]

Intrusive surveillance is different. This may be authorised only on one of three grounds: where necessary in the interests of national security; for the purpose of preventing or detecting serious crime; or in the interests of the economic well-being of the United Kingdom. Again, the authorisation must be proportionate to the end to be achieved by carrying it out (s 32). Authorising officers include chief constables, provosts marshal, HM Revenue and Customs, and the National Crime Agency (ibid). In the case of *intrusive* surveillance by the police, revenue and customs, immigration officers or the Competition and Markets Authority, an authorisation does not take effect unless approved by a judicial commissioner (s 36).[37]

A person who is the subject of improper surveillance of any of the foregoing kinds may make a complaint to the Investigatory Powers Tribunal.[38] In *Kinloch* v *H M Advocate*,[39] it was argued that unauthorised covert surveillance breached ECHR, art 8 and that evidence obtained against a person accused of money laundering should be inadmissible as a result. The Supreme Court held that the police surveillance – which took the form of following the accused in public places – did not constitute a breach of Convention rights, on the ground that he had no reasonable expectation of privacy. According to Lord Hope, the accused was watched

> in places where he was open to public view by neighbours, by persons in the street or by anyone else who happened to be watching what was going on. He took the risk of being seen and of his movements being noted down. The criminal nature of what he was doing, if that was what it was found to be, was not an aspect of his private life that he was entitled to keep private.[40]

---

[34] *AKJ* v *Metropolitan Police Commissioner* [2013] EWHC 32 (QB); *DIL* v *MPC* 2014 EWHC 2184 (QB).

[35] HC 837 (2012–13).

[36] Information about the inquiry is available on its dedicated website.

[37] Concerns have been expressed about the failure of the procedures for the retention, use and storage of information obtained by intrusive surveillance to comply with ECHR, art 8, with unfavourable comparisons being drawn with the procedures relating to the interception of communications, discussed below: *R E* v *United Kingdom* [2015] ECHR 947, (2016) 63 EHRR 2.

[38] On which, see Investigatory Powers Tribunal, *Report 2010* (2011), and in particular *Paton* v *Poole Borough Council* (IPT/09/01, 02, 03, 04 and 05), a notorious case of directed surveillance of a family to determine whether they genuinely resided within the catchment area of a popular and over-subscribed school (ibid, p 28).

[39] [2012] UKSC 62, [2013] 2 WLR 141.

[40] Ibid, para 21.

Overlapping regimes

A great deal of the activity which is authorised by the Police Act 1997, Part III, would also fall within the definition of intrusive surveillance in the RIPA 2000 and the Regulation of Investigatory Powers (Scotland) Act 2000. So while the Police Act 1997 allows the use of surveillance devices in vehicles on the authorisation of the police alone, RIPA 2000 would require such activity to be approved by a judicial commissioner. As a result, prior approval by a judicial commissioner will normally be required for many forms of surveillance: in the case of dwellings, hotel bedrooms and offices, it would be required by the Police Act; and in the case of vehicles, it would be required by RIPA 2000.

In practice, combined warrants are issued to authorise intrusive surveillance and interference with property (as defined by the 1997 Act). Only exceptionally could bugging devices be used on the word of the police alone: one example would be the bugging of a known meeting place of suspected criminals (such as a warehouse or a pub). It should be emphasised, however, that other forms of police surveillance (such as watching someone (directed surveillance), or using informants or infiltrating organisations (covert human intelligence)) would not require prior judicial approval.

There are restrictions on the use of the Police Act 1997 procedures to engage in conduct which could be authorised by a targeted equipment interference warrant under the Investigatory Powers Act 2016.[41]

C. Communications and communications data

A particular form of surveillance operated for many years by various agencies is the interception of mail and phone calls. This is an area of the law which has grown exponentially in recent years, in terms of its volume, complexity and sophistication. Even as late as the 1980s, there was virtually no law, apart from the need to obtain a warrant to intercept mail,[42] since when the position has changed unrecognizably, partly as a result of the demands of the ECtHR and the CJEU (both of which have a more developed sense of the rule of law than the common law),[43] but just as importantly because of the fast pace of development in the area of information technology.

The principal legislation is now the Investigatory Powers Act 2016, a formidable statute of some 291 pages, which was the subject of intense pre-legislative scrutiny,[44] as well as some well-informed criticism from various sources.[45] A novel feature of the Act is Part 1, which sets out principles of privacy by which the Act is to be construed, highlighting parliamentary and wider concerns about the potential impact of the legislation. These principles apply particularly in relation to discretionary powers (such as the granting of a warrant under the Act) and include a duty to consider whether less intrusive means could be used, and the public interest in the protection of privacy (s 2).

----

[41] Investigatory Powers Act 2016, s 14.

[42] Post Office Act 1953, s 58, and subsequently Postal Services Act 2000, ss 83 and 84.

[43] For the CJEU, see *Joined Cases C-293/12 and 594/12, Digital Rights Ireland and Seitlinger*, 8 April 2014. See also *Joined Cases C-203/15 and C-698/15, Tele2 Sverige AB v Post-och telestyrelsen and Home Secretary v Watson*, 21 December 2016. The *Digital Rights Ireland* case led to the Digital Rights and Investigatory Powers Act 2014, which was a short-term measure to protect the ability of law enforcement, security and intelligence agencies to secure access to 'communications data' (on which see below), and which had a 'sunset clause' in the Act itself of 31 December 2016, on which date the Act was repealed. The issues covered by the 2014 Act are now governed by the Investigatory Powers Act 2016.

[44] See HL 93, HC 651 (2015–16) (Joint Committee on Draft Investigatory Powers Bill).

[45] HC 255 (2015–16), SG 2016/68 (Interception Commissioner); HL Paper 6, HC 104 (2016–17) (JCHR).

The following is necessarily a brief outline of some of the salient features of the Act. Those seeking more detailed information should consult more specialist works.

Interception of communications

The general principles of the old regime (as set out initially in the Interception of Communications Act 1985 and then RIPA 2000) are largely retained in the 2016 Act, though as suggested, the arrangements are now more complex and much of the language highly technical. It continues to be a criminal offence to intercept communications without lawful authority (s 3),[46] which can be provided either by a warrant or in one of a number of the circumstances specifically authorized by the Act (s 6).[47] Warrants are of three kinds: targeted, mutual assistance or bulk interception warrants respectively; targeted warrants in turn are of two kinds: interception and examination respectively (s 6).

Part 2, ch 1 of the 2016 Act makes provision for targeted and mutual assistance warrants (s 15), which may be sought by various intelligence and law enforcement agencies (s 18). An application may be made to an appropriate minister (usually the Home Secretary or the Scottish ministers) (s 19), whose decision must now be approved by a Judicial Commissioner appointed under the Act (s 23).[48] The latter is a major innovation, successive governments having resisted until now the demand that warrants to intercept communications should be approved judicially. Continuing ministerial involvement in these matters is not easy to justify.[49]

In terms of the grounds on which a targeted interception warrant may be issued, these are recognizable from the earlier legislation. Thus, warrants may be issued where necessary in the interests of national security, for the purpose of preventing or detecting serious crime, or in the interests of the economic well-being of the United Kingdom (but in this last case only where these interests are 'relevant' to the interests of national security, and only where the information considered necessary to obtain relates to the acts or intentions of people outside the British Isles) (s 20). A mutual assistance warrant may be issued where necessary to give effect to an international agreement relating to the prevention or detection of serious crime (s 20(3)).[50]

The role of the Judicial Commissioner is to consider whether the warrant is 'necessary' for the purpose for which it was granted, and if it was 'proportionate', both requirements reflecting the demands of the ECHR, article 8 (s 23(1)). In reviewing the granting of a warrant, the Judicial Commissioner must apply the principles of judicial review that would be applied by a court, and notably must also take care to ensure that he or she complies with the general duties relating to privacy set out in section 2 of the Act (and referred to above) (s 23(2)).

---

[46] 'Interception' is defined widely to include 'monitoring transmissions' (s 4).

[47] Here we are concerned mainly with interceptions authorised by a warrant. The interceptions authorised by the Act without the need for a warrant relate to situations where there is consent, where it is undertaken by businesses for monitoring purposes, or where it relates to certain institutions such as prisons, psychiatric hospitals and immigration detention facilities (ss 44–52).

[48] On the appointment of judicial commissioners, see IPA 2016, ss 227–28. The Investigatory Powers Commissioner and the judicial commissioners replace the various oversight bodies appointed under RIPA 2000 and the Police Act 1997 (the Interception of Communications Commissioner, the Intelligence Commissioner and the Chief Surveillance Commissioner).

[49] In another departure from the past, special safeguards have been introduced for MPs (warrant to be granted only by the Prime Minister) (s 26), and for material subject to legal privilege (warrant only to be granted in 'exceptional and compelling circumstances') (s 27), as well as confidential journalistic material (the need for secure arrangements for handling and disposal of such material) (s 28).

[50] Serious crime is widely defined to mean either (*a*) a crime which could reasonably lead to imprisonment for at least three years if committed by someone over the age of 18 (or 21 in Scotland) convicted of a first offence; or (*b*) conduct that 'involves the use of violence, results in substantial financial gain or is conduct by a large number of persons in pursuit of a common purpose' (s 263).

Written reasons must be given where approval is refused, and an appeal lies by the *applicant* to the Investigatory Powers Commissioner (s 23(4),(5)).[51]

So far as the procedures are concerned, it remains the case that warrants must be signed by the minister personally (s 30(2)), except in urgent cases when the minister must nevertheless have agreed (presumably by phone or otherwise) (s 23(4)). There can be no delegation under the *Carltona* principle,[52] which makes this a formidable obligation in view of the volume of warrants granted annually. The Interception of Communications Commissioners who had oversight responsibilities for the law under the 1985 and 2000 Acts revealed in their annual reports a steep upward trajectory in the number of warrants granted annually, from a total of 519 reported in 1988 to 3,059 in 2015 (involving a larger number of agencies).[53]

This means that the Home Secretary (principally responsible for the granting of warrants) must spend a considerable amount of time each day dealing with warrants, the 3,059 warrants issued annually representing almost 12 warrants every working day.[54] This is a burden of time that can only increase under the 2016 Act, which introduces a wider range of factors to be considered before warrants may be issued, with the possibility that the need for judicial approval will require more care to be taken before decisions are made. That said, although the warrant must be signed by the minister, the case for doing so will likely be set out clearly in advice from senior officials.[55]

Once granted, the warrant not only *authorizes* the applicant to make the interception, but also imposes duties on operators to *give effect* to the warrant (s 43).

Obtaining and retaining communications data

Provision was made in the Regulation of Investigatory Powers Act 2000 to deal with the situation where it is deemed necessary for public authorities to secure access to 'communications data'.[56] Until RIPA 2000 came into force, access to this information was governed by a voluntary regime set up under the Telecommunications Act 1984 and the Data Protection Act 1998. It was thought that this 'loosely regulated' regime was 'unacceptable in terms of human rights and because, in certain cases, it has led to unacceptably high demands on the public telecommunications operators'.[57]

As a result, Chapter 2 of Part I of RIPA 2000 introduced a statutory procedure whereby the law enforcement and other agencies could require service providers to supply communications data in defined circumstances.[58] These powers (revisited by the Digital Rights and Investigatory Powers Act 2014) are now to be found in the Investigatory Powers Act 2016, the Explanatory Notes to which refer to communications data as 'the 'who', 'when', 'where' and 'how' of a communication, but not its content. It is a way of enabling the authorities to identify networks and contacts, rather than the detail of what is being said.

Under the 2016 Act (as under RIPA 2000), authorisations to obtain communications data may be (i) sought by a wider category of officials, and (ii) for a wider range of purposes than in the

---

[51] There is obviously no appeal by the person against whom the warrant has been issued, who will necessarily be unaware that the application has been made.

[52] See pp 291–2 above.

[53] HC 255 (2015–16), SG 2016/68, para 6.39. Ministers are reported as having refused requests for warrants in only six cases in 2015: ibid, para 6.41.

[54] It is not clear how much time is spent by ministers considering these applications, but given their other responsibilities, it cannot be very much.

[55] The latter are likely to filter carefully what appears before the minister, and may be the de facto source of authority as a result.

[56] For the formal definition, see IPA 2016, s 261.

[57] HC Deb, 6 March 2000, col 773 (Mr Jack Straw).

[58] RIPA 2000, s 22.

case of interception warrants, perhaps reflecting the belief that access to communications data is a less intrusive violation of privacy than the interception of communications. These authorisations may thus be granted by the 'designated senior officer' in a 'relevant public authority' (s 61(1)), of which there are 48 categories extensively listed in Schedule 4, including law enforcement bodies, security and intelligence agencies and government departments.[59] Local authorities are also a relevant public authority (s 73).

An authorization to demand disclosure of communications data from anyone in possession of it may be granted where necessary for one of ten purposes set out in the Act (s 61(7)), and that obtaining the data is proportionate to what is sought to be achieved (s 61(1)(c)). These purposes relate to national security; preventing or detecting crime, or preventing disorder; the economic well-being of the United Kingdom; public safety; public health; assessing or collecting taxes; prevention of death or injury; to assist investigations into miscarriages of justice; to assist in identifying someone who has died; and the regulation of financial services or stability (s 61(7)). No doubt others will be added in due course.

Unlike interception warrants, there is no need for judicial approval of this kind of surveillance, which seems hard to justify, particularly as the surveillance is targeted on individuals, as a heading in the Act makes clear. There is an exception for local authority authorisations, which must be authorised by a justice of the peace in England and Wales or a sheriff in Scotland, raising questions about why this should not be required in all cases (s 75).[60] There is also an exception relating to journalistic material (s 77), with the authorization not to take effect until approved by a judicial commissioner.[61] Judicial scrutiny in all cases might help to ensure confidence in a practice annual reports of the Interceptions of Communications Commissioner suggest is extensively used.[62]

In addition to the question of access to communications data, the 2016 Act empowers the government to require internet service providers and other holders of communications data to retain the data for up to a year (s 87(3)). This may be done by means of a retention notice, which may be issued where necessary and appropriate for any of the purposes for which an authorization to obtain communications data may be granted (s 87(1)(a)). A retention notice (which may be addressed to one or more telecommunications operators) must be approved by a Judicial Commissioner (s 87(1)(b)). The data are stored with a view to access for the purposes outlined above.

The purpose here is clearly to prevent the destruction of material that may at some later stage be evidence implicating a targeted individual. It is nevertheless curious that judicial authorization should be required to store but not access data.

Bulk data and bulk data warrants

The most controversial feature of the 2016 Act, and the one thought most likely to give rise to human rights concerns (and which was therefore of greatest concern to the JCHR and others), are the provisions relating to bulk warrants.[63] This is because 'their exercise will result in the acquisition of large volumes of untargeted data about a large number of people, most of whom will not be of intelligence interest'.[64] In other words, bulk data access authorizes mass

---

[59] Others include regulatory bodies such as the Gambling Commission and the Food Standards Agency.

[60] This bears comparison with the Coalition government's initiatives to contain the powers of local authorities under the Protection of Freedoms of Act 2010, which introduced the need for judicial approval.

[61] The definition of journalistic material is set out in IPA 2016, s 264, which is not the same as the definition in PACE 1984, ch 15 above.

[62] HC 255 (2015–16), SG 2016/68: 761,702 items of communications acquired by public authorities during 2015 (para 7.23).

[63] HL Paper 6, HC 104 (2016–17), pp 9–15.

[64] Ibid, para 2.2.

surveillance by the security and intelligence services. There are thus two issues here: the collection and the examination of data.[65]

Bulk datasets can be obtained by the security and intelligence services from a number of sources, including government departments, commercial organisations and law enforcement agencies.[66] The information about individuals obtained in this way will include data about travel, communications and finance, and as already pointed out will include information about individuals who are of no interest to the intelligence services.[67] Nevertheless, MI5 argues that access to this information enables it to 'make the right connections between disparate pieces of information'.[68] The use of such data nonetheless raises major privacy concerns.[69]

The 2016 Act makes provision for different kinds of warrant relating to bulk data: (i) interception of bulk data (ss 136–57), (ii) acquisition of bulk data (ss 158–75), (iii) bulk equipment interference (ss 176–98) and (iv) bulk personal dataset warrants (ss 199–226), all of which may be issued by the Home Secretary only at the request of the head of an intelligence service (defined to mean MI5, MI6 and GCHQ). In all four cases, warrants may be granted where necessary and proportionate (i) in the interests of national security; or (ii) preventing or detecting serious crime, or (iii) in the interests of the economic well-being of the United Kingdom (ss 138, 158, 178, 204 and 205).

So far as the purposes for which warrants may be granted, the 2016 Act provides that:

- a bulk interception warrant may be granted to intercept overseas-related communications or to obtain secondary data from such communications (s 136), secondary data being data attached to or logically associated with the communication (s 137);

- a bulk acquisition warrant may be granted to require the disclosure of any communications data for the operational purposes of the intelligence services as specified in the warrant, and is not confined to overseas persons or activities (s 158(6));[70]

- a bulk equipment interference warrant authorizes the interference with communications equipment (including computers) for communications, equipment data and 'any other information', where the main purpose is to obtain overseas related information (s 176); and

- a bulk dataset warrant authorises the retention of a dataset which the intelligence service in question has 'acquired' by means unspecified (s 199), but which includes personal data relating to a number of individuals, the majority of whom are not, and are unlikely to become, of interest to the service in the exercise of its functions (s 199(1) (a), (b)).

These are highly technical and complex provisions which mask formidable and extraordinary powers of surveillance. In all cases the approval of Judicial Commissioner is required. But quite whether that is enough to allay concerns is another matter, even though the Commissioner is required before giving approval to be satisfied about the necessity and proportionality of the warrant, applying the principles of judicial review as would be applied by a court. Although not expressly stated, the judicial commissioner is also bound to ensure that

---

[65] A good account of the practice and its operation is to be found in the evidence of the security and intelligence services in *Privacy International* v *Foreign Secretary* [2016] UKIPTrib 15_110-CH.

[66] Ibid.

[67] Ibid.

[68] Ibid, para 7.

[69] As made clear in *Privacy International* v *Foreign Secretary*, ibid.

[70] A bulk acquisition warrant may relate to data whether or not in existence at the time of the issuing of the warrant.

Convention rights are respected.[71]

In each of these cases the decision to grant the warrant has to be taken by the minister personally and must be signed by him or her. In cases of urgency, however, warrants may be issued without judicial approval in advance. Should this happen, the approval of a judicial commissioner must be obtained subsequently, but if it is refused there is a right to have the matter reviewed by the Investigatory Powers Commissioner. But if still refused, the improper granting of the warrant will not normally affect the legality of anything done thereunder.[72]

Judicial oversight and role of the courts

Despite the requirement of judicial warrants introduced by the IPA 2016, the system of general judicial oversight has been retained by the 2016 Act. The Investigatory Powers Commissioner (IPC) and the judicial commissioners are appointed by the Prime Minister on the recommendation of the Lord Chancellor and senior judges (s 227).[73] Both the IPC and the commissioners must have held high judicial office, while the IPC alone is responsible for keeping under review ('including by way of audit, inspection and investigation' (s 229)) the exercise by public authorities of various statutory functions and powers, including those under related legislation such as RIPA 2000 and the Police Act 1997, Part III.[74]

Also continuing with established practice, there are tight restrictions on the use of intercepted material in legal proceedings. There should be no disclosure of interception-related content or any evidence that tends to suggest that interception-related conduct may have occurred (s 56). The legislation thus continues to prevent 'the asking of questions suggesting that a warrant to intercept communications has been or is to be issued',[75] so that 'neither the existence of a telephone intercept under warrant nor the result thereof are to be disclosed in evidence'.[76] In this country, 'the content of interceptions may inform police investigations but may not form part of the evidence at any subsequent trial'.[77]

The position under IPA 2016, s 56 compares with evidence obtained from listening devices and other forms of surveillance by the intelligence services and the police, which may be disclosed not only for the purpose of preventing or detecting serious crime, but also for the purpose of criminal proceedings.[78] Although the total exclusion of interception evidence in many cases may benefit the defence,[79] equally there are circumstances where the accused is

---

[71] The commissioner must also ensure that the general duties relating to privacy set out in s 2 of the Act are respected.

[72] See e.g., IPA 2016, s 25. Note also the duty on the part of the IPC to inform a person of any error, but only where the error is serious and reporting would be in the public interest. To be serious, the error must have caused significant prejudice or harm, but the fact that it is a breach of Convention rights is not sufficient to establish that the error is serious. The IPC must publish annually all the errors that have been brought to his or her attention. It is not clear what an error is for these purposes. Does it include a warrant granted but not subsequently approved?

[73] The appointment of judicial commissioners also requires the approval of the Investigatory Powers Commissioner, as well as the Lord Chancellor and senior judges (IPA 2016, s 227).

[74] The IPC has wide powers of investigation, which can be undertaken at his or her own initiative, and may be directed by the Prime Minister (at the request of the Investigatory Powers Commissioner, the Intelligence and Security Committee of Parliament (on which see below), or otherwise) to keep certain matters under review (s 230).

[75] *R v Preston* [1994] 2 AC 130, at p 144 (Lord Jauncey). There are, however, qualifications in IPA 2016, Sch 3 whereby interception material may be disclosed in what are referred to as exceptional circumstances, though these now cover a wide range of legal proceedings, many of which are terrorist related.

[76] *R v Preston*, ibid.

[77] *R v E* [2004] EWCA Crim 1243, [2004] 1 WLR 3279, at p 3289 (Hughes J).

[78] *R v Khan* [1997] AC 558, at 576 (Lord Nolan). See also *R v E*, above.

precluded from relying on evidence of the interception to rebut the case against him or her.[80] Proposals to relax the rules prohibiting the use of interception evidence in criminal prosecutions were vigorously opposed by the Interception Commissioner.[81]

A potentially important form of accountability is lost as a result.

D. Data protection: storing and processing information

The storage and use of information about individuals is an issue which has assumed much greater significance as a result of the computer revolution and the greater capacity now to store and process personal information:

> One of the less welcome consequences of the information technology revolution has been the ease with which it has become possible to invade the privacy of the individual. No longer is it necessary to peep through keyholes or listen under the eaves. Instead, more reliable information can be obtained in greater comfort and safety by using the concealed surveillance camera, the telephoto lens, the hidden microphone and the telephone bug. No longer is it necessary to open letters, pry into files or conduct elaborate inquiries to discover the intimate details of a person's business or financial affairs, his health, family, leisure interests or dealings with central or local government. Vast amounts of information about everyone are stored on computers, capable of instant transmission anywhere in the world and accessible at the touch of a keyboard. The right to keep oneself to oneself, to tell other people that certain things are none of their business, is under technological threat.[82]

But we should not overlook the fact that the storage and use of personal information in different forms had occurred for many years before the invention of the computer. Obvious examples include the files maintained by the intelligence services about people deemed to be politically subversive;[83] the disclosure of medical information to insurance companies and employers;[84] and the blacklisting of trade unionists conducted by organisations sympathetic to employers.

It goes without saying that the common law proved of little value to regulate much of this activity and indeed failed to develop any tools to deal with it. The use of this material did not attract liability for conspiracy to injure,[85] although there might be liability in defamation if the information was distributed – but only if it were untrue. The Security Service Act 1989 provided a limited opportunity for individuals to complain to the tribunal established by that Act about inquiries conducted about them by the security service, and about the disclosure of information 'for use in determining whether [they] should be employed'.[86] These complaints are now made to the Investigatory Powers Tribunal, and it is not known whether any of the very few complaints ever upheld by that tribunal relates to vetting or surveillance by the security service.

----

[79] But there is no restriction on using evidence discovered as a result of interception.

[80] *R* v *Preston* (note 75 above).

[81] Cm 7324, 2008 (proposals by a Committee of Privy Counsellors chaired by Sir John Chilcot), and HC 901 (2008–9), SG/2009/138, para 2.7 (response of the Interception Commissioner). See previously HC 315 (2006–7).

[82] *R* v *Brown* [1996] 1 AC 541, at p 556 per Lord Hoffmann.

[83] See Lustgarten and Leigh, above, ch 5.

[84] See Access to Health Records Act 1990 by which the practice is now regulated, although in a manner which arguably permits access to too much information by employers and insurance companies, albeit with the 'consent' of the individual.

[85] *McKenzie* v *Iron Trades Employers' Insurance Association* 1910 SC 79.

[86] Security Service Act 1989, Sch 1(2) and (3): see Lustgarten and Leigh, above, pp 153–6.

Data Protection Act 1998

Data protection in the United Kingdom has been governed principally by Council Directive 95/46/EC, which provided in art 1 that its objective is to 'protect the fundamental rights and freedoms of natural persons, and in particular their right to privacy with respect to the processing of personal data'. The lengthy recitals to the Directive made clear that it was underpinned by the requirements of the ECHR, art 8,[87] and inspired also by the need to ensure that in the interests of fair competition between member states and the free flow of data, common standards of protection should be applied. In the ambitious words of the first recital, 'data-processing systems are designed to serve man'.

Directive 95/46/EC was implemented in domestic law by the Data Protection Act 1998. The latter replaced the 1984 Act of the same name, which applied only to computer-related data.[88] It has been held that the Directive did not violate Community obligations relating to freedom of expression, and that member states were expected to have regard to freedom of expression considerations when implementing the Directive.[89] At the same time, however, the Act is to be construed in a purposive way to give effect to the Directive,[90] the primary objective of which as we have seen was to protect individuals' fundamental rights, notably the right to privacy and accuracy of their personal data held by others.[91]

Data for the purposes of the 1998 Act are defined as 'information', which is recorded or processed by computer; as well as any other information recorded as part of a relevant filing system.[92] A difficult practical issue in the definition of personal data has been identified by the courts as whether the data 'relate to' an individual, which has been read in effect to mean data about an individual, but not necessarily all data in which an individual was mentioned (despite the recognised fact that a name is itself personal data).[93] It does not mean all data 'in which factual elements relating to a data subject are embedded'.[94] The Act applies to anyone who processes data (both public and private sector),[95] though in the case of public bodies there are overlaps with the Freedom of Information Act 2000.[96]

Some data are described as being 'sensitive personal data', a subset, or a species, of 'personal data',[97] and defined to mean personal data consisting of any of the following information about the data subject: racial or ethnic origin, political opinions, religious belief, trade

---

[87] On the need to comply with which was emphasised in *South Lanarkshire Council* v *Scottish Information Commissioner* [2013] UKSC 55, [2013] 1 WLR 2421.

[88] The following is a necessarily condensed account, which highlights the main features of the Act.

[89] *Case C-101/01, Criminal Proceedings Against Lindqvist* [2004] QB 1014.

[90] *Campbell* v *MGN* [2002] EWCA Civ 1373, [2003] QB 633, Lord Phillips, at para 96. See also *Deer* v *Oxford University* [2017] EWCA Civ 121.

[91] *Durant* v *Financial Services Authority* [2003] EWCA Civ 1746, [2004] FSR 28 (Auld LJ). Also *South Lanarkshire Council* v *Scottish Information Commissioner*, above (Baroness Hale).

[92] A relevant filing system is defined to mean 'any set of information relating to individuals to the extent that, although the information is not processed by means of equipment operating automatically in response to instructions given for that purpose, the set is structured, either by reference to individuals or by reference to criteria relating to individuals, in such a way that specific information relating to a particular individual is readily accessible': Data Protection Act 1998, s 1(1).

[93] See the discussion in *Deer* v *Oxford University*, above, and in *Edem* v *Information Commissioner* [2014] EWCA Civ 92.

[94] Ibid, in *Deer*, referring to the Opinion of Advocate General Sharpston in *Cases C-141/12, C-372/12 YS* v *Minister voor Immigratie* [2015] 1 WLR 609, CJEU.

[95] Processing itself is defined extremely broadly in both the Directive and domestic law; it essentially means any use of the data at all, including simply retaining or storing it.

[96] See above, pp 209–306.

[97] *Common Services Agency* v *Scottish Information Commissioner*, above, para 37 (Lord Hope).

union status, physical or mental health or condition,[98] sexual life, the commission or alleged commission of an offence, and any criminal proceedings brought against him or her (s 2).[99] Where data fall into one of these categories, additional protections are afforded to that data by the legislation. Another key concept in the Act is 'the special purposes'. Defined to mean journalism, artistic purposes or literary purposes (s 3), data held for these purposes enjoy special protection from some of the law enforcement powers considered below.

Underpinning the Act are the eight data protection principles, with which data controllers must comply (s 4(4)). These are set out in Sch 1 as follows: (i) personal data shall be fairly and lawfully processed; (ii) they shall be obtained only for a specified and lawful purpose; (iii) they shall be 'adequate, relevant and not excessive' in relation to the purposes for which they are processed; (iv) they shall be accurate and kept up to date; (v) they shall not be kept longer than necessary for the purpose for which the data are processed; (vi) they shall be processed in accordance with the rights of the data subject; (vii) appropriate measures are to be taken against unauthorised or unlawful processing of personal data; and (viii) they shall not be transferred outside the European Economic Area.

These principles are subject to detailed interpretation in the Act itself and, in the case of the first, it is provided additionally that at least one of the six conditions in Sch 2 must be met. This provides that data are to be processed only if the data subject consents, or if the processing is necessary for one of a number of purposes which include the administration of justice and the exercise of any functions of the Crown, a minister of the Crown or a government department. The other conditions specified are that the processing is necessary for the purposes of a contract to which the data subject is a party; to comply with any legal obligation to which the data controller is subject; to protect the vital interests of the data subject; or for 'the purposes of legitimate interests pursued by the data controller or by the third party or parties to whom the data are disclosed'.[100]

Where the data are 'sensitive personal data', at least one of the eleven conditions in Sch 3 (as amended) must also be met.[101] As might be expected from the more sensitive nature of the data, the Sch 3 conditions (including the additional ones made in secondary legislation) are narrower and more restrictive than those in Sch 2.

Data subjects and data controllers

The first of two key substantive aspects of the Act relate to the rights of the data subject, that is to say the person whose personal data are being stored and used by another. Under the Act

---

[98] On which see *Common Services Agency*, ibid.

[99] See *R (A) v Chief Constable of C* [2001] 1 WLR 461.

[100] This last condition, which is the most commonly used in practice because it is the most generalised, was considered in *South Lanarkshire Council v Scottish Information Commissioner*, above, where it was held that the test of necessity could not be used to defeat a freedom of information application about the general wage levels of the Council's employees, in which no individual employee would be identified. The condition essentially imposes a test of proportionality on the processing of the data controller.

[101] These are (i) the data subject has given 'his explicit consent'; (ii) the processing is necessary for the purposes of exercising any right or duty of the data controller in connection with employment; (iii) the processing is necessary to protect the vital interests of the data subject; (iv) the processing is carried out in the course of the legitimate activities of a non–profit-making association; (v) the information contained in the personal data has been made public as a result of steps deliberately taken by the data subject; (vi) the processing is necessary for purposes relating to legal proceedings; (vii) the processing is necessary for the administration of justice, the exercise of a statutory duty or the exercise of any functions of the Crown, a minister or a government department; (viii) the processing takes the form of the disclosure of sensitive personal data by an anti-fraud organisation and is necessary to prevent fraud; (ix) the processing is necessary for medical purposes and is undertaken by a health professional or another person who owes an equivalent duty of confidentiality; (x) the processing is undertaken for the purpose of ethnic monitoring; and (xi) any other circumstances specified in an order made by the Secretary of State.

the data subject is entitled on request and in writing to be (*a*) informed by any data controller whether any personal data are being processed by the data controller; (*b*) given a description of the personal data and the purposes for which they are being used, as well as the people to whom they may be disclosed; and (*c*) supplied with the information which is being processed and informed of the logic of any decision taken in relation to him or her (such as performance at work) which is based solely on the 'processing by automatic means of personal data' (s 7).[102] This is known as the right of subject access, and such requests are an increasingly common litigation and investigation tool.

This last is designed to protect people excluded credit because of their postal code or workers refused employment or promotion because of psychometric testing. There are a number of exceptions to this subject access request right (particularly where it would necessarily involve disclosing confidential information about another person), and provision is made as to the manner in which the information should be disclosed. In some circumstances, the data subject is entitled by giving notice in writing to require the data controller to stop processing his or her personal data (s 10). Enforcement of these rights of access provisions is by the ordinary civil courts,[103] namely the county court or High Court in England and Wales and the sheriff court or Court of Session in Scotland (s 15).

The second of the two main substantive provisions of the Data Protection Act 1998 relates to the responsibilities of data controllers. Personal data are not to be processed unless the data controller has first registered with the Information Commissioner (s 17), a post created by the Act (s 6), on which see below. Those applying for registration with the Information Commissioner must describe the personal data to be processed, the purposes for which they are to be processed and the persons to whom the data controller intends to disclose the data (s 16). Applicants for registration must also provide a 'general description of measures to be taken for the purpose of complying with the seventh data protection principle' (referred to above) (s 18(2)(b)). There is in addition a duty to notify the Commissioner of any material changes to the practice of the data controller with regard to personal data (s 20). It is an offence to process data without being registered and to fail to notify any relevant changes (s 21).

An individual who suffers damage, as a result of a breach of any of the provisions of the Act by a data controller, is entitled to recover compensation from the latter (s 13). As drafted, s 13 required a two-stage process, whereby compensation for non-pecuniary loss, such as distress, could only be recovered where the data subject could also establish damage in the form of pecuniary loss. Given that in most cases a breach of the Act is likely to be upsetting but will not have caused financial harm, that posed a very significant bar to data subjects vindicating their rights. In *Google Inc* v *Vidal-Hall*,[104] the Court of Appeal held that s 13 had failed properly to give effect to the Directive by imposing such a bar, and had also breached the right to an effective remedy in art 47 of the European Charter of Fundamental Rights. As a result, it struck down the limiting words of s 13(1), although they still appear on the face of the legislation.

Perhaps predictably, there are a number of situations where the Act does not apply or where its application is diluted, in order to allow data controllers to perform their functions and carry on their businesses. There are at least ten such general categories of exempt data, the first of which are data where exemption is required for the purpose of safeguarding national security (s 28). These are exempt from all the data protection principles. A ministerial

---

[102] The motive with which data are sought is irrelevant, and an application may be made not only to check their accuracy but also for a collateral purpose such as litigation: *Deer* v *Oxford University*, above. But the motive could be a factor in refusing a remedy under s 7(9), below.

[103] See DPA, s 7(9), on which see *Dawson-Damer* v *Taylor Wessing* [2017] EWCA Civ 74, and *Deer* v *Oxford University*, above, on the factors to be taken into account by a court in exercising its discretion under s 7(9).

[104] [2015] EWCA Civ 311, [2016] QB 1003.

certificate stating that the exemption is required is enough for this purpose, though any person affected by the issuing of the certificate may appeal to the Administrative Appeals Chamber of the Upper Tribunal (previously the Information Tribunal National Security Appeals Panel) against the certificate (s 28(4)).

In an important decision, the then Information Tribunal – sitting to deal with national security appeals – overruled a blanket certificate of the Home Secretary exempting the Security Service from much of the Act. The Liberal Democrat MP Norman Baker wrote to the Service asking if it was processing personal data of his and if so what such data were. The Service would neither confirm nor deny.

The decision of the Tribunal was confined to the duty of a data controller under s 7(1)(a) of the 1998 Act to inform people from whom a request is made whether or not their personal data are being processed. The Tribunal held that the ministerial certificate was too wide because it would 'exempt the Service from the obligation to respond positively to any request made to it under section 7(1)(a) of the Act, regardless of whether national security would be harmed by a positive response in a particular case'.[105] Following this decision the Home Secretary issued a fresh certificate under s 28 of the 1998 Act, which removed the blanket exemption of the Security Service.

Individuals may now make an application to the Service, which may be refused on the grounds of national security only on a case-by-case basis. The new certificate provides that 'no data shall be exempt from the provisions of section 7(1)(a) of the Data Protection Act 1998 if the Security Service, after considering any request by a data subject for access to relevant personal data, determines that adherence to the principle of neither confirming nor denying whether the Security Service holds data about an individual is not required for the purpose of safeguarding national security'.

However, it has not proved to be any easier for individuals to determine whether the Security Service processes their personal data. In *Hitchens v Home Secretary*,[106] the Information Tribunal dismissed an appeal from a journalist who had asked the Security Service if it processed data about him and for access to the files he believed that it held on him about his time as 'an extreme left-wing student' in the 1970s. The tribunal upheld the Security Service's decision not to confirm or deny whether such files existed.[107]

Special exemptions from various aspects of the Act (affecting both subject access and the duties of the data processor) apply to data processed for the prevention or detection of crime or for the assessment or collection of tax (s 29),[108] and for personal data relating to the physical or mental health of the data subject (s 30). Other exemptions apply to the activities of regulatory bodies (s 31); journalism, literature or art (s 32);[109] research purposes (including historical research) (s 33); and manual data held by local authorities (s 33A). Otherwise there are exemptions for personal data the data controller is obliged to make available to the public by statute (s 34), or disclose by virtue of any legal obligation or court order (s 35). Finally,

---

[105] *Baker v Home Secretary* [2001] UKHRR 1275.
[106] [2003] UKIT NSA 4.
[107] See also *Hilton v Home Secretary* [2005] UKIT NSA 5.
[108] For consideration of the wide scope of s 29, see *Zaw Lin v Metropolitan Police Commissioner* [2015] EWHC 2484 (QB).
[109] This exemption was widely construed by the Court of Appeal in *Campbell v MGN Ltd*, note 90 above. For proposals that it should be more tightly drawn, see HC 779 (2012–13) (Leveson report). The latter report also recommended the removal of other journalistic protections.

there are exemptions to avoid infringing parliamentary privilege (s 35A), for personal data processed for domestic purposes (s 36) and for other miscellaneous purposes (s 37).

> The section 35 exemption was considered by the Supreme Court in *Rugby Football Union* v *Consolidated Information Services Ltd*,[110] where it was said that 'before a Court makes an order requiring disclosure of personal data, which would attract the exemption under section 35(1), it must first take into account and weigh in the balance the right to privacy with respect to the processing of personal data which is protected by article 1(1) of the Directive'.[111]
>
> The issue in the RFU case was effectively whether an order under the Data Protection Act 1998, s 35 was consistent with the EU Charter of Fundamental Rights, art 8. The RFU was concerned that tickets for rugby matches were being sold unlawfully and was granted a court order (a so-called *Norwich Pharmacal* order),[112] to require a ticketing agency to disclose information that would enable the RFU to identify who had been buying and selling tickets in breach of the rules.
>
> The Supreme Court held that the making of such an order did not violate the EU Charter in circumstances where 'the impact that can reasonably be apprehended on the individuals whose personal data are sought is simply not of the type that could possibly offset the interests of the RFU in obtaining that information'.[113] The interest of the RFU lay in finding the identity of people who were buying and selling tickets in stark breach of the terms of the conditions by which it supplied them.

Information Commissioner

Enforcement of the Act is principally by means of the Information Commissioner and the First-tier Tribunal (Information Rights) (formerly the Information Tribunal) (s 6). The Commissioner is a continuation of the office of Data Protection Registrar under the Data Protection Act 1984, and is appointed by the government ('Her Majesty by Letters Patent' according to the statutory form) (s 6); but neither the Commissioner nor his or her staff are to be regarded as Crown servants.[114] Following changes made by the Protection of Freedoms Act 2012, appointments are now for non-renewable fixed terms of up to seven years.

Once appointed, a Commissioner can be removed within the term only after an address from both Houses of Parliament for one of a number of prescribed reasons. The Tribunal in contrast is appointed by the Lord Chancellor, to include a legally qualified chairman and deputy chairmen, as well as persons to represent the interests of data subjects and data controllers respectively. National security cases are now heard by the Administrative Appeals Chamber of the Upper Tribunal, a superior court of record, which consists of three judicial members for these purposes. This replaces the National Security Appeals Panel of the Information Tribunal.[115]

The Commissioner – whose powers were enhanced by the Coroners and Justice Act 2009 – may issue an enforcement notice to a data controller if satisfied that the data controller is breaching the data protection principles (s 40). The notice may require the data controller to

---

[110] [2012] UKSC 55, [2012] 1 WLR 3333.

[111] Ibid, para 25.

[112] *Norwich Pharmacal Co* v *Customs and Excise Commissioners* [1974] AC 133, where the House of Lords recognised the right of a prospective claimant to obtain information in order to seek redress for an arguable wrong: *Rugby Football Union*, above, para 14.

[113] *Rugby Football Union*, above, para 46 (Lord Kerr).

[114] Formally the Information Commissioner is an NDPB: see ch 12 above, esp pp 312–3.

[115] SI 2008 No 2698 (L 15), esp reg 14(10).

take steps specified in the notice or to refrain from conduct specified in the notice. This might include the erasing of inaccurate data. The new provisions of the DPA, s 41A enable the Commissioner effectively to initiate an investigation of government departments and other public authorities by way of an assessment notice, designed to enable the Commissioner to determine whether a data controller has complied or is complying with the data protection principles.

An assessment notice issued under the Data Protection Act 1998, s 41A requires the data processor to permit the Commissioner to enter specified premises and to have access to and copies of specified documents. This is in addition to the original provisions of the DPA, s 42 which permits any person directly affected by the processing of any data to seek an assessment from the Commissioner as to whether the processing is likely to be in accordance with the Act. Where such a request has been made, the Commissioner may serve the data controller with an information notice requiring the data controller to furnish the Commissioner with specified information within a specified time (s 43).

Apart from the power to issue these and other notices (which may be appealed by the recipient to the First-tier Tribunal (Information Rights)), the Commissioner may also apply to a circuit judge or a district judge (magistrates' courts) for a warrant where there are reasonable grounds to suspect that a data controller is contravening the data protection principles or that an offence against the Act has been committed (s 50, Sch 9). No warrant is to be issued in respect of any personal data processed for 'special purposes' except in limited circumstances. Unless in cases of urgency or in order not to defeat the purpose of the entry, a warrant should normally be granted only if the data processor has refused access to the Commissioner.

The Commissioner also has the power to impose monetary penalties on data controllers, where there is a serious and deliberate breach of the data protection principles (s 55A). The maximum amount of such penalty is £500,000. The data controller must be given notice of intent in advance and an opportunity to make representations before the penalty is imposed (s 55B).[116] Prosecutions under the Act may be brought only by the Commissioner or the DPP, and may be tried either summarily or on indictment (s 60). A recent high-profile example was the prosecution and conviction of an individual involved in the blacklisting of trade unionists, for failing to register as a data controller.[117] Despite the wide powers of the Commissioner, concerns have been expressed about enforcement of the Act in practice.[118]

Reform

As we have seen, this is an area of the law that has been greatly influenced by EU law. Apart from the Directive, reference should also be made to the EU Charter of Fundamental Freedoms of 2000, the importance of which was enhanced by the Lisbon Treaty in 2007. Art 8(1) of the Charter provides that 'Everyone has the right to the protection of personal data concerning him or her', with art 8(2) providing further that 'such data must be processed fairly for specified purposes and on the basis of the consent of the person concerned or some other legitimate basis laid down by law'. While it is true that these provisions are not unqualified,[119] they will nevertheless be lost to British law as a result of Brexit.[120]

---

[116] See *Central London Community Healthcare NHS Trust* v *Information Commissioner* [2013] UKUT (AAC) 551 (first exercise of this power). There have now been a substantial number of penalties issued for breach of the Act, most commonly in cases of data breaches or data losses involving large numbers of data subjects. All of the notices issued by the Commissioner are published on her website.
[117] See Ewing, *Ruined Lives*, above. The affair has attracted widespread interest and was the subject of investigation by the Scottish Affairs Select Committee: HC 1071 (2012–13).
[118] See HC 779 (2012–13) (Leveson report).
[119] *Rugby Football Union* v *Consolidated Information Services Ltd* [2012] UKSC 55, [2012] 1 WLR 3333.
[120] For the influence of the Charter on domestic litigation in this area, see *Google Inc*, above.

The importance of EU law as a source of British law is thus overwhelming, its importance reinforced by the requirement that the DPA must be construed consistently with Directive 95/46/EC. This is highlighted by *Google Inc* v *Vidal-Hall*[121] above, where as we have seen, the Court of Appeal found the restriction on damages in the DPA 1998, s 13 (to those who suffered economic loss only), to be in breach of the requirements of the Directive that non-economic loss should be recoverable. Unable to construe domestic law consistently with the Directive by applying the *Marleasing* principle, the Court was of the view that the offending provisions should be disapplied. There will be no more of that in the future.

Directive 95/46/EC is/was repealed with effect from 25 May 2018, being replaced by the General Data Protection Regulation (GDPR),[122] which, as a regulation, will have direct effect pending Brexit. At the time of writing, the government had introduced legislation to give and maintain effect to the GDPR in the form of a Data Protection Bill of some 200 clauses and 18 detailed schedules, to come into force by 25 May 2018, well before Brexit. This will avoid the need to rely upon the EU Withdrawal Bill to maintain the GDPR's effectiveness in domestic law, and its continued application has been agreed by all parties to be essential and positively desirable, given the importance of cross-border data flows to inter-state trade.[123]

Following Brexit, it will be for the UKSC and not the CJEU to resolve any problems of conflict between the GDPR and the Data Protection Bill, once enacted.[124] But as introduced, the Bill is not only unwieldy, it also creates a number of slightly different regimes, including (i) the direct application of the GDPR, (ii) situations to which the GDPR is to be treated as applying, (iii) a parallel but different regime applying to law enforcement agencies, and (iv) a much narrower regime applying to the intelligence agencies.

E. Police databases

The concerns expressed above about the storage and use of information have increased in intensity in recent years as a result of the expansion of databases held by various government departments and other public authorities. These include the National Domestic Extremism Database, the DNA database, the Police National Computer and the NHS patients' database.[125] Databases of these kinds are controversial not least because they tend to emerge without any formal legal authority or statutory mandate, and because there is a lack of confidence that the databases created will be properly managed, or that the information collected about individuals will not be misused.

Otherwise, there are concerns about (i) how and why some people appear on databases, particularly those where entry will carry a stigma or have potentially adverse consequences (such as the Police National Computer), (ii) what use is made of the personal information which may be recorded on databases maintained by government departments (with whom is the information shared and under what conditions?); and (iii) the right of access to the information by the individual whose information is recorded, if only to ensure that there are no mistakes and that any mistakes are corrected.

Here we provide examples of three such databases (with an account of their function), each being progressively less exclusive.

---

[121] Ibid.

[122] Regulation (EU) 2016/679.

[123] On the EU Withdrawal Bill, see ch 6 above.

[124] The government's intention at the time of writing is that the former (UKSC) will not to be bound by the latter (CJEU) in the interpretation of the Regulation.

[125] See HC 153 (2008–9) (Public Accounts Committee).

National Domestic Extremism Database

The existence of the National Domestic Extremism Database came to public attention following the litigation in *Catt* v *Metropolitan Police Commissioner*,[126] where the applicant sought the removal of his personal records from the database. The database is maintained under 'statutory authority', in the sense that the Police Act 1996, s 39 and s 39A authorise the Home Secretary to issue codes of practice relating to policing. A Code of Practice on the Management of Policing Information was issued under this legislation in 2005,[127] along with accompanying guidance to police forces now published by the College of Policing.[128] The catalyst for these developments was not public disorder but the need for the police to improve the management of information, a need identified following the murder of two Soham schoolchildren in 2002.

The Code provides that chief constables and other senior police officers have a duty to 'obtain and manage' information needed for 'police purposes'.[129] The latter term is defined to mean '(a) protecting life and property; (b) preserving order; (c) preventing the commission of offences; (d) bringing offenders to justice; and (e) any duty or responsibility of the police arising from common or statute law'.[130] Apparently under this authority, the NDED has been established to enable the police 'to respond and prevent, reduce and disrupt public disorder and criminal activity associated with 'domestic extremism' and single issue campaigning in England and Wales'.[131] Although there is no definition of 'domestic extremism', it is used by the police 'to describe the activity of individuals or groups who carry out criminal acts of direct action to further their protest campaign, outside the democratic process'.[132]

The NDED was 'maintained by the National Public Order Intelligence Unit (NPOIU) under the command of the National Coordinator for Domestic Extremism (NCDE)', both of which are now 'subsumed' within the National Domestic Extremism Unit (NDEU) under the authority of the Metropolitan Police.[133] According to press reports based on freedom of information requests, there were almost 9,000 people on the database, with information based on 'surveillance techniques, including undercover police, paid informants and intercepts, against political campaigners from across the spectrum'.[134] In the *Catt* case it was held that the entry on the database of the personal details of an 85-year-old political activist – who had never been convicted of any offence – was not a violation of his Convention rights, the Supreme Court holding that the surveillance of protesters was necessary in a democratic society.[135]

DNA database

The Protection of Freedoms Act 2012 introduced important changes to the law relating to the retention of fingerprints and DNA profiles of people who have been arrested by the police but not charged, or who have been charged but acquitted. It was previously the case that once

---

[126] [2012] EWHC 1471 (Admin), [2012] HRLR 23, overruled [2013] EWCA Civ 192, [2013] WLR(D) 108, overruled in turn [2015] UKSC 9.

[127] For a copy of the Code, visit http://www.cleveland.police.uk/downloads/Code_of_Practice_on_MoPI.pdf.

[128] *R (Catt)* v *Metropolitan Police Commissioner* [2015] UKSC 9, para 10.

[129] Home Office, Code of Practice on the Management of Policing Information (2005), para 4.1.1.

[130] Ibid, para 2.2.2.

[131] *Catt* v *Metropolitan Police Commissioner* [2012] EWHC 1471 (Admin), [2012] HRLR 23, para 5.

[132] Ibid.

[133] As explained in *Catt*, ibid, paras 1, 5. Now the National Domestic Extremism and Intelligence Unit: *R (Catt)* v *Metropolitan Police Commissioner* [2015] UKSC 9, para 20.

[134] *The Guardian*, 26 June 2013.

[135] *R (Catt)* v *Metropolitan Police Commissioner* [2015] UKSC 9, overturning the Court of Appeal.

taken, samples and profiles could be retained indefinitely, even in the case of those who were innocent. The *Coalition Programme for Government* included a commitment to 'adopt the protections of the Scottish model for the DNA database', a commitment to change the existing law being required as a result of the decision of the ECtHR in *S and Marper* v *United Kingdom*.[136] There it was held that the English practice at the time of retaining the DNA profiles of anyone arrested or charged with an offence (as well as those convicted) failed to meet the requirements of the ECHR, art 8, the Strasbourg court contradicting the unanimous view of the House of Lords.

The legislation implementing *S and Marper* takes the form of a series of amendments to PACE 1984, in what is a complex regulatory framework. At its simplest, however:

- the DNA profile of someone convicted of a recordable offence may be retained indefinitely;[137]

- where the individual has been charged but not convicted for a 'qualifying' offence (typically serious offences), the profile may be retained for up to three years;[138]

- where the individual has been arrested but not charged with a 'qualifying' offence, the profile may be retained with the approval of the Commissioner for the Retention of Biometric Material.

In this last case, the individual in question has a right to be heard in advance of any decision being made by the Commissioner.

Information about the National DNA Database (NDNAD) is to be found in the annual reports of the Biometrics Commissioner, where a number of concerns have been raised about updating and accessing the database. The reports also reveal that a small number of applications are made to include the data of people arrested but not charged of a qualifying offence. Perhaps most interesting, however, is the context provided by the Commissioner about the number of people whose data are held on the database. In 2016 it was reported that the details of some 4.7 million people were held in England and Wales, with 5.2 million being held nationally. This represents 8 per cent of the population. While the number of new entries is declining year on year (because of the fall in crime and the number of persistent offenders being re-arrested), there were nevertheless 246,400 new profiles added in 2016.[139]

Police National Database

A third prominent database maintained by the state is the Police National Computer. The legal authority for the latter appears to be an obscure subsection in PACE 1984, in a section dealing with the 'fingerprinting of certain offenders'. Thus by virtue of PACE 1984, s 27(4), the Home Secretary 'may by regulations make provision for recording in national police records convictions for such offences as are specified in the regulations'. The regulations apply to (*a*) convictions for, and (*b*) cautions, reprimands and warnings given, in respect of any offence punishable with imprisonment and any offence specified in the Schedule to the National Police Records (Recordable Offences) Regulations 2000 (as amended).[140]

---

[136] [2008] ECHR 1581, (2009) 48 EHRR 50. See subsequently *R (GC)* v *Metropolitan Police Commissioner* [2011] UKSC 21, [2011] 1 WLR 1230. See also *R (RMC)* v *Metropolitan Police Commissioner* [2012] EWHC 1681 (Admin) (retention of photographs).

[137] A 'recordable' offence is one that by virtue of PACE 1984, s 27 is recordable on the national police computer (on which see below).

[138] A 'qualifying' offence is an offence listed in the PACE 1984, s 65A which includes offences such as murder, manslaughter, sexual offences and terrorist offences, but also many others.

[139] Commissioner for the Retention and Use of Biometric Material, *Annual Report* (2016), para 15.

[140] SI 2000 No 1139.

Ironically, the Protection of Freedoms Act 2012 extended the recording of convictions in PACE 1984, s 27(4) to include cautions, reprimands and warnings, thereby giving retrospective effect to provisions in the 2000 regulations for which there was otherwise no authority in primary legislation. As pointed out in the Explanatory Notes to the 2012 Act, the primary purpose of the recording of this information is to enable criminal record checks to be conducted. A procedure for making such checks was established by the Police Act 1997, enabling employers (particularly those whose activity involves employees working closely with children or vulnerable adults) to require checks before engaging people in certain jobs. These checks are now made for employers by the Disclosure and Barring Service (DBS), which is the successor body to the Criminal Records Bureau and the Independent Safeguarding Authority.

As amended in 2005, the Police Act 1997 creates two different kinds of checks. The first are standard criminal record checks which list the recorded offences committed by the individual in question, as well as cautions, reprimands and warnings received. If there are no such offences or other recorded information, this should be stated in the certificate. The second are enhanced criminal record checks, which should include the foregoing matters, but also any other relevant information about the individual held by the police, which the chief officer 'reasonably believes to be relevant' and ought to be provided.[141] In including non-conviction information of this latter kind, the police must have regard to Home Office guidance. These procedures have been introduced principally for reasons of public safety, with the need for effective procedures being highlighted by the Soham murders referred to above.[142]

Protection of the individual

It has been noticed judicially that use of these measures to obtain an enhanced check 'has increased substantially since the scheme was first devised', and that the number of disclosures of information by means of enhanced checks had reached 215,640 for 2007–8 and 274,877 for 2008–9. Moreover, 'not far short of ten per cent of these disclosures [had additional 'relevant information' on them] (17,560 for 2007/2008; 21,045 for 2008/2009)', with 'the release of sensitive information of this kind' in the context of increasing use of the procedure generally being said to be 'a cause of very real public concern'.[143] This is because of the impact on (i) employment opportunities, (ii) the opportunity to engage in unpaid work in the community, and (iii) the opportunity to 'establish and develop relations with others'.

It is not surprising that aspects of the procedure should be found to violate Convention rights, as a result of the disproportionate amount of information required in some cases.[144] On the other hand, in *R(L)* v *Metropolitan Police Commissioner*,[145] the applicant had been offered employment as a primary school assistant, which would involve close contact with children. Although she had no criminal convictions, an enhanced criminal record check revealed that her son had been placed on a child protection register because of neglect and disruptive behaviour at school. The applicant was refused the job, and claimed that the disclosure of this information violated ECHR, art 8. The Supreme Court rejected the argument that art 8 was 'not engaged' in this case, and held that any disclosure would have to be justified under art 8(2).

---

[141] Police Act 1997, ss 113A, 113B. This of course rather begs the question why the police should be holding such information in the first place. See above in relation to the NDED.

[142] See HC 653 (2003–4) (Bichard Report).

[143] *R(L)* v *Metropolitan Police Commissioner* [2009] UKSC 3, [2009] 3 WLR 1056, para 42 (Lord Hope).

[144] *R(T)* v *Greater Manchester Chief Constable* [2013] EWCA Civ 25, [2013] 2 All ER 813 (declaration of incompatibility granted, upheld *R(T)* v *Home Secretary* [2014] UKSC 35, [2014] 3 WLR 96).

[145] [2009] UKSC 3, [2009] 3 WLR 1056.

The Supreme Court also held, however, that questions of compatibility with Convention rights could be assessed within the framework of the existing legislation, which in this case did not need to be declared incompatible with these rights.[146] Notwithstanding the concerns expressed about this procedure, it was nevertheless held on the facts of this case that there was no ground to challenge the decision to release the information about the appellant. Amendments introduced by the Protection of Freedoms Act 2012 now enable individuals to have the inclusion of non-conviction material on an enhanced certificate reviewed by an independent monitor,[147] while further amendments in 2013 reduce the risk of spent convictions being disclosed.[148]

F. Privacy and the press

The emphasis in this chapter so far has been on state interference with privacy. But as already pointed out, private parties may also be responsible for infringing the privacy of individuals. These private parties may include employers, insurance companies and newspaper proprietors.[149]

It is true that some of the antics of the press will be caught by some of the measures already discussed, most notably telephone tapping or phone hacking,[150] which may be an offence unless there is consent under s 3 of the IPA 2016. The use of surveillance devices by journalists will not require authorisation under the RIPA 2000 and may be unlawful if a trespass is involved. But a 'sting' operation – in a hotel bedroom, for example – may take place with the consent of the owner of the property.[151] And as far as data protection is concerned, we have seen that by s 32 the 1998 Act expressly protects journalistic material.

Yet the invasion of privacy and abuse of power by the increasingly multinational newspaper industry has been a concern for many years. Following a high-profile inquiry on press culture, practices and ethics,[152] Sir Brian Leveson reported in 2012 that sections of the press had been acting 'outrageously' in clear breach of their own Press Complaints Commission Code of Practice. Nevertheless, Sir Brian's proposals for a new independent and legally grounded regulator were fiercely resisted by the newspaper industry, which set about reforming its own system of self-regulation, thereby managing again to escape more credible forms of supervision and accountability.

As a result, the government's Leveson-based scheme applies only to a small number of the minnows in the industry, which enjoy an exclusive statutory protection from exemplary damages as a result of their participation.[153]

---

[146] Compare *R(T)* v *Home Secretary* , above, which dealt with different facts.

[147] Police Act 1997, s 117A.

[148] SI 2013 No 1200, giving effect to *R(T)* v *Greater Manchester Chief Constable*, above and considered by the Supreme Court in the appeal above. But for continuing concerns about the rights of the individual whose information is being passed on, see *R(P)* v *Home Secretary* [2017] EWCA Civ 321.

[149] See *McGowan* v *Scottish Water* [2005] IRLR 167, and *Martin* v *McGuiness* 2003 SLT 1424.

[150] On which see HC 375 (2006–7), HC 362 (2009–10), paras 339–495 (dealing largely with the *News of the World*).

[151] *Grobbelaar* v *News Group Newspapers Ltd* [2001] 1 WLR 3024.

[152] HC 779 (2012–13).

[153] Crime and Courts Act 2013, s 34. See *R (News Media Association)* v *Press Recognition Panel* [2017] EWHC 2527 (Admin) – an unsuccessful judicial review of the decision by the PRP to recognize Impress as the regulator. For an account of the Leveson saga, which is simply the latest investigation from which the press have emerged largely unscathed, see P Wragg [2015] PL 290. For previous press scandals, see note 167 below (Calcutt report).

Breach of confidence

The starting point of any discussion of legal liability of the press is the equitable doctrine of breach of confidence.[154] The genesis of the modern action is *Prince Albert* v *Strange*,[155] which related to a number of etchings which the Prince had made of close members of his family. The defendant had obtained a copy of the etchings from an employee of a printer to whom they had been given by the Prince so that they could be reproduced. The Prince secured an injunction to restrain the defendant from exhibiting the etchings. In somewhat tendentious terms, the Lord Chancellor rejected the defendant's claim that he was 'entitled to publish a catalogue of the etchings, that is to say, to publish a description or list of works or compositions of another, made and kept for the private use of that other, the publication of which was never authorised, and the possession of copies of which could only have been obtained by surreptitious and improper means'.[156]

In *Argyll* v *Argyll*,[157] the court restrained the publication of confidential marital secrets and in doing so made clear that 'the court in the exercise of its equitable jurisdiction will restrain a breach of confidence independently of any right of law'. The publication of confidential information can thus be restrained, even though there is no breach of contract or any violation of property rights.[158] Actions for breach of confidence have been brought on a number of occasions since *Argyll* v *Argyll* to restrain confidential information of a wide and varied kind.[159] In one case, it was held that an action could be brought where the defendant disclosed the existence of a sexual relationship between the applicant and another woman (a murder victim) which the applicant had told the defendant in confidence.[160] In another, it was held that a newspaper could be restrained from publishing a story to the effect that two unnamed doctors with AIDS were employed by a particular health authority and were continuing to practise despite their condition.[161]

It has been held that there was a breach of confidence involved in the tapping of the applicant's telephone by a newspaper;[162] but that there was no breach of confidence when it was done by the police investigating criminal offences.[163] Thus although there is a public interest in protecting confidential information, there may be circumstances where a more compelling public interest favours disclosure.[164] As will be discussed below, liability for breach of confidence has evolved quickly in recent years to encapsulate a wider liability for invasion of privacy, which is now likely often to be a feature of cases involving press disclosures of unwanted publicity. There remain circumstances, however, where an action based on the ground of breach of confidence alone may continue to be appropriate,[165] or where the confidential nature of information is itself an important ingredient in action based principally on other grounds.[166]

[154] See Gurry, *Breach of Confidence*, H Fenwick and G Phillipson [1996] CLJ 447 and (2000) 63 MLR 660, and G Phillipson (2003) 66 MLR 726.

[155] (1849) 1 Mac&G 25. See also *Pollard* v *Photographic Co* (1888) 40 Ch D 345.

[156] Ibid, at p 42.

[157] [1967] Ch 302. The protection of confidentiality does not apply to sexual relationships outside marriage in the same way: *A* v *B plc* [2002] EWCA Civ 337, [2003] QB 195.

[158] The ingredients required to establish a breach of confidence are set out in *Coco* v *A N Clark Engineers Ltd* [1969] RPC 41, at p 47, and in *Attorney-General* v *Guardian Newspapers (No 2)* [1990] AC 109, at p 281.

[159] See *Saltman Engineering Co Ltd* v *Campbell Engineering Co Ltd* [1963] 3 All ER 413; *Fraser* v *Evans* [1969] 1 QB 349; *Lion Laboratories Ltd* v *Evans* [1985] QB 526.

[160] *Stephens* v *Avery* [1988] Ch 449. Also *Barrymore* v *News Group Newspapers Ltd* [1997] FSR 600.

[161] *X* v *Y* [1988] 2 All ER 648.

[162] *Francome* v *Mirror Group Newspapers Ltd* [1984] 2 All ER 408.

[163] *Malone* v *Metropolitan Police Commissioner* [1979] Ch 344.

[164] *Attorney-General* v *Guardian Newspapers (No 2)*, note 158 above.

[165] *Napier* v *Pressdram Ltd* [2009] EWCA Civ 445, [2010] 1 WLR 934, and now *R (Ingenious Media Holdings plc)* v *HMRC* [2016] UKSC 54, [2016] 1 WLR 4164.

[166] *Associated Newspapers Ltd* v *Prince of Wales* [2006] EWCA Civ 1776, [2008] Ch 57.

'Reformed' self-regulation

Press self-regulation has undergone several iterations since the creation of the Press Council in 1953, which gave way to the Press Complaints Commission in 1991,[167] replaced in turn by the Independent Press Standards Organisation (IPSO) in 2014 in the wake of Leveson's stinging rebuke to the industry. Established and funded by newspaper publishers, IPSO – which represents the great bulk of the industry and which boycotted the government's post-Leveson scheme – adjudicates on complaints that a newspaper has violated the Editors' Code of Practice, which it is the responsibility of IPSO to enforce.[168]

The Editors' Code – which came into force in 2016 – includes a section on privacy, which is virtually identical to the Code of Practice previously administered by the PCC. The Editor's Code provides as follows:

2 Privacy

(i) Everyone is entitled to respect for his or her private and family life, home, health and correspondence, including digital communications.

(ii) Editors will be expected to justify intrusions into any individual's private life without consent. Account will be taken of the complainant's own public disclosures of information.

(iii) It is unacceptable to photograph individuals, without their consent, in public or private places where there is a reasonable expectation of privacy.

Under the Code, this provision along with others may be overridden in the public interest, which is defined in the Code, to which we return in more detail in Chapter 17 below.

IPSO is not a statutory body and the Editors' Code is not legally enforceable (save perhaps between the newspaper companies who are members and bound as such by contractual obligations). Nevertheless, failure to comply with the Editors' Code (like the PCC Code before it) may have legal effects, in the sense that a court may be more likely to restrain a publication on privacy grounds if the publication in question has failed to follow either the Editors' Code or a corresponding broadcasting code.

The Human Rights Act 1998 provides that courts must give due weight to freedom of expression (s 12(4)) – which they would surely be required to do anyway.[169] But it also provides that in proceedings which relate to journalistic, literary or artistic material, the court must ask – among other matters – whether it would be in the public interest for the material to be published, as well as whether 'any relevant privacy code' has been followed. This is most likely to arise in proceedings to restrain a publication which relates to the private life of the applicant.[170]

If the answer to both questions is 'yes', then the courts are less likely to restrain publication than if the answer is 'no'. In the words of Brooke LJ in *Douglas* v *Hello! Ltd*, when referring to the privacy provisions of the PCC Code: 'A newspaper which flouts cl 3 of the code is likely in those circumstances to have its claim to an entitlement to freedom of expression

---

[167] For background, see Cm 1102, 1990 (Calcutt report), and subsequently Cm 2135, 1993. The Commission had an independent chair as well as independent members and representatives of the national and regional press.

[168] According to the court in *R (News Media Association)* v *Press Recognition Panel*, above, IPSO 'regulated some 2600 newspaper and magazine titles in print and online, approximately 90% by circulation of the UK's national, regional and local press, approximately 80% of the UK's magazine publishers'.

[169] Cf *Douglas* v *Hello! Ltd*, ibid, at p 1004 (Sedley LJ).

[170] As pointed out in a different context in *Marine A* v *Guardian News and Media* [2013] EWCA Crim 2367, issues arise about 'journalists who are not bound by any relevant privacy code (including for example foreign journalists, and publishers of weblogs) or by writers of books on current affairs' (para 67).

trumped by article 10(2) considerations of privacy.'[171] In *AAA* v *Associated Newspapers Ltd*,[172] an injunction was refused in circumstances where there had been compliance with the code.

Compliance with the code cannot be conclusive: the fact that a newspaper has followed the code will not be a decisive factor if, for example, the courts take the view that the code or the way in which it is applied falls short of Convention rights as protected by art 8, or fails to comply with any other legal obligation.[173] Most IPSO complaints are about accuracy rather than privacy, and many complaints are resolved by mediation. Where a complaint is upheld by adjudication, the newspaper may be required to publish the adjudication.

The remedies under the IPSO complaints process are very limited, and indeed a publication of an adjudication that a breach of privacy has taken place may serve only to draw further attention to the hapless complainant.

Misuse of private information

Although the Human Rights Act does not permit an individual to sue a newspaper for a violation of privacy, the Act has nevertheless significantly advanced the cause of those who have argued that self-regulation of the newspaper industry is not a secure enough basis for the protection of privacy.[174] It is true that there is no duty on the part of the courts to 'create a free standing cause of action based on the Convention', but there is nevertheless a duty 'to act compatibly with Convention rights in adjudicating upon existing common law causes of action',[175] leading to claims that the English courts should 'so far as possible, develop the common law in such a way as to give effect to Convention rights', and that 'in this way horizontal effect is given to the Convention'.[176]

Since the Human Rights Act came into force in 2000, there have been a number of high-profile cases brought by 'celebrities' and other people in the public eye challenging the publication in the press of information about their private lives. In dealing with these cases of alleged breach of private life, the courts responded initially by absorbing Convention rights 'into the long established action for breach of confidence'.[177] With the passage of time, however, it appears that a new tort of breach of privacy is emerging under the shadow of the Human Rights Act, which is related to and overlaps with (but is independent of) liability in equity for breach of confidence.[178]

Perhaps the landmark case in this process is the House of Lords decision in *Campbell* v *MGN Ltd*,[179] where a fashion model claimed successfully in part that her privacy had been violated by a newspaper which revealed details of her drug addiction. The House of Lords held that the newspaper had been entitled to disclose that the appellant was a drug addict who was receiving treatment, but not the details of the treatment she was receiving. The

---

[171] *Douglas* v *Hello! Ltd*, above, at p 994. See also *A* v *B plc* [2002] EWCA Civ 337, [2003] QB 195, and now *PJS* v *News Group Newspapers Ltd* [2016] UKSC 26, specifically in relation to IPSO.

[172] [2013] EWCA Civ 554, [2013] WLR (D) 189

[173] See *Venables* v *News Group Newspapers Ltd* [2001] EWHC 32 (QB), [2001] Fam 430.

[174] For a good discussion, see HC 362 (2009–10) (Culture, Media and Sport Select Committee).

[175] *Venables* v *News Group Newspapers Ltd* (note 173 above), at p 446.

[176] *Associated Newspapers Ltd* v *Prince of Wales* [2006] EWCA Civ 1776, [2008] Ch 57, at para 25 (Lord Phillips).

[177] *A* v *B plc*, note 157 above, at para [4] (Woolf LCJ). See G Phillipson (2003) 66 MLR 726.

[178] For a discussion of this issue, see *Mosley* v *NGN* [2008] EWHC 1777 (QB), [2008] EMLR 20. See also R Buxton (2009) 29 OJLS 413.

[179] *Campbell* v *MGN Ltd* [2004] UKHL 22, [2004] 2 AC 457; and subsequently *Campbell* v *MGN Ltd* (No 2) [2005] UKHL 61, [2005] 1 WLR 3394.

House of Lords also held that this conclusion was reinforced by clause 3(i) of the Press Complaints Commission's Code of Practice. In explaining the developing law of confidence, Lord Nicholls said:

> The continuing use of the phrase 'duty of confidence' and the description of the information as 'confidential' is not altogether comfortable. Information about a person's private life would not, in ordinary usage, be described as 'confidential'. The more natural description today is that the information is private. *The essence of the tort is better encapsulated now as misuse of private information.*[180]

Under the guidance of these developments, it was held that the private journals of the Prince of Wales commenting on the handover of Hong Kong to China were confidential and that the *Daily Mail* had acted unlawfully in publishing them. The journals in question had been leaked by a former employee of the Prince, and the Court of Appeal addressed the situation where publication 'involves a breach of a relationship of confidence, an interference with privacy or both', reinforcing the sense that privacy is emerging as a separate but overlapping cause of action.[181] In *Associated Newspapers Ltd* v *Prince of Wales*,[182] the Court of Appeal also emphasised the importance of art 10, a matter given little consideration in the past in determining whether a publication should be restrained on public interest grounds.

Where no breach of a confidential relationship is involved, a balance will have to be struck between art 8 and art 10 rights and 'will usually involve weighing the nature and consequences of the breach of privacy against the public interest, if any, in the disclosure of private information'.[183] Where, however, there is also a breach of confidence involved, this will tilt the balance more in the direction of restraining the publication, as in this case where it was said that 'those who engage employees, or who enter into other relationships that carry with them a duty of confidence, ought to be able to be confident that they can disclose, without risk of wider publication, information that it is legitimate for them to wish to keep confidential'.[184]

The most interesting development in recent years, however, has been the recognition by the Supreme Court that this remarkable legal journey has now reached a fork in the road, in the sense that a claim based on 'the tort of privacy' or 'misuse of personal information' (which appear to be synonyms) is one that attracts greater protection than one based in breach of confidence alone.[185] It was also emphasised that the claim is based on intrusion and distress, so that the fact the information is already in the public domain is not a reason for refusing an injunction to stop any repetition of the distress. In the *RJS* case an injunction was granted to stop the publication of details of the applicant's private life even though the information had been published in newspapers and magazines elsewhere in the world, and was available on the internet:

> (i) there is not, without more, any public interest in a legal sense in the disclosure or publication of purely private sexual encounters, even though they involve adultery or more than one person at the same time, (ii) any such disclosure or publication will on the face of it constitute the tort of invasion of privacy, (iii) repetition of such a disclosure or publication on further occasions is capable of constituting a further tort of invasion of privacy, even in relation to persons to whom disclosure or publication was previously made – especially if it occurs in a different medium.[186]

---

[180] *Campbell* v *MGN Ltd* [2004] UKHL 22, [2004] 2 AC 457, at para 14. Emphasis added. In *Mosley* (above), it was explained that this cause of action applies 'even in circumstances where there is no pre-existing relationship giving rise of itself to an enforceable duty of confidence' (para 7).

[181] See also *Lord Browne* v *Associated Newspapers Ltd* [2007] EWCA Civ 295, [2007] 3 WLR 289; *Mosley* v *NGN Ltd*, above; and *Terry* v *Persons Unknown* [2010] EWHC 119 (QB), [2010] Fam Law 453.

[182] [2006] EWCA Civ 1776, [2008] Ch 57.

[183] Ibid, para 65.

[184] Ibid, para 67.

[185] *PJS* v *News Group Newspapers Ltd* [2016] UKSC 26, para 25

[186] Ibid.

G. Conclusion

By virtue of the Human Rights Act, art 8 is now enforceable in the domestic courts against public authorities.[187] This means that the exercise of different powers referred to in sections B and C of this chapter may now be challenged under the Human Rights Act and indeed that it may be possible to challenge some of the statutory provisions as being incompatible with Convention rights. But although the legislation cannot be presumed to be watertight, it is most unlikely that many challenges will succeed, though it is possible that gaps will continue to be exposed in the regulatory framework for the interception of communications.[188]

There are also unlikely to be many cases where the Human Rights Act will add much in practice to the legal armoury of the individual concerned that powers of surveillance and interception have been improperly exercised. By virtue of their different supervisory roles, senior and retired judges are now directly involved in the supervision and management of the different schemes, with the substance of which they seem broadly content, rarely upholding complaints that the exercise of a power to infringe privacy has been improperly authorised.

The legal powers of government and others relating to the storage and use of information in section D above are about to be substantially revised, but they have so far largely avoided any serious conflict with fundamental rights. This has been less true of the various police databases discussed in section E, where the approach of the courts has been mixed. Moreover, it has not been easy to challenge other powers on privacy grounds, such as sharing NHS data with other government departments,[189] taking photographs of protesters,[190] releasing photographs of suspects[191] or advising the owners of caravan sites about convicted paedophiles.[192]

The weight of any right to privacy derived from the Human Rights Act may have been felt most acutely in the field of private law, to protect the individual's right to privacy from the exercise of private rather than state power, particularly that exercised by the press. But although the HRA has helped to drive important changes to the common law, here too the practical effects should not be exaggerated, the changes seriously inhibited by the costs associated with access to justice, which puts enforcement of these new common law rights well beyond the reach of most victims.

So while we should acknowledge the great steps that have been taken in relation to privacy since the enactment of the Human Rights Act 1998, we should be cautious about its impact in the face of continuing threats by both public and private power, neither of which governments for various reasons seem inclined effectively to contain.

---

[187] See ch 14.

[188] See, e.g., *Liberty v United Kingdom* (2009) 48 EHRR 1 (in relation to the interception of up to 10,000 telephone calls coming from Dublin to London between 1990 and 1997); *R E v United Kingdom* [2015] ECHR 947, (2016) 63 EHRR 2.

[189] *R (W) v Health Secretary* [2015] EWCA Civ 1034, [2016] WLR 698.

[190] *Wood v Metropolitan Police Commissioner* [2009] EWCA Civ 414, [2010] 1 WLR 123 (but unjustifiable retention and storage of photographs may breach Convention rights). See now *R (Catt) v Metropolitan Police Commissioner* [2015] UKSC 9, and *JR38 for Judicial Review (Northern Ireland)* [2015] UKSC 42.

[191] *Hellewell v Derbyshire Chief Constable* [1995] 1 WLR 804 (pre HRA); *JR38 for Judicial Review (Northern Ireland)*, ibid.

[192] *R v North Wales Police Chief Constable, ex p Thorpe* [1999] QB 396 (pre HRA, but ECHR considered).

CHAPTER 17

Right to freedom of expression

The right to freedom of expression, in the words of art 10 of the European Convention on Human Rights, includes freedom to hold opinions 'and to receive and impart information and ideas without interference by public authority and regardless of frontiers'. This freedom is fundamental to the individual's life in a democratic society.[1] In the first place, it has a specific political content. The freedom to receive and express political opinions, both publicly and privately, is linked closely with the freedom to organise for political purposes and to take part in free elections:

> Without free elections the people cannot make a choice of policies. Without freedom of speech the appeal to reason which is the basis of democracy cannot be made. Without freedom of association, electors and elected representatives cannot bind themselves into parties for the formulation of common policies and the attainment of common ends.[2]

So does freedom of expression closely affect freedom of religion.[3] Lawyers remember *Bushell's* case in 1670 as having established the right of the jury to acquit an accused 'against full and manifest evidence' and against the direction of the judge: they should also remember that Bushell was foreman of the jury which acquitted the Quakers William Penn and William Mead on charges of having preached to a large crowd in a London street contrary to the Conventicle Act.[4] Moreover, liberty of expression is an integral part of artistic, cultural and intellectual freedom – the freedom to publish books or produce works of art, however disconcerting they may be to the prevailing orthodoxy.[5]

A. The nature of legal protection

Rights and restraints

It has been said that freedom of expression is a 'sinew of the common law'.[6] Individuals are thus free to speak and write what they like, provided that what they say is not otherwise unlawful. In addition, the law of parliamentary privilege provides protection for proceedings in Parliament,[7] and there is a growing body of legislation that in different ways

---

[1] For a compelling statement, see *R* v *Shayler* [2002] UKHL 11, [2003] 1 AC 247, at para [21].

[2] Jennings, *Cabinet Government*, p 14. See also Laski, *A Grammar of Politics*, ch 3.

[3] The right to freedom of religion is separately protected by ECHR, art 9 and in an increasingly secular society raises new questions about freedom of religious expression: see *R (National Secular Society) v Bideford Town Council* [2012] EWHC 175 (QB), [2012] 2 All ER 1175 (local authority no power to say prayers at council meetings). See now Local Government (Religious etc Observances) Act 2015.

[4] *R* v *Penn and Mead* (1670) 6 St Tr 951.

[5] See also *R* v *Home Secretary, ex p Simms* [2000] 2 AC 115, at p 126, per Lord Steyn. For a good account of some of the issues discussed in this chapter, see Barendt, *Freedom of Speech*.

[6] *R* v *Advertising Standards Authority, ex p Vernons* [1993] 2 All ER 202 (Laws J). For a good if random example of its influence in this sense, see *Rhodes* v *OPO* [2015] UKSC 32.

[7] See ch 9. But the protection of parliamentary privilege may be lost if comments in Parliament are repeated outside: *Buchanan* v *Jennings* [2004] UKPC 36, [2005] 1 AC 115. See further pp **482–3** below.

promotes and protects free speech in its widest sense. A statutory right to information is to be found in the Data Protection Act 1998 and the Freedom of Information Act 2000.[8] Both of these measures aid the work of the investigative journalist, whose role has been acknowledged judicially.[9]

Also important is the Contempt of Court Act 1981, s 10, which protects the journalist from having to reveal his or her sources, although as discussed in Chapter 13 above, this provision has been narrowly construed against the journalists by the courts.[10] It was also shown little respect by the Foreign Affairs Select Committee in 2003, when it was interrogating the journalist Andrew Gilligan about the sources for his report that government documents relating to the Iraq war had been 'sexed up'.[11] In addition to the foregoing, the Public Interest Disclosure Act 1998 provides a limited protection for 'whistleblowers', that is to say workers who bring into the public domain serious concerns about the conduct of their employer's business.[12]

It remains the case nevertheless that freedom of expression is subject to a wide range of restrictions, many of which are long-standing. These restrictions are of two kinds: the first is censorship or prior restraint of material by state authorities before it is published or displayed. Restrictions of this kind have often been viewed with great suspicion, and have been strongly deprecated by the US Supreme Court in cases arising under the free speech guarantee in the First Amendment. Yet despite Blackstone's insistence that free speech meant 'laying no previous restraints upon publication',[13] there have been concerns about censorship in Britain,[14] while the use of injunctions and so-called 'super-injunctions' to restrain publications has seen a controversial revival in recent years.

So far as restrictions of the second kind are concerned, these take the form of the imposition of penalties or the granting of redress in the case of someone specifically harmed by the material, after the event. There is a wide range of criminal offences which restrict free speech. These offences exist to protect public order; to protect public morality by punishing the publication of obscene material; and by virtue of the law on contempt of court, to maintain the authority and impartiality of the judiciary. Restrictions imposed by the recently reformed law of defamation exist to protect the rights and reputations of others, while the developing law on breach of confidence may help to protect the privacy of individuals from unwanted intrusion.

Human Rights Act

The right to freedom of expression has been formally strengthened by the Human Rights Act 1998, although even before the enactment and coming into force of this measure, the right to freedom of expression was winning a new prominence in the case law, being supported by a

---

[8] See chs 16 and 11 respectively.

[9] *Loutchansky* v *Times Newspapers Ltd* [2001] EWCA Civ 536, [2002] QB 321. Compare *Hayes* v *Willoughby* [2013] UKSC 17, [2013] 1 WLR 935 (esp per Lord Reed).

[10] Note also the limited protections for journalistic material in the Police and Criminal Evidence Act 1984 (ch 15), and the Investigatory Powers Act 2016 (ch 16).

[11] HC 1044 (2002–3).

[12] See J Gobert and M Punch (2000) 63 MLR 25; and Hobby, *Whistleblowing and the Public Interest Disclosure Act 1998*. There are, however, serious concerns about the lack of protection for whistleblowers in the NHS in particular. See HC 898 (2012–13) (Francis Report).

[13] *Commentaries*, 9th edn, IV, p 151.

[14] The classic legal study of censorship is O'Higgins, *Censorship in Britain*.

number of powerful judicial dicta and extra-judicial statements.[15] It is true that the bold assertion of freedom of expression in art 10 of the ECHR is subject

> to such formalities, conditions, restrictions or penalties as are prescribed by law and are necessary in a democratic society, in the interests of national security, territorial integrity or public safety, for the prevention of disorder or crime, for the protection of health or morals, for the protection of the reputation or rights of others, for preventing the disclosure of information received in confidence, or for maintaining the authority and impartiality of the judiciary.

In this sense freedom of expression is the most heavily qualified of all the Convention rights, paradoxically perhaps in light of Lord Steyn's acknowledgement of freedom of expression as 'the lifeblood of democracy'.[16]

Nevertheless, the Human Rights Act contains special protection in the sense that no remedy is to be granted which affects the exercise of the Convention right to freedom of expression without ensuring that the respondent has been notified of the proceedings and given an opportunity to reply (s 12(2)).[17] This is particularly important in the context of an application for an interim injunction to restrain a publication. So too is the parallel requirement that interim relief is not to be granted before a trial 'unless the court is satisfied that the applicant is likely to establish that publication should not be allowed' (s 12(3)).[18] In all cases 'the court must have particular regard to the importance of the Convention right to freedom of expression' (s 12(4)).[19]

But the courts seem to have taken a cautious approach to these provisions, which are said not to require them 'to treat freedom of expression as paramount'.[20] In fact the Human Rights Act has made only a limited impact in the field of freedom of expression, despite the very robust judicial dicta in its defence to which we have already referred. Part of the reason for this limited impact is that 'the courts emphasised the importance of freedom of expression or speech long before the enactment of the 1998 Act'.[21] Indeed, a number of important decisions have been taken in recent years to extend the boundaries of free speech quite independently of the Human Rights Act (although clearly within its shadow),[22] but perhaps not as far as many would like.

Another reason has been the willingness on the part of the courts to have the fullest regard for the rights and freedoms of others.[23] So we find that the rights of the press – and others – have been subordinated to the demands of copyright, defamation, 'public morality', national security, and confidentiality. Indeed, as discussed in Chapter 16, the Act may have helped fashion a new restraint on press freedom by encouraging the development of an enforceable right to privacy on the back of the equitable doctrine of breach of confidence. These developments reflect an appreciation on the part of the judges that large newspapers can be engines of oppression, an appreciation most vividly expressed in Sir Brian Leveson's inquiry into the culture, practices and ethics of the press.[24]

---

[15] See *Reynolds* v *Times Newspapers Ltd* [2001] 2 AC 127, *McCartan Turkington Breen* v *Times Newspapers Ltd* [2001] 2 AC 277, *Loutchansky* v *Times Newspapers Ltd*, above, and *R* v *Shayler*, above.

[16] *R* v *Home Secretary, ex p Simms* [2000] 2 AC 115, at p 126.

[17] This does not apply where an application is made under the Contempt of Court Act 1981, section 11 to allow a name or other matter to be withheld from the public in proceedings before the court: *A* v *BBC* [2014] UKSC 25. On the 1981 Act, see ch 13 above.

[18] On the operation of this provision, see *BHAM* v *Person or Persons Unknown* [2017] EWHC 644 (QB), where there is also a discussion of some of the leading cases on freedom of expression.

[19] See ch 14 above.

[20] *Imutran Ltd* v *Uncaged Campaigns Ltd* [2001] 2 All ER 385, at p 391.

[21] Ibid.

[22] For example, *Reynolds* v *Times Newspapers Ltd* [2001] AC 127.

[23] As illustrated by *R (Pro-Life Alliance)* v *BBC* [2003] UKHL 23, [2004] 1 AC 185.

[24] HC 779 (2012–13).

B. Prior restraint: censorship and ownership

Censorship

For many years dramatic and operatic performances in Great Britain were subject to the prior censorship of the Lord Chamberlain, an officer of the royal household. The Theatres Act 1968 abolished the requirement that plays should receive a licence before being performed (s 1).[25] In place of censorship, rules against obscenity similar to those in the Obscene Publications Act 1959 are applied to the performance of plays (s 2), subject to a defence of public good (s 3). Other criminal restraints placed on theatrical performances are in respect of the use of threatening, abusive or insulting words or behaviour intended or likely to stir up racial hatred,[26] or occasion a breach of the peace.[27]

Prosecutions for these various offences, including obscenity, require the consent of the Attorney General in England and Wales, though there have been proposals to transfer this responsibility to the DPP or some other public official.[28] Unusually, the Theatres Act 1968, s 2(3) prescribes that 'proceedings on indictment for presenting or directing an obscene performance cannot be commenced more than two years after the commission of the offence'.[29] In addition, there may be no prosecution at common law for any offence the essence of which is that a performance of a play is 'obscene, indecent, offensive, disgusting or injurious to morality'; nor may there be prosecutions under various statutes relating to indecency (1968 Act, s 2(4)), an important safeguard against moral censorship.

Censorship of films originated unintentionally with the Cinematograph Act 1909, which authorised local authorities to license cinemas in the interests of public safety, mainly against fire. In fact, with the approval of the courts,[30] local authorities extended the scope of licensing to other matters to include the approval of the films shown in licensed cinemas.[31] In the Cinematograph Act 1952, and more recently in the Cinemas Act 1985, Parliament confirmed the power of local authorities to license the films shown and required licensing authorities to impose conditions restricting children from seeing unsuitable films. The main work of censorship of films is undertaken by the British Board of Film Classification, a non-statutory body set up by the film industry, with the approval of central and local government.

The board is responsible for the classification of films with special reference to the admission of young children and others under 18. Although a licensing authority normally allows the showing of films that have been classified by the board (which was established to promote uniformity in classification practices throughout the country), the authority may not transfer its functions and must retain power to review board decisions.[32] Thus it may refuse a local showing to a film classified by the board; it may vary a classification; or it may grant permission to a film refused a certificate. Powers of local censorship are not popular with the film industry, but a case can be made for maintaining some local variation in issues of public morality.

---

[25] For the background, see HC 503 (1966–7). See also Findlater, *Banned!*

[26] Public Order Act 1986, s 20.

[27] Theatres Act 1968, s 6.

[28] Private prosecutions may be launched on other grounds, as in 2007 when a private prosecution for blasphemy was brought unsuccessfully by a Christian group in relation to 'Jerry Springer – the Opera'. Blasphemy has since been abolished. See below, p 469.

[29] *R v J* [2004] UKHL 42, [2005] 1 AC 562, at para 55.

[30] *LCC v Bermondsey Bioscope Ltd* [1911] 1 KB 445.

[31] See generally, Hunnings, *Film Censors and the Law*; Williams Report on Obscenity and Film Censorship, Cmnd 7772, 1979.

[32] *Ellis v Dubowski* [1921] 3 KB 621; *Mills v LCC* [1925] 1 KB 213.

The Video Recordings Act 1984 established a scheme for the censorship of video recordings,[33] under which it is an offence to supply (whether or not for reward) any recording for which no classification certificate has been issued (s 9). Certain recordings are exempt from this requirement (such as those concerned with sport, religion or music and those designed to be educational) (s 2), and so are certain kinds of supply (s 4). A video work may not, however, be an exempted work if to any extent it depicts or is designed to encourage such matters as sexual or violent activity (s 2(2)).[34] Nor is it exempt if to any extent it depicts criminal activity which is likely to any significant extent to stimulate or encourage the commission of an offence (s 2(3)).

Classification is conducted by the British Board of Film Classification, which may certify that a video work is suitable for general viewing, suitable only for persons over the age of 18,[35] or that it is to be supplied only in a licensed sex shop.[36] Although not an enforcement agency, the BBFC's website reveals that it assists public authorities concerned with the illegal supply of videos, and also plays a part in the enforcement of the Video Recordings Act 1984, working with local enforcement agencies (such as trading standards officers) for this purpose. The main concerns here are the sale of material to people under the age of 18, the distribution and sale of unclassified material, and the unauthorised sale of restricted material in an unlicensed sex shop.

There is no censorship of the internet, though the Digital Economy Act 2017 introduced restrictions designed to control access by children to pornographic material. These provisions are discussed below.

Ownership and self-regulation

The historic freedom of the press means that, subject to the civil and criminal restraints on publication which will be considered later, any person or company may publish a newspaper or magazine without getting official approval in advance, provided they have the financial means to do so. For economic reasons, this liberty is unlikely to be exercised effectively on a national basis except by a very few newspaper publishers. Fears of a movement towards monopoly conditions in sectors of the press led to the enactment of provisions to ensure that newspaper mergers above a certain scale did not take place in a manner contrary to the public interest.

This is not so much a restraint as a device to ensure diversity in opinion, and is a problem compounded by the same global companies playing a large part in both the television and newspaper industries. In the interests of diversity, it is important to ensure that there is not over-concentration of media ownership in a few hands, and important also to ensure that private media owners do not misuse the considerable power that ownership bestows. Britain has not, however, followed the route of some countries (notably Sweden) by subsidising newspaper owners in order more actively to promote competition and diversity.[37]

The current regulatory regime is now to be found in the Enterprise Act 2002, which was extended with modifications to media mergers by the Communications Act 2003. This replaced the procedure that operated under the Fair Trading Act 1973. Media mergers may involve advice, assessment and judgment by the Office of Communications (OFCOM)

---

[33] The Act was unusually repealed and revived in its entirety by the Video Recordings Act 2010 (without amendment), to comply with overlooked obligations under EU law.

[34] See *Kent CC v Multi Media Marketing*, *The Times*, 9 May 1995.

[35] On which see *Tesco Stores Ltd v Brent London Borough Council* [1993] 1 WLR 1037.

[36] For the procedures adopted by the Board, see *Wingrove v UK* (1996) 24 EHRR 1. For appeals to the Video Appeals Committee, see S Edwards [2001] Crim LR 305. On the implications of judicial review, see C Munro [2006] Crim Law Rev 957.

[37] Questions of media concentration and competition are discussed in HC 779 (2012–13) (Leveson report). See also HL Paper 122 (2007–8).

and the Competition and Markets Authority (previously the Competition Commission),[38] and ultimately a merger may be blocked or modified by the Secretary of State on public interest grounds. These grounds relate to the need for accurate presentation of news in newspapers, free expression of opinion in newspapers, and a sufficient plurality of views in the newspaper market.[39]

The operation of these measures gives rise to acute political difficulty from time to time, with the demands of politically powerful media proprietors often putting ministers in uncomfortable positions. Perhaps as a result, the British newspaper industry remains heavily concentrated in the hands of a few proprietors with four principal newspaper publishers dominating both the daily and Sunday circulation. While they play an important role probing the conduct of government, it is not to be forgotten that most newspapers are commercial enterprises whose first duty is one arising under private law to maximise shareholder return. Press demands for special regulatory immunity should always be treated with caution.

Since 1953 newspaper proprietors have accepted a measure of self-regulation to deal with abuse on the part of their editors and journalists. The Press Complaints Commission was created in 1991, to replace the Press Council, the Commission being funded by a voluntary levy of newspaper and magazine publishers. Apart from the independent chair, the Commission included members with no press connections, as well as senior editors drawn from the national and regional newspapers and magazines. Its primary responsibilities included the handling of complaints of alleged violations of the Code of Practice which was published in 1991 (by the newspaper industry) to regulate its conduct on a range of matters dealing mainly with accuracy and privacy.

Following a number of highly publicised abuses, in 2012 Sir Brian Leveson proposed a new regulatory model. While sympathetic to the principle of press self-regulation, Sir Brian reported that a new body should be established by the industry, but that it should be independent and underpinned by statute.[40] Accepting the need for change, the government proposed a variation, in the shape of a regulatory body established by royal charter rather than statute, with powers to award fines but with an immunity for participating newspapers from exemplary damages.[41] As discussed in Chapter 16, however, the newspaper industry boycotted the government scheme with impunity, and rebranded the Press Complaints Commission as the Independent Press Standards Organisation.[42]

C. Regulation of television and radio[43]

The BBC

In the case of broadcasting, technical reasons have so far prevented access being open to all comers as in the case of the press. Even if all broadcasting were to be provided by privately owned companies, it would still be necessary for a regulatory agency to allocate channels and frequencies to them. Until 1954, the British Broadcasting Corporation enjoyed a public

---

[38] See OFCOM, *Measurement Framework for Media Plurality* (2015).

[39] Enterprise Act 2002, s 58(2A) and (2B), as inserted by the Communications Act 2003. See *British Sky Broadcasting Group plc* v *Competition Commission* [2010] EWCA Civ 2, [2010] 2 All ER 97.

[40] HC 779 (2012–13).

[41] Crime and Courts Act 2013, s 34 et seq. In addition, the royal charter is subject to change only if both Houses of Parliament approve a draft of the change, in each case with the support of two-thirds of those voting.

[42] See *R (News Media Association)* v *Press Recognition Panel* [2017] EWHC 2527 (Admin).

[43] Barendt, *Broadcasting Law*; Craufurd Smith, *Broadcasting Law and Fundamental Rights*.

monopoly of all broadcasting in the United Kingdom, and it still provides a large share of broadcasting services. The BBC is a corporation set up by royal charter and it operates under the strategic direction of the BBC Board.

The BBC's charter was renewed in 2017 for a period of ten years,[44] together with a new agreement between the corporation and the government whereby the broadcaster is subject to a number of duties.[45] These are similar in terms to those imposed on the commercial broadcasters by legislation. The charter is debated by both Houses of Parliament before it is granted by the Queen in Council, though it is open to question whether the BBC should be regulated by legislation rather than royal prerogative.[46] In terms of income, the BBC is mainly financed by a grant from the exchequer, based on the net revenue of television licence fees, though the structure of the BBC seeks generally to maintain its independence of the government of the day.

The BBC has a number of public purposes set out in the Royal Charter, including a duty to provide 'accurate and impartial news, current affairs and factual programming', which includes the 'championing of freedom of expression'. The charter requires the Corporation to act in the 'public interest', observe high standards of openness and seek to maximize transparency and accountability; and exercise 'rigorous stewardship of public money' in accordance with principles in the charter. Otherwise the BBC is subject for the first time to regulatory supervision by OFCOM,[47] and to financial scrutiny – including value for money inquiries – by the Comptroller and Auditor General.

For reasons of defence or in circumstances of emergency, the government may request the BBC to broadcast certain specified material, and may also request that it does not broadcast other specified material, requests which under the terms of the agreement must be met. Apart from these specific powers, the government may not control the BBC's programmes, although it may bring great pressure to bear, and disputes may erupt between the government and the BBC, as in 2003 when the government vigorously contested a claim by a BBC journalist that it had deliberately exaggerated Saddam Hussein's weapons capabilities in the run up to the invasion of Iraq in that year.[48]

Commercial television and radio

Television and radio services financed by advertising are now governed by the Broadcasting Acts 1990 and 1996, and by the Communications Act 2003. The Office of Communications (OFCOM) is the regulatory authority, replacing a number of bodies which previously performed a regulatory role, including the Independent Television Commission and the Broadcasting Standards Commission. As such, OFCOM is one of a growing number of regulators operating in British public life with what is by now a familiar mixture of roles and responsibilities, sometimes performing duties (such as the issuing and renewal of licences) that in the past were the responsibility of the Secretary of State.[49]

---

[44] Cm 9365, 2016.

[45] Cm 9366, 2016.

[46] See HC 82 (2004–5) (Culture, Media and Sport Committee).

[47] Under the BBC Licence and Agreement, OFCOM is required to 'prepare and publish an Operating Framework which must contain provisions OFCOM consider appropriate to secure the effective regulation of the activities of the BBC as set out in the Charter and this Agreement'. This is an interesting (and perhaps unique) example of a statutory body (OFCOM) being directed by a prerogative instrument (the BBC Licence and Agreement) addressed principally to a third party (BBC).

[48] See Lord Hutton, Report of the Inquiry into the Circumstances Surrounding the Death of Dr David Kelly, CMG (2004).

[49] ch 12 above.

OFCOM is required to ensure the 'availability throughout the United Kingdom of a wide range of television and radio services which (taken as a whole) are both of high quality and calculated to appeal to a variety of tastes and interests'.[50] It is also required to ensure that there is a 'sufficient plurality of providers of different television and radio services', as well as the application of standards to protect the public from the inclusion of 'offensive and harmful material' in broadcasting services.[51] These obligations are in addition to the duty to ensure that standards are in place to provide adequate protection to the public 'and all other persons' from both unfair treatment in programmes and unwarranted infringements of privacy by broadcasters.[52]

Curiously, OFCOM has only an oblique statutory duty to promote or uphold the right to freedom of expression, and indeed many of the foregoing duties are about restraints on free speech. But as a public authority, OFCOM is clearly bound by the obligations of the Human Rights Act and art 10 of the ECHR. OFCOM is, however, required to produce a code to promote certain statutory standards objectives to be included in both television and radio services. There are twelve standards objectives covering programme content, including a requirement of impartiality on matters of political or industrial controversy, a requirement that news is reported with 'due accuracy', and a requirement that the public are protected from harmful and offensive material.[53]

The main restraint on advertising relates to political advertising. This is widely defined to mean (*a*) an advertisement inserted by or on behalf of a political organisation; (*b*) an advertisement directed towards a political end; or (*c*) an advertisement that has a connection with an industrial dispute.[54] Licence holders are required to comply with the standards code and OFCOM is required to establish procedures to deal with complaints that the standards have been breached.[55] OFCOM also has the duty to ensure that licence holders comply with the fairness code issued under the Broadcasting Act 1996,[56] an obligation transferred to OFCOM by the 2003 Act.[57] There is now a single code, which deals with both standards and fairness.[58]

Broadcasting Code

OFCOM's Broadcasting Code – which applies in part to the BBC as well as the other broadcasters – is designed to balance the broadcasters' rights to freedom of expression with various rights of viewers and listeners (as well as programme participants and subjects). The code thus purports to set boundaries for the broadcaster, including those which relate to (*a*) standards, and (*b*) fairness. The standards' requirements amplify the matters specified in the legislation and give guidance on protecting young people, on protecting all members of the public from harmful and offensive material, and on ensuring that material likely to encourage disorder or crime is not included in broadcasts.

The guidance also seeks to ensure that broadcasters exercise responsibility in dealing with religion, and it indicates what is needed to comply with obligations relating to due impartiality.

[50] Communications Act 2003, s 3(2)(c).

[51] Ibid, s 3(2)(d) and (e).

[52] Ibid, s 3(2)(f).

[53] Ibid, s 319.

[54] Ibid, s 321 (*R (Animal Defenders' International)* v *Secretary of State for Culture, Media and Sport* [2008] UKHL 15, [2008] 1 AC 1312; *Animal Defenders International* v *United Kingdom* [2013] ECHR 1362 (GC), (2013) 57 EHRR 21). On political advertising, see ch 7 above.

[55] Communications Act 2003, s 325.

[56] Ibid, s 326.

[57] Ibid, Sch 1, para 14.

[58] OFCOM, *Broadcasting Code* (2017).

A separate chapter on elections and referendums reminds the broadcasters about various legal obligations but also advises them that due weight must be given to 'the coverage of parties and independent candidates during the election period'. It is further provided that in determining the appropriate level of coverage to be given to parties and independent candidates, 'broadcasters must take into account evidence of past electoral support and/or current support'.

So far as the fairness provisions are concerned, these emphasise the need to deal fairly with contributors to programmes and the need to obtain 'informed consent' from those who take part. This means that contributors should be told 'the nature and purpose of the programme, what the programme is about and be given a clear explanation of why they were asked to contribute'. It is also provided that guarantees about confidentiality and anonymity 'should normally be honoured'. A related chapter of the Code on privacy provides that any breach of privacy must be warranted, and if the reason for breach of privacy is based on the public interest, the broadcaster must be able to demonstrate that the public interest outweighs the right to privacy.

Anyone affected by an alleged breach of the fairness or privacy provisions of the Code (or anyone authorized on their behalf), may complain to OFCOM. Complaints may be made by legal as well as natural persons, a court taking the view that 'A company does have activities of a private nature which need protection from unwarranted intrusion'.[59] OFCOM may refuse to entertain a fairness complaint relating to unjust or unfair treatment if the person making the complaint does not have sufficiently direct interest.[60] Other restrictions on complaints mean that they cannot be considered where the matter complained of is the subject of court proceedings, or if it appears to OFCOM that the person affected has a remedy by way of legal action in a court of law.[61]

Role of the courts

A few attempts have been made to challenge broadcasting content in the courts. A difficulty with the BBC, however, is that it was established under the prerogative and, at least until the *CCSU* case,[62] it was unclear to what extent those exercising power under the prerogative were subject to judicial review. As late as 1983, the High Court in Northern Ireland was unwilling to enforce the BBC's policy of political impartiality in an action brought by the Workers' Party contesting election broadcasting.[63]

It is now well accepted, however, that the BBC is subject to judicial review.[64] So in *Houston* v *BBC*,[65] an interim interdict was granted to restrain the corporation from broadcasting in Scotland an extended interview with the Prime Minister three days before the local government elections. It was held that the pursuers had established a prima facie case that the broadcast would violate the BBC's duty, under the terms of its licence, to treat controversial subjects with due impartiality and that the programme should not be broadcast until after the close of the poll. The BBC is a public authority for the purposes of the Human Rights Act, so that it not only enjoys Convention rights, but also must respect the Convention rights of others.

---

[59] See *R* v *Broadcasting Standards Commission, ex p BBC* [2001] QB 885.

[60] Broadcasting Act 1996, s 111. Cf *R* v *Broadcasting Complaints Commission, ex p Channel Four Television, The Times*, 6 January 1995 (the term 'direct interest' had to be broadly construed, even if it meant that 'too many complaints' would be made). But cf *R* v *Broadcasting Complaints Commission, ex p BBC, The Times*, 24 February 1995 (complaint by National Council for One Parent Families refused on the ground that it did not have a sufficiently direct interest in a *Panorama* programme which was said to build up a false picture of lone parents by using misleading and false information).

[61] Broadcasting Act 1996, s 114.

[62] *Council of Civil Service Unions* v *Minister for the Civil Service* [1985] AC 374. See ch 10 above

[63] *Lynch* v *BBC* [1983] NILR 193.

[64] *R (Pro-Life Alliance)* v *BBC* [2003] UKHL 23, [2004] 1 AC 185.

[65] 1995 SLT 1305. See also *R* v *BBC, ex p Referendum Party, The Times*, 29 April 1997.

In *R (Pro-Life Alliance) v BBC*[66] the broadcasting authorities refused to carry the pictures of a party election broadcast which had been submitted by the Alliance. The broadcast contained 'prolonged and deeply disturbing' images of an aborted foetus which the broadcasters believed to be contrary to their obligations to maintain taste and decency. It was argued for the Alliance in legal proceedings that this 'censorship' of the broadcast by the broadcasters violated art 10 of the ECHR. In reversing a decision of the Court of Appeal, the House of Lords (by a majority) disagreed, with Lord Hoffmann in a robust speech expressing the view that it is not unreasonable to require political parties to comply with standards of taste and decency which are 'not particularly exacting'.

In contrast to the position of the BBC, there has never been much scope for disputing that – as statutory bodies – the commercial television and radio sector is subject to judicial review. This would be particularly true of the regulatory authorities such as OFCOM and its predecessor bodies such as the Independent Television Authority and the Independent Broadcasting Authority. But although the IBA like everyone else was required to observe the law, and although the IBA's decisions were subject to judicial review, the courts did not show a desire to assume the role of censor.[67] A similar restraint has been shown in the (now many) cases brought to challenge party election broadcasts (more fully explained in Chapter 7 D), and more recently the operation of the statutory restrictions on political advertising,[68] although there are exceptions to such restraint.[69] As already indicated, regulatory bodies such as OFCOM are public authorities for the purposes of the Human Rights Act 1998.

Turning from the regulators in the commercial sector, (unlike the BBC) it is unlikely that the commercial broadcasters will be the subject of judicial review. There are nevertheless cases where the television or radio company itself may be the subject of legal proceedings on other grounds, and they would almost certainly be open to challenge were they to flout statutory or common law duties.

In *R v Central Independent Television plc*[70] the respondents were due to broadcast a programme on the work of the obscene publications squad of Scotland Yard and in particular about the work of detectives engaged in tracing a man who was imprisoned on two charges of indecency. The man had previously been married to Mrs R who was the mother of his child and there was concern that the programme contained scenes which would identify the mother and the child, causing the latter distress. Invoking the parental jurisdiction of the court, the mother moved successfully to have the moving pictures of the father obscured, a decision reversed by the Court of Appeal which held that the press and broadcasters were entitled to publish the results of criminal proceedings, even though 'the families of those convicted had a heavy burden to bear and the effect of publicity on small children might be very serious'.

....

[66] Note 64 above. For a critique, see E Barendt [2003] PL 580; J Jowell [2003] PL 592; and A Scott (2003) 66 MLR 224. But compare *Aston Cantlow and Wilmcote with Billesley Parochial Church Council v Wallbank* [2003] UKHL 37, [2004] 1 AC 546; ch 14 above.

[67] *Attorney-General, ex rel McWhirter v IBA* [1973] QB 629.

[68] *R v Radio Authority, ex p Bull* [1997] 2 All ER 561; *R (Animal Defenders' International) v Secretary of State for Culture, Media and Sport*, note 54 above; *Animal Defenders International v United Kingdom*, note 54 above.

[69] *Wilson v Independent Broadcasting Authority* 1979 SLT 279. Cf *Wilson v Independent Broadcasting Authority* 1988 SLT 276. Also C Munro, *New Law Journal*, 4 October 1996, p 1433, and *New Law Journal*, 11 April 1997, p 528.

[70] [1994] Fam 192.

In a robust defence of freedom of expression, in a case where it was perhaps unnecessary, Hoffmann LJ said:

> Publication may cause needless pain, distress and damage to individuals or harm to other aspects of the public interest. But a freedom which is restricted to what judges think to be responsible or in the public interest is no freedom. Freedom means the right to publish things which government and judges, however well motivated, think should not be published. It means the right to say things which 'right-thinking people' regard as dangerous or irresponsible. This freedom is subject only to clearly defined exceptions laid down by common law or statute.

It is to a consideration of some of the exceptions referred to by Hoffmann LJ that we now turn.

D. Offences against public order

Changing nature of criminal law

By section 73, the Criminal Justice and Coroners Act 2009 abolished the common law offences of seditious libel and blasphemous libel, offences that were covered in earlier editions of this text. The former made it an offence to create political discontent and disaffection (and as such was a handy tool against the pioneering socialists in the late nineteenth and early twentieth centuries),[71] while the latter made it an offence to outrage and insult a Christian's feelings (and as such was a handy tool to be used against those who linked Jesus Christ to homosexuality).[72]

Blasphemy was also used by the British Board of Film Classification when it refused to issue a classification certificate under the Video Recordings Act 1984 for a film entitled *Visions of Ecstasy*. The film included an 'intense erotic' moment between St Teresa and Jesus Christ, the decision being taken on the ground that the film was blasphemous. Nevertheless, these offences were increasingly anomalous at a time of greater political plurality and vigour in public debate, and at a time when cultural diversity made it inappropriate to single out one religion (albeit that of the established church) for special treatment.[73]

The abolition of these offences should not be taken as a retreat of the criminal law as a source of restraint on free speech. There are two reasons for this, the first being that many other chapters in this text reveal a wide range of criminal constraints on freedom of expression. These include contempt of court restricting the publication of material calculated to prejudice a fair trial or interfere with the administration of justice (Chapter 13), and official secrecy and associated common law offences (misconduct in a public office) which deal with the disclosure and reporting of material dealing with certain kinds of government information (Chapter 19).

Secondly, however, while the common law offences of sedition and blasphemy have been abolished, legislation remains on the statute book addressing in modern form the kind of mischief to which both of these offences were principally addressed. Thus it might be argued that statutory measures dealing with incitement to religious hatred are a more wide-ranging restriction on free speech than that imposed in modern times by blasphemy, while the offence

---

[71] *R v Burns* (1886) 16 Cox CC 355, *R v Aldred* (1909) 22 Cox CC 1. More recently, see *R v Chief Metropolitan Stipendiary Magistrate, ex p Choudhury* [1991] QB 429. And see Williams, *Keeping the Peace*, ch 8, and E C S Wade (1948) 64 LQR 203.

[72] *R v Lemon* [1979] AC 617. And see *Gay News Ltd v UK* (1982) 5 EHRR 123.

[73] With the abolition of blasphemy as an offence, the BBFC has reclassified a film, *Multiple Maniacs*, having previously insisted on cuts on blasphemy grounds, and allowed the film to be shown with these cuts restored: BBFC, *Annual Report 2016*, p 43.

of inducing terrorism is a more precise and targeted way of addressing the concerns of sedition in a contemporary context (there being significant overlap between this statutory offence introduced in 2008 and the common law offence abolished in 2009).

So far as restraints on free speech in the interests of public order are concerned, these restrictions tend to be responses to particular problems at particular times, and the issues considered here overlap with those considered in Chapters 18 and 20. If, however, sedition was a crime of the 18th and 19th centuries in particular, incitement to disaffection is a restriction introduced to deal with the activities of the Communist party in the 1930s as it tried to encourage soldiers and sailors to disaffect. Similarly, the law relating to the incitement to racial hatred is a restriction introduced to deal with the menace of far-right parties with racist views at a time of growing ethnic diversity.

Finally, the offence of inciting terrorism is a response to the more recent problem of political violence in Northern Ireland, and the emergence of terrorism on a global scale. The offence is directed specifically at the activities of some supporters of national and international terrorist organisations (widely defined) and their willingness publicly to express that support. In other words, the legal restrictions on freedom of expression discussed here are symptoms of temporal problems, which – at least in the case of incitement to disaffection – are allowed to remain on the statute book long after the mischief to which they were directed has gone.

Incitement to disaffection[74]

Parliament has on several occasions legislated to prevent the spread of disaffection, mainly to protect members of the armed forces, who might otherwise be exposed to attempts to persuade them to disobey their orders. The Incitement to Mutiny Act 1797, passed following the Nore mutiny, made it a felony maliciously and advisedly to endeavour to seduce members of the armed forces from their duty and allegiance to the Crown or to incite members to commit any act of mutiny. Although the 1797 Act has been repealed (and although seditious libel has been abolished), the Aliens Restriction (Amendment) Act 1919, s 3, still prohibits an alien from causing sedition or disaffection among the civil population as well as among the armed forces.

It is an offence under the 1919 Act, s 3 for any alien to promote or interfere in an industrial dispute in any industry in which he or she has not been bona fide engaged in the United Kingdom for at least two years preceding an alleged offence. The Police Act 1996, s 91, replacing legislation first passed in 1919 at a time of serious unrest within the police, prohibits acts calculated to cause disaffection among police officers or to induce them to withhold their services or commit breaches of discipline. Under the Incitement to Disaffection Act 1934, which passed through Parliament against severe criticism from a variety of quarters, it is an offence maliciously and advisedly to endeavour to seduce a member of the armed forces from that person's duty or allegiance.

The 1934 Act contains wide-ranging provisions for the prevention and detection of the offence. These include wide powers of search on reasonable suspicion, though a warrant may be issued only by a High Court judge. Moreover, it is an offence for any person, with intent to commit or to aid, counsel or procure commission of the main offence, to have in his or her possession or under his or her control any document of such a nature that the distribution of copies among members of the forces would constitute that offence. Notwithstanding the safeguards in the Act, it does restrain certain forms of political propaganda; and it could be used to suppress or interfere with the distribution of pacifist literature.

Prosecutions under the Act in England require the consent of the Director of Public Prosecutions. This consent was given between 1973 and 1975 in relation to members of a campaign

---

[74] Bunyan, *The Political Police in Britain*, pp 28–36; Ewing and Gearty, *The Struggle for Civil Liberties*, chs 2–5.

for the withdrawal of British troops from Northern Ireland, who were convicted for the leaflets they had prepared, one of the convictions being upheld by the Court of Appeal.[75] The accused has a right to jury trial: it would be a matter for the jury to decide whether a leaflet which gave information to a soldier about procedures for leaving the army and his or her rights as a soldier was an attempt to seduce that person from duty or allegiance to the Crown. There have been calls for the offence to be abolished, and it appears currently to serve little useful purpose.

Incitement to racial hatred

It has long been recognised that the preservation of public order justifies the imposition of criminal sanctions on those who utter threats, abuse or insults in public places, which are likely to give rise to a breach of the peace.[76] In 1965, when Parliament first created machinery to deal with racial discrimination, an offence of incitement to racial hatred was created which was not dependent on proof of an immediate threat to public order. This reflected the belief that racial hatred itself contains the seeds of violence.[77] The position is now governed by the Public Order Act 1986, dealing specifically with 'racial hatred', taken to mean 'hatred against a group of persons defined by reference to colour, race, nationality (including citizenship) or ethnic or national origins' (s 17).

The provisions in the Public Order Act 1986, s 17 replace measures enacted earlier in the Race Relations Act 1976 and before that in the Race Relations Act 1965. By s 18 of the 1986 Act, it is an offence for a person to use threatening, abusive or insulting words or behaviour or to display any material which is threatening, abusive or insulting if he or she does so with intent to stir up racial hatred or if in the circumstances racial hatred is likely to be stirred up.[78] The 1986 Act also applies to publicising or distributing such material (s 19), theatrical performances (s 20), the distribution, showing or playing of a recording of visual images or sounds (s 21), and television and radio broadcasts (s 22).

The offence in s 23 of the Act relates to the possession of material which if published or displayed would amount to an offence under the Act. Where there are reasonable grounds for suspecting that a person has possession of such material, a justice of the peace may grant a warrant to a police constable authorising the entry and search of premises for the material in question. It is not an offence to publish a fair and accurate report of proceedings in Parliament (or the Scottish Parliament or the Welsh Assembly), or of proceedings publicly heard before a tribunal or court where the report is published contemporaneously with the proceedings (s 26).

A prosecution in England and Wales may not occur without the consent of the Attorney General (s 27). Although these are wide-ranging restrictions, they are justifiable primarily because a serious threat to personal security and dignity, not to mention public order, is inherent in certain forms of political and social expression. Nevertheless, controversy was sparked when in 2006 these provisions were extended to apply also to incitement to religious hatred, this being 'hatred against a group of persons defined by reference to

---

[75] *R v Arrowsmith* [1975] QB 678; and see *Arrowsmith* v *UK* (1978) 3 EHRR 218 (no infringement of European Convention on Human Rights).

[76] ch 18.

[77] See D G T Williams [1966] Crim LR 320; Lester and Bindman, *Race and Law*, ch 10; and P M Leopold [1977] PL 389.

[78] It is not now necessary, as it was under the 1965 Act, to prove that the accused intended to stir up racial hatred: in practice, such proof had been too stringent a requirement for the law to be an effective restraint on racist propaganda. See also W J Wolffe [1987] PL 85 and S Poulter [1991] PL 371.

religious belief or lack of religious belief'.[79] The law was later extended to cover incitement to hatred on grounds of sexual orientation.[80]

Incitement to terrorism

The Terrorism Act 2006 introduced a third public order restriction on free speech, a highly contentious measure politically at the time of its introduction, attracting opposition from both government and opposition benches. By section 1, this applies to a statement that is likely to be understood by some or all of the members of the public to whom it is published as 'a direct or indirect encouragement or other inducement to them to the commission, preparation or instigation of acts of terrorism'. For this (and other purposes in the Act) 'public' is defined to mean 'the public of any part of the United Kingdom or of a country or territory outside the United Kingdom, or any section of the public' (s 20(3)(a)).[81]

It is an offence – punishable by up to seven years' imprisonment – to publish a statement to which the foregoing applies if at the time the statement is published the accused intends members of the public to be directly or indirectly encouraged to commit acts of terrorism, or is reckless as to whether they will be so encouraged or induced (s 1(2)). Statements are likely to be understood as indirectly encouraging the commission of acts of terrorism if they glorify the commission or preparation of acts of terrorism, provided it can reasonably be inferred that what is being glorified is 'being glorified as conduct that should be emulated' (s 1(3)). Other provisions in the Act define glorification to include 'any form of praise or celebration' (s 20(2)).

Related to the above, section 2 creates a separate offence in relation to terrorist publications, which is the offence of dissemination of such publications. The question of what is a terrorist publication is surprisingly complex, and the term needs carefully to be dissected. First, it is necessary to determine what is meant by *terrorist* for these purposes (a question which also arises in relation to the section 1 offence referred to above). The answer lies in the Terrorism Act 2000, s 1, where terrorism is defined widely to mean action or the threat of action involving serious violence or serious damage to property, which is designed to influence the government or intimidate the public or a section of the public, and is undertaken to advance an ideological cause.[82]

For these latter purposes the government to be influenced need not be the UK government, but could be a foreign government, and the activity being planned could be planned to be undertaken overseas. This leads to the second question of what is meant by a *publication* for these purposes. Here s 2(13) defines it to mean an article or record of any description that contains matter to be read, listened to, or looked at or watched, which means that it covers traditional printed material (such as leaflets and pamphlets) as well as more sophisticated internet-based material (in relation to which powers are given to the police by s 3 to require people to remove terrorism-related material from internet sites).

Having thus defined *terrorist* and *publication*, the third question arises after putting both together: what is a *terrorist publication*? Here, s 2(3) provides that the term applies to publications likely to be understood by those or some of those to whom the material becomes available to be 'a direct or indirect encouragement or other inducement to them to the commission,

---

[79] Racial and Religious Hatred Act 2006, s 1, inserting new Public Order Act 1986, ss 29A–29N.

[80] Criminal Justice and Immigration Act 2008, s 74, Sch 16; amending Public Order Act 1986. On disability hate crime, see College of Policing, *Hate Crime Operational Guidance* (2014).

[81] It also applies to public meetings, whether entry is on payment of a fee or not (s 20(3)(b)).

[82] This is a definition which overlaps with the now abolished offence of seditious libel, which also emphasised (i) an intention to change the constitution, by (ii) violent means. See *R v Burns*, above, and *R v Aldred*, above. The common law offence was probably wider and more elastic in principle, though it had probably become unusable in practice, having been designed for a different age.

preparation or instigation of acts of terrorism', or to be 'useful' in the commission or preparation of such acts. As in the case of the s 1 offence referred to above, 'matter that is likely to be understood by a person as indirectly encouraging the commission or preparation of acts of terrorism includes any matter which [glorifies terrorism]' (s 2(4)).

The section 2 offence is committed only if the dissemination (for example by circulation, sale or loan) takes place with the intention that the dissemination will have the effect of directly or indirectly encouraging or inducing the commission, preparation or instigation of acts of terrorism (s 2(1)). This is a complicated offence, which requires an intention to encourage or induce acts of terrorism by the dissemination of a publication which encourages or induces acts of terrorism. Like section 1, the section 2 offence carries a penalty of up to seven years' imprisonment if convicted on indictment (s 2(11)).[83] Despite its controversial nature, the CPS website records a number of convictions under the 2006 Act in most years since its introduction.[84]

E. Obscene publications

Before the Obscene Publications Act 1959

It resulted from the development of the law concerning the printing of books that, as with seditious, blasphemous and other libels, it became an offence punishable by the common law courts to publish obscene material. This jurisdiction was exercised for the first time in *Curl*'s case when the court held that it was an offence to publish a book which tended to corrupt morals and was against the King's peace.[85] The flourishing business of pornography in the Victorian underworld led to the Obscene Publications Act 1857. This Act gave the police power to search premises, seize obscene publications kept for sale, and bring them before a magistrates' court for destruction.

The Act did not define 'obscene' but its sponsor, Lord Campbell, stated that it was to apply 'exclusively to works written for the single purpose of corrupting the morals of youth, and of a nature calculated to shock the common feelings of decency in any well regulated mind'.[86] In 1868, in *R* v *Hicklin*, Cockburn CJ declared the test for obscenity to be:

> whether the tendency of the matter charged as obscenity is to deprave and corrupt those whose minds are open to such immoral influences and into whose hands a publication of this sort may fall.[87]

This test came to dominate the English law of obscenity, and as we will see, the legacy of the common law continues to be found on the statute book, despite so far forlorn attempts to find a new approach. As developed, this test of obscenity required account to be taken of the circumstances of publication: in *Hicklin*'s case, Cockburn CJ said that immunity for a medical treatise depended on the circumstances, since the publication of some medical details would not be fit for boys and girls to see. But the test did not permit the author's intention to be taken into account. Although the tendency to deprave and corrupt was often assumed from the character of a book, who might the potential readers be?

....

[83] For guidance, see *R* v *Rahman* [2008] EWCA Crim 1465, [2008] 4 All ER 661.
[84] It also reveals tough sentences in recent cases involving support for Daesch.
[85] (1727) 17 St Tr 153; Robertson, *Obscenity*, ch 2.
[86] HL Deb, 25 June 1857, col 329.
[87] (1868) LR 3 QB 360, 371.

In 1954, in *R v Reiter*, the Court of Criminal Appeal took the view that a jury should direct their attention to the result of a book falling into the hands of young people.[88] But a few months later, in *R v Martin Secker Warburg Ltd*, Stable J asked: 'Are we to take our literary standards as being the level of something that is suitable for the decently brought up young female aged 14?'.[89] Other difficulties in the law included the use of the 1857 Act against serious literature; the failure of the 1857 Act to enable a publisher or author to defend a work against destruction; and the tendency of prosecutors to take selected passages of a book out of context. A lengthy campaign by publishers and authors led to the Obscene Publications Act 1959.[90]

Obscene Publications Acts 1959 and 1964

The 1959 Act, which does not apply to Scotland, sought both to provide for the protection of literature and to strengthen the law against pornography. For the purposes of the 1959 Act (but not of other Acts in which the word 'obscene' is used):[91]

> an article shall be deemed to be obscene if its effect or (where the article comprises two or more distinct items) the effect of any one of its items is, if taken as a whole, such as to tend to deprave and corrupt persons who are likely, having regard to all relevant circumstances, to read, see or hear the matter contained or embodied in it (s 1(1)).[92]

A wide definition of 'article' (s 1(2)) includes books, pictures, films, records and such things as film negatives used in producing obscene articles,[93] and video cassettes.[94] It is an offence to publish an obscene article, whether for gain or not, or to have obscene articles in one's possession, ownership or control for the purpose of publication for gain or with a view to such publication,[95] whether for sale within Britain or abroad.[96] The definition of 'publishing' includes distributing, circulating, selling, hiring and, for example, showing pictures or playing records; since 1991 it includes television and sound broadcasting,[97] and since 1994 it has included the transmitting of electronically stored data.[98] It is a defence to prove that publication of an obscene article is justified 'as being for the public good on the ground that it is in the interests of science, literature, art or learning or other objects of general concern'. Expert evidence on the literary, artistic, scientific or other merits of an article is admissible to establish or negative the defence of public good.[99]

The 1959 Act, s 3, confers search, seizure and forfeiture powers similar to those in the 1857 Act. A warrant may be obtained by a constable (or the DPP) from a magistrate for the search of specified premises, stalls or vehicles, where there is reasonable suspicion that obscene articles are kept for publication for gain. When a search is made, articles believed to be obscene and also documents relating to a trade or business may be seized. The seized articles must be brought before a magistrate. When notice has been given to the occupier of the

---

[88] [1954] 2 QB 16.

[89] [1954] 2 All ER 683, 686 (Kauffmann's *The Philanderer*).

[90] See HC 123 (1957–58); and Robertson, *Obscenity*, pp 40–4.

[91] *R v Anderson* [1972] 1 QB 304, 317 (*Oz, School Kids Issue*).

[92] On the item by item test, see *R v Anderson*, ibid, at p 312.

[93] 1964 Act, s 2, the sequel to *Straker v DPP* [1963] 1 QB 926.

[94] *A-G's Reference (No 5 of 1980)* [1980] 3 All ER 816.

[95] 1959 Act, s 2(1), as amended in 1964. See *R v Taylor* [1995] 1 Cr App R 131 (publication where films depicting obscene acts are developed, printed and returned to the owner).

[96] *Gold Star Publications Ltd v DPP* [1981] 2 All ER 257; and see (1983) 5 EHRR 591.

[97] Broadcasting Act 1990, s 162, amending 1959 Act, by inserting s 1(4)–(6).

[98] Criminal Justice and Public Order Act 1994, s 168(1). See *R v Perrin* [2002] EWCA (Crim) 747.

[99] 1959 Act, s 4.

premises to show cause why the articles should not be forfeited, the magistrates' court may order forfeiture if satisfied that the articles are obscene and were kept for publication for gain. The owner, author or maker of the articles may also appear to defend them against forfeiture. The defence that publication is for the public good is available and expert evidence relating to the merits of the articles may be called. In these proceedings there is no right to the decision of a jury, but there are rights of appeal to the Crown Court or the High Court. Because of certain defects in the 1959 Act, the Act of 1964 was passed to strengthen the law against publishing obscene matter. The latter added the offence of having an obscene article for publication for the purposes of gain,[100] and authorised a forfeiture order to be made following a conviction under the 1959 Act.

One difficulty is the 1959 Act's definition of obscenity as 'a tendency to deprave and corrupt'. The definition makes it impossible to rely on such synonyms as 'repulsive', 'filthy', 'loathsome' or 'lewd',[101] and requires the jury to consider whether the effect of a book is to tend to deprave and corrupt a significant proportion of those likely to read it. 'What is a significant proportion is entirely for the jury to decide.'[102] In cases relating to the internet in particular, however, it may not be appropriate for 'the task of the jury [to] be complicated by a direction that the effect of the article must be such as to tend to deprave and corrupt a significant proportion, or more than a negligible number of likely viewers'.[103] Lord Wilberforce has said: 'An article cannot be considered as obscene in itself: it can only be so in relation to its likely readers.'[104] Experienced police officers may for practical purposes not be susceptible to being depraved and corrupted,[105] but it seems that a man may be corrupted more than once.[106] Although the circumstances in which articles are sold are relevant, it is no defence for booksellers to prove that most of their sales are made to middle-aged men who are already addicted to pornography; articles may 'deprave and corrupt' the mind without any overt sexual activity by the reader resulting.[107] Obscenity is not confined to sexual matters: a book dealing with the effects of drug taking may be obscene,[108] as may cards depicting violence when sold to children.[109]

Common law offences

In *Shaw* v *DPP*,[110] the appellant had published the *Ladies' Directory*, an illustrated magazine containing names, addresses and other details of prostitutes and their services. The House of Lords upheld Shaw's conviction for the offence of conspiracy to corrupt public morals. Lord Simonds accepted that the law must be related to the changing standards of life, having regard to fundamental human values and the purposes of society; he said that 'there remains in the courts of law a residual power to enforce the supreme and fundamental purpose of the

---

[100] Cf *Mella* v *Monahan* [1961] Crim LR 175.

[101] *R* v *Anderson* [1972] 1 QB 304; cf the perceptive analysis by Windeyer J in *Crowe* v *Grahame* (1968) 41 AJLR 402, 409.

[102] *R* v *Calder & Boyars Ltd* [1969] 1 QB 151, 168. But it is 'more than a negligible number' (*R* v *O'Sullivan* (1995) 1 Cr App R 455).

[103] *R* v *Perrin* [2002] EWCA (Crim) 747. According to the court, 'such a direction is all too likely to give rise to a request for further assistance as to what proportion is significant, or what number is negligible'.

[104] *DPP* v *Whyte* [1972] AC 849, 860.

[105] *R* v *Clayton and Halsey* [1963] 1 QB 163.

[106] *Shaw* v *DPP* [1962] AC 220, 228 (CCA).

[107] *DPP* v *Whyte* [1972] AC 849, 867.

[108] *Calder (Publications) Ltd* v *Powell* [1965] 1 QB 509; *R* v *Skirving* [1985] QB 819.

[109] *DPP* v *A & BC Chewing Gum Ltd* [1968] 1 QB 159.

[110] [1962] AC 220.

law, to conserve not only the safety and order but also the moral welfare of the State'.[111] It was the jury which provided a safeguard against the launching of prosecutions to suppress unpopular or unorthodox views. Lord Reid, dissenting, rejected the view that the court was guardian of public morals. This controversial decision derived in part from the supposed offence of conspiracy to effect a public mischief, which was later held not to be part of criminal law.[112] Although Shaw was also convicted for having published an obscene book, contrary to the 1959 Act, *Shaw*'s case enabled prosecutions to be brought at common law for conspiracy rather than for breaches of the 1959 Act. Thereafter the Law Officers assured the House of Commons that a conspiracy to corrupt public morals would not be charged so as to circumvent the 'public good' defence in the 1959 Act.[113]

In *Knuller Ltd v DPP*,[114] however, the House of Lords reaffirmed the decision in *Shaw*, in a case in which the appellants had published a magazine containing advertisements by male homosexuals seeking to meet other homosexuals. The Lords upheld a conviction of the appellants for conspiracy to corrupt public morals, rejecting a defence based on the Sexual Offences Act 1967 by which homosexual acts between adult males in private had ceased to be an offence. A second conviction for conspiracy 'to outrage public decency' was quashed on the ground of misdirection, but a majority of the House held that at common law it was an offence to outrage public decency and also to conspire to outrage public decency; and that such a conspiracy could take the form of an agreement to insert outrageously indecent matter on the inside pages of a magazine sold in public.[115] Lords Reid and Diplock did not agree that 'outraging public decency' was an offence; Lord Reid said, 'To recognise this new crime would go contrary to the whole trend of public policy followed by Parliament in recent times.'[116] Nevertheless, the abolition of common law conspiracy with the introduction of new statutory offences in the Criminal Law Act 1977 was stated expressly not to affect a conspiracy that involves an agreement to engage in conduct which tends to corrupt public morals or outrages public decency.[117]

Although the common law offence has thus been recognised and preserved by statute,[118] prosecutions for (i) conspiracy to corrupt public morals, or (ii) to outrage public decency are unusual. One such case, however, is *R v Gibson*,[119] in which both the owner of an art gallery and an artist were convicted for exhibiting a model's head to the ears of which were attached earrings made out of a freeze-dried human foetus of three or four months' gestation. The case raised the question whether a prosecution at common law to outrage public decency was precluded by s 2(4) of the Obscene Publications Act 1959, whereby common law proceedings are not to be brought where 'it is of the essence of the offence that the matter is obscene'. The Court of Appeal held that there are two broad types of offence involving obscenity and that the 1959 Act applied only in respect of one (those involving the corruption of public morals) but not the other (those which involve an outrage on public decency, whether or not public morals are involved). This decision may make it easier for the Crown to bring prosecutions at common law, thereby circumventing the defences which would otherwise be available in a prosecution brought under the Act. Of these, the most important

---

[111] Ibid, p 268. See D Seaborne Davies (1962) 6 JSPTL 104, J E Hall Williams (1961) 24 MLR 626 and Robertson, *Obscenity*, ch 8.
[112] *DPP v Withers* [1975] AC 842.
[113] HC Deb, 3 June 1964, col 1212.
[114] [1973] AC 435.
[115] See now *R v Walker* [1996] 1 Cr App R 111.
[116] *Knuller Ltd v DPP* [1973] AC 435, 459.
[117] Criminal Law Act 1977, s 5(3); cf s 53(3).
[118] See also Theatres Act 1968, s 2(4).
[119] [1990] 2 QB 619; M Childs [1991] PL 20.

is undoubtedly the public good defence in s 4. However, the offence can only be committed in public and only if seen by others.[120]

Reform of the law

It has been reported that the 1959 Act is used in about 70 cases annually, though its value was called into question in 2012, following the acquittal of the accused by a London jury in a high-profile pornography case. The CPS Guidelines suggest that charges will be brought only in what some might consider to be serious if not 'extreme' cases, and not in cases which in the past would almost certainly have attracted prosecution. Account is also taken of the form in which the material is presented (films and photographs more serious than the printed word), as well as the type and scale of any commercial venture involved, and whether children are likely to have access.

There is, however, little prospect of the law being liberalized, as had once been proposed in a different era,[121] with the Criminal Justice and Immigration Act 2008 not only increasing the penalties under the Obscene Publications Act 1959 (to five years), but also introducing a new offence of possessing extreme pornographic images. The latter is expressed to (i) relate to defined activities listed in the Act, and (ii) to be 'grossly offensive, disgusting or otherwise of an obscene character' (s 63), though there is no definition of obscene (or 'disgusting') for these purposes. The Human Rights Act has yet to have an impact here, though the Strasbourg Court has generally taken a back seat on the control of pornographic 'expression'.[122]

One of the main challenges in this area at the present time relates to the internet, where there is a real concern about images of child sexual abuse, as well as problems of access by children to unsuitable material. Internet service providers and internet users are subject to ordinary civil and criminal liabilities, including the law relating to obscene publications, defamation and incitement to racial hatred.[123] The Digital Economy Act 2017 now introduces a regulatory regime addressed to those who make pornography available on the internet on a commercial basis, and who must now ensure that the material is not normally accessible by people under the age of 18.

In addition, an important role is performed by the Internet Watch Foundation which was established in 1996 by UK internet service providers to advise internet users about how best to restrict access to harmful or offensive content on the internet generally.[124] The Foundation is independent of government and, although working very closely with the police, it has no statutory powers. The IWF website emphasizes its role in relation to child sex abuse in particular, providing a forum for internet users to report material which they believe to be criminal. If on investigation the material is thought to be criminal, the internet service provider will be issued with a 'takedown notice', and the information will be passed to the police.

---

[120] *R v Hamilton* [2007] EWCA Crim 2062, [2008] 2 WLR 107. See now Law Commission, *Simplification of Criminal Law: Public Nuisance and Outraging Public Decency* (Law Com No 358, 2015), where it is reported that the offence is used mainly to deal with offensive sexual activity in public.

[121] Cmnd 7772, 1979 (Williams report). See Simpson, *Pornography and Politics – the Williams Report in Retrospect*.

[122] *Handyside v UK* (1976) 1 EHRR 737. Cf *Belfast City Council v Miss Behavin' Ltd* [2007] UKHL 19, [2007] 1 WLR 1420.

[123] See *Godfrey v Demon Internet Ltd* [2001] QB 201 (defamation), and *R v Perrin* [2002] EWCA Crim 747 (obscene publications).

[124] See www.iwf.org.uk.

F. Defamation

Nature of liability

Libel was at one time punishable by the criminal law. Although rarely used in modern times, criminal libel was not finally abolished by the Coroners and Justice Act 2009.[125] However, defamation continues to give rise to civil liability, the law being designed to protect the reputation of the claimant from improper attack.[126] In principle, the law provides a remedy for false statements which 'substantially affect in an adverse manner the attitude of other people towards the claimant, or have a tendency so to do'.[127] For this purpose words are to be given 'the natural and ordinary meaning [they] would have conveyed to the ordinary reasonable reader'.[128]

Defamation takes two main forms: (*a*) slander (defamation in a transitory form by spoken word or gesture), and (*b*) libel (defamation in a permanent form such as the written or printed word). By statute, words used in the course of broadcasting and of public performances in a theatre are treated as publication in permanent form and may be libellous.[129] In the interest of free speech, neither local authorities (and by inference central government departments) nor political parties may bring an action in defamation.[130] It is thus an anomaly of English law that corporations may sue in libel, particularly in view of the increasing role of corporations in the delivery of public services, defamation thus a major chill on efforts to hold corporations to account.[131]

Freedom of expression ought not to be a licence gratuitously to besmirch the reputations of politicians or anyone else, and it is the role of the law to ensure that powerful newspaper companies and others do not abuse freedom of expression in this way.[132] That said, it is nevertheless difficult to exaggerate the extent to which defamation law is an important restraint on freedom of expression and the ability of the press and political activists to hold politicians and others to account.[133] Although giving rise to rights and remedies in private law, the importance of defamation for public law is nevertheless to be seen in the high-profile cases brought by politicians, sometimes ill-advisedly and with disastrous consequences for the individuals concerned.

Growing concern about the effect of defamation law on freedom of expression gave way to the Defamation Act 2013,[134] which makes a number of important changes that ought to benefit publishers and campaigners. A statement is now not to be treated as defamatory unless its

---

[125] A move warmly welcomed in an impressive report on *Press Standards, Privacy and Libel* by the House of Commons Culture, Media and Sport Committee of the House of Commons: HC 362 (2009–10), para 235.

[126] See *Reynolds* v *Times Newspapers Ltd* [2001] 2 AC 127, at p 201 (Lord Nicholls) and *Kearns* v *Bar Council* [2003] EWCA Civ 331, [2003] 1 WLR 1357, at p 1373 (Simon Brown LJ). For fuller accounts of the law of defamation, see textbooks on the law of tort and Mitchell, *The Making of the Modern Law of Defamation*.

[127] *Lord McAlpine* v *Bercow* [2013] EWHC 1342 (QB). For an action to succeed, the publication must be read as a whole, rather than one or more isolated passages. See *Charleston* v *News Group Newspapers Ltd* [1995] 2 AC 65.

[128] *Bonnick* v *Morris* [2002] UKPC 31, [2003] 1 AC 300.

[129] Broadcasting Act 1990, s 166; and Theatres Act 1968, s 4.

[130] See respectively *Derbyshire County Council* v *Times Newspapers Ltd* [1993] AC 534 and *Goldsmith* v *Bhoyrul* [1998] QB 459; E Barendt [1993] PL 449. Public servants may sue for libel: *Gough* v *Local Sunday Newspapers (North) Ltd* [2003] EWCA Civ 297, [2003] 1 WLR 1836 (borough solicitor accused of incompetence).

[131] *Steel* v *McDonald's Corporation* [1999] EWCA Civ 1144; *Tesco Stores Ltd* v *Guardian* [2008] EWHC 14 (QB), [2009] EMLR 5; *Jameel* v *Wall Street Journal* [2006] UKHL 44, [2007] 1 AC 359. The position is all the more anomalous for the fact that trade unions cannot sue for defamation: *EETPU* v *Times Newspapers* [1980] 1 All ER 1097.

[132] See the discussion in *Reynolds* v *Times Newspapers Ltd*, above. Compare Loveland, *Political Libels*.

[133] For a good account from a serious journalist's perspective, see Palast, *The Best Democracy Money Can Buy*.

[134] See A Mullis and A Scott (2014) 77 MLR 87.

publication has 'caused or is likely to cause serious harm to the reputation of the claimant' (s 1(1)).[135] While defamation continues to protect corporations, it is now provided that 'harm to the reputation of a body that trades for profit is not 'serious harm' unless it has caused or is likely to cause the body serious financial loss' (s 1(2)),[136] though this alone is unlikely to be enough to stop defamation being used as a weapon by companies against those who would hold them to account.

New statutory defences

The Defamation Act 2013 does not only address the nature of the harm that must be established for the purposes of libel, but it also amends the law relating to defences, with section 2 abolishing the common law defence of justification[137] and replacing it with a new truth-based defence, which applies where the 'imputation conveyed by the statement complained of is substantially true' (s 2(1)).[138] Where a statement is capable of two or more distinct imputations, the defence applies if one is substantially true and any other is not, provided that the latter does not cause any substantial harm.

In addition to abolishing the defence of justification, the 2013 Act also abolishes the common law defence of fair comment, replacing it with a new statutory defence of honest opinion (s 3(1)).[139] The latter defence applies where three conditions are met: the statement complained of was a statement of opinion (s 3(2)); the statement complained of indicated the basis of the opinion (s 3(3)); and the opinion is one that could have been held by an honest person on the basis of any fact existing at the time of the publication, or anything asserted as a fact in a privileged statement (s 3(4)).

Section 4 of the Defamation Act 2013 abolishes the eponymous *Reynolds* defence, after the decision in which it was established.[140] The defence is essentially a form of qualified privilege (on which see below), which applies where the publication can be justified in the public interest. In applying this test, Lord Nicholls said that courts should have regard to ten factors. These were: the seriousness of the allegation; the nature of the information; the source of the information; steps taken to verify the information; the status of the information; the urgency of the matter; whether comment was sought from the claimant; whether the article contained the gist of the claimant's side of the story; the tone of the article; and the circumstances and timing of the article.

In developing these principles (said to be non-exhaustive), Lord Nicholls said that 'the common law does not seek to set a higher standard than that of responsible journalism, a standard the media themselves espouse'.[141] Although in the *Reynolds* case the defence of

---

[135] A statement for these purposes is defined to mean 'words, pictures, visual images, gestures or any other method of signifying meaning'. On serious harm, see *Cooke* v *MGN* [2014] EWHC 2831 (QB); *Monroe* v *Hopkins* [2017] EWHC 433 (QB) (defamation by twitter); *Lachaux* v *Independent Print Ltd* [2017] EWCA Civ 1334) (no defence to serious harm that others had also libelled the applicant, following *Dingle* v *Associated Newspapers Ltd* [1961] 2 QB 162, [1964] AC 371).

[136] For useful background to this change, see HC 362 (2009–10), paras 164–78.

[137] On the common law defence, see *Rothschild* v *Associated Newspapers Ltd* [2013] EWCA Civ 197, and *Cruddas* v *Calvert* [2015] EWCA Civ171

[138] Cf *Rothschild*, ibid, where Laws LJ cites with approval the following passage from the judgment of Tugendhat J in the court below: 'In a case where a defendant is not able to prove the whole of the defamatory allegation he has made, the law is that he may nevertheless succeed if he can prove, on the balance of probabilities, that what he has alleged is substantially true.'

[139] See *Joseph* v *Spiller* [2010] UKSC 53, [2011] 1 AC 852, where it was thought that the then common law defence of fair comment should be renamed honest comment. For the position in Scotland, see *Massie* v *McCaig*, 2013 CSIH 13 (allegedly defamatory remarks about the purpose of a political donation).

[140] *Reynolds* v *Times Newspapers Ltd* [2001] 2 AC 127.

[141] Ibid at p 202.

qualified privilege was not made out (the newspaper having failed to carry an account of the claimant's side of the story),[142] the defence has nevertheless become well established albeit judges were encouraged not to apply it rigidly.[143] Indeed, the *Reynolds* defence was thought to provide a firm basis for investigative journalism, the House of Lords accepting that there was both a duty and an interest on the part of the press to impart information for the benefit of the democratic process.

A statutory defence has, however, replaced the *Reynolds* defence, designed to codify the common law rules in force at the time of enactment.[144] The new defence may be engaged where a contested statement (*a*) was, or formed part of, a statement on a matter of public interest, which (*b*) the defendant reasonably believed was in the public interest to publish. There is no definition of the public interest for these purposes, though the Explanatory Notes accompanying the Act make clear that 'the current case law would constitute a helpful (albeit not binding) guide to interpreting how the new statutory defence should be applied. It is expected the courts would take the existing case law into consideration where appropriate' (para 35).

The scope of the statutory defence is said to reflect the common law defence it replaced, and to embrace both an objective (part (a)) and a subjective (part (b)) element. In determining 'whether it was reasonable for the defendant to believe that publishing the statement complained of was in the public interest' (part (b)), the court is required to 'make such allowance for editorial judgment as it considers appropriate' (s 4(4)). It is also provided 'for the avoidance of doubt' that the new defence under s 4 may be relied upon 'irrespective of whether the statement complained of is a statement of fact or a statement of opinion' (s 4(5)). Despite its origins, the *Reynolds* test does not apply only to categories of political information.[145]

Modern forms of communication have presented new problems for defamation law. In *Godrey* v *Demon Internet Service*,[146] it was held that internet service providers may be liable in defamation for defamatory messages posted by internet users, internet posting constituting a publication for these purposes. The Defamation Act 2013 provides a specific defence for internet operators, who may escape liability if they can show that they did not post the offending statement, though the defence may be defeated if the operator fails to remove it (s 5).

Messages posted on Twitter have also been found to be subject to the law of defamation, as revealed in a high-profile case involving Ms Sally Bercow (wife of the House of Commons Speaker) who was found to have defamed a former treasurer of the Conservative party.[147] There is no special defence for Twitter users, the law of defamation applying subsequently in a high-profile case involving intemperate tweets by a journalist, the court rejecting claims that the nature of Twitter was such that normal rules of defamation did not apply.[148] Defamation law applies also to Facebook and YouTube.[149]

---

[142] See also *Galloway* v *Daily Telegraph* [2006] EWCA Civ 17, [2006] EMLR 221; Cf *Bonnick* v *Morris* [2002] UKPC 31, [2003] 1 AC 300.

[143] *Jameel* v *Wall Street Journal Europe* [2006] UKHL 44, [2007] 1 AC 359. And see *Roberts* v *Gable* [2007] EWCA Civ 721, [2008] QB 502; *Charman* v *Orion Publishing Group Ltd* [2007] EWCA Civ 972, [2008] 1 All ER 750.

[144] Defamation Act 2013, s 4.

[145] It is important to note, however, that *Reynolds* provides a defence not only in relation to claims brought by politicians: see *Flood* v *Times Newspapers Ltd* [2012] UKSC 11, [2012] 2 AC 273.

[146] [2001] QB 201.

[147] *Lord McAlpine* v *Bercow* [2013] EWHC 1342 (QB).

[148] *Monroe* v *Hopkins*, above, for which Monroe was awarded £24,000 damages. The judgment is interesting also for an appendix on 'How Twitter Works'.

[149] See *Suresh* v *Samed* [2017] EWHC 173 (QB). Cf *Richardson* v *Facebook and Google (UK) Ltd* [2015] EWHC 3154 (QB) and *CG* v *Facebook Ireland Ltd* [2016] NICA 54.

Absolute, qualified and parliamentary privilege

Reynolds was about creating a new head of 'qualified privilege' whereby it will be a defence to an action for libel that the publication was in the public interest and without malice. Although *Reynolds* revealed that the categories of privilege at common law are not closed,[150] it was already the case that most common law categories of privilege were the subject of statutory privilege, following the Defamation Act 1996. Absolute privilege includes:

(a) statements made during parliamentary proceedings and statements in the official reports of debates or in other papers published by order of either House of Parliament;[151] (b) statements made by one officer of state to another in the course of his or her official duty, a privilege which in absolute form applies only to certain communications at a high level;[152] (c) reports by and statements to the Parliamentary Ombudsman;[153] (d) the internal documents of a foreign embassy;[154] and (e) the fair and accurate report of proceedings in public before a court anywhere in the world (including an international court) if published contemporaneously with the proceedings. For this purpose a court includes any tribunal or body exercising the judicial power of the state.[155]

Qualified privilege, unlike absolute privilege, is destroyed as a defence if the claimant proves malice on the part of the defendant.[156] Under the Defamation Act 1996, Sch 1, such privilege arises in two types of case. The first comprises reports privileged without 'explanation or contradiction'.

This first category applies to the fair and accurate report of public proceedings of a legislature or international organisation anywhere in the world;[157] a court anywhere in the world (to the extent not protected by absolute privilege);[158] or a person appointed to hold a public inquiry by a government or legislature anywhere in the world.[159] It also applies to the fair and accurate report of any public document and of any material published by or on the authority of a government or legislature anywhere in the world,[160] as well as to any matter published anywhere in the world by an international organisation or conference.[161]

The second category of qualified privilege comprises reports privileged subject to explanation or contradiction, in the sense that there is no defence if the plaintiff shows that the defendant failed following a request, 'to publish in a suitable manner a reasonable letter or statement by way of explanation or contradiction'.[162]

This second category includes 'a copy, extract from or summary of a notice or other matter issued for the information of the public' by a legislature or government anywhere in the

---

[150] *Reynolds*, above, at p 197.

[151] ch 9.

[152] E.g. *Chatterton* v *Secretary of State of India* [1895] 2 QB 189.

[153] Parliamentary Commissioner Act 1967, s 10(5); ch 23.

[154] *Al-Fayed* v *Al-Tajir* [1988] QB 712.

[155] Defamation Act 1996, s 14(3), as amended by the Defamation Act 2013.

[156] Ibid, s 15(1). But carelessness, impulsiveness or irrationality do not amount to malice: *Horrocks* v *Lowe* [1975] AC 135, though any of these may 'cost a journalist dear' in an action against the press – *Loutchansky* v *Times Newspapers (Nos 2–5)* [2001] EWCA Civ 536, [2002] QB 321. See also, on qualified privilege, *Kearns* v *Bar Council* [2003] EWCA Civ 331, [2003] 1 WLR 1357.

[157] See also ch 9.

[158] See also ch 13, and *Webb* v *Times Publishing Co* [1960] 2 QB 535.

[159] See *Tsikata* v *Newspaper Publishing plc* [1997] 1 All ER 655 (report need not be a contemporary report).

[160] See *Curistan* v *Times Newspapers Ltd* [2008] EWCA Civ 432, [2008] 3 All ER 923 (privilege not lost because of the publication in the same article of extraneous material not privileged).

[161] Defamation Act 1996, Sch 1, Part 1.

[162] Ibid, s 15(2)(a).

world, or any authority carrying out governmental functions (expressly defined to include police functions).

The second category also includes a fair and accurate report of proceedings at any public meeting in the United Kingdom of (*a*) a local authority or local authority committee; (*b*) a justice of the peace acting otherwise than as a court exercising judicial functions; (*c*) a commission or tribunal; (*d*) a local authority inquiry; or (*e*) any other statutory tribunal, board or inquiry.

An amendment introduced in 2013 now explicitly includes a fair and accurate report of proceedings at a press conference held anywhere in the world for the discussion of a matter of public interest.[163] This is in addition to the fair and accurate report of a number of other matters specified in the Schedule, the substance of many of which was expanded by the 2013 Act.[164]

Turning to the question of parliamentary privilege, this is usually seen as an important source of protection for free speech, as a result of the operation of art 9 of the Bill of Rights of 1689. *Prebble* v *Television New Zealand Ltd*,[165] revealed, however, that the latter provision could have consequences probably never intended. The plaintiff was a New Zealand cabinet minister who claimed to have been defamed by the television company. The defendant wished to demonstrate the truth of the allegations by relying on things said or done in Parliament, but was confronted by the Bill of Rights. In upholding the lower courts, the Privy Council said that: 'Parties to litigation, by whomsoever commenced, cannot bring into question anything said or done in the House (whether by direct evidence, cross-examination, inference or submission) that the actions or words were inspired by improper motives or were untrue or misleading.'

But on a second point, the Privy Council reversed a decision of the lower court to stay the proceedings in the light of the apparent disadvantage to the defendant, on the ground that although there 'may be cases in which the exclusion of material on the grounds of parliamentary privilege makes it quite impossible fairly to determine the issues between the parties', on the facts this was not one of them. Where, however, 'the whole subject matter of the alleged libel relates to the plaintiff's conduct in the House so that the effect of parliamentary privilege is to exclude virtually all the evidence necessary to justify the libel', the proceedings should be stayed not only to prevent an injustice to the defendant, but also to avoid the 'real danger' that 'the media would be forced to abstain from the truthful disclosure of a member's misbehaviour in Parliament'.

Although the plaintiff in *Prebble* was permitted to proceed with his action on the facts, the impact of the decision was immediately felt in this country by two Conservative members of Parliament.

In the case of Rupert Allason MP,[166] an action against *Today* newspaper was stayed, the defendant seeking to show that which was prohibited, namely that 'early day motions were at least inspired by improper motives'. To enforce parliamentary privilege but to refuse a stay would be unjust to the defendant, who would be deprived of their only defence 'while allowing the plaintiff to continue on an unsatisfactory and unfair basis'. In the view of Owen J, MPs 'had to take the ill consequences together with the good consequences' of parliamentary privilege'.

---

[163] This is for clarification. The House of Lords had already held that a press conference was covered under other heads to which qualified privilege applies under the Act: *McCartan Turkington Breen* v *Times Newspapers Ltd* [2001] 2 AC 277.

[164] See Defamation Act 1996, Sch 1, Part 2, the content of which is too detailed for a full account here.

[165] [1995] 1 AC 321. G Marshall [1994] PL 509, M Harris (1996) 8 *Auckland UL Rev* 45.

[166] *Allason* v *Haines*, *The Times*, 25 July 1995.

In the case of Neil Hamilton MP, it was claimed by the plaintiff that he had been libelled by *The Guardian* which alleged that he had received money from a businessman in return for asking ministers questions which were intended to further that businessman's interests. On this basis it was ruled by May J that the case could not proceed as the evidence directly involved proceedings in Parliament.[167] This case provided a catalyst for legislative reform, a number of people at the time believing Mr Hamilton to have been placed in an invidious position.

The *Prebble* case and its progeny in the United Kingdom were thought to create a real injustice, and an amendment was introduced to the Defamation Bill in 1996.[168] As a result, the art 9 protection may be waived, overcoming the *Prebble* problem in the following way: a claimant may bring an action in defamation to vindicate his or her reputation provided the claimant is willing to permit the defence to refer to proceedings in Parliament to justify what it had written. If the claimant is not prepared to waive the protection of art 9, then *Prebble* will continue to apply and the action may be stayed, on the ground that the newspaper must be allowed to prove that what it said was true. Newspapers would otherwise be 'reluctant to criticise what anyone said in Parliament if it meant that they could be sued while they had to stand with their hands tied behind their backs'[169].

Returning to the case of Mr Neil Hamilton, Hamilton dropped his case against *The Guardian* despite the fact that the 1996 Act, s 13 allowed him to continue. But not only did he discontinue the legal proceedings, but also the House of Commons Standards and Privileges Committee found that he had received money from the businessman Mr Al Fayed for lobbying services, and he lost his parliamentary seat at the general election in 1997. In a second libel case brought by Hamilton, this time against Mr Al Fayed about allegations made by him on television, the defence sought to have the trial stayed on the ground of parliamentary privilege. But Mr Hamilton invoked the 1996 Act, s 13 to waive parliamentary privilege, and this was found by the House of Lords to provide a complete answer to the attempt by the defence to have the action stayed, though Hamilton's action was nevertheless ultimately unsuccessful.[170]

Procedure and remedies

While much of the Defamation Act 2013 is concerned with the substance of the law, other provisions of the same Act also address procedural points. The latter are designed in part to respond to concerns about 'libel tourism', whereby someone with a remote connection with the United Kingdom brings claims for defamation in the English courts on the ground that what may be only a few copies of an allegedly defamatory article have been published in this country. Steps to tighten up on this are to be found in the 2013 Act, s 9, following which a defamation action may not be brought unless 'the court is satisfied that, of all the places in which the statement complained of has been published, England and Wales is clearly the most appropriate place in which to bring an action in respect of the statement' (s 9(2)).

This means that 'where a statement has been published in this jurisdiction and also abroad the court will be required to consider the overall global picture to consider where it would be most appropriate for a claim to be heard'.[171] By way of example, a statement 'published

---

[167] For details, see HL Deb, 7 May 1996, cols 24–5. See also cols 42–3 (regarding Mr Ian Greer).

[168] Ibid, col 24.

[169] Ibid, col 251.

[170] *Hamilton* v *Al Fayed* [2001] 1 AC 395. See A W Bradley [2000] PL 556.

[171] Defamation Act 2013, Explanatory Notes.

100,000 times in Australia and only 5,000 times in England' would be 'a good basis on which to conclude that the most appropriate jurisdiction in which to bring an action in respect of the statement was Australia rather than England'. However, a number of factors would have to be taken into account in addition to the number of times a statement was published in different jurisdictions, 'including, for example, the amount of damage to the claimant's reputation in this jurisdiction compared to elsewhere'.[172]

Three other procedural changes are also significant. The first is the abolition of jury trial in defamation cases (s 11), an issue that has been a major concern for publishers over many years. Actions for defamation were one of the few surviving forms of civil action where either party had a right to insist on trial by jury.[173] When the judge ruled that a statement was capable of being regarded as defamatory, it was the jury that decided whether the applicant had been defamed and if so the damages that he or she should recover. The provisions of the 2013 Act, s 11 are the end of a process in recent years in which the role of the jury has been diminished, a process triggered by the extravagant award of damages in some cases.[174] The removal of the jury nevertheless removes an important aspect of popular control over the conduct of the press.

The second additional procedural change is the power of the court to require a summary of its judgment in a defamation case to be published by the defendant. Where the parties are unable to agree the content of the summary, the dispute may be resolved by the court (s 12(3)), which is also empowered to give directions about 'the time, manner, form or place of publication' if necessary (s 12(4)).[175] The third procedural change is to be found in s 13, which applies where a court gives judgment for the claimant, in circumstances where the defendant may not be in a position to require the offending material to be withdrawn from circulation (as where it is on internet site, or where it is being distributed by others). In such cases, the court may order a number of steps to be taken, including the removal of a defamatory statement from a website (s 13(1)).

G. Breach of confidence

Government information

We turn finally to consider the role of breach of confidence as a restraint on freedom of expression. As with defamation, liability here arises under civil law rather than criminal law, which means that actions may be brought by individuals and companies as well as by the state. We have already seen in Chapter 16 how the action for breach of confidence has provided the basis for the emerging right to privacy. But the law relating to confidentiality does not apply only to protect information relating to the private life of the individual.

---

[172] Ibid.

[173] Senior Courts Act 1981, s 69.

[174] See *Tolstoy Miloslavsky* v *UK* (1995) 20 EHRR 442 (excessive damages awards inconsistent with defendant's Convention rights), and *John* v *Mirror Group Newspapers* [1997] QB 586 (judges to give greater guidance to juries about damages).

[175] Section 12 complements and extends generally the provisions of the Defamation Act 1996, s 8, which enables the court in some circumstances to deal with defamation cases by way of summary judgment. In these cases the court could order the defendant to publish a suitable correction and apology (s 9(1)(b)). If the parties are unable to agree the content of any such correction or apology, 'the court may direct the defendant to publish or cause to be published a summary of the court's judgment agreed by the parties or settled by the court in accordance with rules of court' (s 9(2)). Where the parties are unable to agree on the time, manner, form or place of publication of the correction and apology, 'the court may direct the defendant to take such reasonable and practicable steps as the court considers appropriate' (ibid).

It may thus be possible in some cases to use breach of confidence to restrain the disclosure of government information. However, the label of 'confidential' applied to a document does not mean that a court will restrain its publication should a copy reach a newspaper. In *Fraser v Evans*, the court refused to ban publication of a confidential report which Fraser, a public relations consultant, had prepared for the Greek government, when the *Sunday Times* had obtained a copy of it from Greek sources: Fraser's contract with the Greek government required him but not the government to keep it confidential.[176]

More recently, the Attorney General invoked the same action in 1975 in his attempt to restrain publication of the Crossman diaries, discussed more fully in Chapter 11 above. This is another case that revealed both the limitations of breach of confidence as a restriction on freedom of expression, as well as its potential scope. In that case an injunction was not granted to restrain the publication of the diaries. Lord Widgery CJ nevertheless ruled that publication of information received by a Cabinet minister prejudicial to Cabinet collective responsibility would be restrained if such restraint was clearly required in the public interest.[177]

Breach of confidence is important because it allows the government to apply for an order to prevent the publication of a document or information.[178] To that extent it is very different from defamation where the courts traditionally have been reluctant to grant injunctions, the victim being left instead to seek a remedy in damages (though this is not to deny the severe chilling effect of a claim in advance of publication that a proposed publication contains potentially defamatory material).[179] It is also very different from the criminal law, which relies on punishment after publication, though it would be possible both to seek an injunction to restrain a publication and to bring a prosecution under the Official Secrets Acts 1911–89.[180]

Spycatcher and national security

It is nevertheless clear that an action for breach of confidence may be brought to restrain the publication of government secrets. In this respect, the action acquired considerable prominence and value for the government as a tool for restraining the disclosure of secret information by disaffected members of the security services. Here, the most sensational attempt to use breach of confidence to protect government information was the *Spycatcher* case.

> Mr Peter Wright, a retired security service officer, wrote a book, *Spycatcher*, in which he claimed to reveal secrets relating to activities of the British security service. The book was due to be published initially in Australia, which the British government sought an injunction to restrain. Two British newspapers (*The Guardian* and *The Observer*) carried accounts of what the book was said to contain, at which point the Attorney General moved for an injunction to restrain the newspapers from carrying any such reports. An interim injunction was granted on the ground that publication would be a breach of confidence. Legal proceedings to

---

[176] [1969] 1 QB 349.

[177] *A-G v Jonathan Cape Ltd* [1976] QB 752. See also *Commonwealth of Australia v John Fairfax and Sons Ltd* (1980) 147 CLR 39.

[178] It is of course not only the government that may apply for an injunction to protect confidential information. See ch 16.

[179] *Herbage v Pressdram Ltd* [1984] 2 All ER 769. This is because of 'the value the court has placed on freedom of speech and … also on freedom of the press, when balancing it against the reputation of a single individual, who … can be compensated in damages' (at p 771).

[180] See ch 19.

restrain publication in Australia failed,[181] and the book was also published in the United States. When copies of the book began freely to enter the United Kingdom, *The Guardian* and *The Observer* moved to have the interim injunctions discharged, on the ground that there was now no public interest in maintaining the injunctions in view of the fact that the contents of the book were widely known and freely available throughout the world. The House of Lords (by a majority of three to two) refused the application on the ground that the restrictions remained necessary in the public interest (for reasons that were neither clear nor convincing).[182]

However, the Attorney General's application for permanent injunctions against the newspapers failed.[183] The House of Lords agreed that security service personnel owe a life-long duty of confidence and that they may be restrained by injunction from disclosing any information which they obtain in the service of the Crown, as may any third party to whom such information is improperly conveyed. However, the availability of the book in the United States fatally undermined the government's claim that the maintenance of the injunctions was necessary in the public interest. In the opinion of Lord Keith, 'general publication in this country would not bring about any significant damage to the public interest beyond what has already been done. All such secrets as the book may contain have been revealed to any intelligence service whose interests are opposed to those of the United Kingdom.'[184] But although the actions for permanent injunctions failed, the punishment of several newspapers for contempt of court was subsequently upheld by the House of Lords. *The Times* had published material which breached the terms of the injunctions against *The Observer* and *The Guardian*, and it was held that by their conduct they had interfered with the administration of justice.[185]

It was subsequently held by the European Court of Human Rights that the refusal of the House of Lords in 1987 to discharge the injunctions violated art 10 of the European Convention on Human Rights on the ground that, after publication of the book in the United States, the material in question was no longer confidential.[186] Breach of confidence has nevertheless become an established basis for regulating the publication of material about the security service,[187] and this continues to be the position, notwithstanding the Human Rights Act.

In *Attorney-General v Times Newspapers* Ltd[188] the newspaper gave an undertaking to the Attorney General not to publish information about the Secret Intelligence Service (SIS) which had been given to it by Richard Tomlinson, a former agent. When his book was subsequently published in Russia, the *Times* successfully applied to the court to have the undertaking varied, to allow it to publish any of Tomlinson's material which was 'generally

---

[181] (1987) 8 NSWLR 341 (Powell J); (1987) 75 ALR 353 (NSW Court of Appeal); (1988) 78 ALR 449 (High Court of Australia). See Turnbull, *The Spycatcher Trial*.

[182] *A-G v Guardian Newspapers Ltd* [1987] 3 All ER 316.

[183] *A-G v Guardian Newspapers Ltd (No 2)* [1990] 1 AC 109.

[184] For a fuller treatment of this intricate affair, see Ewing and Gearty, *Freedom under Thatcher*, pp 152–69. See also D G T Williams (1989) 12 Dalhousie LJ 209; and A W Bradley [1988] All ER Rev 55.

[185] *A-G v Times Newspapers Ltd* [1992] 1 AC 191.

[186] *The Observer v UK* (1992) 14 EHRR 153. And see I Leigh [1992] PL 200.

[187] See *Lord Advocate v Scotsman Publications Ltd* [1990] 1 AC 812; N Walker [1990] PL 354.

[188] [2001] 1 WLR 885.

accessible to the public at large'. The Attorney General thought that this variation was too wide, but the Court of Appeal overruled his objections and also rejected his claim that any publication should be approved in advance either by himself or by the court. Having regard to the Human Rights Act the court did not think it right that the newspaper 'should seek confirmation from the Attorney General or the court that facts that they intend to republish have been sufficiently brought into the public domain by prior publication so as to remove from them the cloak of confidentiality'. But the court emphasised that the newspaper was bound by confidentiality, the effect of the decision being that the newspaper alone should be responsible for determining when it thought the boundaries had been reached. Should it break the obligation, it would be 'subject to the sanctions that exist for contempt of court'.

So although Times Newspapers succeeded in having the undertaking varied, the result was hardly a ringing endorsement of freedom of expression, despite the Human Rights Act. The court also stated: 'It is desirable that there should usually be consultation between a newspaper and representatives of SIS before the newspaper published information that may include matters capable of damaging the service or endangering those who serve in it.' Such consultation does, in fact, take place. Where a publication is made in breach of confidence, the agent may be required to account for his or her profits.[189]

'Super-injunctions' and parliamentary privilege

As we have seen in Chapter 16, liability for breach of confidence has developed under the Human Rights Act, which has not led to an unequivocal vindication of free speech in this area. This is partly because Convention rights include the right to respect for one's private life, a provision that has to be balanced against the Convention right to freedom of expression. Breach of confidence continues to provide a basis of restraint of information that has political implications, as well as information that deals with personal or commercial secrets. One such example discussed in Chapter 16 relates to the journals of the Prince of Wales in which there was criticism of Chinese government officials at the time of the handover of Hong Kong by the United Kingdom.[190]

An even more controversial example of the use of injunctions to restrain the publication of confidential information is provided by the Trafigura affair, which raises questions also about the use of so-called 'super-injunctions' to prevent discussion of matters of public interest. Although the case was about restraining the publication of material subject to legal privilege,[191] the issues were similar in principle to questions that might arise in relation to breach of confidence. The matter erupted when Paul Farrelly MP tabled a parliamentary question about Trafigura which had obtained an injunction preventing the disclosure of an internal document relating to 'the alleged dumping of toxic waste in the Ivory Coast'.[192] The problem arose because a month earlier an injunction had been granted against *The Guardian* (and 'persons unknown') preventing it from publishing details of the report.

The latter injunction also prohibited publication of the fact that the injunction had been obtained, stating in terms that the respondent must not communicate or disclose 'the information that the Applicants have obtained an injunction'. A 'third level of secrecy was granted

---

[189] *Attorney-General* v *Blake* [2001] AC 268.
[190] *Associated Newspapers Ltd* v *Prince of Wales* [2006] EWCA Civ 1776, [2008] QB 57.
[191] Neuberger, *Report of the Committee on Super-Injunctions* (2011), para 5.10.
[192] HC 362 (2009–10), para 94.

by the judge in that Trafigura and subsidiary's identities as claimants were replaced by the random initials "RJW" and "SJW"'.[193] The gravity of this matter was increased still further when Trafigura informed *The Guardian* that it would be in breach of the injunction if it reported Mr Farrelly's question, which led the newspaper to report on its front page that it was unable to report a parliamentary question.[194] On this occasion, the Lord Chief Justice issued an unprecedented statement a week later doubting whether the injunction could prevent discussion of the matter in Parliament,[195] a view supported by the Speaker who resisted calls on behalf of the company for a debate on libel to be halted on *sub judice* grounds.[196]

In the course of that debate, the Parliamentary Under-Secretary of State for Justice agreed that reporting of any such matter in Parliament was protected by the Parliamentary Papers Act 1840, s 3, and that *The Guardian* was free to report Mr Farrelly's question.[197] The injunction was eventually withdrawn, and the position of *The Guardian* was thus vindicated.[198] However, doubts have since been expressed about the extent to which media reporting of parliamentary proceedings is in fact protected from the risk of legal liability.[199]

H. Conclusion

The Trafigura affair highlights the different potential threats to freedom of expression, with attempts to use the law directly to prevent the publication of a report, the identity of applicants for an injunction, and the existence of an injunction; as well as indirectly to prevent the press reporting of a parliamentary question, and a debate in Parliament. While the drama also revealed the continuing importance of parliamentary privilege as a means of protecting freedom of expression, the conclusion of the affair left a number of outstanding questions unresolved, not least the use of 'super-injunctions' to restrain publicity, as a new form of prior restraint.[200]

In the meantime, much has been done to remove redundant laws (seditious, blasphemous, obscene and criminal libel), though in some cases these have been replaced by legislation that occupies much the same territory. A great deal has also been done by decision to contain the scope of libel law, though again other restraints on freedom of expression have been fashioned to protect the privacy of individuals. As pointed out in the Court of Appeal in relation to the ECHR: 'the prominence nowadays to be given to Article 10 is matched by the prominence nowadays to be given to Article 8 and to the fact that an individual's reputation is an important part of his social identity'.[201]

These contrasts and contradictions are a reminder that there will always be those who wish to impose restraints on the speech of others, and that freedom of expression will never be unlimited.

---

[193] Ibid, para 95.

[194] *The Guardian*, 13 October 2009.

[195] HC 362 (2009–10), para 97.

[196] Ibid, paras 98, 102.

[197] See ch 9 above.

[198] The use of super-injunctions was also the subject of investigation by a committee chaired by Lord Neuberger, following which their use was discouraged though not prohibited. See Neuberger, *Report of the Committee on Super-Injunctions*, above. Chapter 6 of the latter report contains a detailed account of the Trafigura affair.

[199] Ibid, paras 6.23–6.24. See ch 9 above.

[200] See also *Terry* v *Persons Unknown* [2010] EWHC 119 (QB), [2010] Fam Law 453.

[201] *Lachaux* v *Independent Print Ltd*, above, para 90 (Davis LJ).

CHAPTER 18

Freedom of association and assembly

This chapter examines the principal features of the law relating to freedom of association and assembly.[1] These freedoms traditionally were protected in the same way as other freedoms in English law; that is to say, people are free to associate and assemble to the extent that their conduct is not otherwise unlawful. The principle is best illustrated in the context of freedom of assembly by the seminal decision in *Beatty* v *Gillbanks*:[2]

> Members of the Salvation Army insisted on marching through the streets of Weston-super-Mare despite violent opposition from the 'Skeleton Army' and despite an order from the magistrates that they should not march. In an attempt to stop the Salvationist marches, the police sought to have their leaders bound over to keep the peace on the ground that they had committed an unlawful assembly. If the Salvationists had not marched there would clearly have been no disturbance of the peace. As previous processions had led to disorder, the Salvationists knew that similar consequences were likely to ensue. The Divisional Court held that the acts of the Salvation Army were lawful and that it was not a necessary and natural consequence of these acts that disorder should have occurred. The court did not accept that a person might be punished for acting lawfully if he knew that his doing so might lead another person to act unlawfully.

Although historically the common law might thus offer some protection, cases in which freedom of assembly triumphed nevertheless tended in practice to be unusual, in view of the wide range of statutory (and common law) 'exceptions' to the legal principle. Protection for freedom of assembly has, however, now been enhanced by the Human Rights Act, with the right to freedom of association and assembly now being expressly protected by art 11 of the ECHR. But as in the case of the common law, these Convention rights are subject to significant qualifications and permitted limitations, provided they are 'prescribed by law' and 'necessary in a democratic society'. There thus continues to be a tension between freedom and restraint, and it is this tension that will be explored in the following pages.

A. Freedom of association[3]

The law generally imposes no restrictions on the freedom of individuals to associate together for political purposes. People are free to form themselves into political parties, pressure groups, community associations and so on, without any official approval. People are also free

---

[1] See Mead, *The New Law of Peaceful Protest* (a major study). See also Ewing and Gearty, *The Struggle for Civil Liberties*, chs 5 and 6; Ewing and Gearty, *Freedom under Thatcher*, ch 4; and Ewing, *Bonfire of the Liberties*, ch 4. Also C A Gearty, in McCrudden and Chambers (eds), *Individual Rights and the Law in Britain*, ch 2. Further, Morgan, *Conflict and Order*, and Townshend, *Making the Peace*. For Scotland, see Ewing and Dale-Risk, *Human Rights in Scotland*, ch 9. See also HL Paper 46, HC 320 (2008–9) (Joint Committee on Human Rights).

[2] (1882) 9 QBD 308. And see Hart and Honoré, *Causation in the Law*, pp 333–5. Compare *Deakin* v *Milne* 1882 10 R (J) 22, and *Hutton* v *Main* 1891 19 R (J) 5.

[3] See K D Ewing, in McCrudden and Chambers (eds), *Individual Rights and the Law in Britain*, ch 8.

to determine with whom they will associate: organisations ought not to be required to accept into membership or to retain individuals who for one reason of another have beliefs that collide with those of the organisation.[4] Trade unions, for example, cannot normally be required to take into membership people (such as members of the British National Party) whose beliefs and conduct are thought to be contrary to the principles of the union.[5] Freedom of association thus swings both ways: it is a right of the individual, but simultaneously a right of individuals in association, and sometimes the exercise of both rights gives rise to an irreconcilable conflict in which only one can prevail.

The first exception to the right to freedom of association relates to the need to promote a politically neutral public service. As we saw above, there continue to be restrictions on the political activities of civil servants, these depending to a great extent on the seniority of the official in question and the nature of the work in which he or she is engaged. Although these restrictions relate mainly to political activities rather than membership of political or other organisations, it would surely be unusual for senior civil servants to align themselves formally with a political party.[6] Similarly, local government officers in politically restricted posts may not actively engage in party politics, though there does not appear to be a restriction on membership of a political party.[7] Police officers may not take any active part in politics,[8] a rule designed 'to prevent a police officer doing anything which affects his impartiality or his appearance of impartiality'.[9] Concerns about external security led to the controversial banning of trade union membership at Government Communications Headquarters (GCHQ) in 1984, a ban not revoked until 1997.[10]

A second exception to the right to freedom of association lies in the banning of certain forms of association, even by people who are not otherwise restricted in their political activities because of their employment in the public service. Under the Public Order Act 1936, s 1, it is an offence for any person in a public place or at a public meeting to wear a uniform signifying association with a political organisation or with the promotion of any political object.[11] Passed in response to the conduct of fascists in the 1930s, s 2 of the same Act makes it an offence (*a*) to organise or train the members or supporters of any association for the purpose of enabling them to be used in usurping the functions of the police or the armed forces, or (*b*) to organise and train (or equip) them, either for enabling them to be employed for the use or display of physical force in promoting any political object, 'or in such manner as to arouse reasonable apprehension that they are organised and either trained or equipped for that purpose'.[12]

More recently, the Terrorism Act 2000 re-enacted wide-ranging restrictions on membership and participation in the activities of terrorist organisations.[13] This Act contains what appears to be the only example of British legislation that makes it an offence simply to be a member of a specific organisation;[14] the proscribed organisations include al-Qaeda and

[4] See *RSPCA* v *Attorney-General* [2001] 3 All ER 530.
[5] Employment Act 2008, s 19, implementing *ASLEF* v *United Kingdom* [2007] IRLR 361; K D Ewing (2007) 36 ILJ 425; (2009) 38 ILJ 50.
[6] See ch 11.
[7] Local Government and Housing Act 1989, ss 1–2 (as amended by the Local Democracy, Economic Development and Construction Act 2009); SI 1990 No 851. These arrangements have been found not to violate the ECHR, art 10: *Ahmed* v *UK* (2000) 29 EHRR 1. See G Morris [1998] PL 25; [1999] PL 211.
[8] SI 2003 No 527, reg 6 and Sch 1. See also Police Act 1996, s 64(1), restrictions on freedom of police officers to join trade unions.
[9] *Champion* v *Chief Constable of Gwent* [1990] 1 All ER 116.
[10] See ch 19 below. Also, Fredman and Morris, *The State as Employer*.
[11] See *O'Moran* v *DPP* [1975] QB 864. See now Terrorism Act 2000, s 13.
[12] *R* v *Jordan and Tyndall* [1963] Crim LR 124; D G T Williams [1970] CLJ 96, 102–4.
[13] Terrorism Act 2000. Part II.
[14] Ewing, note 1 above.

Hamas, as well as proscribed 'Irish Groups'. There are, in fact, 14 proscribed organisations listed in the Terrorism Act 2000, Sch 2; the Act contains a power for more to be added (s 3), as a result of which another 85 have now been proscribed.[15]

B. The right of public meeting

Public meetings may be held in the open air in places to which the public have free access. However, it is usually necessary to get the prior consent of the owners of the land, which is a significant issue as much public space is privately owned.[16] Many local authorities have made by-laws governing the use of parks for various purposes, including public meetings,[17] with fresh statutory powers to make public spaces protection orders having a potential application to public assemblies.[18] Otherwise, it may be possible to hold an assembly on the highway without the need for prior consent.[19] But the scope of this right is very limited: the assembly must be 'reasonable and non-obstructive, taking into account its size, duration and the nature of the highway'. It must, moreover, be 'not inconsistent with the primary right of the public to pass and repass'.[20] As we shall see, it may be very difficult to hold an assembly on the highway without inadvertently acting unlawfully.

In the case of Trafalgar Square in London, statutory regulations have been made under which approval is required from the Greater London Authority and the Mayor acting on its behalf.[21] Similarly, in the case of Hyde Park, no meetings may be held as of right:[22] although Speaker's Corner is available for any who wish to speak, the law is applied there 'as fully as anywhere else'.[23] More recently, the Police Reform and Social Responsibility Act 2011 introduced new controls on activities in Parliament Square.[24] With the activities of anti-war protesters clearly in mind,[25] the Act is designed to stop the unauthorised use of loudspeakers and loudhailers, and the use of tents and sleeping equipment in the controlled area. Police officers have wide powers to give directions to individuals to cease a prohibited activity, failure to comply with which is an offence.[26] These measures have since been extended to a controlled area in the vicinity of the Palace of Westminster.[27]

For meetings, rallies or assemblies which are not held in the open air, a major practical restriction is the need to find premises for them, to say nothing of the cost of hiring a hall and dealing with security.[28] The organisers of an unpopular cause may find it difficult to hire

---

[15] See ch 20 below.

[16] Rowbottom, *Democracy Distorted*. The problem is compounded by a lack of transparency about what public space is privately owned and the conditions imposed by developers or owners on the use of the space: *The Guardian*, 26 September 2017.

[17] *De Morgan* v *Metropolitan Board of Works* (1880) 5 QBD 155; *Aldred* v *Miller* 1925 JC 21; *Aldred* v *Langmuir* 1932 JC 22. And see *R* v *Barnet Council, ex p Johnson* (1990) 89 LGR 581 (condition excluding 'political activity' at community festival held invalid).

[18] Anti-social Behaviour, Crime and Policing Act 2014, s 59. See note 193 below.

[19] *DPP* v *Jones* [1999] 2 AC 240. See pp 495–6 below.

[20] Ibid, per Lord Chancellor (Irvine).

[21] Greater London Authority Act 1999, ss 383–5. See Trafalgar Square Bye-Laws 2012.

[22] *Bailey* v *Williamson* (1873) 8 QBD 118; Royal Parks and Other Open Spaces Regulations 1997, SI 1997 No 1639 (as amended).

[23] *Redmond-Bate* v *DPP* [2000] HRLR 249.

[24] Police Reform and Social Responsibility Act 2011, ss 142–9.

[25] On whom, see *R (Haw)* v *Home Secretary* [2006] EWCA Civ 532, [2006] QB 780; *DPP* v *Haw* [2007] EWHC 1931 (Admin), [2008] 1 WLR 379.

[26] On the scope of the powers, see 2011 Act above, ss 144, 145.

[27] Anti-social Behaviour, Crime and Policing Act 2014, s 153, inserting new Police Reform and Social Responsibility Act 2011, s 142A.

[28] Under the Criminal Justice and Public Order Act 1994, s 170, the security costs of political party conferences may be met by the Treasury.

suitable venues, whether these are owned by private individuals or by public authorities such as a local council. However, candidates at local, parliamentary and assembly elections are entitled to the use of schools and other public rooms for the purpose of holding election meetings.[29] Otherwise local authorities appear to have a wide discretion in deciding to whom to let their premises, although this discretion is subject to law and may now be open to challenge on the ground of illegality under the Human Rights Act 1998.[30] But not even the Human Rights Act has fully met the argument that local authorities in particular should be under a general duty to make their halls available to all groups, whether popular or unpopular, without discriminating between them on political or other grounds.[31]

Such a duty applies to universities and higher and further education institutions under the Education (No 2) Act 1986. By s 43, the governing bodies of such establishments must 'take such steps as are reasonably practicable to ensure that freedom of speech within the law is secured for members, students and employees of the establishment and for visiting speakers'. Governing bodies must issue and keep up to date a code of practice to facilitate the discharge of these duties. However, the foregoing measures must now be read along with the Counter Terrorism and Security Act 2015, which requires universities (and others) to have 'due regard to the need to prevent people from being drawn into terrorism'. Although provision is made in the 2015 Act to respect freedom of expression (s 31); consistently with this latter duty, universities have nevertheless made it clear that some speakers will not be welcome on campus,[32] in a manner that sits uncomfortably with the duties under the 1986 Act.[33]

In *R v University of Liverpool, ex p Caesar-Gordon*,[34] the university authorities refused permission for a meeting at the university to be addressed by two first secretaries from the South African Embassy. This was done because of fear that in the event of the meeting taking place public violence would erupt in Toxteth, the residential area adjacent to the university. On an application for judicial review by the chairman of the student Conservative Association, the Divisional Court held that, on a true construction of s 43(1), the duty imposed on the university is local to the members of the university and its premises. Its duty is to ensure, so far as is reasonably practical, that those whom it may control, that is to say its members, students and employees, do not prevent the exercise of freedom of speech within the law by other members, students and employees and by visiting speakers in places under its control. But under s 43(1), the university was not entitled to take into account threats of 'public disorder' outside the confines of the university by persons not within its control. A declaration was granted that the university acted ultra vires in denying permission to hold the meeting. The court suggested, however, that had the university authorities confined their reasons when refusing permission 'to the risk of disorder on university premises and among university members', then no objection could have been taken to their decisions.

---

[29] Representation of the People Act 1983, ss 95, 96. See *Webster* v *Southwark Council* [1983] QB 698; *Ettridge* v *Morrell* (1986) 85 LGR 100.

[30] Such decisions may also be open to challenge if the refusal to let a hall is unreasonable in the *Wednesbury* sense: *Wheeler* v *Leicester City Council* [1985] AC 1054. Cf *Verrall* v *Great Yarmouth BC* [1981] QB 202.

[31] Street, *Freedom, the Individual and the Law* (5th edn), p 56.

[32] See for example, University of Cambridge, University Statement on Freedom of Speech, 13 June 2016: http://www.registrarysoffice.admin.cam.ac.uk/governance-and-strategy/university-statement-freedom-speech.

[33] The 1986 Act most notably includes an obligation 'to ensure, so far as is reasonably practicable, that the use of any premises of the establishment is not denied to any individual or body of persons on any ground connected with (*a*) the beliefs or views of that individual or of any member of that body; or (*b*) the policy or objectives of that body' (s 43).

[34] See E Barendt [1987] PL 344.

C. Public processions and assemblies

Public processions

By contrast with static meetings on the highway, at common law a procession in the streets is prima facie lawful, being no more than the collective exercise of the public right to use the highway for its primary purpose.[35] This does not mean that it would be a reasonable use of the highway for a dozen demonstrators to link arms and proceed down a street so as to interfere with the right of others to use the highway, or for a large group of demonstrators to decide to obstruct a street: a procession would become a nuisance 'if the right was exercised unreasonably or with reckless regard of the rights of others'.[36] It might also be held to be an obstruction of the highway.

But because processions were prima facie lawful, statutory powers were needed if the police were to control them. General powers were contained in the Public Order Act 1936, passed at a time when fascist marches in the East End of London were a serious threat to order. These powers were extended by the Public Order Act 1986. The first major change was the introduction of a requirement that the organisers of a public procession should give advance notice to the police (s 11). The duty applies in respect of processions designed (*a*) to demonstrate support for or opposition to the views or actions of any person or body of persons; (*b*) to publicise a cause or campaign; or (*c*) to mark or commemorate an event. There are a few exclusions from the duty to notify,[37] but most processions for political purposes will be caught by these requirements. The notice, which must specify the proposed time, date and route, must be delivered to a police station (in the area where the procession is to start) at least six clear days in advance.

In addition to this notice requirement, the 1986 Act extends the grounds for which conditions can be imposed on public processions, as well as the circumstances whereby such processions may be banned. So in addition to the original ground of 'serious public disorder' in the 1936 Act, a senior police officer may impose conditions where he or she reasonably believes that the procession may result in serious damage to property or serious disruption to the life of the community. The officer may also impose conditions where the purpose of the organisers of the procession is to intimidate others (s 12). The conditions may be such as appear necessary to prevent disorder, damage, disruption or intimidation, including conditions prescribing the route and prohibiting entry to a specified public place. Unlike the 1936 Act, there is no restriction on the giving of directions relating to the display of flags, banners or emblems. If these powers to impose conditions are not enough to prevent serious public disorder, the chief officer of police may apply to the local authority (or in London the Home Secretary) for a banning order under what is now s 13 of the 1986 Act. The power to issue a banning order is restricted to serious public disorder; the section does not permit an order to be made on the wider grounds on which conditions may be imposed.

Similar powers in Scotland are in the Civic Government (Scotland) Act 1982.[38] By s 62, the organisers of a public procession must notify (at least 28 days in advance) both the Scottish police and the local authority in whose area the procession is to be held. After consulting the

---

[35] A Goodhart (1937) 6 CLJ 161, 169.

[36] *Lowdens* v *Keaveney* [1903] 2 IR 82, 90 (Gibson J); and see *R* v *Clark (No 2)* [1964] 2 QB 315.

[37] By s 11(2), there is no duty to notify where 'the procession is one commonly or customarily held in the police area (or areas) in which it is proposed to be held or is a funeral procession organised by a funeral director acting in the normal course of his business'. A monthly cycle ride by large numbers of cyclists through the streets of London which did not follow any particular route was held to fall within s 11(2): *Kay* v *Metropolitan Police Commissioner* [2008] UKHL 69, [2008] 1 WLR 2723.

[38] See Ewing and Dale-Risk, note 1 above, ch 9. See also W Finnie, in Finnie, Himsworth and Walker (eds), *Edinburgh Essays in Public Law*, pp 251–77.

chief constable, the local authority may then prohibit the holding of the procession or impose conditions upon it. This may be done having regard to the likely effect of the procession in relation to public safety, public order, damage to property and disruption to the life of the community, while the local authority should also have regard to any 'excessive burden on the police'.[39] It thus appears not only that a local authority in Scotland could ban a specific march (whereas in England and Wales the ban must be on the holding of all public processions or of any class of public processions specified in the order), but also that the grounds for imposing a ban (or conditions) are both different and wider.

Another important difference between Scots law and the 1986 Act is the appeal procedure in the Civic Government (Scotland) Act 1982, s 64. Thus, a person who has given notice of a procession under s 62 may appeal within 14 days to the sheriff against an order prohibiting or imposing conditions on the procession. The grounds of appeal are limited by the statute to error of law, mistake of fact, unreasonable exercise of discretion or that the local authority have 'otherwise acted beyond their powers'. There is no comparable provision in the Public Order Act 1986. It is true that the organiser of a procession could seek judicial review of a banning order or of an order to impose conditions.[40] But, unlike in Scotland, this would be review and not an appeal, and it would be in the High Court under the judicial review procedure and not in the local sheriff court. In any event, the Court of Appeal has made clear that, in a case involving a banning order under s 3(2) of the 1936 Act, it is not willing to encourage such applications.[41] There is also the practical problem of securing judicial review in enough time before the procession is due to be held.

There is no duty on the police to give notice of the conditions 'as early as possible', as there is on the local authority in Scotland.[42] If the police exercise their powers unreasonably, it may be possible for anyone arrested for violating the conditions to challenge the legality of any conditions as a defence in criminal proceedings. But this will not restore their right to participate in the procession, or the right to conduct the procession as initially conceived.

Public assemblies

Police powers specifically to regulate public assemblies were introduced in the Public Order Act 1986 (s 14). The senior police officer present at an assembly (or the chief constable in the case of an assembly intended to be held) may impose conditions as to its location and duration, as well as the number of people who may be present. These conditions may be issued where it is reasonably believed (*a*) that the assembly may result in serious public disorder, serious damage to property, or serious disruption to the life of the community; or (*b*) that the purpose of organising the assembly is to intimidate others. A public assembly is defined to mean an assembly of two or more people in a public place which is wholly or partly open to the air (s 16).[43]

There is no procedure in the Act for challenging instructions issued under this power, although if they are issued long enough in advance, judicial review is available in principle. The only other means of challenging any directions would be collaterally, as a defence in

---

[39] Police, Public Order and Criminal Justice (Scotland) Act 2006, s 71, amending Civic Government (Scotland) Act 1982, s 63.

[40] Judicial review was also available in principle to challenge banning orders under s 3(2) of the Public Order Act 1936. See *Kent* v *Metropolitan Police Commissioner*, *The Times*, 15 May 1981. For the position under the ECHR, see *Plattform 'Ärzte für das Leben'* v *Austria* (1988) 13 EHRR 204.

[41] *Kent* v *Metropolitan Police Commissioner*, above. That may have to be re-assessed, however, in light of the Human Rights Act 1998.

[42] Civic Government (Scotland) Act 1982, s 63.

[43] As amended by the Anti-social Behaviour Act 2003, s 57. Before then a public assembly for this purpose was defined as meaning an assembly of at least 20 people.

criminal proceedings for violating a direction given under the Act. It could be argued that the police had exceeded their powers, for example, because the purpose of an assembly was to cause inconvenience and embarrassment to third parties, rather than to intimidate them.[44] Nevertheless, the section gives the police wide powers to control public assemblies, and by the power to issue directions, to frustrate the purpose of the assembly. In a report on the G20 protests in 2009 (at which a bystander died after an incident with a police officer), the House of Commons Home Affairs Committee noted concerns about the way in which this power is now being used, drawing attention in particular to an alleged failure of the police properly to communicate their use of section 14, so that to 'the protesters being dispersed it seemed as if the police, without warning had began to use force to clear a peaceful protest'.[45]

The Criminal Justice and Public Order Act 1994 added new powers in respect of public assemblies, corresponding to the powers relating to public processions in s 13 of the 1986 Act.[46] These powers apply to 'trespassory assemblies', that is to say an assembly 'on land to which the public has no right of access or only a limited right of access', a wide definition of uncertain scope, as considered below. The power of the police – in what is now the Public Order Act 1986, s 14A – is activated where a chief officer 'reasonably believes' that such an assembly of 20 or more people (*a*) is likely to be held without the permission of the occupier of the land, and (*b*) may result in serious disruption to the life of the community or significant damage to land, a building or monument of historical, architectural, archaeological or scientific importance.

If these conditions are met, the chief officer of police may apply to the local authority for an order prohibiting all 'trespassory assemblies' in the district or part of it, for a specified period of up to four days in an area within five miles' radius of a specified centre. The order, which may be varied or revoked before it expires, may be made after consulting the Secretary of State (who must give consent before an order may be made), and the order may be made as requested, or with modifications. In Scotland there is no need for ministerial approval to the making of the order (or in granting it with varied terms), while in London the order may be issued by the Metropolitan Police Commissioner with the consent of the Home Secretary. It is an offence to organise or take part in an assembly which is known to be prohibited, and a constable in uniform may stop any person reasonably believed to be on the way to an assembly 'likely to be an assembly which is prohibited', and 'direct him [or her] not to proceed in the direction of the assembly'. It is an offence to fail to comply with a direction.

In *DPP* v *Jones*[47] an order had been made prohibiting the holding of assemblies within a four-mile radius of Stonehenge from 29 May to 1 June 1995. While the order was in force, a peaceful assembly was held within the area covered by the order. When those present refused to disperse, they were arrested and convicted of trespassory assembly. The conviction was overturned by the Crown Court, and on an appeal by way of case stated it was held that conduct could constitute a trespassory assembly even though the conduct complained of was peaceful and did not obstruct the highway.

On a further appeal to the House of Lords, the question was whether the assembly exceeded the public's right of access to the highway for the purposes of the definition of a 'trespassory assembly': if the public had the right to use the highway in this way, there would

---

[44] *Police* v *Lorna Reid* [1987] Crim LR 702.
[45] HC 418 (2009–10), para 27. The same report also expressed concerns about the use of section 14 against journalists covering protests.
[46] On the 1994 Act, see M J Allen and S Cooper (1995) 59 MLR 364.
[47] [1999] 2 AC 240; G Clayton (2000) 63 MLR 252.

be no 'trespass' under the 1986 Act as amended. The House of Lords (dividing 3–2) reinstated the decision of the Crown Court. The Lord Chancellor said that the right to use the highway was not limited to passage and repassage: 'the public highway is a public place which the public may enjoy for any reasonable purpose, provided the activity in question does not amount to a public or private nuisance and does not obstruct the highway by unreasonably impeding the primary right of the public to pass and repass: within these qualifications there is a public right of peaceful assembly on the highway'.[48]

D. Freedom of assembly and private property rights

Picketing

The purpose of picketing is to enable pickets to impart information to those entering or leaving premises, or in some cases to seek to persuade them not to enter in the first place. It has been said that the Human Rights Act 'arguably has created a "right to picket" to the extent that the right to peaceful assembly has been guaranteed by article 11 of the [ECHR]'.[49] However, those who picket may be subject to directions issued by the police under s 14 of the Public Order Act 1986. The police may also issue directions to prevent a breach of the peace; failure to comply with such directions may lead to an arrest for obstructing a police officer.[50] But even if a picket is perfectly peaceful and is not subject to regulation by the police in these ways, those who participate may in law be committing offences for which they can be arrested without a warrant provided the conditions for making an arrest are met.

1. Criminal and civil liability

The offence most obviously committed in the past by those engaged in peaceful picketing is obstruction of the highway under the Highways Act 1980, s 137, for the purposes of which the highway includes the pavement as well as the road. A picket is no more a lawful or unlawful use of the highway than is any other kind of assembly.[51] Under the Trade Union and Labour Relations (Consolidation) Act 1992, s 241 (a measure originally contained in the Conspiracy and Protection of Property Act 1875, s 7), it is an offence for a person 'wrongfully and without legal authority' to 'watch and beset' premises where a person works or happens to be, with a view to compelling him or her to abstain from doing something which he or she is entitled to do. This is an offence introduced to deal with the workplace, but there is no reason why its application should be so limited. Having apparently fallen into disuse, what is now s 241 was revived during the miners' strike of 1984–5 as one of the weapons in the police armoury for dealing with the large-scale picketing that took place.[52]

Apart from possible criminal liability, those who organise a picket may also face civil liability. There is authority for the view that picketing premises may constitute a private nuisance against the owner or occupier of these premises. The law is sufficiently unclear that an interim injunction may be granted on an application to stop the picketing.

[48] Ibid, at p 257.
[49] *Gate Gourmet London Ltd* v *TGWU* [2005] EWHC 1889 (QB), [2005] IRLR 881, para 22 (Fulford J).
[50] See pp 512–3 below.
[51] See *Broome* v *DPP* [1974] AC 587; *Kavanagh* v *Hiscock* [1974] QB 600; and *Hirst* v *Chief Constable of West Yorkshire* (1987) 85 Cr App R 143.
[52] See P Wallington (1985) 14 ILJ 145.

In *Hubbard* v *Pitt*, a community action group organised a peaceful picket outside the offices of estate agents in Islington, distributing leaflets and displaying placards to protest against the firm's part in improving property at the expense of working-class residents. On the issue of whether an interim injunction should be issued to the firm against the pickets, Forbes J held that the picketing was unlawful since it was not in contemplation or furtherance of a trade dispute (on the significance of which, see below) and was inconsistent with the public right to use the highway for passage and repassage.

But in the Court of Appeal, the majority upheld the interim injunction on quite different grounds, holding only that the plaintiffs had a real prospect of establishing at the eventual trial that the protesters were committing a private nuisance against them and that the balance of convenience lay in favour of the picketing being stopped until the main hearing of the action. Lord Denning MR dissented, holding that the use of the highway for the picket was not unreasonable and did not constitute a nuisance at common law; he considered that picketing other than for trade disputes was lawful so long as it was done merely to obtain or communicate information or for peaceful persuasion.[53]

During the miners' strike of 1984–5 an attempt was made – successfully in the short term – to extend the tort of private nuisance. So in *Thomas* v *NUM (South Wales Area)*,[54] Scott J held that pickets would be liable not only to the owner or occupier of the premises being picketed, but also to workers (and presumably others) who were 'unreasonably harassed' in entering the premises. This extension of tortious liability was subsequently rejected, in relation to an industrial dispute at Wapping in 1985–6.[55]

2. Special rules for trade disputes

Special rules govern picketing in the case of trade disputes. As now provided by the Trade Union and Labour Relations (Consolidation) Act 1992, s 220:

It shall be lawful for a person in contemplation or furtherance of a trade dispute[56] to attend

(a) at or near his own place of work; or

(b) if he is an official of a trade union, at or near the place of work of a member of that union whom he is accompanying and whom he represents

for the purpose only of peacefully obtaining or communicating information or peacefully persuading any person to work or abstain from working.[57]

This provision, unlike its predecessors, restricts the freedom to picket in a trade dispute to one's own place of work.[58] There is no restriction in the Act on the number of people who may picket in this way, but a Code of Practice on Picketing issued with parliamentary approval recommends no more than six people at any particular site.[59]

---

[53] [1976] QB 142. See P Wallington [1976] CLJ 82. But picketing is not necessarily a nuisance: see K Miller and C Woolfson (1994) 23 ILJ 209, at pp 216–17.

[54] [1986] Ch 20 (K D Ewing [1985] CLJ 374). See now Protection from Harassment Act 1997, and *Hunter* v *Canary Wharf* [1997] AC 655.

[55] *News Group Newspapers Ltd* v *SOGAT 1982 (No 2)* [1987] ICR 181.

[56] For the meaning of the term 'trade dispute', see Trade Union and Labour Relations (Consolidation) Act 1992, s 244.

[57] See also the Code of Practice on Picketing issued under the 1992 Act.

[58] As to secondary action under the old law, see *Duport Steels Ltd* v *Sirs* [1980] 1 All ER 529.

[59] SI 1992 No 476. Failure to comply with the code does not render any person liable to proceedings, but it may be taken into account by a court or tribunal. See e.g. *Thomas* v *NUM (South Wales Area)*, above.

The Trade Union Act 2016 introduced additional restrictions requiring greater trade union supervision of pickets.[60]

Even if these requirements are met, there is no right on the part of pickets to stop vehicles and to compel drivers and their occupants to listen to what they have to say. In *Broome v DPP*,[61] the House of Lords refused to read such a right into a statutory predecessor of the current law on the ground that it would involve reading into the Act words which in their view would seriously diminish the liberty of the subject. Everyone has the right to use the highway free from the risk of being compulsorily stopped by any private citizen and compelled to listen to what he or she does not want to hear.[62] Pickets thus have a right to seek to communicate information or to seek peacefully to persuade, but not to stop persons or vehicles.

The purpose of the special provisions relating to picketing in trade disputes is to give workers and trade union officials a limited protection from both criminal and civil liability. So far as the criminal law is concerned, those who picket peacefully for the permitted purposes will not be liable under either the Highways Act 1980, s 137, or the Trade Union and Labour Relations (Consolidation) Act 1992, s 241. This is because the latter, by s 220 (providing that picketing 'shall be lawful'), gives limited legal authority to obstruct the highway and to watch and beset. If, however, the purpose of the picket is deemed to be the causing of an obstruction rather than peaceful persuasion or the peaceful communication of information, then s 220 of the 1992 Act will not prevent those involved from being arrested and charged.

So far as civil liability is concerned, s 220 provides an immunity from liability for private nuisance where the pickets are acting peacefully.[63] But it does not provide immunity where the purpose of the picket is adjudged to be to harass others, as in *Thomas v NUM (South Wales Area)*.[64] Together with s 219 of the 1992 Act, s 220 also gives pickets immunity in tort for conspiracy, inducing breach of contract, and intimidation.[65] In this case, however, the protection is of qualified value, for it applies only where the increasingly tight restrictions on the conduct of industrial action have been complied with, including the holding of a secret ballot, in some cases the meeting of ballot thresholds, and the giving of appropriate notice to employers.

There may be circumstances where picketing in the course of a trade dispute does not involve the commission of a tort and where as a result the immunity is unnecessary. Although such cases are rare, they are not unknown.

In *Middlebrook Mushrooms Ltd* v *Transport and General Workers' Union*,[66] the plaintiff employers were in dispute with some of their employees who went on strike and were subsequently dismissed. The employees then organised a campaign to distribute leaflets outside supermarkets to persuade shoppers not to buy the plaintiff's mushrooms. An injunction was granted at first instance to restrain the defendants from directly interfering with the employer's contracts, but was discharged on appeal.

---

[60] Trade Union Act 2016, s 10, introducing a new Trade Union and Labour Relations (Consolidation) Act 1992, s 220A. See R Dukes and N Kountouris (2016) 45 ILJ 337.

[61] [1974] AC 587. Also *Kavanagh v Hiscock* [1974] QB 600.

[62] Ibid, at p 603.

[63] *Hubbard v Pitt* [1976] QB 142.

[64] [1986] Ch 20.

[65] For full consideration of these questions, reference should be made to the labour law texts, e.g. Collins, Ewing and McColgan, *Labour Law*; Deakin and Morris, *Labour Law*; and Smith and Baker, *Smith and Wood's Employment Law*.

[66] [1993] ICR 612.

Neither party relied on the 1992 Act and it was held that in order for the defendants' action to be tortious, the persuasion had to be directed at one of the parties to the contracts allegedly interfered with (in this case between the supermarket and the employers). Here the 'suggested influence was exerted, if at all, through the actions or the anticipated actions of third parties who were free to make up their own minds'. The leaflets were directed at customers and contained no message which was directed at the supermarket managers.

Sit-ins, squatting and forcible entry

In recent years the expression of protest has often taken the form of entry onto private land, most notably by animal rights protesters and environmental activists, the former protesting about field sports and vivisection, the latter about fracking or the building of new motorways, power stations or airports, which in the process spoil or destroy the natural or built environment. Other groups to engage in this type of activity are workers protesting about the threat of job losses, and peace campaigners anxious about nuclear weapons or the role of British troops in Afghanistan or Iraq.

1. Criminal liability

There is no right to enter private property for these purposes,[67] and this form of protest action may fall foul of some of the measures already discussed, although there are other provisions that may be relevant. So in *Chandler* v *DPP*,[68] an attempt by nuclear disarmers to enter and sit down outside an RAF base was held to be a conspiracy to commit a breach of the Official Secrets Act 1911, s 1(1), which makes it an offence for any purpose prejudicial to the safety of the state to approach or enter 'any prohibited place'. In *Galt* v *Philp*,[69] a sit-in at a hospital laboratory by scientific officers was held to be a breach of s 7 of the Conspiracy and Protection of Property Act 1875 (now s 241 of the Trade Union and Labour Relations (Consolidation) Act 1992).

Action of this type is also governed to some extent by the Criminal Law Act 1977, which extensively reformed the law following the recommendation of the Law Commission.[70] Part I creates a statutory offence of conspiracy, which was charged in *R* v *Jones*[71] where the accused entered an RAF base with the intent to cause criminal damage to military equipment at the time of the Iraq war. It was no defence that the events in Iraq were unlawful under international law, the court rejecting a claim to this effect based on the Criminal Damage Act 1971. Part II of the 1977 Act created various offences relating to entering and remaining on property. These include (*a*) without lawful authority, to use or threaten violence for the purpose of securing entry into any premises on which another person is present and against the will of that person (s 6); (*b*) to remain on residential premises as a trespasser after being required to leave by or on behalf of a displaced residential occupier of the premises (s 7); (*c*) without lawful authority, to have offensive weapons on premises after having entered them as a trespasser (s 8); (*d*) to enter as a trespasser any foreign embassies and other diplomatic premises (s 9); and (*e*) to resist or obstruct a sheriff or bailiff seeking to enforce a court order for possession (s 10).

---

[67] *Appleby* v *United Kingdom* (2003) 37 EHRR 38 (exclusion of protesters from a shopping centre not a breach of the ECHR). See J Rowbottom [2005] EHRLR 186, and same author, *Democracy Distorted*, ch 6.

[68] [1964] AC 763. Prosecutions have also been brought for breach of regulations made under the Military Lands Act 1892: *Francis* v *Cardle* 1988 SLT 578.

[69] [1984] IRLR 156. See K Miller (1984) 13 ILJ 111. For the offence under the 1992 Act, see p 496 above.

[70] HC 176 (1975–6). Cf *Kamara* v *DPP* [1974] AC 104.

[71] [2006] UKHL 16, [2007] 1 AC 136.

Additional measures directed at trespassing on private land were introduced by the Criminal Justice and Public Order Act 1994. Indeed, Part V of the Act is entitled 'Public Order: Collective Trespass or Nuisance on Land', but deals with a wide range of different issues, not all of which are concerned with freedom of assembly. This part of the Act deals, for example, with people trespassing on land, 'with the common purpose of residing there for any period' (s 61),[72] gatherings on land in the open air of 20 or more persons (whether or not trespassers) at which amplified music is played during the night (so-called raves) (s 63),[73] the removal of squatters (ss 75–6), and unauthorised campers residing on land, without the consent of the occupier (s 77). The Act does, however, deal expressly with questions of freedom of assembly and public protest, not least in the provision it makes for 'trespassory assemblies', the terms of which we have already encountered.

Otherwise s 68 deals with what are referred to as 'disruptive trespassers', the main targets being animal rights' activists who trespassed on land to disrupt fox-hunting events. But s 68 is not confined to such activity, the government declining to accept an Opposition amendment to limit its scope to country sports, on the ground that there is no reason why events such as church fêtes, public race meetings or open-air political meetings 'should suffer the invasion of others who intend to intimidate, obstruct or disrupt these proceedings'.[74] Thus it is an offence (of aggravated trespass) for any person to trespass on land to intimidate persons taking part in lawful activities or to obstruct or disrupt such activity.[75] The senior police officer present at the scene is empowered to require anyone committing or participating in aggravated trespass to leave the land in question; failure to do so is an offence.[76]

More recent concerns about demonstrations at or near royal palaces led to the introduction of a new criminal offence to enter or be on any designated site as a trespasser.[77] A designated site is one designated by the Secretary of State and may include any Crown land, any land owned privately by the Queen or the Prince of Wales, and any land designated in the interests of national security.

2. Civil liability and injunctions

As in the case of picketing outside private property,[78] civil law has an important role to play in relation to those who take their protest into or onto private property.

> In *Department of Transport* v *Williams*,[79] an application was made for injunctions to restrain protesters from action designed to disrupt the building of the M3 extension over Twyford Down. Interim injunctions were granted by Alliott J to restrain the defendants from (i) entering upon land specified in the order, (ii) interfering with the use of the highway specified in the order, and (iii) interfering with the carrying on of work authorised by the M3 Motorway Scheme (SI 1990 No 463).

....
[72] See *R (Fuller)* v *Dorset Chief Constable* [2002] EWHC Admin 1057, [2003] QB 480.

[73] As amended by the Anti-social Behaviour Act 2003, s 58.

[74] Official Report, Standing Committee B, 8 February 1994, col 614.

[75] See *Winder* v *DPP*, *The Times*, 14 August 1996 (Schiemann LJ); *DPP* v *Barnard*, *The Times*, 9 November 1999 (Laws LJ); *DPP* v *Tilly* [2002] Crim LR 128; and *McAdam* v *Urquhart* 2004 SLT 790. It is no defence to a charge under s 68 (by virtue of s 68(2)) that the activities being disrupted were unlawful under international law: *R* v *Jones* [2006] UKHL 16, [2007] 1 AC 136. See also *Richardson* v *DPP* [2014] UKSC 8 on the limited scope of the s 68(2) defence,

[76] It is no defence to a charge under s 68 that the accused (in this case protesters against genetically modified crops who disrupted the drilling of maize) had an honest and genuine belief about the dangers of such crops: *DPP* v *Bayer* [2003] EWHC 2567 (Admin), [2004] 1 WLR 2856 (DC).

[77] Serious Organised Crime and Police Act 2005, s 128.

[78] *Hubbard* v *Pitt*, above.

[79] *The Times*, 7 December 1993.

> In the case of the first injunctions, it was subsequently held that these could be granted on the ground of trespass, but that the second should be set aside because they added nothing to the first. The third required there to be a basis in law for holding that it was tortious to prevent or interfere with the department's carrying out of works under the authorisation in the statutory instrument. It was held that in such a case an injunction could be grounded in the tort of wrongful interference with business; the unlawful means for the purposes of establishing this was found in the Highways Act 1980, which provides by s 303 that it is an offence wilfully to obstruct any person carrying out his lawful duties under the Act.[80]

The risk of civil liability is particularly serious in view of the principle in *American Cyanamid Co* v *Ethicon Ltd*[81] that an interim injunction may be granted on the ground that there is a serious issue to be tried and that the balance of convenience is in favour of relief, pending the trial of the action.[82] The defendant thus need not be acting unlawfully to be restrained, it being possible and indeed likely that the balance of convenience will lie in favour of the plaintiff where disorder is threatened. On the other hand, it has been held that *American Cyanamid Co* does not deal with the situation where the granting or otherwise of the interim injunction is likely to dispose finally of the matter,[83] as in the case of a protest, the cause of which may well have passed before the matter comes to trial. In these cases, it has been held that 'the degree of likelihood the plaintiff would have succeeded in establishing his right to an injunction if the action had gone to trial, is a factor to be brought into the balance'.[84]

Applications for injunctions to restrain assemblies of various kinds are likely to encounter claims based on the Human Rights Act 1998 to the extent that the injunction will undermine the right to freedom of assembly. In these circumstances the courts ought to give more weight to the respondent's defence than might otherwise have been the case.[85]

E. Public order offences

Riot and violent disorder

As well as the rules relating to assemblies and processions, there are several ways in which a breach of public order may constitute an offence. Such offences were initially developed through the common law, but following Law Commission recommendations in 1983[86] these common law offences were abolished and replaced with new offences in the Public Order Act 1986.[87]

The first of these is *riot*, defined by s 1 of the 1986 Act to apply where 12 or more persons who are present together use or threaten unlawful violence for a common purpose in

---

[80] See also *CIN Properties Ltd* v *Rawlins, The Times*, 9 February 1995; and *Phestos Shipping Co Ltd* v *Kurmiawan* 1983 SLT 388.
[81] [1975] AC 396.
[82] For the similar position in Scotland, see *McIntyre* v *Sheridan* 1993 SLT 412.
[83] *NWL Ltd* v *Woods* [1979] ICR 867 (a trade dispute case, where the *American Cyanamid Co* rule was modified by statute).
[84] Ibid, at p 881 (Lord Diplock).
[85] See *Gate Gourmet London Ltd*, above. Where the case raises freedom of expression issues, see Human Rights Act 1998, s 12, discussed in ch 14 C above.
[86] Criminal Law: Offences Relating to Public Order (Law Commission 123).
[87] 1986 Act, Part I. For the background to the 1986 Act, see Cmnd 7891, 1980; HC 756 (1978–80); Cmnd 9510, 1985. Also Law Commission, Criminal Law: Offences Relating to Public Order (above).

circumstances where their conduct 'would cause a person of reasonable firmness present at the scene to fear for his personal safety'.[88] The scope of the offence is widened considerably, since no person of reasonable firmness need actually be present at the scene and since, unlike at common law, a riot may be committed in private as well as in a public place.[89] Charges of riot are unusual today (at least in the context of political and industrial protest).[90] But such charges were brought during the miners' strike of 1984–5, though many of the prosecutions collapsed in controversial circumstances.[91]

When a riot is in progress, the police and other citizens may use such force as is reasonable in the circumstances to suppress it.[92] Anyone convicted of riot is liable to imprisonment of up to ten years or a fine, or both,[93] while a victim who suffers damage, destruction or theft to uninsured property may bring a claim for compensation against the local policing body under the Riot Compensation Act 2016, where a riot is defined in the same way as in the Public Order Act 1986. The 2016 Act replaces the antiquated scheme that had been in force under the Riot (Damages) Act 1886,[94] following a government review commissioned in 2013. The latter was ordered after widespread civil disorder in London, Manchester and Birmingham in August 2011, which had revealed difficulties in the administration of the 1886 Act in modern conditions.[95]

Section 2 of the Public Order Act 1986 replaces the old common law offence of unlawful assembly with an offence of *violent disorder*. The history of unlawful assembly is an important part of the history of the law of public order. After the lapse of the Seditious Meetings Act 1817, it fell to the courts to develop the definition of an unlawful assembly, upon which depended the powers of the police to control and disperse such assemblies.[96] The statutory offence clears up some of the confusion of the old law.[97] Violent disorder is committed where three or more persons who are present together use or threaten unlawful violence and their conduct (taken together) is such as would cause a person of reasonable firmness present at the scene to fear for his or her personal safety. As with riot, no person of reasonable firmness need actually be present, and the offence may be committed in private as well as in public places.

As with the old common law rules, a meeting which begins as a lawful gathering may become an unlawful assembly if disorder takes place, weapons are produced, or if language inciting an

---

[88] For the common law definition, see *Field v Metropolitan Police Receiver* [1907] 2 KB 853. At common law riot could be committed by three or more people. For a general account of the law in practice, see Vogler, *Reading the Riot Act*.

[89] Public Order Act 1986, s 1(5).

[90] Charges of mobbing and rioting were unsuccessfully brought in Scotland during the miners' strike in 1972, when strikers used force to prevent supplies of coal reaching a power station. See P Wallington (1972) 1 ILJ 219.

[91] See McCabe and Wallington, *The Police, Public Order and Civil Liberties*, p 163.

[92] Criminal Law Act 1967, s 3. The Riot Act 1714 has now been repealed, both for England and Wales, and Scotland.

[93] Public Order Act 1986, s 1(6).

[94] See *Mayor's Office for Policing and Crime v Mitsui Sumitomo Insurance (Europe) Co* [2016] UKSC 18 for discussion of the origins of the 1886 Act. Entitlement to compensation was narrowly construed to mean only physical damage and not also consequential losses such as loss of profit.

[95] HC Debs, 9 May 2013, col 171. See also HC 1456 (2010–12), concerns expressed by Home Affairs Select Committee on the delays in paying compensation after the disorder in August 2011. On the disorder, see K D Ewing, 'The Sound of Silence – Human Rights, the Rule of Law and the "Riots"', UK Const. L. Blog (31 August 2011) (available at http://ukconstitutionallaw.org). In Scotland, compensation is payable under the Riotous Assemblies (Scotland) Act 1822, s 10 (as amended by the Local Government etc. (Scotland) Act 1994).

[96] Leading cases included *R v Vincent* (1839) 9 C & P 91, and *R v Fursey* (1833) 6 C & P 80. See also Hawkins, *Pleas of the Crown*, c 63, s 9.

[97] See *R v Chief Constable of Devon and Cornwall, ex p CEGB* [1982] QB 458. See also HC 85 (1983–4), p 38.

offence is used by speakers. But unlike the common law, under the statutory offence, when this transformation occurs persons present who do not share the unlawful purpose are not guilty of violent disorder. A person is guilty of violent disorder only if he or she intends to use or threaten violence or is aware that his or her conduct may be violent or threaten violence.[98] Such a person is liable on conviction on indictment to imprisonment for up to five years and on summary conviction to imprisonment for up to six months.[99] In both cases a fine may be imposed rather than or as well as imprisonment. At common law when an unlawful assembly was in progress, it was the duty of every citizen to assist in restoring order, for example by dispersing or by going to the assistance of the police.[100] Presumably the duty survives the abolition of the common law offence and its replacement with violent disorder,[101] even if it is likely to be impossible to enforce.

While rare, prosecutions for unlawful assembly and violent disorder are not unknown in modern times. When serious disorder occurred at a demonstration protesting against a Greek dinner at the Garden House Hotel in Cambridge (at a time when the Greek government was unpopular in radical circles) students in the forefront of the disorder were convicted of riot and unlawful assembly.[102] In *Kamara* v *DPP*,[103] students from Sierra Leone occupied the Sierra Leone High Commission in London, locking the staff in a room and threatening them with an imitation gun. Their conviction for, inter alia, unlawful assembly was upheld by the House of Lords, which ruled that it was not necessary to show that an unlawful assembly had occurred in a public place. As we have seen, this ruling has been given statutory force for the purposes of violent disorder.[104]

Unlawful assembly charges were brought during the miners' strike of 1984–5, reflecting 'a specific prosecution policy intended to have a deterrent effect even before charges were proved and sentence pronounced'. However, many charges were dropped before the first hearing and, of those which did proceed, only 'a few indictments for unlawful assembly resulted in conviction'.[105] A few charges of *affray* were also brought during the strike. This ancient offence consists of unlawful fighting or a display of force by one or more persons in a public place or on private premises, involving a degree of violence calculated to terrify persons present who are of reasonably firm character.[106] The Public Order Act 1986 placed this offence on a statutory footing (s 3).[107]

Threatening, abusive and insulting behaviour

Apart from riot, violent disorder and affray, the other category of offences dealt with by the Public Order Act 1986 relates to threatening, abusive and insulting behaviour. This offence – which appears to correspond to the Scottish common law offence of breach of the peace – was originally

---

[98] Public Order Act 1986, s 6(2). The same is true for riot, see s 6(1).

[99] Ibid, s 2(5).

[100] Charge to the Bristol Grand Jury (1832) 5 C & P 261; *R* v *Brown* (1841) Car & M 314. And see *Devlin* v *Armstrong* [1971] NILR 13.

[101] Cf *A-G for Northern Ireland's Reference (No 1 of 1975)* [1977] AC 105.

[102] *R* v *Caird* (1970) 54 Cr App R 499. And see *The Listener*, 8 October (S Sedley) and 26 November 1970 (A W Bradley).

[103] [1974] AC 104. For unlawful assembly during an industrial dispute, see *R* v *Jones* (1974) 59 Cr App R 120.

[104] Public Order Act 1986, s 2(4).

[105] McCabe and Wallington, above, pp 99–100.

[106] *Button* v *DPP* [1966] AC 591; *Taylor* v *DPP* [1973] AC 964.

[107] By s 3 of the 1986 Act, a person is guilty of *affray* if he or she uses or threatens unlawful violence towards another and his or her conduct is such as would cause a person of reasonable firmness present at the scene to fear for his or her personal safety. Where two or more persons use or threaten the unlawful violence, it is their conduct taken together that must be considered. See *I* v *DPP* [2001] UKHL 10, [2002] 1 AC 285 (brandishing petrol bombs constitutes an offence; but it must be directed towards a person or persons present at the scene).

enacted in the Public Order Act 1936, s 5. This provided that it was an offence to use threatening, abusive or insulting words or behaviour with intent to provoke a breach of the peace or whereby a breach of the peace was likely to be occasioned. If the purpose of ss 1–4 of the 1936 Act was to regulate the conduct of fascist demonstrators in the 1930s, the purpose of s 5 was, it seems, to deal with communist counter-demonstrators who would disrupt fascist rallies.

Section 5 of the 1936 Act has been replaced by ss 4, 4A and 5 of the Public Order Act 1986. By s 4:

A person is guilty of an offence if he –

(a) uses towards another person threatening, abusive or insulting words or behaviour, or

(b) distributes or displays to another person any writing, sign or other visible representation which is threatening, abusive or insulting,

with intent to cause that person to believe that immediate unlawful violence will be used against him or another by any person, or to provoke the immediate use of unlawful violence by that person or another, or whereby that person is likely to believe that such violence will be used or it is likely that such violence will be provoked.

This provision of the 1986 Act was supplemented by a new s 4A inserted by the Criminal Justice and Public Order Act 1994. This provides that it is an offence for a person with intent to cause another person harassment, alarm or distress to (a) use 'threatening, abusive or insulting words or behaviour, or disorderly behaviour'; or (b) display any writing, sign or other visible representation which is threatening, abusive or insulting, thereby causing that person or another person [who need not be the intended target of the conduct] 'harassment, alarm or distress'. This complements s 5 of the 1986 Act by which it is an offence for any person to use threatening or abusive (but not now insulting) words or behaviour, or disorderly behaviour, or display threatening or abusive (but not now insulting) material of the kind referred to in s 4 (b) within the hearing of any person 'likely to be caused harassment, alarm or distress thereby'.[108]

By virtue of the Crime and Courts Act 2013, s 57, it is no longer an offence under the Public Order Act 1986, s 5, to use 'insulting' words or behaviour, or to distribute or display writing, signs, or other visible representations on the ground only that they are 'insulting'. This small change to the 1986 Act was initiated in the House of Lords and was initially resisted by the government, which thought it useful as a way to deal with people who desecrated poppies on Remembrance day or swore at police officers, while it was also used against Christian fundamentalists who railed against homosexuality.

The power under s 5 to prosecute for insulting behaviour only was thought by some to be an unjustifiable restraint on free speech, though it was defended by the police as being a valuable tool to help them keep the peace and maintain public order, while others saw it as a way of protecting minorities. But although the government accepted this amendment to the 1986 Act, it is to be emphasised that the use of insulting words or behaviour and the delivery of insults by means of writing, signs or other visible representations continues to be unlawful where it falls within the 1986 Act, sections 4 and 4A.

All three offences (ss 4, 4A and 5) may be committed in a public or private place, though no offence is committed in a private place where the words or behaviour are used by a person

---

[108] The threat of violence is not a requirement of s 5 (nor indeed of s 4A), and 'a police officer can be a person who is likely to be caused harassment and so on' (*DPP v Orum* [1988] 3 All ER 449).

within a dwelling, and the person harassed, alarmed or distressed is also inside the dwelling. It is a defence under ss 4A and 5 that the accused's conduct took place inside a dwelling and that he or she had no reason to believe that it would be seen or heard outside. It is also a defence under ss 4A and 5 that the accused's conduct was reasonable,[109] and additionally under s 5 that he or she had no reason to believe that there was any person within hearing or sight who was likely to be caused harassment, alarm or distress.[110] Moreover, a person is guilty of an offence under ss 4 and 5 only if he or she intends or is aware that the conduct is threatening, abusive, insulting or disorderly (s 6).[111]

As with s 5 of the 1936 Act, the crucial words 'threatening, abusive or insulting' are not defined.[112] Decisions under s 5 of the 1936 Act may thus be helpful in the construction of ss 4, 4A and 5 of the 1986 Act. On what is meant by insulting, the leading case is *Brutus* v *Cozens*.[113]

> During a Wimbledon tennis match, Brutus and other anti-apartheid protesters went on to the court, distributed leaflets and sat down. The spectators strongly resented the interruption of play. Brutus was prosecuted for using insulting behaviour whereby a breach of the peace was likely to be occasioned. The justices dismissed the charge, finding that the conduct was not insulting. On appeal by the prosecutor, the Divisional Court directed the justices that behaviour was insulting if it affronted other people and evidenced a disrespect or contempt for their rights, and thereby was likely to cause the resentment which the spectators had expressed at Wimbledon. The House of Lords unanimously allowed an appeal by Brutus against this direction, holding that 'insulting' was to be given its ordinary meaning and that the question whether certain behaviour had been insulting was one of fact for the justices to determine. Lord Reid pointed out that s 5 of the 1936 Act did not prohibit *all* speech or conduct likely to occasion a breach of the peace. Vigorous, distasteful and unmannerly speech was not prohibited. There could be no definition of insult: 'an ordinary sensible man knows an insult when he sees or hears it'.

It is not enough that the accused's conduct is insulting. Under the Act it must, for example in the case of s 4, be likely to provoke violence. This corresponds with the requirement in s 5 of the 1936 Act that the accused's conduct be likely to provoke a breach of the peace. In *Jordan* v *Burgoyne*,[114] the accused was convicted under s 5 because a speech he made in Trafalgar Square was provocative 'beyond endurance' to Jews, blacks and ex-servicemen in the crowd. It was held that the words used were insulting, and the Divisional Court rejected the

---

[109] On which see *DPP* v *Percy* [2002] Crim LR 835, which considers the relationship between the reasonableness defence and Convention rights, notably art 10. In that case a conviction for desecrating the American flag in the presence of American soldiers was overturned because the district judge had not given adequate weight to Convention rights. But it seems clear that had he more fully considered this defence, he could quite properly have convicted. See *Hammond* v *DPP* [2004] Crim LR 851.

[110] See *Morrow, Geach and Thomas* v *DPP* [1994] Crim LR 58 (defence not made out in a case of a protest outside an abortion clinic – 'shouting slogans, waving banners, and preventing staff and patients from entering', thereby causing distress to patients).

[111] See *DPP* v *Clarke* (1992) 94 Cr App R 359 (defendants displaying pictures outside an abortion clinic: pictures abusive for the purposes of s 5 and caused distressed; but it did not follow that the defendants intended them to be threatening, abusive or insulting, or were aware that they might be so). On the other hand, it is unnecessary for the purpose of s 5 that anyone has suffered harassment, alarm or distress: *Norwood* v *DPP* [2003] Crim LR 888.

[112] [1973] AC 854.

[113] Ibid. Cf *Coleman* v *Power* (2004) 209 ALR 182 (High Ct of Australia).

[114] [1963] 2 QB 744.

interpretation of the court below that the words used by the defendant were not likely to lead ordinary, reasonable persons to commit breaches of the peace. In the view of the court the defendant must 'take his audience as he finds them, and if those words to that audience or that part of the audience are likely to provoke a breach of the peace, then the speaker is guilty of an offence'.[115] A similar conclusion would be reached under the 1986 Act.

An important issue under s 4 of the 1986 Act relates to the question of how soon after insulting conduct must the violence be likely to take place. Section 5 of the 1936 Act 'did not require that the breach of the peace which was either intended or likely to be occasioned should follow immediately upon the actions of the defendant'. The question whether such a requirement now exists was considered in *R v Horseferry Road Magistrate, ex p Siadatan*.[116]

> The applicant laid an information against Penguin Books and Mr Salman Rushdie, the publishers and author of *The Satanic Verses*, which many devout Muslims found offensive. It was alleged that the respondents had distributed copies contrary to s 4(1) of the 1986 Act on the ground that the book contained abusive and insulting writing whereby it was likely that unlawful violence would be provoked. On a strict construction of the Act, the Divisional Court held that the magistrate was correct in refusing to issue a summons. In the view of the court, the requirement in the Act that the insulted person should be 'likely to believe that such violence will be used' means that the insulted person is likely to believe that the violence will be used immediately. Watkins LJ observed: 'A consequence of construing the words "such violence" in s 4(1) as meaning "immediate unlawful violence" will be that leaders of an extremist movement who prepare pamphlets or banners to be distributed or carried in public places by adherents to that movement will not be committing any offence under s 4(1) albeit that they intend the words in the pamphlet or on the banners to be threatening, abusive and insulting and it is likely that unlawful violence will be provoked by the words in the pamphlet or on the banner.'[117]

Although s 4 of the 1986 Act thus appears to be narrower than the corresponding provisions of the 1936 Act, the police have other powers which may go some way towards closing any 'gap in the law which did not exist under the 1936 Act'.[118] These include the powers conferred by the Police Act 1996, s 89(2), which is discussed below. It is a separate offence if any of the foregoing offences under ss 4, 4A or 5 of the 1986 Act are racially or religiously aggravated,[119] a provision widely construed by the House of Lords.[120]

Other offences

1. Obstruction of the highway

As already pointed out, it is an offence under the Highways Act 1980, s 137 if 'a person without lawful authority or excuse in any way wilfully obstructs the free passage along a highway'. An obstruction in this sense is caused when a meeting or assembly is held on the highway

---

[115] Ibid, at p 749.

[116] [1991] 1 QB 260.

[117] Compare *DPP v Ramos* [2000] Crim LR 768.

[118] [1991] 1 QB 260, at p 266.

[119] Crime and Disorder Act 1998, s 31, as amended by Anti-terrorism, Crime and Security Act 2001, s 39. On the meaning of racially or religiously aggravated: s 28, considered in *Norwood v DPP*, above, and *DPP v M* [2004] EWHC 1453 (Admin), [2004] 1 WLR 2758. Indecent or 'racialist' chanting at designated football matches is also an offence: Football Offences Act 1991, s 3.

[120] *R v Rogers* [2007] UKHL 8, [2007] 2 WLR 280.

(which for this purpose includes the pavement as well as the road). It is no defence that the obstruction affected only part of the highway leaving the other part clear.[121] Nor is it a defence that the arrested person was only one of a number of people causing the obstruction,[122] or that the defendant believed that she was entitled to hold meetings at the place in question, or that other meetings had been held there.[123]

The offence thus gives wide powers to the police to disperse what may be a peaceful assembly, and it has been widely used. Following *DPP* v *Jones*,[124] however, it is now recognised that the highway may lawfully be used for some political purposes where this does not interfere with the primary purpose of the highway, which is passage and repassage. Such use will provide a lawful excuse to any charge of obstruction. This is a conclusion which had been reached already in *Hirst* v *Chief Constable of West Yorkshire*[125] by the Divisional Court in relation to the Highways Act 1980, a decision which was expressly approved in *Jones*.

> In *Hirst*, a group of animal rights supporters were demonstrating outside a furrier's shop and handing out leaflets. They were convicted of obstruction of the highway, contrary to the Highways Act 1980, s 137. In reversing the convictions Glidewell LJ said that the question whether someone was causing an obstruction without lawful excuse was to be answered by deciding whether the activity in which the defendant was engaged was or was not a reasonable user of the highway. This would be for the magistrates to decide, but it was clearly anticipated that the distribution of handbills could be a reasonable user.

In 2002, Westminster City Council was unable to obtain an injunction to stop an anti-war protest by a single individual (Brian Haw), who maintained a vigil over many years in Parliament Square.[126] Apart from the Highways Act 1980, obstruction of the highway is a public nuisance, which may be prosecuted as an indictable offence at common law.[127] Although still in use, the Law Commission has reported that the conduct previously dealt with as public nuisance is likely to be dealt with by a variety of other offences and procedures. It nevertheless recommended that the offence should be retained but in statutory rather than common law form.[128]

2. Protection from harassment

Closely associated with the Public Order Act 1986, ss 4, 4A and 5 is the Protection from Harassment Act 1997, which has been said to be concerned with 'serious and persistent' forms of harassment.[129] The Act is considered briefly in this chapter because it has been used against protesters (particularly animal rights but also environmental protesters), and as a way of regulating the exercise of the right to freedom of assembly.

It is unlawful to pursue a course of conduct which amounts to the harassment of another and which the person pursuing the conduct knows or ought to know amounts to harassment

---

[121] *Homer* v *Cadman* (1886) 16 Cox CC 51.
[122] *Arrowsmith* v *Jenkins* [1963] 2 QB 561.
[123] Ibid. Cf *Cambs CC* v *Rust* [1972] 2 QB 426.
[124] [1999] AC 240; pp 495–6 above.
[125] (1987) 85 Cr App R 143. See S Bailey [1987] PL 495.
[126] *The Guardian*, 5 October 2002. See now Serious Organised Crime and Police Act 2005, ss 132–8.
[127] *R v Clark (No 2)* [1964] 2 QB 315. See also *News Group Newspapers Ltd* v *SOGAT 82 (No 2)* [1987] ICR 181. On public nuisance and the ECHR, see *R v Rimmington* [2005] UKHL 63, [2006] 1 AC 459.
[128] Law Commission, *Simplification of Criminal Law: Public Nuisance and Outraging Public Decency* (Law Com No 358, 2015).
[129] *Ferguson* v *British Gas* [2009] EWCA Civ 46, [2009] 3 All ER 304, at para [53] (Sedley LJ).

(s 1(1)). This has been extended so that a person must not pursue a course of conduct which involves (*a*) knowingly harassing two or more persons, with (*b*) intent to persuade another person 'not to do something that he is entitled or required to do', or 'to do something that he is not under any obligation to do' (s 1(1A)).[130] It is a defence that the course of conduct was pursued for the purpose of preventing or detecting crime,[131] or that it was reasonable in the circumstances (s 1(3)).[132]

Apart from being an offence to pursue a course of conduct in breach of ss 1 or 1(1A) (s 2), civil proceedings may be brought by a victim for an injunction to restrain an unlawful course of conduct and for damages suffered as a result (s 3).[133] An injunction may also be sought where there is a breach of s 1(1A) (s 3A), on this occasion by either the target of the harassment or the persons who are being persuaded to do or not to do something as an instrument of the harassment. It is, moreover, an offence under s 4 to engage in a course of conduct which causes another person to fear on at least two occasions that violence will be used against him or her.

Where a person has been convicted of an offence, a court may issue a restraining order against the person concerned, prohibiting the defendant from doing anything specified in the order which amounts to harassment or which will cause a fear of violence (s 5). A similar power has been introduced in relation to people who have been acquitted (s 5A). Breach of an order is an offence under the Act,[134] which has been adapted for application to Scotland (s 8). As pointed out by the Supreme Court, 'the Act is capable of applying to any form of harassment', including (i) the repeated offensive publications in a newspaper;[135] (ii) victimisation in the workplace;[136] and (iii) campaigns against the employees of an arms manufacturer by political protesters.[137]

> The scope of the powers under the 1997 Act (as amended) is illustrated by the well-publicised decision in *Oxford University* v *Broughton*.[138]
>
> The university obtained injunctions under the Act against a number of leading animal rights activists and animal rights organisations. The conduct of the defendants was jeopardising the completion of new laboratories where it was believed experiments would be conducted on animals. The order prohibited protesters from harassing protected persons and from entering an exclusion zone around the construction site except once a week at a time approved in the injunction.
>
> The most controversial feature of the injunction was the definition of 'protected persons'. This extended to the members and employees of the university and their families, the

---

[130] As inserted by Serious Organised Crime and Police Act 2005, s 125. See also s 126 (similar provisions in relation to harassment of a person in his or her home). The Act was extended by the Protection of Freedoms Act 2012, which introduced a new offence of stalking to the 1997 Act. These provisions are not dealt with here.

[131] The defence has been held to apply only if the conduct of the defendant is rational: *Hayes* v *Willoughby* [2013] UKSC 17, [2013] 1 WLR 935.

[132] See *DPP* v *Selvanayagam*, *The Times*, 23 June 1999 (conduct cannot be reasonable if in breach of a court injunction).

[133] See *Huntingdon Life Sciences Ltd* v *Curtin*, *The Times*, 11 December 1997; *Daiichi Pharmaceuticals UK Ltd* v *Stop Huntingdon Animal Cruelty* [2003] EWHC 2337 (QB), [2004] 1 WLR 1503; and *Oxford University* v *Broughton* [2004] EWHC 2543 (QB).

[134] See *R* v *Evans* [2004] EWCA Crim 3102, [2005] 1 WLR 1435.

[135] *Thomas* v *News Group Newspapers Ltd* [2001] EWCA Civ 1233, [2002] EMLR 4.

[136] *Majrowski* v *Guy's and St. Thomas's NHS Trust* [2006] UKHL 34, [2007] 1 AC 224.

[137] *EDO MBM Technology Ltd* v *Campaign to Smash EDO* [2005] EWHC 837 (QB) Compare *Hayes* v *Willoughby* [2011] EWCA Civ 1541, [2012] 1 WLR 1510.

[138] [2004] EWHC 2543 (QB).

employees and shareholders of the contractor, as well as their families, servants or agents, and any person seeking to visit the laboratory or any premises or home belonging to or occupied by a protected person. The High Court rejected a claim that these restraints amounted to an unjustifiable restriction on Convention rights.

Additional restraints on demonstrating outside someone's home were introduced by the Criminal Justice and Police Act 2001 – as amended in 2005[139] – in response to the activities of animal rights protesters who picketed the homes of directors and employees of companies said to be engaged in vivisection.[140] Still further restraints on animal rights groups are to be found in the Serious Organised Crime and Police Act 2005, s 145. These have the effect of making it an offence to interfere with commercial relationships in a manner designed to harm animal research.

3. Breach of the peace

In English law there is no offence of breach of the peace, though the apprehension of a breach of the peace provides grounds for an arrest,[141] and for the exercise of police powers under the Police Act 1996, s 89(3) (on which see below).[142] The position is different in Scotland, where the long-established common law offence of breach of the peace applies broadly to include the use of violent and threatening language in public, and breaches of public order and decorum.

In a leading case to which reference is still made, it was said that the offence involves conduct which 'will reasonably produce alarm in the minds of the lieges, not necessarily in the sense of personal fear, but alarm lest if what is going on is allowed to continue it will lead to the breaking up of the social peace'.[143] The broad nature of this offence probably explains why, on facts very similar to those in *Beatty* v *Gillbanks*, the Scottish courts convicted the local leaders of a Salvation Army procession of breach of the peace.[144] Breach of the peace is commonly used by the police in public order situations. During the miners' strike of 1984–5, of the 1,046 charges brought in Scotland, no fewer than 678 of these were for breach of the peace.[145]

Although used to deal with a wide range of anti-social behaviour, this offence may serve as a flexible and adaptable restraint on different forms of political activity and public protest. It is used not only against pickets in trade disputes, but also in response to (i) the selling of a National Front newspaper outside a football ground (Tynecastle Park, Edinburgh),[146] (ii) the provocative conduct of participants in an Orange march,[147] (iii) the activities of environmental

---

[139] Serious Organised Crime and Police Act 2005, ss 126, 127.

[140] Criminal Justice and Police Act 2001, s 42. The same Act also permits directors of such companies not to publish their home addresses.

[141] *Albert* v *Lavin* [1982] AC 546; *R (Laporte)* v *Chief Constable of Gloucestershire Constabulary* [2007] 2 AC 105; and *R (Hicks)* v *Metropolitan Police Commissioner* [2017] UKHL 9.

[142] See also *Lansbury* v *Riley* [1914] 3 KB 229 (power of magistrates to bind over to keep the peace when it is apprehended that someone may breach the peace; but power not exercisable unless a breach of the peace is anticipated: *Percy* v *DPP* [1995] 3 All ER 124 (a non-violent peace protest). This is a useful restraint to be used against those engaged in on-going and persistent campaigns.

[143] *Ferguson* v *Carnochan* (1889) 2 White 278. See *Smith* v *Donnelly*, below, where *Ferguson* is cited with approval and explained on the basis that 'it is clear that what is required to constitute the crime of breach of the peace is "conduct severe enough to cause alarm to ordinary people and threaten serious disturbance to the community"' (Lord Coulsfield).

[144] *Deakin* v *Milne* (1882) 10 R(J) 22.

[145] McCabe and Wallington, above, p 164.

[146] *Alexander* v *Smith* 1984 SLT 176.

[147] *McAvoy* v *Jessop* 1989 SCCR 301.

protesters (sitting in a tree to prevent it being felled by motorway contractors),[148] (iv) the actions of peace movement activists at the Faslane naval base,[149] and (v) a noisy demonstration in the Scottish Parliament.[150]

The incorporation of Convention rights provided an opportunity to argue before the Scottish courts that the indeterminacy of the offence of breach of the peace violates art 7 of the ECHR. But the argument failed,[151] as have other challenges to breach of the peace convictions based on arts 10 and 11 of the Convention. In *Jones* v *Carnegie*,[152] the High Court of Justiciary rejected an attempt to restrict the scope of the offence to cases where there was 'evidence of actual alarm or annoyance'. It is enough that the conduct is 'genuinely alarming and disturbing to any reasonable person'.

Nevertheless, the substance of the offence has been narrowed by recent decisions (it is no longer enough to show that the conduct of the accused is annoying, and the offence can no longer be committed in private without any 'public' element).[153] On the other hand, the courts have emphasised that the test of whether a breach of the peace has taken place is an objective one and that it is not necessary to show that anyone has actually been alarmed or disturbed.[154] In such circumstances, however, the conduct must be 'flagrant', a requirement which is 'not always helpful'.[155]

Recent cases have shown the courts unwilling to convict for peaceful protest where no one was alarmed or distressed.[156] More recently still, however, in *Maguire* v *Procurator Fiscal, Glasgow*,[157] the wearing of a provocative shirt – with a pro-INLA, anti-Remembrance Day, and pro-Bloody Sunday remembrance message while attending a Rangers v Celtic football match – was held to be a breach of the peace. The offending conduct was 'not part of a legitimate protest', and was 'genuinely alarmingly and disturbing to any reasonable person'. What is a 'legitimate' protest is, however, highly contestable, and dangerous territory for a court to enter.

F. Preventive powers of the police

Entry into meetings

In a public place like Trafalgar Square, there can be no doubt of the power of the police to be present and to deal with outbreaks of disorder if they occur. Where a public meeting is held on private premises, the power of the police to attend is less certain. At one time the official view of the Home Office was that except when the promoters of a meeting asked the police to be present in the meeting, they could not go in, unless they had reason to believe that an

---

[148] *Colhoun* v *Friel* 1996 SCCR 497.

[149] *Smith* v *Donnelly* 2001 SLT 1007; *Jones* v *Carnegie* 2004 SLT 609.

[150] *Jones* v *Carnegie*, ibid.

[151] *Smith* v *Donnelly*, above.

[152] Note 150 above. The court approved *Alexander* v *Smith*, above, and *McAvoy* v *Jessop*, above, though it also said that 'peaceful protest, in which the accused did no more than hand out leaflets and hold up a banner and where that did not involve any provocation . . . would be unlikely to justify a conviction for breach of the peace' (p 616). For discussion of the wider issues, see P Ferguson (2001) 5 *Edin Law Rev* 145.

[153] See *Harris* v *H M Advocate* [2009] HCJAC 80, 2009 SLT 1078. See now Criminal Justice and Licensing (Scotland) Act 2010, s 38 (threatening or abusive behaviour which applies also in private).

[154] *Jones* v *Carnegie*, above.

[155] *Dyer* v *Brady* [2006] HCJAC 72, 2006 SCCR 629.

[156] Ibid.

[157] [2013] HCJAC 36. See subsequently *Maguire* v *United Kingdom*, Appn No 58060/13, 3 March 2015 (no breach of Convention rights).

actual breach of the peace was being committed in the meeting.[158] This view was stated after disorder occurred at a fascist meeting at Olympia in London, when the stewards inflicted physical violence on dissentients in the audience. No police were stationed on the premises, although large numbers had been assembled in nearby streets. Within a year, the court disapproved of the Home Office view of the law.

In *Thomas* v *Sawkins*[159] a meeting had been advertised in a Welsh town (*a*) to protest against the Incitement to Disaffection Bill which was then before Parliament, and (*b*) to demand the dismissal of the Chief Constable of Glamorgan. The meeting was open to the public without payment, and the police arranged for some of their number to attend. The promoter requested the police officers to leave.

A constable committed a technical assault on the promoter thinking that the promoter was on the point of employing force to remove a police officer from the room. There was no allegation that any criminal offence had been committed at the meeting or that any breach of the peace had occurred. When the promoter prosecuted the constable for assault, the magistrates' court found that the police had reasonable grounds for believing that if they were not present there would be seditious speeches and other incitement to violence, and that breaches of the peace would occur; that the police were entitled to enter and remain in the hall throughout the meeting; and that consequently the constable did not unlawfully assault the promoter.

In the Divisional Court these findings were upheld. Lord Hewart CJ was of opinion that the police have powers to enter and to remain on private premises when they have reasonable grounds for believing that an offence is imminent or likely to be committed; nor did he limit this statement to offences involving a breach of the peace. In the opinion of Avory J, 'the justices had before them material on which they could probably hold that the police officers in question had reasonable grounds for believing that, if they were not present, seditious speeches would be made and/or that a breach of the peace would take place. To prevent any such offence or a breach of the peace the police were entitled to enter and remain on the premises.'[160]

Although the second objective of the meeting in *Thomas* v *Sawkins* was admittedly provocative to the local police, it did not suggest an incitement to violence, which was a necessary element in the offence of sedition. Nor does protest against a Bill involve a breach of the peace. It is unclear whether Lord Hewart's opinion is confined to public meetings on private premises or whether it also applies to private meetings and other activities on private premises. May the police enter any private premises if they reasonably believe that any offence is imminent or is likely to be committed? The judgments in the case gave scant consideration to the argument that as soon as the promoter asked the police to withdraw from the premises, this rescinded the open invitation given to the public (including the police) to attend. Did this not make the officers trespassers on private premises from that point onwards?[161] It may be that it is in the public interest that the police should be entitled to enter and remain in any public meeting: but why should a similar right apply to private meetings? Doubts as to the width of *Thomas* v *Sawkins* are resolved by the Police and Criminal Evidence Act 1984, which preserves the power of the police to enter premises to deal with or prevent a breach of the peace, but otherwise abolishes all common law powers of the police to enter premises without a warrant.[162]

....
[158] HC Deb, 14 June 1934, col 1968.
[159] [1935] 2 KB 249. See Ewing and Gearty, *The Struggle for Civil Liberties*, ch 6.
[160] Ibid, at p 256.
[161] *Davis* v *Lisle* [1936] 2 KB 434; *Robson* v *Hallett* [1967] 2 QB 939.
[162] 1984 Act, s 17(5), (6); ch 15.

Obstruction of the police

The statutory offence of obstructing the police in the execution of their duty activates a common law power of arrest.[163] It is particularly important in the law of public order. The leading case is *Duncan* v *Jones*[164] in 1936, which gave rise to fears about the uses to which the offence could be put.

> Mrs Duncan was forbidden by Jones, a police officer, to hold a street meeting at a place opposite a training centre for the unemployed. She refused to hold the meeting in another street 175 yards away. Fourteen months previously, Mrs Duncan had held a meeting at the same spot, which had been followed by a disturbance in the centre attributed by the superintendent of the centre to the meeting. Mrs Duncan mounted a box on the highway to start the meeting but was arrested and charged with obstructing a police officer in the execution of his duty. There was no allegation of obstruction of the highway or of inciting any breach of the peace.
>
> The lower court found (a) that Mrs Duncan must have known of the probable consequences of her holding the meeting, viz, a disturbance and possibly a breach of the peace, and was not unwilling that such consequences should ensue, (b) that Jones reasonably apprehended a breach of the peace, (c) that in law it therefore became his duty to prevent the holding of the meeting, and (d) that by attempting to hold the meeting, Mrs Duncan obstructed Jones when in the execution of his duty. The Divisional Court upheld the conviction. Humphreys J remarked that on the facts as found, Jones reasonably apprehended a breach of the peace: it then became his duty 'to prevent anything which in his view would cause that breach of the peace'.

The decision has been strongly criticised on several grounds. First, for reasons of principle. Goodhart remarked:

> At first sight it may seem unreasonable to say that a police officer cannot take steps to prevent an act which, when committed becomes a punishable offence. But it is on this distinction between prevention and punishment that freedom of speech, freedom of public meeting and freedom of the press are founded.[165]

Second, the decision gave rise to concern about the nature of the power extended to police officers. On one view, it would give a police officer power to prevent the holding of a lawful meeting if he or she suspected not that the meeting itself might be disorderly, but that breaches of the peace might occur as a result of the meeting, whether committed by supporters or opponents of the speakers at the meeting. The reasoning of Humphreys J brings forward in time and widens the preventive powers of the police to a degree that could lead to intolerable restrictions on the liberty of meeting. On this basis the police could forbid a meeting in the students' union of a college from taking place merely because a 'disturbance' had previously occurred in the college after a similar meeting.

Yet despite this criticism and concern, the offence of obstructing a police officer is now an important weapon in the armoury of police powers for controlling public protest. Although *Duncan* v *Jones* illustrates the power to issue directions as to location where this is considered necessary to maintain the peace, other cases illustrate that the power may be used to issue directions as to numbers. In *Piddington* v *Bates*,[166] a police officer gave instructions that during

---

[163] Police Act 1996, s 89(2).
[164] [1936] 1 KB 218; Ewing and Gearty, *The Struggle for Civil Liberties*, ch 5.
[165] (1937) 6 CLJ 22, 30. See also E C S Wade (1937) 6 CLJ 175, and T C Daintith [1966] PL 248.
[166] [1960] 3 All ER 660.

a trade dispute at a factory in North London only two pickets would be permitted outside each entrance. When the appellant insisted on joining the pickets, despite a police officer's instructions not to do so, he was arrested for obstruction. The Divisional Court dismissed his appeal against the conviction, in which it was argued that a restriction to two pickets was arbitrary and unlawful. In the view of Lord Parker CJ, 'a police officer charged with the duty of preserving the Queen's peace must be left to take such steps as, on the evidence before him, he thinks are proper'.[167]

But apart from this wide power to give directions as to how a demonstration or picket is conducted, more recent developments indicate that the power permits the police to give directions not only to disperse a demonstration but also effectively to ban or to prevent one from being held in the first place. In *Moss* v *McLachlan*,[168] the defendants were stopped at a motorway exit by police officers who suspected that they were travelling to attend a picket line at one of a number of collieries several miles away. When they refused to turn back, the defendants arrested for obstructing a police officer in the execution of his duty. Their appeals against conviction were dismissed, with Skinner J observing that 'The situation has to be assessed by the senior police officers present. Provided they honestly and reasonably form the opinion that there is a real risk of a breach of the peace in the sense that it is in close proximity both in place and time, then the conditions exist for reasonable preventive action including, if necessary, the measures taken in this case.'[169]

The exercise of this power was considered by the House of Lords for the first time in *R (Laporte)* v *Gloucester Chief Constable*,[170] where a coach carrying demonstrators was travelling to RAF Fairford.

The coach was stopped by the police some three miles short of its destination, and its occupants prevented by the police from travelling to the site of the demonstration. These steps had been taken because the police suspected that there were a number of hard-line protesters on the coach, which was returned to London along with its occupants under police escort.

It was held that the action taken against the applicant Laporte was unlawful and could not be justified; there was no evidence that a breach of the peace was 'imminent', though the position may have been different if the police had intervened at a later stage in the journey, provided the evidence on the ground would have justified such intervention.[171]

In the course of its decision, the House of Lords rejected the existence of a wider common law power claimed by the police that they could do whatever was reasonable to prevent a breach of the peace.[172]

Containment and 'kettling' of demonstrators

A practice of containment by the police that has emerged in recent years is sometimes referred to as 'kettling'. This involves detaining protesters in large groups for long periods of time until any risk of violence perceived to exist by the police has passed. Apart from the fact that

---

[167] Ibid, at p 663.

[168] [1985] IRLR 76. See G S Morris (1983) 14 ILJ 109. Also *O'Kelly* v *Harvey* (1883) 15 Cox CC 435.

[169] [1985] IRLR 76, at p 78. For evidence of the practice being adopted by the Scottish police (although inevitably on a different legal base, possibly breach of the peace), see Miller and Woolfson, above, at pp 220–1.

[170] [2006] UKHL 55, [2007] 2 AC 105.

[171] A point reinforced by *R (Moos)* v *Metropolitan Police Commissioner* [2012] EWCA Civ 12.

[172] The case was said to be very different from *Moss* v *McLachlan* (above), a decision approved though said to have 'carried the notion of imminence to extreme limits'.

people are being detained against their wishes in this way, there are the additional problems of people being detained for long periods of time in adverse weather conditions, in situations of great discomfort and without access to food, medicines and other facilities.

It is unclear how long this routine has been used as a standard practice by the police, but its use as a policing tool shot to prominence during May Day protests in 2001, and again at the G20 protests in the City of London eight years later. The use of the practice at the 2001 event led to legal proceedings on the part of two of those who were 'kettled', the question arising whether the police conduct could be justified as an application of the power to take steps to prevent a breach of the peace, and if so whether it violated the Convention rights of the individuals concerned.

In *Austin* v *Metropolitan Police Commissioner*,[173] the police detained a large number of protesters on May Day 2001, for up to seven hours in Oxford Circus, London. It was contended that those detained were without sufficient toilet facilities or food and drink. In proceedings against the police for false imprisonment and violation of ECHR art 5, one applicant complained that she was refused permission to leave the scene to pick up her child, while another was refused permission to leave despite not being a protester yet caught up in the police response.

Following a detailed analysis of the speeches in the *Laporte* case (above), the Court of Appeal held that the conduct of the police was justified as being necessary to prevent a breach of the peace which they believed to be imminent.[174] So far as the detention of people who were not protesters is concerned, the Court of Appeal held that 'where (and only where) there is a reasonable belief that there are no other means whatsoever whereby a breach or imminent breach of the peace can be obviated, the lawful exercise by third parties of their rights may be curtailed by the police'.[175]

The House of Lords agreed. Although it was noted that art 5 (on the right to liberty) is a Convention right which is not qualified in the same way as other Convention rights, Lord Neuberger took the view that it was unrealistic to contend that art 5 came into play at all. The decision of the House of Lords is, however, subject to a requirement that the police conduct is proportionate and reasonable,[176] though clearly there will be scope for debate about when that boundary is reached, especially as it was held in *Austin* that a seven-hour detention in cold weather did not violate that standard.[177]

> The House of Lords decision in *Austin* was surprisingly upheld in *Austin* v *United Kingdom*.[178] The ECtHR held by a majority that there was no breach of ECHR, art 5, on the ground that the detention of the protesters (and others) was a restriction on freedom of movement rather than a deprivation of liberty. It is true that the majority accepted that 'the coercive nature of the containment within the cordon; its duration; and its effect on the applicants, in terms of physical discomfort and inability to leave Oxford Circus, point towards a deprivation of liberty' (para 64).

---

[173] [2009] UKHL 5, [2009] 1 AC 564. (H Fenwick [2009] PL 737).

[174] [2007] EWCA Civ 989, [2008] QB 660. The Court of Appeal has subsequently emphasised that the legality of containment is to be determined by whether the police officer authorising it had reasonable grounds to believe that a breach of the peace was imminent. It is not whether the court reasonably believed it to be imminent: *R (Moos)* v *Metropolitan Police Commissioner*, above.

[175] This was said to be 'a test of necessity' which 'can only be justified in truly extreme and exceptional circumstances', and the action taken in such circumstances 'must be both reasonably necessary and proportionate'.

[176] This is a requirement of both the decision to contain, and the conditions of containment.

[177] See subsequently, *R (Moos)* v *Metropolitan Police Commissioner*, above.

[178] [2012] ECHR 459, (2012) 55 EHRR 14.

But the Court also accepted that it must take into account 'the context in which the measure was imposed', noting that 'the measure was imposed to isolate and contain a large crowd, in volatile and dangerous conditions', and that 'the police decided to make use of a measure of containment to control the crowd, rather than having resort to more robust methods, which might have given rise to a greater risk of injury to people within the crowd' (para 66). The decision that there was no deprivation of liberty was 'based on the specific and exceptional facts' of the case (para 68).

The complainants in *Austin* v *United Kingdom* did not argue that there had been a breach of their rights under arts 10 and 11 of the ECHR; but the majority nevertheless reiterated that 'measures of crowd control should not be used by the national authorities directly or indirectly to stifle or discourage protest, given the fundamental importance of freedom of expression and assembly in all democratic societies'.[179] The Home Affairs Select Committee took a more critical view of police practice in the aftermath of the G20 protests in 2009, where it was said that kettling should only be used 'sparingly' and in 'clearly defined circumstances' which should be 'codified'.[180]

The domestic litigation in *Gillan and Quinton* and *Austin* (above) was followed by *Hicks*,[181] in which the Supreme Court upheld the right of the police to arrest and detain a group of individuals on the day of a royal wedding, at which it was anticipated they would engage in protests that would lead to a breach of the peace.

The individuals in question were released shortly after the event had passed, without having been brought before any court to be bound over to keep the peace. Such conduct of the police would clearly frustrate the right to freedom of assembly, though the matter was contested not on the basis that the police action violated ECHR, art 11, but again that it violated art 5 on the right to liberty.

In protecting the right to liberty, the latter permits its restriction only in carefully limited circumstances, which are proving to be too tight for public authorities in the contemporary world.[182] The only applicable restriction that would have justified the action of the police in this case was the power in art 5(1)(c), which allows for the deprivation of liberty 'for the purpose of bringing the individual before the competent legal authority on reasonable suspicion of having committed an offence or when it is reasonably considered necessary to prevent his committing an offence'.

The latter was said to be 'implicitly dependent on the cause for detention continuing long enough for the person to be brought before the court'. Although that was not the position here, the arrested person's interests were nevertheless adequately served by being able to challenge the legality of the arrest and detention after the event.[183] What the Supreme Court has thus done, however, has been to create a power of preventive arrest, of much greater constitutional significance than the issues that have exercised public lawyers since *Duncan* v *Jones*.[184]

---

[179] Ibid, at para 68.

[180] HC 418 (2008–9). Compare *R (the Moos)* v *Metropolitan Police Commissioner*, above.

[181] *R (Hicks)* v *Metropolitan Police Commissioner* [2017] UKSC 9. *Laporte* points in the other direction.

[182] See also the control order cases discussed in ch 20 below.

[183] Ibid, para 38.

[184] See note 164 above. *Hicks* is also impossible to reconcile with *Hassan* v *United Kingdom* [2014] ECHR 1145, where it is said that 'It has long been established that the list of grounds of permissible detention in Article 5(1) does not include internment or preventive detention where there is no intention to bring criminal charges within a reasonable time' (para 97).

This is an extraordinary power to give to the police. The power not only bypasses the ancient power of the police to apply to a court for a binding over order, an ancient power designed specifically to ensure that 'troublemakers' do not breach the peace.[185] It also transfers the onus from the police (no longer required to justify in advance the imposition of restrictions on liberty) to the citizen (now required to chase a claim of illegality after the event).

G. Conclusion

At the time of the introduction of the Human Rights Act 1998, there appeared to be a growing recognition on the part of the courts of the importance of freedom of assembly,[186] with a number of cases making bold claims about its value.[187] These cases were thought to reflect a significant change in judicial attitude that previously had been concerned in a rather one-dimensional way with public order to the neglect of other considerations. It is particularly significant that, in the leading case on freedom of assembly, the then Lord Chancellor should consider the 'public's rights of access to the public highway' as 'an issue of fundamental constitutional importance'.[188]

Changing judicial attitudes were demonstrated initially by a recognition that passage and repassage are not the only lawful uses of the highway. As we have seen, it was acknowledged in *DPP* v *Jones* that 'the holding of a public assembly on a highway can constitute a reasonable user of the highway and accordingly will not constitute a trespass', even if it did not follow that 'a peaceful and non-obstructive public assembly on a highway is always a reasonable user and is therefore not a trespass'.[189] This recognition at the highest level of the right of lawful assembly on the highway is accompanied by a preparedness on the part of the courts sometimes to read down legislation that is being used to impose an unwarranted restraint on freedom of assembly.[190]

There also appeared to be a greater willingness on the part of at least some judges to challenge the exercise of discretion by police officers who take steps, including arrest, to disperse an assembly in order to prevent a breach of the peace. In the *Redmond-Bate* case, it was said:

Free speech includes not only the inoffensive but the irritating, the contentious, the eccentric, the heretical, the unwelcome and the provocative provided it does not tend to provoke violence. Freedom only to speak inoffensively is not worth having.

But it should not be overlooked that this last passage is from a case concerned with individuals who had been arrested for refusing to stop preaching on the steps of Wakefield Cathedral when instructed to do so by the police. The same vigorous approach to freedom of assembly has not always been adopted in other cases involving large numbers of noisy anti-globalisation or angry anti-war protesters.

---

[185] On which, see *Lansbury* v *Riley* [1914] 3 KB 229.
[186] On which see H Fenwick (1999) 62 MLR 491, esp pp 492–5.
[187] *Redmond-Bate* v *DPP* [2000] HRLR 249, and *DPP* v *Jones*, above.
[188] *DPP* v *Jones*, above, at p 251.
[189] Ibid, per Lord Hutton, at p 293.
[190] *Huntingdon Life Sciences Ltd* v *Curtin, The Times*, 11 December 1997. See also *Gate Gourmet London Ltd* v *TGWU*, above. But cf *Oxford University* v *Broughton*, above. Also *Hayes* v *Willoughby*, above, where concerns are expressed by Lord Reed in dissent that the 1997 Act may now be a threat to investigative journalism in light of the Supreme Court's narrow reading of the defence in s 1(3). But see *Trimingham* v *Associated Newspapers* [2012] EWHC 1296 (QB) – 1997 Act not such a threat to the press.

In these cases, Convention rights have often yielded to other concerns, notably the need to maintain public order under common law rules created long before the enactment of the Human Rights Act 1998.[191] It is thus still premature to draw too many conclusions about the liberalising effect of the Human Rights Act, especially as we continue to be reminded that 'in a democratic society the protection of public order lies at the heart of good government'.[192] Together with new local authority powers with potential application in relation to freedom of assembly,[193] such remarks tend to suggest that the main impact of Convention rights in this area will not be to call into question the substantive law, but to constrain the manner of its exercise.[194]

This means that the public authorities – local authorities and the police – will be bound to have regard to arts 10 and 11 when exercising discretionary powers. That said, recent cases in both the Strasbourg Court and the UKSC have shown a remarkable indulgence to the police. The recognition of wide common law powers and the bending of Convention rights in the interests of the State suggests that the principles that informed *DPP v Jones* and *Laporte* respectively have been largely eclipsed. That claim is reinforced by *DB v PSI Chief Constable*,[195] where it was said that in exercising 'operational discretion' in policing public protest officers must have regard to the Convention rights (such as art 8) of third parties, thereby presenting the ironic twist of the HRA being yet another source of *restraint* on the right to freedom of assembly.

---

[191] *Austin v Metropolitan Police Commissioner*, above, and *R (McClure) v Metropolitan Police Commissioner*, above.

[192] *R (McCann) v Manchester Crown Court* [2002] UKHL 39, [2003] 1 AC 787, at para [41] (Lord Hope). See also *R (Hicks) v Metropolitan Police Commissioner*, above, and *DB v PSI Chief Constable*, below.

[193] Notably the public spaces protection orders introduced by the Anti-social Behaviour, Crime and Policing Act 2014, s 59. Used initially to deal with a wide range of anti-social behaviour such as aggressive begging, keeping dogs under control, and touting (punts in Cambridge), its potential use in the context of public protest (initially outside abortion clinics) has not gone unnoticed. The express provision in the Act (s 72) that in making such orders local authorities must have regard to ECHR arts 10 and 11 is not so much a reassurance that this power will not be used as a restraint on assembly as a warning that it almost certainly will be so used.

[194] For a very sober account of the practical impact of the Human Rights Act on freedom of assembly, see A Geddis [2004] PL 853.

[195] [2017] UKSC 7, esp para 72 ('The area of discretion available to the police was also constrained by the positive obligation to protect the appellant's article 8 rights'). *DB* was decided two weeks before *Hicks*; only Lords Reed and Dyson sat in both cases.

CHAPTER 19

State security and official secrets

In the liberal constitution, the protection of liberty is a primary duty of the government. But so too is the protection of the security of the state, whether from external aggression or internal subversion. An uneasy tension exists between personal liberty and national security, and it is the duty of the constitutional lawyer to ensure that the demands of the latter do not become an excuse for unnecessary restrictions on the former.

Although the common law may at first sight appear to take little account of state necessity,[1] national security is a matter to which the courts nevertheless attach considerable importance.[2] But this does not mean that the judges should withdraw at the mere mention of national security: to do so would seriously compromise the rule of law.[3] The terrorist attacks in the United States in September 2001 ('9/11') appeared initially to have induced British judges to move further into the background when national security was raised.[4] But the House of Lords subsequently made it clear that the 'war on terror' will not be accepted as an excuse for the discriminatory violation of Convention rights or the breach of basic common law rules prohibiting the use of evidence obtained by torture.[5]

Today state security, or more commonly national security, is mentioned in a large number of statutes, which typically make special provision for matters relating to national security. Thus the Parliamentary Ombudsman may not investigate action taken with the authority of the Secretary of State for the purposes of protecting the security of the state,[6] and rights under the Data Protection Act 1998 may be excluded for the purpose of safeguarding national security.[7] The right of journalists to protect their sources may have to yield to the interests of national security,[8] as may the right of access to official information under the Freedom of Information Act 2000.[9] And in some litigation where national security considerations are being contested, the matter may be held in camera, with the citizen assigned a lawyer approved by the state.[10]

A. Security and intelligence

There are three principal security and intelligence agencies operating in the United Kingdom, with overlapping responsibilities. These are the Security Service, the Secret Intelligence Service, and GCHQ; the Defence Intelligence Staff also has intelligence functions. The costs

---

[1] *Entick* v *Carrington* (1765) 19 St Tr 1030.

[2] See *Conway* v *Rimmer* [1968] AC 910, at pp 955, 993; *A–G* v *Jonathan Cape Ltd* [1976] QB 752, at p 768.

[3] For a powerful statement of the judicial role in national security cases, see A Barak (2002) 116 Harv L Rev 19.

[4] *Home Secretary* v *Rehman* [2001] UKHL 47, [2003] 1 AC 153. A Tomkins (2002) 118 LQR 200.

[6] Parliamentary Commissioner Act 1967, Sch 3(5).

[5] *A* v *Home Secretary* [2004] UKHL 56, [2005] 2 AC 68 (ch 14); and *A* v *Home Secretary (No 2)* [2005] UKHL 71, [2006] 1 All ER 575 (ch 14). See also Lord Bingham (2003) 52 ICLQ 841, Lord Steyn (2004) 53 ICLQ 1, and Lord Hope (2004) 53 ICLQ 807. But compare *Home Secretary* v *Rehman*, above, esp per Lord Hoffmann.

[7] See ch 16.

[8] Contempt of Court Act 1981, s 10; *Secretary of State for Defence* v *Guardian Newspapers Ltd* [1985] AC 339.

[9] See ch 11.

[10] See Justice and Security Act 2013, Pt 2 (reversing *Al Rawi* v *Security Service* [2011] UKHL 34, [2012] 1 AC 531), and *Tariq* v *Home Office* [2011] UKSC 35, [2012] 1 AC 452.

of this machinery have increased sharply in recent years, the published costs of the three agencies now accounting for about £2.5 billion and rising.[11]

Formal machinery for these agencies to bring intelligence to the attention of government is provided by the Joint Intelligence Committee, which was established in 1936 as a sub-committee of the Committee of Imperial Defence.[12] Part of the Cabinet Office since 1957, the JIC meets frequently, its main function being to provide ministers and senior officials with 'coordinated intelligence assessments on a range of issues of immediate and long-term importance to national interests, primarily in the fields of security, defence and foreign affairs'.[13]

As well as the intelligence agencies (the 'producers'), the JIC includes officials from various intelligence 'users', notably the Ministry of Defence and the Foreign Office, the Treasury, the Department for International Development, and the Home Office. Other departments may also attend when relevant, as also may representatives of the intelligence agencies of the United States, Canada and Australia. The JIC is a committee of officials whose chairman is responsible for supervising its work and for ensuring that its 'warning and monitoring role is discharged effectively'.[14] According to the Butler Committee in 2004,

> The JIC thus brings together in regular meetings the most senior people responsible for intelligence collection, for intelligence assessment and for the use of intelligence in the main departments for which it is collected, in order to construct and issue assessments on the subjects of greatest current concern. The process is robust, and the assessments that result are respected and used at all levels of government.[15]

The collection of this information at home and abroad gives rise to questions about effective legal and political accountability for security measures. In recent years, however, there has been a welcome lifting of the veil of secrecy which has for so long surrounded the security and intelligence services. This is reflected in part by the open discussion of the JIC and its intelligence assessments in the Butler inquiry, appointed in 2004 to investigate the intelligence coverage available in respect of weapons of mass destruction at the time of the invasion of Iraq. It is reflected more notably in the greater role of legislation in regulating the affairs of the Security Services, and in particular by the extension of the principle of judicial oversight, and with it the publication of annual reports by the judicial commissioners.

Much of that legislation has been driven by the European Convention on Human Rights. As we have seen,[16] many of the rights set out in the Convention allow for exceptions and these generally include national security, provided that the restriction is prescribed by law and necessary in a democratic society. This is true, for example, of arts 8, 9, 10 and 11. One of the difficulties with the procedures and practices traditionally operating in this country was their relative informality, and the lack of clear legal rules setting out the functions and powers of the security and intelligence services.[17] So to the extent that the activities of the Security Services violate the private life of the individual, it could not be said that these activities were 'prescribed by law'. At best, it might be said that they were not 'prohibited by law'.

---

[11] HC 444 (2015–16). To put it into perspective the reported income is more than double the total annual income of British trade unions. See Annual Report of the Certification Officer for Trade Unions and Employers' Associations 2016–17 (2017) (trade union income of £1,2 billion).

[12] Lord Butler (Chair), Review of Intelligence on Weapons of Mass Destruction: Report of a Committee of Privy Counsellors, HC 898 (2003–4), para 41.

[13] Ibid, para 43.

[14] https://www.gov.uk/government/groups/joint-intelligence-committee.

[15] Butler, above, para 43.

[16] See ch 14.

[17] *Malone* v *UK* (1984) 7 EHRR 14; *Hewitt and Harman* v *UK* (1992) 14 EHRR 657; and *Khan* v *UK* (2001) 31 EHRR 1016.

B. Security and intelligence services

The modern security and intelligence services have their origins in the early years of the 20th century, and are concerned mainly with surveillance and the gathering of intelligence at home and overseas. Different methods are used for these purposes, though they have become much more sophisticated with the passage of time and the development of new technology. The main security and intelligence services are MI5 and MI6, though we also give an account below of the work of GCHQ, and Defence Intelligence, as well as Counter Terrorism Command. Although CTC is a police unit, it does have some security responsibilities.

Security Service

The Security Service was created in the War Office in 1909 to deal with the fears about German espionage in the period immediately before the First World War. The unit was called MO5, and later MI5. In 1935, MI5 was amalgamated with the section of the Metropolitan Police dealing with counter-subversion, and in that year it changed its name to the Security Service.[18] The domestic security service is, however, still referred to as MI5.

A remarkable feature of these developments is that they took place without statutory authority. The service was set up by executive decision, with functions determined by the executive, the service accountable only to the executive. In his report on the Security Service following the Profumo scandal in 1963, Lord Denning wrote:

> The Security Service in this country is not established by Statute nor is it recognised by Common Law. Even the Official Secrets Acts do not acknowledge its existence. The members of the Service are, in the eye of the law, ordinary citizens with no powers greater than anyone else. They have no special powers of arrest such as the police have. No special powers of search are given to them. They cannot enter premises without the consent of the householder, even though they may suspect a spy is there. If a spy is fleeing the country, they cannot tap him on the shoulder and say he is not to go. They have, in short, no executive powers. They have managed very well without them. We would rather have it so, than have anything in the nature of a 'secret police'.[19]

According to Lord Denning, this absence of legal powers was made up for by the close cooperation between the Security Service and the police, particularly the Special Branch.[20] The Security Service would make all the initial investigations, relying on its technical resources and specialised field force. But as soon as an arrest was possible, the police were called into consultation and from that point onwards both forces worked as a team. Because of the lack of executive power of the Security Service, an arrest would be made by the police and if a search warrant were needed, this too would be obtained by the police.[21]

Before the enactment of the Security Service Act 1989, the Security Service was governed by a directive issued by the Home Secretary (Sir David Maxwell Fyfe) in 1952. Addressed to the Director General of MI5,[22] this provided that, although the Security Service was not a part of the Home Office, the Director General would be responsible to the Home Secretary personally, with

---

[18] For a full account of its origins from non-official histories, see Andrew, *Secret Service*. See also West, *MI5: British Security Service Operations 1909–45*; and *A Matter of Trust: MI5, 1945–72*. For further analyses, see Ewing and Gearty, *The Struggle for Civil Liberties*, ch 2; Gill, *Policing Politics*; Lustgarten and Leigh, *In from the Cold*; Williams, *Not in the Public Interest*, part 2; and Bunyan, *The Political Police in Britain*, chs 3, 4.

[19] Cmnd 2152, 1963.

[20] See p 523 below.

[21] Cmnd 2152, 1963, para 273.

[22] Reproduced in *R v Home Secretary, ex p Hosenball* [1977] 3 All ER 452 in the judgment of Lord Denning MR.

a right on appropriate occasions of direct access to the Prime Minister. The directive also stated that the service 'is part of the Defence Forces of the country', and that 'its task is the Defence of the Realm as a whole, from external and internal dangers arising from attempts at espionage and sabotage, or from actions of persons and organisations whether directed from within or without the country, which may be judged to be subversive of the state'. The work of the service was to be strictly limited to what is necessary for these purposes and was expressly required to be kept absolutely free from any political bias or influence.

Questions of the political responsibilities of the service were clarified by Lord Denning in his famous 1963 report.[23] Although the function of the service is the defence of the realm, political responsibility did not (and does not) lie with the Secretary of State for Defence, but with the Home Secretary and the Prime Minister, who is advised on security matters by the Cabinet Secretary.[24] However, it has been an open question for many years just what degree of political responsibility has existed, particularly in view of the convention that ministers 'do not concern themselves with the detailed information which may be obtained by the Security Services in particular cases, but are furnished with such information only as may be necessary for the determination of any issue on which guidance is sought'.[25]

Since 1989 the work of the service has changed in response to the new and evolving international position, and the so-called 'war on terror' in particular. During the Cold War the service was concerned largely with counter-subversion and counter-espionage. So far as the former is concerned, it was reported in 1995 that the threat from subversive organisations had decreased to the point where it was assessed as being 'low'. The Communist Party of Great Britain (CPGB) no longer existed, while the main surviving organisation (the Communist Party of Britain) was assessed to be only about 1,100 strong, compared to 25,000–30,000 in the CPGB in the 1970s and 56,000 at its peak in 1942.[26] According to the Security Commission, it had been agreed inter-departmentally that the investigation of subversive organisations should be reduced,[27] and in 1992 the service assumed a new responsibility in the form of 'Irish republican terrorism', which was transferred from the Special Branch.

Although this step seems clearly to have been inspired by the need to fill the gap in the work of the service caused by the end of the Cold War, it was explained in Parliament that the service already had responsibility for Irish loyalist and international terrorism and for Irish republican terrorism overseas.[28] Indeed, it was only the accident of history which had given the police the leading responsibility for Irish republican terrorism, a decision which had been taken in 1883 when the Special Irish Branch was formed to track down Fenians who at the time were placing bombs in London. The Security Service is now greatly concerned with the domestic implications of international terrorism (notably ISIL and al-Qaeda), as well as domestic extremism (usually of a right-wing variety), and cyber-crime. Otherwise, espionage from Russian and Chinese agents continues to be a concern, with the Security Service reporting that the number of Russian agents has not fallen since the Soviet days.

Secret Intelligence Service, GCHQ and Defence Intelligence

The existence of the Secret Intelligence Service (SIS, or MI6 as it is more commonly known) was first officially acknowledged in May 1992, although it was founded in 1909, albeit not in its modern form. Despite the ending of the Cold War, the government is nevertheless of the

---

[23] See also Wilson, *The Labour Government 1964–70*, p 481.

[24] Cmnd 2152, 1963, para 238.

[25] Ibid.

[26] Pelling, *The British Communist Party*, p 192.

[27] Cm 2930, 1995.

[28] HC Deb, 8 May 1992, cols 297–306.

view that there is a role for the security and intelligence services 'alongside the armed services and diplomatic services in protecting and furthering the interests of Britain and its citizens at home and abroad'.[29] The threats which are said to make the continued existence of these agencies necessary 'include nuclear, chemical, biological and conventional proliferation of weapons', as well as 'terrorism and the threat to our armed forces in times of conflict, serious crime, espionage and sabotage'.[30]

According to postings on the SIS website now removed,[31] the Service 'mounts covert operations overseas in support of British government objectives' and 'collects intelligence subject to requirements and priorities established by the JIC and approved by ministers'. It uses 'human and technical' sources for these purposes, and works with a wide range of foreign intelligence and security services, as well as other British agencies such as GCHQ, the Security Service (MI5), the armed forces, the Foreign Office, the Home Office, the Ministry of Defence, and HM Revenue and Customs. The service is required to work within the law as laid down by the Intelligence Services Act 1994, and has a key role in the implementation of the government's National Security Strategy.[32]

Although it had been operating at least since 1947, Government Communications' Headquarters (GCHQ) was not publicly acknowledged to exist until the trial of Geoffrey Prime, an official who was convicted under s 1 of the Official Secrets Act 1911 in 1982 for passing information to the Soviet Union. This was followed by a report of the Security Commission which not only revealed the existence of the centre but also gave an account of the security procedures in operation there, including those for physical and document security.[33] It came more prominently to the fore in 1984 when controversially the government announced a trade union ban at the establishment,[34] one irony of which is that as a result GCHQ 'has become as well known in political circles as MI5 and MI6'.[35]

Officially, GCHQ 'provides government with information' to 'support policy-making and operations in the fields of national security, military operations, law enforcement and economic well being',[36] and in doing so works closely with overseas agencies such as the National Security Agency in the United States. According to its website, the role of GCHQ is to 'defend Government systems from cyber threat, provide support to the Armed Forces and strive to keep the public safe, in real life and online', with terrorism being an important preoccupation. The Director of GCHQ, like the Chief of SIS, is personally responsible to the Foreign Secretary by whom he is appointed, subject to the overall responsibility of the Prime Minister for security and intelligence matters. Like SIS, GCHQ has been placed on a statutory footing by the Intelligence Services Act 1994 (on which see below).

Established as Defence Intelligence Staff (DIS) in 1964 following the creation by statute of a unified Ministry of Defence, Defence Intelligence (DI) is run by the Chief of Defence Intelligence. The work of DI includes intelligence collection, and like the other agencies it contributes to the work of the JIC.[37] An 'integral part' of the Ministry of Defence,[38] DI provides intelligence for the armed forces and other government departments, and analyses information from a wide variety of sources, both overt and covert. Also initially having a

---

[29] HC Deb, 22 February 1994, col 155 (Mr Douglas Hurd).

[30] Ibid (giving examples of the work of MI6 in the then contemporary world).

[31] http://www.sis.gov.uk/.

[32] Ibid. For the National Security Strategy, see Cm 9161, 2015.

[33] Cmnd 8876, 1983.

[34] See p 270 above.

[35] Official Report, Standing Committee E, 15 March 1994, col 115.

[36] HM Government, *National Intelligence Machinery* (2010), p 8.

[37] See also HC 115 (1995–6) (Scott Report), para C 2.26.

[38] https://www.gov.uk/government/groups/defence-intelligence.

Cold War role, website postings since removed indicate a shift of DI's focus 'towards providing intelligence support to operations overseas, countering the proliferation of weapons of mass destruction, and supporting the global war on terrorism'.

The Chief of Defence Intelligence is a serving military officer who according to website postings now removed reports to the Chief of the Defence Staff and the Permanent Secretary of the MOD. Funded from the Defence Vote, DI does not fall within the statutory definition of the intelligence services (which is confined to the Security Service, the Secret Intelligence Service and GCHQ). This means that DI is not governed by the Intelligence Services Act 1994, and therefore not subject to the various processes of scrutiny and accountability in the Act. Nevertheless, under the Investigatory Powers Act 2016, the Chief of Defence Intelligence may apply for an interception warrant,[39] and it appears that DI may use the various forms of surveillance authorised by the Regulation of Investigatory Powers Act 2000.[40]

All the security and intelligence agencies now emphasise the importance of cyber-crime and internet-based activity as part of their concerns.

Special Branch and Counter-Terrorism Command[41]

Although not an official security and intelligence service, another agency engaged in work related to state security has emerged from what was previously the police Special Branch, which as we have seen was formed in 1883 in response to a Fenian bombing campaign in London. After three years the word 'Irish' was dropped from the Branch's title, and it was expanded to deal with other security problems. After 1945 provincial police forces established their own permanent Special Branch, 'primarily to acquire intelligence, to assess its potential operational value, and to contribute more generally to its interpretation'.[42] There is now more formal national co-ordination of Special Branch activity, with some Special Branches known as counter-terrorism branches.

In this way the Special Branch assists both the Security Service and the Secret Intelligence Service in carrying out their statutory duties. Home Office guidelines revised in 2004 (and not again since) emphasised that the acquisition of high-grade intelligence is vital to the work of the Special Branch and explained the different ways by which information is obtained: 'the handling of covert human intelligence sources, intelligence gathering, field enquiries, intelligence passed on from other parts of the police service, and surveillance by conventional and technical means'.[43] Although terrorism is the 'key priority' for the Special Branch,[44] there is also an acknowledgement that Special Branches in most police forces have responsibility for gathering intelligence on threats to public order and community safety from individuals 'motivated by racial hatred or political conviction'. In addition, the Special Branch gathers intelligence on 'political and animal rights extremist activity, anti-globalisation and environmental extremism'.[45]

Following the London terrorist bombings in 2005, the Metropolitan Police Special Branch was merged with the Anti-Terrorist Branch to form Counter-Terrorism Command (also known as SO 15), which combines the intelligence-gathering role of the former with the investigation role of the latter.[46] Counter-Terrorism Command (CTC) is said now to be 'the

---

[39] Investigatory Powers Act 2016, s 18; see ch 16.

[40] Regulation of Investigatory Powers Act 2000, s 41.

[41] See Bunyan (note 18 above), and Allason, *The Branch: A History of the Metropolitan Police Special Branch 1883–1983*.

[42] *Home Office Guidelines on Special Branch Work in the United Kingdom* (2004), para 18.

[43] Ibid, para 19.

[44] Ibid, para 20.

[45] Ibid, para 27.

[46] *The Times*, 3 October 2006.

primary police resource for countering terrorism', and is a 'very large and complex command', with a headcount then of approximately 1,500 which was 'still growing'.[47] As such the CTC has a number of responsibilities, which, according to information on the Metropolitan Police website which has been removed, include 'detecting, investigating and preventing terrorist threats and networks'. Here CTC works closely with the security and intelligence services. In addition, CTC 'has the national lead for domestic extremism, a role undertaken by the National Domestic Extremism Unit', and also deals with 'sensitive national security investigations, such as Official Secrets Act enquiries'.

Although the Metropolitan Police Service was designated by the National Police Chiefs' Council as the lead force for what is now the National Domestic Extremism and Disorder Intelligence Unit, the latter 'remains a national policing unit'. As such, it 'supports all police forces to help reduce the criminal threat from domestic extremism across the UK', with a key responsibility being intelligence gathering on 'domestic extremism' and public order issues.[48] In the recent past 'domestic extremism' was categorised for policing purposes into five themes: animal rights, extreme right-wing, extreme left-wing, environmental and emerging trends. These terms are not defined, though it has been claimed that 'domestic extremism' only applies to individuals or groups 'who carry out criminal acts of direct action to further their protest campaign, outside the democratic process'.[49]

The CTC thus stands at the apex of a complex National Counter-Terrorism Network of police units of various kinds, explained as follows:

> The sort of coalface of countering terrorism is essentially every police force because all officers and staff have a role to be aware and to make contributions to a national effort. Then you have the local force special branches in each force, then the next level up is the counter-terrorism intelligence units, the next level up is the counter-terrorism units, the five larger ones, and at the top, I guess, is the Counter-Terrorism Command in London.[50]

Special Branches thus continue to play an important part as local intelligence gatherers.[51] It is important to emphasise, however, that Special Branch officers are police officers with no additional powers.

Not being officially part of the formal security and intelligence apparatus of the state, CTC is not governed by the procedures discussed in the following part of this chapter.

C. Legal framework of security and intelligence services

As explained above, it has been necessary to place the security and intelligence services, and the work they do, on a firm statutory base, with some form of statutory oversight. But of course, it is not enough that there should be legal authority for the work of the security and intelligence services. Also important is the nature and quality of the law and the manner of its exercise: to satisfy the Convention any restriction on Convention rights by the security and intelligence services must be proportionate to the objective which it is sought to be achieved.

---

[47] HC 212 (2008–09), Minutes of Evidence, 12 February 2009, Q 97 (Mr Bob Quick QPM).
[48] http://www.npcc.police.uk/NationalPolicing/NDEDIU/AboutNDEDIU.aspx.
[49] *Catt* v *Metropolitan Police Commissioner* [2012] EWHC 1471 (Admin), [2012] HRLR 23, para 5. The *Catt* case has tended to suggest that such assurances are hollow, and that 'peaceful protestors' are also swept up in the surveillance work of the NDEU. See further *R (Catt)* v *Metropolitan Police Commissioner* [2015] UKSC 9. See further ch 16 above.
[50] Ibid, Q 98.
[51] Ibid.

Security Service Act 1989[52]

The Security Service is now governed to some extent by the Security Service Act 1989, which creates a legal basis for the Service and some of its powers (though other legal powers and controls are to be found in the Regulation of Investigatory Powers Act 2000 (RIPA) and the Investigatory Powers Act 2016 (IPA) considered in Chapter 16).[53] It is also the case that the security and intelligence services operate within boundaries defined by the ECHR, which ought to have implications for the Human Rights Act 1998.

1. Statutory functions and powers

In providing for the continuation of the Security Service (MI5), the Security Service Act 1989 defines its function to be 'the protection of national security and, in particular, its protection against threats from espionage, terrorism and sabotage, from the activities of agents of foreign powers and from actions intended to overthrow or undermine parliamentary democracy by political, industrial or violent means' (s 1(2)). The term 'national security' is not defined, although it has been said to be wider than the particular heads specified in the Act.[54] The service also has the task of safeguarding the economic well-being of the country against threats posed by the actions or intentions of persons outside the United Kingdom (s 1(3)).

By an amendment to the 1989 Act introduced by the Security Service Act 1996, it is also a function of the service to act in support of the activities of police forces and other law enforcement agencies in the prevention and detection of serious crime. According to the government, this last provision reflects 'the firm intention' that the service 'should be deployed against organised crime' and that the 'drug traffickers, the money launderers and the racketeers' are to become the service's new targets. The role of the service is to be 'a supporting one' in this capacity, the legislation reflecting fully 'the principle that the public and the law enforcement agencies will retain the primary responsibility'.[55] Nevertheless, these provisions were extremely controversial and gave rise to concern in Parliament and elsewhere.

According to its website, the Service has suspended activity concerned with serious crime, and did so following the creation of the Serious Organised Crime Agency in 2006 (a body now replaced by the National Crime Agency) at a time when resources were required elsewhere. So far as the other statutory functions of the service are concerned, it appears that it is now preoccupied with espionage and terrorism. The latter relates mainly to international terrorist groups linked to al-Qaeda and ISIL, and to Northern Ireland. Although 'domestic extremist' groups may aspire to the use of violence, they are thought to present more of a threat to public order than to national security and are thus the responsibility of the National Domestic Extremism and Intelligence Unit based in the Metropolitan Police, and referred to above.

In exercising its wide powers, the service continues to be under the operational control of the Director General, who is appointed by the Home Secretary (s 2(4)). The duties of the Director General, who must make an annual report to the Prime Minister and the Home Secretary (s 2), include taking steps to ensure that the service does not take any action to further the interests of any political party (s 2(2)(b)). This is narrower than the rule contained in the Maxwell Fyfe directive which required the service to be kept free from 'any political

[52] See I Leigh and L Lustgarten (1989) 52 MLR 801; also Ewing and Gearty, *Freedom under Thatcher*, pp 175–88.
[53] For arrangements in other countries, see Lee, Hanks and Morabito, *In the Name of National Security* (Australia), and Lustgarten and Leigh, above, which is strong on Australian and Canadian developments.
[54] Cm 1480, 1991. Although not 'easily defined', it 'includes the defence of the realm and the government's defence and foreign policies involving the protection of vital national interests at home and abroad'. What is a vital national interest is 'a question of fact and degree', more 'easily recognised when being considered than defined in advance'.
[55] HL Deb, 14 May 1996, cols 398–9 (Baroness Blatch). The meaning of detection for these purposes is widely defined: s 1(5), as inserted by the RIPA 2000, s 82(1).

bias or influence', a rule which it is claimed did not prevent the surveillance of the Campaign for Nuclear Disarmament or trade unions involved in pay disputes.[56]

The 1989 Act conferred a new power on the service. This was the power to apply to the Home Secretary for a warrant authorising 'entry on or interference with property' (s 3).[57] Hitherto there was no power to grant any such warrant, but the service may not have been unduly impeded by the absence of such a power. Indeed, in *Attorney-General* v *Guardian Newspapers (No 2)* Lord Donaldson MR appeared willing to turn a blind eye to the unauthorised entry of private property by the Security Services, referring to it as a 'covert invasion of privacy', which might be considered excusable in the defence of the realm.[58] This power to apply for a Home Office warrant introduced in 1989, was replaced by comparable provisions in the Intelligence Services Act 1994, on which see below.

2. *Statutory accountability*

The 1989 Act is significant for having introduced new statutory procedures for the supervision of the Security Service. These are modelled on procedures introduced in the Interception of Communications Act 1985, which gave way to the Regulation of Investigatory Powers Act 2000 (RIPA) and in due course to the Investigatory Powers Act 2016 (IPA). The 1989 Act made provision for the appointment of a Security Service Commissioner, being someone who holds or has held high judicial office (s 4); and also a Security Service Tribunal to hear complaints against the service (s 5). The Commissioner was required to keep under review the power of the Home Secretary to issue warrants to the service.

The practice of the Commissioner was to review all the s 3 warrants issued, reviewed and cancelled,[59] and in some cases the products obtained by the operation.[60] In all the cases examined, the Commissioner found the procedures to have been in good order and warrants to have been properly issued. An exception was in 1999 when in one case an application was said to be 'thin and lacking in particularity'. After interviewing the responsible officers, the Commissioner was able to conclude that the application had been properly made and the officers in question were asked to make a supplementary written statement to the Secretary of State to clarify the position.[61]

The Regulation of Investigatory Powers Act 2000 abolished the office of Security Service Commissioner, with a new Intelligence Services Commissioner given oversight for all the intelligence services (including in some cases those attached to the Ministry of Defence).[62] The Intelligence Services Commissioner was required to keep under review the way in which both ministers and members of the intelligence services exercise their powers under Parts II and III of the Regulation of Investigatory Powers Act 2000, in so far as the powers related to the intelligence services. These included powers connected with surveillance.

The Intelligence Services Commissioner was abolished in turn by the Investigatory Powers Act 2016, which creates a new office of Investigatory Powers Commissioner, which together with a body of judicial commissioners is to have responsibility for oversight of the

---

[56] Allegations to this effect were made by a retired MI5 officer, Cathy Massiter, in a Channel 4 television programme. For the unsuccessful challenge to the legality of this activity, see *R* v *Home Secretary, ex p Ruddock* [1987] 2 All ER 518.

[57] On the way this power is exercised, see Cm 1480, 1991, para 3. Section 3 was replaced by ss 5 and 6 of the Intelligence Services Act 1994 (on which see below).

[58] [1990] AC 109, at 190. Cf *Entick* v *Carrington*, above.

[59] Cm 4002, 1998, para 5; Cm 4365, 1999, para 7; and Cm 4779, 2000, para 15.

[60] Cm 4365, 1999, para 7.

[61] Notwithstanding this apparent irregularity, the Commissioner was nevertheless able to report that the 'Secretaries of State have been properly advised', and that they 'have exercised their powers under the Act correctly': Cm 4779, 2000, paras 16 and 17.

[62] Regulation of Investigatory Powers Act 2000, s 59(2).

intelligence services as well as the use of investigatory powers by other agencies.[63] The focus is thus now on the powers rather than the agencies exercising them, with responsibilities for the latter depending on the Prime Minister specifically directing the Commissioner to keep under review the carrying out of any aspect of the functions of an intelligence service (or its head), or any part of the armed forces of the Ministry of Defence relating to intelligence activities.[64]

In addition to oversight by the Investigatory Powers Commissioner (who must report annually to the Prime Minister),[65] the Regulation of Investigatory Powers Act 2000 provides that the Investigatory Powers Tribunal established by s 65 of the Act may hear complaints against any of the intelligence services, this replacing the jurisdiction of the tribunal created by the 1989 Act to deal only with MI5.[66] The IPT has exclusive jurisdiction to deal with all complaints concerned with the conduct of the intelligence services, which relates to the complainant, his or her property or his or her communications. It is also the only body to deal with complaints about the violation of Convention rights in relation to the security and intelligence services, though a right of appeal from the IPT on points of law was introduced by the IPA 2016.[67]

Serious concerns have been expressed about the procedural rules under which the IPT operates, these departing markedly from normal standards for the conduct of civil litigation. Drafted by the Home Secretary under the authority of RIPA, these require high levels of secrecy in the conduct of the proceedings, in terms of the hearing of the complaint, the disclosure of evidence and the giving of reasons, though the tribunal makes much of the claim that legal questions may be heard in public on assumed facts.[68] The procedures were held by the ECtHR to be consistent with the ECHR, art 6, 'bearing in mind the importance' of secret surveillance measures 'to the fight against terrorism and serious crime'.[69]

Intelligence Services Act 1994

So far as the Secret Intelligence Service is concerned, its activities are governed by the Intelligence Services Act 1994, which also applies to GCHQ. As in the case of the Security Service (above), other legal powers and controls are to be found in the Regulation of Investigatory Powers Act 2000 (RIPA) and the Investigatory Powers Act 2016 (IPA), considered in Chapter 16. It is also the case here that the security and intelligence services operate within boundaries defined by the ECHR, which ought to have implications for the Human Rights Act 1998.

1. Statutory functions

The functions of SIS are stated by s 1(1) to be (*a*) the obtaining and providing of information relating to the actions or intentions of persons outside the British Islands, and (*b*) the performing of 'other tasks relating to the actions or intentions of such persons'. These extraordinarily wide provisions are constrained by s 1(2) which provides that the statutory functions are exercisable only (*a*) in the interests of national security (with 'particular reference to the

---

[63] See ch 16.

[64] Investigatory Powers Act 2016, s 230.

[65] Ibid, s 234.

[66] A total of 338 complaints were made to the 1989 Act tribunal between 1989 and 1999: Cm 4779, 2000, para 37. In 42 of these cases it appears that the complainant was the subject of a personal file kept by the Security Service.

[67] Now Regulation of Investigatory Powers Act 2000, s 67A, inserted by IPA 2016, s 242. Previously a wide ouster clause (on which see ch 25 below) protected the IPT, from which the only recourse was to Strasbourg. See *A* v *B* [2009] UKSC 12, [2010] 2 AC 1; and *R (Privacy International)* v *IPT* [2017] EWHC 114 (Admin). On the ouster of jurisdiction, see P F Scott [2017] PL 115.

[68] Investigatory Powers Tribunal, *Report 2010–15*, p 22. In fact only 27 per cent of cases are heard in open court.

[69] *Kennedy* v *United Kingdom* [2010] ECHR 682, (2011) 52 EHRR 4.

defence and foreign policies of Her Majesty's Government'), (*b*) in the interests of the economic well-being of the United Kingdom, or (*c*) in support of the prevention or detection of serious crime.[70]

The 'interests of national security' are not otherwise defined, nor (more surprisingly) is what constitutes 'serious crime'.[71] And although 'a well-worn provision', it was acknowledged that a power to take action 'in the interests of the economic well-being' of the United Kingdom 'sometimes causes puzzlement as to what it can mean'.[72] It was explained, however, that the power 'might be useful' where 'substantial British economic interests were at stake or where there was a crisis or a huge difficulty about the continued supply of a commodity on which our economy depended'.[73] At the very least this appears to authorise the SIS role in gathering economic intelligence to inform policy.

The Act also places GCHQ on a statutory footing, under the authority of the Foreign Secretary. By virtue of s 3, its functions are to:

- 'monitor or interfere with electromagnetic, acoustic and other emissions and any equipment producing such emissions';
- 'obtain and provide information derived from or related to such emissions or equipment'; and
- provide advice and assistance about language and cryptology to the armed forces, government departments or any other organisation approved by the Prime Minister.

As in the case of SIS the foregoing functions are exercisable only in the interests of national security (with particular reference to the defence and foreign policies of the government); or the interests of the economic well-being of the United Kingdom. These measures were strongly criticised in standing committee as providing a mandate which is 'wide and sweeping', inadequately constrained by the 'partial stricture' that it be exercised in the interests of national security.[74] It was pointed out in reply, however, that there were a number of safeguards in the Act to prevent the abuse of power (according to the minister there were eleven in total).

So far as the duty of GCHQ to assist in the prevention and detection of crime is concerned, this was said not to be new, but had been going on for 'decades'. It was reported then that GCHQ intervenes when criminals use 'sophisticated communications devices to commit a crime' and assists in the deciphering of diaries and notebooks kept by criminals in sophisticated codes.[75] The GCHQ website provides detail of the wide range of activities now undertaken by the agency in relation to serious crime, which includes matters as varied as the protection of children from sexual exploitation on the one hand, and cyber-crime on the other.

2. Statutory powers

By section 5, the Intelligence Services Act 1994 authorises 'entry on or interference with property or with wireless telegraphy' by each of the three security and intelligence agencies, provided that any such action is taken with the authority of a warrant issued by the Secretary of State (or in some cases the Scottish Ministers);[76] otherwise the action is 'unlawful'.[77] This replaces the power first introduced by the 1989 Act, s 3, which applied only to the Security

---

[70] The meaning of detection and prevention for these purposes is widely defined: s 11(1A), as inserted by RIPA 2000, s 82.

[71] See Cm 3288, 1996, para 8.

[72] HC Deb, 22 February 1994, col 157 (Mr Hurd).

[73] Ibid.

[74] Official Report, Standing Committee E, 15 March 1994, col 117.

[75] Ibid, col 132.

[76] Note that the double lock mechanism (ministerial warrant and judicial approval) introduced by the Investigatory Powers Act 2016 (ch 16 above) does not apply to these s 5 powers (or to the s 7 powers discussed below).

[77] But unlike the unauthorised interception of communications it is not an offence (IPA 2016, s 3).

Service. A warrant may be issued if the Secretary of State 'thinks it necessary' for the purpose of assisting the agency making the application in carrying out any of its functions, provided that the taking of the action is proportionate to what the action seeks to achieve.

A warrant issued on the application of either the SIS or GCHQ may not relate to British property, unlike warrants issued to the Security Service, which may be issued for two such purposes:

- the first relates to the traditional functions of the service, as defined in s 1(2) and (3) of the Security Service Act 1989, in which case it may relate to property in Britain, without further qualification;

- the second relates to the function of the service added by the Security Service Act 1996, namely to act in support of the police and law enforcement agencies in the prevention and detection of serious crime.

In the latter case the warrant may authorise action in respect of property in Britain, but only if the action is to be taken in relation to offences that involve violence, result in substantial financial gain, or constitute conduct by a large number of persons in pursuit of a common purpose, or if the offence is one which carries a term of three years' imprisonment on conviction for the first time.[78] Warrants are normally to be issued by a Secretary of State (or in some cases a member of the Scottish government) and are valid for up to six months, although they may (but need not) be cancelled before the period of six months expires (s 6).

Apart from the power to interfere with property (albeit with the authority of a warrant), by section 7, the 1994 Act also contains a remarkable power for the Secretary of State to authorise a person to commit an act 'outside the British Islands' which would be unlawful 'under the criminal or civil law of any part of the United Kingdom'. The effect of an authorisation under this so-called 'James Bond clause'[79] is to give the individual committing an offence (or other unlawful act) immunity from legal liability in this country (but not in the country in which the crime or unlawful act may be committed). Authorisation should be given only where the acts to be done are 'necessary for the proper discharge of a function of the Intelligence Service or GCHQ'.

> There is no need for authorisation where GCHQ provides information about the location of a foreign national to the intelligence agencies of a foreign power, which then uses the information to seek and kill an enemy suspect. So in *R (Khan)* v *Foreign Secretary*,[80] it was held that there was no criminal liability on the part of GCHQ when information was passed to the CIA to enable the United States to kill applicant's father in Pakistan (along with a number of others) in a targeted drone strike.

Understandably, these powers gave rise to some concern in Parliament, with one Opposition member pointing out that they grant

the Secretary of State complete power to authorise activities that violate the law of other states as well as that of the United Kingdom. There is no limit on what can be authorised. In extreme cases the use of lethal force will be allowed.[81]

Ministers were, however, rather coy about the way in which the powers would be used, and appeared to think it enough to reassure the House that 'certain actions can be undertaken by

---

[78] 1994 Act, s 5, as amended by Security Service Act 1996.
[79] HL Paper 152, HC 230 (2008–9), para 53. The government will not reveal the number of occasions on which this power has been used.
[80] [2014] EWCA Civ 24.
[81] Official Report, Standing Committee E, 17 March 1994, col 174.

the agencies under the specific authority of ministers only.'[82] They were unwilling to contemplate even an obligation to report annually to the Intelligence and Security Committee (on which see below) on the number and general description of all acts authorised under this section, on the ground that provision was made for the appointment of a judicial commissioner to ensure that the ministers' powers were exercised properly.[83]

The annual reports of the commissioner provide little information about the use of this power.[84]

3. Statutory accountability

Political responsibility for the agencies (other than MI5) was said to be 'primarily' that of the Foreign Secretary 'under the Prime Minister'.[85] Under the Act, however, the operations of the SIS continue to be under the control of the Chief of the Intelligence Service (s 2), while the operations of GCHQ continue to be under the control of its Director (s 4).

Each of the foregoing is responsible for ensuring the efficiency of the respective services, and that no information is obtained by their organisations except so far as is necessary for the proper discharge of their functions. They must also ensure that information is not disclosed by their organisations except 'so far as necessary' for the proper discharge of their functions, and that the respective agencies do not take 'any action to further the interests of any United Kingdom political party' (ss 2(2)(b), 4(2)(b)). By a strange quirk of drafting (although it may not be unintended), either service may disclose information even though it is not necessary for it to do so in 'the proper discharge of its functions'.

Thus the SIS may disclose material (without violating the duty of the Chief of the Intelligence Service) on the additional (but not necessarily consequential) ground that it is in the interests of national security, for the prevention or detection of serious crime, or for the purpose of any criminal proceedings (s 2(2)(a)). GCHQ may disclose information falling into the last of these three categories, even though, again, disclosure is not necessary for the proper discharge of its functions, a much narrower incidental power than that possessed by SIS. Both the Chief of Intelligence Service and the Director of GCHQ are required to make an annual report to the Prime Minister and the Foreign Secretary (ss 2(4) and 4(4)).

Following the precedents established in 1985 and 1989, the 1994 Act made provision for the creation of an Intelligence Services Commissioner (appointed by the Prime Minister and being a person who held or had held high judicial office) and a tribunal for the investigation of complaints about the SIS or GCHQ. The decisions of both the Commissioner and the tribunal (including decisions as to jurisdiction) were not subject to appeal and were not liable to be questioned in any court of law. However, the RIPA 2000 merged the jurisdictions of the Intelligence Services Commissioner and the Security Service Commissioner, and transferred the jurisdiction of the security and intelligence tribunal to the investigatory powers tribunal.

From 2000 to 2006, Lord Brown of Eaton-under-Heywood (a Lord of Appeal in Ordinary since 2004) occupied the office of Intelligence Services Commissioner. As Simon Brown LJ, he had also been the first President of the security and intelligence tribunal appointed under the 1994 Act above. Sir Peter Gibson replaced Lord Brown as Commissioner, Sir Peter being a retired member of the Court of Appeal, who like his predecessor appears generally to have

---

[82] HC Deb, 22 February 1994, col 160.

[83] Official Report, Standing Committee E, 17 March 1994, col 175.

[84] See HC 459 (2015–16), SG/2016/96: 'Oversight of section 7 can be particularly challenging because of the multitude of possible acts that could be authorised. Some section 7s have a standard consideration of necessity and proportionality while in others there is no intrusion into privacy but they may require a lengthy legal consideration' (p 21).

[85] HC Deb, 22 February 1994, col 154.

been satisfied with the operation of the procedures under the Act.[86] In common with his predecessor, however, Sir Peter was unwilling to reveal how many warrants are issued or authorisations granted under the 1994 Act.

Sir Mark Waller, also a retired Court of Appeal judge, succeeded Sir Peter as Commissioner in 2010. Sir Mark broke with earlier practice by publishing details of the number of warrants and authorisations issued to the security and intelligence services annually.[87] The figures published cover both the 1994 Act and RIPA, but the statistics are not broken down by service or power. So far as complaints to the investigatory powers tribunal are concerned, although we know that just over a third of complaints relate to the security and intelligence services, there is no detailed information about the grounds for these complaints or of their disposal.[88] Complaints to the IPT against the security and intelligence services (or anyone else) were rarely successful.[89]

As explained above, the office of the Intelligence Services Commissioner was abolished by the IPA 2016, with many of the responsibilities transferred to the Investigatory Powers Commissioner established by that Act.

D. Protection for state secrets and national security

Much of the foregoing has been concerned principally with the surveillance and intelligence-gathering activities of the state agencies responsible for national security. But the protection of national security is also about protecting classified information from falling into the wrong hands. This may be information of a wide and varied kind, relating to defence and foreign affairs on the one hand, and the work of the security and intelligence services on the other. In this part, we consider some of the different methods adopted to protect such information.

Security Service and employment law

Staff employed by the security and intelligence services were traditionally denied the rights normally extended to other workers.[90] The Trade Union and Labour Relations (Consolidation)

---

[86] HC 902 (2008–9), SG/2009/139, para 31. For a strong defence of the system of judicial supervision after the event and its effectiveness, see the report of the Commissioner (Sir Mark Waller) for 2015: HC 459 (2015–16), SG/2016/96, pp 6–7. The Commissioners have, however, drawn attention to a number of 'errors' where no valid warrant or authorisation had been issued in relation to covert activity. In 2008, for example, there were 18 such cases: HC 902 (2008–9), SG/2009/139, p 47, rising to 83 in 2015: HC 459 (2015–16), SG/2016/96, p 49.

[87] In 2015, there were 1,560 warrants and authorisations not including renewals: HC 459 (2015–16), SG/2016/96, p 52.

[88] Investigatory Powers Tribunal, *Report 2010–15*, p 20. There were 968 complaints decided between 2010 and 2015, of which only ten were in favour of the complainant (eight of these in 2015). It is not known how many of these related to the security and intelligence services, and how many to other bodies (such as local authorities) subject to the tribunal's jurisdiction. As the tribunal said: the 'mere fact of an investigation or receipt of a complaint must not be seen as any indication of unlawful behaviour' (ibid).

[89] But see *Liberty* v *GCHQ* [2014] UKIPTrib 13_77-H, [2015] 3 All ER 142 – the first case in which a claim against the security and intelligence services has succeeded. This unusual decision (albeit with limited impact) was met with a palpable gasp of relief that the IPT may be worthwhile. See subsequently to the same effect: *Belhadj* v *Security Service* [2015] UKIPTrib 13, and *Privacy International* v *Foreign Secretary* [2016] UKIPTrib 15_110-CH, [2017] 3 All ER 647. However, in these cases the IPT narrowly construed Convention rights, avoiding any remedy for the complainants, and elegantly creating 'hollow' rather than 'historic' victories: N Simonsen, *UK Human Rights Blog*, 16 February 2015, commenting on *Liberty* v *GCHQ*, ibid.

[90] For a full account of public service employment law generally, including the position of civil servants, see Fredman and Morris, *The State as Employer*.

Act 1992 gives rights in relation to trade union membership, among other things; the Employment Rights Act 1996 covers a larger area, including rights relating to unfair dismissal. Both of these statutes apply to Crown servants,[91] but in both cases an exception was made for those in Crown employment in respect of whom there was a ministerial certificate exempting the employment from the protection of the legislation 'for the purpose of safeguarding national security'.[92]

Certificates were issued excluding the members of the Security Services and subsequently the staff at GCHQ, where rights in respect of trade union membership were unilaterally withdrawn in controversial circumstances in 1984.[93] This rather foolish decision did more than anything to draw attention to GCHQ and the work it does, as well as generating international criticism for breaching the freedom of association guarantees in International Labour Organization Convention 87, an international treaty to which the United Kingdom is a party.[94] Trade union rights at GCHQ were substantially (but not wholly) restored in 1997.[95]

1. Employment rights

The position now under the Employment Relations Act 1999 is that almost all employment rights apply to members of the security and intelligence services, with a number of exceptions and qualifications.[96] It is expressly provided that the protections for whistleblowing extended by the Public Interest Disclosure Act 1998 do not apply in relation to employment in the Security Service, SIS or GCHQ. There are, however, procedures introduced after the *Spycatcher* affair designed to enable members of the security and intelligence services to raise concerns internally.[97] But the right of workers to be accompanied by a trade union official in grievance or disciplinary matters at the workplace does not apply to the members of the security and intelligence services.[98]

It is also provided that in some circumstances an employment-related complaint must be dismissed by the employment tribunal where it is shown that the action complained of was taken for the purpose of safeguarding national security. This applies specifically to cases where the complainant is alleging that he or she has been subjected to a detriment because of trade union membership or activities; or that he or she has been unfairly dismissed.[99] But it is not only where an individual has been dismissed for reasons of national security that sensitive security matters may be raised in tribunal proceedings. There is a fear that security matters could be ventilated in a hearing where someone has been dismissed because of misconduct, or alleges that he or she has been discriminated against on grounds of race or sex.

2. Procedural exceptions

The Employment Relations Act 1999 introduced a number of procedural changes to address such concerns, although the changes were mildly controversial and led to criticism of the government by the parliamentary Intelligence and Security Committee (for not going far

---

[91] Trade Union and Labour Relations (Consolidation) Act 1992, s 273; Employment Rights Act 1996, s 191. And see ch 26 B.

[92] Trade Union and Labour Relations (Consolidation) Act 1992, s 275; Employment Rights Act 1996, s 193.

[93] See *Council of Civil Service Unions* v *Minister for the Civil Service* [1985] AC 374; G S Morris [1985] PL 177.

[94] But it did not breach the ECHR, art 11: *CCSU* v *UK* (1988) 10 EHRR 269; S Fredman and G S Morris (1988) 17 ILJ 105.

[95] For a fuller account, see the 12th edition of this work, pp 647–8; also Ewing, *Britain and the ILO*.

[96] See Employment Relations Act 1999, Sch 8, amending the 1992 and 1996 Acts respectively.

[97] See *R* v *Shayler* [2002] UKHL 11, [2003] 1 AC 247. See also Rimington, *Open Secret*, pp 176–7.

[98] Employment Relations Act 1999, s 15. See HL Deb, 8 July 1999, col 1101. The government claimed that 'the security and intelligence services already have good grievance and disciplinary procedures in place' (col 1101).

[99] Employment Tribunals Act 1996, s 10(1), as inserted by the Employment Relations Act 1999, Sch 8. But see *B* v *BAA plc* [2005] IRLR 927 for the narrowing of the operation of this provision.

enough to protect the officials).[100] These changes related first to the tripartite structure of the tribunal, with the Secretary of State empowered to make regulations to alter the normal composition of the employment tribunal (i) in cases relating to Crown employment proceedings, where (ii) it is expedient to do so in the interests of national security. Further, they relate to the procedure adopted by the tribunal, with the Secretary of State again empowered to make regulations authorising him or her to issue directions to an employment tribunal in Crown employment proceedings where it is expedient in the interests of national security to do so.

The directions may require a tribunal to sit in private, to exclude the applicant or his or her representative from all or part of the proceedings, to take steps to conceal the identity of a particular witness, or to keep the reasons for its decision secret. If either of the last two directions is given, it is an offence to publish anything likely to lead to the identification of the witness, or the reasons for the tribunal's decision.[101] Regulations made under these powers – which also allow for the appointment of a special advocate to represent the interests of someone (including an applicant) excluded from any proceedings – have been held to be consistent with Convention rights, the Supreme Court holding that they do not breach art 6 (right to a fair trial).[102] Lord Kerr dissented on the ground that the procedure violated both Convention rights and the common law right to a fair trial.

Security procedures in the civil service[103]

Since 1948 various procedures have been in place to seek to exclude from sensitive positions in the civil service those who are perceived to be a threat to national security. The first of these procedures, the so-called purge procedure, was announced in 1948, having been introduced some time before. The aim was to ensure that 'no one who is known to be a member of the Communist Party, or to be associated with it in such a way as to raise legitimate doubts about his or her reliability, is employed in connection with work, the nature of which is vital to the security of the state'.[104]

1. Development of vetting procedures

The purge procedure was accompanied by the announcement of positive vetting in 1952, which had been on the agenda at least since the arrest and conviction of Klaus Fuchs in 1950 for communicating atomic secrets to the Soviet Union, for which he was sentenced to 14 years' imprisonment. Its announcement was a direct consequence of the defection of Donald Maclean and Guy Burgess to Moscow, in the aftermath of which the Foreign Secretary set up a committee under the chairmanship of Sir Alexander Cadogan to examine all aspects of the security arrangements in the Foreign Office. The committee reported in November 1951, approving plans for positive vetting which had already been prepared, and recommending that it should apply widely within the Foreign Service.

The committee proposed that vetting should cover not only 'political unreliability' but also 'the problem of character defects, which might lay an officer open to blackmail, or otherwise undermine his loyalty and sense of responsibility'. The practice of positive vetting was thus introduced as a 'regular system' at the beginning of 1952, but without recourse to legislation,

---

[100] Cm 4532, 1999. Also Cm 4777, 2000.

[101] Employment Tribunals Act 1996, s 10B, as inserted by the Employment Relations Act 1999, Sch 8.

[102] See *Tariq v Home Office*, above. For the relevant regulations, see SI 2004 No 1861, esp Sch 2. It should be emphasised, however, that the provisions of the Regulations meet Convention obligations only if construed consistently with these obligations. See *Tariq*, above, and *AB v Ministry of Defence*, UKEAT 0101_09_2407.

[103] See Fredman and Morris, above, pp 232–6; Street, *Freedom, the Individual and the Law*, pp 148–52.

[104] HC Deb, 25 March 1948, cols 3417–26. See M L Joelson [1963] PL 51. The procedure was applied also to fascists, although communists were the real target.

or without even informing or seeking the approval of Parliament.[105] It has since been extended well beyond the Foreign Service, and made more transparent, with a number of safeguards introduced to enable vetting decisions to be challenged by aggrieved individuals adversely affected by the process. The procedures were revised in 1985, again in 1990, 1994 and 2010,[106] and most recently in 2017.[107]

2. Current vetting procedures

As with previous vetting procedures, the existing arrangements are not to be found in legislation. Indeed it is not clear that they have even been approved by Parliament. The first question, however, is to be clear why vetting is necessary, with the government explaining that there is a need to protect against the threats of 'terrorism, espionage, or other actions that could threaten the United Kingdom', with reference also being made to the 'requirements of international agreements concerning the protection of allies' information'.[108] These being the concerns with which national security vetting is principally concerned, the need then is to identify and exclude from certain forms of employment those individuals who by their access to sensitive assets (physical, personnel or information) could present a risk.

Security vetting applies not only to full-time civil servants but also to part-time staff and to contractors, and takes three different forms: Counter Terrorist Check (CTC), Security Check (SC) and Developed Vetting (DV), with the level of vetting depending on the nature of the risk. Checks will be made of employee records, criminal records for previous convictions, Security Service records, and credit rating agencies for any financial irregularities. Checks will also be made for personality traits that may make the individual unsuitable. Reasons for the latter include 'potential conflicts of interest; vulnerability (direct or indirect) to pressure, instances of irresponsible behaviour; poor judgment and lack of maturity; extreme beliefs; and serious physical or mental ill health'.[109]

The most recent statement on security vetting states that security clearance may be refused or withdrawn where: (*a*) there are security concerns related to an individual's involvement or connection with compromising activities, organisations or individuals; (*b*) personal circumstances, defined as current or past conduct indicating that an individual may be susceptible to pressure or improper influence; (*c*) instances of dishonesty or lack of integrity casting doubt upon an individual's reliability; and (*d*) other behaviours or circumstances indicating unreliability. Employees will normally have an opportunity to 'discuss, comment on and challenge any adverse information', unless the opportunity to do so 'could compromise national security, the public interest or third party confidentiality'.

3. Vetting appeals

These non-statutory procedures are complemented by an extra-statutory appeals mechanism announced in 1997.[110] The Security Vetting Appeals Panel (an NDPB chaired by a retired judge) now hears appeals against the refusal or withdrawal of security clearance.[111] The Panel

---

[105] 'Not surprisingly the purge procedure has been regarded as of dwindling importance since Positive Vetting has been applied to new entrants to sensitive posts in the civil service for more than thirty years': Lustgarten and Leigh, p 131.

[106] HC Deb, 27 July 2010, col 90WS (Prime Minister).

[107] https://www.gov.uk/guidance/security-vetting-and-clearance. The 2017 changes were concerned principally 'to establish a single provider of government National Security Vetting Services' following recommendations in the Strategic Defence and Security Review 2015 (Cm, 9161, 2015), para 7.17.

[108] HC Deb, 27 July 2010, col 90WS (Prime Minister).

[109] Ibid.

[110] For an account of the procedures operating before then, see Lustgarten and Leigh, pp 139–49; Fredman and Morris, p 233.

[111] On NDPBs, see ch 12 above.

has no jurisdiction in cases involving new recruits, nor does it apply to members of the security and intelligence services. But it is otherwise 'available to hear appeals from individuals in government departments, the armed forces and other organisations, or their contractors, who have exhausted the internal appeals process and remain dissatisfied with the outcome'. A complaint may be made in writing to the Panel setting out the reasons; the respondent department will reply in writing; and an oral hearing may then be held.

Despite its composition, the SVAP is an advisory and not a judicial body, which makes recommendations to ministers. It has no power to ensure that its recommendations are carried out, and no power to award compensation. Proceedings of the Panel are in principle subject to judicial review.[112] As explained above, the SVAP has no authority over the security and intelligence services, though staff and contractors of the latter who have a grievance about their security clearance could complain to the IPT, as indeed could anyone else who believes that a refusal to grant them clearance was as a result of the actions of one of these services. Apart from complaints to the SVAP, a refusal or withdrawal of security clearance could be challenged in statutory proceedings, for example in an employment tribunal where there is alleged race discrimination.[113]

Official Secrets Act 1911[114]

The Official Secrets Act 1911 served two distinct but related purposes:

(*a*) to protect the interests of the state against espionage and the gathering of information which might be useful to an enemy and therefore injurious to state security;

(*b*) to guard against the unauthorised disclosure of information which is held by officials of the state, whether or not the information has any direct reference to state security as such.

The legal sanctions under (*b*) help to support the sanctions against espionage, since it may in a particular case be possible to prove unauthorised disclosure of information without being able to prove elements of espionage. But they may also serve to protect the corridors of power against disclosure of information and publicity which a government might find politically embarrassing or inconvenient. The Official Secrets Act 1911, on which later Acts have been built, was passed rapidly through Parliament in circumstances in which ministers emphasised purpose (*a*) as the primary object of the Act, and did not mention purpose (*b*).

1. Section 1

Section 1(1) of the 1911 Act creates a group of offences, mainly connected with espionage. It is an offence, punishable with 14 years' imprisonment:

if any person *for any purpose prejudicial to the safety or interests of the State* –

(*a*) approaches, inspects, passes over or is in the neighbourhood of, or enters any prohibited place within the meaning of this Act; or

(*b*) makes any sketch, plan, model, or note which . . . might be or is intended to be directly or indirectly useful to an enemy; or

---

[112] *R v Director of GCHQ, ex p Hodges*, The Times, 26 July 1988. See also *R v Home Secretary, ex p Hosenball* [1977] 3 All ER 452, 460. Ministerial decisions in response to a panel's advice would also be subject to judicial review.

[113] *Tariq v Home Office*, above.

[114] Ewing and Gearty, *The Struggle for Civil Liberties*, ch 2; Bailey, Harris and Jones, *Civil Liberties: Cases and Materials*, ch 8; Andrew, *Secret Service*; Williams, *Not in the Public Interest*, part 1.

(*c*) obtains, collects, records, or publishes or communicates to any other person any secret official code word, or pass word, or any sketch, plan, model, article, or note, or other document or information which . . . might be or is intended to be directly or indirectly useful to an enemy.

The italicised phrase caused difficulties when charges under s 1 were brought following a non-violent political demonstration against an RAF base, in *Chandler v DPP*.[115]

> Anti-nuclear demonstrators sought to immobilise an RAF bomber base by sitting down on the runway. They were arrested as they approached the base and charged with conspiring to enter a prohibited place for a purpose prejudicial to the safety or interests of the state, contrary to s 1 of the 1911 Act. The trial judge refused to allow the accused to bring evidence to show that it would be beneficial to the United Kingdom if the government's nuclear policy were abandoned. For a variety of interlocking reasons, the House of Lords unanimously upheld the conviction. The demonstrators admittedly wished to obstruct the use of the airbase and it was immaterial that they believed that such obstruction would ultimately benefit the country. The offences created by the 1911 Act, s 1 were not confined to spying but included sabotage and other acts of physical interference.

During an official secrets trial in 1978, Mars-Jones J indicated that the use of s 1 in situations that fell short of spying and sabotage could be oppressive.[116] Cases since then have been concerned mainly with spying, including the convictions of Geoffrey Prime in 1983,[117] Michael Bettaney in 1984[118] and Michael Smith in 1993,[119] all of whom had communicated secret information to the USSR. The other celebrated s 1 prosecution in the 1980s was that of eight signals intelligence officers based in Cyprus.[120] But unlike the cases of Prime, Bettaney and Smith, the prosecution failed. A subsequent inquiry by David Calcutt QC revealed that the accused had been unlawfully and oppressively detained while investigations were being conducted by the police and Security Service.[121]

2. Section 2

It is said that section 2 of the 1911 Act created a plethora of over 2,000 different offences related to the misuse of official information.[122] In particular, by s 2(1) it was an offence punishable by two years' imprisonment

> if any person having in his possession or control . . . any document or information . . . which has been entrusted in confidence to him by any person holding office under Her Majesty . . . communicates the . . . document or information to any person, other than a person to whom he is authorised to communicate it or a person to whom it is in the interests of the State his duty to communicate it.[123]

---

[115] [1964] AC 763. For a full account of this important case, see K D Ewing, in Campbell, Ewing and Tomkins (eds), *The Legal Protection of Human Rights: Sceptical Essays*, ch 8.

[116] A Nicol [1979] Crim LR 284; Aubrey, *Who's Watching You?*

[117] *R v Prime* (1983) 5 Cr App R (S) 127.

[118] *R v Bettaney* [1985] Crim LR 104.

[119] Cm 2903, 1995.

[120] See A W Bradley [1986] PL 363. See also Cmnd 9923, 1986.

[121] Cmnd 9781, 1986.

[122] Cmnd 5104, 1972, para 16.

[123] In *R v Ponting* [1985] Crim LR 318 the trial judge, McCowan J, directed the jury that the interests of the state are the interests of state as determined by the government of the day.

Other offences included the unauthorised retention of documents and failure to take reasonable care of documents.

Section 2 plainly extended to the disclosure of information which bore no relation to national security.[124] An offence could be committed even though the information was not secret,[125] and even though it was disclosed in order to promote rather than undermine British interests abroad.[126] The scope of the section – well described as a 'catch all'[127] – was, however, mitigated in two ways. First, as with all offences under the Official Secrets Acts, the consent of the Attorney General in England (or the Lord Advocate in Scotland) was necessary before any prosecution could be brought.[128] Second, the authorisation which prevented disclosure of information being an offence could be wholly informal and could be implicit in the circumstances of disclosure.

Ministers and many senior civil servants, by what was known as the practice of self-authorisation, were able to decide for themselves how much information to disclose, at least in matters relating to their own duties.[129] Thus, if an off-the-record briefing was given to a journalist (for example, to enable him or her to 'leak' the contents of a Bill before it was published in Parliament) no breach of the Official Secrets Acts would have occurred. More than once it had been stressed that s 2 of the 1911 Act was not to be blamed for secrecy in government, since at any time ministers could adopt a more open approach.[130] Nonetheless, the form of the 1911 Act often presented journalists with a real difficulty in knowing what they might safely publish.

3. Other provisions

Other notable provisions of the Official Secrets Acts include section 6 of the 1920 Act, which effectively removes a suspect's right of silence in a case brought under s 1 of the 1911 Act, by providing that a Secretary of State may authorise the police to call a prospective witness for questioning about a s 1 offence, and in this event refusal to attend or to give information is itself an offence.[131] Also notable is s 7 of the 1920 Act, under which it is an offence to attempt to commit any offence under the Acts or to endeavour to persuade another person to commit such an offence, or to aid and abet or to do *any act preparatory* to the commission of such an offence. Under the 1920 Act, s 8, a court may exclude the public from the trial of an offence under the Acts if the prosecution applies for this on the ground that the publication of evidence would be prejudicial to national safety.

This latter measure, which is employed in s 1 prosecutions[132] and which has also been employed in s 2 cases,[133] is an important departure from the general rule of 'the English system of administering justice' that 'it be done in public'.[134] For if

> 'the way the courts behave cannot be hidden from the public ear and eye this provides a safeguard against judicial arbitrariness or idiosyncrasy and maintains the public confidence in the administration of justice'.[135]

---

[124] See *Loat* v *James* [1986] Crim LR 744.

[125] *R* v *Crisp* (1919) 83 JP 121.

[126] *R* v *Fell* [1963] Crim LR 207.

[127] Cmnd 5104, 1972, para 17.

[128] Official Secrets Act 1911, s 8.

[129] Cmnd 5104, 1972, para 18.

[130] E.g. Cmnd 4089, 1969, p 11; Cmnd 5104, 1972, ch 5.

[131] Before the Official Secrets Act 1939 amended the 1920 Act, s 6, refusal on demand by a police inspector to disclose the source of information obtained in breach of the Acts was itself an offence (*Lewis* v *Cattle* [1938] 2 KB 454).

[132] As in the cases of *Bettaney*, note 118 above, and the Cyprus intelligence personnel, pp 524–5 above.

[133] As in the *Ponting* case, note 123 above.

[134] *A-G* v *Leveller Magazine Ltd* [1979] AC 440, at pp 449–50.

[135] Ibid, at p 450.

However, even if a prosecution is held behind closed doors, the accused and his or her law-yer may not be excluded and sentence must be delivered in open court.[136] Moreover, s 9 of the 1911 Act confers wide powers of search and seizure, authorising a magistrate to grant a search warrant permitting the police to enter and search premises 'and every person found therein', and to seize anything which is evidence of an offence under the Act 'having been or being about to be committed'.

In cases of 'great emergency' where in the interests of the state immediate action is neces-sary, written authority for such a search under s 9 may be granted by a superintendent of police.

> In January 1987 it was reported that the BBC had decided not to broadcast a programme about the Zircon spy satellite in the interests of national security. In so doing the Corpora-tion denied that there had been any government pressure. Two days later, an injunction was obtained by the Attorney General restraining the journalist responsible for the pro-gramme, Duncan Campbell, from talking or writing about the contents of the film. He could not be found, however, to be served with the injunction, whereupon the *New Statesman* published details about the programmes.
>
> The foregoing was followed by a Special Branch raid of the *New Statesman*'s offices, and subsequently of the BBC's premises in Glasgow. The latter raid – which lasted for 28 hours – was conducted under the authority of a warrant granted under s 9 of the 1911 Act.[137] The police filled several police vans with documents, discarded film clips and over 200 contain-ers of film. It was never entirely clear what the police were looking for, and no prosecutions followed. The episode illustrates the extent to which the 1911 Act may be used oppres-sively, even without a prosecution taking place.[138]

Official Secrets Act 1989

The operation of the Official Secrets Act 1911, s 2, was examined closely by a committee chaired by Lord Franks which reported in 1972.[139] The committee had been appointed after an unsuccessful prosecution of the *Sunday Telegraph* for publishing Foreign Office docu-ments relating to the Labour government's policy towards the Nigerian civil war.[140]

1. Background to the Act

The Franks committee reported that the law then in force was unsatisfactory and that there should be a new Official Information Act, to protect only certain forms of information, namely:

(*a*) classified information relating to defence or internal security, or to foreign relations, or to the currency or to the reserves, the unauthorised disclosure of which would cause serious injury to the interests of the nation;

(*b*) information likely to assist criminal activities or to impede law enforcement;

(*c*) Cabinet documents (in the interests of collective responsibility);[141]

---

[136] Official Secrets Act 1920, s 8(2).

[137] The warrant was arguably unlawful, having been issued by a sheriff, not by a justice of the peace: R Black (1987) *J of the Law Society of Scotland* 138.

[138] For fuller details, see Ewing and Gearty, *Freedom under Thatcher*, pp 147–52. See also A W Bradley [1987] PL 1, 488.

[139] Cmnd 5104, 1972.

[140] See Aitken, *Officially Secret*.

[141] See ch 11.

(*d*) information which has been entrusted to the government by a private individual or concern (for example, for tax or social security purposes or in a census).

The requirement that information of the kind specified in (*a*) must be classified would make necessary a new system of classifying documents which, unlike the existing system, would have legal consequences. Offences under the proposed new Act were recommended to include the communication by a Crown servant, contrary to his or her official duty, of information subject to the Act; the communication by any person of information of the kinds set out in (*a*), (*b*) and (*c*) which that person reasonably believed had reached him or her as a result of a breach of the Act; and the use of official information of any kind for purposes of private gain.

The Franks committee therefore recommended that protection of official information by criminal sanctions should continue only where the public interest clearly required this. But no reform of the Official Secrets Acts was forthcoming at that time, although other weaknesses in the law became evident during the so-called ABC trial in 1978.[142] In 1979 the Conservative government introduced not a Freedom of Information Bill but a Protection of Official Information Bill. This sought to give absolute protection to information regarding security and intelligence, regardless of whether that information was already available to the public.[143]

But the Bill was abandoned by the government in the political controversy surrounding the disclosure at that time that the famous art historian Sir Anthony Blunt had been a Russian spy as a younger man. Pressure for reform was maintained in the 1980s, with interest fuelled by some controversial prosecutions. These included the cases of Sarah Tisdall, a Foreign Office clerk, who was convicted for leaking to *The Guardian* a secret document relating to the delivery of cruise missiles to Greenham Common;[144] and Clive Ponting, a senior official in the Ministry of Defence, who was acquitted for leaking to an MP documents relating to the sinking of the Argentinian vessel, the *General Belgrano*, during the Falklands War.[145]

2. Substance of the Act

The pressure for reform culminated in the Official Secrets Act 1989, which many would argue does not go far enough.[146] While repealing s 2 of the 1911 Act, the 1989 Act introduced new restrictions on the unauthorised disclosure of an admittedly narrower range of information.

One category of information protected from disclosure relates to security and intelligence. Section 1 of the 1989 Act provides that it is an offence for security and intelligence staff without lawful authority to disclose any information obtained in the course of employment in the service. Where permission is refused, it may be necessary to take legal action to secure the necessary consent. In *A* v *B*,[147] a former intelligence officer refused permission to publish his memoirs sought to challenge the refusal in judicial review proceedings, claiming a breach of his Convention rights (notably art 10 – freedom of expression). The action failed, the Supreme Court holding that the Investigatory Powers Tribunal established by RIPA 2000 had exclusive jurisdiction to consider such matters.

Section 1 also deals with disclosures without lawful authority by civil servants and government contractors, unauthorised disclosure by whom is unlawful only if 'damaging' to the work of the security and intelligence services. Sections 2 and 3 make it an offence for a civil servant or government contractor, without lawful authority, to disclose any information

---

[142] A Nicol [1979] Crim LR 284.

[143] HL Deb, 5 November 1979, col 612; cf Cmnd 7285, 1978, para 31.

[144] For the circumstances, see *Secretary of State for Defence* v *Guardian Newspapers Ltd* [1985] AC 339.

[145] See Ponting, *The Right to Know*.

[146] For background, see Cm 408, 1988. For analyses, see S Palmer [1990] PL 243; Birkinshaw, *Reforming the Secret State*.

[147] [2009] UKSC 12, [2010] 2 AC 1.

relating to defence or international affairs if the disclosure is damaging. In the case of defence, disclosure is defined as being damaging if it damages the capability of the armed forces to carry out their tasks, while in both cases disclosure is damaging if it endangers the interests of the United Kingdom abroad or endangers the safety of British citizens abroad (s 2(2)).[148]

It is an offence by s 4 for a civil servant or a government contractor to disclose without lawful authority any information if this results in the commission of an offence, facilitates an escape from legal custody, or impedes the prevention or detection of offences or the apprehension or prosecution of suspects. Section 4 further provides that it is an offence to disclose information 'relating to the obtaining of information' (as well as any information obtained) as a result of warrants issued under the Interception of Communications Act 1985, the Regulation of Investigatory Powers Act 2000, s 5 (phone tapping), the Intelligence Services Act 1994 (interference with property or unlawful acts done outside the United Kingdom), or the Investigatory Powers Act 2016. It is thus not an offence under s 4 to disclose information obtained unlawfully without a warrant, although it might be an offence under s 1.

The offences under the Act are committed only where disclosure is made without lawful authority. This corresponds to the former s 2 of the 1911 Act, whereby the offence was committed only if the disclosure was unauthorised. The question of when a Crown servant was authorised to disclose information is, as we have seen, one that gave rise to considerable difficulty, particularly in the case of Cabinet ministers and senior officials.[149] By s 7 of the 1989 Act, a disclosure is authorised if it is made in accordance with the official duty of the minister or civil servant concerned, though any refusal of a request by a member of the Security Services to disclose protected information is (in principle) subject to judicial scrutiny.[150]

An offence may be committed not only by the official disclosing the information, but also by a third party, such as a newspaper, which reports it. Although it is no longer an offence to receive information protected against disclosure (as it was under s 2 of the 1911 Act), it is an offence for the recipient to disclose the information without lawful authority, knowing or having reasonable cause to believe that it is protected from disclosure (s 5). In effect, it is an offence for a newspaper to publish protected information which has been leaked without authority. Controversially, there is no public interest defence available in this or indeed in other cases, the government having rejected such a measure.[151]

In these circumstances, however, a newspaper is liable only if the disclosure is damaging and is made knowing or having reasonable cause to believe that it is damaging. There have been no prosecutions of newspapers since the Act was introduced.

Official secrets and human rights

Many of the offences under the Official Secrets Acts are associated with the publication of information. Many prosecutions have been for the same reason.

The question that now arises is whether these measures are consistent with the guarantees of freedom of expression in the ECHR and whether the Human Rights Act provides a defence to anyone prosecuted under the Official Secrets Acts 1911–89. This question has

---

[148] Section 3 was used successfully against David Keogh, an official in the Whitehall communications centre, who leaked a document setting out the details of a meeting between George Bush and Tony Blair in 2004 about the war in Iraq dealing in particular with the US assault on the Iraqi city of Fallujah. Keogh passed the document to Leo O'Connor, an assistant to a Labour MP. O'Connor was charged and convicted under section 5 of the Act (see below). The trials took place in 2007, and both Keogh and O'Connor received jail sentences. See Ewing, *Bonfire of the Liberties*, pp 154–8.

[149] See Cmnd 5104, 1972, para 18.

[150] See *R v Shayler* [2002] UKHL 11, [2003] 1 AC 247.

[151] Cm 408, 1988.

become more urgent in recent years following another spate of unauthorised disclosures by former members of the security and intelligence services in the late 1990s. These include Richard Tomlinson, who published a book in Russia and also material on the internet identifying individuals who recruited for the security and intelligence services.

They also include David Shayler, who fled to France after a number of high-profile revelations about the activities of the Security Service. On his return from France, Mr Shayler was charged, convicted and imprisoned under the Official Secrets Act 1989. In some of the preliminary litigation, the House of Lords held that although Mr Shayler was entitled to the protection of freedom of expression under the Human Rights Act, the Official Secrets Act was designed to protect national security, and the restriction it imposed on freedom of expression was justified.[152] No proceedings were brought against a former director of MI5 who published her memoirs in 2001 in a blaze of publicity, the book also being serialised in *The Guardian* newspaper in the same year.

The question whether the Official Secrets Acts are compatible with the Human Rights Act was raised in *Attorney-General* v *Blake*,[153] where it was held that the Attorney General was entitled to an account of profits earned by a former member of the security and intelligence services for a publication which was made in breach of a contractual obligation not to disclose material obtained as a result of his employment. In the course of the case it was argued that s 1 of the Official Secrets Act 1989 is 'drawn too widely' because it criminalises disclosure of information when no damage results, by focusing on the 'status of the individual who makes the disclosure, rather than on the nature of the information itself'.

But although the House of Lords preferred not to deal with this point, Lord Nicholls drew attention to another factor which appears to be decisive in an action where the Human Rights Act is relied on by a member of the security and intelligence services. This was the undertaking not to disclose information that Blake had voluntarily given when he joined the service. According to Lord Nicholls, neither Blake nor any other member of the service should have an incentive to break this undertaking. He continued:

> It is of paramount importance that members of the service should have complete confidence in all their dealings with each other, and that those recruited as informers should have the like confidence. Undermining the willingness of prospective informers to co-operate with the services, or undermining the morale and trust between members of the services when engaged on secret and dangerous operations, would jeopardise the effectiveness of the service. An absolute rule against disclosure, visible to all, makes good sense.[154]

It is unclear when – if ever – the prosecution of a disclosure in breach of the Official Secrets Act 1989 would be regarded as a disproportionate protection of national security. But in the *Shayler* case, the House of Lords seemed satisfied that there were adequate internal safeguards to enable a member of the Security Service to bring wrongdoing to the attention of the authorities without the need for unauthorised public disclosure in the press. Although the Human Rights Act thus may not present a serious obstacle to prosecutions under the Official Secrets Act 1989, political circumstances nevertheless may make it difficult to proceed with such a charge, as highlighted by the case of Kathryn Gun, a GCHQ official who was charged under the 1989 Act for allegedly leaking an email from US spies to their British counterparts.

It was claimed that the email – sent on 31 January 2003 and published by *The Observer* – tended to show that the Americans wanted British support to find out the voting intentions and negotiating positions of some UN Security Council member states on the forthcoming

---

[152] *R* v *Shayler*, above. The affair has generated a body of case law. See also *Attorney-General* v *Punch* [2002] UKHL 50, [2003] 1 AC 1046, and *R (Bright)* v *Central Criminal Court* [2001] 2 All ER 244.

[153] [2001] 1 AC 268.

[154] Ibid, at p 287.

resolutions about Iraq. The charges were subsequently withdrawn, in the face of Ms Gun's defence that she leaked the email 'to save lives from being lost in a war'. Reports at the time suggested that the government was not motivated by a desire to uphold the right to freedom of expression, but by a fear that a potential jury would be moved by an anti-war sentiment, that the respondent would be acquitted, and that the Official Secrets Act 1989 would be brought into permanent disrepute, in the same way as its predecessors.[155]

Defence and security media advisory notices

The Official Secrets Acts impose important restrictions on press freedom in the sense that they effectively control the information which might be made available. And as we saw in Chapter 17 G, the action in equity for breach of confidence has the capacity to do much the same. Indeed, it was this which formed the basis for controlling the press during the so-called *Spycatcher* affair in 1987. But there are other restrictions and fetters on press freedom, which have been introduced in the interests of national security. One of these is the system of 'D' notices,[156] a form of extra-legal censorship in which the press cooperates with the government.

A 'D' notice is a means of providing advice and guidance to the media about the defence and counter-terrorist information, the publication of which would be damaging to national security. They are issued by what was the Defence, Press and Broadcasting Committee, an advisory body composed of senior civil servants and editors from national and regional newspapers, periodicals, news agencies, television and radio. The committee was chaired by a senior civil servant from the Ministry of Defence, and included representatives of government departments responsible for national security, as well as representatives of the press and broadcasters.

The system was overhauled in 1993 (following an internal review in the light of international changes (in particular the break-up of the Soviet Union), and the increased emphasis on openness in government. As a result, the number of 'D' notices was reduced from eight to six, and their content and style revised to make them more relevant and user-friendly. It was as a result of this review that the name of the notices was changed from 'D' to 'DA' notices and that of the committee to Defence, Press and Broadcasting Advisory Committee (DPBAC), 'better to reflect the voluntary and advisory nature of the system'.[157] The number of notices has since been reduced to five.

In 2015 the system was the subject of a review under the chairmanship of the Vice Chancellor of Essex University, following a number of high-profile leaks of intelligence information (first in 2010 involving Julian Assange, and then in 2013 by Edward Snowden). The review broadly supported the existing arrangements and concluded that 'the purpose of the system should remain that of preventing inadvertent disclosure of information that would compromise UK military and intelligence operations and methods, or put at risk the safety of those involved in such operations, or lead to attacks that would damage the critical national infrastructure and/or endanger lives' (p 19).[158]

Following the 2015 review (which was not uncritical of certain aspects of the operation of the scheme), 'DA' Notices were renamed again (Defence and Security Media Advisory Notices), as was the DPBAC (now DSMAC). The five DSMA Notices deal respectively with Military Operations, Plans and Capabilities (DSMA Notice 1); Nuclear and Non-Nuclear Weapon Systems and Equipment (DSMA Notice 2); Military Counter-Terrorist

---

[155] For an account of this episode, see Ewing, *Bonfire of the Liberties*, ch 5.
[156] D Fairley (1990) 10 OJLS 430; Williams, *Not in the Public Interest*, ch 4.
[157] HC Deb, 23 July 1993, col 454 (WA).
[158] A copy of the review and the government's response are available on the website of the DSMA Notice System: www.dsma.uk.

Forces, Special Forces and Intelligence Agency Operations, Activities Communication Methods and Techniques (DSMA Notice 3); Physical Property and Assets (DSMA Notice 4); and Personnel and their Families (DSMA Notice 5).[159]

Each of these notices gives details of the kind of information which editors are requested not to publish, usually information which relates to defence or anti-terrorist capabilities, or to individuals who might be a terrorist target. The notices also include an explanation of their purpose. The secretary of the committee plays a key role in advising the media on the interpretation of the notices, and is available to government departments as well as the media to give advice on the system. In September 2001 he advised the media to minimise speculation about imminent military action in Afghanistan for fear of helping the 'enemy'.[160]

It is a problem that DSMA Notices are inevitably drafted in general terms, although it is the application of a DSMA Notice to a particular set of circumstances on which the secretary is expected to give guidance, after consultation with government departments as appropriate. This advice is also sometimes referred to as a 'DSMA Notice' rather than advice given under the authority of a DSMA Notice. It was claimed in 2009 that 'since 1997 there have been 30 occasions where the committee secretary has written to specific editors when a breach in the D-Notice guidelines is judged to have occurred', with editors being reminded of the 'content of the code'.[161]

The committee has made clear in the past, however, that the secretary is not 'invested with the authority to give rulings nor to advise on considerations other than national security'; and, on the other hand, that the 'notices have no legal standing and advice offered within their framework may be accepted or rejected partly or wholly'.[162] Compliance with the DSMA Notice system does not relieve the editor of responsibilities under the Official Secrets Acts; nor indeed will it necessarily prevent legal proceedings being brought to restrain any publication or broadcast.[163] Correspondence between the secretary and journalists is intended to be confidential.[164]

The Defence Select Committee reviewed the 'D' notice system as long ago as 1980 and concluded (with reservations) that 'D' notices should be maintained, despite sharp divisions within the press about the value of the scheme which, judged in legal terms, is manifestly imperfect and imprecise.[165]

E. Political scrutiny

One of the main questions relating to security and intelligence services in any country is one of accountability. Such agencies inevitably operate in the shadows, and will understandably avoid any attempt to shine a spotlight on their activities. Accountability is nevertheless

---

[159] See www.dmsa.uk, where the full text of all five notices may be found.

[160] *The Independent*, 27 September 2001. In April 2009 it was reported that the Committee contacted the media about photographs that had been taken of a senior police officer as he entered No 10 Downing Street. The photographs showed in some detail the contents of a document the police officer had been carrying, revealing information about a sensitive police undercover operation in a terrorist investigation: *Daily Telegraph*, 9 April 2009.

[161] http://www.defenceviewpoints.co.uk/articles-and-analysis/d-notices-uk-s-defence-self-censorship-system. A more recent example is reported in *The Guardian*, 17 June 2013. Moreover, the 2015 review referred to above states that there were 624 requests for guidance between 2011 and 2014.

[162] The work of the secretariat was, however, warmly praised by the 2015 review, above.

[163] See *A-G v BBC*, *The Times*, 18 December 1987 regarding the broadcast by the BBC of a radio series (*My Country Right or Wrong*) about the Security Service.

[164] *The Guardian*, 17 June 2013.

[165] HC 773 (1979–80); J Jaconelli [1982] PL 37.

important, not only to ensure that the agencies in question act within boundaries of their legal mandate, but also to re-assure the public on behalf of whom they act that their conduct underpins rather than subverts the liberal values they are entrusted to defend. We have already encountered some forms of accountability in the form of the Commissioners appointed under RIPA and the IPA. There is also a question of parliamentary scrutiny.

Home Affairs Committee

In 1992 the Home Affairs Select Committee invited the Director General of the Security Service to appear before it, possibly in private. In a series of remarkable exchanges, the invitation was declined after consultation with the Home Secretary, who later said that he would consider whether the committee might meet her informally, 'perhaps over lunch'. This stance was adopted following the convention 'under which information on matters of security and intelligence is not placed before Parliament', which the Home Secretary regarded 'as binding in relation to Departmental Select Committees no less than in relation to Parliament itself'.

In the Home Secretary's view, the Security Service was not to be regarded as falling within the ambit of any select committee, although this need not 'prevent the Director General from having a meeting with [the Chairman of the Committee] and one or two senior members on an informal basis to discuss the work of the Security Service in general terms providing that the Government's position is understood'. Mrs Rimington (the then Director General) was said to share this view and would 'accordingly be in touch with [the Chairman] to invite [him] and a couple of [his] senior colleagues to lunch'.

As the Home Affairs Committee said, however, an informal lunch with Mrs Rimington (who was 'permitted to lunch with the press'), 'while a welcome move towards openness', was 'no substitute for formal parliamentary scrutiny of the Security Service'. The Committee was of the view that the service fell within its terms of reference and that 'the value-for-money of the Security Service and its general policy are proper subjects for parliamentary scrutiny as long as such scrutiny does not damage the effectiveness of the Service'. Thus thwarted, the committee then reviewed the various options for enhanced parliamentary scrutiny of the service.[166]

Notwithstanding the compelling case for scrutiny, the government responded by saying that in 1989 Parliament had considered very carefully the question of oversight.[167] It had concluded in favour of preserving the existing approach to accountability, by which the Director General of the Security Service is responsible to the Home Secretary of the day, who is himself or herself accountable to Parliament for the work of the Security Service. (It is, however, a strange kind of accountability which labours under a convention which prevents matters relating to security and intelligence from being placed before Parliament.)

The government also referred to the procedures for judicial oversight of the service by means of a commissioner and a tribunal under the Security Service Act 1989. In the government's view, this system had worked well in the three-and-a-half years since the 1989 Act had come into force, although, once again, it is a strange kind of oversight which examines only the exercise of specific statutory powers rather than the work of the service as a whole. Nevertheless, in the face of this intervention the government accepted that the position should be examined afresh.

An opportunity to do just that was provided by the Intelligence Services Act 1994, where important concessions in the direction of democratic accountability were made, although it is still open to question whether they go far enough. Thus in 1998 the then Home Secretary (Mr Jack Straw) refused a request from the Home Affairs Select Committee to take evidence

---

[166] HC 265 (1992–3).
[167] Cm 2197, 1993.

from the Director General of the Security Service in a public session, offering instead a brief-ing from the Director General.[168] Reporting in 1999, the Committee concluded that 'the accountability of the security and intelligence services to Parliament ought to be a fundamen-tal principle in a democracy'.[169]

Nevertheless the Home Affairs Committee met a similar response in 2013, when again it invited the Director General of the Security Service to appear before it.[170] This time the Home Secretary's intervention was all the more unfortunate for the fact that the Director General had only recently appeared before another parliamentary committee, the Intelligence and Security Committee (ISC) (on which see below), along with the heads of SIS and GCHQ.[171] Although an unprecedented event, the latter was criticised by some for 'deferential' question-ing on the part of the parliamentarians, with the more robust Home Affairs Select Committee having follow-up questions it would have liked to put to the Director General.

It is reported that the Home Affairs Committee particularly wanted to question the Direc-tor General about claims that *The Guardian* had endangered national security by publishing information leaked by whistleblower Edward Snowden (on which see below). But although the Director General agreed in principle to appear before the Committee, the Home Secre-tary intervened on the ground that she did not believe 'it would be appropriate or necessary for the oversight provided by the ISC to be duplicated by another committee'. It is now up to the Home Affairs Committee to flex whatever muscles it has to insist on its right to call wit-nesses rather than continue to complain that 'Ministers should take care not to dictate to parliamentary committees which witnesses can be called and for what reasons'.[172]

Intelligence and Security Committee[173]

One of the reasons given by successive Home Secretaries for refusing the Home Affairs Com-mittee's request to examine security chiefs was that Parliament had 'given' responsibility for overseeing the Security Service to the Intelligence and Security Committee. This is a most curious committee which is modelled on the Select Committee system, but which has a num-ber of important differences, beginning with the fact that it is established by statute – the Intelligence Services Act 1994 – rather than by the Standing Orders of the House of Com-mons (or House of Lords). Any changes to the operation of the committee must thus be sanctioned by statute, and this was done most recently in the Justice and Security Act 2013.[174]

The ISC consists of nine members drawn from both the House of Commons and the House of Lords (although none may be a minister of the Crown). Each member of the ISC is

---

[168] HC 291 (1998–9), app 1.

[169] Ibid, para 48. The best the Home Affairs Committee had been able to secure had been a private briefing from Director General of the Security Service in 2007 about the government's Counter-Terrorism pro-posals (after he had addressed the Society of Editors on the same subject): HC 43 (2007–8). The HAC did not report the briefing's content as evidence, and although it is acknowledged that the briefing 'informed' the committee's report, it is not clear how. On the speech to the Society of Editors, see J Evans, 'Defending the Realm', Speech by Director General of the Security Service, 15 October 2009; see also HL Paper 152, HC 230 (2008–9), paras 55–56.

[170] *The Guardian*, 4, 11 December 2013, on which this account draws. For an account of the Home Secretary's subsequent appearance before the Home Affairs Committee (on 16 December 2013), see *The Guardian*, 16 December 2013 (Andrew Sparrow).

[171] Intelligence and Security Committee, Uncorrected Transcript of Evidence, 7 November 2013.

[172] *The Guardian*, 11 December 2013.

[173] See M Supperstone [1994] PL 329.

[174] The evolving statutory base of this Committee raises nice questions about the potential for judicial review, questions that so far show no evidence of having been contemplated. This could arise in a most interesting way in relation to the powers of the Committee, were it ever to seek to maximise its statutory powers.

appointed by the House of which he or she is a member, but only after being nominated by the Prime Minister, after consulting the Leader of the Opposition. The main functions of the ISC are set out in the Justice and Security Act 2013, s 2, which provides that the committee may examine or otherwise oversee the 'expenditure, administration and operations' of the three main security services. It may also examine and oversee other security and intelligence work of the government, in accordance with a Memorandum of Understanding agreed with the Prime Minister.[175]

Although the 2013 Act was largely a progressive measure in terms of enhancing the role of the committee, it nevertheless remains the case that the government thus continues to have greater control over the ISC than over the other select committees, and that the recent reforms to the latter have largely washed over this committee.[176] Indeed, apart from the foregoing, the Prime Minister has a statutory right to veto the committee's examination of ongoing operational matters,[177] while the power of the committee to call for papers is subject to a statutory veto of the Home Secretary, even though this veto may only be exercised where the information is 'sensitive' (as defined) and should not as a result be disclosed in the interests of national security.[178]

In 2017 the committee was chaired by a former Attorney General (Dominic Grieve QC) and included among its other eight members two members of the House of Lords as well as MPs from three major political parties (including the SNP). The secretariat of the committee is drawn from the Cabinet Office, not from Parliament.[179] The committee has been required by statute since 1994 to make an annual report on the discharge of its functions to the Prime Minister, which must then be laid before Parliament, although parts of the report may be held back, after consultation with the committee, if it appears to the Prime Minister that the publication of any matter would be prejudicial to any of the agencies.[180] Some of the reports are badly disfigured by redaction, to the point of futility on some issues.[181]

In its first report, the committee commented that because of the nature of its work 'it must have access to national security information', with the result that committee members 'have all been notified under the Official Secrets Act 1989'. The constitutional position was that the committee was 'now operating within the "ring of secrecy"', reporting directly to the Prime Minister on its work and, through him or her, to Parliament. An important development reported in 1999 was the appointment of an investigator by the committee to enable it more fully to examine different aspects of agencies' activities.[182] The committee's annual reports reveal that it has examined a wide range of issues. These include the priorities and plans of the agencies, their financing, and personnel management issues.

An important issue raised in the annual reports for 1997–8 and 1998–9 respectively relates to the destruction of Security Service files. It was noted in 1998 that 110,000 files had been destroyed since 1992, the vast majority of which related to subversion, on targets about whom the service was no longer conducting any investigations. For historians of the British state this was a tragedy and ensures that there can be no accountability of the Security Service even long after the event. Following concerns that the service was solely responsible for the review and destruction of files and that some form of 'independent check should be built into

---

[175] Justice and Security Act 2013, s 1(5)). The Memorandum of Understanding must be laid before but not necessarily approved by Parliament (s 1(6)).

[176] See ch 8 above.

[177] 2013 Act, s 2(3), on which see HC 1152 (2016–17). The relationship between the Committee and the Prime Minister is set out in a Memorandum of Understanding: HC 794 (2013–14).

[178] 2013 Act, above, Sch 4. See HC 1152 (2016–17).

[179] Ibid.

[180] Ibid, s 3.

[181] See Cm 4309, 1999 (Sierra Leone).

[182] Cm 4532, 1999; and see Cm 4073, 1998; also HC 291 (1998–9), para 14.

the process', it was agreed that Public Record Office officials should be involved in the examination of files identified by the Security Service for destruction.[183]

The committee has also issued specific reports on a number of contentious issues, including most notably the publication of the so-called Mitrokhin Archive. This consisted of material held by the KGB which Mr Mitrokhin had removed from Russia and which identified a number of British citizens as Soviet agents. A number of these individuals were subsequently named in public, although none was prosecuted, their identities having been known to the authorities for many years. The report of the ISC in fact provides a fascinating insight into the working of the intelligence services at a number of levels. It was revealed, for example, that the Security Service had failed to consult the Law Officers about whether one of the alleged spies should be prosecuted, taking the view that prosecution would not be in the public interest.

As the ISC pointed out, however, this was a decision that ought to have been for the Attorney General to make. More recent international events have led the committee to investigate the adequacy and assessment of the evidence relating to 'weapons of mass destruction' claimed to have been held by Iraq in the period before the invasion of that country in 2003.[184] In a separate report, some light was cast on the role of British agents in the detention of British nationals by the United States in Afghanistan and Guantanamo Bay, as well as Iraq, though there were obvious constraints on the ability of the committee to conduct a meaningful investigation. Nevertheless, the committee found evidence of some concerns being expressed by British intelligence officers, and also revealed that intelligence officers had interviewed detainees without the knowledge of ministers.[185]

The Committee has been concerned most recently with the legality of the use of drones to kill British citizens in Syria, 'the first time outside participation in a military campaign that the UK had conducted a lethal drone strike against a terrorist target'.[186] However, the Committee has been unable properly to assess government action as a result of ministerial failure to release crucial intelligence assessments, with important implications for the effectiveness of the Committee's work.[187] As it pointed out

> Oversight and scrutiny depend on primary evidence: without sight of the actual documents provided to Ministers we cannot ourselves be sure – nor offer an assurance to Parliament or the public – that we have indeed been given the full facts surrounding the authorisation process for the lethal strike.[188]

F. Conclusion

The transparency and accountability of the security and intelligence services have been greatly strengthened since the publication of earlier editions of this text, when the very existence of these bodies was barely known. (Indeed, the existence of GCHQ was only officially

---

[183] Cm 4073, 1998, and Cm 4532, 1999. For more recent annual reports giving an account of other concerns (such as security vetting, the Official Secrets Act, relationships with the media, the use of interception evidence in legal proceedings, document security, torture and rendition, cyber security, and greater government access to communications data), see Cm 5542, 2002; Cm 5837, 2003; Cm 6240, 2004; Cm 6510, 2005; Cm 7299, 2008; Cm 7542, 2009; Cm 7807, 2010; Cm 7844, 2010; Cm 8114, 2011; Cm 8403, 2012; and HC 547, 2013. The 2016 report contains some interesting information about the financing of the security and intelligence services: HC 444 (2015–16).

[184] Cm 5972, 2003.

[185] Cm 6469, 2005.

[186] HC 444 (2015–16), para 3. See also HL Paper 141, HC 574 (2015–16) (powerful report on human rights dimension of the same subject by JCHR).

[187] HC 444 (2015–16), para 30.

[188] Ibid, para 72.

recognised in the 1980s.) The same is true of the legal framework by which these bodies are governed, with statutory regulation from the 1980s onwards having been driven in large part by the demands of the ECHR, and the developing jurisprudence of the ECtHR.

But while it is important to acknowledge steps in the direction of greater transparency, accountability and legality, it is also important to acknowledge the limitations of these developments. There is constant concern that the security and intelligence services stray beyond their brief, with confidence in the adequacy of the existing legal and political structures having been shaken by two developments in particular. The first relates to persistent allegations about the complicity of British security and intelligence personnel in the mistreatment of terrorist suspects by foreign governments. These allegations, the subject of important litigation,[189] were given credibility by Sir Peter Gibson who reported in 2013 that 'UK intelligence officers were aware of inappropriate interrogation techniques and mistreatment'.[190]

The other cause for concern relates to the allegations by the whistleblower Edward Snowden, a former employee of the National Security Agency in the United States. Among the many troubling disclosures are those relating to the alleged involvement of GCHQ in a covert operation to intercept, store and analyse the data of millions of people. As reported in *The Guardian* newspaper, this secret project code-named *Tempora* enables GCHQ to have access to the phone calls, email messages, internet use and social media activity, thereby permitting GCHQ 'to access and process vast quantities of communications between entirely innocent people'.[191] The audacity of the programme has raised serious questions about the effectiveness of the political scrutiny of GCHQ, as well as the robustness of the legal framework by which it is governed.[192]

---

[189] These cases are dealt with elsewhere in this text. See *R (Binyam Mohamed) v Foreign Secretary* [2010] EWCA Civ 65, [2011] QB 218 (ch 26 below); *Al Rawi v Security Service* [2011] UKSC 34, [2012] 1 AC 131 (ch 26 below).

[190] Sir Peter Gibson (chair), *Report of the Detainee Inquiry* (2013), para 7.6. Also important is the powerful JCHR report on complicity in torture: HL Paper 152, HC 230 (2008–9). The latter report also highlights the unwillingness of ministers to account to Parliament for the work of the Security Services.

[191] *The Guardian*, 21 June 2013 ('GCHQ taps fibre-optic cables for secret access to world's communications').

[192] *Privacy International v Foreign Secretary*, above.

CHAPTER 20

Special and emergency powers

In times of grave national emergency, normal constitutional principles may have to give way to the overriding need to deal with the emergency. As Lord Pearce once said, 'the flame of individual right and justice must burn more palely when it is ringed by the more dramatic light of bombed buildings'.[1]

Thus, the European Convention on Human Rights, art 15, permits a member state to take measures derogating from its obligations under the Convention 'in time of war or other public emergency threatening the life of the nation'. The UK government has exercised the right of derogation in respect of events in Northern Ireland, and more recently in response to international terrorism in the aftermath of events in the United States on 11 September 2001.[2]

But even under such circumstances no derogation is permitted from art 2 (which protects the right to life) except in the case of deaths resulting from lawful acts of war, art 3 (which prohibits the use of torture), art 4(1) (which prohibits slavery) and art 7 (which bars retrospective criminal laws). Thus, despite the existence of a grave emergency, there are limits beyond which a state may not go, and it is open to question whether and how far 'the desirability of an effective remedy for judicial review must yield to the higher interests of the State'.[3]

Emergencies come in different guises, and the extent to which normal rules should be qualified is never clear. There is a constant battle between government and the courts in determining what restrictions are permissible and in what circumstances. A major concern now of a continuing nature is how best to deal with the threat of terrorism and the implications for human rights and other legal standards. In a recent expression of the judicial role, Lords Neuberger and Dyson said that 'the two most fundamental and well-established functions of any government are the defence of the realm from external attack and the maintenance of the rule of law internally'. They added:

> The executive is, or at any rate should be, particularly well informed and experienced in assessing any risks to national security and how to deal with them, whereas the courts are not. However, this does not mean that the court should simply wave through any such legislation: the rule of law crucially requires the court to be vigilant when assessing the necessity or proportionality of both the contents and the implementation of any statute which interferes with human rights.[4]

This chapter is concerned with special or emergency powers to deal with special or emergency circumstances. We begin with (i) the use of troops to assist the civil authorities (as was the case in Northern Ireland from 1969 to 2007),[5] progressing to (ii) the enactment of legislation introducing special powers to deal with terrorism, legislation justified initially as being 'temporary' and as such to require renewal every five years. It is now 'permanent', with 'special' powers

---

[1] *Conway* v *Rimmer* [1968] AC 910, at p 982.

[2] See ch 14 B. But it did not do so in relation to the conflict in Iraq and Afghanistan, on which see *al-Waheed* v *Ministry of Defence* [2017] UKSC 2. *Quaere* in any event whether the conditions for making a derogation were met.

[3] *R* v *Home Secretary, ex p Adams* [1995] All ER (EC) 177, at p 185 (Steyn LJ). See *R* v *Home Secretary, ex p Cheblak* [1991] 2 All ER 319 where judicial review yielded rather too easily. Compare the thoughtful discussion of this issue by Sedley J in *R* v *Home Secretary, ex p McQuillan* [1995] 4 All ER 400, at pp 420–1.

[4] *Beghal v DPP* [2015] UKSC 49, para 75.

[5] For details, see the 14th edition of this text, pp 628–9.

having been normalised. We conclude with (iii) a consideration of emergency powers taken in war-time and now available in peace-time conditions, though it has been a long time since emergency powers of these kinds have had to be introduced or used.

A. Use of troops in assisting the police

Authority for use of troops

In Chapter 18 we examined the main powers available to the police in maintaining public order. But in the 19th century and earlier, when there was less political freedom and police forces were weaker, the local magistrates were expected to call in detachments of soldiers to restore order when necessary. By contrast with 19th-century practice, the 'civil power' that may call in the armed forces today appears no longer to be the local magistracy, but the Home Secretary, acting on a request from a chief officer of police.[6] It would then be for the Secretary of State for Defence to respond to the call.

For the last 100 years or so, the police, with greater or less difficulty depending on the circumstances, have been able to control and contain public protest in Great Britain, though not in Northern Ireland. Apart from unrest in Glasgow in 1919, it has not been necessary to deploy troops for peace-keeping activities in Great Britain on any occasion since the First World War.[7] They have been required, however, to maintain essential services during strikes (for example, the firefighters' strike in 2003),[8] and on occasion to deal with extreme terrorist action (for example, the occupation of the Iranian embassy in London in May 1980), as well as to assist with the disposal of carcasses during the foot and mouth epidemic on British farms in 2001.[9]

> The use of the troops for peace-keeping activities may be illustrated by a rather late example, the Featherstone riots in 1893.[10] When the police were engaged elsewhere, a small detachment of soldiers was summoned to protect a colliery against a riotous crowd, which broke windows and set buildings on fire.
>
> As darkness was falling, a magistrate called on the crowd to disperse and he read the proclamation from the Riot Act. When the crowd did not disperse, the magistrate authorised the soldiers to fire and their officer decided that the only way to protect the colliery was to fire on the crowd. Two members of the crowd were killed. A committee of inquiry held that the action of the troops was justified in law, though it is difficult to see how such a conclusion could be justified today.

A decision to call in the troops to restore order was, in the past at least, a decision enabling firearms to be used to repress the disturbances. But in modern times the police are trained to use and equipped with firearms 'to deal with armed criminals and political terrorists not posing any extraordinary problem or capable of posing a limited threat'.[11] The

---

[6] HC Deb, 8 April 1976, col 617.

[7] See Williams, *Keeping the Peace*, pp 32–5.

[8] Cm 3223, 1996, pp 27–8.

[9] The armed forces provide assistance to other departments in a number of ways: apart from counter-drug activities, it includes fishing protection and assistance in natural emergencies: Cm 5109, 2001, p 3. See also Cm 6041, 2003, para 1.6. Some legal cover for this activity will be provide by the Emergency Powers Act 1964, s 2, authorising the use of troops for urgent work of national importance.

[10] Report of the Committee on the Disturbances at Featherstone, C 7234, 1893. And see HC 236 (1908).

[11] Cmnd 6496, 1976, p 95. For a sobering account of a police operation using firearms, see *R (Duggan) v Assistant Deputy Coroner* [2017] EWCA Civ 142. According to Home Office statistics, there were 15,705 police firearms operations in the year ending 31 March 2017, ten incidents in which police firearms were discharged, and 6,278 firearms officers.

occasions on which firearms may be carried are governed by police rules, and this may involve the use of lethal force, as was tragically revealed by the death of Jean-Charles de Menezes in the aftermath of the London terrorist bombings in July 2005.[12] An error of judgment on the part of a police officer could lead to criminal proceedings, liability in tort, a coroner's investigation,[13] as well as an examination by the Independent Police Complaints Commission.[14]

Matters would thus now have to be exceptionally grave before the armed forces were called upon to restore and maintain order, as emphasised by events such as the miners' strike of 1984–5 and the fuel protests of September 2000.[15] Despite large-scale public disturbances, national coordination of policing, together with new training and operational methods, meant that it was unnecessary to deploy the army in either of these situations for peace-keeping purposes.[16] It is now clear, however, that the use of troops during the miners' strike was nevertheless contemplated, though there is no evidence that they would have been used for peace-keeping purposes.[17]

Legal authority for use of force

Reference has been made politically to 'the limitations on the availability of military support to the civil power in Great Britain'.[18] But whatever may be the rules today that govern the decision that the armed forces should be called in, their legal authority to act in a situation of riot seems to rest on no statutory or prerogative powers of the Crown, but simply on the duty of all citizens to aid in the suppression of riot and on the duty of the armed forces to come to the aid of the civil authorities.[19]

In place of the common law rules on the use of force in the prevention of crime, s 3 of the Criminal Law Act 1967 now provides:

> A person may use such force as is reasonable in the circumstances in the prevention of crime, or in effecting or assisting in the lawful arrest of offenders or suspected offenders or of persons unlawfully at large.

Thus, the use of firearms must be justified by the necessity of the situation and does not become legal by reason of the decision to call in the troops. Indeed, the use of excessive force or the premature use of firearms would render the officer in command and the individual soldiers personally responsible for death or injuries caused. Issues of liability are decided by the criminal or civil courts after the event,[20] and may give rise to court-martial proceedings,[21] as well as a coroner's investigation as already suggested.

One of the most notorious examples in modern times of the use of excessive force by the troops was in Derry/Londonderry on 30 January 1972, when 13 citizens were shot dead, and another 14 were wounded, one fatally. A lengthy inquiry (which took 12 years to complete) conducted by Lord Saville concluded in 2010 that none of the victims 'was posing a threat of

---

[12] *Da Silva* v *United Kingdom* [2016] ECHR 314.

[13] Coroners and Justice Act 2009, s 1. See *R (Duggan)* v *Assistant Deputy Coroner*, above. Someone who uses lethal force may also be able to rely on the defence of self-defence (*Duggan*, ibid, where the authorities are discussed).

[14] See ch 15 above.

[15] On which see H Fenwick and G Phillipson (2001) 21 LS 535.

[16] See McCabe and Wallington, *The Police, Public Order and Civil Liberties*, pp 49–50.

[17] *The Guardian*, 3 January 2014.

[18] HC Deb, 8 April 1976, col 617 (Mr Roy Jenkins, Home Secretary).

[19] *Charge to Bristol Grand Jury* (1832) 5 C . . . P 261.

[20] See *R* v *Clegg* [1995] 1 AC 482, and *Bici* v *Ministry of Defence* [2004] EWHC 786 (QB).

[21] Armed Forces Act 2006, Pt 2.

causing death or serious injury, or indeed was doing anything else that could on any view justify their shooting'.[22] But although the soldiers in question were identified by the inquiry (though they remain anonymous), none has been prosecuted, and it is unlikely for a number of reasons that they ever will be.[23]

In modern conditions, the proposition that to call in the troops makes possible the use of firearms needs to be qualified in the sense that it is no longer correct, as was said in 1893, that a soldier can act only by using deadly weapons.[24] To call in the army to deal with civil unrest would indeed be of incalculable political significance. But the British army's experience in Northern Ireland suggests that there are many other ways of dealing with hostile crowds which are more effective and less deadly than firing into them – batons, riot shields, water cannon, rubber bullets and even CS gas – and the armed forces do not have a monopoly on the use of CS gas.[25]

Legal liability for excessive force

The use of the troops to assist the civil authorities for a sustained period of time arose most recently in relation to events in Northern Ireland. These events also tested the legal authority of the soldier when deployed in such circumstances, and it has been suggested that the legal position of the soldier called to assist the civil authorities in Northern Ireland to contain terrorist or political violence may not be the same as that of his or her counterpart called to assist the civil authorities elsewhere for other purposes:

> There is little authority in English law concerning the rights and duties of a member of the armed forces of the Crown when acting in aid of the civil power; and what little authority there is relates almost entirely to the duties of soldiers when troops are called upon to assist in controlling a riotous assembly. Where used for such temporary purposes it may not be inaccurate to describe the legal rights and duties of a soldier as being no more than those of an ordinary citizen in uniform. But such a description is in my view misleading in the circumstances in which the army is currently employed in aid of the civil power in Northern Ireland . . .
>
> In theory it may be the duty of every citizen when an arrestable offence is about to be committed in his presence to take whatever reasonable measures are available to him to prevent the commission of the crime; but the duty is one of imperfect obligation and does not place him under any obligation to do anything by which he would expose himself to the risk of personal injury . . . In contrast to this a soldier who is employed in aid of the civil power in Northern Ireland is under a duty, enforceable under military law, to search for criminals if so ordered by his superior officer and to risk his own life should this be necessary in preventing terrorist acts. For the performance of this duty he is armed with a firearm, a self-loading rifle, from which a bullet, if it hits the human body, is almost certain to cause serious injury if not death.[26]

It has been said by the government, however, that 'service personnel are given certain specific powers under the law (for example, to make arrests and carry out searches) in order to enable them to carry out effective support to the RUC [now the Police Service of Northern

---

[22] The Bloody Sunday Inquiry Report (2010). See earlier HC 220 (1971–2) (Widgery Report), on which see C A Gearty (1994) 47 CLP 19, at p 33.

[23] There was, however, unusually an apology from the government delivered to the House of Commons by the Prime Minister. See subsequently *R (B) v Chief Constable of the PSNI* [2015] EWHC 3691 (Admin).

[24] C 7234, 1893, pp 10, 12.

[25] On the power to make it available to the police, see ch 10 above.

[26] *A–G for Northern Ireland's Reference (No 1 of 1975)* [1977] AC 105, at pp 136–7 (Lord Diplock).

Ireland]'. In exercising these powers and in seeking to uphold the law, service personnel remain accountable to the law at all times. They have no immunity, nor do they receive special treatment. If service personnel breach the law, they are liable to arrest and prosecution under the law. This applies equally to the use of force, including lethal force.'[27] Arrest and other powers were extended to members of the armed forces by legislation applying only in Northern Ireland.[28]

Considerable controversy has, nevertheless, arisen from time to time as a result of the use of firearms by the military, not only in relation to the events in Derry/Londonderry referred to above. Between 1969 and 1994 the security forces are said to have been responsible for 357 deaths in Northern Ireland, including 141 who were republican 'military activists', 13 who were loyalist equivalents and 194 who were civilians. Eighteen of these deaths led to criminal charges, with a total of six convictions being secured, one for attempted murder, one for manslaughter and four for murder.[29]

In *Attorney-General for Northern Ireland Reference (No 1 of 1975),*[30] the accused was a soldier on foot patrol who shot and killed a young man in an open field in a country area in daylight. The shot had not been preceded by a warning shot and the rifle was fired after the deceased ran off after having been told to halt. The area was one in which troops had been attacked and killed by the IRA and where a surprise attack was a real threat. When the accused fired, he believed that he was dealing with a member of the IRA, but he had no belief at all as to whether the deceased had been involved or was likely to be involved in any act of terrorism. In fact, the deceased was an 'entirely innocent person who was in no way involved in terrorist activity'.

After the soldier's acquittal for murder, the House of Lords held that the stated circumstances (where 'he fires to kill or seriously wound an unarmed person because he honestly and reasonably believes that person is a member of a proscribed organisation [in this case the Provisional IRA] who is seeking to run away, and the soldier's shot kills that person') raised an issue for the tribunal of fact as to whether the Crown had established beyond reasonable doubt that the shooting constituted unreasonable force. According to Lord Diplock, 'there is material upon which a jury might take the view that the accused had reasonable grounds for apprehension of imminent danger to himself and other members of the patrol if the deceased were allowed to get away . . . and that the time available to the accused to make up his mind was so short that even a reasonable man could only act intuitively'.[31]

On the other hand, in *R v Clegg*[32] it was held that a soldier who used excessive force in self-defence leading to the death of the victim was guilty of murder rather than manslaughter.

---

[27] Statement on the Defence Estimates 1994, p 36.

[28] Justice and Security (Northern Ireland Act) 2007, ss 21 (powers of stop and question), 22 (powers of arrest), 23 (powers of entry), 25 (powers of search of detained persons). These powers are additional to any existing common law or statutory powers and are 'not to be taken to affect those powers **or Her Majesty's prerogative**' (emphasis added), to which we may ask: what prerogative?

[29] Gearty and Kimbell, *Terrorism and the Rule of Law*, pp 57–8.

[30] [1977] AC 105. See also *Farrell v Defence Secretary* [1980] 1 All ER 166; *R v Bohan and Temperley* (1979) (5) BNIL; *R v Robinson* (1984) (4) BNIL 34; *R v McAuley* (1985) (10) BNIL 14. See also R J Spjut [1986] PL 38 and [1987] PL 35.

[31] [1977] AC 105, at p 138.

[32] [1995] 1 AC 482.

'Shoot to kill' allegations

The use of firearms by the authorities in Northern Ireland gave rise to allegations of a shoot-to-kill policy, these being directed at both the RUC and the armed forces.[33] The allegations were sufficiently serious that an inquiry was appointed in the 1980s under the chairmanship of Mr John Stalker, the Deputy Chief Constable of Greater Manchester.[34] Mr Stalker was removed from the inquiry in controversial circumstances, and it was completed by the Chief Constable of West Yorkshire, but no evidence was published to substantiate the allegations.[35]

The controversy was revived following the decision of the European Court of Human Rights in *McCann* v *United Kingdom*,[36] which concerned the fatal shooting of three IRA activists in Gibraltar in 1987.

Three known IRA personnel were shot by four SAS officers while it was thought that they were about to detonate a bomb, to the danger of life on Gibraltar.

It transpired that this belief was erroneous and that the suspects were not only unarmed, but also that they were not in possession of bomb equipment at the time of their deaths. They were nevertheless shot 29 times (one suspect being shot 16 times). By a majority of 10 to 9, the Court held that there had been a breach of art 2 which in protecting the right to life was said to rank as 'one of the most fundamental provisions in the Convention'.[37] There was no evidence of 'an execution plot at the highest level of command in the Ministry of Defence or in the Government'; although 'all four soldiers shot to kill', on the facts and in the circumstances the actions of the soldiers did not in themselves give rise to a violation of art 2.

But it was held that the operation as a whole was controlled and organised in a manner that failed to respect art 2, and that the information and instructions given to the soldiers rendered inevitable the use of lethal force in a manner which failed to take adequately into consideration the right to life of the three suspects. Having regard 'to the decision not to prevent the suspects from travelling into Gibraltar, to the failure of the authorities to make sufficient allowances for the possibility that their intelligence assessments might in some respects, at least, be erroneous, and to the automatic recourse to lethal force when the soldiers opened fire', the Court was not persuaded that 'the killing of the three terrorists constituted the force which was no more than absolutely necessary in defence of persons from unlawful violence'.[38]

Allegations of a shoot-to-kill policy of the security forces in Northern Ireland gave rise to litigation – in the European Court of Human Rights and in the domestic courts under the Human Rights Act – at the instance of bereaved families concerned that adequate steps

---

[33] See *Farrell* v *UK* (1983) 5 EHRR 466, *McCann* v *UK* (1995) 21 EHRR 97, *McKerr* v *UK* (2002) 34 EHRR 20; *Jordan* v *UK* (2003) 37 EHRR 2; *Finucane* v *UK* (2004) 37 EHRR 656; and *Kelly* v *United Kingdom*, *App No* 30054/96. See also *In re McKerr* [2004] UKHL 12, [2004] 1 WLR 807.

[34] See Stalker, *Stalker*.

[35] See HC Deb, 25 January 1988, cols 21–35.

[36] (1995) 21 EHRR 97.

[37] Art 2(1) provides that 'Everyone's life shall be protected by law', while art 2(2) provides by way of qualification that 'Deprivation of life shall not be regarded as inflicted in contravention of this article when it results from the use of force which is no more than absolutely necessary: (a) in defence of any person from unlawful violence . . .'

[38] The political reaction to the decision was very critical of the Court: see e.g. HL Deb, 29 January 1996, col 1225. Compare C Gearty, 'After Gibraltar', *London Review of Books*, 16 November 1995.

have not been taken to investigate the deaths of people allegedly killed by the RUC.[39] Although critical of government conduct that served only to 'add fuel to fears of sinister motives',[40] the ECtHR has yet to find evidence of a shoot-to-kill policy. Nor did the Saville inquiry, before which it had been submitted that the use of lethal force was encouraged or tolerated by the State.[41]

That said, in 2012, the then Prime Minister (David Cameron) apologised to the family of the murdered Belfast lawyer Pat Finucane and agreed that there was state collusion in his murder, involving police officers and soldiers with his loyalist killers.[42]

B. Legislative responses to terrorism – what is terrorism?

Legal origins

Special legislation dealing with terrorism was first introduced in Britain in 1974, following the Birmingham pub bombings in that year.[43] Although said by its author to be 'drastic',[44] the Prevention of Terrorism (Temporary Provisions) Act 1974 was at least subject to the formality of annual renewal by Parliament, while subsequent Prevention of Terrorism (Temporary Provisions) Acts expired after five years: hence the reference to temporary provisions in their short titles.

Confined to the situation in Northern Ireland, the early anti-terrorism legislation was controversial because of its threat to civil liberties. Critics were concerned by its 'proscription' of the IRA, and its introduction of exclusion orders, preventing British citizens resident in Northern Ireland from travelling to the rest of the country. But although a short and tightly drawn measure, it was only the start and its focus on the IRA soon expanded as anti-terrorism powers extended.

Perhaps inevitably, these temporary provisions became permanent, with the Terrorism Act 2000 being designed to implement the recommendations of an *Inquiry into Legislation Against Terrorism* conducted by Lord Lloyd of Berwick in 1996.[45] Passed just after the Belfast Agreement in 1999, and just before the 9/11 attacks in New York and Washington in 2001, the 2000 Act has become a cornerstone in the government's response to international as well as domestic terrorism.

The Belfast Agreement was thus not the occasion to repeal special powers to deal with terrorism. On the contrary, the 9/11 attacks on the United States by individuals linked to al-Qaeda led to the introduction of additional powers in the United Kingdom addressed specifically to international terrorism, though many of these powers – contained in the Anti-terrorism, Crime and Security Act 2001 – were to prove even more contentious than the provisions of the Terrorism Act 2000 they complement.[46]

---

[39] See cases referred to in note 33 above.

[40] *Jordan* v *United Kingdom*, above, para 144. Also *Kelly* v *United Kingdom*, above.

[41] The Bloody Sunday Inquiry Report, above.

[42] *The Guardian*, 12 December 2012.

[43] Special powers to deal with threats to security in Northern Ireland are, however, almost as old as the Province itself. See Civil Authorities (Special Powers) Act 1922, replaced by Northern Ireland (Emergency Provisions) Act 1973, amended in 1975 and 1977 and re-enacted in 1978, 1987, 1991 and 1996. On the 1922 Act, see Calvert, *Constitutional Law in Northern Ireland*, ch 20; Campbell, *Emergency Law in Ireland 1918–1925*; and Ewing and Gearty, *The Struggle for Civil Liberties*, ch 7. The 1973 Act was preceded by the Diplock Report, Cmnd 5185, 1972.

[44] Jenkins, *A Life at the Centre*, p 394.

[45] Cm 3420, 1996. See also the important report by Gearty and Kimbell, *Terrorism and the Rule of Law*.

[46] See A Tomkins [2002] PL 205 and H Fenwick (2002) 65 MLR 724.

Counter-terrorism powers have nevertheless continued to increase as the nature of the terrorist threat continues to change,[47] with the main contemporary sources in the United Kingdom being Daesh (otherwise referred to as ISIS, ISIL or Islamic State) and al-Qaeda,[48] while the risk in Northern Ireland is still assessed as 'severe'.[49] Financial and personnel resources devoted to counter-terrorism (including police and security and intelligence services) continue to rise steeply.[50]

Terrorism defined

Special powers to deal with terrorism having thus gradually expanded, the first question for consideration is simply this: to what activity do the restrictions apply? Here, one of the most controversial features of the Terrorism Act 2000 is the wide definition of terrorism in s 1 to mean action or the threat of action which (*a*) falls within s 1(2); (*b*) is designed to influence a government (or an international governmental organisation), or to intimidate the public or a section of the public; and (*c*) is made for the purpose of advancing a political, religious, racial or ideological cause.

Much of the concern relates to the wide scope of the action falling within s 1(2), which applies not only to serious violence, serious damage to property and the endangering of human life, but also to creating 'a serious risk to the health or safety of the public or a section of the public', as well as seriously interfering with or seriously disrupting an electronic system. Section 1 also makes it clear that the Act applies to terrorist activity overseas, as well as that directed at the British government. The action to which the section applies may be action outside the United Kingdom and the government it is designed to influence may be the government of the United Kingdom (or a part thereof), or of a country other than the United Kingdom.[51]

This wide definition gave rise to a great deal of comment, and a number of difficult questions were raised as the Bill was passing through Parliament. A good example is the following by Mr Douglas Hogg:

> If someone decided to break into a mink farm in order to release the mink from their cages, or to break into a research station and destroy the animals' cages, that would clearly be an act of serious violence. It would be a criminal act – and one that I deplore. But why should such organisations be classified as terrorist under [section] 1?[52]

There was also the case of the women who attacked the Hawk aircraft with hammers, as well as the case of the Trident Ploughshares 2000 organisation, which attacked the Trident submarine.[53]

The Home Secretary conceded that this conduct might well fall under s 1, but felt that the answer to the potentially wide scope of the legislation lay in the self-restraint of the prosecuting authorities. According to Mr Straw, 'we must have some confidence in the law enforcement agencies and the courts. If we look back at the past 25 years, we can see that the powers have been used proportionately in the face of an horrific threat from terrorism in Ireland and from international terrorism'.[54] Not everyone would feel so sanguine. The Home Secretary

---

[47] On the context for the expansion of these powers, see D Anderson, *The Terrorism Acts in 2015 – Report of the Independent Reviewer on the Operation of the Terrorism Act 2000 and Part 1 of the Terrorism Act 2006* (2016), para 2.1.

[48] Ibid, paras 2.2, 2.5

[49] Ibid, para 2.13.

[50] Ibid, para 3.4–3.14.

[51] See *R* v *F* [2007] EWCA (Crim) 243, [2007] 2 All ER 193.

[52] HC Deb, 14 Dec 1999, col 155.

[53] Ibid, col 200.

[54] Ibid, col 155. See also at col 165 (stressing independence of the police, the DPP and the Attorney General). The consent of the DPP is necessary before any prosecution (s 117).

also drew attention to the Human Rights Act 1998 and to arts 5 and 6 of the ECHR as a 'profound safeguard against the disproportionate use of the powers' in the Act.[55]

It was some time before these concerns about the scope of the definition were judicially acknowledged, though they had been identified for some time by the government's independent reviewer of terrorism legislation.[56] In *Miranda* v *Home Office*,[57] however, the Court of Appeal cited the 'example of a newspaper article, politically motivated and aimed at influencing the Government, whose publication is said to endanger lives'. The court continued:

> It would follow on the literal interpretation that (i) the possession of any article for a purpose connected with the publication, or of any document likely to be useful to persons publishing material of that kind would be punishable by up to 15 years or 10 years imprisonment (sections 57 and 58 of TACT respectively); (ii) acts preparatory to publication would be punishable by up to life imprisonment (section 5 of the Terrorism Act 2006); (iii) anyone who encouraged the writing of similar articles, or circulated such encouragement to others could be imprisoned for up to seven years (sections 1 and 2 of the Terrorism Act 2006); and (iv) the newspaper in question could be proscribed (with the consent of Parliament) as an organisation concerned in terrorism (section 3)

The issue in *Miranda* was whether powers under the Terrorism Act 2000 could be used to stop and question Mr Miranda who was the spouse of a *Guardian* journalist, Kent Greenwald. Mr Greenwald had been given encrypted data by Edward Snowden 'which had been stolen from the National Security Agency (NSA) of the United States'.[58] Although the Court of Appeal took fully into account criticisms of the statutory definition of terrorism, the application of the definition to a case such as this appears not to have been one of the 'unpalatable consequences' of the Act to which the court had referred,[59] when expressing concern about the breadth of the definition. Nevertheless, the application of the definition to a case such as *Miranda* suggests that the concerns raised when the Act was passed were fully justified.[60]

Terrorist organisations

Having identified 'terrorism' in Part I, the Terrorism Act 2000 retains and expands in Part II the power to proscribe terrorist organisations. Reflecting the political origins of the 2000 Act, the 14 bodies initially proscribed are all connected with events in Northern Ireland.

Rather fortuitously in light of events post-enactment, however, there is a power in the 2000 Act to add to the list by order (s 3). This power has been exercised frequently and there are now another 70 organisations on the list, said to be involved in terrorist activities in different parts of the world, but thought to operate in or from this country.[61] Before an organisation may be added to the list, the Secretary of State must believe that it is 'concerned in terrorism' (s 3(4)), which means not only that it commits or prepares acts of terrorism, but also that it promotes or encourages terrorism or is 'otherwise concerned in terrorism' (s 3(5)). To promote or encourage for these purposes may include to glorify.[62]

....

[55] Ibid, col 160. It was also claimed by a former minister from the Opposition benches that 'the integrity of Ministers is often bolstered by the knowledge of the existence of judicial review' (HC Deb, 14 Dec 1999, Mr Tom King).

[56] D Anderson, *The Terrorism Acts in 2013 – Report of the Independent Reviewer on the Operation of the Terrorism Act 2000 and Part 1 of the Terrorism Act 2006* (2014), para 4.2

[57] [2016] EWCA Civ 6.

[58] Ibid, para 6.

[59] Ibid, para 51.

[60] See also *R* v *Gul* [2014] UKSC 64.

[61] See Anderson, *The Terrorism Acts in 2015*, above, para 5.4. See also Home Office, *Proscribed Terrorist Groups or Organisations* (2017). The list also includes extreme right-wing organisations based in the United Kingdom.

[62] Terrorism Act 2006, s 21, amending 2000 Act, s 3 by inserting new s 3(5A)–3(5C).

The Secretary of State also has the power to remove an organisation by order from the proscribed list, following an application by the organisation or any person affected by the organisation's proscription (s 4). If the Secretary of State refuses the application, an appeal may be made to the Proscribed Organisations Appeal Commission, which is required to apply the principles of judicial review (s 5), with a right of appeal from the Commission on a point of law to the Court of Appeal, Court of Session or Court of Appeal in Northern Ireland, as appropriate (s 6).[63] The de-proscription procedures have been strongly criticized by the government's independent reviewer of terrorism, who claims that a number of organisations are wrongly proscribed.[64]

In general, a decision to proscribe an organisation is not subject to judicial review, with a proscribed organisation being expected by the courts to use the statutory de-proscription procedure,[65] where it may be represented by a special advocate appointed by one of the government's law officers.[66]

> In *R v Z*[67] the question was whether the Real IRA was a proscribed organisation. The proscribed organisations in the Schedule include the IRA but not the Real IRA, a newly formed splinter group that did not accept the peace process. Reading the legislation very widely, the House of Lords held that the term IRA applied to an organisation 'whatever relationship (if any) it has to any other organisation of the same name'. Although there was a risk that 'a group within the extended IRA family would be proscribed which was currently non-violent', Lord Bingham concluded that 'it might well have been thought unlikely that a body bearing the name IRA or any variant of it would be at all friendly to parliamentary democracy'.[68]

It is an offence to be a member (or to profess membership) of a proscribed organisation (s 11), a measure said to be of 'extraordinary breadth'.[69] It is a defence under s 11(2) if the defendant can prove that the organisation was not proscribed while he or she was a member, a burden read down by the House of Lords to be evidential rather than legal. This is despite the fact that Parliament had clearly intended otherwise when enacting the 2000 Act, providing a nice example of how the Human Rights Act, s 3 is binding on future or subsequently enacted legislation.[70] It is an offence to invite support for such an organisation (s 12), or to organise a meeting (whether in public or private) in support of such an organisation. Breach of these provisions could lead to imprisonment of up to ten years or to a fine, or both, after a conviction on indictment (s 12(6)).

In addition to the foregoing, it is an offence under s 13 for a person in a public place to wear an item of clothing or wear, carry or display an article 'in such a way or in such circumstances as to arouse reasonable apprehension that he is a member or supporter of a proscribed

---

[63] See *Lord Alton of Liverpool v Home Secretary* [2008] EWCA Civ 443, [2008] 1 WLR 2341, which together with the decision of the POAC which the Court of Appeal upholds, gives a good insight into the proscription procedure in the Home Office.

[64] Anderson, *The Terrorism Acts in 2015*, above, para 5.13.

[65] *R (Kurdistan Workers' Party) v Home Secretary* [2002] EWHC (Admin) 644.

[66] 2000 Act, Sch 3, para 7.

[67] [2005] UKHL 35, [2005] 2 AC 645.

[68] Ibid, para [20]. See also Terrorism Act 2006, s 22, inserting new Terrorism Act 2000, s 3(6)–(11).

[69] *Attorney-General's Reference No 4 of 2002* [2004] UKHL 43, [2005] 1 AC 264, para [47] (Lord Bingham).

[70] Ibid.

organisation' (s 13(1)). Conduct violating s 13 may also be unlawful under the Public Order Act 1936, s 1, whereby it is an offence to wear a political uniform in public. Although the 1936 Act was designed initially for use against Mosley's blackshirts, it was used successfully in 1975 against IRA pall-bearers at a funeral in Coventry, dressed in dark pullovers, dark berets and dark glasses.[71] The restrictions in the Terrorism Act 2000 are wider, there being no need to show that the demonstration of support amounts to the wearing of a uniform: an emblem such as a ring is enough.

Terrorist funds

Part III of the Terrorism Act 2000 (as amended in 2001) deals with terrorist property, defined to mean both money and property likely to be used for the purposes of terrorism, including any resources of a proscribed organisation (s 14). It is an offence to solicit, receive or give money or property for terrorist purposes (s 15). The Act contains additional measures first introduced in 1989 'to strike at the financial roots of terrorism',[72] at a time when it was thought that the IRA (then the main target) had an annual income of £3–4 million, generated not only by robbery and extortion, but also by apparently legitimate business activity which gave the organisation 'an assured income and a firmer base'.[73]

So, apart from the direct financing of terrorism, it is an offence to use or possess money or property for terrorist purposes (s 16). Although property for this purpose includes magazines and other literature, it has been held that s 16 does not violate the ECHR, art 10, since it falls well within art 10(2).[74] It is also an offence to be involved in 'an arrangement' whereby money or property is made available for terrorist purposes (s 17).[75] This is intended to cover various banking transactions, including an arrangement whereby money or other property is made available to a lawful business and either that money, or the profits of that activity, is 'intended to be used for terrorist purposes'.

Section 18 contains the so-called laundering offence, making it unlawful to enter into an arrangement 'which facilitates the retention or control by or on behalf of another person of terrorist property', by concealment, removal from the jurisdiction, transfer to nominees or 'in any other way'. This is an extremely wide provision, in the sense that 'an estate agent collecting rent from office premises might be totally unaware that the ultimate beneficiaries of the profits are a company operating for the benefit of a terrorist organisation'. Moreover, 'if charged, the statutory defence made available under section 18(2) would place a reverse burden upon [the accused]'.[76]

Where someone suspects that another person has committed an offence under ss 15–18, it is an offence to fail to inform the police as soon as reasonably practicable (s 19).[77] There is an exception for employees who have informed their employer in accordance with any procedure for reporting concerns of this kind (although if the employer has no procedure, there would be no defence for failing to notify the police). There is also an exception for lawyers in relation to information obtained from a client in connection with the provision of legal advice.

---

[71] *O'Moran* v *DPP* [1975] QB 864.

[72] HC Deb, 6 Dec 1988, col 212 (Mr Douglas Hurd).

[73] Ibid, col 213.

[74] *O'Driscoll* v *Home Secretary* [2002] EWHC 2477 (Admin).

[75] Section 17A (introduced by the Counter-Terrorism and Security Act 2015) makes it an offence for an insurer to pay out for the loss of property handed over in response to a terrorist demand.

[76] Lord Carlile, *Report on the Operation in 2004 of the Terrorism Act 2000* (2005), para 42. Lord Carlile was the government's independent reviewer of terrorism legislation. He was replaced in 2011 by David Anderson QC referred to above, who in turn was replaced by Max Hill QC. The reviewer is appointed under Terrorism Act 2006, s 36, and his powers have recently been extended.

[77] Amended by the Counter-Terrorism Act 2008, s 77.

But there is no exception for journalists,[78] although there is a general defence of reasonableness from which journalists might benefit.[79]

Section 21 deals with the position of police informers, so that it is not an offence for a person to withhold information under ss 15–18 if acting with the express consent of the police; nor is it an offence to be involved in a money-laundering arrangement after informing the police that the money or other property in question is terrorist property. The latter provision would protect the bank or other body which is the medium for the unlawful action and also give the police access to information about the arrangement. Additional measures introduced by the Anti-terrorism, Crime and Security Act 2001 – ss 21A and 21B – impose duties of disclosure on the financial services industry.

Where a person is convicted of an offence under ss 15–18, a court may make an order for the forfeiture of money or property destined for terrorist use or which was the subject of an arrangement for handling or laundering terrorist funds (s 23). There are powers for the seizure, detention and forfeiture in civil proceedings of cash intended to be used for terrorist purposes, as well as cash which represents the resources of a proscribed organisation or property obtained through terrorism. The powers of forfeiture may be exercised even though no criminal proceedings have previously been brought in connection with the cash.[80]

Perhaps more important than the foregoing are statutory powers to freeze the assets of terrorist suspects under the UN Charter, which are given effect by both EU law (Council Regulation 881/2002) and domestic law (United Nations Act 1946).[81]

C. Legislative responses to terrorism – terrorist investigations, police powers and terrorist offences

Terrorist investigations

Part IV of the 2000 Act deals with 'terrorist investigations' defined to mean the investigation of one of five matters: the commission, preparation or instigation of acts of terrorism; an act which appears to have been done for the purposes of terrorism; the resources of a proscribed organisation; the possibility of making a proscription order under s 3; and the commission, preparation or instigation of an offence under the Terrorism Act 2000 itself, or the Terrorism Act 2006, Part 1 (s 32).

Sections 33–6 empower the police to impose *cordons* for up to 28 days in the course of terrorist investigations and to order people to leave the area, to leave premises in the cordoned area and to remove vehicles from the area. An order designating a cordoned area may be made by a police officer of the rank of superintendent or above, although it may also be made by an officer of lesser rank where necessary 'by reason of urgency' (s 34(2)). There are few formalities associated with the exercise of this power.[82]

---

[78] A point raised in Parliament at Second Reading in the Commons: HC Deb, 14 Dec 1999, col 181 (Fiona Mactaggart). See also J J Rowe [2001] Crim LR 527, at pp 537–8.

[79] HL Deb, 23 May 2000, col 653 (Lord Bassam).

[80] Anti-terrorism, Crime and Security Act 2001, s 1 and Sch 1.

[81] *Ahmed* v *HM Treasury* [2010] UKSC 2; [2010] 2 AC 534; *Youssef v Foreign Secretary* [2016] UKSC 3. The powers are said to be 'draconian', 'drastic', 'oppressive', 'devastating', making designated persons 'effectively prisoners of the state', 'without access to funds or other economic resources'. See the discussion in *Youssef v Foreign Secretary* [2013] EWCA Civ 1301, [2014] QB 728.

[82] Thus, if made orally, the designation is to be confirmed in writing as soon as reasonably practicable; and it can only be made for 14 days in the first instance, to be renewed as necessary. There is no reporting to the Home Secretary or to anyone else on the exercise of this power, and not even an annual reporting obligation on the number of times the power is exercised. These powers may also be exercised in some circumstances by the British Transport Police and by the Ministry of Defence Police following amendments introduced by the 2001 Act.

There are extensive powers conferred on the police to obtain *information for the purposes of a terrorist investigation*. By virtue of s 37 and Sch 5,[83] a justice of the peace may issue a search warrant (all premises or specific premises), if there are reasonable grounds for believing that there is material on the premises to which the application relates which is likely to be of substantial value to the investigation (Sch 5, para 1(5)), and does not consist of items subject to legal privilege or excluded or special procedure material (as defined by PACE) (para 4).[84]

In the case of excluded or special procedure material, a constable may apply to a circuit judge or a district judge (magistrates' court) for an order requiring the person in possession to produce it for the constable to take away or have access to it (paras 5–10). For these purposes, documents may be taken away and examined to determine if they should be seized, provisions which do not apply to items subject to legal privilege.[85] There is no provision in the Terrorism Act 2000 requiring the application for an order to be made *inter partes*.

Where an order is not complied with or where access to the material is needed more immediately, the constable may apply to a circuit judge or a district judge (magistrates' court) for a warrant to search the premises (again specific premises or all premises) for the excluded or special procedure material (paras 11 and 12). A circuit judge or a district judge (magistrates' court) may also issue an order requiring a person to provide an explanation of any material which has been produced or seized under the foregoing provisions (para 13).

In cases 'of great emergency', a police officer of the rank of superintendent or above may by written order authorise conduct which would otherwise require a judicial warrant (para 15).[86] Amendments introduced in 2001 make it an offence to fail to provide information to the police if the person in question 'knows or believes' that the information 'might be of material assistance' in preventing the commission by another person of an act of terrorism.[87]

Police powers

Police powers of arrest, search, and stop and search are dealt with in Part V of the Terrorism Act 2000. They apply to someone who is *a terrorist*, defined to mean not only someone who has committed an offence under the Act, but also someone who has been 'concerned in the commission, preparation or instigation of acts of terrorism'. For this purpose terrorism carries the meaning set out in s 1 (s 40).

Section 41 gives a power to a constable to *arrest without a warrant* a person whom 'he reasonably suspects to be a terrorist'.[88] A person so arrested may be detained for up to 48 hours,

---

[83] As amended by the Terrorism Act 2006.

[84] For legal privilege or excluded or special procedure material, see ch 15 above. Separate provisions deal with police access to confidential customer information held by banks, extended in 2001 to include a police power to monitor bank accounts (with the authority of a circuit judge or sheriff) and to freeze accounts. See Terrorism Act 2000, Sch 6 and Anti-terrorism, Crime and Security Act 2001, ss 4–16, and Schs 2 and 3.

[85] Counter-Terrorism Act 2008, ss 1–9. The same applies to the search powers under the 2000 Act, s 43. See below.

[86] In cases of great emergency, such a police officer may also require a person to provide an explanation of any material seized in pursuance of an order under para 15 (para 16).

[87] Anti-terrorism, Crime and Security Act 2001, s 117, inserting a new s 38B into the Terrorism Act 2000.

[88] See *O'Hara* v *Chief Constable of the RUC* [1997] 1 All ER 129. Section 41 does not appear to meet the objections raised about its predecessors, namely that they permitted the police to arrest and detain someone who has not and is not suspected of having committed an offence. This remains the case and doubt has been raised about whether this power is consistent with art 5 of the ECHR. See J J Rowe [2001] Crim LR 527, esp pp 532–3 where the author refers to concerns raised in Parliament by Lord Lloyd as the Bill was being enacted.

in contrast to the normal 24 or 36 hours. A lawful arrest is a precondition of any such detention.[89] Further detention must be authorised by a warrant issued by a judicial authority (a district judge (magistrates' courts) in England and Wales; a sheriff in Scotland; or a county court judge or resident magistrate in Northern Ireland).[90]

A person should not be *detained without charge* for more than 14 days in total from the time of arrest.[91] Controversial amendments introduced by the Terrorism Act 2006 extended the period of 14 days to 28 days with appropriate judicial authority (ss 23–5). But this was reversed by the Protection of Freedoms Act 2012, though there are also provisions to enable the 28-day period to be reinstated in urgent circumstances when Parliament is dissolved, there apparently being no need for such powers when Parliament is in session.[92]

In addition to powers of arrest and detention, a police officer may apply to a justice of the peace for a warrant to *enter and search* any premises on reasonable suspicion that a person concerned with the commission, preparation or instigation of acts of terrorism will be found there (s 42). (The Terrorism Act 2006 also authorises a police constable to apply to a justice of the peace for a warrant to enter and search premises for terrorist publications prohibited by section 2 of the 2006 Act (publications that encourage or glorify terrorism).)

Moreover, the 2000 Act authorises a police officer to *stop and search* a person whom 'he reasonably suspects to be a terrorist'. This may be done in order 'to discover whether he has in his possession anything which may constitute evidence that he is a terrorist' (s 43(1)). A police officer may also *search* a person arrested under s 41 'to discover whether he has in his possession anything which may constitute evidence that he is a terrorist' (s 43(2)).

Other – highly controversial – *stop and search powers* were contained in s 44,[93] which are much wider than the more limited powers in s 43. These will be considered in the following section. Otherwise, Part V includes wide-ranging powers to *stop, detain and question individuals at ports and borders* with a view to determine whether the individuals in question are or have been 'concerned in the commission, preparation or instigation of acts of terrorism'.[94] There is also a power to search the person and his or her property, and to seize property. These powers may be exercised without any reasonable suspicion of involvement in a terrorist offence.[95]

The Sch 7 power was considered in two important cases. In *Beghal* v *DPP*,[96] the appellant was stopped at East Midlands airport after visiting her husband who was detained on terrorist charges in France. She was stopped and questioned about her movements but refused to cooperate, and was charged and convicted of an offence under Sch 7, and appealed claiming that her conviction violated her right to liberty (art 5), fair trial (art 6) and private life (art 8). The Supreme Court dismissed the claim, with Lord Kerr dissenting.

---

[89] *Forbes* v *HM Advocate* 1990 SCR 69.

[90] On which see *Magee* v *United Kingdom* [2015] ECHR 478. The detained person may be excluded from the proceedings in which such an application is made: see *Ward* v *Police Service of Northern Ireland* [2007] UKHL 50, [2007] 1 WLR 3013.

[91] As originally enacted, the period of detention was seven days; the increase to 14 days was made by the Criminal Justice Act 2003, s 306.

[92] Protection of Freedoms Act 2012, inserting a new Terrorism Act 2000, Sch 8, Part 4. A number of safeguards have been introduced to contain the exercise of this power should it ever be reinstated.

[93] This provision has its origins in Prevention of Terrorism (Temporary Provisions) Act 1989, s 13A (inserted by the Criminal Justice and Public Order Act 1994, s 81); and s 13B (inserted by the Prevention of Terrorism (Additional Powers) Act 1996).

[94] Terrorism Act 2000, s 53, and Sch 7.

[95] For criticism in relation to a controversial use of Sch 7 (in the case of David Miranda, on which see below), see A W Bradley, *The Guardian*, 21 August 2013 (letter to editor).

[96] *Beghal v DPP* [2015] UKSC 49

In *Miranda* v *Home Secretary*,[97] the appellant was carrying encrypted data while travelling through Heathrow airport, where he was stopped and questioned about it at the request of MI5. The exercise of Sch 7 powers in this case was held to be lawful, but Sch 7 was held to be incompatible with ECHR, art 10 (freedom of expression), a matter that had not been considered in *Beghal*. A declaration of incompatibility was granted insofar as the Schedule applied to journalistic material.

In the meantime, Sch 7 had been amended in 2014 to provide greater safeguards for those stopped and questioned. Express provision is made for time limits, periodic reviews of detentions under the Schedule, the manner of exercise of the search power, and the right of the person detained to have someone informed and to consult a solicitor. At the time of writing, there has been no legislative response to *Miranda*, though the code of practice governing the use of Sch 7 has been amended to take account of the decision.[98]

Police powers of stop and search

Now repealed, the power in the Terrorism Act 2000, s 44 referred to immediately above enabled a senior police officer to grant an 'authorisation' for renewable periods of 28 days, which in turn 'authorised' a constable in uniform in the area or place specified in the authorisation to stop and search vehicles and pedestrians. An authorisation – which ceased to have effect within 48 hours unless approved by the Secretary of State (s 46(4)) – could only be given if 'expedient for the prevention of acts of terrorism'.

The overuse of the foregoing stop and search powers was widely criticised, with 8,000–10,000 uses each month in 2008 being said by the government's independent reviewer of terrorist legislation to be 'alarming'.[99] They were also found (eventually) to breach Convention rights:

In *Gillan and Quinton* v *United Kingdom*, the House of Lords held that the exercise of this power against a student and a journalist at an arms fair in East London did not breach their Convention rights.[100] This was despite the fact that the Metropolitan Police had turned what were enacted as temporary powers into permanent powers, with each 28-day authorisation being renewed on its expiry, so that there was a rolling series of authorisations.

The European Court of Human Rights took a different view, holding that the s 44 powers violated the right to private life in art 8 of the ECHR, and that the arbitrary nature of the powers were such that they could not be said to be in accordance with law for the purposes of justification under art 8(2).[101] In the House of Lords in contrast, Lord Bingham had doubted whether 'an ordinary superficial search of the person can be said to show a lack of respect for private life'.

The offending provisions of the 2000 Act were duly repealed and replaced, by a more tightly drawn power the government presumably believes is consistent with its Convention obligations.[102] The replacement power provides that stop and search may be invoked by the authorisation of a senior police officer who (*a*) 'reasonably suspects that an act of terrorism will take place', and (*b*) 'reasonably considers' that the authorisation is 'necessary to prevent such an act'. There are tighter geographical and temporal factors now to be considered in

---

[97] [2016] EWCA Civ 6.
[98] See Anderson, *The Terrorism Acts in 2015*, above, paras 7.27–7.31.
[99] Lord Carlile, *Report on the Operation in 2008 of the Terrorism Act 2000 and of Part 1 of the Terrorism Act 2006* (2009), para 147.
[100] *R (Gillan)* v *Metropolitan Police Commissioner* [2006] UKHL 12, [2006] 2 AC 307.
[101] *Gillan and Quinton* v *United Kingdom* [2009] ECHR 28, (2010) 50 EHRR 45.
[102] Protection of Freedoms Act 2012, s 59.

making an authorisation, in the sense that the area covered must be no greater than necessary to prevent the suspected act of terrorism, while the duration of the authorisation must be no longer than necessary (s 47A(1)).

Once made, the authorisation empowers a constable in uniform to stop and search a vehicle, its driver and passengers, and anything else in the vehicle (s 47A(2)). Once made, an authorisation also enables a constable in uniform to stop and search a pedestrian, and to search anything the pedestrian may be carrying (s 47A(3)). In both cases, the replacement power retains an equivalent to the original legislation restricting the power of stop and search to 'be exercised only for the purpose of searching for articles of a kind which could be used in connection with terrorism' (s 47A(4)). Crucially, however, 'the power conferred by such an authorisation may be exercised whether or not the constable reasonably suspects that there is such evidence' (s 47A(5)).

It is thus the case that the 2012 amendments retain the power of random stop and search, which was perhaps the greatest departure in the Terrorism Act 2000, s 45 from what was referred to by Lord Brown in *Gillan* as 'our traditional understanding of the limits of police power'.[103] Further provisions relating to the exercise of the power of stop and search are to be found in the Terrorism Act 2000, Sch 6B, also introduced by the 2012 Act (s 61(2), Sch 5). This deals with the way in which the power is exercised (no removal of any clothing in public except for headgear, footwear, an outer coat, a jacket or gloves); and the obligation to provide a written statement relating to the exercise of the power (to be provided only on request within 12 months of the incident).

The replacement powers also provide that an authorisation is valid for up to 14 days, unlike the previous provisions by which the authorisation was valid for up to 28 days. Like the provisions it replaces, however, the new law provides for a power of renewal of an authorisation, provided the tighter grounds for invoking the power have been met. It ought also to be noted that consistently with the requirements of the replaced provisions, an authorisation by a senior police officer is valid for only 48 hours unless confirmed (with or without modifications) by the Home Secretary.

The original stop and search powers having been extensively used before *Gillan and Quinton*, the revised powers were never invoked in 2015.[104] The powers were not so necessary after all.

Terrorist offences

Part VI of the 2000 Act contains a number of offences designed to frustrate terrorist activity, beginning with section 54 which deals with 'weapons training'. Thus, it is an offence to provide or receive instruction or training in the making or use of firearms, radioactive material, explosives or chemical, biological or nuclear weapons. However, it is a defence if the accused can 'prove that his action or involvement was wholly for a purpose other than assisting, preparing for or participating in terrorism' (s 54(3)).

It is also an offence to direct the activities of an organisation which is concerned in the commission of acts of terrorism (s 56), and to possess any article for a purpose connected with the commission, preparation or instigation of acts of terrorism (s 57). It is a defence to prove that the article was not in the possession of the individual for a terrorist purpose, and while the burden of proof is on the defendant (s 57(2)), it has been said that this is 'evidential rather than persuasive or legal'.[105] Sufficient evidence of possession may be established where the accused and the article in question are both present on the premises (s 57(3)).[106]

---

[103] [2006] UKHL 12, [2006] 2 AC 307.

[104] Anderson, *The Terrorism Acts in 2015*, above, para 6.9.

[105] See HL Deb, 23 May 2000, col 754 (Lord Bassam). Sufficient evidence of possession may be established where the accused and the article in question are both present on the premises (s 57(3)).

[106] Compare *R v DPP, ex p Kebeline* [2000] 2 AC 326.

Moving on, sections 58 and 58A of the 2000 Act deal with intelligence gathering for terrorist purposes. The former – found not to violate Convention rights[107] – makes it an offence for a person to collect or record any information of a kind likely to be useful to a person committing or preparing an act of terrorism. The latter – inserted by the Counter-Terrorism Act 2008 – is designed to protect conspicuous high-risk potential targets of terrorist activity and is thus apparently unexceptionable.

The section 58A offence thus applies to conduct by the accused which elicits or attempts to elicit information about an individual who is or who has been a member of the armed forces, the intelligence services or the police. The offence is committed in respect of information of a kind that is likely to be useful to someone committing or preparing an act of terrorism. It is also an offence to publish or communicate such information.

One problem with s 58A is that it has emerged – perhaps unwittingly – as a serious threat to free speech, with journalists and photographers claiming that it was being used by the police to prevent them from taking photographs of police officers in particular. It would be unfortunate if the press were to be prevented by this or any other measure from photographing police officers while performing their duties, particularly where they are recording examples of excessive force.

Admittedly, section 58A(2) does provide that it is a 'defence for a person charged with an offence under this section to prove that they had a reasonable excuse for their action'. Nevertheless, this is a matter that attracted the attention of the government's independent reviewer of terrorist legislation, who expressed the following concern:

> It should be emphasised that photography of the police by the media or amateurs remains as legitimate as before, unless the photograph is *likely* to be of use to a terrorist. This is a high bar. It is inexcusable for police officers ever to use this provision to interfere with the rights of individuals to take photographs. The police must adjust to the undoubted fact that the scrutiny of them by members of the public is at least proportional to any increase in police powers – given the ubiquity of photograph and video enabled mobile phones.[108]

By virtue of s 59 it is an offence to incite terrorism overseas, a measure designed to 'deter those who use the United Kingdom as a base from which to promote terrorist acts abroad'.[109]

A number of other offences were created by the Terrorism Act 2006. Chief amongst those, not considered elsewhere in this text,[110] are those relating to preparing for terrorism and training for terrorism (ss 5, 6), all the more notable for the fact that they were made extra-territorial by the Serious Crimes Act 2015 (s 81), designed to deal with people who travel to Syria to engage in conduct caught by these provisions.[111]

D. Legislative responses to terrorism – detention without trial, control orders, TPIMs and secret justice

Detention without trial

One of the most symbolically important provisions of the Terrorism Act 2000 was the repeal of the provisions in the Northern Ireland (Emergency Provisions) Act 1996 dealing with the detention without trial – or internment – of terrorist suspects. Although the power to intern

---

[107] *Jobe v United Kingdom*, App No 48279/09, 14 June 2011.
[108] Lord Carlile, *Report on the Operation in 2008 of the Terrorism Act 2000 and of Part 1 of the Terrorism Act 2006* (2009), para 197.
[109] HC Deb, 14 Dec 1999, col 162.
[110] See pp 472–3 (encouragement to terrorism).
[111] Anderson, *The Terrorism Acts in 2015*, above, para 1.7.

was retained until the commencement of the 2000 Act,[112] it was in practice discontinued in 1975, having proved to be not only highly controversial but also of questionable effect.[113] In *Ireland* v *United Kingdom*,[114] the European Court of Human Rights held that these procedures violated art 5 of the ECHR, but that derogation could be justified under art 15.[115]

A fresh derogation was made to authorise new powers of detention without trial contained in Part 4 of the Anti-terrorism, Crime and Security Act 2001. These highly contentious measures provided that the Secretary of State could issue a certificate in respect of an individual whose presence in the United Kingdom was reasonably believed to present a risk to national security and who was reasonably suspected of being a terrorist (s 21(1)). A terrorist for this purpose was defined with reference to international terrorism (s 21(2)), and terrorism carried the same meaning for this Act as it did for the Terrorism Act 2000.

Where a certificate was issued that someone was a suspected international terrorist, the individual could be refused leave to enter or remain in the United Kingdom, or deported or removed in accordance with immigration law (s 22). But there might be circumstances where removal or deportation was prevented by 'a point of law which wholly or partly relates to an international agreement' or to 'a practical consideration' (s 23). An example of the former would be art 3 of the ECHR which – as construed by the Strasbourg Court – prevents the deportation of individuals to countries where they might suffer inhuman or degrading treatment or punishment.[116]

In these cases the 2001 Act provided that the suspected international terrorist could be detained indefinitely without trial (s 23). An appeal lay to the Special Immigration Appeals Commission by someone who had been certified as a suspected international terrorist (s 25) and the Commission was required to cancel a certificate if it concluded that there were no reasonable grounds for the suspicion. The Commission was required to review any certificate after six months and at three-monthly intervals thereafter.[117] There was an appeal on a point of law to the Court of Appeal or the Court of Session (s 27).[118]

In *A* v *Home Secretary*[119] these provisions relating to detention were dealt a fatal blow by the House of Lords. Proceedings were brought by nine foreign nationals who were being or who had been detained indefinitely without trial.[120] The Special Immigration Appeals Commission upheld the government's decision to derogate from the Convention but also granted a declaration that the legislation was incompatible with art 14 of the ECHR to the extent that it discriminated against foreign nationals. The government's appeal on this latter point was upheld by the Court of Appeal, but the declaration was reinstated by the House of Lords in a majority decision of 8-1.

---

[112] See HC Deb, 9 January 1996, col 37. Cf Cm 2706, 1995, p 33.

[113] For background, see Cm 1115, 1990. A full account of the procedures is given in *Ireland* v *UK* (1978) 2 EHRR 25.

[114] (1978) 2 EHRR 25.

[115] It was also held, however, that the techniques employed to interrogate interned suspects violated art 3 as inhuman and degrading treatment.

[116] See *Chahal* v *UK* (1996) 23 EHRR 413.

[117] A review could also be conducted at the request of the certified individual if the Commission considered that the review should be held because of a change of circumstances (s 26).

[118] By virtue of an amendment made by the 2001 Act, the Special Immigration Appeals Commission is now a superior court of record (s 27).

[119] [2004] UKHL 56, [2005] 2 AC 68. See A Tomkins [2005] PL 259; M Arden (2005) 121 LQR 604; M Elliott (2010) 8 *Int J of Const Law* 131.

[120] A number of detainees left the country, while several others were released either unconditionally or on bail, and another was transferred to Broadmoor hospital on mental health grounds.

The House of Lords agreed that there was a public emergency threatening the life of the nation, thereby justifying the derogation from art 5 of the Convention. But the House of Lords also concluded that the steps taken against foreign nationals were disproportionate and discriminatory. As a result, the derogation order was quashed.[121] Moreover, a declaration was issued under the Human Rights Act 1998 that s 23 of the 2001 Act was incompatible with art 5 and 14 of the ECHR, 'in so far as it is disproportionate and permits detention of suspected international terrorists in a way that discriminates on the ground of nationality or immigration status'.

The *A* case is a good example of the limitations of the Human Rights Act, in the sense that although declared incompatible with Convention rights, the offending provisions nevertheless remained on the statute book and in force. Equally, although the Convention rights of the individuals were clearly violated by their detention without trial, the House of Lords had no power to compensate them for the losses they suffered and continued to suffer. Sections 21–32 of the 2001 Act were not repealed until the Prevention of Terrorism Act 2005 was passed, and detainees were required to bring subsequent proceedings in the European Court of Human Rights to recover compensation for the violation of their Convention rights.[122]

Control orders

In removing the power of indefinite detention (albeit in a 'prison with three walls' – in the sense that the detainees were always free to leave the United Kingdom), the Prevention of Terrorism Act 2005 introduced new powers of executive restraint.[123] These were called control orders, with a control order being defined as 'an order against an individual that imposes obligations on him for purposes connected with protecting members of the public from a risk of terrorism' (s 1(1)).

The 2005 Act provided for two kinds of control orders: (i) non-derogating control orders made by the Home Secretary, which were not to impose obligations inconsistent with the individual's right to liberty under ECHR, art 5; and (ii) derogating control orders which could impose obligations inconsistent with art 5, made only by a court on an application by the Home Secretary. Before the power to make derogating control orders could be invoked, procedures set out in the 2005 Act, s 6 had first to be complied with.

But these latter powers were never invoked, so that only non-derogating control orders were ever made. This, however, was not a significant constraint, as there was wide scope for making non-derogating control orders, where 'necessary for purposes connected with preventing or restricting involvement by that individual in terrorism-related activity' (s 1(3)). The conditions that could be imposed on individuals merit careful reading. By virtue of s 1(4), they were as follows:

- a prohibition or restriction on his possession or use of specified articles or substances;

- a prohibition or restriction on his use of specified services or specified facilities, or on his carrying on specified activities;

- a restriction in respect of his work or other occupation, or in respect of his business;

---

[121] See subsequently SI 2005 No 1071.

[122] *A v United Kingdom* [2009] ECHR 301, (2009) 49 EHRR 29.

[123] The Bill was bitterly contested in Parliament and the government had to make a number of concessions to secure its passage. See J Hiebert (2005) 68 MLR 676.

- a restriction on his association or communications with specified persons or with other persons generally;

- a restriction in respect of his place of residence or on the persons to whom he gives access to his place of residence;

- a prohibition on his being at specified places or within a specified area at specified times or on specified days;

- a prohibition or restriction on his movements to, from or within the United Kingdom, a specified part of the United Kingdom or a specified place or area within the United Kingdom;

- a requirement on him to comply with such other prohibitions or restrictions on his movements as may be imposed, for a period not exceeding 24 hours, by directions given to him in the specified manner, by a specified person and for the purpose of securing compliance with other obligations imposed by or under the order;

- a requirement on him to surrender his passport, or anything in his possession to which a prohibition or restriction imposed by the order relates, to a specified person for a period not exceeding the period for which the order remains in force;

- a requirement on him to give access to specified persons to his place of residence or to other premises to which he has power to grant access;

- a requirement on him to allow specified persons to search that place or any such premises for the purpose of ascertaining whether obligations imposed by or under the order have been, are being or are about to be contravened;

- a requirement on him to allow specified persons, either for that purpose or for the purpose of securing that the order is complied with, to remove anything found in that place or on any such premises and to subject it to tests or to retain it for a period not exceeding the period for which the order remains in force;

- a requirement on him to allow himself to be photographed;

- a requirement on him to cooperate with specified arrangements for enabling his movements, communications or other activities to be monitored by electronic or other means;

- a requirement on him to comply with a demand made in the specified manner to provide information to a specified person in accordance with the demand;

- a requirement on him to report to a specified person at specified times and places.

These provisions were used to impose what has been described as a form of house arrest,[124] and questions were inevitably raised about whether the tight conditions imposed under ostensibly non-derogating control orders were consistent with Convention obligations.[125] This is a matter on which the House of Lords disagreed sharply, with Lord Brown occupying the middle ground in holding that a control order imposing detention at home for up to 16 hours a day is the maximum that could be imposed consistently with the right to liberty under art 5 of the ECHR.[126]

In *Home Secretary* v *AP*,[127] the person subject to a control order with a 16-hour detention requirement was subsequently required to live some 150 miles away from his family to avoid contact with 'radical elements'. The Supreme Court upheld a Divisional Court decision to quash this requirement, holding that restrictions on private life can be taken into account in determining that in exceptional cases the circumstances give rise to a violation

---

[124] For details (drawn from evidence to the JCHR), see K D Ewing and J-C Tham [2008] PL 668.

[125] For a sceptical view of whether the constraints on liberty under non-derogating orders were compatible with art 5, see HL Paper 122, HC 915 (2005–6) (Joint Committee on Human Rights).

[126] *Home Secretary* v *JJ* [2007] UKHL 45, [2008] AC 385.

[127] [2010] UKSC 24, [2011] 2 AC 1.

of ECHR, art 5. Control orders were abolished in 2011, following a commitment in the Coalition agreement 'urgently' to review the regime as part of a wider review of counter-terrorism legislation.

While the control order regime was perhaps less restrictive of liberty than indefinite detention in prison without trial, nevertheless more people were the subject of control orders than were ever detained under the 2001 Act, the control order regime – unlike the detention regime – applying equally to British nationals as to the nationals of other countries.[128]

Terrorism protection and investigation measures

Although control orders have been abolished, the Terrorism Protection and Investigation Measures Act 2011 reintroduced provisions very similar, though not quite as restrictive. Under the replacement provisions the Secretary of State may issue a notice of terrorism protection and investigation measures (a 'TPIM notice'), provided conditions A to E in section 3 are met. These are respectively that:

- the Secretary of State is satisfied on the balance of probabilities that the individual is, or has been, involved in terrorism-related activity (the 'relevant activity') (Condition A);
- some or all of the relevant activity is new terrorism-related activity (Condition B);
- the Secretary of State reasonably considers that it is necessary, for purposes connected with protecting members of the public from a risk of terrorism, for TPIMs to be imposed on the individual (Condition C);
- the Secretary of State reasonably considers that it is necessary, for purposes connected with preventing or restricting the individual's involvement in terrorism-related activity, for the specified TPIMs to be imposed on the individual (Condition D);
- a court gives the Secretary of State permission to impose a TPIM notice, unless he or she reasonably considers that on grounds of urgency TPIMs should be imposed without such permission (Condition E).

TPIM notices may be imposed for a period of up to a year, though they may be renewed by the Home Secretary (on one occasion only), provided that conditions A, C and D above are met. The normal procedure for the imposition of a TPIM is for an application to be made by the Home Secretary to the High Court, which must consider whether any decisions of the minister relating to the application are 'obviously flawed',[129] and whether to grant permission for the measures to be imposed on the individual. It is expressly provided that the court may consider the application in the absence of the individual; without the individual having been notified of the application; and without the individual having been given an opportunity of making any representations to the court (s 6(4)).

It is then provided that in determining an application for a TPIM, 'the court must apply the principles applicable on an application for judicial review' (s 6(6)), having just enacted that the proceedings can be conducted in breach of one of these principles, namely the requirement of procedural propriety. Although an application may be granted only if the court concludes that the Home Secretary's decisions in relation to Conditions A, B and C are not 'obviously flawed', nevertheless a finding that a decision in relation to Condition D is obviously flawed does not mean that the

---

[128] A total of 18 orders had been made in the first year of the scheme's operation. Of these, 11 were made against people who had been detained under the 2001 Act, but nine of these were removed after five-and-a-half months when the individuals in question were served with notice of intention to deport. By the end of 2010, a total of 48 people had been the subject of a control order. For details, see Lord Carlile, *Sixth Report of the Independent Reviewer Pursuant to Section 14(3) of the Prevention of Terrorism Act 2005* (2010), para 15.

[129] Specifically, the decisions relating to Conditions A, B, C and D.

application cannot be granted, with the court empowered to give directions to the Home Secretary about the measures to be imposed on the individual (s 6(10)).

Although a TPIM notice may thus be issued in the absence of the respondent, provision is made for the review of such notices by a court in the presence of the respondent, this to be held 'as soon as reasonably practicable' (s 8). The purpose is to review the decisions of the Home Secretary that 'the relevant conditions were met and continue to be met' (s 9(1)). In performing this role, the court must again comply with the principles of judicial review (s 9(2)), and in doing so may quash the TPIM notice; quash measures specified in the TPIM notice; or give directions to the Home Secretary in relation to the revocation of the TPIM notice, or the variation of measures specified therein (s 9(5)).

Otherwise, the court must decide that the notice is to continue in force (s 9(6)). These powers may be exercised only after the Home Secretary has consulted the police about the possibility of criminal charges being brought against a person in respect of whom TPIM measures are contemplated (s 10). Where a TPIM notice is issued, the police should be informed by the Home Secretary, and steps should be taken by the police to 'secure that the investigation of the individual's conduct, with a view to a prosecution of the individual for an offence relating to terrorism, is kept under review throughout the period the TPIM notice is in force' (s 10(5)(a)).

Although the 2011 Act includes ostensibly more robust safeguards for the individual than the control order regime it replaced, no one should be under any illusions about the substance of the powers conferred on the minister. The 14 categories of restraint provided for in the Act relate to what are referred to as overnight residence measures, travel measures, exclusion measures, movement directions measures, financial services measures, property measures, weapons and explosive measures, electronic communication device measures, association measures, work or study measures, reporting measures, appointments measures, photography measures, and monitoring measures. These are largely self-explanatory, though a fair amount of detail relating to the scope of each is provided for in the Act.[130]

It would not be appropriate necessarily to apply all of these measures to everyone who is the subject of a TPIM notice: to do so would be a violation of Condition D and would invite more carefully targeted measures being imposed by the High Court (though of course it is always open to a minister to test the court by taking measures greater than might be required by the circumstances). But they are nonetheless formidable powers,[131] which are in addition to existing powers (such as prerogative powers to cancel passports), which are unaffected by the TPIM regime.[132]

Special advocates and secret trials

Returning to the now replaced non-derogating control order regime, these were also made by the Home Secretary with the permission of a High Court judge, which usually had to be granted before the control order was made (2005 Act, s 3(1)(a)). In urgent cases (or in the case of the people who had been detained under the repealed provisions of the 2001 Act), such permission was not required, though all control orders in these cases had to be referred immediately to the High Court for confirmation (s 3(1)(b), (c)). Confirmation

---

[130] The 2011 Act was amended by the Counter-Terrorism and Security Act 2015, increasing the number of categories to 14 from 12.

[131] D Anderson, *Report on Terrorism Prevention and Investigation Measures Act 2011 in 2012 (2013)*, where it is reported that ten men were subject to TPIMs, none of whom were British citizens. It was reported in 2016 that there were six people subject to TPIMs, all but one of whom were British. This was said to mark a revival in use which had declined after 2013 with only one or two people being subject to such orders annually: *The Guardian*, 20 October 2016.

[132] *R (XH)* v *Home Secretary* [2017] EWCA Civ 41, [2017] 2 WLR 1437

could be refused where the Home Secretary's decision to make a control order had been 'obviously flawed' (s 3(3)(b)).

Although the government was thus required by political pressure to provide for judicial involvement in the control order system, the proceedings were nevertheless conducted largely in secret, in order to prevent the disclosure of evidence that would be contrary to the public interest. Much of the evidence against an individual who was the subject of a control order would be based on intelligence reports, the releasing of which (even to the subject of the control order) might reveal details about the work of the security and intelligence services or the identity of informers that the government would rather keep quiet.

Under the Civil Procedure Rules governing control order cases, the subject of a control order could be (i) excluded from part of the proceedings; (ii) denied access to all the evidence being used against him or her; and (iii) be refused a copy of the full decision of the Court if the public interest so required.[133] It is true that a Special Advocate could be appointed to represent his or her interests before the court, but this would be a person not chosen by the person subject to a control order, and in any event there were restrictions in the procedural rules on the ability of the Special Advocate to communicate with the controlled person or his or her legal representative.[134]

This curious procedure was nevertheless upheld by the House of Lords (again divided), which rejected a challenge that the procedure violated ECHR, art 6, with Baroness Hale taking the view that it would be possible for the courts to provide the controlled person with sufficient procedural protection.[135] Following the decision of the Strasbourg court in the *A* case,[136] the House of Lords (sitting as a bench of nine) subsequently held that the Civil Procedure Rules were to be read in such a way as to ensure that the controlled person has 'sufficient information about the allegations against him to give effective instructions to the Special Advocate'.[137]

In light of the foregoing, it is thus not surprising that similar procedural measures apply to applications for TPIMs as they did for control orders. With the authority of the 2011 Act above, the Civil Procedure Rules make similar if not identical provision for (i) the making of anonymity orders, (ii) the holding of hearings in private, (iii) the withholding of evidence from the respondent and his or her legal representatives ('closed material'), (iv) the appointment of a special advocate, (v) prohibiting the special advocate from communicating with the respondent and his or her legal representatives, and (vi) withholding reasons from the respondent.[138]

E. Legislative responses to terrorism – travel restrictions and preventative measures

Seizure of travel documents

A prominent feature of government concerns has been the travel of British citizens to conflict zones allegedly to engage with forces hostile to the United Kingdom, and in some cases allegedly plotting terrorist activity in the United Kingdom. An obvious way to address these concerns is to restrict the right of British citizens to travel to conflict zones in the first place, with the government having the power under the prerogative to withdraw a passport for an

---

[133] For a discussion, see Ewing, *Bonfire of the Liberties*, ch 7.
[134] On the rise and spread of the special advocate, see J Ip [2008] PL 717.
[135] *MB and AF* v *Home Secretary* [2007] UKHL 46, [2007] 3 WLR 681. See K D Ewing and J-C Tham, above.
[136] *A* v *United Kingdom*, above.
[137] *Home Secretary* v *AF* [2009] UKHL 28, [2009] 3 All ER 643, at para 81 (Lord Hope).
[138] CPR, Part 80.

indefinite period, as in the case of the individuals whose passports were cancelled to prevent them travelling to Syria, where it was suspected they would engage in terrorist activity.[139]

The Counter-Terrorism and Security Act 2015 confers extensive new powers for police officers at ports and airports in relation to people who are suspected of being there (*a*) 'with the intention of leaving Great Britain for the purpose of involvement in terrorism-related activity outside the United Kingdom', or (*b*) have 'arrived in Great Britain with the intention of leaving it soon for that purpose' (Sch 1(2)).[140] Where a constable suspects that an individual has any such purpose, he or she may require the individual in question to hand over all travel documents. It is an offence to fail to do so (Sch 1(15)), though the constable may otherwise search for, inspect and retain all such documents (Sch 2(7))).[141]

These are significant powers, which are widely defined: travel documents for example include not only passports and tickets, but also the passports of any country or territory outside the United Kingdom (the power to confiscate which would not be governed by the prerogative) (Sch 1(6) – definition of travel documents).[142] Once exercised, a senior police officer may then authorize the retention of the documents, while (i) the Home Secretary considers whether to cancel the passport (in the case of a British passport holder),[143] (ii) consideration is given to the possibility of criminal proceedings, or (iii) consideration is given to the imposition of other measures on the individual in question (Sch 1(5)).[144]

The authorities may retain documents for these purposes initially for 14 days (during which time a review must take place after 72 hours) (Sch 1(5)(2)), which may be extended for up to 30 days (from the time the documents were seized) with the authority of a District Judge (Magistrates Court) or a Sheriff (Sch 1(8)). The individual whose documents were seized has the right to be present at the judicial hearing and to make representations (Sch 1(9)(1), though the court has the power to exclude both the individual and his or her legal representatives (Sch 1(9)(3)).[145] There is no power to detain the individual while inquiries are being conducted, though the 30-day extension must be granted if the authorities are acting 'diligently and expeditiously' (Sch 1(8)(4)).

No provision is made to compensate as of right anyone who is inconvenienced by the exercise of these powers, even where the suspicion is ill-founded.[146]

Temporary exclusion orders

The foregoing powers are designed to prevent people leaving the United Kingdom to engage in terrorist activity elsewhere. The new power of the Home Secretary to impose temporary

[139] *R (XH)* v *Home Secretary* [2017] EWCA Civ 41, [2017] 2 WLR 1437.

[140] See J. Blackbourn and C. Walker (2016) 79 MLR 840. Other travel restrictions are to be found in the Counter-Terrorism Act 2008, s 58: those convicted of a terrorist offence may be required to register with the police and be subject to travel restrictions.

[141] The search may be carried out by a designated customs or immigration officer.

[142] Although the powers are exercisable by 'constables', the use of the powers is likely to be intelligence led, used against individuals who have been under close surveillance, with the 'constable' being the last in the chain of command. On MI5/police co-operation in a different context but relating to travel, see *Miranda* v *Home Office* [2016] EWCA Civ 6.

[143] This is a notable example of statutory and prerogative powers operating in a complementary manner.

[144] See also Home Office, *Code of Practice for Officers Exercising Functions under Schedule 1 of the Counter-Terrorism and Security Act 2015 in Connection with Seizing and Retaining Travel Documents* (2015).

[145] Specified information may also be withheld on a wide range of grounds from the individual who is the subject of the proceedings (Sch 1(10)).

[146] The JCHR had recommended that compensation should be recoverable: HL Paper 86, HC 859 (2014–15) (Joint Committee on Human Rights). The minister does, however, have the power to 'make whatever arrangements he or she thinks appropriate in relation to the person . . . on the relevant period coming to an end' (Sch 1(14)).

exclusion orders is designed to prevent people from travelling to the United Kingdom where there is a fear that they may engage in terrorist activity here. These powers may be exercised where five statutory conditions are met, of which the most important are the first two, namely that the Home Secretary reasonably

- suspects that the individual has been engaged in terrorist-related activity outside the United Kingdom; and
- considers that it is necessary for 'purposes connected with protecting members of the public in the United Kingdom' from a 'risk of terrorism'.

The third condition is that the individual is outside the United Kingdom, and the fourth is that he or she has a right of abode in the United Kingdom, which would appear to include British citizens as well as others who have close family in the United Kingdom. The final and crucial condition is that a court has given permission for the imposition of a TEO, except in cases of urgency where the approval may be given after the event (s 2). The court may consider the matter in the absence of the individual in question, and is expected to apply the principles of judicial review, though to the lower standards by asking whether any decision of the minister is 'obviously flawed' (s 3).

The substantive and procedural standards are thus very low, with only the Secretary of State having a right of appeal (s 2(9)). The order comes into force when the excluded person is notified and is informed also of the procedures for seeking a permit to return to the United Kingdom under s 6 of the 2015 Act. Valid for two years unless revoked by the Home Secretary (s 4(3)), the temporary exclusion order is renewable. (s 4(8)).[147] While a temporary exclusion order is in force, the excluded person's British passport is invalid (s 4(9)), though as already indicated, a person subject to such an order may be granted a permit to return (s 5), an arrangement which previously operated informally when passports expired and were not renewed.

A permit to return will only be granted if conditions specified in the permit are met (relating mainly to travel arrangements) (s 5(2)). Given the reasons for making a temporary exclusion order, a person granted a permit to return is likely to be of interest to the police and to be at real risk of prosecution.[148] The granting of a permit to return can be made conditional on an interview with a police officer or immigration official (presumably in a third country) (s 6(2)). In some cases, however, the Home Secretary must issue such a permit without a request having been made, as where he or she 'considers' that the individual in question is to be deported to the United Kingdom, or where for reasons of urgency it is expedient to do so (s 7).

Prevent

In addition to the ever-growing array of coercive preventive measures such as TPIMs and travel bans on the one hand, and specifically targeted terrorist offences on the other, a third strategy in response to recent terrorist activity is the government's so called 'Prevent strategy'.[149] The Counter-Terrorism and Security Act 2015 contains statutory measures integral to what is an otherwise administrative process, addressed principally to a number of public sector institutions (notably local authorities; the prison service; schools, colleges and universities; NHS bodies; and the police),[150] with a view to preventing mainly young people being drawn to the terrorist cause.

---

[147] It is also revocable: s 4(4).
[148] As it is, a person who returns on a permit may be subject to TPIM like restrictions (s 9).
[149] For background, see Cm 8092, 2011.
[150] The authorities to which the Act applies are set out in Sch 6.

These latter bodies are required in the exercise of their functions to 'have due regard to the need to prevent people from being drawn into terrorism' (s 26). To this end the Home Secretary is empowered to 'issue guidance to specified authorities about the exercise of their duty', the nature of which may vary according to the type of body to whom the guidance is addressed (s 29). By clumsy legislative drafting, the guidance need not be approved by Parliament, though the date from which it takes effect must be set out in a statutory instrument, which must be laid before Parliament in draft (s 29(5)). Six different guidance documents have now been issued.[151]

The foregoing are serious obligations, by which the State intrudes deeply into the autonomy of higher education institutions in particular. In addition to the power to provide guidance, the appropriate minister may give directions to any authority which is not carrying out its duties under s 26 (s 30), directions which may be enforced by a mandatory judicial order on an application by the minister (s 30(2)). As we discussed in Chapter 18 above, in the case of higher education institutions the exercise of these powers is constrained by a need on the part of the institution in the case of s 26 and the minister in the case of ss 29 and 30 to have regard to freedom of speech on the one hand, and academic freedom on the other (s 31(2)).[152]

Otherwise, additional powers exist uniquely in relation to universities and other further education bodies in the sense that they are subject to monitoring by the Secretary of State or someone designated by him or her (s 32), which in the case of the universities is the Higher Education Funding Council. Under the 2015 Act these institutions must give to the monitoring authority any information that the monitoring authority may require for the purposes of monitoring that body's performance in discharging the duty imposed by section 26(1)' (s 32(2)). This is a duty enforceable by a direction from the minister, and ultimately a court order (s 33).

Universities report annually to Higher Education Funding Council (Hefce) about compliance.

Prevent, the rule of law and universities

The government's guidance (which generally leaves much to be desired) curiously states that s 26 does not impose any new functions on specified authorities,[153] though surely it creates the function of complying with the duty. The scope of that duty is widened by an administrative sleight of hand with the legislation defining terrorism for the purposes of s 26 consistently with the Terrorism Act 2000, s 1,[154] whereas the guidance extends this to include extremism. The latter is defined in turn, without any reference to statutory authority, to mean 'vocal or active opposition to fundamental British values, including democracy, the rule of law, individual liberty and mutual respect and tolerance for those with different faiths and beliefs'.[155]

---

[151] Two of these are general documents, and four are directed specifically to universities and further education institutions respectively.

[152] It is expressly provided that 'the duty to ensure freedom of speech' means the duty imposed by s 43(1) of the Education (No 2) Act 1986; and that 'academic freedom' means the freedom referred to in s 202(2)(a) of the Education Reform Act 1988' (s 31(5)). If nothing else, the 2015 Act gives visibility to the latter provision, which seems largely to be unknown.

[153] HM Government, *Revised Prevent Duty Guidelines for England and Wales* (2015), para 4.

[154] Counter-Terrorism and Security Act 2015, s 35.

[155] HM Government, *Revised Prevent Duty Guidelines*, above, para 7. For these purposes, extremism is not confined to violent extremism: 'RHEBs will be expected to carry out a risk assessment for their institution which assesses where and how their students might be at risk of being drawn into terrorism. This includes not just violent extremism but also non-violent extremism, which can create an atmosphere conducive to terrorism and can popularise views which terrorists exploit': HM Government, *Prevent Duty Guidance for Higher Education Institutions in England and Wales* (2015), para 19. RHEB is the acronym for Relevant Higher Education Bodies, which universities have now become.

This is both a defence of the rule of law as well as a threat to it. Wide though it is, there is (wisely) no reference in the statutory definition of terrorism to 'British values', 'democracy', or 'the rule of law', all highly contestable ideas, which like subversion in an earlier era can be twisted to suit the interests of government.[156] If this approach had been adopted in the past, would universities have been required to exclude Chartists, suffragettes and communists? And today – to take randomly a live issue at the time of writing – does it mean that Catalan independence supporters are 'extremists', in view of reported decisions of the Spanish courts that the demands for self-determination are 'unconstitutional'?

Apart from the casual administrative extension of the definition of terrorism for these purposes, the other notable feature about the guidance is the level of surveillance of students and others that seems to be required, to say nothing of the level of monitoring of universities, as is laid bare on the Hefce website. Thus, the guidance states that 'Prevent work depends on effective partnership'.[157] and that 'to demonstrate effective compliance with the duty, specified authorities must demonstrate evidence of productive co-operation, in particular with local Prevent co-ordinators, the police and local authorities, and co-ordination through existing multi-agency forums, for example Community Safety Partnerships'.[158]

So Hefce proudly reports as a positive case study that the 'university's Prevent lead is also an active member of the local Counter-Terrorism Strategy (CONTEST) Board'.[159] Moreover, the Home Office (which effectively runs the programme) 'expects' what it refers to as 'active engagement from senior management of the university (including, where appropriate, vice chancellors) with other partners including police and [BEIS] regional higher and further education'.[160] While 'the *Prevent* programme must not involve any covert activity against people or communities',[161] specified authorities nevertheless 'may need to share personal information'.[162]

It is true of course that all of this is coloured by the statutory obligation (s 31) to have regard to academic freedom and freedom of speech. But the fact that these matters need expressly to be addressed is itself an acknowledgement of the threat that this programme otherwise presents.[163].

F. Emergency powers

Emergency powers in the First World War

Before the mid-19th century it was the practice in times of national danger to pass what were often known as Habeas Corpus Suspension Acts.[164] Such Acts took various forms. Some prevented the use of habeas corpus for securing speedy trial or the right to bail in the case of persons charged with treason or other offences. Others conferred wide powers of arrest and detention which would not normally have been acceptable. After the danger was over, it was

---

[156] On which see Lustgarten and Leigh, *In from the Cold*, pp 395–410.
[157] HM Government, *Revised Prevent Duty Guidelines*, above, para 17.
[158] Ibid.
[159] On the Hefce webpage 'Monitoring the Prevent Duty', and then the 'effective practice hub'.
[160] HM Government, *Prevent Duty Guidance for Higher Education Institutions*, above, para 12.
[161] HM Government, *Revised Prevent Duty Guidelines*, above, para 21.
[162] Ibid. See also HM Government, *Prevent Duty Guidance for Higher Education Institutions*, above, para 10: 'Where appropriate and legal to do so, an institution should also have procedures in place for the sharing of information about speakers with other institutions and partners.'
[163] The guidance is also woefully short of detail about what draws people into terrorism or what it means to be radicalised. For a powerful argument that universities should be removed from these provisions, see HL Paper 86, HC 859 (2014–15) (Joint Committee on Human Rights).

often the practice to pass an Indemnity Act to protect officials retrospectively from liability for illegal acts which they might have committed.

During the two world wars, however, habeas corpus was not suspended but extremely wide powers were conferred on the executive. The Defence of the Realm Acts 1914–15 empowered the Crown to make regulations by Order in Council for securing public safety or for the defence of the realm.[165] In *R v Halliday, ex p Zadig*, the House of Lords held that this general power was wide enough to support a regulation authorising the Secretary of State to detain persons without trial on the grounds of their hostile origins or associations.[166] In a powerful and memorable dissent, Lord Shaw of Dunfermline declined to infer from the delegation of a general power to make regulations for public safety and defence the right to authorise the detention of a man without trial and without being accused of any offence.

Although the powers of the executive were wide, it was still possible to challenge defence regulations in the courts.

In *Attorney-General v Wilts United Dairies Ltd*,[167] an attempt by the Food Controller to impose a charge of two pence a gallon as a condition of issuing licences for the supply of milk was held invalid, on the ground that the Food Controller's power under defence regulations to regulate the supply of milk did not confer power to impose charges upon the subject. Doubt was also expressed whether a regulation conferring such a power would have been within the general power to make regulations for the public safety or the defence of the realm.

In *Chester v Bateson*[168] a defence regulation empowered the Minister of Munitions to declare an area in which munitions were manufactured to be a special area. The intended effect of such a declaration was to prevent any person without the consent of the minister from taking proceedings to recover possession of any dwelling-house in the area, if a munitions worker was living in it and duly paying rent. It was held that Parliament had not deliberately deprived the citizen of access to the courts and that the regulation was invalid, since it could not be shown to be a necessary or even reasonable way of securing the public safety or the defence of the realm.

Such decisions explain the passing after the war of the wide Indemnity Act 1920 and a separate Act relating to illegal charges, the War Charges Validity Act 1925.

Emergency powers in the Second World War

Following the declaration of the Second World War, the Emergency Powers (Defence) Act 1939 empowered the making of regulations by Order in Council which appeared necessary or expedient for the public safety, the defence of the realm, the maintenance of public order, the efficient prosecution of any war in which His Majesty might be engaged and the maintenance of supplies and services essential for the life of the community. There followed a list of particular purposes for which regulations could be made, including the detention of persons in

---

[164] Dicey, *The Law of the Constitution*, pp 229–37.
[165] For a fascinating account of these powers and their operation, see Rubin, *Private Property, Government Requisition and the Constitution, 1914–1927*. See also Ewing and Gearty, *The Struggle for Civil Liberties*, ch 2.
[166] [1917] AC 260. See D Foxton (2003) 119 LQR 455.
[167] (1921) 37 TLR 884.
[168] [1920] 1 KB 829.

the interests of public safety or the defence of the realm. To avoid another *Wilts United Dairies* case, the Treasury was empowered to impose charges in connection with any scheme of control under Defence Regulations.[169]

Provision was made for laying regulations before Parliament after they were made, and for their annulment by negative resolution within 28 days.[170] Compulsory military service was imposed by separate National Service Acts, and compulsory direction of labour to essential war work was authorised by the Emergency Powers (Defence) (No 2) Act 1940. Although access to the courts was not barred, the scope for judicial review of executive action was limited. Thus the courts could not consider whether a particular regulation was necessary or expedient for the purposes of the Act which authorised it.[171] The courts could, however, hold an act to be illegal as being not authorised by the regulation relied on to justify it.[172]

Special problems of judicial control arose in relation to the power of the executive to authorise detention without trial in the interests of public safety or the defence of the realm. Under Defence Regulation 18 B, the Home Secretary was empowered to detain those whom he had reasonable cause to believe came within specified categories (including persons of hostile origin or association) and over whom it was necessary to exercise control. Persons detained could make objections to an advisory committee appointed by the Home Secretary. The Home Secretary had to report monthly to Parliament on the number of persons detained and the number of cases in which he had not followed the advice of the committee.

It was open to a detainee to apply for habeas corpus, but such applications had little chance of success in view of the decision of the House of Lords in *Liversidge* v *Anderson*.[173]

> Despite a powerful dissenting judgment by Lord Atkin, in that case the House took the view that the power to detain could not be controlled by the courts, if only because considerations of security forbade proof of the evidence on which detention was ordered. The words 'had reasonable cause to believe' only meant that the Home Secretary must have a belief which in his mind was reasonable. The courts would not inquire into the grounds for his belief, although apparently they might examine positive evidence of mala fides or mistaken identity.[174] Stress was laid on the responsibility of the Home Secretary to Parliament.

In only one case did a person who had been detained under the regulation secure his release by habeas corpus proceedings, the individual in question having been wrongly informed of the reason for his detention.[175]

---

[169] Treasury regulations imposing charges required confirmation by an affirmative resolution of the House of Commons.

[170] On parliamentary control of delegated legislation, see generally ch 22.

[171] *R* v *Comptroller-General of Patents, ex p Bayer Products* [1941] 2 KB 306. See also *Pollok School* v *Glasgow Town Clerk* 1946 SC 373.

[172] *Fowler, John, & Co (Leeds) Ltd* v *Duncan* [1941] Ch 450.

[173] [1942] AC 206; and see C K Allen (1942) 58 LQR 232 and R F V Heuston (1970) 86 LQR 33.

[174] Lord Wright, at p 261. The majority decision in *Liversidge* v *Anderson* cannot now be relied on as an authority, either on the point of construction or in its declaration of legal principle: *R* v *Home Secretary, ex p Khawaja* [1984] AC 74, at p 110 (Lord Scarman), and see *Ridge* v *Baldwin* [1964] AC 40, at p 73 (Lord Reid).

[175] *R* v *Home Secretary, ex p Budd* [1942] 2 KB 14. The Divisional Court ordered Budd's release, but the Home Secretary thereupon made a new order for his detention. On Regulation 18B generally, see Simpson, *In the Highest Degree Odious*.

Emergency powers in peace-time

A distinguishing feature of the war-time powers described above is that they were ad hoc measures, repealed shortly after the wars ended. Emergencies of different kinds may arise in peace-time. Until quite recently the concern of governments was with the consequences of large-scale industrial action organised by trade unions, which might disrupt the supply of essential services. It was for this reason that provision was made in the Emergency Powers Act 1920 for declarations of a state of emergency and the making of emergency regulations.[176] These powers applied where there were events of such a nature as to deprive the community or a substantial part of the community of the essentials of life.

Although designed principally to deal with industrial action, the Emergency Powers Act 1920 was also capable of being used where an emergency was caused in other ways, such as natural disaster or a serious nuclear accident.[177] In practice, however, the Act was used only in response to strikes by coalminers, dockers and power workers, and was last used in 1974. In all it was used on 12 occasions,[178] and it has now been repealed with new emergency powers to be found in Part II of the Civil Contingencies Act 2004, an altogether much more wide-ranging measure. The 2004 Act extends the circumstances in which emergency powers may be used.

An emergency is now defined to mean an event or situation that threatens human welfare, the environment, or the security of the United Kingdom (s 19). These terms are widely defined to include matters such as loss of life and damage to property; contamination of land, water or air and flooding; and war and terrorism. As a result, it ought not to be necessary for governments to take additional ad hoc powers to deal with war should such an event arise, though equally the taking of such powers would hardly be a surprise. Unlike the 1920 Act, the 2004 Act's emergency powers can be invoked without a state of emergency being declared and without the need to invoke the Act being considered by Parliament.

There will, however, be an opportunity for Parliament to consider the emergency regulations which are made by the government to deal with the emergency (s 20). These regulations may be made by the Queen in Council (s 20(1)), but in some circumstances it may be possible for the regulations to be made by a senior minister, defined to include the Prime Minister, Foreign Secretary, Home Secretary and Chancellor of the Exchequer (s 20(2)). Regulations may be made where it is necessary to prevent, control or mitigate the effect of the emergency, provided the measures in question are in 'due proportion' to the situation they are designed to address (s 21). The power to make regulations under the 2004 Act has yet to be invoked.

Emergency powers and emergency regulations

The emergency regulations may be made for a wide range of purposes, such as protecting human life, health and safety, and protecting or restoring property (s 22). There are in fact no fewer than 12 purposes for which the regulations may be made. In addressing these purposes, extensive powers may be taken in the regulations. These include the requisition or destruction of property (with or without compensation), and prohibiting freedom of movement or freedom of assembly (s 22(3)). Some of the powers are vague and open-ended, such as the power to prohibit 'other specified activities' (s 22(3)(h)).[179]

Also wide is the power to confer jurisdiction on a court or tribunal (including a court or tribunal established by the regulations) (s 22(3)(n)). Other powers relate to the deployment

---

[176] See Ewing and Gearty, *The Struggle for Civil Liberties*, chs 2 and 4.
[177] See HC Deb, 14 February 1996, col 629 (WA).
[178] For a full account, see Morris, *Strikes in Essential Services*; also G S Morris [1980] PL 317 and C Whelan (1979) 8 ILJ 222.
[179] Defined in turn to mean 'specified by, or to be specified in accordance with, the regulations': s 22(4).

of the armed forces (s 22(3)(l)). But emergency regulations may not impose military conscription or prohibit strikes or other industrial action (s 23(3)). There are also limits on the power to create criminal offences by emergency regulations, on the penalties that may be imposed for such offences, and on the ability to alter criminal procedure (s 23(4)). All such offences must be tried in the magistrates' court in England and Wales or in the Sheriff Court in Scotland (s 23(4)).

The emergency regulations may apply without parliamentary approval for up to seven days, but lapse thereafter if such approval is not forthcoming (s 27). They may be amended by Parliament (s 27(3)). Once approved, the regulations are valid for 30 days unless revoked (s 26), but they may be renewed for further periods of up to 30 days (s 27(4)). The emergency regulations will not apply to Scotland or Wales unless the First Minister or the Welsh Assembly respectively has been consulted (s 29). Once made, the regulations may be subject to judicial review, including under the Human Rights Act.

The government had originally proposed that emergency regulations should have the status of primary legislation in what appeared as an attempt to limit the scope for judicial review. According to the Joint Committee established to consider the draft Bill, however, there was no need to exclude human rights protection in this way, given that the judges are not overly activist in dealing with challenges to emergency powers, and are unlikely to prevent government taking action to protect public safety.[180] The government accepted these criticisms and the Bill was amended so that emergency regulations are to be treated as what they are, namely secondary legislation for the purposes of the Human Rights Act.

G. Conclusion

It should thus be clear that there is a wide range of special and emergency powers available to the government and law enforcement agencies, starting with the use of the troops to assist the civil power, through to the special powers taken to deal with terrorism, through to the taking of more serious emergency powers, to the introduction of martial law. It has not been necessary in modern times to contemplate taking steps at the latter end of the continuum, though martial law was declared in Ireland in the early 20th century at a time when it was part of the United Kingdom.[181]

The main change that has taken place in this field, however, has been the normalisation of special powers to deal with terrorism. These were powers that started as emergency powers, which have not only gradually expanded but have also become permanent. The response to terrorism has thus been at a considerable cost to traditional liberties formally protected by the common law, the ECHR, and the Human Rights Act, and a constant challenge to the rule of law, the preservation of which is often their justification. Freedoms lost are rarely recovered.

We have seen measures which compromise in varying degrees of severity the right to liberty (art 5), the right to a fair trial (art 6), the right to privacy (art 8), the right to freedom of expression (art 10), and the right to freedom of association (art 11), as well as the right to private property (First Protocol, art 1). It has also led to permanent changes to the criminal justice system, for although the special provisions of the Terrorism Act 2000 (Part VII) relating to Northern Ireland have lapsed,[182] key provisions have been re-enacted in another form, albeit with modifications.[183]

[180] HL Paper 184, HC 1074 (2002–3), para 149.
[181] For a fuller account of what has been a static area of the law for almost 100 years, see the 16th edition of this text, pp 561–5.
[182] See the 14th edition of this text, pp 646–9, for an account of these measures.
[183] Justice and Security (Northern Ireland) Act 2007.

Yet the foregoing measures by no means exhaust the restraints that have been introduced since 9/11 in particular, with further restrictions on freedom of expression,[184] and the additional restraints on private property.[185] Other departures from standard practice include the provisions authorising the post-charge questioning of terrorist suspects,[186] the requirement that those convicted of a terrorist offence register with the police (under notification procedures),[187] and the growing range of measures restricting foreign travel, which were considered but rejected during the Cold War.[188]

As was pointed out in the introduction to this chapter, the ever-expanding scope of these powers requires judicial vigilance both as to the powers themselves and the manner of their exercise. It is a matter of fierce academic debate about just how vigilant the courts have been, as the number of unsuccessful legal challenges appear to grow. But so long as terrorist atrocities continue to cause death and serious injury, there are few who would be prepared to criticize the courts for any failure to push the boundaries of human rights to their limits.

---

[184] See pp 564–5. above.
[185] See Counter-Terrorism Act 2008, ss 62–73, and Terrorist Asset-Freezing etc Act 2010.
[186] Counter-Terrorism Act 2008, s 22.
[187] Ibid, ss 40–61.
[188] Ibid, s 58. See also pp 571–3, above.

PART IV

Administrative law

CHAPTER 21

What is administrative law?

The role of the courts in securing judicial review of the decisions of public authorities is a feature of government in the United Kingdom of great constitutional significance. This significance has increased during the last 25 years, both because of the number of cases coming to the courts[1] and the content of the leading cases. This may be why judicial review is sometimes thought to be the only part of administrative law that lawyers need to know. But this is no more correct than to say that employment lawyers need study only the law of unfair dismissal or tort lawyers the law of negligence. Certainly, the law of judicial review, outlined in Chapters 24 and 25, is a vital part of administrative law, but the part must not be mistaken for the whole.

A formal definition of administrative law is that it is a branch of public law concerned with the composition, procedures, powers, duties, rights and liabilities of the various organs of government that are engaged in administering public policies. These policies are either laid down by Parliament in legislation or developed by the government and other authorities in the exercise of their executive powers. On this approach, administrative law includes at one end the principles and institutions of constitutional law outlined in earlier chapters; and at the other the detailed rules in statutes and secondary legislation that govern the provision of complex social services (such as social security and education), the regulation of economic activities (such as financial services), the control of immigration, and environmental law. The constitutional theorist would focus on the former; the practitioner the latter.

It will be evident that there is no 'bright line' demarcating constitutional and administrative law. Building on the account of constitutional principles already given, this part of the text deals with aspects of administrative law relevant to all areas of government. These are the powers of the executive to make secondary, or delegated, legislation; the system of administrative justice whereby tribunals and inquiries and the Parliamentary Ombudsman make decisions or provide redress for individual grievances; judicial review; and the liability of public authorities, notably central government, to be sued for damages. The aim will be to identify the key rules and processes that help to ensure that lawful and just standards of public administration are observed.[2]

A. The functions and development of administrative law

Functions of administrative law

One important function of administrative law is to enable the tasks of government to be performed, including by recognising administrative agencies and their powers to act on behalf of

---

[1] In 1981, 533 applications for judicial review were made, of which 376 were allowed; in 1994, 3,208 were made and 1,260 allowed: Bridges, Meszaros and Sunkin, *Judicial Review in Perspective*, app 1. In 2008, 7,093 claims were made and permission was granted in 914 cases (*Judicial and Court Statistics 2008*). In 2016, 4,300 claims were made, with permission being granted in 661 cases (including on the papers and after an oral renewal hearing) (*Civil Justice Statistics 2016*). The hiving off of most immigration and asylum work to the Immigration and Asylum Chamber of the Upper Tribunal in late 2013 has considerably reduced the workload of the Administrative Court.

[2] For fuller accounts, see the textbooks on administrative law by (respectively) Cane, Craig, Endicott, and Wade and Forsyth. Also Richardson and Genn (eds), *Administrative Law and Government Action*; Harlow and Rawlings, *Law and Administration*; Taggart (ed.), *The Province of Administrative Law*; and Beatson, Matthews and Elliott, *Administrative Law: Text and Materials*.

the state and of the community at large. A second function is to govern the relations between public bodies, for example, between the Secretary of State and a local authority or between two local authorities.[3] A third function is to govern the relations between a public agency and the individuals or private bodies over whose affairs the agency exercises power. We have seen that at the heart of the 'rule of law' is the principle of government according to law.[4] Since every public agency needs legal powers to perform its tasks, it necessarily follows that the agency must not act outside its powers. The content and extent of powers granted will reflect the social, economic and political values recognised in society. The granting of powers is subject both to express conditions or limitations, and also to implied requirements, such as the duty to exercise powers in good faith.

Individuals are affected by administrative powers in many ways, sometimes to their benefit and sometimes to their detriment. An individual's rights are seldom absolute: thus a landowner whose farm is required for a new reservoir does not have an absolute right to prevent acquisition of the land for a lawful purpose that is considered to be in the public interest. Nor do parents with a seriously ill child have an absolute right to medical treatment for him or her in the NHS when this is not recommended on clinical grounds.[5] Conversely, the powers of public authorities should not themselves be regarded as absolute. Private individuals, local communities and minority groups, all have a right to legal protection when confronted with the coercive powers of the state. Since there are few absolutes, the law has to determine the form and extent of that protection and the basis on which disputes may be resolved. The more fundamental the rights of the individual affected, the greater ought to be the degree of protection.[6]

The constitutional background to administrative law

Earlier chapters described the structure of central government; the responsibility of ministers to Parliament; the use of public bodies to regulate public utilities; and the effect of public powers on the individual's rights and liberties. The legislative supremacy of Parliament is relevant to administrative law, since (except where a conflict with EU law arises) no court can hold that the powers of an agency created by Act of Parliament are invalid or inoperative, although the Human Rights Act 1998 permits a statute to be declared incompatible with Convention rights. Where an agency's powers do not come from an Act of Parliament, but from other legislative measures (such as legislation enacted in Northern Ireland, Scotland or Wales, or ministerial regulations) the courts may review the legality of the agency's powers, as well as the decisions taken in reliance on those powers.

In a modern legal system, the way that disputes arising out of administration are handled is of constitutional significance. Where, as in Germany, there are separate superior courts, one entrusted with interpreting the constitution and one dealing with disputes between the citizen and the administration, a distinction between constitutional and administrative law can be based on the actual work done by the two courts. In the United Kingdom such a distinction cannot be drawn: although the section of the High Court in England and Wales dealing with judicial review is the Administrative Court, appeals from the court go along with other civil cases to the Court of Appeal and thence the Supreme Court. Issues of constitutional significance may arise from civil cases brought against public officials[7] as well as from cases involving

---

[3] See respectively *R (Luton BC) v Secretary of State for Education* [2011] EWHC 217 (Admin), [2011] LGR 553; *Bromley BC v Greater London Council* [1983] AC 768.

[4] Ch 4.

[5] *R v Cambridge Health Authority, ex p B* [1995] 2 All ER 129.

[6] This principle was expressly approved in respect of judicial review in *R v Ministry of Defence, ex p Smith* [1996] QB 517, 554.

[7] E.g. *Austin v Metropolitan Police Commissioner* [2009] UKHL 5, [2009] 1 AC 564.

criminal justice[8] and judicial review.[9] The fact that the Human Rights Act makes it unlawful for public authorities to act inconsistently with the Convention rights is another reason why administrative and constitutional cases cannot be separated. The criminal law as such falls outside administrative law, but the operations of the police and the penal system often give rise to disputes about the exercise of powers (for example, over the rights of convicted prisoners against the prison authorities).[10] The procedures of Parliament fall outside administrative law, but the rules of public audit affect the working of government departments,[11] and parliamentary procedures for the scrutiny of delegated legislation may be relevant in cases of judicial review.[12]

Historical origins of administrative law[13]

During the 19th century the Court of King's Bench extended its controlling jurisdiction beyond the justices of the peace to the new administrative bodies springing up in the form of councils and boards. Since they exercised statutory powers, disputes about the limits of their power could be settled by means of the prerogative writs. These procedures for judicial control over inferior courts were used to review the exercise of powers by local authorities and, in the 20th century, by ministers of the Crown.[14] Given the scale of government in the 21st century, the need for judicial review of executive decisions to be available is undiminished.

Inevitably, the supervisory role of the courts has developed as patterns of government have changed. Judicial review of decisions by ministers is complementary to, not a substitute for, ministerial responsibility to Parliament. Remarkably, in the three legal systems of the United Kingdom, the grounds of judicial control have never been defined in legislation. However, by the common law doctrine of precedent, principles have developed both for policing the limits of powers and for reviewing the use of discretionary powers. In 2010, Lord Bingham, the leading judge of our time, declared this principle as being at the heart of the rule of law.[15]

> Ministers and public officers at all levels must exercise the powers conferred on them in good faith, fairly, for the purposes for which the powers were conferred, without exceeding the limits of such powers and not unreasonably.

This principle applies whenever public power is exercised, regardless of whether it is derived from legislation or, as a matter of common law, from the royal prerogative.[16] It is the detailed application of this general principle that we will examine in Chapter 24 and 25.

In Scotland, the detailed history is different, but the general form of the development has been similar. The remedies for controlling inferior tribunals and administrative agencies

---

[8] E.g. *Boddington* v *British Transport Police* [1992] 2 AC 143.

[9] E.g. *R (Purdy)* v *DPP* [2009] UKHL 45, [2009] 4 All ER 1147.

[10] E.g. *R (Daly)* v *Home Secretary* [2001] 2 AC 532; and see *Roberts* v *Parole Board* [2005] UKHL 45, [2005] 2 AC 738.

[11] See Turpin, *Government Procurement and Contracts*; Davies, *The Public Law of Government Contracts*.

[12] Ch 22; and see *HM Treasury* v *Ahmed* [2010] UKSC 2, [2010] 2 AC 534.

[13] History is particularly important to understanding the development of English administrative law: J W F Allison [2013] CLJ 526; (same) *The English Historical Constitution*.

[14] See e.g. *R* v *Glamorganshire Inhabitants* (1700) 1 Ld Raym 580 (review of rates levied by county justices to pay for repairs to bridge), *Board of Education* v *Rice* [1911] AC 179 and *Local Government Board* v *Arlidge* [1915] AC 120, on which see Dicey, *The Law of the Constitution*, app 2.

[15] Bingham, *The Rule of Law*, p 60.

[16] E.g. *CCSU* v *Minister for Civil Service* [1985] AC 374; *R (Bancoult)* v *Foreign Secretary (No 2)* [2008] UKHL 61, [2009] 1 AC 453; *R (Miller)* v *Secretary of State for Exiting the European Union* [2017] UKSC 5, [2017] 2 WLR 583.

were obtained from the Court of Session by the procedures used for civil litigation between private parties. But the principles upon which judicial control was founded were remarkably similar to those developed in English law.[17] The sheriff court exercised an important role in enabling many local administrative disputes to be settled judicially.[18] Since 1900, much of the development in government has been by statute law applying both in England and Scotland; the response of the Scottish courts has been similar to that of the English courts.

In Scotland, as well as Northern Ireland and Wales, there is now a layer of devolved government to which administrative law applies. Apart from questions as to the extent of the devolved powers, which must be decided in accordance with the devolution legislation,[19] decisions by the devolved governments are subject to the same process of judicial review as are decisions of other public bodies.

Dicey's misconception

The study of administrative law in Britain was formerly impeded by a misleading comparison which the constitutional writer, A V Dicey, drew over a hundred years ago between the law in France (*droit administratif*), under which separate administrative courts (headed by the Conseil d'Etat) determined disputes concerning the exercise of administrative power, and the common law in England.[20] Dicey contrasted what he saw as the disadvantages in the French system of administrative courts with the advantages enjoyed in Britain where the common law, as Dicey saw it, subjected executive actions to control by the same courts and on the same principles as governed relationships between private citizens. Dicey believed that the common law gave the citizen better protection against the executive than the French system. Unfortunately, he overlooked the weaknesses of the archaic law that then protected the Crown and government departments from being sued.[21] Moreover, his denial that *droit administratif* existed in England led many to suppose that there was no such thing as administrative law in the United Kingdom. In the landmark decision of *Ridge v Baldwin* in 1964, Lord Reid said: 'We do not have a developed system of administrative law – perhaps because until fairly recently we did not need it'.[22] Lord Diplock described the rapid development of 'a rational and comprehensive system of administrative law' as having been 'the greatest achievement of the English courts' in his judicial lifetime.[23] Another judge has written that in this area of common law, 'the judges have in the last 30 years changed the face of the United Kingdom's constitution'.[24]

Administrative law in Europe is today a fertile ground for comparative research and analysis.[25] Despite many developments on both sides of the English Channel that have occurred since Dicey wrote, the French system of *le contentieux administratif* is based on the use of separate

[17] See e.g. *Moss Empires Ltd v Glasgow Assessor* 1917 SC (HL) 1. Also *Stair Memorial Encyclopaedia, The Laws of Scotland*, vol 1, title Administrative Law (reissue 2000); Clyde and Edwards, *Judicial Review*.

[18] *Brown v Hamilton DC* 1983 SC (HL) 1.

[19] Ch 2 B.

[20] *The Law of the Constitution*, ch 12 and app 2. For critiques of Dicey's approach, see F H Lawson (1959) 7 *Political Studies* 109, 207; and H W Arthurs (1979) 17 *Osgoode Hall LJ* 1. See also Brown and Bell, *French Administrative Law* and, for a recent appraisal of the French system, J-M Sauvé [2008] PL 531.

[21] These defects were very evident after the First World War: see J Jacob [1992] PL 452.

[22] [1964] AC 40, 72.

[23] *Re Racal Communications Ltd* [1981] AC 374, 382; and *R v Inland Revenue Commissioners, ex p National Federation of Self-Employed* [1982] AC 617, 641. And see Lord Diplock [1974] CLJ 233; Lord Scarman [1990] PL 490.

[24] S Sedley, in Richardson and Genn (note 2 above), p 36.

[25] See e.g. Schwarze, *European Administrative Law*; Craig, *UK, EU and Global Administrative Law: Foundations and Challenges*.

administrative courts, whereas the British system relies heavily on the superior civil courts. In both systems, the essential principles of judicial control are judge-made and do not derive from codes or statutes. In France, the price paid for a separate administrative jurisdiction is a complex body of law at the divide between the civil and administrative courts; and conflicts between the two systems of courts must (if necessary) be settled by the *Tribunal des conflits* or by legislation. But the French system has developed rules of procedure (for example, regarding the obtaining of evidence from government departments) and rules of substantive liability (for example, regarding liability for harm caused by official acts) which take account of the public setting of the disputes. The latter rules often impose special duties upon public authorities (for example, liability without fault in some circumstances),[26] not merely immunities.

By contrast, the British approach (as we shall see in Chapter 26) has been to apply the same general principles of liability in contract and tort to public bodies as well as to private citizens.[27] The position is different regarding judicial review of official decisions, since this jurisdiction has no direct counterpart in private law. The Administrative Court is able to provide a fair and effective decision when the legality of official acts is challenged, and in cases of urgency it may act very quickly indeed.

The development of administrative law

The explosion of government in the 20th century did not wait for lawyers and academic writers in Britain to acquire an understanding of administrative law. The first books on the subject by that name appeared in the late 1920s.[28] At that time a narrow approach was taken to the subject, confining it to delegated legislation and the exercise of judicial powers by administrative bodies.

The judicial review of government decisions was marked during the middle years of the 20th century by what has been called the 'great depression' or the 'long sleep'[29] – when the judiciary appeared to acquiesce in an unjustified diminution of their role. When in the late 1960s the senior judges became willing to make greater use of their powers, attention concentrated on the archaic and highly technical processes by which judicial review had to be obtained. In 1976, the English Law Commission recommended major procedural reforms;[30] these were implemented between 1977 and 1981, creating the procedure of application for judicial review.[31] A similar but not identical procedure was introduced into Scots law in 1985.[32]

In 2000, some changes made to the process of judicial review included the re-labelling of historic remedies and the naming of the Administrative Court.[33] At the same time, the Human Rights Act 1998 came into effect with far-reaching implications for administrative law, since it introduced new rules of statutory interpretation, required public authorities to act consistently with Convention rights and thereby created new grounds of judicial

---

[26] R Errera [1986] CLP 157.

[27] *Dorset Yacht Co v Home Office* [1970] AC 1004; ch 26 A. And see Fairgrieve, Andenas and Bell (eds), *Tort Liability of Public Authorities in Comparative Perspective*.

[28] Robson, *Justice and Administrative Law*, and Port, *Administrative Law*. And see G Drewry, in Supperstone, Goudie and Walker (eds), *Judicial Review*, ch 2. For a different approach, see Willis, *The Parliamentary Powers of English Government Departments*.

[29] See respectively Wade and Forsyth, *Administrative Law*, p 12; S Sedley in Andenas and Fairgrieve (eds), *Tom Bingham and the Transformation of the Law*, p 183.

[30] Cmnd 6407, 1976; cf Scottish Law Commission, *Remedies in Administrative Law*, 1971.

[31] Ch 25.

[32] See works cited in note 17. Also T Mullen, K Pick and T Prosser [1995] PL 52; and CMG Himsworth in Supperstone, Goudie and Walker (eds), *Judicial Review*, ch 22.

[33] See *Review of the Crown Office List* (Bowman report), 2000; Civil Procedure Rules, Part 54.

review.[34] While initially it could be claimed that the effect of the Human Rights Act was merely to reinforce existing rules of the common law, in reality the House of Lords (and since October 2009 the Supreme Court) has given much attention to claims that would have failed apart from the Act.[35]

B. Law and the administrative process

The principle that government must be conducted according to law means that for every act performed in the course of government there must be legal authority.[36] That authority is usually derived expressly or by implication from statute or sometimes from the royal prerogative. Moreover, the Crown has at common law the same capacity as any other person to make contracts, own property, etc.[37] A public body must be able to show that it is acting in accordance with legal authority when its action (for example, the levying of a tax) adversely affects the rights or interests of a private individual.

It is not possible to describe the administrative process in terms of law alone. There are many tasks (for example, budgeting and coordination) to which law is not of primary relevance. The creation of executive agencies, like many developments within the civil service, has not been authorised by legislation, being regarded as essentially a form of departmental management. Many politicians and administrators are likely to view law instrumentally as a means of achieving social or economic policies. In areas of government such as taxation, the detailed rules are found in statutes or in judicial decisions interpreting the statutes. Even so, those rules may not provide the complete picture, since from time to time the revenue authorities exercise an extra-statutory discretion not to enforce payment of tax in a situation which neither Parliament nor the government can have foreseen. But the practice of granting extra-statutory concessions would defeat the whole purpose of imposing taxes by law if it became widespread; by the nature of a tax concession, it may escape challenge in a court of law.[38]

By contrast with taxation, in many areas of government the nature of the legal framework is deliberately skeletal, to allow for a flexible discretion on the part of the department concerned in promoting policies that are nowhere laid down in statutory rules. Thus the department responsible for promoting international development has a broad power to provide economic or humanitarian assistance to overseas countries,[39] that can be used to promote widely differing policies. Wide discretion is found in many areas of government, such as the control of immigration or the granting of permission for the development of land. In principle, the exercise of discretion is subject to control by the courts if it is exercised unlawfully.

---

[34] See ch 14.

[35] S Shah and T Poole [2009] PL 347.

[36] The contrary view, expressed in *Malone v Metropolitan Police Commissioner* [1979] Ch 344, was disapproved in *R v Somerset CC, ex p Fewings* [1995] 3 All ER 20, and would conflict with the ECHR. See Harris, O'Boyle and Warbrick, *Law of the ECHR*, pp 344–8, 399–407.

[37] B V Harris (1992) 108 LQR 626, and (2007) 123 LQR 225. The Crown's power to make or recover payments without statutory authority may not be used when this would contradict the clear intention of Parliament: *R (Wilkinson) v IRC* [2005] UKHL 30, [2006] 1 All ER 529; *R (Child Poverty Action Group) v Secretary of State for Work and Pensions* [2010] UKSC 54, [2011] 2 AC 15.

[38] But not necessarily: *R (Davies) v HMRC* [2011] UKSC 47, [2011] 1 WLR 2625. And there may still be judicial criticism: *Vestey v IRC* [1980] AC 1148. For comment that extra-statutory concessions appeared contrary to the prohibition on dispensing powers found in the Bill of Rights 1689, see S Sedley, *Lions under the Throne*, p 130.

[39] International Development Act 2002. And see *R v Foreign Secretary, ex p World Development Movement* [1995] 1 All ER 611.

In practice, the use of discretion is often closely controlled through policy decisions taken by ministers or departmental rules which lay down how officials should exercise their powers.[40] At one time, such policies and rules were often protected from publication outside Whitehall, but today's more open approach to government usually requires disclosure of all policies and rules that are relevant to decision-making in individual cases.[41]

Many officials are therefore concerned with administering government policies rather than with administering the law as such. It is often difficult to separate administration of an existing policy from the making of a new policy. When a department is exercising discretionary powers and a case arises that raises new features, a decision on the facts will serve as a precedent for future decisions of a similar kind. Thus the process gives rise to the formulation of a more detailed policy than had previously existed.

Decision-making within a department is very different from the process by which a court settles a dispute. A civil case, for example, is decided by the judge after hearing evidence and legal arguments brought before the court by the parties in an adversary procedure. Oral proceedings take place in public before the judge, in the presence of the parties and their lawyers. A reasoned decision is announced in open court; when made it can be challenged only by appeal to a higher court. By contrast, departmental decisions are typically taken in private, without an adversary procedure. Often it is not known at what level in the department the decision has been taken. Political pressure may be brought to bear both before and after the decision. Except where a statute so requires, or where it would be unfair for reasons to be withheld, reasons for the decision are not in law required to be given. The decision-making may be subject to disclosure under the Freedom of Information Act 2000, but there are numerous exemptions which allow the information to be withheld in the public interest.

Although the two processes of administrative and judicial decision-making are different, we should not assume that one method is superior to the other or suppose that a department should always try to adopt the methods of a court. Much depends on the type and number of decisions to be made and on the results which it is desired to achieve from a particular scheme. Few ordinary citizens would welcome the delay and expense involved were all public decision-making to resemble judicial proceedings. Decisions made on the basis of general rules and after a procedure that enables the facts to be ascertained and competing considerations to be assessed are likely to be fairer than if made without such aids to decision-making. Thus many classes of decisions that are taken by civil servants at first instance (in such areas as taxation, social security and immigration) are subject to an appeal to independent tribunals, which apply a modified form of judicial procedure in making decisions.

Powers, duties and discretion

A recurring feature in administrative law is the interplay between powers, duties and discretion. If someone satisfies the legal rules that govern who may vote in parliamentary elections, then he or she has a right to be entered on the electoral register and a right to vote in the area where he or she is registered. The relevant officials are under a correlative duty to give effect to these rights. Many situations that arise in the course of public administration are less clear-cut. Thus a minister may be under a duty to achieve certain broad policy objectives without in law being required to take action of any particular kind.

---

[40] On departmental rules and 'quasi-legislation', see ch 22. For the relevance of policies in planning decisions, see *R (Alconbury Developments Ltd)* v *Environment Secretary* [2001] UKHL 23, [2003] 2 AC 295.

[41] *R (Lumba)* v *Secretary of State for the Home Department* [2011] UKSC 12, [2012] 1 AC 245; *R (Justice for Health Ltd)* v *Secretary of State for Health* [2016] EWHC 2338 (Admin).

Clearly, steps taken in the performance of such a duty involve the exercise of discretion. As Lord Diplock said:

> The very concept of administrative discretion involves a right to choose more than one possible course of action on which there is room for reasonable people to hold differing opinions as to which is to be preferred.[42]

Where an Act confers authority to administer a branch of government, it may confer a broad duty on the minister and other public authorities to fulfil certain policy objectives. It may impose specific duties on the minister to act when certain conditions exist and it will probably confer powers on the authorities concerned. In administrative law, 'power' has two meanings, which are not always distinguished: (*a*) the capacity to act in a certain way (for example, power to provide a library service or to purchase land by agreement for a sports field); and (*b*) authority to restrict or take away the rights of others (for example, power to regulate the mini-cab trade in a city or to buy land compulsorily that is needed for a public purpose). Since it is inherent in the nature of a power that it may be exercised in various ways, use of a power invariably requires the exercise of discretion; and power and discretion are often used interchangeably. Often there is a duty to exercise a discretion. When an official decides to perform a duty or to exercise a power or discretion in a certain way, the decision may delight some persons and disappoint others. Within a democracy, important choices of this kind should be made by those who have political responsibility for them, not by judges.[43] Those whose rights or interests are adversely affected by an administrative decision may wish to challenge it, whether by taking any political action to get it changed if that is still possible, by using any rights of appeal that exist, or by seeking judicial review.

Classification of powers

Under a written constitution founded on a formal separation of powers, it may be necessary for a court to decide whether legislative or executive action has improperly infringed the judicial power.[44] Although this is not the case in the United Kingdom, there are several purposes in administrative law for which it may be needed to classify the powers of government as being legislative, administrative or judicial in character. Under the Statutory Instruments Act 1946 in its application to earlier statutes, a distinction was drawn between instruments that were *legislative* and those that were *executive* in character.[45] The jurisdiction of the Parliamentary Ombudsman applies to 'action taken in the exercise of *administrative* functions' by a government department, which may mean that it does not extend to the functions of departments which are legislative in character.[46] Under the Crown Proceedings Act 1947, s 2(5), the Crown is not liable for the acts of any person who is discharging responsibilities of a *judicial* nature.[47] This absolute rule of non-liability has now been altered by the Human Rights Act 1998, s 9, under which the Crown must in some circumstances compensate those who have lost their liberty by reason of a judicial act.[48]

---

[42] *Secretary of State for Education* v *Tameside MBC* [1977] AC 1014, 1064. And see Davis, *Discretionary Justice*, and Galligan, *Discretionary Powers*.

[43] See the *Alconbury* case (above), esp paras [48] (Lord Slynn), [70] (Lord Hoffmann), [139]–[141] (Lord Clyde).

[44] *Liyanage* v *R* [1967] 1 AC 259; *Independent Jamaica Council for Human Rights (1998) Ltd* v *Marshall-Burnett* [2005] UKPC 3, [2005] 2 AC 356. And ch 4 C.

[45] SI 1948/1, reg 2(1); ch 22.

[46] Parliamentary Commissioner Act 1967, s 5(1); ch 23 D.

[47] Ch 26. See *Quinland* v *Governor of Swaleside Prison* [2002] EWCA Civ 174, [2003] QB 306.

[48] The 'judicial act of a court' includes 'an act done on the instructions, or on behalf, of a judge' (Human Rights Act 1998, s 9(5)).

While many powers may be described without difficulty as legislative (in particular, a power to make regulations), administrative (for instance, power to decide where a government office should be located) or judicial (for example, power to decide the meaning of a disputed statute), other powers are so classifiable, if at all, only with difficulty. Laws are not always general in application: legislative form may be used to give effect to the government's decision of an individual case.[49] Government departments exercise both formal and informal powers of rulemaking: is the delegation of executive powers to be regarded as a legislative act?[50] How should we classify, for instance, the decision to build a motorway?[51] Does a decision change its character from being judicial to administrative if it is transferred from a court to a government department?[52]

Today, administrative functions are subject to judicial review without it being necessary for a court first to apply a classificatory label. Public authorities are under a general duty to act fairly, even though the precise content of 'fairness' varies according to the context.[53] Public authorities are required by the Human Rights Act to exercise their functions consistently with rights under the ECHR.

Public and private law

A different classification problem comes from the tendency that the courts adopted after 1980 of resolving questions about jurisdiction, liability and procedure by asking whether the matter was one of private or public law. This formal distinction is reflected in the structure of many European legal systems. Thus in France many public law disputes are decided by the administrative courts; private law is a matter for the civil courts. By contrast, in Britain the superior civil courts exercise an undivided jurisdiction over all justiciable disputes, whether they concern private citizens or public authorities.[54]

Lord Woolf has described public law as 'the system which enforces the proper performance by public bodies of the duties which they owe to the public'; and private law as 'the system which protects the private rights of private individuals or the private rights of public bodies'.[55] On this basis, the emphasis in public law is on holding public authorities to account for their conduct, and in private law on safeguarding individual rights. This analysis may help to explain some essential differences between applying for judicial review (a matter of 'public law') and bringing an action in tort ('private law'). But the distinction is deceptively simple. For one thing, Lord Woolf's two systems overlap to a significant extent. In the common law tradition, the system which protects the private rights of individuals *is* to an important extent the system which enforces the performance by public bodies of the duties which they owe to the public, at least if the public is regarded as comprising all private individuals.[56] Personal liberty, for example, is protected both by the law of habeas corpus[57] and by the law of tort (action for false imprisonment): does habeas corpus come within public law (as the aim is to get the court to order the detainee's release if the detention is unlawful) and the tort remedy within private law (as it may lead to damages being paid to the wrongly detained person)? If so, why? Similarly, a landowner may take action to protect his property against trespass, whether the trespasser is a

---

[49] *Hoffmann-La Roche & Co* v *Trade Secretary* [1975] AC 295.

[50] Cf *Blackpool Corpn* v *Locker* [1948] 1 KB 349.

[51] *Bushell* v *Environment Secretary* [1981] AC 75.

[52] Cf *Local Government Board* v *Arlidge* [1915] AC 120.

[53] See ch 24.

[54] Cf J D B Mitchell [1965] PL 95, advocating the creation of a new public law jurisdiction.

[55] [1986] PL 220, 221. Also Lord Woolf [1995] PL 57, 60–5.

[56] E.g. *Entick* v *Carrington* (1765) 19 St Tr 1030; *Cooper* v *Wandsworth Board of Works* (1863) 14 CB (NS) 180. Also Allison, *A Continental Distinction in the Common Law*.

[57] See ch 25 D.

government department or a neighbouring owner. Should the classification depend on the identity of the defendant? Why should that distinction matter? Comparable questions arise under the Human Rights Act, which protects the individual's Convention rights as well as imposing a duty on public authorities not to infringe those rights.[58] When someone seeks to protect her Convention right to privacy against a public authority, should the proceedings be classed as being a matter of public or private law? Could the answer depend on whether the individual is seeking the (private law) remedy of damages, or the (public law) remedy of quashing the authority's decision? In either event, the claimant may want to restrain further breaches of privacy by the authority, a remedy that is available both in 'public' and 'private' proceedings.

Very often when a private claimant (C) is in dispute with a public authority (P), P's position is founded on a power or duty that has been conferred on it by Parliament. This form of legal justification is not usually available to a private person. In this situation, to overcome P's reliance on statutory authority, C may seek to show that P has (for instance) acted outside the statute or has not followed the correct procedure.[59] This requires the court to review the validity of P's defence, but this is in essence the same task as when a judge must decide in a case against the police whether they had lawful authority for entering and searching private property or making an arrest. What the common law tradition stresses is that, even if there was always a clear-cut demarcation between public bodies and private persons,[60] the acts of public officials are (apart from the effects of statute) in principle subject to the ordinary law that applies to private persons.[61]

The courts have two broad tasks in administrative law. The first (which we may call 'judicial review') arises when an individual challenges the legality of a decision taken by a public authority and the court must, in exercising a supervisory jurisdiction, decide whether to uphold or set aside the decision. This task has no exact equivalent in private law, although in areas such as trusts, company and trade union law, disputes may arise as to the validity of decisions by trustees, company directors and trade union committees, and supervisory principles may be applied in the process of review.[62] The second broad task (which we may call 'governmental liability') arises when individuals seek compensation or damages for loss caused by a public authority's unlawful acts. This task has much in common with the general law of tort, contract and restitution, which applies to public and private entities alike.

The Human Rights Act 1998 makes it no easier for a clear distinction to be drawn between private and public law. The scheme of the Act (by s 6(1)) is to impose a duty to act compatibly with Convention rights in relation to *all* the functions of a 'core' public authority (such as a local council or a government department), whether the nature of a specific act is public or private. And by s 6(5) of the Act, bodies that are not public authorities for all purposes ('hybrid' bodies, with a mixture of public and private functions) have duties under the Act only in respect of acts that are public in their nature. The courts found it difficult to determine whether private companies that are paid by public authorities to provide services (such as care of the elderly) are themselves to be regarded as 'public authorities'; and the leading decision on this question has been reversed as to its particular context by Parliament.[63] The importance of

---

[58] Human Rights Act 1998, s 6.

[59] This was the situation in the iconic *Cooper* v *Wandsworth Board of Works* (p 660 below).

[60] And see *YL* v *Birmingham Council* (below).

[61] See ch 26. Sir William Wade's argument in (1985) 101 LQR 180, 195–7, that *CCSU* v *Minister for the Civil Service* [1985] AC 374 concerned private law issues has received no support.

[62] See Oliver, *Common Values and the Public–Private Divide*; and Craig, in Taggart (ed.), *The Province of Administrative Law*, ch 10.

[63] See *YL* v *Birmingham Council* [2007] UKHL 27, [2008] AC 95 (J Landau [2007] PL 630 and A Williams [2008] EHRLR 524). Earlier cases included *Poplar Housing Association Ltd* v *Donoghue* [2001] EWCA Civ 595, [2002] QB 48 and *R (Heather)* v *Leonard Cheshire Foundation* [2002] EWCA Civ 366, [2002] 2 All ER 936. See D Oliver [2000] PL 476 and [2004] PL 329, M Sunkin [2004] PL 643, H Quane [2006] PL 106. For the sequel to the *YL* case, see Health and Social Care Act 2008, s 145.

identifying public authorities under the 1998 Act is to an extent offset by the rule that courts and tribunals are themselves public authorities for the purposes of the Act; they thus have a duty to act consistently with Convention rights in adjudicating on disputes that arise between private parties.[64]

We have seen that the broad purposes served by judicial review are the same in both English law and the law of Scotland. However, the law in Scotland has escaped the difficulties discussed in this section almost entirely, since the supervisory jurisdiction of the Court of Session does not depend on the private law/public law distinction.[65]

Local government – a note

The emphasis in this book is on the constitutional structures that underlie the democratic government of the United Kingdom. In the context of administrative law, we are concerned with how public bodies provide services, exercise regulatory powers and so on. At a national level, the government's tasks include oversight of the economy, control of the physical environment, provision or oversight of services such as health and education, management of the state's revenues, promotion of 'law and order' and maintenance of the judicial system. As the case of the police shows, it is neither necessary nor desirable that all public services should be provided directly from Whitehall. Moreover, given privatisation of the public utilities and the involvement of private companies in many sectors of government, not all public services are provided directly by public authorities.

In the history of public administration in the United Kingdom, local authorities have played an important role, second in importance only to central government, and they have featured prominently in the evolution of administrative law. Since the 19th century, local councils have been affected by such doctrines of public law as the *ultra vires* rule, whereby a council, with power to levy local taxes and impose charges for services, and receiving grants from central government, may incur expenditure only for purposes authorised by statute. More recently, local government has been subjected to a bewildering quantity of legislative changes (including reorganisation of areas, new forms of local taxation and novel methods of management within councils).[66] Following the Localism Act 2011, local authorities have power to do anything that individuals generally may do (s 1(1)). Elected councils continue to promote local democracy, as well as providing or enabling social services and administering regulatory systems and licensing at a local level. But the vast structure and operation of local government is outside the scope of this text.

In view of the conflicting demands made on local authorities and their limited fund-raising powers, they are often involved in the contentious side of administrative law, whether seeking judicial review against central government[67] or other local authorities,[68] defending claims for judicial review brought by individuals,[69] regulatory agencies[70] or central government[71] or

---

[64] Ch 14. And see e.g. *Campbell* v *MGN Ltd* [2004] UKHL 22, [2004] 2 AC 457. Also H W R Wade (2000) 116 LQR 217; M Hunt [1998] PL 423.

[65] *West* v *Secretary of State for Scotland* 1992 SLT 636; and see CMG Himsworth in Supperstone, Goudie and Walker (eds), *Judicial Review*, ch 22.

[66] See Bailey (ed.), *Cross on Local Government Law*, and Himsworth, *Local Government Law in Scotland*. See also Loughlin, *Local Government in the Modern State*; and (the same) *Legality and Locality: The Role of Law in Central–Local Government Relations*.

[67] E.g. *R* v *Environment Secretary, ex p Hammersmith BC* [1991] 1 AC 521.

[68] E.g. *Bromley Council* v *GLC* [1983] 1 AC 768.

[69] E.g. *R* v *Gloucestershire CC, ex p Barry* [1997] AC 584; *Miss Behavin' Ltd* v *Belfast Council* [2007] UKHL 19, [2007] 3 All ER 1007. On the use of judicial review against local authorities, see M Sunkin et al. [2007] PL 545.

[70] E.g. *R* v *Birmingham Council, ex p EOC* [1989] AC 1155.

[71] E.g. *Lord Advocate* v *Dumbarton DC* [1990] 2 AC 580.

resisting actions for damages in tort resulting from alleged failures of duty.[72] Local councils have never had the privileges and immunities that government departments enjoy as agents of the Crown.[73] Local administrators are not civil servants and management methods are often very different from those in central government.[74] Councillors operate in a political context and the legality of party groups has been recognised,[75] but they are subject to mechanisms for securing public accountability and proper standards of conduct.

Finally, local councils are 'public authorities' for purposes of the Human Rights Act 1998. Every local authority must exercise its functions in a way that is compatible with the Convention rights, except where, as a result of primary legislation, it is unable to act differently or has acted to give effect to primary legislation that could not be read in a manner compatible with the Convention rights.[76]

C. Conclusion

This chapter has been a summary of the form and development of administrative law: what administrative law is. It does not readily lend itself to further abbreviation. It is not always easy to understand why the study of how a branch of law developed is worth knowing, let alone necessary to know. Administrative law is different. As will be seen in subsequent chapters, many of the day-to-day practical problems of administrative law only make sense if it is understood how the law has arrived at the situation it has. The origins and development of the judicial control of administrative powers, of the various kinds, is an essential compass for navigating the doctrinal thickets of matters such as the, extremely thorny, difference between public and private law. If our starting point is to define administrative law as a branch of public law concerned with the composition, procedures, powers, duties, rights and liabilities of the various organs of government that are engaged in administering public policies, then the remainder of this final part of the text explores how administrative law goes about doing so.

---

[72] *X (Minors)* v *Bedfordshire CC* [1995] 2 AC 633; *Barrett* v *Enfield Council* [2001] 2 AC 550.

[73] E.g. *Mersey Docks Trustees* v *Gibbs* (1866) LR 1 HL 93.

[74] The principle in *Carltona Ltd* v *Commissioners of Works* [1943] 2 All ER 560 does not apply in local government.

[75] *R* v *Waltham Forest BC, ex p Baxter* [1988] QB 419; and see I Leigh [1988] PL 304.

[76] Human Rights Act 1998, s 6(1), (2)(a).

CHAPTER 22

Delegated legislation

We saw in Chapter 21 that during the 20th century it came to be realised that the operation of government is carried on to a large extent not directly through laws made by Parliament, but by means of rules made by members of the executive under powers delegated to them by Parliament. This vast body of rules is known as delegated legislation, but it may also be described as secondary (or subordinate) legislation, by comparison with the primary legislation found in Acts of Parliament. In a few areas (especially in the conduct of foreign policy) government still relies not on statutory powers, but on the royal prerogative, that is, the common law powers that are exclusive to the Crown. Orders in Council made under the prerogative are, at least technically, a form of primary legislation. However, so far as the power to legislate is concerned, it was held long ago in the *Case of Proclamations*[1] that the Crown had no residual power to legislate so as to impose obligations or restrictions on the people, or to remove their rights. Over 300 years later it was held that this fundamental principle did not prevent the Crown having power under the prerogative to confer financial benefits on the victims of criminal violence.[2]

The term statute law covers both Acts of Parliament and delegated legislation. The main distinction between the two levels of statute law is that delegated legislation, unlike an Act of Parliament, is not the work of a supreme Parliament and is subject to judicial review. Nevertheless, the combined effect of the two levels is to set up public bodies to perform the tasks of government, and to equip them with the detailed powers needed for operating public services. It is very rare for an Act to contain all the provisions which are essential if a complex service is to be provided. An Act frequently does no more than outline the main features of the scheme, leaving many details to be filled in by subordinate legislation. In complex areas of government such as education, planning and immigration, there are often publications which bring together primary and subordinate legislation, along with codes of practice, ministerial circulars and sometimes a digest of the case law. The bulk of statutory instruments is formidable. From the Westminster Parliament alone in 2012, there were enacted 23 Public General Acts (the lowest total since 1957) and in 2014 3,485 statutory instruments were issued (the highest total on record). For 2016, the equivalent figures were 25 Public General Acts and just 1,243 statutory instruments.

A. The need for delegated legislation

Historical development

The formal process by which a Bill becomes an Act has never been the sole method of legislation. In the earliest years of Parliament, it was difficult to distinguish between enactment by

---

[1] (1611) 12 Co Rep 74, p 50 above; *R (Miller)* v *Secretary of State for Exiting the European Union* [2017] UKSC 5, [2017] 2 WLR 583. The Crown retains prerogative power to legislate for certain overseas possessions, but subject to judicial review: *R (Bancoult)* v *Foreign Secretary (No 2)* [2008] UKHL 61, [2009] 1 AC 453; *R (Barclay)* v *Justice Secretary* [2014] UKSC 54, [2015] AC 276; and ch 10.
[2] *R* v *Criminal Injuries Compensation Board, ex p Lain* [1967] 2 QB 864.

the King in Parliament and legislation by the King in Council. Even when legislation by Parliament had become a distinct process, broad power to legislate by proclamation remained with the Crown. In 1539, by Henry VIII's Statute of Proclamations, royal power to issue proclamations 'for the good order and governance' of the country was recognised to exist and such proclamations were to be enforced as if made by Act of Parliament. One reason given for the Act was that sudden occasions might arise when speedy remedies were needed which could not wait for the meeting of Parliament; the Act contained saving words to protect the common law, life and property. The repeal of the statute in 1547 made little difference to the Tudor use of proclamations, and Henry VIII's name remains associated with the controversial practice of delegating power to the executive to amend Acts of Parliament.

After 1918, some lawyers and politicians became concerned at the wide legislative powers of government departments. The inquiry by the Committee on Ministers' Powers (the Donoughmore Committee)[3] concluded that unless Parliament was willing to delegate law-making powers, it would be unable to pass the kind or quantity of legislation which modern public opinion required. The committee drew attention to certain dangers in delegated legislation and proposed greater safeguards against abuse. In 1946, the Statutory Instruments Act replaced the Rules Publication Act 1893 and promoted a greater uniformity of procedure. Since 1944, a scrutinising committee has been regularly appointed by Parliament, first by the Commons and today by the Commons and Lords jointly. The practice of delegated legislation has been reviewed by many parliamentary committees,[4] but the flood of subordinate legislation shows no sign of abating. The content of those instruments is also important: one committee said in 1986, 'Instead of simply implementing the "nuts and bolts" of Government policy, statutory instruments have increasingly been used to change policy, sometimes in ways that were not envisaged when the enabling primary legislation was passed.'[5]

In 1996, another committee concluded that 'there is ... too great a readiness in Parliament to delegate wide legislative powers to Ministers, and no lack of enthusiasm on their part to take such powers'.[6] Such committees have criticised the way in which Parliament gives 'second-rate' consideration to secondary legislation.[7] One of the areas in which considerable concern has been expressed as a result of Brexit is the likely desire of government to award to itself swingeing powers to amend all manner of laws, including primary legislation and important legal rights, through delegated legislation alone.[8] The publication of the draft European Union (Withdrawal) Bill in July 2017 did not allay those fears.[9]

Why delegated legislation is important

Most constitutions today recognise the need for legislation to exist at several levels within the legal system. Sometimes the need arises from the desire to devolve powers from the centre to

---

[3] Cmd 4060, 1932 ('MPC'). Ch 21.

[4] HC 310 (1952–3); HL 184, HC 475 (1971–2); HL 204, HC 468 (1972–3); HC 588–1 (1977–8), ch 3; HC 152 (1995–6); and HC 48 (1999–2000).

[5] HC 31–xxxvii (1985–6), p 2.

[6] HC 152 (1995–6), para 14, endorsed in HC 48 (1999–2000), para 26.

[7] P Tudor (2000) 21 *Statute Law Review* 149, 150. See too: Greenberg, *Laying Down the Law*.

[8] See, e.g., Lord Judge, 'A Judge's View on the Rule of Law' (Bingham Lecture, 2017) (available at https://www.biicl.org/documents/1637_2017_05_11transcript_of_lord_judges_speech_3. pdf?showdocument=1).

[9] The precise form in which the Bill is eventually passed is likely to vary significantly from that of its original draft, and will, regrettably, post-date this text. It is sufficient to note for present purposes that it is inevitable that any Bill preserving EU law within domestic law upon exiting the EU will require the inclusion of substantial powers to amend those laws by way of delegated legislation. The critical area of debate will be around the safeguards placed on such powers.

the regions or to elected councils within local government areas. Even if the Scottish Parliament and the Welsh Assembly make laws for Scotland and Wales respectively, the cities in those countries need some local laws that differ from those in rural areas.

A more general reason for delegated legislation is that the time available to Parliament for legislation is limited. If Parliament attempted to enact all new statutory rules itself, the legislative machine would clog up, unless the procedure for considering Bills was streamlined to a point at which detailed scrutiny by the legislators would be impossible. Even if the United Kingdom recognised a strict doctrine of separation of powers,[10] this would not create a bright line to distinguish between the laws that *should* be contained in primary legislation and the more detailed or technical rules that can properly be entrusted to the section of government that is administering a public service. Power to make detailed regulations on, for instance, road traffic or social security may be entrusted to the relevant government department, provided that there are procedures to ensure that some oversight is exercised by Parliament over the use made of the power.[11]

Another factor is that much delegated legislation deals with technical matters that are best regulated by a process in which the experience of relevant experts, professional bodies and commercial interests can be fully utilised. The greater the technicality involved in the content of such rules, the less suitable they are for consideration by the usual legislative process and the less likely they are to generate enough political interest to be included in the government's legislative programme.

An important justification for the existence of secondary legislation is that in many areas of government, especially when new services or schemes are established, it is not possible to foresee every difficulty that may arise in practice and detailed rules may be needed to accompany the parent Act.[12] Delegated legislation makes it possible to amend such rules as it is discovered how they are operating. There are also practical reasons why many new Acts should not come into effect as soon as the royal assent is given. It is common today for an Act to delegate power to a minister to make commencement orders, bringing into operation all or successive parts of the Act. There is no duty on the minister to exercise a commencement power, but the minister must not act so as to defeat Parliament's expectation that the Act will come into operation.[13]

Delegated legislation may also be needed in times of emergency when a government has to take action quickly and in excess of its normal powers. Many written constitutions include provision in emergency for suspending formal guarantees of individual liberty. In the United Kingdom, the Civil Contingencies Act 2004 (replacing the Emergency Powers Act 1920) makes permanent provision enabling the executive to legislate subject to parliamentary safeguards in certain emergencies.[14] Under the little-known United Nations Act 1946, by Orders in Council the government may make such provision as appears necessary to give effect to decisions by the UN Security Council calling for sanctions (but not the use of armed force) to preserve international peace and security.[15] Some powers to make delegated legislation

---

[10] See ch 4 C.

[11] In 2016–17, the House of Commons debated just 10 statutory instruments subject to affirmative resolution (of 172), and none of those subject to negative procedure (*Sessional Returns* (HC 1, 2017–19)). These figures do not include the time spent on statutory instruments by committees of the Commons and Lords.

[12] When the community charge, or poll tax, was brought in by the Local Government Finance Act 1988, no fewer than 47 sets of regulations were made in the years 1989–91.

[13] *R v Home Secretary, ex p Fire Brigades Union* [1995] 2 AC 513. It is customary for commencement orders not to be subject to any parliamentary process, in either the positive or negative forms. Cf *R (Haw) v Home Secretary* [2006] EWCA Civ 532, [2006] QB 780.

[14] Ch 20 C.

[15] In *Ahmed v HM Treasury* [2010] UKSC 2, [2010] 2 AC 534 the Supreme Court quashed as ultra vires of the 1946 Act Orders in Council that froze the assets of persons suspected of being involved in international terrorism. The Orders were retrospectively validated by the Terrorist Asset-Freezing (Temporary Provisions) Act 2010.

without parliamentary oversight are potentially extraordinary; for example, under section 40 of the British Nationality Act 1981 (as amended), the Secretary of State may, by order, deprive an individual of his British citizenship if convinced that to do so would be 'conducive to the public good'.

The Cabinet Office has produced guidance to civil servants and parliamentary draughtsmen on the type of factors which may suggest where matters of detail should be contained in the body of the Bill, and when they should be dealt with in secondary legislation.[16] However, sponsoring departments may often make decisions for reasons of political expediency, or even tactics in relation to how best to steer a Bill through Parliament.[17]

B. Types of delegated legislation

While much delegated legislation is essential, governments are often tempted to obtain from Parliament greater powers than they should be given. Criticism centres on particular types of delegated legislation.

Matters of principle

There is a clear threat to parliamentary government if power is delegated to legislate on matters of general policy or if so wide a discretion is conferred that it is impossible to be sure what limit the legislature intended to impose. In practice Acts of Parliament frequently confer legislative powers in wide terms. One reason for this is that if powers are phrased more narrowly, this will make it more likely that the department will need to seek increased powers from Parliament in future. A proposal that Parliament should adopt a policy of passing framework legislation, with all details left to delegated legislation, was rightly rejected by the House of Commons Committee on Procedure in 1978, on the ground that this would further weaken parliamentary control.[18] Nonetheless, governments sometimes propose Bills that have been described as 'skeleton Bills' , Bills that are 'little more than a licence to legislate'.[19] Such Bills can operate only when extensive regulations are made and MPs may ask to see the proposed regulations before approving a Bill in this form. But there are few absolutes in this area and legislative practice is often a compromise between different attitudes to delegation.

Delegation of taxing power

We have seen how vital to the development of parliamentary government was the insistence that Parliament alone could authorise taxation.[20] This insistence survives in an attenuated form, but modern pressures, particularly associated with the economy, require Parliament to delegate some powers in relation to taxation. In particular, the working of a system of customs duties combined with the development of the European Union has made necessary the delegation of power to give exemptions and reliefs from such duties.[21] The government also has power to vary certain classes of indirect taxation by order of the Treasury.[22] These powers are

---

[16] Cabinet Office, *Guide to Making Legislation* (2017).

[17] Greenberg, *Laying Down the Law*, ch 23.

[18] HC 588-I (1977–8), ch 2.

[19] See Tudor (note 7 above), p 152.

[20] Ch 3 A.

[21] European Communities Act 1972, s 5; Customs and Excise Duties (General Reliefs) Act 1979.

[22] Excise Duties (Surcharges or Rebates) Act 1979.

subject to parliamentary control in that orders imposing import duties or varying indirect taxation cease to have effect unless they are confirmed by a resolution of the House of Commons within a limited time. One surprising instance of taxation by delegated legislation was the Community Infrastructure Levy – a wholly new tax which was entirely set up by delegated legislation under Part 11 of the Planning Act 2008.

Sub-delegation

When a statute delegates legislative power to a minister, exercisable by statutory instrument, it may be assumed that Parliament intends the statutory instrument itself to contain the rules. Is it a proper use of such powers for the instrument to sub-delegate legislative power, by authorising rules to be made by another body or by another procedure? The legal maxim, *delegatus non potest delegare*, means that a delegate may not sub-delegate his or her power, but the parent Act may always override this by authorising sub-delegation, as did the Emergency Powers (Defence) Act 1939. Without express authority in the parent Act, it is doubtful whether sub-delegation of legislative powers is valid. However, emergency regulations under the Civil Contingencies Act 2004 may 'make provision of any kind that could be made by Act of Parliament' (s 22(3)), and the breadth of this power may authorise sub-delegation. Where sub-delegation occurs, control by Parliament becomes more difficult. In 1978, the Joint Committee on Statutory Instruments criticised the recurring tendency of departments to seek to bypass Parliament by omitting necessary detail from statutory instruments and vesting a wide discretion in ministers to vary the rules without making further statutory instruments.[23] Under the European Communities Act 1972, sub-delegation is prohibited except for rules of procedure for courts or tribunals.[24]

Retrospective operation

It follows from the supremacy of Parliament that Acts may have retrospective operation.[25] If on occasion retrospective legislation is considered necessary, this must either be done in express words by Parliament itself or, if done through delegated legislation, only on the express authority of a statute.[26] By reason of art 7, ECHR, applied by the Human Rights Act 1998, delegated legislation may not retrospectively create new offences or impose additional penalties.

Exclusion of the jurisdiction of the courts

The power of the courts in reviewing delegated legislation is confined to declaring it *ultra vires*, whether on grounds of substance or procedure,[27] a power that is now subject to the court's duty where possible of protecting rights under the Human Rights Act. While control over the merits of delegated legislation is a matter for ministers and for Parliament, the

---

[23] HL 51, HC 579 (1977–8), p 10; and see *Customs and Excise Commissioners v J H Corbitt (Numismatists) Ltd* [1981] AC 22.

[24] European Communities Act 1972, s 2(2) and Sch 2. This might, in principle, be an arguable precedent to justify sub-delegation within the European Union (Withdrawal) Bill.

[25] Ch 8 B.

[26] See e.g. *R (Stellato) v Home Secretary* [2007] UKHL 5, [2007] 2 AC 70. Cf the unsatisfactory decision in *R v Social Security Secretary, ex p Britnell* [1991] 2 All ER 726 (upholding 'transitional provisions' that had a retrospective effect).

[27] See pp 608–11 below.

possibility of control by the courts should not be excluded. It should never be for a minister to determine the limits of his or her own powers.[28]

Authority to modify an Act of Parliament

However undesirable this might appear in principle, Parliament has for long been known to delegate to ministers power to amend Acts of Parliament.[29] The term 'Henry VIII clause' is given[30] to such provisions, and numerous examples are found in the Scotland Act 1998 and the Government of Wales Act 2006.[31] When the power in a new Act is restricted to amending earlier Acts that are directly affected by the new reforms, the power is less objectionable than when it extends to amending the very Act that contains the power.[32] Yet some Acts dealing with schemes of social and industrial control empower a minister to broaden or narrow the scope of the schemes in the light of experience.[33] Moreover, some statutes confer on ministers power to modify not merely existing but also future Acts.[34]

Three instances of delegated power to modify Acts of Parliament may be given. The European Communities Act 1972, by s 2(2), authorises the making of Orders in Council and ministerial regulations to implement Community obligations of the United Kingdom, to enable rights under the European treaties to be exercised and 'for the purpose of dealing with matters arising out of or related to any such obligations or rights'. Schedule 2 to the Act excludes certain matters from the general power, including the imposition of taxes, retroactive legislation and the sub-delegation of legislative power (other than power to make rules of procedure for any court or tribunal). Subject to these limitations, measures made under s 2(2) may make 'any such provision (of any such extent) as might be made by Act of Parliament' (s 2(4)). The intention in using such wide language must have been to exclude the possibility of judicial review on grounds of vires in the case of instruments made under s 2(2).[35]

An unusual power to amend primary legislation was created by the Human Rights Act 1998, s 10.[36] This authorises ministers or the Queen in Council to make remedial orders when a superior court has declared primary legislation incompatible with a Convention right or the European Court of Human Rights has made a similar finding. The aim of a remedial order is to amend the offending legislation so as to remove the incompatibility. As with orders

---

[28] Yet under the Counter-Inflation Act 1973, Sch 3, para 1, an order made under Part II of the Act could 'define any expressions used in the provisions under which it is made'. And see *Jackson* v *Hall* [1980] AC 854.

[29] MPR, pp 36–8; Carr, *Concerning English Administrative Law*, pp 41–7.

[30] Quite possibly unfairly, given the arguable misinterpretation of the Statute of Proclamations 1539: see Lord Judge, 'Ceding Power to the Executive; the Resurrection of Henry VIII' (King's College London Lecture, 2016) (available at: https://www.kcl.ac.uk/law/newsevents/newsrecords/2015-16/Ceding-Power-to-the-Executive---Lord-Judge---130416.pdf).

[31] See in the Scotland Act 1998, ss 30(2), 79, 89, 104–8, 113(5), 114, 124 and Sch 7. These powers were considered necessary to enable ministers to implement devolution (see HL 101, 124, 146 (1997–8)). They are not to be confused with the power of the Scottish Parliament to make laws for Scotland, that necessarily includes power to amend Westminster Acts on devolved matters.

[32] See e.g. Freedom of Information Act 2000, s 75 (Secretary of State may by order repeal or amend any statutory provision which appears to him to be capable of preventing the disclosure of information).

[33] Health and Safety at Work etc. Act 1974, ss 15 and 80; Sex Discrimination Act 1975, s 80, esp sub-s (3).

[34] See N W Barber and A L Young [2003] PL 112. Also Delegated Powers and Regulatory Reform Committee, *Guidance for Departments* (2007), para 16.

[35] See HL Deb, 17 February 1976, cols 399–417, and HL 51, HC 169 (1977–8), pp 17–18. Cf *R* v *HM Treasury, ex p Smedley* [1985] QB 657.

[36] See ch 14 C.

under the Legislative and Regulatory Reform Act (below), the making of an order is subject to an unusually full form of parliamentary supervision.[37]

The third instance of power to amend primary legislation is found in the Legislative and Regulatory Reform Act 2006. Replacing an earlier Act of 2001, this enables ministers to amend or repeal existing Acts with the aim of removing or reducing any burden resulting from that legislation, in respect of such matters as financial cost, administrative inconvenience and obstacles to efficiency (s 1). This power is subject to many conditions and qualifications: thus the new provision must not impose, abolish or vary any tax (s 5(1)); may not create new offences punishable with imprisonment for more than two years (s 6(1)); must not authorise any forcible entry, search or seizure (s 7(1)); and may not amend the Human Rights Act 1998 (s 8).[38] A power such as this provides an alternative to legislation by Bill, and new procedures within Parliament have become necessary for preventing their misuse.[39]

Despite constitutional criticism, the Public Bodies Act 2011, giving effect to a Cabinet Office review of public bodies in 2010, is a further controversial example of this practice.[40] It conferred power on ministers to abolish bodies specified in Schedule 1 to the Act and to transfer their powers to 'eligible persons' such as UK ministers, Scottish and Welsh ministers and 'any other person exercising public functions' (s 1). Schedule 1 to the Act included bodies such as the Administrative Justice and Tribunals Council, the Commission for Rural Communities, the Inland Waterways Advisory Council, the Library Advisory Council for England, and the National Consumer Council. The Act conferred power to merge bodies listed in Schedule 2 (including the Competition Commission and the Office of Fair Trading) and to change the constitutions of other public bodies. The Act includes several restrictions on use of the powers: s 7 seeks to protect functions such as judicial and enforcements powers that must be exercised independently of ministers, s 10 requires prior consultation, and s 11 enables use of the Act to be subject to a super-affirmative procedure that can be triggered by either House, similar to that in the Legislative and Regulatory Reform Act 2006. Unusually, s 12 also imposed a sunset clause of five years, after which time bodies listed in Schedule 5 could not be affected by order.

Nomenclature

Despite the Statutory Instruments Act 1946, terminology is often confusing. The term 'statutory instrument' is a comprehensive expression to describe all forms of subordinate legislation subject to the 1946 Act.[41] Within the scope of the Act are many powers conferred on ministers by Acts dating back from before the 1946 Act. As regards Acts passed thereafter, there are two categories of statutory instrument: (*a*) legislative powers conferred on the

---

[37] See below, page 607.

[38] While the new measure must 'make the law more accessible or more easily understood' (s 3(4)), it is puzzling that it must not 'remove any necessary protection' , nor must it be 'of constitutional significance' (s 3(2), (d) and (f)). What this latter category means is not explained.

[39] On earlier legislation preceding the 2006 Act, see [1995] PL 21 (M Freedland) and 34 (C M G Himsworth). On how the government's Bill for the 2006 Act was cut down in Parliament, see P Davis, [2007] PL 677. It originally included a remarkably broad power that would have enabled the government to abolish long-established rules of the common law (Davis, at 685). The mammoth Company Law Reform Bill, 2005–6, included a super-affirmative clause (later abandoned) the avowed intention of which was to make it unnecessary for any future reforms of company law to be made by Parliament!

[40] For criticism of the original Bill, see 6th report, Select Committee on the Constitution (HL 51, 2010–12). See also 50th report, Merits of Statutory Instruments Committee (HL 250, 2010–12). And Cabinet Office, *Using the Public Bodies Act 2011*, March 2012.

[41] The official abbreviation for statutory instruments is SI followed by the year and number, e.g. SI 2004 No 252 (or SI 2004/252).

Queen in Council and stated in the parent Act to be exercisable by Order in Council; (*b*) legislative powers conferred on a minister of the Crown and stated to be exercisable by statutory instrument. The first of these, the statutory Order in Council, must be distinguished from prerogative Orders in Council, which are not statutory instruments at all, though some of these are published in the annual volumes of statutory instruments. One reason why some powers are vested in the Queen in Council is that the more prestigious formality of an Order in Council may seem appropriate to some classes of legislation.[42] In the past powers were occasionally vested in a named minister, but today powers are generally vested in 'the Secretary of State' ; this means that the powers may in law be exercised by any holder of the office of Secretary of State. Many statutory instruments apply only in one locality, but the term does not include local by-laws or such matters as the confirmation of compulsory purchase orders. Confusingly, some kinds of rule made under statutory authority are not statutory instruments, for example immigration rules under the Immigration Act 1971 and regulations made by the Electoral Commission under the Political Parties, Elections and Referendums Act 2000.

Although statutory instrument is the generic term, various names are applied to the schemes of rules made by statutory instrument: orders, regulations, warrants, schemes, directions and so on. Several of these terms may be used in a single Act to distinguish different procedures for different purposes. In practice, the term 'regulation' is used mainly for matters of wide general importance. Where the legislation deals with procedure, rules are generally enacted, for example, the Civil Procedure Rules. With the term 'order' there is less uniformity; thus a commencement order may bring into effect all or part of an Act of Parliament and in town planning law a general development order contains detailed rules for the control of development.

To add to the scope for confusion, statutes may authorise the making of codes of practice, guidance and other forms of rules and provide sanctions of various kinds if they are not followed.[43] These measures must be distinguished from informal administrative rules (guidelines, circulars, etc.), which are made without express statutory authority; they are considered later in this chapter.

The Human Rights Act 1998 draws a distinction between what it defines as 'primary legislation' and 'subordinate legislation'.[44] The reason for the distinction is to protect Acts of Parliament from being set aside or invalidated by the courts for inconsistency with Convention rights. But the demarcation line drawn is unsatisfactory in that the Act includes in 'primary legislation' various measures that are not Acts of Parliament. These include measures of the Church Assembly, instruments made under primary legislation that amend Acts of Parliament and Orders in Council made under the Crown's prerogative.[45] There is no good reason why, if a minister uses a Henry VIII clause to amend a statute, and thereby creates inconsistency with a Convention right, the minister's action should be treated as if it were an Act of Parliament.

If delegated legislation is a necessary phenomenon in the modern state, then it is essential (1) that the process by which it is made should include the consultation of interests; (2) that Parliament should retain the ability to oversee and supervise the use of delegated powers; (3) that delegated legislation should be published; and (4) that it is subject to challenge in the courts should reasons for this arise.

---

[42] No discussion of an Order takes place in the Privy Council when it is made: and ministers have the same responsibility to Parliament for Orders in Council as for other statutory instruments.

[43] For an official definition of codes of practice, see p 612 below.

[44] Human Rights Act 1998, ss 3(2), 4, 21 (1). And see ch 14 C. The Interpretation Act 1978 also draws a distinction between 'primary' and 'subordinate legislation' , but does not define the distinction in the same way: s 21(1).

[45] See P Billings and B Pontin [2001] PL 21.

C. Control and supervision by Parliament

To what extent does Parliament control or supervise the making of delegated legislation? An answer to this difficult question must deal with the following matters: (*a*) the powers conferred; (*b*) procedures for making statutory instruments; (*c*) the role of the House of Lords; (*d*) technical scrutiny of statutory instruments; and (*e*) considering the merits of statutory instruments.

The conferment of powers

Since all delegated legislative powers stem from statute, there is always, at least in theory, an opportunity at the committee stage of a Bill to examine clauses that seek to delegate legislative powers. It was only in 1992 that the House of Lords appointed a committee to consider clauses in Bills proposing to delegate legislative powers and to receive for each Bill a government memorandum justifying the proposals. By reporting promptly on such proposals, the committee (now named the Committee on Delegated Powers and Regulatory Reform) aims to discourage the granting of excessive powers and to ensure that an appropriate level of scrutiny is included in the parent legislation. Its reports receive no media attention, but it has often persuaded the government to accept its views on such questions as the choice of procedure for parliamentary scrutiny in relation to a specific Bill.[46]

Procedures for making statutory instruments

In delegating legislative powers to government, Parliament typically provides for some parliamentary control or oversight to be built into the use of specific powers. However, two basic reasons for delegating legislative power are pressure on Parliament's time and the technical nature of the subject-matter; the very object of delegation would be frustrated if Parliament had to approve each instrument in detail. The procedure through which a statutory instrument must pass depends on the terms of the parent Act. The principal procedures are the following:

(*a*) laying of the draft instrument before Parliament, and requiring affirmative resolution before instrument can be 'made' ;

(*b*) laying of the instrument after it has been made, to come into effect only when approved by affirmative resolution;

(*c*) laying of the instrument that takes immediate effect, but requires approval by affirmative resolution within a stated period as a condition of continuance;

(*d*) laying of the instrument that takes immediate effect, subject to annulment by resolution of either House;

(*e*) laying in draft, subject to resolution that no further proceedings be taken – in effect a direction to the minister not to 'make' the instrument;

(*f*) laying before Parliament, with no further provision for control.[47]

In a few instances, examples of which were discussed above, a 'super-affirmative procedure has been created to deal with exceptional forms of delegated legislation, or particularly controversial

---

[46] See C M G Himsworth [1995] PL 34, P Tudor (2000) 21 *Statute Law Review* 149, HL 112 (1998–9) and HL 110 (2004–5), ch 2. The Committee's *Guidance for Departments* (2009), outlines criteria for deciding whether proposals for delegation and proposed levels of parliamentary supervision are 'appropriate'.

[47] It is customary for commencement orders to be subject to no parliamentary control; and see *R (Stellato)* v *Home Secretary* [2007] UKHL 5, [2007] 2 AC 270. In such cases, there could be a motion to 'take note' of the instrument: see HC SO 118(4)(b).

subject areas;[48] at the other extreme, some statutory instruments are not required to be laid before Parliament at all (as will be the case if the parent Act is silent on laying before Parliament).

In cases (*a*)–(*c*) (*positive procedure*), an affirmative resolution of each House (or in the case of financial instruments, of the Commons alone) is needed if the instrument is to come into force or to remain in operation. In cases (*d*) and (*e*) (*negative procedure*), no action need be taken in either House unless there is some opposition to the instrument.

Of these procedures, by far the most common is case (*d*) (subject to annulment); the most common of the positive procedures is case (*a*). Under the positive procedure, the government must secure an affirmative resolution in each House and, if necessary, it must allot time in the Commons for such a resolution; current practice in the Commons is for the instrument to be debated, however briefly, in a 'delegated legislation committee'.[49] Under the negative procedure, any member who so wishes may 'pray' that the instrument be annulled. It was formerly impossible for time to be found to debate all prayers for annulment which had been tabled.[50] The situation has been eased by the use of delegated legislation committees and by changes in the timetabling of Commons business,[51] but it would be a very rare event indeed for the House to adopt a motion to annul a statutory instrument.

A novel provision made by the European Communities Act 1972 was that a statutory instrument made under s 2(2) should be subject to annulment by a resolution of either House unless a draft of the instrument had been approved by each House before the instrument was made.[52] Thus the government may choose whether the negative or positive procedure should be used. That choice is very often made with an eye on tactical decisions based around the ease with which the Bill may be passed. One increasingly common approach has been to require the affirmative resolution procedure for the first exercise of a power and the negative procedure thereafter. This has proved surprisingly attractive to the scrutiny committees, despite it not being obviously clear why subsequent uses should logically require any less oversight.[53]

An Act that delegates legislative powers will specify the parliamentary procedures that are to apply. In addition, the Statutory Instruments Acts 1946 contains some general requirements. By s 4, where an instrument must be laid in Parliament after being made, it must in general be laid before it comes into operation; the heading of such an instrument must state three dates, showing (i) when it was made, (ii) when it was laid in Parliament and (iii) when it came into operation. What constitutes laying before Parliament is governed by the practice of each House,[54] and an instrument may be laid when Parliament is not sitting. The rule that an instrument must be laid before it comes into operation is clear, subject to statutory provision for immediate operation in cases of urgency. Although there is no binding judicial authority on the matter, it is submitted that failure to lay an instrument prevents it from coming into operation.[55] While under the 1946 Act an interval of one day between laying and operation is in law sufficient, departments are urged to ensure that the interval is not less than 21 days.[56]

[48] The Public Bodies Act 2011 and Legislative and Regulatory Reform Act 2006 are examples of the former; the inclusion of a super-affirmative procedure for regulations under the Investigatory Powers Act 2016 (s 268) is an example of the latter.

[49] See HC SO 118.

[50] A Beith (1981) 34 *Parliamentary Affairs* 165; Griffith and Ryle (eds), *Parliament*, pp 345–52.

[51] See HC SO 17 and 118.

[52] European Communities Act 1972, Sch 2, para 2.

[53] Greenberg, *Laying Down the Law*, ch 23.

[54] Laying of Documents before Parliament (Interpretation) Act 1948. See HL SO 71, HC SO 159. Also *R v Immigration Appeal Tribunal, ex p Joyles* [1972] 3 All ER 213.

[55] Cf A I L Campbell [1983] PL 43. The point was assumed but not decided in *R v Social Services Secretary, ex p Camden BC* [1987] 2 All ER 560 (A I L Campbell [1987] PL 328).

[56] HL 51, HC 169 (1977–8), pp 11–12; and *Statutory Instrument Practice* (Cabinet Office, 2006), 4.13.

By s 5 of the 1946 Act, where an instrument is subject to annulment, as in procedure (*d*) above, there is a uniform period of 40 days during which a prayer for annulment may be moved, exclusive of any time during which Parliament is adjourned for more than four days or is prorogued or dissolved. Where, as in procedure (*e*), an instrument is laid in draft but subject to the negative procedure, the same period of 40 days applies. In the case of instruments which need an affirmative resolution before they can come into operation (procedure (*b*)), no set period is provided as the government in each case must decide how urgently the instrument is needed. Under procedure (*c*) the period for obtaining the affirmative resolution is stated in the parent Act.

The role of the House of Lords

Although a parent Act may expressly confine control of statutory instruments to the Commons, the House of Lords is usually granted the same powers of control as the Commons. Moreover, the procedure under the Parliament Acts 1911 and 1949 for bypassing the Lords applies to Bills and not to statutory instruments. But it is extremely rare for the House of Lords to exercise its veto over subordinate legislation. When on 18 June 1968 the House rejected an order containing sanctions against the Rhodesian government made under the Southern Rhodesia Act 1965,[57] this caused the Labour government to propose (unsuccessfully) to abolish the power of the Lords to veto statutory instruments.[58] In 1994 the House declared that it had an 'unfettered freedom to vote on any subordinate legislation submitted for its consideration'.[59] In 2000, the House exercised this freedom, rejecting the Greater London Election Rules because of a disagreement over granting candidates a free postal delivery.[60] The Lords thus have the power to veto all instruments, except financial instruments that are laid only in the Commons. They sometimes adopt a resolution disapproving of an instrument without rejecting it, to induce the government to think again. In 2006, after a full examination of this issue, a joint committee of both Houses found that while the upper House should not regularly reject statutory instruments, 'in exceptional circumstances it may be appropriate for it to do so'. This conclusion was accepted by the government.[61]

The issue of the role of the Lords regained political prominence when, in October 2015, it withheld agreement, on a deferred basis, to the Tax Credits (Income Thresholds and Determination of Rates) (Amendment) Regulations 2015, which was subject to the affirmative resolution procedure. The Regulations intended to reduce the threshold at which tax credits would begin to be withdrawn from recipients. The government considered that this was a statutory instrument dealing with financial matters, covered by the budget, to which the Commons had already given its approval, and that it was therefore unprecedented for the Lords to withhold consent. The view was expressed that it was a convention that the Lords would not withhold consent to such instruments. The Prime Minister commissioned Lord Strathclyde to carry out a review of the role of the House of Lords in respect of statutory instructions, which was published in December 2015 and recommended a new statutory procedure restricting the Lords to an invitation to the Commons to reconsider the matter, preserving and ensuring Commons primacy.[62] A number of House of Lords committees responded robustly defending both the effectiveness and propriety of the scrutiny provided by the Lords, and explaining that the constitutional convention was in terms which permitted the Lords to

---

[57] A month later, on 18 July 1968, an identical order was approved by the Lords.

[58] Cmnd 3799, 1969, pp 22–3; Parliament (No 2) Bill 1969, clauses 13–15.

[59] HL Deb, 20 October 1994, col 356.

[60] HL Deb, 22 February 2000, cols 136 and 182. Equivalent rules were later approved: HL Deb, 6 March 2000, col 849.

[61] See HL 265, HC 1212 (2005–6), ch 6; and the government response, Cm 6997, 2006, paras 36–47.

[62] Strathclyde Review: Secondary legislation and the primacy of the House of Commons (2015, Cm 9177).

withhold approval of a statutory instrument approved by the Commons in exceptional circumstances.[63] The government indicated that it did not intend to legislate, but that it may do so if the issue arose again.[64] It did not respond in any detail to the various Lords Committee responses.[65] The position of the Lords accordingly remains unchanged, as does the view of the House of Lords as to the scope of the convention governing its role.

The technical scrutiny of statutory instruments

In the oversight of subordinate legislation, both Houses depend on the work of committees advised by qualified persons. All general statutory instruments laid before Parliament, as well as other statutory orders, come under scrutiny by the Joint Committee on Statutory Instruments, consisting of seven members appointed from each House. The members from the Commons meet separately to scrutinise those instruments which are laid only in the Commons. The joint committee is advised by the Speaker's Counsel and by Counsel to the Lord Chairman of committees.

The committee must consider whether the attention of the Houses should be drawn to an instrument on various legal and procedural grounds. In summary, these are:

(*a*) that an instrument imposes a charge on public revenues or requires payments to be made to any government department or public authority or sets the amount of such charge or payments;

(*b*) that it has been made under an Act that excludes it from challenge in the courts;

(*c*) that it appears to have retrospective effect without the express authorisation of the parent Act;

(*d*) that there has been unjustifiable delay by the department (in publishing it, laying it in Parliament or in giving notice that it has come into operation before being laid);

(*e*) that there is doubt as to whether there is a power to make it or that it makes unusual or unexpected use of the delegated powers;

(*f*) that for any reason its form or meaning need to be explained;

(*g*) that its drafting appears to be defective; or

(*h*) 'on any other ground which does not go to its merits or the policy behind it'.[66]

Around 1,500 instruments are examined by the committee each year, but relatively few instruments are reported to the two Houses. Before such a report is made, the department concerned will have sent to the committee an explanation of the position. An adverse report does not in itself have any effect on the instrument; in particular, if the committee expresses doubts about the vires of an instrument, that is a question that only the courts may decide.

Considering the merits of statutory instruments[67]

The Joint Committee on Statutory Instruments does not examine the merits or policy of an instrument. Occasionally, these matters may be discussed by the whole House of Commons

---

[63] See: HL 116, HL 119, HL 128 (2015–16).

[64] Government Response to the Strathclyde Review: Secondary legislation and the primacy of the House of Commons and the related Select Committee Reports (2016, Cm 9363).

[65] As to which, see HL 90 (2016–17).

[66] HC SO 151; HL SO 74.

[67] This account of secondary legislation is confined to the Westminster Parliament and does not deal with procedures in Edinburgh, Cardiff and Belfast for dealing with measures that are subordinate to the legislation adopted by the devolved Parliament or Assembly: see e.g. Scotland Act 1998, ss 52, 117, 118, and Sch 4, para 11; Standing Orders of the Scottish Parliament, ch 10.

on an affirmative resolution or on a prayer for annulment, but in general such debates are held in delegated legislation committees. Several such committees are regularly appointed, on the lines of the Public Bill committees used for the committee stage of Bills.[68] The committee debate enables important issues to be ventilated, but many such debates are no more than a formality.

Certain delegated measures that require the particularly close attention of Parliament form the new category of 'super-affirmative' instruments that has been created to legitimise the exercise of new 'Henry VIII' powers by ministers to amend primary legislation. Two instances of these instruments may be mentioned.

One, under the Human Rights Act 1998, s 10, is the 'remedial order' by which the government amends primary legislation to remove an inconsistency with a Convention right. The other, under the Legislative and Regulatory Reform Act 2006, amends primary legislation for such purposes as to ease the burden of a regulatory scheme.[69] The procedure laid down by these two Acts provides for greater scrutiny than is usual and requires each House to accept that the statutory conditions for making the order are satisfied; and the period for parliamentary action is 60 days rather than the usual 40. In the former case, the Joint Committee on Human Rights has the primary task of scrutinising remedial orders.[70] Under the 2006 Act, this is entrusted to the Regulatory Reform Committee (Commons)[71] and the Delegated Powers and Regulatory Reform Committee (Lords). Cabinet Office guidance states that use of the super-affirmative procedure should be avoided by departments as it adds to the complexity of parliamentary handling.[72]

In order that each House may inform itself about EU secondary legislation, committees of the two Houses exercise functions comparable with those of the committees which deal with statutory instruments.[73]

Publication of statutory instruments

Although it is desirable that all legislation should be publicised before it takes effect, there are some matters, for example changes in indirect taxation, where the object of the legislation might be defeated if it had to be made known to the public in advance. The Statutory Instruments Act allows that for essential reasons a statutory instrument may come into operation even before it is laid before Parliament, with the safeguard that the Lord Chancellor and the Speaker must be provided with an immediate explanation. More generally, it provides a uniform procedure for numbering, printing and publishing statutory instruments.[74] It is a defence in proceedings for breach of a statutory instrument to prove that it had not been issued by the Stationery Office at the date of the alleged breach, unless it is shown by the prosecutor that reasonable steps had been taken to bring the purport of the instrument to the notice of the public, or of persons likely to be affected by it, or of the person charged.[75] Thus ignorance of a statutory instrument is no defence, but in certain circumstances failure to issue an instrument may be.

---

[68] Ch 8 C.

[69] And see above, p 601.

[70] For the procedure, see Human Rights Act 1998, sch 2; and also HC SO 152B.

[71] See HC SO 14.

[72] *Cabinet Office Guide to Making Legislation* (2017), para 16.6.

[73] Ch 6 C.

[74] Statutory Instruments Act 1946, s 2, amended by the Statutory Instruments (Production and Sale) Act 1996.

[75] Statutory Instruments Act 1946, s 3(2); *R v Sheer Metalcraft Ltd* [1954] 1 QB 586. For the argument that at common law delegated legislation must be published before it can come into force, see D J Lanham (1974) 37 MLR 510 and [1983] PL 395; cf A I L Campbell [1982] PL 569.

D. Challenge in the courts

Although the Supreme Court has expressed the view that the classification of primary and secondary legislation is not determinative of its susceptibility to judicial review, the general rule is that primary legislation cannot be challenged but that delegated legislation may be.[76]

If made in accordance with the prescribed procedure, and within the powers conferred by the parent Act, a statutory instrument is as much part of the law as the statute itself. The essential difference between statute and statutory instrument is that, unlike Parliament, a minister's powers are limited. Consequently, if a department attempts to enforce a statutory instrument against an individual, the individual may as a defence question the validity of the instrument. The courts have power to decide this question even though the instrument has been approved by resolution of each House of Parliament.[77]

The validity of a statutory instrument may be challenged on two main grounds: (*a*) that the content or substance of the instrument is ultra vires the parent Act; (*b*) that the correct procedure has not been followed in making the instrument. The chances of success in such a challenge depend essentially on the terms of the parent Act, as interpreted by the court.[78] The duty under the Human Rights Act 1998, s 3(1), to interpret legislation consistently with Convention rights where this is possible, significantly widens the scope for challenging the validity of delegated legislation. Except where the parent Act expressly or by necessary implication authorises regulations to be made that infringe Convention rights, a general power to make regulations on a given subject must be interpreted as *excluding* power to make regulations that infringe Convention rights.[79] The Human Rights Act thus requires the courts to strike down a secondary instrument where it is not possible to interpret it as being consistent with Convention rights, even though apart from the 1998 Act the regulation would have been valid.[80] But the court may not strike down secondary legislation where primary legislation prevents the secondary legislation being made in any other terms.[81] In the latter case, the court may, under the 1998 Act, s 4, declare that the regulation is incompatible with a Convention right. Moreover, the interpretation and enforcement of delegated legislation may be subject to the requirements of EU law.[82] However, it is a well-established principle that delegated legislation should be construed in a way which falls within the conferring power where possible.[83]

Quite apart from human rights and EU law, there is a long-established presumption of interpretation that Parliament does not intend delegated powers to be exercised for certain purposes unless by express words or by necessary implication it has clearly authorised them. The principles that no one should be deprived of access to the courts except by clear words

---

[76] *AXA General Insurance Ltd* v *HM Advocate* [2011] UKSC 46, [2012] 1 AC 868 at [41]. That case concerned the susceptibility of an Act of the Scottish Parliament to judicial review, and the Supreme Court accepted that, on narrow grounds, review was possible. Orders in Council, although primary legislation, are also amenable to judicial review: *R (Bancoult)* v *Foreign Secretary (No 2)* [2008] UKHL 61, [2009] 1 AC 453.

[77] *R* v *Home Secretary, ex p Javed* [2001] EWCA 789, [2002] QB 129; *Hoffmann-La Roche* v *Trade Secretary* [1975] AC 295.

[78] See *R* v *Environment Secretary, ex p Spath Holme Ltd* [2001] 2 AC 349.

[79] See A W Bradley, R Allen and P Sales [2000] PL 358; D Squires [2000] EHRLR 116.

[80] Although there may be unusual cases in which the courts accept that it would be contrary to good administration to strike down the entirety of a statutory instrument, despite finding it to be in breach of Convention rights: *R (T)* v *Greater Manchester Police* [2014] UKSC 35, [2015] AC 49.

[81] Human Rights Act 1998, s 3(2). And ch 14 C.

[82] See e.g. *R (Barker)* v *Bromley Council* [2006] UKHL 52, [2007] 1 AC 470 (failure of planning regulations properly to implement a European directive).

[83] *R (Petsafe Ltd)* v *Welsh Ministers* [2010] EWHC 2908 (Admin), [2011] EuLR 270.

of Parliament and that there is no power to levy a tax without clear authority have been repeatedly illustrated. Two recent examples will suffice. In *R (Public Law Project) v Lord Chancellor*, the Supreme Court expressly endorsed a restrictive approach to delegated powers where Parliament might not have contemplated the outcome, striking down an order which proposed to remove the availability of civil legal aid from persons who failed a residence test.[84] The constitutional importance of access to the courts was reaffirmed in even starker terms by the Supreme Court in *R (Unison) v Lord Chancellor*.

> The Employment Tribunals and the Employment Appeal Tribunal Fees Order 2013 introduced a fees regime for bringing and continuing claims in employment tribunals and the Employment Appeal Tribunal. Its introduction was followed by a dramatic reduction in claims being brought in the tribunals, by some 66–70 per cent. *Held* that any hindrance of the constitutional right of access to the courts, which was of benefit to society as a whole, required clear parliamentary authorisation. The statistics, and the level at which the fees were set bearing in mind income levels and what could be reasonably afforded, posed a real risk that access to justice would be effectively prevented because of the deterrent effect the fees regime had.[85]

By similar reasoning a court might declare invalid a statutory instrument which purported to have retrospective effect in the absence of clear authority from Parliament. In Scotland, the Court of Session quashed a regulation made by the Secretary of State which removed from qualified teachers the right to continue teaching without first registering with a statutory Teaching Council.[86] The Home Secretary's power to make rules for the management of prisons did not permit him to make rules fettering a prisoner's right of access to the courts.[87] Relevant considerations must be borne in mind by the relevant minister.[88] Social security regulations which deprived certain asylum seekers of benefits while their appeals for asylum were pending were unlawful because their effect was to prevent the right to appeal from being exercised.[89] Furthermore, delegated legislation must add something. Where regulations may be made to prescribe a description of a type of benefits scheme, those regulations must actually contain a description which goes beyond that in the primary legislation.[90]

There have been a series of cases at the highest level arising out of the various legislative regimes for designating certain individuals or institutions because of alleged links to terrorism or rogue states. That designation will result in the freezing of assets and the prevention of trade with others; a potentially draconian outcome. In *Ahmed v HM Treasury*, the Supreme Court held ultra vires clauses in Orders in Council made under the United Nations Act 1946 that sought to implement resolutions of the UN Security Council requiring states to freeze the assets of persons who commit or attempt to commit terrorist acts.[91] One reason why the orders were ultra vires was that they went wider than the Security Council resolutions by

[84] [2016] UKSC 39, [2016] AC 1531.
[85] [2017] UKSC 51. The Supreme Court also held that the order was in breach of EU law. For an earlier example of similar reasoning to similar effect, see *R v Lord Chancellor, ex p Witham* [1998] QB 575.
[86] *Malloch v Aberdeen Corpn* 1974 SLT 253; and see Education (Scotland) Act 1973.
[87] *Raymond v Honey* [1983] AC 1 and *R v Home Secretary, ex p Leech* [1994] QB 198.
[88] *Badger Trust v Welsh Ministers* [2010] EWCA Civ 807.
[89] *R v Social Security Secretary, ex p Joint Council for Welfare of Immigrants* [1996] 4 All ER 385.
[90] *R (Reilly) v Work and Pensions Secretary* [2013] UKSC 68, [2013] 3 WLR 1276.
[91] [2010] UKSC 2, [2010] 2 AC 534.

being stated to apply where there were 'reasonable grounds for suspecting' that someone was or might be a terrorist; also, the effect of one order was to deprive an individual of the chance to seek judicial review of his listing as a terrorist. In *R* v *Forsyth*, concerning another Order in Council made under the 1946 Act, it was claimed that the order was invalid because it had been made ten years after the Security Council had asked governments to prevent funds being made available to Iraq.[92] The Supreme Court held that, while urgent measures would often be required by the Security Council, the lapse of time did not prevent the government from implementing this Security Council resolution. In a case arising from a Security Council resolution concerning the supply of military equipment to Iraq, an Order in Council was held not to be effective, since an essential definition of the banned equipment could not be found in other delegated legislation; criticising government departments for not keeping proper records of their legislation, the Court of Appeal refused to supply its own definition to fill the gap in the prosecution's case.[93] Most recently, an Iranian bank suspected of being involved in financing Iran's nuclear programme challenged an Order made under the Counter-Terrorism Act 2008 that effectively excluded the bank from the UK financial market.[94] The majority of the Supreme Court held that it was irrational and arbitrary to designate the bank where the risk did not arise from the bank specifically, but the banking sector generally. It was also procedurally unfair that the bank had not had the opportunity to make representations on the decision to designate it. The Court held that the fact that the designation took the form of delegated legislation requiring parliamentary approval did not affect the duty of fairness.

The courts do not lightly review the substantive legality of a statutory instrument, but if necessary they apply a test of unreasonableness where a regulation is so unreasonable that Parliament cannot be taken as having authorised it to be made under the Act in question.[95] However, where an order by the Environment Secretary 'capping' local councils' expenditure was subject to approval by resolution of the Commons, the House of Lords held that if the order came within the 'four corners' of the parent statute, it was subject to review for unreasonableness only on the extreme grounds of bad faith, improper motive or manifest absurdity.[96]

A serious procedural error by the department concerned could lead to an instrument being set aside. Where there was a duty to consult interested organisations before regulations were made, it was held that the mere sending of a letter to an organisation did not amount to consultation;[97] and no effective consultation occurred when a department failed to allow sufficient time for this.[98] But not every procedural error vitiates the statutory instrument, and if there has been substantial compliance with a prescribed procedure, minor irregularities may be overlooked.

Where because of its content or procedure an instrument is to an extent defective, this does not necessarily mean that the whole instrument is a nullity; it may still be operative to its lawful extent or bind persons not affected by the defect of procedure.[99] To decide when such 'severance' is permissible may involve a textual, or 'blue pencil' test (does deletion of the

---

[92] [2011] UKSC 9, [2011] 2 AC 69.

[93] *R* v *D* [2011] EWCA Crim 2082, [2012] 1 All ER 1108.

[94] *Bank Mellat* v *HM Treasury (No 2)* [2013] UKSC 39, [2014] AC 700.

[95] *Maynard* v *Osmond* [1977] QB 240; *Cinnamond* v *British Airports Authority* [1980] 2 All ER 368; *R* v *Home Secretary, ex p Javed* [2001] EWCA 789, [2002] QB 129.

[96] *R* v *Environment Secretary, ex p Hammersmith BC* [1991] 1 AC 521, applying *Nottinghamshire CC* v *Environment Secretary* [1986] AC 240 (C M G Himsworth [1986] PL 374, [1991] PL 76).

[97] *Mushrooms Ltd Agricultural Industry Training Board* v *Aylesbury* [1972] 1 WLR 190.

[98] *R* v *Social Services Secretary, ex p Association of Metropolitan Authorities* [1986] 1 All ER 164. See also *Howker* v *Work and Pensions Secretary* [2002] EWCA Civ 1623, [2003] ICR 405.

[99] *Dunkley* v *Evans* [1981] 3 All ER 285; the *Aylesbury Mushrooms* case, note 97 above.

offending phrase or sentence leave a grammatical and coherent text?) and also a test of whether, after deletion of the unlawful part, the substance of the provision remains essentially unchanged in purpose and effect from what had been intended.[100]

Where the parent Act provides that regulations when made should have effect 'as if enacted in this Act', the correct view has long been that this expression in the parent Act adds nothing to the binding effect of a properly made instrument.[101] Where a tribunal must adjudicate on the rights of an individual and the extent of those rights is directly affected by a regulation, the tribunal must if necessary decide whether the regulation is valid;[102] its decision on this issue will be subject to appeal. And if someone is prosecuted for breach of a regulation or by-law, it is always a good defence in law for the defendant to show that the instrument in question is invalid.[103]

By-laws are a form of delegated legislation that generally applies only in a particular locality or certain public places (for example, airports). They are usually made by a local council or a statutory undertaking and are subject to ministerial confirmation before they take effect. The courts have traditionally shown less deference in respect of by-laws than over departmental regulations,[104] but there are principled suggestions that any law made by a democratically accountable body should be accorded respect by the court.[105]

E. Administrative rule-making

Legislation by statutory instrument is more flexible than primary legislation, since the law can be changed without the need for a Bill to pass through Parliament. Nonetheless, statutory instrument procedures are complex and the instruments are expressed in formal language. In government today, many less formal methods of rule-making are used. Such methods are sometimes directly authorised by Act of Parliament, but rules so made may have an uncertain legal status, for example, immigration rules made under the Immigration Act 1971. In *Odelola* v *Home Secretary*,[106] Lord Hoffmann referred to the 'rather unusual' status of the immigration rules and the House of Lords held that they were not delegated legislation. In *Pankina* v *Home Secretary*[107] the Home Office had issued 'policy guidance' that added an increased financial requirement to what the Immigration Rules said must be shown by students of UK universities who had come to study in the United Kingdom and wished to remain to do skilled work after graduating. The Court of Appeal held this requirement to be unlawful, since (as Sedley LJ said), the immigration rules 'have ceased to be policy and have acquired a status akin to law'. That additional requirement should have been laid before Parliament as an amendment to the Immigration Rules.

Not surprisingly, the implications of this decision were examined in a stream of other cases, culminating in two decisions by the Supreme Court. In *R (Munir)* v *Home Secretary* a

---

[100] *DPP* v *Hutchinson* [1990] 2 AC 783 (A W Bradley [1990] PL 293); and *R* v *IRC, ex p Woolwich Building Society* [1991] 4 All ER 92. Cf *R (Confederation of Passenger Transport)* v *Humber Bridge Board* [2003] EWCA 842, [2004] QB 310 (power of court to remedy evident mistake in statutory instrument).

[101] *Minister of Health* v *R* [1931] AC 494.

[102] *Chief Adjudication Officer* v *Foster* [1993] AC 754 (D Feldman (1992) 108 LQR 45; A W Bradley [1992] PL 185). See also: *Work and Pensions Secretary* v *Carmichael* [2017] UKUT 174 (AAC).

[103] E.g. *R* v *Reading Crown Court, ex p Hutchinson* [1988] QB 384; *Boddington* v *British Transport Police* [1999] 2 AC 143.

[104] See *Kruse* v *Johnson* [1898] 2 QB 91; *Cinnamond* v *British Airports Authority* [1980] 2 All ER 368.

[105] *R (Petsafe Ltd)* v *Welsh Ministers* [2010] EWHC 2908 (Admin), [2011] EuLR 270.

[106] [2009] UKHL 25, [2009] 1 WLR 1230.

[107] [2010] EWCA Civ 7191, [2011] QB 376.

Bangladeshi citizen and his wife and children were adversely affected by the withdrawal of a policy introduced in 1996 that enabled a family to remain in the United Kingdom where the children had had more than seven years' continuous residence.[108] The policy and its withdrawal had never been included in Immigration Rules. The Supreme Court rejected arguments for the Home Secretary that the power to make immigration rules was derived from the royal prerogative, finding that they were delegated legislation and that *Odelola* was obiter and wrong. The policy in question did not have the nature of a rule and that neither the policy nor its withdrawal had to be included in the Immigration Rules. In the linked case of *R (Alvi)* v *Home Secretary* the same court, grappling with the difficult borderline between what is and is not a rule that must be included in the Immigration Rules, held that 'the Immigration Rules should include all those provisions which set out criteria which are or may be determinative of an application for leave to enter or remain'.[109] Since some aspects of the 'points based system' for granting admission for certain occupations were determinative of whether Alvi, an assistant physiotherapist, would be admitted, they should have been included in the Immigration Rules and not merely included in ancillary codes of practice.[110] Unhelpfully, Lord Hope appears to have approved the *Odelola* line that the Rules are not delegated legislation, despite the Court's clear judgment in *Munir*.[111]

Two forms of rule-making that are often authorised by statute are codes of practice and administrative guidelines or notes of guidance.[112] In 2017, the Cabinet Office defined codes of practice in the following way.

> A code of practice is an authoritative statement of practice to be followed in some field. It typically differs from legislation in that it offers guidance rather than imposing requirements: its prescriptions are not hard and fast rules but guidelines which may allow considerable latitude in their practical application and may be departed from in appropriate circumstances. The provisions of a code are not directly enforceable by legal proceedings, which is not to say that they may not have significant legal effects. A code of practice, unlike a legislative text, may also contain explanatory material and argument.[113]

Such codes of practice are often found in branches of law such as that on the use of police powers and employment disputes. Although codes of practice and guidance do not have the force of delegated legislation and generally do not have a mandatory effect,[114] the issuing department may be expected either to observe them or take steps to change them.[115] A local authority or a body such as an NHS trust must follow statutory guidance from central government except where it can state good reasons for not doing so.[116]

Depending on the parent Act, these rules may totally evade the procedures for parliamentary control described earlier. In fact, many administrative rules are issued without direct statutory authority. This phenomenon was once described as 'administrative

---

[108] [2012] UKSC 32, [2012] 1 WLR 2192.

[109] [2012] UKSC 33, [2012] 1 WLR 2208 at [97].

[110] The Supreme Court promptly had to return to the effect of *Munir* and *Alvi* in *R (New London College Ltd)* v *Home Secretary* [2013] UKSC 51, [2013] 1 WLR 2858.

[111] [2012] UKSC 33, [2012] 1 WLR 2208 at [9].

[112] See e.g. Police and Criminal Evidence Act 1984, Part VI; Freedom of Information Act 2000, ss 45 and 46.

[113] *Cabinet Office Guide to Making Legislation* (2017), App D.

[114] See e.g. *Laker Airways* v *Department of Trade* [1977] QB 643.

[115] *R* v *Home Secretary, ex p Khan* [1985] 1 All ER 40 (A R Mowbray [1985] PL 558).

[116] *R* v *Islington Council, ex p Rixon* [1997] ELR 66; *R (Munjaz)* v *Ashworth Hospital Authority* [2005] UKHL 58, [2006] 2 AC 148 (hospital's policy on detention of mental patients upheld despite departing from code of practice). Also *R (Daniel Thwaites plc)* v *Wirral Magistrates* [2008] EWHC 838 (Admin), [2009] 1 All ER 239 (duty of licensing authority to 'have regard to' guidance from Secretary of State).

quasi-legislation',[117] when it was related to the practice of issuing the official interpretation of doubtful points in statutes and of stating concessions that would be made in individual cases. The practice has continued, for the revenue authorities often choose to waive the application of over-harsh laws rather than seek changes in the legislation. In 1979, the then Inland Revenue's use of executive discretion rather than a statutory basis for assessing tax was described by the House of Lords as unconstitutional.[118] As Walton J had said: 'One should be taxed by law, and not be untaxed by concession.'[119]

In many areas of government, such as town planning, housing, education and health, ministerial statements of policy and circulars to local authorities have a practical effect which falls little short of declaring or modifying the law. On matters of general policy where controversial issues are involved, government by circular is not a satisfactory substitute for legislation. Nor can such circulars require the performance of unlawful acts.[120]

F. Conclusion

Understanding of the legislative process, and the ways by which delegated legislation are made, is rarely high on the constitutional and administrative lawyer's agenda. However, as this chapter has shown, understanding delegated legislation is essential for two principal reasons.

First, the making and passing of delegated legislation is a fundamental aspect of our constitutional arrangements. Delegated legislation, as we have discussed, is now a far greater proportion of the law that guides our everyday lives than it was even 20 years ago. Any constitutional lawyer must be able to understand when it can be made, how it is made, how (and the extent to which) it is scrutinised and how it is different from the primary legislation under which it is made.

Secondly, delegated legislation can be the subject of an administrative law challenge in the courts. It can be declared ultra vires and it can be struck down. Understanding how it has been made, and the particular considerations the courts will apply to the evaluation of delegated legislation, is essential for any challenge to be brought or a legal judgment evaluated.

---

[117] R E Megarry (1944) 60 LQR 125; Ganz, *Quasi-Legislation*; R Baldwin and J Houghton [1986] PL 239. Informal administrative rules may be termed 'tertiary rules' (Baldwin, *Rules and Government*, ch 4) or, in the European context, 'soft law' : K Wellens and G Borchardt (1989) 14 EL Rev 267.

[118] *Vestey* v *IRC (No 2)* [1980] AC 1148.

[119] *Vestey* v *IRC* [1979] Ch 177, 197. See *R (Wilkinson)* v *IRC* [2005] UKHL 30, [2006] 1 All ER 529 (extra-statutory concession could not be made to grant widowers a tax allowance that Parliament had granted only to widows) and *R (Davies)* v *HMRC* [2011] UKSC 47, [2011] 1 WLR 2625 (whether guidance on non-domicile rules having benevolent interpretation or are inconsistent with practice). For adverse comment, see S Sedley, *Lions under the Throne*, p 130. See too the unsuccessful judicial review of the Revenue's decisions to reach settlements with major corporations which had considerable tax liabilities: *UK Uncut Legal Action Ltd* v *HMRC* [2013] EHWC 1283 (Admin).

[120] *Royal College of Nursing* v *DHSS* [1981] AC 800; *Gillick* v *West Norfolk Health Authority* [1986] AC 112.

CHAPTER 23

Administrative justice

The title of this chapter may seem a contradiction in terms: there are such marked differences between the way in which decisions are made by civil servants and ministers on the one hand, and by the courts on the other, that the two systems, administration and justice, should be kept quite separate. However, as we will see in relation to judicial review, there is a strong tendency in administrative law for principles derived from the courts, such as the doctrine of natural justice, to be applied to official decisions. The same tendency applies to developing institutions within government. In his seminal book, *Justice and Administrative Law*, first published in 1928, Robson described the extent to which 'trial by Whitehall' had developed in the British constitution. He argued that the judicial powers given to administrative bodies promoted the welfare of society and that administrative justice could become 'as well-founded and broad-based as any other kind of justice now known to us and embodied in human institutions'.[1] Today, the influence of administrative justice is seen in decisions of the European Court of Human Rights interpreting art 6 of the European Convention.[2]

In this chapter, we examine various institutions and procedures that are located within a broad territory somewhere between the world of government departments on one hand and that of the law courts on the other. This territory is liable to be the site of diverse struggles for possession between competing interests from the administrative and legal worlds. In one sector of the territory that was formerly under strong departmental influence, namely administrative tribunals, the judicial model of decision-making now holds undoubted sway. Indeed, the British system of tribunals must no longer be referred to with the adjective 'administrative'. The system will be outlined in section A of this chapter, but in truth specialist tribunals are now a vital element in the garden of justice, with their own maze of case law and procedural rules.

In another sector, that of public inquiries (section B), government departments exercise the dominant influence over the decision-making, but key aspects of the procedures exist to promote the fairness and openness of the process. section C deals with inquiries appointed under the Inquiries Act 2005 (which replaced older legislation). This Act provides a formal process of impartial fact-finding for discovering what happened when things have gone seriously wrong in government or major scandals and disasters have occurred. section D is concerned with Ombudsmen. The function of these officials is to investigate individual complaints about government or public authority action and to discover whether injustice has been caused by official error. Ombudsmen carry out this function by investigatory means which owe little to court procedures, and their powers fall short of requiring a remedy to be provided, although an acceptable remedy is usually the result when the Ombudsman decides that injustice has occurred.

---

[1] Robson, *Justice and Administrative Law*, p 515.
[2] See e.g. C Harlow in Alston (ed.), *The EU and Human Rights*, ch 7; R Barrett & P Engelman, in Supperstone, Goudie and Walker (eds), *Judicial Review*, pp 74–78. Also Harris and Partington (eds), *Administrative Justice in the 21st Century*, pt 5; and Adler (ed.), *Administrative Justice in Context*.

A. Tribunals[3]

Reasons for creation of tribunals

For many centuries Britain has had specialised courts in addition to the courts of general jurisdiction. Mediaeval merchants had their courts of pie poudre; the tin miners of Devon and Cornwall had their courts of Stannaries.[4] From the early 19th century until they were abolished in 2009, the General Commissioners of Income Tax provided a local court for resolving disputes about the amount of tax that an individual should pay. The growth of the modern state led to the creation of many new procedures for settling the disputes that arose from the impact of public powers and duties on the rights and interests of private persons. The National Insurance Act 1911, in creating the first British social insurance scheme, provided for individual disputes that arose to be decided on appeal by an independent panel. Indeed, the history of social security appeals is central to the history of tribunals in the 20th century: after 1945, the structure of appeals became a notable feature of the welfare state.[5]

When Parliament creates new public services or regulatory schemes, questions and disputes will inevitably arise from operation of the legislation. There are three main means of enabling such questions and disputes to be settled: (*a*) by conferring new jurisdiction on the ordinary courts; (*b*) by creating new machinery in the form of a tribunal, sometimes with the right of appeal to a higher tribunal or to the courts; or (*c*) by leaving decisions to be made by the administrative bodies responsible for the scheme. Possible variants in solution (*c*) include (i) allowing an individual to seek review at a higher level within the same public body of a decision that he or she does not accept; (ii) providing for an appeal to another administrative body (for example, from a local council to central government), or (iii) requiring a hearing or public inquiry to be held before certain decisions are made. Whether or not any provision of these kinds is made, the procedure of judicial review is potentially available to supervise the legality of decisions. But judicial review, which should be an exceptional remedy, does not provide a right of appeal and is unable to ensure the quality of numerous decisions at first instance.

In 1955 the Committee on Administrative Tribunals and Inquiries (the Franks committee) was appointed to review (*a*) the constitution and working of statutory tribunals appointed in connection with the functions of ministers and (*b*) the operation of administrative procedures that included the holding of public inquiries or hearings on behalf of ministers, especially in relation to the compulsory purchase of land. One achievement of the Franks committee, which reported in 1957, was to make clear that tribunals and inquiries differed in their constitutional status and functions. No tribunal ought to be seen as part of the structure of a government department, for tribunals exercised functions which were essentially judicial in character, although of a specialised nature. As the Franks committee stated in words of great significance:

> We consider that tribunals should properly be regarded as machinery provided by Parliament for adjudication rather than as part of the machinery of administration. The essential point is that in all these cases Parliament has deliberately provided for a decision outside and independent of the Department concerned.[6]

---

[3] See report of the Franks committee, Cmnd 218, 1957, parts II and III; Richardson and Genn (eds), *Administrative Law and Government Action*, part II; Harlow and Rawlings, *Law and Administration*, ch 11; Leggatt, *Tribunals for Users*; and Jacobs, *Tribunal Practice and Procedure*.

[4] See *R v East Powder Justices, ex p Lampshire* [1979] QB 616.

[5] On these tribunals, see Baldwin, Wikeley and Young, *Judging Social Security*; Adler and Bradley (eds), *Justice, Discretion and Poverty*; cf R Sainsbury, in Harris and Partington (eds), *Administrative Justice in the 21st Century*, ch 22.

[6] Cmnd 218, 1957, p 9.

In contrast, the public inquiry, while it granted those affected by official proposals with some safeguards against ill-informed and hasty decisions, was essentially a step in a complex process leading to a departmental decision for which a minister was responsible to Parliament.

The constitutional logic of the view that tribunals are 'machinery provided by Parliament for adjudication' reached its culmination 50 years after the Franks report, in the Tribunals, Courts and Enforcement Act 2007. We shall see that this Act deals with tribunals as a vital part of the machinery of justice, operating alongside the ordinary civil courts.

Court and tribunals – some comparisons

Although there is today no doubt about the judicial role of tribunals, the existence of tribunals was sometimes in the past thought to weaken the judiciary and the authority of the ordinary courts.[7] In fact, the machinery of the courts is not suited for settling all disputes arising out of the work of government. One reason for this is the need for specialised knowledge (in areas such as taxation, social security or immigration) if disputes are to be settled expeditiously and consistently. Another reason is the large volume of appeals that arise from first-instance decisions in such areas. Further, while policy decisions and oversight of a department's work are entrusted to ministers, the efficient administration of many areas of government depends on there being a body of rules which officials can apply without constant recourse to a minister.[8] The right of appeal against an official's decision at first instance is a better remedy for the aggrieved individual than the principle of ministerial responsibility, since it provides a means of discovering whether the rules have been correctly applied or whether a decision has been made that is contrary to the department's professed policies.

Factors favouring the use of tribunals have included the need for procedure which avoids the formality of the courts; the need, if a new social policy is introduced, for the speedy, cheap and decentralised decision of many cases; and the need for expert knowledge in the tribunal, whose members may include both lawyers and also other professionals or lay persons. Another factor has been that the legal profession has no monopoly of the right to represent parties to tribunal proceedings: there is a value in enabling the individual affected to be heard in person by the tribunal.[9] Certainly, most tribunals are concerned with disputes between a private individual and a public authority (these may be termed, disputes between *citizen and the state*). This does not apply to employment tribunals, which deal with disputes between the parties to the employment relationship. However, even with this exception there is a striking overlap in the decisions made by courts and tribunals.[10] For instance, in hearing claims for unlawful discrimination brought against employers, employment tribunals make decisions that other legal systems entrust to a labour court; and cases alleging unlawful discrimination against bodies other than employers are, under the Equality Act 2010, brought in the county court.

The essentials of good adjudication apply to both tribunals and courts. The right under art 6(1) ECHR to a fair hearing before an independent and impartial court or tribunal does not depend on the label applied to the decision-maker. It is fundamental that neither judges nor tribunal members should be subject to dismissal when a government department is dissatisfied with their decisions. Procedure in a tribunal is often said to be informal. But informality is difficult to reconcile with the need for legal precision,[11] not to mention fairness to all parties, and tribunal procedures are not always less formal than procedures in a comparable court.

---

[7] See e.g. Lord Scarman, *English Law – the New Dimension*, part III. For a historical critique, see Arthurs, *Without the Law: Administrative Justice and Legal Pluralism in the 19th Century*.

[8] This fact underlies the present use in Whitehall of executive agencies: see ch 11 D.

[9] See G Richardson and H Genn [2007] PL 116, re-assessing the right to an oral hearing.

[10] A very different distinction is drawn in Australia between 'administrative tribunals' and the courts: see P Cane [2009] PL 479 and (same author) *Administrative Tribunals and Adjudication*.

[11] H Genn, in Richardson and Genn (eds), ch 11 (note 3 above).

Although some tribunals do exercise jurisdiction at first instance (this is true of employ-ment tribunals), the right to go to a tribunal usually arises only where a public body or official has first made a decision that the individual disputes. The need for individuals to appeal will depend to a large extent on whether the public body in question has taken reasonable steps to ensure that they 'get decisions right first time'.[12]

A safeguard common to all tribunals is that it should be possible to challenge their deci-sions on points of law, whether by appeal to a higher court or tribunal or by judicial review. Until the reform of the tribunal system made in 2007, the confusing lack of system in rela-tion to tribunals extended to the piecemeal provision made for appeals.[13] Where no right of appeal is provided in the legislation, the decisions and procedures of a tribunal are subject to judicial review.[14]

The Leggatt review of tribunals

In 2001, for the first time since the Franks report of 1957, a review of all tribunals was con-ducted. It was undertaken for the Lord Chancellor by a retired Court of Appeal judge, Sir Andrew Leggatt, assisted by an expert panel.[15] He found that, leaving regulatory bodies to one side, there were some 70 different tribunals in England and Wales, between them dispos-ing of nearly a million cases each year. But of the 70 tribunals, only 20 heard more than 500 cases a year: many of the tribunals were defunct and some had never had any cases to decide. Leggatt criticised the lack of system in tribunals, commenting that tribunals had grown up in a haphazard way, created piecemeal by legislation and separately administered by govern-ment departments with wide variations of approach, in a way that (in his view) took more account of departmental needs than the convenience of tribunal users. He proposed the crea-tion of what would indeed be a system of administrative justice, 'a single, overarching struc-ture' that would give the individual improved access to all tribunals. Although this would involve reorganising the structure and servicing of tribunals, many tribunals, particularly those with large caseloads, would continue to function with little practical change in their decision-making being necessary.

The Leggatt review proposed that there should be a single tribunal system, administered by an integrated tribunal service, and operating in divisions according to subject matter. The divisions proposed by Leggatt would have brought together existing tribunals under nine headings: (*a*) education; (*b*) employment; (*c*) finance and revenue; (*d*) health and care; (*e*) immigration and asylum; (*f*) property, land and valuation; (*g*) social security, pensions and criminal injury compensation; (*h*) transport; and (*i*) aspects of trade, competition, patents and copyright. Leggatt also proposed the creation of a general tribunal to hear appeals from the first tier of tribunal decisions, since the 'tribunal maze' extended to a bewildering variety in the rights of appeal.

Tribunals, Courts and Enforcement Act 2007

A main aim of the Act was to carry through the complex reform of tribunals initiated by the Leggatt review.[16] Part 1 of the Act set up two new general tribunals, with the function of replacing the great majority of the former first-instance and appellate tribunals: the First-tier Tribunal to make first-instance decisions, and the Upper Tribunal to hear appeals from the

---

[12] *Transforming Public Services*, Cmd 6243, 2004, para 3.9.

[13] See Lord Woolf (1988) 7 CJQ 44; Law Commission, *Administrative Law: Judicial Review and Statutory Appeals* (HC 669, 1993–4), part XII.

[14] See chs 24, 25.

[15] See Leggatt, *Tribunals for Users*, and comment by A W Bradley [2002] PL 200.

[16] See R Carnwath [2009] PL 48.

First-tier Tribunal (s 3). The Act created the office of Senior President of Tribunals, appointed by the Queen on the advice of the Lord Chancellor (s 2). The first Senior President was Carnwath LJ. The Act envisages that his successors would also be drawn from the Court of Appeal or from the appellate courts in Scotland and Northern Ireland,[17] and upon his appointment to the Supreme Court in 2012, Sullivan LJ was appointed the Senior President. Ryder LJ was appointed in 2015. In a statement of principle that reinforces the assimilation of tribunals to the courts, the guarantee of judicial independence given in the Constitutional Reform Act 2005[18] for judges in the civil and criminal courts was extended to those holding judicial office in the new tribunals (s 1).

The Senior President must take account of the need for tribunals to be accessible, for their proceedings to be fair, quick and efficient, for tribunals to have available suitable expertise to deal with specialised areas of law, and for the development of new informal methods of resolving disputes (s 2). The Senior President reports each year to the Lord Chancellor on matters relevant to cases coming before the First-tier and Upper Tribunals (s 43), has authority to make representations to Parliament, and is required to represent the views of all tribunal members (sch 1, paras 13, 14). The two tribunals comprise persons who are legally qualified and are known as judges, as well as non-legal members who may have professional qualifications (for instance, in medicine or valuation) or be lay persons with relevant experience.

The First-tier Tribunal is organised in a system of chambers, each headed by a judge as president. The Lord Chancellor has power by order to transfer the functions of many tribunals to the appropriate chamber, whereupon the former tribunals are abolished. The First-tier Tribunal comprises six divisions: (*a*) the General Regulatory Chamber (whose multifarious functions include consumer credit and estate agent appeals, charity appeals, information disputes, appeals concerning the micro-chipping of dogs and driving standards agency appeals); (*b*) the Social Entitlement Chamber (dealing with social security, child support, asylum support and criminal injuries compensation); (*c*) the Health, Education and Social Care Chamber (mental health review, special educational needs and disability, and care standards); (*d*) the War Pensions and Armed Forces Compensation Chamber: (*e*) the Tax Chamber (income tax, VAT and duties); (*f*) the Immigration and Asylum Chamber;[19] and (*g*) the Property Chamber (residential property, rent functions, leasehold valuation and agricultural lands). Members of the First-tier Tribunal may sit in more than one chamber. Employment tribunals, and some other smaller jurisdictions, are outside this structure, but like the First-tier Tribunal chambers they are administered by the general Courts and Tribunals Service.

The Upper Tribunal is organised in a smaller number of chambers: (1) the Administrative Appeals Chamber; (2) the Tax and Chancery Chamber; (3) the Lands Chamber; and (4) the Immigration and Asylum Chamber. The president of each chamber is a High Court judge. In outline, each chamber hears appeals from one or more chambers of the First-tier Tribunal, although certain limited types of case may be heard directly by the Upper Tribunal. However, the First-tier Tribunal has power to review its own decisions (exercisable once only in any case) and it may then take a fresh decision, may refer the case to the Upper Tribunal or may decide that no action is needed.[20] The purpose of this review is to deal rapidly with decisions that are considered to be clearly wrong, so avoiding the need for an appeal. The parties

---

[17] If it is not possible to appoint a judge at appellate level, the Judicial Appointments Commission will operate a selection process: sch 1, parts 1 and 2.

[18] See ch 13 B.

[19] The functions of the former Asylum and Immigration Tribunal have been divided between this chamber of the First-tier Tribunal and the related chamber in the Upper Tribunal.

[20] 2007 Act, s 9. The Upper Tribunal has a similar power (s 10).

to a decision by the First-tier Tribunal have a right of appeal to the Upper Tribunal, but only on a point of law and only with the leave of either Tribunal. A novel feature of the scheme is that the Upper Tribunal may in specified classes of case exercise a so-called 'judicial review' jurisdiction, closely modelled on judicial review proceedings in the Administrative Court; and certain proceedings may be transferred from the Administrative Court to the Upper Tribunal, and vice versa (ss 15–21). From the Upper Tribunal, there is a right of appeal with leave to the Court of Appeal (in Scotland, to the Inner House of the Court of Session) (ss 13–14).[21]

In two Supreme Court cases heard together in 2011, *R (Cart)* v *Upper Tribunal*[22] and *Eba* v *Advocate General for Scotland*,[23] the question arose of whether, if leave to appeal is refused by both First-tier and Upper Tribunals, that refusal is subject to judicial review. A refusal of permission to appeal is an excluded decision within the meaning of the Act and cannot be appealed (ss 11(4) and 13(8)). The Supreme Court in *Cart* held that (*a*) the Upper Tribunal's decisions were subject to judicial review, but (*b*) in light of the tribunal structure under the 2007 Act, it was reasonable to restrict judicial review by applying criteria that now apply to limit the making of a 'second-tier appeal' to the Court of Appeal, and also to appeals from the Upper Tribunal to the Court of Appeal. These criteria are (*a*) that the appeal raises an important point of principle or practice or (*b*) that there is some other compelling reason for the appeal to be heard. In reaching this decision, the Supreme Court emphasised both the importance of entrusting the courts with authority to uphold the law, and the need for courts to remember that even in the administration of justice, resources are limited. As a result of this decision, and in response to suggestions from members of the Court, the Civil Procedure Rules were amended to provide for the test set out in *Cart*.[24] In addition, the judicial review time limit has been reduced to 16 days after the date on which the Upper Tribunal's decision was sent to the applicant (r 54.7A(3)), and unlike with normal judicial review claims, there is no right to request an oral reconsideration if permission is refused on the papers (r 54.7A(8)). In *Eba* v *Advocate General for Scotland*, a similar conclusion was reached for Scotland; and the Supreme Court ruled that, contrary to what was held in *Watt* v *Lord Advocate*,[25] the Scottish courts may correct an error of law made by a statutory tribunal even if the error might be said to be 'within jurisdiction'. Lord Hope observed that, while the position of tribunals in Scotland has not been identical with their position in English law, the 2007 Act did apply to Scotland and there were common factors (such as the need to respect the expertise of specialist tribunals) that indicated that Scots law and English law should now be aligned.

One valuable result of the two-tier structure is to rationalise the diverging procedures that separate tribunals had used. This task has been carried out by the Tribunal Procedure Committee. The aims of the procedure rules include that of ensuring that in tribunal proceedings 'justice is done'; that the tribunal system is 'accessible and fair'; that proceedings are 'handled quickly and efficiently'; and that the rules are 'both simple and clearly expressed'.[26]

All appointments to the First-tier and Upper Tribunals are made by the Judicial Appointments Commission. The 2007 Act contains rules of eligibility for appointment to

---

[21] On the meaning attached to errors of law at this level, and the desirability of interpreting the concept flexibly, see Carnwath (note 16 above) at 61–4 and *R (Jones)* v *First-tier Tribunal* [2013] UKSC 19, [2013] 2 AC 48, [43]–[47]. For a more sceptical approach, see *Criminal Injuries Compensation Authority* v *Hutton* [2016] EWCA Civ 1305.

[22] [2011] UKSC 28, [2012] 1 AC 663.

[23] [2011] UKSC 29, 2011 SLT 768.

[24] Civil Procedure (Amendment No.2) Rules 2012 (SI No 2012/2208).

[25] 1979 SC 120.

[26] 2007 Act, s 22(4). The rules take account of the specialist needs of each chamber. All the procedure rules are listed on the justice.gov.uk website.

the Tribunals that may encourage greater diversity in their membership.[27] The flexible and wide-ranging jurisdiction of the two Tribunals should mean that no other tribunals need be created in future: if as a result of legislation new decisions are to be made that require a right of appeal, power to decide the appeals can be conferred on the First-tier Tribunal, and then assigned to an appropriate chamber, as has not infrequently occurred.

Some tribunals continue to exist outside the two-tier scheme created by the Act of 2007. They include the Investigatory Powers Tribunal, created by the Regulation of Investigatory Powers Act 2000, the Proscribed Organisations Appeal Commission, created under the Terrorism Act 2000, and the Competition Appeal Tribunal, created by the Enterprise Act 2002. Tribunals that are now outside the two-tier tribunal structure may be brought within the scheme, provided that they exist under statutory authority. This means that private and domestic tribunals must remain outside the scheme, but bodies that hear appeals from decisions made by local councils may in future be added to it.

Conclusion

The constitutional position of tribunals has been transformed by the reforms initiated by the Leggatt review and given effect by Parliament in 2007.[28] Most issues over tribunals that arose between 1957 and 2007 are now of historical interest alone. The legislative changes have had to be matched by an extensive re-deployment of administrative and judicial resources. The full benefits of having a system of tribunals that is assimilated to the system of courts are still being felt, but the allocation of decision-making to the First-tier and Upper Tribunals has made possible a flexible and effective interface between these tribunals, and the Administrative Court and Court of Appeal. In the immigration and asylum field, the allocation of the vast majority of such cases to the specialist tribunal chambers has vastly reduced the workload of the Administrative Court. The First-tier and Upper Tribunals comply fully with the standards of judicial decision-making required by art 6(1) ECHR, although not necessarily every substantive underlying area of law determined by those tribunals engages civil rights and obligations within the meaning of art 6(1).[29] It is unlikely (unless Parliament were to go back on the Act of 2007) that tribunals could come under covert political influence or control. To take one example, the creation of the Immigration and Asylum chambers within the two-tier structure should prove to last longer than other attempts to structure decision-making in this controversial area. The commitment of the 2007 Act to the wider landscape of administrative justice, including the principle of proportionate dispute resolution, should ensure that tribunal procedures are not raised to a level of formality that prevents decisions being made in a manner that is accessible, effective and understood by the public, although there has been an inevitable array of Upper Tribunal case law interpreting the procedural rules.[30]

B. Public inquiries

As we have seen in section A, the status of tribunals in the United Kingdom is now largely assimilated to that of the courts: the legally qualified members of the First-tier and Upper Tribunals are termed judges, and the tribunals have a close relationship with

---

[27] 2007 Act, schs 2, 3; Qualifications for Appointment of Members to the First-tier Tribunal and Upper Tribunal Order 2008 (SI No 2692/2008), as amended.

[28] As was convincingly argued by Carnwath LJ in his first annual report as Senior President of Tribunals: *Tribunals Transfers*, 2010.

[29] See e.g. *Browning* v *Information Commissioner* [2013] UKUT 236 (AAC) at [82] in relation to appeals under the Freedom of Information Act 2000.

[30] As to which, see Jacobs, *Tribunal Practice and Procedure*.

the Administrative Court and Court of Appeal. The nature of public inquiries is different. The public inquiry is an administrative process that became widespread during the 20th century as government departments acquired power to intervene in matters of local government such as housing, public health, compulsory purchase and town planning. The issues that caused central government to become involved often arose out of a conflict between a local authority's policies and the rights and interests of individuals. Public inquiries of this kind (conducted locally by an official of central government, most commonly designated an 'inspector')[31] should not be confused with inquiries investigating matters of national concern, that may be held under the Inquiries Act 2005; these are considered in section C below.

Two views on the nature of inquiries have often been expressed. As seen by the Franks committee in 1957, the 'administrative' view was to regard the inquiry as a step leading to a ministerial decision in the exercise of discretion, for which the minister was responsible only to Parliament. By contrast, on the 'judicial' view, the inquiry appeared 'to take on something of the nature of a trial and the inspector to assume the guise of a judge', so that the ensuing decision must be based directly on the evidence presented at the inquiry.[32]

The Franks committee rejected these two extreme interpretations. In the committee's view, the objects of the inquiry procedure were (*a*) to protect the interests of the citizens most directly affected by a governmental proposal by granting them a right to be heard in support of their objections; and (*b*) to ensure that thereby the minister would be better informed of the whole facts of the case before the final decision was made.[33]

The inquiries examined by the Franks committee mostly concerned such matters as the compulsory purchase of land for public purposes (such as a new town, a power station or a motorway), and disputes under planning law about the use and development of land. Inquiries and similar procedures serve many other purposes, for example to inquire into electoral boundaries[34] or to investigate the failure by a local authority to maintain proper standards of care in relation to children.[35]

Rules of procedure for public inquiries

Under the Tribunals and Inquiries Act 1992, s 9, as amended, the Lord Chancellor may make rules regulating the procedure at statutory inquiries. Rules have been made in respect of inquiries held for many purposes, including inquiries into compulsory purchase orders, appeals against the refusal of planning permission; and inquiries into development plans and major infrastructure projects.[36] Subject to the rules, procedure at the inquiry is determined by the inspector. The degree of formality depends on the circumstances of the inquiry, particularly the extent of legal representation. The inspector's report must include his or her conclusions and recommendations, if any; it will be sent to the parties when the minister's decision is notified to them.

....

[31] In Scotland, the commonly used term is that of 'reporter'.

[32] Cmnd 218, 1957, p 58.

[33] 'The purpose of an inquiry is two-fold: it is both to reach a rational planning decision and to allow the various parties to have their concerns heard': HC 364 (1999–2000), para 34 (Committee on Environment, Transport and Regional Affairs).

[34] Ch 7 B.

[35] See Justice/All Souls report, *Administrative Justice*, pp 312–27; S Sedley (1989) 52 MLR 469; L Blom-Cooper [1993] CLP 204 and e.g. the (Laming) report of inquiry into the death of Victoria Climbié, Cm 5730, 2003. Also SOLACE, *Getting It Right: Guidance on the Conduct of Effective and Fair Ad Hoc Inquiries* (2002). And section C below.

[36] See, for example, Town and Country Planning Appeals (Determination by Inspectors) (Inquiries Procedure) (England) Rules 2000 (SI No 2000/1625) (as amended).

One important rule deals with the situation where the minister, after considering the inspector's report, either differs from the inspector on a finding of fact or, after the close of the inquiry, 'takes into consideration any new evidence or new matter of fact (not being a matter of government policy)'. In such a case, if the minister proposes not to follow the inspector's recommendation because of this new material, the public authority and objectors must be informed, and they have the right to require the inquiry to be reopened. The background to this lies in what was known as the chalk-pit affair:[37] after an inquiry into a controversial application to extract chalk in the Essex countryside, the department that conducted the inquiry consulted privately with the Ministry of Agriculture about the harm that the chalk working would cause to neighbouring property. This secret consultation was defended at the time, but today it would breach the inquiry rules.

The aim of the procedure rules is to protect the fairness and openness of the inquiry process: the rules are enforceable in the courts, and the requirement to observe them exists alongside duties at common law derived from the principle of natural justice.[38] If a particular inquiry is not governed by statutory rules of procedure, there is in any event a duty to observe common law rules of natural justice or fairness.[39] Although the procedure rules define those who are entitled to notice of an inquiry and to take part, they give the inspector a discretion to allow other persons to appear at the inquiry. In practice, community associations and other interest groups are permitted to take part and thereby they acquire a right to come to the Administrative Court if it is alleged that the procedure rules have not been observed.[40]

If there has been a departure from proper procedure, the Administrative Court may give an effective remedy to those aggrieved by setting aside the inquiry. Alternatively, where someone is adversely affected by the improper conduct of an inquiry, or by acts of the department related to the inquiry, he or she may take the complaint to the Parliamentary Ombudsman, who can make a full investigation into the matter and may recommend the department to provide a remedy.[41]

The changing use of public inquiries

The public inquiry continues to be a part of the process by which certain decisions are made, especially those concerning use of land for developments of environmental significance, but its role has diminished. Increased involvement of the legal profession in inquiries put pressure on the planning process, and led to delays and over-centralisation of decision-making on many local issues. Many steps have been taken to restrict the use of the public inquiry and to encourage the use of speedier procedures. For instance, the Planning and Compulsory Purchase Act 2004, ss 100–1, authorised the use in connection with compulsory purchase of a *written representations* procedure that has long been available for planning appeals,[42] but only if the objectors consent to this; if consent is not given, then either a public inquiry must be held or they must be given a *hearing*, in each case before a member of the Planning Inspectorate.[43]

[37] See J A G Griffith (1961) 39 *Public Administration* 369; and *Buxton* v *Minister of Housing* [1961] 1 QB 278.

[38] Ch 24 C.

[39] *Fairmount Investments Ltd* v *Environment Secretary* [1976] 2 All ER 865; *Bushell* v *Environment Secretary* [1981] AC 95.

[40] *Turner* v *Environment Secretary* (1973) 72 LGR 380.

[41] Section D below.

[42] Town and Country Planning (Appeals) (Written Representations Procedure) (England) Regulations 2009 (SI No. 2009/452).

[43] See: The Town and Country Planning (Hearings Procedure) (England) Rules 2000 (SI No. 2000/1626) (as amended).

As regards the control of development, delay has been reduced by transferring the power to decide planning appeals from the Secretary of State to the inspectorate. All appeals regarding applications for planning permission and all appeals against enforcement notices may be decided by an inspector;[44] however, the Secretary of State retains power to decide certain appeals and may 'call in' applications for decision.[45] An inspector's decision is subject to review in the courts, but the Secretary of State is not responsible to Parliament for it. In their decision-making, inspectors must take account of published planning policies, at the national, regional or local level, as well as all other material considerations and views of the parties.

The leading judicial examination of a planning inquiry is that made in *Bushell* v *Environment Secretary*.[46]

During a lengthy inquiry held concerning the M40 extension near Birmingham, the inspector allowed objectors to bring evidence challenging estimates of future traffic growth, but refused to allow civil servants to be cross-examined on these. After the inquiry and before the minister made a decision, the department revised its traffic estimates, but the minister did not allow the inquiry to be reopened to examine the new estimates. The objectors claimed that natural justice entitled them (*a*) to cross-examine officials on the traffic predictions and (*b*) to a re-opening of the inquiry. The House of Lords upheld the motorway orders, holding that natural justice had not been infringed. The judges stressed that an inquiry was quite unlike civil litigation. An inspector had wide discretion to disallow cross-examination if it would serve no relevant purpose. The methods of predicting future traffic growth were an essential element in national policy for motorways, and were not suitable for investigation at local inquiries. Lord Edmund-Davies, dissenting, held that the objectors had been denied 'a fair crack of the whip'.[47]

This decision was a reminder that a public inquiry into a controversial proposal put forward by a government department is only part of a political process in which the minister cannot be expected to assume a cloak of judicial impartiality. A similar reminder was given in *R (Alconbury Developments Ltd)* v *Environment Secretary*.[48]

A Human Rights Act challenge was made to the minister's power to determine planning appeals which, instead of being decided by an inspector, had been 'called in' for the minister to decide. Similar challenges were made to the minister's power to approve a compulsory purchase order under the Highways Act 1980 and a new rail link under the Transport and Works Act 1992. The claimants argued that (1) the decisions affected their civil rights; (2) by art 6(1) ECHR, such questions must be determined by an independent and impartial tribunal, failing which a decision must be subject to review by a court with full jurisdiction to consider its legality; (3) the Secretary of State was not such a tribunal; and (4) there was insufficient judicial control of the decisions to satisfy art 6(1) ECHR, since the statutory appeals available did not provide for a rehearing on the merits. The House of Lords broadly

---

[44] Town and Country Planning Act 1990, Sch 6 and Town and Country Planning (Determination of Appeals by Appointed Persons) (Prescribed Classes) Regulations 1997 (SI No. 1997/420) (as amended).

[45] 1990 Act, ss 77–79. And see the *Alconbury* case (note 48 below).

[46] [1981] AC 75. And see *R* v *Transport Secretary, ex p Gwent CC* [1988] QB 429.

[47] [1981] AC 75, 118.

[48] [2001] UKHL 23, [2003] 2 AC 295. See D Elvin and J Maurici [2001] JPL 883.

> approved points (1)–(3) but rejected point (4), holding that art 6(1) ECHR did not require a court to rehear the merits of the decisions; the statutory appeals to the High Court provided sufficient review of their legality. Lord Clyde said: 'We are concerned with an administrative process and an administrative decision. Planning is a matter for the formation and application of policy. The policy is not a matter for the courts but for the executive' (para 139).

Earlier, in *Bryan* v *United Kingdom*,[49] the Strasbourg Court had held that no breach of art 6(1) ECHR occurred where an inspector's decision on a planning appeal was subject to an appeal to the High Court that extended to all grounds of judicial review; such control by the national court overcame the fact that the position of the inspector was not an independent court or tribunal for the purposes of art 6(1). Because of *Bryan* v *United Kingdom*, the challenge in *Alconbury* focused on the fact that the decisions were made by the minister, not by an inspector.

The Planning and Compulsory Purchase Act 2004, s 44, gave power to the Secretary of State to deal with infrastructure projects of national or regional importance. The minister could appoint an inspector as 'lead inspector', to conduct a public inquiry into aspects of the project, with power to set a timetable for the inquiry and to appoint additional inspectors to conduct concurrent sessions of the inquiry into specific matters.

Following reviews of the planning system and of the handling of major transport proposals,[50] further changes were made by the Planning Act 2008. This introduced a new system for major infrastructure projects, to exclude altogether any future public inquiry. Instead, national policy statements that affect the projects may be adopted by the Secretary of State, subject to prior consultation and publicity; the statements must be laid before Parliament and are subject to approval from the House of Commons (s 9). Where such statements have been adopted, the Secretary of State decides whether to approve the project, but must do so in accordance with the policy statement.[51]

The public examination of such a project is in principle to be dealt with by written representations (s 90). But a hearing may be held on specific issues (s 91), and a hearing must be held if the proposal involves compulsory acquisition and an owner asks to be heard (s 92). The Act does not authorise a public inquiry at any stage, but an 'open-floor hearing' may be held at which any interested persons may make representations (s 93). All hearings must be in public, but time limits may be imposed, and cross-examination of witnesses is strictly limited. Nevertheless, the inspector may allow oral questioning if necessary to ensure that representations are adequately tested, or that an individual has a 'fair chance' to put his or her case (s 94 (7)). Significantly, 'representations relating to the merits of a policy set out in a national policy statement' are excluded (s 98(4)). An order to permit the development may be challenged by judicial review but, in keeping with the desire to reduce delay, the period for challenge is restricted to six weeks from publication of the order or (if later) from publication of the reasons for the order (s 118).[52]

---

[49] (1995) 21 EHRR 342, applying *Albert and Le Compte* v *Belgium* (1983) 5 EHRR 533.

[50] See K Barker, *Review of Land Use Planning* (2006), and R Eddington, *Transport Study* (2006), which were followed by the white paper, *Planning for a Sustainable Future*, Cm 7120, 2007.

[51] The Planning Act 2008 had created an Infrastructure Planning Commission, but this was abolished, and its functions reallocated to the Secretary of State, by the Localism Act 2011, s 128 and Sch 13.

[52] In general, judicial review must be sought within three months of the decision challenged. However, in 2013, the Civil Procedure Rules were amended to reduce the period of challenge to decisions taken under the planning acts (principally the Town and Country Planning Act 1990) to six weeks: r 54.5. This aligns the position with statutory review of planning and similar decisions, which has long been subject to a six-week limitation period. See p 683 below.

One problem under this process is that campaigners against particular projects will find it difficult to accept that the issues can be fairly examined by the Secretary of State, especially if the national policy statement is site-specific as to a new reservoir, wind farm or power station. For this and other reasons, objectors are likely to seek judicial review of proceedings under the 2008 Act,[53] even if the disputed issues are essentially policy questions which (the framers of the Act would argue) should be decided by ministers.

This account of the changing use of public inquiries may suggest that we need to differentiate between two broad categories (while recognising that an intermediate 'grey' category exists between them): (*a*) decisions (such as the approval of major wind farms, high-speed rail links or power stations) that have a high content of national policy, are controversial, environmentally sensitive and cannot be decided by adjudication, but only by a governmental decision for which there must be political accountability; and (*b*) more routine matters, such as small-scale planning applications, which are decided in accordance with national, regional and local policies, initially by local authorities but with a right of appeal to the Planning Inspectorate. In this second category, discretion must still be exercised by the decision-makers, although sometimes the outcome depends on application of rules. When a planning inspector deals with this second category of questions, then this function is arguably comparable with that of the tribunals that we considered in section A – which cannot be said of the duties of ministers in deciding whether, for instance, nuclear power is in the national interest.

C. The Inquiries Act 2005

Both tribunals and inquiries form part of the regular structure of administrative justice and numerous decisions are made each year by these procedures. This section deals with something different – the legal provision for enabling a national disaster or major scandal to be the subject of investigation, with a view to finding out the reasons for the event, whether individuals or public authorities were responsible for it, and the lessons to be learnt. When such inquiries are held, it is essential that they are conducted impartially and with full regard to the evidence given to them. For this reason, serving judges have in the past been appointed to conduct such inquiries, but today retired judges are often preferred.[54] The government nearly always has a direct interest in these inquiries, since the ministers and civil servants concerned may thereby come under close public scrutiny. MPs have a strong interest in inquiries as a means of allaying concern and establishing accountability; and the inquiries are paid for by the taxpayer. Some inquiries are concerned with questions of human rights, especially where deaths have occurred.[55] Many inquiries are held without statutory authority; others are conducted under legislation specific to the subject matter (whether, for instance, it concerns

---

[53] J Maurici [2009] JPL 446. For an example of a challenge to a high-profile major infrastructure planning project (the High Speed 2 rail line) which failed on all the substantive policy challenges and succeeded only on one consultation issue, see: *R (Buckingham CC)* v *Transport Secretary* [2013] EWHC 481 (Admin); and on appeal: [2014] UKSC 3, [2014] 1 WLR 324.

[54] Although whether this is always appropriate in principle is a matter for debate: see J Beatson (2005) 121 LQR 221 and Lord Thomas [2015] PL 225. The suitability of a judicial appointment, individually or as the chair of a panel, has been the subject of controversy in individual cases: e.g. the (eventual) appointment of non-lawyer Professor Alexis Jay to lead the Independent Inquiry into Child Sexual Abuse, and the appointment of retired appellate judge Sir Martin Moore-Bick to lead the Grenfell Tower Inquiry.

[55] Under art 2, ECHR, the state must investigate unnatural deaths, including deaths in which the state may be implicated: *Jordan* v *UK* (2003) 37 EHRR 2. This duty has increased the significance of inquests and (in Scotland) fatal accident inquiries. See also *R (Hurst)* v *North London Coroner* [2007] UKHL 13, [2007] 2 AC 189; *R (Middleton)* v *West Somerset Coroner* [2004] UKHL 10, [2004] 2 AC 182; and *R (Smith)* v *Oxfordshire Assistant Deputy Coroner* [2010] UKSC 29, [2011] 1 AC 1.

policing, rail accidents, or failures in the NHS). We deal first with the inquiries which, until its repeal in 2005, were held under the Tribunals of Inquiry (Evidence) Act 1921.

The Tribunals of Inquiry (Evidence) Act 1921

In the 19th century, parliamentary committees were occasionally appointed to inquire into matters of concern, such as alleged corruption in government. Use of these committees was discredited in 1913 when a Commons committee investigated the conduct of members of the Liberal government in the Marconi affair and the committee produced three conflicting reports.[56] The 1921 Act provided a more reliable way of securing an impartial investigation into major events. When the government had decided that a formal inquiry was necessary with powers of obtaining evidence, the two Houses would resolve that a 'tribunal of inquiry' be appointed to inquire into a matter of 'urgent public importance'; this enabled the tribunal to be appointed by the government. The tribunal would be granted all the powers of the High Court (in Scotland, of the Court of Session) to examine witnesses and require production of documents. When a person summoned as a witness failed to attend or refused to answer questions which the tribunal had power to ask, the chairman of the tribunal could report the matter to the High Court or Court of Session for inquiry and punishment as a contempt of court.[57]

In more than 80 years, only 24 tribunals of inquiry were appointed. Serious allegations of corrupt or improper conduct in the public service that were inquired into included a leakage of Budget secrets (1936), alleged bribery of ministers and civil servants (1948), premature disclosure of information relating to the raising of the bank rate (1957) and the disastrous financial operations of the Crown Agents (1978).[58] Other matters of public anxiety were the tragic Aberfan disaster (1966), the Dunblane shootings (1996), abuse of children in care in North Wales (1999), and the 'Bloody Sunday' shootings in Londonderry (1972 and 2010).[59]

Such tribunals of inquiry usually consisted of a senior judge, assisted by one or two additional members or expert assessors. The tribunal would hear witnesses in public, called to the inquiry by counsel instructed by the Treasury Solicitor. Witnesses were entitled to be legally represented and their costs could be met from public funds. They would be cross-examined by lawyers appearing at the tribunal and questioned by the tribunal. Because of the inquisitorial proceedings, steps might be needed to protect witnesses from being inculpated in giving evidence on charges which had not been formulated in advance and which they had no chance of contesting.[60] The Attorney General could assure witnesses that no criminal charges would be brought against them in respect of their evidence.

Other forms of inquiry

The public procedures of a tribunal of inquiry were not considered suitable for a review of events leading to the Falkland Islands hostilities that involved access to secret diplomatic and intelligence documents; instead, Lord Franks was appointed to chair a committee of Privy Counsellors. A similar method was adopted for the Butler review of intelligence on weapons

---

[56] See Donaldson, *The Marconi Scandal*.

[57] See *A-G v Mulholland and Foster* [1963] 2 QB 477 (imprisonment of journalists for refusing to disclose their sources).

[58] See Cmd 5184, 1936; Cmd 7616, 1948; Cmnd 350, 1957; HC 364 (1981–2). See Keeton, *Trial by Tribunal*; and Z Segal [1984] PL 206.

[59] HC 553 (1966–7); Cm 3386, 1996; HC 201 (1999–2000); HC 220 (1971–2) and HC 29-I (2009–10). As to the latter, see L Blom-Cooper, *Public Inquiries: Wrong Route on Bloody Sunday*.

[60] This criticism was made of the tribunal which investigated the collapse of the Vehicle and General Insurance Company: HC 133 (1971–2).

of mass destruction in Iraq.[61] In 2009, Sir John Chilcot and other Privy Counsellors were appointed by the Prime Minister, after consulting opposition parties, to examine British involvement in Iraq from 2001 until July 2009. Chilcot's broad terms of reference were to establish as accurately as possible the way government decisions were made before and during the conflict, and to identify the lessons to be learnt. The committee decided to hear as much evidence as possible in public; witnesses were questioned by the committee, and lawyers were absent from the public proceedings.[62]

Other inquiries have been held under subject-specific legislation, for example into the conduct of the police or health authorities, or rail accidents.[63] Other inquiries have been conducted less formally and without statutory powers (including Lord Denning's dramatic inquiry into the Profumo affair in 1963).[64] As well as the Franks, Butler and Chilcot inquiries already mentioned, other non-statutory inquiries have included Sir Richard Scott's inquiry (1992–6) into the export of arms to Iraq,[65] and Lord Hutton's inquiry into the death of Dr David Kelly.[66] Such inquiries are 'judicial' in that they are conducted by a judge, although similar inquiries are conducted by other persons (for instance, the Bichard inquiry into the background to the Soham murders).[67] Their procedure is investigative and they have no power to compel witnesses to attend. Since they are not protected by the law of contempt of court, the subject matter can be discussed freely in the media. In the arms for Iraq inquiry, the inquisitorial procedure for taking evidence in public was criticised for its effect on witnesses, who were permitted legal assistance but not representation.[68]

The Inquiries Act 2005

Against this background, the Inquiries Act 2005 provides a new legal framework for inquiries, but it does not affect the power of a government to appoint non-statutory inquiries. The Act repealed the 1921 Act and the legislation for subject-specific inquiries of the kind already mentioned.[69]

In outline, the Act empowers any minister in the UK government[70] to appoint an inquiry when 'particular events' have caused or may cause public concern, or 'there is public concern that particular events may have occurred' (s 1(1)). Such an inquiry may not determine a person's civil or criminal liability, but may find facts from which it is likely that liability may be inferred (s 2). The minister appoints the chairman of the inquiry, either to act alone, or with other members appointed by the minister after consulting the chairman (ss 3, 4). In making appointments, the minister must take into account the expertise of the panel, the need for balance and the services of assessors (ss 8, 11). The inquiry's terms of reference are settled and may be amended by the minister, after consulting the chairman or proposed chairman (s 5(3), (4)). Parliament must be informed of the inquiry, but is not required to approve the

---

[61] See the Butler report, HC 898 (2003–4).
[62] HC 264 (2016–17).
[63] See respectively the (Macpherson) inquiry into the killing of Stephen Lawrence, Cm 4262, 1998; the (Kennedy) inquiry into the Bristol Royal Infirmary, Cm 5207, 2001; and the (Cullen) inquiry into the Paddington rail disaster (*The Ladbroke Grove Rail Inquiry, Parts 1 & 2*, Health and Safety Executive, 2001).
[64] Cmnd 2152, 1963; and Cmnd 3121, 1966, pp 19–21.
[65] See HC 115 (1995–6). Also I Leigh and L Lustgarten (1996) 59 MLR 695; and A W Bradley, in Manson and Mullan (eds), *Commissions of Inquiry*, ch 2.
[66] HC 247 (2003–4). For his reply to media criticism of the report, see Lord Hutton [2006] PL 807.
[67] The Bichard inquiry report, HC 653 (2003–4).
[68] See Lord Howe [1996] PL 445; and Scott report, app A, part D. Also B K Winetrobe [1997] PL 18; L Blom-Cooper [1993] CLP 204 and [1994] PL 1; C Clothier [1996] PL 384; M C Harris [1996] PL 508; Leigh and Lustgarten (note 65 above), pp 694–701; and H Grant [2001] PL 377.
[69] For the repealed statutes, see Sched 3.
[70] The Act confers similar powers on the devolved authorities in Scotland, Wales and Northern Ireland.

minister's decision (s 6). No member of the inquiry panel may have a direct interest in the subject matter or a close association with an interested party, except where this could not reasonably be regarded as affecting the impartiality of the panel (s 9). If the minister proposes to appoint a judge to serve on an inquiry, he or she must consult the president of the court concerned; for judges in England and Wales, this will be the Lord Chief Justice; in Scotland, the Lord President of the Court of Session; and for the Supreme Court, the president of the court (s 10, as amended). But the Act does not prevent the minister from appointing a judge who is willing to be appointed, even if the president does not consent to the appointment. In some circumstances, the minister may suspend an inquiry, but only after consulting the chairman, and notice of the suspension with reasons must be laid before Parliament (s 13); the minister may even bring the inquiry to an end before it has reported, subject to consulting the chairman and notifying Parliament (s 14).

The procedure and conduct of an inquiry are to be as directed by the chairman, subject to fairness and the need to avoid unnecessary costs (s 17). The chairman must take reasonable steps to ensure public access to the inquiry and the evidence, but restrictions on access may be imposed by the minister or the chairman, for instance for the purpose of reducing 'harm or damage' that would otherwise be caused (ss 18, 19). The 'harm or damage' includes damage to national security or international relations, damage to economic interests of the United Kingdom and damage caused by disclosure of commercially sensitive information (s 19(5)).[71] The chairman may require witnesses to attend the inquiry and produce relevant documents (s 21), subject to the exclusion of privileged information (s 22).[72] It is for the minister, or in some circumstances the chairman, to arrange for publication of the full report, subject to the omission of material that might cause 'harm or damage' of the kind mentioned (s 25). Reports when published are laid before Parliament (s 26).

The Act makes it an offence (s 35) to fail to comply with notices from the chairman under s 21, and such notices may be enforced in the High Court (in Scotland, the Court of Session) as if they had been issued in civil proceedings (s 36). Anyone who wishes to challenge decisions of the minister in relation to the inquiry or decisions by the panel has only 14 days from becoming aware of a decision in which to seek judicial review (although the court may extend the period) (s 38). The costs of the inquiry are to be borne by the minister, but the minister may notify the panel if it is going outside the terms of reference and the minister need not bear future costs if the panel ignores this warning (s 39). Rules of procedure and evidence may be made by the Lord Chancellor (s 41). A non-statutory inquiry can be converted into a 2005 Act inquiry.[73]

While there was certainly a good case to be made for further general legislation on inquiries, aspects of the Act are controversial. By eliminating altogether the need for Parliament to approve proposed inquiries, as required by the 1921 Act, the Act is open to the criticism that while inquiries often involve the acts and decisions of government departments, it is ministers who decide to hold an inquiry, appoint the chairman and panel members, settle and enforce the terms of reference, restrict public access to the inquiry and impose restrictions on publication. However, the Northern Ireland Court of Appeal held that the ability of a minister to stop an inquiry did not have a direct impact on its independence.[74] It will be important for parliamentary and public opinion to uphold the highest standards of integrity in the recourse made by governments to the Inquiries Act. The use of public resources for inquiries cannot be justified unless the findings made by inquiries are likely to allay public concern.[75]

---

[71] See also s 23 (risk of damage to the economy).
[72] The law of public interest immunity in civil proceedings (see ch 26 D) applies to inquiries: s 22(2).
[73] See *R (D) v SSHD* [2006] EWCA Civ 143, [2006] 3 All ER 946, [43]–[46].
[74] *Re Application by David Wright for Judicial Review* [2007] NICA 24.
[75] This is a factor that the Act rightly refers to in two places: ss 19(4)(a) and 25(5)(a).

Since the enactment of the 2005 Act a number of public inquiries have been held under it, most prominently the Mid Staffordshire NHS Foundation Trust Inquiry, chaired by Robert Francis QC, the Leveson Inquiry into the Culture, Practice and Ethics of the Press, chaired by Leveson LJ, and the ongoing Independent Inquiry into Child Sexual Abuse.[76] Both the Francis and Leveson inquiries – probably the most high-profile under the new system – can be said to have met the test of allaying public concern, both leading to significant public debate about legal and political reforms of the NHS and press regulation respectively. Whether the Child Sexual Abuse Inquiry is able to do the same remains to be seen.

D. Ombudsmen

Although the idea derived from the Ombudsman in Scandinavian countries and New Zealand,[77] the British model was designed to fit alongside other means of remedying citizens' grievances, such as challenge in the courts (in the 1960s judicial review was a little-used remedy), appeal to tribunals, the right to be heard at a public inquiry, and parliamentary means, such as an MP's letter or question to the minister concerned. Although each remedy may be effective in the appropriate situation, each has its particular limitations.[78] By comparison with those remedies, the value of the ombudsman model is that it provides an accessible, cheap (from the viewpoint of someone with a complaint against officialdom), non-legalistic and general-purpose remedy which may take a variety of forms, by which an individual can get his or her grievance examined by an independent and impartial person, experienced in the ways of government and able to distinguish good from bad administration. The ombudsmen acting in the public sector are also much more generally willing to engage with the substance of a complaint, rather than the traditional procedural focus and the high-level scrutiny of policy decisions found in the courts on judicial review.[79]

The focus in this section will be on the Parliamentary Ombudsman (now known as the Parliamentary and Health Service Ombudsman). After more than 40 years of that office, we can see that its success, admittedly within a structure that now seems overly rigid, led to similar initiatives in Britain in local government, the NHS and other areas of the public sector. The use of ombudsman-type procedures has also taken root in the regulated private sector, including financial and legal services. Commitment to the ombudsman concept within a large organisation (whether governmental or commercial) is to accept the principle that individuals need effective redress against the mistakes, inefficiencies and other failings that occur in corporate conduct.

The Parliamentary Ombudsman

When the office of 'Parliamentary Commissioner for Administration' was created in 1967, it was indicative of the caution with which this was done that the word 'ombudsman' was not allowed to appear in the legislation. The statutory title just stated has always been cumbrous, and in 1994 the government agreed that 'at the first opportunity' of legislation it would be changed to 'Parliamentary Ombudsman'.[80] No such opportunity has apparently arisen since. In

---

[76] HC 375-I (2013–14); and HC 780-I (2012–13).

[77] On comparative aspects, the earlier literature includes Rowat (ed.), *The Ombudsman*; Gellhorn, *Ombudsmen and Others*; Hill, *The Model Ombudsman*; Stacey, *Ombudsmen Compared*.

[78] Cf *The Citizen and the Administration* (the Whyatt report), 1961 and Cmnd 2767, 1965.

[79] Moules, *Actions against Public Officials: Legitimate Expectations, Misstatements and Misconduct*, ch 10.

[80] See HC 619 (1993–4).

fact, the present holder of the office, Rob Behrens CBE, describes himself as the 'Parliamentary and Health Service Ombudsman'.[81] While the Parliamentary Ombudsman has close links with the executive, the office was designed as an extension of Parliament; and it has virtually no links with the judicial system. As Sir Cecil Clothier, then the Ombudsman, said in 1984:

> The office . . . stands curiously poised between the legislative and the executive, while discharging an almost judicial function in the citizen's dispute with his government; and yet it forms no part of the judiciary.[82]

It may not matter that it is difficult to locate the Ombudsman within a formal separation of powers, but it is important that the Ombudsman should be recognised as having a constitutional role that can help to maintain the electorate's faith in democracy and strengthen the principle of accountable government: yet this dimension is often absent from discussion of constitutional reform.[83] On one view, the essence of the ombudsman idea for the ordinary person is accessibility, flexibility, informality and humanity. On another view, the Ombudsman provides an authoritative means of 'judging' the conduct of faceless officials and bureaucracies, thus helping to develop administrative practices that are both humane and effective. In the British version of the Ombudsman, both aspects of the role are seen at work.

Status and jurisdiction[84]

The Parliamentary Ombudsman is appointed by the Crown and holds office for not more than seven years, without the possibility of reappointment; she may be removed by the Crown for misbehaviour, following addresses by both Houses (s 1, as amended).[85] Originally, the appointment was solely a matter for the government, but the chairman of the Commons committee on the Ombudsman (currently the Public Administration Committee) is now consulted before an appointment is made.[86] The Ombudsman's salary is charged on the Consolidated Fund (s 2). She appoints the staff of the office, subject to Treasury consent as to numbers and conditions of service (s 3). Of the seven Ombudsmen who served between 1967 and 2002, five came to the post after civil service careers and two were Queen's Counsel; the present Ombudsman (Rob Behrens CBE, appointed in 2017) came from a complaints and regulatory background, having been the Independent Adjudicator for Higher Education (essentially, the universities ombudsman). Before him, Ms Ann Abraham had worked in public sector housing, and Dame Julie Mellor had been an accountant in private practice and chair of the Equal Opportunities Commission.

The formal task of the Ombudsman is to investigate complaints by private persons that they have suffered injustice in consequence of maladministration by government departments and many non-departmental public bodies, in the exercise of their administrative functions (s 5). The area of jurisdiction is defined by the 1967 Act, Sch 2 of which lists the departments and other bodies subject to investigation. This list may be amended by Order in

---

[81] Because the same person is appointed under both the Parliamentary Commissioner Act 1967 and the Health Service Commissioners Act 1993.

[82] Report for 1983 (HC 322 (1983–4)), p 1.

[83] See the valuable series of articles by Ann Abraham in (2008) 61 *Parliamentary Affairs* at 206, 370, 535, 681 and in [2008] PL 1. Also R Kirkham, B Thompson and T Buck, (2009) 62 *Parliamentary Affairs* 600.

[84] References in the text are to the Parliamentary Commissioner Act 1967, as amended. The literature includes Gregory and Hutchesson, *The Parliamentary Ombudsman*; Seneviratne, *Ombudsmen: Public Services and Administrative Justice*; Harlow and Rawlings, *Law and Administration*, ch 12; A W Bradley [1980] CLJ 304; C Clothier [1986] PL 204; G Drewry and C Harlow (1990) 53 MLR 745; N O'Brien [2009] PL 466.

[85] 1967 Act.

[86] Cmnd 6764, 1977. See HC 619 (1993–4) for the government's agreement to amend the law to provide for appointment following an address by the Commons moved after consultation with the Opposition: the law has not been amended.

Council (s 4), and this is done whenever bodies are abolished or created. Section 4 restricts the bodies which may be entered in Sch 2 to (*a*) government departments; (*b*) bodies exercising functions on behalf of the Crown; (*c*) bodies established under the prerogative, an Act of Parliament or Order in Council, or by a minister, that fulfil certain criteria as to the source of their income and the power of appointment to them.[87]

The Ombudsman has no jurisdiction over the devolved authorities in Scotland or Wales, nor over bodies which are outside central government, for example, local authorities, the police and universities, although she may investigate complaints about the way in which central departments have discharged their functions in these fields. Many matters are excluded from investigation for which ministers are or may be responsible to Parliament (s 5(3) and Sch 3). Thus the Ombudsman may not investigate:

(*a*) action taken in matters certified by a Secretary of State to affect relations between the UK government and other governments, or international organisations;

(*b*) action taken outside the United Kingdom by any officer representing or acting under the authority of the Crown;[88]

(*c*) administration of dependent territories outside the United Kingdom;

(*d*) action taken by a Secretary of State under the Extradition Acts;

(*e*) action taken by or with the authority of a Secretary of State for investigating crime or protecting the security of the state, including action so taken with respect to passports;

(*f*) (1) the commencement or conduct of civil or criminal proceedings before any UK court, court-martial or international court; (2) action taken by persons appointed by the Lord Chancellor as administrative staff of courts or tribunals, being action taken on the authority of persons acting in a judicial capacity;

(*g*) an exercise of the prerogative of mercy;

(*h*) action taken on behalf of central government by authorities in the NHS;

(*i*) matters relating to contractual or other commercial transactions on the part of central government;[89]

(*j*) appointments, discipline and other personnel matters in relation to the civil service and the armed forces, and decisions of ministers and departments in respect of other branches of the public service;

(*k*) the grant of honours, awards or privileges within the gift of the Crown.

It was these restrictions that led to criticism that the 1967 Act sought to carve up areas of possible grievances in an arbitrary way.[90] The exclusion of the NHS was later put right by the creation of an Ombudsman for the Health Service, a post that for England has always been held by the Parliamentary Ombudsman. The restrictions which have been most criticised are in (*i*) and (*j*) above. The government may by Order in Council revoke any of these restrictions (s 5(4)), but despite frequent recommendations from the Commons committee mentioned above, successive governments have refused to revoke the restriction on personnel matters in (*j*).[91]

---

[87] The numerous bodies within jurisdiction include the Arts Council, Charity Commission, English Nature, National Gallery, Sport England, OFSTED and utility regulators such as OFCOM.

[88] The acts of British consuls abroad, other than honorary consuls, are within jurisdiction, if the complainant is resident or has a right of abode in the United Kingdom: 1967 Act, s 6(5).

[89] This is subject to an exception for transactions relating to land bought compulsorily or under threat of compulsory powers. But for this exception, a latter-day Crichel Down affair (ch 5 C) would be outside the Ombudsman's jurisdiction.

[90] HC Deb, 18 October 1966, col 67 (Quintin Hogg MP). Cf report by Justice, *Our Fettered Ombudsman* (1977).

[91] See e.g. HC 615 (1977–8); and Cmnd 7449, 1979.

A limitation of a different kind is that the Ombudsman may not normally investigate any action in respect of which the complainant has or had a right of recourse to a tribunal or a remedy in a court of law, although she may do so if in a particular case the citizen could not reasonably be expected to exercise the right (s 5(2)).[92] Thus, if an individual wishes to challenge a decision about tax or social security, he or she should appeal to the relevant tribunal. But the Ombudsman often accepts that a complainant cannot be reasonably expected to embark on the hazardous course of litigation.[93]

The complainant need not be a British citizen, but in general must be resident in the United Kingdom or have been present in the United Kingdom when the offending action occurred, or the action concerned must relate to rights or obligations arising in the United Kingdom (s 6(4)).

There is a time bar: the Ombudsman may investigate a complaint only if it is made to an MP within 12 months from the date when the citizen first had notice of the matter complained of, except where circumstances justify the Ombudsman in accepting a complaint made later than this (s 6(3)).

It is for the Ombudsman to determine whether a complaint is duly made under the Act; in practice, many complaints identify the injustice that has been suffered more closely than the maladministration that caused it.[94] The Ombudsman has an express discretion to decide whether to investigate a complaint;[95] there is no duty to do so and the courts will not readily interfere with a decision not to investigate.[96] His decisions are in principle subject to judicial review on the usual grounds, if those grounds for the Administrative Court to intervene can be shown. Thus, if he were to investigate a complaint that is outside his jurisdiction, the decision could be quashed;[97] and no one could be liable for refusing to supply information to him (s 9). There are no prescribed standards of fairness applicable to an investigation, but a claimed lack of procedural fairness can be considered by the Court.[98] However, it would be unsatisfactory if the acts of someone charged to promote the resolution of grievances were to generate a mass of satellite litigation. Recognising this, the courts have accepted that it will be rare for a judge to find the Ombudsman to have acted perversely, and that it is not for the courts to usurp the role of the Ombudsman.[99] The extent of the Ombudsman's powers may involve difficult legal issues, and because the Ombudsman considers maladministration rather than pure legality, he need not be strictly be bound by what the law requires as a court would be.[100] Where the Ombudsman has to exercise a discretion under the 1967 Act, the court will not intervene except where it is satisfied that the discretion has been exercised unlawfully.[101]

---

[92] However, the Ombudsman may legitimately refuse to investigate a complaint which has already been the subject of judicial review, and so it may be important for an individual to pursue his case with the Ombudsman first: *R (Scholarstica Umo) v Commissioner for Local Administration in England* [2003] EWHC 3202 (Admin), [2004] ELR 265.

[93] Cf *R v Commissioner for Local Administration, ex p Croydon BC* [1989] 1 All ER 1033, 1044–5. See HC 735 (2005–6), paras 18–20 on use of this discretion.

[94] Cf *R v Local Commissioner for Administration, ex p Bradford Council* [1979] QB 287, 313.

[95] 1967 Act, s 5(5). And see *Re Fletcher's Application* [1970] 2 All ER 527.

[96] *R (Rapp) v Parliamentary and Health Service Ombudsman* [2015] EWHC 1344 (Admin).

[97] See *R (Cavanagh) v Health Service Commissioner* [2005] EWCA Civ 1578, [2006] 3 All ER 543 (Health Service Ombudsman 'has no power of investigation at large').

[98] *R (Miller) v Parliamentary and Health Service Ombudsman* [2015] EWHC 2981 (Admin) (in which the challenge was rejected, including by reference to what the complainant would have been well aware of).

[99] *R (Doy) v Commissioner for Local Administration* [2001] EWHC (Admin) 361, [2002] Env LR 11.

[100] If the Ombudsman does not follow the law, however, the courts expect to see clear reasons being given as to why not: *R (Aviva Life and Pensions) v Financial Ombudsman Service* [2017] EWHC 352 (Admin).

[101] *R v Parliamentary Commissioner for Administration, ex p Dyer* [1994] 1 All ER 375. In *R v PCA, ex p Balchin* [1998] 1 PLR 1 (Sedley J), (*the same*) *No 2* [2000] 2 LGR 87 (Dyson J) and (*the same*) [2002] EWHC 1876 (Admin) (Harrison J), decisions by successive Ombudsmen rejecting a complaint against the Department of Transport were quashed; see P Giddings [2000] PL 201. See also *R (Attwood) v Health Service Commissioner* [2008] EWHC 2315 (Admin), [2009] 1 All ER 415.

Procedure

One important feature of the ombudsman idea is that the Ombudsman should be accessible to the individual. But in Britain the citizen has no right to present a complaint to the Parliamentary Ombudsman. A complaint must first be addressed to an MP by the person who claims to have suffered injustice (s 5(1)). It is for the MP to decide whether to refer the complaint to the Ombudsman.[102] Usually complainants will take their complaint to their constituency MP, but the Act does not require this. Very many inquiries and complaints are received directly by the Ombudsman, whose staff advise the individual what action may be open, including the advice that a complaint within the Ombudsman's remit cannot be considered unless it is forwarded by an MP.[103] In 1993 retention of the 'MP filter' was supported by a Commons committee, but many MPs (including the present successor to that committee) now wish the filter to be abolished.[104]

The 1967 Act lays down a formal procedure by which the Ombudsman first decides whether a complaint received via an MP falls within jurisdiction. If it does, he must decide whether a full investigation would be justified, and there may be practical factors that make this unnecessary (if for instance it is unlikely that an investigation will lead to a worthwhile outcome, or if it is likely that an informal intervention with the relevant department will resolve the complaint).[105] If he decides to make a full investigation, the department and persons named in the complaint must have an opportunity to comment (s 7(1)). The investigation, carried out in private, will generally involve examining departmental records. The Ombudsman may compel witnesses to give evidence and produce documents (s 8). Investigations are not restricted by public interest immunity (s 8(3)),[106] but he may not see documents which are certified by the Secretary of the Cabinet, with the Prime Minister's approval, as relating to proceedings of the Cabinet or a Cabinet committee (s 8(4)). When a formal investigation is completed, the Ombudsman sends the MP concerned a report on the investigation (s 10(1)). If it appears that injustice was caused through maladministration and has not been remedied, he may lay a special report before Parliament (s 10(3)). Reports relating to an investigation are absolutely privileged in the law of defamation (s 10(5)). A minister may not veto an investigation, but may require the Ombudsman to omit from a report information that would prejudice the safety of the state or be against the public interest (s 11(3)).

These powers of investigation give the Ombudsman a formidable instrument for scrutinising departmental action should it be necessary, but there is little value in a prolonged scrutiny of cases in which it is rapidly apparent (and accepted by the department) that mistakes were made in handling the individual's affairs. Recent Ombudsmen have developed the use of flexible procedures that are more focused on the needs of the complainant than in the past.[107] The aim is to find the most effective way of resolving the complaint, if possible by informal means; the staff maintain a dialogue with the complainant, and encourage departments to provide an appropriate outcome without delay when this is justified.

Despite his power to investigate and report on complaints, the Ombudsman has no power to enforce provision of a remedy. Thus he cannot alter a departmental decision or award compensation to a citizen, although he may suggest an outcome that he would regard as acceptable. In the very great majority of cases, departments agree to such an outcome, but in exceptional cases a department may refuse and may argue that the Ombudsman's conclusions are mistaken.

---

[102] This decision is not amenable to judicial review: *R (Murray)* v *Parliamentary Commissioner for Administration* [2002] EWCA Civ 1472.

[103] Cf Report of PCA for 1978 (HC 205 (1978–9)), p 4.

[104] See HC 33–I (1993–4), pp xv–xx; M Elliott [2006] PL 84, 90–2; and HC 107 (2009–10).

[105] See the Ombudsman's report for 2008–9 (HC 786, 2008–9), pp 8–9.

[106] See ch 26 D.

[107] See the report for 2004–5, HC 348 (2005–6), pp 36–41; and for 2008–9 (above), pp 9–10.

In *R (Bradley) v Work and Pensions Secretary*,[108] the Department of Work and Pensions refused to accept certain findings by the Ombudsman of maladministration regarding information given to members of certain final salary pension schemes that later collapsed. When several affected persons sought judicial review of the refusal, the court examined the Ombudsman's findings in great detail. The Court of Appeal held that the minister was not bound to accept the Ombudsman's findings of maladministration and might come to his own conclusion about what had occurred. However, the minister's decision could be set aside if it was irrational, in the sense that it was not supported by 'cogent reasons' for rejecting the Ombudsman's conclusions. In a later case, the Divisional Court held that the government's reasons for rejecting several findings by the Ombudsman concerning the Equitable Life affair lacked cogency and reasoning.[109]

A minister is usually under a strong obligation to accept the Ombudsman's findings, but a report may have such political implications that a minister could come under pressure not to do so;[110] and if there has been a systemic failure affecting hundreds or thousands of persons, the costs of providing a remedy may be large. To support the Ombudsman in this situation, and to oversee the office, the Public Administration Committee in the Commons examines his reports and takes evidence from departments that he has criticised. The committee has made valuable studies of such matters as the powers and remit of the Ombudsman, the meaning of maladministration, remedies and the need for reform of the various public sector ombudsmen.[111]

The Ombudsman's casework

What is meant by the phrase, 'injustice to the person aggrieved in consequence of maladministration' (s 10(3))? No definition and no illustrations of maladministration and injustice are given in the Act. It is for the Ombudsman to interpret what the concept includes.[112] Maladministration includes such defects as 'neglect, inattention, delay, incompetence, ineptitude, perversity, and arbitrariness'.[113] Many examples of maladministration are found in the Ombudsman's reports. They include failure to give effect to assurances given to a citizen;[114] incorrect advice and delay in dealing with a benefit claim;[115] failure to treat someone with respect;[116] failure to give proper effect to a department's policy guidance;[117] dilatory enforcement of regulations

---

[108] [2008] EWCA Civ 36, [2009] QB 114. And see R Kirkham, B Thompson and T Buck [2008] PL 510; JNE Varuhas (2009) 72 MLR 102. After the Court of Appeal's decision, the Secretary of State proposed a modified form of compensation that the Ombudsman considered acceptable.

[109] *R (Equitable Members Action Group) v HM Treasury* [2009] EWHC 2495 (Admin).

[110] In 1975, the government was supported by the Commons in rejecting the Ombudsman's finding that the government had some responsibility for holidaymakers' losses arising from collapse of the Court Line group: HC Deb, 6 August 1975, col 532.

[111] See HC 33–I (1993–4); HC 619 (1993–4); HC 112 and 316 (1994–5); HC 612 (1999–2000); HC 448 (2002–3); HC 107 (2009–10).

[112] *R v Local Commissioner for Administration, ex p Bradford Council* [1979] 1 QB 287, 311; *R (Doy) v Commissioner for Local Administration* [2001] EWHC (Admin) 361, [2002] Env LR 11.

[113] HC Deb, 18 October 1966, col 51 (R H S Crossman MP). For a similar list see Lord Denning MR's judgment in *R v Local Commissioner for Administration, ex p Bradford Council* [1979] 1 QB 287, 311.

[114] See A W Bradley [1981] CLP 1, 8–11.

[115] See e.g. HC 348 (2005–6), pp 26–7.

[116] Ibid, p 25.

[117] A R Mowbray [1987] PL 570. See also A R Mowbray [1990] PL 68 and P Brown, in Richardson and Genn (note 3 above), ch 13 (remedies for misinformation).

against asbestosis;[118] failure to make departmental policy known in the press;[119] and even the making of misleading statements by a minister in Parliament.[120] Maladministration is not, however, a synonym for unlawful conduct: it is wider.[121]

Even if maladministration has occurred, this does not mean that injustice has thereby been caused to the individual. Conversely, injustice or hardship may exist, caused not by maladministration but by legislation or a judicial decision. Injustice for this purpose means not merely injury of a kind that a court may remedy, but includes 'the sense of outrage aroused by unfair or incompetent administration, even where the complainant has suffered no actual loss'.[122] It is not restricted to a concept such as damage within the meaning of tort law.[123]

One cause of difficulty has been the relation between maladministration and discretionary decisions. The Ombudsman may not question the merits of a discretionary decision taken without maladministration (s 12(3)). Where errors have been made in the procedures leading to a discretionary decision, he can report accordingly. But what if a discretionary decision has caused manifest hardship to the individual, but no identifiable defect has occurred in the procedures leading up to it? In such a case, the Ombudsman may infer an element of maladministration from the very decision itself or may inquire into harsh decisions based on the over-rigorous application of departmental policies.[124] An account of maladministration prepared in 1993 by Sir William Reid, then Ombudsman, included 'unwillingness to treat the complainant as a person with rights' and 'failure to mitigate the effects of rigid adherence to the letter of the law where that produces manifestly inequitable treatment'.[125]

Three leading examples of the Ombudsman's investigations may be given. The Sachsenhausen case was the first occasion on which a department was found to be seriously at fault.[126]

Under the Anglo-German Agreement of 1964, the German government provided £1 million for compensating UK citizens who suffered from Nazi persecution during World War Two. Distribution of this money was left to the discretion of the UK government. In 1964, the Foreign Secretary (Mr Butler) approved rules for distributing it. Later the Foreign Office withheld compensation from 12 persons who claimed under the rules because they had been detained within the Sachsenhausen concentration camp. Pressure from many MPs failed to get this decision reversed and a complaint was referred to the Ombudsman. By this time the whole of the £1 million had been distributed to other claimants. After an extensive investigation, the Ombudsman reported that there were defects in the procedure by which the Foreign Office reached its decisions and subsequently defended them, and that this maladministration had damaged the reputation of the claimants. When this report was debated in the Commons, the Foreign Secretary (Mr George Brown) assumed personal responsibility for the decisions, which he maintained were correct. He nonetheless made available an additional £25,000 in order that the claimants might receive the same rate of compensation as successful claimants on the fund.[127]

[118] HC 259 (1975–6), p 189. On the Ombudsman's response to official delay, see S N McMurtrie [1997] PL 159.

[119] HC 680 (1974–5).

[120] HC 498 (1974–5).

[121] *R v Local Commissioner for Administration, ex p Liverpool City Council* [2000] EWCA Civ 54, [2001] 1 All ER 462.

[122] Both judgments in *R v PCA, ex p Balchin*, note 101 above, approved this quotation from Mr Crossman's speech to Parliament in 1966.

[123] *R v Commissioner for Local Administration, ex p S* (1999) 1 LGR 633.

[124] HC 9 (1968–9); HC 350 (1967–8), and see G Marshall [1973] PL 32.

[125] Report of PCA for 1993, HC 290 (1993–4), p 4.

[126] HC 54 (1967–8); HC 258 (1967–8); G K Fry [1970] PL 336; Gregory and Hutchesson (note 84), ch 11.

[127] HC Deb, 5 February 1968, cols 105–17.

At that time, the prevailing view was that the 'Butler rules' were not enforceable in law since they conferred no rights on the claimants, but on similar facts today the claimants could seek judicial review of the Foreign Office decisions, based on the legitimate expectations created by the rules.[128]

An extremely extensive investigation was undertaken by the Ombudsman into the Barlow Clowes affair, referred to him by no fewer than 159 MPs.[129]

> In 1988, the Barlow Clowes investment business collapsed, leaving millions of pounds owing to investors, many of whom were older persons of modest means. The Department of Trade and Industry had licensed the business under the Prevention of Fraud (Investments) Act 1958 (later replaced by the more rigorous Financial Services Act 1986), though there were indications that the business was not properly conducted. The Ombudsman found that there had been maladministration by civil servants in five respects. As a result, the losses to investors exceeded what they would have been had the department exercised its regulatory powers with a 'sufficiently rigorous and enquiring approach'.[130]

The government took the unusual course of rejecting the findings of maladministration, but nonetheless undertook *ex gratia* to provide £150 million to compensate investors for up to 90 per cent of their loss. Had the investors attempted to sue the DTI in negligence, they would almost certainly have failed to establish in law that the department owed them a duty of care.[131]

The third example has striking resemblances to the Sachsenhausen case above.

> In 2000, the Ministry of Defence announced an *ex gratia* scheme for compensating British military and civilian persons interned by the Japanese during World War Two. Professor Hayward, a British citizen who had been interned as a boy, was refused payment because neither he, his parents nor grandparents had been born in the United Kingdom. The Ombudsman (Ann Abraham) found that the MoD embarked on the scheme before it had worked out the rules of eligibility; it had developed new criteria after payments had begun without checking that they were compatible with those already used; and it could not show that the scheme had been administered correctly. She recommended that the government should apologise to those affected, review operation of the scheme and reconsider the claims of Hayward and others so placed. The MoD agreed to apologise, but refused to review the scheme or to reconsider. It was only when the Commons Committee on Public Administration called the Minister for Veterans from the MoD to give evidence that the MoD began a review – having just 'discovered' that inconsistent criteria had been used.[132] Three months later, the MoD widened the scheme to include British citizens with 20 years' residence in the United Kingdom.

---

[128] Ch 24 B.

[129] See PCA, HC 76 (1989–90); HC 671 (1987–8) (the Le Quesne report); HC 99 (1989–90); and R Gregory and G Drewry [1991] PL 192, 408.

[130] HC 76 (1989–90), para 8.12.

[131] *Yuen-Kun Yeu v A G of Hong Kong* [1988] AC 175 and *Davis v Radcliffe* [1990] 2 All ER 536; ch 26 A.

[132] See *A Debt of Honour*, HC 324 (2005–6); and HC 735 (2005–6). See also *R (Association of British Civilian Internees in the Far East) v Defence Secretary* [2003] EWCA Civ 473, [2003] QB 1397; R Kirkham (2006) 69 MLR 792.

At one time, the services of the Ombudsman had little publicity and were under-used. During the 1990s, the number of complaints made rose from 801 in 1991 to a record figure of 1,933 in 1996 before falling back slightly. In 2000–1, 1,721 new complaints were received and the Ombudsman disposed of 1,787 cases.[133] Since then, the level of complaints has risen, although recent statistics are difficult to compare with earlier years. In 2016–17, the Parliamentary Ombudsman received over 123,000 informal inquiries, leading to over 6,900 complaints against government departments and other public bodies. The great majority of these complaints were rejected as resulting in no case to answer, and others were concluded by means of an informal intervention with the department. Only 470 were accepted for investigation, of which around 50 per cent of complaints were fully or partially upheld.

The extent to which any Ombudsman is able to perform his or her functions is dependent upon being properly resourced, invariably out of budgets allotted to the bodies whose maladministration he considers. Chronic under-funding can prevent an ombudsman carrying out his public functions. If the situation is sufficiently extreme, that under-funding may be an unlawful act on the part of the public body which provides the funding, as was found to be the case in relation to the Northern Ireland Police Ombudsman.[134]

Other Ombudsmen in the public sector[135]

The ombudsman model has been applied in other areas of government. Although complaints about the NHS were excluded from the remit of the Parliamentary Ombudsman, a scheme of Health Service Ombudsmen for England, Wales and Scotland was later introduced.[136] Complaints about health authorities, NHS trusts and other bodies may be referred directly to the Ombudsman by a member of the public. There is no 'MP filter', but complaints must be first raised with the appropriate NHS body. In 1996, the scope of NHS complaints was enlarged to include complaints in respect of primary health functions such as general medical and dental services, and by the removal of a statutory bar which had prevented the Ombudsman from investigating complaints about clinical judgment.[137] From 2004 to 2009, complainants who were not satisfied with the initial answer that they received had to notify them for review to the Healthcare Commission. In April 2009, this body was abolished and complaints by way of review now come to the Health Service Ombudsman. The Parliamentary Ombudsman was formerly appointed Health Service Ombudsman in Scotland and Wales as well as in England. Today, as the health service is devolved in Scotland and Wales, NHS complaints in those countries are handled by the Scottish and Welsh Ombudsmen respectively. Although the legislation remains separate, the present Ombudsman organises his resources as a single office, producing a composite annual report. As Health Service Ombudsman, he has published special reports dealing with the problems of NHS funding for long-term care of elderly and disabled people.[138]

As far as local government is concerned, there is a Commission for Local Administration in England (of which the Parliamentary Ombudsman is an *ex officio* member).[139] The scheme resembles the Parliamentary Ombudsman model, but with differences. Individuals may

---

[133] Report of PCA for 2000–1 (HC 5 (2001–2)).

[134] *Bell's Application for Judicial Review* [2017] NIQB 38.

[135] See Seneviratne, *Ombudsmen: Public Services and Administrative Justice*.

[136] See the consolidating Health Service Commissioners Act 1993.

[137] Health Service Commissioners (Amendment) Act 1996.

[138] See HC 399 (2002–3) and HC 144 (2004–5).

[139] Local Government Act 1973, Part III, as amended. On the many changes made by the Local Government and Public Involvement in Health Act 2007, see M Seneviratne [2008] PL 627.

complain to one of the two Local Government Ombudsmen regarding maladministration by local authorities, joint boards, police authorities and other bodies, and (since 2008) concerning failures in service and failures to provide a service. Since 1988, it has been possible to complain either directly to an Ombudsman or by referring the matter to a member of the body in question; but before the Ombudsman may investigate, the complaint must have been brought to the notice of the authority in question. The complainant must specify the conduct which he or she considers to be maladministration, or at least identify the matter giving rise to complaint.[140] Certain matters are excluded from investigation, for instance complaints about action which affects all or most of the inhabitants in the local area. As with the Parliamentary Ombudsman, the local Ombudsman has no means of compelling the provision of a remedy, but a council has power to pay compensation where the Ombudsman reports in favour of a complaint.[141] If no satisfactory response is made by the council to the Ombudsman's first report, he or she may issue a second report that recommends the action to be taken, including measures to remedy a matter and to prevent its recurrence in the future, and (where relevant) to provide a remedy for injustice caused; the report may require local publicity to be given to the affair.[142] A strong case may be made for imposing a legal obligation on a council to provide a remedy in such circumstances.[143] The courts have interpreted the legislative framework as intending local authorities to loyally accept Ombudsman reports and that they should carry out their statutory duties in relation to them unless they have judicially reviewed the report as legally flawed.[144] The Court of Appeal has described the situation as involving a 'convention that local authorities will be bound by the findings' of the Ombudsman.[145] However, there is no legal obligation to implement a report, but any reasoned decision for a refusal is subject to judicial review.[146]

Devolution to Scotland and Wales has made possible the creation of an integrated office of Ombudsman in each country.[147] The Scottish Public Services Ombudsman provides a 'one stop shop' to receive complaints regarding the Scottish executive, the NHS, higher and further education institutions, local government and many other public bodies.[148] For Wales, the Westminster Parliament created the office of Public Services Ombudsman for Wales, with jurisdiction broadly corresponding to that of the Scottish Ombudsman, but subject to the many differences in the two schemes of devolution.[149] In both Wales and Scotland, the Parliamentary Ombudsman retains powers in relation to areas of government (such as immigration, taxation and social security) that are not devolved.

In April 2000, a Cabinet Office review of public sector ombudsmen in England[150] concluded that the legislation needed a radical overhaul: integrated arrangements for complaints of maladministration should be made for central and local government, the NHS and other

---

[140] *R v Local Commissioner, ex p Bradford Council* [1979] QB 287.

[141] Local Government Act 1974, s 31(3), as amended.

[142] Ibid, s 31(1)–(2H), as amended by the Local Government and Housing Act 1989.

[143] Cf Commissioner for Complaints Act 1969 (Northern Ireland), s 7 (power of county court to award damages). See also HC 448 (1985–6), C M G Himsworth [1986] PL 546 and Justice/All Souls Committee report, *Administrative Justice – Some Necessary Reforms*, ch 5.

[144] *R v Local Commissioner for Administration, ex p Eastleigh Borough Council* [1988] QB 855; M Jones [1988] PL 608.

[145] *R (Bradley) v Work and Pensions Secretary* [2008] EWCA Civ 36, [2009] QB 114, [139].

[146] *R (Gallagher) v Basildon District Council* [2010] EWHC 2824 (Admin), [2011] PTSR 731; *R (Westwood Homes) v South Hallam DC* [2014] EWHC 863 (Admin).

[147] See M Elliott [2006] PL 84.

[148] The office was created by the Scottish Public Services Ombudsman Act 2002 (Scotland). Complaints about cross-border public authorities that relate to devolved matters may be investigated.

[149] M Seneviratne [2006] PL 6; Public Services Ombudsman (Wales) Act 2005.

[150] Cabinet Office, *Review of Public Sector Ombudsmen in England* (2000) (the Collcutt review).

bodies. Individuals should have a common right of access to the new-style Ombudsmen. The review was welcomed by the select committee on public administration.[151] Instead of primary legislation, for which no time could be found, the outcome was an order under the Regulatory Reform Act 2001.[152] This enabled the various ombudsmen to collaborate fully in investigations, to delegate functions to each other's staff, to issue advice and guidance on good administrative practice, and to resolve complaints informally.[153] The Cabinet Office returned to the topic in 2016, publishing a draft Bill which would abolish the Parliamentary Ombudsman, the Health Service Ombudsman, the Local Government Ombudsman and (potentially) the Housing Ombudsman, unifying them into a single Public Service Ombudsman role.[154] Complaints would be able to be made directly to the new Ombudsman, who would be given increased powers to investigate and to share information, and the Ombudsman would be given a new role in publishing complaints guidance and training for the public sector. Progress on the Bill was restricted by the 2017 general election, and it is yet to be laid before Parliament, but its having been drafted indicates widespread agreement that an overhaul of the ombudsman system would be of benefit.

The desire for joined-up Ombudsmen is not easy to satisfy in a simple way, given the increasing complexity of levels of government and forms of public administration. In response to the Citizen's Charter initiative in 1991,[155] some departments appointed so-called 'lay adjudicators' to deal promptly with grievances that had not been dealt with satisfactorily by the officials concerned. Thus the Inland Revenue appointed a Revenue Adjudicator;[156] and the Home Office appointed a Prisons Ombudsman for England and Wales,[157] whose onerous tasks include dealing with the complaints of prisoners and immigration detainees, and investigating the deaths of persons in detention. There is also a Housing Ombudsman, whose functions were amended under the Localism Act 2011 (Part 7, Chapter 6). Further, the European Parliament appoints an Ombudsman to hear complaints from EU citizens of maladministration on the part of European institutions, except for the Court of Justice and the General Court acting in their judicial role.[158]

Although the ombudsman concept originated as a safeguard against abuses in government, it has spread in a variety of forms to the private sector, with banks, building societies, insurance companies and many others appointing ombudsmen to deal with complaints from dissatisfied customers; their position is generally founded upon contract, but in the case of the legal profession, the Legal Services Ombudsman was created by statute.[159] These processes are outside the scope of this text, but their success will have an impact on the ombudsman model in the public sector, encouraging further progress being made towards prompt, accessible and cost-effective remedies, including ensuring that public authorities respect the human rights of the individuals whose lives they are affecting.[160]

---

[151] See HC 612 (1999–2000).

[152] The Regulatory Reform (Collaboration etc. between Ombudsmen) Order 2007 (SI 2007 No 1889).

[153] See e.g. the valuable report, *Six lives: the provision of public services to people with learning disabilities* (HC 203, 2008–9) by the Parliamentary and Local Government Ombudsmen.

[154] *Draft Public Service Ombudsman Bill* (2016, Cmnd 9374).

[155] See Cm 1599, 1991; HC 158 (1991–2). Also A W Bradley [1992] PL 353; A Barron and C Scott (1992) 55 MLR 526.

[156] See P Morris [1996] PL 309.

[157] The title is inappropriate, because of potential confusion with the Parliamentary Ombudsman: see HC 33–I (1993–4), p x. See also *R (D) v Home Secretary* [2006] EWCA Civ 143, [2006] 3 All ER 946 and note 73 above.

[158] For the work of the EU Ombudsman, see HL 117 (2005–6). See also EU Charter of Fundamental Rights (2000), art 43 and TFEU, art 228.

[159] Courts and Legal Services Act 1990, ss 21–6. And cf the Judicial Appointments and Conduct Ombudsman, created by the Constitutional Reform Act 2005, s 62.

[160] See N O'Brien [2009] PL 466 for a perceptive discussion of this question.

E. Conclusion

We have seen in this chapter an array of different mechanisms by which administrative justice may be secured. The tribunal system unified under the Tribunals, Courts and Enforcement Act 2007 has brought together an eclectic mix of different jurisdictions and reveals just how wide the range of subject matters covered by the tribunals have become. Tribunals are increasingly court-like in their approach to adjudication and the procedural rules adopted to govern their functioning. It is a matter for debate the extent to which the judicialisation of tribunals helps the citizen for whom they are intended, or moves too far away from the original intent of tribunals as a quick and cheap administrative remedy.

Although the term 'inquiries' is used in both Sections B and C of this chapter, it can have a very different meaning. An administrative inquiry into, say, a planning matter is an entirely different creature from an inquiry set up under the Inquiries Act 2005. Again, the difference which can be readily identified is between a formal procedure which is very close to a court-like experience (under the Act), and a more informal process whereby an administrator takes a policy-driven decision.

The final part of this chapter considered the increasing number of Ombudsmen. They remain the overlooked remedial tool of administrative law, perhaps because Ombudsmen have so far managed to continue to go about their work without the judicial formality of tribunals and inquiries. Although lawyers invariably focus on courts as the remedy for all administrative ills, it is in many cases the Ombudsmen who can provide an affordable route of complaint which may even result in monetary compensation.

CHAPTER 24

Judicial review I: the grounds of review

Judicial review of administrative action is an essential process in a constitutional democracy founded upon the rule of law. Whatever statutory provision is made for appealing against official decisions, it is salutary that all decision-makers exercising public power should know that the courts exercise jurisdiction over the *legality* of their decisions, on such matters as the extent of their powers and the proper observance of procedure. Certainly, judicial review is no substitute for administrative or political control of the *merits*, *expediency* or *efficiency* of decisions; and matters such as the level of expenditure that should be permitted to local councils are not inherently suitable for decision by a court.[1] But the courts can ensure that decisions made by public authorities conform to the law and that standards of fair procedure are observed.

In exercising this jurisdiction, the courts take account of both the legislation that applies to the subject of the dispute and the principles of administrative law that have developed from judicial decisions. The role of the judiciary is first to determine the legal rules that apply and then to decide on the facts whether the rules have been breached. While the background of common law rules does not change overnight, 'Parliament, understandably and indeed inevitably, tends to lay down different rules for different situations'; the judges 'are continually being faced with the need to study, interpret and apply new versions of the rules'.[2]

The legislation that applies to public authorities is made up of innumerable different Acts, varying widely in the powers conferred, the agencies in whom powers are vested and the extent of protection for private interests. Because of this, judicial review always has a tendency to fragment into disparate branches of law, such as education, housing and immigration law. Yet general principles have emerged from numerous judicial decisions affecting public authorities, and awareness of those principles is essential when specific statutes are before the court.

Judicial review of administrative action involves the judges in developing legal principles against a complex and often changing legislative background. Lord Diplock warned in 1981 that 'judicial statements on matters of public law if made before 1950' were likely to be a misleading guide to the current law.[3] Since 1981 changes in the law have continued to occur, as the coverage of government by judicial review has spread and the depth of review has intensified. It was formerly said that judicial review of administrative action 'is inevitably sporadic and peripheral' when set against the entire administrative process.[4] But the general principles which emerge from the judicial process should not be haphazard, incoherent or contradictory.[5]

The legal solution to many administrative disputes inevitably involves the reviewing court in choosing between the merits of the opposing arguments,[6] and the outcome is often unpredictable. Even if the relevant principles are clear, their application to particular facts is seldom

---

[1] *R v Environment Secretary, ex p Hammersmith Council* [1991] 1 AC 521, 662.

[2] Ibid, at 561 (Lord Donaldson MR).

[3] *R v IRC, ex p National Federation of Self-Employed* [1982] AC 617, 640.

[4] Woolf, Jowell and Le Sueur, *De Smith's Judicial Review*, p 8 (the authors of the present edition not maintaining that view originally expressed by Professor De Smith in 1980).

[5] For a perceptive critique of the underlying theories, see D J Galligan (1982) 2 OJLS 257.

[6] See e.g. the acute difference of judicial opinion in the controversial decision of the Law Lords by 3–2 in *R (Bancoult) v Foreign Secretary (No 2)* [2008] UKHL 61, [2009] 1 AC 453 and M Elliott and A Perreau-Saussine [2009] PL 697.

clear-cut, which is why the bare statement that courts in judicial review proceedings are not fact-finders can be misleading. Since the court's decision may have a political impact when it concerns the cherished policy of a minister or local authority, this may lead to criticism of the judges for political bias.[7] A particularly prominent instance of this occurred in 2016, when the challenge to the intention of the government to commence the process of leaving the European Union under prerogative powers and not by Act of Parliament, provoked fierce public and press criticism of both the claimants and the government. The judgment of the Divisional Court (comprising the Lord Chief Justice, the Master of the Rolls and a senior Lord Justice) unanimously found against the government,[8] causing *The Daily Mail* to infamously headline its front page 'Enemies of the People' over photographs of the three judges. The press coverage of the Supreme Court's decision, by 8–3, to dismiss the government's appeal was happily more muted;[9] possibly because by that point it was apparent that there was no political appetite to block leaving the EU. Many cases of judicial review (for instance, in relation to immigration policy or anti-terrorist measures) give rise to political controversy, but it is fundamental that the judges should decide such cases on legal grounds, not for reasons relating to their own political views. Unjustified and lazy charges that the judges have their own covert agenda for obstructing government policies have sometimes been made not only by the press but also by ministers whose decisions have been set aside.[10] The landmark decision in *M v Home Office*[11] that the Home Secretary (Kenneth Baker) was in contempt of court over the removal from Britain of a Zairean asylum seeker may indeed have had an impact on Mr Baker's political standing: but the decision owed nothing to party politics and everything to what the judges considered should be the proper relationship between the executive, the courts and the individual.

This chapter outlines the grounds on which courts exercise the function of judicial review.[12] Some are of long standing in the common law, such as the rule against bias and the right to a fair hearing; others, such as proportionality and legitimate expectations, are still developing. Before we consider these grounds, three preliminary matters must be mentioned.

First, the foundations of judicial review have been the subject of vigorous scholarly debate.[13] In the background to the debate is the historical growth of public law in an unwritten constitution. The theoretical base for the system of judicial review is difficult to find, given the questions raised by the interface between the supremacy of Parliament and the rule of law.[14] One approach (styled the 'ultra vires' theory) emphasises that the ultra vires doctrine is fundamental to the principles of judicial review; since these principles have developed through statutory interpretation, they depend for their legitimacy on the intention of Parliament. Since Parliament has not prohibited the evolution of judicial review, its intention must have been to authorise it. Ultra vires has traditionally been the language of public law.

By contrast, the 'common law' theory stresses the common law foundations of judicial review. It does not dispute the authority of legislation by Parliament, but argues that the grounds of review are judge-made, have never been the subject of comprehensive legislation, and include principles of fair and just administration far beyond anything that Parliament has expressly authorised. Many successful judicial review claims do not involve a public authority acting outside the scope of its express statutory powers. Further, judicial review extends

---

[7] E.g. Griffith, *The Politics of the Judiciary*, chs 3–7.

[8] *R (Miller) v Secretary of State for Exiting the EU* [2016] EWHC 2768 (Admin); [2017] 1 All ER 158.

[9] *R (Miller) v Secretary of State for Exiting the EU* [2017] UKSC 5, [2017] 2 WLR 583.

[10] For a stark example involving the then Home Secretary David Blunkett, see: A W Bradley [2003] PL 397.

[11] *M v Home Office* [1994] 1 AC 377.

[12] For the procedure of judicial review, see ch 25.

[13] See the valuable collection of articles in Forsyth (ed.), *Judicial Review and the Constitution*.

[14] Chs 3 and 4.

to non-statutory powers. It is not founded on a fiction of parliamentary intent but is an aspect of the rule of law, a principle that is of co-ordinate authority with the supremacy of Parliament. In response to this 'common law' theory, a 'modified ultra vires theory' has been advanced.[15] Instead of relying on the direct and specific intent of Parliament, this view attributes to Parliament a generalised and indirect intent that the rule of law should be upheld; thus judicial review may be said to accord with the intent of Parliament.

Underlying this debate are concerns about the supremacy of Parliament, and about the authority of the judiciary should a political crisis develop regarding judicial review. All sides accept that Parliament has authority to legislate on the scope of judicial review, whether to enlarge it or to restrict it in specific ways;[16] but some 'common law' theorists are less willing than the 'ultra vires' adherents to accept that Parliament has absolute authority to exclude judicial review.

More recent judicial expressions of the justification for judicial review have referred to the enforcement of the rule of law as the 'ultimate controlling factor on which our constitution is based'. Whether this provides any more practical guidance than the ultra vires doctrine is open to question, but it avoids some of the artificiality inherent in focusing on an unexpressed and implied intention of Parliament.[17]

The second matter relates to classification of the grounds of judicial review. In the GCHQ case in 1984, Lord Diplock classified the grounds on which administrative action is subject to judicial control under three heads, namely illegality, irrationality and procedural impropriety; he accepted that further grounds (for example, proportionality) might be added as the law developed.[18] In 1986, the President of the New Zealand Court of Appeal commented that 'the substantive principles of judicial review are simply that the decision-maker must act in accordance with law, fairly and reasonably'.[19] This is an admirable summary of the policy behind the law, but a great deal needs to be known about the meaning attached to each of its three strands if it is to serve as a guide to decision-making.

The third matter is the remarkable impact of the Human Rights Act 1998 upon judicial review.[20] In brief, by s 3, the Act requires every court, where it is possible to do so, to apply and interpret legislation compatibly with Convention rights. By s 6(1), it is unlawful for public authorities (except where they are required to do so by primary legislation) to act in a way which is incompatible with Convention rights. And by ss 6–7, judicial review is the residual procedure for protecting Convention rights if there are no other proceedings in which the issue of human rights may be raised. Accordingly, the 1998 Act extended the existing grounds of judicial review by a requirement of great breadth and complexity, namely that all public authorities must act consistently with Convention rights.

A. Judicial review on substantive grounds

This section is concerned with grounds of review relating to the substance or content of the official decision or action that is under review; grounds relating to the procedure by which a decision was made are considered later in the chapter. Although the emphasis is

---

[15] See Elliott, *The Constitutional Foundations of Judicial Review*, P Craig and N Bamforth [2001] PL 763; T R S Allan [2002] CLJ 87; C F Forsyth and M Elliott [2003] PL 286.

[16] See ch 25 C.

[17] *R (Jackson)* v *Attorney General* [2005] UKHL 56, [2006] 1 AC 262 at [107] (Lord Hope); and *AXA General Insurance Ltd* v *Lord Advocate* [2011] UKSC 46, [2012] 1 AC 868 at [51] (Lord Hope) and [142]–[143] (Lord Reed). See also: Constitutional Reform Act 2005, s 1 and Lord Steyn [2002] EHRLR 723.

[18] *CCSU* v *Minister for Civil Service* [1985] AC 374, 410; cf 414 (Lord Roskill).

[19] Sir Robin Cooke, in Taggart (ed.), *Judicial Review of Administrative Action in the 1980s*, p 5.

[20] See p 662 below and ch 14 C.

on English law, the principles of judicial review in the law of Scotland are very similar.[21] Substantive judicial review has always proved to be the area of most concern to both courts and government; it has the potential to raise constitutional questions about the appropriate role of the courts in regulating executive action which is subject to democratic oversight. Judicial review of policy throws into sharp relief the nature of judicial review as a legal and a political tool to attack unfavourable policy decisions. As a result, the courts have been traditionally slow to intervene.

The ultra vires rule (excess of powers)

When a public authority is intending to exercise a power vested in it by legislation, it must do so in accordance with the legislation, both as regards the limits of the power and as regards any detailed conditions that must be observed when the power is used. If a public authority acts beyond the limits of the power, its acts are to that extent invalid as being ultra vires. The ultra vires doctrine cannot be used to question the validity of an Act of Parliament; but provides the foundation enabling the court to intervene when a public authority has departed from the legislation. (The ultra vires doctrine also applies to the rare cases in which a government department may be seeking to exercise a power stemming from the royal prerogative at common law.)[22] The simplest instance of the rule is where a local council, whose capacity to act and to regulate private activities is derived from statute, acts outside the scope of that authority. Two examples may be given.

In *R v Richmond Council, ex p McCarthy and Stone Ltd*, a local planning authority began charging a fee of £25 for informal consultations between its planning officers and developers intending to seek planning permission for new development. The council was required by law to determine all applications for planning permission that were made, whether or not such informal consultations had been held. *Held*, by the House of Lords, while it was conducive or incidental to the council's planning functions that its officers should have informal consultations with intending developers, the fee of £25 was not lawful, since making such a charge was not incidental to those functions. The House applied the principle that no charge on the public can be levied by a public body without clear statutory authority.[23]

In *Hazell v Hammersmith Council*, the local authority (as other councils had done) in 1983 established a fund for conducting transactions in the capital money market, by which the council could benefit from future movements in interest rates. These transactions included interest rate swaps, options to make such swaps, forward rate agreements and so on. If interest rates fell, the council would benefit; in fact, rates went up and large capital losses were made by the council. In a second stage of the policy, the council made further swaps, but solely to limit the extent of its losses while extricating itself from the market. The district auditor applied for a declaration that all the transactions were unlawful. *Held*, the council had no power to enter into interest swap transactions, which by their nature involved speculation in future interest rates, since they were inconsistent with the statutory borrowing powers of the council and were not 'conducive or incidental to' those powers.[24]

---

[21] See *Stair Memorial Encyclopedia of the Laws of Scotland*, vol 1, Administrative Law (reissue, 2000); Clyde and Edwards, *Judicial Review*; C Himsworth in Supperstone, Goudie and Walker (eds), *Judicial Review*, ch 22; and see *Eba v Advocate General for Scotland* [2011] UKSC 29, [2012] 1 AC 710.

[22] *R (Miller) v Secretary of State for Exiting the EU* [2017] UKSC 5, [2017] 2 WLR 583. And see ch 10 E.

[23] [1992] 2 AC 48.

[24] [1992] 2 AC 1; and see M Loughlin [1990] PL 372, [1991] PL 568.

As these cases illustrate, the powers of an authority include not only those expressly conferred by statute but also those which are reasonably incidental to those expressly conferred.[25] The courts are often required to decide whether a general power to do X includes by implication or interpretation a specific power to do Y.[26] A local council's implied powers do not include what on other grounds is objectionable.

> In *Crédit Suisse* v *Allerdale Council*, the council set up a company to provide a leisure pool complex (which was plainly within the council's powers) together with time-share accommodation (which eventually was held not to be); since the council was restricted from itself borrowing the necessary capital, it guaranteed repayment of a loan of £6 million made by the plaintiff bank to the company. The company did not earn enough from selling time-shares to repay the loan. *Held*, the guarantee was void and unenforceable, as the legislation had provided a comprehensive code of borrowing powers. The project was 'an ingenious scheme designed to circumvent the no doubt irksome controls imposed by central government'.[27]

The rule requiring statutes to be observed applies to all public authorities, but its application in any case necessarily depends on the powers vested in the public body. Government departments benefit from the rule that the Crown as a legal person is not created by statute and has capacity at common law to own property, enter into contracts, employ staff, etc.[28] However, a department that is exercising statutory powers of regulation may not use them so as to conflict with other statutes or exceed its powers in other ways.

> In *R* v *Social Security Secretary, ex p Joint Council for the Welfare of Immigrants*[29] the minister had power under the Social Security Contributions and Benefits Act 1992 to make regulations regarding eligibility for income support. To discourage asylum seekers from coming to the United Kingdom, the minister made regulations that barred certain asylum seekers from receiving income support, although they were entitled to remain in the country while their appeals under the Asylum and Immigration Appeals Act 1993 were determined. The Court of Appeal held, by 2–1, that the regulations would, for some asylum seekers, render nugatory their appeal rights; as they conflicted with the 1993 Act, the regulations were ultra vires.

Nor may a department incur expenditure which does not meet the relevant conditions imposed by Parliament.[30] When a public body's conduct is challenged as ultra vires or

---

[25] As regards local authorities, see Local Government Act 1972, s 111 (as amended) and now the general power of competence in the Localism Act 2011, s 1. The general power of competence is designed to avoid the sort of litigation noted above by giving local authorities the power to do anything an individual may do; see A Bowes and J Stanton [2014] PL 392.

[26] See e.g. *R (W)* v *Metropolitan Police Commissioner* [2006] EWCA Civ 458, [2007] QB 399 (whether statutory power at night to 'remove' a person under 16 from a dispersal area to his home included power to use coercion).

[27] [1997] QB 306 (Neill LJ); and see *Crédit Suisse* v *Waltham Forest Council* [1997] QB 362.

[28] See B V Harris (1992) 108 LQR 626 and (2007) 123 LQR 225; A Perry (2015) 131 LQR 652. Also *R* v *Health Secretary, ex p C* [2000] 1 FCR 471 and *R (Shrewsbury Council)* v *Communities and Local Government Secretary* [2008] EWCA Civ 148, [2008] 3 All ER 548.

[29] [1996] 4 All ER 385. And see *R (BAPIO)* v *Home Secretary* [2008] UKHL 27, [2008] AC 1003: NHS guidance restricting employment of foreign doctors held unlawful (by Lords Bingham and Carswell) as aim could be achieved only by amending Immigration Rules.

[30] *R* v *Foreign Secretary, ex p World Development Movement* [1995] 1 All ER 611.

contrary to statute, the court's attention focuses on the Act which is claimed to be the source of its authority. But the process of judicial review is far from being a narrow exercise in statutory interpretation. One reason for this is that acts taken under the prerogative or from another non-statutory source may themselves be subject to judicial review.[31] A second reason is that many statutes confer broad discretion on public authorities; judicial control of such discretion goes well beyond statutory interpretation.[32]

The concept of jurisdiction[33]

In many cases use is made of the language of jurisdiction, rather than of vires. Often it makes no difference which terminology is used, except that the language of jurisdiction is more appropriate when used in relation to an inferior court or tribunal. Supervision by the higher courts did not provide a fresh decision on the merits, but sought to ensure that the body in question had observed the rules upon which its power to make decisions depended. According to a famous dictum in *R* v *Nat Bell Liquors*:

> That supervision goes to two points: one is the area of the inferior judgment and the qualifications and conditions of its exercise; the other is the observance of the law in the course of its exercise.[34]

This approach distinguished between the rules that limited the powers of the lower court or tribunal, and the rules that it had to observe in deciding a matter within its powers. Thus a tribunal could be dealing with a matter that was 'within its jurisdiction' but while doing so could make an error of law. For procedural reasons, many older cases were concerned with the elusive distinction between (*a*) an error made by a tribunal on a point of jurisdiction and (*b*) an error of law made by a tribunal 'within jurisdiction'.

Today, the law has fortunately developed to a point at which we need no longer struggle with the concept of an 'error of law within jurisdiction', for the reason that all errors of law made by a tribunal now give rise to judicial review. The recent pages of this history begin with a House of Lords decision that illustrates the difficulties of distinguishing between jurisdictional and non-jurisdictional matters: *Anisminic Ltd* v *Foreign Compensation Commission*.[35]

The Foreign Compensation Commission was a tribunal created by the Foreign Compensation Act 1950. It had rejected a claim made by a British company (Anisminic) under a scheme for compensating British subjects who had lost property in Egypt during the Suez affair in 1956. The reason for rejection was that, on the commission's interpretation of the relevant Order in Council, it was fatal to the claim that Anisminic's assets in Egypt had after 1956 been acquired by an Egyptian company, since the order required that any 'successor in title' to the British claimant had to be of British nationality. In the absence of any right to appeal, Anisminic had to establish not only that the commission's interpretation of the order was erroneous, but also that the commission's decision rejecting the claim was a nullity, since the 1950 Act excluded the power of the High Court to review errors of law made within the jurisdiction of the commission. *Held*, by a majority in the House of Lords, the

---

[31] See *CCSU* v *Minister for the Civil Service* [1985] AC 374; *R* v *Panel on Take-overs, ex p Datafin plc* [1987] QB 815.

[32] J Jowell and A Lester [1987] PL 368.

[33] Wade and Forsyth, *Administrative Law*, ch 8; and Craig, *Administrative Law*, ch 16.

[34] [1922] 2 AC 128, 156.

[35] [1969] 2 AC 147; and see H W R Wade (1969) 85 LQR 198, B C Gould [1970] PL 358, L H Leigh [1980] PL 34, J Beatson (1984) 4 OJLS 22.

> commission's interpretation of the Order in Council was wrong (since the Egyptian company was not Anisminic's 'successor in title'); this error had caused the commission to take into account a factor (nationality of the Egyptian company) which was irrelevant to Anisminic's claim. Thus the commission had exceeded the limits of its jurisdiction and the decision rejecting the claim was a nullity.

The main issue for present purposes is whether *Anisminic* established the rule that *all* errors of law made by a tribunal cause the tribunal to exceed its jurisdiction. On a reading of the speeches in *Anisminic*, this does not seem to have been intended, but in *Pearlman* v *Keepers and Governors of Harrow School*, Lord Denning MR said that the distinction between an error which entails absence of jurisdiction and an error made within the jurisdiction should be abandoned, and that the new rule should be that 'no court or tribunal has any jurisdiction to make an error of law on which the decision of the case depends'.[36]

This position was confirmed when, in *R* v *Hull University Visitor, ex p Page*, the House of Lords held unanimously that *Anisminic* had established that all errors of law made by a tribunal were subject to judicial review 'by extending the doctrine of ultra vires'. Parliament must be taken to have conferred power on a tribunal subject to it being exercised 'on the correct legal basis'; a misdirection in law in making the decision rendered the decision ultra vires.[37]

An important proposition that is not affected by the *Anisminic* and *Hull University* cases is that no tribunal or other decision-maker has power conclusively to determine the limits of its own jurisdiction.[38] Lord Mustill has said that the question of jurisdiction is 'a hard-edged question. There is no room for legitimate disagreement.'[39]

What has been called the doctrine of jurisdictional fact arises when a decision-maker's jurisdiction depends on a 'precedent fact' which must if necessary be established by the court and not by the decision-maker.[40] To take the example of the Home Secretary's power to deport an alien when this would be conducive to the public good: if X is detained under this power with a view to deportation and claims that she is not subject to deportation as she is a British citizen, the court must examine the relevant evidence and must decide the matter for itself; on this issue the court is not confined to a supervisory role.

This fundamental principle was re-established by the House of Lords in *R* v *Home Secretary, ex p Khawaja*.[41] The case concerned the power of the Home Secretary to remove from the United Kingdom those who were 'illegal entrants' under the Immigration Act 1971. The

---

[36] [1979] QB 56, 70. This was supported by Lord Diplock in *Re Racal Communications Ltd* [1981] AC 374, 383; P Daly (2011) 74 MLR 694.

[37] [1993] AC 682, 701.

[38] The word to be emphasised here is 'conclusively'. When a new claim comes to a tribunal, the tribunal may at the outset have a duty to decide whether it is within its jurisdiction: such a decision may, depending on the legislation, be challenged by exercising a right of appeal (if there is one) and/or by judicial review. The Supreme Court firmly rejected the reintroduction of errors of law within jurisdiction in respect of the First-tier and Upper Tribunal structure in *R (Cart)* v *Upper Tribunal* [2011] UKSC 28, [2012] 1 AC 663, instead imposing a more stringent second appeals criteria taken from the Civil Procedure Rules: namely that the proposed appeal would raise some important point of principle or practice; or there is some other compelling reason for the relevant appellate court to hear the appeal.

[39] *R* v *Monopolies and Mergers Commission, ex p South Yorkshire Transport Ltd* [1993] 1 All ER 289, 293. Lord Mustill accepted that a criterion on which a body's jurisdiction depends may be 'broad enough to call for the exercise of judgment', which will be assessed by reference to irrationality: *Moyna* v *Work and Pensions Secretary* [2003] UKHL 44, [2003] 1 WLR 1929.

[40] See R Williams [2007] PL 793 for a re-assessment of jurisdictional review of errors of law and fact.

[41] [1984] AC 74, reversing *R* v *Home Secretary, ex p Zamir* [1980] AC 930.

House applied the principle that (in Lord Scarman's words) 'where the exercise of an executive power depends upon the precedent establishment of an objective fact, it is for the court, if there be a challenge by way of judicial review, to decide whether the precedent requirement has been satisfied'.[42] On this test, it was not sufficient that the immigration officers reasonably believed Khawaja to be an illegal entrant; his status as an illegal entrant had to be established by evidence before the power to remove him could be exercised. Similarly, it is a precedent fact to which there is a right or wrong answer whether or not an individual is a child to whom duties are owed under the Children Act 1989.[43]

Unlawful use of discretionary powers[44]

We have already seen that the concept of a discretion involves the possibility of choosing between several decisions or courses of action, each of which may be lawful.[45] However, in exercising a discretion, an official or public body may (intentionally or inadvertently) make a decision or embark on action which the court considers to be unlawful. For centuries, the courts have supervised such decisions.[46] While the court will not substitute its own decision for the decision made by the official or body to whom the law entrusts the discretion, it may intervene where a discretion appears not to have been lawfully exercised. To stand in the shoes of the decision-maker would be to extend the role of the courts beyond its proper constitutional limits. Even if the language of a statute seems to confer an absolute discretion, the courts will be very reluctant to hold that their power to review the action taken is excluded. As was said in a leading Canadian case on the improper cancellation of a liquor licence, 'In public regulation of this sort there is no such thing as absolute or untrammelled "discretion" [by which] . . . action can be taken on any ground or for any reason that be suggested to the mind of the administrator'.[47] The attitude of the courts to claims that a minister has unlimited discretion is shown in *Padfield* v *Minister of Agriculture*.

> Under the Agricultural Marketing Act 1958, the milk marketing scheme included a complaints procedure by which a committee of investigation examined any complaint made about the operation of the scheme 'if the Minister in any case so directs'. Padfield, a farmer in south-east England, complained about the prices paid to farmers in that region by the Milk Marketing Board. The minister refused to direct that the complaint be referred to the committee of investigation, and claimed that he had an unfettered discretion in deciding whether or not to refer such complaints. *Held*, the minister would be directed to deal with the complaint according to law. The reasons given by the minister for his refusal were not good reasons in law and showed that he had not exercised his discretion in a manner which promoted the intention and objects of the Act. Lord Reid said: 'the policy and objects of the Act must be determined by construing the Act as a whole, and construction is always a matter of law for the court.'[48]

---

[42] [1984] AC 74, 108.

[43] *R (A)* v *Croydon London Borough Council* [2009] UKSC 8, [2009] 1 WLR 2557.

[44] See Auburn, Moffett and Sharland, *Judicial Review: Principles and Procedure*, chs 11–14, 16–18; Wade and Forsyth, *Administrative Law*, chs 10, 11; Craig, *Administrative Law*, chs 16–19. And see Galligan, *Discretionary Powers*.

[45] See ch 21, text at notes 42–3.

[46] See e.g. *Rooke*'s case (1598) 5 Co Rep 99b: '"Discretion" means . . . that something is to be done according to the rules of reason and justice, not according to private opinion.'

[47] Rand J in *Roncarelli* v *Duplessis* (1959) 16 DLR (2d) 689, 705.

[48] [1968] AC 997, 1030 (Lord Reid). In *R* v *Environment Secretary, ex p Spath Holme Ltd* [2001] 2 AC 349, 396, Lord Nicholls said: 'The discretion given by Parliament is never absolute or unfettered.'

This decision was also significant in that the judges, after examining the reasons given by the minister to see whether they conformed to the Act, were prepared to assume that he had no better reasons for his decision. The willingness of the judges to impose limits upon the minister's discretion in *Padfield* matches the way in which they have frequently cut down the width of local authority discretions. Thus a local planning authority may grant planning permission 'subject to such conditions as they think fit', but the courts have severely limited the apparent width of this power.[49]

The distrust of excessive discretion explains why the power to refuse naturalisation to an alien without giving reasons was held subject to a procedural requirement of fairness;[50] and why a power to grant what would otherwise be a 'conclusive' certificate may be reviewed if the power is inconsistent with EU law.[51] In the past the courts were readier to accept that executive discretion was immune from judicial review than they are today. A notorious instance of the courts' refusal to review executive discretion arose during the Second World War: in *Liversidge* v *Anderson*,[52] the House of Lords, Lord Atkin dissenting, held that the power of the Home Secretary to detain anyone whom he had reasonable cause to consider to be of hostile origin or association was a matter for executive discretion and that the courts must accept a statement by the Home Secretary that he believed he had cause to order the detention. This is an example of extreme judicial deference to executive decision-making, best explained by the context of wartime, and it has no authority beyond its own specific context.[53]

There are various substantive grounds on which the exercise of discretion may be reviewed by the courts. In practice, these grounds overlap and a decision may be defective on several grounds.

1. Error of law

As we have seen, any error of law by a public authority is outwith its jurisdiction and a matter over which the courts will exercise control. An authority which is entrusted with a discretion must direct itself properly on the law or its decision may be declared invalid.

> In *R* v *Home Secretary, ex p Venables*, the Home Secretary increased from 10 to 15 years the 'tariff period' which two young murderers would have to serve before being considered for release. The Home Secretary stated that young offenders sentenced to detention during Her Majesty's pleasure would be dealt with on the same basis as adult offenders on whom mandatory life sentences had been imposed. *Held*, by 3–2, the Home Secretary by this statement misdirected himself in law. 'His legal premise was wrong: the two sentences are different. A sentence of detention during Her Majesty's pleasure requires the Home Secretary to decide from time to time . . . whether detention is still justified. The Home Secretary misunderstood his duty. This misdirection by itself renders his decision unlawful.'[54]

So too, when a county council decided to ban deer hunting over its land, but without considering the extent of its powers, the policy was quashed.[55] Decisions such as these illustrate Lord Diplock's statement that 'the decision-maker must understand correctly the law that regulates his decision-making power and must give effect to it'.[56]

....
[49] E.g. *R* v *Hillingdon Council, ex p Royco Homes Ltd* [1974] QB 720.
[50] *R* v *Home Secretary, ex p Fayed* [1997] 1 All ER 228.
[51] E.g. Case C-222/84, *Johnston* v *Chief Constable, RUC* [1987] QB 129.
[52] [1942] AC 206. See R F V Heuston (1970) 86 LQR 33, (1971) 87 LQR 161; Simpson, *In the Highest Degree Odious*.
[53] *Nakkuda Ali* v *MF de S Jaywatne* [1951] AC 66.
[54] *R* v *Home Secretary, ex p Venables* [1998] AC 407, 518–19 (Lord Steyn).
[55] *R* v *Somerset CC, ex p Fewings* [1995] 3 All ER 20.
[56] *Council of Civil Service Unions* v *Minister for the Civil Service* [1985] AC 374, 408.

The notion of error of law goes wider than a mere mistake of statutory interpretation. A minister commits an error of law if (inter alia) he or she acts when there is no evidence to support the action or comes to a conclusion to which, on the evidence, he or she could not reasonably have come.[57] These principles were highlighted in 1976 when a Labour Secretary of State and a Conservative council clashed over the re-organisation of secondary education.

> Under a power now contained in s 496 of the Education Act 1996, if the Secretary of State was satisfied that an education authority was proposing to act unreasonably, he or she could issue such directions to the authority as appeared expedient. When in May 1976 the newly elected Tameside council proposed, contrary to an earlier plan, to continue selection for entry to five grammar schools in the coming September, the Secretary of State directed the council to adhere to the earlier plan. The House of Lords refused to enforce this direction, holding that it was valid only if the Secretary of State had been satisfied that no reasonable authority could act as the council was proposing to. 'Unreasonable' did not mean conduct which the Secretary of State thought was wrong. On the facts, there was no material on which the Secretary of State could have been satisfied that the council was acting unreasonably. He must therefore have misdirected himself as to the grounds on which he could act.[58]

Reliance on error of law as a ground for controlling discretion places the courts in a position of strength vis-à-vis the administration since it is peculiarly for the courts to identify errors of law. As the *Tameside* case indicated, error of law is a sufficiently pliable concept to enable the judges, if they feel it is necessary, to make a very close scrutiny of the reasons for a decision and the facts on which it was based.

2. Error of fact

Apart from the jurisdictional fact doctrine mentioned above, an attempt to seek judicial review of a decision based on the claim that the decision-maker made an error of fact will generally be met by the reply that judicial review does not provide a right of appeal. This is more likely if there was some evidence for and some against the disputed finding, since the claimant is, in effect, asking the court to substitute itself for the decision-maker in deciding an issue of fact.[59] But suppose that there has been an evident mistake in a finding of fact that is directly material to the decision? In *R v Criminal Injuries Compensation Board, ex p A*,[60] four members of the House of Lords accepted that a decision could be quashed for a material error of fact. In 2004 the Court of Appeal held that a mistake of fact giving rise to unfairness is a separate head of challenge where there is an appeal on a point of law.[61] There are four

---

[57] *Edwards* v *Bairstow* [1956] AC 14; applied to ministers' decisions in *Coleen Properties Ltd* v *Minister of Housing* [1971] 1 All ER 1049. On error of law generally, see J Beatson (1984) 4 OJLS 22.

[58] *Education Secretary* v *Tameside Council* [1977] AC 1014 (D Bull (1987) 50 MLR 307).

[59] On the law/fact distinction, see W A Wilson (1963) 26 MLR 609, (1969) 32 MLR 361; E Mureinik (1982) 98 LQR 587 and T Endicott (1998) 114 LQR 292. And see text at note 57 above; and *Edwards* v *Bairstow* [1956] AC 14 (error of law where factual findings unsupported by any evidence).

[60] [1999] 2 AC 330 (on a matter of 'crucial importance' to A's claim for compensation, the Board proceeded on basis of inaccurate police evidence about a medical examination). See T H Jones [1990] PL 507 on the earlier authorities.

[61] *E* v *Home Secretary* [2004] EWCA Civ 49, [2004] QB 1044. See P Craig [2004] PL 788, R Williams (note 40 above) who examines the effects of different forms of error of fact and CF Forsyth in Forsyth, Elliott, Jhaveri, Scully-Hill and Ramsden (eds), *Effective Judicial Review*, ch 15. For the application of *E* to a decision not to prosecute see: *R (D)* v *DPP* [2017] EWHC 1768 (Admin).

conditions to this jurisdiction. First, there must have been a mistake as to an existing fact. Second, the existence of the fact must be uncontentious and objectively verifiable. Third, the claimant should not have been responsible for the mistake. Fourth, the mistake must have been material to the earlier decision, though it need not necessarily have been decisive. Related to this is the consideration that if, for the purposes of art 6(1) ECHR, an official decision affects an individual's civil rights, a reviewing court must be able to control essential findings of fact, although it is not required to provide a rehearing on every evidentiary issue.[62]

3. Irrelevant considerations

Powers are not lawfully exercised if the decision-maker takes into account factors that in law are irrelevant, or leaves out of account relevant matters. Thus the Home Secretary acted unlawfully when, in deciding whether it was justified to release from prison two young men who as children had been convicted of murder, he took into account an irrelevant matter (public petitions demanding that the murderers be imprisoned for life) and refused to take account of a relevant matter (their progress and development in detention).[63] A decision to award a council house to a councillor, enabling her to go in front of others on the housing list, was unlawful, having been influenced by the view of the chairman of the housing committee that it would help her to be re-elected.[64] Where rates of over £50,000 had been overpaid to a council on an unoccupied warehouse, the council did not lawfully exercise its statutory discretion to refund overpaid rates when it refused to do so for reasons which disregarded the statutory purpose of the discretion.[65]

The court's power to rule that certain considerations are irrelevant may severely limit the scope of general words in a statute,[66] but the courts do not always interpret statutory discretion narrowly.[67] The converse of the proposition that an authority must not take into account irrelevant considerations is that it must take into account relevant considerations. However, to invalidate a decision it is not enough that considerations have been ignored which *could* have been taken into account: it is only when the statute 'expressly or impliedly identifies considerations *required to be taken into account* by the authority as a matter of legal obligation' that a decision will be invalid because relevant considerations were ignored.[68] Thus there are factors which the decision-maker *may* take into account, but need not do so.[69] While it is for the court to rule whether particular factors are relevant or irrelevant and whether they were taken into consideration, it is generally for the decision-maker to decide what weight to give to a relevant consideration that is taken into account.[70] However, if undue weight is given to one factor, this may cause the decision to be reviewed on grounds of reasonableness or proportionality.[71]

[62] *R (Alconbury Developments Ltd)* v *Environment Secretary* [2001] UKHL 23, [2003] 2 AC 295, esp Lord Slynn at [53] and Lord Nolan at [61].

[63] *R* v *Home Secretary, ex p Venables* [1998] AC 407.

[64] *R* v *Port Talbot Council, ex p Jones* [1988] 2 All ER 207.

[65] *R* v *Tower Hamlets Council, ex p Chetnik Developments Ltd* [1988] AC 858.

[66] See e.g. *Mixnam's Properties Ltd* v *Chertsey UDC* [1965] AC 735 (G Ganz (1964) 27 MLR 611).

[67] E.g. *Roberton* v *Environment Secretary* [1976] 1 All ER 689 (risk of assassination of Prime Minister relevant to diversion of footpath on Chequers Estate); *R* v *Westminster Council, ex p Monahan* [1990] 1 QB 87 (relevant to permission for office development near Covent Garden that profits would fund improvements in opera house).

[68] *CREEDNZ Inc* v *Governor-General* [1981] 1 NZLR 172, 183 (Cooke J) (emphasis supplied), approved in *Re Findlay* [1985] AC 318, 333.

[69] See *R* v *Somerset CC, ex p Fewings* [1995] 3 All ER 20, at 32 (Simon Brown LJ). (By 2–1, ban on hunting deer on council's land held unlawful as council had not based ban on its powers of land management; but belief that deer hunting was cruel was not necessarily irrelevant.)

[70] *Tesco Stores* v *Environment Secretary* [1995] 2 All ER 636; *R (Sainsbury's Supermarkets Ltd)* v *Wolverhampton City Council* [2010] UKSC 20, [2011] 1 AC 437; *R* v *Cambridge Health Authority, ex p B* [1995] 2 All ER 129.

[71] See pp 655–662 below.

The case law has not always been clear as to the effect of a decision-maker having taken into account an irrelevant consideration, or failed to take into account a relevant one. Such a decision should always be unlawful, but where it can be shown that it made no difference to the decision the courts need not quash the decision.[72] The *Tameside* case, above, is also authority for the proposition that a decision-maker is required not only to direct himself correctly in relation to the scope of the relevant function, but is also obliged to take reasonable steps to acquaint himself with relevant considerations in order to exercise that function.[73]

4. Improper purposes

The exercise of a power for an improper purpose is invalid. Improper purposes include malice or personal dishonesty on the part of the officials making the decision, but examples of this kind are rare. Most instances of improper purpose have arisen out of a mistaken interpretation by a public authority of its powers, sometimes contributed to by an excess of zeal in the public interest. Thus a city council which was empowered to buy land compulsorily for the purpose of extending streets or improving the city could not validly buy land for the purpose of taking advantage of an anticipated increase in value of the land.[74] In *Congreve* v *Home Office*, where the Home Office had threatened certain holders of television licences that their licences would be revoked by the Home Secretary if they did not each pay an extra £6, the Court of Appeal held that it was an improper exercise of the Home Secretary's power of revocation 'to use a threat to exercise that power as a means of extracting money which Parliament had given the Executive no mandate to demand'.[75] In *Porter* v *Magill*,[76] it was unlawful for the Conservative majority on the Westminster council to adopt a policy of selling council houses in certain parts of the city in the belief that home owners were more likely than council tenants to vote Conservative. The House of Lords accepted that councillors are elected and in due course may stand for re-election, but stressed that a council's powers must be used for the purposes for which they were conferred, not to promote the electoral advantage of a political party.

Difficulty arises when the public body is motivated by both lawful and unlawful purposes.

In *Westminster Corporation* v *London and North Western Railway Co*, the Corporation was empowered to provide public conveniences but not pedestrian subways. Underground conveniences were designed so that the subway leading to them provided a means of crossing a busy street. It was sought to stop the scheme on the ground that the real object was the provision of a crossing and not public conveniences. The court refused to intervene. 'It is not enough to show that the corporation contemplated that the public might use the subway as a means of crossing the street. In order to make out a case of bad faith, it must be shown that the corporation constructed the subway as a means of crossing the street under colour and pretence of providing public conveniences not really wanted.'[77]

---

[72] *R* v *Rochdale MBC, ex p Cromer Ring Mill Ltd* [1982] 3 All ER 761; *R (FDA)* v *Work and Pensions Secretary* [2012] EWCA Civ 332, [2013] 1 WLR 444.

[73] *Education Secretary* v *Tameside MBC* [1977] AC 1014.

[74] *Municipal Council of Sydney* v *Campbell* [1925] AC 338. In *Crédit Suisse* v *Allerdale Council* (above), the scheme was designed to evade a statutory borrowing restriction.

[75] [1976] QB 629, 662 (Geoffrey Lane LJ).

[76] [2001] UKHL 67, [2002] 2 AC 357. See also *R* v *Lewisham Council, ex p Shell UK Ltd* [1988] 1 All ER 938.

[77] *Westminster Corpn* v *London and North Western Railway Co* [1905] AC 426, 432 (Lord Macnaghten); cf *Webb* v *Minister of Housing* [1965] 2 All ER 193.

Although the case law is not always consistent, the weight of authority supports an approach whereby the court considers the dominant purpose of the decision, and if this was improper, the decision is unlawful. If the dominant purpose was a proper one, improper subsidiary purposes will not invalidate the decision.[78] As a result, it can be rather difficult in practice to categorise a case as being about irrelevant considerations or improper purposes,[79] although doing so may matter at the stage of considering the remedial effect of the unlawful decision and whether it should be quashed.

5. Unauthorised delegation

A body to which the exercise of discretion has been entrusted by statute may not delegate the exercise of that discretion to another person or body unless the statute can be read as having authorised such delegation. In general, a statute that authorises one level of delegation does not thereby authorise further delegation. In *Barnard* v *National Dock Labour Board*, the national board lawfully delegated disciplinary functions over registered dockers to local boards; a local board acted unlawfully when it sub-delegated the power to suspend dockers to the port manager.[80]

The rule against unauthorised delegation of powers might seem to require all powers vested in a minister to be exercised by him or her personally. However, in the case of central government the courts have accepted that powers and duties conferred on a minister may properly be exercised by officials for whom the minister is responsible to Parliament or by a junior minister.[81] Constitutional fiction sees the decision of the official as the decision of the minister,[82] even if in practice the minister has no awareness of the matter at all. Accordingly, information available to officials advising a minister is deemed to be information taken into account by the minister.[83] But where a statutory duty is vested in one minister, he or she may not adopt a policy by which the decision is effectively made by another minister.[84] And, where a discretion is vested in a subordinate officer, it may not be taken away by orders from a superior.[85]

Similar principles apply to statutory agencies, save that there is no scope for the application of principle equating officials with ministers responsible for them.[86] Outside of central government, the analytical focus is likely to be a power to delegate which can be implied from the statutory scheme.[87] The Police Complaints Board could not adopt a rule of taking no action on complaints which the Director of Public Prosecutions had decided should not lead to criminal proceedings;[88] but the Commission for Racial Equality could delegate to its staff

---

[78] *Westminster Corporation* (above); *R* v *Southwark Crown Court, ex p Bowles* [1998] AC 641; *Re Kelly's Application for Judicial Review* [2000] NI 103.

[79] As to which, see G D S Taylor [1976] CLJ 272.

[80] [1953] 2 QB 18. And e.g. *Young* v *Fife Regional Council* 1986 SLT 331.

[81] *Carltona Ltd* v *Commissioners of Works* [1943] 2 All ER 560; *Re Golden Chemical Products* [1976] Ch 300. See also *R* v *Home Secretary, ex p Oladehinde* [1991] 1 AC 254; D Lanham (1984) 100 LQR 587; *R* v *Home Secretary, ex p Doody* [1994] 1 AC 531, 566 (power of Home Secretary to determine penal element of life sentence for murder); and ch 11 D.

[82] *R (Bourgass)* v *Justice Secretary* [2015] UKSC 54, [2016] AC 384 at [49] (Lord Reed) (prison governors hold independent office and do not fall within the *Carltona* principle).

[83] *National Association of Health Stores* v *Health Secretary* [2005] EWCA Civ 154.

[84] *Lavender & Son Ltd* v *Minister of Housing* [1970] 3 All ER 871, distinguished in *Audit Commission* v *Ealing Council* [2005] EWCA Civ 556; J Braier [2005] JR 216.

[85] *Simms Motor Units Ltd* v *Minister of Labour* [1946] 2 All ER 201.

[86] *DPP* v *Haw* [2007] EWHC 1931 (Admin), [2008] 1 WLR 379.

[87] R Gregson [2017] PL 408.

[88] *R* v *Police Complaints Board, ex p Madden* [1983] 2 All ER 353.

the task of conducting formal investigations into alleged discrimination,[89] and the Conservators of the River Cam could delegate to their River Manager the conduct of prosecutions for the breach of by-laws.[90] Whether there is a power to delegate beyond the statutorily designated decision-maker will depend upon the nature of the power or duty in issue and, in the light of practicalities, what Parliament can have intended.[91] In local government, there is now wide authority for councils to delegate their functions to committees, sub-committees and officers.[92]

6. Discretion may not be fettered

The powers of public bodies typically include making discretionary decisions, whether in granting a benefit sought by an individual – be it planning permission, a licence, or admission to a school – or imposing a penalty (such as revoking a licence or excluding a pupil for misconduct). In law, the decision-maker must consider the matter 'on its merits', taking into account all relevant circumstances. It is impossible to assess the merits of an individual case without considering general matters, such as relevant standards, current policies and decisions made in other cases. These principles apply to the exercise of discretionary powers vested in government departments, but departments cannot function effectively unless they formulate policies as to how a particular discretion will be exercised. Such policies may not be treated as binding rules.

> Under a scheme for discretionary investment grants to industry, the Board of Trade applied a rule that grants could not be paid in respect of items costing less than £25 and refused to pay a grant to a firm which had spent over £4 million on gas cylinders costing £20 each: the House of Lords accepted that the department was entitled to make such a rule or policy, provided that it was prepared to listen to arguments for the exercise of individual discretion.[93]

In such a case, individuals may find it very difficult to persuade officials that they should receive preferential treatment. Their right might be more realistically described as a right to ask that the general policy should be changed.[94] Good administration would seem to require that public authorities should be able to adopt definite policies without this interfering with the proper exercise of discretion.[95] Four general types of fettering case can be analysed.[96]

The first is where legislation requires the decision-maker to have and operate a policy, the operation of which is challengeable only on the ordinary principles of judicial review.[97] Second, the exercise of a common law power – i.e. not one derived from statute – is not subject to the fetter principle.[98] Alternatively, this second category could be considered an exception to the first category.

[89] *R v Commission for Racial Equality, ex p Cottrell & Rothon* [1980] 3 All ER 265. Cf *Financial Ombudsman Service v Heather Moor and Edgecomb Ltd* [2008] EWCA Civ 643, [2009] 1 All ER 328. M Freedland [1996] PL 19.
[90] *Noon v Matthews* [2014] EWHC 4330 (Admin).
[91] *DPP v Haw* [2007] EWHC 1931 (Admin), [2008] 1 WLR 379 (Metropolitan Police Commissioner cannot have been intended to have to personally consider all applications to demonstrate in London, and decide on the appropriate conditions, given that thousands of such applications are made).
[92] Local Government Act 1972, s 101.
[93] *British Oxygen Co v Board of Trade* [1971] AC 610.
[94] Ibid, at 631 (Lord Dilhorne).
[95] Cf *A-G ex rel Tilley v Wandsworth BC* [1981] 1 All ER 1162 and *R v Rochdale BC, ex p Cromer Ring Mill Ltd* [1982] 3 All ER 761.
[96] CJS Knight [2009] JR 73.
[97] *R (Nicholds) v Security Industry Authority* [2006] EWHC 1792 (Admin), [2007] 1 WLR 2067.
[98] *R (Sandiford) v Foreign Secretary* [2014] UKSC 44, [2014] 1 WLR 2697; *R (Elias) v Defence Secretary* [2006] EWCA Civ 1293, [2006] 1 WLR 3213. For a contrary argument, see: A Perry [2017] CLJ 375.

The third type of situation is the most common: fettering in law. The *British Oxygen* case above is the classic example. It occurs when a decision-maker adopts a policy as to the exercise of a discretion, but applies it in an over-rigid manner. The decision-maker may adopt a general policy and indicate that it will be applied in the absence of exceptional circumstances,[99] but may not have a rule that certain applications will always be refused.[100]

The fourth type of case is fettering in fact, where a policy admits of exceptions but is actually operated so rigidly as to constitute a fetter.[101] There is a clear overlap here with a case of failing to take account of relevant considerations. A decision-maker may be required to set out the exceptional circumstances the policy allows for.[102] Public authorities that have adopted policies must take steps to see that they are applied consistently, and must bring them to the notice of the actual decision-makers.[103] A government department that adopts and applies a policy which is contrary to its published policy is acting unlawfully.[104]

7. Unreasonableness (irrationality)

A judge may not on judicial review set aside an official decision merely because he or she considers that the matter should have been decided differently. Judicial review does not provide a right to appeal on the merits of the decision. However, in exceptional circumstances a decision may be set aside for unreasonableness, and if this ground for review is raised, the court will have the difficult task of considering whether a decision that is otherwise within the powers of the authority may be said to be 'unreasonable'.

> *Associated Provincial Picture Houses Ltd* v *Wednesbury Corporation*[105] concerned the Sunday Entertainments Act 1932, that gave a local council power to permit cinemas to open on Sundays, 'subject to such conditions as the [council] think fit to impose'. The Wednesbury council allowed cinemas to show films on Sundays, on condition that no children under 15 should be admitted to the performances, with or without an adult. Very many councils permitted children to go to the cinema on a Sunday if they were accompanied by an adult. The condition in Wednesbury was challenged by one of the cinemas. *Held*, the condition was neither ultra vires nor unreasonable.

In his oft-quoted judgment, Lord Greene MR set out what is now termed the *Wednesbury* test, namely that a court may set aside a decision for unreasonableness only when the authority has come to a conclusion 'so unreasonable that no reasonable authority could ever have come to it'.[106]

---

[99] See e.g. *R* v *Home Secretary, ex p P and Q* [2001] 2 FLR 383 (policy of allowing mothers in prison to keep babies with them under the age of 18 months).

[100] *R* v *Port of London Authority, ex p Kynoch* [1919] 1 KB 176, 184 (dictum of Bankes LJ). See D J Galligan [1976] PL 332. Also *R* v *Home Secretary, ex p Venables* [1998] AC 407 (discretion fettered by rigid policy of ignoring child's development in prison) and *R* v *Home Secretary, ex p Hindley* [2001] 1 AC 410 (Home Secretary prepared to reconsider decision on whole life tariff at any time).

[101] *R* v *North West Lancashire Health Authority, ex p A* [2000] 1 WLR 977; *R* v *Southwark London Borough Council, ex p Melak* (1997) 29 HLR 223.

[102] *R (Rogers)* v *Swindon NHS PCT* [2006] EWCA Civ 392, [2006] 1 WLR 2649.

[103] *R (Rashid)* v *Home Secretary* [2005] EWCA Civ 744; and see M Elliott [2005] JR 281.

[104] *R (Lumba)* v *Home Secretary* [2011] UKSC 12, [2012] 1 AC 245.

[105] [1948] 1 KB 223.

[106] On the principles of *Wednesbury* review, see J Jowell and A Lester [1987] PL 368; Lord Irvine [1996] PL 59; R Carnwath [1996] PL 245; J Laws in Forsyth and Hare (eds), *The Golden Metwand and the Crooked Cord*, pp 185–201; A Le Sueur [2005] JR 32; M Fordham [2008] JR 266; P Daly [2011] PL 238; P P Craig [2013] CLP 1; P P Craig [2015] PL 60; R Williams [2017] PL 99.

The judgment emphasised that unreasonableness is closely related to other grounds of review, such as irrelevant considerations, improper purposes and error of law. It is important to remember that unreasonableness operates as both a self-standing head of substantive review *and* as the standard of review (the level of scrutiny the court adopts) in certain types of case.

The meaning of 'unreasonable' was central to the *Tameside* case, as we have seen. Lord Diplock said there that 'unreasonable' denotes 'conduct which no sensible authority acting with due appreciation of its responsibilities would have decided to adopt'.[107] In the GCHQ case, the same judge made the test more exacting by calling the test one of irrationality: it meant 'a decision which is so outrageous in its defiance of logic or of accepted moral standards that no sensible person who had applied his mind to the question to be decided could have arrived at it'.[108] In 1998, Lord Cooke regretted that some *Wednesbury* phrases had become 'established incantations'; he preferred 'the simple test' of whether the decision under review 'was one which a reasonable authority could reach'.[109]

What can now be seen is that the test of unreasonableness does not apply uniformly to all kinds of decision. There are some decisions (for instance, allocating financial resources to local councils) where the court would intervene for unreasonableness only in exceptional circumstances.[110] These include the allocation of scarce resources, the exercise of specialist expertise, or inherently policy-driven or political judgments.[111]

By contrast, if fundamental human rights are in issue, as where the life of an asylum seeker may be at risk, 'the basis of the decision must surely call for the most anxious scrutiny'.[112] In 1996, the Court of Appeal held that an unreasonable decision was

> one beyond the range of responses open to a reasonable decision-maker. But in judging whether the decision-maker has exceeded this margin of appreciation the human rights context is important. The more substantial the interference with human rights, the more the court will require by way of justification before it is satisfied that the decision is reasonable in the sense outlined above.[113]

Despite this significant development, the court upheld the government's policy that banned homosexuals from serving in the armed forces. However, the policy later failed the test of proportionality in European human rights law, because of its effect on the claimants' right to respect for their private lives.[114]

The *Wednesbury* test has often been said to present too high a hurdle in the way of a challenge to official action, and critics have argued that the European test of proportionality provided a better approach to the control of discretion. In 1991, an attempt to get British courts to adopt the test of proportionality was made in *R v Home Secretary, ex p Brind*.[115] The House of Lords held that, without incorporation of the European Convention on Human Rights (and except when rights in EU law were affected),[116] British courts could not

---

[107] *Education Secretary v Tameside Council* [1977] AC 1014, at 1064.

[108] *Council of Civil Service Unions v Minister for the Civil Service* [1985] AC 374, 410.

[109] *R v Chief Constable of Sussex, ex p International Trader's Ferry Ltd* [1999] 2 AC 418, 452.

[110] *R v Environment Secretary, ex p Nottinghamshire CC* [1986] AC 240.

[111] Respectively: *Nottinghamshire* (above), *R (London and Continental Railway) v The Rail Regulator* [2013] EWHC 2607 (Admin); *R (Corner House Research) v Director of the Serious Fraud Office* [2008] UKHL 60, [2009] 1 AC 756.

[112] *R v Home Secretary, ex p Bugdaycay* [1987] AC 514, 531. The impact on an individual is relevant to the level of scrutiny: *R (KM) v Cambridgeshire County Council* [2012] UKSC 23, [2012] PTSR 1189.

[113] *R v Ministry of Defence, ex p Smith* [1996] QB 517, 554 (Sir Thomas Bingham MR).

[114] *Lustig-Prean v UK* (1999) 29 EHRR 548.

[115] [1991] 1 AC 696.

[116] As in the *International Trader's Ferry* case (above).

review executive decisions on the basis of proportionality. Applying the *Wednesbury* test, the House upheld a government ban on the broadcasting of direct statements by representatives of proscribed organisations in Northern Ireland.

In 2001, Lord Cooke described the *Wednesbury* case as 'an unfortunately retrogressive decision' in that it 'suggested that there are degrees of unreasonableness and that only a very extreme degree can bring an administrative decision within the legitimate scope of judicial invalidation'.[117] Yet decisions have continued to be based on the *Wednesbury* test. The Home Secretary's decision to include Pakistan in a 'white list' of countries in which persecution of individuals was unlikely to occur was held irrational.[118] The dismissal of a chief constable following the Hillsborough inquest verdicts for issuing a press release which was not, read reasonably, objectionable was held to be irrational.[119] A decision by the NHS to refuse to fund a drug which would treat a child with a rare condition was found to be irrational.[120] By contrast, a scheme for compensating British civilians interned by the Japanese during the Second World War was upheld: it was considered reasonable for British citizens who claimed compensation to be required to show that they had a close link with the United Kingdom and the introduction of proportionality was rejected.[121]

The position of the Supreme Court over recent years has not helped clarity on the status of rationality or proportionality as the standard of review in substantive challenges. In *Kennedy* v *Charity Commission*, Lord Mance explained that *Wednesbury* review was not a rigid standard, and the intensity of scrutiny varied depending on the context.[122] In *Pham* v *Home Secretary*, various members of the Court affirmed that rationality review could vary significantly in its intensity and may not differ significantly from proportionality at least in outcomes,[123] whilst also cautioning about whether it was appropriate to move away from irrationality outside of a context of individual rights.[124] In *R (Keyu)* v *Foreign Secretary* the Court confirmed that proportionality was not a free-standing ground of review in English law, and would require a nine-judge court to alter that position, whilst also emphasising the flexibility of rationality review.[125]

The application of irrationality has led to a number of areas which can either be seen as sub-categories of irrationality as a head of review, or as separate heads of review for which irrationality is the standard: for instance, cases producing arbitrary or discriminatory results, and cases of alleged conspicuous unfairness.[126]

8. Proportionality

Proportionality is not the same as *Wednesbury* unreasonableness. It requires a structured analysis by the court of the decision challenged and the justification of the decision-maker for that challenge. The general standard of review under Human Rights Act claims is proportionality,[127] as it is under EU law. (Proportionality generally means the same thing in both the

---

[117] *R (Daly)* v *Home Secretary* [2001] UKHL 26, [2001] 2 AC 532, at [32].

[118] *R* v *Home Secretary, ex p Javed* [2001] EWCA Civ 789, [2002] QB 129.

[119] *R (Crompton)* v *South Yorkshire Police and Crime Commissioner* [2017] EWHC 1349 (Admin).

[120] *R (SB)* v *NHS England* [2017] EWHC 2000 (Admin).

[121] *R (ABCIFER)* v *Defence Secretary* [2002] EWCA Civ 473, [2003] QB 1397. In a later decision, the scheme was held to be indirectly discriminatory under the Race Relations Act 1976: [2006] EWCA Civ 1293, [2006] 1 WLR 3213.

[122] *Kennedy* v *Information Commissioner* [2014] UKSC 20, [2015] AC 455 at [51]–[54] (Lord Mance).

[123] *Pham* v *Home Secretary* [2015] UKSC 19, [2015] 1 WLR 1591.

[124] See the judgment of Lord Reed in particular.

[125] *R (Keyu)* v *Foreign Secretary* [2015] UKSC 69, [2016] AC 1355 at [271]–[283] (Lord Kerr).

[126] Respectively: *Matadeen* v *Pointu* [1999] 1 AC 98 and *R (Lewisham LBC)* v *AQA* [2013] EWHC 211 (Admin).

[127] *R* v *Home Secretary, ex p Daly* [2001] UKHL 26, [2001] 2 AC 532.

human rights and EU law context, but the precise approach taken may be different.[128]) Even anxious scrutiny *Wednesbury* review is insufficiently intensive.[129] In many cases, the outcome under *Wednesbury* and proportionality will be the same, but not in all. Proportionality requires the court to take additional steps and engage with the challenged decision in much greater depth.[130]

Lord Steyn famously set out the difference between the two tests in *Daly*:

> The starting point is that there is an overlap between the traditional grounds of review and the approach of proportionality. Most cases would be decided in the same way whichever approach is adopted. But the intensity of review is somewhat greater under the proportionality approach. Making due allowance for important structural differences between various convention rights, which I do not propose to discuss, a few generalisations are perhaps permissible. I would mention three concrete differences without suggesting that my statement is exhaustive. First, the doctrine of proportionality may require the reviewing court to assess the balance which the decision maker has struck, not merely whether it is within the range of rational or reasonable decisions. Secondly, the proportionality test may go further than the traditional grounds of review inasmuch as it may require attention to be directed to the relative weight accorded to interests and considerations. Thirdly, even the heightened scrutiny test developed in *R v Ministry of Defence ex p Smith* [1996] QB 517, 554 is not necessarily appropriate to the protection of human rights . . . In other words, the intensity of the review, in similar cases, is guaranteed by the twin requirements that the limitation of the right was necessary in a democratic society, in the sense of meeting a pressing social need, and the question whether the interference was really proportionate to the legitimate aim being pursued. The differences in approach between the traditional grounds of review and the proportionality approach may therefore sometimes yield different results. It is therefore important that cases involving convention rights must be analysed in the correct way.[131]

It is quite possible that in time proportionality will be recognised as a ground of judicial review, or as the standard of review in substantive challenges, in purely domestic judicial review cases which have no connection to either the HRA or EU law. However, at the moment, proportionality is not fully a part of domestic judicial review and it has not supplanted *Wednesbury*.[132] The Supreme Court has confirmed that it would require a case in which the need for proportionality was squarely in issue, and where the Court was sitting with nine members, for such a step to be taken.[133]

The proportionality test adopted by the English courts has been set out by the Privy Council in *de Freitas v Permanent Secretary of Ministry of Agriculture, Fisheries, Lands and Housing* as a carefully structured analysis.[134] The court must ask whether: (1) the legislative objective is sufficiently important to justify limiting a fundamental right; (2) the measures

---

[128] *R (Rotherham MBC) v Business Secretary* [2015] UKSC 6, [2015] PTSR 322.

[129] *Smith & Grady v UK* (1999) 29 EHRR 493.

[130] M Elliott in Forsyth, Elliott, Jhaveri, Scully-Hill and Ramsden (eds), *Effective Judicial Review*, ch 16.

[131] *Daly* (above) at [27]–[28].

[132] Lord Hoffmann in Ellis (ed.), *The Principle of Proportionality in the Laws of Europe*; Schwarze, *European Administrative Law*, ch 5; M Elliott [2001] CLJ 301; J Rivers [2006] CLJ 174; T Hickman [2008] PL 694; Dame Mary Arden [2013] PL 498; Sir Phillip Sales (2013) 129 LQR 223. Note, however, the majority judgments in *Kennedy v Charity Commission* [2014] UKSC 20, [2014] 2 WLR 808, esp [51]–[55] (Lord Mance).

[133] *R (Keyu) v Foreign Secretary* [2015] UKSC 69, [2016] AC 1355.

[134] [1999] 1 AC 69.

designed to meet the legislative objective are rationally connected to it; and (3) the means used to impair the right or freedom are no more than is necessary to accomplish the objective. The House of Lords in *Huang* v *Home Secretary* added the following fourth step, that the analysis must: 'always involve the striking of a fair balance between the rights of the individual and the interests of the community which is inherent in the whole of the Convention. The severity and consequences of the interference will call for careful assessment at this stage.'[135]

In truth, the fourth step rolls back into the third, but it broadens the scope of the exercise under step three. That broader third step is the balancing test, where the court must assess whether a fair balance has been struck between the factors which the parties rely on. The addition from *Huang* makes clear that the third step is not to ask whether a less restrictive approach was possible, although that is relevant to consider; but whether the decision as a whole has struck a fair balance, taking into account the importance of the right and any other possible methods of achieving the legitimate aim. The addition of the fourth stage is now well-established, having been repeatedly approved and applied by the Supreme Court.[136]

What proportionality adds to unreasonableness, beyond the sense of fair balance, is a need for structured justification. Once the claimant has shown that there is an interference with a right (that the facts fall within the scope of an ECHR right), it will be for the claimant to prove that there is no legitimate aim, and that there is no rational connection. These two stages will invariably be difficult to prove and are rarely met. But it is for the public authority to prove the key third stage (and fourth, following *Huang*) that the impairment of the right has been no more than necessary. The bulk of the work of proportionality is done at the third stage (particularly in the European Court of Human Rights), and the burden being on the public authority requires the court to closely engage with the justifications put forward by the authority.

It is important that the proportionality analysis be conducted properly and in a structured manner in each case in which it is raised. In certain types of case lower courts and tribunals have learnt from long experience that particular arguments are often run but that they will almost never succeed under the existing law. There is a consequent, and understandable, tendency on the part of those courts and tribunals to simply apply a test of 'exceptionality': does this case have something about it which takes it out of the ordinary? Such an approach is not permitted. The proportionality analysis must always be gone through carefully and cautiously. It may in fact be only in exceptional cases that the infringement of the right will be disproportionate (for example, article 8 ECHR rights overcoming deportation of those with no right to be in the United Kingdom), but this cannot be converted into a legal test, and the wording of 'exceptionality' is best avoided altogether. The Supreme Court has stressed and re-stressed in a variety of contexts that there can be no test of exceptionality.[137] Exceptionality must be the outcome of the test, not the threshold.

Much judicial and academic ink has been spilt on the subjects of margins of appreciation for, discretionary areas of judgment of, and deference to, the decision-maker.[138] This involves the court in some way recognising that the decision-maker's justifications and reasoning may

---

[135] [2007] UKHL 11, [2007] 2 AC 167 at [19].

[136] *R (Quila)* v *Home Secretary* [2011] UKSC 45, [2012] 1 AC 6; *Bank Mellat* v *HM Treasury (No. 2)* [2013] UKSC 39, [2014] AC 700.

[137] *Huang* (above); *Norris* v *Government of the USA* [2010] UKSC 9, [2010] 2 WLR 572; *Re W (Children)* [2010] UKSC 12, [2010] 1 WLR 701.

[138] See Lord Hoffmann's criticism of deference in *R (Pro-Life Alliance)* v *BBC* [2003] UKHL 23, [2004] 1 AC 185 at [74]–[77]; R Clayton [2004] PL 33; R Edwards (2002) 65 MLR 859; J Jowell [2000] PL 671, [2003] PL 592, and ch 4 in Craig and Rawlings (eds), *Law and Administration in Europe*; Lord Steyn [2005] PL 346; M Hunt in Bamforth and Leyland (eds), *Public Law in a Multi-Layered Constitution*, ch 13; T R S Allan [2006] CLJ 671; A L Young (2009) 72 MLR 554; A Kavanagh (2010) 126 LQR 222; T R S Allan (2011) 127 LQR 96.

have advantages over the legal process. These advantages, as acknowledged in the case law, may be constitutional – in the sense that the decision-maker has been specifically allocated its function by Parliament, or where primary legislation is challenged under the HRA the decision-maker may be Parliament itself – or it may be institutional – in the sense that the decision-maker is best placed to undertake the balancing exercise because it has particular expertise in the area. It is undoubtedly the case that, despite considerable academic debate, the courts have always been willing to afford the decision-maker a degree of latitude in the choices made, in a similar manner to the European Court of Human Rights affording a margin of appreciation to individual states. In *Huang* the House of Lords, in a single opinion, took the whole debate back to basics:

> Much argument was directed on the hearing of these appeals, and much authority cited, on the appellate immigration authority's proper approach to its task, due deference, discretionary areas of judgment, the margin of appreciation, democratic accountability, relative institutional competence, a distinction drawn by the Court of Appeal between decisions based on policy and decisions not so based, and so on. We think, with respect, that there has been a tendency, both in the arguments addressed to the courts and in the judgments of the courts, to complicate and mystify what is not, in principle, a hard task to define, however difficult the task is, in practice, to perform . . . The giving of weight to factors such as these is not, in our opinion, aptly described as deference: it is performance of the ordinary judicial task of weighing up the competing considerations on each side and according appropriate weight to the judgment of a person with responsibility for a given subject matter and access to special sources of knowledge and advice. That is how any rational judicial decision-maker is likely to proceed.[139]

Proportionality is ultimately, like all legal tests, a matter for the court.[140]

When an infringement of a Convention right is alleged, it is for the court to make the determination. The House of Lords in *R (SB)* v *Governors of Denbigh High School* stressed that what matters is the result.[141] The fact that the decision-maker has taken into account Convention rights in reaching its conclusion will not save that decision if the court finds it to be disproportionate. Equally, where no apparent balancing exercise has taken place, this will not prove to be a ground of illegality under the Human Rights Act 1998 unless the decision in substance infringes a Convention right. The decision-maker 'cannot be expected to make such decisions with textbooks on human rights law at their elbows'.[142] In *Belfast City Council* v *Miss Behavin' Ltd* it was suggested that where the balancing exercise had been undertaken it would be accorded due weight.[143] If a 'good' rights balance made by the decision-maker is relevant to the court's adjudication, why is a 'bad' or a non-existent one not relevant, too? If conducting their own proportionality exercise is to be accorded some weight in deciding that the decision actually was proportionate, the fact that the decision-maker has not conducted that exercise should logically be accorded at least some weight on the question of whether the decision itself is held to be proportionate.

The better view is that consideration should be given to the decision-making process adopted in reviewing the human rights compliance of a discretionary decision. It is, for the

---

[139] *Huang* (above) at [14]–[16].
[140] *R (Lord Carlile)* v *Home Secretary* [2014] UKSC 60, [2015] AC 945.
[141] [2006] UKHL 15, [2007] 1 AC 100.
[142] *Denbigh* (above) at [68] (Lord Hoffmann).
[143] [2007] UKHL 19, [2007] 1 WLR 1420.

purposes of the court, irrelevant. It may be useful for the decision-maker to consider the matter in a judicial manner (i.e. to have acted as though it were a court, with the accompanying procedural protections and emphasis on law), but only instrumentally in that it will increase the likelihood of reaching the same answer as the court will. However, the two are separate factors. The court must be entirely unconcerned with whether or not the decision-maker has 'talked the rights talk'. It is the job of the court to assess whether or not the decision-maker has 'walked the rights walk'. A case which falls into an area where the courts would ordinarily show a certain degree of deference to the primary decision-maker may be treated differently. Where they would do so, it may be relevant in reaching a judgment on whether the decision-maker has 'walked the rights walk' to take into account whether it has persuasively 'talked the rights talk'. It is relevant in this type of case because the court is already concerned with what the decision-maker is saying, as well as what they are doing. Thus, in *Denbigh* and *Miss Behavin'*, if the decision-makers had balanced the rights themselves that would have been a relevant factor to consider, providing one accepts that some deference is due in the areas of uniform policy and free speech restrictions in cases of pornography.[144]

In outline, if action to achieve a lawful objective is taken in a situation where it will restrict a fundamental right, the effect on the right must not be disproportionate to the public purpose sought to be achieved. The test applies in respect of European Convention rights, many of which (for instance, the right to freedom of expression) are subject to such restrictions 'as are prescribed by law and are necessary in a democratic society' for specified public purposes.[145] A restriction cannot be regarded as 'necessary in a democratic society' unless it is proportionate to the legitimate aim pursued.[146] If in a given situation there is a need for public action to restrict the right, the restriction 'must be necessary and proportionate to the damage which the restriction is designed to prevent'.[147] Any further restriction is unjustifiable.

One striking effect of the Human Rights Act has been to require the courts to apply the test of proportionality in almost every case when a claim for judicial review is based on an infringement or restriction of a Convention right. The test may be applied in challenges to Acts of Parliament or to the exercise of discretion,[148] and whether the remedy is sought by judicial review or by appeal.[149] In *R (Daly)* v *Home Secretary*,[150] a prison policy that barred a prisoner in a closed prison from being present while his cell was searched, even when letters between him and his solicitor were examined, was held by the House of Lords to be unlawful on common law grounds. It was also held to infringe Daly's right under art 8(1) ECHR to respect for his correspondence to a greater extent than was necessary. Lord Steyn commented that proportionality was likely to mean a greater intensity of review than the *Wednesbury* test or even the heightened scrutiny test applied in *R* v *Ministry of Defence, ex p Smith*,[151] but he denied that this meant there had been a shift to 'merits review'.

The fact that proportionality is now a key mechanism in the protection of Convention rights raises difficult questions about the extent to which the courts may substitute their views for decisions taken by ministers, Parliament or, for instance, the broadcasting authorities.[152] Must

144 CJS Knight [2007] JR 221; D Mead [2012] PL 61; A Kavanagh (2014) 130 LQR 235.
145 Art 10(2) ECHR. See *Sunday Times* v *UK* (1979) 2 EHRR 245; and ch 4 C.
146 As in *Dudgeon* v *UK* (1981) 4 EHRR 149.
147 *R* v *Home Secretary, ex p Brind* [1991] 1 AC 696, 751 (Lord Templeman).
148 See, respectively, *A* v *Home Secretary* [2004] UKHL 56, [2005] 2 AC 68; *R (Farrakhan)* v *Home Secretary* [2002] EWCA Civ 606, [2002] QB 1391.
149 On recourse by way of appeal, see *Huang* v *Home Secretary* [2007] UKHL 11, [2007] 2 AC 167.
150 [2001] UKHL 26, [2001] 2 AC 532.
151 See text at note 113.
152 As in *R (Pro-Life Alliance)* v *BBC* [2003] UKHL 23, [2004] 1 AC 185.

the courts decide every human rights case by applying their view of what they regard as correct? As we have seen, the court is required by the Human Rights Act to decide whether there has actually been a violation of the Convention, and must not find that there has been a breach merely because the decision-maker has not used words that refer to the ECHR.[153] But this does not mean that a considered assessment of the implications by a responsible decision-maker must be ignored by the court. Depending on the context, issues of constitutional respect and institutional competence may arise. When in 2004 the Law Lords held indefinite detention for suspected terrorists to be incompatible with the Convention right to liberty,[154] the decision cannot be said to have been deferential to Parliament or the government, even though the context of national security might have called for this.[155]

Acting incompatibly with Convention rights

The Human Rights Act 1998, s 6(1), provides: 'It is unlawful for a public authority to act in a way which is incompatible with a Convention right.' An act for this purpose includes a failure to act – but not a failure to make any primary legislation (s 6(6)). And the act of a public authority is not unlawful if, as a result of primary legislation, the authority could not have acted differently or if it gives effect to legislation that cannot be read in a way compatible with Convention rights.

While issues as to the lawfulness of a public authority's act under s 6(1) may be raised in any court or tribunal proceedings to which they are relevant (s 7(1)), the scheme of the Act extends the scope of judicial review into the broad expanse of all Convention rights, including the right to life (art 2), the right to a fair hearing (art 6(1)), the right to respect for private and family life (art 8) and freedom of expression (art 10). It follows that decisions of public authorities are subject to judicial review and may be held unlawful, even if apart from the Act no such claim could have been made. In practice, applicants for judicial review may seek to rely both on Convention rights and on the grounds for review that are available at common law. In some cases, the human rights claims do not affect the outcome; in others, as we have seen in respect of proportionality, they may be decisive in the claimant's favour because of the different standard of review applied by the courts.

Judges in the United Kingdom dealing with judicial review must (because of the Human Rights Act, s 2) take account of case law from Strasbourg, which may mean applying that case law even if they consider it to be unsatisfactory.[156] When decisions by a public authority are under review, it does not matter that the authority did not expressly deal with Convention issues in making its decision,[157] for the task of the reviewing court is to decide whether the actual outcome on the facts was a breach of Convention rights. However, a public authority that ignores its obligations under the Act must obviously be at greater risk of its decisions being challenged as unlawful.

[153] See *R (Begum)* v *Denbigh High School* [2006] UKHL 15, [2007] 1 AC 100; *Belfast Council* v *Miss Behavin' Ltd* [2007] UKHL 19, [2007] 3 All ER 1007.

[154] *A* v *Home Secretary*, note 148 above.

[155] Cf *Home Secretary* v *Rehman* [2001] UKHL 47, [2003] 1 AC 153, [62] (Lord Hoffmann). And see A Kavanagh [2009] PL 287.

[156] See *Home Secretary* v *AF (No 3)* [2009] UKHL 28, [2009] 3 All ER 643, applying *A* v *UK* (2009) 26 BHRC 1 (use of special advocates); see esp speeches of Lords Hoffmann and Rodger ([98]: 'Even though we are dealing with a UK statute, in reality, we have no choice'). Contrast with *R* v *Horncastle* [2009] UKSC 14, [2010] 2 AC 373 rejecting the European Court's approach to hearsay evidence in criminal trials.

[157] See cases cited in notes 141–3 above.

B. Legitimate expectations

A ground of judicial review linked with fairness that has undergone rapid development since the 1980s is that of legitimate expectations.[158] It now has both substantive and procedural content and is consequently best placed between the two other sections of this chapter. The protection of legitimate expectations exists in other systems of law (including those of Canada, Germany and the EU)[159] and is an aspect of legal certainty. In their dealings with public agencies, private persons need to know if they can rely on statements by officials or on decisions that have been notified to them, and when those can be departed from.

Five broad types of case should be considered. First, where there has been the revocation of an existing favourable decision. Secondly, a procedural entitlement said to arise from a representation that a particular procedure will be followed. Thirdly, a procedural entitlement said to arise out of an interest in a substantive benefit which cannot fairly be withdrawn without some right to comment. Fourth, a representation as to a substantive entitlement. Finally, cases which arise out of representations that are held to be ultra vires.

Revocation of an existing decision

We deal first with the unusual situation in which a public body has made a *decision* conferring a benefit upon an individual that it later tries to revoke and replace with a fresh decision that is less favourable to the individual. If the agency took the first decision properly and told the individual of it, without qualifying it as 'provisional' or 'subject to review', a court will hold that the agency has exercised its discretion and may not alter the decision to the individual's disadvantage.[160] This position is subject to express statutory provision. Apart from legislation, an authority that has conferred a continuing benefit on someone under a mistake of fact may revoke the benefit for the future when it discovers the true position.[161] And when the original benefit was based on a mistake of law, the authority may make a fresh decision based on a correct view of the law.[162]

When a legitimate expectation may arise

For the remaining categories of case, it is necessary to consider when a legitimate expectation can arise. The easiest case is that of an *express assurance*. When the Hong Kong government gave a public assurance to illegal entrants into the colony who had come from Macao that they would be interviewed and their merits considered before it would be decided whether to deport them, the Judicial Committee explained why this assurance should be enforced:

> When a public authority has promised to follow a certain procedure, it is in the interest of good administration that it should act fairly and implement its promise, so long as implementation does not interfere with its statutory duty.[163]

---

[158] See R Baldwin and D Horne (1986) 49 MLR 685; C F Forsyth [1988] CLJ 238; P P Craig (1992) 108 LQR 79; C J S Knight [2009] PL 15; R Williams (2016) 132 LQR 639 (offering a slightly different categorisation than set out here). For an account of the law, see Auburn, Moffett and Sharland, *Judicial Review: Principles and Procedure*, ch 19.

[159] Schwarze, *European Administrative Law*, ch 6; Schønberg, *Legitimate Expectations in Administrative Law*; Moules, *Actions against Public Officials*, ch 3.

[160] *Re 56 Denton Road Twickenham* [1953] Ch 51.

[161] *Rootkin v Kent CC* [1981] 2 All ER 227.

[162] *Cheung v Herts CC, The Times*, 4 April 1986; C Lewis [1987] PL 21.

[163] *A-G of Hong Kong v Ng Yuen Shiu* [1983] AC 629, 638 (Lord Fraser). And see *R v Liverpool Corporation, ex p Liverpool Taxis Association* [1972] 2 QB 299.

For an assurance of this kind to be enforceable, the official statement must have been 'clear, unambiguous and devoid of relevant qualification'.[164] Whether an assurance meets this test is determined by reference to how, on a fair reading of the promise as made, it would reasonably have been understood by those to whom it was made.[165]

It is common practice for a public authority to make known the policy that it intends to follow on a given subject: while that policy is in place, individuals may reasonably expect that the policy will be applied to them and will not be simply ignored.[166] When the Home Secretary had issued process instructions to immigration officials to give a visa applicant a chance to rectify missing information, it was unlawful not to follow those instructions and reject the application without giving the applicant that chance.[167] If there is a *change of policy*, especially if this is done without any warning or publicity, individuals may be disappointed not to receive the benefit that they had expected. All public authorities must be able to change their policies from time to time, and the courts have held that while individuals may hope to get the benefit of an existing policy or legal rule, they do not ordinarily have a legitimate expectation that the policy or rule will not be changed.[168] But in certain circumstances, the change in policy which resiles from a legitimate expectation may be subjected to procedural requirements or even substantively prevented. A general policy statement can create a legitimate expectation, but only where that policy has a 'pressing and focused' impact will a legitimate expectation arise in favour of a procedural remedy. Only if the policy amounts to a pressing and focused assurance of the continuation of the policy will a substantive legitimate expectation be found.[169]

A legitimate expectation may arise even in the absence of an assurance, where a public agency has followed a *consistent practice* of acting in a certain way, and then suddenly changes the practice without any warning. In the GCHQ case,[170] the invariable practice of the government had been to consult with civil service unions before changing terms of employment for civil servants; because of this, the unions had a legitimate expectation of being consulted before the Thatcher government withdrew from staff at GCHQ the right to join a union. However, there was some evidence from the Cabinet Secretary that the government decided against consultation for reasons of national security; this factor was held to prevail over the unions' legitimate expectation. In another case, for 25 years the Revenue had accepted tax refund claims without taking any notice of a statutory time limit: it was held that the Revenue could not without notice begin to refuse refunds on the basis that the claims were late.[171] The test for such cases set out by the Supreme Court is that the practice must have been 'so unambiguous, so widespread, so well-established and so well-recognised as to carry with it a commitment to a group'.[172]

The ability of the court to enforce an expectation may be affected by other factors affecting the public interest. In a similar case, where tax officials had told taxpayers that an element in proposed dealings would be treated as capital and not as income, but later dealt with it as income, Bingham LJ said:

> If a public authority so conducts itself as to create a legitimate expectation that a certain course will be followed it would often be unfair if the authority were permitted to follow a different

[164] *R v IRC, ex p MFK Ltd* [1990] 1 All ER 91, 110; approved in *R (Bancoult) v Foreign Secretary (No. 2)* [2008] UKHL 61, [2009] AC 453.

[165] *Paponette v AG of Trinidad and Tobago* [2010] UKSC 32, [2012] 1 AC 1.

[166] As it was in *R (Rashid) v Home Secretary* [2005] EWCA Civ 744.

[167] *Mandalia v Home Secretary* [2015] UKSC 59, [2015] 1 WLR 4546.

[168] See *Re Findlay* [1985] AC 318; and *Hughes v DHSS* [1985] AC 776 (civil servants hoping for benefit of favourable retirement age, but age raised before they could retire).

[169] *R (Bhatt Murphy) v Independent Assessor* [2008] EWCA Civ 755.

[170] *Council of Civil Service Unions v Minister for the Civil Service* [1985] AC 375.

[171] *R v IRC, ex p Unilever plc* [1996] STC 681.

[172] *R (Davies) v HMRC* [2011] UKSC 47, [2011] 1 WLR 2625 at [49] (Lord Wilson).

course to the detriment of one who entertained the expectation . . . But fairness is not a one-way street. It imports the notion of equitableness, of fair and open dealing, to which the authority is as much entitled as the citizen. The Revenue's discretion . . . is limited. Fairness requires that its exercise should be on a basis of full disclosure.[173]

Thus, for the Revenue's assurance to be enforced, the taxpayer must have 'put all his cards face upwards on the table'.[174] And the individual's claim to a legitimate expectation may yield to a broader notion of fairness, taking account of the public interest and the principle of legality.[175]

Procedural remedies from procedural expectations

Where the individual has an expectation of a particular procedure which will be followed – for example, an assurance of consistent practice of consultation before any change in policy of consultation – this is the 'paradigm case' of a legitimate expectation.[176] It will only be defeated if there are overriding reasons to resile from it. Because the expectation only imposes a procedural requirement on the public authority, the courts are slow to permit such expectations to be bypassed, although they may be if, for example, time was too limited to carry out a consultation exercise.[177]

Procedural remedies from substantive interests

The cases in which an individual has substantive interest, such as the benefit of a licence, to which the courts will attach a procedural remedy without there being a representation of such a procedure are rare. One example arose from the closure of a residential care home, in which case the court found that a long-standing resident had a legitimate expectation that she would be consulted because of her substantive interest in what had become her home.[178]

When a legitimate expectation may lead to a substantive remedy

The judgment in *R* v *Ministry of Agriculture, ex p Hamble Fisheries Ltd* broke new ground by holding (*a*) that a legitimate expectation might lead to the award of a substantive benefit; and (*b*) that the court must conduct a balancing exercise in considering whether the effect of a changed policy was 'fair', or amounted to an abuse of power, not merely whether the policy met the *Wednesbury* test of unreasonableness.[179] The *Hamble Fisheries* judgment (initially described by the Court of Appeal as heresy),[180] was approved in *R* v *North Devon Health Authority, ex p Coughlan*.[181]

In 1993, a health authority moved seriously disabled patients into a new facility after assuring them that they could live there for as long as they chose. In 1998, the authority decided to close the facility and transfer the patients to local authority care. *Held*, the decision to terminate care in the NHS was based on a mistaken view of the legislation. The promise to the patients had created a legitimate expectation of a substantive benefit, the frustration of which would be so unfair as to amount to an abuse of power. There was no 'overriding public interest' to justify departure from the promise.

---

[173] *R* v *IRC, ex p MFK Ltd*, 110–1.
[174] See *R* v *IRC, ex p MFK Ltd* above.
[175] See the estoppel cases mentioned at page 667 below.
[176] *R (Bhatt Murphy)* v *Independent Assessor* [2008] EWCA Civ 755 at [49] (Laws LJ).
[177] *R (Cheshire East Council)* v *Environment Secretary* [2011] EWHC 1975 (Admin).
[178] *R* v *Devon County Council, ex p Baker* [1995] 1 All ER 73.
[179] [1995] 2 All ER 714.
[180] *R* v *Home Secretary, ex p Hargreaves* [1997] 1 WLR 906.
[181] [2001] QB 213, distinguishing *Hargreaves*.

The court's reasoning in *Coughlan* raised difficult questions as to what criteria should be applied by the court in appraising the new policy and assessing the implications for the public authority in granting a substantive remedy. One result of *Coughlan* was a surge in the number of cases in which claims based on legitimate expectations were made, seldom with the success that was achieved in *Coughlan*. In *R (Bibi)* v *Newham Council*, the court made a valuable analysis of what such a claim involves:

> In all legitimate expectation cases, whether substantive or procedural, three practical questions arise. The first question is to what has the public authority, whether by practice or by promise, committed itself; the second is whether the authority has acted or proposed to act unlawfully in relation to its commitment; the third is what the court should do.[182]

It is particularly difficult for the court to grant a substantive remedy when an assurance has been given to the claimant about the granting of something from a limited stock of resources (e.g. housing) on which there are many competing claims.[183]

One of the most difficult issues has been what standard of review is applied by the courts in assessing the fairness of resiling from a substantive expectation. In *Nadarajah*, Laws LJ suggested that the standard of review was proportionality rather than *Wednesbury*.[184] This has been approved by the Privy Council,[185] the weight of authority supports it[186] and it provides the flexible and variable intensity required in such fact-sensitive situations.[187]

In many cases of legitimate expectation, claimants can show that they have relied to their detriment upon the policy or statement under review, and this may strengthen their case for a substantive remedy. But proof of such reliance is not an invariable requirement.[188]

Unlawful representations and estoppel

An area in which there remains considerable scope for development of the law is an expectation based upon a representation which was not lawfully made. The courts have consistently held that no *legitimate* expectation can arise from an unlawful representation.[189] This is a deeply unsatisfactory position for two reasons. First, it is difficult to see why it should be the innocent individual who pays the price for the initial illegality of the public body's action.[190] Secondly, English law is apparently inconsistent with the position taken by the European Court of Human Rights, which treats ultra vires expectations as a possession such as to invoke the right to property in article 1 of the First Protocol, which can only be proportionately interfered with.[191] The unhappy disjunction in protection is, however, understandable: it is hard in

---

[182] [2001] EWCA Civ 607, [2002] 1 WLR 237. On the implications of this approach, see I Steele (2005) 121 LQR 300; also P Sales and K Steyn [2004] PL 564.

[183] As in *R (Bibi)* v *Newham Council* (above).

[184] *R (Nadarajah)* v *Home Secretary* [2005] EWCA Civ 1363.

[185] *Paponette* v *AG of Trinidad and Tobago* [2010] UKPC 32, [2012] 1 AC 1 at [38] (Lord Dyson).

[186] *Bhatt Murphy* (above); *R (Cheshire East Council)* v *Environment Secretary* [2011] EWHC 1975 (Admin); *R (Wood)* v *Education Secretary* [2011] EWHC 3256 (Admin), [2012] ELR 172; *R (Lumba)* v *Home Secretary* [2011] UKSC 12, [2012] 1 AC 245 at [311]–[312] (Lord Phillips, dissenting). The more macro-political the subject-matter, the lesser the intensity of review: *R* v *Education Secretary, ex p Begbie* [2000] 1 WLR 1115.

[187] See P Craig and S Schønberg [2000] PL 684, 698–700; C J S Knight [2007] JR 117; cf M Elliott [2000] JR 27, arguing that *Wednesbury* provides the proper standard of review.

[188] See *R (Bibi)* v *Newham Council* (above).

[189] *AG of Hong Kong* v *Ng Yuen Shiu* [1983] 2 AC 629; *Rowland* v *Environment Agency* [2003] EWCA Civ 1885, [2005] Ch 1.

[190] *Rowland* (above); Craig, *Administrative Law*, ch 22; and Y Vanderman [2012] PL 85, cf S Hannett and L Busch [2005] PL 729.

[191] *Pine Valley* v *Ireland* (1993) 16 EHRR 379; *Stretch* v *UK* (2004) 38 EHRR 12.

a system based upon legality for a court to justify ordering a public body to do something contrary to law.[192]

At an earlier time, the courts rejected the use of the private law doctrine of estoppel in easing the plight of someone who had relied on an assurance from an official only to find that it was not binding because it was thought to allow officials to play fast and loose with legal rules and the limits of a public authority's powers, duties or jurisdiction.[193] Thus estoppel could not affect the obligation to perform a statutory duty. The House of Lords reconsidered the issue in 2002, in which Lord Hoffmann said:

> It seems to me that in this area, public law has already absorbed what is useful from the moral values which underlie the private law concept of estoppel and the time has come for [public law] to stand upon its own two feet.[194]

As a result, the analogy between legitimate expectations and estoppel is not one which is likely to be of any utility in the near future.

C. Review on procedural grounds

Although the content of a public body's decision may be within the powers of the body taking it, exercise of the power may be lawful only if the proper procedure for making the decision has been observed. Procedural review is about examining the process by which a decision has been reached. If there is a failure to observe essential procedural requirements, then the decision will be invalid. These requirements are often found in the legislation which confers the power in question. Others are derived from the common law doctrine of natural justice or, as it is now widely known, the doctrine of fairness. Fundamentally, as will be seen, natural justice and procedural fairness impose no concrete rules: what is fair depends upon – and varies significantly between – the circumstances of each case.

Statutory requirements

Where statute authorises a decision to be made after a certain procedure has been followed, failure to observe the procedure may result in the purported decision being declared a nullity.

> In *Ridge* v *Baldwin*, the Brighton police committee summarily dismissed their chief constable following his trial at the Central Criminal Court on charges of conspiracy; his acquittal had been accompanied by serious criticism of his conduct by the trial judge. Disciplinary regulations under the Police Act 1919 required a formal inquiry to be held into charges brought against a chief constable before he could be dismissed. The committee contended that this procedure did not apply to a power of dismissal authorised by an earlier Act. The House of Lords *held* that the disciplinary regulations applied to the dismissal: 'inasmuch as the decision was arrived at in complete disregard of the regulations it must be regarded as void and of no effect'.[195]

---

[192] *Rainbow Insurance Company Ltd* v *Financial Services Commission* [2015] UKPC 15 at [51]–[53] (Lord Hodge); *R (Sovio Wines Ltd)* v *Food Standards Agency* [2009] EWHC 382 (Admin) at [95]–[98] (Dobbs J).

[193] *Maritime Electric Co* v *General Dairies Ltd* [1937] AC 610; *Rhyl UDC* v *Rhyl Amusements Ltd* [1959] 1 All ER 257; *Essex Congregational Union* v *Essex CC* [1963] AC 808.

[194] *R (Reprotech (Pebsham) Ltd)* v *East Sussex CC* [2002] UKHL 8, [2002] 4 All ER 58. A W Bradley [2002] PL 597 and M Elliott [2003] JR 71.

[195] [1964] AC 40, 117 (Lord Morris of Borth-y-Gest).

But not every procedural error invalidates administrative action. The courts have often distinguished between procedural requirements which are mandatory (breach invalidates) and those which are directory (breach does not invalidate). This seemingly clear distinction takes no account of whether there has been a total or partial failure to observe the procedure; nor of whether the procedural defect caused actual prejudice to anyone.[196] However, as we will see in Chapter 25, it is important to consider this case law – and procedural fairness challenges generally – in the light of the changes made by the Criminal Justice and Courts Act 2015 which require the court to refuse relief to a claimant where it is highly likely that there would have been no substantial difference to the outcome without the unlawful act or failure. That provision has most significant impact where the complaint is that a particular process was not followed.

In 1979, Lord Hailsham suggested that the courts in this area are faced with 'not so much a stark choice of alternatives but a spectrum of possibilities'. He continued: 'The jurisdiction is inherently discretionary, and the court is frequently in the presence of differences of degree which merge almost imperceptibly into differences of kind.'[197] In that case, a planning authority failed to notify landowners of their right of appeal to the Secretary of State against a decision that adversely affected them: this failure invalidated the decision. In 2005, the House of Lords held in *R v Soneji* that the mandatory/directory distinction was not useful: the emphasis ought to be on examining the effects of non-compliance and on appraising the intention of the legislature in laying down the procedures to be followed.[198] In several cases thereafter, the judges took a more relaxed view of incorrect procedure, so much so that doubts were raised about the value of having rules that need not be observed. Where a fundamental rule of criminal procedure had not been observed, Lord Bingham emphasised that the effect of the 'sea change wrought by *Soneji*' had been exaggerated and did not warrant 'a wholesale jettisoning of all rules affecting procedure'.[199] The Court of Appeal has since held that the test for invalidity was whether there had been substantial compliance with the relevant statutory requirements.[200] Good administration will not be encouraged if statutory procedures can be lightly set aside.

Natural justice

The origin of natural justice is to be found in certain assumptions made in the past by judges about the procedures that should be followed if justice is to be done; those assumptions have led to the emergence of rules, and such rules continue to evolve today. Many aspects of natural justice at common law are reinforced under the Human Rights Act 1998 by the right to a fair hearing under art 6(1) ECHR:

> In the determination of his civil rights and obligations or of any criminal charge against him, everyone shall be entitled to a fair and public hearing within a reasonable time by an independent and impartial tribunal established by law.

The common law rules are generally consistent with the Convention right to a fair hearing, and the Supreme Court has robustly reminded us that a focus on the Convention for standards of procedural fairness underplays the significance and breadth of protection offered

---

[196] Compare *Coney* v *Choyce* [1975] 1 All ER 979 (no prejudice from failure to notify school closure at school entrance) with *Bradbury* v *London Borough of Enfield* [1967] 3 All ER 434 (complete failure to notify proposed changes in composition of schools).

[197] *London and Clydeside Estates Ltd* v *Aberdeen DC* [1979] 3 All ER 876, 883.

[198] [2005] UKHL 49, [2006] 1 AC 340.

[199] *R* v *Clarke* [2008] UKHL 8, [2008] 2 All E 665, [20].

[200] *R (Herron)* v *Parking Adjudicator* [2011] EWCA Civ 905, [2012] 1 All ER 709.

by the common law.[201] But the two systems are not always identical. On the one hand, common law rules are at the mercy of legislation by Parliament, which may lay down procedures that on any showing are unfair; but under the Human Rights Act, such legislation may be declared incompatible with art 6(1).[202] Also, art 6(1) requires the hearing to be before an 'independent and impartial tribunal', and this enables issues to be raised about guarantees for judicial independence that are outside the scope of natural justice.[203] On the other hand, the European meaning of 'civil rights and obligations' in art 6(1) does not include important areas of public law, such as taxation and immigration, even though natural justice applies to them as a matter of national law.[204]

Before considering natural justice as a principle of administrative law, two of the main rules of natural justice can be illustrated.

1. The rule against bias

The essence of a fair judicial decision is that it has been made by an impartial judge. This has been the subject of many decisions at common law, to which can now be added decisions of the European Court of Human Rights, interpreting the right under art 6(1) ECHR to a determination by an 'independent and impartial tribunal'.[205] In very rare cases, a judge may actually be biased against a party, in the sense of being partial or prejudiced. But the main rule against bias is that a judge may be disqualified from acting in a case on two grounds, the first being where he or she has a direct pecuniary interest, however small, in the subject matter of the case; thus a judge who is a shareholder in a company appearing as a litigant must decline to hear the case, except with consent of the parties.[206] The automatic disqualification of a judge also applies where there is no financial interest, but the decision of the case between the parties would affect the promotion of a cause by one party with which the judge is closely involved.[207] This situation arose when, as one of five Law Lords who heard an appeal concerning General Pinochet's extradition, Lord Hoffmann was director of a charity associated with Amnesty International, that had argued at the appeal in support of the extradition and was thus in the position of being a party to the case. The judge's involvement with the charity was not disclosed during the hearing. It was held that the decision could not stand, and the appeal was heard again by a different panel of Law Lords.

Secondly, apart from a pecuniary interest or identification with one of the parties, a judge is disqualified when (in Lord Hope's words) 'the fair-minded and informed observer, having considered the facts [relating to an allegation of bias], would conclude that there was a real possibility that the tribunal was biased'.[208] Under this form of the test, disqualification is not automatic but depends on whether an informed observer would conclude there was a 'real possibility of bias' once the facts had been ascertained.

Three comments may be made on the test. First, where bias is alleged, the reviewing court does not have to decide whether the judge was in fact biased, since 'bias operates in such an

---

[201] *R (Osborn)* v *Parole Board* [2013] UKSC 61, [2014] AC 1115 at [54]–[63] (Lord Reed).

[202] E.g. *R (Wright)* v *Health Secretary* [2009] UKHL 3, [2009] 2 All ER 129 (statute authorising suspension of nurse's right to work but without a prior right to be heard).

[203] See e.g. *Starrs* v *Ruxton* 2000 JC 208; (1999) 8 BHRC 1.

[204] See e.g. *R (Smith and West)* v *Parole Board* [2005] UKHL 1, [2005] 1 All ER 755. On the interaction of art 6(1) and fairness, see M Westgate [2006] JR 57; P Craig [2003] PL 753.

[205] The leading Convention cases on judicial bias were reviewed in *Hoekstra* v *HM Advocate* 2001 SLT 28. And see D Williams [2000] PL 45 and K Malleson (2002) 22 LS 53.

[206] *Dimes* v *Grand Junction Canal (Proprietors of)* (1852) 3 HLC 759. And see R Cranston [1979] PL 237.

[207] *R* v *Bow Street Magistrate, ex p Pinochet Ugarte (No 2)* [2000] 1 AC 119. For comment on 'automatic disqualification', see T Jones [1999] PL 391 and A Olowofoyeku [2000] PL 456.

[208] *Porter* v *Magill* [2001] UKHL 67, [2002] 2 AC 357, at [103] (Lord Hope).

insidious manner that the person alleged to be biased may be quite unconscious of its effect'.[209] Second, the test acknowledges that 'in any case where the impartiality of a judge is in question the appearance of the matter is just as important as the reality'.[210] Lord Hewart's dictum, that it is 'of fundamental importance that justice should not only be done but also should manifestly and undoubtedly be seen to be done', comes from *R v Sussex Justices, ex p McCarthy*:

> The acting clerk to the justices was a member of a firm of solicitors who were to represent the plaintiff in civil proceedings as a result of a collision in connection with which the applicant was summoned for a road traffic offence. The acting clerk retired with the bench, but was not asked to advise the justices on their decision to convict the applicant. *Held*, that, as the clerk's firm was connected with the case in the civil action, he ought not to advise the justices in the criminal matter and therefore could not properly discharge his duties as clerk. The conviction was quashed, despite the fact that he had taken no part in the decision.[211]

Third, the test for judicial bias approved in *Porter v Magill* resolves long-standing uncertainty as to whether in establishing bias it was enough that an observer had a 'reasonable suspicion' that a tribunal might be biased, or whether it must beyond this be shown that in fact there was a 'real likelihood' or 'real danger' of bias. On this issue there had been divergence between the English and Scottish courts. An earlier formula adopted by the House of Lords, that sought to lay down a single test for all purposes,[212] was not followed in some Commonwealth decisions.[213] Nor was it consistent with the Strasbourg case law on art 6(1) ECHR, which favours an objective test of the risk of bias in the light of all factors known to the court.[214]

In *Locabail (UK) Ltd v Bayfield Properties Ltd*,[215] the Court of Appeal dealt with five cases in which bias was alleged in respect of such matters as a judge's opinions, social relationships and former professional activities. The court stressed the importance of full disclosure. A judge 'would be as wrong to yield to a tenuous or frivolous objection as he would to ignore an objection of substance'; but 'if in any case there is real ground for doubt, that doubt should be resolved in favour of recusal'.[216] Questions often arise about the impartiality of members of courts and tribunals, and juries.[217] Situations in which there was held to be a 'real possibility of bias' include the following:

(*a*) a Scottish judge heard a case brought by a prisoner that challenged the interpretation placed on a statute by the government, when the judge had earlier (while sitting in Parliament as a minister) upheld that interpretation as being the correct view;[218]

---

[209] *R v Gough* [1993] AC 646, 672 (Lord Woolf).

[210] *Ex p Pinochet Ugarte (No 2)*, at 139 (Lord Nolan).

[211] [1924] 1 KB 256.

[212] *R v Gough* [1993] AC 646.

[213] E.g. *Webb v R* (1994) 181 CLR 41.

[214] *Piersack v Belgium* (1982) 5 EHRR 169 and decisions cited by Lord Hope in *Porter v Magill*, [99]–[102].

[215] [2000] QB 451.

[216] *Locabail*, at [21] and [25].

[217] *R v Abdroikov* [2007] UKHL 37, [2008] 1 All ER 315; *R v Khan* [2008] EWCA Crim 531, [2008] 3 All ER 502 (circumstances in which police officers, prosecuting solicitors and prison officers may not sit as jurors).

[218] *Davidson v Scottish Ministers* [2004] UKHL 34, [2004] UKHRR 1079. Cf *R (Al-Hasan) v Home Secretary* [2005] UKHL 13, [2005] 1 WLR 688.

(*b*) during a lengthy hearing in the Restrictive Practices Court, the economist member of the court asked economic consultants, who were giving expert evidence for one party in the case, about the prospects of obtaining employment with them;[219]

(*c*) shortly before hearing a long commercial case, a High Court judge realised that a principal witness for one side was planned to be a friend whom he had known for 30 years, but he decided to hear the case after ascertaining that his friend would not in fact be called; the Court of Appeal required the judge to recuse himself, even though this would delay the hearing.[220]

But there was held to be no 'real possibility of bias' when

(i) it was claimed that the medically qualified member of a disability tribunal, who had long experience of providing medical reports to the Department of Work and Pensions, would be unconsciously biased because of this;[221] and

(ii) a Scottish judge refused to withdraw from an immigration case concerning a Palestinian asylum-seeker, formerly active in the Palestine Liberation Organisation, who claimed that the judge could not be impartial because of her membership of the International Association of Jewish Lawyers.[222]

In exceptional circumstances of necessity, a judge may have to deal with a case where the law makes no provision for any other person to do so.[223]

2. The right to a fair hearing

It is fundamental to a just decision that each party should have the opportunity of knowing the case against him or her and of replying to this. The principle of open justice is fundamental to the constitution, the administration of justice and the rule of law.[224] Both parties must have the chance to present their version of the facts and to make submissions on the relevant rules of law. Each side must be able to comment on all material considered by the judge, and neither side must communicate with the judge behind the other's back. Although the court's rules of procedure embody these principles, the unwritten right to a hearing may operate even in the courts. Thus the High Court could not order a solicitor personally to bear costs caused by his misconduct without giving him an opportunity to deal with the complaint.[225] However, the requirements of natural justice are not invariable: although a party to civil proceedings is normally entitled to know all the material considered by the judge, there may be exceptional circumstances, particularly regarding the welfare of children, when a court may take into account material that has not been seen by all the parties.[226] In a controversial decision, the House of Lords held by 3–2 that the Parole Board (which in some cases must give an oral hearing to a prisoner whose release on licence has been revoked)[227] need not disclose to a prisoner or his lawyer sensitive material directly affecting

---

[219] *In re Medicaments and Related Classes of Goods* [2001] 1 WLR 700.

[220] *AWG Group Ltd* v *Morrison* [2006] EWCA 6, [2006] 1 All ER 967. Cf *Taylor* v *Lawrence* [2002] EWCA Civ 90, [2003] QB 528.

[221] *Gillies* v *Work and Pensions Secretary* [2006] UKHL 2, [2006] 1 All ER 731.

[222] *Helow* v *Home Secretary* [2008] UKHL 62, [2009] 2 All ER 1031 (no evidence that the judge endorsed some views expressed in the Association's publications). And see L Blom-Cooper [2009] PL 199.

[223] *Jeffs* v *New Zealand Dairy Board* [1967] 1 AC 551. But cf *Kingsley* v *UK* (2001) 33 EHRR 288; and I Leigh [2002] PL 407.

[224] *Scott* v *Scott* [1913] AC 417; *Ahmed* v *HM Treasury (No.1)* [2010] UKSC 1, [2012] 2 AC 697.

[225] *Abraham* v *Jutsun* [1963] 2 All ER 402.

[226] See *Re K (Infants)* [1965] AC 201. Contrast *McMichael* v *UK* (1995) 20 EHRR 205.

[227] *R (West)* v *Parole Board* [2005] UKHL 1, [2005] 1 All ER 755.

his release on licence, but could make it available to a special advocate on condition that it was not disclosed to the prisoner or his lawyer.[228]

Natural justice and administrative authorities

The rules of natural justice have been applied to many decisions made outside the courts. From those rules has developed what is now a universal rule that public authorities must act fairly in making decisions, and this has contributed to a greater openness in government. Before that rule developed, a court would ask whether in relation to a particular decision there was a duty to observe natural justice (a duty to 'act judicially'). If the power to decide affected a person's rights, property or character, it was more likely to be subject to natural justice; so was a decision made by a procedure involving a choice between two opposing views, in a manner resembling litigation.[229] The essential rules of natural justice (including the individual's right to know the charges against him, and a right to reply to them) applied to the use of disciplinary powers, including such penalties as expulsion, by bodies such as universities[230] and trade unions.[231] The same rules were applied in a classic 19th-century decision to action by a local authority directed against an individual's property.

> In *Cooper* v *Wandsworth Board of Works*, the plaintiff sued the board for damages in trespass for demolishing his partly built house. He had failed to notify his intention to build the house to the board, which thereupon had a statutory power to demolish the building. *Held*, that the board should have given a hearing to the plaintiff before exercising their statutory power of demolition. 'Although there are no positive words in a statute requiring that the party shall be heard, yet the justice of the common law shall supply the omission of the legislature.'[232]

The rule against bias has also been applied to local authorities. When the Barnsley markets committee revoked a stallholder's licence for a trivial and isolated misdemeanour, that decision was quashed. Not only did the committee hear the evidence of the market manager (who was in the position of a prosecutor) in the absence of the stallholder, but also the manager was present throughout the committee's deliberations.[233] When the grant of permission for a superstore was challenged by an environmental group because of the private interests of members of the planning authority (only some of which had been declared), it was held that the rules of bias arising from personal interest were not limited to judicial bodies but applied generally in public law, albeit with adjustments for the statutory context in question.[234] In a development of particular significance in the policy context, if the fair-minded and informed observer, knowing the facts, would consider that there was a real possibility that the decision-maker had predetermined the matter, then the public authority will have acted unlawfully.[235] This is a delicate line to tread: public authority decision-makers will inevitably have some

[228] *R (Roberts)* v *Parole Board* [2005] UKHL 45, [2005] 2 AC 738 (note the powerful dissenting speeches by Lords Bingham and Steyn). See ch 26 D.

[229] See R B Cooke [1954] CLJ 14. Cf *Durayappah* v *Fernando* [1967] 2 AC 337, 349.

[230] *Dr Bentley*'s case (1723) 1 Stra 557; cf *Ceylon University* v *Fernando* [1960] 1 All ER 631.

[231] *Annamunthodo* v *Oilfield Workers' TU* [1961] AC 945; cf *Breen* v *AEU* [1971] 2 QB 175.

[232] (1863) 14 CB (NS) 180, 194 (Byles J).

[233] *R* v *Barnsley Council, ex p Hook* [1976] 3 All ER 452.

[234] *R* v *Environment Secretary, ex p Kirkstall Valley Campaign Ltd* [1996] 3 All ER 304.

[235] *R (Lewis)* v *Redcar and Cleveland Borough Council* [2008] EWCA Civ 746, [2009] 1 WLR 83.

sort of policy view, and may have been elected or appointed with a particular policy mandate, and the courts have sought not to prevent such individuals expressing strongly held views. The Localism Act 2011, s 25, provides that decision-makers of local authorities are not to be taken to have closed their minds simply because of the expression of a prior view.

The scope of natural justice

The importance of natural justice in judicial review of administrative action has not been in doubt since the landmark decision of the House of Lords in *Ridge* v *Baldwin*, the facts of which we have already seen in relation to statutory procedures.

> The power of the Brighton police committee under an Act of 1882 was to dismiss 'any constable whom they think negligent in the exercise of his duty or otherwise unfit for the same'. Claiming to act under this power, they dismissed the chief constable without giving him a hearing. The Court of Appeal held that in dismissing the chief constable, 'the defendants were acting in an administrative or executive capacity just as they did when they appointed him'.[236] The House of Lords overruled this view: quite apart from the procedure laid down by the discipline regulations, natural justice required that a hearing should have been given before the committee exercised its power. The failure to give a hearing invalidated the dismissal, and the subsequent hearing given to Ridge's solicitor did not cure the earlier defect.[237]

This decision could have been regarded narrowly as one based on an interpretation of specific legislation. In fact, *Ridge* v *Baldwin* was the first of a group of House of Lords decisions during the 1960s that began to lay the foundations for judicial review today. Especially important was the holding in *Ridge* that the duty to observe natural justice was not confined to powers classified as 'judicial' or 'quasi-judicial'. This enabled the courts to apply natural justice in a very wide variety of situations. In 1970, Megarry J remarked that the courts were tending to apply natural justice to all powers of decision unless the circumstances indicated to the contrary.[238] The benefits of *Ridge* v *Baldwin* spread to many persons, including students,[239] police officers,[240] school teachers,[241] market stallholders,[242] residents of local authority homes at risk of closure,[243] those affected by decisions of self-regulatory bodies[244] and,

---

[236] [1963] 1 QB 539, 576 (Harman LJ).

[237] [1964] AC 40; and see A W Bradley [1964] CLJ 83.

[238] *Gaiman* v *National Association for Mental Health* [1971] Ch 317, 333 (power to expel members of company limited by guarantee). In *Bates* v *Lord Hailsham* [1972] 3 All ER 1019, the same judge held (in an extempore response to an ex parte application) that a general duty of fairness does not arise in respect of delegated legislation. The Supreme Court's firm upholding of the principles of natural justice to a statutory instrument designating an Iranian bank for financial sanctions in *Bank Mellat* v *HM Treasury (No. 2)* [2013] UKSC 39, [2014] AC 700 confirms that *Bates* states far too absolute a proposition.

[239] E.g. *R* v *Aston University Senate, ex p Roffey* [1969] 2 QB 538; and *Glynn* v *Keele University* [1971] 2 All ER 89.

[240] *R* v *Kent Police Authority, ex p Godden* [1971] 2 QB 662; *Chief Constable of North Wales* v *Evans* [1982] 3 All ER 141.

[241] *Hannam* v *Bradford Corpn* [1970] 2 All ER 690; *Malloch* v *Aberdeen Corpn* [1971] 2 All ER 1278.

[242] *R* v *Barnsley Council, ex p Hook* [1976] 3 All ER 452; *R* v *Wear Valley Council, ex p Binks* [1985] 2 All ER 699.

[243] *R* v *Devon CC, ex p Baker* [1995] 1 All ER 73.

[244] *R* v *LAUTRO, ex p Ross* [1993] QB 17.

most notably, convicted prisoners in respect of prison discipline and the parole system.[245] In 1980, on an appeal from the Bahamas concerning refusal of an individual's constitutional right to citizenship, the Judicial Committee held that natural justice must be observed by any person with authority to determine questions affecting the rights of individuals.[246] But natural justice, now more commonly referred to as fairness, is not limited to situations in which private rights are affected, and the courts protect a wide variety of individual interests against unfair action by public bodies.

Fairness and natural justice

The scope of natural justice is best understood against the broad perception that it is the duty of the courts to ensure that *all* administrative powers are exercised fairly, that is, in accordance with principles of fair procedure. It has never been possible to describe the contents of natural justice except in general terms. Today, the essence of natural justice may be explained simply in terms of fairness. In 1994, a challenge by mandatory life prisoners to the procedure for making parole decisions led to the following analysis by Lord Mustill, who derived six principles from the authorities in answer to the question, 'What does fairness require in the present case?':

> (1) Where an Act of Parliament confers an administrative power there is a presumption that it will be exercised in a manner which is fair in all the circumstances. (2) The standards of fairness are not immutable. They may change with the passage of time, both in the general and in their application to decisions of a particular type. (3) The principles of fairness are not to be applied by rote identically in every situation. What fairness demands is dependent on the context of the decision, and this is to be taken into account in all its aspects. (4) An essential feature of the context is the statute which creates the discretion, as regards both its language and the shape of the legal and administrative system within which the decision is taken. (5) Fairness will very often require that a person who may be adversely affected by the decision will have an opportunity to make representations on his own behalf, either before the decision is taken, with a view to producing a favourable result; or after it is taken, with a view to procuring its modification; or both. (6) Since the person affected usually cannot make worthwhile representations without knowing what factors may weigh against his interests fairness will very often require that he is informed of the gist of the case which he has to answer.[247]

The procedural effects of natural justice and fairness

On the basis that a public authority must act fairly in making its decisions, and remembering that fairness is concerned with procedural matters, not with the substance of a decision, what in practical terms must the public authority do? Much depends on the nature of the decision. In a situation where a public office or other benefit is being withdrawn for reasons of misconduct or incompetence, the 'irreducible minimum' at the core of natural justice is (*a*) the right to a decision by an unbiased tribunal; (*b*) the right to have notice of the charges against the individual; and (*c*) the right to be heard in answer to those charges.[248]

In cases where no misconduct is alleged (for example, in the case of school or residential home closures, where parents or residents must in fairness be consulted by the local authority),

---

[245] E.g. *R* v *Hull Prison Visitors, ex p St Germain* [1979] QB 425 and (the same) *(No 2)* [1979] 3 All ER 545; *Leech* v *Deputy Governor of Parkhurst Prison* [1988] AC 533; *R* v *Home Secretary, ex p Doody* [1994] 1 AC 531.

[246] *A-G* v *Ryan* [1980] AC 718.

[247] *R* v *Home Secretary, ex p Doody* [1994] 1 AC 531, 557 (establishing the right of prisoners to be informed of relevant material and reasons for decisions affecting their release on parole).

[248] Lord Hodson in *Ridge* v *Baldwin* [1964] AC 40, at 132.

then (*a*) consultation must take place at a time when the proposals are at a formative stage; (*b*) sufficient reasons must be given for the proposal to permit intelligent consideration and response; (*c*) adequate time must be allowed; and (*d*) the product of consultation must be conscientiously taken into account when the ultimate decision is taken.[249] Although a failure to consult can be an important route of challenge to a policy decision, there is no general duty to consult.[250]

Many detailed procedural questions arise to which there are no general answers. In some contexts individuals do not have the right of an oral hearing,[251] but if the body in question has to decide questions as to someone's conduct or competence, the individual is entitled to know what evidence is given against him or her and must have a fair opportunity to rebut it.[252] In *R (Osborn)* v *Parole Board*, Lord Reed provided a detailed analysis of the sorts of considerations which should affect whether procedural fairness requires an oral hearing, or whether written process will be sufficient.[253] He warned that an oral hearing served not only the purpose of the public authority reaching the best decision (an instrumentalist view), but also served the normative need of the individual to feel that they have participated. Although *Osborn* emphasised a greater need for oral hearings than had previously been granted by the Parole Board, the judgment is careful not to suggest that they are necessary in all cases. A fair procedure is not a uniform procedure, and what is required is always a matter of context. [254]

Regulatory bodies that expect officials to do preliminary work for them must nonetheless be in a position to come to their own decisions.[255] Where a soldier claimed that he had been subject to racial harassment, members of the Army Board could not decide on the complaint judicially without meeting to consider the matter; and the soldier was entitled to see all the material on which the board reached its decision, other than documents for which public interest immunity was properly claimed.[256] An individual has no universal right to be legally represented regardless of the nature of the proceedings in question,[257] but in some circumstances a body with power to permit legal representation may not reasonably refuse it.[258]

There is no absolute rule that natural justice does not apply in the case of preliminary investigations, inspections or suspensions pending a final decision,[259] but the right to a hearing is often excluded or restricted because of the need for urgent action or because of the individual's rights will be observed at a later stage.[260]

---

[249] Known as the *Gunning* requirements: *R* v *Brent LBC, ex p Gunning* (1985) 84 LGR 168, approved by the Supreme Court in *R (Moseley)* v *Haringey LBC* [2014 UKSC 56, [2014] 1 WLR 3947. See too: *R* v *North Devon Health Authority, ex p Coughlan* [2001] QB 213, at [108] (Lord Woolf MR) and *R* v *Devon CC, ex p Baker* [1995] 1 All ER 73. On consultation generally, see C Knight in Supperstone, Goudie and Walker, *Judicial Review*, ch 10.

[250] E.g. *R (Harrow Community Support Ltd)* v *Defence Secretary* [2012] EWHC 1921 (Admin) (placement of surface-to-air missiles on a residential tower block during the Olympics without consultation of residents lawful).

[251] *Lloyd* v *McMahon* [1987] AC 625. Also *R (Smith)* v *Parole Board (No 2)* [2005] UKHL 1, [2005] 1 All ER 755 (Board need not give oral hearing in every case, but must do so in some cases); *R (Hammond)* v *Home Secretary* [2005] UKHL 69, [2006] 1 AC 603.

[252] *Chief Constable of North Wales* v *Evans* [1982] 3 All ER 141.

[253] [2013] UKSC 61, [2014] AC 1115.

[254] *Lloyd* v *McMahon* [1987] 1 AC 625, 702 (Lord Bridge).

[255] *R* v *Commission for Racial Equality, ex p Cottrell and Rothon* [1980] 3 All ER 265.

[256] *R* v *Army Board of Defence Council, ex p Anderson* [1992] QB 169. And see ch 26 D.

[257] *R* v *Maze Prison Visitors, ex p Hone* [1988] AC 379.

[258] *R* v *Home Secretary, ex p Tarrant* [1985] QB 251.

[259] *Rees* v *Crane* [1994] 2 AC 173 (Trinidad judge entitled to notice of complaints against him at initial stage of dismissal procedure).

[260] *Wiseman* v *Borneman* [1971] AC 297; *Furnell* v *Whangarei High Schools Board* [1973] AC 660; *Norwest Holst Ltd* v *Trade Secretary* [1978] Ch 201.

Many aspects of procedure raise issues of fairness: thus it may be unfair for a tribunal to refuse adjournment of a hearing.[261] The manner in which evidence is obtained by tribunals is subject to constraints of natural justice,[262] but hearsay evidence is usually permitted.[263] An individual may be entitled to cross-examine those giving evidence against him or her[264] or obtain the names of potential witnesses from the other side.[265] But it is sometimes sufficient that only the gist of allegations against an individual is made known.[266] It was held contrary to natural justice for a commission with investigative powers to make findings of fact that individuals had been guilty of serious misconduct, when the findings were supported by no evidence of probative value and there had been no opportunity to rebut them.[267]

Considerations of national security may seriously reduce the scope for natural justice.[268] The current practice of appointing 'special advocates' to deal with sensitive matters affecting national security enables allegations and evidence to be withheld from the individual. The use of special advocates 'is an attempt to resolve the tension between due process and national security'[269] and this limited way of protecting the right to fair procedure is arguably better than nothing; but the special advocate cannot in the ordinary sense of the word be said to be 'representing' the individual.

Three matters may be mentioned briefly. First, if fairness or natural justice would entitle someone to be heard, a court should be slow to brush aside that right on the ground that a hearing would make no difference to the outcome.[270] The second matter is whether the failure by an authority to give a hearing to which the individual is entitled is cured by a full and fair hearing given later by an appellate body. No absolute rule applies: sometimes the appeal proceedings may take the form of a full rehearing and this may cure the earlier defect, but in other situations the individual may be entitled to a fair hearing at both stages. In intermediate cases, the court must decide 'whether, at the end of the day, there has been a fair result, reached by fair methods'.[271]

The third matter concerns the legal effect, if any, of a decision reached in breach of natural justice. When a breach of natural justice is established, then on the authority of *Ridge* v *Baldwin* the decision in question is void and a nullity.[272] However, until such a decision is declared to be void by a court, it is capable of having some effect in law and it may be the basis of an appeal to a higher body.[273]

....

[261] *R* v *Cheshire CC, ex p C* [1998] ELR 66.

[262] *R* v *Deputy Industrial Injuries Commissioner, ex p Moore* [1965] 1 QB 456; *Crompton* v *General Medical Council* [1982] 1 All ER 35.

[263] *T A Miller Ltd* v *Minister of Housing* [1968] 2 All ER 633.

[264] *R* v *Board of Visitors, ex p St Germain (No 2)* [1979] 3 All ER 545. Cf *R* v *Commission for Racial Equality, ex p Cottrell and Rothon* (note 232).

[265] *R* v *Blundeston Board of Visitors, ex p Fox-Taylor* [1982] 1 All ER 646.

[266] *R* v *Gaming Board, ex p Benaim and Khaida* [1970] 2 QB 417; *Maxwell* v *Dept of Trade* [1974] QB 523.

[267] *Mahon* v *Air New Zealand Ltd* [1984] AC 808.

[268] *R* v *Home Secretary, ex p Hosenball* [1977] 3 All ER 452; *R* v *Home Secretary, ex p Cheblak* [1991] 2 All ER 319.

[269] J Ip, [2008] PL 717, 741. See ch 26 D.

[270] *John* v *Rees* [1970] Ch 345, 402; *R* v *Chief Constable, Thames Valley, ex p Cotton* [1990] IRLR 344, 352; and *R (Osborn)* v *Parole Board* [2013] UKSC 61, [2014] AC 1115. And see Lord Bingham [1991] PL 64.

[271] *Calvin* v *Carr* [1980] AC 574.

[272] The holding in *Durayappah* v *Fernando* [1967] 2 AC 337 that failure to give a hearing made the decision voidable and not void was contrary to legal principle: see H W R Wade (1967) 83 LQR 499 and (1968) 84 LQR 95.

[273] *Calvin* v *Carr* (above). And see S Sedley [1989] PL 32.

Does fairness require reasons to be given?

Although the giving of reasons 'is one of the fundamentals of good administration',[274] at common law there is no general duty to give reasons for decisions.[275] In many situations, legislation requires reasons to be given, whether only if requested or in all cases (for instance, whenever planning permission is refused). Despite the absence of a general duty to give reasons, the courts do often require reasons to be given. Thus, reasons must be stated for a discretionary decision, if a right of appeal is valueless without this.[276] Fairness may require the giving of reasons, because of the impact of the decision on the individual.[277] Thus a prisoner sentenced to a mandatory life sentence was entitled to know the reasons for the Home Secretary's decision as to the minimum period that he must serve. In the leading case, Lord Mustill said:

> The giving of reasons may be inconvenient, but I can see no grounds at all why it should be against the public interest: indeed, rather the reverse. That being so, I would ask simply: Is refusal to give reasons fair? I would answer without hesitation that it is not.[278]

This approach applies to many decisions that closely affect the individual. Moreover, reasons must be given if a decision in the absence of explanation may appear arbitrary, harsh, mistaken or unreasonable:[279]

> if all other known facts and circumstances appear to point overwhelmingly in favour of a different decision, the decision-maker who has given no reasons cannot complain if the court draws the inference that he had no rational reason for his decision.[280]

Even when a statute excluded the giving of reasons for the refusal of naturalisation, the Home Secretary's duty to act fairly was held to mean that he must give sufficient information on the matters that concerned him to enable the applicants to make such representations as they could on those matters.[281]

Although the courts indirectly require the giving of reasons in many situations, they have not held that reasons should be given for all decisions.[282] Indeed, the exceptions to the rule have arguably almost swallowed the general rule itself. A general ruling to this effect is overdue,[283] even if it were accompanied by an exception for situations in which public interest considerations had to prevail over the general rule.

As it is, the procedure of judicial review supports the giving of reasons. If an individual receives no reasons for a decision and obtains permission for judicial review, the decision-maker will be expected to disclose relevant information so that the court can properly decide the claim for review.[284] A court is likely to hold that there must have been some operative

----

[274] *Breen* v *AEU* [1971] 2 QB 175, 191 (Lord Denning MR). See also G Richardson [1986] PL 437; P Neill, in Forsyth and Hare (eds), *The Golden Metwand and the Crooked Cord*, pp 161–84; P P Craig [1994] CLJ 282.

[275] *R* v *Trade Secretary, ex p Lonrho plc* [1989] 2 All ER 609; *R* v *Higher Education Funding Council, ex p Institute of Dental Surgery* [1994] 1 All ER 651; *Hasan* v *Trade and Industry Secretary* [2008] EWCA Civ 1311, [2009] 3 All ER 539.

[276] *Minister of National Revenue* v *Wright's Canadian Ropes* [1947] AC 109.

[277] *R* v *Home Secretary, ex p Doody* [1994] 1 AC 531.

[278] Ibid, at 564–5.

[279] *R* v *Civil Service Board, ex p Cunningham* [1991] 1 All ER 310 (J Herberg [1991] PL 340).

[280] *R* v *Trade Secretary, ex p Lonrho plc* [1989] 2 All ER 609, 620 (Lord Keith).

[281] *R* v *Home Secretary, ex p Al Fayed* [1997] 1 All ER 228.

[282] See *Stefan* v *General Medical Council* [1999] 1 WLR 1293. And see Lord Bingham's summary of the law in *R* v *Ministry of Defence, ex p Murray* [1998] COD 134.

[283] M Elliott [2011] PL 56.

[284] Cf *R* v *Lancashire CC, ex p Huddleston* [1986] 2 All ER 941 (and A W Bradley [1986] PL 508).

reasons at the time the decision was made and will wish to discover what these were; little weight may be attached to reasons created after the decision was made.[285] The court may sometimes accept evidence as to the reasoning of the decision-maker even if it was not explained at the time, but breach of a statutory duty to give reasons with the decision may cause the court to quash the decision for error of law.[286] Where there is a duty to give reasons, 'proper and adequate reasons must be given' which are intelligible and deal with the substantial points in issue. Concise reasons may be enough,[287] but a general formula that does not deal with the disputed issues in a case is unlikely to be acceptable.

European Union law requires that reasons be given when this is necessary to secure effective protection of an EU right.[288] Where art 6(1) ECHR entitles the individual to a fair hearing before an independent and impartial court or tribunal, the court or tribunal is expected to give reasons for its decision, so that the parties and the public may understand the basis for it.[289]

The public sector equality duty

Although generally overlooked by academic commentators,[290] the public sector equality duty has proved to be a fruitful and vital tool for practitioners and claimants seeking to attack policy decisions which cannot be defeated on substantive grounds, most commonly because they involve the difficult allocation of scarce resources or are large-scale political decisions. The content of the duty is both simple and complex. Section 149 of the Equality Act 2010[291] requires public authorities to have 'due regard' to the statutory needs to eliminate the forms of discrimination prohibited in the Act, advance equality of opportunity and foster good relations between those who share protected characteristics (such as race) and those who do not. This opens the door to a multitude of scenarios of potential relevance.

The duty is a procedural one.[292] It allows the courts to consider the manner by which the public authority reached its decision, not the substance of that decision itself. As Laws LJ put the point:

> the discipline of the PSED lies in the required quality, not the outcome, of the decision-making process. This is well borne out by the learning; but in my judgment it reflects a more general constitutional balance. Much of our modern law, judge-made and statutory, makes increasing demands on public decision-makers in the name of liberal values: the protection of minorities, equality of treatment, non-discrimination, and the quietus of old prejudices. The law has been enriched accordingly. But it is not generally for the courts to resolve the controversies which this insistence involves. That is for elected government. The cause of constitutional rights is not best served by an ambitious expansion of judicial territory, for the courts are not the proper arbiters of political controversy. In this sense judicial restraint is an ally of the s 149 duty, for it keeps it in its proper place, which is the process and not the outcome of public decisions.[293]

---

[285] See A Schaeffer [2004] JR 151 and *R (Nash)* v *Chelsea College of Art and Design* [2001] EWHC 538 (Admin).

[286] *R* v *Westminster City Council, ex p Ermakov* [1996] 2 All ER 302. See also *R (Richardson)* v *North Yorkshire CC* [2003] EWCA Civ 1869, [2004] 2 All ER 31, [31]–[42].

[287] *Re Poyser and Mills' Arbitration* [1964] 2 QB 467, 478. On the adequacy of reasons for a planning decision, see *South Bucks DC* v *Porter (No 2)* [2004] UKHL 33, [2004] 4 All ER 775.

[288] See e.g. *Case 222/86, UNECTEF* v *Heylens* [1989] 1 CMLR 901.

[289] *Hadjianastassiou* v *Greece* (1992) 16 EHRR 219.

[290] T Hickman [2013] PL 325; S Fredman [2011] ILJ 405; Sir Philip Sales [2011] JR 1; A McColgan (2015) 35 OJLS 453.

[291] Previous versions were contained in the Race Relations Act 1976, the Sex Discrimination Act 1975 and the Disability Discrimination Act 1995, all as amended.

[292] Although one major work treats it as a substantive ground of review: Auburn, Moffett and Sharland, *Judicial Review: Principles and Procedure*, ch 15.

[293] *R (MA)* v *Work and Pensions Secretary* [2013] EWHC 2213 (Admin).

The effect is that so long as the public authority has regard to the fact that the policy may, for example, disproportionately impact on disabled people or on women, it may nonetheless lawfully adopt the policy.

Due regard means only the regard which is appropriate in all the circumstances. The decision-maker must be aware of his duty (although it need not be specifically be mentioned); the duty must be fulfilled before and at the time that the decision is considered; it must be exercised in substance, with rigour and an open mind, rather than as a tick-box exercise; the duty is a non-delegable one (although this does not exclude reliance on the work of officials); it is a continuing duty; and an accurate record, usually but not necessary in the form of an Equality Impact Assessment, should be kept to evidence the consideration given.[294]

Following an upsurge in s 149 cases to challenge austerity measures, the courts have more recently sought to reduce the ease with which a public authority can be challenged on the basis of a scenario it had failed to appreciate. Three points may be used by way of illustration. First, it has been held that the process should not be subjected to the level of forensic scrutiny a QC would deploy in court.[295] Secondly, the courts have settled into accepting that the weight to be applied to any of the statutory needs is a matter to be assessed on *Wednesbury* grounds (above, in section A) alone.[296] Thirdly, there has been an increased recognition that the considerable number of potential protected characteristics, forms of discrimination and needs the s 149 duty relates to means that the decision-maker need only have due regard to matters which are likely to arise; purely speculative cases need not be considered.[297] As a result, a balance is usually reached between avoiding the depth of scrutiny which strays into examining the merits of the decision and imposing an unreasonable administrative burden, whilst holding the public authority to compliance with an important legal and constitutional duty.

D. Conclusion

Judicial review is an essential tool by which executive power can be checked. It ensures that administrative decision-making, which may affect a few individuals or almost the entirety of the population, is held to particular standards. As we have seen, those standards go to both the substance of the decision or action, and the process by which that decision was reached.

In the former type of case, substantive challenges, the courts have generally been reluctant to take too interventionist an approach. The court has no mandate to determine policy. Its role is to review the policy adopted by the decision-maker against a series of tests that derive from the general principles of administrative law. A decision or policy should be reached which has not got the law wrong; it should take into account relevant matters and not irrelevant ones; a power should be used for a purpose for which it was granted; and the decision ought not to be so unreasonable that it defies logic or is otherwise irrational. In cases involving human rights law, or European Union law, or, possibly, some areas of domestic law, the court may subject the decision or policy choice to a more structured and searching examination, requiring the decision-maker to justify what it has done whilst recognising the particular expertise that the decision-maker is likely to possess.

---

[294] *R (Brown)* v *Work and Pensions Secretary* [2008] EWHC 3158 (Admin), [2009] PTSR 1506; *R (Baker)* v *Local Government Secretary* [2008] EWCA Civ 141, [2008] LGR 239; summarised in *R (Luton BC)* v *Education Secretary* [2011] EWHC 217 (Admin), [2011] ELR 222 and *R (Essex CC)* v *Education Secretary* [2012] EWHC 1460 (Admin).

[295] *R (Bailey)* v *Brent London Borough Council* [2011] EWCA Civ 1586, [2012] LGR 530 at [102] (Davis LJ).

[296] *Luton BC* (above); *R (Hurley)* v *Business Secretary* [2012] EWHC 201 (Admin), [2012] EqLR 447.

[297] *Bailey* (above); *R (Greenwich Community Law Centre)* v *Greenwich LBC* [2012] EWCA Civ 496, [2012] EqLR 72; *R (Lewisham LBC)* v *AQA* [2013] EWHC 211 (Admin).

Complying with a fair process is similarly a matter of what most would consider basic fairness. A decision-maker ought not to be biased against an individual; where a major policy is being determined, consultation with interested parties may be appropriate; individual decisions should not be taken without the individual having the chance to make representations; and in some sorts of situation, reasons for the decision ought to be given.

The development of the principle of legitimate expectation has been one of the major changes in administrative law over the last decade. The principle has grown considerably, in size, scope and complexity. It is an area of the law in which court decisions are often difficult to understand because of a lack of rigour in analysing which type of legitimate expectation has arisen. But as we have seen, it is at its heart another example of judicial review seeking to ensure fairness in the administrative process: if citizens justifiably believe that a decision-maker will act in a certain way – because he has said that he will, or because he always has – the decision-maker ought to be required to put forward good reasons why that expectation should be overridden.

Although judicial review has a morass of principles, rules and case law, it can be summarised very straightforwardly: the purpose of judicial review is to ensure that administrative policy and decision-making is carried out fairly and in accordance with the law.

CHAPTER 25

Judicial review II: procedure and remedies

In Chapter 24 we considered the principles which the courts apply to the exercise of administrative powers by public authorities. We now examine the procedures by which the courts exercise their supervisory jurisdiction.[1] Review may take place indirectly, when an issue as to the validity of administrative action is decided in the course of ordinary civil or criminal proceedings. So too, the validity of action by a public authority may be relevant to a private law action in contract or tort (Chapter 26). But here we are mainly concerned with the procedures by which the acts and decisions of public authorities are subject to direct judicial review by the courts.

The primary procedure in English law[2] is that of a claim for judicial review, often referred to in short as 'judicial review'. It was created by reforms between 1977 and 1982 which, like many procedural reforms of the common law, did not seek to change the jurisdiction of the High Court in reviewing the legality of the work of public authorities. The relief sought in judicial review proceedings is most commonly a quashing order (previously certiorari), a mandatory order (mandamus) or a prohibitory order (prohibition): the three prerogative remedies. Judicial review has derived benefits from reforms in the general procedure of civil litigation, but there are still reasons for maintaining a distinctive procedure for judicial review.[3] This chapter will look first at the relevant procedure, then in section B at the case law establishing the scope and extent of judicial review and its exclusivity. Section C will consider forms of limitation and exclusion of judicial review. Section D will set out the various remedies which can be obtained, including a brief consideration of habeas corpus and the differences in Scotland.

A. The judicial review procedure

The creation of applications for judicial review

We turn now to examine the procedure by which the remedies considered above may be obtained. The procedure today presents a remarkable contrast with the position in the 1970s, when there was an urgent need for reform in the remedies available in administrative law. The procedural difficulties were such that the success of a case often depended on the choice of remedy, and there were many procedural differences between the prerogative orders on the one hand, and declarations and injunctions on the other. These matters provided serious obstacles to a court's ability to deal with the substantive issues of public law that might arise.[4] In 1977, a new Rule of the Supreme Court (Order 53), created the procedure of 'application for judicial review' and this reform was confirmed by Parliament in 1981. In 2000, Order 53 was replaced by Part 54 of the Civil Procedure Rules, substituting the terminology of a

---

[1] The leading book dealing with the topics in this chapter is Lewis, *Judicial Remedies in Public Law*. See also the works on administrative law that have already been cited.

[2] A similar but not identical procedure was created in Scotland in 1985; p 707 below. For Northern Ireland, see P Maguire, in Hadfield (ed.), *Judicial Review, A Thematic Approach*, app.

[3] For arguments to the contrary, see D Oliver [2002] PL 91.

[4] Report on Remedies in Administrative Law, Cmnd 6407, 1976.

'claim' for judicial review rather than an 'application' (aligning it with other proceedings);[5] and the court in which sit the High Court judges designated to hear claims for judicial review and related cases was named the Administrative Court.[6]

Claims for judicial review: the procedure

By s 31 of the Senior Courts Act 1981 (previously known as the Supreme Court Act 1981), as amended, claims to the High Court for mandatory, prohibiting and quashing orders[7] (and for an injunction restraining a person from acting in a public office to which he or she is not entitled) *must* be made, in accordance with rules of court, by a claim for judicial review. The High Court also has power (1981 Act, s 31(2)) to make a declaration or grant an injunction whenever a claim for judicial review has been made seeking that relief, if it would be 'just and convenient' to do so. In exercising this discretion the court must have regard among other things to the nature of the matters in respect of which the prerogative orders apply, the nature of the persons and bodies against whom the orders lie, and all the circumstances. Thus, if account is taken of the scope of the prerogative orders, declarations and injunctions *may* be granted on a claim for judicial review. The Act does not state whether within this field a claim for judicial review is to be the sole means of obtaining an injunction or declaration.

Permission of the court is needed for every claim for judicial review (s 31(3)). By this rule, derived from earlier procedure for the prerogative orders, a two-stage process exists: (*a*) the court decides whether to permit a claim for review to proceed and, if so, (*b*) a substantive hearing of the claim takes place.

The first step in the procedure before any claim is filed with the court is that a prospective claimant should if possible comply with the pre-action protocol.[8] In outline, this involves a letter to the public authority or official whose act or decision is in question containing sufficient information to enable a reasoned reply to be given, in the hope that the issues may be identified and litigation avoided. If it cannot be avoided, the claimant must file a claim form with the Administrative Court,[9] stating the act or decision to be reviewed, the relevant facts and grounds, and the remedy sought. Notice is given to the defendant and other interested parties, who must within 21 days state whether they intend to contest the claim and, if so, must give a summary of the grounds they will rely on. The granting of permission is generally decided on the papers by a single judge,[10] but the judge may request a short hearing in open court. A hearing is usually held if interim relief is sought. If permission is refused or granted subject to conditions, the claimant may ask for a hearing to renew the application for

---

[5] A claim for judicial review is, in civil procedure terms, essentially a specialised form of a claim brought under the CPR Part 8 procedure (as opposed to the Part 7 procedure, requiring Particulars of Claim, a Defence, and a trial with witness evidence). The older terminology of an application, still seen in the Senior Courts Act 1981, stems from the fact that permission to seek judicial review was formerly made by way of ex parte application (i.e. without notice to the other side). Nothing of any real importance turns on the difference in language, but a 'claim for judicial review' is the correct usage.

[6] CPR, Part 54.

[7] These orders may for convenience be referred to as 'the prerogative orders'. The change of names in 2004 did not affect the jurisdiction of the High Court to make them.

[8] Civil Procedure Rules, Pre-Action Protocol for Judicial Review.

[9] This will mostly be in the High Court in London, but may be filed and heard in Birmingham, Cardiff, Leeds or Manchester. There are some types of claim, particularly terrorism-related, which can only be heard in London. See Practice Direction 54D (and S Nason [2009] PL 440).

[10] In 2013, over 50 High Court judges were designated to sit in the Administrative Court and in addition very many permission applications are determined by Deputy High Court judges. (The list no longer appears to be published, but practical experience suggests the numbers are not much altered.)

permission.[11] If permission is still withheld, the claimant may appeal to the Court of Appeal.[12] In the past, the 'filter' stage operated very unevenly, but it is a safeguard against a flood of 'hopeless' cases and vexatious challenges.[13] Once permission has been granted, the defendant may expand on its grounds of resistance and file further evidence. The substantive hearing takes place before a single judge or, for criminal matters or important cases, a divisional court (that usually consists of a Lord Justice of Appeal, sitting with a High Court judge).

Claims for judicial review must be made promptly and 'in any event not later than three months after the grounds to make the claim first arose', but the period may be shorter for a particular claim if legislation so provides.[14] If the court considers that the case is one which requires urgent action (for instance, a challenge to school admission decisions or where third parties are affected),[15] it may refuse permission for a claim that is not made promptly, even within the three-month period. The court may extend time if there is a good reason to do so, but the parties may not extend time by agreement.[16] In practice, where there is a 'clear-cut' case on the merits, the courts are not minded to allow the potential illegality to continue unchallenged for such apparently formalistic procedural reasons.[17]

The promptness requirement has been the subject of considerable dispute following the decision of the Court of Justice of the EU in *Uniplex (UK) Ltd* v *NHS Business Services Authority*[18] which held that the requirement to bring procurement proceedings promptly breached the EU law principles of legal certainty and access to an effective remedy. The Court of Appeal subsequently held that the application of *Uniplex* was not clear, but that the promptness requirement should not be applied in claims asserting rights under EU law. The majority considered that it should still apply to claims not within the scope of EU law, even when brought at the same time as an EU law claim.[19] The European Court of Human Rights held that promptness was compatible with art 6 ECHR, but this is an issue which may resurface at some stage as a result of *Uniplex*.[20]

Under the Senior Courts Act 1981, s 31(6), the court may refuse to grant leave for a claim or may refuse relief sought by the claimant if it considers that the granting of the relief

[11] This right has been excluded from judicial reviews of decisions of the Upper Tribunal: CPR r 54.7A, and see ch 23 A.

[12] CPR, r 52.8. If the Court of Appeal also refuses leave, the Supreme Court has no jurisdiction to grant leave: *Lane* v *Esdaile* [1891] AC 210. And see *R (Burkett)* v *Hammersmith LBC* [2002] UKHL 23, [2002] 3 All ER 97 (HL has jurisdiction if CA grants leave but rejects claim on its merits). Applications for permission to appeal from a refusal of permission to judicially review a decision of the Upper Tribunal are considered on the papers only, and the appellant is not entitled to an oral hearing to consider leave to appeal.

[13] See A Le Sueur and M Sunkin [1992] PL 102; Bridges, Meszaros and Sunkin, *Judicial Review in Perspective*, chs 7, 8 and (same authors) [2000] PL 651.

[14] CPR, r 54.5. For the operation of these rules, see *R (Burkett)* v *Hammersmith LBC* (above); *R (Nash)* v *Barnet London Borough Council* [2013] EWCA Civ 1004 and M J Beloff, in Forsyth and Hare (eds), *The Golden Metwand and the Crooked Cord*, pp 267–95. A shorter period of six weeks for planning cases and 30 days for public procurement cases was introduced in 2013 with the aims of reducing challenges and increasing certainty in areas where considerable amounts of money are expended. No promptness requirement applies: r 54.5 as amended.

[15] *R* v *Rochdale Metropolitan Borough Council, ex p B* [2000] Ed CR 117 and *R (Camelot UK Lotteries Ltd)* v *Gambling Commission* [2012] EWHC 2391 (Admin) respectively as examples.

[16] CPR, rr 3.1(2)(a); 54.5(2).

[17] *R (Finn-Kelcey)* v *Milton Keynes Borough Council* [2008] EWCA Civ 1067, [2009] Env LR 17; C J S Knight [2009] JR 113.

[18] Case C-406/08 [2010] 2 CMLR 47; C J S Knight [2010] CJQ 297.

[19] *R (Berky)* v *Newport City Council* [2012] EWCA Civ 378, [2012] LGR 592. See too: *R (Powell)* v *Brighton Marina Co Ltd* [2014] EWHC 2136 (Admin).

[20] *Lam* v *UK* (ECtHR, 5 July 2001); *Hardy* v *Pembrokeshire County Council* [2006] EWCA Civ 240, [2006] Env LR 28; but see now: *R (Macrae)* v *County of Herefordshire District Council* [2012] EWCA Civ 457, [2012] JPL 1356.

'would be likely to cause substantial hardship to, or substantially prejudice the rights of, any person or would be detrimental to good administration'. Despite some difficulty arising from the interaction of this provision with the procedure rules, it is now established that where permission has been granted for judicial review, the court at the substantive hearing may not set aside that permission on the ground that there had been unjustified delay in the claim being made; however, delay may be a reason for withholding relief that would otherwise be justified.[21]

If permission to proceed with a claim for judicial review is given, the court may order a stay of proceedings to which the claim relates.[22] The court may grant other interim relief, including mandatory orders and interim declarations,[23] applying the test of balance of convenience that is appropriate in civil proceedings generally,[24] but with regard to special considerations applicable to public law litigation.[25]

The 1981 Act did not expressly provide for interim relief against the Crown, but in *M v Home Office*[26] it was held that the language of s 31 enabled coercive orders (including interim injunctions) to be made against ministers and officers of the Crown in judicial review proceedings.

On a claim for judicial review, the court may award damages, restitution or the recovery of money if such an award has been claimed and the court is satisfied that it could have been obtained by an action brought for the purpose.[27] But this does not alter the basic principle of English administrative law that an unlawful act of a public authority does not, of itself, give rise to a right to damages.[28] Thus even successful applicants for judicial review are seldom able to obtain damages. However, under the Human Rights Act 1998, s 8, the court may grant compensation if it is satisfied that this is 'necessary to afford just satisfaction' to the person whose Convention rights have been infringed.[29]

A claim for judicial review must be supported by such written evidence as is available and a witness statement confirming the truth of the facts relied on; the defendant may file evidence in reply. The claimant owes a duty to the court to disclose all relevant material of which he or she is aware, even if it weakens the claim; the defendant has a similar 'duty of candour' to disclose relevant material the existence of which may be unknown to the claimant.[30] The court may order disclosure of specific documents, further information and, very exceptionally, cross-examination of witnesses, except where the defendant establishes that certain evidence

---

[21] See *R v Criminal Injuries Compensation Board, ex p A* [1999] 2 AC 330; *R v Dairy Produce Tribunal, ex p Caswell* [1990] 2 AC 738 (and A Lindsay [1995] PL 417). However, the effect of *Uniplex* (above) appears to be that in cases asserting EU law rights it would breach legal certainty and the right to an effective remedy to refuse relief in the discretion of the court: *R (Berky)* (above), by a majority, and *AG Quidnet Hounslow v London Borough of Hounslow* [2012] EWHC 2639 (TCC), [2013] PTSR 828.

[22] CPR, r 54.10. Under the former RSC Order 53, r 10, 'stay of proceedings' was interpreted broadly in *R v Education Secretary, ex p Avon Council* [1991] 1 QB 558.

[23] CPR, r 25.1(1). This power was not formerly available: *R v IRC, ex p Rossminster Ltd* [1980] AC 952.

[24] *American Cyanamid Co v Ethicon Ltd* [1975] AC 396.

[25] See *BACONGO v Department of Environment of Belize* [2003] UKPC 63, [2013] 1 WLR 2839 and *R v Transport Secretary, ex parte Factortame Ltd (No 2)* [1991] 1 AC 603, 672-3 (Lord Goff) (adequacy of damages in a public law challenge rarely relevant).

[26] [1994] 1 AC 377 (H W R Wade (1991) 107 LQR 4; M Gould [1993] PL 368). For the Crown Proceedings Act 1947, s 21, see ch 26 C.

[27] Senior Courts Act 1981, s 31(4).

[28] Ch 26 A; e.g. *Dunlop v Woollahra Council* [1982] AC 158.

[29] And see page 723 below.

[30] See O Sanders [2008] JR 244, discussing effect of *Tweed v Parades Commission for Northern Ireland* [2006] UKHL 53, [2007] 1 AC 650. The focus of the duty of candour is invariably on the public authority, for the obvious reason that it (and not the claimant) will be more likely have access to information relevant to the success of the claim which would otherwise be unknown. For particularly egregious failings, see *R (Al-Sweady) v Defence Secretary* [2009] EWHC 1687 (Admin) and [2009] EWHC 2387 (Admin), [2010] HRLR 2.

is protected by public interest immunity.[31] In practice, many cases turn on the documents that record the decision-making process. It is often said that a claim for judicial review is unsuitable for resolving disputes of fact. However, the court must decide issues of fact that are essential to a claim (such as whether a decision-maker was biased, or whether proper consultation took place); and questions requiring disclosure may well arise on issues of proportionality on a claim under the Human Rights Act.[32]

Where the court decides to quash the decision under review, it generally remits the matter to the decision-maker, with an appropriate direction, but if there is no purpose in remitting it the court may take the decision itself.[33] The Civil Procedure Rules permit claims begun by ordinary procedure to be transferred, with permission of the court, into a claim for judicial review and, conversely, a claim for judicial review may be transferred into an ordinary claim.[34]

Standing to apply for judicial review

At the stage when leave is sought for a claim for judicial review, the court must not grant leave 'unless it considers that the applicant has a sufficient interest in the matter to which the application relates'.[35] The test of 'sufficient interest' allows the court significant discretion to decide what may constitute it.

In *R v Inland Revenue Commissioners, ex p National Federation of Self-employed*, a body of taxpayers challenged arrangements made by the Commissioners for levying tax on wages paid to casual employees on Fleet Street newspapers. For many years the employees had given fictitious names to evade tax, but the Commissioners agreed with the employers and unions on a scheme for collecting tax in future and for two previous years, in return for an undertaking by the Commissioners not to investigate any earlier years. The Federation, complaining that their members were never treated so favourably, applied for a declaration that the arrangement was unlawful, and a mandamus ordering the Commissioners to collect tax as required by law. The Court of Appeal held, assuming the agreement to be unlawful, that the Federation had sufficient interest in the matter for their application to be heard. The House of Lords *held* that the question of sufficient interest was not merely a preliminary issue to be decided when leave was being sought on an application for judicial review, but had to be resolved in relation to what was known by the court of the matter under review. On the evidence, the tax agreement was a lawful exercise of the Commissioners' discretion. In general, unlike local ratepayers, a taxpayer did not have an interest in challenging decisions concerning other taxpayers. In the circumstances, the Federation did not have sufficient interest to challenge the Commissioners' decisions.[36]

The speeches in this case contain a wide diversity of opinions about the test of 'sufficient interest'. The above account is based on the views of three judges (Lords Wilberforce, Fraser and Roskill), although Lord Fraser also stressed that the test of 'sufficient interest' was a logically prior question which had to be answered before any question of the merits arose.

---

[31] See ch 26 C.
[32] And see *Tweed* v *Parades Commission* (above), [32], [38]–[40] (Lord Carswell); [56]–[57] (Lord Brown).
[33] Senior Courts Act 1981, s 31(5); and CPR, r 54.19.
[34] CPR, Part 30 and r 54.20. For effect of this on the 'exclusive remedy' issue, see p 691 below.
[35] Senior Courts Act 1981, s 31(3).
[36] [1982] AC 617; P Cane [1981] PL 322.

Lord Scarman paid lip-service to the existence of a test of standing separate from the merits, but his conclusion (that the Federation had no sufficient interest *because* they had not shown that the tax authorities had failed in their duties) virtually eliminated any prior test of standing separate from the merits. Lord Diplock, emphasising the utility of the then new procedure of application for judicial review, argued for a very broad test of standing; he was alone in holding that the Federation had sufficient interest to seek review, but that the case for review failed on its merits.

What emerges from the case is that at the permission stage, the court has a discretion to turn away those without a legitimate concern ('in other words a busybody'),[37] but at the substantive hearing other questions of standing may be raised. A court should not refuse permission for lack of sufficient interest unless it knows enough of the legal and factual context to be sure that this is justified; in advance of examining the merits, the court may be unable to make a surgical separation between 'sufficient interest' and the essence of the case.

In most claims for judicial review, the question of sufficient interest presents no problems, although for the parties not to raise the issue does not confer on the court jurisdiction that is otherwise absent.[38] An ordinary taxpayer had interest to challenge the government's proposal to designate as a 'Community treaty' a treaty providing extra funds to the EU.[39] The Equal Opportunities Commission had standing to challenge statutory provisions which discriminated against women employees in breach of their EU law rights.[40] Trade unions acting in their members' interests and environmental groups have standing to challenge decisions on relevant issues,[41] but difficulties may arise when a claimant is not personally affected by a decision and is acting in the public interest. Thus a non–profit-making company formed to protect the site of a Shakespearian theatre had no standing to review a minister's decision refusing to schedule the site as a historic monument.[42] Relatives of a child who was killed by two young boys had no standing to seek review of a decision by the Lord Chief Justice as to the minimum period in detention that the two youths should serve.[43] However, as with time limits, the courts will be very reluctant to refuse permission on standing grounds where they see a meritorious claim, in order to assess potential wrongdoing on the part of a public authority.[44] Proposals to tighten the law on standing were floated by the government in 2013 but dropped in the face of strong opposition, including from the judiciary.[45]

A different test of standing was created by the Human Rights Act 1998, s 7: a claim that a public authority acted incompatibly with a Convention right (in breach of s 6) may be brought only by someone who is a 'victim' of the act within the meaning of art 34 ECHR. Strasbourg case law does not permit cases to be brought by representative bodies and pressure groups

---

[37] *R v Somerset CC, ex p Dixon* [1998] Env LR 111. And see *R (Edwards) v Environment Agency* [2003] EWHC 736 (Admin), [2004] 3 All ER 21. In the Fleet Street case, above, Lord Scarman referred to the exclusion of 'busybodies, cranks and mischief-makers' but it may not always be obvious whether a claimant is a mischief-maker or a champion of liberty. They may, of course, be both.

[38] *R v Social Services Secretary, ex p CPAG* [1990] 2 QB 540.

[39] *R v HM Treasury, ex p Smedley* [1985] QB 657; *R v Foreign Secretary, ex p Rees-Mogg* [1994] QB 552. See also *R v Felixstowe Justices, ex p Leigh* [1987] QB 582.

[40] *R v Employment Secretary, ex p EOC* [1995] 1 AC 1.

[41] *R v Inspectorate of Pollution, ex p Greenpeace Ltd (No 2)* [1994] 4 All ER 329; *R v Home Secretary, ex p Fire Brigades Union* [1995] 2 AC 513; *R v Foreign Secretary, ex p World Development Movement* [1995] 1 All ER 611. See: P Cane [1995] PL 276 and C Harlow (2002) 65 MLR 1.

[42] *R v Environment Secretary, ex p Rose Theatre Trust Co* [1990] 1 QB 504. See K Schiemann [1990] PL 342 and P Cane [1990] PL 307.

[43] *R (Bulger) v Home Secretary* [2001] EWHC 119 (Admin), [2001] 3 All ER 449. The claim was also rejected on its merits.

[44] *World Development Movement* (above); *R v Somerset County Council, ex p Dixon* [1998] Env LR 111.

[45] A Mills [2015] PL 583, 584–6.

unless they themselves are victims of a breach of their Convention rights.[46] Such bodies must thus ensure that one or more 'victims' are claimants for judicial review in order to rely on s 6 of the 1998 Act. There is no victim test for persons who wish to rely on other provisions of the Act, such as the requirement by s 3 that legislation must be interpreted consistently with the Convention, wherever this is possible.

Alternative remedies[47]

Another issue considered at the permission stage stems from the principle that the prerogative orders are a residual remedy. In a leading 19th-century case, mandamus was refused where a statute created both a duty and a specific remedy for enforcing it (complaint to central government).[48] Today, an individual must use an express right of appeal if this will meet the substance of the complaint.[49] Tribunals exist for deciding claims to social security, disputes over tax, immigration claims and so on. Judicial review is not an optional substitute for an appeal to a tribunal with relevant jurisdiction.[50] The existence of an alternative remedy does not deprive the Administrative Court of jurisdiction, but requires the court to exercise its discretion: whether leave for judicial review to proceed is granted will depend on whether the statutory remedy is a satisfactory and effective alternative to review.[51] Thus, the default powers of ministers concerning social service complaints may deal with the factual issues raised by a complaint, but do not enable important points of law to be resolved.[52] Sometimes the reason for withholding permission is merely that the application for judicial review is premature, as, for instance, where a right of appeal is open to the individual. In other cases, a judicial remedy may be justified, if the decision at first instance is manifestly ultra vires[53] or there has been abuse of statutory procedure by the authority.[54] In such cases, the court considers such matters as the comparative speed, expense and finality of the alternative processes, the need for fact-finding and the desirability of an authoritative ruling on points of law.[55]

B. The extent of judicial review

Scope and extent of judicial review

If an application for review concerns decisions of a public authority or official, the courts readily accept jurisdiction in judicial review, except if a reason to the contrary is shown.[56] Thus, decisions taken under prerogative powers are subject to review, unless the court considers

....
[46] See Harris, O'Boyle and Warbrick, *Law of the ECHR*, 790–99; J Miles [2000] CLJ 133. For an example, see: *R (Children's Rights Alliance for England) v Justice Secretary* [2013] EWCA Civ 34, [2013] 1 WLR 3667. The Equality and Human Rights Commission has a statutory exemption from the need to satisfy the victim test: Equality Act 2006, s 30(3)(a).

[47] See C Lewis [1992] CLJ 138 and (same author) *Judicial Remedies in Public Law*, ch 11 G.

[48] *Pasmore v Oswaldtwistle Council* [1898] AC 387. And see *Barraclough v Brown* [1897] AC 615 (declarations).

[49] *R v Paddington Valuation Officer, ex p Peachey Property Co* [1966] 1 QB 380; *R (Davies) v Financial Services Authority* [2003] EWCA Civ 1128, [2003] 4 All ER 1196.

[50] *R (G) v Immigration Appeal Tribunal* [2004] EWCA Civ 1731, [2005] 2 All ER 165.

[51] *Leech v Deputy Governor of Parkhurst Prison* [1988] AC 533. If an appeal against an immigration decision can be brought only from outside the United Kingdom, this may not be a satisfactory alternative to judicial review; cf *Chikwamba v Home Secretary* [2008] UKHL 40, [2009] 1 All ER 363.

[52] *R v Devon CC, ex p Baker* [1995] 1 All ER 73. Cf *R (Cowl) v Plymouth Council* (below, note 38).

[53] *R v Hillingdon Council, ex p Royco Homes Ltd* [1974] 1 QB 720.

[54] *R v Chief Constable, Merseyside, ex p Calveley* [1986] QB 424.

[55] *R v Falmouth Port Health Authority, ex p South West Water Ltd* [2001] QB 445.

[56] See Auburn, Moffett and Sharland, *Judicial Review: Principles and Procedure*, ch 2; Lewis, *Judicial Remedies in Public Law*, chs 2, 4.

their subject matter to be non-justiciable.[57] Also reviewable are decisions by local authorities in controlling access to public property, initiating legal proceedings and matters preliminary to the award of contracts.[58] Two broad exceptions to the availability of judicial review exist. First, some decisions are subject to statutory appeals and similar procedures which, to a greater or lesser extent, exclude judicial review.[59] Second, public authorities are in general subject to the ordinary law of contract, tort and property. Since *O'Reilly* v *Mackman*,[60] such branches of law are said to fall within private law, to distinguish them from the rules of public law applied on judicial review. A claim for judicial review may not be used in place of an ordinary action in contract or tort, just because the defendant is a public authority.

Thus, when such an authority dismisses an employee, the employee's primary remedy is a claim for unfair dismissal or a claim under the contract of employment.[61] However, depending on the circumstances, decisions by public authorities as employers may stem from or involve issues of public law.[62] Public sector employees such as NHS hospital staff[63] and civil servants[64] must generally use procedures open to them in employment law rather than seek judicial review. This does not necessarily apply to holders of public office such as police and prison officers[65] whose position is based on statute. Judicial review may be available if an employment dispute raises issues as to the powers of the public authority or other matters suitable for redress by judicial review.[66]

A difficult question is what constitutes a 'public law dispute' for judicial review purposes. The prerogative orders were not, and judicial review is not, available against bodies such as trade unions or commercial companies.[67] Membership of a trade union is based on contract. If a trade unionist complains that her expulsion from the union was in breach of union rules or infringed natural justice, she may sue the union for damages and an injunction. Bodies such as the National Greyhound Racing Club and the Jockey Club are not subject to judicial review, even if they regulate major areas of sport, but contractual remedies will often be available.[68] The same is true of political parties, which are contractual

---

[57] See the *CCSU* case, below; *R* v *Ministry of Defence, ex p Smith* [1996] QB 517; *R (Bancoult)* v *Foreign Secretary (No 2)* [2008] UKHL 61, [2009] 1 AC 453. Cf *Reckley* v *Minister of Public Safety (No 2)* [1996] AC 527.

[58] Respectively *Wheeler* v *Leicester City Council* [1985] AC 1054; *Avon CC* v *Buscott* [1988] QB 656; and *R* v *Enfield Council, ex p TF Unwin (Roydon) Ltd* [1989] 1 Admin LR 51.

[59] See p 687 above.

[60] [1983] 2 AC 237, p 690 below.

[61] *R* v *BBC, ex p Lavelle* [1983] 1 All ER 241.

[62] E.g. *CCSU* v *Minister for Civil Service* [1985] AC 374; cf H W R Wade (1985) 101 LQR 180, 190–6 and see now *R (Shoesmith)* v *Ofstead* [2011] EWCA Civ 642, [2011] PTSR 1459.

[63] *R* v *East Berks Health Authority, ex p Walsh* [1985] QB 152.

[64] *R* v *Lord Chancellor's Department, ex p Nangle* [1992] 1 All ER 897.

[65] *R* v *Home Secretary, ex p Benwell* [1985] QB 554. By the Criminal Justice and Public Order Act 1994, s 126, prison officers acquired the same employment rights as other civil servants: G S Morris [1994] PL 535. Contrast *R (Tucker)* v *National Crime Squad* [2003] EWCA Civ 2, [2003] ICR 599 (no judicial review of decision to end police secondment) with *R (Simpson)* v *Chief Constable of Greater Manchester* [2013] EWHC 1858 (Admin) (selection pool for promotion of police officers raised policy issues amenable to judicial review).

[66] See *McLaren* v *Home Office* [1990] ICR 824. Also S Fredman and G Morris [1988] PL 58, [1991] PL 484, (1991) 107 LQR 298.

[67] *R (West)* v *Lloyd's of London* [2004] EWCA 506, [2004] 3 All ER 251 (Lloyd's underwriting syndicates not within public law); *R (Holmcroft Properties)* v *KPMG LLP* [2016] EWHC 323 (Admin) (no review of an accountancy firm appointed as independent overseer of a redress scheme agreed between the claimant and the Financial Conduct Authority).

[68] *Law* v *National Greyhound Racing Club Ltd* [1983] 3 All ER 300; *R* v *Disciplinary Committee of the Jockey Club, ex p Aga Khan* [1993] 2 All ER 853. And see M Beloff [1989] PL 95; N Bamforth [1993] PL 239. Cf *Finnigan* v *New Zealand Rugby Football Union Inc* [1985] 2 NZLR 159 (private association exercising function of major national importance).

membership bodies.[69] Nor are decisions by religious bodies subject to judicial review,[70] including bell-ringing organisations.[71] The position of the universities is more complex. In older colleges and universities that have a visitor, academic staff or students with grievances against the institution had to refer them to the visitor, whose decisions are subject to judicial review, but only on certain grounds.[72] Legislation has now excluded from the visitor's jurisdiction employment disputes involving academic staff, and complaints by students and former students.[73] Many of the newer universities and colleges have no visitor and their decisions are subject to judicial review on the usual grounds.[74]

The most difficult case is that of regulatory bodies which derive their powers neither directly from statute[75] nor from contract. Despite having no formal legal status, the City Panel on Takeovers and Mergers is subject to judicial review, since its functions 'de facto' are in the nature of public law powers and are indirectly supported by statutory sanctions.[76] Publicly owned undertakings are subject to judicial review in respect of some of their functions.[77] The effect of privatisation and 'market testing' of public services has produced some conflicting decisions.[78] However, the courts have settled into applying a multi-factoral test which can be difficult to predict but which considers such matters as the source of the power being exercised, the nature of the body (i.e. whether it is underpinned by statute, or is part of a system of public regulation), whether monopoly control is exercised and whether it receives public funding.[79] Private profit-making companies who set GCSE examinations have been held to be subject to judicial review, because of the very significant public importance potentially affecting the life chances of candidates in those examinations.[80] It was not contested that the regulator of auditors was amenable to judicial review because there was some statutory underpinning to its functions and without it the state would have to intervene.[81] In contrast, the Insurance Ombudsman was held not to be amendable to judicial review because it arose entirely out of industry agreements, with no governmental involvement or oversight.[82]

Inferior courts, such as magistrates' courts and county courts, are subject to judicial review. So is the Crown Court, 'other than its jurisdiction in matters relating to trial on indictment'.[83] This limitation expresses an important principle that makes it necessary to distinguish between those decisions of the Crown Court that are subject to judicial review

[69] *Evangelou* v *McNicol* [2016] EWCA Civ 817 (challenge to restriction of voting rights in Labour party leadership election).

[70] *R* v *Chief Rabbi, ex p Wachmann* [1993] 2 All ER 249.

[71] *TH* v *Chapter of Worcester Cathedral* [2016] EWHC 1117 (Admin).

[72] *R* v *Hull University Visitor, ex p Page* [1993] AC 682.

[73] See respectively Education Reform Act 1988, s 206 and Higher Education Act 2004, s 20.

[74] See *R* v *Metropolitan University of Manchester, ex p Nolan* [1994] ELR 380 and cf *Clark* v *University of Lincolnshire* [2000] 3 All ER 752.

[75] Unlike the Law Society; see e.g. *Swain* v *Law Society* [1983] 1 AC 598.

[76] *R* v *Panel on Take-overs and Mergers, ex p Datafin plc* [1987] QB 817 (C F Forsyth [1987] PL 356; D Oliver [1987] PL 543); *R* v *Advertising Standards Agency, ex p Insurance Service plc* (1990) 2 Admin LR 77.

[77] *R* v *British Coal Corpn, ex p Vardy* [1993] ICR 720. See ch 12 E.

[78] Compare *R* v *Lord Chancellor, ex p Hibbit & Saunders* [1993] COD 326 (D Oliver [1993] PL 214) and *R* v *Legal Aid Board, ex p Donn & Co* [1996] 3 All ER 1.

[79] See variously: *Datafin* (above); *Aga Khan* (above); *R (Siborurema)* v *Office of Independent Adjudicator* [2007] EWCA Civ 1365, [2008] ELR 209; *R (Beer (t/a Hammer Trout Farm))* v *Hampshire Farmer's Market Ltd* [2003] EWCA Civ 1056, [2004] 1 WLR 233; J W F Allison [2007] CLJ 698; C D Campbell [2009] CLJ 90 and (2009) 123 LQR 491. That the test is expressly multi-factoral was emphasised by *R (Weaver)* v *London & Quadrant Housing Trust* [2009] EWCA Civ 587; [2010] 1 WLR 363, at [119] (Rix LJ).

[80] *R (Lewisham LBC)* v *Assessment and Qualifications Alliance* [2013] EWHC 211 (Admin), [2013] ELR 281.

[81] *R (Baker Tilly UK Audit LLP)* v *Financial Reporting Council* [2015] EWHC 1398 (Admin).

[82] *R* v *Insurance Ombudsman Bureau, ex p Aegon Life Assurance Ltd* [1994] CLC 88.

[83] Supreme Court Act 1981, s 29(3); R Ward [1990] PL 50; *In re Ashton* [1994] 1 AC 9 and *R* v *Manchester Crown Court, ex p DPP* [1993] 4 All ER 928.

and others which can be challenged only by appeal after a trial. A somewhat similar situation arises when the legislation setting up a particular tribunal indicates that judicial review is available in respect of some but not all decisions by the tribunal.[84]

This discussion has not yet taken account of the effects of the Human Rights Act 1998. As we have seen,[85] the Act obliges public authorities (and bodies that exercise functions both of a public nature and of a private nature) to act consistently with Convention rights. The defining of public authorities under the 1998 Act has given rise to difficult decisions.[86] It has been observed that the case law on the scope of judicial review is not determinative of whether a body is a public authority for the purposes of the Act,[87] but the two bodies of case law must not be developed in isolation from each other.

Does judicial review provide an exclusive procedure?[88]

Although the House of Lords failed to sound a clear note in the *National Federation* case, the House in two later cases was unanimous in holding that litigants who wished to challenge official decisions must do so by applying for judicial review. The question arose because the Senior Courts Act 1981 did not expressly exclude someone from suing in public law cases for an injunction or declaration, or for damages for breach of statutory duty. The issue had arisen in numerous cases concerning immigrants, prisoners, homeless persons and others.

In *O'Reilly* v *Mackman*, convicted prisoners who had lost remission of sentence in disciplinary proceedings after riots at Hull prison sued for a declaration that the decisions were null and void because of breaches of natural justice.[89] The defendants applied to have the action struck out on the ground that the decisions in question could be challenged only by an application for judicial review. *Held* (House of Lords) while the court had jurisdiction to grant the declarations sought, the prisoners' case was based solely on rights and obligations arising under public law. Order 53, by its requirement of leave from the court and by its time limit, protected public authorities against groundless or delayed attacks. It would 'as a general rule be contrary to public policy, and as such an abuse of the process of the court, to permit a person seeking to establish that a decision of a public authority infringed rights to which he was entitled to protection under public law to proceed by way of ordinary action and by this means to evade the provision of Order 53 for the protection of such authorities' (Lord Diplock).[90] And in *Cocks* v *Thanet DC*, the House held that a homeless person who challenged a decision by a local authority that he was not entitled to permanent accommodation must do so under Order 53, not by suing in the county court for a declaration and damages for breach of statutory duty.[91]

---

[84] See *R (Cart)* v *Upper Tribunal* [2011] UKSC 28, [2012] 1 AC 663.

[85] See ch 14 C.

[86] Including *Poplar Housing Association Ltd* v *Donohue* [2001] EWCA Civ 595, [2002] QB 48; *Aston Cantlow PCC* v *Wallbank* [2003] UKHL 37, [2004] 1 AC 546; *YL* v *Birmingham Council* [2007] UKHL 27, [2008] AC 95. The articles include D Oliver [2000] PL 476, [2004] PL 329; M Sunkin [2004] PL 643; C Donnelly [2005] PL 785; J Landau [2007] PL 630; A Williams [2011] PL 139.

[87] *Aston Cantlow PCC* v *Wallbank* (above), [52] (Lord Hope).

[88] See Auburn, Moffett and Sharland, *Judicial Review: Principles and Procedure*, ch 23; Wade and Forsyth, *Administrative Law*, pp 568–83; Craig, *Administrative Law*, ch 27.

[89] See *R* v *Board of Visitors of Hull Prison, ex p St Germain* [1979] QB 425.

[90] [1983] 2 AC 237, 285. And see C F Forsyth [1985] CLJ 415; and Justice/All Souls Report, *Administrative Justice*, ch 6.

[91] [1983] 2 AC 286. In *O'Rourke* v *Camden Council* [1998] AC 188, the decision in *Cocks* was applied but other aspects of the case were disapproved.

These two decisions left no doubt that the Law Lords wished to take further than Parliament had done the issue of exclusivity. The step taken in *O'Reilly* was justified on practical grounds, namely that litigants could be required to use the judicial review procedure as the former defects in the prerogative orders had been cured. But in seeking to protect public authorities from a flood of litigation,[92] *O'Reilly* relied heavily on the public law/private law distinction, despite the difficulties that this presents in English law.

One consequence of *O'Reilly* was that much expensive (and entirely arid) litigation ensued in testing the procedural choices made by litigants, rather than in deciding the merits of their grievances. Sir William Wade's view in 2000 was dramatic: 'The need for law reform is clearly greater now than it was before 1977.'[93] This view arguably understated the general benefits that resulted from the reforms in 1977–82. Moreover, several decisions by the Lords after *O'Reilly* showed that there is no absolute rule of procedural exclusivity.[94] In *O'Reilly*, Lord Diplock had stated that an exception to the rule might exist where the invalidity of an official decision arose 'as a collateral issue in a claim for infringement of a right of the plaintiff arising under private law'.[95] The converse of this situation arose when a local council sued one of its tenants for non-payment of rent and the tenant raised the defence that rent increases made by the council were ultra vires. Although the tenant could have sought judicial review of the increases (and had not done so), the defence was held to be a proper defence of the tenant's private rights.[96]

In 1992, Lord Diplock's suggested exception was applied directly in *Roy* v *Kensington Family Practitioner Committee*. An NHS committee, acting under statutory powers, had deducted 20 per cent from money due to Dr Roy for providing medical services to the NHS. Dr Roy sued by ordinary action for the full amount. He was granted a declaration that the deduction had not been properly made, and judicial review of the deduction was not required.[97] This decision by the Lords was a significant step in reassessing the limits of the exclusivity rule. Lords Bridge and Lowry favoured restricting the *O'Reilly* rule to situations in which the individual's *sole* aim was to challenge a public law act or decision; thus the rule would not apply when an action to vindicate private rights *might* involve some questions as to the validity of a public law decision.[98] In 1995, the Lords further limited the effect of *O'Reilly*, holding that a regulatory decision interpreting a statutory licence might be questioned by proceedings in the Commercial Court.[99] Subsequent decisions reinforced the trend towards greater procedural flexibility and discouraged reliance on procedural defences.[100]

The modern outcome of this trend is that the Civil Procedure Rules permit transfer into and out of judicial review proceedings: a transfer in either direction will be decided by a judge designated to sit in the Administrative Court, who will consider if the claim raises issues of public law to which Part 54 CPR should apply.[101] Since the time limit that applies to

[92] See Woolf, *Protection of the Public – A New Challenge*, ch 1; and (the same) [1986] PL 220; [1992] PL 221, 231.

[93] Wade and Forsyth, *Administrative Law* (8th edn, 2000), p 653.

[94] *Davy* v *Spelthorne Council* [1984] AC 262 (action in negligence relating to disputed enforcement notice).

[95] [1983] 2 AC 237, 285.

[96] *Wandsworth Council* v *Winder* [1985] AC 461.

[97] [1992] 1 AC 624 (P Cane [1992] PL 193).

[98] [1992] 1 AC 624, at 629 and 653 respectively.

[99] *Mercury Communications Ltd* v *Director General of Telecommunications* [1996] 1 All ER 575.

[100] See *Rye (Dennis) Pension Fund* v *Sheffield Council* [1997] 4 All ER 747 (county court action to secure payment of housing grant); *Steed* v *Home Secretary* [2000] 3 All ER 226 (HL); *Clark* v *University of Lincolnshire* [2000] 3 All ER 752; *D* v *Home Office* [2005] EWCA Civ 38, [2006] 1 All ER 183 (detained immigrants entitled to sue for damages on basis that their detention unlawful and not bound to seek judicial review); *Bunney* v *Burns Anderson* [2007] EWHC 1240 (Ch), [2007] 4 All ER 246.

[101] CPR, Part 30; CPR r 54.20. Where necessary, the same judge can hear both public and private law aspects of the same case by reconstituting herself as the Administrative Court or the Queen's Bench Division as applicable.

judicial review is much shorter than for most civil claims,[102] a case that begins as a claim for judicial review is unlikely to strike a problem of limitation if it is transferred into ordinary procedure. In the converse situation, where the judicial review time limit has not been observed even though the claim is solely concerned with public law issues, the judge may refuse to transfer the claim into judicial review procedure, and this may cause the claim to fail for abuse of process.[103] In general terms, the move from rigid, technical and arguably moribund procedural distinctions to ensuring that disputes are dealt with by the court in the manner which best suits the issues is clearly in the interests of substantive justice. Access to justice is not best achieved when the procedural steps taken to reach it are too readily misunderstood or are rendered unnecessarily difficult.

We have seen that in *O'Reilly*, Lord Diplock said that an exception to the rule of exclusivity could exist where the invalidity of an official decision arose 'as a collateral issue in a claim for infringement of a right of the plaintiff arising under private law'.[104] One form of collateral review occurs when tribunals whose task it is to decide whether a particular benefit should be paid to an individual under a statutory scheme are able to decide on the validity of the relevant regulations.[105] The issue of procedural exclusivity was raised when individuals sought to defend themselves against enforcement action by public authorities. It is now settled that an individual prosecuted for breach of subordinate legislation such as by-laws can as a defence plead that the legislation is invalid, and is not barred from doing so by failure to seek judicial review.[106] But under certain statutory schemes (for instance, the licensing of sex shops or the enforcement of planning control),[107] someone adversely affected by a public authority's decision may have no choice but to seek judicial review if he or she wishes to raise issues that will be outside the scope of a criminal court to determine.

C. The limitation and exclusion of judicial review

Statutory machinery for challenge

The technicalities of the prerogative remedies in their unreformed state often led in the past to legislation providing a simpler procedure for securing judicial review. Such legislation always related to specific powers of government and usually included provisions excluding other forms of judicial review.

An important example is provided by the standard procedure for the compulsory purchase of land. After a compulsory purchase order has been made by the local authority and, if objections have been raised, an inquiry has been held into the order, the minister must decide whether to confirm the order. If it is confirmed, there is a period of six weeks from the confirmation during which any person aggrieved by the purchase order may challenge the validity of the order in the High Court[108] on two grounds: (1) that the order is not within the powers of the enabling Act; or (2) that the requirements of the Act have not been complied

---

[102] See p 683 above.
[103] And see *Clark* v *University of Lincolnshire* (above).
[104] Page 690 above.
[105] *Chief Adjudication Officer* v *Foster* [1993] 1 All ER 705 (D Feldman (1992) 108 LQR 45 and A W Bradley [1992] PL 185).
[106] *Boddington* v *British Transport Police* [1999] 2 AC 143 (C Forsyth [1998] PL 364).
[107] Respectively *Quietlynn Ltd* v *Plymouth Council* [1988] QB 114; *R* v *Wicks* [1998] AC 92. And see A W Bradley [1997] PL 365.
[108] Or in Scotland in the Court of Session. On when the six weeks begin to run, see *Griffiths* v *Environment Secretary* [1983] 2 AC 51.

with and that the objector's interests have been substantially prejudiced thereby.[109] These grounds have been interpreted as covering all grounds upon which judicial review may be sought, including in (1) matters affecting vires, abuse of discretion and natural justice, and in (2) observance of all relevant statutory procedures.[110] When an aggrieved person makes an application to the High Court, the court may make an interim order suspending the purchase order, either generally or so far as it affects the applicant's property. If the order is not challenged in the High Court during the six-week period, the order is statutorily protected from challenge; any other form of judicial review of the order is excluded, before or after the confirmation of the order.[111]

This method of challenge, which first appeared in the Housing Act 1930, was a distinct improvement on legislative attempts to exclude judicial review of ministers' actions altogether and the remedy it provided was much more effective than reliance on the prerogative orders at common law. Today, it provides a statutory form of review in respect of many decisions relating to the control of land.[112] Use of this remedy has enabled the High Court to give its entire attention to the principles of judicial review in issue, uncomplicated by procedural or jurisdictional questions. The time limit on the right of challenge is necessary in order that, if no objection is taken promptly, the authorities concerned can put the decision into effect. By enabling there to be judicial review of executive decisions, they help to satisfy the requirements of art 6 ECHR.[113] In 2013, any judicial review of a decision under planning legislation was made subject to a six-week time limit (CPR, r 54.5(5)).

A tight time limit for bringing proceedings can be justified where the challenger is likely to have been involved in the events leading up to the challenge. Six weeks is tight but not unreasonable. Of more concern is the 30 days introduced for a judicial review of a public procurement matter (r. 54.5(6)), although this does align the position in judicial review with the time limit for proceedings brought directly under the Public Contracts Regulations 2006. There must, however, be a point at which a time limit becomes an effective bar to the bringing of any challenge. Where that point lies is likely to depend on the context in which the issue arises, including the importance of the rights and interests involved.

Statutory exclusion of judicial control[114]

When judges are interpreting legislation, they apply a strong presumption that the legislature does not intend access to the courts to be denied.[115] Where Parliament has appointed a specific tribunal for the enforcement of new rights and duties, it is necessary to have recourse to that tribunal in the first instance. In principle, the tribunal's decisions will be subject to judicial review, if rights of appeal are not provided instead. But many statutes have contained words intended to oust the jurisdiction of the courts. Such provisions have long been interpreted by the judges so as to leave, if possible, their supervisory powers intact.[116] One frequent clause was that a particular decision 'shall be final', but this does not exclude

---

[109] Acquisition of Land Act 1981, s 23 (consolidating earlier Acts).

[110] *Ashbridge Investments Ltd* v *Minister of Housing* [1965] 3 All ER 371; *Coleen Properties Ltd* v *Minister of Housing* [1971] 1 All ER 1049.

[111] Acquisition of Land Act 1981, s 23; and see p 694 below.

[112] E.g. Town and Country Planning Act 1990, ss 284–8; Planning and Compulsory Purchase Act 2004, s 113.

[113] See *R (Alconbury Developments Ltd)* v *Environment Secretary* [2001] UKHL 23, [2003] 2 AC 295 and *Bryan* v *UK* (1995) 21 EHRR 342.

[114] Wade and Forsyth, *Administrative Law*, pp 608–32; Craig, *Administrative Law*, ch 28.

[115] *R (Unison)* v *Lord Chancellor* [2017] UKSC 51 at [66]–[85] (Lord Reed) (employment tribunal fees unlawfully preventing access to justice and quashed as ultra vires).

[116] E.g. *Colonial Bank of Australasia* v *Willan* (1874) 5 PC 417 (express exclusion of certiorari not effective where manifest defect of jurisdiction).

judicial review.[117] Such a clause means simply that there is no right of appeal from the decision. Another clause which does not deprive the courts of supervisory jurisdiction is where a statutory order when made shall have effect 'as if enacted in the Act' which authorised it; the court may nonetheless hold the order to be invalid if it conflicts with provisions of the Act.[118] The fact that a tribunal is described by statute as a 'superior court of record' is not sufficient to exclude the supervisory jurisdiction of the High Court.[119]

It is then only by an exceptionally strong formula that Parliament can deprive the High Court or the Court of Session of supervisory jurisdiction over inferior tribunals and public authorities. As we have seen, exclusion clauses frequently accompany the granting of an express right to challenge the validity of an order or decision during a limited time. Thus, subject to the possibility of challenge to the order within six weeks of its confirmation, a compulsory purchase order 'shall not, either before or after it has been confirmed, made or given, be questioned in any legal proceedings whatsoever . . .'[120]

In *Smith* v *East Elloe Council* the plaintiff, whose land had been taken compulsorily for the building of council houses nearly six years previously, alleged that the making of the order had been caused by wrongful action and bad faith on the part of the council and its clerk. She submitted that the exclusion clause did not exclude the court's power in cases of fraud and bad faith. The House of Lords held by 3–2 that the effect of the Act was to protect compulsory purchase orders from judicial review except by statutory challenge during the six-week period. Although the validity of the order could no longer be challenged, the action against the clerk of the council for damages could proceed.[121]

A rather different attitude towards an exclusion clause was taken by the House of Lords in 1968 in a decision which we have already considered in relation to jurisdictional control.

In *Anisminic Ltd* v *Foreign Compensation Commission*, the Foreign Compensation Act 1950, s 4(4), provided that the determination by the commission of any application made under the Act 'shall not be called in question in any court of law'. The commission was a judicial body responsible for distributing funds supplied by foreign governments as compensation to British subjects. It rejected a claim made by Anisminic, for a reason which the company submitted was erroneous in law and exceeded the commission's jurisdiction. *Held*, by a majority, s 4(4) did not debar a court from inquiring whether the commission had made in law a correct decision on the question of eligibility to claim. 'Determination' meant a real determination, not a purported determination. By taking into account a factor which in the view of the majority was irrelevant to the scheme, the commission's decision was a nullity. Lord Wilberforce said, 'What would be the purpose of defining by statute the limits of a tribunal's powers, if by means of a clause inserted in the instrument of definition, those limits could safely be passed?'[122]

---

[117] *R* v *Medical Appeal Tribunal, ex p Gilmore* [1957] 1 QB 574.

[118] *Minister of Health* v *R* [1931] AC 494.

[119] *R (Cart)* v *Upper Tribunal* [2009] EWHC 3052 (Admin), [2010] 2 WLR 1012 (but note the distinction in respect of judicial review drawn between the Special Immigration Appeals Commission and the Upper Tribunal). The point was not discussed to the same degree in the Supreme Court: [2011] UKSC 28, [2012] 1 AC 663.

[120] Acquisition of Land Act 1981, s 25.

[121] [1956] AC 736.

[122] [1969] 2 AC 147, 208 (and ch 24 A above). For the legislative sequel, see Foreign Compensation Act 1969, s 3.

The decision is a striking example of the ability of the courts to interpret privative clauses in such a way as to maintain the possibility of judicial review. Although the authority of *Smith* v *East Elloe Council* was questioned in the *Anisminic* case, it was not overruled: indeed, the issues involved in considering the finality of a compulsory purchase order are different from those involved in considering whether an award of compensation should be subject to review. A further distinction is between a statute that seeks to exclude the jurisdiction of the courts entirely (as in *Anisminic*) and a statute that confers a right to apply to the courts for review within a stated time (as in the case of a compulsory purchase order) but excludes judicial review thereafter. In 1976, the statutory bar on attempts to challenge the validity of a purchase order after the six-week period was held to be absolute: an aggrieved owner could not bring such a challenge some months later, even though he alleged that the order had been vitiated by a breach of natural justice and good faith which he had only discovered after the six-week period.[123] Even if the purchase order must stand, this will not prevent the owner from seeking compensation from those responsible for acts which engage liability in tort.

In *A* v *B (Investigatory Powers Tribunal)*[124] a former member of the Security Service wished to publish a book about his work and had to seek consent from the Service to do so. Permission to publish parts of the manuscript was refused and he sought judicial review of that refusal, relying on his rights under article 10 ECHR. The Supreme Court held that, under the Regulation of Investigatory Powers Act 2000, only the Investigatory Powers Tribunal had jurisdiction to deal with the case. The 2000 Act said expressly that the Investigatory Powers Tribunal was 'the only appropriate tribunal' for the purposes of proceedings against the Security Service that relied on the Human Rights Act. The effect of the relevant legislation was to bring A's claim within the principle applied in *Barraclough* v *Brown*[125] and (distinguishing *Anisminic*) it was not open to the court to interpret the legislation so as to maintain the possibility of judicial review. Lord Brown concluded that: 'Parliament has not ousted judicial scrutiny of the acts of the intelligence services; it has simply allocated them to the Investigatory Powers Tribunal'.[126]

A slightly different issue arose in *R (Evans)* v *Attorney General*, under the Freedom of Information Act 2000.[127] Section 53 of that Act grants to ministers the power to issue a certificate overriding the decision of the Information Commissioner or judgment of a court or tribunal that certain information should be disclosed under the Act. That certificate can be challenged by way of judicial review, but the allocation to the executive of a power to veto a judicial decision is, as the Divisional Court put it, a 'constitutional aberration'.[128] In the Supreme Court, a judicial review of the certificate issued to prevent disclosure of letters written to ministers by the Prince of Wales succeeded. The judgment of Lord Neuberger drew a parallel with the principle established in *Anisminic* that any decision of the executive should be subject to review by the courts, holding that this logically extended to the insulation of the judicial decision from override by any actor other than Parliament.[129]

---

[123] *R* v *Environment Secretary, ex p Ostler* [1977] QB 122 (N P Gravells (1978) 41 MLR 383 and J E Alder (1980) 43 MLR 670). Also *R* v *Cornwall CC, ex p Huntington* [1994] 1 All ER 694.

[124] [2009] UKSC 9, [2010] 2 AC 1.

[125] [1897] AC 615 (statute creating a duty and providing a means of enforcing it).

[126] [2009] UKSC 9, [2010] 2 AC 1 at [23].

[127] [2015] UKSC 21, [2015] AC 1787; M Elliott [2015] PL 539.

[128] [2013] EWHC 1960 (Admin) at [2] (Lord Judge CJ); C J S Knight (2014) 130 LQR 38.

[129] The majority of the Supreme Court did not, however, adopt such a broad approach to s 53, which had after all been expressly adopted by Parliament. The basis upon which the certificate was quashed was a narrower complaint about the quality of the reasons and analysis adopted by the Attorney General in differing from the judicial decision he was purporting to veto: see C J S Knight (2015) 131 LQR 548.

Parliamentary authority to exclude judicial review

We have seen that in the debate about the foundations of judicial review even those who denied that parliamentary intent was the basis of judicial review accepted that Parliament could restrict or exclude judicial review in specific instances.[130] Today, an attempt by Parliament to do so might conflict with European law. Thus a certificate issued by the Secretary of State for Northern Ireland that purported to be 'conclusive evidence' that a police decision was taken for reasons of national security was held to be contrary to the principle of effective judicial control in EU law.[131] Employment tribunal fees which disproportionately prevented access to justice were not only a breach of common law principles, but were also in breach of EU law because many employment rights which would be vindicated in the tribunal are derived from EU law.[132] Where a matter concerns 'civil rights and obligations', exclusion of access to a court will violate art 6(1).[133] According to the Strasbourg case law, a national legislature may impose reasonable time limits on access to a court, but such restrictions must not impair the essence of the right.[134] The rule that judicial review must be sought promptly and in any event within three months would be likely to comply with art 6; so in most cases would the six-week rule on challenges to planning and compulsory purchase decisions. But an absolute exclusion of review after six weeks might be disproportionate in a case where relevant information is concealed by officials until after the right of access to a court has lapsed. No issues as to art 6 of the ECHR are raised by the exclusion of judicial review on matters that do not necessarily involve an individual's 'civil rights and obligations', such as the validity of an Act of the Scottish Parliament[135] or a Speaker's certificate under the Parliament Act 1911.[136]

Parliament has an uneven record in relation to the exclusion of the courts. The Franks committee in 1957 recommended that no statute should oust the prerogative orders. In response, the Tribunals and Inquiries Act 1958 (re-enacted in 1992, s 12) provided that:

(a) any provision in an Act passed before 1 August 1958 that any order or determination shall not be called into question in any court; or

(b) any provision in such an Act which by similar words excludes any of the powers of the High Court

shall not prevent the remedies of certiorari or mandamus (now quashing and mandatory orders) from being available. A more general provision protects the supervisory jurisdiction of the Court of Session. These provisions do not apply: (i) to an order or determination of a court of law, or (ii) where an Act makes provision for application to the High Court within a stated time (for example, the power to challenge a purchase order within six weeks, as in *Smith* v *East Elloe Council*).[137]

For several reasons, s 12 of the 1992 Act is far from being a sufficient response to the problem of ouster clauses. Section 12 has been held not to apply to 'conclusive evidence' clauses.[138] Given the developments in relation to judicial review in European law, there is a case to be made for a statute that would create a strong rule of interpretation to preserve the possibility of judicial review that would apply to all legislation, whenever enacted, on the lines of the

---

[130] Ch 24, at p 642.
[131] Case 222/84 *Johnston* v *Chief Constable RUC* [1987] QB 129.
[132] *R (Unison)* v *Lord Chancellor* [2017] UKSC 51.
[133] See e.g. *Zander* v *Sweden* (1993) 18 EHRR 175 and *Fayed* v *UK* (1994) 18 EHRR 393.
[134] *Stubbings* v *UK* (1996) 23 EHRR 213.
[135] Scotland Act 1998, s 28(5).
[136] Parliament Act 1911, s 3.
[137] *Hamilton* v *Scottish Secretary* 1972 SLT 233.
[138] *R* v *Registrar of Companies, ex p Central Bank of India* [1986] QB 1114. A different view of 'conclusive evidence' clauses might be taken in other contexts.

Human Rights Act 1998, s 3. Such a rule would not block a determined attempt by the executive to remove judicial review from one or more areas of government. But if such an attempt were made in Parliament, it might help to ensure that the two Houses would rigorously scrutinise the government's proposals and motivation.[139]

The need for such scrutiny was tested by a remarkable attempted ouster clause in the Asylum and Immigration (Treatment of Claimants etc.) Bill 2004. The government sought to remove the right to judicial review of decisions by the proposed Asylum and Immigration Tribunal, and of deportation and removal decisions made by the Home Secretary and officials. The clause expressly excluded a court from considering proceedings to determine whether a purported determination or decision was a nullity by reason of lack of jurisdiction, irregularity, error of law, breach of natural justice or any other matter; limited provision was made for review in case of bad faith or if Convention rights were affected.[140] The clause passed through a complaisant House of Commons but was withdrawn by the government before it was debated in the Lords. It raised fundamental questions about the authority of Parliament to dispense with an independent and impartial scheme of judicial review.[141]

D. Remedies and relief

Remedial discretion in judicial review proceedings

It has been said that judicial discretion is at the heart of administrative law.[142] Certainly, a judge has discretion to exercise at the permission stage, for instance relating to an issue of delay or alternative remedy. A study of how this discretion is exercised has shown that, especially since 2000, when permission became generally a matter to be decided on the papers (which may include the defendant's response), there has been a decline in the percentage of claims for which permission is granted.[143] In *R (Cowl) v Plymouth Council*,[144] the Court of Appeal drew attention to the importance of avoiding litigation whenever possible, and held that in the early stages of a claim for judicial review, the parties and (if necessary at the permission stage) the judge should actively consider alternative ways of resolving the dispute, whether by use of alternative procedures such as a statutory complaints procedure, or of other means such as mediation that are available under the Civil Procedure Rules.[145]

At the substantive hearing, the court exercises further discretion in deciding whether to grant relief even if grounds for review have been established. Although a judge may be reluctant to withhold relief in such a case,[146] relief has been denied for reasons such as the applicant's

---

[139] For consideration of legislation that removed or substantially impaired the role of the High Court in judicial review, see Lord Woolf [1995] PL 57, 68; cf the comments of Lord Irvine [1996] PL 59, 75–8.

[140] The text of the clause is at [2004] JR 97, with related articles and parliamentary materials. See also Lord Woolf [2004] CLJ 317; A Le Sueur [2004] PL 225; and ch 20 B.

[141] See the discussion of ouster clauses in *Jackson* v *Attorney General* [2005] UKHL 56; [2006] 1 AC 262.

[142] See Lord Cooke, in Forsyth and Hare (eds), *The Golden Metwand and the Crooked Cord*, pp 203–20. Also Lewis, *Judicial Remedies in Public Law*, ch 11.

[143] V Bondy and M Sunkin [2008] PL 647. In 2006, the success rate in non-immigration civil cases of judicial review was 35 per cent and in asylum and immigration cases, 14 per cent. Overall it was 22 per cent.

[144] [2001] EWCA Civ 1935, [2002] 1 WLR 803. Although pursuit of alternative dispute resolution or pre-action correspondence does not provide a reason the claim could not be brought within time: *R (Finn-Kelcey) v Milton Keynes Council* [2008] EWCA Civ 1067, [2009] Env LR 17.

[145] On the use of alternative dispute resolution in administrative law, see M Supperstone, D Stilitz and C Sheldon [2006] PL 299 and S Boyron [2006] PL 247. On the increasing likelihood that claims for judicial review will be settled by consent, not by adjudication, see V Bondy and M Sunkin [2009] PL 237.

[146] See T Bingham [1991] PL 64. Also S Sedley [1989] PL 32 (criticising the use of discretion in *R v Chief Constable of North Wales, e p Evans* [1982] 3 All ER 141).

conduct and motives[147] and the public inconvenience that a remedy might entail.[148] Relief was withheld where planning permission had been granted on the basis of a factual error, but the court was satisfied that it would have been granted apart from this.[149] Similar flexibility was shown when, in reviewing decisions of the City's Take-over Panel, the Court of Appeal stated that in that context the court would see its role as 'historic rather than contemporaneous', i.e. that the court would seek to guide the panel in its future conduct of affairs, not to intervene in ongoing takeover battles.[150] It is one thing to hold that the findings of the court speak for themselves and that no declaration is needed,[151] but it is much less justifiable, when a claimant has made out his or her case, for the court in its discretion to discover reasons for withholding relief. Although there have been suggestions that the courts should ordinarily decline to quash an ultra vires statutory instrument,[152] Buxton LJ firmly restated the correct position in *R (C)* v *Justice Secretary*:

> the court has discretion to withhold relief if there are pressing reasons for not disturbing the status quo. It is, however, wrong to think that delegated legislation has some specially protected position in that respect. If anything, the imperative that public life should be conducted lawfully suggests that it is more important to correct unlawful legislation, that until quashed is universally binding and used by the public as a guide to conduct, than it is to correct a single decision, that affects only a limited range of people.[153]

There will, however, be circumstances in which the scale of the impact of a quashing order on a statutory scheme will go so far beyond the facts of the particular case that only declaratory relief should be granted, to avoid a detrimental effect on public administration. This may be particularly true for claims against secondary legislation under the Human Rights Act 1998.[154]

Section 31 of the Senior Courts Act 1981 was amended by the Criminal Justice and Courts Act 2015 to introduce a new restriction concerning relief. Under s 31(2A), the court must refuse to grant relief 'if it appears to the court to be highly likely that the outcome for the applicant would not have been substantially different if the conduct complained of had not occurred'.[155] There is an exception where the court considers that relief would nonetheless be in the 'exceptional public interest': s 31(2B). This is of particular importance in claims which allege procedural failings; the avoidance of so-called 'technical' errors which would be unlikely to affect the substantive outcome was precisely the point of the amendment.[156] The provision has been regularly applied to such cases, albeit with relatively limited detailed judicial consideration of each element of the statutory wording. Where reliance on the new provision has failed, it has been because the court cannot be sufficiently clear

---

[147] E.g. *R* v *Commissioners of Customs and Excise, ex p Cooke* [1970] 1 All ER 1068.

[148] *R* v *Social Services Secretary, ex p Association of Metropolitan Authorities* [1986] 1 All ER 164.

[149] *R* v *North Somerset Council, ex p Cadbury Garden Centre Ltd, The Times*, 22 November 2000.

[150] *R* v *Panel on Take-overs and Mergers, ex p Datafin plc* [1987] QB 815. And see C Lewis [1988] PL 78.

[151] Although in *R (Hunt)* v *North Somerset Council* [2015] UKSC 51, [2015] 1 WLR 3575, the Supreme Court indicated that a declaration would usually be appropriate where no other relief was granted, but that where experienced counsel had not asked for a declaration, one was not required. The form of the relief would not usually alter the position as to costs.

[152] *R* v *Social Services Secretary, ex p Association of Metropolitan Authorities* [1986] 1 All ER 164.

[153] [2008] EWCA Civ 882, [2009] QB 657 at [41]. For an example of a refusal to quash for minor procedural breaches see: *R (Hurley)* v *Business Secretary* [2012] EWHC 201 (Admin), [2012] HRLR 13.

[154] See *R (T)* v *Greater Manchester Police* [2014] UKSC 35; [2015] AC 49, in which the criminal records and rehabilitation of offenders legislation was left in place.

[155] If the court considers that this test is met when it is considering permission on the papers, it must refuse permission: s 31(3C)–(3D). That applies whether or not it has been raised by the parties.

[156] A Mills [2015] PL 583, 586–8.

about whether a correctly adopted procedure, such as a consultation, would make a substantive difference to the outcome.[157] Simply because a statutory duty which is important has not been complied with, that is not sufficient to engage an exceptional public interest.[158] Use of the test can give rise to difficult tactical decisions for a public authority: if evidence is tendered to the effect that conducting the process again without the alleged fault would make no difference, the decision-maker exposes themselves to the risk of an accusation of having pre-emptively shut their eyes to any new information or representations, or of having pre-determined the matter.

Forms of relief

When the action or decision of a public authority or official is challenged by judicial review, the claimant may ask the court to provide one or more of the following forms of relief against the defendant:

(a) to quash, or set aside as a nullity, a decision that is ultra vires or otherwise unlawful;

(b) to restrain the defendant from acting ultra vires or otherwise unlawfully;

(c) to order the defendant to perform its lawful duties;

(d) to declare the rights and duties of the parties;

(e) to order the defendant to pay compensation for loss or injury suffered; and

(f) to secure temporary relief, pending the outcome of the proceedings.

The main defect in English law used to be that while procedures existed for all these forms of relief to be obtained, there was no single procedure for doing so. Often the procedures for obtaining one or more of these reliefs were mutually incompatible and the law was fragmented into the law of different remedies. The main effect of the reforms was that certain remedies which had long been available – namely the prerogative orders (mandamus, prohibition and certiorari), injunctions and declarations – became forms of relief[159] obtainable by the single procedure of application for judicial review. In 2004, more re-naming took place when the prerogative orders lost their historic names: they are now known as mandatory orders, prohibiting orders and quashing orders.[160] Here references to the present procedure will wherever possible use this terminology.

The prerogative orders

The prerogative writs of mandamus, prohibition and certiorari (later restyled orders)[161] were the principal means by which the former Court of King's Bench exercised jurisdiction over local justices and other bodies.[162] Although the writs issued on the application of private persons, the word 'prerogative' was apt because they had sprung from the right of the Crown to ensure that justice was done by inferior courts and tribunals. The Crown as such played no part in the proceedings, and orders could be sought by or against a minister or a government department. Since the prerogative orders upheld the public interest in the administration of

---

[157] See, e.g.: *Public and Commercial Services Union v Minister for the Cabinet Office* [2017] EWHC 1787 (Admin); *R (Bokrosova) v Lambeth LBC* [2015] EWHC 3386 (Admin), [2016] PTSR 355.

[158] *R (Hawke) v Justice Secretary* [2015] EWHC 4093 (Admin).

[159] Senior Courts Act 1981, s 31(1). This Act was enacted as the Supreme Court Act 1981 but it was re-named by the Constitutional Reform Act 2005, which created the present Supreme Court.

[160] Senior Courts Act 1981, ss 29 and 31, as amended.

[161] Administration of Justice (Miscellaneous Provisions) Acts 1933, s 5, and 1938, s 7.

[162] Henderson, *Foundations of English Administrative Law*.

justice, aspects of the procedure (in particular, the need for leave from the court, the summary procedure and the discretionary remedies) were significantly different from litigation that protected an individual's private rights.

A *mandatory order* is an order from the High Court commanding a public authority or official to perform a public duty, in the performance of which the applicant has a sufficient legal interest. The order does not lie against the Crown as such. However, it may enforce performance of a duty imposed by statute on a minister or on a department or on named civil servants, provided that the duty is one which is owed to the applicant and not merely to the Crown.[163]

A mandatory order will not lie if the authority has complete discretion whether to act or not. But there may be a duty to exercise a discretion or to make a decision, such as the duty of a tribunal to hear and determine a case within its jurisdiction. Thus the Home Secretary was required by mandamus to determine an application by the wife of a UK citizen for a certificate to which she was entitled, and which would enable her to enter the United Kingdom.[164] So too the statutory duty of a tribunal to give reasons for its decisions may be enforced in this way. The DPP was required to promulgate a policy identifying the facts and circumstances he considered relevant to any decision to prosecute an individual for aiding and abetting suicide, but the Law Lords stopped short of mandating what those issues should be.[165] Failure to comply is a contempt of court and is punishable accordingly.

A *prohibiting order* is an order issued to prevent a public body from exceeding its jurisdiction, or acting contrary to the rules of natural justice, where something remains to be done which can be prohibited. It must be possible to identify an act or decision the public body might take which should be prohibited.

A *quashing order* (formerly certiorari) is today a means of quashing decisions by public authorities where one or more grounds for judicial review exist. By setting aside a defective decision, a quashing order enables a fresh decision to be taken, albeit that the decision-maker's freedom is likely to be heavily circumscribed by the judgment of the court.[166] A quashing order will usually have the effect that the act was always of no legal effect[167] and it must attach to a specific identified act or decision. Although there are suggestions that an ultra vires act is a nullity such that no quashing order is required, the better view is that the order should be granted, if only to ensure clarity.[168]

A combination of the orders may be sought in the same proceedings, such as when a decision in excess of jurisdiction has already been made and other similar decisions have yet to be made,[169] or in order to quash a decision in excess of jurisdiction and then to compel the tribunal to hear and determine the case according to law.[170]

Although both certiorari and prohibition originated as means of supervising inferior courts and tribunals, they have long been available against ministers, departments, local authorities and other administrative bodies. In 1988, the House of Lords held that the governor of a

---

[163] *R v Special Commissioners for Income Tax* (1888) 21 QBD 313, 317. Cf *R v Lords of the Treasury* (1872) LR 7 QB 387.

[164] *R v Home Secretary, ex p Phansopkar* [1976] QB 606.

[165] *R (Purdy) v Director of Public Prosecutions* [2009] UKHL 45, [2010] 1 AC 345.

[166] E.g. *R (A) v Lord Saville of Newdigate (No.2)* [2001] EWCA Civ 2048, [2002] 1 WLR 1249.

[167] *Mossell (Jamaica) Ltd v Office of Utilities Regulation* [2010] UKPC 1 at [44] (Lord Phillips); *Ahmed v HM Treasury* [2010] UKSC 5, [2010] 2 AC 534; V S Nadhamuni [2015] PL 596.

[168] Contrast *R v Dorking Justices, ex p Harrington* [1984] AC 743, 753 with *R v Hendon Justices, ex p DPP* [1994] QB 167, 178 and Lewis, *Judicial Remedies in Public Law*, p 229. For an interesting attack on the nullity theory, see T Adams [2017] CLJ 289.

[169] *R v Paddington Rent Tribunal, ex p Bell Properties Ltd* [1949] 1 KB 666.

[170] E.g. *R v Hammersmith Coroner, ex p Peach* [1980] QB 211.

prison was also subject to judicial review and Lord Bridge spoke in terms that made clear how much the language of debate had changed:

> The principle is now as well established as any principle can be in the developing field of public law that where any person or body exercises a power conferred by statute which affects the rights or legitimate expectations of citizens and is of a kind which the law requires to be exercised in accordance with natural justice, the court has jurisdiction to review the exercise of that power.[171]

In other words, if the power to make such decisions existed, no separate issue arose as to the availability of a remedy. These decisions concerned the exercise of statutory powers, but the supervisory jurisdiction extended also to prerogative powers and to certain regulatory powers, even if they did not derive from statute.[172]

Injunctions[173]

While the prerogative orders enabled the courts to exercise a supervisory jurisdiction over inferior tribunals and public authorities, the injunction is an equitable remedy available in all branches of law, public and private, to protect a person's rights against unlawful infringement. It is an order which may require or prohibit a person from doing something. Given the obvious overlap with the prerogative remedies, there are not many cases in which a final injunction is sought in judicial review proceedings.

Nonetheless, certain aspects of the law on injunctions may be noted. First, injunctions are not available against 'the Crown' as a legal entity, and they are not available in private law proceedings brought directly against the Crown.[174] In place of an injunction in private law proceedings against the Crown, the court may make an order declaring the rights of the parties, and if necessary the court may grant an interim declaration, which the Crown would be expected to observe.[175] However, EU law may require injunctive relief to be available against the Crown.[176] In 1994, the House of Lords cut down the immunity of the Crown as an entity by holding that an injunction may be issued in judicial review proceedings against government departments, ministers and civil servants.[177]

A second matter concerns the historic procedure known as the 'relator action'. This name was given to an action by a private person seeking an injunction on a matter of public right (such as a public nuisance caused by obstruction of a highway) in which he or she did not have a personal right or interest sufficient to sue in his or her name.[178] This difficulty was overcome by the Attorney General, as guardian of the public interest, consenting to his name being used as nominal plaintiff. Relator actions are now very rare indeed, mainly for the reason that judicial review will nearly always be available (by the usual procedure) whenever a claimant wishes to restrain unlawful action by a public authority. Relator actions have occasionally been used in a different way to enforce the criminal law, when existing penalties are inadequate to deter breaches of the law, for example when planning controls or fire precautions are ignored by those who find it profitable to break the law.[179] Another reason for the

---

[171] *Leech* v *Deputy Governor of Parkhurst Prison* [1988] AC 533, 561.

[172] Respectively *R* v *Criminal Injuries Compensation Board, ex p Lain* [1967] 2 QB 864; and *R* v *Panel on Takeovers, ex p Datafin plc* [1987] QB 815.

[173] Lewis, *Judicial Remedies in Public Law*, ch 8; Wade and Forsyth, *Administrative Law*, pp 478–83.

[174] Crown Proceedings Act 1947, s 21; ch 26 D.

[175] Civil Procedure Rules, r 25.1(1). For the former position, see *R* v *IRC, ex p Rossminster Ltd* [1980] AC 952.

[176] *R* v *Transport Secretary, ex p Factortame Ltd* [1990] 2 AC 85; (The same) *(No 2)* [1991] 1 AC 603.

[177] *M* v *Home Office* [1994] 1 AC 377.

[178] See *Benjamin* v *Storr* (1874) LR 9 CP 400; *Boyce* v *Paddington BC* [1903] 1 Ch 109; *Barrs* v *Bethell* [1982] Ch 294.

[179] *A-G* v *Bastow* [1957] 1 QB 514; *A-G* v *Harris* [1961] 1 QB 74; *A-G* v *Chaudry* [1971] 3 All ER 938.

rarity of relator actions is that a local authority may under the Local Government Act 1972, s 222, institute proceedings in its own name when it considers it expedient to do so for promoting the interests of local inhabitants.[180] Significantly, there is no recorded instance of a relator action against a government department.

Finally, the High Court may grant an injunction to restrain a person from acting in an office to which he or she is not entitled and may declare the office to be vacant. This procedure takes the place of the ancient process of an information in the nature of a writ of *quo warranto*.[181]

Declaratory relief[182]

Declaratory relief is a form of order which merely declares the legal relationship of the parties and is not accompanied by any sanction or means of enforcement. The authority of a court's ruling on law is such that declaratory relief will normally be enough to restrain both the Crown and public authorities from illegal conduct, although it may not impose a particular time period within which corrective steps are required. Under the Civil Procedure Rules, r 40.20: 'The courts may make binding declarations whether or not any other remedy is claimed.' A declaration may be granted when a prerogative remedy would not be.[183]

It is convenient in some public law disputes for the law to be determined in relation to particular facts without a need to seek a coercive remedy. An early example arose in *Dyson v Attorney-General*, where a taxpayer obtained a declaration against the Crown that the tax authorities had no power to request certain information from him on pain of a £50 penalty for disobedience.[184] The jurisdiction to grant declarations is as wide as the law itself, except that the judges may as a matter of discretion impose limits on its use. Thus an action for a declaration must be based on a concrete case which has arisen. The courts are reluctant to grant a bare declaration that can have no legal consequences[185] and will not give answers to hypothetical questions that have been raised in the absence of any genuine dispute about the subject matter.[186] However, courts have reviewed the legality of advisory guidance that in itself has no legal effect.[187] The courts have been understandably reluctant to be forced into making a declaration on matters of high policy about which there is much controversy; for example, a declaration that the invasion of Iraq in 2003 was unlawful in international law was refused as contrary to the public interest.[188]

The court will not give a declaratory opinion in civil proceedings as to a matter that is in issue in concurrent criminal proceedings[189] and, even at the request of the Attorney General,

---

[180] *Stoke-on-Trent Council v B & Q (Retail) Ltd* [1984] AC 754; *Kirklees Council v Wickes Building Supplies Ltd* [1993] AC 227. And see B Hough [1992] PL 130.

[181] Senior Courts Act 1981, s 30; cf Local Government Act 1972, s 92.

[182] Lewis, *Judicial Remedies in Public Law*, ch 7; Zamir and Woolf, *The Declaratory Judgment*. Although the term 'declaratory judgment' is often used, it is appropriate to distinguish declaratory relief (i.e. an order issued by the court which formally declares a particular legal outcome) and a declaratory judgment (in which the reasoning makes clear the legal position but no formal relief is set out in the order).

[183] *R v Employment Secretary, ex p Equal Opportunities Commission* [1995] 1 AC 1; Senior Courts Act 1981, s 31(2).

[184] [1912] 1 Ch 158.

[185] *Maxwell v Dept of Trade* [1974] QB 523.

[186] *R (Rusbridger) v A-G* [2003] UKHL 38, [2004] 1 AC 357.

[187] E.g. *Gillick v West Norfolk Health Authority* [1986] AC 112. In 1994, the Law Commission recommended that the High Court be authorised in its judicial review jurisdiction to make advisory declarations on points of general importance: Law Com No 226, pp 74–6. And see J Laws (1994) 57 MLR 213.

[188] *R (Campaign for Nuclear Disarmament) v Prime Minister* [2002] EWHC 2777 (Admin).

[189] *Imperial Tobacco Ltd v A-G* [1981] AC 718.

will not grant a declaration that conduct would be criminal except in a very clear case.[190] Where a statute both creates a duty and provides the procedure for enforcing it, this may exclude declaratory proceedings.[191] But the existence of a statutory procedure for obtaining a decision on whether planning permission was needed did not prevent a landowner from coming to court for a declaration as to the extent of existing development rights.[192]

The Human Rights Act 1998, by enlarging the jurisdiction of the courts in protecting European Convention rights, has necessarily broadened the potential scope of declarations. A special feature of the Act is the power that it gives to a superior court to declare that a statutory provision that cannot be interpreted in a way that is consistent with a Convention right is incompatible with the right. A 'declaration of incompatibility' of this kind has distinctive features that do not apply to the declaratory relief discussed above. In particular, a declaration of incompatibility does not affect the validity, operation or enforcement of the statutory provision to which it relates, and it 'is not binding on the parties to the proceedings in which it is made'.[193] These unusual limitations do not apply when the court makes a declaration in customary form regarding the powers of a public authority, in a case that does not require the court to rule on the compatibility of primary legislation with Convention rights.

Habeas corpus[194]

The prerogative writ of habeas corpus is in English law an important remedy in respect of public or private action which takes away individual liberty. It was formerly used as the means of securing judicial control of executive acts in extradition law,[195] and it is still used to a lesser extent in other areas involving detention, such as immigration control,[196] mental health,[197] child care[198] and criminal procedure.[199] Unlike the prerogative orders, the writ has not been the subject of recent legislative reform. The writ originally enabled a court of common law to summon persons whose presence was necessary for pending proceedings. In the 15th and 16th centuries, King's Bench and Common Pleas used habeas corpus to assert their authority over rival courts and to release persons imprisoned by such courts in excess of their jurisdiction. In the 17th century, the writ was used to check arbitrary arrest by order of the King or the King's Council.[200]

It was of the essence of habeas corpus that it was a procedure by which the court could determine the legality of an individual's detention, effectively and without delay. Habeas Corpus Acts were enacted in 1679, 1816 and 1862,[201] not to widen the jurisdiction of the courts but to enhance the effectiveness of the writ and to ensure that applications were dealt

---

[190] *A–G v Able* [1984] QB 795. Special considerations arise in medical cases where a patient cannot consent to treatment: e.g. *F (Mental Patient: Sterilisation)* [1990] 2 AC 1; *Airedale NHS Trust v Bland* [1993] AC 789; cf *R (Pretty) v DPP* [2001] UKHL 61, [2002] 1 AC 800.

[191] *Barraclough v Brown* [1897] AC 615.

[192] *Pyx Granite Co Ltd v Ministry of Housing* [1960] AC 260.

[193] Human Rights Act 1998, s 4(5).

[194] See Farbey, Sharpe and Atrill, *The Law of Habeas Corpus*; Clark and McCoy, *The Most Fundamental Legal Right*; Lewis, *Judicial Remedies in Public Law*, ch 12. See also S Brown [2000] PL 31.

[195] On the exclusion of habeas corpus by the Extradition Act 2003, see *R (Hilali) v Governor of Whitemoor Prison* [2008] UKHL 3, [2008] AC 805.

[196] E.g. *R v Durham Prison (Governor), ex p Hardial Singh* [1984] 1 All ER 983; and *Tan Te Lam v Superintendent of Tai A Chau Detention Centre* [1997] AC 97.

[197] E.g. *Re S–C (mental patient)* [1996] QB 599; *GD v Edgware Community Hospital* [2008] EWHC 3572 (Admin).

[198] *LM v Essex CC* (1999) 1 FLR 988.

[199] *R (Bentham) v Governor of Wandsworth Prison* [2006] EWHC 121 (QB).

[200] For *Darnel*'s case and the Petition of Right, see ch 10 D.

[201] For the detail, see Taswell-Langmead, *English Constitutional History*, pp 432–6.

with promptly. Thus the 1679 Act prohibited evasion of habeas corpus by transfer of prisoners detained for 'any criminal or supposed criminal matter' to places outside the jurisdiction of the English courts on pain of heavy penalties. The 1816 Act gave the judge power in civil cases to inquire summarily into the truth of the facts stated in the gaoler's return to the writ, even though the return was 'good and sufficient in law'.[202] The 1862 Act provided that the writ was not to issue from a court in England into any colony or foreign dominion of the Crown where there were courts having authority to grant habeas corpus. Detention within Northern Ireland and Scotland is a matter for the courts in those jurisdictions.[203]

Habeas corpus is described as a writ of right which is granted *ex debito justitiae*. This means that a prima facie case must be shown before it is issued but, unlike the prerogative orders, it is not a discretionary remedy and it may not be refused merely because an alternative remedy exists.[204] Habeas corpus is a remedy against *unlawful* detention: thus it enabled the court to decide whether a profoundly retarded and autistic person incapable of giving consent could be detained under the Mental Health Act 1983 without an order being made for compulsory detention.[205] This decision concerned the limits of a hospital trust's statutory powers of detention. It is more difficult to know whether habeas corpus is a remedy for correcting every error made by a body with power to detain.

Certainly, the writ does not provide a right of appeal for those detained by order of a court or tribunal. It might be supposed that habeas corpus lies whenever there are grounds for judicial review of a decision to detain someone, but the position is much less clear-cut than this. Indeed, the reforms in judicial review procedure that we have considered in this chapter did not apply to habeas corpus, and the two procedures remain separate. In *Rutty*'s case,[206] the High Court, acting under the Habeas Corpus Act 1816 to examine the truth of the facts stated in the return, held that there had been no evidence before the magistrate eight years earlier to justify an order that an 18-year-old woman with learning difficulties be detained. But in a line of immigration cases during the 1970s, the courts were most reluctant to make effective use of habeas corpus as a means of reviewing executive decisions, for example in the case of someone about to be removed from the country as an illegal entrant.[207] We have seen that in *Khawaja*'s case the House of Lords reversed this trend.[208]

During the 1990s, the Court of Appeal distinguished between the scope of habeas corpus and the grounds of judicial review, holding that habeas corpus could mount a challenge to the jurisdiction or vires of a detention decision, but not if the decision was 'within the powers' of the decision-maker yet was defective for reasons such as procedural error, mistake of law, or unreasonableness. The reason given for this limitation on habeas corpus was that, in the latter class of cases, the decision was lawful until it had been quashed.[209] However, this approach seems deeply flawed: it is based on an outdated distinction (between 'errors as to jurisdiction' and 'errors within jurisdiction') which has ceased to apply in judicial review generally. It is now settled that breaches of natural justice, errors of law and so on cause a decision to be ultra vires:[210] how then can such a decision be held to be 'within powers' in the law of habeas corpus? When individual liberty is at stake, it would be unjust for the court to refuse habeas

---

[202] See e.g. *R v Board of Control, ex p Rutty* [1956] 2 QB 109.

[203] *Re Keenan* [1972] 1 QB 533; *Re McElduff* [1972] NILR 1; *R v Cowle* (1759) 2 Burr 834, 856.

[204] *R v Governor of Pentonville Prison, ex p Azam* [1974] AC 18, 31 (CA).

[205] *R v Bournewood NHS Trust, ex p L* [1999] 1 AC 458.

[206] Note 202 above.

[207] The decisions include *R v Home Secretary, ex p Mughal* [1974] 1 QB 313 and *R v Home Secretary, ex p Zamir* [1980] AC 930. And see C Newdick [1982] PL 89.

[208] *R v Home Secretary, ex p Khawaja* [1984] AC 74 and ch 26 A.

[209] *R v Home Secretary, ex p Cheblak* [1991] 2 All ER 319; *R v Home Secretary, ex p Muboyayi* [1992] 1 QB 244.

[210] See *Ridge v Baldwin* [1964] AC 40; *Anisminic Ltd v Foreign Compensation Commission* [1969] 2 AC 147; *R v Hull University Visitor, ex p Page* [1993] AC 682.

corpus to someone who had shown that the decision to detain him or her was ultra vires but first required to be quashed by certiorari: to avoid the injustice, the court would need to grant the detainee permission to apply for judicial review and to quash the decision concerned forthwith. Although this approach has been authoritatively criticised for eroding habeas corpus,[211] it was applied in 1996 where young persons had been wrongly imprisoned for non-payment of fines, and the court held that their detention could be challenged by judicial review, but not by habeas corpus.[212]

This uncertainty affecting habeas corpus is reflected in case law at Strasbourg: the European Court of Human Rights held in the case of a mental patient that habeas corpus did not enable the English court to determine both the substantive and formal legality of the detention,[213] but reached the opposite conclusion in the case of persons suspected of terrorist offences.[214] By art 5(4) ECHR, every person who is detained is entitled to take proceedings by which the lawfulness of the detention is decided speedily by a court, and release is ordered if the detention is unlawful. This is one of the most fundamental of all human rights and art 5(4) is known in Europe as 'the habeas corpus provision'.[215] The awkward interface that has developed in English law between habeas corpus and judicial review needs to be resolved.[216] One possible reform would be to amend the Senior Courts Act 1981, s 31, to add an order of habeas corpus to the forms of relief that may be granted on judicial review, and this would leave intact the law on the writ of habeas corpus. In practice, it is already possible for an applicant to apply both for habeas corpus and, in the alternative, by judicial review for a mandatory order directing release on conditions.[217]

One consequence at a global level of the fears for national security arising from the 11 September attacks on the United States in 2001 is the practice of 'extraordinary rendition', by which persons suspected of links with terrorism are transferred between states and may be held for years without trial. The ancient process of habeas corpus has been invoked both in the United States[218] and in the United Kingdom in attempts to subject rendition to the rule of law. In *Rahmatullah* v *Foreign Secretary* a citizen of Pakistan had in February 2004 been detained by British forces serving in Iraq.[219]

> He was handed over to American forces and taken to the Bagram airbase in Afghanistan, where he was detained. In 2010, a US review board determined that he was not 'an enduring security threat' and that he should be released to Pakistan. But by October 2012, he was still detained. On Rahmatullah's behalf, habeas corpus was sought in the English courts against the British Foreign and Defence Secretaries; it was argued that his detention was unlawful and that the government retained had a sufficient degree of control over him to

---

[211] Law Commission, Law Com No 226, part XI; H W R Wade (1997) 113 LQR 55. Also A Le Sueur [1992] PL 13; M Shrimpton [1993] PL 24.

[212] *R* v *Oldham Justices, ex p Cawley* [1997] QB 1. And see S Brown [2000] PL 31. Cf *Re S-C (mental patient)* [1996] QB 599 (habeas corpus granted when social worker's application for S-C's detention was untruthful).

[213] *X* v *UK* (1981) 4 EHRR 188.

[214] *Brogan* v *UK* (1988) 11 EHRR 117.

[215] Harris, O'Boyle and Warbrick, *Law of the ECHR*, pp 182–96.

[216] See e.g. *B* v *Barking, Havering and Brentwood NHS Trust* (1999) 1 FLR 106; *Sheikh* v *Home Secretary* [2001] ACD 93; and O Davies [1997] JR 11. Although it was observed in passing in *R (Shields-McKinley)* v *Justice Secretary* [2017] EWHC 658 (Admin) at [95] (Holroyde J) that claims for the two were 'interlinked, with a number of features in common'.

[217] See *R (A and others)* v *Home Secretary* [2007] EWHC 142 (Admin).

[218] See *Boumediene* v *Bush* (2008) 553 US 723.

[219] [2012] UKSC 48, [2013] 1 AC 614; H Hooper [2013] PL 213.

> secure his release. This degree of control arose from a Memorandum of Understanding between the US, UK and Australian governments in 2003 which stated that transfer of prisoners of war and civilian detainees between the three states must comply with the relevant Geneva Conventions; it provided that someone such as Rahmatullah, detained by UK forces, 'will be returned' by the United States to the United Kingdom 'without delay upon request' by the United Kingdom.

The Supreme Court held unanimously that there was prima facie evidence that Rahmatullah was illegally detained and that, even though the Secretaries of State did not have physical control of him, there were grounds on which they could claim to assert control, such that there was a reasonable prospect that they could produce him to the court. These grounds arose from the Memorandum of Understanding in 2003 and the United Kingdom's obligations under the Geneva Conventions. For the court to order the Secretaries of State to make a return to the writ of habeas corpus did not involve the court in intruding upon issues of foreign policy and diplomacy. However, it was also held (by 5–2) that a sufficient return to the writ had already been made by the Secretaries of State, as they had made clear the US view that the continued detention was lawful and that if he were to be released, he would be released to Pakistan. Lady Hale and Lord Carnwath dissented: in their view, the strength of habeas corpus is its simplicity; if Rahmatullah had not been handed over to the US forces, he would have been released long ago. 'Where liberty is at stake, it is not the court's job to speculate as to the political sensitivities which may be in play'.[220] In this minority view, the Secretaries of State should have been ordered to request the US authorities to transfer Rahmatullah back to UK custody, in conformity with the Memorandum of Understanding of 2003.

The outcome was that the UK courts, whilst reinvigorating habeas corpus in theory, provided no tangible support for someone detained without trial for over eight years, most of that time outside the UK jurisdiction. A key question not addressed in the judgments is how the Memorandum of Understanding could create rights and obligations in the absence of an Act of Parliament to give it the force of law. But the judges must have had in mind the Geneva Conventions Act 1957, s 1, that makes a grave breach of the relevant Conventions a criminal offence.

Normally the applicant for habeas corpus will be the person detained, but a relative or other person may apply on his or her behalf if the detainee cannot do so. Application is made to the High Court ex parte (that is, without the other side being heard) supported by an affidavit or statement of fact.[221] If prima facie grounds are shown, the court ordinarily directs that notice of motion be given to the person having control of the person detained (for example, a prison governor) but notice may also be served on a minister (for example, the Home Secretary) who is responsible for the detention and who may file evidence in reply. On the day named, the merits of the application will be argued. If the court decides that the writ should issue, it orders the prisoner's release forthwith. Under this practice the respondent need not produce the prisoner in court at the hearing: exceptionally, an applicant may be allowed to present his or her case in person.[222] No return to the writ is made as the writ itself has not been issued. In exceptional cases the court may order the issue of the writ on the ex parte application if, for example, the detainee is at risk of being taken outside the jurisdiction. Disobedience to the writ is punishable by fine or imprisonment for contempt of court, and there may be penalties under the Act of 1679. Officers of the Crown are subject to the writ.[223]

---

[220] [2012] UKSC 48, [2013] 1 AC 614 at [121], [129].
[221] RSC, Ord 54 (kept in being by the Civil Procedure Rules).
[222] *Re Wring* [1960] 1 All ER 536. And see *M v Home Office* [1994] 1 AC 377.
[223] *Re Thompson* (1889) 5 TLR 565; *Secretary of State v O'Brien* [1923] AC 603.

Remedies in Scots administrative law[224]

The prerogative orders were never part of Scots law, except to the extent that they were introduced into Scotland by legislation for the purposes of revenue law, nor did a separate court of equity develop in Scotland. Apart from statutory remedies like the six-week right to challenge a compulsory purchase order, which apply both in Scotland and England, administrative law remedies in Scotland are essentially the same remedies as are available in private law to enforce matters of civil obligation. The most important of these remedies (which are now available subject to procedural changes made in 1985 and subsequently) are (*a*) the ancient remedy of *reduction*, by which any document (including decisions of tribunals, local by-laws, the dismissal of public servants and disciplinary decisions) may be quashed as being in excess of jurisdiction, in breach of natural justice or in other ways contrary to law;[225] (*b*) the no less ancient remedy of *declarator*, from which the English declaration of right was derived; (*c*) the remedies of *suspension* and *interdict*, which together serve broadly the same purposes as prohibition and injunction in English law; (*d*) the action for damages for breach of civil obligation; and (*e*) a summary remedy to enforce performance of statutory duties, comparable with but not identical to mandatory orders.[226] By contrast with the former English law, all relevant forms of relief may be sought in the same proceedings.[227]

Although there have been various differences between Scots and English judicial review procedure, the two were much more closely aligned in 2015 when the Courts Reform (Scotland) Act 2014, enacted by the Scottish Parliament, was brought into force. Section 89 of the 2014 Act made various amendments to the Court of Sessions Act 1988 concerning judicial review procedure in the Court of Session.

First, the new section 27A imposed a three-month time limit to bring a judicial review claim, beginning with the date on which the grounds first arose, subject to a power to extend time where the court considers it equitable. There is no promptness requirement introduced. Prior to section 27A, there was no time limit on petitions for judicial review, but under general principles of Scots law a petition could fail on a plea of *mora* (delay), taciturnity and acquiescence.[228]

Second, a permission stage has been introduced by a new section 27B. It may decide on permission on the papers: s 27B(5). If permission is refused on the papers, or is granted subject to conditions, the applicant may seek to renew the application at an oral hearing within seven days, and the matter will be considered by a different judge: s 27C. An appeal against a refusal of permission at an oral renewal hearing lies to the Inner House of the Court of Session: s 27D. This process is deliberately aligned with the English approach.

However, *third*, the test applied for the grant of permission is different. In English law, the test is one of simple arguability.[229] Section 27B(2)(b) requires the applicant to show that the application has a 'real prospect of success', undoubtedly a higher threshold. Where the judicial review is against the Upper Tribunal for Scotland, the test is akin to that in CPR r 54.7A, where in addition to showing a real prospect of success (not required in England) the

[224] *Stair Encyclopedia of the Laws of Scotland*, vol I, reissue, part 4; C M G Himsworth, in Supperstone, Goudie and Walker (eds), *Judicial Review*, ch 21; Clyde and Edwards, *Judicial Review*, part 5.

[225] See e.g. *Malloch v Aberdeen Corpn* [1971] 2 All ER 1278; *Barrs v British Wool Marketing Board* 1957 SC 72.

[226] Court of Session Act 1988, s 45(b); *T Docherty Ltd v Burgh of Monifieth* 1971 SLT 12. Other remedies include an order *ad factum praestandum* (for performance of a specific duty) and a decree of repetition (that could for instance issue to recover money paid over in response to an ultra vires demand).

[227] E.g. *Macbeth v Ashley* (1874) LR 2 HL (Sc) 352.

[228] *Stair Encyclopedia*, para 121; see *Hanlon v Traffic Commissioners* 1988 SLT 802; *Uprichard v Fife Council* 2000 SCLR 949; and *Somerville v Scottish Ministers* [2006] CSIH 52, 2007 SLT 96, [90]–[94].

[229] *Sharma v Brown-Antoine* [2006] UKPC 57, [2007] 1 WLR 780 at [14] (Lord Bingham).

applicant must also show that there is an important point of principle or practice, or that there is some other compelling reason. This approach to Upper Tribunal challenges is derived from the Supreme Court's decision that there is, in principle, no difference between the law of England and Scots law as to the substantive grounds on which a decision by a tribunal which acts within its jurisdiction may be open to review.[230] In doing so, the Court overturned the decision in *Watt* v *Lord Advocate* that while the remedy of reduction may be used to quash decisions of tribunals which are in excess of their jurisdiction, it is not available to review errors of law made by a tribunal within jurisdiction.[231]

The *fourth* change made by the 2014 Act is also found in s 27B(2), which creates a new test of standing, requiring that the applicant 'demonstrate a sufficient interest in the subject matter of the application'. This is a legislative recognition of the development of the common law, as the Supreme Court had already sought to align Scots law with the English test. In Scots law there had traditionally been a strict approach to standing, requiring the claimant to show 'title and interest' to sue.[232] This was the subject of considerable criticism by comparison to the more relaxed English test,[233] and in *AXA General Insurance Ltd* v *Lord Advocate* the Supreme Court held that 'title and interest' had no place in public law proceedings. Instead the concept of standing should be based on whether there was a sufficient interest, in the sense of a person being directly affected, grounded in the concept of interests rather than rights.[234] The new legislation confirms that approach.

The power of the Court of Session to exercise an extraordinary equitable jurisdiction in the form of the *nobile officium* of the court has not been affected by the 2014 Act.[235]

One problem that has arisen, and which is not addressed by the 2014 Act alterations to the procedure, is that the 'supervisory jurisdiction' of the Court of Session is not defined in legislation, though it has often been described in judgments.[236] It cannot be defined by reference to the remedies that may be granted on a successful application for judicial review since those remedies are available throughout the civil law. The Court of Session in *West* v *Scottish Secretary*[237] robustly rejected the public law/private law distinction. It held that the court has power under its supervisory jurisdiction 'to regulate the process by which decisions are taken by any person or body to whom a jurisdiction, power or authority has been delegated or entrusted by statute, agreement or any other instrument', in particular where there was a 'tripartite relationship' between the decision-maker, the individual affected and the person or body from whom the power to decide was derived. The court's approach to jurisdiction was based on an analysis of the process of decision-making and its review. Later judgments have doubted whether a 'tripartite relationship' is always essential.[238] Since there is no divergence between the substantive grounds of judicial review in English and Scots law, *West* may enable the Scottish courts to apply supervisory jurisdiction to regulatory and similar powers of private organisations, when in English law this would be impeded by the private/public distinction.

---

[230] *Eba* v *Advocate General for Scotland* [2011] UKSC 29, [2012] 1 AC 710.

[231] 1979 SC 120.

[232] *D & J Nicol* v *Dundee Harbour Trustees* 1915 SC (HL) 7.

[233] See Lord Hope [2001] PL 294, discussing *Rape Crisis Centre* v *Home Secretary* 2000 SC 527 (petitioners had no title to review Home Secretary's decision to admit an American boxer and convicted rapist to fight in Glasgow).

[234] [2011] UKSC 46, [2012] 1 AC 868 at [62]–[63] (Lord Hope) and [169]–[170] (Lord Reed).

[235] *Ferguson, Petitioners* 1965 SC 16.

[236] E.g. *Moss Empires Ltd* v *Glasgow Assessor* 1917 SC (HL) 1.

[237] 1992 SLT 636. See W J Wolffe [1992] PL 625; *Stair Encyclopedia*, para 115; Clyde and Edwards, *Judicial Review*, pp 344–7.

[238] See *Naik* v *Stirling University* above; *McIntosh* v *Aberdeenshire Council* 1999 SLT 93, 97; and cf *Blair* v *Lochaber Council* 1995 SLT 407.

E. Conclusion

If, as we saw in the previous chapter, judicial review is about ensuring standards of fairness and legality, the application of the procedural and remedial rules of judicial review is much less straightforward to summarise. Procedure can involve difficult issues in all areas of the law, but in administrative law access to the courts is surprisingly theoretical. Procedural exclusivity and the exclusion of judicial review by statute are areas upon which books can be (and have been) written.

Much of the conceptual difficulty stems from the piecemeal evolution of administrative law over the last century. The historical background to judicial review as a cause of action in part explains why, as judicial review began to grow in the 1960s and 1970s, much judicial ink was spilt in reconciling old restrictive doctrines with a new and growing desire to hold the executive to account.

One theme that can be extracted is that many of the technical rules are interpreted broadly by the courts so as to ensure good challenges are not lost. The rules of standing and time limits are classic examples of control mechanisms which the courts are willing to adjust as necessary in the circumstances of particular cases.

The discretionary award of remedies is another. The old prerogative writs are now a matter of legal history, but their origins explain the oddities of when they can be used and why, even now, judicial review is unique in that a case can be won but no remedy awarded. The range of remedies has increased under the CPR procedure, but administrative lawyers await the next major remedial development: the grant of damages for breach of administrative law.

CHAPTER 26

Liability of public authorities

In Chapters 24 and 25, we examined the law that enables the courts to review the decisions of public authorities on grounds such as ultra vires, error of law and breach of natural justice. We now consider the position of public authorities in relation to civil liability.[1] In principle, public authorities in English law are subject to the same rules of liability in tort and contract as apply to private individuals. There is no separate law of administrative liability for wrongful acts.[2] However, to maintain public services and perform regulatory functions, public authorities require powers which are not available to private individuals. Many public works, such as motorways and power stations, could not be created unless there was power in the public interest to override private rights that might be affected. Parliament legislates to enable public authorities to intervene in private economic activities through regulation or licensing, and in private and family life in the interests of protecting children, the mentally ill and other vulnerable persons. Such powers are often accompanied by statutory protection against liability.

At several points in this chapter, the position of the Crown will be examined. In the past, important distinctions were drawn between (*a*) the Crown, including departments of central government, and (*b*) other public bodies, such as local authorities and statutory corporations. While many of these distinctions have been removed, notably by the Crown Proceedings Act 1947, others remain in being. This chapter deals, in section A, with the liability of public authorities and the Crown in tort and, in section B, with contractual liability. Section C briefly outlines the application of the law of restitution to public authorities, and section D deals with other aspects of the law relating to the Crown, including procedural immunities and privileges and the growing use of closed material procedures.

As with many aspects of public law, the liability of public authorities has been much affected by European law. The liability of EU organs under art 240 TFEU to compensate for serious breaches of EU law that they commit is paralleled by the duty of member states 'to make good loss and damage caused to individuals by breaches of Community law for which they can be held responsible',[3] for example by failure to implement an EU directive. We have already seen the impact of EU law on the supremacy of Parliament that was manifest in the *Factortame* litigation concerning the Merchant Shipping Act 1988, enacted to protect British fishing interests.[4] Later in the same affair, the House of Lords held, after analysing the decision-making that lay behind the 1988 Act, that the Act was a 'sufficiently serious infringement' of EU law to justify the award of compensatory damages.[5] The criteria which led to this decision were derived from EU law,

---

[1] Wade and Forsyth, *Administrative Law*, chs 20, 21; Craig, *Administrative Law*, chs 29, 30; Hogg, Monahan and Wright, *Liability of the Crown*; Harlow, *State Liability – Tort Law and Beyond*; Fairgrieve, *State Liability in Tort*; Fairgrieve, Andenas and Bell (eds), *Tort Liability of Public Authorities in Comparative Perspective*; Kneebone, *Tort Liability of Public Authorities*; Cornford, *Towards a Public Law of Tort*; Lewis, *Judicial Remedies in Public Law*, ch 14.

[2] As was stressed in Dicey's account of the 'rule of law': ch 4.

[3] *Cases C-6/90* and *C-9/90, Francovitch v Italy* [1991] I-ECR 5357, at [37]. Also *Cases C-46/93, Brasserie du Pêcheur SA v Germany* and *C-48/93, R v Transport Secretary, ex p Factortame Ltd* [1996] ECR I-1029; P Craig (1993) 109 LQR 595 and (1997) 113 LQR 67; and C Lewis, in Forsyth and Hare (eds), *The Golden Metwand and the Crooked Cord*, p 319.

[4] See ch 6 C.

[5] *R v Transport Secretary, ex p Factortame Ltd (No 5)* [2000] 1 AC 524.

which requires, for a finding that a breach is 'sufficiently serious', that a member state has 'manifestly and gravely disregarded the limits on the exercise of its discretion'. But the procedural aspects of such a claim in damages may be governed by national law, provided that this does not discriminate against EU law and does not prevent individuals from enforcing their European rights.[6] State liability may arise under EU law even for decisions of the highest national courts.[7]

In respect of human rights, by art 41 ECHR, where a Convention right has been violated and national law does not allow full reparation to be made, the Strasbourg Court 'shall, if necessary, afford just satisfaction to the injured party', by requiring the state to pay compensation. We will consider below the manner in which the Human Rights Act 1998 makes it possible to obtain such compensation in national courts.

The impact of the rules in EU and human rights law continues to be felt at a time when key principles of the liability of public authorities in the United Kingdom remain in flux. In 2004, Lord Steyn made comments on the law on negligence and statutory duties that apply generally to the law of state liability:

> This is a subject of great complexity and very much an evolving area of law. No single decision is capable of providing a comprehensive analysis. It is a subject on which an intense focus on the particular facts and on the particular statutory background, seen in the context of the contours of our social welfare state, is necessary. On the one hand, the courts must not contribute to the creation of a society bent on litigation, which is premised on the illusion that for every misfortune there is a remedy. On the other hand, there are cases where the courts must recognise on principled grounds the compelling demands of corrective justice . . .[8]

The evolving nature of the law is seen in decisions by the highest courts including four that Lord Steyn described as 'milestone' decisions.[9] No more than an outline of the main aspects of the law can be given here.

A. Liability of public authorities and the Crown in tort

Individual liability

In the absence of statutory immunity, every person is liable for wrongful acts that he or she commits and for omissions that give rise to actions in tort at common law or for breach of statutory duty. This applies even if an officer representing the Crown claims to be acting out of executive necessity.

In *Entick* v *Carrington*[10] the King's Messengers were held liable in an action of trespass for breaking and entering the plaintiff's house and seizing his papers, even though they were acting in obedience to a warrant issued by the Secretary of State. This was in law no defence as the Secretary had no legal authority to issue such a warrant.

---

[6] See e.g. rejection of the EU law claim in *Three Rivers DC* v *Bank of England (No 3)* [2001] UKHL 16, [2003] 2 AC 1.

[7] See e.g. *Case C-224/01, Köbler* v *Austrian Republic* [2004] QB 848. No English case has yet held the State liable for a decision of the English courts. The closest so far has been *Cooper* v *Attorney General* [2010] EWCA Civ 464, [2011] QB 976.

[8] *Gorringe* v *Calderdale Council* [2004] UKHL 15, [2004] 2 All ER 326, at [2].

[9] *X* v *Bedfordshire CC* [1995] 2 AC 633; *Stovin* v *Wise* [1996] AC 923; *Barrett* v *Enfield Council* [2001] 2 AC 550; and *Phelps* v *Hillingdon Council* [2001] 2 AC 619.

[10] (1765) 19 St Tr 1030; ch 4 A.

Obedience to orders is not normally a defence whether the orders are those of the Crown, a local authority,[11] a company or an individual employer.[12] The principle that superior orders are no defence to an action in tort would, if unqualified, have placed too heavy a burden on many subordinate officials. At common law an officer of the court, such as a sheriff, who executes an order of the court is protected from personal liability unless the order is on its face clearly outside the jurisdiction of the court.[13] Moreover, it has been found necessary to provide protection for certain classes of official. Thus some statutes exempt officials from being sued in respect of acts done bona fide in the course of duty.[14] The Constables Protection Act 1750 protects constables who act in obedience to the warrant of a magistrate, though the magistrate acted without jurisdiction in issuing the warrant. The Mental Health Act 1983, s 139, affords constables and hospital staff protection against civil and criminal liability in respect of acts such as the compulsory detention of a mental patient, unless the act was done in bad faith or without reasonable care.[15] The liability of individual officials will therefore turn both on the powers which they may exercise and on their privileges and immunities. But no general immunity is enjoyed by officers or servants of the Crown.[16]

Vicarious liability of public authorities

The individual liability of public officials was historically important in establishing that public authorities were themselves subject to the law, but individual liability is not today a sufficient basis for the liability of large organisations, whether in the private or public sectors. It is now essential to be able to sue an individual's employer, if only because the employer is a more substantial defendant: a successful claimant wants the certainty of knowing that any damages and costs awarded will in fact be paid.

In cases not involving the Crown, it has long been the law that a public authority is, like any other employer, liable for the wrongful acts of its servants or agents committed in the course of their employment. It was established in 1866 that the liability of a public body whose servants negligently execute their duties is identical with that of a private trading company.

In *Mersey Docks and Harbour Board Trustees* v *Gibbs*,[17] a ship and its cargo were damaged on entering a dock by reason of a mud bank left negligently at the entrance. The trustees were held liable and appealed to the House of Lords on the ground that they were not a company deriving benefit from the traffic, but a public body of trustees constituted by Parliament for the purpose of maintaining the docks. That purpose involved authority to collect tolls for maintenance and repair of the docks, for paying off capital charges and ultimately for reducing the tolls for the benefit of the public. It was held that these public purposes did not absolve the trustees from the duty to take reasonable care that the docks were in such a state that those who navigated them might do so without danger.

---

[11] *Mill* v *Hawker* (1875) LR 10 Ex 92.

[12] For the position of the armed forces, see ch 20.

[13] *The Case of the Marshalsea* (1613) 10 Co Rep 76a.

[14] E.g. Public Health Act 1875, s 265; Financial Services and Markets Act 2000, s 222; Banking Act 2009, s 244.

[15] The leave of the court is required to bring proceedings: s 139(2). That threshold is a low one and is to be interpreted in accordance with the claimant's Convention rights: *DD* v *Durham County Council* [2011] EWCA Civ 96; *Seal* v *Chief Constable of South Wales* [2007] UKHL 31, [2007] 4 All ER 177; and *TTM* v *Hackney London Borough Council* [2011] EWCA Civ 4, [2011] 1 WLR 2873.

[16] The suggestion to the contrary in *R* v *Transport Secretary, ex p Factortame Ltd* [1990] 2 AC 85, 145 was rightly and authoritatively disapproved in *M* v *Home Office* [1994] 1 AC 377. And see *D* v *Home Office* [2005] EWCA Civ 38, [2006] 1 All ER 183.

[17] (1866) LR 1 HL 93 (discussed in Kneebone (note 1 above), ch 2).

In spite of the argument that a corporation should not be liable for a wrongful act, since a wrongful act must be beyond its powers, a corporation is, like any other employer, liable for the torts of its employees acting in the course of their employment. There must be a relationship between the tortfeasor and the party said to be vicariously liable capable of triggering the doctrine, and the tort committed must be connected with that relationship.[18] Where a prisoner is ill-treated by prison officers, the Home Office may be vicariously liable even if those acts amount to misfeasance in public office, when the ill-treatment is a misguided or unauthorised method of performing their duties.[19] Indeed, it has been held that injury caused by a prisoner to a prison catering manager, during the course of paid work done by the prisoner as part of his rehabilitation, is sufficient to render the Ministry of Justice vicariously liable.[20] An exception to vicarious liability may arise when an official, although appointed and employed by a local authority, carries out functions under the control of a central authority or in the exercise of a distinct public duty imposed by the law.[21] There was formerly no vicarious liability in respect of police officers, but the chief constable is now liable for their acts committed in the performance of their functions.[22]

Tort liability of the Crown

Until 1948 there were two main rules which governed the liability of the Crown: (*a*) the rule of substantive law that the King could do no wrong; (*b*) the procedural rule derived from feudal principles that the King could not be sued in his own courts. The survival of these rules into modern times meant that before 1948 the Crown could be sued neither in respect of wrongs that had been expressly authorised nor in respect of wrongs such as negligence committed by Crown servants in the course of their employment.[23] Nor were government ministers vicariously liable for the staff in their departments, since in law ministers and civil servants are alike servants of the Crown.[24] The law was at last placed on a new basis by the Crown Proceedings Act 1947.

With important exceptions, this Act (which applies only to proceedings by and against the Crown 'in right of Her Majesty's Government in the United Kingdom')[25] established the principle that the Crown is subject to the same liabilities in tort as if it were a private person of full age and capacity in respect of (*a*) torts committed by its servants or agents, (*b*) the duties which an employer at common law owes to his or her servants or agents, and (*c*) any breach of the common law duties of an owner or occupier of property (s 2(1)). The Crown is thus vicariously liable for the torts of its servants or agents.

The Crown is also liable for breach of a statutory duty, provided that the statute is one which binds the Crown as well as private persons (s 2(2)), such as the Occupiers' Liability Act 1984. The Act of 1947 imposes no liability enforceable by action in the case of statutory duties which bind only the Crown or its officers.

---

[18] *Various Claimants* v *Institute of the Brothers of the Christian Schools* [2012] UKSC 56, [2012] 3 WLR 1319.

[19] *Racz* v *Home Office* [1994] 2 AC 45; and p 723 below.

[20] *Cox* v *Ministry of Justice* [2016] UKSC 10; [2016] AC 660.

[21] *Stanbury* v *Exeter Corpn* [1905] 2 KB 838.

[22] Police Act 1996, s 88; see also Police Reform Act 2002, s 47 (civilian staff).

[23] See e.g. *Viscount Canterbury* v *A-G* (1842) 1 Ph 306 (negligence of Crown servants causing Houses of Parliament to burn down).

[24] *Raleigh* v *Goschen* [1898] 1 Ch 73; *Bainbridge* v *Postmaster-General* [1906] 1 KB 178. And see *M* v *Home Office* [1994] 1 AC 377, 408–9.

[25] S 40(2)(b), (c). See *Tito* v *Waddell (No 2)* [1977] Ch 106; *Mutasa* v *A-G* [1980] QB 114; *R* v *Foreign Secretary, ex p Indian Assn of Alberta* [1982] QB 892; and *R (Quark Fishing Ltd)* v *Foreign Secretary* [2005] UKHL 57, [2006] 1 AC 529.

The 1947 Act elaborates the principle of Crown liability in some detail. Thus the Crown's vicarious liability is restricted to the torts of its officers as defined (s 2(6)). This definition requires that the officer shall be (*a*) appointed directly or indirectly by the Crown and (*b*) paid in respect of his duties as an officer of the Crown at the material time wholly out of the Consolidated Fund,[26] moneys provided by Parliament or a fund certified by the Treasury. This excludes, for example, the police. There is no vicarious liability for officers acting in a judicial capacity or in execution of judicial process (s 2(5)),[27] or for acts or omissions of a Crown servant unless apart from the Act the servant would have been personally liable in tort (s 2(1)). The general law relating to indemnity and contribution applies to the Crown as if it were a private person (s 4). The Act does not authorise proceedings against the Sovereign in her personal capacity (s 40(1)) and does not abolish any prerogative or statutory powers of the Crown, in particular those relating to defence of the realm and the armed forces (s 11(1)).

Under the 1947 Act, there were formerly two exceptions from liability in tort. The first related to the armed forces. By s 10, neither the Crown nor a member of the armed forces was liable in tort in respect of acts causing death or personal injury which were committed by a member of the armed forces while on duty, where (*a*) the victim was a member of the armed forces on duty at the time or, if not on duty as such, was on any land, premises, ship, aircraft or vehicle being used for purposes of the armed forces, and (*b*) the injury was certified by the Secretary of State as attributable to service for purposes of pension entitlement. This certificate did not guarantee an award of a pension unless the conditions for entitlement were fulfilled.[28] There certainly must be a public scheme for compensating members of the armed forces who suffer injury or death during their service. But should this exclude the right to sue for common law damages? In 1987, Parliament legislated to put into suspense s 10 of the 1947 Act.[29] Section 10 can be revived if it appears to the Secretary of State necessary or expedient to do so, for example by reason of imminent national danger or for warlike operations outside the United Kingdom. Until it is so revived, and it was not as regards operations in Iraq and Afghanistan, members of the armed forces (and in the event of death, their dependants) may sue fellow members (and the Crown vicariously) in respect of injuries or death arising out of their service. When a soldier sued for personal injury caused during the Gulf operations in 1991 (for which s 10 was not revived), the Court of Appeal held that no duty of care was owed to him by his fellow soldiers during battle conditions, applying the defence of combat immunity on the basis that battlefield decisions are non-justiciable areas for the courts.[30] However, the Supreme Court, by a majority, refused to strike out claims brought by relatives of deceased soldiers who died in Iraq, allegedly due to negligent failures in the equipment they were provided. The Court held that combat immunity must be construed narrowly and that it did not extend to matters of planning and preparation long before hostilities began. The Court left open as a question for trial whether it would be fair, just and reasonable to impose a duty of care on the Ministry of Defence in such circumstances.[31]

---

[26] Ch 9 B.

[27] See *Jones* v *Department of Employment* [1989] QB 1 and *Welsh* v *Chief Constable of Merseyside* [1993] 1 All ER 692. For the position under the Human Rights Act 1998, s 9, see p 725 below. Also I Olowofoyeku [1998] PL 444.

[28] *Adams* v *War Office* [1955] 3 All ER 245. On s 10, see also *Pearce* v *Defence Secretary* [1988] AC 755.

[29] Crown Proceedings (Armed Forces) Act 1987; see F C Boyd [1989] PL 237. The 1987 Act was not retrospective: *Matthews* v *Ministry of Defence* [2003] UKHL 4, [2003] 1 AC 1163 (Crown's former immunity compatible with art 6(1) ECHR). See also National Audit Office, *Ministry of Defence Compensation Claims* (HC 957, 2002–3).

[30] *Mulcahy* v *Ministry of Defence* [1996] QB 732; and ch 16. On liability for off-duty activities, see *Ministry of Defence* v *Radclyffe* [2009] EWCA Civ 635.

[31] *Smith* v *Ministry of Defence* [2013] UKSC 41, [2013] 3 WLR 69. The Court also held, unanimously, that the ECHR did extend to actions of and affecting British armed forces serving abroad, following *Al-Skeini* v *UK* (2011) 53 EHRR 18 and overturning its own earlier judgment in *R (Smith)* v *Oxfordshire Assistant Deputy Coroner* [2010] UKSC 29, [2011] 1 AC 1.

The second exception from liability for tort formerly applied to the Post Office when it was a government department, for acts or omissions in relation to postal packets or telephonic communications (s 9). Nor was there any liability in contract.[32] When the Post Office became a public corporation, the existing limitations on liability for postal and telephone services were continued.[33]

Subject to these exceptions, the Crown Proceedings Act assimilated the tortious liabilities of the Crown to those of a private person. However, in many situations involving the potential liability of the government, the analogy of private liability is not directly helpful. Some claims against the Crown have been held to be non-justiciable,[34] but in general the courts seek to apply to governmental action rules derived from, for example, the common law of negligence.

Statutory authority as a defence

Where acts of a public body interfere with an individual's rights (whether these concern property, contract or liberty), those acts will be unlawful unless legal authority for them exists. Such authority may be found in legislation or in common law. Where Parliament expressly authorises something to be done, it cannot be wrongful to act in accordance with that authority. It will depend on the legislation whether compensation is payable for the rights which Parliament has authorised to be taken away. Construction of public works affecting private rights of property may be subject to detailed rules of compensation in the relevant legislation, but express provision for compensation is not always made. It is then for the court in interpreting the legislation to decide what powers are authorised and whether any compensation is payable. In the process of interpretation, the court will assume that, when discretionary power is given to a public body, there is no intention to interfere with private rights, unless the power is expressed in such a way as to make interference inevitable.

> In *Metropolitan Asylum District* v *Hill*, hospital trustees were empowered by statute to build hospitals in London. A smallpox hospital was built at Hampstead in such a way as to be a nuisance at common law. *Held*, in the absence of express words or necessary implication in the statute authorising the trustees to commit a nuisance, building of the hospital was unlawful. 'Where the terms of the statute are not imperative, but permissive, when it is left to the discretion of the persons empowered to determine whether the general powers committed to them shall be put into execution or not, . . . the fair inference is that the Legislature intended that discretion to be exercised in strict conformity with private rights and did not intend to confer licence to commit nuisance in any place which might be selected for the purpose.'[35]

If, however, the exercise of a statutory power or duty necessarily involves injury to private rights, there is no remedy unless the statute provides compensation.[36]

> In *Allen* v *Gulf Oil Refining Ltd*, the House of Lords held that a local Act which envisaged the building of an oil refinery at Milford Haven, though it gave the company no express power

---

[32] *Triefus & Co Ltd* v *Post Office* [1957] 2 QB 352.
[33] Post Office Act 1969, ss 6(5), 29, 30; British Telecommunications Act 1981, s 70. And see Postal Services Act 2000, s 90.
[34] E.g. *Tito* v *Waddell (No 2)* and *Mutasa* v *A-G* (note 25 above).
[35] (1881) 6 App Cas 193, 212–13 (Lord Watson).
[36] *Hammersmith Rly Co* v *Brand* (1869) LR 4 HL 171.

> to construct the refinery and did not define the site, did give authority for construction and use of the refinery. Such authority protected the company against liability for nuisance to neighbouring owners which was the inevitable result of the construction of the refinery, though the Act gave the owners no compensation for the loss of their rights.[37]

The courts have sometimes placed a heavy onus on the defendant to show that a nuisance that has occurred is an inevitable consequence of the statute. But in *Marcic* v *Thames Water Utilities Ltd*,[38] where a house in London suffered repeated flooding by overflowing sewage, the statutory undertaking responsible for sewerage was not liable to the owner for this serious nuisance. The duties of the defendant were held to be enforceable only by the regulator under the Water Industry Act 1991: despite the malfunctioning of the statutory scheme, the right to sue in nuisance had been taken away by the Act.[39]

Even where, as in the cases of *Allen* and *Marcic*, the right to sue in nuisance is taken away, this does not relieve a body exercising statutory powers of the duty to use reasonable care to avoid causing unnecessary injury. As an old dictum of Lord Blackburn put it,

> . . . no action will lie for doing that which the legislature has authorised, if it be done without negligence, although it does occasion damage to anyone; but an action does lie for doing that which the legislature has authorised, if it be done negligently.[40]

This statement must be read in context: it applies only where a statute authorises an act to be done which will necessarily cause some injury to private rights, and where the act is performed carelessly so causing unnecessary injury to those rights.[41] Such additional injury is outside the protection given by the statute. However, if a public authority which merely has a power to act, and not a duty, decides to take action but acts inefficiently, it is not liable unless the inefficiency causes extra damage to an individual. This was so held in the difficult case of *East Suffolk Catchment Board* v *Kent*, when the use by a river board of an ineffective method of removing flood water from a farmer's land was held to create no liability towards the farmer.[42] In *Barr* v *Biffa Waste Services* the Court of Appeal held that claimants who lived near a landfill site, where a statutory permit for tipping 'pre-treated waste' had been issued by the Environment Agency, were entitled to sue the operators in nuisance when the process at the site created seriously unpleasant smells that interfered with the claimants' comfortable enjoyment of their land.[43] The court applied established principles of the law of nuisance, and rejected the argument that use of the landfill site was reasonable and that the operators could be liable only if they were shown to be negligent in conduct of the site.

Statutory duties[44]

It was at one time the view that anyone harmed by failure to perform a statutory duty could bring an action for damages against the person or body liable to perform it.[45] This has long

---

[37] [1981] AC 1001.

[38] [2003] UKHL 66, [2004] 2 AC 42. The statutory scheme was held to comply with the ECHR.

[39] But the Act did not protect Thames Water from being sued for negligence: *Dobson* v *Thames Water Utilities* [2009] EWCA Civ 28, [2009] 3 All ER 319.

[40] *Geddis* v *Proprietors of Bann Reservoir* (1878) 3 App Cas 430, 455–6.

[41] *X* v *Bedfordshire CC* [1995] 2 AC 633, 733.

[42] [1941] AC 74. And see M J Bowman and S H Bailey [1984] PL 277. Cf *Fellowes* v *Rother DC* [1983] 1 All ER 513, 522 and *Stovin* v *Wise* [1996] AC 923.

[43] [2012] EWCA Civ 312, [2012] 3 All ER 380. See also: M Lee [2015] CLJ 329.

[44] Stanton et al., *Statutory Torts*, ch 2; Harding, *Public Duties and Public Law*, ch 7.

[45] See *Atkinson* v *Newcastle Waterworks Co* (1877) 2 Ex D 441.

since ceased to be the law, since the enormous variety of duties imposed by statute means that there can be no single method of enforcing public duties. Some duties, for example the duty of the Secretary of State for Education to promote the education of the people of England and Wales,[46] are effectively unenforceable by legal proceedings of any kind.[47] Some duties are enforceable only by recourse to statutory compensation. Very many duties may, as we have seen, be enforced by a mandatory order obtained by judicial review.[48] Some statutes provide for a criminal penalty in the event of a breach of duty. Where the statute that creates a duty provides a specific sanction for breach (for example, prosecution) or a remedy for those affected to use, the courts may hold that no other means of enforcing the duty exists.[49]

In some situations, particularly where the statutory duty closely parallels a common law duty (for example, to use care not to cause personal injury) the breach of statutory duty gives rise to a private right of action for damages; such an action is akin to an action for negligence, except that liability depends on breach of the duty itself, not on there being a lack of care.[50] An action for breach exists if it can be shown by interpreting the statute that the duty was imposed for the protection of a certain class and that the legislature intended to confer on members of that class the benefit of a right of action.[51] It is notoriously difficult to evaluate all the factors that are relevant when a court is deciding whether a statutory duty is enforceable by an action for damages and the statute is silent on the point.[52] Where a public authority fails to perform a statutory duty imposed upon it, an individual who is adversely affected may in principle seek judicial review. Laying emphasis on the use of judicial review, recent judicial decisions have limited the availability of damages as a remedy for breach of public duties.

> In *X (minors)* v *Bedfordshire Council*,[53] the House of Lords considered a group of claims for damages arising from the defective performance by local councils of duties relating to the education and welfare of children. The alleged breaches included the failure of a social service authority to take children into care who were badly in need of protection against abuse; a converse error by social workers in taking a child into care believed to be at risk of sexual abuse, when the identity of her abuser was mistaken; and failures by education authorities to identify the special educational needs of children and to provide appropriate schooling. The councils applied to have these claims struck out as disclosing no cause of action. *Held*, so far as the actions were based on breach of statutory duty, they were disallowed. The duties in question gave rise to no private rights of action; nor were the councils under a duty of care in performing them. The education cases were allowed to proceed so far as they were based on the councils' vicarious liability for the professional negligence of teachers and educational psychologists; there was no such vicarious liability for social workers and psychiatrists reporting to the councils on alleged child abuse.

The House of Lords later confirmed that there was no claim for breach of statutory duty against an education authority for failure to diagnose a child's special needs, but that the

---

[46] Education Act 1996, s 10.

[47] For a discussion of judicial review, see ch 24.

[48] Ch 25.

[49] See *Cutler* v *Wandsworth Stadium Ltd* [1949] AC 398; *Lonrho Ltd* v *Shell Petroleum Co Ltd* [1982] AC 173, 185; *Scally* v *Southern Health Board* [1992] 1 AC 294. Cf *Marcic* v *Thames Water Utilities Ltd* (above, note 38) (duties enforceable only by regulator).

[50] E.g. *Reffell* v *Surrey CC* [1964] 1 All ER 743.

[51] See *X* v *Bedfordshire CC* [1995] 2 AC 633, 731.

[52] See Bennion, *Statutory Interpretation*, Code, s 14 (pp 67–85).

[53] [1995] 2 AC 633; see P Cane (1996) 112 LQR 13; L Edwards (1996) 1 Edin LR 115.

authority was liable vicariously for the failure of its employee (an educational psychologist) to show the professional skill that could reasonably have been expected.[54] In a similar welfare context, a homeless person denied temporary housing by a local authority in breach of its duty could enforce the statute by judicial review, but could not recover damages for the breach.[55]

> In *Cullen* v *Chief Constable of the RUC*, the main issue was whether anti-terrorism legislation granting a detained person the right to consult a solicitor conferred a right to sue for damages when the police wrongly prevented a detainee from having access to a solicitor, even though he suffered no direct injury or harm because of this. The Lords held by 3–2 that the aim of the legislation was to create a 'quasi-constitutional' right for the benefit of the public at large, not for the protection of a particular class of individuals: the appropriate remedy was judicial review. In a strong dissenting judgment, Lords Bingham and Steyn were in no doubt that Parliament had intended to create 'a new and remedial provision for the conferment on detainees of a statutory right of access to solicitors'; the statutory language was 'entirely apt to create private law rights'.[56]

It is evident from these and many other decisions[57] that different policy considerations apply to (*a*) the public law remedies obtainable by judicial review, and (*b*) the private law remedy of damages. The interaction between public law concepts and the common law of negligence has caused continuing difficulties in regard to the liability of public authorities, some of which are outlined in the next section.

Public authorities and liability for negligence

Although the Crown Proceedings Act 1947 assimilated the tort liability of the Crown to that of a private person, the duties of government give rise to issues of liability which are not easily resolved by applying legal principles that mainly govern the acts of private persons. Most actions by public authorities stem from legislation. And many disputes as to liability turn directly on the relationship between (*a*) common law rules on the duty of care; (*b*) the legislation, which broadly will confer either a duty or a power to act; and (*c*) the rules of administrative law that apply when judicial review is sought.

> In *Dorset Yacht Co* v *Home Office*,[58] the Home Office was sued for the value of a yacht which had been damaged when seven Borstal boys absconded at night from a Borstal summer camp on an island in Poole harbour. The plaintiffs alleged that the boys were able to abscond because of the negligence of their officers. The Home Office argued that the system of open Borstals would be jeopardised if any liability was imposed on the government for the wrongful acts of those who absconded. The House of Lords held, Lord Dilhorne dissenting, that the Home Office was liable for the negligence of the officers; in the circumstances the officers owed a duty of care to the yacht owners, the damage to the yacht being reasonably foreseeable as the direct consequence of a failure by the officers to take reasonable care.

---

[54] *Phelps* v *Hillingdon Council* [2001] 2 AC 619.

[55] *O'Rourke* v *Camden Council* [1998] AC 188. And see R Carnwath [1998] PL 407.

[56] [2003] UKHL 39, [2004] 2 All ER 237.

[57] See e.g. *Hill* v *Chief Constable of West Yorkshire* [1989] AC 53; *Elguzouli-Daf* v *Commissioner of Metropolitan Police* [1995] QB 335; *Stovin* v *Wise* [1996] AC 923; and *St John Poulton's Trustee in Bankruptcy* v *Ministry of Justice* [2010] EWCA Civ 392, [2011] Ch 1.

[58] [1970] AC 1004. And see Booth and Squires, *The Negligence Liability of Public Authorities*.

This decision had broad consequences for the developing law of negligence, but it was based on the finding of negligence by the officers, and it did not extend to the situation in which it was claimed that an executive discretion (for example, to transfer someone to an open prison) had been improperly exercised. Lord Diplock in *Dorset Yacht* suggested that questions of liability for the exercise of discretion were to be settled by applying the public law concept of ultra vires rather than the civil law concept of negligence.[59] This influential suggestion led to an immense amount of litigation, in particular concerning the exercise of discretion by a public authority in deciding whether to use its regulatory powers. One approach taken was to distinguish between (*a*) decisions that involved policy questions (for instance, use of an authority's resources) and were likely to be unsuitable for judicial determination, and (*b*) the operational tasks performed by the authority once it decided to use its regulatory powers, a task which would be more suitable for judicial appraisal.[60] But this distinction between policy questions and operational tasks proved an elusive way of deciding whether a public authority was liable for a particular misfortune.

In 1990, in *Caparo Industries plc* v *Dickman*,[61] which concerned the duty of care owed by company auditors to potential investors in the company, the Lords adopted a three-part test applying to new situations in which it was sought to establish liability for negligence: (1) whether the harm to the claimant was foreseeable; (2) whether the parties were in a relationship of proximity; and (3) whether it was 'fair, just and reasonable' that the defendant should owe a duty of care to the claimant. This decision confirmed[62] that 'novel categories of negligence' would develop 'incrementally and by analogy with established categories, rather than by a massive extension of a prima facie duty of care', restrained only by indefinable policy considerations seeking to limit the scope of the duty of care. When criterion (3) is applied to novel claims brought against a public body, judges exercise a broad discretion in assessing the consequences for public policy of holding the body liable.

The courts have restricted the imposition of liability in several contexts, particularly as regards claims for economic loss arising out of regulatory functions[63] and claims seeking to impose a private law duty of care on the public functions of the police.[64] Inevitably, the outcome of judicial policy-making is uncertain.

In *Stovin* v *Wise*, a county council as highway authority had statutory power to remove an earth bank that it knew restricted visibility at a dangerous road junction, but it failed to do so. When an accident occurred at the junction, was the council liable for failure to exercise its power? The House of Lords held (by 3-2) that a duty of care to users of the highway to remove the bank arose only if (*a*) it was 'irrational' (in the public law sense) for the power *not*

---

[59] [1970] AC 1004, at 1067.

[60] The application of this principle in *Anns* v *Merton Council* [1978] AC 728 was for wider reasons held to be wrong in *Murphy* v *Brentwood Council* [1991] 1 AC 398.

[61] [1990] 2 AC 605. However, the majority judgment in *Michael* v *Chief Constable of South Wales Police* [2015] UKSC 2, [2015] AC 1732, at [106], made a point of emphasising that the three-part test was not intended to be a blueprint for all future cases.

[62] Quoting from *Sutherland Shire Council* v *Heyman* (1985) 60 ALR 1, 43–4 (Brennan J).

[63] *Yuen Kun-yeu* v *A-G of Hong Kong* [1988] AC 175; *Davis* v *Radcliffe* [1990] 2 All ER 536. And see H McLean (1988) 8 OJLS 442.

[64] *Hill* v *Chief Constable of West Yorkshire* [1989] AC 53; *Brooks* v *Commissioner of Police of the Metropolis* [2005] UKHL 24; [2005] 1 WLR 1495; *Chief Constable of Hertfordshire* v *Van Colle* [2008] UKHL 50, [2009] 1 AC 225; *Desmond* v *Chief Constable of Nottinghamshire* [2011] EWCA Civ 3, [2011] PTSR 1369. But cf *Swinney* v *Chief Constable of Northumbria* [1997] QB 464 and *Waters* v *Commissioner of Metropolitan Police* [2000] 4 All ER 934. And see discussion below of the *Osman* litigation.

to be used and (*b*) there were exceptional factors indicating that the policy of the legislation was to confer a right to sue on a person injured when the power was not exercised. The majority held that neither condition was satisfied, adding that it was 'important, before extending the duty of care owed by public authorities, to consider the cost to the community of the defensive measures which they are likely to take to avoid liability'.[65] The dissenting judges held that, being aware of the danger, the council was under a common law duty of care towards road users to use its powers to remove the cause of the danger.

As can be seen in the judgments in *Stovin* v *Wise*, one difficulty in applying the three-part test in *Caparo Industries* was the presumed need in cases against public authorities to reconcile this with the rules of ultra vires. Must the court, when concerned with the careless exercise of statutory functions, decide first that the acts in question were ultra vires, for instance on the ground of *Wednesbury* unreasonableness?[66] In *X* v *Bedfordshire Council*,[67] on a claim that a public authority had been negligent in exercising a statutory discretion, it was held that the first requirement was to show that its decision was 'outside the ambit of the discretion altogether': if it was not outside that ambit, the public authority could not be in breach of any duty of care owed to the claimant.

In later decisions, the Lords have taken a different view. *Barrett* v *Enfield Council* concerned a claim that a social services authority had breached a common law duty of care that it owed to the claimant while he had been in its care as a child. Lord Slynn stated that acts done pursuant to the lawful exercise of discretion may be subject to a duty of care, even if some element of discretion is involved.[68] Lord Hutton said that, in a case involving personal injuries but not policy issues that the courts were ill-equipped to decide, it was preferable for the court to proceed 'by applying directly the common law concept of negligence than by applying as a preliminary test the public law concept of *Wednesbury* unreasonableness . . .'.[69] In 2004, when the failure of a highway authority to use its powers was again before the Lords, Lord Steyn commented that the analysis made by Lord Hoffmann in *Stovin* had been qualified by the intervening decisions of the House.[70] The application of a duty of care on a public authority in circumstances where it has failed to act have repeatedly caused judicial and academic anguish.[71]

Judicial reluctance to impose duties of care on public authorities has caused some claimants to have recourse to Strasbourg. In *Osman* v *Ferguson*, despite strong facts, the Court of Appeal struck out a claim against the police for negligently failing to prevent a fatal attack, holding that the claim was 'doomed to failure';[72] the court applied the ruling in *Hill* v *Chief Constable of West Yorkshire*[73] that it would be against public policy for the police to be under

---

[65] [1996] AC 923, 958 (Lord Hoffmann). And see S H Bailey and M J Bowman [2000] CLJ 85, 101–19.

[66] See ch 24 A.

[67] Note 51 above.

[68] [2001] 2 AC 550, 571. This point was confirmed in *Phelps* v *Hillingdon Council* [2001] 2 AC 619, 653. See: P Craig & D Fairgrieve [1999] PL 626; D Fairgrieve [2002] PL 288; D Nolan [2013] CLJ 651.

[69] [2001] 2 AC 550 at 586.

[70] *Gorringe* v *Calderdale Council* [2004] UKHL 14, [2004] 2 All ER 326; T Hickman [2004] CLJ 166; C J S Knight [2007] JR 165.

[71] D Nolan (2011) 127 LQR 260; S Tofaris & S Steel [2016] CLJ 128; *Furnell* v *Flaherty* [2013] EWHC 377 (QB); D Nolan (2014) 130 LQR 21.

[72] [1993] 4 All ER 344, 354. A 15-year-old boy and his family for months suffered extreme harassment from the boy's former teacher, culminating when he fired at them, severely injuring the boy and killing his father. The police knew of the harassment and of threats by the assailant before the fatal attack occurred.

[73] [1989] AC 53 (a case brought by the family of the last victim of the 'Yorkshire Ripper').

any liability to the victims of crimes committed by those whom the police failed to apprehend. The Strasbourg court held in 1998 that this decision to strike out *Osman* v *Ferguson* was in breach of art 6(1) ECHR, since the effect was to give the police a blanket immunity from being sued in respect of their acts and omissions relating to criminal offences.[74]

This decision at Strasbourg was criticised for having transformed the right to a fair hearing under art 6(1) into an evaluation of the substantive rights that should exist in national law.[75] Three years later, in *Z* v *UK*,[76] a sequel to the Lords' decision in *X* v *Bedfordshire Council*, the Strasbourg court changed its position, holding by 12–5 that for an English court to strike out an action did not breach art 6(1) since there would have been a full and fair hearing, argued in law on the basis that all facts were as claimed by the claimants. However, on the evidence in *Z* v *UK* the court held that for young children to have been left by the local authority to live with cruel and abusive parents for over four years breached their right under art 3 ECHR to be protected against inhuman or degrading treatment; further, the claimants' right under art 13 ECHR to an effective remedy had been breached by the English legal system. In this serious case, the court ordered the UK government to pay substantial compensation to the claimants.

The appellate case law has maintained a distinct reluctance in imposing duties of care on public authorities. In *D* v *East Berkshire NHS Trust*,[77] the Lords held that where doctors suspected that children had been abused by their parents, it would not be fair, just and reasonable to impose on the doctors a common law duty of care towards the parents, although they owed such a duty to the children (just as local authorities owed a duty to the children in performing their statutory duties of protection); but it was accepted that there might be exceptional circumstances in which a different conclusion might be justified.[78] In a very different context, no duty of care was owed to the owners of a nursing home by a health authority in obtaining a magistrate's order to close down the home without notice, even though it was established later that the closure was wholly unjustified.[79] In *Brooks* v *Metropolitan Police Commissioner*,[80] where a public inquiry had established that a police investigation into serious racist crimes had been badly conducted, the Lords upheld the rule that in exercising functions of crime prevention and detection, the police owed no duty of care to the victims and witnesses of crime.

Most recently, the Supreme Court (by a 5–2 majority) resoundingly reiterated the approach taken in *Hill* and in *Brooks*, holding in *Michael* v *Chief Constable of South Wales* that the police owed no duty of care to prevent harm coming to a victim of crime, even where the police knew the identity of both the victim and perpetrator in advance.[81] Lord Toulson, for the majority, did not focus in his reasoning on the sorts of policy reasoning seen in the 1990s case law. Instead, he emphasised the ordinary negligence rule that there could not be a duty of care owed to control the actions of a third party. Although Lord Kerr and Lady Hale gave strong dissents, *Michael* reflects a continuing reluctance on the part of the highest courts to use the law of negligence as a way to remedy injustice.

---

[74] *Osman* v *UK* (1998) 29 EHRR 245.

[75] See e.g. C A Gearty (2001) 64 MLR 159.

[76] (2001) 34 EHRR 3; see C A Gearty (2002) 65 MLR 87. The applicant children complained that the council had delayed for four years before taking them into care, despite extreme circumstances, and that this had caused them serious physical and emotional harm.

[77] [2005] UKHL 23, [2005] 2 AC 373; S H Bailey (2006) 26 LS 155.

[78] Ibid, at [91] (Lord Nicholls). Lord Bingham, dissenting, refused to strike out the claim without fuller inquiry into the facts. See also *Carty* v *Croydon Council* [2005] EWCA Civ 19, [2005] 2 All ER 517.

[79] *Jain* v *Trent Health Authority* [2009] UKHL 4, [2009] 1 AC 853.

[80] [2005] UKHL 24, [2005] 2 All ER 489 (a sequel to the killing of Stephen Lawrence).

[81] [2015] UKSC 2, [2015] AC 1732; J Goudkamp (2015) 131 LQR 519.

By contrast with the judges' reluctance to impose a new duty of care on a public body in discharging its statutory functions, some aspects of negligence are readily applied in the public sector. Thus, under *Hedley Byrne & Co v Heller*,[82] someone who relies to his or her detriment on inaccurate statements made by an official in the course of the latter's duties may have a remedy in negligence for loss suffered: and a local authority was liable when an environmental health officer, acting in an advisory role, negligently required expensive and unnecessary alterations to be made to a farm guesthouse.[83] When a county council was excessively slow to use statutory powers of taking over management of a school that was suffering acute dissension within its governing body, the council was held liable for having caused personal injury (through extreme stress) to the headteacher because of the delay: the council's common law duty of care to the headteacher was held to 'march together with' the proper discharge of its statutory functions.[84]

Misfeasance in public office[85]

It is a fundamental assumption of the law that those who exercise public functions should do so in good faith and without malicious or spiteful motives. Bad faith must not, of course, be assumed merely because a public body has made a decision that is corrected by judicial review. But where it is shown that a body or official was not acting in good faith, liability in tort may exist.[86] Instances of the tort do not often occur, and claimants have what may be the difficult task of proving that named individuals within a public authority acted in bad faith and were not motivated by acceptable reasons.[87] Unusually, in *Bourgoin SA v Ministry of Agriculture*, it was conceded that the minister knew that he did not have the powers that he purported to exercise: it was held that liability for misfeasance would arise.[88]

The tort arises only from the conduct of a public officer in relation to his or her official functions. Liability depends on the state of mind of the officer and takes two forms:

> First there is the case of targeted malice by a public officer, i.e. conduct specifically intended to injure a person or persons. This type of case involves bad faith in the sense of the exercise of public power for an improper or ulterior motive. The second form is where a public officer acts knowing that there is no power to do the act complained of (or reckless as to whether there is) and that the act will probably injure the plaintiff. It involves bad faith inasmuch as the public officer does not have the honest belief that his act is lawful.[89]

The tort is founded upon the dishonest conduct of the official and is one of the intentional torts: an omission to act is not sufficient, unless this arose from a dishonest decision not to

---

[82] [1964] AC 465. [1964] AC 465.

[83] *Welton v North Cornwall DC* [1997] 1 WLR 570. See also *Harris v Wyre Forest DC* [1990] 1 AC 831 and *T (minor) v Surrey CC* [1994] 4 All ER 577.

[84] *Connor v Surrey Council* [2010] EWCA Civ 286, [2010] 3 WLR 1302. The judgment of Laws LJ contains a valuable review of the extensive case law since *Dorset Yacht*, note 58 above.

[85] For consideration of the various ways in which this cause of action remains underdeveloped, see: M Aronson (2016) 132 LQR 427.

[86] See *Roncarelli v Duplessis* (1959) 16 DLR (2d) 689; *David v Abdul Cader* [1963] 3 All ER 579 (malicious refusal of licence) (A W Bradley [1964] CLJ 4); *Micosta SA v Shetland Islands Council* 1986 SLT 193. Also J McBride [1979] CLJ 323, and Moules, *Actions Against Public Officials*, ch 5.

[87] See *Weir v Transport Secretary* [2005] EWHC 2192 (Ch) (claim by shareholders arising from minister's decision to send Railtrack into liquidation).

[88] [1986] QB 716.

[89] *Three Rivers Council v Bank of England (No 3)* [2001] UKHL 16, [2003] 2 AC 1 (Lord Steyn). For a review of the case law, see Clarke J in this case [1996] 3 All ER 558 (and C Hadjiemmanuil [1997] PL 32). The Lords refused by 3–2 to strike out the case: [2003] 2 AC 1, 237. After a prolonged trial, the case collapsed, there being no evidence of dishonesty: [2006] EWHC 816 (Comm).

act. The tort is not actionable unless the claimant can prove that he or she has suffered material damage, including financial loss and physical or mental injury, and it is not enough to show distress, injured feelings or annoyance.[90] As regards the first form of the tort, targeted malice, it makes no difference whether the official exceeds his or her power or complies with the letter of the power.[91] It appears that local councillors could be liable for misfeasance if, intending to damage the interests of a particular lessee, they voted for a resolution requiring the council's rights as owner of property to be exercised against the lessee.[92] Misfeasance in public office was committed when the corporate officer of the House of Commons breached the rules that governed the placing of a contract to provide the windows of a costly new building for the House.[93] Vicarious liability may arise for misfeasance in office where this is an improper way of performing an officer's duties or is very closely connected with the performance of those duties.[94] Exemplary damages may be payable for misfeasance in public office.[95]

Tort liability, compensation and the Human Rights Act

It is outside the scope of this text to enumerate all the duties, both positive and negative, deriving from the ECHR that the Human Rights Act (HRA) imposes on public authorities. But in outline we may consider whether the ECHR will strengthen the protection that the law of torts gives to individuals against arbitrary, careless or oppressive acts by public authorities.[96]

By the HRA, s 6, a public authority must act consistently with Convention rights, except where primary legislation makes this impossible.[97] As we saw in Chapter 24, public authorities that use their powers in a way that infringes Convention rights are acting unlawfully; if they do, their actions are subject to judicial review. Is there also a remedy in tort?

Under art 41 ECHR, the Strasbourg court shall 'if necessary' afford 'just satisfaction' to someone whose rights have been infringed where full reparation has not been paid at the national level.[98] Under the HRA s 8, a civil court or tribunal with power to award damages has a similar power to award damages to someone whose Convention rights have been infringed if this would be 'just and appropriate' and is necessary to afford 'just satisfaction'; and the court must take account of the practice of the Strasbourg court. Those who hoped that this would open the door to many new claims for compensation have been disappointed. *Anufrijeva* v *Southwark Council*[99] concerned breaches of art 8 (right to respect for private and family life) occurring through inefficiency and delay by local authorities and the Home Office. The Court of Appeal held that damages were not recoverable as of right, even where a Convention right had been breached: a balance had to be struck between the interests of the claimant and the public as a whole; claimants should seek any damages that might be payable

---

[90] *Watkins* v *Home Secretary* [2006] UKHL 17, [2006] 2 AC 395 (bad faith of prison officers in opening prisoner's confidential legal correspondence: no material damage). A prisoner removed from an open to a secure prison suffers material damage: *Karagozlu* v *Metropolitan Police Commissioner* [2006] EWCA Civ 1691, [2007] 2 All ER 1055.

[91] *Three Rivers Council* v *Bank of England (No 3)* [2003] 2 AC 1, 235 (Lord Millett, citing *Jones* v *Swansea Council* [1989] 3 All ER 162).

[92] *Jones* v *Swansea Council* [1990] 3 All ER 737.

[93] *Harmon CFEM Facades (UK) Ltd* v *Corporate Officer of the House of Commons* (2000) 67 Con LR 1.

[94] *Racz* v *Home Office* [1994] 2 AC 45.

[95] *Kuddus* v *Chief Constable of Leicestershire* [2001] UKHL 29, [2002] 2 AC 122; C J S Knight [2011] JR 49.

[96] See Dame Mary Arden [2010] PL 140.

[97] See ch 14 C.

[98] See A R Mowbray [1997] PL 647; Law Commission, *Damages under the Human Rights Act 1998* (Cm 4853); J Hartshorne [2004] EHRLR 660; T R Hickman, in Fairgrieve, Andenas and Bell (eds) (above, note 1), ch 2; D Fairgrieve, (the same), ch 4.

[99] [2003] EWCA Civ 1406, [2004] QB 1124.

by attaching the request to a claim for judicial review. Even so, the judges were concerned that a claim for compensation if brought by adversary proceedings would probably cost more than the amount of any award.

The Court of Appeal's decision in *Anufrijeva* was influential in *R (TG) v Lambeth Council*,[100] where the council had acted wrongly in dealing with the claimant under housing legislation (and not under the Children Act 1989) at a time when he was under 18. The court granted judicial review of the council's decision as to TG's current status, but it refused to permit TG to proceed with a claim for compensation based on article 8 ECHR, holding that the Strasbourg case law did not in general support such a claim when this arose from a state's failure to provide a home or other financial support for the claimant.

In *R (Greenfield) v Home Secretary*,[101] a convicted prisoner had been required to serve extra days for a drug offence within the prison, and he had not had a fair hearing under art 6(1) ECHR. The House of Lords rejected his claim for compensation, holding there to be no right under the 1998 Act to compensation for every infringement of Convention rights; the power to order compensation was not central to protection of human rights; procedural faults of the kind in Greenfield's case would not attract compensation unless the claimant could show a causal link between the procedure and the actual outcome; and the courts must not follow national scales of damages. Lord Bingham said, 'the 1998 Act is not a tort statute. Its objects are different and broader'; he warned of the 'risk of error if Strasbourg decisions given in relation to one article of the Convention are read across as applicable to another'.[102]

In *Rabone v Pennine Care NHS Trust*, the Supreme Court awarded compensation under the Human Rights Act 1998, s 8, by way of 'just satisfaction' of a claim by parents for breach of article 2 ECHR when their daughter, an informal psychiatric patient considered to be at 'moderate to high' risk of suicide, was released from hospital on home leave (against the wishes of her parents) and hanged herself a day later.[103] In *R (Faulkner) v Justice Secretary*,[104] the Supreme Court considered cases involving prisoners who were subject to indeterminate sentences, and whose tariff periods had expired. The consideration of their cases by the Parole Board was delayed because of lack of resources. The Court reiterated that the courts should be guided, following *Greenfield*, primarily by any clear and consistent practice of the European Court of Human Rights and that the amount of any such award should reflect the levels of awards made in Strasbourg in comparable cases brought by applicants from the United Kingdom or other countries with a similar cost of living. This echoes the terms of section 8(4) of the HRA. Lord Reed noted that courts should not apply domestic measures of damages. So, in a case where there is no guideline case in Strasbourg, it is necessary for domestic courts to do their best in the light of such guidance as can be gleaned from the Strasbourg decisions in other cases. 'The over-arching duty of the court under section 8(1) is . . . to grant such relief or remedy as it considers just and appropriate; and that duty exists even where no clear or consistent European practice can be discerned.'[105]

Accordingly, a claimant who alleges that her Convention rights have been infringed by a public authority (and nothing more than this) may not sue in tort but must proceed under s 7 HRA; it is then for the court to decide whether a payment by way of 'just satisfaction' should be made. However, the restrictive principles in *Greenfield* will not arise where there has been a breach of Convention rights (for instance, of art 3 ECHR (prohibition of torture) or of art 5 (right to liberty)) and on the same facts it can be shown that the authority has committed

---

[100] [2011] EWCA Civ 526, [2011] 4 All ER 453.

[101] [2005] UKHL 14, [2005] 2 All ER 240. And see R Clayton [2005] PL 429.

[102] *R (Greenfield) v Home Secretary* (above), at [19] and [7].

[103] [2012] UKSC 2, [2012] AC 72.

[104] [2013] UKSC 23, [2013] 2 AC 254.

[105] *R (Faulkner) v Justice Secretary* (above), at [36].

torts in relation to the torture or false imprisonment. In these instances, damages in tort may be recovered and compensation under the 1998 Act is unlikely to be necessary.

When it is claimed that a public authority, either through positive action or an omission to act, has infringed an individual's Convention rights, and where it is not disputed that a duty of care arises in national law, then the courts may be willing to decide the extent of that duty of care by reference to case law under the Convention.[106] By contrast, where a duty of care of relevant scope is not clearly recognised in national law and where it is uncertain whether the claimant's case would be protected at Strasbourg, a claim may be allowed to proceed in the law of tort and not under the Convention.[107] Another decision by the Lords has been said to be 'an example of a situation in which the court has used a Convention right as a launch pad for a possible development in the future'.[108]

When the breach of a Convention right results from a judicial act, an award of damages may be made under the HRA, s 9, only (*a*) if the act is not done in good faith, or (*b*) if an award is necessary under art 5(5) ECHR to compensate for unlawful detention. Any award will be made against the Crown, not against the judge. Successful reliance on s 9 has, unsurprisingly, been rare, but for a disturbing case in which a Family High Court judge wrongly committed a man to prison for contempt, see *LL* v *Lord Chancellor*.[109]

Other forms of tort liability

Other forms of tort liability may be briefly mentioned. First, public authorities, and particularly the Home Office and prison authorities, are regularly sued for the tort of false imprisonment, where an individual has been detained without legal authority.[110] Secondly, the Privy Council has confirmed that the tort of malicious prosecution extends to the bringing of civil proceedings.[111] At least in theory, a public authority could be liable for bringing proceedings without reasonable or probable cause but with malice, as the Crown has been traditionally so liable for the malicious prosecution of criminal proceedings. Thirdly, the Court of Appeal has confirmed that the tort of abuse of process does not extend to a claim action for pure economic loss allegedly suffered as a result of bringing judicial review proceedings.[112] It was considered that a claimant should not be discouraged from pursuing judicial review proceedings after permission has been given by the court.

It is also relevant to note the development of the remedies available for tortious liability. Ever since the general warrant cases in the 1760s in which exemplary damages were awarded for unlawful search and seizure, the courts have had power to award exemplary damages for oppressive, arbitrary or unconstitutional acts in the exercise of public power.[113] It was formerly considered that the power was limited to certain torts for which exemplary damages had been awarded before 1964,[114] but in 2001, in a case of alleged misfeasance in public office

---

[106] See *Savage* v *South Essex Partnership NHS Trust* [2008] UKHL 74, [2009] 1 AC 681 (failure by psychiatric hospital to take reasonable operational measures to prevent suicide of patient where a real and immediate risk of that event).

[107] *Mitchell* v *Glasgow Council* [2009] UKHL 11, [2009] 3 All ER 205.

[108] Arden (note 96 above) at p 152, referring to the speech of Lord Scott in *Ashley* v *Chief Constable of Sussex* [2008] UKHL 25, [2008] 1 AC 962.

[109] [2017] EWCA Civ 237.

[110] The leading authority on damages for false imprisonment is *R (Lumba)* v *Home Secretary* [2011] UKSC 12; [2012] 1 AC 245.

[111] *Crawford Adjusters* v *Sagicor General Insurance (Cayman) Ltd* [2013] UKPC 17, [2014] AC 366.

[112] *Land Securities Plc* v *Fladgate Fielder* [2009] EWCA Civ 1402, [2010] Ch 467.

[113] *Wilkes* v *Wood* (1763) Lofft 1; *Rookes* v *Barnard* [1964] AC 1129, 1226. And see *Lancashire CC* v *Municipal Mutual Insurance Ltd* [1997] QB 897.

[114] *AB* v *South West Water Services Ltd* [1993] QB 507, applying *Broome* v *Cassell and Co Ltd* [1972] AC 1027.

by a police officer, the House of Lords held that this limitation was not justified and that such a rigid rule would limit the future development of the law.[115] Juries considering the award of exemplary damages against the police must be directed by the trial judge as to the permissible range of such awards.[116] For a particularly egregious example of potential misfeasance one should consider the facts of *Muuse* v *Home Secretary*.[117] In brief, immigration officials unlawfully detained Muuse; disobeyed an order of the court to release him; made no enquiries about the nationality of Muuse although he repeatedly told them he was Dutch and although the Prison Service held all the relevant documentation to prove this having confiscated it from him; issued an unlawful deportation order to Somalia (a failed state); failed to conduct any investigation into matters raised with them and failed to allow Muuse time to appeal his deportation; failed to revoke the deportation order even after being provided with the documentation showing Dutch nationality, continuing to detain Muuse without any authority; and subjected Muuse to racist remarks. The Court of Appeal upheld an award of exemplary damages of £27,500 for the tort of false imprisonment.

Tort liability and judicial review

In an era when the use of judicial review has expanded dramatically, as has liability for breach of duties owed in EU law, the UK courts have resisted an equivalent expansion in the liability of public bodies to be sued for damages. We have seen that in France both the judicial review of decisions and the power to award compensation for wrongful acts committed by public authorities are entrusted to the administrative courts.[118] Under the French system, rules of public liability have developed which differ from the rules of liability in civil law. In English law, by contrast, public authorities and officials are in principle subject to the same law of civil liability as private persons. Thus a claim in damages against a public authority must be based on an existing tort (including negligence, nuisance, trespass to the person, false imprisonment[119] and misfeasance in public office) or on a specific right of action created by statute. Yet the existing categories of tort do not include all instances in which a public body may cause loss to an individual through acts or omissions that as a matter of public law are in some way wrongful.

In particular, English law does not accept that an individual has a right to be indemnified for loss caused by invalid or ultra vires administrative action.[120] Although a claimant for judicial review may seek damages or restitution together with quashing, mandatory, declaratory and restraining orders, this has not changed the substantive rules of liability.[121] Thus a prisoner may seek judicial review of a decision to put him in solitary confinement for 28 days, but has no right to sue the governor or the Home Office for damages, whether for breach of prison rules or for false imprisonment.[122]

The Supreme Court's decision in *R (Lumba) (Congo)* v *Home Secretary* held unanimously that it was unlawful in public law for the Secretary of State to operate an unpublished policy

---

[115] *Kuddus* v *Chief Constable of Leicestershire* [2001] UKHL 29, [2002] 2 AC 122.

[116] *Thompson* v *Metropolitan Police Commissioner* [1998] QB 498.

[117] [2010] EWCA Civ 453.

[118] Ch 21. Brown and Bell, *French Administrative Law*, ch 8. Also Markesinis et al., *Tortious Liability of Statutory Bodies* (comparing English, French and German law).

[119] See *R* v *Governor of Brockhill Prison (No 2)* [2001] 2 AC 19 (damages for detention beyond lawful date of release).

[120] *Hoffmann-La Roche* v *Secretary of State for Trade* [1975] AC 295, 358 (Lord Wilberforce); *Financial Services Authority* v *Sinaloa Gold* [2013] UKSC 13, [2013] 2 AC 28 at [31] (Lord Mance).

[121] See ch 25; and see e.g. *Page Motors Ltd* v *Epsom and Ewell BC* (1982) 80 LGR 337, and P Cane [1983] PL 202; *Davy* v *Spelthorne BC* [1984] AC 262.

[122] *R* v *Deputy Governor of Parkhurst Prison, ex p Hague* [1992] 1 AC 58.

which was inconsistent with published policy, but the court was divided on the consequences of this.[123] The majority (six judges) held that the actual detention had been unlawful and gave rise to an award of damages. However, three of these judges (Lords Collins, Kerr and Dyson) held that, since the detainees would have been lawfully detained anyway, they had suffered no loss and should recover only nominal damages of £1 each. The other three of the majority judges (Lord Hope, Lord Walker and Lady Hale) held that damages should be awarded of a 'conventional' amount that would reflect the importance of the right of liberty and the seriousness of the infringement (payments of £500 or £1,000 to each claimant were suggested). A minority of three judges (Lords Phillips, Brown and Rodger) held that, because the claimants would have been lawfully detained in any event, there was no liability for false imprisonment. The judgments in this case included wide-ranging discussion of the principles of public law that applied and of the various forms of damages that are available (i.e. nominal, vindictive, exemplary, conventional). In a case concerning similar facts, *R (Kambadzi)* v *Home Secretary*,[124] the Home Office failed to conduct regular reviews of the detention pending deportation of a Zimbabwean, who had completed a prison sentence for serious offences; the Home Office's published policy required regular review and said that 'to be lawful', detention must conform with the stated policy. By 3–2, the Supreme Court held that the executive's failure to adhere to its published policy without good reason amounted to an abuse of power that rendered the detention itself unlawful.

When a trader's licence for a market stall is cancelled in breach of natural justice, he or she may by judicial review recover the licence[125] but has no right to compensation for the intervening loss of income unless, exceptionally, he can make out the misfeasance tort discussed above. It is well established that a public authority's decision may be invalid, in the sense of being ultra vires, without this giving rise to a right to damages.[126]

> In *Jain* v *Trent Health Authority*,[127] the claimants' nursing home was suddenly closed down when, without giving notice to the owners, the registration authority obtained a closing order from a magistrate. Five months later, a tribunal upheld the owners' appeal and found that the immediate closure of the home was not justified. But by then the business had been ruined. The owners sued the health authority for economic damage caused by negligence. *Held*, the health authority's powers of registration and inspection were intended to protect the interests of the residents of the homes. The fact that the statutory procedures were insufficient to prevent damage to the owners did not mean that the health authority owed them a duty of care.

In matters not covered by EU law or the HRA, those who suffer loss caused by unlawful, unfair or unreasonable decisions by a public authority have a genuine complaint about the state of the law. In some circumstances, where maladministration by central or local government has caused individuals to suffer injustice, they may be able to obtain compensation by complaining to the appropriate Ombudsman; but the authority is not at risk of being sued for damages.[128] In 1988, the Justice/All Souls committee on administrative law recommended

---

[123] [2012] UKSC 19, [2012] AC 245. For discussion of the cases applying *Lumba*, see: C Dobson & A Ruck Keene [2012] PL 628.

[124] [2011] UKSC 23, [2011] 1 WLR 1299.

[125] *R* v *Barnsley Council, ex p Hook* [1976] 3 All ER 452.

[126] See e.g. *Dunlop* v *Woolahra Council* [1982] AC 158.

[127] [2009] UKHL 4, [2009] 1 AC 853.

[128] Ch 23 D; and *R* v *Knowsley BC, ex p Maguire* (1992) 90 LGR 653. And see M Amos [2000] PL 21.

that the law should provide for compensation to be paid to one who sustains loss as a result of acts or decisions that are wrongful or contrary to law or are a result of excessive delay.[129] Not surprisingly, no government since 1988 has endorsed this proposal.

In 2008, the Law Commission issued a consultation paper, *Administrative Redress: Public Bodies and the Citizen*.[130] This reviewed the range of remedies available when substandard administration occurs, and argued that radical reform was needed in respect of the remedies obtainable through the courts, since negligence actions against public bodies were 'uncertain and unprincipled' and the torts of misfeasance in public office and breach of statutory duty were unsuitable 'in the modern era'. The particular reform suggested would involve defining the 'truly public' functions of public authorities; these would not be subject to the law of negligence and would give rise to compensation only for 'serious fault' and on a discretionary basis. This proposal was never very likely to be adopted, and was dropped in 2010.[131] A more practical step would be a limited reform enabling the Administrative Court on judicial review to grant compensation to an individual who has suffered serious economic loss from an invalid administrative act.[132]

B. Contractual liability[133]

The making of contracts is the means whereby an infinite number of transactions occur in a market economy, and many contracts are made by public authorities. Legislation is the primary means of creating duties and rights in public law, such as the duty to pay taxes or the right to receive free medical services. Often government has a choice to make in deciding whether to rely on legislative commands or contract to achieve a certain goal: thus, to recruit the armed forces, the policy may be to employ a wholly professional army based on recruiting volunteers in return for pay or to compel all persons of a certain age to serve alongside a nucleus of regular soldiers. Legislation is needed both to authorise conscription and to levy taxation to pay for the armed forces, but a significant distinction may be drawn in achieving certain ends between (*a*) reliance on legislative commands (*imperium*) and (*b*) use of government's economic resources (*dominium*).[134]

The government, formerly the monarch, has long met many of its needs by exercising *dominium* and making contracts.[135] Trends in public policy since 1979 have expanded the purposes for which contracts are used, from the procurement of labour, goods and other assets to the contracts placed by the Home Office for companies to manage prisons and detention centres;[136] the authority given by Parliament for 'contracting out' statutory functions;[137] and the privatisation of

---

[129] *Administrative Justice, Some Necessary Reforms*, ch 11.

[130] Earlier publications by the Commission were a discussion paper, *Monetary Remedies in Public Law* (2004), and a scoping paper, *Remedies Against Public Bodies* (2006). See R Bagshaw (2006) 26 LS 4.

[131] See M Fordham [2009] PL 1 and T Cornford [2009] PL 70.

[132] Cf Harlow, *State Liability – Tort Law and Beyond*, pp 115–16: proposal for the Administrative Court to have an equitable power to award compensation for administrative fault when abnormal loss or a gross violation of human rights has occurred.

[133] Street, *Governmental Liability*, ch 3; Mitchell, *The Contracts of Public Authorities*; Turpin, *Government Procurement and Contracts*; Hogg, Monahan and Wright, *Liability of the Crown*, ch 9; Davies, *The Public Law of Government Contracts*.

[134] This distinction is developed by T C Daintith [1979] CLP 41 and (same author) in Jowell and Oliver (eds), *The Changing Constitution* (1994), ch 8.

[135] See e.g. *The Bankers' Case* (1695) Skin 601. A later monarch, George IV, rented jewels to display in his crown that he could not afford to buy.

[136] Criminal Justice Act 1991, ss 84–91, Sch 10; Criminal Justice and Public Order Act 1994, ss 7–15.

[137] Deregulation and Contracting Out Act 1994, part II.

public utilities.[138] Sometimes the shell of a contract is used, without legal content, as with the creation of the 'internal market' in the NHS in 1990[139] and the use of 'framework agreements' to govern executive agencies.[140] The 'private finance initiative' and public–private partnerships enable new projects to be financed and managed, to a greater or lesser extent, jointly by the public and private sectors.[141] One commentator has written: 'The techniques of public administration have been refashioned in the mould of the private commercial sector . . . Contract has replaced command and control as the paradigm of regulation.'[142] A French lawyer has remarked on the tendency 'in all major industrialised countries' to 'a growing contractualisation of relations between administrative bodies and society, as well as among administrative bodies themselves'.[143]

In English law, the contracts of public authorities are in principle subject to the same law that governs contracts between private persons. There is no separate jurisdiction governing administrative contracts, as there is in France.[144] Nevertheless, these generalisations must be qualified. First, contracts made on behalf of the Crown are subject to some exceptional rules, which were modified but not necessarily abolished by the Crown Proceedings Act 1947 (below). Apart from these rules, it might appear that the Crown has unlimited power at common law to enter into contracts,[145] but this is subject to statute: where the Crown or ministers have statutory power to take certain action (for instance, managing the prison system) through officials acting under direction from ministers, legislation is needed if power is to be conferred on a private company and exercised by its employees.

Secondly, we have seen that statutory bodies such as local authorities are subject to legal control exercised through the rules of ultra vires, as regards the substance of action that they may take and the procedure by which decisions are made. A contract which is beyond the power of a local authority to make is void and unenforceable.[146] A contract made by a public authority may be held void on the ground that it seeks to fetter the future use of the authority's discretionary powers.[147] Thus, where a planning authority in Cheshire agreed with Manchester University to discourage new development within the vicinity of the Jodrell Bank radio telescope, the purported agreement was without legal effect.[148] And the fact that a local authority has contracted with a company for certain services does not prevent the authority from using a statutory power to make by-laws, even if the by-laws make the future performance of the contract impossible or unprofitable for the contractor.[149] A full account of the making of contracts in local government would examine the effect of a council's standing orders on awarding contracts, public audit, and statutes that impose objectives such as 'best value' in the placing of contracts.[150]

---

[138] See ch 14.

[139] See D Longley [1990] PL 527 and J Jacob [1991] PL 255.

[140] On the role of contracts in government generally, see Harden, *The Contracting State*; Craig, *Administrative Law*, ch 5; Harlow and Rawlings, *Law and Administration*, chs 8, 9.

[141] See M Freedland [1994] PL 86, [1998] PL 288; Y Marique, *Public-Private Partnerships and the Law*.

[142] M Hunt, in Taggart (ed.), *The Province of Administrative Law*, p 21.

[143] J-B Auby [2007] PL 40, 42.

[144] Mitchell, *Contracts of Public Authorities*, ch 4; Brown and Bell, *French Administrative Law*, pp 202–11.

[145] See B V Harris (1992) 108 LQR 626, (2007) 123 LQR 225.

[146] *Rhyl UDC* v *Rhyl Amusements Ltd* [1959] 1 All ER 257; *Hazell* v *Hammersmith Council* [1992] 2 AC 1; *Crédit Suisse* v *Allerdale Council* [1997] QB 306. Although see now: *Charles Terence Estates* v *Cornwall Council* [2012] EWCA Civ 1439, [2013] 1 WLR 466.

[147] *Ayr Harbour Trustees* v *Oswald* (1883) 8 App Cas 623; *Triggs* v *Staines UDC* [1969] 1 Ch 10; *Dowty Boulton Paul Ltd* v *Wolverhampton Corpn (No 2)* [1973] Ch 94.

[148] *Stringer* v *Minister of Housing* [1971] 1 All ER 65.

[149] *William Cory & Son Ltd* v *City of London* [1951] 2 KB 476. And see text to notes 163–6 below.

[150] See respectively *R* v *Enfield Council, ex p Unwin (Roydon) Ltd* (1989) 1 Admin LR 51; *Porter* v *Magill* [2001] UKHL 67, [2002] 2 AC 357; and the Local Government Act 1999.

An underlying question of great difficulty concerns the use of judicial review as a remedy regarding the contractual decisions of public authorities. It is often uncertain whether there is a 'sufficient public law element' in a dispute to justify use of judicial review. Judicial review should not be used when it is merely claimed that a public body is in breach of contract.[151] But contractual situations may well involve issues as to the abuse of public power, so that judicial review would be appropriate.[152]

The economic importance of public procurement contracts has long been recognised in EU law, and the European directives on this matter are implemented by delegated legislation within the United Kingdom, creating rights and duties enforceable in the ordinary courts.[153] The public procurement rules require authorities that enter into certain contracts to follow open procedures for the tendering process for contracts above a stated value, to observe certain criteria in awarding the contract, to specify lawful policy objectives, and to state reasons for choosing a particular contractor. If these duties are breached, a company whose tender has not succeeded may sue the authority for damages.[154]

Contractual liability of the Crown

By s 1 of the Crown Proceedings Act 1947 it is possible to sue the appropriate government department or, where no department is named for the purpose, the Attorney General, by ordinary process either in the High Court or in a county court. The 1947 Act generally repealed the pre-existing Petitions of Right Act 1860, but the old regime appears to remain in place for proceedings in matters of contract or property against the Sovereign personally.[155] The 1947 Act applies only to proceedings against the Crown in right of the government of the United Kingdom, not to claims that arise in respect of the Crown's overseas territories.[156]

In Scotland the petition of right procedure had never existed, since it was always possible to sue the Crown in the Court of Session on contractual claims or for the recovery of property.[157] Accordingly, s 1 of the 1947 Act does not apply to Scotland.

In general the ordinary rules of contract apply to the Crown: thus an agent need have only ostensible authority to bind the Crown and there is no rule requiring the actual authority of the Crown.[158] Those who make contracts on behalf of the Crown, as its agents, are in accordance with the general rule not liable personally.[159] Statutory authority is not needed before

---

[151] Ch 25 B.

[152] See S H Bailey [2007] PL 444.

[153] See Directives 2004/17/EC and 2004/18/EC of the European Parliament and Council; Public Contracts Regulations 2006 (SI 2006/5) and Utilities Contracts Regulations 2006 (SI 2006/6). And see Arrowsmith, *The Law of Public and Utilities Procurement*. The relationships between different public bodies can sometimes give rise to difficult issues: *Edenred (UK) Group v HM Treasury* [2015] UKSC 45, [2015] PTSR 1088.

[154] In *Energy Solutions v Nuclear Decommissioning Agency* [2016] EWHC 1988 (TCC) a judgment of nearly 950 paragraphs was required to consider the liability issues, in a claim reported to be worth (before it was settled after the judgment) into the billions of pounds. In *Harmon CFEM Facades (UK) Ltd v Corporate Officer, House of Commons* (2000) 67 Con LR 1, 72 Con LR 21, the claimant submitted the lowest tender but was not awarded the contract; it won substantial damages for breaches of duty (including failure to state relevant criteria and unlawful post-tender negotiations) and breach of implied contract.

[155] Crown Proceedings Act 1947, s 40(1); *Franklin v A-G* [1974] QB 185, 194.

[156] Before Rhodesia achieved lawful independence as Zimbabwe, difficulties as to Crown proceedings arose over the non-payment of interest to holders of Rhodesian government stock; see *Franklin v A-G* [1974] QB 185; *Franklin v R* [1974] QB 202.

[157] Mitchell, *Constitutional Law*, p 304.

[158] See *A-G for Ceylon v Silva* [1953] AC 461 on the difficulties of establishing ostensible authority in relation to the Crown. Cf *Re Selectmove Ltd* [1995] 2 All ER 531.

[159] *Macbeath v Haldimand* (1786) 1 TR 172; and see *Town Investments Ltd v Department of the Environment* [1978] AC 359.

the Crown can make a contract, but payments due under the Crown's contracts come from money provided by Parliament; if Parliament exceptionally provides that no money is payable to a certain contractor, payments that would otherwise be due may not be enforced.[160] If a contract expressly provides that payments are to be conditional on Parliament appropriating the money, the Crown is not liable if Parliament does not do so. But, in general, 'the prior provision of funds by Parliament is not a condition preliminary to the obligation of the contract'.[161] Payments due under contract are made out of the general appropriation for the class of service to which the contract relates and not from funds specifically appropriated to a particular contract. It is usually accepted that the Crown has full contractual capacity as a matter of common law,[162] but this cannot entitle the Crown to make contracts which are contrary to statute. Moreover, there is a rule of law, the exact extent of which it is not easy to determine, that the Crown cannot bind itself so as to fetter its future executive action.

In *Rederiaktiebolaget Amphitrite* v *R*, a Swedish shipping company, Sweden being a neutral in the First World War, was aware that neutral ships were liable to be detained in British ports. They obtained an undertaking from the British government that a particular ship, if sent to this country with certain cargo, would not be detained. Accordingly, the ship was sent with such a cargo, but the government withdrew the undertaking and refused clearance for the ship. On trial of a petition of right, *held*, the undertaking of the government was not enforceable as the Crown was not competent to make a contract which would have the effect of limiting its power of executive action in the future.[163]

It has been suggested that the defence of executive necessity only 'avails the Crown where there is an implied term to that effect or that is the true meaning of the contract';[164] or again that the defence has no application to ordinary commercial contracts. A preferable view is that the *Amphitrite* case illustrates a general principle that the Crown, or any public authority, cannot be prevented by an existing contract from exercising powers which are vested in it either by statute or common law for the protection of the public interest.[165]

In *Commissioners of Crown Lands* v *Page*, the Crown sued for arrears of rent due under a lease of Crown land that had been assigned to the defendant. The defence was that the land had been requisitioned by a government department and that this constituted eviction by the Crown as landlord. The Court of Appeal held that the arrears were payable. Devlin LJ said: 'When the Crown, in dealing with one of its subjects, is dealing as if it too were a private person, and is granting leases or buying and selling as ordinary persons do, it is absurd to suppose that it is making any promise about the way in which it will conduct the affairs of the nation.'[166]

---

[160] *Churchward* v *R* (1865) LR 1 QB 173. Of course, today such a step would inevitably lead to a challenge under the Human Rights Act 1998 for breach of Article 1 of Protocol 1 ECHR.

[161] *New South Wales* v *Bardolph* (1934) 52 CLR 455, 510 (Dixon J); Street, *Governmental Liability*, pp 84–92.

[162] See B V Harris (1992) 108 LQR 626; cf M Freedland [1994] PL 86, 91–5.

[163] [1921] 3 KB 500.

[164] *Robertson* v *Minister of Pensions* [1949] 1 KB 227, 237 (Denning J).

[165] Street, *Governmental Liability*, pp 98–9; Mitchell, *The Contracts of Public Authorities*, pp 27–32, 52–65.

[166] [1960] 2 QB 274, 292; see also *William Cory & Son Ltd* v *City of London* [1951] 2 KB 476.

As we have seen, some problems arise in relation to the contracts of public authorities to which English law provides no certain answer, for instance concerning the power of a public body to decide with whom to contract and whom to remove from its list of approved contractors.[167] This power was used by the Labour government in 1975–8 to require companies who were granted contracts to observe a non-statutory pay policy.[168] This is an example of a government's ability to achieve public goals without recourse to legislation.[169]

We have also seen that where European rules on public procurement apply, the pre-contractual procedures observed by public authorities are controlled, with recourse to the courts if the rules are breached. Where these rules do not apply, the legal regime is uncertain. In one case, the Lord Chancellor's Department was held to have acted unfairly in awarding a contract, but the process was held not to be subject to judicial review.[170] The courts should, however, uphold fairness and legitimate expectations in this situation. Thus, the National Lottery Commission acted unlawfully in deciding not to award the next licence for the Lottery to the existing licensee (Camelot) but to enter into negotiations with the rival bidder (the People's Lottery).[171] In Northern Ireland, the right not to be discriminated against on religious grounds was held by the Strasbourg Court to apply to public procurement decisions.[172] Control over government contracts is exercised by the Comptroller and Auditor General. Much government practice in placing and administering contracts derives from rulings of the Public Accounts Committee of the House of Commons.[173] In view of the numerous government contracts awarded each year, relatively few disputes arising from them reach the courts. Disputes are resolved by various forms of consultation, negotiation or arbitration. Government contracts are excluded from the jurisdiction of the Parliamentary Ombudsman.[174]

Service under the Crown

Service under the Crown has long been an instance of the special contractual position of the Crown; it is generally held to be part of the prerogative that the Crown employs its servants at its pleasure, whether in the civil service or the armed forces.[175] The Crown formerly claimed that its freedom to dismiss its servants at will was necessary in the public interest, and this claim was accepted in the older case law. Thus, in the absence of statutory provision,[176] no Crown servant had a remedy for wrongful dismissal. Even when a colonial servant had been engaged for three years certain, only for the appointment to be terminated prematurely, the

---

[167] Turpin, *Government Procurement and Contracts*, ch 4.

[168] G Ganz [1978] PL 333. Whether this will always be a lawful use of power will depend on the circumstances, particularly if statutory powers are relevant; see, for example, *R (Palestine Solidarity Campaign Ltd) v Secretary of State for Communities and Local Government* [2017] EWHC 1502 (Admin) and *Wheeler v Leicester City Council* [1985] AC 1054 for the improper use of public powers to further political campaigns (concerning pension investments and use of local authority sports facilities respectively).

[169] T C Daintith [1979] CLP 41.

[170] *R v Lord Chancellor, ex p Hibbit & Saunders* [1993] COD 326 (D Oliver [1993] PL 214). Cf *R v Legal Aid Board, ex p Donn & Co* [1996] 3 All ER 1. Also S Arrowsmith (1990) 106 LQR 277; A Davies (2006) 122 LQR 98.

[171] *R v National Lottery Commission, ex p Camelot Group plc* [2001] EMLR 43.

[172] *Tinnelly & Sons Ltd v UK* (1998) 27 EHRR 249.

[173] See, for example, HC 777 (2013–14), on contracting out public services.

[174] Ch 23 D.

[175] See *CCSU v Minister for the Civil Service* [1985] AC 374 and cf Sir William Wade (1985) 101 LQR 180.

[176] E.g. the rule that judges hold office during good behaviour (ch 13 C), *Gould v Stuart* [1896] AC 575 and *Reilly v R* [1934] AC 176.

court reasoned that it was 'essential for the public good that it should be capable of being determined at the pleasure of the Crown'.[177]

While at common law civil servants lacked tenure of office, in practice they enjoyed a high degree of security. This security depended on convention rather than law, and the collective agreements on conditions of service which were applied to civil servants did not give rise to contractual rights.[178] Indeed, it was for a long time uncertain whether Crown service was a contractual relationship at all, and it was doubtful whether civil servants could even sue for arrears of pay.[179] Today, most provisions of the Employment Rights Act 1996 apply to civil servants, and they are protected against unfair dismissal.[180] They are also protected against discrimination in relation to their employment.[181]

In 1991, a newer look was given to the common law when it was held that civil servants are employed by the Crown under contracts of employment, since the incidents of a contract are present and the civil service pay and conditions code deals in detail with the relationship. Although the code states that the relationship is governed by the prerogative and that civil servants may be dismissed at pleasure, neither the Crown nor civil servants intend the contents of the code to be merely voluntary.[182] In many cases the courts have held that an aggrieved civil servant cannot seek judicial review of a dismissal or other action because of the private law nature of the claim.[183] However, where the remedies in the employment tribunal would be insufficient and where significant issues would fall outside the jurisdiction of the tribunal, a judicial review of a dismissal has been allowed to proceed.[184]

The law on Crown service is thus more contractual than it once was. However, some limitations on employment rights are likely to bear more heavily on civil servants than on other employees, such as the rule that employment tribunals may not consider a complaint of unfair dismissal where the dismissal was for reasons related to national security. Moreover, in cases involving Crown employees, special procedures may be adopted by the tribunals in dealing with issues affecting national security.[185]

In 2010, by part 1 of the Constitutional Reform and Governance Act, the employment and management of the civil and diplomatic service was placed on a statutory basis, but this has had little apparent impact on the matters discussed in this section.

Members of the armed forces have less protection in law than civil servants, and the system of command and discipline stands in the way of assimilating military service to civilian employment. Some statutory employment rights apply to the armed forces.[186] In respect of discrimination on grounds of race, sex, sexual orientation and religion or belief, a member of the forces has a right of recourse to an employment tribunal.[187] They may pursue a complaint by means of the internal redress of complaints procedure.[188] Members of the armed forces,

---

[177] *Dunn v R* [1896] 1 QB 116; G Nettheim [1975] CLJ 253. Cf *Dunn v MacDonald* [1897] 1 QB 401.

[178] *Rodwell v Thomas* [1944] KB 596; cf *CCSU v Minister for the Civil Service* (above).

[179] *Kodeeswaran v A-G of Ceylon* [1970] AC 1111; cf *Cameron v Lord Advocate* 1952 SC 165.

[180] Employment Rights Act 1996, s 191.

[181] Equality Act 2010, s 83(2).

[182] *R v Lord Chancellor's Department, ex p Nangle* [1992] 1 All ER 897 (see S Fredman and G Morris [1991] PL 485 and (1991) 107 LQR 298).

[183] For which see text to notes 178–9 above.

[184] *R (Shoesmith) v Ofsted* [2011] EWCA Civ 642, [2011] ICR 1195 (dismissal of local government employee on instructions of the Secretary of State following a public outcry over the death of Baby P).

[185] Employment Rights Act 1996, ss 10, 193; Employment Relations Act 1999, Sch 8. See *Tariq v Home Office* [2011] UKSC 35, [2012] 1 AC 452 (and discussion below).

[186] Employment Rights Act 1996, s 192, amended by Armed Forces Act 1996, s 26.

[187] Equality Act 2010, s 83(3), subject to certain exceptions in para 4 of Schedule 9.

[188] Armed Forces (Redress of Individual Grievances) Regulations 2007 (SI 2007/3353), and see *Crosbie v Secretary of State for Defence* [2011] EWHC 879 (Admin).

like all other persons, may seek protection for their Convention rights under the Human Rights Act 1998,[189] although the extent of their rights may be affected by their duties. Police officers are not Crown servants, being officers of the peace. They have no right to join a trade union and cannot complain of unfair dismissal.[190] The Court of Appeal has held that the exclusion of parks police officers from collective bargaining rights is a breach of their Article 11 ECHR rights, although it affirmed that the exclusion from unfair dismissal rights, while unsatisfactory, was not a breach of Article 8 ECHR.[191] Police officers do, however, have protection against discrimination.[192] A chief officer of police who is required to resign or retire by his or her police and crime commissioner under s 38 of the Police Reform and Social Responsibility Act 2011 must challenge that removal decision by way of judicial review.[193]

C. Restitution and public authorities[194]

A claim for restitution may now be included in a claim for judicial review.[195] The law of restitution was applied by the House of Lords in resolving a fundamental question as to the obligations of public authorities in *Woolwich Building Society v Inland Revenue Commissioners (No 2)*.[196] Nearly £57 million in tax had been paid under protest by the society under regulations which were held to be ultra vires.[197] The House held by 3–2 that there was a general restitutionary principle by which money paid pursuant to an ultra vires demand by a public authority was recoverable as of right, not at the discretion of the authority. This, said the majority, was required both by common justice and by the principle in the Bill of Rights that taxes should not be levied without the authority of Parliament.[198] Among the questions left open by Lord Goff's speech was whether the same principle applies if taxes are levied wrongly because the tax inspector misconstrued a statute or regulation. On this point Lord Goff commented that 'it would be strange if the right of the citizen to recover overpaid charges were to be more restricted under domestic law than it is under Community law'.[199] The House of Lords subsequently confirmed that an individual may seek restitution of monies paid under a mistake of fact or law.[200] In *Test Claimants in the Franked Investment Income Group Litigation v Revenue and Customs Commissioners*, the Supreme Court restated the principle in *Woolwich* in the context of a complicated case concerning the compatibility of UK tax statutes with EU law.[201] On this issue, holding that it was not necessary to show that a demand had been made, Lord Walker said: 'We should restate the *Woolwich* principle to cover all sums paid to a public

---

[189] Cf *R v Ministry of Defence, ex p Smith* [1996] QB 517; and *Smith v UK* (2000) 29 EHRR 493.

[190] Employment Relations Act 1996, s 200.

[191] *Wandsworth London Borough Council v Vining* [2017] EWCA Civ 1092.

[192] Equality Act 2010, s 42.

[193] The first completed use of the s 38 power was successfully challenged on irrationality grounds in *R (Crompton) v South Yorkshire Police and Crime Commissioner* [2017] EWHC 1349 (Admin).

[194] Williams, *Unjust Enrichment and Public Law: A Comparative Study of England, France and the EU*; P B H Birks [1980] CLP 191; J Adler (2002) 22 LS 165; G Virgo [2006] JR 370; A Burrows, in Burrows (ed.), *Essays on the Law of Restitution*.

[195] Senior Courts Act 1981, s 31(4).

[196] [1993] AC 70. See P B H Birks [1992] PL 580; J Beatson (1993) 109 LQR 401.

[197] *R v IRC, ex p Woolwich Building Society* [1991] 4 All ER 92.

[198] See ch 1 B.

[199] [1993] AC 70, at 177; and Goff and Jones, *The Law of Unjust Enrichment*, ch 22.

[200] *Kleinwort Benson Ltd v Lincoln City Council* [1999] 2 AC 349; *Deutsche Morgan Grenfell plc v Inland Revenue Commissioners* [2006] UKHL 49, [2007] 1 AC 558.

[201] [2012] UKSC 19, [2012] AC 245.

authority (and sufficiently causally connected with) an apparent statutory authority to pay tax which (in fact and in law) is not lawfully due.'[202]

The law of restitution works both ways. Where a public authority has made ultra vires payments to private parties, it is entitled to seek to recover them.[203] Such a claim is subject only to the defence of change of position, i.e. where the innocent receiver of the money unlawfully paid out has changed his position by spending the money. In *R (Child Poverty Action Group)* v *Work and Pensions Secretary*, it was held that the Secretary of State had no power based on the common law of restitution to recover any payments of social security benefit that were found to have been overpaid; the reason for this was that the social security legislation was intended to provide an exclusive scheme for recovering over-payments of benefit, and statutory changes in that scheme had not revived the common law in this area of social provision.[204]

D. The Crown in litigation: privileges and immunities

As we have already seen,[205] 'the Crown' is a convenient term in law for the collectivity that now comprises the monarch in her governmental capacity, ministers, civil servants and the armed forces. Lord Templeman said in 1993: 'The expression "the Crown" has two meanings, namely the monarch and the executive.'[206] When the monarch governed in person, royal officials properly benefited from the monarch's immunities and privileges. But despite the ending of personal government, the institutions of central government continued to benefit from Crown status. The shield of the Crown extended to what was described as the general government of the country or 'the province of government',[207] but not to local authorities or to other public corporations. Notwithstanding the Crown Proceedings Act 1947, for several reasons it may be necessary to know whether a public authority has Crown status.[208] It is very common for an Act which creates a new public body to state whether and to what extent it should enjoy Crown status,[209] but this does not always happen. Whether because of express legislation or judicial interpretation, a public agency may be regarded as having Crown status for some purposes, but not for others.

As we have seen, under the 1947 Act the Crown may be sued for breach of statutory duty. But nothing in the Act affects 'any presumption relating to the extent to which the Crown is bound by an Act of Parliament' (s 40(2)(f)). The rule that Acts do not bind the Crown, that is, that the Crown's rights and interests are not prejudiced by legislation unless a statute so enacts by express words or by necessary implication, significantly limits governmental liability for breach of statutory duty. It is by this rule, for example, that Crown property is in law exempt from taxation and much environmental legislation. This immunity of central government from regulation that applies to private persons goes much further than is justifiable in the

---

[202] [2012] UKSC 19, [2012] AC 245 at [79].
[203] *Auckland Harbour Board* v *R* [1924] AC 318; *Charles Terence Estates* v *Cornwall Council* [2011] EWHC 2542 (QB), [2012] PTSR 790; Goff and Jones, *The Law of Unjust Enrichment*, ch 23.
[204] [2010] UKSC 54, [2011] 2 AC 15.
[205] Ch 10, text at notes 4–8. And see in Sunkin and Payne (eds), *The Nature of the Crown*, ch 2 (Sir W Wade) and ch 3 (M Loughlin).
[206] *M* v *Home Office* [1994] 1 AC 377, 395.
[207] *Mersey Docks Trustees* v *Cameron* (1861) 11 HLC 443, 508; *BBC* v *Johns* [1965] Ch 32.
[208] E.g. liability to taxation and the criminal law; whether staff are Crown servants (*R* v *Barrett* [1976] 3 All ER 895). And see ch 12.
[209] See e.g. Parliamentary Standards Act 2009, Sch 1, para 9 (Independent Parliamentary Standards Authority not to be regarded as servant or agent of Crown).

modern age. In 1947, the Privy Council took a strict view of the test of 'necessary implication', holding that in the absence of express words the Crown is bound by a statute only if the purpose of the statute would be 'wholly frustrated' if the Crown were not bound.[210] In 1989, in *Lord Advocate* v *Dumbarton Council*, the House of Lords for the first time considered the legal basis of Crown immunity. The House held that the Crown is not bound by any statutory provision 'unless there can somehow be gathered from the terms of the relevant Act an intention to that effect'.[211] For an Act to bind the Crown, it is sufficient for it to be shown that if the Act did not do so its purpose would be frustrated in a material respect, not that its purpose would be wholly frustrated. Where an Act does not apply to the Crown or its servants acting in the course of duty, a Crown servant is not liable criminally if he or she disregards the statute.[212] But these rules do not prevent the Crown deriving benefits from legislation. Even though the Crown is not named in an Act, the Crown may take advantage of rights conferred by the Act.[213]

Procedure

Where the Act of 1947 enables proceedings to be brought against the Crown in English courts, whether in tort or contract or for the recovery of property, in principle the normal procedure of litigation applies. The action is brought against the appropriate department, the Minister for the Civil Service being responsible for publishing a list of departments and naming the solicitor for each department to accept process on its behalf; in cases not covered by the list, the Attorney General may be made defendant. The trial follows that of an ordinary civil action, but differences arise in respect of remedies and enforcement. The most important is that in place of an injunction or a decree of specific performance, the court makes an order declaring the rights of the parties (s 21(1)); and no injunction may be granted against an officer of the Crown if the effect 'would be to give any relief against the Crown which could not have been obtained in proceedings against the Crown' (s 21(2)).

The court may grant injunctive relief where necessary to protect rights under EU law.[214] The House of Lords held in *M* v *Home Office*, applying ss 23(2) and 38(2) of the 1947 Act, that the restrictions on injunctive relief do not apply to applications for judicial review, which are not 'proceedings against the Crown' for the purposes of the 1947 Act.[215] It was also held in *M* v *Home Office* that s 21(2) of the 1947 Act does not prevent injunctive relief being granted against officers of the Crown (including ministers) who have personally committed or authorised a tort and applies only in respect of duties laid on the Crown itself. As Lord Woolf said, 'it is only in those situations where prior to the Act no injunctive relief could be obtained that s 21 prevents an injunction being granted'.[216] But he added that declaratory relief against officers of the Crown should normally be the appropriate remedy.

Other provisions maintaining the special position of the Crown include the rule that judgment against a department cannot be enforced by the ordinary methods of levying execution or attachment; the department is required by the Act to pay the amount certified to be due as

---

[210] *Province of Bombay* v *Municipal Corpn of Bombay* [1947] AC 58 and *Madras Electric Supply Co Ltd* v *Boarland* [1955] AC 667.

[211] [1990] 2 AC 580, 604 (ch 10 D and J Wolffe [1990] PL 14). Contrast *Bropho* v *State of Western Australia* (1990) 171 CLR 1 (and S Kneebone [1991] PL 361). See now: *R (Black)* v *Justice Secretary* [2017] UKSC 81.

[212] *Cooper* v *Hawkins* [1904] 2 KB 164. See now Road Traffic Regulation Act 1984, s 130. On the Crown's 'axiomatic' immunity in criminal law, M Sunkin [2003] PL 716; M Andenas and D Fairgrieve [2003] PL 730.

[213] Crown Proceedings Act 1947, s 31.

[214] *Case C-213/89, R* v *Transport Secretary, ex p Factortame Ltd (No 2)* [1991] 1 AC 603; ch 6 D.

[215] [1994] 1 AC 377; S Sedley, in Forsyth and Hare (eds), *The Golden Metwand and the Crooked Cord*, pp 253–66; T Cornford, in Sunkin and Payne (eds), *The Nature of the Crown*, ch 9.

[216] [1994] 1 AC 377, 413, disapproving *Merricks* v *Heathcoat-Amory* [1955] Ch 567; and see H W R Wade (1991) 107 LQR 4.

damages and costs (s 25);[217] and that there can be no order for restitution of property, but the court may declare the claimant entitled as against the Crown (s 21(1)).

An action for a declaration may be brought against the Crown without claiming other relief, for example where a wrong is threatened,[218] but not to determine hypothetical questions which may never arise, for example, as to whether there is a contingent liability to a tax.[219]

In civil litigation, when the claimant seeks an interim injunction against the defendant to maintain the status quo pending the final decision, the court grants such a request only if the claimant gives an undertaking as to damages, so that the defendant's loss may be made good if the action ultimately fails. When the Crown is seeking to assert rights of property or contract, the Crown may be expected to give such an undertaking. But when the Crown takes proceedings to enforce the law, an undertaking as to damages is generally not appropriate.[220]

In Scotland, which has a distinct system of civil procedure, actions in respect of British or UK departments (like the Ministry of Defence or HM Revenue and Customs) may be brought against the Advocate General for Scotland, an office created by the Scotland Act 1998; in respect of departments of the devolved Scottish Administration, actions are brought against the Lord Advocate.[221] Actions may be raised by and against the Crown in either the Court of Session or the sheriff court. So far as remedies against the Crown are concerned, the decision in *M* v *Home Office* did not in terms extend to Scotland, given that separate provision applying to Scottish civil procedure had been made in the Crown Proceedings Act 1947. In *Davidson* v *Scottish Ministers*[222] the House of Lords had to decide whether the Court of Session had power to grant interim or final interdicts against the Crown in cases brought by way of judicial review, or whether s 21(1)(a) of the 1947 Act, which appeared to rule this out, applied only to proceedings against the Crown to enforce private rights. Overruling earlier Scottish authority to the contrary, the Lords held that the 1947 Act had never been intended to prevent the Scottish courts granting interim or final interdicts against the Crown in proceedings (analogous to judicial review) that invoked the 'supervisory jurisdiction' in relation to acts of the Crown or its officers. In broad terms, this confirmed that the benefit of the principle in *M* v *Home Office* could extend to Scotland. When the devolved prison service in Scotland broke an undertaking it had given to the court not to open certain mail being received by a prisoner, the Lords held that in relation to contempt of court, ministers and civil servants in the Scottish government are in the same position as their counterparts in Whitehall.[223]

Non-disclosure of evidence: public interest immunity

Disclosure of documents in civil litigation (formerly termed discovery) is a procedure by which a party may inspect all documents in the possession or control of an opponent which relate to the matters in dispute. By s 28 of the 1947 Act, the court may order discovery against the Crown and may require the Crown to answer interrogatories, that is, written questions to obtain information from the other party on material facts. But the Act expressly

[217] Cf *Gairy* v *A-G of Grenada* [2001] UKPC 30, [2002] 1 AC 167 (rule of no coercive relief against Crown yields to G's constitutional right not to be deprived of property without compensation).
[218] *Dyson* v *A-G* [1912] 1 Ch 158.
[219] *Argosam Finance Co* v *Oxby* [1965] Ch 390.
[220] *Hoffmann-La Roche & Co* v *Trade Secretary* [1975] AC 295 (enforcement of price control for drugs). And see *Kirklees Council* v *Wickes Building Supplies Ltd* [1993] AC 227. For the approach to interim relief in judicial review proceedings see: *BACONGO* v *Department of Environment of Belize* [2003] UKPC 63, [2013] 1 WLR 2839 and *R* v *Transport Secretary, ex parte Factortame Ltd (No 2)* [1991] 1 AC 603, 672–3 (Lord Goff) (adequacy of damages in a public law challenge rarely relevant).
[221] Crown Suits (Scotland) Act 1857 as amended by the Scotland Act 1998, Sch 8, para 2.
[222] [2005] UKHL 74, 2005 SLT 110, overruling *McDonald* v *Secretary of State for Scotland* 1994 SLT 692.
[223] See *Beggs* v *Scottish Ministers* [2007] UKHL 3, [2007] 1 WLR 455.

preserves the existing rule of law (formerly known as 'Crown privilege') that the Crown may refuse to disclose any document or to answer any question on the ground that this would be injurious to the public interest; the Act even protects the Crown from disclosing the mere existence of a document on the same ground. Public interest immunity (which became known as PII in the wake of the Matrix Churchill trial in 1992 discussed below) is not restricted to proceedings in which the Crown is a party and may apply also to civil proceedings between private individuals. Although PII is important for the police, its main function is as a means of keeping secret information held by central government. Vital defence and security interests must be protected against the harmful exposure of information in judicial proceedings. But who should decide in a particular situation what must not be disclosed? It is not surprising that ministers and officials may be tempted to exaggerate the harm that would be done by disclosing information they wish to keep secret. But even if they were always to resist the temptation, they are not in a position to assess the harm to the system of justice if the court is barred from seeing relevant information. That being so, the courts have a vital role to play in balancing the need for secrecy against the demands made by the law makers. This role of the courts saw a remarkable development over the second half of the 20th century, and the challenge to the system of justice continues today.

1. The leading cases

We can start at the height of the Second World War with the decision in *Duncan* v *Cammell Laird & Co.*[224]

> Early in 1939 a new submarine sank while on trial with the loss of 99 lives, including civilian workmen. Many families of those who died brought actions in negligence against the company which had built the submarine under contract with the Admiralty. In a test action, the company objected to producing documents relating to the design of the submarine. The First Lord of the Admiralty directed the company not to produce the documents on the ground of Crown privilege, since disclosure would be injurious to national defence. *Held* (House of Lords) the documents should not be disclosed. Although a validly taken objection to disclosure was conclusive, and should be taken by the minister himself, the decision ruling out such documents was that of the judge. In deciding whether it was his duty to object, a minister should withhold production only where the public interest would be harmed, for example, where disclosure would be injurious to national defence or to good diplomatic relations, 'or where the practice of keeping a class of documents secret is necessary for the proper functioning of the public service'.[225]

On this basis, documents might be withheld either because the *contents* of those documents must be kept secret (as in *Duncan*'s case itself) or on the much wider ground that they belonged to a *class* of document which must be treated as confidential, for example civil service memoranda and minutes, to guarantee candour of communication on public matters within government. Thereafter, the practice developed of withholding documents simply on the minister's assertion that they belonged to a class of documents which it was necessary to withhold 'in the public interest for the proper functioning of the public service'.[226] It seemed that the courts could not overrule the minister's objection if taken in correct form.

[224] [1942] AC 624. For the subsequent history, see J Jacob [1993] PL 121.
[225] [1942] AC 624, 642.
[226] See *Ellis* v *Home Office* [1953] 2 QB 135 and *Broome* v *Broome* [1955] P 190 for the harsh operation of the rule; and J E S Simon [1955] CLJ 62.

In 1968, in a landmark decision, the Lords overruled an objection by the Home Secretary to production of certain police reports.

In *Conway* v *Rimmer*[227] a former probationary constable, C, sued a police superintendent for malicious prosecution after an incident of a missing electric torch had led to C being acquitted of theft and then dismissed from the police. The Home Secretary claimed privilege for (*a*) probationary reports on C and (*b*) the defendant's report on the investigation into the incident. He certified that these were confidential reports within a class of documents production of which would be injurious to the public interest. *Held*, the court has jurisdiction to order the production of documents for which immunity is claimed. The court will give full weight to a minister's view, but this need not prevail if the relevant considerations are such that the judges have the experience to weigh them.

The House of Lords thus established that it is for the courts to hold the balance in the contest between secrecy and disclosure. It opened the way for further decisions on issues that included (*a*) the use as evidence of material which is subject to constraints of confidentiality; (*b*) disclosure of documents relating to the formulation of government policy; (*c*) the grounds which must be shown before the court will inspect documents; and (*d*) the use of public interest immunity in criminal proceedings.

The fact that documents are regarded as confidential by their authors is no reason why they should as a class be immune from disclosure on grounds of public interest. Where a government department holds material supplied in confidence by companies regarding commercial activities, the court's decision on disclosure will depend on an assessment of factors such as the reasons for disclosure and the harm that disclosure might cause to the public interest.[228] In *Science Research Council* v *Nassé*,[229] the House of Lords held that on an employee's complaint of unlawful discrimination, no question of public interest immunity (PII) could arise in respect of confidential reports on other employees held by the employer. Lord Scarman stated that PII was restricted 'to what must be kept secret for the protection of government at the highest levels and in the truly sensitive areas of executive responsibility'.[230]

In *Conway* v *Rimmer*, Lord Reid had said that Cabinet minutes and documents concerned with policy-making were protected against disclosure, as the inner working of government should not be exposed to ill-informed and biased criticism.[231] In *Burmah Oil Co Ltd* v *Bank of England*,[232] the issue arose of whether such high-level documents were always protected from disclosure.

In 1975 Burmah Oil had with government approval agreed to sell its holdings in BP stock to the Bank of England as part of an arrangement protecting the company from liquidation. Later the company sued to have the sale set aside as unconscionable and inequitable. It wished to see documents held by the bank, including (*a*) minutes of meetings attended by

---

[227] [1968] AC 910; D H Clark (1969) 32 MLR 142.
[228] Compare *Crompton Amusement Machines Ltd* v *Commissioners of Customs and Excise* [1974] AC 405 and *Norwich Pharmacal Co* v *Commissioners of Customs and Excise* [1974] AC 133.
[229] [1980] AC 1028.
[230] Ibid, at 1088.
[231] [1968] AC 910, 952; see also Lord Upjohn at 993.
[232] [1980] AC 1090; D G T Williams [1980] CLJ 1.

> ministers and (b) communications between senior civil servants on policy matters. The Crown contended that it was 'necessary for the proper functioning of the public service' that the documents be withheld. The House of Lords *held* that the Crown's claim of immunity was not conclusive. If it was likely (or reasonably probable) that the documents contained matter that was material to the issues in the case, the court might inspect them to determine where the balance lay between the competing public interests. Having inspected the documents, the Lords ordered that they be not produced since they did not contain material necessary for disposing fairly of the case.

In *Burmah Oil*, the judges had moved far beyond the position in *Conway* v *Rimmer*, accepting that there might be circumstances in which a high-level governmental interest must give way before the interests of justice. Even Cabinet papers are not immune from disclosure in an exceptional case where the interests of justice so require.[233]

The assessment of PII cannot sensibly be done without sight of the documents in issue. Yet, in *Air Canada* v *Trade Secretary*[234] the House of Lords upheld the Secretary of State's claim for immunity and refused to inspect the documents. The majority held that for a court to exercise the power of inspection, it was not sufficient that the documents *might* contain information relevant to the issues in dispute; the party seeking access to the documents must show that it was *reasonably probable* that the documents were likely to help his or her case. A speculative belief to this effect was not enough. This decision was a reminder that even in judicial review proceedings, the court does not have a power at will to inspect all relevant documents held within government. A particularly stark effect of how a successful claim to PII can insulate the government from challenge can be seen from *AHK* v *Home Secretary*.[235] In that case, the claimant had been refused naturalisation on national security grounds and the Home Secretary withheld the reasons for and basis of her decision as immune from disclosure under PII. Ouseley J accepted the claim of PII and made clear that the claimant's challenge was accordingly doomed to fail, because he would be unable to dispute the rationality or legality of the reasoning (because he could not see it). On no view could this be thought to be an entirely satisfactory position.

Although PII arose in the context of civil litigation, immunity from disclosure extends to criminal proceedings, albeit in a different form.[236] Plainly the public interest in keeping material secret can be damaged by disclosure wherever it occurs, but the public interest in the administration of justice is at its strongest when, if evidence is withheld from production in a criminal trial, this may prevent the accused from establishing a defence.[237]

In November 1992, the trial of three Matrix Churchill executives for the unlawful export of arms to Iraq brought these issues to public notice. Before the trial, four ministers had signed PII certificates withholding documents that concerned whether the defendants' purpose in

....

[233] As in the Australian case of *Sankey* v *Whitlam* (1978) 21 ALR 505. See also *Air Canada* v *Trade Secretary* [1983] 2 AC 394, 432 (Lord Fraser); I G Eagles [1980] PL 263. See now the qualified exemption from disclosure for Ministerial communications, including Cabinet papers, where the public interest does not favour disclosure: Freedom of Information Act 2000, s 35.

[234] [1983] 2 AC 394; Lord Mackay (1983) 2 CJQ 337 and T R S Allan (1985) 101 LQR 200.

[235] [2012] EWHC 1117 (Admin) and [2013] EWHC 1426 (Admin).

[236] *R* v *Ward* [1993] 2 All ER 577, *R* v *Davis* [1993] 2 All ER 643. And see *Rowe* v *UK* (2000) 8 BHRC 325. The present rules on disclosure in criminal procedure are outside the scope of this work; but see *R* v *H* [2004] UKHL 3, [2004] 2 AC 134.

[237] Non-disclosure by the prosecution, with the judge's approval, of relevant evidence by reason of PII may cause a trial to be unfair in breach of art 6(1) ECHR: see *Edwards and Lewis* v *UK* (2003) 15 BHRC 189 (evidence re entrapment), distinguishing *Jasper* v *UK* (2000) 30 EHRR 441.

exporting machinery to Iraq was known to the Security Services and thus to the government. PII was claimed on 'class' grounds that included protecting the functioning of government and maintaining the secrecy of intelligence operations. Having inspected the documents, the trial judge ordered disclosure, and the trial collapsed.[238] Sir Richard Scott's inquiry into 'arms for Iraq' made a penetrating study of the use of PII certificates in the case.[239] Among his criticisms were that 'class' claims for PII had been made which ought to have had no place in a criminal trial, that the claims extended to documents 'of which no more could be said than that they were confidential', and that inadequate and misleading advice had been given to ministers when they were asked to sign PII certificates.[240] This included advice that in effect left ministers with no option but to claim immunity on a class basis, even if the public interest did not require such a claim to be made. This view of the law was corrected in *R v Chief Constable of West Midlands Police, ex p Wiley*, where the Lords held that documents which are relevant to litigation *should* be produced unless disclosure would cause substantial harm. 'A rubber stamp approach to public interest immunity by the holder of a document is neither necessary nor appropriate.'[241] It is now settled that when ministers have claimed PII for evidence in civil litigation, it is for the judge to whom such a claim is made to study the evidence and decide whether the public interest in keeping the material secret is outweighed by the interests of justice.[242]

2. The development of public interest immunity into a closed material procedure
The law has come a very long way since *Duncan v Cammell Laird* distinguished between 'contents' and 'class' as a basis for withholding documents in the public interest. But the potential for tension between executive secrecy and open justice has intensified since the September 2001 attacks, as the effects of the 'war against terror' have impacted upon basic human rights.

One indication of this is the increasing use of procedure whereby the executive appoints special advocates to 'represent' an individual when the court is dealing with secret material that cannot be disclosed to the individual. This is known as a 'closed material procedure', or CMP. Special advocates were authorised by the Special Immigration Appeals Commission Act 1997 for certain immigration appeals, but the model was applied without statutory authority by the Parole Board.[243] In exceptional cases, the criminal courts accept the use of specially appointed advocates to make submissions to the judge about the material to be protected, on condition that no information is passed to the defendant or the defendant's representatives.[244] The issue of a PII certificate in judicial review proceedings is not in itself a reason for the appointment of a special advocate to deal with material that cannot be disclosed to the claimant, since it is primarily for the judge to decide where the balance of interests may lie.[245] The use of special advocates does not necessarily ensure that the individual has a fair hearing that satisfies art 6(1) ECHR.[246]

[238] See A W Bradley [1992] PL 514, A T H Smith [1993] CLJ 1, I Leigh [1993] PL 630. On the Scott report, see [1996] PL 357–507; also I Leigh and L Lustgarten (1996) 59 MLR 695.

[239] In the Scott report (HC 115, 1995–6), see on PII vol III, chs G.10–15 and G.18; vol IV, ch K.6. Also R Scott [1996] PL 427; Tomkins, *The Constitution after Scott*, ch 5; I Leigh, in Thompson and Ridley (eds), *Under the Scott-light*, pp 55–70.

[240] Scott report, para G18.104.

[241] [1995] 1 AC 274, 281 (Lord Templeman). And see *Savage v Chief Constable of Hampshire* [1997] 2 All ER 631.

[242] In *Somerville v Scottish Ministers* [2007] 1 UKHL 44, [2007] 1 WLR 2734, the Lords reminded the Scottish courts that this was the duty of the judge at first instance.

[243] *R (Roberts) v Parole Board* [2005] UKHL 45, [2005] 2 AC 738.

[244] See *R v H* [2004] UKHL 3, [2004] 2 AC 134, [10]–[39].

[245] *Murungaru v Home Secretary* [2008] EWCA Civ 1015; *Home Secretary v AHK* [2009] EWCA Civ 287, [2009] 1 WLR 2049.

[246] *Home Secretary v AF (No 3)* [2009] UKHL 28, [2009] 3 WLR 74, applying *A v UK* (2009) 49 EHRR 625. For an illuminating commentary by a special advocate, see: M Chamberlain (2009) CJQ 314 and 448.

Another repercussion of the 'war on terror' on the protection of human rights is seen in *R (Binyam Mohamed)* v *Foreign Secretary*.[247]

> A former detainee at Guantanamo Bay sought judicial review of a refusal by the Foreign Secretary to provide information relevant to his trial on terrorist charges in the United States. After protracted hearings over material withheld by the Foreign Secretary, and after dealing with much of this material in closed proceedings, the Divisional Court decided to include in its published judgment seven brief paragraphs confirming that the claimant had suffered, at the least, cruel, inhuman and degrading treatment at the hands of the US authorities. The Foreign Secretary argued that publication of the court's conclusions would prejudice co-operation between the British and US Security Services. The Court of Appeal held that the claim to PII was not justified in the context of the litigation: the paragraphs did not reveal information that would be of interest to a terrorist or harmful to national security, and the information was already in the public domain. The argument to censor the published judgment engaged 'concepts of democratic accountability and, ultimately, the rule of law itself'.[248]

That case formed part of a complex history of litigation brought by former detainees at Guantanamo Bay in which they sought damages from the UK government for illegal acts that they claimed occurred when they were detained, and during their rendition, interrogation and detention in American custody. To resist a further set of these claims, and arguing that it was impractical to go through the PII process, the government urged the court to order a 'closed material procedure' by which sensitive security material in its possession could be made known to special advocates, appointed to act for the claimants, so that part of the defence case would not be revealed to the claimants or to their lawyers. While a CMP is always less than a perfect ideal of open justice, it would at least have the potential to remedy the sort of outcome seen in *AHK* (above) where the effect of PII meant that the claim was bound to fail. The central issue of principle came to the Supreme Court. In *Al Rawi* v *Security Service*,[249] nine judges were unanimous that the courts have no power simply to replace the normal process of PII with a closed material procedure. A majority of six judges further held that after the PII process has been completed, the court has no power at common law to introduce a closed material procedure, appointing special advocates and so on, since this would be a radical departure from the principles of open and natural justice, and would deny parties their common law right to a fair trial. In the majority view, existing exceptions to the principle that justice must be done in open court (for instance, to protect the interests of a child or in intellectual property law to keep secret a commercial interest) did not justify introducing a controversial new rule in all civil litigation. Such a fundamental change in civil procedure, if it were to be made, must be made by Parliament. A minority of three judges (Lord Mance, Lord Clarke and Lady Hale) were less categorical than the majority, holding that in some circumstances the court may have power to order a closed material procedure where difficulties remain after the PII process has been completed.

---

[247] [2010] EWCA Civ 65 and [2010] EWCA Civ 158, [2011] QB 218.

[248] Ibid, [56]. For stringent judicial criticism of failings by the Ministry of Defence in regard to PII certificates, see *Al-Sweady* v *Defence Secretary* [2009] EWHC 1687 (Admin) and [2009] EWHC 2387 (Admin), [2010] HRLR 2.

[249] [2011] UKSC 34, [2012] 1 AC 531, M Chamberlain [2011] CJQ 360; J Ip (2012) 75 MLR 606. The decision has not stopped the courts adopting a 'confidentiality ring' procedure, only permitting disclosure to the claimant's lawyers and not the claimant himself: *R (Mohammed)* v *Defence Secretary* [2012] EWHC 3454 (Admin); [2013] 2 All ER 897.

Alongside *Al Rawi*, the Supreme Court also decided *Home Office* v *Tariq.*[250] The Employment Tribunals Act 1996 authorises the Secretary of State to make regulations authorising employment tribunals to adopt a closed material procedure if the interests of national security so require. Tariq, an immigration officer who had been suspended on security grounds, challenged an order applying closed material to his claim against the Home Office for discrimination on grounds of race and religion, relying on the ECHR and on EU law. By 8–1, the Supreme Court upheld the closed material procedure in employment cases, holding that the system contains sufficient safeguards to protect the claimant's interests. In dissent, Lord Kerr held that withholding of information from a claimant is a breach of the common law right to a fair trial, and also a breach of the right to a fair trial under article 6(1) ECHR.[251]

The Supreme Court had to return to the issue of CMPs in *Bank Mellat* v *HM Treasury (No. 1)* where it held – against the context of an asset freezing regime under the Counter-Terrorism Act 2008 which permitted a CMP to be adopted – by a 6–3 majority that the Supreme Court could itself adopt a CMP on an appeal.[252] The Court nonetheless made it very clear that it was extremely unhappy about requests to use a CMP, and the use of a CMP had, in that case, been wholly unnecessary. Lord Neuberger also set out clear guidance to be adopted by any court considering using a CMP and issuing a judgment which was partially closed, or secret.[253]

The Supreme Court's decision in *Al Rawi* that the courts had no power to introduce a closed material procedure in civil proceedings caused the government to introduce legislation to give the courts that novel power.[254] The resulting Bill met very strong criticism, particularly in the House of Lords,[255] and some limitations on the government's original proposals were adopted. Part 2 of the Justice and Security Act 2013 authorises the High Court, Court of Session and higher courts in the course of civil proceedings to decide (on the application of the Secretary of State, any party to the proceedings, or of its own motion) that a 'closed material procedure' (CMP) may be followed. Such procedure applies where 'sensitive material' (defined as 'material the disclosure of which would be damaging to the interests of national security', s 6(11)) would otherwise require to be disclosed (or withheld) by the party in question and where 'it is in the interests of the fair and effective administration of justice' that the procedure should apply (s 6(5)). Before applying to the court, the Secretary of State must have considered whether a claim for public interest immunity (PII) should be made (s 6(7)). The decision of the court authorising a CMP must be kept under review by the court and may be revoked if the 'fair and effective administration of justice' no longer requires it (s 7(3)). Before the court authorises a CMP, a 'special advocate' must be appointed by a law officer of the Crown to represent the interests of the party adversely affected by the CMP (s 9(1)): the litigant and his or her regular legal representatives cannot be informed of the material in question. When a CMP is authorised by the court, proceedings involving the sensitive material take place in strict secrecy but in the presence of the special advocate; the eventual judgment of the court will need to be in two parts, one an open judgment covering matters

---

[250] [2011] UKSC 35, [2012] 1 AC 452.

[251] Lord Kerr considered to be anomalous the decision of the Strasbourg court in *Kennedy* v *UK* (2011) 52 EHRR 4 which, in a case of suspected telephone tapping brought under the Regulation of Investigatory Powers Act 2000, held that Kennedy had no absolute right to see all relevant evidence and that the UK legislation did not breach articles 6(1) and 8 ECHR.

[252] [2013] UKSC 38, [2013] 3 WLR 179.

[253] [2013] UKSC 38, [2013] 3 WLR 179 at [68]–[74].

[254] See the Green Paper, *Justice and Security* (Cm 8194, 2011); and observations by the Joint Committee on Human Rights (24th report, HL 286, HC 1777, 2010–12).

[255] House of Lords Constitution Committee, *Justice and Security Bill* (3rd report, HL 18, 2012–13). See too: M Chamberlain [2012] CJQ 424; M Fordham [2012] JR 187; T Otty [2012] EHRLR 267.

dealt with in open court, and the other a secret judgment that cannot be published or disclosed to the litigant, and can be seen only by the Secretary of State and the special advocates. It remains to be seen whether the structure for decision-making contained in the Act will enable the courts to make decisions independently of the executive on matters that may have a bearing on national security, but may also (as with rendition and prolonged detention in Guantanamo Bay) have a drastic effect on the individual's rights and liberties and on the due process of law. The case law over the early years of the 2013 Act's operation has adopted an approach of cautious approval of the s 6 conditions for a CMP, respecting the balance struck by Parliament between the competing needs of open justice and national security, and agreeing to CMPs in some high-profile cases.[256]

E. Conclusion

Judicial review is a branch of law which applies only to public authorities. In other areas of the law, so it was traditionally said, the Crown (or other public authorities) had no special or particular protection beyond that of any other litigant. As we have seen in this chapter, that was never true and it is certainly not true now.

The status of an individual party as a public authority has a series of effects. It may mean that they are subject to torts which do not apply to private individuals (misfeasance in public office, breach of the Human Rights Act 1998). It may mean that particular types of proceedings cannot be brought at all because of the Crown Proceedings Act 1947. It may mean that in particular cases information can be withheld on public interest immunity grounds, or the claimant is excluded from large sections of the proceedings altogether by the application of a closed material procedure.

Even in 'ordinary' cases of breaches of obligations – tort, contract, restitution – the fact that the defendant is a public authority means that the law may react differently. Imposing a new duty of care on a public authority in negligence has given rise to a contradictory and evolving body of case law; the freedom of public bodies to act in the public interest has meant that they may escape contractual obligations more readily; and large sections of the law of restitution have been developed in the context of recovery of overpaid tax revenue.

As a result, it must not be forgotten that administrative law is more than just judicial review. Judicial review is only one way in which the State may be held to account, and it is only one branch of law in which the involvement of public authorities as a party to litigation means that special considerations or rules may apply.

---

[256] See in particular: *R (Sarkandi)* v *Foreign Secretary* [2015] EWCA Civ 687, [2016] 3 All ER 837; *R (K)* v *Defence Secretary* [2016] EWCA Civ 1149, [2017] 1 WLR 1671 (Afghan intelligence sources aiding British troops); *Belhaj v Straw* [2017] EWHC 1861 (trial of tort claims arising out of allegations of extraordinary rendition to Libya). And see: E Nanopoulos (2015) 78 MLR 913.

BIBLIOGRAPHY

Ackerman, B, *We the People: Foundations*, 1991

Adler, M (ed.), *Administrative Justice in Context*, 2010

Adler, M, & Bradley, A W (eds), *Justice, Discretion and Poverty*, 1976

Aitken, J, *Officially Secret*, 1971

Alderman, R K, & Cross, J A, *The Tactics of Resignation*, 1967

Alexander, L (ed.), *Constitutionalism: Philosophical Foundations*, 1998

Allan, T R S, *Constitutional Justice: A Liberal Theory of the Rule of Law*, 2001

Allan, T R S, *Law, Liberty and Justice: The Legal Foundations of British Constitutionalism*, 1993

Allan, T R S, *The Sovereignty of Law*, 2013

Allason, R, *The Branch: A History of the Metropolitan Police Special Branch 1883–1983*, 1988

Allison, J W F, *A Continental Distinction in the Common Law: A Historical and Comparative Perspective on English Public Law*, rev edn, 2000

Allison, J W F, *The English Historical Constitution: Continuity, Change and European Effects*, 2007

Alston, P (ed.), *The EU and Human Rights*, 1999

Amery, L S, *Thoughts on the Constitution*, 2nd edn, 1953

Amos, M, *Human Rights Law*, 2006

Andenas, M, & Fairgrieve, D (eds), *Tom Bingham and the Transformation of the Law*, 2009

Andrew, C, *Secret Service: The Making of the British Intelligence Community*, 1985

Andrews, J A (ed.), *Welsh Studies in Public Law*, 1970

Anson, W R, *The Law and Custom of the Constitution*, vol. I, *Parliament* (ed. M L Gwyer), 5th edn, 1922; vol. II, *The Crown* (ed. A B Keith), 4th edn, 1935

Arlidge, A and Lord Judge, *Magna Carta Uncovered*, 2014

Arnstein, W L, *The Bradlaugh Case*, 1965

Arnull, A, *The European Union and its Court of Justice*, 2nd edn, 2006

Arrowsmith, S, *The Law of Public and Utilities Procurement*, 3rd edn, 2014

Arthurs, H W, *Without the Law: Administrative Justice and Legal Pluralism in the 19th Century*, 1985

Aubrey, C, *Who's Watching You?*, 1981

Auburn, J, Moffett, J & Sharland, A, *Judicial Review: Principles and Procedure*, 2013

Austin, J, *The Province of Jurisprudence Determined* (ed. H L A Hart), 1954

Bagehot, W, *The English Constitution* (introduction R H S Crossman), 1963

Bailey, S H (ed.), *Cross on Local Government Law*, looseleaf

Bailey, S H, Harris, D, & Jones, T, *Civil Liberties: Cases and Materials* (6th edn by S H Bailey and N Taylor), 2009

Baldwin, J R, Wikeley, N, & Young, R, *Judging Social Security: The Adjudication of Claims for Benefit in Britain*, 1992

Baldwin, R, *Rules and Government*, 1995

Bamforth, N, & Leyland, P (eds), *Accountability in the Modern Constitution*, 2014

Bamforth, N & Leyland, P (eds), *Public Law in a Multi-layered Constitution*, 2013

Barber, N W, *The Constitutional State*, 2012

Barendt, E, *Broadcasting Law: A Comparative Study*, 1993

Barendt, E, *Freedom of Speech*, 2nd edn, 2007

Barnett, A, *This Time: Our Constitutional Revolution*, 1997

Barnett, A (ed.), *Power and the Throne: The Monarchy Debate*, 1994

Bassett, R G, *1931: Political Crisis*, 1958

Bates, E, *The Evolution of the European Convention on Human Rights*, 2010

Beatson, J, & Cripps, Y (eds), *Freedom of Expression and Freedom of Information*, 2000

Beatson, J, Matthews, M H, & Elliott M, *Administrative Law: Text and Materials* (5th edn by M Elliott and J N E Varuhas), 2016

Beer, S H, *Modern British Politics*, 1965

Beer, S H, *Treasury Control*, 2nd edn, 1957

Bell, J S, *French Constitutional Law*, 1992

Bellamy, R, *Political Constitutionalism: A Republican Defence of the Constitutionality of Democracy*, 2007

Bennion, F, *Statutory Interpretation* (ed. D Bailey & L Norbury), 7th edn, 2017

Bentham, J, *Handbook of Political Fallacies* (ed. H A Larrabee), 1962

Bercusson, B, *European Labour Law*, 2nd edn, 2009

Berger, R, *Impeachment*, 1973

Berkeley, H, *The Power of the Prime Minister*, 1968

Bingham, T, *The Rule of Law*, 2010

Birkinshaw, P, *Freedom of Information: The Law, the Practice and the Ideal*, 2010

Birkinshaw, P, *Reforming the Secret State*, 1991

Birrell, D, & Murie, A, *Policy and Government in Northern Ireland: Lessons of Devolution*, 1980

Blackburn, R, *The Electoral System in Britain*, 1995

Blackburn, R, *King and Country: Monarchy and the Future King Charles III*, 2006

Blackburn, R, *The Meeting of Parliament*, 1990

Blackburn, R, & Plant, R (eds), *Constitutional Reform: The Labour Government's Constitutional Reform Agenda*, 1999

Blackburn, R, & Polakiewicz, J (eds), *Fundamental Rights in Europe: The European Convention on Human Rights and Its Member States 1950–2000*, 2001

Blackstone, *Commentaries on the Laws of England*, 10th edn, 1787; 14th edn, 1803

Blick, A, *Beyond Magna Carta: A Constitution for the UK*, 2015

Blom-Cooper, L, *Public Inquiries: Wrong Route on Bloody Sunday*, 2017.

Blom-Cooper, L, Drewry G, & Dickson, B (eds), *The Judicial House of Lords, 1876–2009*, 2009

Blom-Cooper, L J, & Drewry, G, *Final Appeal*, 1972

Bogdanor, V, *Devolution in the United Kingdom*, 1999

Bogdanor, V, *Multi-party Politics and the Constitution*, 1983

Bogdanor, V, *Politics and the Constitution*, 1996

Bogdanor, V, *The Monarchy and the Constitution*, 1995

Bogdanor, V, *The New British Constitution*, 2009

Bogdanor, V, *The People and the Party System*, 1981

Bogdanor, V (ed.), *The British Constitution in the Twentieth Century*, 2003

Bolingbroke, H St J, *Political Writings* (ed. D Armitage), 1997

Booth, C, & Squires, D, *The Negligence Liability of Public Authorities*, 2006

Brady, A D P, *Proportionality and Deference under the UK Human Rights Act*, 2012

Bragg, B, *A Genuine Expression of the Will of the People*, 2001

Brazier, R, *Constitutional Practice: The Foundations of British Government*, 3rd edn, 1999

Brazier, R, *Constitutional Reform: Re-shaping the British Political System*, 3rd edn, 2008

Brazier, R, *Ministers of the Crown*, 1997

Bridges, Lord, *The Treasury*, 2nd edn, 1966

Bridges, L, Meszaros, G, & Sunkin, M, *Judicial Review in Perspective*, 2nd edn, 1995

Bromhead, P A, *Private Members' Bills in the British Parliament*, 1956

Brown, L N, & Bell, J S, *French Administrative Law*, 5th edn, 1998

Brown, L N, & Kennedy, T, *The Court of Justice of the European Communities*, 5th edn, 2000

Brownlie, I, *Principles of Public International Law* (ed. J Crawford), 8th edn, 2012

Brownlie, I, & Goodwin-Gill, G S, *Basic Documents on Human Rights*, 6th edn, 2010

Bryant, C (ed.), *Towards a New Constitutional Settlement*, 2007

Bryce, J, *Studies in History and Jurisprudence*, 1901

Buckland, P, *The Factory of Grievances*, 1979

Bunyan, T, *The Political Police in Britain*, 1976

Burrows, A (ed.), *Essays in the Law of Restitution*, 1991

Butler, D, *Governing without a Majority: Dilemmas for Hung Parliaments in Britain*, 1983

Butler, D (ed.), *Coalitions in British Politics*, 1978

Butler, D E, *The Electoral System in Britain since 1918*, 2nd edn, 1963

Calvert, H, *Constitutional Law in Northern Ireland*, 1968

Campbell, C, *Emergency Law in Ireland 1918–1925*, 1994

Campbell, T D, Ewing, K D, & Tomkins, A (eds), *Sceptical Essays on Human Rights*, 2001

Campbell, T D, Ewing, K D, & Tomkins, A (eds), *The Legal Protection of Human Rights: Sceptical Essays*, 2011

Cane, P, *Administrative Law*, 5th edn, 2009

Cane, P, *Administrative Tribunals and Adjudication*, 2009

Card, R, *Public Order Law*, 2000

Carmichael, P, & Dickson, B, *The House of Lords*, 1999

Carnall, G, & Nicholson, C (eds), *The Impeachment of Warren Hastings*, 1989

Carpenter, D, *Magna Carta*, 2015

Carr, C, *Concerning English Administrative Law*, 1941

Cartwright, T J, *Royal Commissions and Departmental Committees in Britain*, 1975

Chester, D N, & Bowring, N, *Questions in Parliament*, 1962

Chitty, J, *Prerogatives of the Crown*, 1820

Clapham, A, *Brierley's Law of Nations: An Introduction to the Role of Law in International Relations*, 7th edn, 2012

Clark, D, & McCoy, G, *The Most Fundamental Legal Right: Habeas Corpus in the Commonwealth*, 2000

Clayton, R, & Tomlinson, H, *Civil Actions against the Police*, 3rd edn, 2003

Clayton, R, & Tomlinson, H, *The Law of Human Rights*, 2nd edn, 2009

Clyde, Lord, & Edwards, D J, *Judicial Review*, 2000

Collins, H, Ewing, K D, & McColgan, A, *Labour Law*, 2012

Convery, J, *The Governance of Scotland*, 2000

Cook, R, *The Point of Departure*, 2003

Cornford, T, *Towards a Public Law of Tort*, 2008

Cosgrove, R A, *The Rule of Law: Albert Venn Dicey, Victorian Jurist*, 1980

Cowley, P (ed.), *Conscience and Parliament*, 1998

Cowley, P, *The Rebels: How Blair Mislaid His Majority*, 2005

Craig, P P, *Administrative Law*, 8th edn, 2016

Craig, P P, *UK, EU and Global Administrative Law*, 2015

Craig, P P, *Public Law and Democracy in the UK and the USA*, 1991

Craig, P P, & De Burca, G, *EU Law: Text, Cases and Materials*, 6th edn, 2015

Craig P P, & Rawlings, R W, *Law and Administration in Europe: Essays in Honour of Carol Harlow*, 2003

Craufurd Smith, R, *Broadcasting Law and Fundamental Rights*, 1997

Crick, B, *The Reform of Parliament*, 2nd edn, 1968

Cripps, Y, *The Legal Implications of Disclosure in the Public Interest*, 2nd edn, 1994

Cross, R, *Precedent in English Law* (eds R Cross & J W Harris), 4th edn, 1991

Cross, R, *Statutory Interpretation* (eds J Bell & G Engle), 1995

Cross, R, & Tapper, C, *Evidence* (ed. C Tapper), 12th edn, 2010

Cygan, A J, *The United Kingdom Parliament and European Union Legislation*, 1998

Dalyell, T, *Devolution, The End of Britain?*, 1977

Davies, A C L, *The Public Law of Government Contracts*, 2008

Davies, P L, & Freedland, M R, *Labour Legislation and Public Policy: A Contemporary History*, 1993

Davis, K C, *Discretionary Justice*, 1969

D'Entreves, A P, *The Notion of the State*, 1967

De Smith, S A, *The New Commonwealth and its Constitutions*, 1964

De Visser, M, *Constitutional Review in Europe*, 2013

Deakin, S, & Morris, G S, *Labour Law*, 6th edn, 2012

Devine, T M, *The Scottish Nation 1700–2000*, 1999

Dicey, A V, *The Law of the Constitution* (ed. E C S Wade), 10th edn, 1959

Dicey, A V, & Rait, R S, *Thoughts on the Union between England and Scotland*, 1920

Dickson, B, *Human Rights and the United Kingdom Supreme Court*, 2013

Donaldson, A G, *Some Comparative Aspects of Irish Law*, 1957

Donaldson, F, *The Marconi Scandal*, 1962

Donaldson, G, *Edinburgh History of Scotland*, vol. 3, *James V–James VII*, 1965

Douglas-Scott, S, *The Constitutional Law of the European Union*, 2002

Drewry, G (ed.), *The New Select Committees*, 2nd edn, 1989

Drucker, H (ed.), *Scottish Government Yearbook 1980*, 1980

Dworkin, R, *Taking Rights Seriously*, 1977

Edwards, J Ll J, *The Law Officers of the Crown*, 1964

Edwards, J Ll J, *The Attorney-General, Politics and the Public Interest*, 1984

Elliott, M, *The Constitutional Foundations of Judicial Review*, 2001

Ellis, E (ed.), *The Principle of Proportionality in the Laws of Europe*, 1999

Elton, G R, *Studies in Tudor and Stuart Politics and Government* (2 vols), 1974

Endicott, T, *Administrative Law*, 3rd edn, 2015

Englefield, D (ed.), *Commons Select Committees*, 1984

Erskine May, *Parliamentary Practice* (*The Law, Privileges, Proceedings and Usage of Parliament*) (ed. M Jack), 24th edn, 2011

Evans, G (ed.), *Labor and the Constitution, 1972–1975*, 1977

Ewing, K D, *Bonfire of the Liberties: New Labour, Human Rights and the Rule of Law*, 2010

Ewing, K D, *Britain and the ILO*, 2nd edn, 1994

Ewing, K D, *Ruined Lives: Blacklisting in the UK Construction Industry*, 2009

Ewing, K D, *Trade Unions, the Labour Party and the Law*, 1983

Ewing, K D, *The Cost of Democracy: Party Funding in Modern British Politics*, 2007

Ewing, K D, *The Funding of Political Parties in Britain*, 1987

Ewing, K D, & Dale-Risk, K, *Human Rights in Scotland – Text, Cases and Materials*, 2004

Ewing, K D, & Gearty, C A, *A Law Too Far: Part III of the Police Bill, 1997*, 1997

Ewing, K D, & Gearty, C A, *Freedom under Thatcher: Civil Liberties in Modern Britain*, 1990

Ewing, K D, & Gearty, C A, *The Struggle for Civil Liberties: Political Freedom and the Rule of Law in Britain, 1914–45*, 2000

Ewing, K D, & Issacharoff, S (eds), *Party Funding and Campaign Financing in International Perspective*, 2006

Ewing, K D, Rowbottom, J & Tham, J-C, *The Funding of Political Parties: Where Now?*, 2011

Fairgrieve, D, *State Liability in Tort*, 2003

Fairgrieve, D, Andenas, M, & Bell, J (eds), *Tort Liability of Public Authorities in Comparative Perspective*, 2002

Fairhurst, J, *Law of the European Union*, 10th edn, 2014

Farbey, J, Sharpe, R J, & Atrill, S, *The Law of Habeas Corpus*, 3rd edn, 2011

Farmer, J A, *Tribunals and Government*, 1974

Feldman, D J, *Civil Liberties and Human Rights in England and Wales*, 2nd edn, 2002

Feldman, D J (ed.), *English Public Law*, 2nd edn, 2009

Fenwick, H, *Civil Rights: New Labour, Freedom and the Human Rights Act*, 2000

Fenwick, H M, Phillipson, G, & Masterman, R M W (eds), *Judicial Reasoning under the UK Human Rights Act*, 2007

Ferguson, W, *Edinburgh History of Scotland*, vol. 4, *1689 to the Present*, 1968

Findlater, R, *Banned!*, 1967

Finnie, W, Himsworth, C, & Walker, N (eds), *Edinburgh Essays in Public Law*, 1991

Fisher, J, *British Political Parties*, 1996

Flinders, M, Gamble, A, Hay, C, & Kenny, C (eds), *The Oxford Handbook of British Politics*, 2009

Foley, M, *The Politics of the British Constitution*, 1999

Foley, M, *The Rise of the British Presidency*, 1993

Foley, M, *The Silence of Constitutions: Gaps, 'Abeyances' and Political Temperament in the Maintenance of Government*, 1989

Ford, P, & Ford, G (ed.), *Luke Graves Hansard's Diary, 1814–1841*, 1962

Forsey, E A, *The Royal Power of Dissolution of Parliament in the British Commonwealth*, 1943

Forsyth, C (ed.), *Judicial Review and the Constitution*, 2000

Forsyth, C, Elliott, M, Jhaveri, S, Scully-Hill, A, & Ramsden, M, (eds), *Effective Judicial Review: A Cornerstone of Good Governance*, 2010

Forsyth, C, & Hare, I (eds), *The Golden Metwand and the Crooked Cord: Essays in Honour of Sir William Wade*, 1998

Foster, C D, *British Government in Crisis*, 2005

Franklin, M N, & Norton, P (eds), *Parliamentary Questions*, 1993

Fredman, S, & Morris, G S, *The State as Employer: Labour Law in the Public Services*, 1989

Fredman, S and Campbell, M (eds), *Social and Economic Rights and Constitutional Law*, 2017

Freeman, E A, *The Growth of the English Constitution*, 1872

Fryde, E B, & Miller, E (eds), *Historical Studies of the English Parliament 1399–1603*, 1970

Fuller, L L, *The Morality of Law*, 1964

Galligan, D J, *Discretionary Powers: A Legal Study of Official Discretion*, 1987

Ganz, G, *Quasi-Legislation: Recent Developments in Secondary Legislation*, 1987

Gardbaum, S, *The New Commonwealth Model of Constitutionalism*, 2013

Gearty, C, *Civil Liberties*, 2007

Gearty, C A, *Principles of Human Rights Adjudication*, 2004

Gearty, C A (ed.), *European Civil Liberties and the European Convention on Human Rights*, 1997

Gearty, C A, & Kimbell, J A, *Terrorism and the Rule of Law*, 1995

Gee, G, & Rackley, E (eds), *Debating Judicial Appointments in an Age of Diversity*, 2017

Gellhorn, W, *Ombudsmen and Others*, 1966

Gerhardt, M J, *The Federal Impeachment Process: A Constitutional and Historical Analysis*, 2nd edn, 2000

Gibbons, T, *Regulating the Media*, 2nd edn, 1997

Giddings, P J (ed.), *Parliamentary Accountability: A Study of Parliament and Executive Agencies*, 1995

Gill, P, *Policing Politics*, 1994

Goff, Lord, & Jones, G H, *The Law of Unjust Enrichment*, 9th edn, 2016

Goldsworthy, J, *Parliamentary Sovereignty Contemporary Debates*, 2010

Goldsworthy, J, *The Sovereignty of Parliament: History and Philosophy*, 1999

Gordon, M, *Parliamentary Sovereignty in the UK Constitution*, 2015

Gordon, R, *Repairing British Politics: A Blueprint for Constitutional Change*, 2010

Gordon, R, & Street, A, *Select Committees and Coercive Powers: Clarity or Confusion?*, 2012

Gough, J W, *Fundamental Law in English Constitutional History*, 1955

Graham, C, *Regulating Public Utilities*, 2000

Grayling, A C, *Towards the Light: The Struggle for Liberty and Right that Made the Modern State*, 2007

Greenberg, *Craies on Legislation*, 11th edn, 2017

Greenberg, D, *Laying Down the Law*, 2011

Gregory, R, & Hutchesson, P G, *The Parliamentary Ombudsman*, 1975

Grey, Earl, *Parliamentary Government*, 1864

Griffith, J A G, *Parliamentary Scrutiny of Government Bills*, 1974

Griffith, J A G, *The Politics of the Judiciary*, 5th edn, 1997

Griffith, J A G, & Ryle, M, *Parliament* (eds R Blackburn and A Kennon), 2nd edn, 2002

Gurry, F, *Breach of Confidence* (eds T Aplin, L Bently, P Johnson & S Malynicz), 2nd edn, 2012

Hadden, T, & Boyle, K, *The Anglo-Irish Agreement*, 1989

Hadfield, B, *The Constitution of Northern Ireland*, 1989

Hadfield, B (ed.), *Judicial Review, A Thematic Approach*, 1995

Hadfield, B (ed.), *Northern Ireland: Politics and the Constitution*, 1992

Hailsham, Lord, *On the Constitution*, 1992

Hailsham, Lord, *The Dilemma of Democracy*, 1978

Halliday, S, *Judicial Review and Compliance with Administrative Law*, 2004

Hanham, H J, *The Nineteenth Century Constitution, 1815–1914*, 1969

Harden, I, *The Contracting State*, 1992

Harding, A J, *Public Duties and Public Law*, 1989

Hardt, S, *Parliamentary Immunity: A Comprehensive Study of the Systems of Parliamentary Immunity in France, the UK and the Netherlands*, 2013

Harlow, C, *State Liability – Tort Law and Beyond*, 2004

Harlow, C, & Rawlings, R, *Law and Administration*, 3rd edn, 2009

Harris, D, & Darcy, J, *The European Social Charter*, 2nd edn, 2001

Harris, D J, O'Boyle, M, & Warbrick, C, *Law of the European Convention on Human Rights* (eds D Harris et al), 3rd edn, 2014

Harris, M, & Partington, M (eds), *Administrative Justice in the 21st Century*, 1999

Hart, H L A, *The Concept of Law*, 2nd edn, 1997

Hart, H L A, & Honoré, A M, *Causation in the Law*, 1959

Hartley, T C, *The Foundations of European Community Law*, 8th edn, 2014

Hawkins, W, *Pleas of the Crown*, 6th edn (by T Leach), 2 vols, 1787

Hayek, F A, *The Constitution of Liberty*, 1963

Hazell, R and Melton J (eds), *Magna Carta and its Modern Legacy*, 2015

Hazell, R (ed.), *The English Question*, 2006

Hazell, R (ed.), *The State of the Nations 2003: The Third Year of Devolution in the United Kingdom*, 2003

Hazell, R, & Rawlings, R W, *Devolution, Law Making and the Constitution*, 2005

Heard, A, *Canadian Constitutional Conventions: The Marriage of Law and Politics*, 1991

Hearn, W E, *The Government of England*, 1867

Hedley, P, & Aynsley, C, *The D-Notice Affair*, 1967

Henderson, E G, *Foundations of English Administrative Law*, 1963

Hendry, I, & Dickson, S, *British Overseas Territory Law*, 2011

Hennessy, P, *Cabinet*, 1986

Hennessy, P, *The Prime Minister: The Office and its Holders Since 1945*, 2000

Hennessy, P, *Whitehall*, rev edn, 1990

Heuschling, L, *Etat de droit, Rechsstaat, Rule of Law*, 2002

Heuston, R F V, *Essays in Constitutional Law*, 2nd edn, 1964

Hewart, Lord, *The New Despotism*, 1929

Hiebert, J L, and Kelly, J B, *Parliamentary Bills of Rights*, 2015

Hill, L B, *The Model Ombudsman*, 1976

Himsworth, C M G, *Local Government Law in Scotland*, 1995

Himsworth, C M G, & Munro, C R, *The Scotland Act 1998*, 2nd edn, 2000

Himsworth, C M G, & O'Neill, C M, *Scotland's Constitution: Law and Practice*, 3rd edn, 2015

Hobby, C, *Whistleblowing and the Public Interest Disclosure Act 1998*, 2001

Hogg, P W, *Constitutional Law of Canada*, 5th edn, 2007; student edn, 2017

Hogg, P W, Monahan, P & Wright, W K, *Liability of the Crown*, 4th edn, 2011

Holdsworth, W, *A History of English Law* (14 vols), 1923–64

Holt, J C, *Magna Carta*, 2nd edn, 1992

Hood Phillips, O, *Reform of the Constitution*, 1970

Hood Phillips, O, & Jackson, P, *Constitutional and Administrative Law*, 8th edn (by P Jackson and P Leonard), 2001

Horne, A, Drewry, G, & Oliver, D (eds), *Parliament and the Law*, 2013

Hunnings, N M, *Film Censors and the Law*, 1967

Hunt, M, *Using Human Rights Law in English Courts*, 1997

Jacobs, E, *Tribunal Practice and Procedure*, 4th edn, 2016

Jacobs, F G, White, R C A, & Ovey, C, *The European Convention on Human Rights* (eds B Rainey, E Wicks & C Ovey), 7th edn, 2017

James, S, *British Cabinet Government*, 1992

Janis, M, Kay, R, & Bradley, A W, *European Human Rights Law: Text and Materials*, 3rd edn, 2008

Jefferson, T, & Grimshaw, R, *Controlling the Constable: Police Accountability in England and Wales*, 1984

Jenkins, R, *A Life at the Centre*, 1991

Jenkins, R, *Mr Balfour's Poodle*, 1954

Jennings, I, *Cabinet Government*, 3rd edn, 1959

Jennings, I, *Parliament*, 2nd edn, 1957

Jennings, I, *The Law and the Constitution*, 5th edn, 1959

Jones, B, Norton, P, & Daddow, O (eds), *Politics UK*, 7th edn, 2018

Jones, T, *Whitehall Diary*, vol. 3 (ed. R K Middlemas), 1971

Joseph, R, *The War Prerogative: History, Reform, and Constitutional Change*, 2013.

Jowell, J L, & Oliver, D H, *The Changing Constitution*, 3rd edn, 1994; 4th edn, 2000; 5th edn, 2004; 6th edn, 2007; 7th edn, 2011

Jowell, J L, Oliver, D H, & O'Cinneide, C (eds), *The Changing Constitution*, 8th edn, 2015

Justice/All Souls Committee, *Administrative Justice: Some Necessary Reforms*, 1988

Kavanagh, A, *Constitutional Review under the UK Human Rights Act 1998*, 2009

Keating, M J, & Midwinter, A, *The Government of Scotland*, 1983

Keeton, G W, *Trial by Tribunal*, 1960

Keir, D L, & Lawson, F H, *Cases in Constitutional Law*, 6th edn, 1979

Kenny, A (ed.), *The Oxford History of Western Philosophy*, 2000

Kerr, J, *Matters for Judgment*, 1979

King, A, *Does the United Kingdom Still Have a Constitution?*, 2001

King, A, *The British Constitution*, 2007

Kinley, D, *The European Convention on Human Rights: Compliance without Incorporation*, 1993

Kneebone, S, *Tort Liability of Public Authorities*, 1998

Kostal, R W, *A Jurisprudence of Power: Victorian Empire and the Rule of Law*, 2005

Lane, J-E, *Constitutions and Political Theory*, 1996

Laski, H J, *A Grammar of Politics*, 5th edn, 1967

Latham, R T E, *The Law and the Commonwealth*, 1949

Laundy, P, *The Office of Speaker*, 1964

Lawrence, R J, *The Government of Northern Ireland*, 1965

Le Sueur, A (ed.), *Building the United Kingdom's Supreme Court – National and Comparative Perspectives*, 2003

Lee, H P (ed.), *Judiciaries in Comparative Perspective*, 2011

Lee, H P, Hanks, P, & Morabito, V, *In the Name of National Security: The Legal Dimensions*, 1995

Leggatt, A P, *Tribunals for Users*, 2001

Legomsky, S H, *Immigration and the Justiciary: Law and Politics in Britain and America*, 1987

Leigh, I, & Masterman, R, *Making Rights Real: The Human Rights Act in Its First Decade*, 2008

Lester, A, & Bindman, G, *Race and Law*, 1972

Lester, A, Pannick, D, & Herberg, J (eds), *Human Rights Law and Practice*, 3rd edn, 2009

Lewis, A, *Make No Law*, 1991

Lewis, C B, *Judicial Remedies in Public Law*, 5th edn, 2014

Linklater, M, & Leigh, D, *Not Without Honour*, 1986

Locke, J, *Two Treatises of Government* (ed. P Laslett), rev edn, 1988

Loughlin, M, *Foundations of Public Law*, 2010

Loughlin, M, *Legality and Locality: The Role of Law in Central–Local Government Relations*, 1996

Loughlin, M, *Local Government in the Modern State*, 1986

Loughlin, M, *Public Law and Political Theory*, 1992

Loughlin, M, *The British Constitution: A Very Short Introduction*, 2013

Loveland, I, *By Due Process of Law? Racial Discrimination and the Right to Vote in South Africa 1850–1960*, 1999

Loveland, I, *Political Libels: A Comparative Study*, 2000

Loveland, I D, *Constitutional Law, Administrative Law and Human Rights*, 6th edn, 2012

Lowell, A L, *The Government of England*, 1912 edn

Lumb, R D, Moens, G A, & Trone, J, *The Constitution of the Commonwealth of Australia* (eds G A Moens & J Trone), 9th edn, 2016

Lustgarten, L, *The Governance of the Police*, 1986

Lustgarten, L, & Leigh, I, *In from the Cold: National Security and Parliamentary Democracy*, 1994

MacCormick, N, *Questioning Sovereignty: Law, State, and Nation in the European Commonwealth*, 1999

McCabe, S, & Wallington, P, *The Police, Public Order and Civil Liberties: Legacies of the Miners' Strike*, 1988

McCrudden, C (ed.), *Regulation and Deregulation: Policy and Practice in the Utilities and Financial Services Industries*, 1999

McCrudden, C, & Chambers, G (eds), *Individual Rights and the Law in Britain*, 1993

McIlwain, C H, *Constitutionalism, Ancient and Modern*, 1947

Mackintosh, J P, *The British Cabinet*, 3rd edn, 1977

Mackintosh, J P, *Specialist Committees in the House of Commons – Have They Failed?* (rev), 1980

McLean, I, *What's Wrong with the British Constitution?*, 2010

Maitland, F W, *The Constitutional History of England*, 1908

Major, J, *The Autobiography*, 1999

Manson, A, & Mullan, D (eds), *Commissions of Inquiry: Praise or Reappraise?*, 2003

Margach, J, *The Abuse of Power*, 1978

Marique, Y, *Public-Private Partnerships and the Law*, 2014

Markesinis, B S, *The Theory and Practice of Dissolution of Parliament*, 1972

Markesinis, B S, Auby, J-B, Coester-Waltjen, D, & Deakin, S F, *Tortious Liability of Statutory Bodies: A Comparative and Economic Analysis of Five English Cases*, 1999

Marshall, G, *Constitutional Conventions*, 1984

Marshall, G, *Constitutional Theory*, 1971

Marshall, G, *Parliamentary Sovereignty and the Commonwealth*, 1957

Marshall, G, *Police and Government*, 1965

Marshall, G, & Moodie, G C, *Some Problems of the Constitution*, 5th edn, 1971

Mathijsen, P S R F, *A Guide to European Union Law* (eds P R S F Mathijsen and P Dyrberg), 11th edn, 2013

Mead, D, *The New Law of Peaceful Protest*, 2010

Middlemas, K, & Barnes, J, *Baldwin*, 1969

Miliband, R, *Capitalist Democracy in Britain*, 1982

Mill, J S, *Representative Government*, 1861

Millett, J D, *The Unemployment Assistance Board*, 1940

Milne, D, *The Scottish Office*, 1957

Minkin, L, *The Blair Supremacy*, 2014

Mitchell, J, *Devolution in the United Kingdom*, 2009

Mitchell, J D B, *Constitutional Law*, 2nd edn, 1968

Mitchell, J D B, *The Contracts of Public Authorities*, 1954

Mitchell, P, *The Making of the Modern Law of Defamation*, 2005

Montesquieu, *The Spirit of the Laws* (eds A M Cohler, B C Miller & H S Stone), 1989

More, J S, *Lectures on the Law of Scotland* (ed. J McLaren), 1864

Morgan, J, *Conflict and Order: The Police and Labour Disputes in England and Wales 1900–39*, 1987

Morison, J, & Livingstone, S, *Reshaping Public Power: Northern Ireland and the British Constitutional Crisis*, 1995

Morris, A (ed.), *The Growth of Parliamentary Scrutiny by Committee*, 1970

Morris, C, *Parliamentary Elections, Representation and the Law*, 2012

Morris, G S, *Strikes in Essential Services*, 1986

Morrison, H, *Government and Parliament*, 3rd edn, 1964

Mosley, R K, *The Story of the Cabinet Office*, 1969

Moules, R, *Actions against Public Officials: Legitimate Expectations, Misstatements and Misconduct*, 2009

Mount, F, *The British Constitution Now: Recovery or Decline?*, 1992

Mowbray, A R, *Cases and Materials on the European Convention on Human Rights*, 3rd edn, 2012

Mowbray, A R, *The Development of Positive Obligations under the ECHR by the European Court of Human Rights*, 2004

Munro, C R, *Studies in Constitutional Law*, 2nd edn, 1999

Munro, J, *Public Law in Scotland*, 2nd edn, 2007

Navot, S, *The Constitutional of Israel – a Contextual Analysis*, 2014

Nicol, D, *EC Membership and Judicialization of British Politics*, 2001

Nicolson, I F, *The Mystery of Crichel Down*, 1986

Nicolson, H, *King George V*, 1952

Nobles, R, & Schiff, D, *Understanding Miscarriages of Justice*, 2000

Nolan, Lord, & Sedley, S, *The Making and Remaking of the British Constitution*, 1997

Normanton, E L, *The Accountability and Audit of Governments*, 1966

Norton, P, *Dissension in the House of Commons 1945–1974*, 1975; *1974–1979*, 1980

Norton, P, *Parliament in British Politics*, 2nd edn, 2005

Norton, P, *The Commons in Perspective*, 1981

O'Higgins, P, *Censorship in Britain*, 1972

Oliver, D, *Common Values and the Public–Private Divide*, 1999

Oliver, D, *Constitutional Reform in the UK*, 2004

Oliver, D, & Drewry, G (eds), *The Law and Parliament*, 1998

Oliver, D, & Fusaro, C, *How Constitutions Change: A Comparative Study*, 2011

Oliver, P C, *The Constitution of Independence: The Development of Constitutional Theory in Australia, Canada and New Zealand*, 2005

Olowofoyeku, A, *Suing Judges: A Study of Judicial Immunity*, 1993

Paine, T, *Rights of Man* (ed. B Kucklick), 1989

Palast, G, *The Best Democracy Money Can Buy*, 2003

Palmer, E, *Judicial Review, Socio-Economic Rights and the Human Rights Act*, 2009

Parris, H, *Constitutional Bureaucracy*, 1969

Paterson, A, *The Law Lords*, 1982

Paterson, A, *Final Judgment: The Law Lords and the Supreme Court*, 2013

Peers, S, & Hervey, T, *The EU Charter of Fundamental Rights*, 2014.

Peers, S, & Ward, A (eds), *The EU Charter of Fundamental Rights: Politics, Law and Policy*, 2004

Pelling, H, *The British Communist Party: A Historical Profile*, 1975

Pickles, E, *Securing the Ballot*, 2016

Pimlott, B, *The Queen: A Biography of Elizabeth II*, 1996

Pinto-Duschinsky, M, *British Political Finance 1830–1980*, 1981

Pollock, F, & Maitland, F W, *History of English Law*, vol. 1, 1898

Polyviou, P G, *Entry, Search and Seizure: Constitutional and Common Law*, 1982

Ponting, C, *The Right to Know: The Inside Story of the Belgrano Affair*, 1985

Port, F J, *Administrative Law*, 1929

Prechal, S, *Directives in EC Law*, 2nd edn, 2005

Price, R, de Silva, N, & Clayton, R, *Parker's Law and Conduct of Elections*, 1996

Prosser, T, *Laws and the Regulators*, 1997

Qvortrup, M (ed.), *The British Constitution: Continuity and Change*, 2013

Rawlings, H F, *The Law and the Electoral Process*, 1988

Rawlings, R, Leyland, P and Young, A (eds), *Sovereignty and the law*, 2013

Rawlings, R W, *Delineating Wales: Constitutional, Legal and Administrative Aspects of National Devolution*, 2003

Raz, J, *Ethics in the Public Domain: Essays in the Morality of Law and Politics*, 1994

Reed, R & Murdoch, J L, *A Guide to Human Rights Law in Scotland* (cd. J L Murdoch), 4th edn, 2017

Reid, G, *The Politics of Financial Control*, 1966

Reiner, R, *The Politics of the Police*, 4th edn, 2010

Richard, I, & Welfare, D, *Unfinished Business: Reforming the House of Lords*, 1999

Richards, P G, *Parliament and Conscience*, 1970

Richards, P G, *Patronage in British Government*, 1963

Richardson, G, & Genn, H (eds), *Administrative Law and Government Action: The Courts and Alternative Mechanisms of Review*, 1994

Riley, P W J, *The Union of England and Scotland*, 1978

Rimington, S, *Open Secret: The Autobiography of the Former Director-General of MI5*, 2001

Roberts, C, *The Growth of Responsible Government in Stuart England*, 1966

Roberts-Wray, K, *Commonwealth and Colonial Law*, 1966

Robertson, G, *Obscenity*, 1979

Robson, W A, *Justice and Administrative Law*, 3rd edn, 1951

Robson, W A, *Nationalised Industries and Public Ownership*, 2nd edn, 1962

Rogers, D, *By Royal Appointment: Tales from the Privy Council*, 2015

Rogers, S (ed.), *The Hutton Inquiry and its Impact*, 2004

Rosenfeld, M & Sajó, A, *The Oxford Handbook of Comparative Constitutional Law*, 2012

Roseveare, H, *The Treasury*, 1969

Rowat, D C, *The Ombudsman*, 2nd edn, 1968

Rowbottom, J, *Democracy Distorted: Wealth, Influence and Democratic Politics*, 2010

Rubin, G R, *Private Property, Government Requisition and the Constitution 1914–1927*, 1994

Runciman, W G, *Hutton and Butler: Lifting the Lid on the Workings of Power*, 2004

Rutter, J, *The Strange Case of Non-Ministerial Departments*, 2013

Ryle, M, & Richards, P G (eds), *The Commons under Scrutiny*, 3rd edn, 1988

Sajó, A, *Limiting Government: An Introduction to Constitutionalism*, 1999

Sampford, C J H, *Retrospectivity and the Rule of Law*, 2006

Sands, P, *Lawless World*, rev edn, 2006

Sands, P, *Torture Team: Uncovering War Crimes in the Land of the Free*, rev edn, 2009

Sawer, G, *Federation under Strain*, 1977

Scarman, Lord, *English Law: The New Dimension*, 1974

Schønberg, S, *Legitimate Expectations in Administrative Law*, 2000

Schwarze, J, *European Administrative Law*, rev edn, 2006

Scutt, J, *Women and the Magna Carta*, 2015

Sedley, S, *Lions under the Throne*, 2015

Seneviratne, M, *Ombudsmen: Public Services and Administrative Justice*, 2002

Shaw, J, *The Transformation of Citizenship in the European Union: Electoral Rights and the Restructuring of Political Space*, 2007

Shaw, M N, *International Law*, 8th edn, 2017

Shell, D, *The House of Lords*, 1988

Shipman, T, *All Out War*, 2017

Sibley, T, & Jeffries, J, *The Shameful Deportation of a Trade Union Leader*, 2008

Simpson, A W B, *Human Rights and the End of Empire: Britain and the Genesis of the European Convention*, 2001

Simpson, A W B, *In the Highest Degree Odious*, 1992

Simpson, A W B, *Pornography and Politics: the Williams Report in Retrospect*, 1983

Singer, P, *Democracy and Disobedience*, 1973

Smith, I T, & Baker, A, *Smith and Wood's Employment Law* (eds I T Smith, A Baker & O Warnock), 13th edn, 2017

Smith, J C, & Hogan, B, *Criminal Law* (ed. D Ormerod), 14th edn, 2015

Smith, T B (ed.), *The Laws of Scotland: Stair Memorial Encyclopedia*, vols 1 & 5, 1987

Stacey, F, *Ombudsmen Compared*, 1978

Stalker, J, *Stalker*, 1988

Stanton, K, Skidmore, P, Harris, M, & Wright, J, *Statutory Torts*, 2003

Steel, D, *A House Divided: The Lib–Lab Pact and the Future of British Politics*, 1980

Stephen, J F, *Digest of Criminal Law*, 1877

Stephen, J F, *History of the Criminal Law of England* (3 vols), 1883

Stevens, R, *Law and Politics: The House of Lords as a Judicial Body, 1800–1976*, 1979

Stevens, R B, *The Independence of the Judiciary: The View from the Lord Chancellor's Office*, 1993

Stewart, J D, *British Pressure Groups*, 1958

Stone, R, *The Law of Entry, Search and Seizure*, 5th edn, 2013

Straw, J, *Aspects of Law Reform: An Insider's Perspective*, 2013.

Street, H, *Freedom, The Individual and the Law*, 5th edn, 1982; 7th edn (G Robertson), 1993

Street, H, *Governmental Liability*, 1953

Sunkin, M, & Payne, S (eds), *The Nature of the Crown: A Legal and Political Analysis*, 1999

Supperstone, M, Goudie, J, & Walker, P (eds), *Judicial Review*, 6th edn, 2017

Sutherland, E et al. (eds), *Law Making in the Scottish Parliament: The Early Years*, 2011

Swinfen, D B, *Imperial Appeal: The Debate on the Appeal to the Privy Council, 1833–1986*, 1987

Taggart, M (ed.), *Judicial Review of Administrative Action in the 1980s*, 1987

Taggart, M (ed.), *The Province of Administrative Law*, 1997

Taswell-Langmead, T P, *English Constitutional History* (ed. T F T Plucknett), 11th edn, 1960

Terry, C S, *The Scottish Parliament 1603–1707*, 1905

Thompson, B, & Ridley, F F (eds), *Under the Scott-light: British Government Seen through the Scott Report*, 1997

Thompson, E P, *Whigs and Hunters: The Origin of the Black Act*, 1975

Thompson, E P, *Writing by Candlelight*, 1980

Tomkins, A and Scott, P (eds), *Entick v Carrington: 250 Years of the Rule of Law*, 2017

Tomkins, A, *Our Republican Constitution*, 2005

Tomkins, A, *The Constitution after Scott: Government Unwrapped*, 1998

Townshend, C, *Making the Peace: Public Order and Public Security in Modern Britain*, 1993

Trench, A (ed.), *Has Devolution Made a Difference? The State of the Nations 2004*, 2004

Trench, A (ed.), *The Dynamics of Devolution: The State of the Nations 2005*, 2005

Trench, A (ed.), *The State of the Nations 2008*, 2008

Tribe, L, *Constitutional Choices*, 1985

Turnbull, M, *The Spycatcher Trial*, 1989

Turpin, C C, *Government Procurement and Contracts*, 1989

Tushnet, M, *The Constitution of the USA: A Contextual Analysis*, 2009

Vile, M J C, *Constitutionalism and the Separation of Powers*, 1967

Vogler, R, *Reading the Riot Act: The Magistracy, the Police and the Army in Civil Disorder*, 1991

Wacks, R, *Personal Information*, 1989

Wacks, R, *The Protection of Privacy*, 1980

Wade, H W R, *Constitutional Fundamentals*, 1980

Wade, H W R, & Forsyth, C F, *Administrative Law*, 11th edn, 2014

Walker, C P, & Starmer, K, *Justice in Error*, 1993

Walker, J, *The Queen has been Pleased*, 1986

Walker, N, *Policing in a Changing Constitutional Order*, 1998

Walker, P G, *The Cabinet*, rev edn, 1972

Walker, S, *In Defense of American Liberties*, 1990

Walkland, S A (ed.), *The House of Commons in the Twentieth Century*, 1979

Watt, B, *UK Election Law: A Critical Examination*, 2006

Webb, P, *The Modern British Party System*, 2000

Weiler, J H H, *The Constitution of Europe: 'Do the New Clothes Have an Emperor?' and Other Essays on European Integration*, 1999

Weir, S, *Unequal Britain*, 2006

Weir, S, & Beetham, D, *Political Power and Democratic Control in Britain*, 1999

West, N, *A Matter of Trust: MI5, 1945–72*, 1982

West, N, *MI5: British Security Service Operations 1909–45*, 1983

Wheare, K C, *Modern Constitutions*, 2nd edn, 1966

Wheeler-Bennett, J, *King George VI*, 1958

White, F, & Hollingsworth, K, *Audit, Accountability and Government*, 1999

Whitlam, G, *The Truth of the Matter*, 1979

Whittington, K E, *Constitutional Construction: Divided Powers and Constitutional Meaning*, 1999

Whitty, N, Murphy, T, & Livingstone, S, *Civil Liberties Law: The Human Rights Act Era*, 2001

Wicks, E, *The Evolution of a Constitution: Eight Key Moments in British Constitutional History*, 2006

Williams, D G T, *Keeping the Peace*, 1967

Williams, D G T, *Not in the Public Interest*, 1965

Williams, E N, *The 18th Century Constitution, 1688–1815*, 1960

Williams, G, *Media Ownership and Democracy*, 2nd edn, 1996

Williams, O C, *The Historical Development of Private Bill Procedure*, 2 vols, 1949

Williams, R, *Unjust Enrichment and Public Law: A Comparative Study of England, France and the EU*, 2010

Willis, J, *The Parliamentary Powers of English Government Departments*, 1933

Wilson, H, *The Governance of Britain*, 1976

Wilson, H, *The Labour Government, 1964–70*, 1974

Wilson, S S, *The Cabinet Office to 1945*, 1975

Winetrobe, B K, *Realising the Vision: A Parliament with a Purpose*, 2001

Wolfe, J N (ed.), *Government and Nationalism in Scotland*, 1969

Woodhouse, D, *The Office of Lord Chancellor*, 2001

Woodhouse, D, *Ministers and Parliament: Accountability in Theory and Practice*, 1994

Woodhouse, D (ed.), *The Pinochet Case: A Legal and Constitutional Analysis*, 2000

Woolf, Sir H, *Protection of the Public: A New Challenge*, 1990

Woolf, Lord, Jowell, J, Le Sueur, A, Donnelly, C & Hare, I, *De Smith's Judicial Review*, 7th edn, 2013

Wyatt, D, & Dashwood, A, *European Union Law* (eds A Dashwood, M Dougan et al.), 6th edn, 2011

Young, A, *Democratic Dialogue and the Constitution*, 2017

Young, A, *Parliamentary Sovereignty and the Human Rights Act*, 2009

Young, H, *The Crossman Affair*, 1976

Zamir, I, Woolf, Lord, & Woolf, J, *The Declaratory Judgment*, 4th edn, 2011

Zander, M, *The Police and Criminal Evidence Act 1984*, 7th edn, 2015

Ziegler, K, Baranger, D, & Bradley, A W, *Constitutionalism and the Role of Parliaments*, 2007

INDEX